Frommer's® Ireland

22nd Edition

by Christi Daugherty & Jack Jewers

WILEY

John Wiley & Sons, Inc.

Published by:
John Wiley & Sons, Inc.
111 River St.
Hoboken, NJ 07030-5774

ISBN 978-1-118-02765-3 (paper); 978-1-118-07697-2 (paper); 978-1-118-14665-1 (ebk); 978-1-118-14666-8 (ebk); 978-1-118-14667-5 (ebk)

Editor: Jamie Ehrlich
Production Editor: Eric T. Schroeder
Cartographer: Andrew Murphy
Photo Editor: Richard Fox
Cover Photo Editor: Richard Fox
Design and Layout by Vertigo Design
Graphics and Prepress by Wiley Indianapolis Composition Services

Front cover photo: An aerial view of Blarney Castle and its grounds © MIVA Stock/SuperStock, Inc. Back cover photos: LEFT: High cross with cathedral © Gareth McCormack/AGE Fotostock, Inc. MIDDLE: Glandore Harbour in County Cork © The Irish Image Collection/Design Pics Inc.—RM Content/Alamy Images. RIGHT: A pint of Guinness in Dublin © Axiom Photographic Limited/SuperStock, Inc.

For information on our other products and services or to obtain technical support, please contact our Customer Care Department within the U.S. at 877/762-2974, outside the U.S. at 317/572-3993 or fax 317/572-4002.

Wiley also publishes its books in a variety of electronic formats. Some content that appears in print may not be available in electronic formats.

Manufactured in China

5 4 3 2 1

CONTENTS

12 MAYO, SLIGO & THE NORTH SHANNON VALLEY 494

13 COUNTY DONEGAL 530

14 NORTHERN IRELAND 562

15 PLANNING YOUR TRIP TO IRELAND 654

Index 674

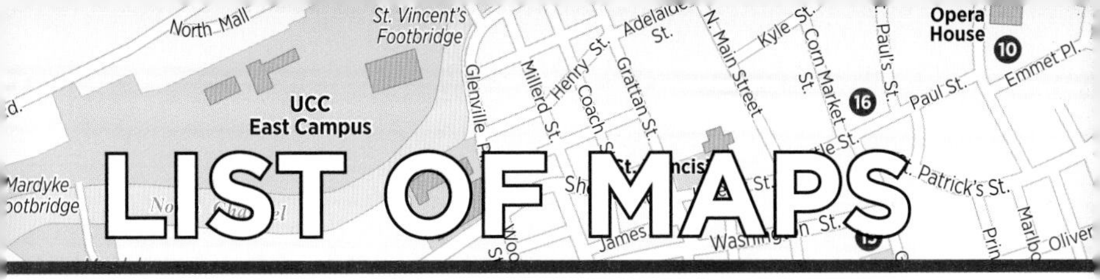
North Mall
St. Vincent's Footbridge
UCC East Campus
Mardyke
Glenville
Millerd St.
Henry St.
Coach St.
Grattan St.
Adelaide St.
N. Main Street
Kyle St.
Corn Market St.
Paul's St.
Paul St.
Opera House
Emmet Pl.
Patrick's St.
James
Oliver
10
16

LIST OF MAPS

ABOUT THE AUTHORS

Christi Daugherty is an expat American. A former journalist, she's the author of several travel books including *Frommer's Paris Day by Day.* She also co-wrote *Frommer's MTV Ireland* and *Frommer's MTV Europe.* She learned everything she knows about Ireland accidentally, while getting lost repeatedly over the course of many years. She likes to think that she gets lost so you don't have to. These days she and her husband and co-writer Jack Jewers spend their spare time traveling around Ireland (she drives, he navigates) looking for new places to explore. She spends whatever time is left over writing unpublished mystery novels.

Jack Jewers has directed films for the BBC, reviewed publications for *Time Out,* and contributed to several guidebooks, including previous editions of *Frommer's Ireland.* He also co-wrote *Frommer's Ireland Day by Day.* Jack grew up listening to his great aunt's tales about living in Dublin during the Civil War. She once leaned out of a window during a late-night battle to tell the gunmen to keep the noise down—people were trying to sleep. Born and raised in England, Jack proposed to his Irish-American wife at a spa in County Kerry. She said yes. That spa gets a great review in this book.

HOW TO CONTACT US

In researching this book, we discovered many wonderful places—hotels, restaurants, shops, and more. We're sure you'll find others. Please tell us about them, so we can share the information with your fellow travelers in upcoming editions. If you were disappointed with a recommendation, we'd love to know that, too. Please write to:

Frommer's Ireland, 22nd Edition
John Wiley & Sons, Inc. • 111 River St. • Hoboken, NJ 07030-5774
frommersfeedback@wiley.com

ADVISORY & DISCLAIMER

FROMMER'S STAR RATINGS, ICONS & ABBREVIATIONS

Every hotel, restaurant, and attraction listing in this guide has been ranked for quality, value, service, amenities, and special features using a **star-rating system.** In country, state, and regional guides, we also rate towns and regions to help you narrow down your choices and budget your time accordingly. Hotels and restaurants are rated on a scale of zero (recommended) to three stars (exceptional). Attractions, shopping, nightlife, towns, and regions are rated according to the following scale: zero stars (recommended), one star (highly recommended), two stars (very highly recommended), and three stars (must-see).

In addition to the star-rating system, we also use **seven feature icons** that point you to the great deals, in-the-know advice, and unique experiences that separate travelers from tourists. Throughout the book, look for:

special finds—those places only insiders know about

fun facts—details that make travelers more informed and their trips more fun

kids—best bets for kids and advice for the whole family

special moments—those experiences that memories are made of

overrated—places or experiences not worth your time or money

insider tips—great ways to save time and money

great values—where to get the best deals

The following abbreviations are used for credit cards:

AE American Express **DISC** Discover **V** Visa

DC Diners Club **MC** MasterCard

TRAVEL RESOURCES AT FROMMERS.COM

Frommer's travel resources don't end with this guide. Frommer's website, **www.frommers.com**, has travel information on more than 4,000 destinations. We update features regularly, giving you access to the most current trip-planning information and the best airfare, lodging, and car-rental bargains. You can also listen to podcasts, connect with other Frommers.com members through our active-reader forums, share your travel photos, read blogs from guidebook editors and fellow travelers, and much more.

1

THE BEST OF IRELAND

Tiny, and with ever-changing scenery, Ireland is an addictive place to explore. Within a few miles you can travel from plunging cliffs to flat pastureland to towering mountains to gloomy peat bog. You can spend the night in ancient castles or state-of-the-art spa hotels, dine on fine Irish cuisine or snack on fish and chips served in a paper bag. The sheer number of sights, little villages, charming pubs, and adorable restaurants and shops is overwhelming—you always feel that you might be missing something. So it's nice to have somebody help you focus, and that's why we've put together this list of some of our favorite places and things in Ireland. We hope that while you're here, you'll find a few of your own.

THE best PICTURE-POSTCARD TOWNS

- **Dalkey** (County Dublin): The cutest of a string of upscale seaside towns in suburban Dublin nicknamed "Bel Eire" (pronounced "Bellaire," get it?) for their wealth, beauty, and density of celebrity residents, Dalkey is both a short drive and a million miles away from the busy city. With a castle, a mountaintop folly, lovely beaches, and some fine restaurants, this is a town that tempts you to settle into its comfortable affluence. See chapter 5.

PREVIOUS PAGE: **Ross Castle in Killarney National Park.** ABOVE: **The colorful cobbled streets of Kinsale, on the coast in County Cork.**

Carlingford, on the Cooley Peninsula in County Louth.

- **Carlingford** (County Louth): The ancient name for this gorgeous little town is *Cuan Aighneach,* which means "Haven of the People with the Perfect Reputation." With its castle ruins overlooking the glassy lough, and pedestrian-friendly lanes filled with colorful shops, cafes, and pubs, this place tends to live up to its reputation. See chapter 6.
- **Inistioge** (County Kilkenny): Nestled in the Nore River valley, surrounded by undulating hills, this riverfront village with two spacious greens and a host of pubs cries out to be photographed. Its rivers and lakes are swimming with fish and attract hosts of anglers. See chapter 7.
- **Kinsale** (County Cork): Kinsale's narrow streets all lead to the sea, dropping steeply from the hills around the harbor, although the crowds of visitors teeming on the sidewalks every summer attest to the fact that the Kinsale secret is out. The walk from Kinsale through Scilly to Charles Fort and Frower Point is breathtaking. Kinsale has the added benefit of being a foodie town, with no shortage of good restaurants. See chapter 8.
- **Dingle/An Daingean** (County Kerry): Dingle is a charming hilltop medieval town. Its stone buildings ramble up and down hills, and its small population is relaxed about visitors. It has lots of little diners and picturesque pubs, and a lovely, historic church. See chapter 9.
- **Kenmare** (County Kerry): It's easy to fall in love with Kenmare, with its stone cottages, colorful gardens, and flowers overflowing from window boxes. It's also home to several elegant hotels, so it makes an enchanting base when exploring the Ring of Kerry. See chapter 9.
- **Athlone** (County Westmeath): Sitting at the edge of the River Shannon, its streets curving around a sturdy, fortresslike castle, Athlone is a charmer. Houses are painted in bright hues, and with its small, funky boutiques and spirit of fun, it has the feel of a busy university town. Good restaurants and lively pubs add to its charms. See chapter 11.
- **Ardara** (County Donegal): On the southwest coast of County Donegal, the tiny town of Ardara looks as if it were carved out of a solid block of granite. Its streets undulate up and down the rocky hills, and are lined with little boutiques and charming arts shops, many selling clothes made of the famed Donegal wool. You can wander its entirety in a few minutes. It's a bite-size place. See chapter 13.

Ireland
SCOTLAND
ATLANTIC OCEAN
North Channel
To Troon
Stranraer
To Douglas, Heysham, Liverpool
To Heysham, Douglas
Ards Peninsula
Portaferry
Strangford
Downpatrick
Ardglass
Dundrum Bay
Newcastle
Annalong
Strangford Lough
Larne
Island Magee
Belfast Lough
Newtownabbey
Bangor
Newtownards
City
Comber
Carrickfergus
BELFAST
Belfast Int'l
Lisburn
Antrim
Lough Neagh
NORTHERN IRELAND
Rathlin I.
Fair Head
Ballycastle
Cushendun
Red Bay
Cushendall
Carnlough
Antrim Mts.
Ballymena
Ballymoney
Bushmills
Giant's Causeway
Coleraine
Portrush
Portstewart
Limavady
Bann
Magherafelt
Randalstown
Maghera
Cookstown
Sperrin Mts.
Derry (Londonderry)
Lough Foyle
Culdaff Bay
Ballygorman
Inishowen
Buncrana
Malin Head
Ballyliffin
Strabane
Sion Mills
Newtownstewart
Omagh
Sixmilecross
Ballygawley
Craigavon
Portadown
Armagh
Banbridge
Mourne Mts.
Carlingford
Dundalk
Dundalk Bay
Dunany Point
Clogherhead
Drogheda
Newgrange
Skerries
Rush
Lambay I.
Malahide
Dublin Int'l
Newry
Warrenpoint
Louth
LOUTH
Inniskeen
Monaghan
MONAGHAN
Ballybay
ULSTER
Cavan
CAVAN
Virginia
Kells (Ceanannus Mor)
Navan
MEATH
Trim
Mullingar
WESTMEATH
Edgeworthstown
Longford
LONGFORD
Lough Sheelin
Lough Ramor
Lough Derravaragh
Lough Owel
Royal Canal
Enniskillen
Upper Lough Erne
Lower Lough Erne
Belturbet
Newtownbutler
Lough Oughter
Arva
Dromore
Lifford
Letterkenny
DONEGAL
Fanad
Milford
Rosguill
Glenveagh National Park
Derryveagh Mts.
Blue Stack Mts.
Donegal
Ballintra
Finn
Lough Derg
Tory I.
Tory Sound
Bloody Foreland
Gola I.
Owey I.
Arranmore I.
Ballintra
Gweebarra Bay
Glenties
Loughros More Bay
Mountcharles
Glencolumbkille
Inver Bay
Donegal Bay
Inishmurray
Cliffoney
Lough Melvin
Lough Macnean
Dromahair
Lough Gill
Lough Allen
Iron Mts.
LEITRIM
Drumsna
Carrick-on-Shannon
Lough Arrow
Lough Key
Lough Gara
Curlew Mts.
Sligo
SLIGO
Sligo Bay
Ballymote
Frenchpark
ROSCOMMON
Castlerea
Roscommon
Ballymahon
Lough Ree
Shannon
Ballygar
Mountbellew
Tuam
CONNACHT
Knock
Charlestown
Foxford
Ox Mts.
Slieve Gamph
Killala Bay
Killala
Ballina
Ballycastle
Bangor Erris
Lough Conn
MAYO
Castlebar
Ballinrobe
Cong
Lough Mask
Lough Corrib
Partry Mts.
Nephin Beg Ra.
Ballycroy National Park
Newport
Westport
Clew Bay
Louisburgh
Sheffrey Hills
Maamturk Mts.
Connemara
Connemara National Park
Ennis Head
Mullet Peninsula
Belmullet
Blacksod Bay
Achill Island
Croaghaun
Achill Head
Clare I.
Inishturk
Inishbofin
Inishshark

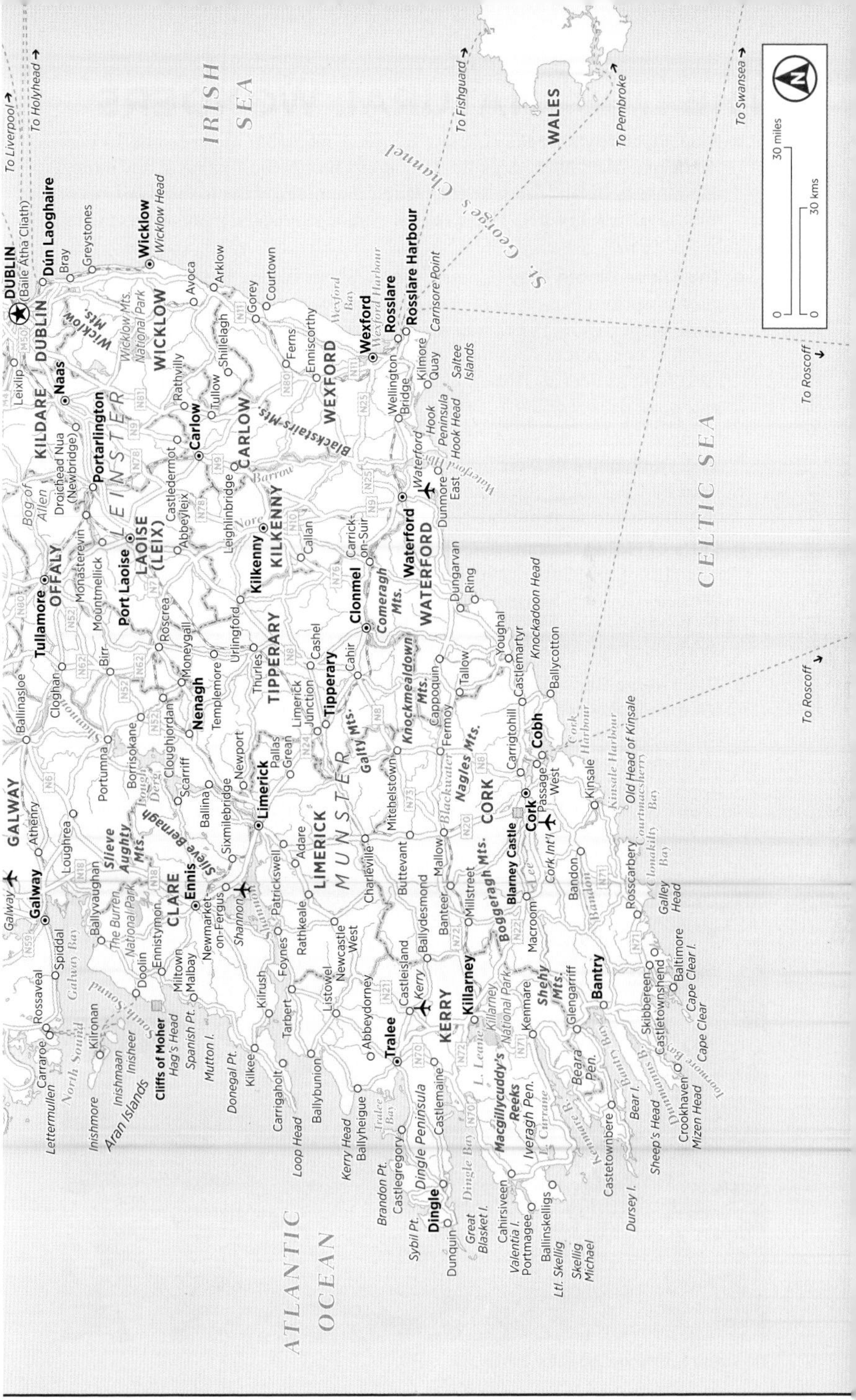
IRISH SEA
To Liverpool
To Holyhead
DUBLIN
(Baile Átha Cliath)
Dún Laoghaire
Bray
Greystones
Wicklow
Wicklow Head
DUBLIN
Wicklow Mts.
Wicklow Mts. National Park
WICKLOW
Avoca
Arklow
Gorey
Courtown
Leixlip
Naas
KILDARE
Droichead Nua (Newbridge)
Portarlington
Bog of Allen
Rathvilly
Tullow
Shillelagh
Ferns
Enniscorthy
WEXFORD
Wexford
Wexford Bay
Wexford Harbour
Rosslare
Rosslare Harbour
Carnsore Point
St. George's Channel
To Fishguard
To Pembroke
WALES
To Swansea
30 miles
30 kms
Carlow
CARLOW
Blackstairs Mts.
Castledermot
Leighlinbridge
Barrow
LEINSTER
Monasterevin
Abbeyleix
LAOISE (LEIX)
Port Laoise
Mountmellick
Tullamore
OFFALY
Kilkenny
KILKENNY
Nore
Callan
Carrick-on-Suir
Wellington Bridge
Kilmore Quay
Saltee Islands
Hook Peninsula
Hook Head
Waterford
Waterford Harbour
Dunmore East
WATERFORD
Dungarvan
Ring
Clonmel
Comeragh Mts.
Knockmealdown Mts.
Cappoquin
Tallow
Youghal
Castlemartyr
Knockadoon Head
Ballycotton
To Roscoff
CELTIC SEA
Ballinasloe
Cloghan
Birr
Roscrea
Moneygall
Urlingford
Thurles
TIPPERARY
Cashel
Cahir
Tipperary
Limerick Junction
Templemore
Nenagh
Cloughjordan
Borrisokane
Portumna
Lough Derg
Shannon
GALWAY
Galway
Athenry
Loughrea
Slieve Aughty Mts.
Slieve Bernagh
Scarriff
Ballina
Newport
Limerick
Pallas Grean
Galty Mts.
MUNSTER
Mitchelstown
Fermoy
Blackwater
Nagles Mts.
Carrigtohill
Cobh
Cork Harbour
Passage West
Cork
Cork Int'l
Kinsale
Kinsale Harbour
Old Head of Kinsale
Courtmacsherry Bay
CORK
Blarney Castle
Boggeragh Mts.
Mallow
Buttevant
Charleville
LIMERICK
Adare
Patrickswell
Sixmilebridge
Ennis
CLARE
Shannon
Newmarket-on-Fergus
Ennistymon
The Burren National Park
Ballyvaughan
Galway Bay
Spiddal
Rossaveal
Carraroe
Lettermullen
North Sound
Kilronan
Inishmore
Inishmaan
Inisheer
Aran Islands
South Sound
Doolin
Cliffs of Moher
Hag's Head
Miltown Malbay
Spanish Pt.
Mutton I.
Donegal Pt.
Kilkee
Kilrush
Foynes
Rathkeale
Newcastle West
Tarbert
Carrigaholt
Loop Head
Ballybunion
Listowel
Abbeydorney
Castleisland
Ballydesmond
Banteer
Millstreet
Macroom
Bandon
Clonakilty Bay
Rosscarbery
Galley Head
Skibbereen
Castletownshend
Baltimore
Cape Clear I.
Cape Clear
Bantry
Bantry Bay
Shehy Mts.
Glengarriff
Kenmare
Killarney
Killarney National Park
Kerry
KERRY
Tralee
Tralee Bay
Ballyheigue
Kerry Head
Castlegregory
Brandon Pt.
Dingle Peninsula
Dingle
Dingle Bay
Castlemaine
L. Leane
Macgillycuddy's Reeks
Iveragh Pen.
Beara Pen.
Kenmare R.
Castletownbere
Bear I.
Dursey I.
Sheep's Head
Dunmanus B.
Crookhaven
Mizen Head
Roaringwater Bay
Cahirsiveen
Valentia I.
Portmagee
Ballinskelligs
Ltl. Skellig
Skellig Michael
Dunquin
Great Blasket I.
Sybil Pt.
ATLANTIC OCEAN

THE best NATURAL WONDERS

- **MacGillycuddy's Reeks** (County Kerry): A mountain range on the Iveragh Peninsula, MacGillycuddy's Reeks not only has the best name of any mountain range in Ireland, but also the highest mountain on the island, Carrantuohill (1,041m/3,414 ft.). The Reeks are among Ireland's greatest spectacles. See p. 365.
- **The Slieve Bloom Way** (County Laois): Slieve Bloom, Ireland's largest and most unspoiled blanket bog, rises gently above the peat fields. Its beauty—gentle slopes, glens, rivers, waterfalls, and bog lands—is subtle but persistent, and it is comparatively untouched. You can have it more or less to yourself, apart from its deer and foxes, and an occasional frolicking otter. See p. 426.
- **The Burren** (County Clare): We can guarantee this: The Burren is one of the strangest landscapes you're likely to see. Its vast limestone grassland is spread with a quilt of wildflowers from as far afield as the Alps, all softening the stark stones jutting out of the ground. Its inhabitants include nearly every species of butterfly found in Ireland. See p. 432.
- **Cliffs of Moher** (County Clare): Rising from Hag's Head to the south, these magnificent sea cliffs reach their full height of 214m (702 ft.) just north of O'Brien's Tower. The views of the open sea, of the Aran Islands, and of the Twelve Bens mountains of Connemara (see below) are spectacular. A walk south along the cliff edge at sunset makes a perfect end to any day. See p. 438.
- **The Twelve Bens** (County Galway): Amid Connemara's central mountains, bogs, and lakes, the rugged Twelve Bens range crowns a spectacular landscape. Some of the peaks are bare and rocky, others clothed in peat. The loftiest, Benbaun, in Connemara National Park, reaches a height of 719m (2,395 ft.). See p. 476.

The craggy karst landscape of the Burren.

Hikers on the Slieve League coastal walk in County Donegal.

Ireland's most curious natural wonder, the UNESCO-inscribed Giant's Causeway, in County Antrim.

- **Croagh Patrick** (County Mayo): Rising steeply 750m (2,460 ft.) above the coast, Croagh Patrick is seen as a holy mountain, where the saint is said to have retreated in penance. Traditionally, barefoot pilgrims climb it the last Sunday of July, but in recent years, hundreds of Nike-shod tourists have been making the ascent daily. The view from above can be breathtaking or nonexistent—the summit is often wrapped in clouds. See p. 498.
- **Slieve League** (County Donegal): The Slieve League peninsula stretches for 48km (30 miles) into the Atlantic. Its pigmented bluffs rise to startlingly high sea cliffs. They can also be walked along, if you dare. See p. 545.
- **Giant's Causeway** (County Antrim): At the foot of a cliff by the sea, this mysterious mass of dark, tightly packed, naturally occurring hexagonal basalt columns are nothing short of astonishing. This volcanic wonder, formed 60 million years ago, looks marvelous from above, even better when negotiated (cautiously) on foot. See p. 610.

Cahir Castle, in County Tipperary.

THE best CASTLES

- **Trim Castle** (County Meath): Trim, also called King John's Castle, restored as a preserved ruin, is a massive Anglo-Norman structure. It was all but impregnable for 4 centuries (late 12th to mid–17th c.). Until it was abandoned and collapsed in the 17th century, it never underwent any significant alteration. For anyone with imagination, Trim is a visual gateway into medieval Ireland. See p. 233.
- **Cahir Castle** (County Tipperary): One of the largest of Ireland's medieval fortresses, this castle is in an extraordinary state of preservation. Tours explain some fascinating features of the military architecture, and then you're free to roam through a maze of tiny chambers, spiral staircases, and dizzying battlements. See p. 396.
- **Kilkenny Castle** (County Kilkenny): Although parts of the castle date from the 13th century, the existing structure has the feel of an 18th-century palace. There have been many modifications since medieval times, including the addition of colorful landscaping, and the old stables now hold numerous art galleries and shops. See p. 276.
- **Blarney Castle** (County Cork): Despite the mobs of tourists who besiege it daily, this majestic tower house is worth a visit. While you're there, check out the Badger Cave and dungeons at the tower's base, as well as the serpentine paths that wind through the castle gardens. Need we mention the Blarney Stone? You sidle in under the upper wall with your head hanging over a 10-story drop. You kiss it. It's a thing people do. See p. 300.
- **Bunratty Castle and Folk Park** (County Clare): This grand old castle has been well restored and filled with a curious assortment of medieval

furnishings, offering a glimpse into the life of its past inhabitants. This is the first stop for many arrivals from Shannon, so expect crowds. See p. 420.

- **Doe Castle** (County Donegal): This picturesque tower house is surrounded on three sides by the waters of Sheep Haven Bay and on the fourth by a moat carved into the bedrock that forms its foundation. It has a remote waterfront setting and sweeping views of the nearby hills. See p. 550.
- **Carrickfergus Castle** (County Antrim): This well-preserved Norman fortress on the bank of Belfast Lough is huge and impressive, with an imposing tower house and a high wall punctuated by corner towers. See p. 597.
- **Dunluce Castle** (County Antrim): These castle ruins surmount a razor-sharp promontory jutting into the sea. This was a highly defensible setting, and the castle wasn't abandoned until a large section collapsed and fell into the breakers. See p. 610.

THE best OF ANCIENT IRELAND

- **Hill of Tara** (County Meath): Of ritual significance from the Stone Age to the Christian period, Tara has seen it all and kept it all a secret. This was the traditional center and seat of Ireland's high kings. Although the hill is only 154m (512 ft.) above sea level, from here you can see each of Ireland's four Celtic provinces on a clear day. The site is mostly unexcavated and tells its story in whispers. It's a place to be walked slowly. See p. 229.
- **Newgrange** (County Meath): One of the archaeological wonders of western Europe, Newgrange is the centerpiece of a megalithic cemetery dating back 5,000 years. Its massive mound and passage tomb are amazing feats of engineering. But the question remains: What was it all for? See p. 232.
- **Loughcrew** (County Meath): At this little-known site, not far from Newgrange, a series of cruciform passage tombs crown two hills. Guided tours of the cairns are offered during the summer, but we prefer to come in the off season, when you can borrow a key and make your own imaginative reconstruction. See p. 231.
- **Lough Gur** (County Limerick): This lakefront site will convince you that the Neolithic farmers of Ireland had an estimable sense of real estate. Inhabited

Newgrange, a UNESCO World Heritage Site, older than the Egyptian pyramids, in County Meath.

Save Money: Buy a Heritage Card

The Heritage Card is a pass that allows you free entry to almost all historic sites owned or managed by the Irish government. Given that these include some of the country's most popular attractions, this can be a big saving. The card costs €21 for adults, €16 for seniors, €8 for children, and €55 for families. You can buy them at any of the site ticket offices, or at www.heritageireland.ie.

Dozens of sights listed in this book take Heritage Cards, including: Aughnanure Castle (p. 476); the Blasket Centre (p. 377); Carrowmore Megalithic Cemetery (p. 517); Céide Fields (p. 500); Charles Fort (p. 311); Clonmacnoise (p. 488); Dublin Castle (p. 146); Fota House (p. 322); Glendalough (p. 204); Glenveagh National Park (p. 551); the Hill of Tara (p. 229); the Iveagh Gardens; Jerpoint Abbey (p. 278); the John F. Kennedy Arboretum (p. 250); Kilmainham Gaol (p. 148); Kilkenny Castle (p. 276); Muckross House (p. 359); the National Botanic Gardens (p. 196); the Rock of Cashel (p. 397); and Trim Castle (p. 233).

for more than 4,000 years, the ancient farming settlement offers a number of prehistoric remains. The most impressive of these is the largest surviving stone circle in Ireland, made up of 113 stones. See p. 413.

- **Dún Aengus** (County Galway): No one knows who built this massive stone fort, or when. The eminent archaeologist George Petrie called Dún Aengus "the most magnificent barbaric monument in Europe." Facing the sea, where its three stone rings meet steep 90m (295-ft.) cliffs, Dún Aengus still stands guard today over the southern coast of the island of Inishmore, the largest of the Aran Islands. See p. 472.
- **Carrowmore and Carrowkeel** (County Sligo): These two megalithic cities of the dead (Europe's largest) may have once contained more than 200 passage tombs. The two together—one in the valley and the other atop a nearby mountain—convey an unequaled sense of the scale and wonder of the ancient peoples' reverence for the dead. Carrowmore is well presented and interpreted, while Carrowkeel is left to itself and to those who seek it out. See p. 516 and 517.
- **Navan Fort** (County Antrim): There is no longer much remaining here to reflect the great past of this fort, though it was once the ritual and royal seat of Ulster. Thankfully, the interpretive center here is nothing short of remarkable, and it offers a great introduction to the myth and archaeology of the fort, known in Irish as *Emain Macha.* See p. 606.

THE best EARLY CHRISTIAN RUINS

- **Glendalough** (County Wicklow): Nestled in "the glen of the two lakes," this atmospheric monastic settlement was founded in the 6th century by St. Kevin, who was looking for seclusion and certainly found it here. The setting is endlessly scenic, with lakes and forests surrounding it. Although quite remote, Glendalough suffered assaults from the Vikings and English forces,

Glendalough, the 6th-century monastic settlement between two lakes surrounded by forest in County Wicklow.

The dizzying climb to the remains of an early Christian settlement atop Skellig Michael, a daunting peak in the Atlantic.

and eventually faded away. Today its stone ruins collude with the countryside to create one of the loveliest spots in Ireland. See p. 204.

- **The Rock of Cashel** (County Tipperary): In name and appearance, "the Rock" suggests a citadel, a place designed more for power than prayer. In fact, Cashel (or *Caiseal*) means "fortress." The rock is a huge outcropping—or an *up*cropping—of limestone topped with spectacularly beautiful ruins, including what was formerly the country's finest Romanesque chapel. This was the seat of clerics and kings, a power center to rival Tara. Now, however, the two sites vie only for the attention of tourists. See p. 397.
- **Jerpoint Abbey** (County Kilkenny): Jerpoint is the finest representative of the many Cistercian abbeys whose ruins dot the Irish landscape. Somehow, hundreds of years of rain and wind have failed to completely wipe away medieval carvings, leaving us a rare chance for a glimpse of how magnificent these abbeys once were. The splendid, richly carved cloister is the best place to spot the carvings, particularly at the top of the many columns. See p. 278.
- **Skellig Michael** (County Kerry): Thirteen kilometers (8 miles) offshore of the Iveragh Peninsula, rising sharply 214m (702 ft.) out of the Atlantic, this is a remote rocky crag dedicated to the archangel Michael. In flight from the world, early Irish monks in pursuit of "white martyrdom" (meaning martyrdom without bloodshed) chose this spot to build their austere hermitage. Today the journey to Skellig, across choppy seas, and the arduous climb to its summit are challenging and unforgettable. See "The Skellig Islands" under "The Iveragh Peninsula" in chapter 9.
- **Clonmacnoise** (County Offaly): This was once one of Ireland's most important religious, artistic, and literary centers, a place of pilgrimage and culture. Founded in the mid–5th century at the axis of the River Shannon and the medieval east-west thoroughfare known as the *Eiscir Riada,* Clonmacnois thrived for centuries until its prime riverfront location brought repeated

violent raids that proved its undoing. Even in ruins, Clonmacnois remains a place of peculiar serenity. See p. 488.

- **Inishmurray** (County Sligo): This uninhabited island off the Sligo coast holds another striking monastic ruin, this one surrounded by what appears to be the walls of an even more ancient stone fort. Despite its remoteness, the Vikings sought out this outpost of peace-seeking monks for destruction in A.D. 807. Today its circular walls and the surrounding sea create a stunning view, well worth the effort required to reach it. See "Exploring the Surrounding Countryside" under "Sligo & Yeats Country" in chapter 12.

THE best LITERARY SPOTS

- **Dublin Writers Museum** (Dublin): With handwritten letters from Brendan Behan to friends back home, and early flyers from the Abbey Theatre when it was run by Lady Gregory and Yeats, this museum is heaven for bookish types. You can spend hours reading the memorabilia and marveling at the trivia. See p. 147.
- **Glasnevin Cemetery** (Dublin): Besides being the setting for part of *Ulysses,* this is the resting place of James Joyce's parents and other members of his family. The English-born poet Gerard Manley Hopkins is buried here, in the Jesuit plot. Maud Gonne, the Irish nationalist and longtime Dublin resident who is said to have inspired Yeats's play *Cathleen ní Houlihan,* is buried in the Republican plot. The writer, drinker, and Irish Republican Brendan Behan is also buried here. See p. 157.
- **Davy Byrnes** (Dublin): In *Ulysses* Joyce describes the main character, Leopold Bloom, stopping in at this Dublin pub for a Gorgonzola sandwich and a glass of burgundy. "He raised his eyes and met the stare of a bilious clock. Two. Pub clock five minutes fast. Time going on. Hands moving. Two. Not yet." Today the clock is kept 5 minutes fast, in honor of Bloom and Joyce. See p. 179.
- **James Joyce Museum** (Dublin): At the edge of the sea in the Dublin suburb of Sandycove, this Martello tower was home to Joyce for a short time, and he based a character on his host, Oliver St. John Gogarty, described in *Ulysses* as "stately, plump Buck Mulligan." The museum was opened in 1962, and its interior has been restored to look as it did when Joyce was here, along with plenty of memorabilia, including Joyce's walking stick and guitar. See p. 192.

Davy Byrnes, a Dublin pub where James Joyce was a regular.

- **St. Patrick's Cathedral** (Dublin): Jonathan Swift tickled and horrified the world with his vicious wit. He shook up political establishments with his sarcasm, and nauseated the English-speaking world with his suggestion that people should dine on Irish babies. While kicking up such a stir, he was dean of St. Patrick's Cathedral, which sponsored and supported him through it all. He is buried here alongside his longtime companion, Stella Johnson. See p. 151.
- **County Sligo:** With its many connections to the beloved poet W. B. Yeats, this county is a pilgrimage destination for Yeats fans. The poet's writing was shaped by the landscape and people in this farming region, and many of its monuments—including Lough Gill, Glencar Lake, Ben Bulben Mountain, and Maeve's tomb—appear in his poetry. There are also several museums housing first editions, photographs, and other memorabilia, and Yeats's dark and somber grave is in Drumcliff. See chapter 12.

THE best GARDENS

- **Powerscourt Gardens** (County Wicklow): This grandiose Irish garden is set amid the natural splendor of the Wicklow Hills just outside of Dublin. The sprawling, manicured gardens and the wild beauty of the Powerscourt waterfall make this a great day's outing, and a respite from the noise and congestion of the city. See p. 207.
- **Japanese Gardens** (County Kildare): On the grounds of the National Stud, this peaceful enclave is based on the traditional designs of Japanese gardens. A Japanese specialist planned the structure and its symbolism, and most of the plants and stones were imported from Japan. See p. 223.
- **Ilnacullin** (County Cork): A ferry conveys visitors from a rhododendron-framed bay in the town of Glengarriff to Garinish Island, the unlikely site of a fine Italianate garden. The formal garden, with the casita at its center, is

Glenveagh National Park, on the banks of Lough Veagh in County Donegal.

linked to a "wild garden" that showcases a collection of rhododendrons, azaleas, and rare trees. See p. 327.

- **Glenveagh National Park** (County Donegal): A castle and its gardens stretch across a strangely barren valley high in the hills of Donegal, along the banks of Lough Veagh. The sprawling park contains a grand statuary garden, a walled garden, and a rhododendron-lined path that leads to a stunning view of the castle and lake. See p. 551.
- **Mount Stewart House Gardens** (County Down): Built upon an elaborate plan, the Mount Stewart House has several gardens of distinctive character. The Ards Peninsula provides a climate conducive to cultivating many subtropical species. The statuary, topiary, and planting designs reflect a touch of whimsy. See p. 600.

THE best FAMILY ACTIVITIES

- **Dublin Zoo in the Phoenix Park** (Dublin): Kids love this sympathetically designed zoo, with its wild creatures, animal-petting corners, and train ride. The surrounding park has room to run, picnic, and explore. See p. 162.
- **Irish National Heritage Park** (County Wexford): Nearly 9,000 years of Irish history come alive here in ways that will fascinate visitors of all ages. The whole family will be captivated by the story of ancient Ireland, from its first inhabitants to its Norman conquerors. See p. 245.
- **Fota Island Wildlife Park** (County Cork): In this wildlife park, rare and endangered animals roam freely. You'll see everything from giraffes and zebras to kangaroos, flamingos, penguins, and monkeys wandering the grassland. Add in a small amusement park for toddlers, a tour train, picnic tables, and a gift shop and you have the makings of a wonderful family outing. See p. 322.
- **Muckross House and Gardens** (Killarney, County Kerry): This huge Victorian mansion with its exquisite gardens is also home to skilled artisans at work. Nearby are a series of reconstructed traditional farms, with animals and docents, providing a gateway to rural Ireland as it was for centuries. See p. 359.
- **Fungie the Dolphin Tours** (Dingle, County Kerry): Every day, fishing boats ferry visitors out into the nearby waters to see Fungie, the friendliest dolphin you're ever likely to meet. Fungie swims right up to the boat, and the boatmen stay out long enough for ample sightings. You can also arrange an early-morning dolphin swim. See p. 377.
- **Bunratty Castle and Folk Park** (County Clare): Kids are enthralled by this well-restored medieval

Dogs at Bunratty Castle and Folk Park, the re-creation of a 19th-century village in County Clare.

castle and re-created 19th-century village. It's complete with a school and loaded with active craftspeople. See p. 420.

- **Marble Arch Caves** (Marlbank, County Fermanagh): Adventurous families are guided by boat through well-lit underground waterways to explore caves and view amazing stone formations. See p. 649.

THE best ACTIVE VACATIONS

- **Sailing Ireland's West Coast:** Spectacular coastal scenery, interesting harbor towns, and an abundance of islands make the west coast a delight for cruising sailors. See "Sailing," in chapter 4.
- **Horseback Riding in Donegal:** The wild and woolly coast of Donegal offers the perfect scenic backdrop for trail riding, and as varied a terrain—beaches, countryside, mountains—as you'll find anywhere. See chapter 13.
- **Sea Kayaking in West Cork:** In Skibbereen, Atlantic Sea Kayaking specializes in accompanied trips along the dramatic, rugged coastline of West Cork. There are trips for various levels, so you can play it as safe or as rough as you want. See p. 332.
- **Bicycling in the Southwest:** The peninsulas and islands of Cork and Kerry are perfect for cycling, with an abundance of beautiful places to visit. Roycroft's Cycles in Skibbereen, County Cork, rent bikes that are a notch above the usual rental equipment. See the "Sports & Outdoor Pursuits" sections in chapters 8 and 9.

Bicycles are the optimal means of taking in the head-spinning views along the Conor Pass in County Kerry.

- **Walking the Donegal Coast:** The rugged headlands of Donegal are the most spectacular in Ireland, and the best way to explore them is on foot. Among the finest walks are Slieve League, Malin Head, and Horn Head. See "The Donegal Bay Coast," in chapter 13.

Kinvara, in County Galway, is one of many snug harbors for sailors along Ireland's rugged west coast.

THE best DRIVING TOURS

- **Antrim Coast:** The Antrim Coast is 97km (60 miles) long, stretching north of **Larne** and west past Bushmills and the Giant's Causeway to Portrush. If you start in gorgeous Glenarm, with its castle walls and barbican gate, and head north along the coast from there, the route takes in sweeping views of midnight-blue sea against gray unforgiving cliffs and deep green hillsides. You often have the road mostly to yourself. See chapter 14.
- **Conor Pass** (Dingle Peninsula): The main road from Tralee to Dingle Town takes you 390m (1,300 ft.) above sea level on a road that seems impossibly narrow and rough, but which offers extraordinary views. You may (as we have done) find yourself above the clouds here, and in places you can see for miles. It's an unforgettable drive, especially in the spring or fall, when the weather can create gorgeous skies. See chapter 9.
- **Slea Head Drive** (Dingle Peninsula): This drive, starting from Dingle Town and heading down the Ventry road, follows the sea past a series of ancient ruins, including the Dunbeg Fort. Taking in deep blue ocean views along the way, it brings you to Dunqiun, where you can embark on boats to the Blasket Islands, with their ancient remains. From there you continue on to Gallarus Oratory, and then back to Dingle Town. See chapter 9.
- **Inishowen Peninsula** (County Donegal): This far-flung promontory in the northern outreaches of Ireland stretches out from Lough Foyle to the east and Lough Swilly to the west toward Malin Head, its farthest point. Around the edges are ancient sites, charming villages, and beautiful beaches surrounded by intimidating rocky coves attacked by crashing waves. At its center are gorgeous views, mountains, and quiet, vivid green pastures. If you are looking to get lost, this is a great place to do it. See chapter 13.

THE best LUXURY ACCOMMODATIONS

- **The Clarence** (Dublin; ✆ **01/407-0800;** www.theclarence.ie): Owned by members of the band U2, the Clarence is a perfect mixture of

The award-winning spa at the Park Hotel Kenmare, on the outskirts of Killarney National Park in County Kerry.

sleek sophistication and coolness. Everything here is designed for subtle elegance, from the soft, neutral color schemes, to the luxurious bed linens and huge beds, to the helpful staff. The Octagon Bar is a relaxing hangout, while the Tea Room restaurant is one of the best eateries in town. Its Relax spa will pummel and facial you into relaxation, while the staff members hurry off to find your favorite red wine. Staying here is a real treat. See p. 115.

The Martyn Suite at Gregans Castle Hotel, serving some of Ireland's finest cuisine, in County Clare.

- **Park Hotel Kenmare** (County Kerry; ✆ **800/323-5463** in the U.S., or 064/664-1200 in Ireland; www.parkkenmare.com): In a palm-tree-lined garden beside Kenmare Bay, this imposing 19th-century hotel is grand and luxurious. In the high-ceilinged sitting rooms, fires crackle in the open fireplaces, oil paintings decorate the walls, and there's a full set of armor at the top of the grand staircase surrounded by tapestries and rare antiques. Guest rooms have Georgian and Victorian furnishings and peaceful waterfront or mountain views. The guest-only, in-house spa is extraordinary. See p. 350.
- **Gregans Castle Hotel** (County Clare; ✆ **800/323-5463** in the U.S., or 065/707-7005 in Ireland; www.gregans.ie): Not a castle at all, but an ivy-covered, stone manor house, this small, family-run hotel is filled with light, and has lovely views of the Burren and Galway Bay. The drawing room and expansive hallways are filled with heirlooms, and the walls are decorated with

Raymond Piper's mural paintings of the Burren. Guest rooms are spacious and elegantly decorated in muted colors with antique pieces, and all have expansive views of the gorgeous countryside. Dinners here are outstanding, and worth every penny. See p. 436.

- **Delphi Lodge** (County Galway; ✆ **095/42222;** www.delphilodge.ie): This was once the country hideaway for the marquis of Sligo, and now it can be yours. Inside, the emphasis is on clean, bright simplicity and perfect taste. It's a different kind of luxury—there's no spa here; instead the spectacular setting, at the edge of a lake and at the foot of a lush, green mountain, provides the beauty and the relaxation. "Tranquillity," "comfort," and, well, "fishing" are the operative words here. Whether or not you're an angler, you will want to stay longer than you'd planned—and by renting one of the cottages for a week or more, you can make the indulgence more affordable. See p. 483.
- **Rathmullan House** (County Donegal; ✆ **800/223-6510** in the U.S., or 074/915-8188 in Ireland; www.rathmullanhouse.com): This getaway lies at the end of a long private drive on the banks of the mirrorlike waters of Lough Swilly. Rooms are big and beautifully detailed, with a soft color scheme, claw-foot tubs, and private patios. There are half a dozen drawing rooms in which you can relax on big leather sofas by open fires. The staff is friendly and open, the hotel restaurant is stellar, and the atmosphere is one of pure rural rest and relaxation. See p. 554.

THE best MODERATELY PRICED ACCOMMODATIONS

- **Moy House** (County Clare; ✆ **065/708-2800;** www.moyhouse.com): This unusual 19th-century tower house atop a hill overlooking the sea is beautiful inside and out. Rooms have comfortable, modern beds covered in crisp Irish linens, and are decorated with original paintings and period antiques. Bathrooms are beautifully designed to combine modern conveniences with the building's old architecture (a glass panel in one room provides a look down into an ancient well). Downstairs, the small, attractive dining room serves up excellent food and has a sea view. It's a snug, warm, friendly place to visit. See p. 443.
- **The Bervie** (County Mayo; ✆ **098/43114;** www.bervie-guesthouse-achill.com): Views really don't get any better than this—right at the edge of the sea, overlooking the cliffs across the bay. This cozy retreat is an ideal place to stay for those exploring Ireland's wild west coast. Owners Elizabeth and John Barrett are charming hosts who greet you with fresh scones and will cook you a delightful dinner if you wish. The house is a former coast guard station—as solid as a rock, and as comforting as a security blanket. See p. 508.
- **Temple House** (County Sligo; ✆ **071/918-3329;** www.templehouse.ie): Not a hotel, yet not quite like any other B&B we've stayed in, Roderick and Helena Perceval's grand manor house is an extraordinary place where ceilings soar to the stratosphere, marble stays solidly underfoot, and the family's working farm stretches out for miles around you. A Templar castle lies in ruins on the banks of their lake. They offer amazing breakfasts, and will cook you a wonderful dinner. You can explore their pond, boat on their lake, and

The grounds of Temple House, in County Sligo, encompass the ruins of a Knights Templar castle and a working family farm.

experience a bit of their country idyll. To spend a few days here is to experience a different world. See p. 521.

- **Iskeroon** (County Kerry; ✆ **066/947-5119;** www.iskeroon.com): This charming place sits amid an arrestingly beautiful natural setting, overlooking the sailboats of Derrynane Harbour and the Skelligs beyond. Inside, the 1930s building has been done in fresh Cape Cod style with locally made furniture and linens. It's now self-catering, but they'll bring you the supplies for a fresh, delicious breakfast. See p. 352.
- **Waterloo House** (Dublin; ✆ **01/660-1888;** www.waterloohouse.ie): A classy guesthouse at the edge of central Dublin, Waterloo House has a lovely Georgian look, with a comfortable sunny drawing room where you can read the papers and fluffy white comforters on the bed in your room. A quiet, peaceful option. See p. 126.

THE best BUDGET ACCOMMODATIONS

- **The Bastion** (County Westmeath; ✆ **090/649-4954;** www.thebastion.net): This simple and peaceful guesthouse in the heart of colorful Athlone is a find. Run by brothers Vinny and Anthony McCay, it has a minimalist approach, with clean white walls and crisp white linens contrasted with dark polished wood. The big, rambling house is comfortable, friendly, and perfectly located for touring Athlone, or as a base for exploring the surrounding countryside. See p. 492.
- **Devondell** (County Galway; ✆ **091/528306**): Definitely one of the best value places to stay in Galway Town, this elegant little B&B sits in an upscale

residential district a short stroll from the sea. Breakfasts here are something else. See p. 459.

- **The Shores** (County Kerry; ✆ **066/713-9196**): It's not often you find a place with a private beach for under €100 per night. Views of Tralee Bay from this guesthouse are stunning, especially on a sunny day. Bedrooms are comfortable and well designed, and the breakfast menu will give you a good start to your day. See p. 390.
- **Glencairn Inn** (County Waterford; ✆ **058/56232;** www.glencairninn.com): A cozy farmhouse with a charming country-chic decor, this is a lovely option where rooms are the color of buttermilk, beds are iron or brass, and bathrooms have big, claw-foot tubs. The French owners also run the outstanding Pastis Bistro, where dinners are an event. See p. 269.
- **Wicklow Way Lodge** (County Wicklow; ✆ **01/281-8489**): Set on a peaceful farm with sweeping views of the surrounding countryside, this is one of those places that you can't quite believe you've found for the money. Hosts Seamus and Marilyn Kinlan could hardly make their guests feel more welcome. See p. 218.
- **Tara Lodge** (Belfast; ✆ **028/9059-0900**): This stylish, comfortable little boutique hotel is an excellent find in Belfast, a city not known for the quality of its budget accommodations. Rooms are comfortable and well designed. Try the homemade porridge at breakfast—it's practically legendary. See p. 589.

THE best RESTAURANTS

- **L'Gueuleton** (Dublin; ✆ **01/675-3708**): This place is worth the effort you'll have to put in to book a table well in advance. The cozy dining room is all candlelight, exposed brick walls, polished wood beams, and Prada-clad

Fishy Fishy Café has become a pilgrimage spot for seafood lovers in Kinsale, County Cork.

The Friday buffet at Ballymaloe House, founded by culinary legend Myrtle Allen, in County Cork.

Oysters from Kinsale, Ireland's first stop for traveling gourmands.

clientele. The Irish-French menu changes constantly, but includes warming options such as whole roast sea bass with new potatoes and chive beurre blanc, or venison casserole with juniper and organic root vegetables. See p. 131.

- **Chapter One** (Dublin; ✆ **01/873-2266**): Arguably the city's most atmospheric restaurant, this remarkable eatery fills the vaulted basement space of the Dublin Writers Museum. Artfully lighted and tastefully decorated, it offers a menu with local, organic ingredients, all cleverly used in dishes like the squab pigeon Wellington style, and the hot cured Clare Island salmon with glazed red pepper and crab. Fabulous! See p. 138.
- **The Chart House** (County Kerry; ✆ **066/915-2255**): In this inviting bistro, everyone comes for the confident, simple cooking. Think wonderful comfort food with a flair, such as steak filet with black pudding mash, or roasted pork with brandied apples. And the service is, as the Irish would say, "spot on." See p. 384.
- **Fishy Fishy Café** (County Cork; ✆ **021/470-0415**): This superfriendly little restaurant is *the* place to go for seafood in Kinsale. No reservations, no fuss, just perfectly prepared food, sourced locally. Really local. As in, the waiter can tell you exactly who caught your dinner. See p. 318.
- **The Wild Geese** (County Limerick; ✆ **061/396451**): The emphasis here is simple, but perfect: Start with superb local ingredients and build on that. This is clear in dishes such as the Irish duck confit served on wontons with sesame dressing, the Clare crabmeat soufflé, or grilled salmon with tempura vegetables. See p. 415.

- **Moira's at the Cromleach Lodge** (County Sligo; ✆ **071/916-5155**): Moira's is well situated in the lovely country house of Cromleach Lodge, with panoramic views of Lough Arrow and environs. The menu changes nightly, depending on what is freshest and best from the sea and garden. It may include such dishes as pan-fried fish of the day with lobster tartare and champagne sauce, or grilled filet of beef with shallot and pancetta ragout and confit garlic mash. See p. 522.
- **James Street South** (Belfast; ✆ **028/9043-4310;** www.jamesstreetsouth.co.uk): This fashionable place in Belfast is a hit because of the terrific cooking, which delivers modern classics with an Irish twist. The lamb is always excellent, and shouldn't be missed. Portions are generous, the wine list very good, the crowd rapturous. See p. 591.
- **Deane's** (Belfast; ✆ **028/9033-1134;** www.michaeldeane.co.uk): Owned and run by Irish celebrity chef Michael Deane, this restaurant offers his unique approach to Irish cuisine. Using seasonal, local produce and meats, he creates Irish food with an international twist. The seafood is outstanding, and the desserts are unforgettable. See p. 590.

THE best PUBS

- **Brazen Head** (Dublin): Nearly qualifying as one of Ireland's ancient sites, the Brazen Head, commissioned by Charles II, is more than 300 years old, but its stout is as fresh as it comes. Among its illustrious alumni are Wolfe Tone, Daniel O'Connell, and Robert Emmet, who planned the Dublin rising of 1803 under the Head's low timbers. See p. 182.
- **Abbey Tavern** (Dublin): A short distance from Dublin center, the Abbey Tavern is the perfect place to recover and refuel after spending a day exploring Dublin. The Abbey is known far and wide for its ballads as well as its brew. See p. 186.
- **The Long Valley** (County Cork): For anyone who knows and loves Cork, this is a place of pilgrimage. There's one endless, low-slung room with a bar running its full length, doors taken from an ocean liner, barmen in white butchers' coats, and a selection of delectable sandwiches. It's a slice of heaven. See p. 308.
- **McGann's** (County Clare): Doolin, a dot of a town on the Clare Coast, is a magnet for traditional Irish musicians—and a wonderful spot to hear impromptu sessions of Irish music. Gus O'Connor's, down the road, is

The 300-year-old Brazen Head is Dublin's oldest operating pub.

The pours are as perfect as the seafood at Moran's Oyster Cottage in County Galway.

more famous (but also thicker with tourists); McGann's remains the genuine article without the hype. See p. 445.

- **Moran's Oyster Cottage** (County Galway): Famed for its seafood, this centuries-old thatched-cottage pub on the weir also draws a perfect pint. This may well be the oyster capital of Ireland. It's 19km (12 miles) out of Galway and well worth the drive—or the walk, for that matter. See p. 470.
- **Crown Liquor Saloon** (Belfast): This National Trust pub, across from the Grand Opera House in Belfast, is a Victorian gem. Your mouth will drop open at its antique publican splendor even before you lift your first pint. See p. 593.

The pints come with unlimited eye candy at the Crown Liquor Saloon in Belfast.

THE best WEBSITES

- **Dublin Tourist Office** (www.visitdublin.com): This site is the most comprehensive resource for visiting the capital. We especially like the last-minute booking service, which lets you find out which hotels and guesthouses have immediate availability, as well as which are offering the best discounts.

- **Irelandhotels.com** (www.irelandhotels.com): What catapults this accommodations database ahead of all the others is its "search by facility" function. Gotta have a gym? Need to find a babysitter? Want in-room Wi-Fi for your laptop? No problem. Plug in your requirements and you'll get a list of hotels and guesthouses that fit the bill.
- **Tourism Ireland** (www.discoverireland.ie): Bord Fáilte's site is easy to navigate and extremely informative. It's an excellent place to gather ideas for your trip.
- **AA Roadwatch** (www.aaroadwatch.ie): Planning on driving? The route-planning feature of the Irish Automobile Association's site is brilliantly simple. Plug in a starting point and destination and you'll get a detailed, no-brainer set of directions from A to B.
- **Entertainment Ireland** (www.entertainment.ie): This handy, exhaustive, searchable database includes just about every event in Ireland, from museum exhibitions and rock concerts to new plays and nightclub theme nights—and there are well-written reviews of them all.
- **Irish Family History Foundation** (www.irishroots.net): This comprehensive genealogy resource contains documentation from all 32 counties. Much of the archived information is free for your perusal, or you can avail yourself of researchers.
- **Newshound** (www.nuzhound.com): Hands down, this is the best single resource for keeping up-to-date on Northern Ireland. It's a searchable library of news articles about developments in the North, including a terrific timeline of key events in the troubles. In addition, there are articles on the Republic, as well as travel and dining reviews.
- **Menu Pages** (www.menupages.ie): This online restaurant guide hosts the latest menus, prices, locations, and customer reviews of restaurants in Ireland's biggest towns. The frank reviews by recent customers can be brutally honest. Also, restaurant special offers are featured on the home page daily.

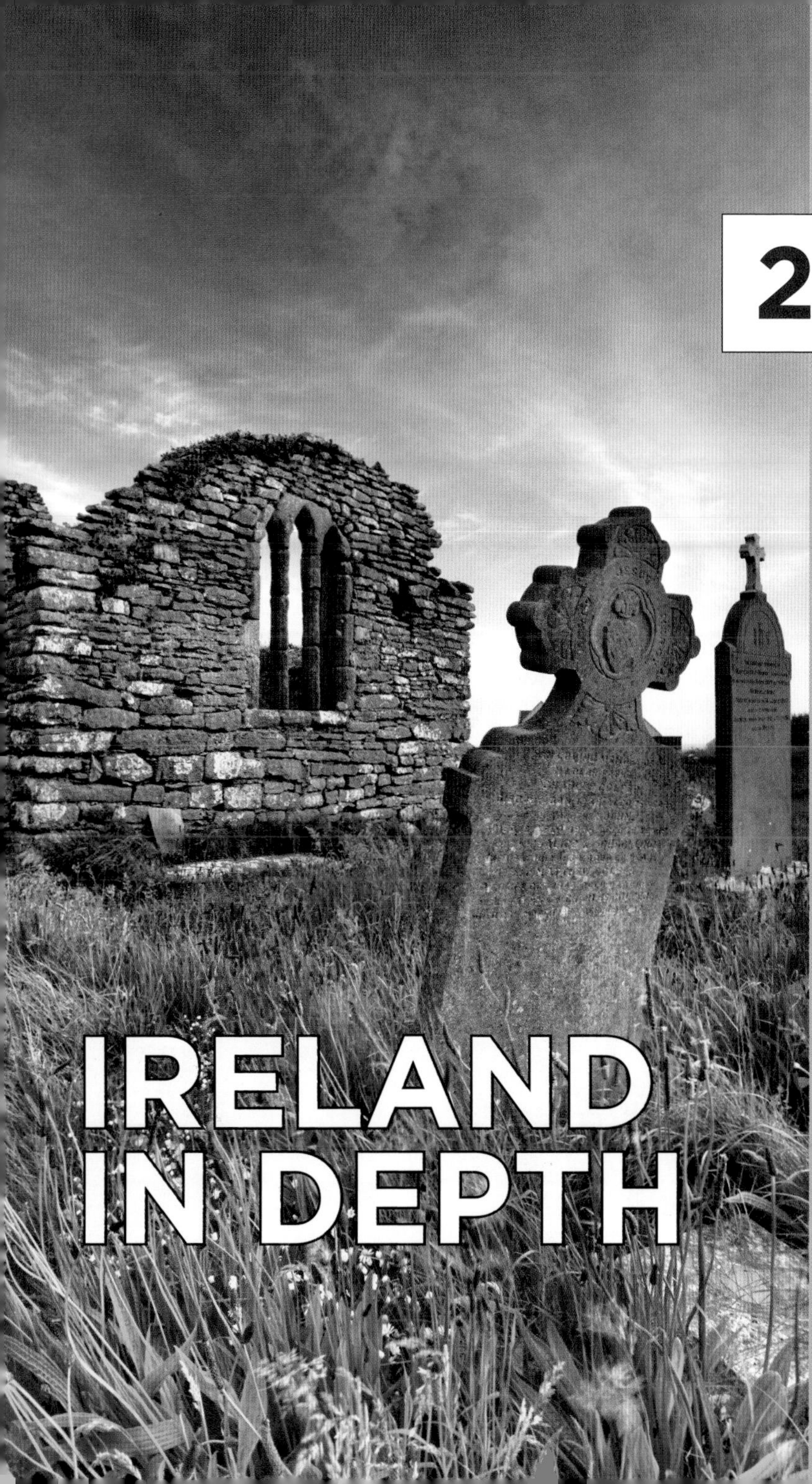

2

IRELAND IN DEPTH

This is a difficult time for Ireland, as it reels from an ongoing economic crisis and struggles to find political and financial equilibrium. In 2011, the country's government collapsed and a new government was elected quickly, but the Irish are clearly worried about where they're headed. A complex, small country with a deeply troubled past, Ireland is rich with history, beauty, and life. Troubled though these days are, this is a fascinating time to visit and see Ireland in transition.

IRELAND TODAY

The Irish boom economy of the late 1990s changed the country monumentally—resulting in an unprecedented spread of unbelievable wealth and a huge amount of property development. The excess associated with the boom—business executives flying from Dublin to Galway in their private helicopters for lunch at a particularly good oyster bar, for example, and small apartments in Dublin selling for millions of euros—always seemed unsustainable. And so it was. As suddenly as the boom started, it ended. Over the course of a few weeks in 2008, the economy crashed, sending the country into an economic and political tailspin. Ireland's

PREVIOUS PAGE: **The grounds of St. Dubhan's Church, on the Hook Peninsula in County Cork.** ABOVE: **A harbinger of Northern Ireland's progress, the renovation of the Merchant Hotel transformed a bank building in downtown Belfast.**

banks were faced with €8 billion worth of bad loans. In a country with only four million residents, that's a catastrophe. The economy continued its freefall in 2009 and 2010. Property prices in Dublin tumbled by 50% over the course of just 18 months. In 2011, the government that led the country into the economic disaster resigned.

This all came as a shock to the Irish, who, after more than 15 years of European investment, had begun to believe their newfound affluence would last forever. As recently as 2007, the country was still pouring money into infrastructure—expanding Dublin's tram system, building new government offices, and improving the national transportation system. The chatter of jackhammers formed a constant aural background in nearly every town in the Republic, and the dump truck seemed to be the national symbol of Ireland, as the huge vehicles trundled along by the dozen, carrying tons of gravel and sand to be used laying new roads and building new neighborhoods. But there was little sense to Ireland's growth mania as construction far outpaced demand. Entire subdivisions were built with nobody to live in them—thousands of new homes sat empty. Developers gambling on future growth built shining new ghost towns. At the same time, property prices were so high, families crowded into tiny two-bedroom apartments, and parents commuted long distances to work in city centers where they couldn't afford to live.

Now, it seems, birdsong is returning to Ireland. But it is a changed country—littered with unneeded subdivisions and apartment complexes, dotted with soulless glass office buildings. For a while, property prices made many Irish people millionaires—at least, on paper. Now the plunging prices have left millions of families in negative equity. The crash was so sudden, tales spread of people driving to unemployment offices in €30,000 sports cars.

At the same time, the peace that had held in the North since 1998 was shattered in 2009 by a series of brutal sectarian murders in the North. In the subsequent years, low-level violence has continued. An IRA splinter group opposed to the peace agreement calling itself "the Real IRA" claimed responsibility for most of the attacks, and several people have been arrested. Although the violence was nowhere near the levels experienced in the 1970s, it still sent a shiver down the spine of those living in both the Republic and the North, as they remembered how fragile peace can be on this island. Even before the recent outbreak, this was always the kind of place where you looked over your shoulder when you talked, even in the most inoffensive terms, about religion or politics.

In 2011, with a new government, and Enda Kenny as new taoiseach, or prime minister, the Irish hoped to put the economic nightmare behind them. Experts think the process could take years, though. Possibly decades. And Ireland may never be as wealthy as it was for a few short years during the boom. But it will survive. It has been through worse.

THE MAKING OF IRELAND

THE FIRST SETTLERS With some degree of confidence, we can place the date of the first human habitation of the island somewhere after the end of the last ice age, around the late 8000s B.C.

Ireland's first colonizers, Mesolithic Homo sapiens, walked, waded, or floated across the narrow strait from what is now Britain in search of flint and, of course, food.

The next momentous prehistoric event was the arrival of Neolithic farmers and herders, sometime around 3500 B.C. The Neolithic "revolution" was the first of many to come to Ireland a bit late, at least 5,000 years after its inception in the ancient Near East. The domestication of the human species—settled life, agriculture, animal husbandry—brought with it a radically increased population, enhanced skills, stability, and all the implications of leisure. Unlike Ireland's Mesolithic hunters, who barely left a trace, this second wave of colonizers began to transform the island at once. They came with stone axes that could fell a good-size elm in less than an hour. Ireland's hardwood forests receded to make room for tilled fields and pastureland. Villages sprang up, and more permanent homes, planked with split oak, appeared at this time.

Far more striking, though, was the appearance of massive megalithic monuments, including court cairns, dolmens (stone tables), round subterranean passage tombs, and wedge tombs. There are thousands of these scattered around Ireland, and to this day only a small percentage of them have been excavated. These megalithic monuments speak volumes about the early Irish. To visit Newgrange and Knowth in the Boyne Valley and Carrowmore in County Sligo is to marvel at the mystical practices of the early Irish. Even today little is known about the meaning of these mysterious stone remnants of their lives.

Early Celtic inhabitants of the island assumed that the tremendous stones and mounds were raised by giants. They called them the people of the *sí,* who eventually became the *Tuatha Dé Danann,* and, finally, fairies. Over many generations of oral tradition, the mythical people were downsized into "little people," who were believed to have led a magical life, mostly underground, in the thousands of *raths,* or earthwork structures, coursing the island like giant mole tunnels. All of these sites were believed to be protected by the fairies, and to tamper with them was believed to bring great bad luck, so nobody ever touched them. Thus they have lasted to this

DATELINE

ca. 8000 B.C. Earliest known human settlers arrive in Ireland.

2000 B.C. First metalworkers come to Ireland.

ca. 700 B.C. Celtic settlement of Ireland begins.

ca. A.D. 100 The Gaels arrive in Ireland, naming one of their biggest settlements *Dubhlinn.*

A.D. 432 Traditional date of St. Patrick's return to Ireland as a Christian missionary.

500–800 Ireland becomes one of the largest centers of Christianity in Europe—often referred to as the "Golden Age."

795 First Viking invasion.

841 Vikings build a sea fort in the area of modern-day Dublin.

853 Danes take possession of the Norse settlement.

1014 Battle of Clontarf. High king of Ireland, Brian Boru, defeats the Vikings.

A glass pyramid marks the site of Céide Fields, a Neolithic farm settlement preserved for 5 millennia under a bog in County Mayo.

day—ungraffitied, undamaged, unprotected by any visible fences or wires, but utterly safe.

THE CELTS Of all the successive waves of outsiders who have, over the years, shaped, cajoled, and pockmarked the timeline of Irish history, none have made quite such a deep-seated impact as that of the Celts. They came in waves, the first perhaps as early as the 6th century B.C. and continuing until the end of the 1st millennium. They fled from the Roman invasion and clung to the edge of Europe—Ireland being, at the time, about as far as you could go to elude a Roman force. In time, they controlled the island and absorbed into their culture everyone they found there. Their ways—and their genes—dominated. They brought iron weapons; chariots; cults and contests; and poetry, music, and other forms of artistic genius, all of which took root and flourished in Irish soil.

1167–71 Forces of English King Henry II seize Dublin and surrounding areas.

1204 Dublin Castle becomes center of English power.

1297 First parliamentary sessions in Dublin.

1300s First great plague kills a third of the population of Dublin.

1500s English rule consolidated across Ireland. Henry VIII proclaims himself king of Ireland.

1534–52 Henry VIII begins suppression of Catholic Church in Ireland.

1558–1603 Reign of Elizabeth I. Ireland proclaimed an Anglican country. The "plantation" of Munster divides Ireland into counties.

1591 Trinity College founded.

1607 The flight of the Irish earls, marking the demise of the old Gaelic order.

1641 Irish Catholic revolt in Ulster led by Sir Phelim O'Neill ends in defeat.

1649 Oliver Cromwell invades and begins the reconquest of Ireland.

continues

The unshakeable remains of Dún Aengus, a prehistoric fort on Inishmore, in the Aran Islands.

Despite their cultural potency, however, the Celts developed little in the way of centralized government, existing instead in a near-perpetual state of division and conflict with one another. The island was divided among as many as 150 tribes, grouped under alliances to five provincial kings. The provinces of Munster, Leinster, Ulster, and Connaught date from this period. They fought fiercely among themselves over cattle (their "currency" and standard of wealth), land, and women. None among them ever ruled the entire island, though not for lack of trying. One of the most impressive monuments from the time of the warring Celts is the stone fortress of Dún

DATELINE *continued*

- **1690** The forces of King James II, a Catholic, are defeated at the Battle of the Boyne, consolidating Protestant order in England.
- **1691** Patrick Sarsfield surrenders Limerick. He and some 14,000 Irish troops, the "Wild Geese," flee to the Continent.
- **1704** Enactment of first Penal Laws. Apartheid comes to Ireland.
- **1778** The Penal Laws are progressively repealed.
- **1782** The Irish Parliament is granted independence.
- **1791** Wolfe Tone founds the Society of the United Irishmen.
- **1796–97** Wolfe Tone launches an invasion from France, fails, is taken captive, and commits suicide.
- **1798** "The Year of the French." A French invasion force is defeated at Killala Bay. General Humbert surrenders to Cornwallis.
- **1801** The Irish Parliament is induced to dissolve itself. Ireland becomes part of the United Kingdom.
- **1803** Twenty-five-year-old Robert Emmet is hanged after his

Aengus, on the wind-swept hills of the Aran Islands.

THE COMING OF CHRISTIANITY The Celtic chiefs neither warmly welcomed nor violently resisted the Christians who came ashore beginning in the 5th century A.D. Although threatened, the pagan Celts settled for a bloodless rivalry with this new religion. In retrospect, this may have been a mistake.

A detail from the Book of Kells, in Trinity Library, Dublin.

Not the first, but eventually the most famous, of these Christian newcomers was a man called Maewyn Succat, a young Roman citizen torn from his Welsh homeland in a Celtic raid and brought to Ireland as a slave, where he was forced to work in a place called the Forest of Foclut (thought to be around modern County Antrim). He escaped on a ship bound for France, where he spent several years as a priest before returning to Ireland as a missionary. He began preaching at sacred Celtic festivals, a tactic that frequently led to confrontations with religious and political leaders, but eventually he became such a popular figure with the people of Ireland that after his death in 461, a dozen clan chiefs fought over the right to bury him. His lasting legacy was, of course, the establishment in Ireland of one of the strongest Christian orthodoxies in Europe—an achievement for which he was later beatified as St. Patrick.

uprising of fewer than 100 men is a tragic failure.

1829 Daniel O'Connell secures passage of the Catholic Emancipation Act. He is later named lord mayor of Dublin.

1845–c.52 The Great Famine. An estimated two million Irish either die or emigrate, mostly to the U.S.

1848 The revolt of the Young Irelanders ends in failure.

1858 The Irish Republican Brotherhood, a secret society known as the Fenians, is founded in New York.

1866 In an imaginative publicity stunt, a minuscule army of Fenians attempts to invade Canada.

1879 Michael Davitt founds the National Land League to support the claims of tenant farmers.

1879–82 The "land war" forces the enactment of reform. The tenant system unravels; land returns to those who work it.

1886 and 1894 Bills for Home Rule are defeated in Parliament.

1893 The Gaelic League is founded to revive the Irish language.

continues

Ireland's conversion to Christianity was a somewhat negotiated process. The church at the time of St. Patrick was, like the man who brought it, Roman. To Ireland, an island then still without a single proper town, the Roman system of dioceses and archdioceses didn't apply to the way they lived. So the Irish adapted the church to their own situation. They built isolated monasteries with extended monastic "families," each more or less autonomous. The pope, like an Irish high king, was to them like an ordained prizefighter—he was expected to defend his title, one challenge after another, or lose it.

Ireland flourished in this fashion for several centuries, and became a center of monastic learning and culture. Monks and scholars were drawn to it in droves, and they were sent out in great numbers as well, to Britain and the Continent as emissaries for the island's way of thinking and praying.

As the historian Thomas Cahill wrote in *How the Irish Saved Civilization* (Nan A. Talese, 1995), "Wherever they went the Irish brought with them their books, many unseen in Europe for centuries and tied to their waists as signs of triumph, just as Irish heroes had once tied to their waists their enemies' heads." And they worked with a fervor; in fact, they worked so hard that the Irish penned more than half the biblical commentaries written worldwide between A.D. 650 and 850.

Like their megalithic ancestors, these monks left traces of their lives behind, and these have become enduring monuments to their spirituality. Early monastic sites such as gorgeous Glendalough in County Wicklow, wind-swept Clonmacnois in County Offaly, and isolated Skellig Michael off the Kerry coast give you an idea of how they lived, while striking examples of their work can be seen at Trinity College (which houses the Book of Kells) and at the Chester Beatty museum at Dublin Castle.

THE VIKING INVASIONS The monastic city-states of early medieval Ireland might have continued to lead the world's intellectual process, but the Vikings came along and ruined everything. After centuries of relative peace, the first

DATELINE *continued*

1904 The Abbey Theatre opens in Dublin.

1905–08 Founding of Sinn Fein ("We Ourselves") with close links to the Irish Republican Brotherhood.

1912 Third Home Rule bill passes in the House of Commons and is defeated by the House of Lords.

1916 Patrick Pearse and James Connolly lead an armed uprising on Easter Monday to proclaim the Irish Republic. Defeat is followed by the execution of 15 leaders of the revolt.

1918 Sinn Fein wins a landslide election victory against the Irish Parliamentary Party.

1919 Sinn Fein, led by Eamon de Valera, constitutes itself as the first Irish Dáil and declares independence.

1919–21 The Irish War of Independence. Michael Collins commands the Irish forces.

1921 Anglo-Irish Treaty. Ireland is partitioned. Twenty-six counties form the Free State; the other six remain a part of the U.K. The Free wave of Viking invaders arrived in A.D. 795. The wealthy nonviolent Irish monasteries were among their first targets. Unprepared and unprotected, the monasteries, which had amassed collections of gold, jewels, and art from followers and thinkers around the world, were decimated. The round towers to which the monks retreated for safety were neither high enough nor strong enough to protect them and their treasures from the onslaught.

Once word spread of the wealth to be had on the small island, the Scandinavian invaders just kept on coming, but much as they were experts in the arts of pillage and plunder, one thing of which they had no knowledge was literature. They didn't know how to read. Therefore, they paid scant attention to the magnificent books they came across, passing them over for more obvious riches. This fortunate quirk of history allowed the monks some means of preserving their dying culture—and their immeasurably valuable work—for the benefit of future generations.

Of course, the Vikings did more than hit and run. They settled down and took over much of the country—securing every major harbor on Ireland's east coast with a fortified town. These were the first real towns in Ireland: In addition to Dublin, they also founded Cork, Waterford, and the river city of Limerick. They had plundered the country fairly thoroughly by the time the Irish, always disinclined to unite, did so at last, and managed to push out the Vikings after a decisive military campaign lead by the army of Brian Boru in 1014. When the Vikings departed, they left their towns behind, forever altering the Irish landscape. The legacy of the Vikings in Ireland is complex, and a visit to Dublin's Wood Quay and the city walls of Waterford is a good introduction to their influence.

With the Vikings gone, Ireland enjoyed something of a renewal in the 11th and 12th centuries. Its towns grew, its regional kings made successive unsuccessful bids to unite the country under a single high kingship, and its church came under increased pressure to conform to the Vatican's rules. All of these factors would play a part in ripening Ireland for the next invasion.

State adopts its first constitution a year later.

1922–23 The Irish civil war, between the government of the Free State and those who opposed the Anglo-Irish treaty. Michael Collins is assassinated by the IRA, who saw the treaty as a sellout.

1932 Eamon de Valera leads Fianna Fáil to victory and becomes head of government.

1937 The Free State adopts a new constitution, abandoning membership of the British Commonwealth and changing the country's official name to Eire.

1939 Dublin is bombed by Germany at start of World War II, but Ireland remains neutral.

1948 The Republic of Ireland Act. Ireland severs its last constitutional links with Britain.

1955 Ireland is admitted into the United Nations.

1963 U.S. President John F. Kennedy visits Dublin.

continues

The Vikings may have been gone, but prosperous and factionalized Ireland made attractive prey to other nations, and it was, tragically, an Irish king who opened the door to the next predator. Diarmait Mac Murchada, king of Leinster, whose ambition was to be king of all of Ireland, decided he could do it, with a little help. So he called on Henry II, the Norman king of England. Diarmait offered Henry a series of incentives in return for military aid: Not only did he bequeath his eldest daughter to whoever led the army, but he also offered them overlordship of the Kingdom of Leinster. To put it bluntly, he made Henry an offer he couldn't refuse. So it was that an expeditionary force, led by the Earl of Pembroke, Richard de Clare—better known as Strongbow—was sent to Diarmait's aid. After the successful invasion and subsequent battles in which Strongbow emerged victorious, he remained in Ireland as governor, and thus gave the English their first foothold in Ireland. What Diarmait did not realize, of course, was that they would never leave.

THE NORMAN INVASION In successive expeditions from 1167 to 1169, the Normans, who had already conquered Britain, crossed the Irish Sea from England with crushing force. The massive Norman fortifications at Trim are a powerful reminder of the sheer power the invaders brought with them. During the next century, the Norman-English settled in, consolidating their power in new towns and cities. Indeed, many settlers grew attached to the island, and did their best to integrate with the local culture. Marriages between the native Irish and the invaders became commonplace. Over the next couple of centuries, they became more Irish and less English in their loyalties.

In 1314 Scotland's Robert the Bruce defeated the English at Bannockburn and set out to fulfill his dream of a united Celtic kingdom. He installed his brother Edward on the Irish throne, but the constant state of war took a heavy toll. Within 2 years, famine and economic disorder had eroded any

DATELINE *continued*

1969 Violence breaks out in Northern Ireland. British troops are called in.

1972 In Derry a peaceful rally turns into "Bloody Sunday." The Northern Irish Parliament is dissolved, and direct rule imposed from Britain.

1973 Ireland joins the European Community.

1986 The Anglo-Irish Agreement gives the Republic a say in the government of Northern Ireland.

1990 Mary Robinson is elected Ireland's first female president.

1994 The IRA announces a cease-fire, and the Protestant paramilitaries follow suit. Commencement of peace talks.

1995 The British and Irish governments issue "A New Framework for Agreement," and U.S. President Bill Clinton makes a historic visit to Ireland, speaking to large crowds in Belfast and Derry. He is received with enthusiasm in the Republic.

1996 The IRA breaks its cease-fire. An IRA bomb in Omagh kills 29. The

The Oliver Cromwell mural on a gable in Belfast.

public support Edward might have enjoyed. By the time he was defeated and killed at Dundalk in 1317, few were prepared to mourn him.

Over the next 2 centuries, attempts to rid Ireland of its English overlords fell short. Independent Gaelic lords in the north and west continued to maintain their territories. By the close of the 15th century, English control of the island was effectively limited to the Pale, a walled and fortified cordon around what is now greater Dublin. (The phrase "beyond the pale" comes from this—meaning anything that is uncontrollable or unacceptable.)

North sees the worst rioting in 15 years.

1997 The IRA declares a new cease-fire. Sinn Fein enters inclusive all-party peace talks designed to bring about a comprehensive settlement.

1998 The all-party peace talks conclude with the so-called Good Friday Agreement, later strongly supported in referendums held on the same day in the Republic and the North. John Hume and David Trimble are awarded the Nobel Peace Prize.

1999 The implementation of the agreement is blocked by a Unionist demand—"in the spirit" but contrary to the letter of the Good Friday Agreement—that IRA decommissioning precede the appointment of a new Northern Ireland executive. The peace process stalls until November, when the new power-sharing Northern Ireland Executive is established.

2000 The IRA issues a statement saying it will decommission its arms. In May, power is restored to the institutions established by the Good Friday Agreement.

continues

ENGLISH POWER & THE FLIGHT OF THE EARLS During the reign of the Tudor monarchs in England (1485–1603), the brutal reconquest of Ireland was set in motion. Henry VIII was the first to proclaim himself king of all Ireland—something even his warlike ancestors had stopped short of doing—but it wasn't until later that century that the claim was backed up by force. Elizabeth I, Henry's daughter, declared that all Gaelic lords in Ireland must surrender their lands to her, with the dubious promise that she would immediately grant them all back again—unsurprisingly, the proposition was hardly welcomed in Ireland, and a rebel army was raised by Hugh O'Neill and "Red" Hugh O'Donnell, two Irish chieftains.

Despite significant victories early on in their decade-long campaign, most notably over a force led by the Earl of Essex, whom Elizabeth had personally sent to subdue them, by 1603 O'Neill was left with few allies and no option but to surrender, which he did on March 23, the day before Elizabeth died. O'Neill had his lands returned, but constant harassment by the English prompted him, along with many of Ireland's other Gaelic lords, to sail for Europe on September 14, 1607, abandoning their lands and their aspirations for freedom.

THE COMING OF CROMWELL By the 1640s, Ireland was effectively an English plantation. Family estates had been seized and foreign (Scottish) labor brought in to work them. A systematic persecution of Catholics, which began with Henry VIII's split from Rome but did not die with him, barred Catholics from practicing their faith. Resentment against the English and their punitive laws led to fierce uprisings in Ulster and Leinster in 1641, and by early 1642 most of Ireland was again under Irish control. Unfortunately for the rebels, any hope of extending the victories was destroyed by internal disunion and by the eventual decision to support the Royalist side in the English civil war. In 1648 King Charles I of England was beheaded, and the victorious commander of the parliamentary forces, Oliver Cromwell, was installed as ruler. Soon his supporters were taking on his enemies

DATELINE *continued*

2001 David Trimble threatens to resign as Ulster Unionist party leader if the IRA does not decommission as promised. The IRA doesn't; Trimble resigns in June. Following a surge of feeling in the wake of the September 11 terrorist attacks on the U.S., IRA decommissioning begins.

2002 The peace process continues amid sectarian violence on both sides.

2004 Irish government passes smoking ban in all public indoor spaces. U.S. President George W. Bush arrives for E.U.-U.S. Summit and is greeted with anti–Iraq War protests.

2005 A £27-million bank robbery in Northern Ireland—thought to be the work of an IRA splinter group—leads to the withdrawal of the region's entire currency stocks. David Trimble loses his parliamentary seat, but hard-line parties Sinn Fein and the Democratic Unionist Party (DUP) do extremely well. The IRA in Ireland. A year later, the Royalists' stand collapsed in defeat at Rathmines, just south of Dublin.

Defeat for the Royalist cause did not, however, mean the end of the war. Cromwell became paranoid that Ireland would be used to launch a French-backed insurgency if it was not brought to heel, and he detested the country's Catholic beliefs. So it was that as the hot, sticky summer of 1649 drew to a close, Cromwell set sail for Dublin, bringing with him an army of 12,000 men, and a battle plan so ruthless that it remains notorious to this day.

In the town of Drogheda, more than 3,552 Irish soldiers were slaughtered in a single night. When a group of men sought sanctuary in the local church, Cromwell ordered the church burned down with them locked inside—an act of such monstrosity that some of his own men risked a charge of mutiny and refused the order. On another day, in Wexford, more than 2,000 were murdered, many of them civilians. The trail of destruction rolled on, devastating counties Galway and Waterford. When asked where the Irish citizens could go to be safe from him, Cromwell famously suggested they could go "to hell or Connaught"—the latter being the most far-flung, rocky, and unfarmable part of Ireland.

After a rampage that lasted 7 months, killing thousands and leaving churches, monasteries and castles in ruins, Cromwell finally left Ireland in the care of his lieutenants and returned to England. Hundreds of years later, the memory and lore of his extraordinary violence lingers painfully in Ireland. In certain parts of the country, people still spit at the mention of his name.

THE PENAL LAWS Cromwell died in 1658, and 2 years later the English monarchy was restored, but the anti-Catholic oppression continued. In 1685, though, something quite remarkable happened. Contrary to the efforts of the English establishment, the new king, James II, refused to relinquish his Catholic faith after ascending to the throne. It looked for a while as if things

decommissioning process is officially declared complete, and the IRA disbands as a paramilitary unit.

2007 A power-sharing executive is put into place in Northern Ireland, bringing together lifelong enemies DUP leader Ian Paisley and Sinn Fein leader Gerry Adams.

2008 Ireland's economy begins to crash as the country becomes the first in the E.U. to officially enter recession.

2009 A series of sectarian murders in Northern Ireland threatens the peace process, though virtually all sides unite in condemnation.

2010 British prime minister David Cameron apologized for "Bloody Sunday"—when British soldiers killed 14 Irish protesters in Bogside, a Catholic neighborhood in Derry, Northern Ireland, in 1972.

2011 Longtime ruling party Fianna Fáil is swept out of office on a wave of voter anger, replaced by Fine Gael. New taoiseach Enda Kenny vows to restore Irish economic stability.

could change in Ireland, and that the Catholics might have found a new ally in the unlikeliest of quarters. However, such hopes were dashed 3 years later, when James was ousted from power, and the Protestant William of Orange installed in his place.

James fled to France to raise support for a rebellion, then sailed to Ireland to launch his attack. He struck first at Derry, to which he laid siege for 15 weeks before finally being defeated by William's forces at the Battle of the Boyne. The battle effectively ended James's cause, and with it, the hopes of Catholic Ireland for the best part of a century.

After James's defeat, English power was once more consolidated across Ireland. Protestant landowners were granted full political power, while laws were enacted to effectively immobilize the Catholic population. Being a Catholic in late-17th-century Ireland was not exactly illegal per se, but in practice life was all but impossible for those who refused to convert to Protestantism. Catholics could not purchase land, and existing landholdings were split up unless the families who owned them became Protestants; Catholic schools were banned, as were priests and all forms of public worship. Catholics were barred from holding any office of state, practicing law, or joining the army. Those who still refused to relinquish their faith were forced to pay a tax to the Anglican church, and by virtue of not being able to own land, the few who previously had been allowed to vote certainly were not anymore.

The new British landlords settled in, planted crops, made laws, and sowed their own seeds. Inevitably, over time, the "Anglos" became the Anglo-Irish. Hyphenated or not, they were Irish, and their loyalties were increasingly unpredictable. After all, an immigrant is only an immigrant for a generation; whatever the birthright of the colonists, their children would be Irish-born and bred. And so it was that an uncomfortable sort of stability set in for a generation or three, albeit of a kind that was very much separate and unequal. There were the haves—the wealthy Protestants—and the have-nots—the deprived and disenfranchised Catholics.

A kind of unhappy peace held for some time. But by the end of the 18th century, the appetite for rebellion was whetted again. To understand why, one need look no further than the intellectual hotbed that flourished among the coffee shops and lecture halls of Europe's newest boomtown: Dublin.

WOLFE TONE, THE UNITED IRISHMEN & THE 1798 REBELLION By the 1770s, Dublin was thriving as never before. As a center for culture and learning, it was rivaled only by Paris and London; thanks to the work of such architects as Henry Gratton (who designed Custom House, the Kings Inns, and the Four Courts), its very streets were being remodeled in a grand, neoclassical style that was more akin to the great cities of southern Italy than of southern Ireland.

However, while the urban classes reveled in their newfound wealth, the stringent Penal Laws that had effectively cut off the Catholic workers from their own countryside forced many of them to turn to the city for work. In Dublin's buzzing intellectual scene political dissent soon brewed, and even after a campaign by Irish politicians led to many of the Penal Laws being repealed in 1783, Dublin was a breeding ground for radicals and political activists. The results were explosive.

When war broke out between Britain and France in the 1790s, the United Irishmen—a nonviolent society formed to lobby for admission of Catholic Irishmen to the Irish Parliament—sent a secret delegation to persuade the French to intervene on Ireland's behalf against the British. Their emissary in this venture was a Dublin lawyer named Wolfe Tone. In 1796 Tone sailed with a French force bound for Ireland and determined to defeat forces loyal to the English crown, but they were turned back by storms.

In 1798, though, full-scale insurrection led by the United Irishmen did spread across much of Ireland, particularly the southwestern counties of Kilkenny and Wexford, where a tiny republic was briefly declared in June. But it was crushed by Loyalist forces, which then went on a murderous spree, killing tens of thousands of men, women, and children, and burning towns to the ground. The nadir of the rebellion came when Wolfe Tone, having raised another French invasion force, sailed into Lough Swilley in Donegal, but was promptly captured by the British. At his trial, wearing a French uniform, Tone requested that he be shot, in accordance with the rights of a foreign soldier, but when the request was refused, he suffered a more gruesome end. While waiting for the gallows, he slit his own throat in jail; however, he missed the jugular vein, instead severing his windpipe, leading to a slow and painful death 8 days later. His last words were reputed to have been: "It appears, sir, that I am but a bad anatomist."

The rebellion was over. In the space of 3 weeks, more than 30,000 Irish had been killed. As a final indignity in what became known as "The Year of the French," the British tricked the Irish Parliament into dissolving itself, and Ireland reverted to strict British rule.

The apprehension of Irish revolutionary Wolfe Tone.

A CONFLICT OF CONFLICTS In 1828 a Catholic lawyer named Daniel O'Connell, who had earlier formed the Catholic Association to represent the interests of tenant farmers, was elected to the British Parliament as Member of Parliament for Dublin. Public opinion was so solidly behind him that he was able to persuade the British prime minister that the only way to avoid a civil war in Ireland was to force the Catholic Emancipation Act through Parliament. He remained an MP until 1841, when he was elected Lord Mayor of Dublin, a platform he used to push for repeal of the direct rule imposed from London after the 1798 rebellion.

O'Connell organized enormous rallies (nicknamed "monster meetings") attended by hundreds of thousands, and provoked an unresponsive conservative government to such an extent that it eventually arrested him on charges of seditious conspiracy. The charges were dropped, but the incident—coupled with growing impatience toward his nonviolent approach of protest and reform—led to the breakdown of his power base. "The Liberator," as he had been known, faded, his health failed, and he died on a trip to Rome.

THE GREAT FAMINE Even after the anti-Catholic legislation began to recede, the vast majority of farmland available to the poor, mostly Catholic population of the countryside was harsh, and difficult to cultivate. One of the few crops that could be grown reliably was the potato, which effectively became the staple diet of the rural poor. So when, in 1845, a fungus destroyed much of the potato crop of Ireland, it is not difficult to understand the scale of the devastation this caused. However, to label the Great Irish Famine of the 1840s and 50s as a "tragedy" would be an incomplete description. It was, of course, tragic—undeniably, overwhelmingly so—but at the same time, the word implies a randomness to the whole sorry, sickening affair that fails to capture its true awfulness. The fact is that what started out as a disaster was turned into a devastating crisis by the callous response of an uninterested British establishment.

As the potato blight worsened, it became apparent to many landlords that their farm tenants would be unable to pay rent. In order to offset their financial losses, they continued to ship grain overseas, in lieu of rent from their now-starving tenants. The British Parliament, meanwhile, was reluctant to send aid, putting the reports of a crisis down to, in the words of Prime Minister Robert Peel, "the Irish tendency to exaggerate."

Of course, as people started to die by the thousands, it became clear to the government that something had to be done, and emergency relief was sent to Ireland in the form of cheap, imported Indian cornmeal. However, this contained virtually no nutrients, and ultimately contributed to the spread of such diseases as typhus and cholera, which were to claim more victims than starvation itself.

To make matters worse, the cornmeal was not simply given to those in need of it. Fearful that handouts would encourage laziness among a population they viewed as prone to that malaise, the British government forced people to work for their food. Entirely pointless make-work projects were initiated, just to give the starving men something to do for their cornmeal; roads were built that led nowhere, for instance, and elaborate follies constructed that served no discernible purpose, some of which still litter the countryside today, memorials to cruelty and ignorance.

AN BHFUIL GAEILGE AGAT? (DO YOU speak IRISH?)

Ireland has two official languages, Irish Gaelic and English. Today English is still the first and most commonly spoken language for the vast majority of the Irish people. But there was at time when that wasn't the case. In 1835 the Irish-speaking population of Ireland was reckoned at four million. The British suppressed the language—forbidding its use and teaching—so thoroughly that soon few could remember it. When the 2002 census was taken, just under 60,000 Irish residents said they spoke Gaelic.

There is a huge and emotional pro-Irish-language movement underway in Ireland right now—one that is disproportionate to the actual number of Irish speakers (although the popularity of the language is growing, particularly among the young, as all Irish children now learn Gaelic in school). All Irish citizens are now entitled by law to conduct any official business with the state (legal proceedings, university interviews, and filing taxes, for example) in Gaelic. Increasingly, street signs are in both Gaelic and English, and many towns are reverting to their Gaelic names (which often bear no resemblance to their old English names).

Areas of the country (counties Kerry, Galway, and Donegal in particular) where Gaelic is widely spoken are Gaelic protection zones called **Gaeltacht,** and in those areas all English words have been removed from road signs, warning signs, and street signs. This has cartographers moving as rapidly as possible (which, unfortunately, isn't *that* fast) to rewrite maps in order to keep up, but the simple fact is you're likely to have a map that still calls the Dingle "Dingle," rather than the name that all the street signs now call it: "An Daingean." And even the cartographers won't tell you the Gaelic word for "Caution."

The growing Gaeltacht movement in Ireland is increasingly aggressive, with a bit of a nationalistic bent, and its proponents want to make no exceptions to the strict anti-English rules on signage for the millions of tourists who visit the island every year. This means that visitors are more likely to find themselves utterly lost—clutching a map in which the town's names are all in English, and standing in a town in which all street names are in Gaelic. Should this happen to you, don't hesitate to ask for help—all Irish residents who speak Gaelic also speak English, and most are very sympathetic to the plight of nonresidents who do not know this complex, ancient language.

One of the most difficult things to comprehend a century and a half later is the sheer futility of it all. For behind the statistics, the memorials, and the endless personal anguish, lies perhaps the most painful truth of all: that the famine was easily preventable. Enormous cargoes of imported corn sat in Irish ports for months, until the British government felt that releasing them to the people would not adversely affect market rates. Meanwhile, huge quantities of meat and grain were exported from Ireland. (Indeed, in 1847, cattle exports went up 33% from the previous year.)

Given the circumstances, it is easy to understand why so many chose to leave Ireland. More than a million emigrated over the next decade, about three-quarters of them to America, the rest to Britain or Europe. They drained the country. In 1841, Ireland's population was 8 million; by 1851 it was 6.5 million.

THE STRUGGLE FOR HOME RULE As the famine waned and life returned to something like normality, the Irish independence movement gained new momentum. New fronts opened up in the struggle for Home Rule, both violent and nonviolent, and, significantly, the Republicans now drew considerable support from overseas—particularly from America. There, groups such as the Fenians fund-raised and published newspapers in support of the Irish cause, while more audacious schemes, such as an 1866 "invasion" of Canada with fewer than 100 men, amounted to little more than publicity stunts, designed to raise awareness for the cause.

The Irish Declaration of Independence, on display in the General Post Office, Dublin.

Back home in Ireland, partial concessions were won in Parliament, and by the 1880s, nationalists such as the MP for Meath, Charles Stewart Parnell, were able to unite various factions of Irish nationalists (including the Fenian Brotherhood in America) to fight for Home Rule. In a tumultuous decade of legislation, he came close, but revelations about his long affair with Kitty O'Shea, the wife of a supporter, brought about his downfall as a politician.

By 1912, a bill to give Ireland Home Rule was passed through the British House of Commons, but was defeated in the House of Lords. Many felt that the political process was still all but unstoppable, and that it was only a matter of time before the bill passed fully into law and effective political independence for Ireland would be secured. However, when the onset of World War I in 1914 forced the issue onto the back burner once again, many in the Home Rule movement grew tired of the political process.

THE EASTER REBELLION On Easter Monday 1916, a group of nationalists occupied the General Post Office in the heart of Dublin, from which they proclaimed the foundation of an Irish Republic. Inside were 1,500 fighters, led by schoolteacher and Gaelic League member Patrick Pearse and Socialist leader James Connolly.

The British, nervous at an armed uprising on its doorstep while it fought a massive war in Europe, responded with overwhelming force. Soldiers were sent in, and a battle raged in the streets of Dublin for 6 days before the leaders of the rebellion were captured and imprisoned. There are still bullet holes in the walls of the post office and the buildings and statues up and down O'Connell Street. Pearse, Connolly, and 12 other leaders were imprisoned, secretly tried, and speedily executed.

Ultimately, though, the British reaction was as counterproductive as it was harsh. The totality with which those involved in organizing the rebellion were pursued and dispatched acted as a lightning rod for many of those who had been undecided about the effectiveness of a purely political struggle. Indeed, a fact that has become somewhat lost in the ensuing hundred or so years since Patrick Pearse stood on the steps of the post office early on that cold Monday morning, reading a treatise on Irish independence, is that a great many Irish didn't support the rebellion at the time. Many either believed that the best course of action was to lie low until the war had ended, when concessions would be won as a result, or that it was simply the wrong thing to do, as long as sons of Ireland were sacrificing their lives in the trenches of Europe.

The aftermath of 1916 all but guaranteed, for better or for worse, that Ireland's future would be decided by the gun.

REBELLION A power vacuum was left at the heart of the nationalist movement after the Easter Rising, and it was filled by two men: Michael Collins and Eamon de Valera. On the surface, both men had much in common; Collins was a Cork man who had returned from Britain in order to join the Irish Volunteers (later to become the Irish Republican Army, or IRA), while de Valera was an Irish-American math teacher who came back to Ireland to set up a new political party, Sinn Fein.

> **Impressions**
>
> ***You cannot conquer Ireland. You cannot extinguish the Irish passion for freedom. If our deed has not been sufficient to win freedom, then our children will win it by a better deed.***
>
> **—Patrick Pearse (1879–1916)**

When de Valera's party won a landslide victory in the general election of 1918, its MPs refused to sit in London, instead proclaiming the first Dáil, or independent parliament, in Dublin. De Valera went to rally support for the cause in America, while Collins stayed to concentrate on his work as head of the Irish Volunteers. Tensions escalated into violence, and for the next 2 years, Irish nationalists fought a tit-for-tat military campaign against the British in Ireland.

The low point of the struggle came in 1920, when Collins ordered 14 British operatives to be murdered in their beds, in response to which British troops opened fire on the audience at a football game at Croke Park in Dublin, randomly killing 12 innocent people. A truce was eventually declared on July 9, 1921, and 6 months later, the Anglo-Irish treaty was signed in London, granting legislative independence to 26 Irish counties (known together as the Irish Free State). The compromise through which that freedom was won, though, was that six counties in the north would remain part of the United Kingdom. Collins knew that compromise would not be accepted by the more strident members of his rebel group. And he knew they would blame him for agreeing to it in the first place. When he signed the treaty he told the people present, "I am signing my own death warrant."

As he feared, nationalists were split between those who accepted the treaty as a platform on which to build, and those, led by the nationalist de Valera, who saw it as a betrayal, and would accept nothing less than

Eamon de Valera beneath a portrait of his rival, Michael Collins.

Tony Blair and Bertie Ahern shake hands after the Good Friday peace talks in Belfast.

immediate and full independence at any cost. Even the withdrawal of British troops from Dublin for the first time in nearly 800 years did not quell their anger. The result was an inexorable slide into civil war. The flashpoint came in April 1922, when violence erupted around the streets of the capital, and rolled on for 8 days until de Valera's supporters were forced to surrender.

The government of the fledgling free state ordered that Republicans be shot on sight, leading to the deaths of 77 people. And Collins had been right about his own fate: Four months later he was assassinated while on a visit to his childhood home.

The fallout from the civil war dominated Irish politics for the next decade. De Valera split from the Republicans to form another party, Fianna Fáil ("the Warriors of Ireland"), which won the election of 1932 and governed for 17 years. Despite his continuing dedication to the Republican ideal, however, de Valera was not to be the one who finally declared Ireland a republic, in 1948; ironically, that distinction went to a coalition led by de Valera's opponent, Douglas Hyde, whose victory in the election of 1947 was attributed to the fact that de Valera had become too obsessed with abstract Republican ideals to govern effectively.

STUCK IN NEUTRAL One of the more controversial, not to say morally ambiguous, decisions that Eamon de Valera made while in office was to stay neutral during World War II, despite the best efforts of Winston Churchill and Franklin Roosevelt to persuade him otherwise. The basis for his decision—a combination of Ireland's size and economic weakness, and the British presence in Northern Ireland—may have made sense to some extent, but it left Ireland in the peculiar position of tacitly favoring one side in the war, but refusing to help it. After the death of Adolf Hitler in April 1945, de Valera alienated the Allies further by sending his personal sympathies to the German ambassador.

His reticence didn't find much favor among the Irish population either. During the war, as many as 300,000 Irish men found ways to enlist in the British or U.S. armies. In the end, more than 50,000 Irish soldiers perished in a war their country had refused to join.

TROUBLE ON THE WAY After the war, 2 decades passed without violence in Ireland, until the late 1960s once more saw the outbreak of sectarian conflict in the North. What started out as a civil rights movement, to demand greater equality for Catholics within Northern Ireland, soon escalated into a cycle of violence that lasted for 30 years.

It would be a terrible oversimplification to say that the Troubles were merely a clear-cut struggle between those who wanted to complete the process of Irish unification and those who wanted to remain part of the United Kingdom, although that was, of course, the crux of the conflict. Factors such as organized crime and terrorism, together with centuries-old conflicts over religious, land, and social issues, make the conflict even harder for outsiders to understand.

The worst of the Troubles came in the 1970s. In 1972, British troops inexplicably opened fire on a peaceful demonstration in Derry, killing 12 people—many of whom were shot while they tended to the wounds of the first people injured. The IRA took advantage of the mood of public outrage to begin a civilian bombing campaign on the British mainland. The cycle of violence continued for 20 years, inexorably and depressingly, while all the while, none of the myriad sides in the conflict would talk to each other. Finally, in the early 1990s, secret talks were opened between the British and the IRA, leading to an IRA cease-fire in 1994 (although the cease-fire held only shakily—an IRA bomb in Omagh 4 years later killed 29, the most to die in any single incident of the Troubles).

The peace process continued throughout the 1990s, helped significantly by the mediation efforts of U.S. President Bill Clinton, who arguably became more involved in Irish affairs than any president before him until, eventually, on Good Friday 1998, a peace accord was finally signed in Belfast. The agreement committed all sides to a peaceful resolution of the conflict in Northern Ireland, and included the reinstatement of full self-government for the region in a power-sharing administration. It stopped short of resolving the territorial issue once and for all—in other words, Northern Ireland is still part of the U.K., and will be for the foreseeable future. On the contrary, to some extent the conflicts rage more bitterly and more divisively than ever before, the difference being that, with notable exceptions, they are fought through the ballot box, rather than the barrel of a gun. In 2005 the IRA fully decommissioned its weapons, and officially dissolved itself as a paramilitary unit.

The peace held until 2009, when violence again broke out in the North, and as this book was going to press, efforts were underway to stop the North from spinning again into a tailspin of attack and counterattack.

But in 2010, after an investigation that took 12 years and cost nearly £195 million, all 13 people killed on Bloody Sunday were officially cleared of any wrongdoing. Britain's new prime minister, David Cameron, said, "There is no doubt. There is nothing equivocal. There are no ambiguities.

What happened on Bloody Sunday was both unjustified and unjustifiable. It was wrong."

While Northern Ireland still struggled to find peace, the Republic of Ireland flourished. The 1990s brought unprecedented wealth and prosperity to the country, thanks in part to European Union subsidies, and partly to a thriving economy, which acquired the nickname "the Celtic Tiger" for its new global strength. But that too came crashing down in 2009, as the property market crashed and the economy crumbled, as detailed in the introduction to this chapter. The country was scrambling to find firm economic ground as this book was being written. But that firm ground was proving awfully hard to find.

IRELAND IN POPULAR CULTURE

Books

FICTION Ireland is one of the most written-about places in the world. If you're looking to read about the country before your trip, you're going to be busy.

If you're especially ambitious, you could bite off James Joyce's *Ulysses,* a classic to be certain, but a famously impenetrable one. Some Joycean classics that are a bit easier to dip into include *Dubliners,* a book of short stories about the titular city, and *A Portrait of the Artist as a Young Man.*

Dive into the absorbing books and plays of Brendan Behan with *Borstal Boy,* his semi-autobiographical book about growing up as a member of the IRA. Also good is his play *Quare Fellow.*

If you're headed out into the Irish countryside, you might want to pick up a copy of W. B. Yeats's *Collected Poems,* since the view you're about to see is the same one that inspired him.

Of modern writers, among the best loved are Maeve Binchy (*Dublin 4*); J.P. Donleavy (whose book *The Ginger Man,* about a drunken Trinity College student, was banned by the Catholic Church); Roddy Doyle (whose book *The Commitments,* about aspiring Irish musicians, became a top-grossing film); and Jennifer Johnston, who addressed the tension between Protestants and Catholics in *How Many Miles to Babylon?* You can also try Edna O'Brien (*The Country Girls*) for bawdy laughs, Flann O'Brien (*At-Swim-Two-Birds*) for hilarious writing about writing, and Liam O'Flaherty, whose *The Informer* is a thriller about a veteran of the civil war.

Respected expat novelists include Irish journalist and novelist Colm Tóibín (*The Heather Blazing* and *The Master*) and Colum McCann (*Let the Great World Spin*).

NONFICTION Two excellent books by Tim Pat Coogan, *The Irish Civil War* (2001) and *The Troubles: Ireland's Ordeal 1966–1996 and the Search for Peace* (1997), are essential reading for anyone wanting to understand the complexities of 21st-century Ireland. For a look at modern Ireland, try John Ardagh's *Ireland and the Irish* (1997), or F. S. Lyons's *Ireland Since the Famine* (2009). To understand more about the famine, try Cecil Woodham-Smith's *The Great Hunger* (1992). It's viewed as the definitive, dispassionate examination of what really happened.

A still from the animated feature film, *The Secret of Kells.*

Film

Although lots of movies have been made about Ireland, not very many *good* movies have been made about Ireland. Here are a few exceptions. *Michael Collins* (directed by Neil Jordan, 1996) is a fine biopic about the Irish rebel, filmed largely on location. *Maeve* (directed by John Davis and Pat Murphy, 1982) is widely viewed as one of Ireland's first proper independent films. It addresses the lives of the young amid sectarian violence. *Veronica Guerin* (directed by Joel Schumacher, 2003) is a dark, fact-based film with Cate Blanchett about a troubled investigative reporter on the trail of a drug boss.

In a cheerier vein, *Wild About Harry* (2000) is a romantic comedy about a philandering TV host, while *Intermission* (2003) is a lively romance featuring Colin Farrell talking in his own accent. *The Commitments* (1990) may be the most famous Irish musical yet made, but *Once* (2007) is a touching, Oscar-winning portrait of two struggling young musicians busking on Dublin's streets.

Music

Music is inescapable in Ireland, and if you hear a band play in a bar and you like them, we strongly advise you to buy a CD from them. Some local faves include Damien Rice *(O)*, who did play in bars until he became a superstar a couple of years ago. The Irish folk singer Christy Moore *(Live at the Point)* is still widely viewed as one of the greatest ever. Barry McCormack has been winning accolades from critics for his *We Drank Our Tears.* David Kitt is one of Dublin's top songwriters; check out his *Big Romance.* The Frames, led by singer/guitarist Glen Hansard, have been playing on the Dublin scene for years, and you can join their devoted followers by buying *Cost.* Finally, Adrian Crowley's *When You Are Here, You Are Family,* is a warm and delightful folksy album worth owning. Obviously, traditional music is still alive and well in Ireland, particularly in close association with Irish step dancing. The folk culture is primarily found outside of Dublin, although some pubs in the city do still showcase traditional music. There's also

A session of traditional Irish music at Auld Dubliner, in the capital.

Cultúrlann na hÉireann, which offers much in the way of traditional Irish performances. Similarly, in Galway the **Taibhdhearc Theatre** offers a program of traditional music, dance, and plays. In County Kerry, **Siamsa Ti** offers a mixture of Irish music, dance, and mime. For a less formal atmosphere, check out local pubs in small towns, which almost always can be counted on to host Irish music and sometimes dancing, too.

EATING & DRINKING IN IRELAND

Restaurants

Restaurants in Ireland have become surprisingly expensive in recent years, and even with the economic crash it's still rather difficult to find good places that do not charge an average of €25 for a main course. On the plus side, restaurants are varied and interesting here—settings range from old-world hotel dining rooms, country mansions, and castles to sky-lit terraces, shop-front bistros, riverside cottages, thatched-roof pubs, and converted houses. Lately, appreciation has grown for creative cooking here, with an emphasis on locally grown produce and meat.

Before you book a table, here are a few things you should know.

RESERVATIONS Except for self-service eateries, informal cafes, and some popular seafood spots, most restaurants encourage reservations; most expensive restaurants require them. In the most popular eateries, Friday and Saturday nights are often booked up a week or more in advance, so have a few options in mind if you're booking at the last minute and want to try out the hot spots.

Tip: If you stop into or phone a restaurant and find that it is booked from 8 or 8:30pm onward, ask if you can dine early (at 6:30 or 7pm), with a promise to leave by 8pm. It works sometimes.

PRICES Meal prices at restaurants include taxes (13.5% VAT in the Republic of Ireland and a 17.5% VAT in Northern Ireland). Many restaurants include the tip as a service charge added automatically to the bill (it's usually listed at the bottom, just before the bill's total). It usually ranges from 10% to 13%.

When no service charge is added, tip around 12% or so, depending on the quality of the service. But do check your bill, as some unscrupulous restaurants do not make it clear that you have already tipped, thus encouraging you to accidentally do so twice.

The price categories used in this book are based on the price of a complete dinner (or lunch, if dinner is not served) for one person, including tax and tip, but not wine or alcoholic beverages:

Very Expensive €50 and up
Expensive €35 to €50
Moderate €17 to €34
Inexpensive Under €17

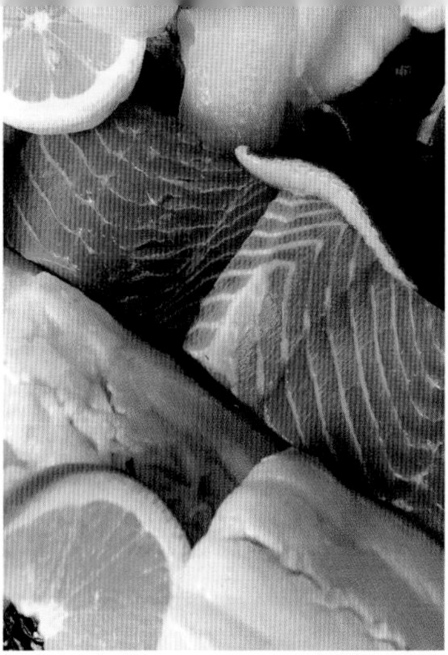
In Kinsale, a spread of fresh fish and seafood—key ingredients in Ireland's culinary renaissance.

DINING TIPS Don't be surprised if you are not ushered to your table as soon as you arrive at some upscale restaurants. This is not a delaying tactic—many of the better dining rooms carry on the old custom of seating you in a lounge while you sip an aperitif and peruse the menu. Your waiter then comes to

Dining Bargains

Despite the economic bust, restaurant prices are still generally absurdly high, largely because of taxes, but partly for reasons of hubris. Nobody is more aware of this than the Irish. Here are some strategies they use (and you can too) to keep meal costs down.

If you want to try a top-rated restaurant but can't afford dinner, have your main meal there in the middle of the day by trying the set-lunch menu. You'll experience the same great cuisine at half the price of a nighttime meal. The latest economic troubles have seen restaurants competing for customers by offering more set-price meals, early-bird specials (sometimes through the whole evening, or every night early in the week), and other discount enticements. Keep an eye out for them.

Alternatively, try an inexpensive lunch in a cafe or a pub. Pub food is usually a lot better than its name suggests; the menu usually includes a mix of sandwiches and traditional Irish food, including stews and meat pies. In recent years, many pubs have converted or expanded into restaurants, serving excellent, unpretentious meals at (somewhat) reasonable prices. ***But beware:*** Some pubs have taken advantage of rising restaurant prices to raise their own prices—check the menu before you sit down at a table (most places post them by their doors).

Supermarkets and grocery stores in Ireland sell good premade sandwiches (these are much better than similar supermarket sandwiches in the U.S.) for a few euros. These can make a good, cheap lunch or dinner. Coffee shops also sell sandwiches for a few euros, and muffins for even less (for a quick, cheap breakfast).

A perfect pour in a National Trust setting at Belfast's Crown Liquor Saloon.

discuss the choices and to take your order. You are not called to the table until the first course is about to be served. You are not under an obligation to have a cocktail, of course. It's perfectly fine to order a soft drink or just a glass of water.

Pubs

The pub continues to be a mainstay of Irish social life. There are pubs in every city, town, and hamlet. Most people have a "local"—a favorite pub near home—where they go for a drink and some conversation with neighbors, family, and friends. Pubs are not bars—they are more about socializing than drinking, and many people you see in the pub are just having a soft drink (lime cordial and soda water is a particular favorite, or orange juice and lemon soda). So feel free to go to the pub, even if you don't drink alcohol. It's a good way to meet locals.

PUB HOURS The Republic of Ireland's drinking hours were extended a couple of years ago, a mere 2 centuries after they were first created. Gone are the days when all pubs closed at 11pm. Now pubs set their own hours. Most still close by 11:30pm, but some stay open until 2am, and most stay open throughout the day (laws previously required pubs to close from 2–4pm). After normal pub hours, nightclubs and discos keep going to the wee hours.

You'll notice that when the dreaded "closing time" comes, nobody clears out of the pub. That's because the term is a misnomer. The "closing time" is actually the time when the barmen must stop serving alcohol, so expect to hear a shout for "Last orders!" or, occasionally, the marvelous if antiquated "Time, gentlemen, please!" Anyone who wants to order his or her last drink does so at that point. The pubs don't actually shut their doors for another 20 to 30 minutes. When the time comes to really close, the bartenders will shout "Time to leave!" lights will be turned up brightly, and people make their way to the doors.

In the North, the laws have also changed recently to allow pubs to stay open later, although most still close at 11pm on Monday to Thursday. On Friday and Saturday nights, many pubs stay open until midnight or 1am, and a few even later than that—particularly in large towns and cities.

WHEN TO GO

A visit to Ireland in the summer is very different from a trip in the winter. Apart from climatic considerations, there are the issues of cost, closures, and crowds. Generally speaking, in summer, airfares, car-rental rates, and hotel prices are highest and crowds at their most intense. But the days are long (6am sunrises and 10pm sunsets), the weather is warm, and every sightseeing attraction and B&B is open. In winter, you can get rock-bottom prices on airfare and hotels. But it will rain and the wind will blow, and many rural sights and a fair proportion of the rural B&Bs and restaurants will be closed.

All things considered, we think the best time to visit is in spring and fall, when weather falls in between bad and good, but you get lower-than-high-season prices and the crowds have yet to descend.

Weather

Rain is the one constant in Irish weather, although a bit of sunshine is usually just around the corner. The best of times and the worst of times are often only hours, or even minutes, apart. It can be chilly in Ireland at any time of year, so think *layers* when you pack.

Winters can be brutal, as the wind blows in off the Atlantic with numbing constancy, and gales are common. But deep snow is rare, and temperatures rarely drop much below freezing. In fact, Ireland is a fairly temperate place: January and February bring frosts but seldom snow, and July and August are very warm, but rarely hot. The Irish consider any temperature over 68°F (20°C) to be "roasting," and below 34°F (1°C) as bone chilling. For a complete online guide to Irish weather, consult **www.ireland.com/weather**.

Average Monthly Temperatures in Dublin

	JAN	FEB	MAR	APR	MAY	JUNE	JULY	AUG	SEPT	OCT	NOV	DEC
TEMP (°F)	36–46	37–48	37–49	38–52	42–57	46–62	51–66	50–65	48–62	44–56	39–49	38–47
TEMP (°C)	2–8	3–9	3–9	3–11	6–14	8–17	11–19	10–18	9–17	7–13	4–9	3–8

Holidays

The Republic observes the following national holidays: New Year's Day (Jan 1); St. Patrick's Day (Mar 17); Easter Monday (variable); May Day (May 1); first Mondays in June and August (summer bank holidays); last Monday in October (autumn bank holiday); Christmas (Dec 25); and St. Stephen's Day (Dec 26). Good Friday (the Fri before Easter) is mostly observed, but not statutory.

In the North, the schedule of holidays is the same as in the Republic, with some exceptions: The North's summer bank holidays fall on the last Monday of May and August; the Battle of the Boyne is celebrated on Orangeman's Day (July 12); and Boxing Day (Dec 26) follows Christmas.

In both Ireland and Northern Ireland, holidays that fall on weekends are celebrated the following Monday.

Ireland Calendar of Events

This sampling of events is drawn from 2011 schedules. Many events had not set their 2012 and 2013 dates at the time this book was being written. The most up-to-date listings of events can be found at **www.discoverireland.ie** and **www.entertainment.ie** for Ireland, and **www.eventguide.ie** and **www.visitdublin.com** for Dublin.

For an exhaustive list of events beyond those listed here, check **http://events.frommers.com**, where you'll find a searchable, up-to-the-minute roster of what's happening in cities all over the world.

JANUARY

Funderland. Royal Dublin Society, Ballsbridge, Dublin 4. An annual indoor fun fair, complete with white-knuckle rides, carnival stalls, and family entertainment (✆ **01/283-8188;** www.funfair.ie). December/January. (Also smaller events in Cork, Limerick, and Belfast later in the year; check the website for details.)

Yeats Winter School. Sligo Park Hotel, Sligo Town. This event offers a weekend of relaxation, lectures, and a tour of Yeats Country (✆ **071/914-2693;** www.yeats-sligo.com). Late January.

FEBRUARY

Dublin International Film Festival. Irish Film Centre, Temple Bar, Dublin 2, and various cinemas in Dublin. More than 100 films are featured, with screenings of the best in Irish and world cinema, plus seminars and lectures on filmmaking, lately sponsored by Jameson whiskey (✆ **01/662-4620;** www.jdiff.com). Late February.

MARCH

St. Patrick's Dublin Festival. Held around St. Patrick's Day itself, this massive 4-day festival is open, free, and accessible to everyone. Street theater, carnival acts, sports, music, fireworks, and other festivities culminate in Ireland's grandest parade, with marching bands, drill teams, floats, and delegations from around the world (✆ **01/676-3205;** www.stpatricksday.ie). On and around March 17.

St. Patrick's Day Parades. Held all over Ireland and Northern Ireland, celebrating Ireland's patron saint. March 17.

APRIL

Pan Celtic Festival. County Donegal. For 5 days, the wider Celtic family (including Cornwall, Isle of Man, Scotland, Wales, and Brittany) unites for culture, song, dance, sports, and parades with marching bands and pipers. There are also lots of fringe events, from nature walks to poetry readings (**www.panceltic.ie**). March/April.

Samhlaíocht Chiarrai/Kerry Arts Festival. Tralee, County Kerry. A spring festival of music, food, literature, crafts, film, performance, and visual art. Running at the same time is the **Bumblebee Festival,** a largely hands-on program of activities for kids (✆ **066/712-9934;**www.samhlaiocht.com). Late April.

World Irish Dancing Championships. Gleneagle Hotel, Killarney. The premier international competition in Irish dancing features more than 4,000 contenders from as far away as New Zealand (✆ **01/814-6298;** www.clrg.ie). April.

MAY

Belfast City Marathon. An epic 42km (26-mile) race of 6,000 international runners through the city. It starts and finishes at Maysfield Leisure Centre (✆ **028/9060-5944;** www.belfastcitymarathon.com). Early May.

May Day Races. Down Royal Racecourse, Maze, Lisburn, County Antrim. One of the major events on the horse-racing calendar (✆ **028/9262-1256;** www.downroyal.com). Early May.

Wicklow Arts Festival. Hot on the heels of the Gardens Festival, this is Wicklow's other big spring event, held over 5 days in Wicklow Town. There are dozens of music, theater, art, and literary events, many of which are free (www.wicklowartsfestival.ie). Early May.

JUNE

Murphy's Cat Laughs Comedy Festival. Various venues in Kilkenny Town. Past performers at this international festival of stand-up comedy include American comics Bill Murray, George Wendt, and Emo Phillips, and Ireland's Dara O'Briain (✆ **056/776-3837;** www.thecatlaughs.com). Early June.

Music Festival in Great Irish Houses. Various venues throughout counties Dublin, Wicklow, and Kildare. This 10-day festival of classical music performed by leading Irish and world-renowned international artists is intimately set in the receiving rooms of stately buildings and mansions (✆ **01/664-2822;** www.musicgreatirishhouses.com). Early June.

Taste of Ireland. Iveagh Gardens, Dublin. Visitors to this 4-day celebration of all things food-related can sample dishes prepared by some of the country's top chefs. Best to book in advance as the event is usually a sellout—and consider wearing elastic-waistband pants (✆ **01/210-9290;** www.tastefestivals.ie). Mid-June.

Bloomsday Festival. Various Dublin venues. This unique day of festivity celebrates Leopold Bloom, the central character of James Joyce's *Ulysses.* Every aspect of the city, including the menus at restaurants and pubs, duplicates the aromas, sights, sounds, and tastes of Joyce's fictitious Dublin on June 16, 1904, the day when all of the action in *Ulysses* takes place. Ceremonies are held at the James Joyce Tower and Museum; guided walks visit Joycean sights. Contact the James Joyce Centre, 35 N. Great George's St., Dublin 1 (✆ **01/878-8547;** www.jamesjoyce.ie). June 16.

Cork Midsummer Arts Festival. Emmet Place, Cork City. The program includes musical performances and traditional Irish *céilí* bands, and always has a strong literary content. Bonfire nights are particularly popular (✆ **021/421-5131;** www.corkfestival.com). Mid- to late June.

Irish Derby. The Curragh, County Kildare. This is Ireland's version of the Kentucky Derby or Royal Ascot and is a fashionable gathering (***hint:*** jackets for men, posh hats for women) of racing fans from all over the world. It's one of the richest and most definitive middle-distance horse races in Europe. Booking recommended (✆ **045/441205;** www.curragh.ie). Late June.

Killarney SummerFest. Fitzgerald Stadium, Killarney, County Kerry. This (mainly rock) music festival gets bigger every year and is one of the highlights of the Irish summer of music. Past performers have included Bryan Adams and Sheryl Crow. Fringe events include street entertainment and art workshops. (✆ **064/71560;** www.killarneysummerfest.com). Late July/early August.

County Wicklow Gardens Festival. In the county known as the "garden of Ireland," stately heritage properties and gardens open their gates to visitors on selected dates. Contact Wicklow County Tourism (✆ **0404/20070;** www.visitwicklow.ie). Entire summer, kicks off in June.

JULY

Oxegen. Punchestown Racecourse, County Kildare. This (mainly rock) music festival is now one of Europe's premier summer music fests, with nearly 100 acts playing on five stages during 1 weekend. Previous headliners have included Coldplay and Eminem. For tickets, contact **www.ticketmaster.ie** or **www.oxegen.ie**. Early July.

The Temple Bar Summer Sensational. Dublin 2. This 4-day festival features street theater, film, photography, and music, all set amid the backdrop of

Dublin's most cultured district (✆ **01/677-2255;** www.templebar.ie). Mid-July.

Battle of the Boyne Commemoration. Belfast and other cities. This annual event, often called Orangeman's Day, recalls the historic battle between two 17th-century kings. It's a national day of parades by Protestants all over Northern Ireland; most have a celebratory atmosphere, although some parades still turn nasty in West Belfast and Derry, so proceed with caution. Contact the House of Orange, 65 Dublin Rd., Belfast BT2 7HE (✆ **028/9032-2801**). July 12.

Galway Arts Festival & Races. Galway City and Racecourse. This 2-week fest is a shining star on the Irish arts scene, featuring international theater, concerts, literary evenings, street shows, arts, parades, music, and more. The famous Galway Races follow, with 5 more days of racing and merriment, music, and song (✆ **091/509700;** www.galwayartsfestival.ie). Mid- to late July.

Lughnasa Fair. Carrickfergus Castle, County Antrim. A spectacular revival with a 12th-century Norman castle and its grounds, this event features people in period costumes, medieval games, traditional food, entertainment, and crafts (✆ **028/9335-1273**). Late July/early August.

AUGUST

Fáilte Ireland Horse Show. RDS Showgrounds, Ballsbridge, Dublin 4. This is the most important equestrian and social event on the Irish national calendar. Aside from the daily dressage and jumping competitions, highlights include a fashionable ladies' day, nightly formal hunt balls, and the awarding of the Aga Khan Trophy and the Nation's Cup (✆ **01/668-0866;** www.dublinhorseshow.ie or www.rds.ie). Early August.

Kilkenny Arts Festival. Kilkenny Town. This weeklong event has it all, from classical and traditional music to plays, one-person shows, readings, films, poetry, and art exhibitions (✆ **056/775-2175;** www.kilkennyarts.ie). August.

Puck Fair. Killorglin, County Kerry. Each year the residents of this tiny Ring of Kerry town capture a wild goat and enthrone it as "king" over 3 days of merrymaking that include open-air concerts, horse fairs, parades, and fireworks. This is one of Ireland's oldest festivals (✆/fax **066/976-2366;** www.puckfair.ie). August 10 to August 12.

Rose of Tralee International Festival. Tralee, County Kerry. A gala atmosphere prevails at this 5-day event, with a full program of concerts, street entertainment, horse races, and a beauty-and-talent pageant leading up to the televised selection of the "Rose of Tralee" (✆ **066/712-1322;** http://roseoftralee.ie). Late August.

National Heritage Week. More than 400 events are held throughout the country—walks, lectures, exhibitions, music recitals, and more (✆ **056/777-0777;** www.heritageweek.ie). Late August.

Fleadh Cheoil na hÉireann. Tullamore, County Offaly. This has been Ireland's premier summer festival of traditional music since 1951, with competitions held to select the all-Ireland champions in all categories of instruments and singing. Note that the website address is year-specific; we presume it will be different for 2012 and 2013 (✆ **087/936-5059;** www.fleadh2011.ie). Late August/early September.

SEPTEMBER

Lisdoonvarna Matchmaking Festival. Lisdoonvarna, County Clare. Still the biggest and best singles' event after all these years, this traditional "bachelor" festival carries on in the lovely spa town of Lisdoonvarna, with lots of wonderful music and dance (✆ **065/707-4005;** www.matchmakerireland.com). September/October.

All-Ireland Hurling & Gaelic Football Finals. Croke Park, Dublin 3. The finals of Ireland's most beloved sports, hurling and Gaelic football, are Ireland's equivalent of the Super Bowl. If you can't be at Croke Park, experience this in the full bonhomie of a pub. You can find information at **www.gaa.ie**, or obtain tickets through Ticketmaster (✆ **01/836-3222;** www.ticketmaster.ie). September.

Irish Antique Dealers' Fair. RDS Showgrounds, Ballsbridge, Dublin 4. Ireland's premier annual antiques fair, with hundreds of dealers from all over the island (✆ **01/679-4147;** www.iada.ie). Late September/early October.

Galway International Oyster Festival. Galway and environs. Find out why London's *Sunday Times* put it on its "Top 12 World's Best Event List." A haven for oyster aficionados from across the globe, its highlights include the World Oyster Opening Championship, a grand opening parade, a yacht race, an art exhibition, a gala banquet, traditional music, and, of course, lots of oyster eating (✆ **091/587992;** www.galwayoysterfest.com). Late September.

Dublin Theatre Festival. Theaters throughout Dublin. Showcases for new plays by every major Irish company (including the Abbey and the Gate), plus a range of productions from abroad (✆ **01/677-8439;** www.dublintheatrefestival.com). Late September/mid-October.

OCTOBER

Kinsale International Gourmet Festival. Kinsale, County Cork. The foodie capital of Ireland hosts this well-respected annual fest, featuring special menus in all the restaurants and plenty of star chefs in town from abroad. (✆ **021/477-3571;** www.kinsalerestaurants.com). October.

Baboró International Arts Festival for Children. Galway. A fun-filled, educational festival geared to kids 3 to 12 years of age, with theater, music, dance, museum exhibitions, and literary events (✆ **091/562667;** www.baboro.ie). Late October.

Guinness Cork Jazz Festival. Cork City. Ireland's second city stages a first-rate festival of jazz, with an international lineup of live acts playing in hotels, concert halls, and pubs (✆ **021/427-8979;** www.guinnessjazzfestival.com). Late October.

Kinsale Fringe Jazz Festival. Meanwhile, not to be outdone, nearby Kinsale plays host to its own concurrent fringe jazz festival (✆ **021/477-2234;** http://kinsale.ie). Late October.

Dublin City Marathon. On the last Monday in October, more than 5,000 runners from both sides of the Atlantic and the Irish Sea participate in this popular run through the streets of the capital (✆ **01/623-2250;** www.dublinmarathon.ie). Late October.

Wexford Festival Opera. Theatre Royal, Wexford City. This is not your average stuffy opera festival. Famous as much for the jubilant, informal atmosphere as for the acclaimed productions of lesser known 18th- and 19th-century operatic masterpieces, the festival also offers classical music concerts, recitals, and more. (✆ **053/912-2144;** www.wexfordopera.com). Late October/early November.

Belfast Festival at Queen's. Queen's University, Belfast. Ireland's largest arts festival attracts enormous crowds each year for its stellar program of drama, opera, music, and film (✆ **028/9097-1197;** www.belfastfestival.com). There's also a concurrent **fringe festival** in the Cathedral Quarter (✆ **028/9027-0466**). October/November.

NOVEMBER

Murphy's Cork International Film Festival. Cinemas throughout Cork. Ireland's oldest film festival offers a plethora of international features, documentaries, short films, and special programs (✆ **021/427-1711;** www.corkfilmfest.org). Mid-November.

DECEMBER

Killarney Christmas Market. Fair Hill, Killarney, County Kerry. Killarney gets very enthusiastic indeed about the festive season, so it's unsurprising that it should host some of the region's best Christmas markets, devoted mainly to quality local crafts and food (✆ **064/663662;** www.christmasinkillarney.com). Various dates in December.

12 Days of Christmas Market. IFSC, Dublin. Now part of the traditional run-up to Christmas in Dublin, this huge event all but takes over Docklands. Mostly it's an opportunity to shop (there are over 100 different traders), but there's also a traditional-style fairground, and festive food and drink aplenty (✆ **01/818-3300;** www.docklands.ie). Mid-December.

Limerick Christmas Racing Festival. Limerick Racecourse, Greenpark, Limerick. Four days of holiday horse racing (✆ **061/320000;** www.limerickraces.ie). Late December.

RESPONSIBLE TRAVEL

Responsible tourism is conscientious travel. It means being careful with the environments you explore, and respecting the communities you visit. Two overlapping components of responsible travel are **eco-tourism** and **ethical tourism.** The **International Ecotourism Society (TIES)** defines eco-tourism as responsible travel to natural areas that conserves the environment and improves the well-being of local people. TIES suggests that eco-tourists follow these principles:

- Minimize environmental impact.
- Build environmental and cultural awareness and respect.
- Provide positive experiences for both visitors and hosts.
- Provide direct financial benefits for conservation and for local people.
- Raise sensitivity to host countries' political, environmental, and social climates.
- Support international human rights and labor agreements.

You can find some eco-friendly travel tips and statistics, as well as touring companies and associations—listed by destination under "Travel Choice"—at the **TIES** website, **www.ecotourism.org**.

Responsible Travel (www.responsibletravel.com) is a great source of sustainable travel ideas; the site is run by a spokesperson for ethical tourism in the travel industry. **Sustainable Travel International** (www.sustainabletravelinternational.org) promotes ethical tourism practices, and manages an extensive directory of sustainable properties and tour operators around the world.

In the U.K., **Tourism Concern** (www.tourismconcern.org.uk) works to reduce social and environmental problems connected to tourism.

Volunteer travel has become increasingly popular among those who want to venture beyond the standard group-tour experience to learn languages, interact with locals, and make a positive difference while on vacation. Volunteer travel usually doesn't require special skills—just a willingness to work hard—and programs vary in length from a few days to a number of weeks. Some programs provide free housing and food, but many require volunteers to pay for travel expenses, which can add up quickly.

For general info on volunteer travel, visit **www.volunteerabroad.org** and **www.idealist.org**.

TOURS

History & Architecture Tours

The Dublin bus company **Dublin Bus** (✆ **01/873-4222;** www.dublinbus.ie) operates several tours focusing on Irish history and architecture, all of which depart from the Dublin Bus office at 59 Upper O'Connell St., Dublin 1. You can buy your ticket from the bus driver or book in advance at the Dublin Bus office or at the Dublin Tourism ticket desk on Suffolk Street.

Gray Line (✆ **01/605-7705;** www.irishcitytours.com) offers a range of full-day and multiple-day excursions from Dublin to the historic monastic site at Glendalough, as well as to the prehistoric remains at Newgrange, and the architecturally significant Powerscourt.

The national bus company, **Bus Éireann** (✆ **091/562000;** www.buseireann.ie), provides a good range of tours throughout Ireland. You can tour Dublin and around to Glendalough or Newgrange by bus, or travel by boat to Waterford, and it also offers good tours of Galway, taking in the Maam Cross, Recess, Roundstone, and Clifden.

For a more historical, intellectual approach to Ireland's famous history, try **Mary Gibbons Tours** (✆ **086/355-1355;** www.newgrangetours.com), which leads absorbing, in-depth tours of Newgrange, Powerscourt, and Glendalough.

Adventure Trips

For touring the Wicklow Mountains and Glendalough, try **Discover Dublin** (✆ **01/280-1899;** www.discoverdublin.ie), which offers a tour it has dubbed the "Wild Wicklow Tour." Wild might be too strong a word, but it is certainly lively and enjoyable, and includes visits to the mountainous area around Avoca and the scenic Sally Gap.

Political Tours

The best tours in Belfast are the extraordinary **Black Taxi Tours ★** (✆ **0800/052-3914** or 0289/064-2264; www.belfasttours.com), which take you through the areas where the Troubles had the most impact, and explain it all in intelligent, compassionate, unbiased, firsthand terms.

3

SUGGESTED IRELAND ITINERARIES

Ireland is such a small island that you can cover a lot of ground in a week, and feel quite at home within two, but even with the best of intentions and all the energy in the world, you'll never see it all on a short visit.

To get the most out of it, you need to know at least in part what you want to see, and that will decide how you should travel. If your ideal Ireland involves wandering through the countryside, visiting small villages, climbing castle walls, hailing history from a ruined abbey, or finding yourself alone on a rocky beach—you simply cannot do those things without a car. Out of the main towns, public transportation exists, but it's slow and limiting. Every major town has car-rental agencies, so give strong consideration to renting a car.

The next step is deciding where to start. That decision can be made for you by where your flight terminates. If you're flying into Shannon Airport, then it makes good geographic sense to start out on the west coast. If you're flying into Dublin, you might as well explore that city first, then either head up to the North and the ruggedly beautiful Antrim Coast, or south down to the Wicklow Mountains, Kilkenny, and the rolling green hills of Wexford and Waterford.

Still, if you fly into Dublin but your heart is in Galway, no worries. You can traverse the width of the country in a few hours (once you get out of Dublin's stultifying sprawl), so if you start early enough, it's doable. Just bear in mind that rural roads are not well lighted or well signposted, so driving at night should be avoided. It's too stressful, and being lost in unfamiliar territory, where it can be many miles between villages, is no fun at all. This is more of an issue in the winter, when it can get dark as early as 4pm, than in the summer, when it often stays light until after 10pm.

So taking all of these factors into consideration, the question remains: *Where do you want to go?* We can't answer that question for you, but we can give you some itineraries that we have used ourselves, which you might enjoy, depending upon your interests.

These might help you focus on ways in which you can orchestrate your journey so that you can get the most out of it with the fewest scheduling worries—the last thing you want to do on vacation is to spend the whole time looking at your watch.

If you've never visited Ireland, Dublin is a good place to start, and the surrounding area holds plenty to keep you busy. If you have been here before, and Dublin and Galway are old hat, you might consider heading north, through County Mayo, County Sligo, and on to the exotic wilds of Donegal and the Antrim Coast.

Take what you find here, and pick and choose the parts that appeal to you, add in your own favorite shopping or scenic drives, and turn it all into a holiday custom-made for yourself.

PREVIOUS PAGE: **The Gap of Dunloe, in Killarney National Park, County Kerry.**

THE REGIONS IN BRIEF

The island is divided into two major political units—Northern Ireland (which, along with England, Scotland, and Wales, is part of the United Kingdom), and the Republic of Ireland. Of Ireland's 32 counties, 26 are in the Republic.

Ireland divided into two separate countries in 1922, when the British government that had occupied Ireland agreed to allow the Republic to become a free state, with the exception of the six northern counties that remained part of the U.K.

The line between north and south is no longer marked, and the only indication on many roads that you've crossed into a different nation is the road signs, which change from metric distances in the Republic to imperial in Northern Ireland.

The ancient Gaelic regions into which Ireland was once divided are still used in conversation and directions: Ulster is north, Munster is south, Leinster is east, and Connaught is west. Each region is divided into counties:

In Ulster (to the north) Cavan, Donegal, and Monaghan in the Republic; Antrim, Armagh, Derry, Down, Fermanagh, and Tyrone in Northern Ireland.

In Munster (to the south) Clare, Cork, Kerry, Limerick, Tipperary, and Waterford.

In Leinster (to the east) Dublin, Carlow, Kildare, Kilkenny, Laois, Longford, Louth, Meath, Offaly, Westmeath, Wexford, and Wicklow.

In Connaught (to the west) Sligo, Mayo, Galway, Roscommon, and Leitrim.

DUBLIN & ENVIRONS With 40% of the Republic's population living within 97km (60 miles) of Dublin, the capital is the center of the profound, high-speed changes that have transformed Ireland into a prosperous and increasingly European country. Within an hour's drive of Dublin are Dalkey, Dún Laoghaire, and many other engaging coastal towns, as well as the rural beauty of the Wicklow Mountains, and the prehistoric ruins in County Meath.

THE SOUTHEAST The southeast offers sandy beaches, Wexford's lush and mountainous countryside, Waterford's famous Crystal Factory, Kilkenny and Cahir's ancient castles, the Rock of Cashel, the Irish National Heritage Park at Ferrycarrig, and Ireland's largest bird sanctuary on the Saltee Islands.

CORK & ENVIRONS Cork, Ireland's second-largest city, feels like a buzzy university town, and provides a congenial gateway to the south and west of the island. Within arm's reach are Blarney Castle (and its famous stone), the culinary and scenic delights of Kinsale, the Drombeg Stone Circle, Sherkin and Clear islands, and Mizen Head. Also in this region is the dazzling landscape of West Cork.

THE SOUTHWEST The once-remote splendor of County Kerry has long since ceased to be a secret, so at least during the high season, be prepared to share the view in this gorgeous section. The Ring of Kerry (less glamorously known as hwys. N70 and N71) encircling the Iveragh Peninsula is the most visited attraction in Ireland after the Book of Kells. That's both a recommendation and a warning. Killarney National Park provides a stunning haven from buses. Killarney is surrounded by natural beauty, but is filled with souvenir shops and tour groups. Marginally less visited highlights include the rugged Dingle Peninsula, and two sets of islands with rich histories: the Skelligs and the Blaskets.

THE WEST The west of Ireland offers a first taste of Ireland's wild beauty and striking diversity for those who fly into Shannon Airport. County Limerick has an array of impressive castles: Knappogue, Bunratty, Ashrod, and (just over the county line in Galway) Dunguaire. County Clare's natural offerings—particularly the lunar landscapes of the Burren—are unforgettable. Farther up the coast to the north, past Galway, County Mayo is the home of the sweet town of Westport on Clew Bay. Achill Island has beaches and stunning cliff views, and is accessible by car.

GALWAY & ENVIRONS Galway Town is busy, colorful, and funky—a youthful, prospering port and university city, and the self-proclaimed arts capital of Ireland with theater, music, dance, and an exciting street life. County Galway is the gateway to Connemara's moody, melancholy, magical landscapes. Here are the Twelve Bens mountains, Kylemore Abbey, and the charming seaside town of Clifden. Offshore lie the mysterious Aran Islands—Inishmore, Inishmaan, and Inisheer—with their irresistible desolation.

THE NORTHWEST In Ireland it's easy to become convinced that isolated austerity is beautiful, and nowhere is this more true than Donegal, with its jagged, desolate coastline that, if you don't mind the cold, offers some fine surfing. Inland, the Glenveagh National Park has as much wilderness as you could want. County Sligo inspired the poetry of W. B. Yeats with its dense collection of megalithic sites: stone circles, passage tombs, dolmens, and cairns at Carrowmore, Knocknarea, and Carrowkeel.

THE MIDLANDS The lush center of Ireland, bisected by the lazy River Shannon, is a land of pastures, rivers, lakes, woods, and gentle mountain slopes, a verdant antidote to the barren beauty of Connemara and a retreat, in high season, from the throngs of tourists who crowd the coasts. The shores and waters of the Shannon and Lough Derg and of their many lesser cousins provide much of the lure.

OUTDOOR PURSUITS—cycling, boating, fishing, and hiking—are the heart of the matter here. The midlands also hold remarkable sites—Birr Castle and its splendid gardens, and Clonmacnois, the evocative ruins of a famous Irish monastic center.

NORTHERN IRELAND Across the border, Northern Ireland's six counties are undergoing a time of intense change. Still one of the most underrated parts of Ireland, the stunning Antrim Coast (particularly Ballycastle and Cushendun), the extraordinary, octagonal basalt columns of the Giant's Causeway, and the Glens of Antrim are unforgettable. The loveliness of the Fermanagh Lake District is written in a minor key. The old city walls of Derry, the past glory of Carrickfergus Castle, and Belfast's elaborate political murals make a trip across the border worthwhile.

THE BEST OF IRELAND IN 1 WEEK

We love to fly into Dublin, knowing that the compact, laid-back city awaits a few miles down the road, with its old-fashioned pubs, its modern restaurants, and its absorbing sights all laid out for walking. If you've never been here, a couple of days in Dublin make for a quick primer on Ireland. It's just enough time to do some shopping on **Grafton Street,** head up O'Connell Street to the **General Post Office,** and discover the Georgian beauty of **St. Stephen's Green** and **Merrion Square.** It's not nearly enough time, but you can give the surface of the city a good brush in a couple of days, and then head south to **Kilkenny** and **Wicklow,** on to **Waterford, Cork,** and **Kerry,** and up to **Clare** for a quick glance before the clock runs out. It is only hitting the high points but, as high points go, they're not bad. This kind of trip is quite high energy, but it's not completely exhausting.

DAYS 1 & 2: Arrive in Dublin ★★★

If it happens that you're arriving from North America, you start with an advantage: Most flights arrive early in the morning, which effectively gives you an extra day's sightseeing. Check into your hotel, say yes to any tea and scones offered, take a minute to relax, and then head out on foot. Get a map from your hotel to augment the ones in this book, and then just start walking. Stay south of the River Liffey, and head down Dame Street to **Dublin Castle** (p. 146), which holds the magical **Chester Beatty Library** (p. 144) with its vast collection of gorgeous illuminated manuscripts. Later take in **St. Patrick's Cathedral** (p. 151) and the vibrant green quadrangles of **Trinity College** (p. 152), before heading down to Merrion Square, with its impressive granite architecture and the ancient gold on display at the **National Museum** (p. 150). It's a short stroll from here down to **St.**

The bustling Temple Bar district, on the banks of the Liffey in Dublin.

The Best of Ireland Itineraries

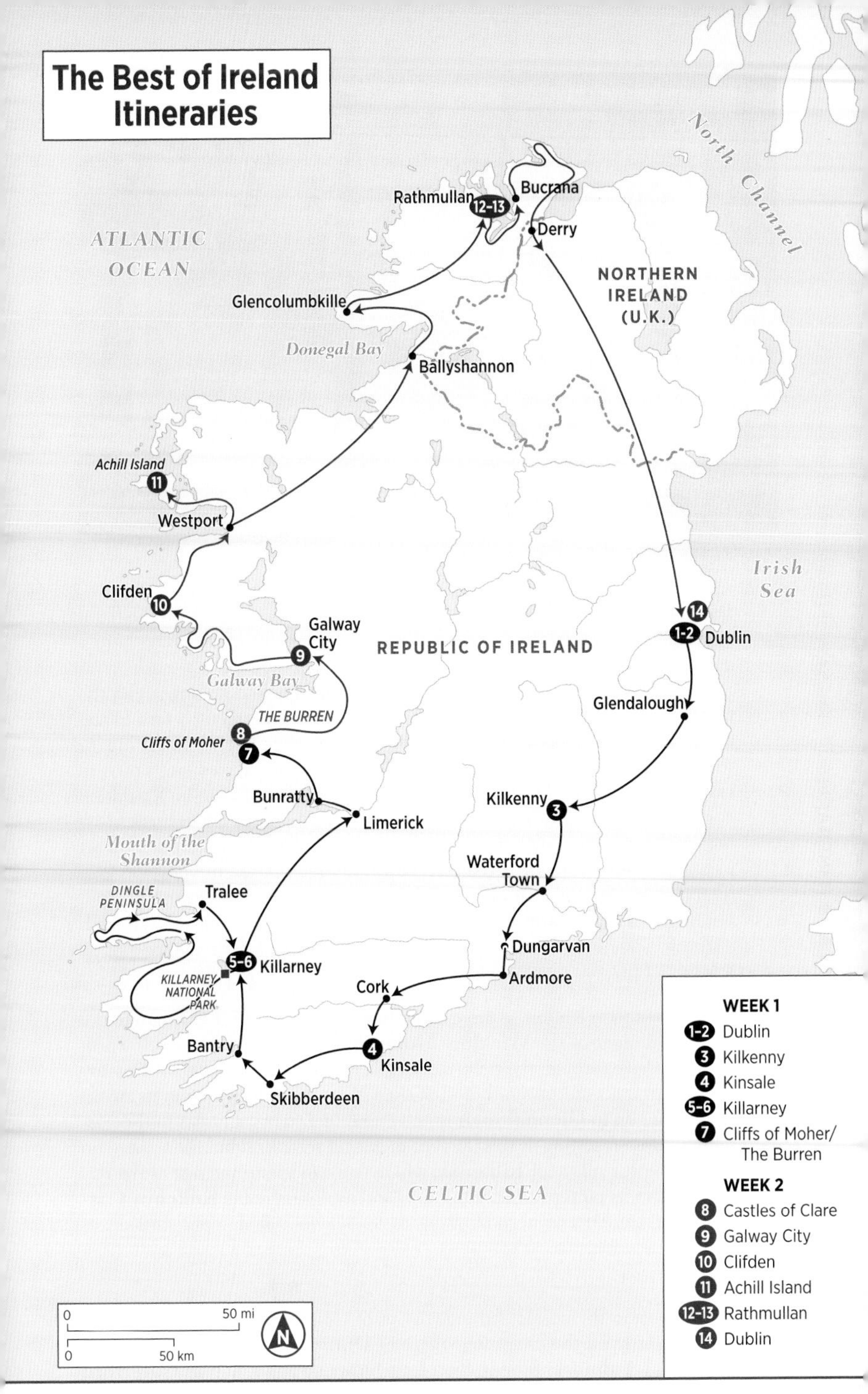

One of Kinsale's many colorful shop fronts, in County Cork.

Patrick's Green, where you can rest your weary toes and soak up the floral view, before strolling up **Grafton Street** for a last bit of shopping before collapsing in your hotel.

On **Day 2,** have a hearty breakfast in your hotel before striking out for the trendy cultural hub of **Temple Bar.** Stroll down Parliament Street to the river, then take a right, and walk along the noisy, vibrant waterfront to the effervescent arc of the **Ha'penny Bridge.** Head across and down to O'Connell Street and walk on up past its many statues to the bullet-ridden columns of the **General Post Office** (p. 159), where the 1916 Easter Rising was based. After exploring its displays, head farther up O'Connell Street to the **Dublin Writers Museum** (p. 147), which bookish types will love for its extensive display of memorabilia. It's a few doors down from the small but mighty **Hugh Lane Gallery** (p. 148), where you can marvel that such a strong collection of classical pieces was ever owned by one man.

DAY 3: South to Wicklow & Kilkenny ★★★

It takes less than 2 hours to drive from the hustle and traffic of Dublin to the peace and quiet of the **Wicklow Mountains** (p. 210), and it's well worth the trip. Drive through the town of Enniskerry to the great estate of **Powerscourt** (p. 207) on the south end of the village. After lunching in its Avoca Café, head on to **Glendalough** (p. 204) and feel your soul relax in the pastoral mountain setting of this ancient monastic retreat. From there drive on to the colorful village of **Kilkenny,** where you can spend the rest of the day shopping in its pottery and crafts shops and exploring noble **Kilkenny Castle** (p. 276). This is a good place to spend your first night outside of Dublin.

DAY 4: West to Waterford & Cork ★★

Set off west to the coastal fishing villages of County Waterford, looking out along the way for the charming village of **Dunmore East** and the alluring beaches of **Ardmore.** Stop in for a little browsing and lunch in **Waterford**

Town, stopping on your way out at the **Waterford Crystal Factory** before heading west to Cork. If castles entice you, stop at **Dungarvan,** midway between Waterford and Cork, and spend some time wandering through the sturdy walls of **King John's Castle** (p. 407). From there, head on to explore the delightful Cork coast. Introduce yourself to busy **Cork City** (p. 290) and smaller, quieter **Kinsale** (p. 309), the self-proclaimed gourmet capital of Ireland. Either one would be an ideal place to spend the night.

DAYS 5 & 6: From Cork to Kerry ★★

Start **Day 5** by heading west to the wilder section of Cork. It's a sprawling, political, complex area, and well worth taking some time to understand. Consider taking a tour of the area in the morning (several good ones are listed in the Cork chapter), to get a more in-depth look at it, although foodies might prefer to indulge in a half-day cooking class at **Ballymaloe Cookery School** (p. 321). Walkers might want to add a day to their journey, in order to spend some time exploring the countryside on foot. There's plenty to do, and even touristy **Blarney Castle** (p. 300) is interesting to explore.

At your own pace, move on into County Kerry, at the southwest tip of the island. Here the most popular place to explore—and one of the busiest tourist spots in Ireland—is the **Ring of Kerry** (see "The Ring of Kerry," in chapter 9). It is a beautiful drive, but because of the preponderance of tourist buses, not everybody will want to make it. Others will brave the masses to see extraordinary countryside, with its plethora of historic sites and tiny villages. If you've the stamina, the entire Ring is doable at a reasonable pace over 2 days, although you'd have to skip pretty much everything else around here to do so.

If it's quiet you're after, you could instead take the short section of the Ring that runs from lovely **Kenmare** (p. 344) to the bucolic peace of **Killarney National Park** (p. 358), where you can indulge in a buggy ride around its lake and leave only your footsteps. Golfers with a bit of money to

The grounds of Ross Castle, in Killarney National Park.

burn will want to play a round at the **Waterville Golf Links** (p. 350), surrounded by soft sand dunes at the edge of the sea. You can then spend the afternoon shopping in Killarney if you're bored with the car by now, or drive around the **Dingle Peninsula.**

DAY 7: County Clare

Time is short now, so you won't be able to see as much of Clare as it deserves. But make a promise to yourself to come back someday, and head for the perilously tall **Cliffs of Moher** (p. 437) where the view seems to stretch all the way to America (although the price to park will make you shiver). You can lunch in the town of **Ennis,** and then decide whether you'd rather spend the rest of the day exploring the touristy but interesting offerings at **Bunratty Castle** (p. 420) or marveling at the otherworldly landscape of the **Burren** (see "The Burren," in chapter 10). If it's the latter, strike out for the R480 road, which offers the best immediate gratification, as it winds its way through the extraordinary limestone landscape. What a way to end your trip!

THE BEST OF IRELAND IN 2 WEEKS

With 2 weeks, your visit to Ireland will be much more relaxed. You can stretch out a bit more in your travels, heading to less crowded counties, with more time to meet the locals. In your second week, head up to Galway, Mayo, and Donegal, taking time to smell the heather along the way.

DAYS 1 THROUGH 7

Follow "The Best of Ireland in 1 Week" itinerary, as outlined above.

DAY 8: County Clare

After spending Day 7 exploring Clare, you'll discover that you need more time to really get the most out of this big, varied place. Wander the castles of Clare—**Bunratty, Dromoland,** and **Knappogue** (p. 420, 426, and 431)—and consider indulging in one of their medieval banquets held nightly in summer. They're unsurprisingly expensive, but can be good fun for families. Abbey lovers should take the time to visit the exquisite **Corcomroe Abbey** (p. 435).

DAY 9: County Clare to Galway City

This morning, drive up from Clare to Galway City (it will take around an hour), and spend a relaxing day walking the delightful streets of this artsy, vibrant town. Shop for stemware at the **Galway Irish Crystal Heritage Centre** (p. 462), and wander the waterfront. Spend the afternoon relaxing and shopping for locally made arts and crafts, or lingering over pints at the sunny **Front Door** pub (p. 467). If you don't need the rest, and you want to stay busy, take a cruise out to the misty **Aran Islands** (see "The Aran Islands," in chapter 11), or head down to explore Yeats's old country home, **Thoor Ballylee** (p. 469).

DAY 10: County Galway

A busker entertains passersby in Galway.

Start early and strike out for the tiny R336, the best road for exploring the craggy Galway coastline. Stop by the pretty little town of **Spiddal,** where plentiful adorable little shops sell Aran sweaters and other Irish knits—our favorite shop is **Standún** (p. 450). Follow signs to the seaside town of **Clifden,** which has spectacular views and lots of good restaurants and pubs, making it a good place to break for lunch, and a spot of crafts shopping at **Fuchsia Crafts** (p. 479). We love to see the countryside from horseback, and **Cleggan Riding Centre** (p. 480) offers great horseback tours.

DAY 11: County Mayo

Driving up from Galway, the scenery is also spectacular in Mayo, where the rocky shoreline plunges to the cobalt sea in glorious fashion. Head to the south Mayo town of **Westport,** which sits at the edge of a picturesque river, and is a delightful, peaceful place to wander. From there, drive across the flatlands, a strangely empty landscape, toward **Achill Island** (p. 498); the drive along the coast and out across a bridge to the island is slow and windy, but the views are fantastic. Spend a relaxing afternoon and evening exploring the island, before climbing into a comfortable bed at the **Bervie** (p. 508), where the sea is right outside the door. Alternatively, if you want to see more of Ireland's ancient past, skip Achill Island and spend the rest of the day exploring County Sligo (see "Exploring Ancient Ireland," later in this chapter). Our favorite place to stay the night in these parts is **Temple House** (p. 521).

DAY 12: County Mayo to Donegal

Drive up through Mayo and the quiet farmland of Sligo to the rugged landscape of Donegal. Head up the coast past Donegal Town until you catch the N15 road, and then follow it around the breathtaking coastline to the busy hill town of **Ballyshannon** (p. 540), which has excellent crafts shops and glorious views from the top of the hill. The adventurous can explore the **Catsby Cave** (p. 542), a picturesque grotto at the edge of the Abbey River. But here the drive is really the thing, so drive on to the darling town of **Glencolumbkille** (p. 545). There's an excellent folk park here that's well worth an hour of your time before you head on to the stone-cut town of Ardara at the foot of a steep hill—it's wall-to-wall arts-and-crafts shops, and is a pleasure to explore. From there it's around an hour's drive to the Fanad, a scenic drive around Lough Swilly. Follow it around to Rathmullan, a quiet, lakefront village, and spend the night there at relaxing **Rathmullan House** (p. 554).

DAY 13: Donegal

You've been traveling a great deal, so today is a rest day. Spend the morning walking along the lake, or take a horseback tour down its sandy beaches (Rathmullan House arranges excellent horseback treks for adults and pony treks for children). In the afternoon, after you've recharged your batteries, drive around the lake and explore the little villages: **Rathmelton** is a picturesque town with stone cottages mirrored in the glassy lake, while **Dunfanaghy** (p. 550) is adorable and has an excellent beach—perfect for an afternoon swim.

Rough surf on Tullan Strand-Bundoran, in County Donegal.

DAY 14: Heading Home

If your flight leaves late, you could rise early and spend the morning driving up to **Malin Head,** the northernmost tip of Ireland; a wild and woolly place just a couple of hours' drive from Rathmullan. From there, expect the drive to the airport to take at least 4 hours, but allow plenty of time in case of traffic backups around Dublin—they're virtually constant.

THE BEST OF IRELAND FOR FAMILIES

Traveling with children is always a bit of an adventure, and you'll want all the help you can get. Luckily Ireland—with its vast open countryside, farm hotels, and castles—is a fairy-tale playground for kids. You'll have trouble finding babysitters outside the major towns, but just take the kids with you—most restaurants, sights, and even pubs (during the day) welcome children. The best part of the country for those traveling with kids is arguably Cork and Kerry, where everything seems to be set up for families, so here's a sample itinerary to give you some ideas.

DAY 1: Cork City

Start with a stroll through the city on foot. You can pick and choose what your kids will like best. There's a pleasantly scary exhibition at the old **Cork City Gaol** (p. 302), where lifelike figures still await their release in the jail cells. Afterward, you can all go shopping at the **Coal Quay Market** (p. 301)—a flea market where you never quite know what to expect amid its colorful stalls. Next, pack a picnic lunch and head outside the city to the **Blarney Castle** (p. 300), where you can easily fill an entire afternoon kissing rocks, climbing castle walls, and exploring Badger Cave and the castle's gloomy dungeons. The sprawling grounds make a perfect place to dine

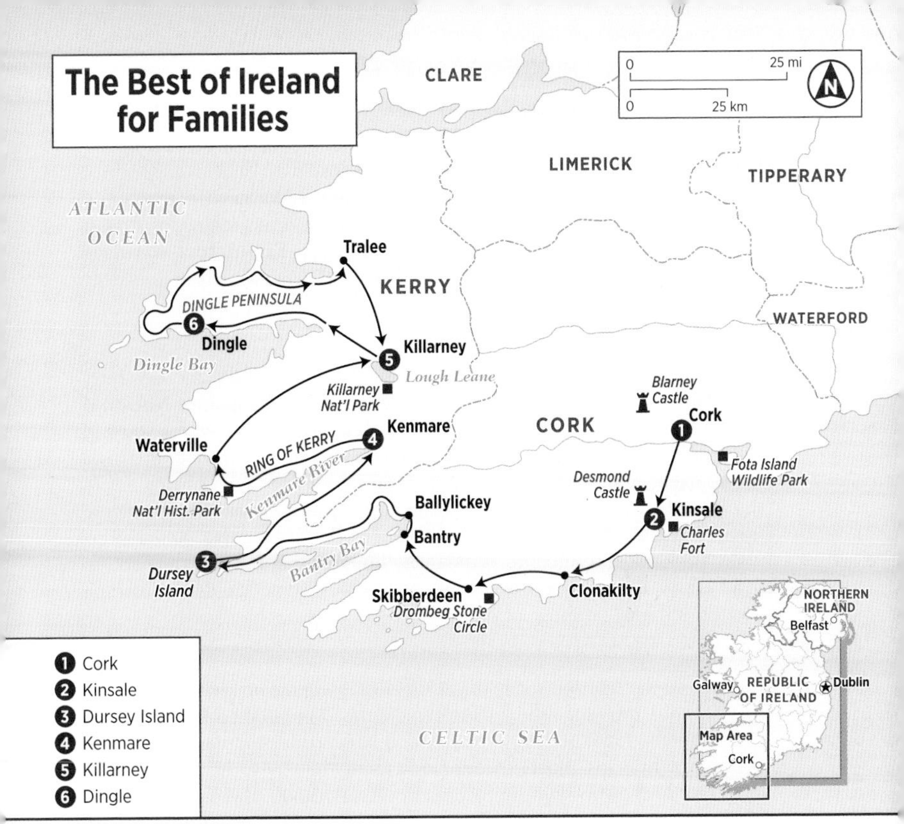

alfresco. If money is no object, spend the night at the **Hayfield Manor Hotel** (p. 296), where the kids will get cookies and milk before bedtime.

DAY 2: Eastern County Cork

In the morning head to the star-shaped **Charles Fort** (p. 311), where the kids can clamber around the ancient walls while you bone up on a little history. You can head for more ancient wall climbing at **Desmond Castle** (p. 311), or, if the kids have had enough historic buildings, indulge them at the **Fota Island Wildlife Park** (p. 322), a zoo without borders, where rare and endangered animals have the run of the place—only cheetahs are behind conventional fencing. You can have another picnic here, as picnic tables are ready and waiting.

DAY 3: Western County Cork

Take the kids on an unforgettable ride in a wooden cable car out to **Dursey Island** (p. 325), which you can easily explore on foot while taking in the sweeping views. Back on the mainland there are plenty of little colorful towns, including Ballydehob, where all the signs for local shops and pubs are done in pictures rather than words. Take them to the **Drombeg Stone Circle** (p. 327) to learn about ancient religions; its strange beauty will bewitch even younger travelers. Take a ferry out to Ilnacullin—just for the ride—or go swimming off Barleycove Beach, where the sand is white and soft.

DAY 4: Kenmare

After driving along a coastal route through a number of tiny beachfront villages, the kids will be ready to hit the water themselves. You can either drive down the Ring of Kerry to the idyllic beach resort of **Waterville,** where you can spend an afternoon swimming, sunbathing, and picnicking, or stop at Kenmare for a seal-watching trip with **Seafari Eco-nature Cruises** (p. 348). The kids will spot everything from frolicking sea otters to sleepy gray seals on the way.

DAY 5: Killarney

Welcome to Ireland's ideal town for families: You could keep the kids busy in Killarney for days. Head straight for the gorgeous **Killarney National Park** (p. 358), stopping first at **Muckross House** (p. 359), where you can get a good park map and a helpful explanation of all of its myriad offerings. Set yourself up near the lakes and spend a relaxing morning rowing out to the **islands,** which hold medieval ruins ripe for exploration. Bring a picnic lunch and relax on the shore, or dine in one of the island cafes. In the afternoon, pack the kids into one of the many **buggies** that traverse the park, or head off to **Kennedy's Pet Farm** (p. 361) for some hands-on learning about traditional farming.

DAY 6: The Dingle Peninsula

It's back to the seafront today to get up close and personal with sea life. In the morning, introduce the kids to Fungie the Dolphin on a **Fungie Tour** (p. 377)—the town mascot is playful and personable, and has a disarming affinity for humans. Boats go out throughout the day to his favorite play area, and he'll swim right up to you. In the afternoon, there's a chance to play with rays, mollusks, and other sea creatures in the hands-on displays in the **Oceanworld Aquarium** (p. 376).

DAY 7: Heading Home

If you have the time, in the morning head to the little town of Blennerville to see its huge working **windmill** (p. 387). If you go inside, you can see it doing its stuff—grinding wheat into flour as it has done for more than 200 years. It's a beautiful way to end your tour of Kerry. From here expect a drive to Shannon Airport to take less than 2 hours, and a drive to Dublin Airport to take 3 to 4 hours.

DISCOVERING THE NORTH

Years of turmoil made the North of Ireland a no-go zone for many tourists, and justifiably so. There was a time when, whatever your perspective on the Troubles, driving around here could be a bit nerve-racking. But times have changed, and while the region still has its problems, more visitors are taking the time to discover this complex but rewarding part of the world. From the travelers' perspective, one legacy of those problems is what makes it so attractive: the North is by far the most untouched section of Ireland. Even today you can explore the restless beauty of the **Antrim Coast** in relative peace, and walk the **Giant's Causeway** alone at sunset. But do it quickly, because word is getting out.

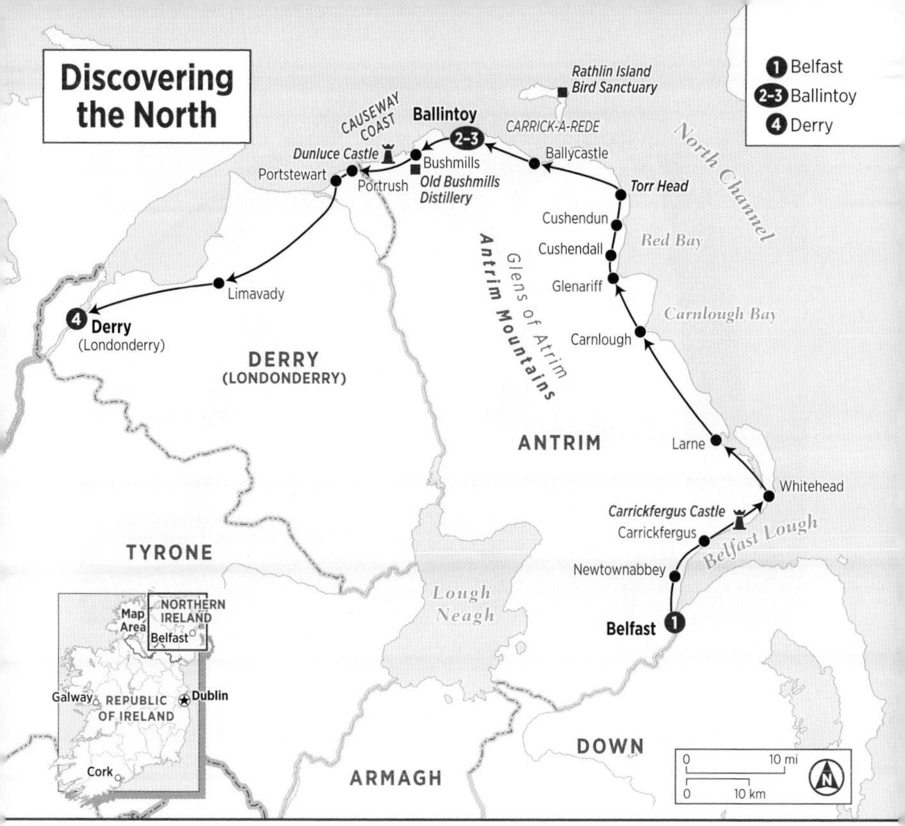

DAY 1: Belfast

Spend the morning getting your bearings, something that is best done by getting out on the street and walking. You can easily see most of Belfast's central sights—tour the grand **City Hall** (p. 578), shop on the small medieval arcades, and stop to view the extraordinary ceiling mosaics at the **Belfast Cathedral** (p. 576). Have lunch at **White's Tavern** (p. 592), a 300-year-old pub where you can get traditional Irish stews, and bangers and mash (sausages and mashed potatoes) in a historic setting. In the afternoon, take a "Black Cab" tour of the Falls and Shankill roads—these one-on-one tours of the areas where the Troubles were the most destructive are an unforgettable chance to hear what happened from those who were there.

DAY 2: Carrickfergus & the Antrim Coast

The noble Norman castle of **Carrickfergus** (p. 597) stands guard about a 15-minute drive from Belfast, and if you head there first thing in the morning, and strike out northward on the A2 road from there, you'll be amid peaceful coastal scenery in about 20 minutes—look out for sweeping views of craggy coastline just after the town of Ballygawley. Stop in the little town of **Glenarm** to explore its castle walls and take in its stone buildings, then head on to **Carnlough,** where you can walk to a waterfall before having a traditional Irish lunch at the **Londonderry Arms** (p. 614). Next, drive on

A mural painted on the gable of a house in Belfast.

to **Cushendun,** to photograph its little stone cottages and have a cup of tea. From there, if you're not afraid of heights, follow signs for the **Torr Head Scenic Road** to **Murlough Bay** for the most spectacular views of the day from the top of a rocky cliff so high that clouds swirl around your ankles. Spend the night at **Whitepark House** (p. 614) overlooking the white crescent of **White Park Bay.**

DAY 3: Ballintoy & the Headlands

After a soul-affirming breakfast, take a brisk walk down the steep hill to **White Park Bay,** and explore for fossils and seashells while soaking up the sea air, then backtrack a few miles on the A2 to the **Carrick-A-Rede Rope Bridge** (but cross it only if you're fine with heights; p. 609). Heading northwest again, follow signs to the **Giant's Causeway** (p. 610), and spend an hour or so exploring its dramatic octagonal pillars. Lunch in **Ballintoy** (or have a picnic on the beach at White Park Bay), then either relax in the countryside or take an afternoon tour of the **Old Bushmills Distillery** (p. 611) in Bushmills. Spend another night at Whitepark House.

DAY 4: Derry

Head inland along the A37 to the busy waterfront town of Derry—about a 40-minute drive. Spend the morning wandering its 17th-century city **walls,** taking in the views and history, and have a pub lunch at **Badger's** (p. 638). In the afternoon, indulge in some shopping in the old city (especially in the **Derry Craft Village;** p. 633), and then take time to explore the **Cathedral of St. Columb** (p. 630), where a 17th-century mortar shell still sits on the porch. In the evening, feast on steaks at **O'Brien's** (p. 638), then meet the locals and catch a traditional Irish band at a pub along **Waterloo Street** (p. 639).

EXPLORING ANCIENT IRELAND

Ireland has treasured and protected its ancient past, and its mysterious stone circles, cairns, and huge stone tables called dolmens are still to be found, perfectly preserved, in pastures and on hillsides all over the island. These are precious connections to our own long-lost pasts, as they provide a window through which we can catch a hazy glimpse of what life was like very long ago. Some of the oldest tombs predate the Egyptian pyramids by centuries, and, in many cases, the sites are preserved but their meaning has long since disappeared, making them intriguing and elusive in equal measures. Exploring these rocky symbols can be the most memorable part of any trip to Ireland.

DAY 1: Knowth & the Boyne Valley

After an early breakfast, head north to the rich rolling Boyne Valley, about an hour's drive north of Dublin off the N2, to the Brú na Bóinne Visitor Centre—the essential center of an extensive Neolithic burial ground. This huge necropolis holds numerous sites, with three open to visitors—**Newgrange** (p. 232), **Knowth** (p. 230), and **Dowth.** Register at the center to tour Newgrange first—a tour here, early in the day before it gets crowded, is spectacular. Next tour the burial ground at Knowth, with its extensive collection of passage-grave art. In the afternoon, head down the N3 to the **Hill of Tara** (p. 229), where mounds and passage graves date from the Bronze Age.

DAY 2: Céide Fields

It will take a couple of hours to drive to the remote location in north County Mayo, but your efforts will be rewarded at this extraordinary ancient site (p. 500) that holds the stony remains of an entire prehistoric farming village on top of a cliff with breathtaking views of the sea and surrounding countryside. Spend the day exploring the 5,000-year-old site, and lunch in the excellent visitor center.

DAY 3: County Sligo

In the morning, drive east to County Sligo. On the N4, south of Sligo Town, visit the **Carrowkeel Passage Tomb Cemetery** (p. 516), on a hilltop overlooking Lough Arrow. It has wide, sweeping views, and its 14 cairns and

One of many ancient tombs at Carrowmore, a Megalithic burial ground in County Sligo.

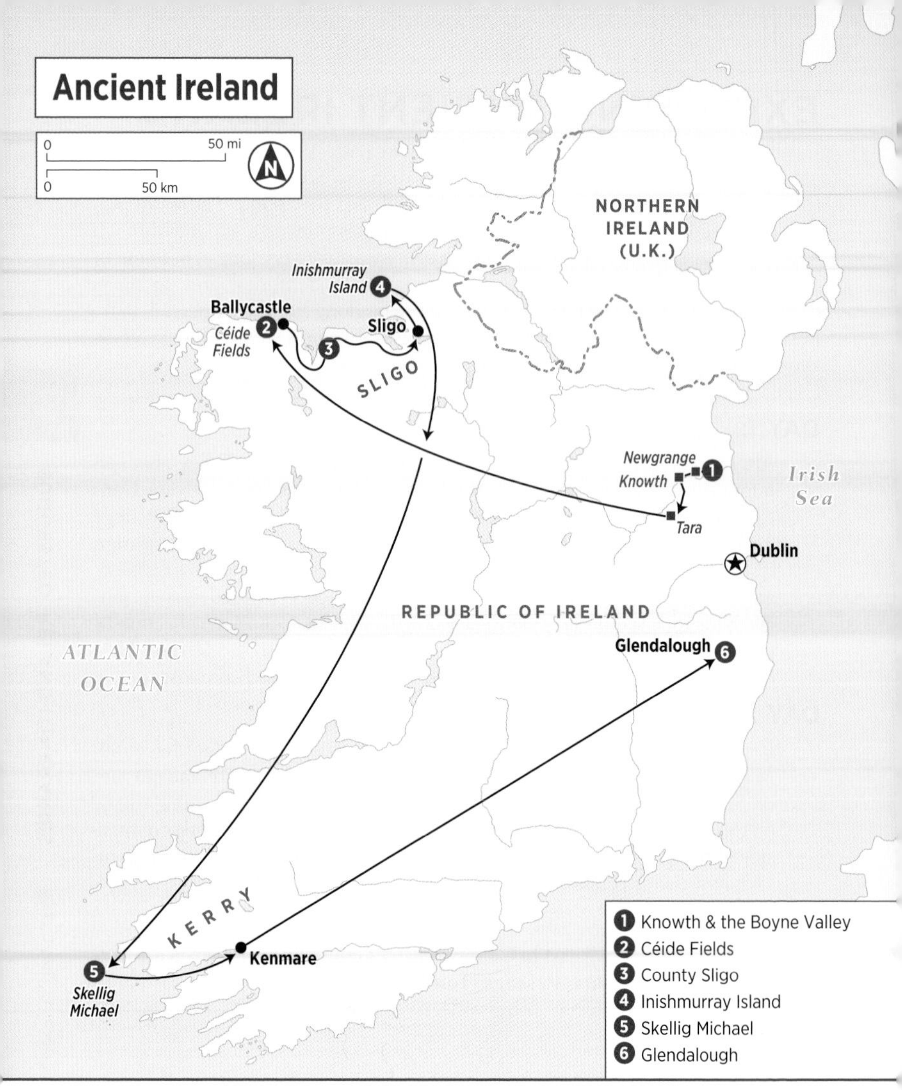

dolmens are often very quiet early in the day—with luck you might have it all to yourself. Then head on to Sligo Town, and follow signs to **Carrowmore Megalithic Cemetery** (p. 517). This extraordinary site has 60 stone circles, passage tombs, and dolmens scattered across acres of green pastures, and is believed to predate Newgrange by nearly a millennium. In the afternoon, if you're feeling energetic, climb to the hilltop cairn of **Knocknarea** nearby—it's believed to be the grave of folklore fairy Queen Maeve.

DAY 4: Inishmurray Island

After a relaxing morning, travel by boat to the island of **Inishmurray** (see "Exploring the Surrounding Countryside" in chapter 12) off the coast of Sligo. There you can spend the day wandering the impressively complete remains of the early monastic settlement founded in the 6th century. You can still make out its chapels and churches, its beehive cells and altars. If the weather is fine, pack a picnic lunch, and eat on the sunny beach.

DAY 5: Skellig Michael

Right after breakfast, head south to County Kerry, where this starkly beautiful island sits 13km (8 miles) offshore, standing sternly as a kind of memorial to the hardy souls who once eked out a living amid its formidable cliffs and stony mountains (see "The Ring of Kerry" in chapter 9). Deeply observant early Christian monks punished their bodies by living here in miserable conditions, and spent their days carving 600 steps into the unyielding stone, so that their walk up to their beehive huts and icy chapels could be made somewhat safer. Today it is an unforgettable landscape, and the ruins of their homes are deeply evocative and profoundly moving. A trip out here by boat, and an afternoon's exploration, will take up much of the day. Once you return to the mainland, reward yourself with a relaxing evening in Kenmare.

DAY 6: Glendalough

Drive east today to County Wicklow, where the evocative ruins of the monastery at **Glendalough** (p. 204) are so large and sprawling, spread around two peaceful lakes on the side of a mountain, that they can fill your entire day. Get a map and information from the visitor center before beginning your exploration of the round towers, chapels, and huts dotted around the wooded site. Don't miss the ancient chapel known as **St. Kevin's Kitchen.** If the weather is warm, bring your lunch and picnic by the lake.

THE BEST DUBLIN PUB-CRAWL

Dublin has a collection of some of the world's best pubs, tucked away on side streets, quietly minding their own business. James Joyce theorized that it was impossible to walk across the city without passing one, and you'd be hard-pressed to do it today. Many of these places have been offering pints of ale to weary travelers for centuries, so touring them is a refreshing way to look at Dublin's history. In a few hours of pub hopping you can take in a lot of city sights, while also taking advantage of the opportunity to meet (and drink with) locals on their home turf. Start in the afternoon or early evening and take your time—3 hours ought to do it (unless you want to make a whole night of it). Make it a relaxing walking tour of central Dublin, stopping for drinks and conversation. Who knows who you'll meet along the way? ***Start:*** *Doheny & Nesbitt, 5 Lower Baggot St., Dublin 2.*

PUB 1: Doheny & Nesbitt

Long popular with politicians, journalists, and (oddly) economists, this pub makes a great start to any stout-based tour of Dublin. Founded in 1850, it's just around the corner from the government buildings. It's said that the seeds of Ireland's economic success of the 1990s and 2000s were planted here, where a band of politicians, civil servants, and economists regularly met and drank in the '80s. Journalists dubbed them "the Doheny & Nesbitt School of Economics."

Heading left out of the pub, Baggot Street soon becomes Merrion Row and runs alongside St. Stephen's Green. Follow it to Grafton Street, just past the Shelbourne Hotel, and turn right. Walk up Grafton to Chatham Street, and turn left. Follow Chatham to Williams Street South, and turn right. The pub is near the corner of Coppinger Row, at 15 William St. S.; it's about a 15-minute walk.

PUB 2: Grogan's Castle Lounge

With its old, wood-paneled walls lined with a ragtag collection of art, this pub is known as one of the city's friendlier joints. It's a favorite with writers and journalists, so it's a great place to eavesdrop on political gossip or hear the latest jokes. Open a newspaper, sit conspicuously near the bar, order a pint of Guinness, and somebody will surely come ask your opinion about something.

Walk left out of the pub and down the alleyway beside it, which brings you to Drury Street; make a left. Follow it to tiny Fade Street, which also looks like an alleyway. Turn right and follow it to the end, which is South Great Georges Street. Make a left and you'll see the pub at 51 S. Great Georges St. The walk should take about 5 minutes.

PUB 3: The Long Hall

Many locals believe this is the city's most handsome pub, and it's easy to see why. Its rich ceiling of red oak, and the titular long bar stretching the length of the building, make it a uniquely atmospheric place in which to sip a pint. The regulars are a mixed group of local professionals and tourists, and the

18th-century McDaid's, where Brendan Behan was a regular.

Dating to 1850, Doheny & Nesbitt packs in contemporary Ireland's movers and shakers.

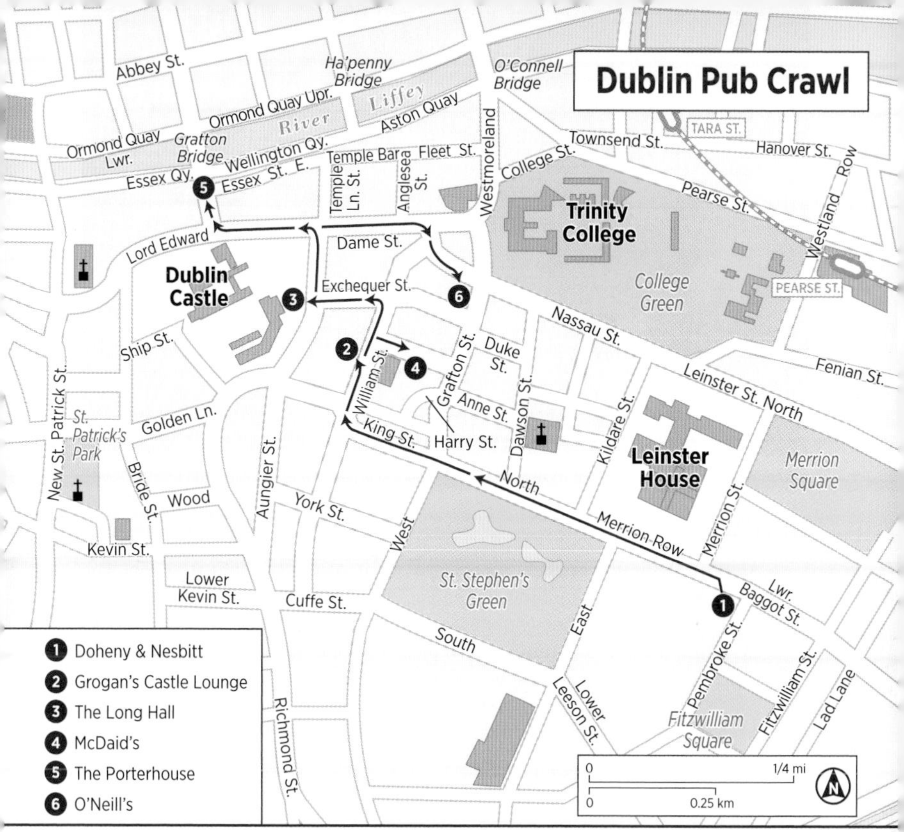

bar staff is friendly. The clock behind the bar mysteriously promising "Correct Time" can be easily ignored, as many a visitor has come for a quick pint but stayed for hours.

Turn left out of the pub, and make an immediate left onto Upper Stephen Street. Follow it for a couple of blocks as it curves around. Turn left on Williams Street South, then make an immediate right onto Chatham Street. Take Chatham to Balfe, and make a left (the Westbury Hotel is on the corner). Balfe curves around to become tiny Harry Street. The pub is at 3 Harry St., and the whole walk should take about 5 minutes.

PUB 4: McDaid's

Just off Grafton Street, McDaid's is one of those rare establishments—able to be all things to all people. Founded in 1779, it's a charming old pub with a long literary history. It was the writer Brendan Behan's favorite pub, and its fame still brings in crowds of tourists, but that doesn't stop the locals from coming, and the colorful mix of Irish regulars and wide-eyed tourists looking for an authentic experience makes for a lively evening. It's packed to the rafters every night.

Walk out of the pub and turn left down Grafton Street, away from St. Stephen's Green. Turn left on Wicklow Street and follow that to South Great Georges Street where you turn right. Follow that to Dame Street, make a left and then a right onto Parliament Street. The pub is at 16 Parliament St., and the walk should take about 10 minutes.

Within its enveloping red walls, the Long Hall has led many a drinking party to third and fourth rounds.

PUB 5: The Porterhouse

After all that pub-crawling, it's time to put some food in your stomach. The Porterhouse is a microbrewery, and it specializes in traditional Irish pub food. You can have a hearty plate of sausages and mash, or a big bowl of Irish stew, and a small half-pint (known just as a "half") of one of their seasonal tasty ales. This is a big, modern pub, with wood floors and lots of tables, so you're likely to get a seat, and you can sit and think about where to go next while filling up on some affordable, quality pub food.

Retrace your steps back up Parliament Street away from the river, and turn left on Dame Street. Follow Dame to College Green, and make a right onto Suffolk Street. The pub is about a block down at 2 Suffolk St. This walk should take about 8 minutes.

PUB 6: O'Neill's

If you've made it this far, then you deserve to finish your night in O'Neill's. This big, blowzy barn of a pub is a lively place to spend an evening. Outside it's a grand, historic Victorian building; inside it's a busy, buzzing space with a lively atmosphere. Bands play most nights, so it's a good place to hear traditional and modern Irish music. It has a band of fiercely loyal regulars who will talk your ear off if you let them. It's a great place to sit back and people-watch into the small hours—but it's certainly not a relaxing spot to wind down.

IRELAND FOR FREE & BY PUBLIC TRANSIT

It's no surprise: Ireland is no longer a cheap country to visit, and hasn't been for some time. Hotels and restaurants are pricey, and in recent years the euro/dollar exchange rate has not been favorable to travelers from the U.S. And that's not even taking into account the global economic conditions that make these uncertain financial times for everybody. But here's the good news: There are a lot of great sites you can visit for free in Ireland, including some of the biggest tourist attractions in the country. You can also save a lot of money by sticking mainly to places that can be reached by public transport, rather than hiring a car (every place we list is easily accessible by train or bus). You'd be surprised how much of Ireland you can see without blowing the budget. (For accommodations, check out the "Moderate" and "Inexpensive" categories in each town and region, and use the tips we give for finding bargain accommodations in chapter 15, "Planning Your Trip to Ireland.") We're starting this tour in Northern Ireland (maybe you got a great deal on a flight to Belfast!), because it's one of the more budget-friendly regions. For more information on train and bus timetables, see **www.irishrail.ie** and **www.buseireann.ie**.

DAYS 1 & 2: Belfast

Finally reinventing itself after many years of stunted growth and political strife, Belfast is a great city to visit right now. It's also full of free visitor attractions. The excellent **Ulster Museum** (p. 582) contains artifacts from across 9,000 years of Irish history, in addition to exhibits more focused on Belfast and her industrial past. Right next door is the **Palm House & Belfast Botanic Gardens** (p. 580), which in turn is a short walk from the campus of **Queen's University** (p. 581). **Belfast City Hall** (p. 578) has free guided tours, while the city's old Victorian swimming baths now contain the **Ormeau Baths Gallery** (p. 581), the region's principal exhibition space for contemporary visual art.

Another exceptional Victorian landmark, **Belfast Castle** (p. 576), is also free to visit; the adjoining **Cave Hill Country Park** (p. 577) is a tranquil place with good walking trails and incredible views of the city. Of course, for all else this city has to offer, it's still most famous for the violence and hardship it endured in the mid– to late 20th century. The epicenter of this was around the **Falls and Shankill roads** (p. 579 and 582). Political murals are still very much a feature of these neighborhoods, which are generally safe for visitors to wander, but you might prefer to splurge £25 on a tour.

Catch a train from Belfast to Dublin (Connolly Station). The trip takes just over 2 hours. The fare (off-peak) for adults is about £10 to £30.

DAYS 3 & 4: Dublin

Ireland's capital is also the number-one destination in the country for free sites. The **Chester Beatty Library** (p. 144) is, for our money, one of the best museums in Ireland. Its collection—which includes illuminated gospels and early copies of the Bible, Torah, and Koran—would easily justify a steep entrance fee, but seeing it won't cost you a penny. Three of the four separate museums that make up the **National Museum of Ireland** are in Dublin, and all are free. The eponymous main site, on Kildare Street (p. 150), contains some of Ireland's greatest archaeological treasures, including a huge horde of Celtic gold. The unique **Natural History Museum** (p. 150) on Merrion Street reopened in May 2010 after a major renovation lasting several years. Also, the former **Collins Barracks** (p. 145) houses the museum's collection of decorative arts.

All of Dublin's major art galleries (at least, those worth visiting) are free. The collection at the **National Gallery of Ireland** (p. 149), though relatively small, includes works by Titian, Vermeer, Monet, and Picasso. Also free are the **Irish Museum of Modern Art** (p. 153), the **Temple Bar Gallery and Studios** (p. 154), the **National Photographic Archive** (p. 161), and the excellent **Hugh Lane Municipal Gallery of Modern Art** (p. 148).

The Crawford Art Gallery in Cork is free to visitors.

Many of Dublin's most historic public buildings don't charge admission. **Áras an Uachtaráin** (the Irish President's House; p. 141) allots entry by tour on a first-come, first-served basis. The **Bank of Ireland Centre/ Parliament House** (p. 158) and the **Four Courts** (p. 159) are also free; **Leinster House** (p. 160) is free, but open by appointment only; while **Custom House** (p. 158) charges just €1.50 to enter its visitor center. The **General Post Office** on O'Connell Street (p. 159) is still a working post office, but has a small number of exhibits devoted to the Easter Rising, including the original Declaration of Independence. Add to this the great public spaces, such as **Phoenix Park** (p. 150), **St. Stephen's Green** (p. 108), and **Trinity College** (p. 152), and it really is possible to spend a full couple of days here without spending a penny on sightseeing.

When you're finished seeing Dublin (but are you ever really finished seeing Dublin?) catch a train from Dublin (Heuston Station) to Galway. You'll get there in just under 3 hours. The off-peak fare for adults is around €25, children €13.

DAY 5: Galway

Ireland's unofficial capital of culture has lots of things you can do for free. The **Galway Arts Centre** (p. 462) usually has good exhibitions, and you can often get cheap tickets for performances. The **Galway City Museum** (p. 462) makes for a good introduction to the region, with a fine collection of artifacts from the medieval period onwards. **St. Nicholas's Collegiate Church,** the oldest church in the city, contains a 12th-century crusader's tomb, among other extraordinary historic pieces. Guided tours are excellent, and cost just €3 (although they should be booked in advance). A little way out of town, the **Galway Irish Crystal Heritage Centre** (p. 462) is an absorbing factory-cum-artisan shop, where you can observe the craftspeople at work on some of the country's trademark crystal creations. This is a great place to offload a little of that money you're saving.

Money-Saving Rail & Bus Passes

For extensive travel by public transport, you can save money by purchasing a rail/bus pass or a rail-only pass. See the box on p. 660 for details on the different passes, where and how you can use them, where to buy them, and current pricing.

Keep your change as you lose track of time on the Mossy Woods Nature Trail in Killarney, County Kerry.

Spend about half a day in Galway, then catch a bus from Galway Bus Station to Cork (Parnell Place Bus Station). In about 4 hours, you'll be in Cork. The off-peak price for adults is around €16, children €13.

DAYS 5 & 6: Cork

County Cork is largely bereft of free sites, but there are enough of them in this lively, bustling city to keep you busy for at least a full day. Start with a trip to the **Old English Market** (p. 303), before heading to the **Cork Public Museum** (p. 302) for an overview of Cork's long and often tumultuous history. Like Dublin, Cork has a couple of first-rate art museums, and most are free to visit. The **Lavit Gallery** (p. 303) showcases work from up-and-coming contemporary artists from the region, while the **Crawford Art Gallery** (p. 302) is quite simply one of the best in the country. The **Mutton Lane Mural** (p. 303) is a more modest artistic offering—but one of the best photo opportunities in the city.

Spend the day, and consider staying over before heading on to Killarney. You can catch a train from Cork to Killarney, changing trains at Mallow, which takes about 3½ hours. The off-peak price for adults is around €25, children €13.

DAYS 6 & 7: Killarney

It's not exactly difficult to reach **Killarney National Park** (p. 358); you just walk toward the cathedral and turn left. This 65-sq.-km (25-sq.-mile) expanse of forest, lakes, and mountains is crisscrossed with several well-thought-out nature trails, plus more challenging routes for serious hikers. A short bus ride will take you to what were formerly the grounds of a great mansion, the **Knockreer Estate** (p. 359), which now contains lovely gardens and beautiful views. Free places to visit in Killarney Town itself include the rather grand neo-Gothic **St. Mary's Cathedral.**

You can stay over in Killarney, or return to Dublin via train. Take the Killarney train to Mallow and then change for Dublin (Heuston Station), which takes about 3½ hours. The off-peak fare is around €20 for adults, children €10.

IRELAND OUTDOORS

4

Ireland is a satisfyingly wild place, where foxes and hares wander in and out of city limits, otters frolic in the rivers, seals bark on the beaches, and wildflowers blanket the countryside so thoroughly it looks like someone spilled the paint. It has spaces of extreme isolation—in Donegal and County Mayo you can drive for long stretches on empty highways and walk for hours along a coastal headland without meeting another human. It can almost be unnerving. But you have to get out of the city to do it.

About a third of Ireland's 4.5 million residents live in Dublin and its sprawling suburbs—and almost half its entire population lives within 97km (60 miles). Apart from a few other small cities, the remaining population spreads thinly across the rest of the island, putting very few demands on the environment. As a result, there are remarkably intact bird and wildlife habitats.

That's the way the locals like it—they love the outdoors and spend as much of their time in it as possible. So what if it rains? That doesn't stop the Irish from golfing, hiking, fishing, and cycling. You're not made of sugar—get outside.

BICYCLING

Bicycling is an ideal way to explore the Irish landscape. The distances are quite manageable, and in a week or two on a bike, you can travel through several of the regions described in this guide or explore one in greater detail. Hostels, B&Bs, and hotels are abundantly available for touring cyclists who don't want to deal with the extra weight of a tent and sleeping bag. Even if you're not game to undertake a full-fledged bike tour, day trips on two wheels are a great way to stretch your legs after spending too much time in the car.

Roads in Ireland are categorized as **M** (Motorway), **N** (National), or **R** (Regional); a few still bear the older **T** (Trunk) and **L** (Link) designations. For reasons of scenery as well as safety, you probably want to avoid motorways and national roads. The R and L are always suitable for cycling, as are the N roads in outlying areas where there isn't too much traffic. The biggest disadvantage of the smaller roads in remote areas is that they often are not signposted, so you should have a good map and compass. In some areas of the west and northwest, *only* the N roads are consistently signposted. Smaller roads are quite narrow and winding, however, which can be somewhat hair-raising.

If you're going to hook up with a cycling outfitter (see below), you probably won't need to bring your own gear. But if you're planning on going it alone, ask your airline how much it will cost to stow your bike in the baggage hold. Be forewarned that airlines are increasingly charging additional fees for "oddly" shaped and bulky items, such as golf bags and bicycles.

Even if you'll be renting a bike, you'll still want to consider bringing a few of your own items. Rental panniers (saddlebags) are often on the flimsy side. If you

PREVIOUS PAGE: **Views from one of Ireland's most transfixing drives, the Conor Pass in County Kerry.**

have cycling shoes and good pedals, you can easily attach them to the rental bike and make your trip immeasurably more enjoyable. With advance notice, most rental shops can outfit a bike with toe clips, bar ends, and water-bottle holders; an advance booking can also improve your chances of reserving the right size bike. Many rental outfits can also arrange a one-way rental over a short distance (up to 161km/100 miles or so). The national companies, such as Eurotrek Raleigh and Ireland Rent-A-Bike (see below), are set up for one-way rentals throughout the country.

> **Mind the Wind**
>
> **If you'll be biking in the west, plan your route from south to north—the same direction as the prevailing winds.**

Anyone cycling in Ireland should be prepared for two inevitable obstacles: wind and hills. Outside the midlands, there are hills just about everywhere, and those on the back roads can have thigh-burning grades. Road engineering is often, well, not very engineered—instead of having switchbacks on a steep slope, roads often climb by the most direct route.

Cyclists have long favored the coastal roads of the southwest, west, and northwest. The quiet roads and rugged scenery of the Beara Peninsula (see chapter 8) make it perfect for a cycling tour, along with the nearby Dingle Peninsula (see chapter 9). The spectacular Causeway Coast and the Glens of Antrim in the North (see chapter 14) are just made for cycling, with quiet roads and dazzling views. Donegal (see chapter 13) is one of the hilliest regions and rewards the energetic cyclist with some of the country's most spectacular coastal and mountain scenery.

Ireland's many islands provide further cycling options—you can bring your bike on all passenger ferries, often for no extra charge, and roads out on the islands have little or no traffic. Some of the best islands with accommodations are Cape Clear, County Cork (see chapter 8); the Aran Islands, County Galway (see chapter 11); and Achill and Clare islands, County Mayo (see chapter 12). There's also some wonderful cycling to be had on Great Blasket Island, County Kerry (see chapter 9), although you'll have to find accommodations on the mainland.

Just one more thing: Remember to cycle on the *left!*

Sheep at Eask Tower in Dingle, County Kerry.

Bicycling Outfitters & Resources

If you're booking from the United States, **Backroads** (✆ **800/462-2848** or 510/527-1555; www.backroads.com) and **VBT** (✆ **800/245-3868;** www.vbt.com) are both well-regarded companies offering all-inclusive bicycle trips in Ireland. Included are bikes, gear, luggage transportation via a support van, good food, and rooms in local inns and hotels of character—everything bundled into one price.

If you want to design your own itinerary and bike independently, several rental agencies with depots nationwide permit one-way rental. They include **Eurotrek Raleigh** (Ireland's largest), Longmile Road, Dublin 12 (✆ **01/465-9659;** www.raleigh.ie); and **Emerald Cycles/Ireland Rent-A-Bike,** Roches Street, Limerick, County Limerick (✆ **061/416983;** www.irelandrentabike.com). Mountain and cross-country bike-rental rates average €20 per day, €80 per week. You can also rent a car bike carrier for €40 per week (good for up to three bikes). On top of the hire price, you'll also have to fork up a refundable deposit of €50 per bike.

If you want your cycling trip to be orchestrated and outfitted by affable local experts, consider **Irish Cycling Safaris,** Belfield Bike Shop, Belfield House, University College Dublin, Dublin 4 (✆ **01/260-0749;** www.cyclingsafaris.com). It offers trips to practically every part of Ireland suitable for two wheels. Group packages include 7 days B&B accommodations and one evening meal and cost €725 (slightly less in off season). If available tour dates don't suit you, or you'd prefer to go it alone, self-guided tours are an option for some locations; they include much the same as group tours (including luggage forwarding) and cost roughly the same as the basic rate plus a €90 supplement. Three- and four-night packages are available to a handful of Ireland's most prime cycling territories, including County Clare and the Burren (see chapter 10).

> **Advance Planning Pays Off**
>
> **Don't wait until you arrive in Ireland to reserve your bike. Places do get booked up, and several outfitters have gone out of business in the past few years due to sky-rocketing insurance costs and the recession. The only way to guarantee you'll have a bike is to prebook.**

For independent cycling adventures in the southeast of Ireland, contact **Celtic Cycling,** 22 Ballybricken, Waterford (✆ **051/850228;** www.celticcycling.com). On the opposite side of the island, **Irish Cycle Tours,** 28 The Anchorage, Tralee, County Kerry (✆ **066/712-8733;** www.irishcycletours.com), offers guided and self-guided tours in the west—specifically Kerry and Connemara—for everyone from honeymooners and families to seniors and singles.

WALKING

Hiking is an increasingly popular activity in Ireland. Since 1982, the network of long-distance, marked trails has grown from 1 to 25, and now stretches across more than 2,414km (1,500 miles). The first to open was the **Wicklow Way,** which begins just outside Dublin and proceeds through rugged hills and serene pastures on its 132km (82-mile) course. Others include the **Beara Peninsula** (see chapter 8), the **Kerry Way** (see chapter 9), the **Dingle Way** (see chapter 9), and the **Ulster Way** (see chapter 14). Most trails are routed so that meals and accommodations—B&Bs, hostels, or hotels—are never more than a day's walk apart. Routes are generally uncrowded, and lots of people tend to walk just part of the trails' lengths.

The Dingle Way.

Though long-distance routes are the best-marked trails in Ireland, the signposting is surprisingly random and inadequate, and a good terrain map is an absolute necessity. Don't expect the kind of close management you'd find on trails in national parks in the U.S., however; the countryside here may be awe-inspiring, but it can get to feel very wild indeed once you're a few miles off the beaten path.

Markers are frequently miles apart and often seem to be lacking at crucial crossroads. Look for a post or cairn on each summit, which usually indicates the way between two peaks. Trees on Irish hillsides rarely impede visibility but a compass becomes crucial when a fog blows in and all landmarks quickly disappear. ***Be warned:*** This can happen quite unexpectedly, and the safest strategy when you can't see your way is to stay exactly where you are until the fog clears.

The walks listed in this guide are on clearly marked trails whenever possible, and otherwise indicated if sections are without markings. We can't give you all the information you need for the walks, so you should consult the local tourist office for advice before setting out. Visitors from Britain—or those who are familiar with their fiercely upheld "rambling" laws—should note that the laws are not the same in Ireland. In parts of the U.K. (*not* including Northern Ireland), walkers have the right of way across most private property when the land is rural and uncultivated, and fences that cross public paths must have places for walkers to pass through. By contrast, in Ireland the laws favor property owners, and farmers are passionate about the privacy of their land. Basically, stay on marked paths, or face the unmitigated wrath of a territorial Irish sheep farmer.

Impressions

Our greatest glory is not in never falling, but in rising every time we fall.

—Oliver Goldsmith (1730–1774)

Luckily, there are some lovely, well-marked paths you can follow without upsetting anybody. For inland hillwalking, try the Wicklow Way (see chapter 6), the Galtee Mountains (see chapter 10), or Glenveagh National Park (see chapter 13). For coastal walks, the best-known kind in this island country, try the Beara Peninsula (see chapter 8), the Inishowen Peninsula (see chapter 13), the Dingle Peninsula (see chapter 9), the Western Way in Connemara (see chapter 11), and the Donegal Bay Coast (see chapter 13).

Walking Resources

Start your research on the Web. Two excellent online resources with plenty of recommended walks are **www.gowalkingireland.com** and **www.walkni.com**. The **Mountaineering Council of Ireland,** which oversees hillwalking on the island, can be visited at **www.mountaineering.ie**.

Before leaving home, you can order maps and guidebooks, including details of available accommodations en route, from **EastWest Mapping,** Clonegal, Enniscorthy, County Wexford (✆ **053/937-7835;** www.eastwestmapping.ie). You can buy maps and guidebooks in local bookshops and outdoor-gear shops across Ireland. Guides can also be obtained from **AnÓige,** the Irish Youth Hostel Association, 61 Mountjoy St., Dublin 1 (✆ **01/830-4555;** www.anoige.ie), or in the North from **Hostelling International Northern Ireland,** 22–32 Donegall Rd., Belfast BT12 5JN (✆ **028/9032-4733;** www.hini.org.uk).

Ordnance Survey maps are available in several scales; the most helpful to the walker is the 1:50,000, or 1¼-inches-to-1-mile, scale. This series is currently available for all of Northern Ireland and a limited number of locations in the Republic. A half-inch-to-1-mile series covers the whole country in 25 maps, available in most shops. These indicate roads, major trails, and historic monuments in exceptional detail. For Ordnance Survey maps, contact **Ordnance Survey Ireland,** Phoenix Park, Dublin 8 (✆ **01/802-5300;** www.osi.ie), or **Ordnance Survey of Northern Ireland,** Colby House, Stranmillis Court,

Wildflower season in the Burren, County Clare.

IRELAND'S NATIONAL parks

Ireland's six **national parks** offer some of the most spectacular scenery and best walking in the country, and all have free admission.

- The **Burren National Park,** Mullaghmore, County Clare (**www.burrennationalpark.ie**), holds fascinating landscapes—a series of limestone beds eroded during the Ice Age to form a barren, lunarlike landscape. The Burren is of particular interest to botanists, since it's the only place in the world where Arctic, Mediterranean, and Alpine species of wildflowers grow side by side in the fissures of the rock.
- **Connemara National Park,** Letterfrack, County Galway (**www.connemaranationalpark.ie**), is a rugged, heather-clad landscape of blanket bog and wet heath, encompassing some of the Twelve Bens mountain range. There are nature trails with accompanying map/booklets (guided walks are available in summer) and a visitor center at Letterfrack.
- **Glenveagh National Park,** near Gweedore, County Donegal (**www.glenveaghnationalpark.ie**), is Ireland's largest national park and also its remotest wilderness—103,600 sq. km (40,000 sq. miles) of mountains, lakes, and natural woodlands that are home to a large red deer population. From the visitor center, you can grab a ride on a minibus along the shores of Lough Veagh to Glenveagh Castle, notable for its outstanding gardens. There are also a self-guided nature trail and a summer program of guided walks.
- **Killarney National Park,** Killarney, County Kerry (**www.killarneynationalpark.ie**), contains nearly 64,750 sq. km (25,000 sq. miles) of spectacular lake and mountain scenery. There are four self-guided trails, a visitor center with a restaurant, and two small lodges with tearooms.
- **Ballycroy National Park,** Ballycroy, County Mayo (**www.ballycroynationalpark.ie**), is the newest of the parks, centered in the Owenduff-Nephinbeg area. It features gorgeous bog landscapes. Along with a visitor center in Ballycroy, there are nature trails galore.
- **Wicklow Mountains National Park,** Glendalough, County Wicklow (**www.wicklowmountainsnationalpark.ie**), is the only park of the six that's not on the west coast. At over 129,500 sq. km (50,000 sq. miles), it contains picturesque woodlands, moors, and mountains, and includes the atmospheric Glendalough monastic site and the Glenealo Valley. There is a park information office at the Upper Lake, near the Glendalough car park.

In addition to national parks, there are 12 **forest reserve parks,** several of which were former private estates. Among the most enchanting is **Lough Key Forest Park** (**www.loughkey.ie**), in County Roscommon, which features a bog-garden, fairy bridge, and archaeological monuments. Contact Tourism Ireland for more information on Ireland's park system.

Hikers on the green road of the Aran islands.

Statuary adorns the gardens at Glenveagh National Park in County Donegal.

Belfast BT9 5BJ (✆ **028/9025-5774;** maps.osni.gov.uk). Tourism Ireland's booklet *Walking Ireland* and the Northern Ireland Tourist Board's *An Information Guide to Walking* are both very helpful. Other excellent resources include *Best Irish Walks,* edited by Joss Lynam (Passport Books, 1995); the similarly named *Best Walks in Ireland* by David Marshall (Frances Lincoln, 2006); *West of Ireland Walks* by Kevin Corcoran (O'Brien Press, 2008); and *Irish Long Distance Walks: A Guide to All the Way-Marked Trails,* by Michael Fewer (Gill and Macmillan, 1993).

In the west of Ireland, there's a wide selection of guided walks in the Burren, from 1 day to a week or more. Contact **Guided Walks and Hikes** (✆ **065/707-6100;** www.burrenguidedwalks.com) for a wide selection of guided walks and hikes of varying lengths. In the southwest, contact **SouthWestWalks Ireland,** 28 The Anchorage, Tralee, County Kerry (✆ **066/712-8733;** www.southwestwalksireland.com). For a full walking holiday package to County Kerry or County Clare and Connemara, consult **Backroads,** 801 Cedar St., Berkeley, CA, 94710 (✆ **800/462-2848;** www.backroads.com).

On the Northern Ireland Tourist Board's website (**www.discovernorthernireland.com/walking**), a walking and hiking page lists self-guided tours, short hikes along the Ulster Way, and names and addresses of organizations offering guided walks throughout the North.

A WALK ON THE wild SIDE

One hazard you won't encounter in the Irish countryside is meeting dangerous animals. Fearsome beasts once common around these parts—including brown bears, wolves, and wildcats—are long since extinct, and we all know the story about St. Patrick banishing the snakes. You may, however, meet European foxes (more the size of large dogs than their American cousins) or badgers, but both are notoriously timid creatures; leave them alone and they'll quite happily follow suit. In fact, if the experience of your authors is anything to go by, the worst you have to fear is an attack of the heebie-jeebies from encountering large spiders (up to 5 or 8cm/2 or 3 inches in length); although these, too, are entirely harmless.

Nope, nothing to fear in the countryside—that is, unless you believe in monsters. **Doyar-Chú** are creatures said to live in the lakes of County Galway. Half-dog, half-fish, and about the size of a crocodile, they supposedly lie in wait for unsuspecting hikers and dog walkers, ready to drag them underwater with their terrifying jaws. Meanwhile, **Muckie** is a Loch Ness monster–type beastie (allegedly) spotted in the Lakes of Killarney. Descriptions range from your average terrifying sea monster to, well, a scary giant black aquatic hog that rises out of the depths of Lough Leane. (That's right. Hog.) Muckie was given an unexpected boost a few years ago when a sonar survey of the lakes showed a large unidentified object that could conceivably have been a living creature, although it vanished instantly. A Japanese TV crew went searching for the beast in 2004, but failed to find anything.

Our advice? Bring a camera. That seems to ensure the monsters will leave you alone given that nobody's ever managed to photograph anything.

BIRD-WATCHING

Ireland is of great interest to birders because of its position on the migration routes of many passerines and seabirds, which find the isle a convenient stopping point on their Atlantic journeys. Opportunities for birding abound, particularly in the 71 **National Nature Reserves.** The network of reserves covers woodlands, bog lands, grasslands, sand dune systems, bird sanctuaries, coastal heath lands, and marine areas.

Most of the important nesting colonies for seabirds are on the west coast, the westernmost promontory of Europe; exceptions are Lambey Island, near Dublin, and Great Saltee in County Wexford. Sandy beaches and tidal flats on the east and west coasts are nesting grounds for large populations of winter waders and smaller, isolated tern colonies. In the North, the largest seabird colony is on Rathlin Island, off the North Antrim Coast.

Until recently, rural Ireland was home to large numbers of a small bird known as the **corncrake** *(Crex crex)*, whose unusual cry during breeding season was a common feature of the early summer night. Sadly, the introduction of heavy machinery for cutting silage has destroyed the protective high-grass environment in which the mother corncrake lays her eggs. (The period for cutting silage coincides with the corncrake breeding period.) Ireland now has only a few areas where the corncrake still breeds. One is the **Shannon Callows ★**, where the bird's cry, which now seems quite mournful, can often be heard in the quiet of nightfall.

Ireland's lakes and wetlands also serve as a **wintering ground** for great numbers of wildfowl from the Arctic and northern Europe. From Greenland, Iceland, and Canada come waders such as knot, golden plover, and black-tailed godwit; flocks of brent, barnacle, and white-fronted geese; and thousands of whooper swans. Every year, as many as 10,000 Greenland white-fronted geese winter on the north shores of Wexford Harbour, making it a mecca for birders. Flooded fields, or "callows," provide habitats for wigeons, whooping swans, and plover; the callows of the Shannon and the Blackwater are especially popular with birders. One of the best winter bird-watching sites is the Wexford Wildfowl Reserve (see chapter 7).

From March onward, mild **spring** weather invites Irish birds to begin nesting early, and their songs fill the woods and hedgerows. The arrival of migrants from Africa can be observed in April and May all along the south coast. Rathlin Island reserve (see chapter 14), home to Northern Ireland's largest seabird colony, is best visited in May and June.

Summer is the time to head to the west of Ireland, where seaside cliffs are an ideal place for large seabird colonies such as puffins and gannets. Some of the best summer birding sites are Great Saltee Island (see chapter 7), Cape Clear Island (see chapter 8), the Skellig Islands (see chapter 9), and Loop Head (see chapter 10).

Autumn is a particularly attractive time for bird-watchers in Ireland, when many rare American waders—mainly sandpipers and plovers—arrive when blown across the Atlantic. A spectacular avian event is the annual fall migration of brent geese. On the shores of Strangford Lough in County Down—Europe's premier brent-watching site—you might see as many as 3,000 on a single day.

Bird-Watching Resources

One of the best sources of information is the **Irish Birding** website (**www.irishbirding.com**), which features links on birding events, sites, and news. Another excellent resource is **BirdWatch Ireland,** Rockingham House, Newcastle, County Wicklow (✆ **01/281-9878;** www.birdwatchireland.ie), an organization devoted to bird conservation in the Republic of Ireland. An equivalent organization in Northern Ireland is the **Royal Society for the Protection of Birds,** Belvoir Park Forest, Belfast BT8 7QT (✆ **028/9049-1547;** www.rspb.org.uk/northernireland).

Wexford Wildfowl Reserve, North Slob, Wexford (✆ **053/912-3406;** www.wexfordwildfowlreserve.ie), has a visitor center with information on local bird-watching sites. The reserve's full-time warden, Chris Wilson, can direct you to other places corresponding to your areas of interest.

The **Altamont Garden,** Tullow, County Wicklow (✆ **059/915-9444;** www.altamontgarden.com), offers weekend courses in ornithology. See chapter 6 for more information.

The bird observatory at the North Harbour, on **Cape Clear Island,** has a warden in residence from March to November and accommodations for bird-watchers. **Ciarán and Mary O'Driscoll** (✆ **028/39153;** www.capeclearisland.com), who operate a B&B on the island, also run boat trips for bird-watchers around the island and have a keen eye for vagrants and rarities.

Northern Ireland has two first-class nature centers for bird enthusiasts, both ideal for families. **Castle Espie,** 78 Ballydrain Rd., Comber, County Down BT23 6EA (✆ **028/9187-4146**), is home to a large collection of ducks, geese, and swans. The **Lough Neagh Discovery Centre,** Oxford Island, Craigavon, County Armagh (✆ **028/3832-2205**), is in the outstanding Oxford Island National Nature Reserve (**www.oxfordisland.com**).

GOLF

Golf is the single biggest sporting attraction in Ireland, with nearly a quarter of a million visitors traveling here specifically to play. The Irish landscape and climate, like those of Scotland, seem almost custom-designed for scenic links, fair fairways, green greens, and dramatic traps—and there is never a shortage of 19th holes. In short, Ireland is a place of golfing pilgrimage.

Best of all, golfing is not confined to those with an Olympian income. Membership fees do not require mortgages, and greens fees for walk-ins are often quite modest, especially on weekdays and at off-peak hours.

See "Sports & Outdoor Pursuits" in each of the sightseeing chapters for a recommended selection of each region's top courses.

Golf Resources

Tourism Ireland has a dedicated golf website with numerous contacts and links (no pun intended) at **www.golf.discoverireland.ie/Home.aspx**.

A host of U.S. companies offer package golf tours. Among them are **Golf International** (✆ **800/833-1389** or 212/986-9176; www.golfinternational.com) and **Wide World of Golf** (✆ **800/214-4653;** www.wideworldofgolf.com).

HORSEBACK RIDING

Ireland is a horse-loving country, with a plethora of stables and equestrian centers offering trail rides and instruction. The **Association of Irish Riding Establishments** (www.aire.ie) is the regulatory body that accredits stables,

Horses and cows are not uncommon on the beaches of Connemara.

Stocky Connemara ponies are built to traverse the region's rugged terrain.

ensuring adequate safety standards and instructor competence. Riding prices range from about €20 to €50 per hour; expect to pay €25 on average. A list of accredited stables throughout the country is available from Tourism Ireland.

Choose your trek or horse ride based on your interests and experience. Pony trekking caters primarily to beginners, and you don't need experience. Long-distance trail riding requires you to trot for extended periods, which can be exhausting (and painful) for a novice. Some horse-riding tours offer meals and lodging as well as riding. Post-to-post trail riding allows a rider to stay at different lodgings each night, riding on trails all day.

Horseback Riding Resources

Tourism Ireland has an informative section on its website about horse riding. Visit **www.discoverireland.com**, click on "Things to see & do," then "Activities," and then select "Equestrian."

Two good riding establishments on the west coast are **Dingle Horse Riding,** Ballinaboula, Dingle, County Kerry (✆ **066/915-2199;** www.dingle horseriding.com), and **Drummindoo Stud & Equestrian Centre,** Knockranny, Westport, County Mayo (✆ **098/25616;** www.drummindoo.com).

In Dublin, you can go trail riding through Phoenix Park with **Ashtown Riding Stables** (✆ **01/838-3807**). They're in the village of Ashtown adjoining the park and only 10 minutes by car or bus (no. 37, 38, 39, or 70) from the city center. Among the other riding centers within easy reach of downtown Dublin are **Carrickmines Equestrian Centre,** Glenamuck Road, Foxrock, Dublin 18 (✆ **01/295-5990;** www.carrickminesequestrian.ie), and **Brennanstown Riding School,** Hollybrook, County Wicklow (✆ **01/286-3778;** www.brennanstownrs.ie). You can

Call Ahead

Always phone ahead to make sure any particular equestrian center is still offering rides. Many have discontinued this service in the past few years due to skyrocketing insurance costs.

see the beaches of Connemara from horseback on a trek with the **Cleggan Riding Centre,** Cleggan, County Galway (✆ **095/44746;** www.clegganriding centre.com). The center offers beach and mountain treks, and the most popular is a 3-hour ride to Omey Island at low tide.

Hidden Trails (✆ **888/9-TRAILS** [987-2457]; www.hiddentrails.com) offers 7-day guided riding tours in several regions in Ireland, including the Wicklow Mountains, West Cork, and Connemara. The tours are graded easy, moderate, or challenging, and include lodging and meals (breakfast, picnic lunch, and dinner).

FISHING

What makes Ireland such a great fishing destination? A coastline of more than 5,603km (3,472 miles), thousands of lakes and ponds, countless creeks, rills, streams, and rivers—those certainly don't hurt. Ireland's temperate climate and low pollution also encourage a high fish population, and low human density has put little pressure on that. It all adds up to fairly ideal fishing conditions.

The sport of fishing—referred to by the Irish as **angling**—is a cherished tradition. Festivals and competitions celebrate the many forms of this sport; for dates and locations, contact Tourism Ireland; you have to sign up well in advance to participate in most of the competitions. Among the festivals are **Killybegs International Sea Angling Festival** in July, the **Baltimore Deep Sea Angling Festival** (www.baltimoreseaangling.com) in August, and the **Cobh International Deep Sea Angling Festival** in September.

In the west and northwest, Killybegs (see chapter 13) is a center for sea angling, while Lough Corrib (see chapter 11) offers much to entice the freshwater angler. The Killarney area (see chapter 9) is a popular angling destination, as are the Blackwater River near Cork and Kinsale (see chapter 8) for sea angling. Also consider the Shannon River and its lakes.

Fishing Resources

The best all-round online resource for fishing in Ireland is the prosaically named **Fishing in Ireland (www.fishinginireland.info)**. In addition to up-to-date details on licenses and permits (see below), it also has a wealth of information on everything from local regulations, weather, and tides to locations suitable for anglers with disabilities. Tourism Ireland devotes a section of its website to fishing. Visit **www.discoverireland.com**, click on "Things to see & do," then "Activities," and then "Fishing."

A helpful brochure, *Angling in Ireland,* detailing what fish can be caught where, is available from the Angling Information Office at the **Central Fisheries Board,** Swords Business Campus, Swords, County Dublin (✆ **01/884-2600;** fax 01/836-0060; www.cfb.ie). Another helpful resource, *The Angler's Guide,* is published by Tourism Ireland. Permits, licenses, and specific information can also be obtained from local outfitters or the Central Fisheries Board.

Fishing seasons are as follows: salmon, January 1 to September 30; brown trout, February 15 to October 12; sea trout, June 1 to September 30; coarse fishing and sea angling, all year. A license is required only for salmon and sea trout angling; the cost is €20 for a day, €46 for 21 days, or €120 annually. For information about permits, visit the Central Fisheries Boards website (www.cfb.ie). You can purchase fishing licenses at most bait and tackle shops. For all private salmon and sea trout fisheries, a permit is required in addition to the license, and it can be considerably more expensive. Prices vary greatly, from €10 to €200 per rod per day (depending on the venue and provider), although most permits run €30 to €40.

Many hotels have exclusive access to lakes and ponds, and will rent boats, gear, and *ghillies* (fishing guides) to their guests. Over a dozen such hotels have formed the **Great Fishing Houses of Ireland** (**www.irelandfishing.com**). Examples include Adare Manor in Limerick (p. 414); the Delphi Lodge in County Galway (p. 483); and Newport House Hotel and Enniscoe House, both in Mayo (p. 507).

In Northern Ireland, you must get a rod license from the **Department for Culture, Arts and Leisure (DCNI),** 1–7 Bedford St., Belfast, County Antrim (✆ **028/9025-8825;** www.dcalni.gov.uk), or in the Derry area from the **Foyle Carlingford Irish Lights Commission,** 22 Victoria Rd., Derry (✆ **028/7134-2100;** www.loughs-agency.org). A permit may also be required; you can obtain information from local outfitters or the DCNI. A rod license costs £3.50 to £24, depending on the license provider and duration of license; day permits cost around £10. You can find a wealth of information in *An Information Guide to Game Fishing,* available from any office of the Northern Ireland Tourist Board.

KAYAKING

This sport has always been popular with the natives—and no wonder, considering the island's 5,603km (3,472 miles) of coastline, plus its numerous lakes and rivers.

In particular, the coastline provides year-round superb sea-kayaking waters, some of which are remote, with spectacular scenery. In a sea kayak, the wonders of the Irish coast can be investigated up close. You'll find caves, tiny inlets, out-of-the-way cliffs, and reefs inhabited by abundant seabirds, colorful crustaceans, seals, and the occasional dolphin. Many islands are within easy reach of the mainland, and with experience and good conditions, a sea kayaker can reach any of Ireland's island outposts.

A number of adventure centers offer kayaking lessons, and a few schools are devoted solely to kayaking. For those new to the sport or unfamiliar with the Irish coast, a guided excursion is the best option.

Kayaking Resources

For a rich source of information about kayaking in Ireland, visit the **Irish Canoe Union** website at **www.canoe.ie**.

Courses and day trips for all levels of experience are available from **Deep Blue Sea Kayaking** (✆ **086/820-5627;** www.deepblueseakayaking.com) and **Shearwater Sea Kayaking** (✆ **086/836-8736** or 087/988-5658; www.shearwaterseakayaking.ie). Although kayaking is mainly a summer activity, the latter also runs special winter excursions to the Skerries and Lambay Island in Dublin Bay. Kayaking vacations are also available at **Delphi Mountain Resort,** Leenane, County Galway (✆ **095/42208;** www.delphimountainresort.com).

SAILING

Whether by cruising from port to port or dinghy sailing on the lakes, many regions of Ireland can best be experienced from the water. The craggy and indented coastline has plenty of safe havens for overnight stops—there are more than 140 between Cork Harbor and the Dingle Peninsula alone. This region of West Cork and Kerry is the most popular coastline for cruising, and several companies offer yacht charters.

Some of the harbors in the southwest that are most popular with sailors include Cork, Kinsale, Glandore, Baltimore, and Bantry. On the **west coast,** Killary Harbour, Westport, and Sligo have sailing clubs and are in areas of great beauty. There are also several sailing clubs and yacht-charter companies in the Dublin area.

Sailing Resources

Sailing schools hold courses for sailors at all levels of experience, and sometimes offer day sailing as well. Ireland also has more than 120 yacht and sailing clubs along the coast and lakes. The best sources for information are Tourism Ireland; the **Irish Sailing Association,** 3 Park Rd., Dún Laoghaire, County Dublin (✆ **01/280-0239;** www.sailing.ie); and *East and North Coasts of Ireland Sailing Directions* and *South and West Coasts of Ireland Sailing Directions* (both published by Imray, Laurie, Norie & Wilson Ltd. of Wych House) from the Irish Cruising Club (**www.irishcruisingclub.com**). The guides give information on harbors, port facilities, tides, and other topics of interest. They are available in bookshops in Ireland or online at www.imray.com.

The **International Sailing Schools Association** is an excellent resource for finding a sailing school; you can find links to members at www.sailingschools.org.

A BIT OF adventure

If you're looking for more from your Ireland trip than just a bit of golf or hiking, you might want to try one of the country's adventure centers. These lively, youthful facilities offer a range of guided activities—from rappelling to kite surfing—in some of the country's most remote and beautiful settings, along with accommodations, food, and all you need for a holiday with like-minded folk.

The **Delphi Mountain Resort,** Leenane, County Galway (✆ **095/42208;** www.delphimountainresort.com), is a popular option deep in the mountains of County Galway. There is almost nothing you can't do here; the resort offers courses in kayaking, windsurfing, and raft building, as well as mountaineering, abseiling, hiking, and archery. Everything is reasonably priced, and the atmosphere is laid-back and friendly.

Another option is **Little Killary Adventure Company,** Leenane, County Galway (✆ **095/43411;** www.killaryadventure.com), which will take you on Hobie Cat sailing trips, or guide you through an exploration of the countryside by kayak, water skis, or on foot on hill- and coastal walking tours, straight up on rock-climbing expeditions, and more.

On the southern shores of Carlingford Lough, an hour's drive north of Dublin, the **Carlingford Adventure Centre** (✆ **042/937-3100;** www.carlingfordadventure.com) offers residential and day courses in canoeing, kayaking, sailing, and windsurfing, as well as land-based activities such as rock climbing, archery, zip wire, and the ominously titled "Leap of Faith."

Sailing Ireland (✆ **053/913-9163;** www.sailingireland.ie) runs a variety of sailing courses, and also offers yacht charters from its base in Bridgetown, County Wexford.

Kinsale Yacht Charters, 2 Castlepark Marina Centre, Kinsale, County Cork (✆ **087/271-0371;** www.kinsaleyachtcharter.com; see chapter 8), is one of the largest charter firms in Ireland and also offers package deals. A full range of yacht sailing options is available from **Sovereign Sailing** (✆ **021/477-4145;** www.sovereignsailing.com). They also offer racing charter packages if money is no object. Yacht charters are also available from **Shannon Sailing Ltd.,** New Harbour, Dromineer, Nenagh, County Tipperary (✆ **067/24499;** www.shannonsailing.com).

DIVING

With visibility averaging 15m (49 ft.) and occasionally reaching 29m (95 ft.), and many wrecks to explore, the west coast of Ireland may be cold, but it's still a pretty good place for divers.

The Irish dive season generally starts in March and ends in October, although specific dates depend on your comfort zone. Outside these months, weather and ocean conditions could make jumping into the sea unappealing. The PADI open-water diver certification is the minimum requirement for all dives; most schools also offer introductory dives for novices.

The rocky coast of West Cork and Kerry is great for diving, with centers in Baltimore (see chapter 8) and Dingle (see chapter 9). On the west coast, there are many great locations, one of which is the deep, sheltered Killary Harbour. Northern Ireland offers many interesting dives, with more than 400 named wrecks off the coast and many in the Irish Sea and in Belfast Lough.

Diving Resources

The **Irish Underwater Council** (**CFT,** or **Comhairle Fo-Thuinn**), 78A Patrick St., Dún Laoghaire, County Dublin (✆ **01/284-4601;** www.cft.ie), is an association of more than 70 Irish diving clubs. Its website lists information on diving and snorkeling, dive centers, and dive hotels (no pun intended) throughout the Republic, and publishes the *CFT Guide to Dive Sites* and other information on exploring the Emerald Isle's emerald waters. The CFT operates under the aegis of the CMAS (Confédération Mondiale des Activités Subaquatiques), the world diving federation.

Sign up for certified level-one and level-two instruction and equipment rental for kayaking, sailing, and windsurfing at the **Surfdock Centre,** Grand Canal Dock Yard, Ringsend, Dublin 4 (✆ **01/668-3945;** www.surfdock.ie). Dublin Bay is filled with sea life and old wrecks, making it ideal for cold-water diving. To try it out, get in touch with **Oceantec Adventures** in Dún Laoghaire (toll-free within Ireland at ✆ **1800/272-822**). It offers a five-star PADI diving school and arranges dive vacations on the west coast.

The **UK Diving** website, **www.ukdiving.co.uk**, features information on diving in the North, including an excellent wreck database you can access either through a conventional listing or by pinpointing on a map.

Irish dive centers and schools include **Discover Scuba,** 20 Terenure Park, Dublin 6 (✆ **01/492-7392;** www.discoverscuba.ie); **Oceantec Adventures,** Dún Laoghaire, County Dublin (✆ **1800/272-822**); **Baltimore Diving**

Centre, Baltimore, County Cork (✆/fax **028/20300;** www.baltimore diving.com); and **Scubadive West,** Renvyle, County Galway (✆ **095/ 43922;** www.scubadivewest.com).

WINDSURFING

Kite surfing is a thrill along Ireland's wind-swept coast.

Windsurfing is increasingly popular in Ireland, and some spots play host to vast flotillas of colorful sails and wet-suited windsurfers when conditions are good. Some of the best locations are in remote areas of the west coast, and those spots are rarely crowded. Windsurfing schools with boards for rent can be found in most regions of the country, with the greatest concentration on the southeast and southwest coasts.

In Dublin the most popular spot is Dollymount Beach; Salthill, behind Dún Laoghaire Harbour, is another good choice. In the Southeast, try Brittas Bay (County Wicklow), Cahore (County Wexford), and Rosslare (County Wexford). Dunmore East (County Waterford), Dungarvan (County Waterford), and Cobh (County Cork) are good in the south. The most challenging waves and winds are in the west, at Brandon Bay on the Dingle Peninsula, Roundstone in Galway, Achill Island in Mayo, and Magheroarty and Rossnowlagh in Donegal.

Because even skilled windsurfers spend a sizable portion of their time in the water, the water quality is surely a concern. The Republic of Ireland has 27 designated European Union Blue Flag beaches and marinas, and Northern Ireland has 12. To find a complete listing or to check out a particular beach in advance, go to **www.blueflag.org**.

Windsurfing Resources

Equipment rental and lessons are widely available on Ireland's coasts and lakes. Try the following centers: the **Surfdock Centre,** Grand Canal Dock Yard, Ringsend, Dublin 4 (✆ **01/668-3945;** www.surfdock.ie); the **Dunmore East Adventure Centre,** Dunmore East, County Waterford (✆ **051/383783;** www.dunmoreadventure.com); the **Oysterhaven Centre,** Oysterhaven, Kinsale, County Cork (✆ **021/477-0738;** www.oysterhaven.com); and, in the North, **Craigavon Watersports Centre,** 1 Lake Rd., Craigavon, County Armagh (✆ **028/3834-2669;** www.craigavonactivity.org).

If kite surfing is your thing, check out the website **www.kitesurfing.ie**. It offers advice on where to buy or rent boards, the best locations, and weather conditions, and it also hooks you up with other kite surfers.

5

DUBLIN

STELLA ARTOIS
Coors
BRAUEREI BECK & CO
BECK'S
VIER
BREMEN GERMANY
SMITHWICK'S
GUINNES

It's easy to fall for charming, crazy, colorful Dublin. The laid-back Irish capital is a somehow harmonious blend of Victorian pubs, rows of elegant Georgian town houses in silvery stone, and glittering modern buildings. With a permanent population of nearly 1.7 million; more than a third of the Irish people either live in or near this city, which explains the great restaurants, bars, and shopping opportunities. Get ready to have a good time.

THINGS TO DO From the **National Museum** and its ancient caches of polished gold, stroll along Georgian terraces around **Merrion Square,** past the homes of literary luminaries like Yeats, Wilde, and Beckett. Nearby is **Dublin Castle,** which houses the **Chester Beatty Library.** You'll find plenty of Dubliners welcoming sunny days on the flower-strewn **St. Stephen's Green.** Take a walk north over the River Liffey and up statue-lined **O'Connell Street** to the **Dublin City Gallery** for Francis Bacon's chaotic studio.

SHOPPING On weekends in **Temple Bar** you can find markets filling its cobbled squares, where stalls are piled high with farmhouse cheeses. Splash out on your favorite Kevin Sharkey abstract painting or Georgian furniture along **Francis Street**'s arts and antique stores. Inside the **Powerscourt Centre,** local young designers sell reworked vintage clothes and delicate silver jewelry. Edge past the buskers on pedestrianized **Grafton Street,** where a top-hatted doorman welcomes you into the elegant, 160-year-old **Brown Thomas** department store.

NIGHTLIFE & ENTERTAINMENT From the storied **Abbey Theatre** to the shining new Daniel Libeskind–designed **Grand Canal Theatre,** Dublin's theatre scene is thriving. Settle down in a wood-paneled booth at a pub for a **traditional music** session with fiddles and pipes, or perch up at the bar where it won't take long for the locals to start a conversation. For sports lovers, you can't beat cheering on the "Dubs" at the mammoth Croke Park stadium at a high-octane hurling match.

RESTAURANTS & DINING Dublin's horizons are widening, from Goan fish curries to top sushi. Stylish seafood restaurants dot the neighborhoods near the Grand Canal. Locals favor fresh Dublin Bay oysters or a hearty lamb-and-Guinness pie at a pub in the city center. On the Liffey's north bank, tucked-away trattorias offer homemade pasta with crusty bread.

ORIENTATION

222km (138 miles) NE of Shannon Airport, 258km (160 miles) NE of Cork, 167km (104 miles) S of Belfast, 309km (192 miles) NE of Killarney, 219km (136 miles) E of Galway, 237km (147 miles) SE of Derry, 142km (88 miles) N of Wexford

PREVIOUS PAGE: **A barkeep at Panti Bar, near the banks of the Liffey.**

Arriving

BY PLANE **Aer Lingus,** Ireland's national airline, operates regularly scheduled, direct flights into Dublin International Airport from Chicago, Boston, Orlando, and New York's JFK. (Aer Lingus no longer operates direct flights to Dublin from the West Coast). **American Airlines** flies to Dublin from Chicago, **Delta Airlines** from Atlanta and New York, **Continental Airlines** from Newark, and **US Airways** from Philadelphia, and also from Charlotte during the summer months. Charters operate from a number of U.S. and Canadian cities. You can also fly from the United States to other European cities and backtrack to Dublin (see "Getting There & Around" in chapter 15). The flight from London takes an hour and a half; from Paris it's 2 hours.

Dublin International Airport (✆ **01/814-1111;** www.dublinairport.com) is 11km (6¾ miles) north of the city center. A travel information desk in the arrivals concourse provides information on public bus and rail services throughout the country.

An excellent airport-to-city shuttle bus service called **AirCoach** operates 24 hours a day, making runs at 15-minute intervals. Its buses run direct from the airport to Dublin's city center and south side, stopping at O'Connell Street, St. Stephen's Green, Merrion Square, Ballsbridge, Donnybrook, and Dalkey—that is, all the key hotel and business districts. Not all the major stops are covered on every service, so do check you've got the right one before you board. The fare is €7 one-way or €12 round-trip for the city center, €8/€14 for Ballsbridge and beyond. Children aged 5 to 12 are €1.50 each way, no matter where you're going. You buy your ticket from the driver. Although AirCoach is slightly more expensive than the Dublin Bus (see below), it makes fewer stops, so it is faster (the journey to the city center takes about 45 min.), and it brings you into the hotel districts. To confirm AirCoach departures and arrivals, call ✆ **01/844-7118** or find it on the Web at **www.aircoach.ie**.

If you need to connect with the Irish bus or rail service, Dublin Bus's **Airlink Express Coach** (✆ **01/844-4265;** www.dublinbus.ie) provides express coach services from the airport into central Dublin and beyond. Routes 747 and 748 go to the city's central bus station, **Busáras,** on Store Street, and on to **Connolly** railway station, and Route 748 makes an additional stop at **Heuston** railway station. Service runs daily from 5:10am until 11:30pm (Sun 7:30am–11:10pm), with departures every 15 to 20 minutes. One-way fare is €6 for adults and €3 for children 11 and under.

Finally, **Dublin Bus** (✆ **01/873-4222;** www.dublinbus.ie) runs daily connections between the airport and the city center from 6am to 11:30pm. The one-way trip takes about 30 minutes, and the fare is €6 adults, €3 children. Bus nos. 16A, 41, 41B, 747, and 748 all serve the city center from Dublin Airport. Consult the travel information desk in the arrivals concourse to figure out which bus takes you closest to your hotel.

For speed and ease—especially if you have a lot of luggage—a **taxi** is the best way to get directly to your hotel or guesthouse. Depending on your destination, fares average between €20 and €30. Surcharges include €.50 for each additional passenger and for each piece of luggage. Depending on traffic, a cab should take between 20 and 45 minutes to get into the city

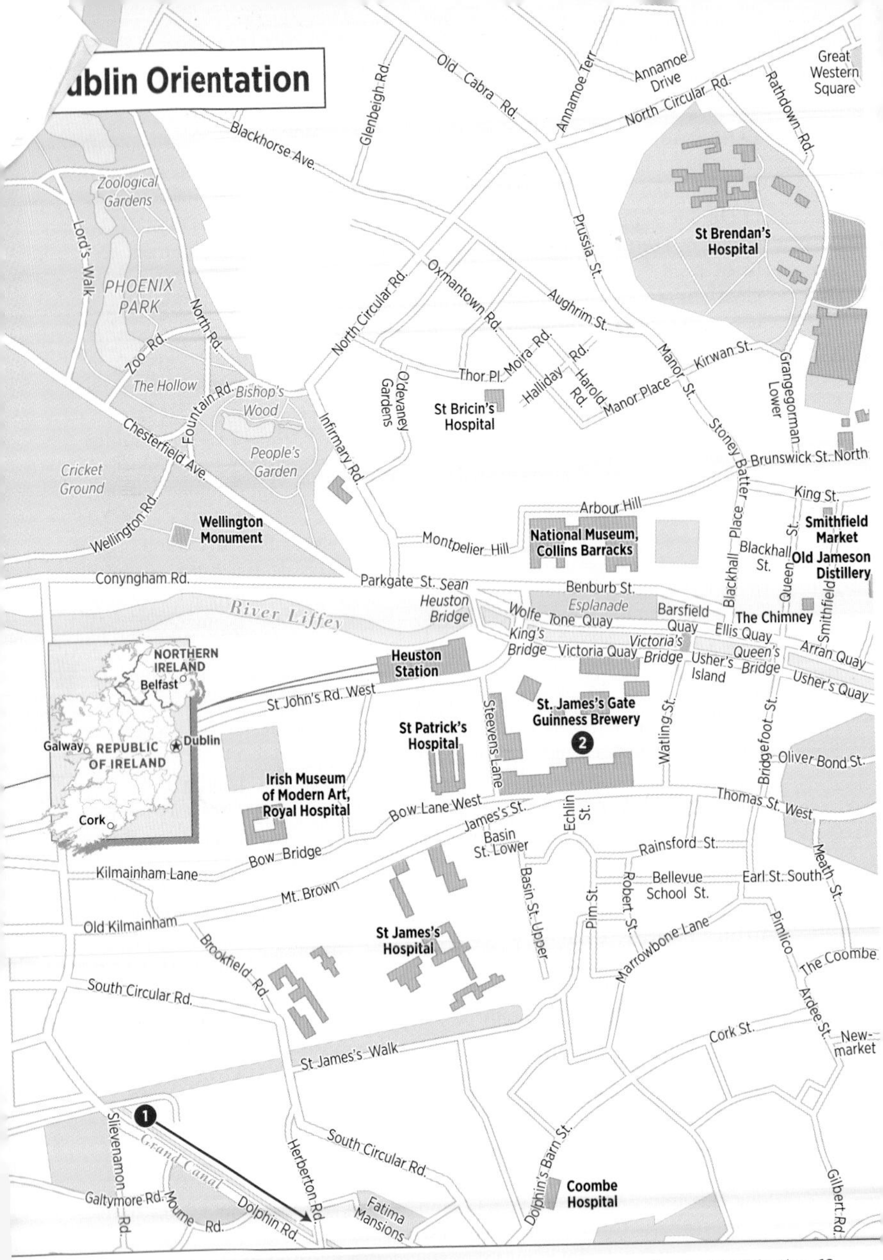

- Busaras/Central Bus Station **5**
- Connolly DART Station **4**
- Dublin Castle/City Hall **9**
- Dublin Tourism Office **10**
- Fitzwilliam Square **17**
- Grafton Street **15**
- Grand Canal **1**
- Guinness Brewery **2**
- Leinster House **14**
- Merrion Square **13**
- O'Connell Street **3**
- Old City/Historic Area **8**
- Pearse DART Station **12**
- St. Stephen's Green **16**
- Tara Street DART Station **6**
- Temple Bar **7**
- Trinity College **11**

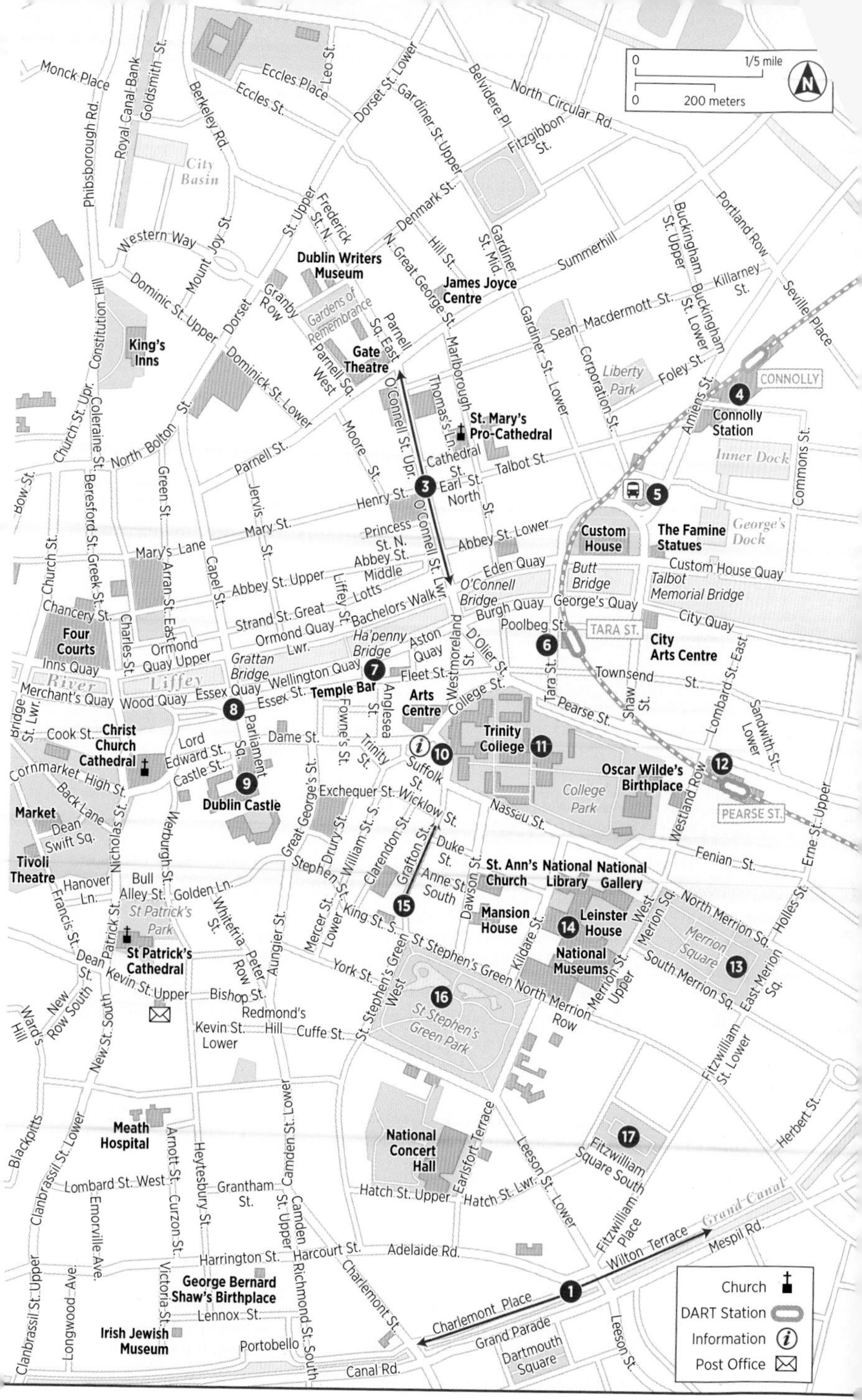

0
1/5 mile
0
200 meters
N
Monck Place
Eccles Place
Eccles St.
Leo St.
Dorset St. Lower
Gardiner St. Upper
Belvidere Pl.
North Circular Rd.
Fitzgibbon St.
Phibsborough Rd.
Royal Canal Bank
Goldsmith St.
Berkeley Rd.
City Basin
Western Way
Mount Joy St.
St. Upper
Frederick St. N.
Denmark St.
Hill St.
N. Great George's St.
Gardiner St. Mid.
Summerhill
Buckingham St. Upper
Portland Row
Dublin Writers Museum
James Joyce Centre
Killarney St.
Seville Place
Constitution Hill
Dominic St. Upper
Dorset St.
Granby Row
Gardens of Remembrance
Parnell Sq. East
Parnell Sq. West
Gate Theatre
Marlborough St.
Sean Macdermott St.
Buckingham St. Lower
King's Inns
Dominick St. Lower
Gardiner St. Lower
Corporation St.
Liberty Park
Foley St.
Amiens St.
CONNOLLY
4
Connolly Station
Church St. Upr.
Coleraine St.
North Bolton St.
Moore St.
O'Connell St. Upr.
Thomas's Ln.
St. Mary's Pro-Cathedral
Cathedral St.
Talbot St.
Inner Dock
Commons St.
Bow St.
Beresford St.
Green St.
Parnell St.
Jervis St.
Henry St.
3
Earl St. North
5
Church St.
Greek St.
Mary's Lane
Arran St. East
Capel St.
Mary St.
Princess St. N.
Abbey St. Middle
O'Connell St. Lwr.
Abbey St. Lower
Custom House
The Famine Statues
George's Dock
Abbey St. Upper
Liffey St.
Lotts
Eden Quay
Butt Bridge
Custom House Quay
Talbot Memorial Bridge
Chancery St.
Charles St.
Four Courts
Ormond Quay Upper
Strand St. Great
Ormond Quay Lwr.
Bachelors Walk
O'Connell Bridge
Burgh Quay
George's Quay
City Quay
Poolbeg St.
TARA ST.
6
City Arts Centre
Inns Quay
River Liffey
Grattan Bridge
Ha'penny Bridge
Aston Quay
Westmoreland St.
D'Olier St.
Tara St.
Townsend St.
Lombard St. East
Merchant's Quay
Wood Quay
Essex Quay
Wellington Quay
7
Fleet St.
Temple Bar
Essex St.
Arts Centre
College St.
Pearse St.
Shaw St.
Sandwith St. Lower
Bridge St. Lwr.
Cook St.
Christ Church Cathedral
8
Lord Edward St.
Parliament Sq.
Dame St.
Fownes St.
Anglesea St.
Trinity St.
10
Trinity College
11
Oscar Wilde's Birthplace
12
Cornmarket
High St.
Castle St.
9
Dublin Castle
Great George's St.
Exchequer St.
Suffolk St.
Wicklow St.
College Park
Nassau St.
Westland Row
PEARSE ST.
Erne St. Upper
Market
Back Lane
Dean Swift Sq.
Nicholas St.
Werburgh St.
Drury St.
William St. S.
Clarendon St.
Grafton St.
Duke St.
Dawson St.
St. Ann's Church
National Library
National Gallery
Fenian St.
Tivoli Theatre
Hanover Ln.
Francis St.
Bull Alley St.
Golden Ln.
Stephen St.
Anne St. South
Mansion House
Leinster House
West Merrion Sq.
North Merrion Sq.
Holles St.
St Patrick's Park
Whitefria St.
Mercer St. Lower
King St. S.
15
Kildare St.
14
Merrion Square
Patrick St.
St Patrick's Cathedral
Peter Row
Aungier St.
York St.
St. Stephen's Green West
St Stephen's Green North
National Museums
Merrion St. Upper
South Merrion Sq.
13
East Merion Sq.
Dean St.
Kevin St. Upper
Bishop St.
16
Merrion Row
New Row South
Ward's Hill
New St. South
Redmond's Hill
Kevin St. Lower
Cuffe St.
St. Stephen's Green Park
Fitzwilliam St. Lower
Herbert St.
Blackpitts
Clanbrassil St. Lower
Meath Hospital
Arnott St.
Heytesbury St.
Camden St. Lower
National Concert Hall
Earlsfort Terrace
Leeson St. Lower
17
Fitzwilliam Square South
Lombard St. West
Emorville Ave.
Curzon St.
Grantham St.
Hatch St. Upper
Hatch St. Lwr.
Grand Canal
Fitzwilliam Place
Wilton Terrace
Mespil Rd.
Clanbrassil St. Upper
Longwood Ave.
Victoria St.
Harrington St.
Camden St. Upper
Harcourt St.
Adelaide Rd.
Charlemont St.
George Bernard Shaw's Birthplace
Lennox St.
Richmond St. South
Irish Jewish Museum
Portobello
Charlemont Place
1
Grand Parade
Dartmouth Square
Leeson St.
Canal Rd.
Church
DART Station
Information
Post Office

center. A tip of a couple of euros is standard. Taxis are lined up at a first-come, first-served taxi stand outside the arrivals terminal.

Major international and local car-rental companies operate desks at Dublin Airport. For a list of companies, see "Getting Around," later in this chapter.

BY FERRY Passenger and car ferries from Britain arrive at the **Dublin Ferryport** (✆ **01/855-5493**), on the eastern end of the North Docks, and at the **Dún Laoghaire Ferryport** (✆ **01/204-7777**). Call **Irish Ferries** (✆ **0818/300-400;** www.irishferries.ie), **P&O Irish Sea** (✆ **01/407-3434;** www.poirishsea.com), or **Stena Line** (✆ **01/204-7777;** www.stenaline.com) for bookings and information. There is bus and taxi service from both ports.

BY TRAIN **Irish Rail** (✆ **1850/366-222;** www.irishrail.ie), also called Iarnród Éireann, operates daily train service to Dublin from Belfast, Northern Ireland, and all major cities in the Irish Republic, including Cork, Galway, Limerick, Killarney, Sligo, Wexford, and Waterford. Trains from the south, west, and southwest arrive at **Heuston Station,** Kingsbridge, off St. John's Road; from the north and northwest at **Connolly Station,** Amiens Street; and from the southeast at **Pearse Station,** Westland Row, Tara Street.

BY BUS **Bus Éireann** (✆ **01/836-6111;** www.buseireann.ie) operates daily express coach and local bus service from all major cities and towns in Ireland into Dublin's central bus station, **Busáras,** Store Street.

BY CAR If you are arriving by car from other parts of Ireland or on a car ferry from Britain, all main roads lead into the heart of Dublin and are well signposted to **An Lar (City Centre).** To bypass the city center, the East Link (toll bridge €1.70) and West Link are signposted, and M50 circuits the city on three sides.

Visitor Information

Dublin Tourism operates six walk-in visitor centers in greater Dublin that are open every day except Christmas. The principal center is on Suffolk Street, Dublin 2, open from June to August Monday to Saturday from 9am to 8:30pm, Sunday and bank holidays 10:30am to 3pm, and the rest of the year Monday to Saturday 9am to 5:30pm, Sunday and bank holidays 10:30am to 3pm. The Suffolk Street office has a currency exchange counter, a car-rental counter, an accommodations-reservations service, bus and rail information desks, a gift shop, and a cafe. For accommodations reservations throughout Ireland by credit card (including some good last-minute deals on Dublin hotels), contact Dublin Tourism at ✆ **01/605-7700** or www.visitdublin.com.

The five other centers are in the **arrivals concourse** of Dublin Airport; **Upper O'Connell Street,** Dublin 1; and the ferry terminal at **Dún Laoghaire Harbor.** All telephone inquiries should be directed to the number listed above, or ✆ **1850/230-330.** All centers are open year-round with at least the following hours: Monday to Friday 9am to 5:30pm and Saturday 9am to 5pm.

For information on Ireland outside of Dublin, call **Bord Fáilte** (✆ **1850/230-330** in Ireland; www.discoverireland.com).

At any of these centers you can pick up the free ***Tourism News.*** The free ***Event Guide,*** a biweekly entertainment guide, is online at **www.eventguide.ie**. ***InDublin,*** a biweekly arts-and-entertainment magazine is available for free at pubs, restaurants, and other entertainment venues, or online at www.indublin.ie.

Grafton Street is bustling with shoppers, buskers, and curious passersby.

City Layout

The city is divided down the middle by the curves of the River Liffey, which empties into the sea at the city's farthest edge. To the north and south, the city center is encircled by canals: The Royal Canal arcs across the north and the Grand Canal through the south. Traditionally, the area south of the river has been Dublin's buzzing, prosperous hub. It still holds most of the best hotels, restaurants, shops, and sights, but the Northside is on the upswing, with hip new bars and hotels giving it a trendy edge. Both north and south, Dublin is compact and easily walked in an hour. In fact, a 45-minute walk from the bucolic peace of St. Stephen's Green, up Grafton Street, and across the Liffey to the top of O'Connell Street offers a good overview of the city's prosperous present and troubled past.

The most interesting suburban towns tend to be along Dublin Bay—these include (heading north along the bay) Drumcondra, Glasnevin, Howth, Clontarf, and Malahide; and (heading south along the bay) Ballsbridge, Blackrock, Dún Laoghaire, Dalkey, Killiney, Rathgar, and Rathmines. Due to the conspicuous wealth and prosperity that came to these towns in the late 1990s, locals have wryly dubbed this area "Bel Eire."

MAIN ARTERIES, STREETS & SQUARES In the town center just south of the river, Dame Street, which changes its name to College Green, Westmoreland Street, and Lord Edward Street at various points, is the main east-west artery connecting Trinity College with Dublin Castle and Christ Church Cathedral. On one side of Dame Street are the winding medieval lanes of Temple Bar, which, with its many pubs and bars, is Dublin's party central. On the other side of Dame Street are lots of tributary streets lined with shops and cafes; the best of these is Great St. George's Street, which arcs off toward the south. Where Dame turns into College Green, the sturdy gray stone walls of Trinity College make an excellent landmark as you get your bearings, and at its southwest corner is the top of Grafton Street—a lively pedestrianized shopping lane crowded with tourists, musicians, and

St. Stephen's Green Park is serene despite the crowds passing through en route to shops and restaurants.

artists, which leads to the bucolic, statue-filled peace of St. Stephen's Green. From there, heading back up via Kildare Street will take you past Leinster House, where the Irish Parliament meets, and a turn to the right brings you to Merrion Square, another of Dublin's extraordinarily well-preserved Georgian squares.

A characteristic Georgian facade on Merrion Square.

To get to the Northside, most visitors choose to walk across the photogenic arch of the Ha'penny Bridge (see "A Toll Tale," below), but most locals take the less attractive O'Connell Bridge nearby. You can be different and cross via the Ha'penny's sleekly modern neighbor, the Millennium Bridge, which is beautifully illuminated after dark. The O'Connell Bridge leads directly onto O'Connell Street, a wide, statue-lined boulevard that is the north's main thruway. O'Connell Street runs north to **Parnell Square,** which holds a couple of marvelous museums and marks the edge of central Dublin. From the bottom to the top, O'Connell Street is lined with statues, starting with an absurdly ornate representation of the titular politician Daniel O'Connell surrounded by angels (which still have bullet holes left from the Easter Rising). The street running along the Liffey's embankment is called the North Quays by all, though its name changes on virtually every block, reflecting the long-gone docks that once lined it.

A Toll Tale

Built in 1816 as one of the earliest cast-iron bridges in Britain and Ireland, the graceful pedestrian-only Ha'penny Bridge (pronounced *Hay*-penny) is the prettiest of Dublin's bridges. Though officially named the Liffey Bridge, it's far better known by the toll once charged to cross it: half a penny. The turnstiles were removed in 1919, when passage was made free.

In the older section of the city, **High Street** is the gateway to medieval and Viking Dublin, from the city's two medieval cathedrals to the old city walls and nearby Dublin Castle. The other noteworthy street in the older part of the city is **Francis Street,** Dublin's antiques row.

Dublin Neighborhoods in Brief

TRINITY COLLEGE AREA On the south side of the River Liffey, Trinity College is an Ivy League–style university with shady quadrangles and atmospheric stone buildings. It's virtually the dead center of the city, and is surrounded by bookstores, shops, and noisy traffic. This area lies in the Dublin 2 postal code.

TEMPLE BAR Wedged between Trinity College and the Old City, this is Dublin's party hub, packed with bars, discos, and pubs. During the day it's quieter and more refined, with good shops, two worthwhile art galleries, recording studios, and theaters. But at night, this is largely the stamping ground of young tourists looking for lots of alcohol, and it's easy to feel over the hill here if you're 25. This area lies in the Dublin 2 and Dublin 8 postal codes.

In the heart of Dublin, Trinity College is Ireland's oldest university, founded by Queen Elizabeth I in 1592.

Lkn 4 a bus?

Dublin Bus has recently launched a handy little service that allows you to get timetable information sent directly to your cellphone as a text message. Text the word "BUS" followed by the route number to 53503. (For example, "BUS 16A" will get you a list of the next buses on route 16A—which runs between the airport and the city center.) The message will also suggest alternatives if there are any. It costs €.30 and you only pay for the outgoing text.

OLD CITY Dating from Viking and medieval times, the cobblestone enclave of the historic Old City includes Dublin Castle, the remnants of the city's original walls, and Christ Church and St. Patrick's cathedrals. Recently, Old City has also gained cachet for its hip boutiques where local designers sell their clothes. It encompasses the Dublin 8 and 2 zones.

LIBERTIES Adjacent to Old City, the Liberties district takes its name from the fact that it was once just outside the city walls, and, therefore, exempt from Dublin's jurisdiction. Although it prospered in its early days, Liberties fell on hard times in the 17th and 18th centuries and has only felt the touch of urban renewal in the last decade or so. Its main claim to fame is the Guinness Brewery. Most of this area is in the Dublin 8 zone.

ST. STEPHEN'S GREEN/GRAFTON STREET AREA The biggest tourist draw in town, this district is home to Dublin's finest hotels, restaurants, and shops. The neighborhood is filled with impressive Georgian architecture, and is primarily a business and shopping zone. It is part of Dublin 2.

FITZWILLIAM & MERRION SQUARES These two little square parks between Trinity College and St. Stephen's Green are surrounded by grand Georgian town houses. Some of Dublin's most famous citizens once lived here; today many of the houses are offices for doctors, lawyers, and government agencies. This area is part of the Dublin 2 zone.

O'CONNELL STREET (NORTH OF THE LIFFEY) The epicenter of Dublin's stormy political struggles, the north was once a fashionable area, but it lost much of its charm as it decayed in the 20th century. Happily, it is now rebounding with high-profile hotels, plenty of shops, and a few top-rated restaurants. With four theaters in walking distance of O'Connell Street, this is Dublin's theater district. It is mostly in Dublin 1.

NORTH QUAYS (the Liffey Riverbanks on the Northside) Once the center of Dublin's shipping industry, this is now a trendy address for hotels, bars, and clubs. The quays are actually a series of streets named after the wharves that once stood at water's edge. The quays start near the mouth of the Liffey and end in the green peace of Phoenix Park. This area is mostly in Dublin 1.

BALLSBRIDGE/EMBASSY ROW Immediately south of the Grand Canal, this upscale suburb is just barely within walking distance of the city center. Primarily a prestigious residential area, it is also home to hotels, restaurants, and embassies, including the U.S. Embassy. This area is part of the Dublin 4 zone.

GETTING AROUND

While driving in the city is intimidating, getting around Dublin is not at all daunting in general. Public transportation is good and getting better, taxis are plentiful and reasonably priced, and your own two feet can easily carry you from one end of town to the other. In fact, with its current traffic and parking problems, it's a city where the foot is mightier than the wheel. If you can avoid it, don't use a car while you're in Dublin.

BY BUS Dublin Bus operates a fleet of green double-deckers and single-deckers, as well as minibuses (the latter charmingly called "imps"). Most originate on or near O'Connell Street, Abbey Street, and Eden Quay on the Northside, and at Aston Quay, College Street, and Fleet Street on the south side. Bus stops, which resemble big blue or green lollipops, are located every few blocks on main thoroughfares. To tell where the bus is going, look at the destination street and bus number above its front window; those heading for the city center indicate that with an odd mix of Latin and Gaelic: VIA AN LAR.

Bus service runs daily throughout the city, starting at 6am (10am on Sun), with the last bus at about 11:30pm. On Friday and Saturday nights, **Nitelink** service runs from the city center to the suburbs from midnight to 4am. Buses operate every 30 minutes for most runs; schedules are posted on revolving notice boards at bus stops.

Inner-city fares are based on distances traveled. The minimum fare is €1.15 (unless you're only going a very short distance within the city center, in which case it's €.50); the maximum fare for journeys in the city center is €2.20, rising to €4.50 if you go as far as the outer suburbs. Children 15 and under pay between €.65 and €1. The Nitelink fare is a flat €5. Buy your tickets from the driver as you enter the bus. Following a rise in robberies of bus drivers in Dublin, all buses (aside from Airlink) now use an "autofare" machine. This means that fares must be paid with coins directly into a fare box next to the driver's cab. Bills are not accepted and no change is given. If you have to pay more than the cost of the ticket, the driver will issue you a refund ticket, which must be presented along with your travel ticket at the Dublin Bus office on Upper O'Connell Street to claim a refund for the difference. Inevitably, this is rarely worth the effort.

If you plan to travel quite a bit by bus, consider purchasing a **bus pass,** or "**rambler**" ticket. Discounted 1-day, 3-day, and 5-day passes are available in advance. The 1-day bus-only pass costs €6, the 3-day pass costs €13, and the 5-day pass goes for €21. Another option worth considering is the **freedom ticket.** Specially designed for tourists, it works like a standard 3-day bus pass, but also includes unlimited travel on the Airlink, Nitelink, and Dublin City Tour buses. The cost is €26 adults and €10 children 13 and under. They can be purchased from most major stores in the city center, any Dublin Tourist Information Office, or in advance from **Ticketmaster** (✆ **011/353-1456-9569** in the U.S.; www.ticketmaster.ie; or follow the link on the Dublin Bus website). There's a charge of €3 to mail freedom tickets to the U.S., and it takes 7 to 10 days to arrive.

For more information, contact **Dublin Bus,** 59 Upper O'Connell St., Dublin 1 (✆ **01/873-4222;** www.dublinbus.ie).

BY DART At this writing, Dublin was about to learn whether it was at last going to get its own subway network—albeit a small one—courtesy of an extension to the existing **DART** (Dublin Area Rapid Transit) system. This is some years off, however, so for now the electric DART trains travel aboveground, linking the city-center stations at **Connolly Station, Tara Street,** and **Pearse Street** with suburbs and seaside communities as far as Malahide to the north and Greystones to the south. Service operates roughly every 10 to 20 minutes Monday to Saturday from around 6am to midnight and Sunday from 9:30am to 11pm. Typical adult fares cost €1.65 for a short single journey in the city center, while a round-trip out to Dalkey or Dún Laoghaire costs €4.20. Combination rail-and-bus tickets, valid all day within the "short hop" zone of the city center, start from €9 adults. One-day, 3-day, and 10-trip passes, as well as student and family tickets, are available at reduced rates from ticket windows in stations. For further information, contact DART, Dublin Pearse Station (✆ **01/703-3592;** www.dart.ie).

BY TRAM The newest addition to Dublin's public transportation network, the sleek, modern (and wheelchair accessible) light-rail tram system known as **LUAS** opened in the summer of 2004. With trams traveling at a maximum speed of 70kmph (44 mph) and departing every 5 minutes in peak hours, LUAS has been popular enough to make at least a small impact on Dublin's appalling traffic congestion. Services run from 5:30am to 12:30am Monday to Friday, 6:30am to 12:30am Saturday, and 7am to 11:30pm on Sunday. The lines link the city center at **Connolly Station** and **St. Stephen's Green** with the suburbs of Tallaght in the southwest and Dundrum and Sandyford to the south. For visitors, one of the handiest reasons to use the LUAS is to get between Connolly and Heuston stations. The one-way fare within the city center is €1.60 adults, €.80 children. You can buy tickets from shops around the city center or from vending machines at stops. You must use your ticket (or the first portion if it's a return) within 90 minutes of purchase. One-day and multiple-day passes are also available. For further information, contact LUAS (✆ **01/800-300-604** or 461-4910; www.luas.ie).

ON FOOT Marvelously compact, Dublin is ideal for walking, as long as you remember to look right and then left (and in the direction opposite your instincts if you're from the U.S. or Canada) before crossing the street. Pedestrians have the right of way at specially marked, zebra-striped crossings (there are usually two flashing lights at these intersections). For some walking-tour suggestions, see "Seeing the Sights," later in this chapter.

BY TAXI It's very difficult to hail a taxi on the street; instead, they line up at taxi stands (called "ranks") outside major hotels, at bus and train stations, and on prime thoroughfares such as Upper O'Connell Street, College Green, and the north side of St. Stephen's Green.

You can also phone for a taxi. Some of the companies that operate a 24-hour radio-call service are **Co-Op** (✆ **01/677–7777**), **National Radio Cabs** (✆ **01/677-2222**), and **VIP/ACE Taxis** (✆ **01/478-3333**). If you need a wake-up call, VIP offers that service, along with especially courteous dependability.

Taxi rates are fixed by law and posted in each vehicle. The following are typical travel costs in the city center: The starting fare for the first kilometer

(⅔ mile) is €4.10 by day and €4.45 at night. For the next 14km (8⅔ miles) the fare is €1.05 per kilometer by day, €1.35 by night, rising to a maximum of €1.77 per kilometer thereafter. You will instead be charged an equivalent price per minute in slow traffic (which runs a minimum €.36 during the day, up to a maximum of €.63 at night). It costs an extra €2 if you order a cab by phone, with €1 extra per passenger. By law taxis have to take the shortest reasonable route to your destination, unless you ask otherwise, so don't be afraid to speak up if you think you're being taken for a longer ride than necessary. ***Be warned:*** At some hotels, staff members will tack on as much as €5 for calling you a cab, although this practice violates city taxi regulations. Ask before you request a taxi if you'll be charged.

BY CAR As mentioned earlier, if you plan to spend all of your time in Dublin, it is unlikely you'll need to rent a car. In fact, getting around the city and its environs is much easier without one.

If you must drive in Dublin, remember to keep to the *left-hand side of the road,* and don't drive in bus lanes. The speed limit within the city is 50kmph (31 mph) although it's very unlikely you'll ever reach it. Seat belts must be worn at all times by driver and passengers.

Most major international **car-rental firms** are represented in Dublin, as are many Irish-based companies. They have desks at the airport, full-service offices downtown, or both. Rates vary greatly according to company, season, type of car, and duration of rental. In high season, the average weekly cost of a subcompact starts at around €200; you'll get the best price if you've made car-rental arrangements well in advance from home. (Also see "By Car" under "Getting Around" in chapter 15.)

International firms represented in Dublin include **Avis,** 35–39 Old Kilmainham, Dublin 8, and at Dublin Airport (✆ 01/605-7500; www.avis.ie); **Budget,** 151 Lower Drumcondra Rd., Dublin 9 (✆ 01/837-9611; www.budget.ie), and at Dublin Airport (✆ 01/844-5150); **Hertz,** 151 S. Circular Rd., Dublin 8 (✆ 01/709-3060; www.hertz.ie), and at Dublin Airport (✆ 01/844-5466); and **Murray's Europcar,** 29 Parkgate St., Dublin 8 (✆ 01/648-5900; www.europcar.ie), and at Dublin Airport (✆ 01/812-2800).

During normal business hours, free parking on Dublin streets is nonexistent. Never park in bus lanes, cycle lanes, or along a curb with double yellow lines. City officials will either clamp ("boot") or tow errant vehicles. To get your car declamped, the fee is around €90, and if your car is towed, it will cost upward of €165 to reclaim it.

Throughout Dublin, you'll find multibay meters and "pay and display" **parking.** If you park on the street, look around for a meter (there's usually one on every block). You insert coins into the machine for however many hours you expect to be there, retrieve a ticket, and then stick that ticket in the front window of your car to prove you've done it. Expect to pay at least €2 per hour. The best places to park are surface parking lots and multistory car parks in central locations such as Kildare Street, Lower Abbey Street, and Marlborough Street. Expect to pay anything from €2 per hour to upwards of €20 for 24 hours. Long-stay bargains are few and far between, but one worth noting is the **St. Stephen's Green Shopping Centre** (St. Stephen's Green West, Dublin 2; ✆ **01/478-0888**), where you can park all day for €10 and overnight for €5.

BY BICYCLE The steady flow of Dublin traffic rushing down one-way streets may be a little intimidating for most cyclists, but there are many opportunities for more relaxed pedaling in residential areas and suburbs, along the seafront, and around Phoenix Park. The Dublin Tourism office can supply you with bicycle touring information and suggested routes.

Bicycle rentals start at around €20 per day, or €100 per week, with a standard deposit of around €200 cash. Bicycles can be rented from **Cycleways,** 185 Parnell St. (just off O'Connell St.), Dublin 1 (✆ **01/873-4748**).

[Fast FACTS] DUBLIN

For countrywide information, see chapter 15, "Planning Your Trip to Ireland."

American Express There's an American Express office at 116 Grafton St. (✆ **01/677-2874**). It's open Monday to Friday from 9am to 5pm and on Saturday from 9am to noon. There's an Amex desk at the **Dublin Tourism Centre** on Suffolk Street (✆ **01/605-7709**). For lost and stolen cards call ✆ **185/088-2028.** The 24-hour assistance number is ✆ **0044/1737-815-086.** This number connects you to the London office, but you pay the same as a call within Ireland. There's also an Amex travel office at **Atlas Travel,** 28 Pearse St. (✆ **01/241-2345**), but it only deals with business customers.

Banks Nearly all banks are open Monday to Friday 10am to 4pm (to 5pm Thurs) and have ATMs that accept Cirrus network cards as well as MasterCard and Visa. Convenient locations include the **Bank of Ireland,** at 2 College Green, Dublin 2, and 6 O'Connell St., Dublin 1, and the **Allied Irish Bank (AIB),** at 100 Grafton St., Dublin 2, and 87 N. Strand, Dublin 3.

Business Hours **Museums and sights** are generally open 10am to 5pm Tuesday to Saturday, and 2 to 5pm Sunday. **Shops** generally open 9am to 6pm Monday to Friday, with late opening on Thursday until 7 or 8pm. Department stores tend to stay open slightly later. In the city center most department stores and many shops are open noon to 6pm on Sunday.

Currency Exchange Currency-exchange services, signposted as BUREAU DE CHANGE, are in most Dublin banks and at many branches of the Irish post office system, known as **An Post.** A bureau de change operates daily during flight arrival and departure times at Dublin Airport; a foreign-currency note-exchanger machine is also available on a 24-hour basis in the arrivals concourse. Some hotels and travel agencies offer bureau de change services, although the best rate of exchange is usually when you use your bank card at an ATM.

Dentists For dental emergencies, your hotel will usually contact a dentist for you; otherwise, try **Molesworth Clinic,** 2 Molesworth Place, Dublin 2 (✆ **01/661-5544**), or **Smiles Dental,** 28 O'Connell St. (✆ **1850/323-323**). See also "Dental Surgeons" in the Golden Pages (Yellow Pages) of the telephone book. The American Embassy (see "Embassies & Consulates," below) can provide a list of dentists in the city. Expect to be charged upfront for services.

Doctors If you need to see a physician, most hotels and guesthouses will contact a house doctor for you. The **American Embassy** (see "Embassies

& Consulates," below) can provide a list of doctors in the city, and you should contact them first. Otherwise, you can call the **Irish Medical Organization** (a doctors' union) at 10 Fitzwilliam Place, Dublin 2 (✆ **01/676-7273;** www.imo.ie). As with dentists, expect to pay for treatment upfront, and contact your insurance company when you return home to find out whether you are eligible for reimbursement.

Embassies & Consulates The **American Embassy** is at 42 Elgin Rd., Ballsbridge, Dublin 4 (✆ **01/668-8777;** http://dublin.usembassy.gov); the **Canadian Embassy** is at 7–8 Wilton Terrace, Dublin 2 (✆ **01/234-4000;** www.canada.ie); the **British Embassy** is at 29 Merrion Rd., Dublin 2 (✆ **01/205-3700;** britishembassyinireland.fco.gov.uk); and the **Australian Embassy** is at Seventh Floor, Fitzwilton House, Wilton Terrace, Dublin 2 (✆ **01/664-5300;** www.ireland.embassy.gov.au). In addition, there is an **American Consulate** at 223 Stranmillis Rd., Belfast BT9 5GR (✆ **028/9038-6100;** belfast.usconsulate.gov).

Emergencies For police, fire, or other emergencies, dial ✆ **999.**

GLBT Resources Contact the **Gay Switchboard Dublin,** Carmichael House, North Brunswick Street, Dublin 7 (✆ **01/872-1055;** http://gayswitchboard.ie); or drop in at the **Outhouse,** 105 Capel St., Dublin 1 (✆ **01/873-4999;** www.outhouse.ie), Dublin's GLBT community resource center.

Hospitals For emergency care, two of the most modern hospitals in Dublin are **St. Vincent's University Hospital,** Elm Park (✆ **01/221-4000**), on the south side of the city, and **Beaumont Hospital,** Beaumont Road (✆ **01/809-3000**), on the Northside.

Hot Lines In Ireland, hot lines are called "helplines." For **emergencies, police, or fire,** dial ✆ **999; Alcoholics Anonymous** (✆ **01/842-0700** daytime; 852-7000 evenings until 10pm and all day Sun; www.alcoholicsanonymous.ie); **Narcotics Anonymous** (✆ **086/862-9308** or 01/672-8000; www.na-ireland.org); **Rape Crisis Centre** (✆ **1800/778-888** or 01/661-4911; www.drcc.ie); and for people suffering from depression, **Samaritans** (✆ **1850/609-090** or 01/872-7700; www.dublinsamaritans.ie).

Information For directory assistance, dial ✆ **11811** or 11850. For visitor information offices, see "Orientation," earlier in this chapter.

Internet Access Internet access is everywhere in Dublin; look for signs in cafes, pubs, shopping malls, hotels, and hostels. Like all of Dublin's public libraries, the **Central Library,** in the ILAC Centre, off Henry Street, Dublin 1 (✆ **01/873-4333**), has a bank of PCs with free Internet access. Centrally located Internet cafes are the **Global Internet Café,** 8 O'Connell St., Dublin 2 (✆ **01/878-0295;** www.globalcafe.ie), and the **Access Cyber Cafe,** 168 Parnell St., Dublin 1 (✆ **01/878-3403**), which also offers a left-luggage service. A half-hour online averages around €2 to €3.

Magazines The leading magazines for upcoming events and happenings are ***InDublin*** (www.indublin.ie), published every 2 weeks and available at newsstands; the ***Dubliner*** (www.thedubliner.ie), published monthly; ***Hot Press*** (www.hotpress.com), also published every 2 weeks with excellent event listings; the ***Journal of Music*** (www.journalofmusic.com) for music information; and the free biweekly ***Event Guide*** (www.eventguide.ie).

Pharmacies Centrally located drugstores—known as pharmacies or chemist shops—include **Boots,** which has branches at 12 Grafton St., Dublin 2 (✆ **01/677-3000**), and St. Stephen's Green, Dublin 2 (✆ **01/478-4368**). A late-night pharmacy is **Hamilton Long & Co.,** 5 Lower O'Connell St. (✆ **01/874-8456**). It closes at 9pm daily.

Police Dial ✆ **999** in an emergency. The metropolitan headquarters for the **Dublin Garda Siochana (Police)** is in Phoenix Park, Dublin 8 (✆ **01/666-0000**).

Post Office The Irish post office is best known by its Gaelic name, **An Post.** The **General Post Office (GPO)** is located on O'Connell Street, Dublin 1 (✆ **01/705-8833;** www.anpost.ie). Hours are Monday to Saturday 8am to 8pm. Branch offices, identified by the sign OIFIG AN POST/POST OFFICE, are open Monday to Saturday only, 9am to 5pm (although some only open half-days on Sat).

Weather Phone ✆ **1550/122113,** or check the Web at www.ireland.com/weather.

Yellow Pages The classified section of the telephone book is called the Golden Pages (**www.goldenpages.ie**).

WHERE TO STAY

With a healthy mix of plush, modern hotels and grand old guesthouses, Dublin excels in providing a place to rest your head at the end of a day. Prices are not cheap, but there are good off-season deals to be had if you book early, particularly in the luxury category—keep an eye on the hotel websites in the months before your trip.

In this guide, we give each hotel zero to three stars, based on overall value. As a result, a fine but expensive hotel may get one star, while an excellent budget choice may get two.

In general, hotel rates in Dublin do not vary as much seasonally as they do in the countryside, although some hotels charge slightly higher prices during special events, such as St. Patrick's Day and the Dublin Horse Show. The money savings here come by the day of the week: If you're looking for the best deal, some hotels cut their rates by as much as 50% on Friday and Saturday nights, when business traffic is low. On the other hand, some hotels offer midweek specials.

It usually pays to book hotels well in advance. Many hotels can be booked through toll-free numbers from North America, and the quoted prices offered can be appreciably (as much as 40%) lower than those offered at the door. Even better, book online—many hotels offer Web-only special deals that can amount to massive savings on the rack rate. Remember, the fact that times are tough in the global economy right now cuts both ways: hotels are at greater risk of closure, but they will also be more eager to secure your business. There are some truly amazing deals out there, if you know where to look. Don't be shy about asking about any available discounts or special offers, and be prepared to shop around. We've found that several hotels have actually *lowered* their prices this year, for the second or third year running—something that was, for much of the last decade, all but unheard of around these parts.

If you arrive in Ireland without a reservation, don't despair. One of the best sources of last-minute rooms (often at a discount) is **www.visitdublin.com**. The website lets you view hotels and guesthouses with immediate availability. Remember, though, that you will have trouble at immigration if you arrive in Ireland without having arranged a place to stay at least for your first night.

Another option is to arrive in person at the nearest **tourist office.** Alternatively, phone them at ✆ **066/979-2030.** This is a nationwide and cross-border "free-phone" facility for credit card bookings, which operates daily from 8am to 11pm (Ireland time). You can access it from North America (✆ **011-66/979-2030**) and on the Web at **www.gulliver.ie**.

Most luxury hotels are on the south side of the river in Temple Bar and around Trinity College, but there are a few on the Northside. Places like the boutique, U2-owned **Clarence** hotel in Temple Bar are stylish indicators of how far Dublin has come, while the celebrity hangout **Morrison** hotel just across the river from it proves that the north bank is on the upswing. There are lots of excellent midrange hotels around St. Stephen's Green, where the small but perfectly formed **Number 31** leads the way. Most budget hotels are in the north, where affordable guesthouses like the **Roxford Lodge** cluster around funky Lower Gardiner Street.

Historic Old City & Temple Bar/Trinity College Area

Temple Bar is the youngest, most vibrant niche in a young, vibrant town. Stay here and you'll be on the doorstep of practically anywhere you'd want to go. That said, it can get *very* noisy at night, so request a room on a top floor or at the rear of the establishment if you want some shut-eye.

VERY EXPENSIVE

The Clarence ★★★ For some, knowing that a hotel is owned by rock stars might not be a selling point—but this is one of the most sophisticated hotels in Dublin. U2's Bono and the Edge bought the place in 1992; it was beautifully renovated, keeping the best of its mid-19th-century charm, but adding layers of contemporary elegance. Rooms are designed with lush fabrics in neutral tones of oatmeal and chocolate, Shaker-style furniture, and exceptionally comfortable, firm, king-size beds. The elegant **Tea Room** restaurant (p. 132) is one of the best in town for contemporary Irish cuisine. The **Octagon Bar** (p. 185) has a good buzz, and the **Study** has the feel of an old-style gentlemen's club; a relaxing place to read the papers and enjoy a glass of wine, or a light meal. There's also a well-equipped gym and health spa, which offers treatments starting from about €100 for an hour.

6–8 Wellington Quay, Dublin 2. www.theclarence.ie. ✆ **01/407-0800.** Fax 01/407-0820. 48 units. €140–€320 double; €370–€470 1-bedroom suite; €450–€550 2-bedroom suite; €390–€570 garden terrace suite. Full Irish breakfast €29. AE, DC, MC, V. Valet parking €25. Bus: 51B, 51C, 68, 69, or 79. **Amenities:** Restaurant; bar; babysitting; concierge; gym; room service; smoke-free rooms; spa. *In room:* A/C, interactive TV, DVD/broadband system, hair dryer, minibar.

The Westin ★★ The Westin makes good use of this building's grand, 19th-century facade (the building was once a bank)—it promises real luxury and the interior easily fulfills it. The elegant lobby is lined with big marble columns and decorated with exquisite plasterwork; one entrance leads down a great hall of mirrors. The spacious rooms have a real sense of modern sophistication, with decor in shades of mahogany and cream, comfortable beds, and

> **A Parking Note**
>
> **Many Dublin hotels do not offer parking; if you have a car, you'll have to find (and pay for) street parking. In this section, we've provided parking information only for the few hotels that do offer parking arrangements or discounts for guests. The more expensive hotels can charge as much as €25 per night to park, so ask about this hidden charge before you book.**

Where to Stay in Dublin

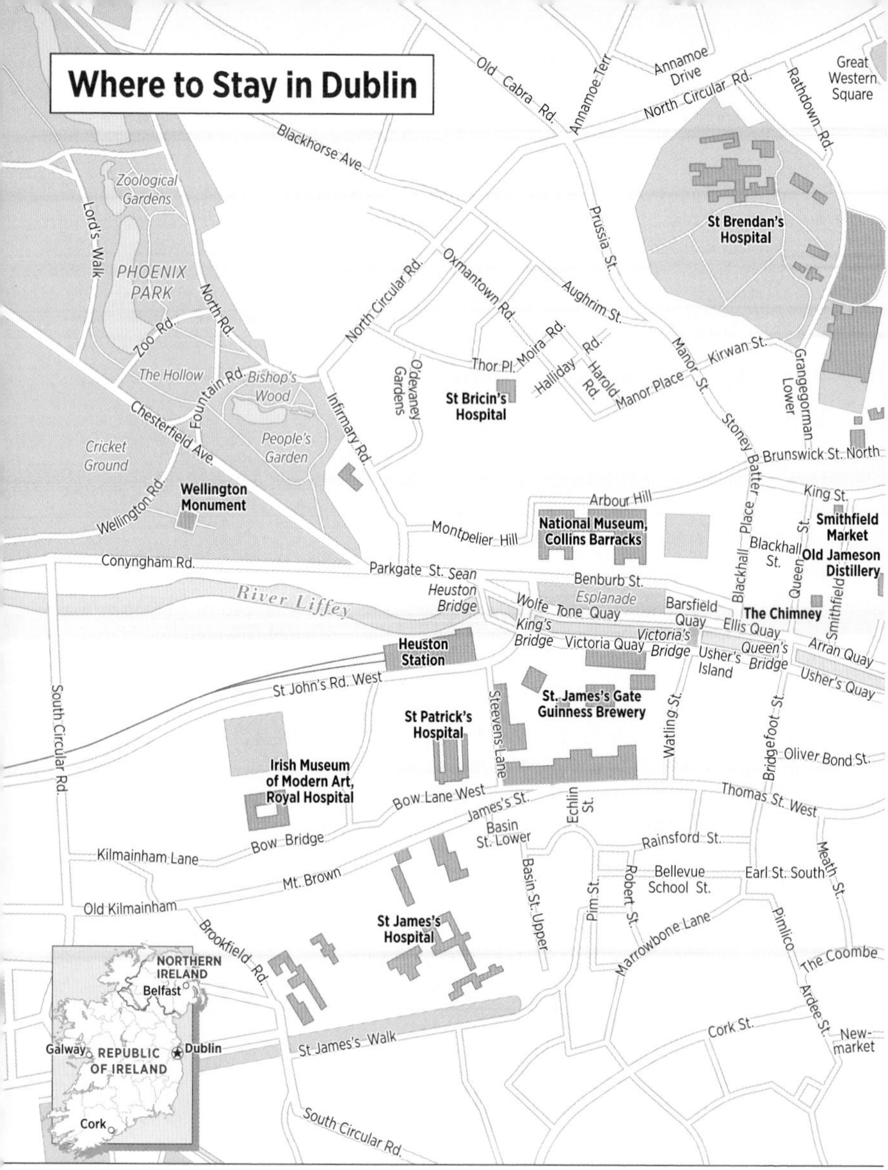

Avalon House **10**
Brooks Hotel **11**
Buswells Hotel **15**
The Clarence **5**
The Clarion Hotel Dublin IFSC **3**
Conrad Hotel **18**
Eliza Lodge **6**
The Fitzwilliam Hotel **12**
The Gresham **1**
Hotel Isaacs **2**
Merrion Hotel **17**
The Morrison **4**
Number 31 **20**
Premier Suites Stephen's Hall **19**
The Shelbourne **16**
Temple Bar Hotel **8**
Trinity Lodge **14**
25 Eustace Street **7**
The Westbury Hotel **13**
The Westin **9**

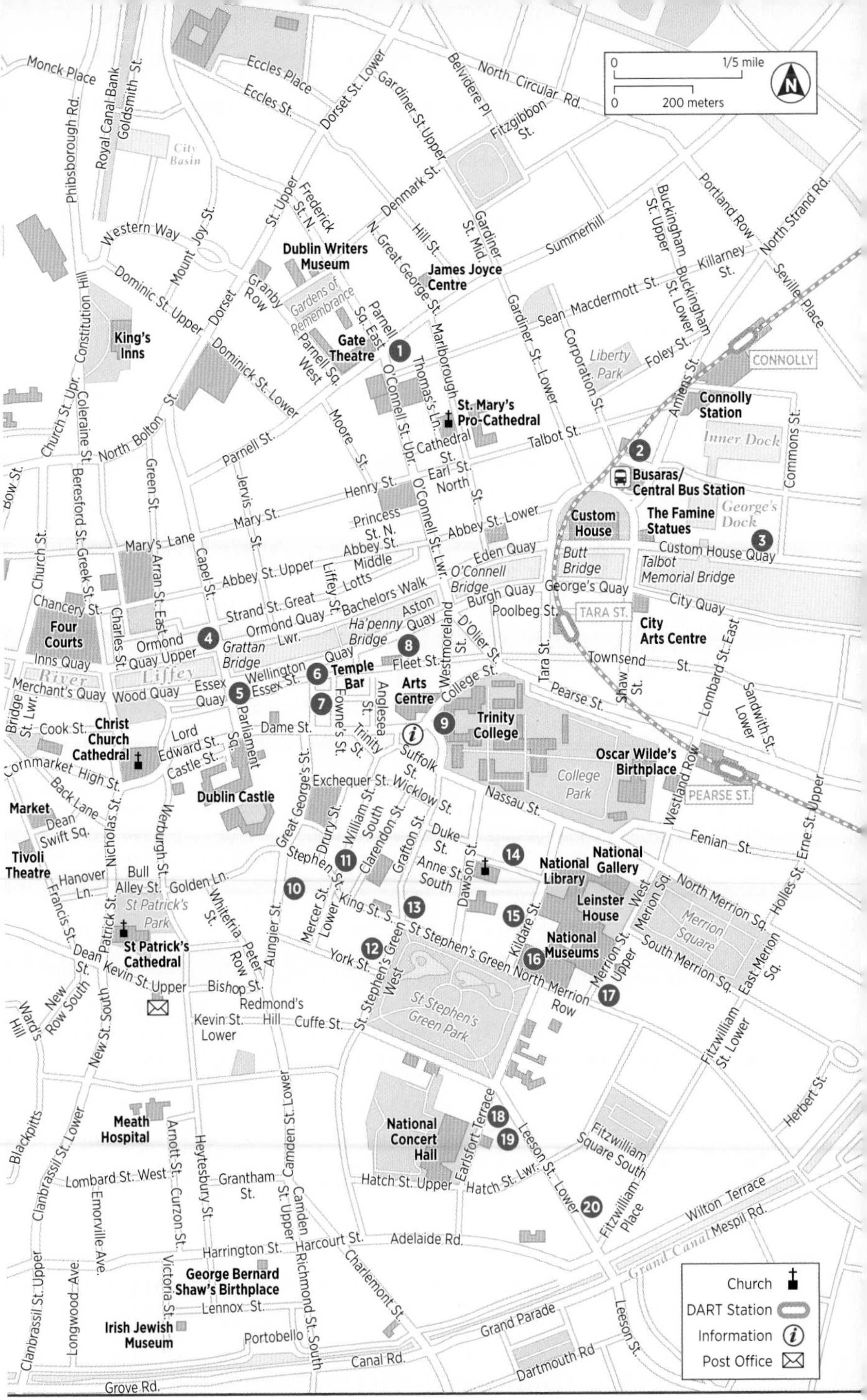

0
1/5 mile
0
200 meters
N
Monck Place
Phibsborough Rd.
Royal Canal Bank
Goldsmith St.
City Basin
Eccles Place
Eccles St.
Dorset St. Lower
Gardiner St. Upper
Belvidere Pl.
North Circular Rd.
Fitzgibbon St.
Denmark St.
Frederick St. N.
St. Upper
Western Way
Joy St.
Mount
Dominic St. Upper
Dorset
Granby Row
Dublin Writers Museum
Gardens of Remembrance
Parnell Sq. East
Parnell Sq. West
N. Great George's St.
Hill St.
James Joyce Centre
Gardiner St. Mid.
Summerhill
Buckingham St. Upper
Buckingham St. Lower
Portland Row
North Strand Rd.
Killarney St.
Seville Place
Sean Macdermott St.
Gardiner St. Lower
Corporation St.
Liberty Park
Foley St.
Amiens St.
CONNOLLY
Connolly Station
Inner Dock
Commons St.
Constitution Hill
King's Inns
Dominick St. Lower
Gate Theatre
1
O'Connell St. Upr.
Thomas's Ln.
Marlborough St.
St. Mary's Pro-Cathedral
Cathedral St.
Talbot St.
2
Busaras/ Central Bus Station
Church St. Upr.
Coleraine St.
North Bolton St.
Parnell St.
Moore St.
Earl St. North
Bow St.
Beresford St.
Green St.
Jervis St.
Henry St.
O'Connell St. Lwr.
Custom House
The Famine Statues
George's Dock
3
Mary St.
Princess St. N.
Abbey St. Lower
Church St.
Mary's Lane
Capel St.
Arran St. East
Abbey St. Upper
Liffey St.
Abbey St. Middle
Lotts
Eden Quay
O'Connell Bridge
Butt Bridge
Custom House Quay
Talbot Memorial Bridge
Greek St.
Chancery St.
Charles St.
Strand St. Great
Ormond Quay Lwr.
Bachelors Walk
Aston Quay
Burgh Quay
George's Quay
City Quay
Poolbeg St.
TARA ST.
Four Courts
Ormond Quay Upper
4
Grattan Bridge
Ha'penny Bridge
8
Westmoreland St.
D'Olier St.
City Arts Centre
Lombard St. East
Inns Quay
River Liffey
Wood Quay
Essex Quay
5
Wellington Quay
Essex St.
6
Temple Bar
Fleet St.
Arts Centre
College St.
Tara St.
Townsend St.
Shaw St.
Merchant's Quay
Bridge St. Lwr.
7
Fowne's St.
Anglesea St.
Pearse St.
Sandwith St. Lower
Cook St.
Christ Church Cathedral
Lord Edward St.
Parliament Sq.
Dame St.
Trinity St.
Suffolk St.
9
Trinity College
Oscar Wilde's Birthplace
Cornmarket
High St.
Castle St.
Dublin Castle
Great George's St.
Exchequer St.
Wicklow St.
College Park
Westland Row
PEARSE ST.
Back Lane
Market
Dean Swift Sq.
Nicholas St.
Werburgh St.
Drury St.
William St. South
Clarendon St.
Grafton St.
Nassau St.
Duke St.
Fenian St.
Erne St. Upper
Tivoli Theatre
Hanover Ln.
Francis St.
Bull Alley St.
Golden Ln.
Stephen St.
11
Anne St. South
Dawson St.
14
National Library
National Gallery
North Merrion Sq.
Holles St.
10
Whitefriar St.
Aungier St.
Mercer St. Lower
King St. S.
13
Leinster House
Merrion Sq. West
Merrion Square
St Patrick's Park
Patrick St.
15
Kildare St.
St Patrick's Cathedral
Dean St.
Kevin St. Upper
Peter Row
York St.
12
St Stephen's Green West
St Stephen's Green North
National Museums
16
Merrion St. Upper
South Merrion Sq.
East Merion Sq.
Ward's Hill
New Row South
New St. South
Bishop St.
Redmond's Hill
Kevin St. Lower
Cuffe St.
St Stephen's Green Park
Merrion Row
17
Fitzwilliam St. Lower
Herbert St.
Blackpitts
Clanbrassil St. Lower
Meath Hospital
Arnott St.
Heytesbury St.
Camden St. Lower
National Concert Hall
Earlsfort Terrace
18
19
Leeson St. Lower
Fitzwilliam Square South
Lombard St. West
Emorville Ave.
Curzon St.
Grantham St.
Camden St. Upper
Hatch St. Upper
Hatch St. Lwr.
20
Fitzwilliam Place
Wilton Terrace
Mespil Rd.
Harrington St.
Harcourt St.
Adelaide Rd.
Charlemont St.
Grand Canal
Clanbrassil St. Upper
Longwood Ave.
Victoria St.
George Bernard Shaw's Birthplace
Lennox St.
Richmond St. South
Church
DART Station
Information
Post Office
Irish Jewish Museum
Portobello
Grand Parade
Leeson St.
Canal Rd.
Dartmouth Rd.
Grove Rd.

soft linens; many have sweeping views of the city. There's also an in-room spa service to help you ease away the jet lag with minimum effort. The hotel's bar, the **Mint** (p. 185), is in the old vaults, and the **Exchange** restaurant is bright and modern. It's well worth a splurge.

College Green, Dublin 2. www.thewestindublin.com. ✆ **01/645-1000.** 163 units. €220–€352 double; €514–€644 suite. AE, DC, MC, V. Parking €20. Bus: All An Lar (cross-city) buses. **Amenities:** Restaurant; lounge; bar; babysitting; concierge; gym; room service; smoke-free floors; spa treatments. *In room:* A/C, TV, minibar, Wi-Fi.

MODERATE

Buswells Hotel ★ This traditional hotel has a wonderful sense of class that saves it from feeling stuffy. The spacious, slightly masculine rooms are spread throughout three Georgian buildings. The fact that the hotel is so sprawling can make it feel a bit idiosyncratic, and finding your room can be a challenge after a few pints of Guinness. But it's worth the wandering, as it has great style and a unique ambience, in part because its location near the Irish government buildings makes its bar and restaurant hotbeds of political intrigue, not to mention a prime spot for eavesdropping. Unusually for Dublin hotels, Buswells offers free overnight parking at a nearby public lot.

What's in a Name?

The "Bar" in Temple Bar has nothing to do with a pub or the law. "Bar" was a Viking word meaning "street," and Dublin was occupied for many of its early years by Viking invaders. Temple Bar, the district, came to be the name for the area around a street that the Irish called Temple.

23–25 Molesworth St., Dublin 2. www.buswells.ie. ✆ **01/614-6500.** Fax 01/676-2090. 69 units. €95–€140 double. AE, DC, MC, V. Free parking (except on some public holidays). DART: Pearse. Bus: 10, 11, 13, or 46A. **Amenities:** Restaurant; bar; babysitting; concierge; gym; room service; smoke-free floors. *In room:* TV, Wi-Fi.

Eliza Lodge ★ This hotel overlooking the Liffey embodies all the exuberance and zest of Temple Bar. The reception rooms aren't much to write home about, and many of the cheaper bedrooms are on the small side, but remember this is a budget rate for Dublin. Guest rooms are simple and attractive, done in neutral creams and blond woods, with big floor-to-ceiling windows—the better to take in the riverside vistas. At the top end, executive rooms have Jacuzzi tubs and bay windows looking out over the quay. But a better-value splurge is the smaller penthouse doubles that have balconies overlooking the river for €170. ***Note:*** The windows are not soundproof, and rooms on the lower floors can get a lot of street noise. Take your breakfast (included in the room rate) in the Liffey-view **Italian Corner** restaurant.

23–24 Wellington Quay, Dublin 2. www.elizalodge.com. ✆ **01/671-8044.** Fax 01/671-8362. 18 units. €80–€170 double. Breakfast €9. AE, MC, V. Bus: 51B, 51C, 68, 69, or 79. **Amenities:** Restaurant; bar; Wi-Fi (downstairs only). *In room:* A/C, TV, hair dryer.

Temple Bar Hotel This trendy, five-story hotel embodies the exuberance and energy of modern Temple Bar. It was developed from a former bank building, and great care was taken to preserve the brick facade and Victorian mansard roof. Guest rooms are not fancy and quite plain, if comfortable. The orthopedic beds are firm, although the smallish rooms are a bit cramped. **Buskers** and **Alchemy,** the hotel's nightclubs, are very popular and *loud*. Bear that in mind before you book—if you're looking for peace and quiet, this is definitely not the place for you, at least on the weekend. Midweek, rooms are quieter and frequently cheaper.

Fleet St., Temple Bar, Dublin 2. www.templebarhotel.com. ✆ **01/612-9200.** Fax 01/677-3088. 129 units. €100–€130 double. Rates include full Irish breakfast. AE, MC, V. DART: Tara St. Bus: 78A or 78B. **Amenities:** Restaurant; 3 bars; babysitting; concierge; access to a nearby health club; room service. *In room:* TV, hair dryer.

SELF-CATERING

25 Eustace Street This wonderfully restored Georgian town house, dating from 1720, was rescued by the Irish Landmark Trust. Today the three-story house has a superb timber-paneled staircase, fireplaces in every room, mahogany furniture, and brass beds. The huge drawing room features a baby grand piano, and there's a full dining room as well as a well-equipped galley kitchen, and three bedrooms (a double, a twin, and a triple). One of the two bathrooms has a cast-iron claw-foot tub. The bookshelves have been thoughtfully stocked with classics by Irish novelists. As with all the Trust's properties, there's no TV. All this, and Temple Bar at your doorstep. Some readers have reported that the house is a little close to Temple Bar's party scene and the noise can be too much on weekends.

25 Eustace St., Dublin 2. Contact the Irish Landmark Trust. www.irishlandmark.com. ✆ **01/670-4733.** Fax 01/670-4887. 1 apt. €900 per week in low season, rising to €2,100 per week during peak months. Weekly bookings only July–Aug; rest of year 3- or 4-night stay. AE, MC, V. Bus: Any An Lar (cross-city) bus. *In room:* Full kitchen, no phone.

St. Stephen's Green/Grafton Street Area

St. Stephen's Green may be only a 10-minute walk from the hustle and bustle of Temple Bar and Trinity College, but it's infinitely calmer and less harried. This is a good area if you're looking for a little peace and quiet.

EXPENSIVE

Brooks Hotel ★ This sophisticated, trendy hotel isn't for everybody, but those who love it, *love* it. The lobby recently had a full makeover, adding cushy sofas, interesting art, and soothingly elegant furnishings. The restaurant and bar have

A Note on Prices

The troubled Irish economy has sent hotel prices swinging. Prices fluctuated wildly while we were writing this book, and they'll keep changing once it's published. Some hotels, desperate for cash, were raising their prices. Others, eager to lure bargain hunters, were dropping prices. Use the prices in this book as a guideline, and check online well in advance of your trip. We are finding discounts in excess of 50% at many four-star hotels if we book more than a month in advance, and packages that include meals, tours, and other enticements. Sometimes this can even make staying at a top-tier hotel cheaper than a "budget" option.

also had a modern face-lift, but the color schemes in the relatively small guest rooms—with their signature colors of red, gold, purple, and brown—won't appeal to everyone. Superior and executive rooms are more spacious and have DVD players and radios. The oak-paneled drawing room is a restful oasis for a cup of tea or a glass of sherry while you peruse the *Irish Times*.

59–62 Drury St., Dublin 2. www.brookshotel.ie. ✆ **01/670-4000.** 98 units. €140–€270 double. AE, DC, MC, V. Discounted overnight parking at adjacent parking lot. DART: Tara St. or Pearse. Bus: 10, 11A, 11B, 13, 14, 15, 15A, 15B, 20B, or 46A. **Amenities:** Restaurant; bar; babysitting; concierge; minigym; room service; smoke-free floors. *In room:* A/C, TV, DVD/DVD player (in superior rooms and up), fax, hair dryer, minibar.

Conrad Hotel ★★ This modern, glass-walled hotel, which sits on one corner of St. Stephen's Green, is a favorite of the international and Irish business travelers, so it has all of the technological gizmos and snazzy extras you'd expect. Bedrooms are nicely done in neutral colors with big windows, with individual temperature controls for the air-conditioning and big, modern bathrooms. The gym is hypermodern, and reduced rates are available for the nearby K Club golf course. The **Alex** restaurant is a sleek, continental place geared to those with comfortable expense accounts.

Earlsfort Terrace, Dublin 2. www.conradhotels.com. ✆ **01/602-8900.** Fax 01/676-5424. 198 units. €150–€280 double; €190–€380 suites. AE, DC, MC, V. Parking €10. Bus: 10, 11, 13, 14, 15, 44, 46A, 47, 48, or 86. **Amenities:** Restaurant; bar; pub; babysitting; concierge; gym; 24-hr. room service; smoke-free floors. *In room:* A/C, TV w/pay movies, CD player, minibar, high-speed Internet.

The Fitzwilliam Hotel ★★★ Take an unbeatable location with sweeping views over the Green, add a Michelin-starred restaurant, throw in contemporary design by Terence Conran, and you have a hit on your hands. Conran has a knack for easygoing sophistication, and in the Fitzwilliam he uses clean lines and a few neutral colors (white, beige, gray) throughout. The beauty is in the detail—attentive staff, big, comfortable beds, sparkling votive candles, a bowl of fresh apples by the elevators, and well-designed storage. Rooms are done in neutral tones with stripped-down furniture. **Thornton's,** the restaurant, is very good, or you could try the more casual **Citron,** or linger over cocktails at the **Inn on the Green** bar. Light sleepers take note: Although St. Stephen's Green is definitely less noisy than Temple Bar, you may want to ask for a room on one of the upper floors.

109 St. Stephen's Green, Dublin 2. www.fitzwilliamhotel.com. ✆ **01/478-7000.** Fax 01/478-7878. 130 units. €165–€270 double. Breakfast €22. AE, DC, MC, V. DART: Pearse. Bus: 10, 11A, 11B, 13, or 20B. **Amenities:** 2 restaurants; bar; babysitting; concierge; room service; smoke-free rooms. *In room:* A/C, TV, DVD, CD player, fax, hair dryer, minibar, high-speed Internet (free).

Number 31 ★ A discreet plaque outside an elegant gate on a tiny side street is your only clue that what lies beyond is an outstanding guesthouse. It's actually two converted buildings—one a grand Georgian town house, the other a more modern coach house—with nice touches, like a sunken living room where seating is arranged around a peat-burning fireplace. In the main house, rooms are large and simply decorated, while in the coach house rooms are elegant and modern. Handmade beds are enveloped in natural linens. Unfortunately, the rack rate doesn't reflect what's available—there's no restaurant, no bar, no room service, and no air-conditioning. The delicious breakfast here is some consolation—cooked to order for you, with organic, seasonal ingredients, and choices ranging from mushroom frittatas to fresh-baked cranberry bread. And keep an eye out for discounted rates.

31 Leeson Close, Lower Leeson St., Dublin 2. www.number31.ie. ✆ **01/676-5011.** 21 units. €190–€220 double. Rates include breakfast. AE, MC, V. Free parking. Bus: 11, 11A, 11B, 13, 13A, or 13B. *In room:* TV, hair dryer, Wi-Fi.

The Shelbourne ★★★ One of Dublin's true *grande dame* hotels, the Shelbourne hotel has played a significant role in Irish history—the constitution was drafted here in 1922, in room no. 112. (If it's not occupied, and you ask nicely, the concierge may let you take a peek). It still attracts Irish politicians, especially to its bars and restaurants. Rooms are decorated in grand, traditional style, with soft yellows and pinks, and the hotel claims to have "Ireland's most luxurious beds." Rooms also have international power sockets, so your appliances shouldn't explode. The bars, restaurant, and lobby are warmed by fireplaces and lighted by Waterford chandeliers, and the **Lord Mayor's Lounge** is ideal for afternoon tea. Each evening guests are greeted with freshly made nibbles (fish cakes one day, brownies the next). If you have a hankering to learn more about your Irish heritage, make an appointment with the in-house **genealogy butler,** Helen Kelly.

27 St. Stephen's Green, Dublin 2. www.marriott.co.uk. ✆ **1-888/236-2427** in the U.S., or 01/663-4500. Fax 01/661-6006. 265 units. €200–€300 double; €340–€460 suite. Breakfast €20–€26. AE, DC, MC, V. Limited free self-parking; off-site parking €30; valet parking €25. DART: Pearse. Bus: 10, 11A, 11B, 13, or 20B. **Amenities:** 2 restaurants; 2 bars; babysitting; concierge; fitness center; room service; beauty and spa treatments. *In room:* A/C, TV, radio, minibar.

The Westbury Hotel ★ This upscale hotel straddles the line between traditional and modern, trying to offer a little something for everyone just off the bustling shopping hub of Grafton Street. The newly refurbished guest rooms have custom-designed furniture and chic tones of oatmeal and mahogany. The hotel recently acquired a trendy new restaurant, **Wilde**, to go alongside its chic cocktail bar and beautifully appointed Gallery Café—as handsome a spot for afternoon tea as you'll find in these parts.

Grafton St., Dublin 2. www.doylecollection.com. ✆ **01/679-1122.** Fax 01/679-7078. 204 units. €180–€280 double; €290–€640 suite. Full Irish breakfast €30. AE, DC, MC, V. Parking €20. Bus: All An Lar (cross-city) buses. **Amenities:** 2 restaurants; bar; babysitting; concierge; 24-hr. room service; smoke-free rooms. *In room:* A/C, interactive TV, DVD/broadband system, hair dryer, minibar.

MODERATE

Premier Suites Stephen's Hall Well located on the southeast corner of St. Stephen's Green in a handsome Georgian town house, this all-suite hotel offers a bit of value for families, visitors who plan an extended stay, or folks who want to entertain or do their own cooking. The building underwent a full renovation a couple of years ago, which renewed each suite in tasteful modern style. Each apartment contains a sitting room, dining area, fully equipped kitchenette, tiled bathroom, and bedroom, and the smallest apartment is just under 150 sq. m (1,615 sq. ft.). On the website there's a link that allows you to pre-order groceries and have them delivered on the day you arrive. If you're not there, the reception staff will also unpack them for you. How suite is that?

14–17 Lower Leeson St., Dublin 2. www.stephens-hall.com. ✆ **01/638-1111.** Fax 01/638-1122. 30 units. €95–€175 studio and 1-bedroom suite; €190–€240 2-bedroom suite. AE, DC, MC, V. Parking

€10. DART: Pearse. Bus: 11, 11A, 11B, 13, 13A, or 13B. **Amenities:** Concierge; smoke-free floor. *In room:* TV, radio, fax, Wi-Fi.

Trinity Lodge In an enormous Georgian town house that feels miles away from the anonymous chain hotels in the city center, the Trinity is a sweet and historic place to stay, a few blocks off Grafton Street. The gray stone building dates from 1785, and its 10 large guest rooms are brightly decorated in keeping with that period, some with paintings by the respected Irish artist Graham Knuttel. The breakfast room downstairs is warmly designed in country-house style. A second building across the street houses six large rooms with a more contemporary edge. The buildings are protected historical structures, so there's no elevator access to their four levels—ask for a ground-floor room if you have mobility problems.

12 S. Frederick St., Dublin 2. www.trinitylodge.com. ✆ **01/617-0900.** Fax 01/617-0999. 16 units. €100–€140 double. Rates include breakfast. MC, V. Bus: All An Lar (cross-city) buses. **Amenities:** Restaurant; bar; room service; smoke-free rooms. *In room:* A/C (some), TV, Wi-Fi.

INEXPENSIVE

Avalon House This warm and friendly hostel in a beautiful old redbrick building is a not-so-well-kept secret among those who travel to Dublin on a budget. Its pine floors, high ceilings, and open fireplace make it a pleasant place in which to relax, and its cafe is a popular hangout for international travelers. Most accommodations are in dorms of varying sizes, with a few single- and twin-bedded rooms available, too. It's not exactly the Clarence, but it's got all you really need—clean, cheerful rooms in a safe location at a cheap price. There are also a few helpful extra touches, such as free Wi-Fi, a left-luggage facility for up to 2 weeks, and its own bureau de change. All in all, this is one of the best budget options in town.

55 Aungier St., Dublin 2. www.avalon-house.ie. ✆ **01/475-0001.** Fax 01/475-0303. 12 units. €25–€46 per person double with private bathroom; €12–€18 dorms. Rates include light continental breakfast. AE, MC, V. Bus: 16, 16A, 19, 22, or 155. No curfew but passes must be shown on entry after 9pm. **Amenities:** Cafe; TV lounge; smoke-free rooms; Wi-Fi.

Fitzwilliam Square/Merrion Square Area

This elegant Georgian neighborhood feels and looks much like nearby St. Stephen's Green, but its streets are less busy and commercialized, and its hotels marginally less expensive. Fitzwilliam Square and Merrion Square are small parks surrounded by Georgian town houses. Many of the houses are offices for doctors, lawyers, and government agencies.

VERY EXPENSIVE

Merrion Hotel ★ Housed in four restored Georgian houses, the Merrion is a deeply feminine, traditionally elegant hotel. Downstairs the lobby and lounges have formal furniture and fires glowing in hearths—the kinds of places where proper afternoon tea seems called for. The impressive contemporary art on the walls is part of one of the country's largest private collections. Service is discreetly omnipresent, and the spacious rooms overlook either the government buildings or the hotel's 18th-century-inspired gardens of acacia and lilac. Pamper yourself in the **Tethra Spa.** Stretch your credit card's limit at the Michelin-starred **Restaurant Patrick Guilbaud** (p. 137) or save a few pennies at the somewhat cheaper and more atmospheric **Cellar** restaurant.

Upper Merrion St., Dublin 2. www.merrionhotel.com. ✆ **01/603-0600.** 142 units. €230–€595 double; €950–€1,600 suite. Breakfast €24–€29. DC, MC, V. Parking €20 per night. DART: Pearse. Bus: 10, 13, or 13A. **Amenities:** 2 restaurants; 2 bars; babysitting; concierge; gym; pool; room service; spa. *In room:* A/C, TV, DVD, minibar, Wi-Fi.

O'Connell Street Area North of the Liffey

The newly hip Northside has much to offer in the way of hotels. With the grand Gresham and the trendy Morrison (see below) leading the way, it's growing in popularity as a place to stay. Best of all, not only is it very central and within walking distance of all the major sights and shops, but hotel rates tend to be lower than they are just across the bridge.

VERY EXPENSIVE

The Morrison ★★ Fashion fans will have no trouble pegging the design of this trendy hotel as the work of the uber-cool John Rocha, who is responsible for everything from the crushed velvet bed throws in blood red or burned Sienna, to the Waterford crystal vases. Rocha uses a palette of neutral colors—cream, chocolate, and black—to achieve a kind of warm minimalism in the guest rooms, which have stereos, Egyptian cotton linens, and cool Portuguese limestone in the bathrooms. Suites are equipped with iMacs. This is really an oversize boutique hotel, with an ideal location just across the Liffey from Temple Bar. The stylish atrium-style restaurant, **Halo,** is one of the most talked-about in town.

Lower Ormond Quay, Dublin 1. www.morrisonhotel.ie. ✆ **01/887-2400.** Fax 01/874-4031. 138 units. €125–€285 double; €170–€320 studios; €285–€1,160 suite. AE, DC, MC, V. DART: Connolly. Bus: 70 or 80. **Amenities:** Restaurant; 2 bars; babysitting; concierge; room service. *In room:* A/C, CD player, MP3 docking station, hair dryer, minibar, Nintendo Wii (suites and studios), iMacs (suites), high-speed Internet.

EXPENSIVE

The Clarion Hotel Dublin IFSC ★ All smooth, straight lines and extra touches, this relaxing, modern hotel is a good option for business travelers. The comfortable rooms are softened by Egyptian cotton bedding, and filled with the latest electronic gadgets, including high-speed Internet and PlayStation units. Bathrooms have nifty steam-free mirrors. The stylish bar and restaurant are workaday but useful. However, this hotel's best offering is arguably its state-of-the-art health club, with its gorgeous low-lit pool that urges you to exercise. There are yoga and aerobics classes for the energetic. Happily, the sauna, steam room, and whirlpool require no physical exertion at all. Rooms at the front have a gorgeous view of the Liffey and Dublin skyline. It can be significantly cheaper to get a room-only rate here and grab breakfast somewhere else; some good alternatives can be found nearby.

International Financial Services Centre, Dublin 1. www.clarionhotelifsc.com. ✆ **01/433-8800.** Fax 01/433-8811. 163 units. €100–€200 double; €180–€230 suite. AE, DC, MC, V. Parking €12. DART: Connolly. Bus: All An Lar (cross-city) buses. **Amenities:** Restaurant; bar; babysitting; concierge; gym; pool; room service; smoke-free floors; spa. *In room:* A/C, TV (satellite/DVD), hair dryer, minibar, high-speed Internet.

The Gresham ★★ This is one of Dublin's top-tier historic hotels, and has welcomed visitors for nearly 200 years. Rooms are generally small, but coolly decorated in neutral tones, with big, firm beds and huge windows. The more upmarket Lavery Rooms are over 33 sq. m (355 sq. ft.) and, thanks to a recent price cut, aren't much of an extra splurge. There's a bright, cheerful bistro, **Toddy's,** and the slightly more traditional **Restaurant 23,** which serves decent European cuisine. The pleasant bar, which overlooks O'Connell Street, also serves light snacks—handy on Sundays, when (in an anachronistic touch that verges on the ridiculous for a place this size) neither of the Gresham's other restaurants are open. The vast lobby is one of the best places in Dublin to have a cup of tea or a cocktail in elegant but relaxed surroundings.

23 Upper O'Connell St., Dublin 1. www.gresham-hotels.com. ✆ **01/878-6881.** Fax 01/878-7175. 288 units. €115–€300 double. Rates include breakfast. AE, DC, MC, V. Parking €15 per night. Bus: 11 or 13. **Amenities:** Restaurant; 2 bars; babysitting; concierge; room service; smoke-free floors. *In room:* A/C, TV, fridge, hair dryer, Wi-Fi.

INEXPENSIVE

Hotel Isaacs This friendly guesthouse has basic, clean and comfortable bedrooms and suites, with polished pine furniture, big-screen TVs—and, by Irish standards, it's cheap. Rooms in the "Georgian wing" are more elegantly designed, and with fancier furnishings, but they cost more. On the downside, the super-central location (by a bus and DART stop) means that it can get noisy on weekends (especially on the lower floors) and management's attitude towards room amenities verges on the parsimonious. Air-conditioning? That'll be an extra €15. How about Wi-Fi? No problem, just pony up another €25, and then pay to actually use the service. Want to reserve one of the parking spaces outside? Another €13, or you have to use the multistory nearby. Once you add all that in, it's not such a bargain. We recommend this place if you're traveling in the high season and can't get a good advance-booking bargain at a better hotel.

Store St., Dublin 1. www.isaacs.ie. ✆ **01/813-4700.** Fax 01/836-5390. 54 units. €95–€13. Room upgrades €25–€50. Rates include breakfast. MC, V. DART: Connolly. All An Lar (cross-city) buses. **Amenities:** Restaurant; cafe/bar; gym. *In room:* Cable TV, Wi-Fi (in Georgian wing).

Ballsbridge & the Southern Suburbs

This is the most prestigious Dublin residential neighborhood, south of the canal, coveted for its leafy streets and historic buildings. Beautiful though it is, it's a good 20- or 30-minute walk to most sights and shops.

VERY EXPENSIVE

Four Seasons ★★★ ☺ If money is no object, the Four Seasons lures you like a De Beers diamond draws a socialite. The beauty is in the details: The indoor pool and whirlpool overlook a sunken garden; the lobby and guest rooms are equally smart and plush; the spa is outstanding and the restaurants elegant. This is an excellent option for families, as there are complimentary cribs, child-proof bedrooms, and a babysitting service. A menu of children's activities will keep the kids occupied while you have a romantic meal or just kick back for some quiet meditation (the better to prepare yourself for the bill). Other useful extras include a free car service to ferry you to the city center. Always check the website's rates before booking; online discounts and package deals can be very good.

Simmonscourt Rd., Ballsbridge, Dublin 4. www.fourseasons.com/dublin. ✆ **800/819-5053** in the U.S., or 01/665-4000. Fax 01/665-4099. 197 units. €210–€250 double; €495–€830 suite. AE, DC, MC, V. Free parking. DART: Sandymount (5-min. walk). Bus: 7, 7A, 7X, 8, or 45. **Amenities:** 2

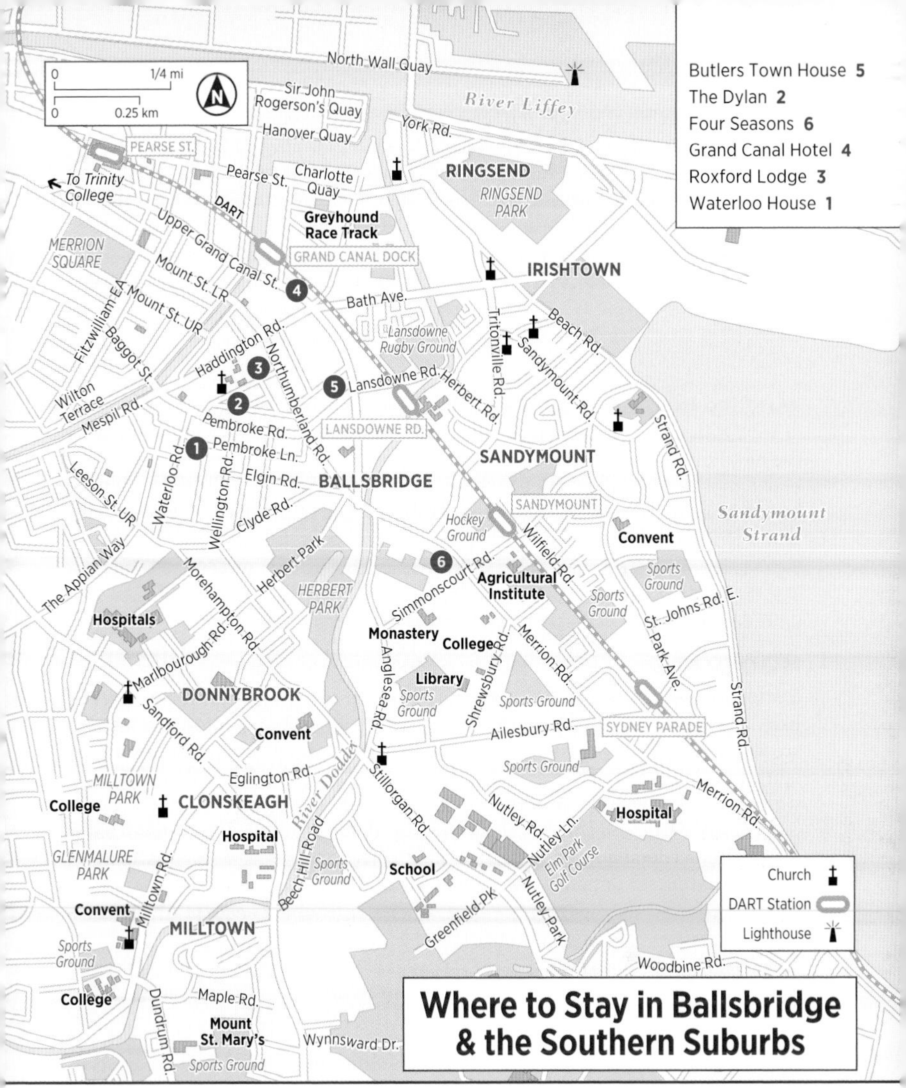

restaurants; lobby lounge; bar; babysitting; children's programs; concierge; health club & spa; whirlpool; indoor pool; room service; smoke-free rooms. *In room:* TV/DVD, CD player available, radio, hair dryer, minibar.

EXPENSIVE

The Dylan ★ If money is no object, and style is everything, this is probably the place for you. A determinedly glamorous boutique hotel, the Dylan has transformed the former Royal Hospital Nurses' Home with vivid colors, bright carpets and curtains, Murano glass chandeliers, studded leather wallpaper, and lime-green sofas. Guest rooms are quite small, and the decor is disco chic, with Frette linens and Divine Dreams beds. Service here is excellent, but beauty's in the eye of the beholder, so this very hip, very adult hotel is certainly not for everyone. Families in particular might find its party-hearty atmosphere a bit off-putting (it has a signature cocktail—vanilla vodka with crème de banana—as well as a thumping club soundtrack). But 20-somethings—at least, those not feeling the pinch of the credit crunch—line up to spend the night.

Eastmoreland Place, Ballsbridge, Dublin 4. www.dylan.ie. ✆ **01/660-3000.** Fax 01/660-3005. 44 units. €270–€440 double; €320–€690 suites. Rates include full breakfast. AE, MC, V. Valet parking €20. Bus: 10, 46A, 46B, 63, or 84. **Amenities:** Restaurant; lounge; bar; nightclub; concierge; room service; smoke-free rooms. *In room:* Plasma TV, CD player, radio, hair dryer, minibar.

Waterloo House ★ This classy guesthouse is charming in an old-world kind of way, with an elegant, high-ceilinged drawing room where you can linger over the morning papers or a good book. Guest rooms are large (some have two double beds), most have fluffy white comforters and walls in lemony yellow. The varied breakfast menu (French toast, waffles, croissant, fish of the day . . .) offers more than the usual Irish fried eggs and bacon. A quiet, peaceful alternative.

8–10 Waterloo Rd., Ballsbridge, Dublin 4. www.waterloohouse.ie. ✆ **01/660-1888.** 17 units. €130–€175 double. Rates include full breakfast. MC, V. Free parking. Closed Christmas week. DART: Lansdowne Rd. Bus: 5, 7, or 8. **Amenities:** Breakfast room. *In room:* TV, hair dryer.

MODERATE

Butlers Town House ★ This beautifully restored Victorian town house feels like a gracious family home. The atmosphere is elegant but comfortable, rooms are richly furnished with four-poster or half-tester beds, and draped in luxurious fabrics in rich colors. The gem here, in our opinion, is the Glendalough Room, with a lovely bay window and small library (you have to request it when you book your room). Afternoon tea is served in the drawing room. Prices here have dropped considerably over the last couple of years, turning what was once a pleasant but pricey option into a genuine slice of affordable luxury.

44 Lansdowne Rd., Ballsbridge, Dublin 4. www.butlers-hotel.com. ✆ **800/44-UTELL** (448-8355) in the U.S., or 01/667-4022. Fax 01/667-3960. www.butlers-hotel.com. 20 units. €100–€110 double. Rates include full breakfast. AE, DC, MC, V. Closed Dec 23–Jan 10. Secure free parking. DART: Lansdowne Rd. Bus: 7, 7A, 8, or 45. **Amenities:** Breakfast room; bar; babysitting; room service; access to off-site gym. *In room:* A/C, TV, hair dryer, Wi-Fi.

Grand Canal Hotel ★ This modern hotel at the edge of Ballsbridge is a clean and pleasant alternative to bustling central Dublin hotels. Its rooms are medium-size, quiet, and comfortable with a bright, contemporary decor and comfortable beds. Executive rooms with balconies are €25 extra. The hotel's **Gasworks Bar** has a friendly pub atmosphere, and is popular with locals (although we have heard a few complaints about noise from the bar bothering light-sleeping hotel guests, so ask for a room as far from the bar as possible). Prices in the hotel's restaurant are noticeably lower than those charged at comparable places a 20-minute walk away in the city center. Check the website for some good package deals, often including tickets to a big show and dinner at bargain rates.

Grand Canal St., Ballsbridge, Dublin 4. www.grandcanalhotel.ie. ✆ **01/646-1000.** 142 units. €80–€175 double. Breakfast €12. AE, MC, V. DART: Grand Canal. **Amenities:** Restaurant; 2 bars; room service; smoke-free rooms. *In room:* TV, CD player (some rooms), hair dryer, Wi-Fi.

Roxford Lodge ★ 🏷 This lovely little hotel is slightly outside of central Dublin (Grafton St. is a 25-min. walk), but about as good as it gets anywhere in the city for the price. Rooms are simple and elegant, with little flourishes that incorporate elements of the original Victorian building, such as corniced ceilings and bay windows. Most bedrooms have their own whirlpool baths and saunas, which sacrifices a little space but raises the luxury quotient. Service is personable and breakfasts are delicious. Guests can help themselves to free coffee all day in the lounge.

46 Northumberland Rd., Ballsbridge, Dublin 4. www.roxfordlodge.ie. ✆ **01/668-8572.** €110–€120 double; €165–€200 suite. Rates include breakfast. AE, MC, V. Bus: 11 or 13. **Amenities:** Lounge. *In room:* TV, DVD, CD player, hair dryer, Wi-Fi.

WHERE TO EAT

The economic upswing of the nineties and noughties brought with it a new generation of international, sophisticated eateries. Ireland is now a nation of foodies, and that's not going away. However, as the economy has gone down, so too has there been a minor resurgence in the popularity of traditional Irish fare, even in expensive restaurants. That's not to say that the food in Dublin has got *worse*—it's just that places seem less inclined to innovate. Even the most fashionable and wealthy diners, it would seem, have need of comfort food right now.

However, Dublin is still a notoriously expensive city in which to eat out. Prices have come down a little, but you're still likely to pay more for a meal here than in a comparable U.S. city, or even in Paris or London. But when the food here is good, it's very good, so if you can afford to splurge once or twice while you're in town, do so—you're in for a treat.

Historic Old City/Liberties & Around

EXPENSIVE

Lord Edward ★★ SEAFOOD Established in 1890 in the heart of the Old City opposite Christ Church Cathedral, this cozy upstairs dining room claims to be Dublin's oldest seafood restaurant. Nine different versions of sole, including au gratin and Veronique, are available. There are also many variations of prawns, from Thermidor to Provençal, and fresh lobster is prepared au naturel or in sauces. Fresh fish—from salmon and sea trout to plaice and turbot—is served grilled, fried, meunière, or poached. Vegetarian dishes are also available. At lunch, the bar sells simpler fare. At best conservative, at worst passé, the Lord Edward isn't Dublin's trendiest restaurant, but it has amassed plenty of fans over the years for its old-fashioned dependability.

23 Christ Church Place, Dublin 8. ✆ **01/454-2420.** www.lordedward.ie. Reservations required. Main courses €18–€39; fixed-price dinner €35. AE, DC, MC, V. Mon–Fri 12:30–2:30pm and 6–10:45pm; Sat 6–10:45pm. Closed Dec 24–Jan 3. Bus: 50, 54A, 56A, 65, 65A, 77, 77A, 123, or 150.

INEXPENSIVE

Govinda's VEGETARIAN The motto of this Hare Krishna–run establishment is healthy square meals on square plates for very good prices. The meals are generous, belly-warming concoctions of vegetables, cheese, rice, and pasta. Every day, 10 main courses are offered cafeteria style. Some are Indian, others are a variety of mainstream staples such as lasagna or macaroni and cheese.

Where to Eat in Dublin

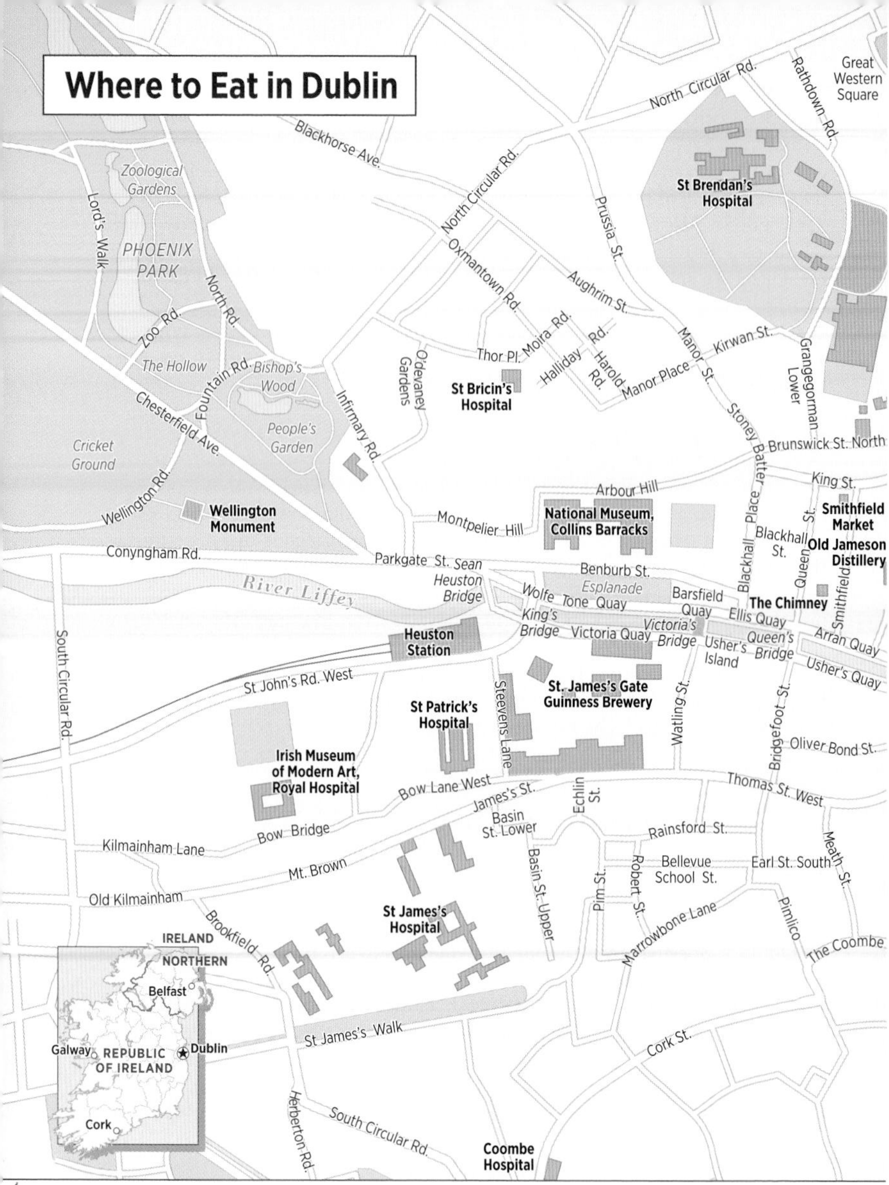

Avoca Café **23**
Bang **33**
Bewley's **25**
Blackboard Bistro **30**
Boojum **4**
Café Mao **26**
Chapter One **1**
Cornucopia Wholefood Restaurant **24**
Dobbins **36**
Eden **17**
Ely Wine Bar **34**
Epicurean Food Hall **3**
Govinda's **21**
Irish Film Centre Cafe Bar **16**
Juice **18**
L'Ecrivain **37**
L'Gueuleton **22**
La Mère Zou **31**
The Larder **13**
Lemon **27**
Leo Burdock's **11**
Les Frères Jacques **15**
Lord Edward **10**

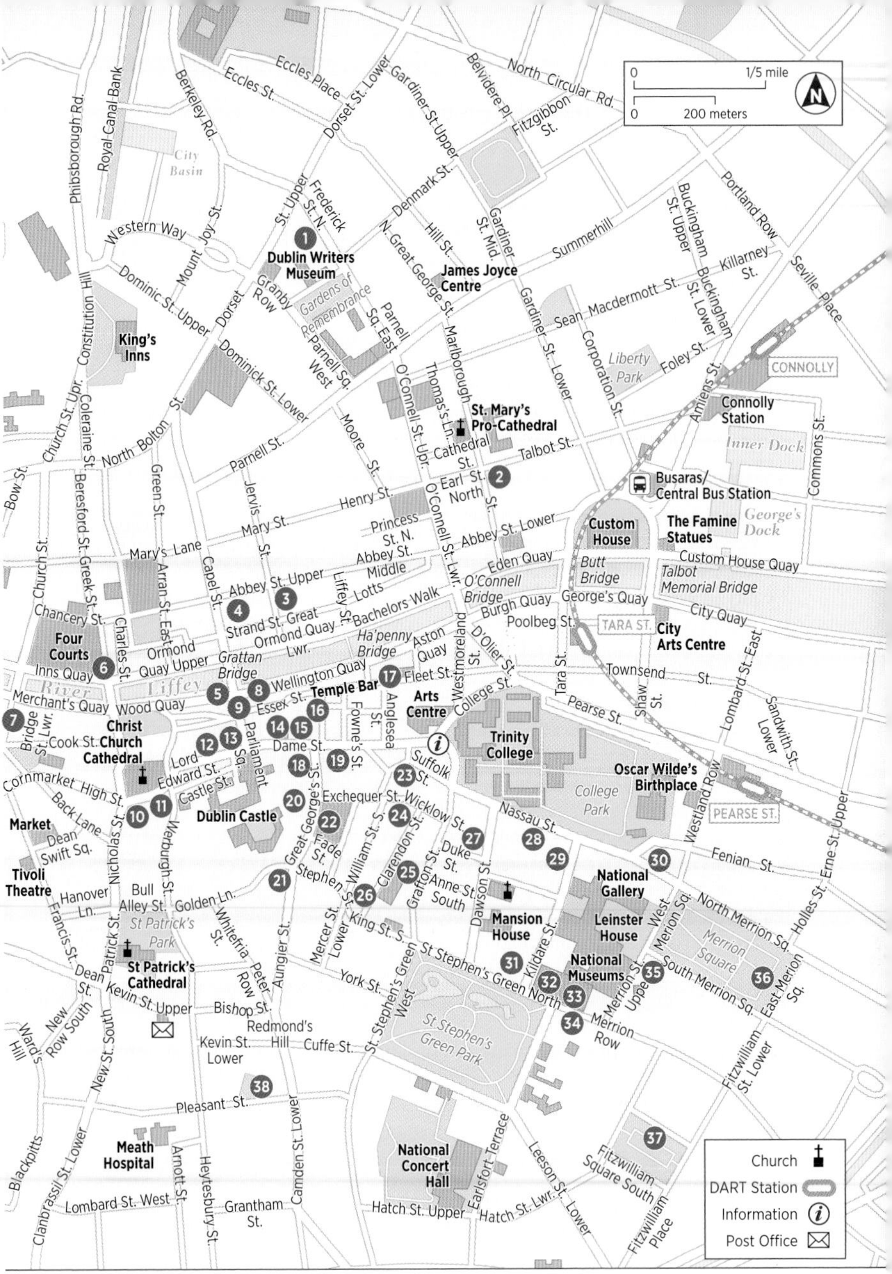

Mermaid Café **14**
101 Talbot **2**
One Pico **29**
O'Shea's Merchant **7**
Peploe's **32**
The Pig's Ear **28**
The Porterhouse **9**
Queen of Tarts **12**
Restaurant Patrick Guilbaud **35**
Sabor Brasil **38**
Soup Dragon **5**
Stag's Head **19**
The Tea Room **8**
Winding Stair **6**
Yamamori Noodles **20**

EATING OUT WITHOUT breaking THE BANK

Although not quite as stratospheric as once they were, prices for food in Dublin are still sky-high. Visitors may find themselves a little shell-shocked when the check arrives—even in comparatively "cheap" places. In other words, unless your pockets jingle with some serious change, you're going to want to get creative sometimes when it comes to eating out.

You can get a cost break in the city's many cafes and tearooms, which offer sandwiches, scones, soup, and hot platters at reasonable prices. The cafe in the tourist information center on Suffolk Street—Fionn McCool's—does good, cheap food for less than €10 (you can also download a voucher for free tea and coffee here at **www.visitdublin.com**). Or you could have your lunch in a pub, where you can get a hearty meal for around €10. The pub option is for lunch only, though, as most pubs don't serve food after 3pm.

If it's summer, cut costs by buying a sandwich at one of the many sandwich shops—or even in grocery chains like Tesco and Dunnes—and have a picnic in a city square or St. Stephen's Green. Store-bought sandwiches are better and fresher than in North America, and they only cost a few euros. Some Spar grocery stores are now making crepes and stir-fries to order for a few euros. And at the Botticelli *gelataria* at 3 Temple Bar you can have a scoop of excellent ice cream for €2.50.

In the winter, though, getting out of the cold can be a priority, so consider popping into a coffee shop and grabbing a sandwich there—usually no more than about €4.

At dinnertime, bargains are harder to come by. However, many restaurants offer "early-bird" or fixed-price menus at about 25% off their normal price—look out for signs in central Dublin.

Definitely take advantage of free breakfasts if your hotel offers them, as that's the best deal on food you're going to get in Dublin. However, if your hotel offers a room-only rate (not all of them do), it's often cheaper to find your own breakfast elsewhere. We mention this in reviews where the saving is a big one.

Veggie burgers are prepared to order. For dessert, try a rich wedge of carrot cake with a dollop of cream or homemade ice cream. There are also branches on Merrion Row and Middle Abbey Street.

4 Aungier St., Dublin 2. ✆ **01/475-0309.** www.govindas.ie. Snacks €1–€5; main courses €7–€11; takeout trays €7–€8. MC, V. Mon–Sat noon–9pm. Closed Dec 24–Jan 2. Bus: 16, 16A, 19, or 22.

Leo Burdock's FISH AND CHIPS Established in 1913, this quintessential Irish takeout shop across from Christ Church Cathedral is a cherished Dublin institution. Cabinet ministers, university students, and Hollywood stars alike (Tom Cruise and Liam Neeson are both fans) can be found at the counter waiting for fish bought fresh that morning and good Irish potatoes, both cooked in "drippings" (none of that modern cooking oil!). There's no seating, but you can sit on a nearby bench or stroll down to the park at St. Patrick's Cathedral.

2 Werburgh St., Dublin 8. ✆ **01/454-0306.** www.leoburdocks.com. Main courses €6–€8. No credit cards. Mon–Sat noon–midnight; Sun 4pm–midnight. Bus: 21A, 50, 50A, 78, 78A, or 78B.

Queen of Tarts ★★ TEA SHOP This tiny tearoom is one of our favorite places to blow a diet on decadent cakes and cookies, with a pot of tea on the side to make it all legal. The cake counter is dizzying—we challenge you to come here and not order something sweet, like the luscious blackberry pie or the rich chocolate cake, with cream bursting from its seams. The scones are tender and light, dusted with powdered sugar, and served with tiny pots of jam. Delicious, hearty breakfasts and light lunches are also served. There's an additional branch just around the corner on Cow's Lane.

4 Corkhill, Dame St., Dublin 2. ✆ **01/670-7499.** www.queenoftarts.ie. Baked goods and cakes €2.50–€6; breakfast €3–€10; lunch €6–€12. No credit cards. Mon–Fri 8am–7pm; Sat 9am–7pm; Sun 10am–6pm. Bus: Any city-center bus.

Temple Bar/Trinity College Area

VERY EXPENSIVE

Les Frères Jacques ★★ FRENCH/SEAFOOD The business crowd loves this friendly, upmarket French restaurant, which brings a touch of haute cuisine to the lower edge of the trendy Temple Bar district. The menu offers such fare as roast monkfish with lobster juice risotto, or Atlantic turbot with black-eye bean and chorizo cassoulet. Lobster is served, according to the menu, "fresh from our shores"—which sounds more romantic than "plucked from the tank," but it literally couldn't be fresher. Although the emphasis is definitely on seafood here, the menu includes plenty to keep carnivores happy, including filet of Irish beef with cognac sauce and lamb with polenta and roasted almonds.

74 Dame St., Dublin 2. ✆ **01/679-4555.** www.lesfreresjacques.com. Reservations recommended. Main courses €32–€38; fixed-price lunch €21–€26; 4-course dinner €42. AE, DC, MC, V. Mon–Fri 12:30–2:30pm and 6–10:30pm; Sat 6–10:30pm. Closed Dec 24–Jan 4. Bus: 50, 50A, 54, 56, or 77.

EXPENSIVE

Eden ★★ MODERN IRISH/INTERNATIONAL This is one of Temple Bar's hippest eateries, a cool minimalist space with an open-plan kitchen overlooking Meeting House Square. The menu focuses on traditional flavors with the hint of a well-traveled, international accent. Irish scallops may be served a potato cake and *sauce vierge* (olive oil, lemon juice, and tomatoes), or the filet of Irish beef alongside spinach and mustard mash and béarnaise sauce. Seafood lovers are may prefer to just to stay closer to home and go straight for the fresh catch of the day. Typical desserts include Tahitian vanilla *panna cotta,* which comes with a deliciously tart strawberry and lime sorbet.

Meeting House Sq. (entrance on Sycamore St.), Dublin 2. ✆ **01/670-5372.** www.edenrestaurant.ie. Main courses €19–€28; fixed-price lunch, 2 courses €18, 3 courses €23. AE, DC, MC, V. Mon–Thurs 12:30–3pm and 6–10pm; Fri–Sat noon–3pm and 6–10:30pm; Sun noon–4pm and 6–9:30pm. Bus: 51B, 51C, 68, 69, or 79.

L'Gueuleton ★★ FRENCH Rated by local critics as one of the best restaurants in Dublin, L'Gueuleton is worth the effort you'll have to put in to book it well in advance. The cozy dining room is all candlelight, exposed brick walls, flagstone floors, polished wood beams, and Prada-clad clientele. The elegant bistro menu changes constantly, but includes warming options like Toulouse sausages with lyonnaise potatoes, or grilled hake with chorizo, clams, and baby spinach.

1 Fade St., Dublin 2. ✆ **01/675-3708.** www.lgueuleton.com. Reservations required. Main courses €16–€27. AE, DC, MC, V. Mon–Sat 12:30–3pm and 6–10pm; Sun 1–3pm and 6–9pm. Bus: Any An Lar (cross-city) buses.

Mermaid Café ★★ MODERN Owned by a chef and an artist, this popular eatery is a mixture of good restaurant and classy hangout. It's a lunchtime favorite of local professionals, and a good place to take a date in the evening. Dishes often found on the frequently changing menu range from the likes of Barnsley chop with new potatoes, fennel and rosemary, to an array of excellent seafood dishes, including a rich seafood casserole. The popular weekend brunch can give you a good idea of the menu at a less wallet-denting price than going for an evening meal.

69–70 Dame St., Dublin 2. ✆ **01/670-8236.** www.mermaid.ie. Reservations required. Fixed-price lunch menu 3-course €20, 2-course €17; early-bird dinner Mon–Fri 6–7pm, 2-course €22, 3-course €27. Main courses: dinner €17–€26; Sun brunch €12–€17. MC, V. Mon–Sat 12:30–3pm and 6–11pm; Sun noon–3:30pm (brunch) and 6–9pm. Bus: 50, 50A, 54, 56A, 77, 77A, or 77B.

The Pig's Ear ★★ MODERN IRISH With its hot pink front door and humbug-striped awning, one only has to see this place to infer a certain playful imagination in the mind of its chef. Stephen McAllister is quite a celebrity in Ireland, although the clientele are far too cool to turn their heads if he puts in an appearance. On the other hand, maybe they're too busy admiring the handsome views of Trinity College from the upstairs dining room. Either way, his menu pitches a sophisticated twist on traditional Irish cuisine. Take dishes such as honey-roasted pork belly, which is served with mini sausage rolls and spiced prunes; or the filet of sea bream cooked in clay with mash and nut brown butter. Desserts include bread and butter ice cream and chocolate tart served with spiced cherries. And if you've still got room, how about rounding it all off with bag of old-fashioned candy, guaranteed to make you feel like a kid again?

4–5 Nassau St., Dublin 2. ✆ **01/670-3865.** www.thepigsear.ie. Reservations required. Main courses €18–€27; fixed-price early-bird menus €20–€25; fixed-price lunch menus €16–€20. AE, DC, MC, V. Mon–Sat 12:30–3pm and 5:30–10pm. DART: Pearse. Bus: 7, 8, 10, 11, or 46A.

The Tea Room ★★★ INTERNATIONAL This ultrasmart restaurant, ensconced in the U2-owned Clarence hotel, is guaranteed to deliver one of your most memorable meals in Ireland. This gorgeous room's soaring yet understated lines are the perfect backdrop for chef Methieu Melin's complex, but accessible approach to food. Honey-glazed breast of duck is served in a sweet-and-sour orange sauce with a hazelnut and goat cheese lollipop, and the filet of sea bass comes with spiced beans and balsamic teriyaki. If you don't feel like being adventurous, that's just fine: Go for the homemade fish and chips perhaps, or just a New York steak with onion rings and garlic butter. The nightly Market Menu offers an unfussy three-course meal at a genuinely reasonable price, given where you are.

In the Clarence, 6–8 Wellington Quay, Dublin 2. ✆ **01/407-0813.** www.theclarence.ie. Reservations required. Main courses €12–€32; Market Menu fixed-price dinners 2-course €20, 3-course €25. AE, MC, V. Mon–Fri noon–5pm; Mon–Wed 6–10pm; Thurs 6–10:30pm. Bus: 51B, 51C, 68, 69, or 79.

MODERATE

Juice VEGETARIAN If nobody told you this was a vegetarian eatery, you'd probably never notice, so interesting is the menu and so tasty is the food. It's a lovely looking place, with soaring 9m (30-ft.) ceilings softened by a suspended

Outdoors Is the New Indoors (for a Smoke)

While Ireland has a reputation as a hard-drinking, heavy-smoking place, it is not above American-style health laws, and thus it has a sweeping antismoking law. Smoking is banned in virtually all public spaces, including restaurants, bars, hotel lobbies—you name it. Therefore, there will be no smoking at the table, and not even any nipping into the bar for a quick drag. It's out into the cold and wet to indulge.

The Irish are not entirely unsympathetic to the addicted among us, and most restaurants and bars have created lavish patios and gardens, usually covered and heated, where smokers can puff away in relative comfort.

sailcloth and muted lighting. Brunch is classic here, with pancakes, huevos rancheros, and French toast topped with fresh fruit or organic maple syrup. The rest of the day, you can sample the homemade dips—hummus, baba ghanouj, tapenade, roasted carrot pâté—with crudités and pita-bread strips. True to its name, there are about 30 kinds of juices and smoothies on offer.

Castle House, 73–83 S. Great Georges St., Dublin 2. ✆ **01/475-7856.** www.juicerestaurant.ie. Reservations recommended Fri–Sat. 3-course early-bird dinner €15; brunch main courses €6–€10; dinner main courses €12–€16. AE, MC, V. Daily 11am–11pm. Bus: 50, 54, 56, or 77.

Yamamori Noodles JAPANESE This place has such a casually exuberant atmosphere that you may just be startled by how good the food is. Prices range from bargain to splurge for dishes such as chili chicken ramen or the *yamamori yaki soba* with its mound of wok-fried noodles, piled high with prawns, squid, chicken, and roast pork. Vegetarians aren't overlooked, as there are plenty of veggie options. Lunch specials are outstanding.

71–72 S. Great George's St., Dublin 2. ✆ **01/475-5001.** www.yamamorinoodles.ie. Reservations only for parties of 4 or more. Dinner main courses €11–€20; sushi, sashimi, and norimaki €4–€9 per piece. MC, V. Sun–Wed 12:15–11pm; Thurs–Sat 12:15–11:30pm. Bus: 50, 50A, 54, 56, or 77.

INEXPENSIVE

Avoca Café ★★ MODERN IRISH Who would think that one of the best places to have lunch in Dublin is on the third floor of a shop? It's true! This polished, casual cafe is perched above the vibrant pinks and reds of the knitted wools and painted doodads in the charming Avoca shop near Trinity College. If you can tear yourself away from the shopping, there are thick homemade soups, fresh salads, and light lunches to keep you going in the buzzing cafe. There's also a cheaper (but equally fresh) deli in the basement. If you've got a room-only rate at your hotel—or just crave some variety—you should earmark the Avoca Café as a spot for breakfast. The selection isn't large, but it's delicious and reasonably priced options include sweet and savory home-baked scones, or French toast served with bacon and maple syrup.

11–13 Suffolk St., Trinity College, Dublin 2. ✆ **01/672-6019.** www.avoca.ie. Main courses €11–€14. MC, V. Mon–Wed and Fri 10am–6pm; Thurs 10am–8pm; Sat 10am–6:30pm; Sun 11am–6pm. Bus: 50, 54, or 56.

Bewley's CAFE In a beautiful Beaux Arts building on Grafton Street, Bewley's was long the city's most famous coffee shop and gathering place. A few years ago, though, it was sold to a chain, and many feared the worst. Happily, it has survived the transition (and been sold again), and emerged as a pleasant cafe and coffee shop. Breakfast is popular (though not cheap), and the lunch menu consists of soups, snacks, and toasted sandwiches, alongside heartier pasta and pizza dishes. Bewley's is best experienced as an atmospheric and elegant place to have a cup of coffee and rest your weary feet in the afternoon—even though it doesn't quite match up to the much-missed original.

78 Grafton St., Dublin 2. ✆ **01/672-7720.** www.bewleys.com. Fixed-price 3-course dinner €15; sandwiches (11am–5pm) €6–€10; main courses €8.50–€16. MC, V. Mon–Wed 8am–10pm; Thurs–Sat 8am–11pm; Sun 9am–10pm. Bus: 50 or 56.

Irish Film Centre Cafe Bar CAFE A trendy drinking spot in Temple Bar, the hip Cafe Bar (in the lobby of the city's coolest place to watch a movie) features an excellent, affordable menu that changes daily. Dishes are simple and well prepared; deli sandwiches are available at lunchtime, alongside a selection of burgers, fish cakes, salads, and the like, which also form the backbone of the dinner menu. Tapas are served after 5pm, and there's a brunch menu every Sunday. The weekend entertainment usually includes music or comedy.

6 Eustace St., Temple Bar, Dublin 2. ✆ **01/677-8788.** www.irishfilm.ie. Lunch and dinner €7–€10. MC, V. Mon–Sat 12:30–9:30pm; Sun noon–4pm. Bus: 21A, 78A, or 78B.

The Larder ★ 🎁 CAFE This tiny place is a modern, creative cafe, focusing on fresh local produce and meats, and innovative dishes. It has a rugged, ancient look, with exposed brick walls, utilitarian metal lights, and red armchairs. Stellar dishes include anything for breakfast (scrambled eggs with smoked salmon, or ricotta cheese pancakes, for instance), or for dinner we suggest classic bistro fare such as rib-eye steak frites, or fish pan Florentine with spinach and new potatoes—all prepared beautifully.

8 Parliament St., Temple Bar, Dublin 2. ✆ **01/633-3581.** www.thelarderbistro.com. Dinner main courses €14–€17. AE, MC, V. Mon–Tues 7:30am–6pm; Wed–Thurs 7:30am–10:30pm; Fri–Sat 10:30am–10:30pm; Sun 9:30am–10:30pm. Bus: 50, 54, 56, or 77.

St. Stephen's Green/Grafton Street Area

VERY EXPENSIVE

One Pico ★★ MODERN EUROPEAN About a 5-minute walk from St. Stephen's Green, on a wee lane off Dawson Street, this is a sophisticated, grown-up place, with excellent service and fantastic food. The food is a mixture of European influences; if you're lucky, you might find the duck confit with red cabbage and beet-root *chiffonade,* or the 28-day aged Hereford rib-eye with celeriac and truffle mash. For dessert, an Amalfi lemon tart is the end to a near-perfect meal. The fixed-price dinner menu is excellent value for those wanting to treat themselves without breaking the bank—although the restaurant is quite strict about how long you can linger over dinner.

5–6 Molesworth Place, Schoolhouse Lane, Dublin 2. ✆ **01/676-0300.** www.onepico.com. Reservations required. Fixed-price 3-course lunch menu €25, dinner €26–€39; tasting menus €65–€85; dinner main courses €13–€17. AE, DC, MC, V. Mon–Sat 12:30–2:30pm and 6–11pm. DART: Pearse. Bus: 10, 11A, 11B, 13, or 20B.

EXPENSIVE

La Mère Zou ★★ FRENCH Imagine a country house in Provence where you could get superb Gallic cooking *en famille*. Chef Eric Tydgadt has created a warm, comfortable, basement-level bistro in which to savor his fresh French country specialties. The emphasis is on perfectly cooked food accompanied by persuasive but "unarmed" sauces served in an unpretentious manner. Mussels are a house specialty, in an irresistible tomato gratin sauce. Other dishes, like the duck confit or the pot-roast pork, are all lavished with the same attention. Unsurprisingly, the excellent wine list favors French wines, with several reasonably priced options. The fixed-price early-bird menu, usually served until 7pm, is available all night on Monday and Tuesday. There's live jazz here on Friday and Saturday nights from 9 to 11pm.

22 St. Stephen's Green, Dublin 2. ✆ **01/661-6669.** www.lamerezou.ie. Reservations recommended. Fixed-price 3-course early-bird menus €25 2 courses, €29 3 courses. Main courses €18–€28. AE, DC, MC, V. Mon–Fri noon–2:30pm; Mon–Sat 6–11pm. DART: Pearse. Bus: 10, 11A, 11B, 13, or 20B.

Peploe's ★ MODERN IRISH In the vast basement of a Georgian building, this wine bar and restaurant is so chic even the waitstaff are nattily attired. Food is on the traditional side, and features local meats and produce—try the venison loin with balsamic *jus*, if it's on offer, or perhaps the monkfish and Dublin bay prawn pie. Prices are a bit eyebrow-raising, but you can get a good deal at lunchtime.

16 St. Stephen's Green, Dublin 2. ✆ **01/676-3144.** www.peploes.com. Reservations recommended. Fixed-price 3-course early-bird menu €25; main courses lunch €12–€29, dinner €13–€33. AE, DC, MC, V. Daily noon–midnight. DART: Pearse. Bus: 10, 11A, 11B, 13, or 20B.

Sabor Brasil BRAZILIAN Another fine place to take refuge when you're bored of all that butter-rich Euro-cuisine, Sabor Brasil is worth the trek from the city center. There's nowhere quite like it that we've been to in Dublin; it's tucked away on a side street, a half-mile or so south of St. Stephen's Green. Inside it's brash, gaudy—and *minuscule*. Don't even think of coming if you haven't made a booking. However, the quality of the food more than rewards the effort. The menu is meat-focused (the steaks are outstanding—if it's on offer, try the *grelhado* sirloin, with a crust of rock salt and garlic), although there are traditional seafood and vegetarian options too. Prices are perhaps a little high, but it's as much the unique experience you're paying for as anything else. We don't suggest you try and find this place without a taxi; it's quite hidden, and not in the city's finest neighborhood.

50 Pleasant St. (off Camden St.), Dublin 8 ✆ **01/475-0304.** Reservations essential. Main courses €21–€25. MC, V. Tues–Sat 6–10:30pm. Bus: 65 or 65X. Suburban rail to Harcourt St.

MODERATE

Café Mao ★ ASIAN This is where to go when you feel like some Asian cooking with an exhilarating attitude. The exposed kitchen lines one entire wall, and the rest of the space is wide open—great for people-watching. The menu reads like a Best of Asia list: Thai fish cakes, *nasi goreng*, chicken hoisin, salmon ramen. Everything is delicious—you can't go wrong. There are also branches in the Pavilion in Dún Laoghaire (✆ **01/214-8090**), and in Civic Square, Dundrum, Dublin 16 (✆ **01/296/2802**).

HOW TO eat LIKE AN IRISHMAN

If you've come to Dublin expecting to find plenty of restaurants still serving "proper" traditional Irish food, you're going to be disappointed. Despite a recent trend away from overfussy modern cuisine, Dublin is still far too chic, and Dubliners far too sophisticated, for the Irish stew, soda bread, and shepherd's pie they grew up eating. The food you cannot escape in the Irish countryside, you cannot find in Dublin.

A number of pricey restaurants do modern, upscale interpretations on Irish cooking; places like **Chapter One** (p. 138) and **Restaurant Patrick Guilbaud** (p. 137) use only Irish ingredients in their complex dishes, for which you will pay a premium. But the simple, basic food that the Irish are known for is not really represented.

Still, you can get around this, as long as you don't mind eating in a pub. Several of the city's traditional pubs still serve plain, hearty Irish food, and as an added benefit, it's certainly much cheaper than what you'll find in the high-and-mighty restaurants. Your best options include the **Porterhouse** microbrewery on Parliament Street in Temple Bar (p. 182), which is an excellent place for a midweek lunch of dishes such as Irish stew with brown bread or "bubble-and-squeak "(made with fried potatoes and cabbage). Not too far away, **O'Shea's Merchant** (12 Bridge St. Lower; ✆ **01/679-3797**) and the **Stag's Head** pub (p. 182) are good places to find real Irish food. Both offer home-cooked, traditional food in pleasant surroundings (just don't try to eat there on busy weekend nights when it's too crowded for comfort).

2 Chatham Row, Dublin 2. ✆ **01/670-4899.** www.cafemao.com. Reservations recommended. Main courses €11–€15. AE, MC, V. Mon–Wed noon–10:30pm; Thurs noon–11pm; Fri–Sat noon–11:30pm; Sun noon–10pm. DART: Pearse. Bus: 10, 11A, 11B, 13, or 20B.

INEXPENSIVE

Cornucopia Wholefood Restaurant VEGETARIAN This little cafe just off Grafton Street is one of the best vegetarian restaurants in the city, and it also serves wholesome meals for people on various restricted diets (vegan, nondairy, low sodium, low fat). Soups are particularly good here, as are the salads and the hot dishes, such as roast squash and fennel with olive polenta. This place is a delicious healthy alternative.

19 Wicklow St., Dublin 2. ✆ **01/677-7583.** Main courses €11–€13. MC, V. Mon–Wed noon–9pm; Thurs–Sat noon–10:30pm; Sun noon–8:30pm. Bus: Any An Lar (city-center) bus.

Lemon ☺ CREPERIE The kids are bound to drag you to this one with its bright orange interior and enticing smell of sizzling batter and the dazzling array of delicious fillings and sauces. Nobody's forcing you to go savory for breakfast. You're under no obligation to have one of the imaginative lunch options, such as pastrami, Cashel blue, and caramelized onion; or perhaps the fabulously named "Vegetarian Powercrepe." Or you could just go straight for the sweet option. European pancakes are thinner than their American counterparts, and in our opinion you can't beat the traditional method of serving them—just lemon and sugar (or, if the sun's over the yard arm, an added splash of Grand Marnier too). However, you can get them almost any way you could possibly want, including banana and Belgian chocolate sauce; powdered sugar and whipped cream; or maple syrup and pecan. Add a cup of excellent coffee on the side, and you can't go wrong.

60 Dawson St., Dublin 2 ✆ **01/672-8898.** www.lemonco.com. Crepes 4€-10€. No credit cards. Mon-Fri 8am-7:30pm; Thurs 8am-9pm; Sat 9am-7:30pm; Sun 10am-6:30pm. DART: Pearse. Bus: 10, 11A, 11B, 13, or 20B.

Fitzwilliam Square/Merrion Square Area

VERY EXPENSIVE

L'Ecrivain ★★ FRENCH This is one of Dublin's truly exceptional restaurants, from start to finish. The atmosphere is relaxed, welcoming, and unpretentious, and chef Derry Clarke's food is extraordinary. Most dishes consist of Irish ingredients, prepared without dense sauces. You might find, on the constantly changing menu, rack of lamb with caramelized sweetbread and roast aubergine, or seared Bere Island scallops with lobster strudel. A great wine list is the cherry on top.

109 Lower Baggot St., Dublin 2. ✆ **01/661-1919.** www.lecrivain.com. Reservations required. Fixed-price 3-course lunch €25-€45; fixed-price 3-course dinner €65; 7-course tasting menu €95; dinner main courses €40-€44. AE, DC, MC, V. Mon-Fri 12:30-2pm; Mon-Sat 6:30-10:30pm. Bus: 10.

Restaurant Patrick Guilbaud ★★ FRENCH/IRISH Ireland's most award-winning restaurant (with two Michelin stars) holds court in elegant quarters at the equally elegant Merrion Hotel. The menu is lavish; roast loin of Wicklow lamb with eggplant caviar and black sole with creamed brown morels are two representative options. However, prices are intense. A starter of game and foie gras terrine with pecan nuts and brioche will set you back €44, and a typical entree costs around €55—and that's before you open the wine list. This is one for the (very) well-heeled gastronomes.

In the Merrion Hotel, 21 Upper Merrion St., Dublin 2. ✆ **01/676-4192.** www.restaurantpatrickguilbaud.ie. Reservations required. Fixed-price 2-course lunch €38; fixed-price 3-course lunch €50; dinner main courses €46-€80. Seasonal tasting menu around €85. AE, DC, MC, V. Tues-Sat 12:30-2:15pm and 7-10:15pm. DART: Westland Row. Bus: 10, 11A, 11B, 13, or 20B.

EXPENSIVE

Bang ★ MODERN IRISH/INTERNATIONAL Almost as much art gallery as eatery, this elegantly bohemian joint is a thing to behold. Set over three floors, the dining rooms are crammed full of gorgeous modern art by local artists; the perfect visual feast to accompany a main of rib-eye steak frites with *pomme anna,* mushrooms and crispy onions, or Claire Island salmon with spinach and red pepper dressing. Don't even think of not having a cocktail—the menu is so imaginative they could almost slap a frame on it and hang it among the paintings.

11 Merrion Row, Dublin 2. ✆ **01/400-4229.** www.bangrestaurant.com. Reservations recommended. Fixed-price lunch menus €17-€27; pretheater menus €22-€27; dinner main courses €19-€28. AE, DC, MC, V. Tues 5:30-10:30pm; Wed-Sat 12:30-10:30pm. Bus: 7, 7A, 8, 10, 11 or 13.

Blackboard Bistro ★ BISTRO This romantic little bistro just around the corner from the National Gallery of Ireland (p. 149) is the kind of place locals recommend to you with a little gasp of delight. Located in the basement of an old Georgian town house, it's certainly snug—come with somebody you don't mind being close to—but the atmosphere is relaxed and the food surpasses expectations. The menu (which changes every few days) is a small but perfectly formed selection of bistro classics—confit de canard with sautéed potatoes, perhaps, or roast chicken with leeks and Dijon cream. The wine list is excellent, but anything else would be unthinkable, surely?

4 Clare St., Dublin 2. ✆ **01/676-6839.** Reservations recommended. Fixed-price menus: 2 courses €19, 3 courses €23; dinner main courses €19–€29. MC, V. Tues–Fri noon–2:30pm and 6–10pm; Sat 6–10pm. DART: Pearse. Bus: 25, 25A, 26, 49X, 50X, 56A, 66, 66A, 66B, 67, 67A, 77X or 123.

Dobbins ★ FRENCH Almost hidden in a lane between Upper and Lower Mount streets, this hip, friendly bistro is a haven for inventive Continental cuisine. The menu changes often, but usually includes such items as duckling with orange-and-port sauce; steamed *paupiette* of black sole with salmon, crab, and prawn filling; pan-fried veal kidneys in pastry; and filet of beef topped with crispy herb bread crumbs with shallot and Madeira sauce.

15 Stephen's Lane (off Upper Mount St.), Dublin 2. ✆ **01/661-9536.** www.dobbins.ie/restaurant. Reservations recommended. Fixed-price 3-course early-bird menu €30; dinner main courses €19–€29. AE, DC, MC, V. Mon–Fri 12:30–2:45pm; Tues–Sat 6–9:45pm; Sun noon–3pm. DART: Pearse. Bus: 5, 7A, 8, 46, or 84.

Ely Winebar ★ ORGANIC IRISH This cosmopolitan, clever place does everything right. The owners get the organic produce from their family farm in County Clare, so everything is absurdly fresh. The food is simple but expertly prepared versions of Irish favorites, the service attentive and helpful. Think gourmet "bangers and mash" (wild boar sausages and mashed spuds), fresh Clare oysters, rich Irish stew, and a vast selection of artisan cheeses. Factor in a smashing wine list and you've got a winner. There are two other Ely venues in town: the **Ely Bar & Brasserie** in Customs House Quay (✆ **01/672-0010**) and the **Ely Gastro Pub** on Hanover Quay (✆ **01/633-9986**).

22 Ely Place (off Merrion Row), Dublin 2. ✆ **01/676-8986.** www.elywinebar.ie. Reservations recommended. Fixed-price early-bird menus: two courses €20, 3 courses €25; dinner main courses €15–€30. AE, DC, MC, V. Mon–Thurs noon–11:30pm; Fri noon–12:30am; Sat 5pm–12:30am. Bus: 7, 7A, 8, 10, 11, or 13.

O'Connell Street Area/North of the Liffey

VERY EXPENSIVE

Chapter One ★★ MODERN IRISH This remarkable eatery fills the vaulted basement space of the Dublin Writers Museum. Artfully lighted and tastefully decorated, it's one of the best restaurants in town, although prices certainly reflect that. Meals are prepared with regional, organic ingredients, all cleverly used in dishes like the Connemara lamb, and the hot hake with red pepper and shrimp *Basquaise* and *coco de Paimpol* beans (a French white bean). If you fancy a bit of culinary theater to go with your food, try and book the chef's table—a single, glass-walled booth located in the kitchen.

18–19 Parnell Sq., Dublin 2. ✆ **01/873-2266.** www.chapteronerestaurant.com. Reservations recommended. Tasting menu €75; 3-course fixed-price lunch/pretheater menu €38; dinner main courses €32–€36. AE, DC, MC, V. Tues–Fri 12:30–2pm and 6–10:30pm; Sat 7:30–10:30pm. Bus: 27A, 31A, 31B, 32A, 32B, 42B, 42C, 43, or 44A.

MODERATE

101 Talbot ★ INTERNATIONAL This modest, second-floor restaurant above a shop may be unassuming, but don't be fooled—it's actually a bright beacon of good cooking on the Northside. The menu features light, healthy food, with a strong emphasis on vegetarian dishes. Dishes change regularly, but mains might be pan-seared tuna with sweet pepper and tomatoes, parsnip and sweet potato *rosti* served with spinach and brie, or a classic chargrilled Irish steak with mushroom and brandy sauce. The dining room is casually funky, with contemporary Irish art and big windows. The staff is endlessly friendly, making it a pleasure to visit.

101 Talbot St. (at Talbot Lane near Marlborough St.), Dublin 1. ✆ **01/874-5011.** www.101talbot.ie. Reservations recommended. Fixed-price 2-course early-bird menu €22; dinner main courses €15–€24. AE, MC, V. Tues–Sat noon–3pm and 5–11pm. DART: Connolly. Bus: 27A, 31A, 31B, 32A, 32B, 42B, 42C, 43, or 44A.

Winding Stair ★★ MODERN IRISH This long-beloved bookstore cafe was reworked a couple of years ago into a sleek, gorgeous restaurant with wood floors, big windows, and stunning river views. It's still in a lovely old bookstore (you can pick up some Joyce on your way to dinner), but it's definitively modern in its cooking style. Dishes are clever interpretations of Irish favorites: Start with the seafood chowder with chorizo and treacle bread, perhaps, before moving on to the steamed mussels and homemade fries with aioli, or pork neck marinated in cider (the alcoholic kind) with roasted rosemary potatoes, shallots, and apple. The wine list is brilliantly chosen; the atmosphere is pure elegant sophistication. This place isn't trendy, it's classic.

40 Lower Ormond Quay, Dublin 1. ✆ **01/872-7320.** www.winding-stair.com. Reservations recommended. Fixed-price early-bird menus: 2 courses €25, 3 courses €30. Main courses €22–€27. AE, DC, MC, V. Daily noon–3pm; Mon–Sat 5:30–10:30pm; Sun 6–9:30pm. Bus: 90, 92, or 151.

INEXPENSIVE

Boojum MEXICAN This is a great place to know about. Just around the corner from the Jervis Shopping Centre (p. 172), the classic tacos, burritos, and fajitas here are good, fast, and *cheap*. This is an order-at-the-bar, stay-or-go kind of place, popular with a younger crowd. The menu is far smaller than you'd expect from a Mexican cantina in America, but it's all good, fresh, and plentiful, and the atmosphere is lively. It's ideal for a cheap and cheerful dinner, or a tasty lunch on the go.

Millennium Walkway, Dublin 1. ✆ **01/872-9499.** www.boojummex.com. Main courses €6.50–€7.50. No credit cards. Mon–Fri 11:30am–9pm; Sat noon–9pm. Bus: 39B or 69X. LUAS: Jervis.

Epicurean Food Hall GOURMET FOOD COURT This wonderful food hall houses a wide variety of artisan produce, local Irish meats, and regional specialties. Favorites include **La Corte,** an Italian deli and coffee stand; **Taco Taco,** a funky little taqueria; **Bagelrush,** for its health-conscious, American-style bagels, soups, and salads; **Moonstar Café** and **Istanbul**, both of which specialize in Turkish and Mediterranean food (particularly kabobs at the latter); **Ramos** for a rapid, sit-down Greek lunch; or the **Asian Fusion** buffet, which offers a mix-and-match of tasty Thai, Chinese, and Indian favorites. If you want to make your foraged meal a little bit fancier, **Layden's Fine Wines** sells wine by the bottle or glass. There is some seating in the hall, and a couple of outlets have their own, but it gets packed during lunch hour on weekdays, so visit at off-peak times if possible.

Middle Abbey St., Dublin 1. ✆ **01/878-7016.** www.epicureanfoodhall.com All items around €3–€15. No credit cards. Mon–Fri 9:45am–7pm, Sat–Sun 11:30am–7pm. Bus: 70 or 80.

Soup Dragon SOUP This place may be tiny, with less than a dozen stools alongside a bar, but it's big on drama: blue walls, black and red mirrors, orange slices and spice sticks flowing out of giant jugs. The menu changes daily, but usually features a few traditional choices (potato and leek, carrot and coriander) as well as the more exotic (Thai green chicken curry, for example). They also serve salads, bagels, sandwiches, and wraps. Breakfast is pretty good here too, offering a nice balance of the healthy (banana bread, muesli, porridge) and the hearty (such as the "dragon breakfast" fry up, which will keep you going for hours).

168 Capel St., Dublin 1. ✆ **01/872-3277.** www.soupdragon.com Breakfast €1.50–€7.50; soup €5.50–€13; other lunch items €4–€7. MC, V. Mon–Fri 8am–5pm; Sun 10–4pm. Bus: 70 or 80.

Ballsbridge/Embassy Row Area

EXPENSIVE

Roly's Bistro IRISH/INTERNATIONAL This two-story, shop-front restaurant is a local institution, beloved for providing the kind of reliably good, tummy-warming food you never tire of: roasted breast of chicken with orzo pasta and wild mushrooms, or braised shank of lamb with root vegetable purée and rosemary *jus,* to name just two. The bright and airy main dining room can be noisy when the house is full, but there's also an enclave of booths for those who prefer a quiet tête-à-tête. Roly's has recently started opening for breakfast, and while the menu veers little from the assorted combinations of egg and bacon you're likely to find at your hotel, you may well find it a cheaper alternative.

7 Ballsbridge Terrace, Dublin 4. ✆ **01/668-2611.** www.rolysbistro.ie. Reservations required. Breakfast €3.50–€12; dinner main courses €20–€35; fixed-price menus: 3-course lunch €23, early-bird €24–€27, dinner €40. AE, DC, MC, V. Mon–Fri 7am–10:30pm; Sat–Sun 9am–10:30pm. DART: Lansdowne Rd. Bus: 5, 6, 7, 8, 18, or 45.

MODERATE

The French Paradox ★★ WINE BAR This darling little bistro and wine bar endears itself to everyone. Wine's the thing here, so relax with a bottle of bordeaux or Côte du Rhône and nibbles from the menu. Tapas is served between 3 and 7pm; typical dishes include superb Iberico hams from Spain and *caviar d'aubergine* with croutons. You could also visit the small dining menu, which offers bistro favorites such as gravlax and blinis.

53 Shelbourne Rd., Dublin 4. ✆ **01/660-4068.** www.thefrenchparadox.com. Reservations recommended. Lunch main courses €8.50–€14; tapas €2.50–€13; dinner main courses €12–€19. AE, MC, V. Mon–Fri noon–3pm and 6pm–midnight; Sat 3pm–midnight. DART: Lansdowne Rd. Bus: 5, 6, 7, 8, or 18.

SEEING THE SIGHTS

Wandering Dublin—just walking down its Georgian streets with a map only in case you get *really* lost—is one of the great pleasures of a visit here. There's almost no way you can go wrong. One minute, you're walking along a quiet, leafy street and suddenly the Irish Parliament appears before you. A few minutes later, it's gorgeous Merrion Square. Then, you're upon the granite buildings of Trinity College—and on and on. So get a sturdy pair of shoes, have your umbrella at the ready, and head out to discover this rewarding city.

The Top Attractions

Áras an Uachtaráin (The Irish President's House) Áras an Uachtaráin was once the Viceregal Lodge, the summer retreat of the British viceroy, whose main digs were in Dublin Castle. From what were never humble beginnings, the original 1751 country house was expanded several times, gradually accumulating splendor. Current Irish President Mary McAleese opened the house to visitors; guided tours originate at the Phoenix Park Visitors Centre every Saturday. After an introductory historical film, a bus brings visitors to and from Áras an Uachtaráin. The focus of the tour is the state reception rooms. The entire tour lasts 1 hour (a little longer in summer, when the gardens are included on the itinerary, weather permitting). Only 525 tickets are given out, first-come, first-served; arrive before 1:30pm, especially in summer.

Note: For security reasons, no backpacks, travel bags, strollers, buggies, cameras, or mobile phones are allowed on the tour.

In Phoenix Park Visitor Centre, Dublin 8. ✆ **01/677-0095.** www.president.ie. Free admission. Sat 10:15am–3:30pm. Closed Dec 24–26. Same-day tickets issued at Phoenix Park Visitor Centre (see p. 150). Bus: 37, 38, 39, or 70.

The Book of Kells This extraordinary hand-drawn manuscript of the four Gospels, dating from the year 800, is one of Ireland's jewels, and with elaborate scripting and colorful illumination, it is undeniably magnificent. It is displayed, along with another early Christian manuscript, at Trinity College's Old Library. Unfortunately, the need to protect the books for future generations means that there's little for you to actually see. The volumes are very small and displayed inside a wooden cabinet shielded by bulletproof glass. So all you really see here are the backs of a lot of tourists, leaning over a small table trying to get a peek at two pages of the ancient books. It's quite anticlimactic, but the Library's **Long Room** goes some way toward making up for that, at least for bibliophiles. The grand, chained library holds many rare works on

A detail from the Book of Kells, Ireland's literary treasure kept under tight wraps at Trinity College.

Dublin Attractions

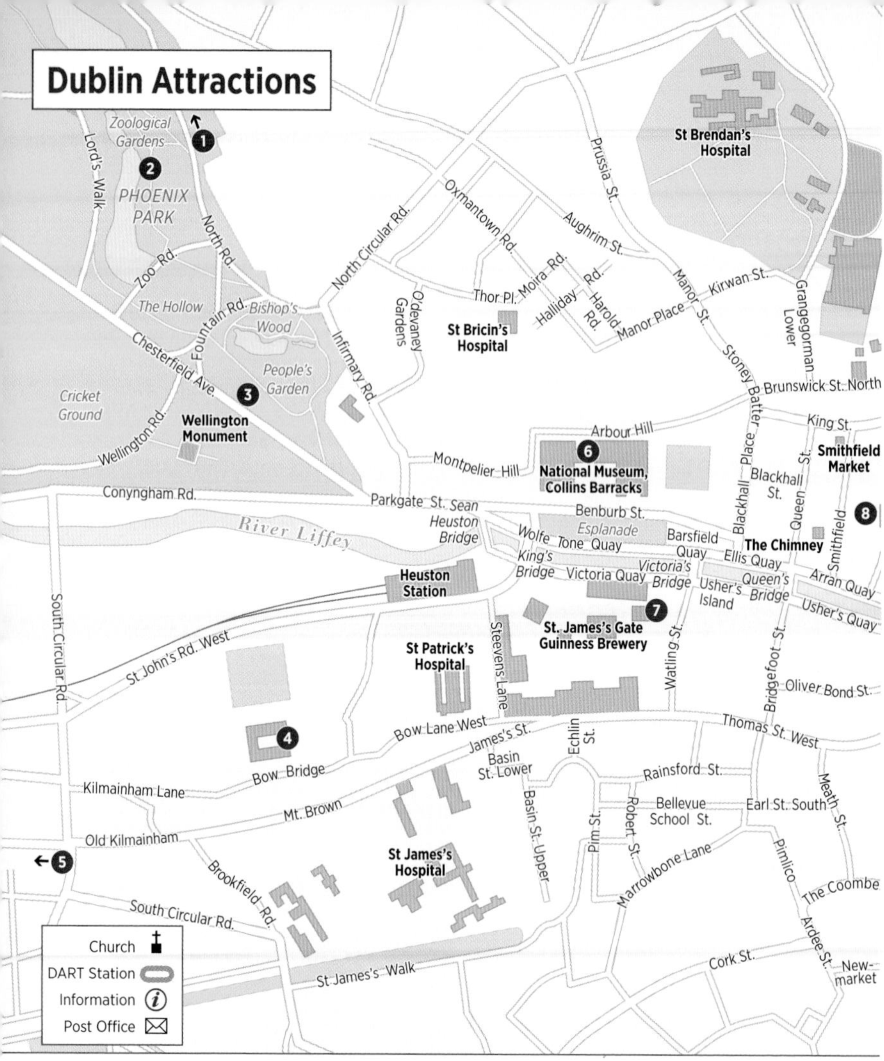

Áras an Uachtaráin **1**
The Ark **42**
Bank of Ireland Centre/ Parliament House **19**
Book of Kells/ Trinity College **20**
Chester Beatty Library **34**
Christ Church Cathedral **41**
Collins Barracks **6**
Custom House **16**
Dublin Castle **38**
Dublin Civic Museum **32**
Dublinia **40**
Dublin Writers Museum **13**
Dublin Zoo **2**
Four Courts **10**
GAA Museum **15**
General Post Office **18**
Glasnevin Cemetery **11**
Guinness Storehouse **7**
Hugh Lane Municipal Gallery **12**
Irish Film Institute **32**
Irish Museum of Modern Art **4**
James Joyce Centre **14**
Kilmainham Gaol **5**
Leinster House **22**
Mansion House **29**
Marsh's Library **36**
National Gallery **21**
National Library of Ireland **23**
National Museum: Archaeology **26**
National Photographic Archive **23**
Natural History Museum **25**
Newman House **28**
Number Twenty Nine **24**
Old Jameson Distillery **8**

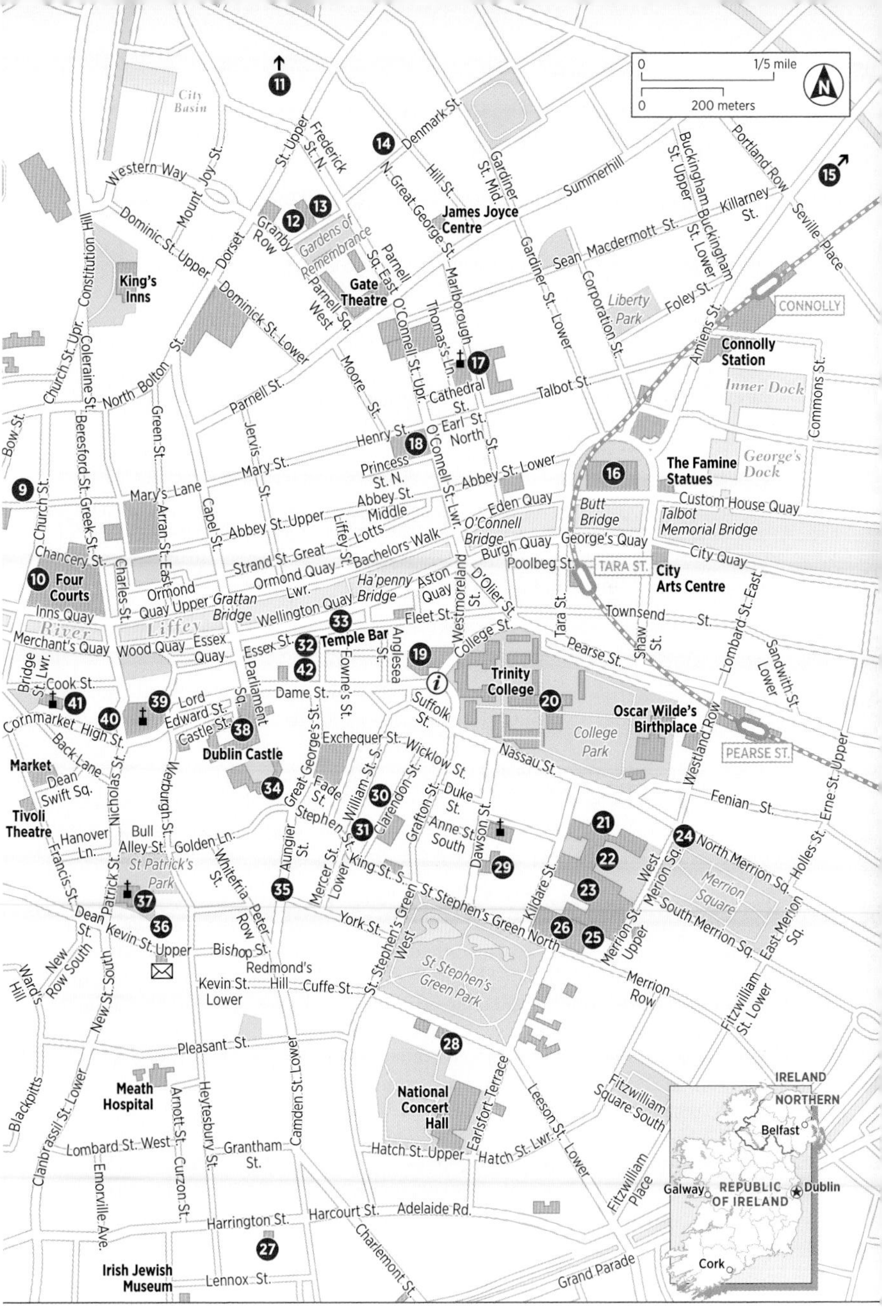

Phoenix Park **3**
St. Audeon's Church **41**
St. Mary's Pro-Cathedral **17**
St. Michan's Church **9**
St. Patrick's Cathedral **37**
St. Teresa's Church **30**
Shaw Birthplace **27**
Temple Bar Gallery **33**
Whitefriar Street Carmelite Church **35**

UNSUNG hero: SIR ALFRED CHESTER BEATTY

Few people embody the term "citizen of the world" as much as Sir Alfred Chester Beatty. Born in New York in 1875, Beatty's American mining business earned him the nickname "the King of Copper"—and a multimillion dollar fortune to boot. This fabulous wealth gave him the means to pursue his passion for ancient manuscripts and works of art, and by the time he was an old man, his collection rivaled some of the world's greatest museums. Beatty became a British citizen in the 1930s and was knighted by Queen Elizabeth in 1954, after he made a generous bequest to the British Museum. However, he left the vast majority of his collection to Ireland—his ancestral home and a place he always loved. In return Beatty was made an honorary citizen in 1957. He died 11 years later in Monaco, but was brought back to Dublin for a state funeral—to date the only civilian to be given this honor. However, despite all this, Beatty is a surprisingly little-known figure in his adoptive home today. Many Dublin tourist guides don't list the Chester Beatty Museum among the city's top attractions, and we've even spoken to locals who had never heard of the museum—or the man himself—at all.

Irish history and showcases frequently changing displays of its holdings. Still, it's hard to say that it's all worth the rather large admission fee. For a cheaper and more fulfilling alternative, try the Chester Beatty Library (below).

College Green, Dublin 2. ✆ **01/608-2320.** www.bookofkells.ie. Admission €9 adults; €8 seniors and students; €18 families; free for children 11 and under. Combination ticket for the Library and Dublin Experience also available. Mon–Sat 9:30am–5pm; Sun 9:30am–4:30pm (opens noon Oct–Apr). Bus: Any An Lar (cross-city) bus.

Chester Beatty Library ★★★ Sir Alfred Chester Beatty was an American of Irish heritage who made a fortune in the mining industry and collected rare manuscripts. In 1956, he bequeathed his extensive collection to Ireland, and this fascinating museum inside the grounds of Dublin Castle was the ultimate result of his largess. The breathtaking array of early illuminated gospels and religious manuscripts outshines the Book of Kells, and there are endless surprises here: ancient editions of the Bible and other religious books, beautiful copies of the Koran, and endless icons from Western, Middle Eastern, and Far Eastern cultures, dating as far back as 2700 B.C. Best of all: It's free. The Library's **Silk Road Café** is an award-winning restaurant that has a devoted local following, offering a menu that features Mediterranean and Near Eastern cuisine.

Clock Tower Bldg., Dublin Castle, Dublin 2. ✆ **01/407-0750.** www.cbl.ie. Free admission. Mon–Fri 10am–5pm (Tues–Fri Oct–Apr); Sat 11am–5pm; Sun 1–5pm. Free guided tours Wed 1pm and Sun 3 and 4pm. Closed Dec 24–26, Jan 1, and Mon public holidays. DART: Sandymount. Bus: 5, 6, 6A, 7A, 8, 10, 46, 46A, 46B, or 64.

Christ Church Cathedral ★ This magnificent cathedral was designed to be seen from the river, so walk to it from the riverside in order to truly appreciate its size. It dates from 1038, when Sitric, Danish king of Dublin, built the first wooden Christ Church here. In 1171, the original foundation was extended into a cruciform and rebuilt in stone by the Norman warrior Strongbow. The present structure dates mainly from 1871 to 1878, when a huge restoration took place—the work done then remains controversial to this day, as much of the building's old detail was destroyed in the process. Still, magnificent stonework and graceful pointed arches survive. There's also a statue of Strongbow inside, and some believe his tomb is here as well, although historians are not convinced. Look out for a heart-shaped iron box in the southeast chapel, which is believed to contain the heart of St. Laurence O'Toole. The best way to get a glimpse of what the original building must have been like is to visit the crypt, which is original to the 12th-century structure.

Christ Church Place, Dublin 8. ✆ **01/677-8099.** www.cccdub.ie. Admission €6 adults; €4 seniors; €3 students and children 14 and under. June–Aug Mon–Sat 9:45–6:15 (may close 5pm for choral services; call ahead), Sun 12:30–2:30pm and 4:30–6:15pm; Sept–Oct Mon–Sat 9:45am–5:15pm, Sun 12:30–2:30pm; Nov–May Mon–Sat 9:45am–4:15pm, Sun 12:30–2:30pm and 4:30–5:15pm. Bus: 21A, 50, 50A, 78, 78A, or 78B.

Collins Barracks Collins Barracks is a splendidly restored, early-18th-century military building, but only worth visiting if you're a fan of the decorative arts, as it's been converted into part of the National Museum of Ireland. Until the acquisition of this vast space, only a fraction of the National Museum's collection could be displayed, but more and more treasures have found their way here. Notable collections include a huge display of Irish silver and furniture; a magnificent collection of rare 19th-century art from Tibet, China, and Japan; and an exhibition devoted to the work of the influential Irish designer and architect Eileen Gray (1878–1976). Collins Barracks is also a prime site for touring exhibitions, so consult the *Event Guide* for details.

Benburb St., Dublin 7. ✆ **01/677-7444.** www.museum.ie Free admission. Tues–Sat 10am–5pm; Sun 2–5pm. Bus: 34, 70, or 80.

Christ Church dates to 1038, but the current cathedral was built in the late 19th century.

SHOULD YOU buy A DUBLIN PASS?

If you're planning a lot of sightseeing in Dublin, the tourism board would like you to consider purchasing its **Dublin Pass,** which offers free admission to most of the city's major sights, as well as free travel from the airport on the AirCoach shuttle, and discounts at a number of shops, bars, and restaurants.

Unfortunately, the pass is a bit pricey, given that so many of Dublin's sights are free, and the Dublin Pass website muddies the water by including free museums (such as the Chester Beatty Library and the national museums) among fee-charging sights. Our advice is this: Buy the pass, but plan carefully how best to use it. For example, consider buying a pass good for 1 or 2 days, and then see all of the city's most expensive sights (the Guinness Storehouse, Kilmainham Gaol, and so forth) on those days. On the other days of your trip, you can devote your time to the museums, parks, and galleries that charge no entrance fee.

An adult pass costs €35 for 1 day, €55 for 2 days, €65 for 3 days, and €95 for 6 days. A child's pass costs €19 for 1 day, €31 for 2 days, €39 for 3 days, and €49 for 6 days.

You can purchase a pass at any Dublin Tourism office, or online at **www.dublinpass.ie**.

Dublin Castle This 13th-century structure was the center of British power in Ireland for more than 7 centuries, until the new Irish government took it over in 1922. You can walk the grounds for free, although this is largely municipal office space now and is disappointingly dominated by parking lots. To see the inside you have to join a tour, although they're reasonably priced; highlights include the 13th-century record tower; the state apartments, once the residence of English viceroys; and the chapel royal, a 19th-century Gothic building with particularly fine plaster decoration and carved-oak gallery fronts and fittings. If it's open, check out the undercroft, an excavated site on the grounds where an early Viking fortress stood, and the treasury, built in the early 18th century. There are also a vaguely interesting on-site craft shop, heritage center, and restaurant.

The crenelated tower and precisely manicured lawn of Dublin Castle.

Palace St. (off Dame St.), Dublin 2. ✆ **01/677-7129.** www.dublincastle.ie. Guided tours €4.50 adults; €3.50 seniors and students; €2 children 11 and under. €1 discount when state apts. aren't available (children go free). Mon–Fri 10am–4:45pm; Sat–Sun and holidays 2–4:45pm. Guided tours every 20–25 min. Bus: 50, 50A, 54, 56A, 77, 77A, or 77B.

Free to the public, the Chester Beatty Library allows guests close access to its extraordinary collection of illuminated gospels and rare manuscripts.

The personal correspondence and effects of Ireland's greatest writers are on public display at the Dublin Writers Museum.

Dublinia ☺ This museum aims to teach the little ones about the Viking and medieval history of Dublin through a series of interactive exhibits. With visual effects, background sounds (some on an annoying loop seem to follow you around repeating the same phrase over and over, until you can still hear it in your sleep weeks later), and aromas ostensibly from that time, it's designed to stimulate, but will probably bore anybody over the age of 14. Still, you and the kids can dress up in medieval garb, be chained up as Viking slaves, and put yourselves in the town stocks. If you plan to visit Dublinia and Christ Church Cathedral on the same day, keep hold of your ticket to claim reduced-price admission.

St. Michael's Hill, Christ Church, Dublin 8. ✆ **01/679-4611.** www.dublinia.ie. Admission €7 adults; €6 seniors; €6 students; €4 children; €20 families. Combination ticket with Christ Church Cathedral €11 adults; €8.50 seniors and students; €26 families. Daily 10am–5pm (last admission 4:15pm; Oct–Mar last admission 4pm). Closed Dec 23–26 and Mar 17. Bus: 50, 78A, or 123.

Dublin Writers Museum ★★ This is an excellent little museum that represents the best of what literary galleries can be, and lovers of Irish literature will find it hard to tear themselves away. The attraction is more than just reading early playbills for the Abbey Theatre when Yeats was involved in running it. The draw is also long letters from Brendan Behan talking about parties he was invited to with the Marx Brothers in Los Angeles after he hit the big time, and scrawled notes from Behan, Joyce, and Beckett about work, life, and love. This museum opens a window and lets in light on Ireland's rich literary heritage, and it is wonderful to walk in that glow. There's a good gift shop with writing-related souvenirs and a selection of books by many classic and modern Irish writers. The museum also hosts occasional literary readings and lectures.

The Hugh Lane Municipal Gallery's modernist treasures include the studio of Irish painter Francis Bacon.

For more than a century, Irish revolutionaries were imprisoned and punished in Kilmainham Gaol.

18–19 Parnell Sq. N., Dublin 1. ✆ **01/872-2077.** www.writersmuseum.com. Admission €7.50 adults; €6.30 seniors and students; €4.70 children; €18 families (2 adults, up to 3 children). Combined ticket with James Joyce Museum or Shaw Birthplace, plus Malahide Castle €12 adults; €9.50 seniors and students; €7.50 children; €29 families. Mon–Sat 10am–5pm; Sun and holidays 11am–5pm. Last admission 45 min. before closing. Hours vary late Dec to early Jan. DART: Connolly Station. Bus: 11, 13, 16, 16A, 22, or 22A.

Hugh Lane Municipal Gallery of Modern Art ★ This little gallery, which celebrated its 100-year anniversary in 2008, has a strong collection of Impressionist works led by Degas's *Sur la Plage* and Manet's *La Musique aux Tuileries,* and also holds sculptures by Rodin, a marvelous collection of Harry Clarke stained glass, and numerous works by modern Irish artists. One room holds the maddeningly cluttered studio of the Irish painter Francis Bacon, which the gallery purchased from London and moved to Dublin piece by piece, where it was reconstructed behind glass. Everything was moved, right down to the dust. It's an excellent, compact art museum, and a great place to spend an afternoon.

Charlemont House, Parnell Sq. N., Dublin 1. ✆ **01/222-5550.** www.hughlane.ie. Free admission. Tues–Thurs 10am–6pm; Fri–Sat 10am–5pm; Sun 11am–5pm. DART: Connolly or Tara stations. Bus: 3, 10, 11, 13, 16, or 19.

Kilmainham Gaol Historical Museum ★★★ This is a key sight for anyone interested in Ireland's struggle for independence from British rule. Within these walls, political prisoners were incarcerated, tortured, and killed from 1796 until 1924. The leaders of the 1916 Easter Rising were executed here, along with many others. Future *taoiseach* (prime minister) Eamon de Valera was its final prisoner. To walk along these corridors, through the grim exercise yard, or into the walled compound is a moving experience that lingers in your memory.

THE tortured TALE OF THE HUGH LANE GALLERY

Hugh Lane was a millionaire and exuberant collector of art. In the early 20th century, he opened his own gallery in Dublin on Harcourt Street, but he soon tired of running it, and offered to donate the whole thing—millions of pounds worth of Impressionist paintings—to the city. His only condition was that the city should build an appropriate structure to hold it all. Dublin agreed, and all seemed well. However, months later, having failed to find a suitable structure, and caught up in wrangling over the cost, the city withdrew from the deal. Lane was furious and, in a temper, made an agreement with the National Gallery in London to give that vast art museum his collection instead.

To the rescue came W. B. Yeats, who was so infuriated by the government's ineptitude that he wrote a series of angry poems lambasting it for its failure to find a place to house such magnificent works. Inspired in part by Yeats's fervor, Lane changed his mind, and decided to leave his collection to Dublin after all. He ordered his will changed, but had not yet had it signed and witnessed when he was killed in 1915 aboard the ocean liner *Lusitania* when it was torpedoed by a German U-boat.

So began a legal stalemate in which the National Gallery and the city of Dublin struggled for the ownerships of the Monets, Courbets, and Manets that a few months earlier Dublin wasn't even sure it wanted.

To an extent, the issue is still unresolved 90 years later, but luckily an agreement is in place by which the main works in the collection are displayed at different times by both galleries. The Hugh Lane Gallery now has a gorgeous home in the classical Charlemont House on Parnell Square.

Mr. Lane would surely approve.

Kilmainham, Dublin 8. ✆ **01/453-5984.** www.heritageireland.ie. Guided tour €6 adults; €4 seniors; €2 children; €14 families. Apr–Sept daily 9:30am–6pm (last admission 5pm); Oct–Mar Mon–Sat 9:30am–5:30pm (last admission 4pm), Sun 10am–6pm (last admission 5pm). Bus: 51B, 78A, or 79.

National Gallery of Ireland ★ This museum houses Ireland's national art collection, as well as a collection of European art spanning the 14th to the 20th centuries. Every major European school of painting is represented, including selections by Italian Renaissance artists (especially Caravaggio's *The Taking of Christ*), French Impressionists, and Dutch 17th-century masters. The highlight of the Irish collection is the room dedicated to the mesmerizing works of Jack B. Yeats, the lesser-known brother of the poet W. B. Yeats. All public areas are wheelchair accessible. The museum has a shop and an excellent self-service **cafe.**

Merrion Sq. W., Dublin 2. ✆ **01/661-5133.** www.nationalgallery.ie. Free admission. Mon–Sat 9:30am–5:30pm (Thurs until 8:30pm); Sun noon–5:30pm. Closed Dec 24–26 and Good Friday. Galleries begin shutdown 15 min. before closing. Free guided tours (meet in the Shaw Room) Sat 2pm and Sun 1 and 2pm (July and Aug also Mon, Wed, and Fri 2pm). DART: Pearse. Bus: 4A, 5, 6, 7, 7A, 10, 13, 13A, 44C, or 48A.

National Museum of Ireland: Archaeology ★★ Established in 1890, this museum is a reflection of Ireland's heritage from 2000 B.C. to the present. The institution actually spans four sites, but for our money, the Museum of Archaeology is the finest of the quartet—not that seeing any of its myriad treasures will cost you a penny. It is the home of many of the country's greatest historical finds, ranging from an extensive collection of Irish Bronze Age gold and the Ardagh Chalice, Tara Brooch, and Cross of Cong. Other highlights include the artifacts from the Wood Quay excavations of the Old Dublin Settlements and an Ancient Egyptian gallery. The only place where it falls flat is on interactive exhibits, which are well thought out and *could* be excellent, but which have tended to be a little neglected on the times we've visited. The museum has a shop and a cafe. ***Note:*** The National Museum's other sites are the Museum of Decorative Arts and History at Collins Barracks (earlier), the newly renovated Natural History Museum on Merrion Street, and the Museum of Country Life in Castlebar, County Mayo.
Kildare St., Dublin 2. ✆ **01/677-7444.** www.museum.ie. Free admission. Tues–Sat 10am–5pm; Sun 2–5pm. Closed Dec 25 and Good Friday. DART: Pearse. Bus: 7, 7A, 8, 10, 11, or 13.

Natural History Museum This unusual museum is not just a museum of science and animals, it's also a museum of museums. Inside its cold, stone walls (recently renovated and returned to their former glory) stuffed and mounted creatures are stored inside polished wooden cabinets and on stone and wooden plinths in precisely the manner in which they would have been displayed in the 19th century. Huge whale skeletons are suspended from the ceiling, in a manner that still seems spectacular. It's a unique and sometimes uncomfortable place in which you can gaze at the bones, or into the lifeless glass eyes, of thousands of species. In addition to presenting the zoological history of Ireland, it contains examples of extinct animals from around the world. It's popular with Irish school groups, so children here seem to travel in herds.
Merrion St., Dublin 2. ✆ **01/677-7444.** www.museum.ie. Free admission. Tues–Sat 10am–5pm; Sun 2–5pm. Closed Dec 25 and Good Friday. DART: Pearse. Bus: 7, 7A, or 8.

Phoenix Park ★ ☺ The vast green expanses of Phoenix Park are Dublin's playground, and it's easy to see why. This is a well-designed, user-friendly park crisscrossed by a network of roads and quiet pedestrian walkways that make its 704 hectares (1,739 acres) easily accessible. Avenues of oaks, beech trees, pines, and chestnut trees are shady hideaways, or you can sun yourself in broad expanses of grassland. It's a relaxing place to spend a restful afternoon, but there's plenty to do here should you feel active. The home of the Irish president (p. 141) is in the park, as is the Dublin Zoo (p. 162). Livestock graze peacefully on pasturelands, deer roam the forested areas, and horses romp on polo fields. The visitor center, adjacent to Ashtown Castle, has information about all the park has to offer. The cafe/restaurant is open 10am to 5pm weekdays, 10am to 6pm weekends. Free parking is adjacent to the center. Also next to the center is the **Victorian Kitchen Walled Garden;** currently being restored to its original 19th-century layout, it can be visited free of charge from 10am to 4:30pm daily. The park is 3km (2 miles) west of the city center on the north bank of the River Liffey.
Phoenix Park, Dublin 8. ✆ **01/677-0095.** www.heritageireland.ie. Free admission. Mid-Mar to Oct daily 10am–5:45pm; Nov to mid-Mar daily 9:30am–5:30pm. Bus: 37, 38, or 39.

St. Patrick's Cathedral ★ This is the largest church in Ireland, and one of the best-loved churches in the world. The present cathedral dates from 1190, but because of a fire and 14th-century rebuilding, not much of the original foundation remains. It is mainly early English in style. A square medieval tower with an 18th-century spire houses the largest ringing peal bells in Ireland. The 90m-long (295-ft.) interior allows for sweeping perspectives of vaulted ceilings and the vast nave. The church's history stretches much further back than the current building, as there were places of worship here as early as the 5th century. Consecrated by its namesake, it also acts as a memorial to Irish war dead (represented in banners and flags throughout the building, some literally rotting away on their poles), and holds a memorial to the Irish soldiers who died fighting in the two world wars (although Ireland was neutral in World War II, at least 50,000 Irish volunteers died fighting with the British army). St. Patrick's is closely associated with the writer Jonathan Swift, who was dean here from 1713 to 1745, and he is buried here alongside his longtime companion, Stella. (Some say they were secretly married.) St. Patrick's is the national cathedral of the Church of Ireland.

Sections of St. Patrick's foundation date to the 12th century.

St. Patrick's houses the remains of its infamous former dean and satirist Jonathan Swift.

HARD TO love: JONATHAN SWIFT

For all his cynicism, the sardonic writer Jonathan Swift loved Dublin and its residents. While dean of St. Patrick's Cathedral from 1713 to 1745, he wrote many of his most controversial works, and he knew that he owed the church and the city a great deal for supporting him when, given that they were often the targets of his barbed wit, they could hardly have been blamed for throwing him out. Heaven knows the English wouldn't have wanted him—he'd already written such sharp polemics about English governmental corruption that he was infamous in that country. In his own way, Swift understood the Irish and the English a bit too well for their comfort. But the Irish kept him on, even after he published his infamous essay "A Modest Proposal," in which he advocated (sarcastically) that the English should eat Irish babies in order to solve Ireland's famine problems.

One of Swift's biggest causes was humane treatment for the mentally ill, which in his time was unheard of. When he died, he bequeathed much of his estate to found St. Patrick's Hospital for the mentally ill.

Typically, though, he couldn't just leave it at that. Instead, he wrote one last caustic verse, as if seeking to guarantee that no Irish person would ever leave flowers on his grave:

"He left the little wealth he had
To build a house for fools and mad;
Showing in one satiric touch
No nation needed it so much."

21-50 Patrick's Close, Patrick St., Dublin 8. ✆ **01/475-4817.** Fax 01/454-6374. www.stpatrickscathedral.ie. Admission €5.50 adults; €4.50 seniors and students; €15 families. Mar–Oct Mon–Fri 9am–5:30pm; Sat 9am–6:30pm; Sun 9–11am, 12:30–3pm and 4:30–6:30pm. Nov–Feb Mon–Sat 9am–5:30pm; Sun 9–11am and 12:30–3pm. Last admission 30 min. before closing. Closed Dec 24–26, except for services. Bus: 49, 49A, 49B, 50, 54A, 56A, 65, 65B, 77, or 77A.

Trinity College ★★ The oldest university in Ireland, Trinity was founded in 1592 by Queen Elizabeth I to offer an education to the children of the upper classes and protect them from the "malign" Catholic influences elsewhere in Europe. Its purpose has changed with the ages, and now it is simply the most well-respected university in Ireland. Among its alumni are Bram Stoker, Jonathan Swift, Oscar Wilde, and Samuel Beckett, as well as an array of rebels and revolutionaries who helped create the Republic of Ireland. The poet and wit Oliver Goldsmith also attended, and his statue stands near the main entrance at College Green, near the statue of the philosopher and fellow Trinity alumnus Robert Burke. The campus spreads across central Dublin just south of the River Liffey, with cobbled squares, gardens, a picturesque quadrangle, and buildings dating from the 17th to the 20th centuries. This is also where you'll find the Book of Kells (p. 141). Between mid-May and September, campus tours take in all of the main sights, with a ticket for the Book of Kells and the Old Library included in the price.

College Green, Dublin 2. ✆ **01/896-1000.** www.tcd.ie. Free admission; tours May to mid Sept daily 10:15am, 10:40am, 11:05 am, 11:35 am, 12:10pm, 12:45pm, 2:15pm, and 3pm; also 3:40pm Mon–Sat.

The Old Library Long Room at Trinity College.

More Attractions

ART GALLERIES & ART MUSEUMS

Irish Film Institute This art-house film institute is a hip hangout for cinephiles in Dublin's artsy Temple Bar district. Refurbished in 2009, it houses three cinemas, the Irish Film Archive, a library, a small but comprehensive bookshop, and a **cafe** (p. 134) that makes a good place for a cup of coffee on a cold afternoon. There's also a busy bar that does banner business. The cinemas show arty, groundbreaking films and are the main attraction here, bar or no bar. Usually about half the films on offer aren't on general release in Ireland, which means you have to become a member before you can buy tickets; but this isn't difficult and costs from €1. The IFI isn't just a place for hip young things; "Wild Strawberries" is the IFI's excellent seniors club, which is open to all. You can see a movie for €4, including tea and coffee. It usually runs on the last Wednesday and Friday of every month at 11am; call the box office for details.

6 Eustace St., Dublin 2. ✆ **01/679-5744,** or 679-3477 for cinema box office. www.irishfilm.ie. Free admission. Cinema tickets €8–€9.50; €6–€8 seniors, students, and children. Center daily 10am–11pm; cinemas daily 1–11pm; cinema box office daily 1–9pm. Bus: 21A, 78A, or 78B.

Irish Museum of Modern Art (IMMA) In the splendidly restored 17th-century edifice known as the Royal Hospital, the IMMA is frequently used as a venue for theatrical and musical events. The small permanent collection contains mostly works by Irish artists, and the big draws are the numerous temporary exhibitions that pass through. Outside, the formal gardens have been restored to stellar condition. ***Note:*** Admission is free, except to some of the temporary exhibitions.

More than 30 artists paint, sculpt, and take photographs at Temple Bar Gallery and Studios.

Panoramic views of Dublin await patrons of the Gravity Bar, in the Guinness Storehouse.

Military Rd., Kilmainham. ✆ **01/612-9900.** www.imma.ie. Free admission. Tues and Thurs–Sat 10am–5:30pm; Wed 10:30am–5:30pm; Sun and holidays noon–5:30pm. Last admission 15 min. before closing. Bus: 51B, 78A, 79, 90, or 123.

Temple Bar Gallery and Studios Founded in 1983 in the heart of Dublin's "Left Bank," this is one of the largest studio and gallery complexes in Europe. More than 30 Irish artists work here at a variety of contemporary visual arts, including sculpture, painting, printing, and photography. Only the gallery section is open to the public, but you can make an appointment in advance to view individual artists at work. The Studios hosts free talks and discussion panels, featuring the great and the good of the Irish arts scene. Call or go online for details.
5-9 Temple Bar, Dublin 2. ✆ **01/671-0073.** www.templebargallery.com. Free admission. Tues-Wed and Fri-Sat 11am–6pm; Thurs 11am–7pm. Bus: 21A, 46A, 46B, 51B, 51C, 68, 69, or 86.

BREWERIES/DISTILLERIES

Guinness Storehouse ★ Founded in 1759, the Guinness Brewery is one of the world's most famous breweries, producing a distinctive dark stout. You can explore the Guinness Hopstore, tour a converted 19th-century building housing the World of Guinness Exhibition, and view a film showing how the stout is made; then move on to the Gilroy Gallery, dedicated to the graphic design work of John Gilroy; and last but not least, stop in at the breathtaking Gravity Bar, where you can sample a glass of the famous brew in the glass-enclosed bar 60m (197 ft.) above the ground, with 360-degree views of the city.
St. James's Gate, Dublin 8. ✆ **01/408-4800.** www.guinness-storehouse.com. Admission €15 adults; €11 seniors and students; €5 children 6–12; €34 families. Daily 9:30am–5pm. Guided tours every half-hour. Bus: 51B, 78A, or 123.

Impressions

Better belly burst than good liquor be lost.
—Jonathan Swift

The Old Jameson Distillery ★ This museum illustrates the history of Irish whiskey, known in Irish as *uisce beatha* (the water of life). Learn as much as you can bear from the film, whiskey-making exhibitions, and right-in-front-of-your-eyes demonstrations. At the conclusion of the tour, you can sip a little firewater and see what you think. A couple of lucky people on each tour are selected to be "tasters" and sample different Irish, Scotch, and American whiskeys.

Bow St., Smithfield Village, Dublin 7. ✆ **01/807-2348.** www.jamesonwhiskey.com. Admission €14 adults; €10 seniors, students, and children; €30 families. Daily 9am–6pm (last tour at 5:30pm). Closed Good Friday and Christmas holidays. Bus: 67, 67A, 68, 69, 79, or 90.

MONUMENTAL humor

Dublin boasts countless public monuments, some modest, others boldly evident. The Irish make a sport of naming them, giving their irrepressible wit and ridicule yet another outlet. A sampler:

Poor **Molly Malone,** who, in song, "wheeled her wheelbarrow through streets broad and narrow," appears with her cockles and mussels at the intersection of Nassau and Grafton streets, across from Trinity College. Due to her ample bosom and plunging neckline, this statue is called "the Tart with the Cart."

Just around the corner from Molly on Dame Street stands another sculpture, a silent frenzy of **trumpeters** and streaming columns of water, proclaiming "You're a nation again"—popularly transliterated as "urination again."

The city's newest major monument is the **Millennium Spire,** a 120m-high (394-ft.) needle thrusting upward in the middle of traffic on O'Connell Street. Made of stainless steel and designed by London architect Ian Ritchie, the spire is intended to reflect the Dublin of the 21st century. (It replaced Nelson's Pillar, a statue of the British Admiral Horatio Nelson, erected under British rule and blown up by the IRA in 1966, on the 50th anniversary of the Easter Rising. Nelson's head was all that survived, and it is now in the Dublin Civic Museum.) Dubliners have had great fun coming up with a suitable nickname for the spire. The favorite is simply "the Spike," although other front-runners include "the Stiletto in the Ghetto" and rather more ribald "Erection at the Intersection."

Then there's the statue of Ireland's great patriot **Wolfe Tone.** Born at 44 Stafford St. in 1763 and graduated from Trinity College, Tone went on to spark a revolutionary fervor among the Irish. He is commemorated in thoroughly modern fashion on the north side of St. Stephen's Green by a semicircle of rough-hewed columns locally known as "Tonehenge."

The best renamed statue, though, is no more. Until a few years ago, **Anna Livia,** James Joyce's mythical personification of the River Liffey, could be found cast in bronze on O'Connell Street across from the General Post Office. The unattractive, hard-to-like statue reclining in streaming water was widely reviled—you'd be hard-pressed to find anybody who didn't hate it. It was nicknamed "the Floozy in the Jacuzzi." Due to its intense unpopularity, it was for many years, but has recently been relocated to the Croppies Acre Memorial Park, next to Collins Barracks (p. 145).

CATHEDRALS & CHURCHES

St. Patrick's Cathedral and Christ Church Cathedral are listed earlier in this chapter, under "The Top Attractions."

St. Audeon's Church Near the only remaining gate of the Old City walls (dating from 1214), this church is said to be the only surviving medieval parish in Dublin. Although it is partly in ruins, significant parts have survived, including the west doorway, which dates from 1190, and the 13th-century nave. It's a Church of Ireland property, but nearby is another St. Audeon's Church, this one Catholic and dating from 1846. It was in the latter church that Father "Flash" Kavanagh used to say the world's fastest Mass so that his congregation was out in time for the football matches. Since 1999, entrance to the ancient church has been through a visitor center. The center's exhibition, relating the history of St. Audeon's, is self-guided; visits to the church itself are by guided tour, and it is only open in high season.

Cornmarket (off High St.), Dublin 8. ✆ **01/677-0088.** Free admission. May–Oct daily 9:30am–5:30pm. Last admission 45 min. before closing. Bus: 21A, 78A, or 78B.

St. Mary's Pro-Cathedral No, there's no pro and amateur league for cathedrals in Ireland—"pro" simply means "temporary." And therein lies a fascinating piece of historical trivia. Contrary to popular belief, Dublin has no Roman Catholic cathedral (St. Patrick's and Christ Church have been part of the Anglican Church of Ireland since the 16th c.) But the Vatican views Christ Church as Dublin's "true" Catholic cathedral. Therefore, St. Mary's has been designated the "temporary" official Catholic cathedral in Dublin, and it has been thus since 1820. It's tucked away on a rather unimpressive back street, but it's nonetheless the heart of the city's Northside. It was built between 1815 and 1825 in Greek Revival Doric style. The exterior portico is modeled on the Temple of Theseus in Athens, with six Doric columns, while the Renaissance-style interior is patterned after the Church of Saint-Philippe du Roule of Paris. The church is noted for its awe-inspiring Palestrina Choir, which sings a Latin Mass every Sunday at 11am (during term times).

83 Marlborough St., Dublin 1. ✆ **01/874-5441.** www.procathedral.ie. Free admission. Mon–Fri 7:30am–6:45pm; Sat 7:30am–7:15pm; Sun 9am–1:45pm and 5:30–7:45pm. DART: Connolly. Bus: 28, 29A, 30, 31A, 31B, 32A, 32B, or 44A.

St. Michan's Church Built on the site of an early Danish chapel (1095), this 17th-century edifice has fine interior woodwork and an organ (dated 1724) on which Handel is said to have played his *Messiah.* A unique (and, let it be noted, macabre) feature of this church is the underground burial vault. Because of the dry atmosphere, mummified bodies have lain for centuries in an extraordinary state of preservation. A few still have their hair and fingernails; on others you can see desiccated internal organs under the skin. The tallest mummy is known as "the Crusader"; his legs were broken in order to fit him into the coffin. Others in residence include "the Nun" and "the Thief"—although their true identities were lost when the church records were destroyed during the Civil War in 1922. It is said that Bram Stoker was inspired to write *Dracula* in part by having visited the vaults as a child. ***Note:*** The church is wheelchair accessible, but the vaults are not.

Church St., Dublin 7. ✆ **01/872-4154.** Free admission. Guided tour of church and vaults €4 adults; €3.50 seniors and students; €3 children 11 and under; €12 families. Nov to mid-Mar

Some guides let intrepid visitors touch the mummies in the crypt at St. Michan's.

Mon–Fri 12:30–3:30pm, Sat 10am–12:45pm; mid-Mar to Oct Mon–Fri 10am–12:45pm and 2–4:45pm, Sat 10am–12:45pm. Closed bank holidays. Bus: 134 (from Abbey St.).

St. Teresa's Church The foundation stone was laid for this building in 1793, and the church was opened in 1810 by the Discalced Carmelite Fathers. After continuous enlargement, it reached its present form in 1876. After years of anti-Catholic legislation, this was the first Catholic church to be legally and openly erected in Dublin, following the Catholic Relief Act of 1793. Among the artistic highlights are John Hogan's *Dead Christ,* a sculpture displayed beneath the altar, and Phyllis Burke's seven beautiful stained-glass windows.

Clarendon St., Dublin 2. ✆ **01/671-8466.** www.clarendonstreet.net. Free admission; donations welcome. Daily 8am–8pm or longer. Bus: 4, 5, 7, 8, 9, 10, 11, 12, 13, 14, 15, 16, 19, 20, 21, 46A, or 74A.

Whitefriar Street Carmelite Church This 19th-century Byzantine-style church is unexpectedly one of the city's most romantic spots. Lovers are drawn here because the church holds the relics of St. Valentine. The pieces of bone are believed to be authentic, and they were given to the church by Pope Gregory XVI in 1836. They're kept in a casket on an altar to the right of the main altar, but once a year (on St. Valentine's Day, of course) are carried out in procession for a special Mass. The church also holds an icon known as **Our Lady of Dublin**, a 15th-century woodcarving that was rescued from a nearby farm where it had been used as a pig trough.

56 Aungier St., Dublin 2. ✆ **01/475-8821.** Free admission. Mon and Wed–Fri 8am–6:30pm; Tues 8am–9:30pm; Sat 8am–7pm; Sun 8am–7:30pm. Bus: 16, 16A, 19, 19A, 83, 122, or 155.

A CEMETERY

Glasnevin Cemetery North of the city center, the Irish national cemetery was founded in 1832 and covers more than 50 hectares (124 acres). Most people buried here were ordinary citizens, but there are also many famous names on the headstones, ranging from former Irish *taoiseach* (prime minister) Eamon de

Valera to other political heroes and rebels including Michael Collins, Daniel O'Connell, Countess Constance Markiewicz, and Charles Stewart Parnell. Literary figures also have their place here, such as writers Christy Brown (immortalized in the film *My Left Foot*) and Brendan Behan (at whose funeral, in 1964, the coffin was escorted by an IRA honor guard from the church). A heritage map, on sale in the flower shop at the entrance, serves as a guide to who's buried where, or you can take a 2-hour guided **tour**. There's also a fully searchable map on the cemetery's website.

Finglas Rd., Dublin 11. ✆ **01/830-1133.** www.glasnevintrust.ie. Free admission. Mon–Fri 9:30am–5pm; Sat 9:30am–1pm. Guided tours €6 offered daily 2:30pm from main gate (except Dec 25–26). Map €3.50. Bus: 19, 19A, 40, 40A, 40B, or 40C.

MORE HISTORIC BUILDINGS

It's not open to the public, but it's worth lingering outside **Mansion House,** Dawson Street, if only because of its fascinating history. The Queen Anne–style building has been the official residence of Dublin's lord mayors since 1715. In 1919, the first Dáil Éireann (House of Representatives) assembled here to adopt Ireland's Declaration of Independence and ratify the Proclamation of the Irish Republic.

Bank of Ireland Centre/Parliament House ★ This building was built in 1729 to house the Irish Parliament, and it did so for less than a century. Then, in 1797, the British Prime Minister William Pitt became convinced that the only way to bring an end to religious violence in Ireland was to close the Irish Parliament and merge it with the English. However, since the Parliament members had purchased their seats at great expense, it was difficult to convince them to agree, so Pitt bought them off with a combination of cash, titles, and promises that anti-Catholic rules would be ended if they only voted themselves out of existence. In 1801 they agreed—one of few Parliaments ever to have done so—and passed the so-called Act of Union. However, King George III disagreed with Pitt's plans to end the anti-Catholic laws and forced Pitt to resign before any such legislation could be passed. The Irish lost their independent government and got nothing in return. After standing empty for 2 years, the building was sold in 1803; the bill of sale required that it be altered so that it could never again be used for governmental gatherings. Today it's a bank, but still has many architectural elements dating from its heyday. Highlights include the windowless front portico, built to avoid distractions from the outside when Parliament was in session, and the grand House of Lords chamber with its Irish oak woodwork, 18th-century tapestries, golden mace, and a sparkling crystal chandelier. Much admired in its day, the building was supposedly an influence on the design of the United States Capitol building in Washington D.C.

This is also the home of the **Bank of Ireland Arts Centre** (✆ **01/671-1488**), accessible via the entrance on Foster Place. It hosts art exhibitions, concerts, and literary readings. Entry to readings, lunchtime recitals, and exhibitions is free.

2 College Green, Dublin 2. ✆ **01/661-5933,** ext. 2265. Free admission. Mon–Wed and Fri 10am–4pm; Thurs 10am–5pm. Guided 45-min. tours of House of Lords chamber Tues 10:30am, 11:30am, and 1:45pm (except holidays). DART: Tara St. Bus: Any An Lar (city-center) bus.

Custom House The Custom House, which sits prominently on the Liffey's North Quays (to the right of the O'Connell Street Bridge if you're coming from the South Bank), is a fine Georgian building. Completed in 1791, it is beautifully proportioned, with a long classical facade of graceful pavilions, arcades, and columns, and a central dome topped by a statue of Commerce. The 14 keystones over the doors and windows are known as the Riverine Heads, because they represent the Atlantic Ocean and the 13 principal rivers of Ireland. Although it burned to a shell in 1921, the building has been masterfully restored, and its bright Portland stone was recently cleaned. Sadly the interior is now closed to the public, but it's still a handsome enough building to warrant a detour.

Custom House Quay, Dublin 1. ✆ **01/888-2538.** DART: Tara St.

> **Impressions**
>
> ***You cannot conquer Ireland. You cannot extinguish the Irish passion for freedom. If our deed has not been sufficient to win freedom, then our children will win it by a better deed.***
>
> **—Patrick Pearse**

Four Courts Home to the Irish law courts since 1796, this fine 18th-century building overlooks the north bank of the Liffey on Dublin's west side. With a sprawling 132m (433-ft.) facade, it was designed by James Gandon (who also designed the Custom House) and is distinguished by its graceful Corinthian columns, massive dome (192m/630 ft. in diameter), and exterior statues of Justice, Mercy, Wisdom, and Moses (sculpted by Edward Smyth). The building was at the center of the fighting during the civil war of 1922 and was badly damaged in the battle, but it was later artfully restored. There are no public tours of the building, although you may be able to get on a schools tour if you contact the office several months in advance. These are designed to teach people about the Irish courts system, however, rather than serve as an architectural tour. There is a public viewing gallery in the courts themselves, however, when in session (see hours below).

Inns Quay, Dublin 8. ✆ **01/872-5555.** Free admission. Usually Mon–Fri 11am–1pm and 2–4pm, but only if court is in session. Call ahead to confirm. Bus: 34, 70, or 80.

General Post Office (GPO) ★ Don't be fooled by the nondescript name: With a facade of Ionic columns and Greco-Roman pilasters 60m long (197 ft.) and 17m high (56 ft.), this is more than a post office—it is the symbol of Irish freedom. Built between 1815 and 1818, it was the main stronghold of the Irish Volunteers during the Easter Rising. On Easter Sunday, 1916, Patrick Pearse stood on its steps and read a proclamation declaring a free Irish Republic, which began, "In every generation the Irish people have asserted their right to national freedom and sovereignty." Then he and an army of supporters barricaded themselves inside the post office. A siege ensued that ultimately involved much of the north of the city, and before it was over, the building was all but destroyed. It had barely been restored before the civil war broke out in 1922 and it was heavily

A statue of mythic warrior in the General Post Office.

damaged again. After that, it remained closed until 1929. It's still a working post office today, although it does house a few exhibits, including the original Declaration of Independence. We rarely bother going inside, though; touching the bullet holes in the walls out front is a far more potent way to experience a sense of this building's history.

O'Connell St., Dublin 1. ✆ **01/705-7000.** www.anpost.ie. Free admission. Mon–Sat 8am–8pm; Sun 10:30am–6:30pm. DART: Connolly. Bus: 25, 26, 34, 37, 38A, 39A, 39B, 66A, or 67A.

Bullet holes still scar the facade of the General Post Office, which served as a fortress against the British during the Easter Rising.

Leinster House The home of the Dáil (Irish House of Representatives) and Seanad (Irish Senate), which together constitute the Oireachtas (National Parliament), this is the center of Irish government. Dating from 1745 and originally known as Kildare House, the building is said to have been the model for Irish-born architect James Hoban's design for the White House in Washington, D.C. It was sold in 1815 to the Royal Dublin Society, which developed it as a cultural center. The National Museum, Library, and Gallery all surround it. The Irish Free State government acquired it in 1924. Tickets are available for guided tours when the Dáil is in session (Oct–May Mon–Fri); tours must be arranged in advance by calling your nation's embassy in Dublin, which will make the arrangements on your behalf. (See p. 666 for a list of numbers.)

Kildare St. and Merrion Sq., Dublin 2. ✆ **01/618-3000.** www.oireachtas.ie. Free admission. By appointment only, Oct–May; times vary but usually 10:30am, 11:30am, 2:30pm, and 3:30pm (also 7 and 8pm while the Dáil is in session). DART: Pearse. Bus: 5, 7A, or 8.

Newman House ★ These fine Georgian town houses on the south side of St. Stephen's Green are the historic seat of the Catholic University of Ireland. Named for Cardinal John Henry Newman, the 19th-century writer, theologian, and the first rector of the university, the buildings date from 1740 and are decorated with outstanding Palladian and rococo plasterwork, marble tiled floors, and wainscot paneling. Room no. 85 has a somber exterior, but inside it has been magnificently restored to its original splendor, with one exception—when the Catholic University took over the buildings in 1865, the fathers must have been put off by the luscious rococo nudes carved into the elaborate plasterwork, for they had clothes painted onto all of the female forms. Most have been blessedly returned to their natural shape, but a figure of Juno is still hidden by a very conservative tunic. ***Note:*** Every other Sunday, Newman House hosts an antiques-and-collectibles fair, where dealers from throughout Ireland sell a wide range of items, including silver, rare books, paintings and prints, coins, stamps, and so forth.

85–86 St. Stephen's Green, Dublin 2. ✆ **01/716-7422.** Guided tours €5 adults; €4 seniors, students, and children 11 and under. June–Aug Tues–Fri tours at 2, 3, and 4pm; Sept–May by appointment only. Bus: 10, 11, 13, 14, 14A, 15A, or 15B.

LIBRARIES

Marsh's Library This caged library, founded in 1701, is the real thing. Unlike Trinity College's Long Room, which is largely for show these days, Marsh's Library is still functioning. Its walls are lined with scholarly volumes, chiefly on theology, medicine, ancient history, maps, and Hebrew, Greek, Latin, and French literature. Wire cages, in which readers would be locked in with the more valuable tomes, still stand anachronistically. The interior—a magnificent example of a 17th-century scholar's library—has remained much the same for 3 centuries. The excellent collection of books by and about Jonathan Swift includes books with his editing comments in the margins. There's also an exhibition space that gets refreshed about once a year. Recent subjects have included "Beware the Jabberwock," a selection of 16th- and 17th-century books on the animal kingdom; and "Hippocrates Revived," covering the (often creepy) history of early medicine.

St. Patrick's Close, Upper Kevin St., Dublin 8. ✆ **01/454-3511.** www.marshlibrary.ie. Donation of €2.50 adults, €1.50 seniors and students requested. Entry free for research (call to arrange). Mon and Wed–Fri 9:30am–1pm and 2–5pm; Sat 10am–1pm. Bus: 50, 54A, or 56A.

National Library of Ireland If you're coming to Ireland to research your roots, this library should be one of your first stops (along with the Heraldic Museum). It has thousands of volumes and records that yield ancestral information, and a specialist genealogy advisory service. Open at this location since 1890, this is the principal library of Irish studies. It's particularly noted for its collection of first editions and the papers of Irish writers and political figures, such as W. B. Yeats, Daniel O'Connell, and Patrick Pearse. It also has an unrivaled collection of maps of Ireland.

Kildare St., Dublin 2. ✆ **01/603-0200.** www.nli.ie. Free admission. Mon–Wed 9:30am–9pm; Thurs–Fri 9:30am–5pm; Sat 9:30am–1pm. Exhibitions close 4:30pm Sat. DART: Pearse. Bus: 10, 11A, 11B, 13, or 20B.

National Photographic Archive Until recently this archive used to house the National Library's 300,000-strong photo collection. Now that has been re-absorbed into the main library, but this building is still used for exhibitions—and a very fine space it is too. Photos are rotated out regularly, so there's always something new to see. In addition to the exhibition area, there is a small gift shop.

Meeting House Sq., Temple Bar, Dublin 2. ✆ **01/603-0374.** www.nli.ie. Free admission. Mon–Sat 10am–5pm; Sun noon–5pm. DART: Tara St. Bus: 21A, 46A, 46B, 51B, 51C, 68, 69, or 86.

LITERARY LANDMARKS

See also "Libraries," above, and the listing for the Dublin Writers Museum (p. 147). You might also be interested in the James Joyce Museum, in nearby Sandycove (p. 192).

James Joyce Centre Just beyond the top of O'Connell Street on the city's Northside, near the Dublin Writers Museum, the Joyce Centre is a small, idiosyncratic gallery in a restored 1784 Georgian town house. There are pros and cons to this place—there's not much in the way of real memorabilia related to Joyce, save for a writing table he used in Paris when he was working on *Finnegan's Wake,* although there are early copies of his work. Overall, it's best to come here if an interesting speaker is scheduled. True Joyce fans, of course, will be in heaven. Call about the James Joyce walking tours.

35 N. Great George's St., Dublin 1. ✆ **01/878-8547.** www.jamesjoyce.ie. Admission €5 adults; €4 seniors, students, and children 9 and under. Separate fees for walking tours and events. Tues–Sat 10am–5pm; Sun noon–5pm. Last admission 30 min. before closing. Closed Dec 24–26. DART: Connolly. Bus: 3, 10, 11, 11A, 13, 16, 16A, 19, 19A, 22, or 22A.

Shaw Birthplace This simple, two-story terraced house near the Grand Canal on the south side was the birthplace in 1856 of George Bernard Shaw, author of *Pygmalion, Man and Superman,* and *John Bull's Other Island,* among many others. Shaw, one of Dublin's three winners of the Nobel Prize for literature, lived here until 1876, when he moved to London. Recently restored, it has been furnished in Victorian style to re-create the atmosphere of Shaw's early days. Rooms on view are the kitchen, the maid's room, the nursery, the drawing room, and a couple of bedrooms, including young Bernard's. The house is a 15-minute walk from St. Stephen's Green.

33 Synge St., Dublin 2. ✆ **01/475-0854.** Admission €6 adults; €5 seniors and students; €4 children; €15 families. Discounted combination ticket with Dublin Writers Museum and James Joyce Museum available. June–Aug Tues–Fri 10am–1pm and 2–5pm; Sat 2–5pm. Bus: 16, 16A, 19, 19A, 22, or 122.

MORE MUSEUMS

See also "Art Galleries & Art Museums," earlier in this chapter. The National Gallery, the National Museum, the Dublin Writers Museum, and Kilmainham Gaol Historical Museum are all listed earlier in this chapter, in "The Top Attractions."

The Ark: A Cultural Centre for Children ★ ☺ Every year, more than 20,000 children visit this cultural center where they are the makers, thinkers, doers, listeners, and watchers. Age-specific programs are geared to small groups of kids from 4 to 14 years old. There are organized minicourses (1–2 hr. long) designed around themes in music, visual arts, and theater, as well as workshops in photography, instrument making, and the art of architecture. The custom-designed arts center has three modern floors that house a theater, a gallery, and a workshop for hands-on learning sessions. Weekdays are often booked for school groups, but Saturday (and sometimes Sun) is kept open for families. Check the current themes and schedule on the Ark's very helpful website and book well ahead.

11a Eustace St., Temple Bar, Dublin 2. ✆ **01/670-7788.** www.ark.ie. Individual activities start at around €10 per child. Workshops Mon–Fri 10am–5pm. Shows as advertised. DART: Tara St. Bus: Any An Lar (cross-city) bus. LUAS: Jervis.

The kids are alright at the Dublin Zoo.

Dublin Zoo ★ ☺ Sprawling across 24 hectares (59 acres) of bucolic Phoenix Park on the north bank of the Liffey, this modern, humane zoo provides a naturally landscaped habitat for more than 235 species of wild animals and tropical birds. Highlights for youngsters include the Children's Pets Corner and a train ride around the zoo. Self-explanatory exhibits include "African Plains," "Fringes of the Arctic," and the "World of Primates." There are playgrounds and gift shops throughout the zoo. A downside: The restaurants within the zoo serve only fast food, but there are plenty of picnic areas for folks who want to bring their own meals.

Phoenix Park, Dublin 8. ✆ **01/677-0095.** www.heritageireland.ie. Free admission. Apr-Sept daily 10am-6pm; Oct daily 10am-5:30pm; Nov-Mar daily 10am-5pm. Zoo: ✆ **1800/924-848.** www.dublinzoo.ie. Admission €15 adults; €8.70 special needs adults; €12 seniors; €13 students; €5.50 special needs child; €11 children 3-16; free for children 2 and under; €44-€52 families, depending on number of children. Mar-Sept daily 9:30am-6pm; Oct daily 9:30am-5:30pm; Nov-Dec daily 9:30am-4pm; Jan daily 9:30am-4pm; Feb daily 9:30am-5pm. Last admission to zoo 1 hr. before closing; to African Plains, 30 min. before closing. Bus: 10, 25, or 26.

GAA Museum On the grounds of Croke Park, principal stadium of the Gaelic Athletic Association, this museum presents the athletic heritage of Ireland. The Gaelic Games (Gaelic football, hurling, handball, and *camogie*) have long been contested on an annual basis between teams representing the various regions of Ireland. Test your skills with interactive exhibits, and peruse the extensive video archive of football finals dating from 1931. The ticket price includes a behind-the-scenes tour of the stadium.

Croke Park, Dublin 3. ✆ **01/819-2323.** http://museum.gaa.ie. Museum and tour €11 adults; €8.50 seniors and students; €7.50 children 11 and under; €30 families. Museum only €6 adults; €4.50 seniors and students; €4 children 11 and under; €16 families. Mon-Sat 9:30am-5pm (July-Aug until 6pm), tours hourly 11am-3pm (July-Aug 10am-4pm); Sun noon-5pm, tours hourly 1-3pm (also at 10am and 4pm, July-Aug.). Bus: 3, 11, 11A, 16, 16A, 51A, or 123.

Genealogy Advisory Service Part of the National Library of Ireland (p. 161), this is an excellent resource for families trying to track down their Irish heritage. Exhibits on display include shields, banners, coins, paintings, porcelain, and stamps depicting Irish coats of arms. The staff are very helpful in answering questions on how to research your family tree, and keep a list of recommended professional genealogists.

2 Kildare St., Dublin 2. ✆ **01/603-0200.** www.nli.ie. Free admission. Mon-Fri 9:30am-5pm; Sat 9:30am-1pm. DART: Pearse. Bus: 5, 7A, 8, 9, 10, 14, or 15.

Number Twenty Nine 🎁 ☺ This little museum in a typical town house on one of the fashionable Georgian streets on Dublin's south side re-creates the lifestyle of a middle-class family from 1790 to 1820. The exhibition is designed to be authentic all the way from the artifacts and artwork of the time to the carpets, curtains, plasterwork, and bell pulls. Tables are set with period dishes and the nursery is filled with toys from the time. It's both educational and particularly beautiful.

29 Lower Fitzwilliam St., Dublin 2. ✆ **01/702-6165.** www.esb.ie/numbertwentynine. Tours only €6 adults; €3 seniors and students; free for children 15 and under. Tues-Sat 10am-5pm; Sun noon-5pm. Closed 2 weeks at Christmas. DART: Pearse. Bus: 7, 8, 10, or 45.

Organized Tours

BUS TOURS

The city bus company, **Dublin Bus** (✆ **01/873-4222;** www.dublinsightseeing.ie), operates several tours of Dublin, all of which depart from the Dublin Bus office at 59 Upper O'Connell St., Dublin 1. You can buy your ticket from the

FAMILY favorites

As with any big(ish) city, Dublin can seem a little kid-unfriendly, but never fear—there's more than enough to do here to keep the little ones happy.

If the weather's fine, Dublin's many parks give families on the go a respite from the city's ruckus. Right in the center at **Merrion Square** and **St. Stephen's Green,** there are lawns for picnicking, ducks to feed, playgrounds for swinging, and gardens for dashing around madly. If you feel like splurging, the whole family can take a carriage ride around the parks (see "Organized Tours," above).

West of Dublin's city center, the vast **Phoenix Park** is paradise for children on a sunny day (p. 150). It holds the **Dublin Zoo** (see above) as well as sports fields, playgrounds, and herds of free-roaming deer. Ice-cream vendors and teahouses are on hand. Those weary of walking can take a trail ride through the park from the **Ashtown Riding Stables** (see below, "Sports & Outdoor Pursuits").

For a lively tour of Dublin's Viking history (well, it's a gentle brush across the surface of Dublin's Viking history, to be honest), the **Viking Splash Tour,** in a reconditioned World War II amphibious "duck" vehicle (see "Organized Tours," above), is more about fun than history.

If they need a little artistic stimulation, the **Ark** (above) offers arts classes and cultural experiences ranging from painting and drawing to theater, while the **Lambert Puppet Theatre** (see below) offers good, clean, old-fashioned fun.

At the edge of town in the suburbs, fresh air, ocean breezes, and castles await their wondering eyes. North of the city is the **Malahide Castle** (p. 195), with a grand, rambling old stone castle, acres of parks and playgrounds, and the incongruous additions of the **Fry Model Railway** exhibit and **Tara's Palace,** filled with antique dollhouses and toys.

The towns south of Dublin are best explored by DART light rail from the city

driver or book in advance at the Dublin Bus office or at the Dublin Tourism ticket desk on Suffolk Street. There are often good discounts if you book online. The following are the best options:

The 75-minute guided **Dublin City Bus Tour** operates on a hop-on, hop-off basis, connecting 23 major points of interest, including museums, art galleries, churches and cathedrals, libraries, and historic sites. Rates are €16 for adults, €14 seniors and students, €6 for children 15 and under. Tours operate daily from 9am to 5pm, roughly every 10 to 15 minutes. Tickets are good for 2 days.

The 2¼-hour **Dublin Ghost Bus** is a spooky evening tour run by Dublin Bus, departing Monday to Thursday at 8pm, and Friday, Saturday and Sunday at 7 and 9:30pm. The tour addresses Dublin's history of felons, fiends, and phantoms. You'll see haunted houses, learn of Dracula's Dublin origins, and even get a crash course in body snatching. It's properly scary, though, and not recommended for children who do not have "teen" in their age. Fares are €28 with no discounts (not recommended for those 13 and under).

The 3-hour **North Coast and Castle Tour** departs daily at 10am and 2pm traveling up the north coast to Malahide and Howth. Fares are €26 for adults, €13 for children 13 and under. Visiting Malahide Castle itself costs extra.

center. You could stop in Monkstown to see a puppet show at the **Lambert Puppet Theatre and Museum** (Clifton Lane; ✆ **01/280-0974;** www.lambertpuppettheatre.com), or, if the kids need a little seaside adventure, go on a few more stops to the heritage village of Dalkey. The **Ferryman** of Coliemore Harbour, just a 10-minute walk from the train, can take the family out to explore **Dalkey Island** and return you a few hours later. After your adventure, reward yourself with a soft-serve ice-cream cone in the village. The park at the top of **Dalkey Hill** offers a memorable view of the town and bay beyond, but it's a very steep climb.

One stop after Dalkey on the DART lies the long pebbled beach of **Killiney.** This is just the place to find the perfect stone for your family collection or to take a beachcombing stroll along the strand. Farther on down the line is the seaside resort town of **Bray,** where Irish water creatures, from starfish to sharks, can be found in the **National Sea Life Centre** (Strand Rd.; ✆ **01/286-6939;** www.sealife.ie; reviewed on p. 207). Along with the aquarium, Bray has arcades, games, and other family amusements along its boardwalk. If you get to Bray with energy and daylight to spare, the hike up **Bray Head** will give you a spectacular view of the Dublin coastline; in summer, it's covered in purple heather and yellow gorse.

Even with so much out there for families to do together, there may be some events—a romantic dinner, perhaps?—to which you'd rather not bring the kids. Dublin parents swear by **Minder Finders** (www.minderfinders.ie), a clued-in agency that uses certified babysitters (many are former nannies or teachers) who arrive armed with a bag full of kid-friendly activities. Each sitter is matched with your kids' ages and interests in mind, to alleviate any "new babysitter" jitters.

The 3¾-hour **South Coast and Gardens Tour** departs daily at 11am and 2pm, traveling south through the seaside town of Dún Laoghaire, through the "Irish Riviera" villages of Dalkey and Killiney, and farther south to visit the vast Powerscourt Estate. The route back to Dublin passes through the Wicklow Mountains. Fares are €28 for adults, €14 for children 13 and under.

Irish City Tours (✆ **01/605-7705;** www.irishcitytours.com) operates its own hop-on, hop-off city tour, covering all the same major sights as the Dublin Bus's Dublin City Tour. It's part of a big global franchise, so the brightly painted double-deckers may well look familiar. The first tours leave at 9:30am from outside the Dublin Tourism office at 14 Upper O'Connell St., and run every 10 to 15 minutes thereafter. The last departures are at 5:30pm in summer, 4:30pm in winter. You can also join the tour at any of a number of pickup points along the route and buy your ticket from the driver. Gray Line's Dublin city tour costs €16 for adults, €14 for seniors and students, and €38 families. Up to 2 kids (14 and under) for every adult go free.

Gray Line also offers a range of full-day excursions from Dublin to such nearby sights as Glendalough, Newgrange, and Powerscourt. Adult fares for their other tours range from about €20 to €40.

Horse-Drawn Carriage Tours

You can tour Dublin in style in a horse-drawn carriage with a driver who will comment on the sights as you travel the city's streets and squares. To arrange a ride, consult one of the drivers stationed with carriages at the Grafton Street side of St. Stephen's Green. Rides range from a short swing around the green to a half-hour Georgian tour or an hour-long Old City tour.

Rides are available on a first-come, first-served basis from April to October (weather permitting) and will run you about €20 to €50 for one to four passengers.

LAND & WATER TOURS

The popular **Viking Splash Tour** ★ (✆ **01/707-6000;** www.vikingsplash.ie) is an unusual way to see Dublin. Aboard a reconditioned American World War II amphibious landing craft, or "duck," this tour starts on land (from Bull Alley St. beside St. Patrick's Cathedral) and eventually splashes into the Grand Canal. Passengers wear horned Viking helmets (a reference to the original settlers of the Dublin area) and are encouraged to issue war cries at appropriate moments. One of the ducks even has bullet holes as evidence of its military service. During summer the tours depart roughly on the half-hour every day 10am to 5:30pm and last an hour and 15 minutes. Off season they're less frequent but do still run, usually about every hour and a half. Tickets are €20 for adults, €10 for children 12 and under, €18 seniors and students, and €60 for a family of five. It runs daily from March to October, and on most days at other times of year, though times tend to vary in winter. Call ahead or check the schedule online.

Leave your fine raiment at home before boarding a Viking Splash Tour.

In addition to a raft of bus tours (see above) Dublin Bus also run a Dublin **River Tour** (✆ **01/473-0000;** www.dublinsightseeing.ie). The zippy little red boats run in all weathers and are wheelchair accessible.

WALKING TOURS

Small and compact, Dublin was made for walking. If you prefer to set off on your own, the **Dublin Tourism** office, St. Andrew's Church, Suffolk Street, Dublin 2, has maps for four tourist trails throughout the city: Old City, Georgian Heritage, Cultural Heritage, and the "Rock 'n Stroll" music tour.

However, if you'd like more guidance, historical background, or just some company, you might want to consider one of the following.

Historical Walking Tours of Dublin ★★ Tours with this award-winning outfit are like 2-hour primers on Dublin's historic landmarks, from medieval walls and Viking remains around Wood Quay, to the architectural splendors of Georgian Dublin, to highlights of Irish history. Guides are historians, and participants are encouraged to ask questions. Tours assemble just inside the front gate of Trinity College; no reservations are needed.

From Trinity College. ✆ **087/688-9412.** www.historicalinsights.ie. Tickets €12 adults; €10 seniors and students; free for children 13 and under. May–Sept daily 11am and 3pm; Apr and Oct daily 11am; Nov–Mar Fri–Sun 11am.

Literary Pub Crawl ★ Walking in the footsteps of Joyce, Behan, Beckett, Shaw, Kavanagh, and other Irish literary greats, this tour visits Dublin's most famous pubs and explores their deep, literary connections. Actors provide humorous performances and commentary between stops. Throughout the night, you can join in a literary quiz—if you win, you'll get a prize. The tour kicks off in the upstairs room of the Duke Pub on Duke Street (off Grafton St.) at 7:30pm, and covers about 1km (½ mile) over 2¼ hours. You can buy tickets on the night or book in advance. No children are allowed, for obvious reasons.

Upstairs at the Duke Pub, 9 Duke St., Dublin 2. ✆ **01/670-5602.** www.dublinpubcrawl.com. Tickets €12 adults; €10 students. Apr–Oct daily 7:30pm; Nov–Mar Thurs–Sun 7:30pm. No tour Mar 17.

1916 Rebellion Walking Tour ★ Dublin was profoundly changed by the rebellion early in the 20th century that became known as the Easter Rising. This tour takes you into the heat of the action at the General Post Office, explaining how the anger rose until the rebellion exploded on Easter Sunday in 1916. The tour is well thought out and run by local historians who wrote a book on the events of that year. Their vast knowledge of the history of Dublin shines through, making this an absorbing experience.

The International Bar, 23 Wicklow St., Dublin 2. ✆ **086/858-3847.** www.1916rising.com. Tickets €12 per person. Mar–Oct Mon–Sat 11:30am; Sun 1pm. No tour Mar 17; start time varies on public holidays.

Traditional Irish Musical Pub Crawl ★★ This tour explores and samples the traditional music scene, and the price includes a songbook. Two professional musicians, who sing as you make your way from one famous pub to another in Temple Bar, lead the tour. The evening is touristy, but the music is good. It lasts 2½ hours.

Leaves from Oliver St. John Gogarty pub and restaurant (upstairs), 57–58 Fleet St. (at Anglesea St.), Temple Bar. ✆ **01/475-3313.** Tickets €12 adults; €10 students and seniors. Apr–Oct daily 7:30pm; Nov–Mar Thurs–Sat 7:30pm. Tickets on sale at 7pm, or in advance from www.discoverdublin.ie, or the Dublin Tourism office.

SPORTS & OUTDOOR PURSUITS

BEACHES Plenty of fine beaches are accessible by city bus or DART, which follows the coast from Howth, north of the city, to Bray, south of the city in County Wicklow. Some popular beaches include **Dollymount,** 5km (3 miles) away; **Sutton,** 11km (6¾ miles) away; **Howth,** 15km (9⅓ miles) away; and **Portmarnock** and **Malahide,** each 11km (6¾ miles) away. In addition, the southern suburb of **Dún Laoghaire,** 11km (6¾ miles) away, offers a beach (at Sandycove) and a long bayfront promenade ideal for strolling in the sea air. For more details, inquire at the Dublin Tourism office.

BIRD-WATCHING The many estuaries, salt marshes, sand flats, and islands near Dublin Bay provide a varied habitat for a number of species. **Rockabill Island,** off the coast at Skerries, is home to an important colony of roseate terns; there is no public access to the island, but the birds can be seen from the shore. **Rogerstown and Malahide estuaries,** on the Northside of Dublin, are wintering grounds for large numbers of brent geese, ducks, and waders. **Sandymount Strand,** on Dublin's south side, has a vast intertidal zone; around dusk in July and August, you can often see large numbers of terns, including visiting roseate terns from Rockabill Island.

Your all-around best bet is a bird sanctuary called Bull Island, also known as the **North Bull,** just north of Dublin city harbor at the suburb of Clontarf. It's not an island at all, but a 3km (2-mile) spit of marshland connected to the mainland by a bridge. It was created by Captain William Bligh, of *Mutiny on the Bounty* fame. Early in the 19th century, he was head of the Port and Docks Board, and he ordered the construction of a harbor wall at the mouth of the River Liffey, in an effort to stop the bay from silting up. In fairly short order, the shifting sands created this small landmass. Its dunes, salt marsh, and extensive intertidal flats provide a unique environment that attracts thousands of seabirds. Hundreds of species have been recorded, and 40,000 birds shelter and nest here. In winter, these figures are boosted by tens of thousands of migrants from the Arctic Circle, and North American spoonbills, little egrets, and sandpipers. Together, they all make a deafening racket. A visitor center is open daily 10:15am to 4:30pm.

FISHING There are plenty of opportunities for freshwater angling on local rivers, reservoirs, and fisheries. A day's catch might include perch, rudd, pike, salmon, sea trout, brown trout, or freshwater eel. The **Irish Tourist Board** operates a good website dedicated to fishing (**www.discoverireland.com/us/ireland-things-to-see-and-do/activities/fishing**). Options for anglers include fishing for brown trout with the River Dodder Anglers' Club (✆ **01/298-2112**) in southwest County Dublin. In addition, the **Dublin Angling Initiative,** Balnagowan, Mobhi Boreen, Glasnevin, Dublin 9 (✆ **087/674-0214**), publishes a free guide—the *Dublin Freshwater Angling Guide*. It's available from the **Eastern Regional Fisheries Board,** 15a Main St., Blackrock, County Dublin (✆ **01/278-7022;** www.fishinginireland.info); or by e-mailing **info@erfb.ie**.

GOLF Dublin is one of the world's great golfing capitals. A quarter of Ireland's courses—including 5 of the top 10—lie within an hour's drive of the city. Visitors are welcome, but phone ahead and make a reservation. The following four courses—two parkland and two links—are among the best 18-hole courses in the Dublin area.

Elm Park Golf & Sports Club ★, Nutley Lane, Donnybrook, Dublin 4 (✆ **01/269-3438;** www.elmparkgolfclub.ie), is in the residential, privileged south side of Dublin. The beautifully manicured parkland, par-69 course is especially popular with visitors because it is within 6km (3¾ miles) of the city center and close to the Jurys, Berkeley Court, and Four Seasons hotels. Greens fees are €70, or €45 before 10am.

Portmarnock Golf Club ★, Portmarnock, County Dublin (✆ **01/846-2968;** www.portmarnockgolfclub.ie), is a respected links course. About 16km (10 miles) from the city center on Dublin's Northside, on a spit of land between the Irish Sea and a tidal inlet, this course opened in 1894. Over the years, the par-72 championship course has been the scene of leading tournaments, including the Dunlop Masters (1959, 1965), Canada Cup (1960), Alcan (1970), St. Andrews Trophy (1968), and many an Irish Open. You won't be surprised, then, to find out that fees are a bit pricey. Greens fees are €180, or €150 before 9am or after 4pm (3pm Sept and Apr) on weekdays.

Royal Dublin Golf Club ★, Bull Island, Dollymount, Dublin 3 (✆ **01/833-6346;** www.theroyaldublingolfclub.com), is often compared to St. Andrews. The century-old, par-73 championship seaside links is on an island in Dublin Bay, 4.8km (3 miles) northeast of the city center. Like Portmarnock, it has been rated among the world's top courses and has played host to several Irish Opens. The home base of Ireland's legendary champion Christy O'Connor, Sr., the Royal Dublin is well known for its fine bunkers, close lies, and subtle trappings. Visitors can play on weekdays except Wednesday, and there are also a few slots held for guests on Saturday 4am to 5:30pm and Sunday 10am to noon. Greens fees are €125; a second round may be played at half price if there's space available.

St. Margaret's Golf & Country Club ★, Skephubble, St. Margaret's, County Dublin (✆ **01/864-0400;** www.stmargaretsgolf.com), is a stunning, par-72 parkland course 4.8km (3 miles) west of Dublin Airport. Greens fees are around €45 Monday to Thursday, €55 Friday to Sunday.

HORSEBACK RIDING Plenty of riding stables are within easy reach of central Dublin, and prices average about €30 to €50 an hour, with or without instruction. Many stables offer guided trail riding, as well as courses in show jumping, dressage, prehunting, eventing, and cross-country riding. For trail riding through Phoenix Park, **Ashtown Riding Stables** (✆ **01/838-3807;** www.ashtownstables.com) is ideal. They're in the village of Ashtown, adjoining the park and only 10 minutes by car or bus (no. 37, 38, 39, or 70) from the city center. Among the other riding centers within easy reach of downtown Dublin is **Carrickmines Equestrian Centre,** Glenamuck Road, Foxrock, Dublin 18 (✆ **01/295-5990;** www.carrickminesequestrian.ie), and **Brennanstown Riding School,** Hollybrook, Kilmacanogue, County Dublin (✆ **01/286-3778;** www.brennanstownrs.ie).

Riding in Phoenix Park.

WALKING For casual walking, the Royal Canal and Grand Canal, which skirt the north and south city centers, respectively, are ideal for seeing the area. Both are marked trails, so you can't get lost, and because they stick to the towpaths of the canals, the paths are flat and easy. Both routes pass a range of small towns and villages that can be used as starting or stopping points.

The walk from Bray (the southern terminus of the DART) to Greystones along the rocky promontory of **Bray Head** is a great excursion, with beautiful views back toward Killiney Bay, Dalkey Island, and Bray. Follow the beachside promenade south through Bray; at the outskirts of town, the promenade turns left and up, beginning the ascent of Bray Head. Shortly after the ascent begins, a trail branches to the left—this is the cliffside walk, which continues another 5km (3 miles) along the coast to Greystones. From the center of Greystones, a train will take you back to Bray. This is an easy walk, about 2 hours each way. Don't attempt this walk in bad weather or strong winds, as the cliffside path will be quite treacherous.

Dalkey Hill and **Killiney Hill** drop steeply into the sea and command great views of Killiney Bay, Bray Head, and Sugarloaf Mountain. To get there, leave the Dalkey DART station, head into the center of Dalkey and then south on Dalkey Avenue (at the post office). About 1km (½ mile) from the post office, you'll pass a road ascending through fields on your left—this is the entrance to the Dalkey Hill Park. From the parking lot, climb a series of steps to the top of Dalkey Hill; from here you can see the expanse of the bay, the Wicklow Hills in the distance, and the obelisk topping nearby Killiney Hill. If you continue on to the obelisk, there is a trail leading from there down the seaward side to Vico Road, another lovely place for a seaside walk. It's about 1km (½ mile) from the parking lot to Killiney Hill.

WATERSPORTS Certified level-one and level-two instruction and equipment rental for three watersports—kayaking, sailing, and windsurfing—are available at the **Surfdock Centre,** Grand Canal Dock Yard, Ringsend, Dublin 4 (✆ **01/668-3945;** www.surfdock.ie). The center has 17 hectares (42 acres) of enclosed fresh water for its courses.

SPECTATOR SPORTS

GAELIC SPORTS If your schedule permits, try to get to a **Gaelic football** or **hurling** match—the only indigenously Irish games and two of the fastest-moving sports around. Gaelic football is vaguely a cross between soccer and American football; you can move the ball with either your hands or feet. **Hurling** is a lightning-speed game in which 30 men use heavy sticks to fling a hard leather ball called a *sliotar*—think field hockey meets lacrosse. Both amateur sports are played every weekend throughout the summer at local fields, culminating in September with the **All-Ireland Finals,** the Irish version of the Super Bowl. For schedules and admission fees, phone the **Gaelic Athletic Association,** Croke Park, Jones Road, Dublin 3 (✆ **01/836-3222;** www.gaa.ie).

GREYHOUND RACING Races are held throughout the year at **Shelbourne Park Greyhound Stadium,** Southlotts Road, Dublin 4 (✆ **01/668-3852**), and **Harold's Cross Stadium,** 151 Harold's Cross Rd., Dublin 6

(✆ **01/497-1081**). For a complete schedule and details for races throughout Ireland, contact **Bord na gCon (Greyhound Board),** Limerick (✆ **061/448000;** www.igb.ie).

Greyhound races take place year-round at Shelbourne Park.

HORSE RACING The closest racecourse to the city center is the **Leopardstown Race Course,** off the Stillorgan road (N11), Foxrock, Dublin 18 (✆ **01/289-0500;** www.leopardstown.com). This modern facility with all-weather, glass-enclosed spectator stands is 9.7km (6 miles) south of the city center. Racing meets—mainly steeplechases, but also a few flats—are scheduled throughout the year, two or three times a month.

POLO With the Dublin Mountains as a backdrop, polo is played from May to mid-September on the green fields of Phoenix Park, on Dublin's west side. Matches take place on Wednesday evenings and Saturday and Sunday afternoons. Admission is free. For full details, contact the **All Ireland Polo Club,** Phoenix Park, Dublin 8 (✆ **01/677-6248;** www.allirelandpoloclub.com), or check the sports pages of the newspapers.

RUGBY & SOCCER The **Aviva Stadium**, 62 Lansdowne Rd., Dublin 4 (✆ **01/238-2300;** www.avivastadium.ie) is, depending on your perspective, either a gleaming new monument to modern Irish sports, or Dublin's newest eyesore. Either way you really can't miss it. This is the official home of both the national rugby and football (soccer) teams.

SHOPPING

In recent years, Dublin has surprised everyone by becoming a good shopping town. Although the recession has inevitably hit small independent shops more acutely than the big chain stores, you can still find excellent craftsmanship in the form of hand-woven wool blankets and clothes in a vivid array of colors, high-quality crafts and antiques, and chic clothes from the seemingly limitless line of Dublin designers.

The hub of mainstream shopping south of the Liffey is **Grafton Street,** crowned by the city's most fashionable department store, Brown Thomas (known as BT), and the jeweler Weirs, but there's much better shopping on the smaller streets radiating out from Grafton, such as **Duke, Dawson, Nassau,** and **Wicklow.** On these streets you'll find small, interesting shops that specialize in books, handicrafts, jewelry, gifts, and clothing. For clothes, look out for tiny **Cow's Lane,** off Lord Edward Street—it is popular with those in the know for its excellent clothing boutiques selling the works of local designers. Also in Grafton's penumbra are **William Street South, Castle Market,** and **Drury Street,** all of which have smart boutiques and irresistible tiny shops. On William Street South, look out for the **Powerscourt Townhouse Centre,** a small, elegant shopping center in a grand Georgian town house. It has relaxing cafes, antiques shops, shoe shops, and the top-floor Design Centre, which sells works by some of Ireland's top designers. Not far away, the **George's Street Arcade** is a marvelous clutter of bohemian jewelry, used books, and vintage clothes.

Generally, Dublin shops are open from 9am to 6pm Monday to Saturday, and Thursday until 9pm. Many larger shops have Sunday hours from noon to 6pm.

Grafton Street is Dublin's main shopping artery.

Major department stores include, on the Northside, **Arnotts,** 12 Henry St., Dublin 1 (✆ **01/805-0400;** http://www.arnotts.ie), and the marvelously traditional **Clerys,** 18–27 Lower O'Connell St., Dublin 1 (✆ **01/878-6000;** www.clerys.com); and on the south side, **Brown Thomas,** 85–95 Grafton St., Dublin 2 (✆ **01/605-6666;** www.brownthomas.com).

Dublin also has several clusters of shops in **multistory malls** or ground-level **arcades,** ideal for indoor shopping on rainy days. On the Northside, these include the **ILAC Centre,** off Henry Street, Dublin 1 (✆ **01/878-2275;** www.ilac.ie), and the **Jervis Shopping Centre** (✆ **01/878-1323;** www.jervis.ie), at 125 Abbey St., Dublin 1. On the south side, there's the **Royal Hibernian Way,** 49–50 Dawson St., Dublin 2 (✆ **01/679-5919**); **St. Stephen's Green Centre,** at the top of Grafton Street, Dublin 2 (✆ **01/478-0888;** www.stephensgreen.com); and the aforementioned **Powerscourt Townhouse Centre,** 59 William St. S., Dublin 2 (✆ **01/679-4144;** www.powerscourtcentre.com).

Art

Combridge Fine Arts In business for more than 100 years, this shop features works by modern Irish artists, as well as quality reproductions of classic Irish art. 17 William St. S., Dublin 2. ✆ **01/677-4652.** www.cfa.ie. DART: Pearse. Bus: 15A, 15B, 15C, 55, or 83.

Green on Red This gallery behind Pearse Street DART station is a little off the tourist track, but it's worth the effort, for some say it's Dublin's finest contemporary art gallery. The gallery represents top local and international contemporary artists including Fergus Feehily, Martin & Hobbs, Gerard Byrne, and Bridget Riley. 26–28 Lombard St., Dublin 2. ✆ **01/671-3414.** www.greenonredgallery.com. DART: Pearse.

Books & Paper

Cathach Books Member of the antiquarian Booksellers Association, this is not the store you head for if you want a bestselling thriller. With secondhand rare books and first editions, and the hushed tone of a library, this is for serious

FIVE COOL souvenirs FOR €5 (OR LESS!) IN DUBLIN

Sure, you can get a keychain shaped like a leprechaun or shamrock, this season's hot T-shirt, or a hat shaped like a pint of Guinness, at any of the many souvenir stores in Dublin. But your friends (unless they *want* a hat shaped like a pint of Guinness), will appreciate these nifty finds, and they don't take up much room in your luggage! (All prices include VAT.)

- **A pennywhistle.** At **Waltons** (69 S. Great Georges St., Dublin 2; ✆ **01/475-0661;** www.waltons.ie; also at 2 N. Frederick St.), which has been in the music business since the 1920s, you'll find sheet music, instructional CDs, and instruments both traditional and modern, ranging from an authentic *bodhrán* (drum) from €13, to harps for €585 and up, and a Dublin tin whistle, complete with instruction booklet and music for 20 songs, for €4.99.
- **Mmmmmarmalade** at Avoca. **Avoca Handweavers** (11–13 Suffolk St., Dublin 2; ✆ **01/677-4215;** www.avoca.ie) is known for its lovely clothing and accessories, but their Dublin location also has a lot of handmade and local sweets and savories in the lower level dining area (not the rooftop cafe). Get a jar of whiskey marmalade for €3.99, strawberry and champagne jam for €4.45, or the rather delightfully named hedgerow jam for €4.45.
- **Mulled Wine Kits.** At the **Oxfam Fair Trade Store** (54 S. King St., Dublin 2; ✆ **01/671-0308;** www.oxfamireland.org), you can find all kinds of food and handicrafts from over 20 different countries, including high-end objets d'art and nifty little gift boxes containing five sachets of spice and sugar that can simply be dropped into a pan of red wine and heated up for a deliciously festive treat.
- **A chic shopping bag.** They don't ask "paper or plastic" at Irish supermarkets; indeed, by law, they can't be given away for free. You're expected to bring your own, and if you don't, you can find sturdy, reusable bags near the checkout for €1 and up. Tesco's basic black bags are good-looking and useful for hauling all your stuff around town, in Dublin and at home. You might also find a designer bag with a cool pattern that costs a bit more (say €3.50), with the proceeds going to charity.
- **Flapjacks.** If you ask for a flapjack in Ireland, you won't get a pancake, but a delightful biscuit (cookie to the North Americans) made from rolled oats, butter, brown sugar, and honey, often with fruit, nuts, or yogurt added. You can get boxes of them in food stores, or grab one in a coffee shop for a euro or two. My friend J., who *loves* them, didn't bring any back the last time we were in Dublin because he said he knew he'd eat his last one and miss them too much. He changed his mind as we waited for our luggage at Newark Airport, and wished he had just one more . . . I pulled one out of my pocket, and he got more than a euro's worth of happiness out of it!

—Kathleen Warnock

bibliophiles. 10 Duke St., Dublin 2. ✆ **01/671-8676.** www.rarebooks.ie. DART: Pearse. Bus: 10, 11A, 11B, 13, or 20B.

Hodges Figgis This enormous bookstore has books on virtually every topic and is Dublin's go-to store for absolutely everything literary. It's so big you can practically get lost in it. It's well worth an afternoon's wander. 56–58 Dawson St., Dublin 2. ✆ **01/677-4754.** DART: Pearse. Bus: 10, 11A, 11B, 13, or 20B.

Noble & Beggarman Based in a handsome old Georgian building just around the corner from St. Stephen's Green, this wonderfully named bookstore is packed full of books on Irish art, photography, architecture, design, and art theory. 28 S. William St., Dublin 2. ✆ **01/633-3568.** www.nobleandbeggarmanbooks.com. Bus: 10, 11A, 11B, 13, 16A, 19A, 20B, 22A, 55, or 83.

The Pen Corner For lovers of fountain pens, this stationery store has been selling stylish writing gear since 1927. It also has a lovely collection of unusual, arty cards, and notepaper. 12 College Green, Dublin 2. ✆ **01/679-3641.** DART: Tara St. Bus: Any An Lar city-center bus.

Craft Stores

Avoca Handweavers This place is a wonderland of vivid colors, soft, intricately woven fabrics, blankets, throws, light woolen sweaters, children's clothes, and toys, all in a delightful shopping environment spread over three floors near Trinity College. All the fabrics are woven in the Vale of Avoca in the Wicklow Mountains. There's also pottery, jewelry, art, food, and adorable little things you really don't need, but can't live without. Hands down, this is one of the best stores in Dublin. The top-floor **cafe** is a great place for lunch (p. 133). 11–13 Suffolk St., Dublin 2. ✆ **01/677-4215.** www.avoca.ie. Bus: All An Lar (cross-city) buses.

The Drawing Room This unusual little place looks like an antiques store until you realize that everything is a reproduction. Lamps, mirrors, funky little gifts, and plenty of unusual photo frames. You can pick up classy and highly individual knickknacks here at a fraction of the price that the genuine article would cost. Whether you tell your admiring friends that your souvenir is the real thing, however, is entirely up to you. 29 Westbury Mall, Dublin 2. ✆ **01/677-2083.** Bus: All An Lar (cross-city) buses.

Powerscourt Townhouse Centre In a restored 1774 town house, this four-story complex consists of a central sky-lit courtyard and more than 60 boutiques, craft shops, art galleries, snack bars, wine bars, and restaurants. The wares include all kinds of crafts, antiques, paintings, prints, ceramics, leatherwork, jewelry, clothing, chocolates, and farmhouse cheeses. You can also book a behind-the-scenes tour to learn more about the history of the house; check the website for details. 59 William St. S., Dublin 2. ✆ **01/679-4144.** www.powerscourtcentre.com. Bus: 10, 11A, 11B, 13, 16A, 19A, 20B, 22A, 55, or 83.

Tower Design Centre Alongside the Grand Canal, this beautifully restored 1862 sugar refinery now houses a nest of craft workshops where you can watch the artisans at work. The merchandise ranges from fine-art greeting cards and hand-marbled stationery to pewter, ceramics, pottery, knitwear, hand-painted silks, copperplate etchings, all-wool wall hangings, silver and gold Celtic jewelry, and heraldic gifts. Pearse St. (off Grand Canal Quay), Dublin 2. ✆ **01/677-5655.** Limited free parking. DART: Pearse. Bus: 2 or 3.

Fashion

See also "Knitwear," on p. 178.

MEN'S FASHION

Alias Tom Still one of Dublin's best small, men's designer clothing stores, the emphasis here is Italian (Gucci, Prada, Armani), but the range also covers other chic designers from the rest of Europe and America. Prices are eye-watering. Duke House, Duke St., Dublin 2. ✆ **01/671-5443.** DART: Pearse. Bus: 10, 11A, 11B, 13, or 20B.

Arnotts Project A new branch of the hardy old Arnotts (p. 172), this vast store in the Jervis Shopping Centre is entirely devoted to youth fashions, urban styles, and designer homeware. Teens and hipsters will be in heaven. Upper Abbey St., Dublin 1. ✆ **01/805-0400.** LUAS: Jervis. Bus: 51.

BT2 Another department store offshoot—this time of the chi-chi Brown Thomas, across the street (p. 172)—this is the one of best shops in Dublin for the coolest designer labels for both men and women. The look is sportier, more casual, and geared to the younger, hopelessly cool set. There are also branches in Dundrum (✆ **01/296-8400**) and Blanchardstown (✆ **01/860-6540**). The prices in all three are nearly as crazy as in BT. 28 Grafton St., Dublin 2. ✆ **01/605-6747.** Bus: All An Lar (cross-city) buses.

Kevin & Howlin For more than a half-century, this has been the best place in town for hand-woven Donegal tweed garments. The selection includes suits, overcoats, jackets, scarves, vests, and myriad hats—everything from Patch caps and Gatsby fedoras to Sherlock Holmes–style deerstalkers and the ubiquitous Paddy hats. 31 Nassau St., Dublin 2. ✆ **01/633-4576.** www.kevinandhowlin.com. DART: Pearse. Bus: 7, 8, 10, 11, or 46A.

WOMEN'S FASHION

BT2 Brown Thomas's sister shop, located across the street, is the best place in town for A-list designer labels. BT2 targets a younger but no less label-conscious crowd than BT—think style-obsessed Trustifarians and yuppies and you've got the clientele in a nutshell. There are two more branches in the Dublin suburbs (see "Men's Fashion" above). 28 Grafton St., Dublin 2. ✆ **01/605-6747.** Bus: All An Lar (cross-city) buses.

Claire Garvey The brightest luminary in Old City is a young Dublin native with a talent for creating romantic, dramatic, and feminine clothing with Celtic flair. Specializing in formalwear, wedding dresses, and debutante gowns (yes, really), Garvey transforms hand-dyed velvet and silk into sumptuous garments that beg to be worn on special occasions. Her one-of-a-kind bijou handbags are a white-hot fashion accessory. 6 Cow's Lane, Dublin 2. ✆ **01/671-7287.** www.clairegarvey.com. Bus: 50, 54A, 56A, 65, 65A, 77, 77A, 123, or 150.

Design Centre This is the city's best one-stop shop if you want to find all of Ireland's hottest contemporary designers—including Louise Kennedy, Mary Gregory, Karen Millen, Mary Grant, and Sharon Hoey—under one roof. Prices are generally high, but there are good bargains to be had during sale seasons and on the seconds rack. Powerscourt Townhouse Centre, Dublin 2. ✆ **01/679-5863** or 679-5718. www.designcentre.ie. DART: Pearse. Bus: 10, 11A, 11B, 13, or 20B.

Jenny Vander This is where actresses and supermodels come to find extraordinary and stylish antique clothing. There are plenty of jeweled frocks, vintage day wear, and stunning costume jewelry filling the clothing racks and display cases. Overall, it's a fabulous place to shop for one-of-a-kind pieces. 20 Market Arcade, S. Great Georges St., Dublin 2. ✆ **01/677-0406.** DART: Pearse. Bus: 10, 11A, 11B, 13, or 20B.

Louise Kennedy This glamorous and sophisticated designer is a longtime favorite of Meryl Streep and former British first lady Cherie Blair. Kennedy's elegant showroom carries her clothing, accessories, and home collections, as well as Philip Treacy hats, Lulu Guinness handbags, Lindley furniture, and other items of perfect taste. 56 Merrion Sq., Dublin 2. ✆ **01/662-0056.** www.louisekennedy.com. DART: Pearse. Bus: 5, 7A, or 8.

Tulle This place is small but mighty when it comes to contemporary clothing designs. It's filled with works by hot new designers like Joanne Hynes and international designers like Pink Soda and Stella Forest. 28 George's St. Arcade, Dublin 2. ✆ **01/679-9115**. Bus: 10, 11A, 11B, or 13.

Jewelry

Costelloe & Costelloe This charming little shop is filled with irresistible little trinkets, handbags, colorful wraps, and jewelry, much of which is heartwarmingly affordable. There's another branch at Level One in Dundrum (✆ **01/296-3120**). 14A Chatham St., Temple Bar, Dublin 2. ✆ **01/671-4209.** www.costelloeandcostelloe.com. DART: Tara St. Bus: 68, 69, or 86.

DESIGNyard This beautiful emporium showcases exquisite, often affordable work from the best contemporary Irish jewelry designers. All exhibited pieces are for sale, and you may also make an appointment to commission an original work of Irish applied art and design. 48–49 Nassau St., Dublin 2. ✆ **01/474-1011.** www.designyardgallery.com. DART: Pearse. Bus: 5, 7A, 8, 15A, 15B, 46, 55, 62, 63, 83, or 84.

Shoppers browse the merchandise at Cow's Lane.

GOING TO market

The traditional Dublin method of buying nearly everything has always been at the weekly market. There were weekly vegetable markets, bread markets, meat markets, fish markets . . . in fact, there was a time when there was almost no need to go to a store at all. Look around sleek, modern, retail-loving, credit card–wielding Dublin, and it appears that things have changed, but don't be fooled. Just underneath that facade the truth can be found—Dubliners still love a good market. In fact, there are great markets around, if you know where to look.

You'll find workaday markets like the **Moore Street Market,** where fruit, vegetables, fish, and bread are sold every weekday from 10am to 2pm, on Moore Street on the Northside. Then there are more upscale, gourmet markets, like the **Temple Bar Food Market** every Saturday from 10am to 4:30pm in Meeting House Square. This is where to go for farmhouse cheeses and fresh, homemade breads, jams, and chutneys. For books, try the **Temple Bar Book Market,** weekends in Temple Bar Square from 11am to 6pm—every imaginable topic is wrapped in its pages, and prices are very good.

Finally, if it's all about fashion for you, try the **Designer Mart at Cow's Lane** in the Old City. Here local designers try out their work on a savvy crowd, who pack in knowing they'll get the clothes at much lower prices than in a boutique. It's held every Saturday from 10am to 5pm.

Gollum's Precious This store with the oh-so-good name is a great place to shop for designer jewelry from all over the world, but especially Paris. It's high fashion and good quality, using unusual materials such as plated glass, and colorful silver designs. There's another branch in Glasthule Village, east of Dún Laoghaire (✆ **01/230-4155**). Ground floor, Powerscourt Centre, Dublin 2. ✆ **01/670-5400.** Bus: 10, 11A, 11B, 13, 16A, 19A, 20B, 22A, 55, or 83.

Rhinestones This shop glitters, but don't be fooled—the reasonable prices let you know it's not really gold. Vivien Walsh is considered Ireland's top designer of costume jewelry, and the shop is a seductive place where her contemporary jewelry with an antique feel shines. 18 St. Andrews St., Dublin 2. ✆ **01/679-0759.** Bus: All An Lar (cross-city) buses.

Weir and Sons Established in 1869, this is the granddaddy of Dublin's fine jewelry shops. It sells new and antique jewelry as well as silver, china, and crystal. There are other branches at the ILAC Centre, Henry Street (✆ **01/872-9588**) and in Dundrum (✆ **01/215-7845**). 96–99 Grafton St., Dublin 2. ✆ **01/677-9678.** www.weirandsons.ie. DART: Pearse. Bus: 10, 11A, 11B, 13, or 20B.

Knitwear

Blarney Woollen Mills This branch of the Cork-based enterprise stands opposite the south side of Trinity College. Known for its competitive prices, it stocks a wide range of woolen knitwear made in Blarney, as well as Irish-made crystal, china, pottery, and souvenirs. 21–23 Nassau St., Dublin 2. ✆ **01/671-0068.** DART: Pearse. Bus: 5, 7A, 8, 15A, 15B, 46, 55, 62, 63, 83, or 84.

Dublin Woollen Mills Since 1888, this shop has been a leading source of Aran sweaters, vests, hats, jackets, and scarves, as well as lamb's-wool sweaters, kilts, ponchos, and tweeds at competitive prices. The shop is on the Northside next to the Ha'penny Bridge. 41–42 Lower Ormond Quay, Dublin 1. ✆ **01/828-0301.** www.woollenmills.ie. Bus: 70 or 80.

Monaghan's Established in 1960 and operated by two generations of the Monaghan family, this store is a prime source of cashmere sweaters for men and women. It has a good selection of colors, sizes, and styles. There are also Aran knits, lamb's wool, crochet, and Shetland wool products. 4–5 Royal Hibernian Way, off Dawson St. ✆ **01/679-4451.** DART: Pearse. Bus: 10, 11A, 11B, 13, or 20B.

Powerscourt Townhouse Centre houses more than 60 high-end vendors.

Traditional Irish Music

The Celtic Note Second only to Claddagh Records (below), this is a terrific source of recorded Irish music in Dublin. The staff are experienced and helpful, and you can listen to a CD before purchasing it. You'll pay full price here, but you're likely to find what you're looking for. 12 Nassau St., Dublin 2. ✆ **01/670-4157.** www.celticnote.com. DART: Pearse. Bus: 5, 7A, 15A, 15B, 46, 55, 62, 63, 83, or 84.

Claddagh Records Renowned among insiders in traditional Irish music circles, this is where to find "the genuine article" in traditional music and perhaps discover a new favorite. Not only are the staff knowledgeable and enthusiastic about new artists, but they're also able to tell you which venues and pubs are hosting the best music sessions that week. 2 Cecilia St., Dublin 2. ✆ **01/677-0262.** www.claddaghrecords.com. Bus: 50, 50A, 54, 56, or 77.

DUBLIN AFTER DARK

Nightlife in Dublin is a mixed bag of traditional old pubs, where the likes of Joyce and Behan once imbibed and where Irish music is often reeling away, and cool modern bars, where the repetitive rhythms of techno now fill the air and the crowd knows more about Prada than the Pogues. There's little in the way of crossover, although there are a couple of quieter bars and a few with a rock music angle, so you take your pick. Aside from the eternal elderly pubs, things change rapidly in the world of Dublin nightlife, so pick up a copy of *InDublin* and the *Event Guide* at local cafes and shops if you're looking for the very latest in the club scene. Both have good listings.

The award-winning website of the ***Irish Times*** (**www.ireland.com**) offers a "what's on" daily guide to cinema, theater, music, and whatever else you're up for. The **Dublin Events Guide,** at **www.dublinevents.com,** also provides a comprehensive listing of the week's entertainment possibilities.

Advance bookings for most large concerts, plays, and so forth can be made through **Ticketmaster Ireland** (✆ **081/871-9300** in Ireland or 353/1485-8010 internationally; www.ticketmaster.ie), with ticket centers in most HMV music stores, as well as at the Dublin Tourism Centre, Suffolk Street, Dublin.

The Pub Scene

In *Ulysses,* James Joyce referred to the puzzle of trying to cross Dublin without passing a pub; his characters quickly abandoned the quest as impossible, and stop to sample a few pints instead. You may want to do the same. Here are some of the city's most distinctive public houses.

PUBS FOR CONVERSATION & ATMOSPHERE

Davy Byrnes ★ In *Ulysses,* Leopold Bloom describes this place as a "moral pub," and stops in for a Gorgonzola sandwich and a glass of burgundy. It has drawn poets, writers, and readers ever since. It dates from 1873, when Davy Byrnes first opened the doors—he presided over it for more than 50 years, and visitors can still see his likeness on one of the turn-of-the-20th-century murals hanging over the bar. 21 Duke St. (off Grafton St.), Dublin 2. ✆ **01/677-5217.** www.davybyrnes.com.

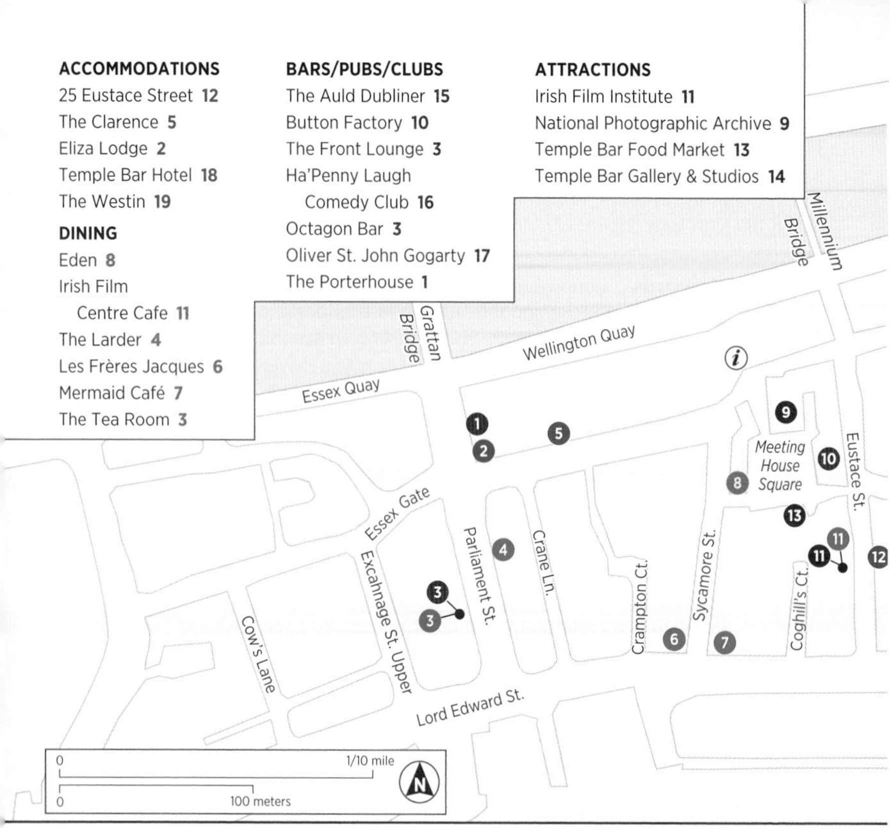

Doheny & Nesbitt ★ Competition is stiff, but this may well be the best-looking traditional pub in town. The Victorian bar houses two fine old "snugs"—small rooms behind the main bar where women could have a drink out of sight of men in days of old—and a restaurant that's good for traditional Irish food. 5 Lower Baggot St., Dublin 2. ✆ **01/676-2945.**

Grogan's Castle Lounge This eclectic place is a bit run-down around the edges, but it's a proper local pub, not heavily frequented by tourists. Its crowd includes local writers and artists (whose work is displayed in higgledy-piggledy fashion on the walls), as well as people who just live around the corner. 15 William St. S., Dublin 2. ✆ **01/677-9320.** www.groganspub.ie.

Kehoe's This tiny traditional bar is best during the day when it's not too crowded

One of Ireland's most handsome pubs, Doheny & Nesbitt features snugs and good traditional Irish food.

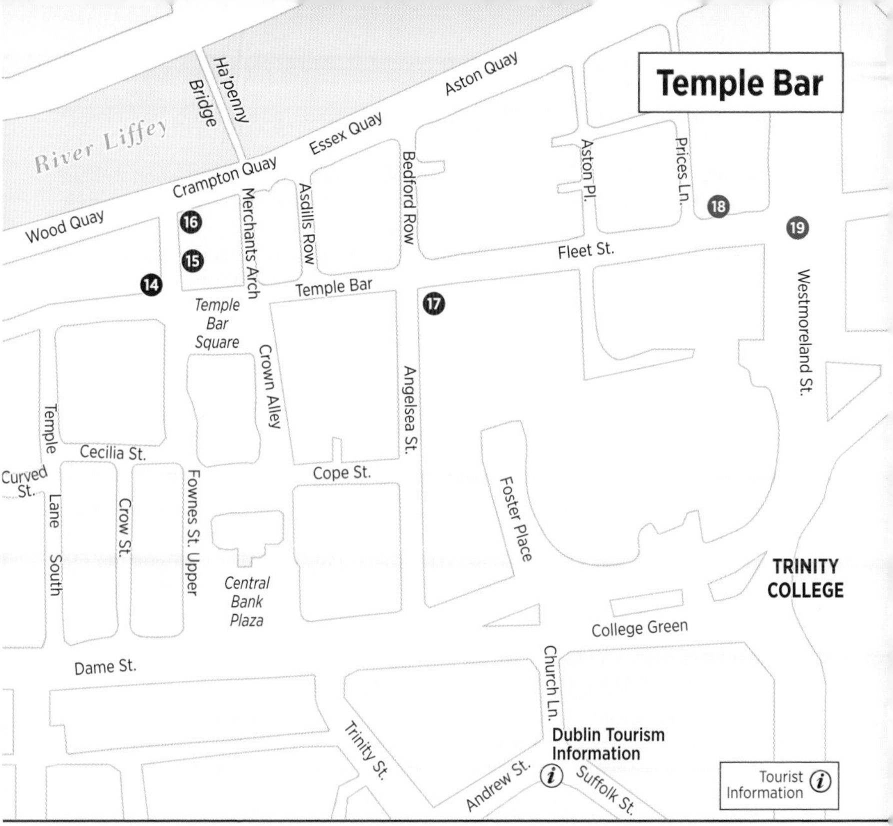

and you can take in its old-fashioned character, eavesdrop on its chatty regulars, and settle in for a pint or two in its comfortable snugs (small private rooms). 9 S. Anne St., Dublin 2. ✆ **01/677-8312.**

The Long Hall This is Doheny & Nesbitt's main competition in the "Prettiest Pub" contest. With a beautiful Victorian decor of filigree-edged mirrors, polished dark woods, and traditional snugs, this place is like a theater of beer. The atmosphere is great and bartenders pour a good pint. 51 S. Great George's St., Dublin 2. ✆ **01/475-1590.**

McDaid's ★ This was Brendan Behan's favorite hangout—well, one of them at least; he had so many back in his Dublin drinking days, and it still has a literary bent. It's well on the tourist track these days, and thus has lost some of its cool cachet. Still, it's got a good atmosphere. 3 Harry St., off Grafton St., Dublin 2. ✆ **01/679-4395.**

Neary's Adjacent to the back door of the Gaiety Theatre, this celebrated enclave is a favorite with stage folk and theatergoers. Its pink-and-gray marble bar and Victorian touches, like the brass

Impressions

I formed a new group called Alcoholics Unanimous. If you don't feel like a drink, you ring another member and he comes over to persuade you.

—Richard Harris

hands that support the globe lanterns by the entrance, give it a touch of class. 1 Chatham St., Dublin 2. ✆ **01/677-8596.**

O'Neill's This friendly place is the pub equivalent of quicksand—you walk in for a quick pint, and before you know it, it's midnight and you've got 20 new best friends. It's big and noisy, but it's made up of a series of smaller rooms and that makes it a pleasant place for conversation. It gets a bit boisterous on the weekends, though. There's live music every night from 9pm. 2 Suffolk St., Dublin 2. ✆ **01/679-3656.** www.oneillsbar.com.

The Porterhouse This was Dublin's first microbrewery pub and it's well worth a visit. Right in the middle of the action in Temple Bar, it offers a constantly changing range of its own ales, lagers, and stouts in a laid-back folksy atmosphere with plenty of room to sit. With a good menu of Irish food (Irish stew, bangers and mash, steak pie) it makes a reasonably priced choice for lunch as well. 16–18 Parliament St., Dublin 2. ✆ **01/679-8847.** www.porterhousebrewco.com.

Stag's Head Mounted stags' heads and eight stag-themed stained-glass windows dominate the decor in this grand old Victorian pub, but it doesn't stop there. There are also wrought-iron chandeliers, polished Aberdeen granite, old barrels, and ceiling-high mirrors. Look for the stag sign inlaid into the sidewalk. This place is a classic. 1 Dame Court (off Dame St.), Dublin 2. ✆ **01/679-3687.** www.louisfitzgerald.com/stagshead.

PUBS FOR TRADITIONAL & FOLK MUSIC

The Auld Dubliner This is a good pub for people who don't normally go to pubs. It's in Temple Bar, so it's central. It's completely relaxed, with bands playing traditional music upstairs, Irish stew on the stove, and quiet pints at the downstairs pub. 24–25 Temple Bar, Dublin 2. ✆ **01/677-0527.**

Brazen Head ★★ In its time, revolutions were plotted in this brass-filled, lantern-lit pub. The Head was licensed in 1661, which makes it one of the oldest pubs in Ireland. (The owners claim it to be *the* oldest, as there was a pub on this site in the 12th c., but it's unclear whether any of the original building is still extant). Nestled on the south bank of the River Liffey, it is at the end of a cobblestone courtyard and was once the meeting place of rebels Robert Emmet and Wolfe Tone. A full a la carte menu is offered and traditional music sessions start at 9:30pm nightly. There's also a popular session from 1:30pm on Sundays, at which customers can get up and sing to a live accompaniment if they're feeling so bold. 20 Lower Bridge St., Dublin 8. ✆ **01/679-9549.** www.brazenhead.com.

Listen to the Music . . .

When you're out for a night of traditional Irish/folk music, you should know that some pubs charge and some do not; if the band is playing informally in the main bar, as often happens, there's no charge, although they will probably pass a hat at some point, and everybody should toss in a few euros. If there is a charge, the music usually happens in a separate room from the main pub, and the charge will be noted on the door; usually it's €5 to €7, and you pay as you go in, cash only. And, don't worry. If they're selling CDs they'll make sure you know about it. (They'll probably autograph them too, after the set.)

From 1661, the Brazen Head is one of Ireland's oldest watering holes.

The Cobblestone This is the most Irish of Irish pubs, with a musicians' corner downstairs where traditional Irish music is played for free every night (and from 2pm Sun), and a proper music hall upstairs where you have to buy tickets, but the bands are top-notch. It's one of the places where the locals go to hear music, so expect to find none of what they call "paddy-whackery." 77 King St. N., Dublin 7. ✆ **01/872-1799.** www.cobblestonepub.ie.

The Merry Ploughboy Well worth the trip into the 'burbs, this popular pub and restaurant is owned and run by the musicians who play there. There's a show with live music and Irish dancing sessions every night at 8:30pm (Mar–Nov; €20, or €55 with dinner and bus transfer to and from the city center). There are also free, informal music sessions in the downstairs bar every Friday and Saturday at 9:30pm until around 12:30am. Traditional Irish food is served in the restaurant, and the *craic* is lively. Make sure you have enough money for a taxi if you stay after midnight—public transport is virtually nonexistent around here in these parts. The bar staff will call you one, or try **Xpert Taxis** (✆ **01/677-0777**), who give a 20% discount for all journeys to and from the pub. Edmondstown Rd., Rathfarnham, Dublin 16. ✆ **01/493-1495.** www.mpbpub.com.

O'Donoghue's Tucked between St. Stephen's Green and Merrion Street, this enclave is widely heralded as the granddaddy of traditional-music pubs. A spontaneous session is likely to erupt at almost any time of the day or night, but it's become very touristy, and we don't consider it local or authentic in terms of clientele. They put on a show for tourists, and it's a bit dull compared to some of the more authentic places. 15 Merrion Row, Dublin 2. ✆ **01/660-7194.** www.odonoghues.ie.

Oliver St. John Gogarty ★ In the heart of Temple Bar and named for one of Ireland's literary greats, this pub has an inviting old-world atmosphere, with shelves of empty bottles, stacks of dusty books, a horseshoe-shaped bar, and old barrels for seats. There are free traditional-music sessions almost every day from 2:30pm to 2am, Monday to Friday. 58–59 Fleet St., Dublin 2. ✆ **01/671-1822.** www.gogartys.ie.

Bars & Nightclubs

Over the last few years, cocktail bars and nightclubs have been springing up around Dublin like daffodils in spring. The nightclub scene is confoundingly

STAYING UP late

Traditionally, pubs close early in Ireland (at 11pm in winter, 11:30pm–12:30am in summer), and for many, that's too soon to call it a night. If you're in that group, you might want to crawl to one of the many late-night pubs and bars. These boozers have received legal permission to remain open after hours, usually until 2 or 3am.

One popular late-nighter for the 18-to-25 set is the **Capitol,** 18 Lower Stephen's St., Dublin 2 (✆ **01/475-7166;** www.capitol.ie).

After-hours pubs that attract the young and hip but are still congenial for those over 25 include **Whelan's,** 25 Wexford St., Dublin 2 (✆ **01/478-0766;** www.whelanslive.com), and the second-oldest pub in Dublin, the **Bleeding Horse,** 24–25 Camden St., Dublin 2 (✆ **01/475-2705**).

For the over-30 late crowd, try **Dakota,** 9 William St., Dublin 2 (✆ **01/672-7696;** www.dakotabar.ie), and **Sinnotts,** South King Street, Dublin 2 (✆ **01/478-4698;** www.sinnotts.ie).

complex. One club could be a gay fetish scene one night and techno-pop dance the next, so you have to stay on your toes. The first rule is to get the latest listings from local sources (see the introduction to "Dublin After Dark" earlier for options).

The hottest clubs have a "strict" (read: unfriendly) door policy of admitting only "regulars." Your chances of getting past the door increase if you're female and wear your hippest clothes.

Cover charges tend to fluctuate from place to place and from night to night and even from person to person (some people can't buy their way in, while others glide in gratis). In other words, clubbing here is pretty much like any other fashionable capital city. Cover charges range from nothing to around €25 and can vary nightly.

Owned by a drag queen named Pandora "Panti" Bliss, the eponymous Panti Bar draws a gay and lesbian crowd, among others.

BARS FOR MIXING, MINGLING & CHATTING

These are modern cocktail bars, where the kind of financially successful, under-40 person who wouldn't be caught dead in a pub goes for a drink.

Ba Mizu This bar draws the young, glamorous set. The clientele includes a regular smattering of models (both male and female) and trendy urbanites. Powerscourt Townhouse Centre, William St. S., Dublin 2. ✆ **01/674-6712.** www.bamizu.com.

The Bank on College Green As the name implies, this bar is in a converted bank building, and that is somehow appropriate, given that the crowd is made up largely of professionals in very expensive shoes—although they tend not to be buying such expensive rounds these days. It's got a good reputation, and it's a gorgeous, vast space. 20–22 College Green, Dublin 2. ✆ **01/677-0677.** www.bankoncollege green.com.

Bruxelles Actually three separate bars in one, Bruxelles is one of Dublin's late-night hangouts, staying open until 2:30am on weekends. Its crowd tends to be well lubricated and therefore overly friendly. This isn't a particularly stylish place, but it's very popular with locals. 7–8 Harry St., off Grafton St., Dublin 2. ✆ **01/677-5362.** www.bruxelles.ie.

Café en Seine This vast bar packs in thousands of young, well-dressed local professionals, and yet it never seems crowded. It's a gorgeous turn-of-the-20th-century building, with plenty of architectural detail, but nobody who comes here regularly cares. They're here for the booze and each other. 40 Dawson St., Dublin 2. ✆ **01/677-4567.** www.cafeenseine.ie.

The Market Bar This is what they call around here a "superpub," but it's really a just a big, laid-back bar, with a soaring ceiling, gorgeous design, a good beer and wine list, and friendly staff. This is the kind of place where you could sit in the late afternoon and have a solitary pint and nobody would bother you. Its no-music policy means that it's quiet enough to hear yourself drink. 14a Fade St., off S. Great George's St., Dublin 2. ✆ **01/613-9094.** www.marketbar.ie.

Mint Bar A sophisticated cocktail bar in the basement of the Westin Hotel, this is suitable for a quiet drink, probably at the end of a long night, as this place stays open until 2am on Friday and Saturday. The cocktail menu is imaginative but pricey; a kind of one-for-the-road with style. The Westin Hotel, College Green, Dublin 2. ✆ **01/645-1322.** www.thewestindublin.com/the-mint-bar.

Octagon Bar This trendy bar on the ground floor of the Clarence hotel is one of the hottest places in town. It's got an eight-sided bar, which the bartenders handle with aplomb, and you don't have to be rich or beautiful to get in. There's a quieter back room and prices are not as high as they could be. It's a favorite celebrity hangout in Dublin, and a blessedly unpretentious one. The Clarence, 6–8 Wellington Quay, Dublin 2. ✆ **01/407-0800.** www.theclarence.ie.

DANCE CLUBS

Howl at the Moon A huge multi-level bar/club, this draws in a fun young crowd with DJs playing popular dance tracks with nothing too techno. There's no cover charge before 11pm on Saturday, 11:30pm on Friday, and all night Thursday. There's a small outdoor terrace and different areas with varied decor, some sofas, and some bar stools, which make it cozy. Open Thursday from 4 to 2:30am, Friday from 4pm to 3am, and on Saturday from 8pm to 3am. Lower Mount St., Dublin 2. ✆ **01/634-5460.** www.howlatthemoon.ie.

Lillie's Bordello With its red walls and (we hope) ironic erotica, this used to be the celeb hangout of choice in

The Octagon Bar in the Clarence hotel draws celebrities, but not to the exclusion of regular folk.

Dublin. In fact, its impact has worn off somewhat, but that's good news for those who don't want to talk their way past doormen; anyone well turned-out will probably get in. It still has its fair share of poseurs and wannabes, but it's a good spot for a cocktail if you go in with an "up for it" attitude. If you don't feel like dancing, head for "the Library," where floor-to-ceiling bookcases and well-worn leather Chesterfields evoke a Victorian gentlemen's club. Open daily 11pm to 2:30am. Adam Court, off Grafton St., Dublin 2. ✆ **01/679-9204.** www.lilliesbordello.ie.

Rí-Rá The name means "uproar" in Irish, and it's appropriate. Though trendy, Rí-Rá has a friendlier door policy than most of its competition, so this may be the place to try first. DJs and bands perform live downstairs, while upstairs is the (marginally) more relaxed Globe Bar. Open Monday to Saturday from 11pm to 2:30am. No cover charge. Dame Court, Dublin 2. ✆ **01/671-1220.** www.rira.ie.

Comedy Clubs

Besides the favorite clubs listed below, **Vicar Street** (see the box, "Smaller Concert Venues," below) tends to get many of the international comics. As always, check the latest listings in magazines for details. Admission ranges from €5 to around €25 depending on the act and the night.

Ha'Penny Laugh Comedy Club Ha'Penny plays host to some of Ireland's funniest people, many of whom are in theater. "The Battle of the Axe" is a weekly show in which comedians, singers, songwriters, musicians, actors, and others storm the open mic in pursuit of the Lucky Duck Award. Tickets cost €9. Ha'penny Bridge Inn, Merchant's Arch, 42 Wellington Quay, Dublin 2. ✆ **086/815-6987.** www.battleoftheaxe.com.

International Bar This legendary bar hosts live comedy on every night of the week. Monday is improv night; new comedy showcases on Tuesdays; on Wednesdays it's the Comedy Cellar (which, you'll be unsurprised to learn, is held upstairs); the International Comedy Club is in residence from Thursday to Saturday; and Sunday is devoted to established comics performing works-in-progress and generally riffing on whatever tickles their fancy. 23 Wicklow St., Dublin 2. ✆ **01/677-9250.** www.international-bar.com.

Dinner Shows & Traditional Irish Entertainment

Abbey Tavern After you've ordered an a la carte dinner, the show—authentic Irish ballad music, with its blend of fiddles, pipes, tin whistles, and spoons—costs €15, which includes an Irish coffee. The price of dinner and show starts at around €42. The box office is open Monday to Saturday from 9am to 5pm. Dinner is at 7pm, and shows start at 9pm. There are shows nightly in summer; in the off season, call ahead for the schedule. Abbey Rd., Howth, County Dublin. ✆ **01/839-0307.** www.abbeytavern.ie. Bus: 31 or 31B.

Cultúrlann na hÉireann This is the home of Comhaltas Ceoltoiri Éireann, an Irish cultural organization that has been the prime mover in encouraging Irish traditional music. The programs include *Céilí* dances, informal recitals, and full-blown music festivals. They also hold regular "tempo sessions" (jam sessions) every Tuesday at 9:15pm, which musicians of all abilities are free to join in (as long as you can hold a tune!). No reservations are necessary for any of the events. 32 Belgrave Sq., Monkstown, County Dublin. ✆ **01/280-0295.** www.comhaltas.com. Tickets for *Céilís* average €5–€10, informal music around €4, shows €20. DART: Monkstown. Bus: 7, 7A, or 8.

The Gay & Lesbian Scene

The gay scene in Dublin has expanded by leaps and bounds in the last decade, from absolutely nothing, to small but sturdy. Due to the country's traditional conservatism, it's unlikely this will ever be an Ibiza-level gay zone, but there are high-quality gay bars and regular gay nights at local dance clubs. Hotels accept same-sex couples without raising an eyebrow. However, the aforementioned conservatism means that it's not a great idea for same-sex couples to hold hands or cuddle on the street, and keeping a low profile when wandering with your gay friends from restaurant to bar isn't a bad idea. Think small-town America, and you'll get the idea.

Cover charges range from €5 to around €20, depending on the club or venue, with discounts for students and seniors.

Check the ***Gay Community News*** (www.gcn.ie) or **Gay Ireland Online** (www.gay-ireland.com) to find out what's going on during your stay. Folks on the helpline **Gay Switchboard Dublin** (✆ **01/872-1055;** www.gayswitchboard.ie) can direct you to activities of particular interest.

Since 1994, LGBTQ people have been stopping by the **Outhouse** (105 Capel St.; ✆ **01/873-4999;** www.outhouse.ie) for information, advice, and a cup of tea or coffee. There's a cafe, meeting rooms (groups from AA to Gay Trekkies meet here), a library, and free Internet access, as well as endless information and a referral service. It's open 7 days a week, and is a vital resource in gay Dublin.

The Dragon ★ This is the biggest, shiniest gay bar in Dublin. It's a two-level affair with a raucous first floor, complete with dance floor and all-ages crowd shouting to be heard over the thumping music, and a quieter upstairs area with lots of cozy nooks for whispering sweet nothings. It has a more upscale crowd than its funkier sister-bar, the George (see below). S. Great Georges St., Dublin 2. ✆ **01/478-1590.**

The Front Lounge This modern bar sprawls across several levels, with wide windows overlooking the hustle and bustle of Temple Bar. The crowd is a friendly, mixed gay/straight clientele. The look here is nice shoes, just the right amount of stubble, and expensive hair gel. You can get a decent mixed drink here, which isn't always the case at the George or the Dragon. 33–34 Parliament St., Temple Bar, Dublin 2. ✆ **01/670-4112.**

The George This is Dublin's most established gay bar, and it tends to be packed most nights with a laid-back, cheerful crowd, mixing mostly locals with savvy tourists. It's a quiet haven during the day, and a good place to sit and have a coffee, but late at night there's a DJ, and tables are pushed back for dancing. If you're gay and visiting Dublin, this is the place you're looking for. 89 S. Great George's St., Dublin 2. ✆ **01/478-2983.** www.capitalbars.com.

Panti Bar This fun, casual joint is run by Pandora "Panti" Bliss, a drag queen with great affection for Dolly Parton. It's a smallish place, with a sort of rec room in the basement and a program of regular events (which the management refers to as "7 Days for Gays") including a cabaret show on Thursday and dance classes on Wednesdays. Panti also has self-catering apartments to rent in central Dublin for €70 per night weekdays, €120 per night weekends; check the website for details. 7–8 Capel St., Dublin 1. ✆ **01/874-0710.** www.pantibar.com.

The Performing Arts

THEATER

With a heritage extending from the likes of George Bernard Shaw, Dublin has a venerable and vital theatrical tradition. Homegrown talent has kept the many theaters here alive, whether it's actors like Colin Farrell or writers like Marina Carr *(By the Bog of Cats)* and Marie Jones *(Stones in His Pockets)*. Complementing the talent are beautiful, historic theaters so vaingloriously gilded that they make every performance an event. Most theaters are within the city's Northside, not far off the river.

There are also numerous theater festivals, ranging from the **Dublin Fringe Festival** each September (**www.fringefest.com**) to the **Dublin Gay Theatre Festival** (**www.gaytheatre.ie**) held the first 2 weeks of May.

The online booking site **Ticketmaster** (www.ticketmaster.ie) is an excellent place to get a quick look at what's playing where and also to buy tickets. In addition to the major theaters listed below, other venues present fewer, although on occasion quite impressive, productions. They also book music, dance, and stand-up comedy performances. They include the **Focus Theatre,** 12 Fade St., Dublin 2 (✆ **01/671-2417;** www.focustheatre.ie); the **Olympia,** 72 Dame St., Dublin 2 (✆ **01/679-3323;** www.mcd.ie); **Project,** 39 E. Essex St., Dublin 2 (✆ **01/881-9613;** www.project.ie); and the **Tivoli,** 135–138 Francis St., opposite Iveagh Market, Dublin 8 (✆ **01/454-4472;** www.tivoli.ie).

Abbey Theatre Since 1903, the Abbey has been the national theater of Ireland. The original theater, destroyed by fire in 1951, was replaced in 1966 by the current functional, although uninspired, 492-seat house. The Abbey's artistic reputation has risen and fallen many times, but is reasonably strong at the moment. In addition to its main stage, the theater also has a 127-seat basement studio, the **Peacock** (see below), where it presents newer/more experimental work. Lower Abbey St., Dublin 1. ✆ **01/878-7222.** www.abbeytheatre.ie. Tickets €15–€40. Senior, student, and children's discounts available Mon–Thurs evening and Sat matinee. Bus: 130, 142, or 33.

Cofounded by William Butler Yeats, the Abby Theatre is still going strong in the 21st century.

Gaiety The elegant little Gaiety holds a varied array of performances, including everything from opera to classical Irish plays to Broadway-style musicals and variety acts. King St. S., Dublin 2. ✆ **01/677-1717.** www.gaietytheatre.com. Tickets €20–€55. LUAS: St. Stephen's Green.

The Gate Just north of O'Connell Street off Parnell Square, this recently restored 370-seat theater was founded in 1928 by Irish actors Hilton Edwards and Michael MacLiammoir to provide a venue for a broad range of plays. That policy prevails today, with a program that includes a blend of modern works and the classics. Although less known by visitors, the Gate is easily as distinguished as the Abbey. 1 Cavendish Row, Dublin 1. ✆ **01/874-4045.** www.gate-theatre.ie. Tickets €15–€35.

The Grand Canal Theatre Dublin's newest major theatre (it debuted in late 2010), the Grand Canal is an intimate venue (seating 2,200) for ballet, classical music, rock 'n' roll—anything that sits well in a glittering new theatre with exquisite acoustics and perfect sightlines. Designed by New York architect Daniel Libeskind, the iconic, crooked theater building slants *louchely* on the edge of the canal in the Docklands. Grand Canal Square, Dublin 1. ✆ **01/677-7999.** www.grandcanaltheatre.ie. Tickets €15–€25.

The Peacock In the same building as the Abbey, this 150-seat theater features contemporary plays and experimental works. It books poetry readings and one-person shows, as well as plays in the Irish language. Lower Abbey St., Dublin 1. ✆ **01/878-7222.** www.abbeytheatre.ie. Tickets €15–€25.

CONCERTS

On any given night, you can find almost anything—rock, pop, jazz, blues, traditional Irish, country, or folk, so check listings magazines to find out what's on where. Music and dance concerts take place in a range of venues—theaters, churches, clubs, museums, stadiums, castles, parks, and universities. While you're more likely to choose your entertainment based on the performer rather than the venue, these institutions stand out.

The Helix This massive auditorium at University College Dublin hosts many concerts throughout the year. The box office is open Monday to Friday 10am to 6pm. Collins Ave., Glasnevin, Dublin 9. ✆ **01/700-7000.** www.helix.ie. Tickets €17–€60. Bus: 11, 11A, 11B, 13, 13A, or 19A.

National Concert Hall This 1,200-seat hall is home to the National Symphony Orchestra and Concert Orchestra, and it hosts dozens of international orchestras and performing artists. In addition to classical music, there are Broadway-style musicals, opera, jazz, and lunchtime concerts. The box office is open Monday to Friday from 10am to 3pm and from 6pm to close of concert. Open

SMALLER CONCERT venues

If you prefer more intimate settings, below are some of the best small venues in Dublin. The Village is among the newest and hottest; Whelan's and Vicar Street are the old favorites. (For what it's worth, Vicar Street was named "live music venue of the year" in 2008 by the prestigious Irish Music organization.) Check local listings, or the individual websites, to find out what's on when you're in town:

- **Button Factory,** Temple Bar, Dublin 2 (✆ **01/670-9202;** www.buttonfactory.ie)
- **Vicar Street,** 58–59 Thomas St., Dublin 8 (✆ **01/454-5533;** www.aikenpromotions.com)
- **Whelan's,** 25 Wexford St., Dublin 2 (✆ **1890/200-078** or 01/478-0766; www.whelanslive.com)
- **Eamonn Doran's,** 3A Crown Alley, Temple Bar, Dublin 2 (✆ **01/679-9114;** eamonndoransbookings@gmail.com)
- **The Village,** 26 Wexford St., Dublin 2 (✆ **1890/200-078** or 01/475-8555; www.thevillagevenue.com)

weekends 1 hour before concerts. Parking is available on the street. Earlsfort Terrace, Dublin 2. ✆ **01/417-0000.** www.nch.ie. Tickets €11–€50. DART: Pearse. Bus: 10, 11, 13, 14, 15, 27C, 44, 46A, 46B, 48A, or 86.

The O2 The venue formerly known as the Point Theatre has been reborn—and rebranded—as this enormous indoor concert space. The face-lift has given the place a new lease on life, and international acts are the name of the game here now. You can also catch big-name stand-up comedy shows and other high-profile events here; it's all top-of-the-bill stuff. All ticket sales are handled by **Ticketmaster** (✆ **081/871-9300**). There is no parking at the O2; the nearest parking lots are at Custom House Quay, the National College of Ireland, and Connolly train station. East Link Bridge, North Wall Quay. ✆ **01/819-8888** for information. www.theo2.ie. Tickets €30–€100. Bus: 53.

SIDE TRIPS FROM DUBLIN

Dublin's suburbs stretch out for miles along the coastline of Dublin Bay. Within a 15- to 20-minute DART ride or a 30-minute drive from the city center, they have ocean breezes and sweeping views of the rocky coastline. They also have lots to see, including castles, museums, and literary sights. If all else fails, you can always spend an afternoon playing in the sand.

Dublin's Southern Suburbs

Heading southward along the bay, the bustling harbor town of **Dún Laoghaire** (pronounced Dun *Lear*-y) is quickly followed by the more upscale seaside towns of **Dalkey** and **Killiney.** All have been collectively nicknamed "Bel Eire" for their beauty and for the density of Irish celebrity residents. You could spend an afternoon wandering all three, or just pick one and linger there for a day. Dún Laoghaire has lots of shopping, as well as a long promenade and a bucolic park. Killiney has a picturesque, cliff-backed expanse of beach. Pretty little Dalkey is a heritage town with two tiny castle towers, a lovely medieval streetscape, and lots of charming pubs, gourmet restaurants, and pricey little boutiques.

If you're traveling to Ireland by ferry from Holyhead, Wales, your first glimpse of Ireland will be the port of Dún Laoghaire. Many people decide to base themselves here and commute into Dublin each day. It's certainly quieter and more picturesque; if you're not staying out late at night (the trains stop running just before midnight, and a taxi will cost quite a lot), you'll save some money over similar luxe accommodations in Central Dublin. And therein lies some really good news for travelers (though not so much for the local economy): hotel prices in these districts have *plummeted* in the last year or two. Top hotels that previously charged hundreds of euros per night, now cost a fraction of that—often under €100, even in high season, which puts some extremely fine places to stay within reach of those without money to burn.

SEEING THE SIGHTS

Dalkey Castle and Heritage Centre Housed in a 15th-century tower house, the center tells the history of this venerable town in a few sweet, if unsophisticated, displays. There are tours, in which guides tell the tale of the building, but the level of detail can be a bit more than you need to know. You might prefer to duck out of the tour and take in the view from the battlements instead. Adjoining the center is a medieval graveyard and the Church of St. Begnet,

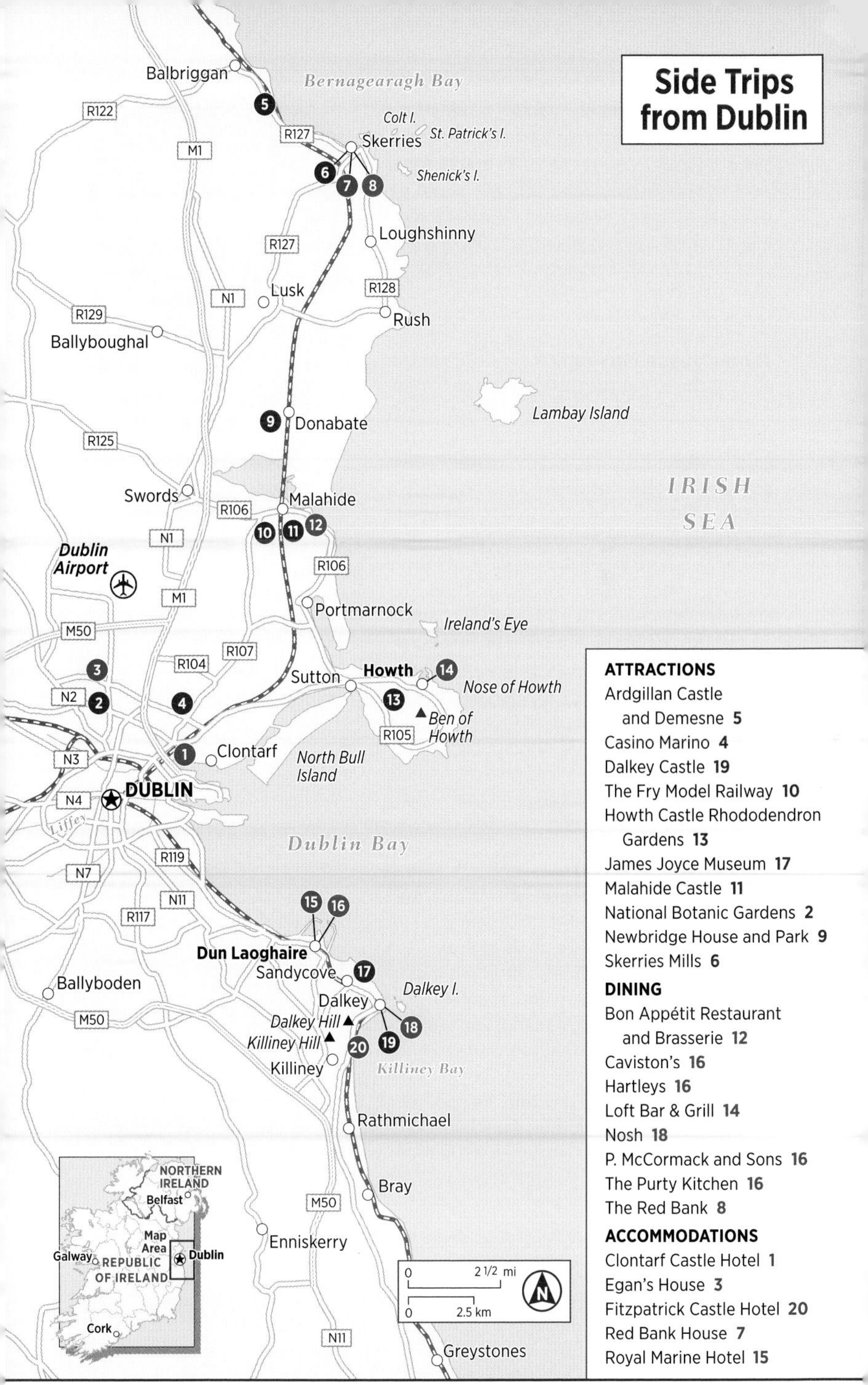
Side Trips from Dublin
Balbriggan
Bernagearagh Bay
R122
M1
R127
Colt I.
St. Patrick's I.
Skerries
Shenick's I.
Loughshinny
R127
N1
Lusk
R128
Rush
R129
Ballyboughal
Lambay Island
Donabate
R125
IRISH SEA
Swords
R106
Malahide
N1
Dublin Airport
R106
M1
Portmarnock
Ireland's Eye
M50
R107
R104
Sutton
Howth
Nose of Howth
N2
Ben of Howth
R105
Clontarf
North Bull Island
N3
N4
DUBLIN
Liffey
Dublin Bay
R119
N7
N11
R117
Dun Laoghaire
Sandycove
Ballyboden
Dalkey
Dalkey I.
M50
Dalkey Hill
Killiney Hill
Killiney
Killiney Bay
Rathmichael
NORTHERN IRELAND
Belfast
Map Area
Galway
REPUBLIC OF IRELAND
Dublin
Cork
M50
Bray
Enniskerry
0 2 1/2 mi
0 2.5 km
N
N11
Greystones
ATTRACTIONS
Ardgillan Castle and Demesne 5
Casino Marino 4
Dalkey Castle 19
The Fry Model Railway 10
Howth Castle Rhododendron Gardens 13
James Joyce Museum 17
Malahide Castle 11
National Botanic Gardens 2
Newbridge House and Park 9
Skerries Mills 6
DINING
Bon Appétit Restaurant and Brasserie 12
Caviston's 16
Hartleys 16
Loft Bar & Grill 14
Nosh 18
P. McCormack and Sons 16
The Purty Kitchen 16
The Red Bank 8
ACCOMMODATIONS
Clontarf Castle Hotel 1
Egan's House 3
Fitzpatrick Castle Hotel 20
Red Bank House 7
Royal Marine Hotel 15

Dalkey's patron saint, whose foundations date back to Ireland's early Christian period.

Castle St., Dalkey, County Dublin. ✆ **01/285-8366.** www.dalkeycastle.com. Admission €6 adults; €5 seniors and students; €4 children; €16 families. May–Aug Mon and Wed–Fri 10am–6pm, Sat–Sun and public holidays 11am–6pm; Sept–Apr Mon–Fri 10am–5pm, Sat–Sun and public holidays 11am–5pm. Last tour 45 min. before closing. DART: Dalkey. Bus: 8.

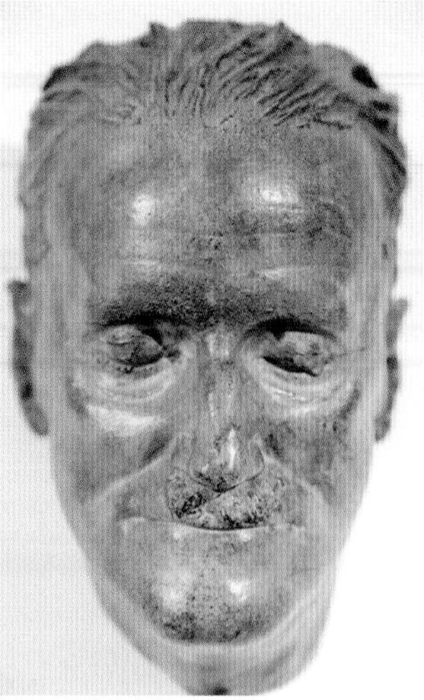

The author of Ulysses once lived and worked in the tower that houses the James Joyce Museum in Sandycove.

James Joyce Museum ★ Sitting on the edge of the bay at the little suburb of Sandycove, this 12m (39-ft.) Martello tower was one of a series of stone structures built in the early 19th century to guard the island against an anticipated invasion by Napoleon's troops. When the threat passed, many of the towers were converted into homes. James Joyce lived here in 1904 as a guest of Oliver Gogarty, who rented the tower from the army for an annual fee of £8 (then about $1.60). Joyce put the tower in the first chapter of *Ulysses* and it has been known as Joyce's Tower ever since. Its collection of memorabilia includes letters, documents, first and rare editions, personal possessions, and photographs. There's a nice small gift shop.

Sandycove, County Dublin. ✆ **01/280-9265.** Admission €6 adults; €5 seniors and students; €4 children 11 and under; €15 families. Combination tickets with Malahide Castle, Fry Model Railway, Dublin Writers Museum, or Shaw Birthplace available. Apr–Aug Tues–Sat 10am–1pm and 2–5pm, Sun 2–6pm; call for off-season hours. DART: Sandycove. Bus: 8.

WHERE TO STAY

Fitzpatrick Castle Hotel ★ With a Victorian facade of turrets, towers, and battlements, this restored 1741 gem is an ideal choice for those who have always wanted to live in a castle. A short drive from the center of the city, it is between Dalkey and Killiney, amid hilltop grounds with clear views of Dublin Bay. It's a marvelous old building, with a wandering lobby that seems to go on forever, filled with comfortable sofas, a piano, and working fireplaces. There's an excellent bar, with leather chairs to sink into, and two good restaurants—**P.J.'s** for upscale dining, and downstairs, the casual and good **Dungeon Restaurant,** for less formal meals. Book online if possible, as good deals are often available. If you prefer more privacy, ask about their guesthouses. Check the website for special offers—as this book was being written, a €400 room was going for €90.

Killiney Hill Rd., Killiney, County Dublin. www.fitzpatrickcastle.com. ✆ **01/230-5400.** Fax 01/230-5430. 113 units. €90–€180 double. Breakfast €12. AE, DC, MC, V. DART: Dalkey. Bus: 59. **Amenities:** 2 restaurants; bar; concierge; guest privileges at nearby 18-hole golf course; gym; indoor pool; room service; saunas; steam room; smoke-free rooms. *In room:* TV, hair dryer.

Royal Marine Hotel ★ 🎁 This grand Victorian hotel (Queen Victoria herself visited it on occasion) reopened in 2009 after a major refurbishment that restored its noble historic structure, and expanded it with a less gorgeous seven-story modern extension. Rooms are simply decorated in contemporary, largely bland style with an emphasis on earth tones, but many have sweeping sea views and balconies. The excellent **sansanaSPA** will work the kinks out, as will a cocktail from the stylish **Pavilion** bar. Locals flock to the weekend breakfast buffet in the restaurant. Its location close to the station makes this a good option for those who want to visit Dublin but not pay five-star Dublin hotel prices. A couple of readers have complained about noise, so you should ask for a quiet room when booking.

Marine Rd., Dún Laoghaire, County Dublin. www.royalmarine.ie. ✆ **01/230-0030.** 227 units. €90–€140 double. AE, MC, V. DART: Dún Laoghaire. **Amenities:** 2 restaurants; 2 bars; concierge; gym; room service; smoke-free rooms; spa. *In room:* TV, hair dryer, free Wi-Fi.

WHERE TO EAT

Expensive

Hartleys INTERNATIONAL This popular restaurant sits squarely in the bustle of Dún Laoghaire's busy seafront. Elegantly converted from the old railway terminal building, it packs in crowds for a varied menu of pasta, salads, steaks, burgers, and grilled seafood. The food can be hit-or-miss, but the atmosphere is unbeatable, and that's what seems to draw in most people.

1 Harbour Rd., Dún Laoghaire, County Dublin. ✆ **01/280-6767.** Reservations required. Fixed-price lunch and evening menu: 2 courses €25, 3 courses €30 (only available until 7:30pm Sat–Sun); dinner main courses €15–€29. AE, DC, MC, V. Mon–Thurs noon–3:30pm and 5:30–10pm; Fri–Sat noon–10pm; Sun noon–9pm. DART: Dún Laoghaire. Bus: 7, 7A, 8, or 46A.

Moderate

Caviston's ★★ SEAFOOD Fresh, fresh fish is the hallmark of this tiny lunch spot in Sandycove, run by the Caviston family, whose neighboring fish shop is legendary. The menu changes daily, but might include roast monkfish with pasta in a saffron-and-basil sauce, chargrilled salmon with béarnaise, or marinated red mullet with roasted red peppers. Three lunchtime sittings can make for frantic service, so your best bet is to arrive at noon sharp, before things get too hectic. Caviston's also has an adjoining deli, the **Food Emporium**—for quality picnic supplies.

59 Glasthule Rd., Sandycove, County Dublin. ✆ **01/280-9245.** www.cavistons.com. Reservations recommended. Main courses €19–€30. DC, MC, V. Tues–Thurs 3 sittings noon–5pm; Fri–Sat 5 sittings noon–10:30pm. DART: Dún Laoghaire.

Nosh ★★ INTERNATIONAL This light, bright, and buzzing restaurant is so laid-back that it has plastic chairs, and yet it delivers the sort of hit-the-spot food that you wish you could get every day: French toast with bacon, bananas, and maple syrup; wonderful soups; and big club sandwiches or salads. For dinner, there may be roast guinea fowl with peanut and sage stuffing, or pan-fried hake with chorizo risotto, plus a short-but-sweet wine list. Weekend brunch is simply fabulous here.

111 Coliemore Rd., Dalkey, County Dublin. ✆ **01/284-0666.** www.nosh.ie. Reservations recommended. Fixed-price early-bird menus (available all night Sun–Thurs): 2 courses €21, 3 courses €24; brunch and lunch dishes €4.50–€15; dinner main courses €17–€28. MC, V. Tues–Sun noon–4pm and 6–10pm. DART: Dalkey.

PUBS

P. McCormack and Sons ★ The main bar at this popular pub has an old-world feel, with globe lamps, stained-glass windows, books, and jugs on the shelves, and lots of nooks and crannies for a quiet drink. In the sky-lit, plant-filled conservatory area, classical music fills the air, and outdoors you'll find a courtyard beer garden. The pub grub here (served noon–3pm and 4–10pm daily) is top-notch, with a varied buffet table of lunchtime salads and meats.

67 Lower Mounttown Rd. (off York Rd.), Dún Laoghaire, County Dublin. ✆ **01/280-5519.** DART: Dún Laoghaire.

The Purty Kitchen ★ Housed in a building that dates from 1728, this old pub is thought to stand at what was once the center of "Dunleery," the old village that all but disappeared when modern Dún Laoghaire was built in the 1820s. The atmosphere is homey, with an open brick fireplace, cozy alcoves, and a large wall mural. There's always something going on—perhaps a session of Irish traditional music in the main bar area, while upstairs in the **Loft** nightclub there could be live blues, or a DJ spinning dance music. The food is great here as well. Call ahead or check the website for entertainment details.

5 Old Dunleary Rd., Dún Laoghaire, County Dublin. ✆ **01/284-3576.** www.purtykitchen.com. No cover for traditional music; cover €6–€10 for blues in the Loft.

Dublin's Northern Suburbs

Dublin's northern suburbs make a convenient base for travelers via **Dublin International Airport,** and there's much to do here, with a delightful assortment of castles, historic buildings, gardens, and the beach to keep you busy. The towns of **Drumcondra** and **Glasnevin** have good hotels.

Just north of Dublin, the picturesque suburbs of **Howth** and **Malahide** offer panoramic views of Dublin Bay, beautiful hillside gardens, and many fine seafood restaurants. Best of all, they are easily reached on the DART. Farther north along the coast, but only 20 minutes from Dublin Airport, lies the bustling and attractive harbor town of **Skerries ★**. Skerries is a convenient and appealing spot to spend your first or last night in Ireland; or stay longer and explore all this area has to offer, including a resident colony of gray seals.

SEEING THE SIGHTS

Ardgillan Castle and Demesne ★ Between Balbriggan and Skerries, this 18th-century castellated country house sits on the coastline on sumptuously manicured lawns. The house was built in 1738 and contains some fine period furnishings and antiques. But the real draw is the setting, at the edge of the wild Irish Sea, with miles of walking paths and coastal views, as well as a rose garden and an herb garden. Behind the lavish rose garden, there's a nice cafe for a quick bite or some ice cream.

Balbriggan, County Dublin. ✆ **01/849-2212.** www.ardgillanskerries.com. Admission to house €7 adults; €5 seniors and students; €14 families. Guided tours June–Aug Thurs 3:30pm. Castle July–Aug daily 11am–6pm; Sept and Apr–June Tues–Sun and public holidays 11am–6pm; Oct–Mar Sun and public holidays 11am–4:30pm. Park daily 10am–dusk. Closed last week in Dec. Free parking. Signposted off N1. Bus: 33.

Casino Marino A casino in the 18th-century sense of the word (meaning "small house"), this charming structure is located in the once-bucolic suburb of Marino, just off the Malahide Road. Designed by Sir William Chambers as a pleasure house for his garden, it is a fine 18th-century neoclassical structure. While it looks tiny from the outside, it somehow manages to contain 16 finely decorated rooms.

Malahide Rd., Marino, Dublin 3. ✆ **01/833-1618.** Admission €3 adults; €2.10 seniors; €1.10 students and children; €8 families. Late Apr to Oct daily 10am–5pm. Last admission 45 min. before closing. Bus: 20A, 20B, 27, 27A, 27B, 42, 42B, or 42C.

The Fry Model Railway ☺ On the grounds of Malahide Castle (see below), this is an exhibit of handmade models of more than 300 Irish trains. The trains were built in the 1920s and 1930s by Cyril Fry, a railway engineer and draftsman. The complex includes items of Irish railway history dating from 1834, and models of stations, bridges, trams, buses, barges, boats, the River Liffey, and the Hill of Howth.

Malahide, County Dublin. ✆ **01/846-3779.** Admission €7.25 adults; €6.10 seniors and students; €4.60 children; €21 families. Apr–Sept Tues–Sat 10am–1pm and 2–5pm; Sun 1–5pm. DART or suburban rail: Malahide. Bus: 42.

Models of more than 300 Irish trains are on display at the Fry Model Railway, on the grounds of Malahide Castle.

Howth Castle Rhododendron Gardens On a steep slope about 13km (8 miles) north of downtown, this 12-hectare (30-acre) garden was first planted in 1875 and is best known for its 2,000 varieties of rhododendrons. Peak bloom time is in May and June. Also on the grounds is the **National Transport Museum of Ireland** (✆ **01/832-0427;** www.nationaltransportmuseum.org), a collection of public-service vehicles from the 1880s to the 1980s. It's probably one for enthusiasts, but charming in its own way. ***Note:*** The footpaths are not properly kept up and can occasionally be treacherous, so you should come prepared for hillwalking, rather than if you were visiting a public park.

Howth, County Dublin. ✆ **01/832-2624.** Free admission to gardens. Apr–June daily 8am–sunset. Transport Museum: €3 adults; €1.25 seniors and children; €8 families. June–Aug Mon–Sat 10am–5pm; Sept–May Sat–Sun and public holidays only 2–5pm. DART: Howth. Bus: 31.

Malahide Castle ★★★ ☺ This crenelated and towered stone castle is satisfyingly complete. Most castles still open to the public in Ireland are ruins, but this one stands so solidly, you get the picture—it's what a castle should be. Founded in the 12th century by Richard Talbot, it was occupied by his descendants until 1973. The fully restored interior is furnished with Irish antiques from the 17th to the 19th centuries. One-of-a-kind historical portraits on loan from the National Gallery line the walls. After touring the house, explore the vast estate, with prized **gardens** filled with more than 5,000 species of plants and flowers—it's the perfect place for a picnic on a sunny day. The Malahide grounds also contain the **Fry Model Railway** museum (see above) and **Tara's Palace,** an antique dollhouse and toy collection. Aspiring ghost hunters may be interested to know that the castle is said to have five resident ghosts, including a jester named Puck, who (while alive) made the mildly threatening vow to haunt the place but harm no one until a male Talbot is no longer in residence.

Malahide, County Dublin. ✆ **01/846-2184.** www.malahidecastle.com. Admission €7.50 adults; €6.30 seniors and students; €4.70 children 11 and under; €18 families; gardens free. Combination tickets with Dublin Writers Museum, James Joyce Museum, Shaw Birthplace, or Fry Model Railway available. AE, MC, V. Year-round daily 10am–5pm (Oct–Mar opens 11am Sun and public holidays). Gardens May–Sept daily 2–5pm. DART: Malahide. Bus: 42.

This 12th-century castle is still exceptionally well preserved, thoughtfully furnished, and open to the general public.

National Botanic Gardens ★ Established by the Royal Dublin Society in 1795 on a rolling 20-hectare (49-acre) expanse of land north of the city center, this is Dublin's horticultural showcase. The attractions include more than 20,000 different plants and cultivars, the Great Yew Walk, a bog garden, a water garden, a rose garden, and an herb garden. A variety of Victorian-style glass houses are filled with tropical plants and exotic species. Remember this spot when you suddenly crave refuge from the bustle of the city. It's a quiet, lovely haven, within a short walk of **Glasnevin Cemetery** (p. 157). All but the rose garden is wheelchair accessible. There's free roadside parking outside the garden gates.

Botanic Rd., Glasnevin, Dublin 9. ✆ **01/804-0300.** www.botanicgardens.ie. Free admission. Prebooked guided tour (groups only) €2. Mid-Feb to mid-Nov daily 9am–6pm; mid-Nov to mid-Feb daily 9:30am–4:30pm. Glasshouses close 1 hr. before garden weekdays, 15 min. on weekends. Bus: 13, 19, or 134.

Newbridge House and Park ★★ ☺ This mansion 19km (12 miles) north of Dublin dates from 1740 and was once the home of Dr. Charles Cobbe, an archbishop of Dublin. Occupied by the Cobbe family until 1984, the house is a showcase of family memorabilia: hand-carved furniture, portraits, daybooks, and dolls, as well as a museum of objects collected on world travels. The Great Drawing Room, in its original state, is one of the finest Georgian interiors in Ireland. The house sits on 140 hectares (346 acres), laid out with picnic areas and walking

Guess Who's Coming to Dinner at Howth Castle?

Although Howth Castle is not itself open to the public (only the grounds are), there is a legend associated with the place that's worth repeating. According to local lore, the pirate Grace O'Malley (see the sidebar "Local Hero: Pirate Grace O'Malley," p. 505) once came to visit the Baron Howth, but the servants would not let her past the gate, as he was eating dinner. This enraged her so much that she kidnapped the baron's grandson, and said she would only let him go when the baron agreed always to lay an extra place at his table, in case a stranger should arrive and need hospitality. To this day, his descendants still honor that agreement at every meal. It pays to be polite.

More than 20,000 types of plants flourish at the National Botanic Gardens.

trails. The grounds also include a working Victorian farm, as well as a craft shop and a coffee shop. There's a terrific, up-to-the-minute playground where children can let off some steam. Donabate, County Dublin. ✆ **01/843-6534.** www.newbridgehouseandfarm.com. House admission €7 adults; €6 seniors and students; €4 children 11 and under; €20 families. Victorian Farm €4 adults; €3 seniors, students, and children; €10 families. Apr–Sept Tues–Sun 10am–5pm, Sun and public holidays 2–6pm; Oct–Mar Tues–Sun and public holidays 11am–4pm. Last tour 1 hr. before closing. Suburban rail to Donabate. Bus: 33B.

The historic seat of the Catholic University of Ireland, Newman House is known for its ornate rococo plasterwork.

Skerries Mills Originally part of an Augustinian Priory, the mill has had many lives (and deaths). Last known as the Old Mill Bakery, providing loaves to the local north coast, it suffered a devastating fire in 1986 and lay in ruins until it was reborn as Skerries Mills in 1999. An ambitious restoration project brought two windmills and a water mill back into operation. There's even an adjoining field of grains—barley, oats, and wheat, all that's needed for the traditional brown loaf—sown, harvested, and threshed using traditional implements and machinery. The result is not only the sweet smell of fresh bread, but also an intriguing glimpse into the past, brought to life by guided tours and the chance to put your hand to the stone and grind flour. If you've worked up an appetite, there's a lovely tearoom and a fine gift shop of Irish crafts. Skerries Mill has quite a schedule of special events year-round, from classical and traditional music concerts to art exhibitions and workshops, including a farmers' market on Saturdays from 10am to 4pm. Call or check the website for details.

Skerries, County Dublin. ✆ **01/849-5208.** www.skerriesmills.org. Guided tours €6.50 adults; €5 seniors and students; €3.50 children; €13 families. Apr–Sept daily 10am–5:30pm; Oct–Mar daily 10am–4:30pm. Last tour 1 hr. before closing. Closed Dec 20–Jan 1. Suburban rail to Skerries. Bus: 33. Skerries town and the Mills signposted north of Dublin off the N1.

WHERE TO STAY

Inexpensive

Clontarf Castle Hotel ★ If you want to be within striking distance of Dublin airport (8km/5 miles away), this hotel in Clontarf is a good option about 10 minutes' drive away. The Norman stone castle that forms the hotel's center dates from 1172, although most of the building is modern. There's still a regal quality to the entrance hall and lobby, which are draped with tapestries and hold a huge fireplace. Guest rooms are in the modern portion of the building, but are nicely done with a mixture of contemporary furniture and antique touches; some have four-poster beds. It's a popular conference center and entertainment venue, so is not really the place for a peaceful getaway. Check for discounts online; the hotel slashed its prices in 2010, and good half-board deals are also available if you book in advance.

Castle Ave., Clontarf, Dublin 3. www.clontarfcastle.ie. ✆ **01/833-2321.** Fax 01/833-0418. 111 units. €90–€300 double. Breakfast €22. AE, DC, MC, V. Free parking. Bus: 130. **Amenities:** Restaurant; 2 bars; babysitting; gym; room service; smoke-free rooms. *In room:* A/C, TV, radio, hair dryer.

Egan's House This two-story, redbrick Victorian guesthouse is in the center of a pleasant residential neighborhood within walking distance of the botanic gardens. Run by Pat and Monica Finn, it has bright if basic rooms in a variety of styles. Some rooms are on the small side, and it won't win any style awards, but this is a friendly, inexpensive option, with a comfortable, lived-in feel. Prices here are pretty reasonable, but be aware that not much is included—from breakfast (€8) to parking (€5) and Wi-Fi (€5) to early check-in (€30)—if you want something here you'll pay for it.

7–9 Iona Park (btw. Botanic and Lower Drumcondra rds.), Glasnevin, Dublin 9. www.eganshouse.com. ✆ **01/830-3611.** Fax 01/830-3312. 23 units. €50–€100 double. 50% reduction for children 5 and under sharing with 2 adults. Breakfast €8. MC, V. Bus: 3, 11, 13, 13A, 16, 19, 19A, 41, 41A, or 41B. **Amenities:** Dining room; lounge; smoke-free rooms. *In room:* TV, hair dryer.

Red Bank House ★★ This invitingly comfortable place in the heart of Skerries town is only 20 to 30 minutes by car from Dublin Airport, so it can provide a convenient first or last night's lodging for your Ireland stay. Better yet, it boasts the award-winning **Red Bank restaurant** (see below), so you are guaranteed a memorable introductory or farewell meal. Guest rooms have a simple, country style—creamy walls, dark woods, crisp white bedspreads and floral drapes. The power showers are just what you need after a long journey. Again, book online for very good discounts.

7 Church St. and Convent Lane, Skerries, County Dublin. www.redbank.ie. ✆ **01/849-1005.** Fax 01/849-1598. 18 units, several with shower only. €44–€88 double. Rates include service and full Irish breakfast. AE, DC, MC, V. Parking on street and lane. Suburban rail to Skerries. Bus: 33. **Amenities:** Restaurant. *In room:* TV, hair dryer.

WHERE TO EAT

Bon Appétit Restaurant and Brasserie ★ FRENCH This chic eatery has two dining rooms; the restaurant is a formal dining extravaganza, complete with walls draped in silk wallpaper. Ingredients are just as luxurious: try the roast turbot with almonds and clams, or the organic lamb with gratin *dauphinoise* and rosemary *jus*. The food has earned top marks from local critics, and now has a Michelin star, so it's packing in the wealthy suburban crowd. Some complain it's a victim of its own success (crowding people in at tiny tables), but the food makes it worth the crush. An altogether more relaxed and informal atmosphere pervades in the brasserie, where the menu is decidedly less fussy (although still far from a budget option, if you order a la carte; a rib-eye steak will cost around €25). Typical dishes include filet of monkfish with lentils and red wine, or slow-roasted duck with black pudding and apple purée.

9 James Terrace, Malahide, County Dublin. ✆ **01/845-0314.** www.bonappetit.ie. Reservations required. Restaurant: fixed-price 3-course dinner €60. Tasting menu (Wed only) 7 courses €65–€80 (must be ordered by entire table). Brasserie: fixed-price 2-course early-bird menu €30; 3-course Sun menu €23; dinner main courses €24–€29. AE, DC, MC, V. Restaurant: Tues–Sat 7–9:30pm; Fri noon–2:30pm. Brasserie: Tues–Sat 6–10:30pm; Sun 1–8pm. Suburban rail to Malahide.

The Loft Bar & Grill BISTRO The upstairs dining room at this cozy, informal restaurant has exposed stone walls and an open fire in one corner lending a homey touch to the otherwise modern design. Food is standard, if slightly retro bistro fare—steaks, chicken supreme, duck with orange sauce—and there are good value early-bird and children's options. Downstairs the **Abbey Tavern** (owned by the same people) serves bar food during the day, and has an oyster-and-mussel bar Saturday lunchtimes from September to April. After your meal, you can join the audience at the Abbey for traditional music, although you'll have to pay an extra €20 to join in the fun (or you could call ahead to book a dinner-and-a-show combo for €45).

Abbey St., Howth, County Dublin. ✆ **01/839-0307.** theloft.abbeytavern.ie. Reservations required. Fixed-price early-bird dinner €25 2 courses, €30 3 courses; main courses €15–€26. MC, V. Mon–Sat 7–11pm. DART: Howth. Bus: 31.

The Red Bank ★★ SEAFOOD The hugely popular Red Bank restaurant has been winning friends, influencing people, and garnering awards for nearly 20 years. The mood here is charmingly old-fashioned and classy. The waiter takes your order in the lounge, where you wait with a drink until the appetizers are ready and you're seated at a table. The fresh seafood is sourced from local waters, and this place is at its best with timeless icons, such as scallops in butter, cream, and white wine; or the classic lobster Thermidor. Service is respectfully old school, highlighted when the dessert cart is wheeled in, laden with an enticing selection of confections. This place is quite generous with its definition of "early-bird;" the (half-price) three-course menu is available until 8pm (7pm on Sun).

5–7 Church St., Skerries, County Dublin. ✆ **01/849-1005.** www.redbank.ie. Reservations required. Fixed-price 3-course early-bird menu €25; dinner main courses €17–€43; fixed-price 3-course dinner €50. AE, DC, MC, V. Mon–Sat 6:30–9:30pm; Sun 12:30–4pm. Suburban rail to Skerries. Bus: 33.

6
AROUND DUBLIN

The area immediately around Dublin is not the most dramatic or beautiful in the country, but if you get off the big, bland motorways, there are treasures in those hills, all within easy reach from the city.

About 30 minutes south of Dublin, you enter the brooding Wicklow Mountains. Home to early religious sites and peaceful river valleys, these hills are perfect for a day trip from Dublin, and make a good starting point to a driving tour of the south of Ireland.

Heading north from Dublin you can see the remnants of ancient civilizations at prehistoric sites Newgrange and Knowth. A short distance away, the green hills around the Boyne Valley are where the Irish kings once reigned with a mixture of mysticism and force.

To the east, the plains of County Kildare start off Ireland's horse country. There's plenty to do and lots of Ireland to see within an hour of Dublin.

COUNTY WICKLOW & COUNTY CARLOW

County Wicklow extends from Bray, 19km (12 miles) S of Dublin, to Arklow, 64km (40 miles) S of Dublin

Sitting at a seaside cafe in the cheerful suburban town of **Bray ★**, you can look off to the southern horizon and see the mountains of County Wicklow casting their shadow your way. Wicklow's northernmost border is just a dozen or so miles south of Dublin, making it one of the easiest day trips from the city. The beauty of the mountains, with their peaceful **Vale of Avoca** and isolated, contemplative monastery site, **Glendalough,** makes this landscape one of the most rewarding views.

Bray is a stylish, upscale town, but it's also busy and bustling, so many people choose to head to County Wicklow by way of the sweet harbor town of **Greystones ★**, a place so charming you might not tell your friends about, for fear of inspiring crowds that could spoil it.

Beyond Greystones, a raised granite ridge runs through the county, peaking at two of the highest mountain passes in Ireland—the **Sally Gap** and the **Wicklow Gap.** Hikers will want to strike out on foot on the well-marked **Wicklow Way** walking path, which wanders for miles past mountain tarns and secluded glens. You can pick up a map at any tourism office, and then choose a stretch of the path to explore. If you're staying in the car, you'll want to track down the picturesque villages of **Roundwood, Laragh,** and **Aughrim.**

Just over the border of County Wicklow lies County Carlow, one of Ireland's smallest counties, bordered to the east by the **Blackstairs Mountains** and to the west by the fertile limestone land of the Barrow Valley and the Killeshin

PREVIOUS PAGE: **Fine specimens from the Irish National Stud farm in Kildare.**

Hills. Its most prominent feature is the 5,000-year-old granite formation known as **Browne's Hill Dolmen.** Its capstone is believed to weigh a colossal 100 tons.

An easy day trip from Dublin, Glendalough is a world apart from the bustling capital.

Essentials

GETTING THERE **Irish Rail** (✆ **01/836-6222;** www.irishrail.ie) provides daily train service between Dublin and Bray and Wicklow.

Bus Éireann (✆ **01/836-6111;** www.buseireann.ie) operates daily express bus service to Arklow, Bray, and Wicklow towns. Both Bus Éireann and **Discover Dublin** (✆ **01/280-1899;** www.discoverdublin.ie) offer an excellent tour that they have dubbed the "Wild Wicklow Tour." It certainly is lively and enjoyable, and hits all the high points, including visits to Avoca and Sally Gap. Another tour option is the **Mary Gibbons Tours** (✆ **086/355-1355;** www.newgrangetours.com), which offers an absorbing, in-depth tour of Glendalough and nearby Powerscourt.

Still, arguably the best way to see Wicklow is by car, as that's the only way that you can take in all the little villages not well served by bus or train. The Dublin Tourist Office has excellent road maps for all of Ireland. Take the N11 south from Dublin City and follow turnoff signs for major attractions.

VISITOR INFORMATION The **Wicklow Tourist Office,** Fitzwilliam Square, Wicklow Town, County Wicklow (✆ **0404/69117;** www.visitwicklow.ie), is open Monday to Saturday year-round from 9:30am to 1pm and 2 to 5:15pm, until 6pm June through September. The **Carlow Tourist Office,** Foresters Hall, College Street, Carlow Town, County Carlow (✆ **059/913-0411;** www.carlowtourism.com), is open Monday to Friday year-round, from 9:30am to 5pm (closed for lunch 1–2pm). It's also open selected Saturdays in the summer; call before you visit.

Seeing the Sights

Altamont Garden The lush, colorful extravagance of Altamont is the result of decades of nurturing. A shadowy avenue of beech trees leads to bright lawns and flowers beneath ancient yew trees. Gravel walks weave around a lake, constructed as a famine-relief project. It's arguably at its best in late May, when spectacular displays of bluebells fill the forest floor on slopes overlooking the River Slaney, but it's always beautiful.

Tullow, County Carlow. ✆ **059/915-9444.** www.altamontgarden.com. Free admission. Mar–Oct daily 9am–7:30pm; Nov and Feb Mon–Thurs and Sat–Sun 9am–4:30pm, Fri 9am–3:30pm; Dec Mon–Thurs 9am–4pm, Fri 9am–3:30pm, Sat–Sun after Christmas only 9am–4:30pm; Jan Mon–Thurs and Sat–Sun 9am–4pm, Fri 9am–3:30pm.

Counties Louth & Meath

Hill of Tara **12**
Holy Trinity Heritage Center **1**
Knowth **8**
Loughcrew **9**
Millmount Museum & Martello Tower **5**
Monasterboice **2**
Newgrange **7**
Old Mellifont Abbey **3**
St. Colmcille's House **10**
St. Peter's Church of Ireland **6**
Slane Castle **4**
Trim Castle **11**

County Kildare

Castletown **13**
The Curragh racetrack **33**
Irish National Stud **35**
Irish Pewtermill **30**
Japanese Gardens **34**
Larchill Arcadian Garden **36**
Moone High Cross **29**
Newbridge Silverware **31**
St. Brigid's Cathedral **32**
Steam Museum **14**

Counties Wicklow & Carlow

Altamont Gardens **26**
Avoca Handweavers **23**
Avondale House & Forest Park **22**
Browne's Hill Dolmen **37**
Glendalough **27**
Glenmacnass Waterfall **20**
Huntington Castle **25**
Killruddery House & Gardens **16**
Mount Usher Gardens **21**
National Sea Life Centre **18**
Powerscourt Gardens, House Exhibition and Waterfall **17**
Russborough House **15**
St. Mullin's Monastery **38**
Vale of Avoca **24**
Wicklow Mountains National Park **28**
Wicklow's Historic Gaol **19**

St. Kevin's Chapel, dedicated to the 6th-century monk who founded the monastic settlement here at Glendalough.

Avondale House & Forest Park ★ ☺ In a fertile valley between Glendalough and the Vale of Avoca, this is the former home of Charles Stewart Parnell (1846–91), one of Ireland's great political leaders. Built in 1779, the house is now a museum dedicated to his memory. The parkland around the house is beautiful, with wooded nature trails along a river, and more formal gardens near the house. There's a cute cafe serving tea and light lunches, as well as homemade breads and pastries, and there's also a playground for children, which should keep them busy for a while. The house's opening hours change regularly, so give them a call before you go.

Off R752, Rathdrum, County Wicklow. ✆ **0404/46111.** Admission €6.50 adults; €6 seniors and students; €4.50 children 11 and under; €19 families. Forest Park daily 8:30am–7pm. Avondale House Apr–May and Sept–Oct Sat–Sun noon–4pm; June–Aug Tues–Sun noon–5pm. Parking €5, free with family ticket.

Browne's Hill Dolmen The purpose of this megalithic stone table has been the subject of conjecture for centuries, but nobody knows for certain. The tomb is an estimated 5,000 years old, and its massive size led earlier Irish residents to believe that it was built by giants. Archaeologists believe the capstone was rolled into place on an earthen ramp constructed for the process and then destroyed. It's likely the dolmen is the burial place of a long-dead king, but it has a rich heritage of myth and legend.

Off Rathvilly Rd., Carlow, County Carlow. Free admission. Daily year-round. Access via parking lot and enclosed pedestrian pathway.

Glendalough ★★★ This evocative, misty glen is a magical place. An ancient, abandoned monastery built on the edge of dark lakes and surrounded by hills and forests, it's a memorable sight. Its name is derived from the Irish *gleann da locha,* meaning "the glen of the two lakes." Things always seem to be in soft focus here as you wander the rocky paths beside the ancient chapels. The ruins date from the 6th century, when a monk who became known as St. Kevin chose this secluded setting, which was already used as a Bronze Age tomb, for his home. For 7 years he fasted, prayed, slept on the hard ground, and ate only what he could catch or find. His self-deprivation and fervor gained attention from passing hunters and peddlers, and soon similarly devout followers found their way here. Over the next 4 centuries, Kevin's church became a center of religious learning, attracting thousands of students from all over Europe. Unfortunately, its success, as with so many early Irish religious sites, was its downfall, and Glendalough soon came to the attention of Vikings, who pillaged it repeatedly between A.D. 775 and 1071. But it was always rebuilt stronger than ever, until 1398, when English forces in Ireland virtually wiped it out. Attempts were made to resuscitate it, and it limped on as just a shadow of all it had been until the 17th century, when it was abandoned altogether.

The combination of so many years of history and such an evocative setting means that there's plenty to see here. Your first step should be to stop by the visitor center behind the Glendalough Hotel near the entrance to the valley, to pick up a map and learn a bit about the lay of the land. There are many walking trails, each one taking in different ruins, as the chapels were scattered over several miles. The oldest ruins, the **Teampall na Slellig,** can be seen across the lake at the foot of towering cliffs, but because there's no boat service, they cannot be visited. There's also a cave known as Kevin's Bed, which is believed to be where the saint lived when he first arrived at Glendalough. Follow the path from the upper lake to the lower lake and walk through the remains of the monastery complex. Although much of the monastic city is in ruins, there's a nearly perfect round tower, 31m (102 ft.) high and 16m (52 ft.) around the base, as well as hundreds of timeworn Celtic crosses and several chapels. One of these is St. Kevin's Chapel, often called St. Kevin's Kitchen, a fine specimen of an early Irish barrel-vaulted oratory with a miniature round belfry rising from a stone roof.

Unfortunately, Glendalough is a victim of its own success, so in the summer it tends to be overrun with tourists, which rather defeats the purpose of visiting such a peaceful place. ***Tip:*** In the high season, it's best to arrive very early in the morning, or after 5pm (it stays light until 9pm at least) in order to see it at its best. (The visitor center closes at 5 or 6pm, but the grounds remain open.)

County Wicklow (11km/6¾ miles east of Wicklow on T7 via Rathdrum). ✆ **0404/45325** or 45352. Admission €3 adults; €2.10 seniors; €1.30 students and children 11 and under; €8 families. Visitor center Mid-Oct to mid-Mar daily 9:30am–5pm; mid-Mar to mid-Oct daily 9:30am–6pm.

Glenmacnass Waterfall ★ The River Glenmacnass flows south across the highest mountain in western Wicklow, Mt. Mullaghcleevaun (848m/2,781 ft.). At one point, it reaches the edge of a plateau and flows off the edge quite spectacularly. There's a parking lot near the top, and a path to the falls, but take care on the rocks, which can be treacherous.

Follow the Military rd. through the Sally Gap and Laragh to the top of Glenmacnass Valley, and then watch for signs to the waterfall. Free admission.

Huntington Castle ★ Built in 1621 on the site of an abbey, which was itself built in the 14th century on the site of a Druid temple, this rambling, crenelated manor house was originally the home of Lord Esmond (on whom the writer Thackeray based his novel *The History of Henry Esmond*). His descendants still occupy the main building. The gardens here are beautiful and as historic as the house—many of the plants date back to the 18th century—and there is an extraordinary walk guarded on either side by ancient yew trees that is not to be missed. It's a rambling, lived-in old house, with vast grounds bounded by the rivers Derry and Slaney. The place is more than a little bit spooky. There's an old temple to the Goddess Isis in the dungeon (heaven knows why), and it's said to be one of the most haunted buildings in Ireland. Stanley Kubrick filmed *Barry Lyndon* here. If you like it so much you can't bear to leave, you can rent one wing of the castle—if you're brave enough—with space for up to five people (from €245–€530 a week, depending on the season); visit **www.shamrockcottages.co.uk** for more information (it's listed under the Wexford section).

Clonegal, County Carlow (off N80, 6.5km/4 miles from Bunclody). ✆ **053/937-7552.** Guided tour €8 adults; €6 seniors, students, and children 7 and older; free for children 6 and under. June–Aug daily 2–6pm. Last tour 5:20pm. Other times by appointment.

Killruddery House & Gardens This grand estate has been the seat of the Earl of Meath since 1618. The noble mansion dates from 1820, and features a later (more frilly) glass Victorian conservatory modeled on the ill-fated Crystal Palace that stood in London at that time. The gardens are a highlight, with a lime avenue, a sylvan theater, exotic plants, twin canals, and a fountain-filled pond edged with beech hedges. The restored walled garden was opened to visitors in 2011, and the traditional kitchen garden is gradually being replanted.

Killruddery, Bray, County Wicklow (off the N11). ✆ **01/286-3405.** www.killruddery.com. House and garden tour €10 adults; €8 seniors and students; €3 children 12 and under; €18 families. Gardens only €6 adults; €5 seniors and students; €2 children 12 and under. House May–June and Sept daily 1–5pm. Gardens Apr Sat–Sun 9:30–5pm; house and gardens May–Sept daily 9:30–5pm.

Mount Usher Gardens ★ Spreading out on 8 hectares (20 acres) at the edge of the River Vartry, this peaceful site was once an ancient lake. These days, it's a riverside garden, designed in a distinctively informal style. Fiery rhododendrons, fragrant eucalyptus trees, giant Tibetan lilies, and snowy camellias compete for your attention. Informal and responsive to their natural setting, these gardens have an almost untended feel—a sort of floral woodland. A spacious cafe, part of

The Curse of Powerscourt House

This grand house in Enniskerry has a history of misfortune. It was designed in the 18th century by Richard Cassels, who also designed Russborough House (see below) and Dublin's Parliament building. The same family lived in the building for 350 years, until the 1950s, but their fortunes gradually declined. By the time they moved out and donated the once magnificent house to the state, it was in terrible condition, and the country had little money to restore it. Its renovation was a painstaking project plagued with financial problems. In the end, the process took 2 decades. Finally, in 1974, the work was done, and a grand reopening was planned. However, it was not meant to be. The day before the event was due to take place a fire broke out, gutting the building. So the slow, painful process of reconstruction began again. This time it's taken even longer—more than 30 years later, most of the house is still unrestored, and only a few rooms have been completed and opened to the public.

The grounds of Powerscourt, a grand 18th-century mansion, include Ireland's highest waterfall.

the very good Avoca chain, overlooks the river and gardens. The courtyard at the entrance to the gardens contains an interesting assortment of shops.

Ashford, County Wicklow (off the N11). ✆ **0404/40205.** www.mountushergardens.ie. Admission €7.50 adults; €6 seniors and students; €3 children 5–16; free for children 4 and under. Mar–Oct daily 10:30am–5:20pm. Cafe and shops 10am–4pm year-round.

National Sea Life Centre ☺ This cleverly designed aquarium at the water's edge in coastal Bray provides a kid-centric introduction to sea life. A labyrinthine path through the aquarium begins with a rock tunnel carved by a freshwater stream; from there, you follow the water's course toward the open sea, from freshwater river to storm-pounded harbor and finally to the briny deep. Along the way, kids use "magic" glasses to read coded questions and find the answers. In the ocean portion, the emphasis is on scary critters, like sharks and octopus. It's well done, and good family fun, but it's a bit pricey considering its size. However, ticket prices are significantly cheaper if purchased in advance online.

Strand Rd., Bray, County Wicklow. ✆ **01/286-6939.** www.sealife.ie. Admission €12 adults; €11 students; €9 children 12 and under. Mar–Oct daily 10am–5pm; Nov–Feb Mon–Fri 11am–4pm, Sat–Sun 10am–5pm.

Powerscourt Gardens, House Exhibition, and Waterfall ★★★ ☺ The 20th century was not kind to this magnificent estate, which was neglected for decades and then gutted by fire. It's taken 30 years to restore the Palladian house to even a glimmer of its former glory. Only a few rooms are now open to the public, and there's an exhibition that tells the history of the building and the long struggle of restoration.

The restored grand ballroom is particularly beautiful, although, mysteriously, it's only open 2 days a week. On other days, even fewer rooms can be seen. Given how little of the house is open to the public, it's hard not to feel a tad disappointed that so much of it is dedicated to shops, even if the retailers (including an Avoca crafts store) are good ones.

Still, the magnificent grounds are really the main attraction here. The gardens are remarkable—graced with classical statuary; filled with little touches like the shady grotto made of petrified moss, the Japanese garden, and an over-the-top fountain from which statues of winged horses rise. The gardens were designed by the landscaper Daniel Robertson between 1745 and 1767. Legend has it that due to terrible gout, he oversaw the work while being carted around in a wheelbarrow, sipping port as he went. When the bottle was dry, work was done for the day.

There's a playground for the kids and plenty of space for them to run around. The Avoca cafe serves rich cakes, hot soups, and healthy salads, alongside a breathtaking view. If you feel energetic, follow the well-marked path over 7km (4⅓ miles) to the picturesque Powerscourt Waterfall—the highest in Ireland (121m/397 ft.). If you're not feeling energetic, you can drive, following signs.

Enniskerry, County Wicklow (off the N11). ✆ **01/204-6000.** www.powerscourt.ie. Gardens €6 adults; €5.50 seniors and students; €3.50 children 5–16; free for kids 4 and under. Waterfall €5 adults; €4.50 seniors and students; €3.50 children 2–16; free for kids 1 and under. Free admission to house. Gardens and house exhibition daily 9:30am–5:30pm (gardens close at dusk in winter); closed Dec 25–26. Ballroom and Garden Rooms year-round Sun 9:30am–1:30pm; May–Sept Mon 9:30am–1:30pm. Waterfall Mar–Apr and Sept–Oct daily 10:30am–5:30pm; May–Aug daily 9:30am–7pm; Nov–Feb daily 10:30am–4pm.

RUSSBOROUGH HOUSE: A LIFE OF crime!

Russborough House sits in a quiet stretch of countryside on a sprawling estate, miles from anywhere in deepest County Wicklow. Given its location, and its low-key reputation (many visitors to Ireland don't even know it's there), you might think that its collection of paintings by Vermeer, Goya, Gainsborough, and Rubens couldn't be safer. You'd be wrong. There have been three major robberies here over the last 30 years in which millions of dollars worth of art have been stolen, damaged, and lost forever.

It all started in 1974 when members of the IRA stole 16 paintings in a sort of crime-based fundraising effort. All of the works were eventually recovered and peace descended, but 10 years later it happened again. That time, a Dublin gangster, Martin Cahill, ordered a number of paintings to be stolen from Russborough to enhance the riches of loyalist paramilitary groups. Only some of those were ever recovered, and many were badly damaged.

In 1986, the owners gave up on the expensive losing game of trying to protect the small but precious collection, and Dublin's National Gallery began managing the collection. Again, all was calm until 2001. This time, thieves smashed a car through the front of the house and drove off with two paintings, including a Gainsborough that had already been stolen twice before. Both were recovered, but after yet another theft (and recovery) of paintings in 2002, the owners decided it would be best to send the most valuable paintings (by Vermeer, Goya, and Gainsborough) to the National Gallery for their own protection. The house still holds an excellent collection of less valuable art (some quality pieces were returned to the house in 2008, improving the collection even more), but expect to be followed around by anxious-looking staff.

18th-century Russborough House was owned by a member of the De Beers family, who amassed a valuable art collection here.

Russborough House ★★ This impressive Palladian villa was built between 1741 and 1751, designed by the great Richard Cassels, who also designed the ill-fated Powerscourt House (above). In the 1950s, the house was purchased by Sir Alfred Beit, a member of the De Beers diamond family. He had inherited a massive collection of art and wanted someplace to keep it, and thought this rural mansion was just the spot. Thus began one of the most exquisite small rural collections in the country, with paintings by Vernet, Vermeer, Goya, Gainsborough, and Rubens. Sadly, after a series of robberies, some of the most valuable paintings in the collection are held in the Beit wing of the National Gallery, but those left behind are still exquisite, and the setting is gorgeous. You can explore the house on your own or by guided tour, and there is certainly a lot to see—stucco ceilings by the Lafranchini brothers, huge marble mantelpieces, inlaid floors, and lavish use of mahogany in doors and staircase, as well as fine displays of silver, porcelain, and fine furniture. If you want to spend more time here, one wing of the museum has been re-developed as a self-catering holiday home.

Blessington, County Wicklow (off N81). ✆ **045/865239.** www.russborough.ie. Admission to house €10 adults; €8 seniors and students; €5 children 15 and under. Garden maze €3. May–Sept daily 10am–6pm; mid-Mar to Apr Sun and national holidays 10am–6pm. Tours given on the hour. Closed Nov–Mar, except by appointment.

St. Mullin's Monastery This little gem is a well-kept secret. On a sunny day, its idyllic setting—in a sleepy hamlet beside the River Barrow, surrounded by soft carpeted hills—is reason enough for a visit. Besides that, this is a fascinating spot, an outdoor museum of sorts, spanning Irish history from the early Christian period to the present, over the course of a few acres. There are the ruins of a monastery founded by St. Moling (Mullin) in roughly A.D. 614. Plundered again and again by the Vikings in the 9th and 10th centuries, it was annexed in the 12th century by a nearby Augustinian abbey. Here, too, are a steep grassy *motte* (grove) and the outline of a bailey (the outer wall or court of a castle) constructed

The highest portions of the Wicklow Way hiking trail cut through Wicklow Mountains National Park.

by the Normans in the 12th century. In the Middle Ages, the monastery ruins were a popular destination, especially during the height of the Black Death in 1348, when pilgrims would cross the river barefoot, circle the burial spot of St. Mullin nine times in prayer, adding small stones to the cairn marking the spot, and drink from the healing waters of the saint's well. These ruins and waters are still the subject of an annual pilgrimage near or on July 25.

Adjoining the monastery buildings is an ancient cemetery still in use, where, contrary to common practice, Protestants and Catholics have long lain side by side. A number of rebels from the 1798 Rising are buried here, including Gen. Thomas Cloney. If the Heritage Centre is closed (it opens at the discretion of the caretaker, Seamus Fitzgerald), there's a map and brief history at the entrance to the cemetery.

On the Barrow Dr., 12km (7½ miles) north of New Ross, St. Mullins, County Carlow. Free admission.

Vale of Avoca ★ Basically a peaceful riverbank, the Vale of Avoca was immortalized in the writings of 19th-century poet Thomas Moore. It's here at the "Meeting of the Waters" that the Avonmore and Avonbeg rivers join to form the Avoca River. It's said that the poet sat under "Tom Moore's Tree" looking for inspiration and penned the lines, "There is not in the wide world a valley so sweet as the vale in whose bosom the bright waters meet. . . ." The tree itself is a sorry sight—nothing left but a stump—but it's still a beautiful place. Two miles away, the charming riverside village of Avoca makes a good stop to do some gift shopping.

Rte. 755, Avoca, County Wicklow.

Wicklow Mountains National Park ★★★ Nearly 20,000 hectares (49,400 acres) of County Wicklow make up this national park. The core area surrounds Glendalough, including the Glendalough Valley and Glendalough Wood Nature Reserves. ***Hikers note:*** The most mountainous stretch of the Wicklow Way cuts through this park (see **www.irishways.com**). In the high season, you'll find an information station at the Upper Lake at Glendalough where you can get maps and route guides for hiking in the Glendalough Valley and surrounding hills. (See "Walking" under "Sports & Outdoor Pursuits," below, for suggestions.) The closest parking is at Upper Lake, where you'll pay €2 per car; or, just walk up from the Glendalough Visitor Centre, where the parking is free. ***Note:*** The Irish

National Parks and Wildlife Service warns that ticks carrying Lyme disease are known to live in the hills. While the risk of contracting the disease is small, you should dress in long sleeves, wear a hat, and avoid hiking in shorts.

Glendalough, County Wicklow. ✆ **0404/45425.** www.wicklowmountainsnationalpark.ie. Information office free admission. No opening restrictions to park. Information office May–Sept daily 10am–6pm; Oct–Nov and Feb–Apr Sat–Sun 10am–5:30pm; Dec–Jan 10am–4pm.

Wicklow's Historic Gaol ★ Given the archaic look of the place, it's impossible to believe that this old jail operated until 1924, the end of a terrifying career that spanned 2 centuries. A visit here is creative and interactive—after passing under the hanging beam, visitors are lined up against the wall of the "day room" and confronted with some dark facts of prison life in 1799, when more than 400 prisoners, most of them rebels, occupied the jail's 42 cells. After years of being fed once every 4 days and allowed to walk in the prison yard for 15 minutes a month, prisoners must have warmed to the idea of the hangman's noose. Within the main cellblock, you can roam the cells and visit informative exhibitions. The impact of these stories is immediate and powerful for children as well as for adults, because this jail held both. Many prisoners were sent from here to penal colonies in Australia and Tasmania; that story, too, is told here, with the help of a stage-set wharf and prison ship. There's an in-house cafe, but if you've still got an appetite after that, you're doing better than us. The jail is said to be very haunted indeed, and a lively, nighttime tour of the Gaol takes place on the last Friday of every month, although this is unsuitable for children.

Kilmantin Hill, Wicklow Town, County Wicklow. ✆ **0404/61599.** www.wicklowshistoricgaol.com. Tour €7.30 adults; €6 seniors and students; €4.50 children 5–15; €19 families with up to 3 children; free for children 4 and under. Daily 10:30am–4:30pm; Sun 11am–4:30pm. Last admission 1 hr. before closing. Night tours last Fri of every month 7–9pm €15, includes glass of wine. Children 15 and under not admitted on night tours.

Shopping

Wicklow and Carlow each have some wonderful craft centers and workshops. Look out for those listed below:

Avoca Handweavers Inside this picturesque cluster of 18th-century whitewashed stone buildings, workers produce the Avoca chain's distinctively bright and cheerful wool throws, scarves, dainty knitwear, and colorful accessories. You can watch the craftspeople weave strands of yarn (made from Irish wool) into desirable throws and blankets, or just head straight to the shops or the excellent **cafe** (p. 221). There are other branches throughout Ireland, including at Powerscourt House, and on the N11 at Kilmacanogue, Bray, County Wicklow (✆ **01/286-7466**). Avoca, County Wicklow. ✆ **0402/35105.** www.avoca.ie.

The beautifully spun, richly colored woolen frocks from Avoca are a strong but soft defense against the damp Irish cold.

Bergin Clarke Studio In this little workshop, Brian Clarke hand-fashions silver jewelry and giftware, and Yvonne Bergin knits stylish, colorful apparel using local yarns. Prices are not cheap, but their work is incredible. Classes in metalwork are offered—book in advance. Open May to September daily 10am to 8pm; October to April Monday to Saturday 10am to 5:30pm. The Old Schoolhouse, Ballinaclash, Rathdrum, County Wicklow. ✆ **0404/46385.**

Glendalough Woollen Mills This long-established crafts shop in a converted farmhouse offers handicrafts from all over Ireland, such as Bantry Pottery and Penrose Glass from Waterford. Books, jewelry, and a large selection of handknits from the area are also sold. Open daily 9:30am to 6:30pm. Glendalough, County Wicklow. ✆ **0404/45156.**

Sports & Outdoor Pursuits

CYCLING The Lorum Old Rectory (p. 217) is also the base for **Celtic Cycling** (✆ **097/977-5282;** www.celticcycling.com/lorum.html), which offers a variety of 1- and 2-week cycling tours, or you can hire the gear you need from them and go it alone. In the summer, this area, with its rolling hills (although things get a bit steep in Wicklow) and gentle breezes, is great cycling country, and this outfit will help you make the most of it. Also, **Cycling Safaris** (✆ **01/260-0749;** www.cyclingsafaris.com) offers a weeklong tour of the area for upward of €670 per person, including rooms and food.

FISHING During brown-trout season (Mar 15–Sept 30), you'll find lots of angling opportunities on the Aughrim River (contact Arie van der Wel; ✆ **0402/36753** or 087/920-2751) and on the Avonmore River (contact Peter Driver in Rathdrum; ✆ **0404/46304** or 087/978-7040). Permits to fish on the Aughrim River are also available from Lawless's Hotel, Aughrim (✆ **0402/36146**) and the Woodenbridge Hotel in the Vale of Avoca (✆ **0402/35146;** www.woodenbridgehotel.com). The Dargle River flows from Enniskerry to the sea at Bray and offers great sea-trout fishing in season from February 1 to October 12 (contact Hugh Duff in Enniskerry; ✆ **01/286-8652**). Shore angling is hugely popular from beaches along the coast; contact the **Irish Federation of Sea Anglers** (✆ **01/280-6873;** www.ifsa.ie) for information on how to obtain permits. ***Note:*** Lovely though it is, the Avoca River south of the Meeting of the Waters is polluted by copper mines and is unsuitable for fishing.

GOLF If you're looking for cachet, head to the championship **Druids Glen Golf Club,** Newtonmountkennedy (✆ **01/287-3600;** www.druidsglen.ie), an inland beauty of a course that bears more than a fleeting resemblance to Augusta and was European Golf Course of the Year in 2000. Greens fees are €150 daily if you arrive after 9am; early-bird greens fees, from 7:30 to 8:50am on weekdays, are €115. It also has a partner course nearby, **Druid's Heath,** which is arguably just as nice, and is much cheaper; green fees are €90 or €70 early-bird. It can be reached at the same phone number. Special rates that include breakfast or a five-course dinner are available at both. For a more affordable day out, try the parkland **Glenmalure Golf Club,** Greenane, Rathdrum (✆ **01/269-6979;** www.glenmalure.com), where greens fees are €25 weekdays and €35 weekends. Lessons are also available for €50 per person, per hour. The **Arklow Golf Club** (✆ **0402/32492;**

www.arklowgolflinks.com), a seaside par-68 course, charges fees of €40 weekdays and €50 Friday and Saturday (closed Sun). In addition to a slightly discounted early-bird price, they also do a twilight rate (after 6pm) of €25.

Irish National Stud, home of many of Ireland's finest thoroughbred race horses.

HORSEBACK RIDING The hillside paths of Wicklow are perfect for horseback riding. More than a dozen stables and equestrian centers offer horses for hire and instructional programs. Rates for horse hire average around €30 to €50 per hour. **Brennanstown Riding School,** Hollybrook, Kilmacanogue (✆ **01/286-3778;** www.brennanstownrs.ie), offers beginner's treks up the picturesque Little Sugar Loaf Mountain, which has views across Dublin Bay. Another leading stables in the area is the **Paulbeg Riding School,** Shillelagh (✆ **053/942-9100**), where experienced riders can explore the surrounding hills, and beginners can receive expert instruction from Sally Duffy, who gives an enthusiastic introduction to the sport.

WALKING Loved by hikers and ramblers for its peace, isolation, and sheer beauty, the **Wicklow Way** is a 132km (82-mile) signposted walking path that follows forest trails, sheep paths, and country roads from the suburbs south of Dublin, up into the Wicklow Mountains, and down through country farmland to Clonegal, where the path ends. It takes about 5 to 7 days to walk its entirety, with overnight stops at B&Bs and hostels along the route. Most people choose to walk sections as day trips.

The grounds of the Irish National Stud farm encompass this tranquil Japanese garden.

You can pick up information and maps at the Wicklow National Park center at Glendalough, or at any local tourist office. Information on less strenuous walks can be found in the ***Wicklow Trail Sheets,*** also from tourist offices. It provides a map and route description for several good short walks along the path.

The most spectacular places to walk in Wicklow are in the north and central parts of the county, and it is traversed by the Wicklow Way and numerous short trails. One lovely walk on the Way begins at the **Deerpark parking lot** near the Dargle River and continues to Luggala, passing Djouce Mountain; the next section, between Luggala and Laragh, traverses some wild country around Lough Dan.

St. Kevin's Way, an ancient pilgrims' route more than 1,000 years old, has recently been restored. The path runs for 30km (19 miles) through scenic countryside from Hollywood to Glendalough, following the route taken by pilgrims who visited the ancient monastic site, and winds its way through roads, forest paths, and open mountainside. It takes in many of the historical sites associated with St. Kevin, who traveled the route in search of a mountain hermitage, as well as areas of geological interest and scenic beauty.

Folks who prefer less strenuous walking can follow the paths around the lakes at **Glendalough,** or join the southern section of the **Wicklow Way,** through Tinahely, Shillelagh, and Clonegal. Not as rugged as the terrain in central Wicklow, the gentle hills roll through peaceful glens. Through much of this section, the path follows country roads chosen for their lack of traffic.

WATERSPORTS & ADVENTURE SPORTS Deep in the Wicklow Mountains, the Blessington Lakes are a 2,000-hectare (4,940-acre) playground of tranquil, clean, speedboat-free water. Less than an hour's drive from Dublin center, and signposted on the N81, the **Blessington Lakes Leisure,** Blessington, County Wicklow (✆ **045/857844**), provides all you need for canoeing, kayaking, sailing, and windsurfing, as well as land-based sports such as archery, orienteering, tennis, and pony trekking.

Where to Stay

VERY EXPENSIVE

BrookLodge & Wells Spa ★★★ BrookLodge is a revolutionary idea—not so much a hotel as a planned village with rooms scattered amid restaurants, pubs, an award-winning spa, a chapel, a bakery, and shops selling wines, homemade jams, and crafts. The property has a comfortable kind of luxury—rooms have firm king-size beds, deep tubs, soft linens, and contemporary furnishings. Service is excellent—the personal touch extends to a decidedly Irish nightly turndown service: chocolates on your pillow and a hot-water bottle between the sheets. The primary restaurant is the **Strawberry Tree** (p. 217)—a gourmet eatery with a passionate dedication to organic cuisine. The hotel's lavish spa, the **Wells,** has made headlines with its Finnish baths, mud suites, hot tubs, indoor and outdoor pools, and innovative therapies. Check the website for good discounts and package deals that include breakfast and dinner.

Macreddin Village (btw. Aughrim and Aghavannagh), County Wicklow. www.brooklodge.com. ✆ **0402/36444.** Fax 0402/36580. 54 units. €250 double. Rates include service charge and full Irish breakfast. Fixed-price 4-course dinner at the Strawberry Tree €65. AE, DC, MC, V. **Amenities:** 3 restaurants; 2 pubs; full-service spa. *In room:* TV, hair dryer.

Rathsallagh House Hotel & Golf Club ★★ Converted from Queen Anne stables in 1798 (the main house was burned in the 1798 uprising), this long, ivy-covered country house sits amid 212 hectares (524 acres) of parkland, which is, in turn, surrounded by Rathsallagh Golf Course (greens fees €40–€50). This is a cheerful place, with log fires roaring in the lounge, and a reviving cup of tea available whenever you need it. Return guests request their favorite rooms by name—the Buttercup, the Romantic, the Over Arch, or the Yellow Room. Rooms are priced according to size, starting with standard rooms, which are rather tiny, and rising to superior rooms, which offer plenty of space. Most rooms have sitting areas, and some have Jacuzzis. The hotel restaurant specializes in local meat and produce, cooked in modern Irish style. Children 11 and under are not allowed here.

Dunlavin, County Wicklow. www.rathsallagh.com. ✆ **800/323-5463** in the U.S., or 045/403112. Fax 045/403343. 31 units. €240–€320 double. Rates include full breakfast. Fixed-price menu €65. AE, DC, MC, V. Closed Dec 23–31. **Amenities:** Restaurant; lounge/bar; 18-hole championship golf course; small indoor pool; sauna; tennis court. *In room:* Wi-Fi, TV/DVD, DVD library, hair dryer.

Ritz-Carlton at Powerscourt ★★ This creamy, crescent-shaped Palladian hotel a sheep's leap from Powerscourt House is a thing of beauty, surrounded by sprawling gardens and golf courses that stretch as far as the eye can see. Throughout the hotel no expense has been spared. Spacious guest rooms are equipped with feather beds, while bathrooms have marble baths and Rainforest showers. Throw in a swimming pool lighted with Swarovski crystal chandeliers and two championship golf courses and you can see why this place attracted attention when it opened in 2008, just before the Irish economic bubble burst. In a way it stands as a monument to that culture of excess. There's an elegant spa should you need help relaxing, and the hotel restaurant, Gordon Ramsey at Powerscourt, comes highly recommended, though it's not cheap (p. 219). Happily, there are four other restaurants and bars in the hotel to choose from.

Powerscourt Estate, Enniskerry, County Wicklow. www.ritzcarlton.com. ✆ **01/274-8888.** Fax 01/274-9999. 200 units. €250–€300 double. Rates include full breakfast and VAT. AE, DC, MC, V. **Amenities:** 3 restaurants; bar; 2 18-hole championship golf courses; indoor pool; sauna; spa; tennis court. *In room:* TV/DVD, hair dryer, minibar, Wi-Fi (free).

Tinakilly Country House & Restaurant ★★ Tinakilly is designed to spoil you with luxurious rooms, sweeping views, and an award-winning restaurant. The building dates from the 1870s when it was the home of a sea captain—its central staircase is said to be the twin of the one on his ship. Rooms are done in Victorian style; many have four-poster or canopy beds. The Captain's Suites are grand, with enormous bathrooms, while standard doubles are small but well decorated, albeit with tiny bathrooms. The **restaurant** (p. 220) is highly rated, so gourmets will want to dine in, rather than heading to the nearby village of Rathnew. Breakfast here earns raves.

On R750, off the Dublin-Wexford rd. (N11), Rathnew, County Wicklow. www.tinakilly.ie. ✆ **800/525-4800** in the U.S., or 0404/69274. Fax 0404/67806. 51 units. €200 double. Rates include full breakfast and VAT. AE, DC, MC, V. **Amenities:** Restaurant; lounge. *In room:* TV, radio, hair dryer.

EXPENSIVE

Glenview Hotel ☺ Located in the poetically named Glen of the Downs, this country hotel is a handy alternative for those looking to get away from it all. A 10-minute drive from Powerscourt House at the edge of the Wicklow Mountains, the hotel is surrounded by gardens and woodlands, perfect for a post-dinner stroll. The spacious bedrooms are decorated in light, pastel tones with marble bathrooms. There are family rooms for those travelling with kids. Deluxe and executive rooms have views of the glen (but you'll pay extra for that), and a full-service spa, the Haven, offers decadent treatments. Its leisure club and pool offer a supervised kids club from 9am to 9pm during the summer—handy for when you want to escape for an hour or two for a massage. Check the website for discounts and package deals.

Glen of the Downs, Delgany, County Wicklow. www.glenviewhotel.com. ✆ **01/287-3399.** Fax 01/287-7511. 70 units. €190–€240 double. Rates include full breakfast. AE, MC, V. **Amenities:** Restaurant; bar; gym; Jacuzzi; pool; steam room; full-service spa. *In room:* AC (in some), TV, hair dryer, Wi-Fi (free).

Kilgraney Country House ★ A striking mix of old and new gives this lovely stone building its flavor. In the public areas, solid, Irish-made antiques are balanced with vivid works of contemporary art and pieces of modern furniture. A tiny spa in a restored apple storehouse offers aromatherapy massage to work out the kinks. Rooms are soothing and minimalist, with lots of creative touches and pieces of modern art. Dinner, served on a long communal table of black Kilkenny marble, is also a fusion of the exotic and the traditional, and the conversation it inspires can last well into the night. Breakfasts are varied—perhaps raisin-and-orange pancakes as a first course, and more standard second-course offerings of scrambled eggs with salmon.

Just off the R705 (L18), 5.6km (3½ miles) from Bagenalstown on the Borris rd., Bagenalstown, County Carlow. www.kilgraneyhouse.com. ✆ **059/977-5283.** 6 units, all with private bathroom, 4 with shower only. €170–€280 double. Rates include full breakfast. 6-course fixed-price dinner €52 (€54 nonguests). AE, MC, V. Closed Nov–Feb. Children 11 and under not accepted. **Amenities:** Lounge; smoke-free rooms; spa. *In room:* TV, hair dryer.

MODERATE

Ballyknocken Guesthouse Hotel & Cookery School ★ The clue's in the name: It's all about the food here. You don't have to take any of owner and TV chef Catherine Byrne's cooking courses during your stay, but you certainly won't want to miss dinner. She prepares mouth-watering, contemporary meals using ingredients from her own garden and the local farm. The bedrooms are midsize and charmingly decorated with a hodgepodge of antiques; in a nice touch, all the bathrooms have original Victorian roll-top tubs. Another alternative is the Milking Parlour, a two-bedroom self-catering loft that sleeps up to six. It's available by the week at a cost of €56 per person, per night. Cooking courses cost around €80 to €100 for a half-day; see the website for the full (extensive) list. Ballyknocken makes a good base for exploring the Wicklow Mountains, and Catherine can provide plenty of information on hiking in the area.

Glenealy, Ashford, County Wicklow. www.ballyknocken.com. ✆ **0404/44627.** 70 units. €139 double. Rates include full breakfast. 4-course dinner Mon–Sat €47. AE, MC, V. *In room:* TV, hair dryer.

The Lord Bagenal ★ 🎁 This storybook country inn begs to be photographed, with its old stone archway and lovely setting at the leafy edge of the Barrow River. Inside, though, it's a bit brutally modern, which can come as a surprise, but rooms are pleasantly decorated in neutral fabrics with fluffy comforters. At night, the award-winning restaurant delivers French-influenced classics created with fresh local produce. Overall, this is a great address to know about when you want to unwind and be comforted.

Main St., Leighlinbridge, County Carlow. www.lordbagenal.com. ✆ **059/977-4000.** 12 units. €90–€150 double. Rates include full breakfast. MC, V. **Amenities:** 2 Restaurants; pub. *In room:* TV, hair dryer, room service, Wi-Fi (free).

Lorum Old Rectory ★ Set well back from the road and surrounded by undulating pastures in the serene Barrow Valley, the Old Rectory is a weathered and welcoming place. The bedrooms are spacious and comfortable, but not at all fancy, although some have big four-poster and canopy beds. Most rooms have calming views of the lush Carlow countryside. There's a small gift shop just for guests, displaying the work of local artists. Good dinners are on offer if you book in advance.

Just off the R705 (L18), 7km (4⅓ miles) from Bagenalstown on the Borris rd., Bagenalstown, County Carlow. www.lorum.com. ✆ **059/977-5282.** Fax 059/977-5455. 5 units, all with private bathroom with shower only. €150–€170 double. Rates include full breakfast. Dinner (must be booked by noon) €48. AE, MC, V. Closed Dec–Feb. *In room:* TV, hair dryer.

INEXPENSIVE

An Óige Glendaloch International Hostel ★ Location, location—this An Óige (Irish Youth Hostel Association) hostel has a prime location right near the Glendalough ruins and lakes, with spectacular views. It was renovated a few years ago, so everything's clean and comfortable, if a tad sterile. There's no curfew, but doors are locked between noon and 5pm. A full breakfast is available for €7.50, and packed lunch for €6. Dinner is a slightly less reliable affair; although it's good value (a three-course meal costs just €13) it's available only to groups of 10 or more. Otherwise, you'll have to head to Laragh, 1.6km (1 mile) away. The Irish Writers' Centre of Dublin hosts traditional music and poetry sessions at the hostel three times a week during the summer months, and live music fills the bar every Saturday night. It's got a great vibe, attracting people of all ages.

Glendalough (follow the signs for Glendalough; the hostel is on the road to the upper lake). www.anoige.ie. ✆ **0404/45342.** €16–€25 per person dorms; €51–€56 per room double, twin. No credit cards. **Amenities:** Restaurant; Internet.

Sherwood Park House This big, grand, 18th-century Georgian country house looms four stories high and has memorable views of the green countryside from every window. Its four guest rooms are all spacious—two on the second floor also have small, adjoining twin rooms, making them perfect for families. Rooms have four-poster and half-tester beds done up in well-chosen fabrics. Bathrooms are a bit out of date, but neat and clean. A peat fire warms the attractive guest sitting room, with its old piano in the corner. Dinner is served in the high-ceilinged dining room; conversation tends to be lively as everyone sits together at one long polished table.

Kilbride, Ballon, County Carlow (off the N80, 3km/2 miles south of Ballon). www.sherwoodparkhouse.ie. ✆ **059/913-9117.** 4 units. €100 double. Dinner €40. AE, MC, V. *In room:* TV.

Tudor Lodge Well located on the slopes of the Wicklow Mountains, this guesthouse makes a good base for ramblers and a peaceful getaway for those who are simply looking to escape the noise of ordinary life. The whitewashed decor is clean and crisp, and most bedrooms are spacious and all are simply decorated—each has a small desk, as well as both a double and a single bed (this makes the smaller rooms a bit of a squeeze). The dining room and living room have large windows overlooking green meadows and mountains. In the summer, you can relax on the stone terrace or riverside patio. At breakfast choose from a small but good selection of options. The restaurants and pubs of Laragh are a short, scenic walk away.

Laragh, County Wicklow. www.tudorlodgeireland.com. ✆ **086/875-9387.** 6 units, all with private bathroom, shower only. €80 double. MC, V. **Amenities:** Smoke-free rooms; Wi-Fi. *In room:* TV, hair dryer.

Tynte House ★ ☺ This handsome 19th-century family farm complex near the tiny town of Dunlavin in western Wicklow has a good mix of rooms, apartment units, and private stone cottages. All are cleverly designed, with bright, tasteful color schemes, light-pine furniture, and spacious tiled bathrooms. The no. 3 mews house and the open-plan apartment are our favorites (for both the light they receive and the country house decor), but none are likely to disappoint. This place is great for families, with a grassy play area and treehouse, a barbecue grill and picnic tables, tennis courts, and a game room with Ping-Pong and pool tables. Prices depend on the season and the size of the cottage.

Dunlavin center, County Wicklow. www.tyntehouse.com. ✆ **045/401561.** Fax 045/401586. 8 units. B&B €70–€110 double; self-catering units €245–€550 per week. Dinner €25. Packed lunches €8. AE, MC, V. *In room:* TV, kitchen.

Wicklow Way Lodge ★★ 🎁 This gorgeous little B&B has some famous fans—Matthew McConaughey stayed here a few years back—and a devoted following among regular visitors to the region. Set amid peaceful farmland just a few miles down the road from Glendalough, the lodge is a modern building, with big windows to take full advantage of the sprawling mountain views (ask for a room at the front). Owners Seamus and Marilyn Kinlan make warm hosts, and the guest rooms are spacious and comfortable, with lots of polished wood, and radiant heating. The only downside is that you can't have dinner here, although the Kinlans can suggest plenty of places nearby. Breakfasts, on the other hand, are legendary—don't even think of not trying the oatmeal. Wicklow Lodge is a wonderful find, less than an hour's drive from Dublin.

Oldbridge, Roundwood, County Wicklow. www.wicklowwaylodge.com. ✆ **01/281-8489.** 5 units. €90 double; €100 double with balcony. AE, MC, V. Rates include full breakfast. *In room:* TV, hair dryer.

SELF-CATERING

Kippure Estate This grand, 96-hectare (240-acre) countryside estate is a kind of peaceful haven of forest and pasture. There are 20 cottages for rent, with some sleeping up to eight people. The cottages are sympathetically designed to blend in with the rustic surroundings, and each is spacious and filled with natural light. Although they are modern and well equipped, each has a wood-burning stove as well. The cottages may be a little close together for those seeking isolation; it's effectively a village, set against a stunning backdrop of trees and mountains. If you prefer, you can stay instead in the main **Kippure Lodge** (€70 per night for a double room). You can take part in a variety of activities on the estate, such as the "Sky Trek," a supervised course involving rope bridges and zip wires (€49 per person).

Manor Kilbride, Blessington, County Wicklow. www.kippure.com. ✆ **01/458-2889.** 20 cottages. €380–€890 per week; €250–€540 weekend. Extra charge for stays that include a bank holiday. AE, MC, V. *In room:* TV, kitchen.

Wicklow Head Lighthouse ★★ 🎁 This 18th-century lighthouse on rocky Wicklow Head makes an unusual getaway. The Irish Landmark Trust (ILT), whose mission is to rescue neglected historic buildings, has transformed the old lighthouse into a kind of coastal show home. The interior is chic rustic with whitewashed walls, pine furniture, brass beds, and well-chosen nautical memorabilia. Each of the six floors holds one octagonal space, including two double bedrooms, and one bathroom. There are 109 calorie-burning steps up to the kitchen, which is on the top floor. Every window has a dazzling ocean view, and the sitting room comes complete with a telescope—great for watching seals frolicking below. As with all ILT properties, there is no TV. ***Note:*** The spiral staircase that corkscrews up the tower is not suitable for people with mobility problems, or for children 4 and under.

Wicklow, County Wicklow. Contact the Irish Landmark Trust at www.irishlandmark.com. ✆ **01/670-4733.** Fax 01/670-4887. €495 for 4 nights in low season, sliding up to €1,575 per week in high season. MC, V.

Where to Eat

EXPENSIVE

Backstage @ Bel's MODERN EUROPEAN There's more than a whiff of showbiz about this theatrical place. You can get breakfast and lunch here, but the real attraction is the evening menu. It's arranged not as the traditional "starter," "main," and "dessert" but "Act One," "Act Two," and so on. It's all in the spirit of fun, and the atmosphere is warm and friendly. Typical mains include wild sea bass with crushed potatoes, and orange and fennel salad, or filet of Wicklow beef with garlic butter, baked field mushrooms, and hand-cut fries. Where possible, the ingredients are sourced locally—and the coffee and tea are fair trade. Desserts are exceptional: Try the hot chocolate fondant with candied orange and pistachio ice cream.

Bel House, Church Rd., Greystones, County Wicklow. ✆ **01/201-6990.** www.bels.ie. Reservations recommended. Fixed-price menu (Tues–Fri 5–7pm) 2 courses €20; main courses €17–€28. MC, V. Daily 9am–10pm (dinner from 5pm).

Chakra by Jaipur ★ INDIAN This place suffers a little from an unromantic location, stuck inside a shopping mall in Greystones' main shopping district, but the food is outstanding. The menu employs the risky strategy of using a touch of Irish ingredients to complement the traditional Indian curries and *biryanis,* but manages not to stray too far from authenticity in doing so. Try the *hyderabadi murgh*—grilled free-range chicken in yogurt and caramelized onion sauce with a touch of lavender, of all things. Or sample the spicy crab chili masala: Dingle bay crab with coriander, green chilies, coconut, and lime.

1st Floor, Meridian Point, Church Rd., Greystones, County Wicklow. ✆ **01/201-7222.** Reservations recommended. Fixed-price menus €30–€45; main courses €15–€26. MC, V. Daily 5–11pm.

Gordon Ramsey at Powerscourt ★ MODERN EUROPEAN Celebrity chef Gordon Ramsey emphasizes fresh local produce at this elegant restaurant in the Ritz-Carlton Powerscourt. Diners can take in lavish views of green Wicklow while they have their every culinary need catered to by Ramsey's famously well-chosen and trained waitstaff. The menu changes daily, but options might include such items as foie gras with almond, chocolate, and cherries; Clare Island salmon with lobster ravioli; fresh local fish with crab, avocado, and mango salad; or king crab with shellfish risotto and mascarpone mousse. You could also have the four-course chef's "surprise" menu (€85), and let the experts decide what's best that night. Make reservations well in advance, as (economic crisis or no) the Dublin glitterati helicopter in for dinner.

Ritz-Carlton Powerscourt, Powerscourt Estate, Enniskerry, County Wicklow. ✆ **01/274-8888.** www.ritzcarlton.com. Reservation recommended. Fixed-price menus €85–€130; main courses €38–€42. AE, MC, V. Daily 11:30am–2pm and 6:30–10pm.

The Strawberry Tree ★★★ GOURMET ORGANIC A past winner of the Irish *Food & Wine*'s best restaurant award, this place has gone from innovative to iconic in a few years. Only wild and organic foods are the ingredients in the memorable meals served in the chic dining room. Starters might include smoked organic beef with wild colts foot, local smoked salmon rillettes with wild sorrel, or wild wood pigeon terrine with strawberry jam. Then there could be beef filet with beets in a balsamic *jus;* or wild guinea fowl with dried fruit compote. If you're feeling sociable, ask to be seated at the "big table," where dishes (from a special, set menu) are presented "feast style" for you and up to 40 other diners to share. From Rathdrum, follow signs for Aughrim and then 3km (2 miles) to Macreddin Village and the BrookLodge & Wells Spa.

BrookLodge, Macreddin Village (btw. Aughrim and Aghavannagh), County Wicklow. ✆ **0402/36444.** www.brooklodge.com. Reservations required. Fixed-price dinner €65; Sun lunch €40. MC, V. Tues–Sat 7–9:30pm; Sun 1:30–3:30pm and 7–9pm. (Closed Mon, Tues, and Wed Nov–Mar)

Tinakilly Country House Hotel ★★ MODERN IRISH This excellent restaurant, which *Bon Appétit* magazine once called "a beacon to restore hope to the traveler's heart," has won as many accolades as the hotel to which it belongs (p. 215). The table d'hôte menu changes daily and is confidently balanced—sophisticated without being fussy. The service, too, is precise and intuitive. Dishes can include pan-fried rump of lamb with roasted vegetables and gratin potato, or duck breast with red-onion marmalade and red currant *jus.* If dinner here is out of your budget, consider coming for a light lunch (1–3pm) or afternoon tea (3–5pm).

In Tinakilly Country House, Rathnew, County Wicklow (on R750, off the N11). ✆ **0404/69274.** www.tinakilly.ie. Reservations recommended. Dinner main courses €28–€34. AE, DC, MC, V. Dinner: Sun–Thurs 6–8:30pm; Fri–Sat 7:30–9:30pm. Lunch: Mon–Fri 12:30–2:30pm; Sat–Sun 1–3:30pm.

MODERATE

Poppies Country Cooking IRISH As the name implies, this is a friendly, casual place to get a bite to eat in Enniskerry. The food is simple fare (stews, sandwiches, soups, and meat pies), but is homemade and a cut above most such fare. The cakes are excellent, so it's worth stopping in for a cup of tea and a scone in the afternoon. A second branch of Poppies is in the Dundrum Town Centre, County Dublin (✆ **01/296-0629**).

The Square, Enniskerry, County Wicklow. ✆ **01/282-8869.** www.poppies.ie. Main courses €13–€20. MC, V. Daily 8:30am–6pm.

Roundwood Inn ★ MODERN IRISH/CONTINENTAL A fixture in tiny Roundwood village for more than 25 years, this cozy old inn is a delightful, snug place with shadowy rooms and huge roaring fires. There are effectively two restaurants here; tasty bar food is served in the main pub area (roast chicken and chips and Westphalian ham and salad are typical dishes) while adjoining is the full-service restaurant. The vibe in here is laid-back and charmingly rough around the edges, while the food is a sophisticated and unusual take on Irish classics, with a Pan-European (mostly German) twist. Mains could include Wicklow lamb, roast suckling pig with schnitzel, or a memorable Irish stew, in addition to impeccably presented seafood, fresh from the bays of Dublin and Galway. In good weather, there's seating in a secluded garden.

Roundwood, County Wicklow. ✆ **01/281-8107.** Reservations required in restaurant. Main courses €9–€19. AE, MC, V. Bar food daily noon–9:30pm. Restaurant Fri–Sat 7:30–9pm; Sun 1-2pm. No children after 6:30pm.

INEXPENSIVE

Avoca Handweavers Tea Shop ★ BISTRO/VEGETARIAN Forget for a moment that this is an informal cafeteria—at a tourist magnet, no less. It is a great place to eat and it delivers a good, healthy meal. The menu changes daily, but starters might include pea-and-mint soup or a crisp Caesar salad. Main courses could be sesame-glazed chicken, honey-roasted ham, Mediterranean sweet frittata, or smoked Wicklow trout. The tea shop attracts a loyal local clientele with its perfect pastries.

Avoca, County Wicklow. ✆ **0402/35105.** Lunch €5–€13. AE, DC, MC, V. Daily 9am–5:30pm (5pm in winter).

Grangecon Café ★ CAFE This is a handy little place to grab a light lunch or a snack. Try one of the beautifully prepared quiches, salads, and sandwiches, or indulge in the fresh cakes and pastries and a cup of tea.

Kilbride Rd., Blessington, County Wicklow. ✆ **045/857892.** Sandwiches, panini, and wraps €8; lunch main courses €9–€13. MC, V. Mon–Wed 9am–4pm; Thurs–Sat 9am–5pm. Closed Sun and bank holidays.

Pubs

The Coach House Adorned with hanging flowerpots, this Tudor-style inn is sweet, surrounded by mountains in picturesque Roundwood. The 18th-century pub is full of local memorabilia, and makes a pleasant stop for pub food and a drink. Guest rooms go for €95 per night. Main St., Roundwood, County Wicklow. ✆ **01/281-8157.** www.thecoachhouse.ie.

Johnnie Fox's This sprawling pub in little Glencullen is endlessly popular. Their 4-hour "Hooley" combines dinner with traditional music and dancing. There's also live music in the bar every night, and a separate restaurant for those who don't want to throw themselves too enthusiastically into the *craic*. It's crowded on weekends, but the food is good and the crowd is friendly. Main St., Rathdrum, County Wicklow. ✆ **01/295-5647.** www.jfp.ie.

The Meetings This quaint country-cottage pub stands idyllically at the "Meeting of the Waters" in the Vale of Avoca. Good pub grub is served daily, with traditional Irish music from April to October, every Sunday afternoon (4–6pm) and weekend nights all year. Avoca, County Wicklow. ✆ **0402/35226.**

COUNTY KILDARE: IRELAND'S HORSE COUNTRY

24–48km (15–30 miles) W of Dublin

The flatlands of Kildare are rich in more ways than one. The soil is lush and fertile, producing miles of green pastures perfect for raising horses, and the population is one of the most affluent in the country, with plenty of cash for buying horses.

Driving through the smooth rolling hills, home to sleek thoroughbreds, you'll notice a similarity to the green grass of Kentucky—in fact, the county is twinned with Lexington, Kentucky. This is the home of the Curragh, the racetrack where the Irish Derby is held, and of smaller tracks at Naas and Punchestown.

Once the stronghold of the Fitzgerald Clan, Kildare comes from the Irish *cill dara,* or "Church of the Oak Tree," a reference to St. Brigid's monastery, which once sat in the county, surrounded by oak trees. Brigid was a bit ahead of her time as an early exponent for women's equality—she founded her coed monastery in the 5th or 6th century.

Essentials

GETTING THERE **Irish Rail** (✆ **01/836-6222;** www.irishrail.ie) provides daily train service to Kildare.

Bus Éireann (✆ **01/836-6111;** www.buseireann.ie) operates daily express bus service to Kildare from Dublin and elsewhere in Ireland.

By car, take the main Dublin-Limerick road (N7) west of Dublin from Kildare, or the main Dublin-Galway road (N4) to Celbridge, turning off on local road R403.

VISITOR INFORMATION Contact the **Wicklow Tourist Office,** Fitzwilliam Square, Wicklow Town (✆ **0404/69117**). It's open year-round Monday to Friday, and Saturday during peak season. You can get general tourist information in the **Kildare Heritage Centre,** Market Square, Kildare Town, County Kildare (✆ **045/530672**).

Seeing the Sights

Castletown ★★ This spectacular Palladian-style mansion has been imitated many times across Ireland over the centuries. It was the first house in this style built in the country (it was built between 1722 and 1729), designed by Italian architect Alessandro Galilei for then-speaker of the Irish House of Commons William Connolly. Today, it's beautifully maintained and the fully restored interior is worth the price of admission. The two glorious follies on the grounds—both commissioned by William Connolly's wife, Louisa, were built as make-work for the starving population during the famine. One is a graceful obelisk, the other is the extraordinarily playful barn, created as a slightly crooked inverted funnel, around which winds a stone staircase. Its name, appropriately enough, is the "Wonderful Barn."

R403, off main Dublin-Galway rd. (N4), Celbridge, County Kildare. ✆ **01/628-8252.** www.castletownhouse.ie. Admission (guided tour only) €4.50 adults; €3.50 seniors, students, and children; €13 families; free for children 4 and under. No cameras. April–Oct Tues–Sun 10am–4:45pm.

The Curragh ★★ This is the country's best-known racetrack, majestically placed at the edge of Ireland's central plain, and home to the **Irish Derby,** held every spring. Races are on at least one Saturday a month from March to October. The track has rail links with all major towns, and Irish Rail runs directly to it from Dublin (Heuston Station) for around €15, including courtesy coach to the main entrance. There's also a "Racing Bus" from Dublin (Busáras) each race day. Call Bus Éireann for details (✆ **01/836-6111;** www.buseireann.ie).

Dublin-Limerick rd. (N7), Curragh, County Kildare. ✆ **045/441205.** www.curragh.ie. Admission €15–€20 for most racing days; €15–€120 on derby days. AE, DC, MC, V. Hours vary; 1st race usually 2pm, but check newspaper sports pages.

From spring through fall, the Curragh hosts weekly horse races, including the annual Irish Derby.

Irish National Stud with Japanese Gardens & St. Fiachra's Garden ★★ Some of Ireland's fastest horses have been bred on the grounds of this government-sponsored stud farm. Horse lovers and racing fans will be in heaven walking around the 383-hectare (946-acre) grounds watching the well-groomed horses being trained. A converted groom's house has exhibits on racing, steeplechase, hunting, and show jumping, plus a rather macabre display featuring the skeleton of Arkle, one of Ireland's most famous horses.

There's a peaceful **Japanese garden ★** dating from 1906, with pagodas, ponds, and trickling streams. There's also a beautifully designed visitor center with a restaurant and shop. The Commemorative Garden of St. Fiachra, in a natural setting of woods, wetlands, lakes, and islands, opened in 1999. The reconstructed hermitage has a Waterford crystal garden of rocks, ferns, and delicate glass orchids.

Off the Dublin-Limerick rd. (N7), Tully, Kildare, County Kildare. ✆ **045/522963.** www.irish-national-stud.ie. Admission €11 adults; €8 seniors and students; €6 children 5–16; €27 families; free for children 4 and under. MC, V. Mid-Feb to late Dec daily 9:30am–5pm. Last admission 3:30pm; parking lot locked at 6:30pm sharp. Bus: From Busáras, Dublin, each morning, returning each evening.

The Irish Pewtermill In an 11th-century mill originally constructed for the nunnery of St. Moling, Ireland's oldest pewter mill makes for a nice diversion. Six skilled craftsmen cast pewter in antique molds, some of which are 300 years old. Casting takes place most days, usually in the morning. The showroom has a wide selection of high-quality, hand-cast pewter gifts for sale, from bowls to brooches, at reasonable prices. There's a set of excellent reproductions of the principal panels from Moone High Cross (see the listing below), with explanatory plaques. They're helpful in further understanding and appreciating the ancient carvings.

Timolin-Moone (signposted off N9 in Moone), County Kildare. ✆ **059/862-4164.** timolinpewter@tinet.ie. Free admission. Mon–Fri 10am–4:30pm; Sat–Sun 11am–4pm.

Larchill Arcadian Garden ★ ☺ 🎁 This unusual farm garden is the only surviving "ornamental farm" in Europe and it was nearly lost forever after it fell into decay in the 1970s and 1980s. Luckily, it was restored in the late 1990s. Products of the Romantic Movement, these hybrid farms were popular in the 18th century, and Larchill is a marvelous example of the movement's art for art's sake ethos. All around the working farm are little things of beauty: a lake dotted with delightful Gothic follies; wooded nature trails; meadows stocked with emus and llamas; a walled garden with geese, and peacocks. There's even a resident ghost haunting a medieval tower. Kids will not be bored here, as there's an adventure trail with traditional games, a playground and sand pit, and guinea pigs and rabbits to pet. Snacks and ice cream are available in the tearoom.

Kilcock, County Kildare (signposted off N4 near Maynooth). ✆ **01/628-7354.** www.larchill.ie. Admission €7.50 adults; €5.50 children; €28 families. May (holiday weekends only, including Mon) and Sept Sat–Sun noon–6pm; June–Aug Thurs–Sun (and holiday weekends Sat–Mon) noon–6pm.

Moone High Cross ★ Amid the picturesque ruins of Moone Abbey, this magnificent high cross is nearly 1,200 years old. The abbey, established by St. Columba in the 6th century, is in evocative ruins around it. The cross features finely crafted Celtic designs as well as biblical scenes: the temptation of Adam and Eve, the sacrifice of Isaac, and Daniel in the lions' den. Among the carvings are several surprises, such as a carving of a Near Eastern fish that reproduces when the male feeds the female her own eggs, which eventually hatch from her mouth.

Moone, County Kildare (signposted off N9 on southern edge of Moone village).

Newbridge Silverware For 60 years, this has been Ireland's leading manufacturer of fine silverware. The visitor center has displays of place settings, bowls, candelabras, trays, frames, and one-of-a-kind items; and if you like it all too much to leave it behind, you can stock up at the shop.

Off Dublin-Limerick rd. (N7), Newbridge, County Kildare. ✆ **045/431301.** Free admission. Mon–Sat 9am–6pm; Sun 11am–5pm.

St. Brigid's Cathedral This 13th-century church stands on the site of St. Brigid's monastery, which was founded in the 5th century. The church, which dominates central Kildare, is a beautiful building with exquisite stained-glass windows portraying Ireland's three great saints: Patrick, Colmcille, and Brigid. The round tower on the grounds dates to the 10th century, and is the second tallest in the country (33m/108 ft.). Somewhere down the line, its pointed roof was replaced by a Norman turret. If the groundskeeper is in, you can climb the stairs to the top for €4. There's a strange-looking stone with a hole at the top near the tower; it's known as the "wishing stone"—according to lore, if you put your arm through the hole and touch your shoulder when you make a wish, then your wish will come true.

Market Sq., Kildare Town, County Kildare. ✆ **045/521229.** Suggested donation €1.50; admission to round tower €4. May–Sept Mon–Sat 10am–1pm and 2–5pm; Sun 2–5pm.

Steam Museum Celebrating the age of steam, this museum contains two collections: The Richard Guinness Hall has prototypical locomotive engines dating from the 18th century, and the Power Hall has rare industrial stationary engines. The engines are turned on fairly regularly—if you're interested, call ahead to find

ST. BRIGID: EARLY feminist

Feminists have embraced this 5th-century saint for decades. Brigid was a headstrong girl who fought against the oppressive rules of her time. When her father picked a husband for her, she refused to marry him. Legend holds that when her father insisted that the wedding should go forward, she pulled out her own eye to prove she was strong enough to resist his plans. He backed down, and the mutilated girl joined a convent, but when she took her vows the bishop accidentally ordained her as a bishop rather than a nun. It is said that as soon as that happened, she was miraculously made beautiful again.

As she grew older, Brigid remained a rebel. She founded a monastery in Kildare, but insisted that it be open to both nuns and monks—something that was extraordinary at that time. Unsurprisingly, word of the monastery, and of its unusual abbess, soon spread throughout Europe and she became a powerful figure in European Christianity. Her followers marked their homes with a plain cross woven from river reeds, and you'll still find crosses, made in precisely that way, in some Irish homes.

One of Brigid's strangest rules for her monastery was that there should always be a fire kept burning, day and night, tended by 20 virgins. Long after she died, the fire at St. Brigid's burned constantly, tended as she said it should be. This continued as late as 1220, when the bishop of Dublin insisted that the tradition, which he viewed as pagan, be stopped. But there is still a fire pit at St. Brigid's Cathedral (p. 224), and a fire is lit in it every February 1, on St. Brigid's feast day.

out times. The museum is inside an old church, outside of which an 18th-century walled garden wanders through several verdant spaces to a delightful rose garden. The shop stocks a variety of recent books and videos on the Irish Railway.

Straffan, County Kildare (signposted off N7 at Kill Village). ✆ **01/627-3155.** www.steam-museum.com. Admission to museum and gardens €7.50 adults; €5 seniors, children, and students; €20 families. June–Aug and public holidays Wed–Sun 2–6pm; May and Sept by arrangement.

Sports & Outdoor Pursuits

CYCLING Kildare's flat-to-rolling landscape is perfect for gentle cycling. Sadly, most organized tours bypass Kildare for regions with more diverse scenery, but you can always plan your own route. Bike rental shops are surprisingly few in County Kildare, but you could try **Cahill Cycles,** Fishery Lane, Naas (✆ **045/881-585**), or **Celbridge Cycle,** Main Street, Celbridge (✆ **01/627-4023**). Alternatively, you could rent a bike in Dublin.

GOLF The flat plains here create excellent parkland layouts, including two 18-hole championship courses. If your wallet is padded, the Arnold Palmer–designed, par-72 **Kildare Hotel & Country Club** (also known as the **K Club**), Straffan (✆ **01/601-7200;** www.kclub.com), has two courses, with greens fees ranging from €90 to €380 for nonresidents in high season, depending on tee time. For a less costly game, the par-70 **Kilkea Castle Golf Club,** Castledermot (✆ **059/914-5555;** www.kilkeacastlegolfresort.ie), charges €40 Monday to Thursday, €50 Friday to Sunday. Kilkea also does four-course golf and meal packages. Or try the par-72 championship course at the **Curragh Golf Club,** Curragh (✆ **045/441714;** www.curraghgolf.com), with greens fees of €25 weekdays, €35 weekends.

HORSEBACK RIDING Visitors can expect to pay an average of €25 per hour for trekking or trail riding in the Kildare countryside. To arrange a ride, contact the **Kill International Equestrian Centre,** Kill (✆ **045/877-333;** www.killinternational.ie).

WALKING The way-marked **Grand Canal Way** is a long-distance walking path that cuts through part of Kildare. Its flatness makes it ideal for beginners and for walkers who lack ambition. The canal passes through plenty of scenic towns, such as Sallins, Robertstown, and Edenderry, where you can find a room and stock up on provisions. For more information, contact the tourist office.

Where to Stay

VERY EXPENSIVE

Kildare Hotel & Country Club ★ The darling of the affluent, sporty set, Kildare is most famous for its 18-hole Arnold Palmer–designed golf course (see above) that hosted the Ryder Cup in 2006. A 45-minute drive from Dublin, this 132-hectare (326-acre), no-expense-spared resort makes a luxurious base from which to visit Dublin and the sights of Kildare. The surroundings are gorgeous and the service excellent, but the atmosphere here is more formal and less relaxed than at some of Ireland's other manor hotels. A Georgian mansion serves as the main hotel, although guest rooms are spread out among several buildings—all sumptuously appointed with luxurious fabrics. The main restaurant, the French-focused **Byerley Turk,** is very formal, but given how much the rooms cost that's no surprise. Men will want a jacket and tie for dinner. You can adjourn for drinks in the library—it's a showcase for an extraordinary collection of Jack B. Yeats paintings.

Straffan, County Kildare. www.kclub.com. ✆ **800/221-1074** in the U.S., or 01/601-7200. Fax 01/601-7297. 95 units. €500–€625 double; €825–€7,500 suite. AE, DC, MC, V. **Amenities:** 3 restaurants; pub; babysitting; concierge; 18-hole golf course; gym; indoor pool; room service; sauna; 2 indoor and 2 outdoor tennis courts. *In room:* A/C, TV, DVD, hair dryer, minibar.

EXPENSIVE

Barberstown Castle ★★ This sturdy castle has overlooked Kildare for more than 750 years. Its five segments—constructed in the 13th, 16th, 18th, 20th, and 21st centuries—somehow form a coherent and pleasing whole. Each luxurious guest room is named after one of the castle's former lords or proprietors. They begin with Nicholas Barby, who constructed the battlemented rectangular castle keep in the 13th century, and include the guitarist Eric Clapton, who once owned the place. All the rooms are warm and cozy, with sitting areas, antiques, and spacious bathrooms. Some have four-poster beds. Two-bedroom family spaces are available, as is a room designed for guests with disabilities.

Straffan, County Kildare. www.barberstowncastle.ie. ✆ **800/323-5463** in the U.S., or 01/628-8157. 58 units. €240–€290 double. Rates include full Irish breakfast. AE, DC, MC, V. Closed Jan–Feb. From Dublin, drive south on N7, take turn for Straffan at Kill; from west on N4, then turn for Straffan at Maynooth. **Amenities:** Restaurant; lounge; smoke-free rooms. *In room:* TV, hair dryer.

INEXPENSIVE

The Courtyard Hotel This is a warm, romantic hotel, where guest rooms are bright and contemporary. It's a little lacking in character, but the huge comfortable beds more than make up for that. If, after whatever journey you've undertaken to arrive here, you happen to feel like a restoring pint of Guinness, then pat yourself on the back for appropriateness. This was the building where Arthur Guinness set up his first brewery in 1756—the bar is named "Arthur" in his honor. ***Tip:*** The bar can get a little loud on weekends, so ask for a quiet room when you book.

Main St., Leixlip, County Kildare. www.courtyard.ie. ✆ **01/629-5100.** 40 units. €110–€140 double; €290 executive suite. Rates include full Irish breakfast. AE, MC, V. **Amenities:** 2 restaurants; bar. *In room:* TV, hair dryer, Wi-Fi.

Westgrove Hotel & Conference Centre This hotel doesn't have a lot of character, but it is a good budget option just a few miles outside Dublin. Set near an unromantic shopping center, the exterior isn't particularly alluring, but inside it's a different story—the decor is sleek and modern, and the staff is welcoming. Bedrooms are spacious, with polished wood furniture and soothing white linens. Beds are comfortable, and the executive apartments are a good size for families with kids. The **Exchange Restaurant** (see below) is a local favorite for dinner, while the hotel spa offers Elemis therapies, and every treatment begins with a warm foot compress.

Clane, Naas, County Kildare. www.westgrovehotel.com. ✆ **045/989-900.** 99 units. €80–€110 double; €150–€180 suite. Rates include full Irish breakfast. AE, MC, V. **Amenities:** 2 restaurants; 3 bars; gym; pool; full-service spa. *In room:* TV, DVD player (executive rooms only), hair dryer, free high-speed Internet.

Where to Eat

MODERATE

Ballymore Inn INTERNATIONAL This may look like a modest country restaurant, but the inspired cooking makes each dish a thing of beauty. The menu is varied yet unpretentious—typical mains might include grilled West Cork dry aged sirloin, or Duncannon salmon with fennel and dill sauce. The pizzas are often the most adventurous thing on the menu, with toppings such as Greek lamb with yogurt and mint winning points for originality. If all this sounds too adventurous, there's a more limited menu on offer in the bar.

Ballymore Eustace, County Kildare (off the N81, southeast of Blessington). ✆ **045/864585.** www.ballymoreinn.com. Reservations required. Main courses €19–€30; fixed-price menu 2 courses €28. MC, V. Restaurant daily 12:30–3pm and 6–9pm. Bar menu Mon–Fri 3–9pm; Sat 2–9pm; Sun 12:30–9pm.

Exchange Restaurant GRILL This long, narrow, bistro-style restaurant in the Westgrove Hotel (see above) is popular with locals for its straightforward, no-nonsense American-style menu, as well as its friendly atmosphere. This is a good place to go if you're feeling like a reasonably priced sirloin steak, a burger, a steaming bowl of seafood chowder, or pan-fried salmon. It's not fancy, but it's reliably good. Its sister restaurant, **Exchange Plus,** also in the Westgrove, is a more sophisticated option.

Westgrove Hotel, Clane, Naas, County Kildare. ✆ **045/989-900.** www.westgrovehotel.com. Main courses €16–€23. MC, V. Sun–Wed 5–10pm; Thurs–Fri 5–11pm; Sat 12:30–11pm.

Silken Thomas GRILL This historic inn is an old-world pub and an atmospheric restaurant with wooden floors and fires crackling in the hearth. The menu offers a good selection of soups, sandwiches, burgers, and salads, as well as steaks, roasts, mixed grills, and fresh seafood platters. **Chapter 16,** an upscale restaurant adjoining the lounge bar, is one of a growing list of side ventures at the Silken Thomas (along with a nightclub and an alcohol-free teen disco). If you can't bear to leave, it has plain-but-nice guest rooms as well (€65 double).
The Square, Kildare, County Kildare. ✆ **045/522232.** www.silkenthomas.com. Reservations recommended for dinner. Main courses €12–€27. AE, MC, V. Mon–Sat 12:30–2:30pm and 6–10pm; Sun 12:30–3pm and 6–9pm.

Pubs

The George Inn The back room of this pub is what makes it special. It was probably the kitchen of the original cottage, which would explain the huge fireplace with warm inglenooks and a brass-and-leather horse harness hanging over the mantel. Seating is random at a hodgepodge of cozy pine tables and chairs, and the atmosphere is welcoming and local. Prosperous, County Kildare. ✆ **045/861041.**

The Moone High Cross Inn This big, 18th-century inn is ideal for a pit stop. There's genuine hospitality and excellent pub food—bacon and cabbage, shepherd's pie, all the classics—not to mention an open fire, finely pulled pints, and convivial conversation. If you really like the place, you can spend the night in one of its five en-suite rooms. Moone, County Kildare. ✆ **059/862-4112.** www.moonehighcrossinnonline.com.

COUNTIES MEATH, LOUTH & THE BOYNE RIVER VALLEY

48–80km (30–50 miles) N and W of Dublin

Less than 48km (30 miles) north of Dublin along Ireland's east coast runs the River Boyne, surrounded by the rich, fertile countryside of counties Meath and Louth. More than any other river in the country, this meandering body of water has been at the center of Irish history.

The banks of the Boyne hold reminders of Ireland's ancient past in the extraordinary and mysterious prehistoric passage tombs of Newgrange and the storied Hill of Tara, once the seat of the high kings. This was the setting for the infamous Battle of the Boyne, when in July 1690, King William III defeated the exiled King James II for the crown of England.

Today its historic treasures are tucked away among miles of farmland, smooth, rolling hills, and modern Dublin suburbs.

Essentials

GETTING THERE **Irish Rail** (✆ **01/836-6222;** www.irishrail.ie) provides daily train service between Dublin and Drogheda.

Bus Éireann (✆ **01/836-6111;** www.buseireann.ie) operates daily express bus service to Slane and Navan in County Meath, and Collon and Drogheda in County Louth. Bus Éireann and **Gray Line Tours** (✆ **01/458-0054;** www.irishcitytours.com) offer seasonal sightseeing tours to Newgrange and the Boyne Valley for around €35 for an adult.

By car, take the N1 north from Dublin City to Drogheda, then the N51 west to Boyne Valley; the N2 northwest to Slane and east on the N51 to Boyne Valley; or the N3 northwest via Hill of Tara to Navan, and then east on the N51 to Boyne Valley.

VISITOR INFORMATION Contact the **Dundalk Tourist Office,** Jocelyn Street, Dundalk, County Louth (✆ **042/933-5484**); the **Drogheda Tourist Office,** Mayoralty Street, Drogheda, County Louth (✆ **041/983-7070**); or the **Bru na Boinne Center,** Newgrange, Donore, County Meath (✆ **041/988-0300**).

County Meath: The Royal County

The verdant pastures and low hills of Meath are Dublin's closest northern neighbor. The farmland here is so rich that there's an old Irish saying that a farm in Meath is worth two in any other county. With sheep grazing peacefully in green fields, Meath may look ordinary, but it holds remnants of Ireland's mysterious past. It is also the site of the **Hill of Tara**—the Olympus of early Ireland where the kings of Ireland ruled.

By then, though, the county was already very old. Meath's rich soil has attracted settlers for more than 8,000 years, and archaeologists have uncovered burial grounds and settlements that give fascinating insight into where and how they lived. The most intriguing of these is **Newgrange,** with its mysterious carvings and huge stone passage tombs. Nearby, the Hill of Slane, a lofty 150m (492-ft.) mound, overlooks one of the loveliest parts of the Boyne Valley. On this hill, tradition has it, Patrick lit the Christian paschal fire in direct defiance of the Irish King Laoghaire, throwing down the gauntlet for a confrontation between Ireland's old and new religious orders.

The chief town of County Meath is **Navan,** but nearby **Kells** is better known to most travelers because of its association with the famous Book of Kells—the hand-illustrated gospel manuscript on display at Trinity College in Dublin (see chapter 5). The town of Kells, known in Gaelic as *Ceanannus Mor* ("Great Residence"), was originally the site of an important 6th-century monastic settlement founded by St. Colmcille. The monastery was dissolved in 1551, and today only ruins and crosses survive.

Less than 40km (25 miles) southeast of Kells, beside the River Boyne, stand the alluring ruins of **Bective Abbey,** a Cistercian monastery founded in 1147. Today it feels more like a castle than a monastery; it is a great ruin, with myriad staircases, passageways, and chambers—a favorite hide-and-seek playground for local children, and perfect for a family picnic.

Even though Meath is primarily an inland county, it is also blessed with a stretch of coastline and two fine sandy beaches, **Bettystown** and **Laytown.** History pops up everywhere in County Meath, even on the beach: The Tara Brooch was found at Bettystown in 1850. Often copied in modern jewelry designs, the brooch is one of Ireland's finest pieces of early Christian gold-filigree work, embellished with amber and glass. It's on view at the National Museum in Dublin.

SEEING THE SIGHTS

Hill of Tara ★ This hill is a sentimental lure to the Irish diaspora, drawn by legends and folklore that place it at the center of early Irish history. Something about this nondescript green hill has always attracted people for spiritual reasons. Ancient tombs have been discovered on the hill that date from the Stone Age.

MODERN motorway CHANGES ANCIENT TARA LANDSCAPE

At the height of the Irish economic boom, the country's insatiable hunger for construction, highways, and speed collided head-on with its ancient history when the government expanded the **M3 motorway** through the middle of the historic Tara Valley. The €1-billion road-building project resulted in passionate protests and extensive legal cases.

From the beginning the project was controversial. In 2007, Ireland's minister for transportation dug a ceremonial shovel of earth at a groundbreaking event, but within weeks, a previously undiscovered ancient archaeological site was found directly in the road's planned path. Many thought that this would stop the government's plans. But it turned out that the government had already amended the National Monuments Act to allow for the demolition of national monuments.

The Tara valley is riddled with ceremonial sites virtually as old as the land itself. Most have yet to be explored by scientists. Archaeologists believe one of them—known as the Mound of the Hostages—dates from 3,000 B.C., making it as old as the pyramids.

It is now alleged that the Irish government has also drawn up plans to expand the N2 highway to within 500 meters of the ancient Newgrange complex. So the protests continue.

In 2010, the Hill of Tara was nominated to UNESCO to be a World Heritage Site, and listed as one of the 100 most endangered sites by the World Monuments Fund.

You can learn the latest on the battle between progress and history around Dublin by reading Irish newspapers or visiting **www.savetara.com**.

Pagans believed that the goddess Maeve lived and reigned from here. By the 3rd century, it was home to the most powerful men in Ireland—the high kings. They had a ceremonial residence on the hill, and ruled as much by myth as by military strength. Every 3 years, a *feis* (a banquet reaching the proportions of a great national assembly) was held there. It's said that more than 1,000 princes, poets, athletes, priests, druids, musicians, and jesters celebrated for a week. A *feis* wasn't all fun and games: Laws were passed, disputes settled, and matters of defense decided. The last *feis* was held in the year 560. After that, Tara went into a decline as the power and popularity of Christianity rose. What's left is not physically impressive—grassy mounds, some ancient pillar stones, and depressions where the Iron Age ring forts stood. All the wooden halls rotted long ago, so you'll have to rely on your imagination. But it's still a magnificent spot, with the hill rising 90m (295 ft.) above the surrounding countryside. A visitor center, with exhibits and a stirring film, is in the old church beside the entrance to the archaeological area. There's no picnicking, but there is a coffee shop/tearoom.

Off the main Dublin rd. (N3), Navan, County Meath. ✆ **046/902-5903.** Admission (visitor center) €3 adults; €2 seniors; €1.10 students and children; €8 families. Late May to mid-Sept daily 10am–6pm.

Knowth ★★ There is some debate over whether this site is more historically important than Newgrange. Both are Stone Age burial grounds, with complex passage tombs. Knowth's tomb was closed to the public for many years as archaeologists explored its depths, but is now open, at least in part. It is a massively long passage—at 34m (112 ft.), it is longer than the one at Newgrange. Then, in 1968, archaeologists discovered a second passage tomb on the opposite side of the mound that was 6m (20 ft.) longer. In the mound itself, scientists found the largest collection of passage tomb art uncovered thus far in Europe, as well as a number of underground chambers and 300 carved slabs. The mound itself is surrounded by 17 satellite graves in a complex pattern. The meaning of it all remains shadowed in mystery, and even now, all of Knowth's secrets have not been uncovered—excavation work is quite constant here, and you may get a chance to see the archaeologists at work. All tickets are issued at the visitor center. Combined tickets with Newgrange are available.

Near Drogheda, County Louth (1.6km/1 mile northwest of Newgrange). ✆ **041/988-0300.** www.knowth.com. Admission to Knowth and Bru na Boinne Centre €5 adults; €3 seniors, students, and children 7 and over; €13 families. Combined ticket with Newrange €11 adults; €8 seniors; €6 children 7 and over; €28 families. Nov–Jan daily 9am–5pm; Feb–Apr and Oct daily 9:30am–5:30pm; May and mid- to late Sept daily 9am–6:30pm; June to mid-Sept daily 9am–7pm. Last admission 45 min. before closing.

Loughcrew ★ The 30 passage tombs of Loughcrew, also known as *Slieve na Calliaghe* or "The Hill of the Witch," crown three hilltops in western Meath. From their summits, the views of the plains of Meath and the lakelands of Cavan are spectacular on a clear day. Two of the cairns—ornamented with Neolithic carvings—can be entered with a key. Guided tours of the cairns are offered from mid-June to mid-September. From mid-September to mid-June, between 10am and 4pm, the keys to both cairns are available from the Loughcrew Coffee Shop, which is in the parking lot. (***Note:*** They ask for an expensive refundable deposit: €50, plus your passport or driver's license.) There are gardens on-site for a fee, but admission is a bit steep. The cairns, however, are free.

Outside Oldcastle, County Meath. ✆ **049/854-1356.** www.loughcrew.com. Cairns free, admission to gardens €8 adults; €5 seniors and students; €4.50 children; €20 families. Apr–Sept daily 10am–6pm; year-round Sun and bank holidays only 1–5pm. Key is available at other times (see

A Stone Age burial ground, Knowth contains Europe's largest collection of passage tomb art.

above). From N3, take R195 through Oldcastle toward Mullingar. 2.4km (1½ miles) out of Oldcastle, look for a signposted left turn. The next left turn into Loughcrew is also signposted.

Newgrange ★★★ Ireland's best-known prehistoric monument is one of the archaeological wonders of western Europe. Built as a burial mound more than 5,000 years ago—long before the Egyptian pyramids or Stonehenge—it sits atop a hill near the Boyne, massive and mysterious. The mound is 11m (36 ft.) tall, and approximately 78m (256 ft.) in diameter. It consists of 200,000 tons of stone, a 6-ton capstone, and other stones weighing up to 16 tons each, many of which were hauled from as far away as County Wicklow and the Mountains of Mourne. Each stone fits perfectly in the overall pattern, and the result is a watertight structure, an amazing feat of engineering. The question remains, though: Who was it for? Even as archaeologists found more elaborate carvings in the stones—spirals, diamonds, and concentric circles—they got no clues as to whether it was for kings, political leaders, or for a long-lost ritual. Inside, a passage 18m (59 ft.) long leads to a central burial chamber that sits in pitch darkness all year, except for 5 days in December. As part of the tour, you can walk down the passage, past elaborately carved stones and into the chamber, which has three sections, each with a basin stone that once held cremated human remains. During the winter solstice (Dec 19–23), a shaft of sunlight travels down the arrow-straight passageway for 17 minutes, until it hits the back wall of the burial chamber. You can register for a lottery to be in the tomb for this extraordinary event.

Tips: Admission to Newgrange is by guided tour only. It's 3.2km (2 miles) east of Slane. Get there early. All tickets are issued at the visitor center, Bru na Boinne. Combined tickets with Knowth (above) are available. Because of the great numbers of visitors, especially in the summer, expect delays; access is not guaranteed. The last tour is given at 4:30pm.

Off N51, Slane, County Meath. ✆ **041/988-0300.** Fax 041/982-3071. www.knowth.com/newgrange.htm. Guided tour and admission to Bru na Boinne Centre €6 adults; €5 seniors; €3 students and children 7 and over; €15 families. Combined ticket with Knowth €11 adults; €8 seniors; €6 children 7 and over; €28 families. Nov–Jan daily 9am–5pm; Feb–Apr and Oct daily 9:30am–5:30pm; May and mid- to late Sept daily 9am–6:30pm; June to mid-Sept daily 9am–7pm.

The entrance stone at Newgrange leads to a passage tomb that lights up in sunlight only during the winter solstice.

Newgrange Farm ☺ After all that history, the kids will thank you for bringing them here to this busy 133-hectare (329-acre) farm where farmer Willie Redhouse and his family will take them on a 1½-hour tour of their farm. You can feed the ducks, groom a calf, and bottle-feed the lambs and kid goats. Children can hold a newborn chick, pet a pony, and play with the pigs. In the aviaries are pheasants and rare birds. You can take a ride on a tractor for an extra €2. The high point of the week (for kids, anyway) occurs at roughly 4pm every Sunday and bank holiday, when the sheep take to the track with teddy bear jockeys for the weekly derby. Demonstrations of sheepdogs working, threshing, and horseshoeing are regularly underway, while in the herb garden, you can get a lesson in picking edible plants and herbs. There is a coffee shop and plenty of picnic space.

Off N51, 3.2km (2 miles) east of Slane (signposted off N51 and directly west of Newgrange monument), County Meath. ✆ **041/982-4119.** www.newgrangefarm.com. Admission €8 per person; €18–€30 families. Daily 10am–5pm. Closed Sept to Good Friday.

St. Colmcille's House Sitting incongruously near more modern houses, like a memory of Ireland's past, St. Colmcille's House is all that's left of an old monastic settlement that once stood where modern homes are now built. Most of the building is 10th century, although the oldest parts predate that by another hundred years. Precisely what the house was built for is unknown, although some experts believe it was once a scriptorium—where monks wrote and illuminated books. The first-floor room still contains the traces of an ancient fireplace and entryway. A narrow metal staircase ascends 4.5m (15 ft.) to a dark vault just under the roof. The small two-chambered space has both a structural and mythical dimension. It is thought to help reinforce the stone arch of the oratory roof and—though this is more conjectural—is also said to be the place where the Book of Kells was completed.

About 180m (about 590 ft.) northwest of St. Columba's Church, Church Lane, Kells, County Meath. No phone. Free admission. Mon–Sat 10am–5pm. Ask for key from caretaker Mrs. B. Carpenter, next door to the oratory on Church Lane.

Slane Castle This 18th-century castle is best known within Ireland for the open-air rock and pop concerts held here in the summertime. For tourists, the big draw is the building itself, a Gothic Revival structure by James Wyatt. The design of the building was made grander in the early 19th century in advance of a visit by the English King George IV to Lady Conyngham, who is believed to have been his mistress (in fact, the Irish claim that the road from Dublin to Slane was built to ease George's journeys to her home). A fire in 1991 burned most of the castle's extensive collection of art and antiques. After extensive renovations, the castle is now open again for visits.

Just west of Slane (signposted off the Navan rd.), County Meath. ✆ **041/988-4400.** www.slanecastle.ie. Admission €7 adults; €5 seniors, students, and children; €20 families. Mid-June to late Aug Sun–Thurs noon–5pm.

Trim Castle ★ This massive Anglo-Norman edifice is a magnificent sight. The Norman lord Hugh de Lacy occupied the site in 1172 and built the enclosed cruciform keep. In the 13th century, his son Walter enlarged the keep, circled it with a many-towered curtain wall, and added a great hall as an upgraded venue for courts, parliaments, and feasts. After the 17th century, it was abandoned and lay in ruins for centuries. Few paid much attention to it until Mel Gibson chose to use it as a setting for the film *Braveheart*. Since then, it's generally overrun with curious visitors in the summertime. The Irish Heritage Service restored it as a "preserved ruin," leaving much of its historic integrity. It's a skeletal reminder of the once-great Anglo-Norman clout. You can take the guided tour, but you'll have to arrive early. It's usually a sellout, but can't be booked in advance. ***Note:*** This

Gruesome Find at Trim Castle

In 1971 when excavation work was underway at Trim Castle, workers made a macabre discovery: While digging to the south of the central keep, they uncovered the remains of 10 headless men. Historians believe that the bodies date from the 15th century. During a time of high crime in 1465, King Edward IV ordered that all robbers should be beheaded, and their heads displayed on spikes to intimidate those who might be thinking of a career in crime. Presumably, these men had all suffered that fate.

tour is unsuitable for small or unruly children, and for anyone unable to maneuver steep climbs or afraid of formidable heights.

Trim, County Meath. ✆ **046/943-8619.** Admission to grounds and tour of keep €4 adults; €3 seniors; €2.30 students and children; €10 families. Admission to grounds only €3 adults; €2 seniors; €1 children and students; €8 families. Easter to mid-Sept daily 10am–6pm; mid-Sept to late Dec Sat–Sun only 10am–5pm. Tours every 30 min. starting at 10:15am; last admission 1 hr. before closing.

SHOPPING

Mary McDonnell Craft Studio Textile artist Mary McDonnell welcomes visitors to watch as she creates leather items, ceramics, jewelry, cushions, and quilts. Her shop stocks the works of local artisans inspired by ancient Celtic designs. Open Tuesday to Saturday from 10:30am to 6pm, Sunday from 3 to 6pm. 4 Newgrange Mall, Slane, County Meath. ✆ **041/982-4722.**

SPORTS & OUTDOOR PURSUITS

CYCLING You can rent bikes by the day from **Clarke's Sports Den** at the back of the Navan Indoor Market (39 Trimgate St., Navan; ✆ **046/902-1130**). Rates are around €15 per day.

GOLF The **Headfort Golf Club,** Kells (✆ **046/924-0146;** www.headfortgolfclub.ie), has two courses and its greens fees are €40 to €50 weekdays, €55 to €70 weekends. Even more reasonably priced is the par-73 **County Meath Golf Club,** Trim (✆ **046/943-1463;** www.countymeathgolfclubtrim.ie), with greens fees of €30 weekdays, €35 weekends. If you prefer links courses, the **Laytown and Bettystown Golf Club,** Bettystown (✆ **041/982-7170;** www.landb.ie), charges greens fees of €50 weekdays, €60 weekends.

HORSEBACK RIDING Visitors can expect to pay an average of €25 per hour for trekking or trail riding in the countryside. To arrange a ride, contact the **Kells Equestrian Centre,** Kells (✆ **046/924-6998;** www.kellsequestrian.com).

WHERE TO STAY & EAT

Trim Castle Hotel A modern hotel close to historic Trim Castle, this place couldn't be more handy for visiting Trim unless it were located atop the castle keep. Rooms are newly done in neutral colors, with big comfortable beds. Some have views of the castle, others overlook gardens. It's all very businesslike here and probably not the type of place where you'll make lifelong friends, but it's a fine place to base yourself while exploring the area. The on-site restaurant and bar are very useful when you're too tired to go out and explore the town in the evening.

Castle St., Trim, County Meath. www.trimcastlehotel.com ✆ **046/948-3000.** 68 units. €95–€150 double. Rates include full breakfast. MC, V. Free parking. **Amenities:** Restaurant; bar. *In room:* TV, hair dryer.

Brogans Bar and Guesthouse This family-run hotel has a devoted following of regulars who forgive it the tiny guest rooms and instead applaud its low prices and good restaurant. Located near the river in central Trim, Brogans is in a 200-year-old stone building within easy walking distance of Trim's main sights. Rooms are, indeed, compact—in some doubles the bed virtually fills the space. But the beds are comfortable and the staff are friendly (although the front desk is often unmanned overnight). The in-house steakhouse offers good, meaty meals at reasonable prices, and the bar regularly features traditional Irish music and a festive *craic*.

High St., Trim, County Meath. www.brogans.ie. ✆ **046/943-1237.** Fax 046/943-7648. 18 units. €50–€95 double. Rates include full breakfast. MC, V. Free parking. **Amenities:** Restaurant; bar. *In room:* TV, hair dryer, Wi-Fi (free).

Vanilla Pod ★ MODERN IRISH In this modern, creative little restaurant in the center of Kells, fresh local ingredients are the center of attention. The menu features light dishes prepared with local poultry and meat. The menu changes with the seasons, but dishes usually include things like warm black pudding, or crab and chili risotto as appetizers, and main courses such as herb-crusted rack of local lamb, and grilled Irish sirloin with balsamic onions. It's all served in a warm and cheerful dining room, with a friendly touch.

At the Headfort Arms Hotel, John St., Kells, County Meath. ✆ **046/924-0084.** Main courses €19–€25. MC, V. Mon–Thurs 5:30–10pm; Fri–Sat 5:30–11pm; Sun noon–3pm and 5–10pm. Early-bird specials until 7:30pm.

County Louth/Cuchulainn Country

Blink and you'll miss it—to the north and east of Meath, little Louth is Ireland's tiniest county at only 824 sq. km (318 sq. miles), and even its largest towns (**Drogheda** and **Dundalk**) are quite small. The heritage town of **Carlingford** ★★ is easily the prettiest, sitting on a spur of the Cooley Mountains, overlooking glassy Carlingford Lough—a photo just waiting to happen. Established by the Vikings, Carlingford still follows its medieval street patterns, and is overseen by a massive 13th-century castle. On the heights above the town, the ancient Irish folk hero Cuchulainn is said to have single-handedly defeated the armies of Ulster in an epic battle.

Drogheda is a busy modern hillside town with a dark history. In 1649, English forces led by Oliver Cromwell sieged the town, which had been held by a small regiment of Irish rebels. Cromwell's forces smashed their way through city walls that had once been thought nearly impregnable. The subsequent indiscriminate massacre of townspeople and Catholic clergy there was so brutal that it remains infamous in Ireland to this day.

SEEING THE SIGHTS

Carlingford Heritage Centre Also known more poetically as the "Holy Trinity Heritage Centre," this museum in a beautifully restored medieval church details Carlingford's history from its Norman origins. If you would like, your visit could include a guided walking tour of the town and a look at King John's Castle, the Mint, the Tholsel (the sole surviving, though altered, gate to the old medieval town), and a Dominican friary. The cost varies according to how much you want to see, but averages about €5. Book a tour in advance at the number below, or through the local tourism office (✆ **042/937-3033**).

Carlingford, County Louth. ✆ **042/9373454.** www.carlingfordheritagecentre.com. Admission €3 adults; €1.50 seniors, students, and children. Sept–May Sat–Sun noon–5pm; June–Aug daily 10am–4:30pm.

Millmount Museum and Martello Tower ★ In the courtyard of 18th-century Millmount Fort, this eclectic little museum tells the history of Drogheda and the Boyne Valley. The collection includes Bronze Age finds, medieval tiles, and a large collection of 19th-century trades-union banners, which the staff will enthusiastically talk your ear off about if business is slow. The mishmash display also includes random domestic items: looms, brewing equipment, gramophones, and, strangely, mousetraps. A geological exhibit contains specimens of stone from every county in Ireland, every country in Europe, and beyond.

Duleek St., off the main Dublin rd. (N1), Drogheda, County Louth. ✆ **041/983-3097.** www.millmount.net. Admission museum and tower €5.50 adults; €3 seniors and children; €4 students; €12 families. Tower only €3 adults; €2 seniors and children; €2.50 students; €6 families. Museum only €3.50 adults; €2.50 seniors and children; €3 students; €8 families. Mon–Sat 9:30am–5:30pm; Sun and bank holidays 2–5pm. Last tour 1 hr. before closing.

HIGH CROSSES: ICONS OF IRELAND

You see them all over Ireland, often in the most picturesque rural surroundings, standing alone like sentries, high Celtic crosses with faded stories carved into every inch of space. They are extraordinary—mournful and unforgettable—but when they were created, they served a useful purpose: They were books, of sorts, in the days when books were rare and precious. Think of the carvings, which inevitably explain the stories of the Bible, as illustrations acting sort of like cartoons explaining the Bible to the uneducated population. When they were created, the crosses were probably brightly painted as well, but the paint has long been lost to the wind and rain.

The **Muiredach Cross ★** at Monasterboice has carvings telling, from the bottom up, the stories of Adam and Eve, Cain and Abel, David and Goliath, and Moses, as well as the wise men bringing gifts to the baby Jesus. At the center of the old cross, the carving is thought to be of Revelation, while, at the top, St. Paul stands alone in the desert. The western side of the cross tells the stories of the New Testament, with, from the top down, a figure praying, the Crucifixion, St. Peter, Doubting Thomas, and, below that, Jesus' arrest. On the base of the cross is an inscription of the sort found often carved on stones in ancient Irish monasteries. It reads in Gaelic, "A prayer for Muiredach for whom the cross was made." Muiredach was the abbot at Monasterboice until 922, so the cross was probably made as a memorial shortly after his death.

Another excellent example of a carved high cross is to be found at the monastery of Clonmacnoise near Shannonbridge (p. 488).

Monasterboice ★ This interesting ancient monastic site holds a peaceful cemetery, one of the tallest round towers in Ireland, ancient church ruins, and two excellent high crosses. The atmosphere here is dreamy, and you get the sense that it was once a peaceful place of prayer. The original site is said to have been founded in the 4th century by a follower of St. Patrick named St. Buithe. The name "Buithe" was corrupted to Boyne over time, and thus the whole region is named after him. The small monastic community thrived here for centuries, until it was seized and occupied by Vikings in the 10th century, but the Vikings were, in turn, defeated by the Irish high king of Tara, Donal, who is said to have single-handedly killed 300 of them. Today there's only a little left, but the Muiredach's High Cross is worth the trip all on its own. Dating from 922, the near-perfect cross is carved with elaborate scenes from the Old and New Testaments. Two other high crosses are more faded, and one was smashed by Cromwell's forces.

Discernible scenes from the Bible adorn the exquisitely preserved 10th-century Muiredach High Cross at Monasterboice.

Off the main Dublin rd. (N1), 9.7km (6 miles) northwest of Drogheda, near Collon, County Louth. Free admission. Daily dawn–dusk.

Old Mellifont Abbey Founded in the 12th century, this was the first Cistercian monastery on the island, and ultimately became the most spectacular. Enough is left of the abbey buildings just a few miles north of Drogheda to give you an idea of what Mellifont was like in its day, when it was the center of Cistercian faith in Ireland, with more than 400 monks living and working within its walls. You can see the outline of the cross-shaped nave, as well as the remains of the cloister, refectory, and warming room, which, because the monks lived lives of suffering, would have been the only part of the monastery with heating. Mellifont was closed in the 16th century during the English dissolution, and a manor house was soon built on the site for an English landlord, using the abbey's stones. A century later, that house would be the last place where Hugh O'Neill, the final Irish chief, stayed before surrendering to the English and then fleeing to Europe in 1607, in the "flight of the Earls." There's a good visitor center next door where you can find out more about the monastery and its complex and lengthy history.

On the banks of the Mattock River, 9.7km (6 miles) west of Drogheda, off T25, Collon, County Louth. ✆ **041/982-6459.** Admission €3 adults; €2 seniors and students; €1 children; €8 families. Late April to late Sept daily 10am–6pm.

Proleek Dolmen Standing around 3.6m (12 ft.) tall, this huge dolmen is said to resemble a giant's finger when viewed from a distance. We've never quite seen the resemblance, but it's an impressive sight nonetheless. The capstone, which looks alarmingly precarious, balanced on top of three smaller stones like a crude, misshapen tripod, weighs a massive 35 tons. The top of the capstone is invariably covered with pebbles, due to a local legend that if you can throw a stone and it stays there, your wish will come true. You can reach the dolmen down a paved footpath from the parking lot of the **Ballymascanlon House Hotel** (see below;

(✆ **042/935-8200;** www.ballymascanlon.com), about 6km (3¾ miles) outside Dundalk. It's about a .4km (¼ mile) walk. To find the hotel from Dublin, take exit 18 for Dundalk North off the M1, then take the N52 off the first roundabout, and the road to Ballymascanlon from the second. The hotel is about 3km (1¾ miles) down this road.

On the grounds of the Ballymascanlon House Hotel, Dundalk, County Louth. Site has no phone; hotel ✆ **042/935-8200.** Free admission.

St. Peter's Church of Ireland This church dating from the 18th century is the latest in a series of churches on this site. It's a low-key but lovely place, approached through frilly, wrought-iron gates. Inside the simple, peaceful nave are several heavily carved tombs, including one spooky carving featuring skeletons wearing shrouds. Some have associated it with the Black Death. St. Peter's is notorious for an incident that occurred here during the battle of Drogheda in 1649. A group of Irish men, fleeing the losing battle, sought refuge in this Protestant church. When Cromwell's forces invaded the church, the men climbed into the steeple. Cromwell's troops used the pews as timber to start a fire, and the men were burned alive, an act so terrible that some of his own men refused the order, risking a charge of mutiny. This is the second rebuilding of St. Peter's since that infamous event.

William St., Drogheda, County Louth. No phone. Free admission. Daily 10am–3pm.

SHOPPING

Celtic Clays This little pottery shop sells the work of Ciaran O'Conboirne. He uses Celtic motifs and rich, earthy tones to create distinctive, collectible pieces that look and feel Irish. Every item is handmade and makes a superb souvenir. You can also watch the potters at work in their studio. Open weekdays 9am to 5:30pm, weekends and holidays noon to 6pm. 2 Riverlane, Carlingford, County Louth. ✆ **042/938-3996.** www.celticclays.com.

WHERE TO STAY & EAT

Ballymascanlon House Hotel This 19th-century Victorian mansion was formerly the home of Baron Plunkett. The house has been enlarged several times with astounding lack of sympathy for the beauty and symmetry of the original building. If you can ignore the unattractiveness of some of the modern structures, you can enjoy the award-winning gardens and grounds forming a peaceful oasis—which includes the impressive Proleek Dolmen (see above). Rooms vary in size, but all are decorated with antiques. The **Terrace Bar** offers live music on Saturday nights, although it's more middle-of-the-road than traditional.

Off the Dublin-Belfast rd. (N1), Dundalk, County Louth. www.ballymascanlon.com. ✆ **042/935-8200.** Fax 042/937-1598. 90 units. €380 double; €590 suite. Rates include full breakfast. AE, DC, MC, V. **Amenities:** Restaurant; pub; golf course; gym; pool; sauna; tennis courts. *In room:* TV, hair dryer.

Ghan House ★★ This 18th-century country house makes a beautiful and quiet retreat overlooking the glassy waters of Carlingford Lough. Some guest rooms are in the main house, while others are in an atmospheric converted dairy next door—all are spacious and have a charmingly old-fashioned feel, with antique beds, floral fabric, and wingback chairs. Little touches—bathrobes, homemade cookies left in your room—convey a small sense of luxury. The Ghan

House restaurant is actually the main draw for most guests. The menu emphasizes local meat and fish cooked in innovative ways; it changes daily but might include Carlingford mussels, Antrim Estate pheasant, or Dromoland Castle venison. If you're coming in the winter months you might even be able to catch one of the festive Georgian-themed nights, with full costume and authentic dishes, but these generally need to be booked well in advance.

Coast Rd., Carlingford, County Louth. www.ghanhouse.com. ✆ **042/937-3682.** Fax 042/937-3772. 12 units. €140–€250 double. Rates include full breakfast. 5-course fixed-price dinner €55. Georgian-themed nights €75 usually twice yearly, Feb/Mar and Nov (call for details). AE, MC, V. **Amenities:** Restaurant. *In room:* TV, hair dryer.

Shalom B&B In a small, modern compound at the edge of the lake in Carlingford, Shalom is a peaceful, tree-shaded place just five minutes walk from the medieval town center. Guest rooms are spacious and homey with comfortable double or twin beds—all have private bathrooms. Owners Kevin and Jackie Woods are eager to share their knowledge about the area, and will happily direct you to their favorite local restaurants and pubs. The compound includes three private one-bedroom self-catering apartments (€95 per night), each with a comfortable living room, kitchen, and bedroom, and little balconies overlooking the lough.

Ghan Rd., Carlingford, County Louth. www.jackiewoods.com. ✆ **042/937-3151.** 7 units. €60 double. Rates include full breakfast. MC, V. **Amenities:** Wi-Fi (free). *In room:* TV, hair dryer.

7

WEXFORD, WATERFORD & KILKENNY

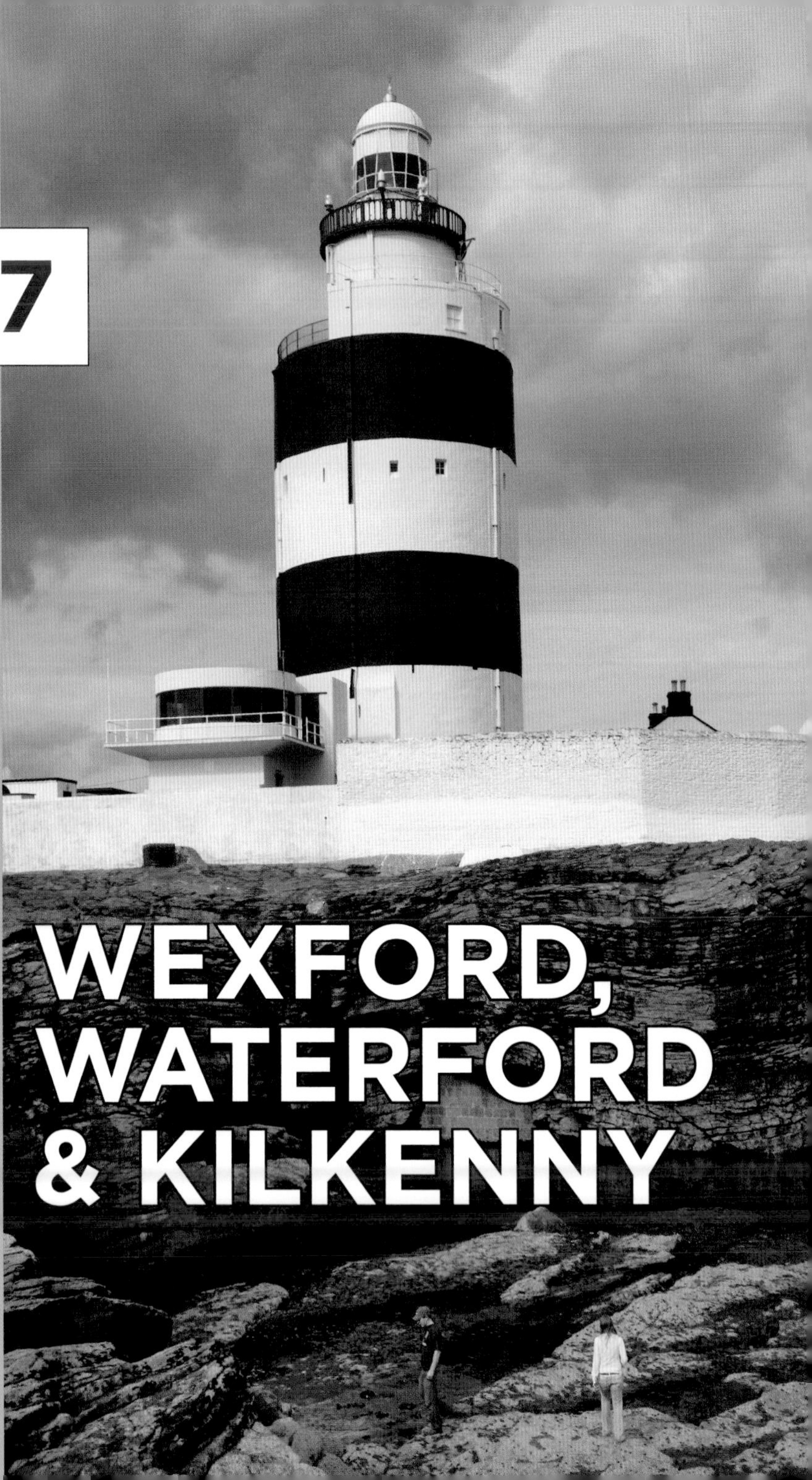

Wexford, Waterford, and Kilkenny combine to form a green, bucolic, easily traversed, and only slightly touristy region just a few hours' drive from Dublin. The local accent down here is particularly musical, almost hypnotic, and it makes even a shopping transaction disproportionately memorable. Expect to do a lot of driving, as there's plenty of space between sights and little in the way of public transportation, and you'll want to see it all—from the windy streets of Waterford, Ireland's oldest city, to the narrow lanes of Wexford, and Kilkenny's mysterious medieval remains.

COUNTY WEXFORD

Wexford Town: 142km (88 miles) S of Dublin, 63km (39 miles) E of Waterford, 90km (56 miles) S of Wicklow, 187km (116 miles) E of Cork, 214km (133 miles) SE of Shannon Airport

Although it's in easy reach of County Wexford, Dublin might as well be hundreds of miles away—this area feels so bucolic and peaceful. Wexford is known for its long stretches of pristine beaches, and for the evocative historic monuments in Wexford Town and on the Hook Peninsula.

The modern English name of Wexford evolved from *Waesfjord,* which is what the Vikings called it when they invaded in the 9th century. The Normans captured the town at the end of the 12th century, and you can still see remnants of their fort at the Irish National Heritage Park.

The next significant conqueror was England, in the form of Cromwell, who arrived in the mid–17th century expecting a pushover, but found that Wexford stood up to him. A bitter battle ensued and he won, as usual, by basis of overwhelming force. Afterward, he handled victory in his usual fashion—gathering together 1,500 of the town's 2,000 residents and slaughtering them. Among the dead were all of Wexford's Franciscan friars. After the massacre, Wexford remained a hotbed of Irish resistance for centuries—in 1798, another uprising against the English left thousands dead here.

With a population of about 10,000, Wexford Town is a hardworking Irish harbor community with a surprisingly sophisticated social calendar, highlighted by its opera festival in late October.

Wexford Town Essentials

GETTING THERE Irish Rail (✆ **1850/366222;** www.irishrail.ie) provides daily train service to Wexford and Rosslare Pier. It serves **O'Hanrahan Station,** Redmond Square, Wexford.

PREVIOUS PAGE: **The lighthouse on the Hook Head peninsula in County Wexford.**

Bus Éireann operates daily bus service to Wexford and Rosslare, into O'Hanrahan Station and Bus Depot, Redmond Square, Wexford (✆ **053/912-2522;** www.buseireann.ie).

If you're driving from Dublin and points north, take the N11 or N80 to Wexford; if you're coming from the west, take the N25 or N8. Two bridges lead into Wexford from the north—the Ferrycarrig Bridge from the main Dublin road (N11) and the Wexford Bridge from R741. The Ferrycarrig Bridge takes you into town from the west. The Wexford Bridge leads right to the heart of town along the quays.

Ferries from Britain run to Rosslare Harbour, 19km (12 miles) south of Wexford Town. **Stena Line** (✆ **01/204-7777;** www.stenaline.com) handles service from Fishguard, Wales. **Irish Ferries** (✆ **0818/300400;** www.irishferries.com) has a route between Rosslare and Pembroke, Wales. (Irish Ferries also provides service from Le Havre and Cherbourg, France.)

If you're traveling between County Wexford and County Waterford, there's a waterborne shortcut. The **Passage East Car Ferry Ltd.,** Barrack Street, Passage East, County Waterford (✆ **051/382488;** www.passage ferry.ie), operates a car-ferry service across Waterford Harbour. It links Passage East, about 16km (10 miles) east of Waterford, with Ballyhack, about 32km (20 miles) southwest of Wexford. The shortcut saves about an hour's driving time between the cities. Crossing time averages 10 minutes. It offers continuous drive-on, drive-off service, with no reservations required. Fares are €8 one-way and €12 round-trip for car and passengers; €2 single trip for foot passengers and €3 round-trip; and €2 one-way and €3 round-trip for cyclists. It operates April to September Monday to Saturday 7am to 10pm, Sunday 9:30am to 10pm; and October to March Monday to Saturday 7am to 8pm, Sunday 9:30am to 8pm.

VISITOR INFORMATION The **Wexford Tourist Office** is on Crescent Quay, Wexford (✆ **053/912-3111**). **Seasonal offices,** open April to September, are found in Enniscorthy town center (✆ **054/34699**) and at New Ross town center (✆ **051/421857**).

TOWN LAYOUT At the edge of the River Slaney, Wexford is a busy, compact town with quaint narrow streets—successors of the 9th-century market trails—lined with 18th-century houses and workaday shop fronts. Four quays (Custom House, Commercial, Paul, and the semicircular Crescent) run beside the water. Crescent Quay marks the center of town. One block inland, Main Street is a long, narrow thoroughfare that you can easily walk. Wexford's shops and businesses are on Main Street and the many smaller streets that fan out from it.

GETTING AROUND Wexford Town is so small that it has no public transportation. **Bus Éireann** (✆ **01/703-2420;** www.buseireann.ie) operates daily service between Wexford and Rosslare. Other local services operate on certain days only to Kilmore Quay, Carne, and Gorey.

The best way to see the town is to walk it. Park your car along the quays; you'll probably need to pay to park, so look for parking meters on the street (marked with big blue P signs) and have some coins ready. Pay first and get a receipt to put in your car window ("pay and display"). There is free parking off Redmond Square, beside the train and bus station. You'll need a car to reach most attractions out of town.

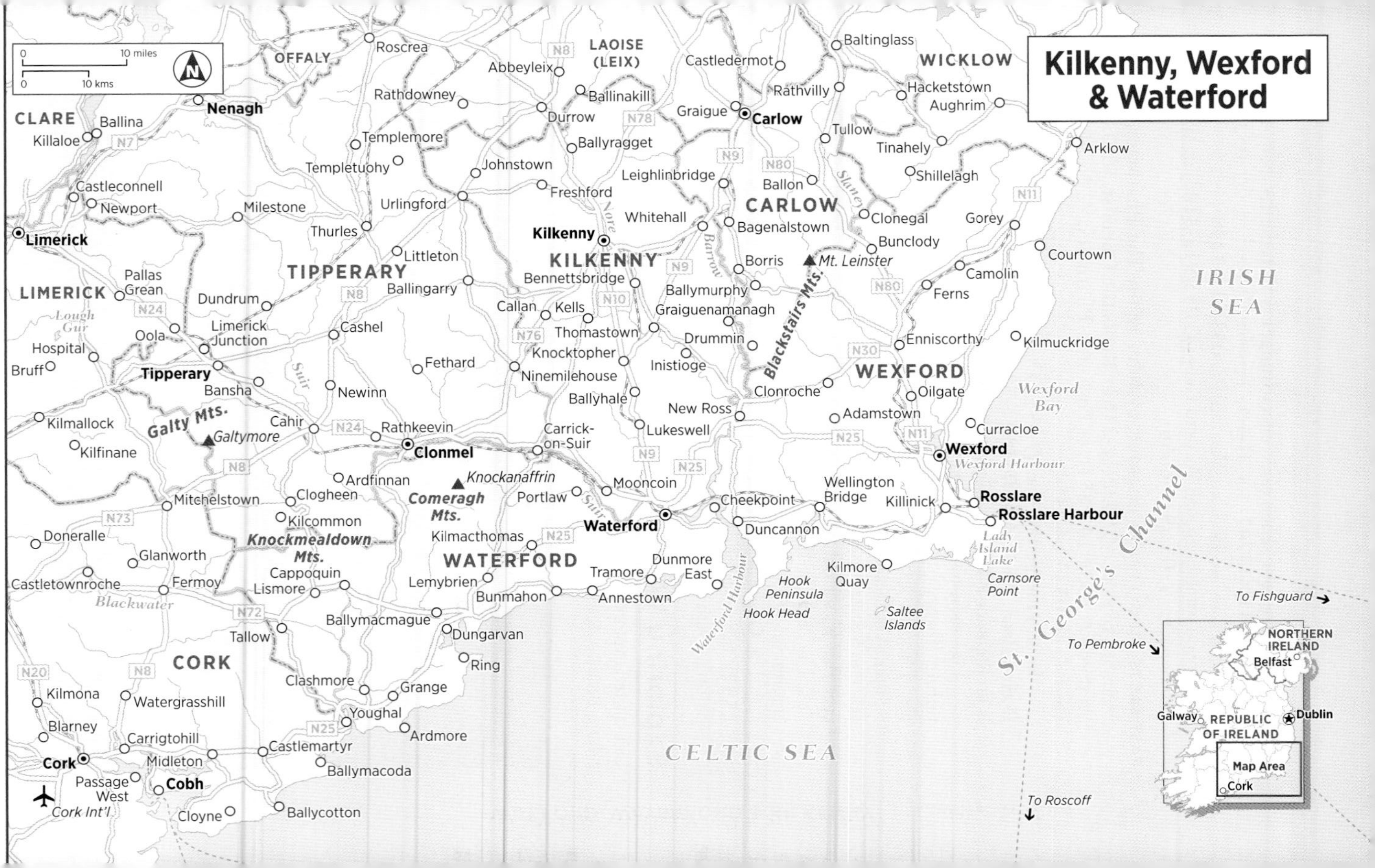
Kilkenny, Wexford & Waterford
0 10 miles
0 10 kms
N
CLARE
LIMERICK
OFFALY
LAOISE (LEIX)
TIPPERARY
KILKENNY
CARLOW
WICKLOW
WEXFORD
WATERFORD
CORK
IRISH SEA
CELTIC SEA
St. George's Channel
Limerick
Killaloe
Ballina
Nenagh
Castleconnell
Newport
Pallas Grean
Lough Gur
Hospital
Bruff
Oola
Limerick Junction
Tipperary
Bansha
Dundrum
Kilmallock
Kilfinane
Galty Mts.
Galtymore
Roscrea
Rathdowney
Templemore
Templetuohy
Milestone
Thurles
Urlingford
Johnstown
Littleton
Ballingarry
Cashel
Fethard
Newinn
Cahir
Rathkeevin
Clonmel
Ardfinnan
Clogheen
Kilcommon
Mitchelstown
Knockmealdown Mts.
Knockanaffrin
Comeragh Mts.
Suir
Abbeyleix
Ballinakill
Durrow
Ballyragget
Freshford
Kilkenny
Nore
Bennettsbridge
Callan
Kells
Thomastown
Knocktopher
Ninemilehouse
Ballyhale
Carrick-on-Suir
Castledermot
Graigue
Carlow
Rathvilly
Leighlinbridge
Ballon
Whitehall
Bagenalstown
Barrow
Borris
Ballymurphy
Graiguenamanagh
Drummin
Inistioge
Mt. Leinster
Blackstairs Mts.
Clonroche
New Ross
Lukeswell
Mooncoin
Portlaw
Waterford
Cheekpoint
Duncannon
Wellington Bridge
Killinick
Baltinglass
Hacketstown
Aughrim
Tullow
Tinahely
Shillelagh
Slaney
Clonegal
Bunclody
Gorey
Arklow
Courtown
Camolin
Ferns
Enniscorthy
Kilmuckridge
Oilgate
Adamstown
Wexford Bay
Curracloe
Wexford
Wexford Harbour
Rosslare
Rosslare Harbour
Lady Island Lake
Carnsore Point
Kilmore Quay
Saltee Islands
Hook Peninsula
Hook Head
Waterford Harbour
Dunmore East
Tramore
Annestown
Bunmahon
Kilmacthomas
Lemybrien
Cappoquin
Lismore
Ballymacmague
Dungarvan
Ring
Tallow
Clashmore
Grange
Youghal
Ardmore
Doneralle
Glanworth
Castletownroche
Fermoy
Blackwater
Kilmona
Watergrasshill
Blarney
Carrigtohill
Cork
Midleton
Castlemartyr
Ballymacoda
Passage West
Cobh
Cloyne
Ballycotton
Cork Int'l
N7
N24
N8
N73
N20
N72
N25
N76
N10
N9
N78
N80
N30
N11
To Fishguard
To Pembroke
To Roscoff
NORTHERN IRELAND
Belfast
Dublin
Galway
REPUBLIC OF IRELAND
Map Area

If you need to rent a car, contact **Budget** at Waterford Airport, Waterford (✆ **051/843747**), or **Hertz,** Ferrybank, Wexford (✆ **053/915-2500**), or Rosslare Harbour, Wexford (✆ **053/913-3238**).

If you want a cab, call Wexford Cabs (✆ **053/912-3123**) or Wexford Taxi Services (✆ **053/914-6666**).

FAST FACTS If you need a drugstore, try **John Fehily/The Pharmacy,** 28 S. Main St., Wexford (✆ **053/912-3163**); **Boots the Chemist,** 56 Main St., Wexford (✆ **053/914-7851**); or **Fortune's Pharmacy,** 82 N. Main St., Wexford (✆ **053/914-2354**).

In an **emergency,** dial ✆ **999.** The **Garda Station** (police) is on Roches Road, Wexford (✆ **053/916-5200**). **Wexford General Hospital** is on Richmond Terrace, Wexford (✆ **053/915-3000**).

Like most towns in Ireland, Wexford offers free Internet access in its **public library** (✆ **053/912-1637**), located in Selskar House, off Redmond Square just in from Commercial Quay. Its hours are Tuesday 1 to 5:30pm, Wednesday 10am to 4:30pm and 6 to 8pm, Thursday and Friday 10am to 5:30pm, and Saturday 10am to 1pm. The demand is so great, however, that it's advisable to call in advance to reserve time on a PC.

The weekly *Wexford People* covers town and county events and entertainment.

The **General Post Office,** on Anne Street, Wexford (✆ **053/912-2587**), is open Monday to Friday 9am to 5:30pm (from 9:30am Tues) and Saturday 9am to 1pm.

Exploring Wexford Town

Get started exploring by walking the length of Main Street, both north and south, taking time to detour up and down the alleys and lanes that crisscross it. The

Overview of Wexford Town, dominated by the steeples of the Church of the Immaculate Conception and the Church of the Assumption.

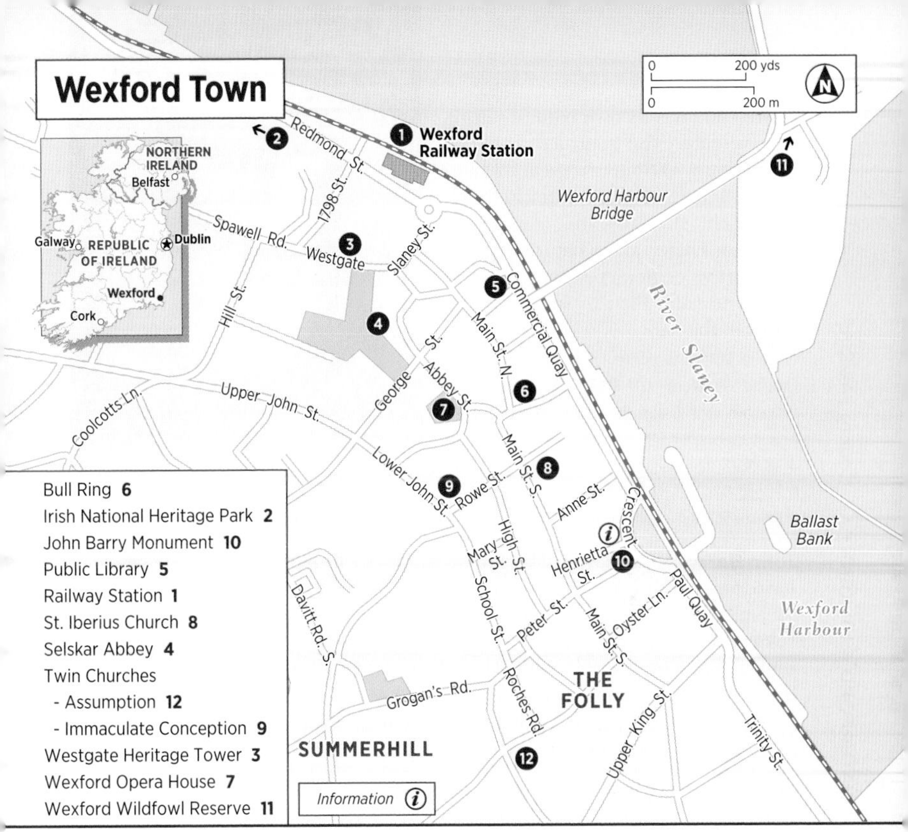

tourist office can supply you with a free map if you want some guidance. You may want to start out by visiting the Westgate Heritage Tower (see below), which will provide you with valuable context and background information before you explore the rest of the city.

The Bull Ring In 1798, the first declaration of an Irish republic was made here, and a statue memorializes the Irish pikemen who fought for the cause. Earlier, in the 17th century, the town square was a venue for bull baiting, a sport introduced by the butcher's guild. Tradition maintained that after a match, the hide of the ill-fated bull was presented to the mayor and the meat was used to feed the poor. Today, activity at the ring is much tamer: a weekly outdoor market, open Friday and Saturday from 10am to 4:30pm.

Off N. Main St., Wexford, County Wexford. Free admission.

Cornmarket Until a century ago, this central marketplace buzzed with the activity of cobblers, publicans, and more than 20 other businesses. Today it's just a wide street dominated by the Wexford Arts Centre, a structure dating from 1775.

Off Upper George's St., Wexford, County Wexford.

Irish National Heritage Park ★ ☺ This 14-hectare (35-acre) living-history park on the banks of the River Slaney outside of Wexford Town provides an ideal introduction for visitors of all ages to life in ancient Ireland, from the Stone Age to the Norman invasion. Each reconstructed glimpse into Irish history is well crafted and has its own natural setting and wildlife. The tour led by head guide Jimmy O'Rourke is great for families with kids—he's a master in bringing each site to life, captivating children. There's also a nature trail and interpretive center, complete with gift shop and cafe. Plan to spend several hours in the park.

Off the Dublin-Wexford rd. (N11), Ferrycarrig, County Wexford. ✆ **053/912-0733.** www.inhp.com. Admission €8 adults; €6.50 seniors and students; €4.50 children 13–16; €4 children 4–12; €20 families. May–Aug daily 9:30am–6:30pm (last admission 5pm); Sept–Apr daily 9:30am–5:30pm (last admission 3:30pm).

The Irish National Heritage Park brings the country's history to life, from the Stone Age through the Norman invasion.

John Barry Monument This bronze statue, a gift from the American people in 1956, faces out to the sea as a tribute to the titular Mr. Barry, a favorite son who became the father of the American Navy. Born at Ballysampson, Tacumshane, 16km (10 miles) southeast of Wexford Town, Barry emigrated to the colonies while in his teens and volunteered to fight in the American Revolution. One of the U.S. Navy's first commissioned officers, he became captain of the *Lexington.* In 1797 George Washington appointed him commander in chief of the U.S. Navy.

Crescent Quay, Wexford, County Wexford.

St. Iberius Church Erected in 1660, St. Iberius was built on hallowed ground—the land has been used for houses of worship since Norse times. The church has a lovely Georgian facade and an interior known for its superb acoustics. Free guided tours are given according to demand.

N. Main St., Wexford, County Wexford. No phone. www.wexford.ferns.anglican.org/iberius.html. Free admission; donations welcome. May–Sept daily 10am–5pm; Oct–Apr Tues–Sat 10am–3pm.

Selskar Abbey This abbey dates from the early 12th century, and it has often been the scene of synods and parliaments. The first Anglo-Irish treaty was signed here in 1169, and it's said that Henry II spent Lent 1172 at the abbey doing penance for having Thomas à Becket beheaded. Although the abbey is mostly in ruins, its choir is part of a Church of Ireland edifice, and a portion of the original tower is a vesting room. The entrance most likely to be open is to the left of Westgate.

Off Temperance Row at Westgate St., Wexford, County Wexford. Free admission.

The Twin Churches: Church of the Assumption and Church of the Immaculate Conception These twin Gothic structures (1851–58) were designed by architect Robert Pierce, a pupil of Augustus Pugin. Their 69m (226-ft.) spires dominate Wexford's skyline. Mosaics on the main doors of both churches give a good bit of local history.

Bride and Rowe sts., Wexford, County Wexford. ✆ **053/912-2055.** Free admission; donations welcome. Daily 8am–6pm.

Westgate Heritage Tower This ancient tollgate once guarded the western entrance of Wexford Town. Sir Stephen Devereux had it built in the 13th century on instructions from King Henry. Like other town gates, it consisted of a toll-taking area, cells for offenders, and rooms for guards. Fully restored as a heritage center, it presents artifacts uncovered around the town, and offers a rather long (nearly 30 min.) informational film, which provides an arguably overly informative look at Wexford's complex and turbulent history.

Westgate St., Wexford, County Wexford. ✆ **053/914-6506.** Audiovisual show €3.20 adults; €1.75 children and students. May–Aug Mon–Fri 10am–6pm, Sat–Sun noon–6pm; Sept–Apr Mon–Fri 10am–5pm.

Wexford Wildfowl Reserve This national nature reserve is part of the unfortunately named North Slob, adjacent to Wexford Harbour, 5km (3 miles) east of Wexford Town. About 10,000 Greenland white-fronted geese—more than one-third of the world's population—winter here, as do brent geese, Bewick's swans, and wigeons. The reserve has a visitor center, an informational film, an exhibition hall, and an observation tower and blinds.

North Slob, Wexford, County Wexford. ✆ **053/912-3129.** www.wexfordwildfowlreserve.ie. Free admission. Daily 9am–5pm.

SIGHTSEEING TOURS

Walking Tours of Wexford Proud of their town's ancient streets and vintage buildings, the people of Wexford began giving tours to visitors more than 30 years ago. The tours are conducted by a local guide with good knowledge about the town and its history. Tours usually depart from outside White's Hotel on Abbey Street at 11am Mondays through Saturdays. Booking is essential. ***Note:*** The tours are run by a very small staff of local guides, so they might occasionally be canceled. Wexford's tourism office is pretty good at communicating if there's a problem, but you may wish to call ahead on the day to confirm, just in case.

Westgate Heritage Centre, Westgate St., Wexford, County Wexford. ✆ **053/916-1155.** Tours €5.

ATTRACTIONS FARTHER AFIELD IN COUNTY WEXFORD

The rounded granite form of **Mount Leinster,** the highest in Wexford, is a landmark throughout the region. This is a popular hang-gliding spot as the summit is always windy. On a clear day, views are sweeping. To get there, follow signs for the Mount Leinster Scenic Drive from the sleepy town of **Kiltealy** on the eastern slopes of the mountain. Soon you will begin climbing the exposed slopes; don't get too distracted by the views, because the road is twisting and quite narrow in places. There's a parking area at the highest point of the auto road, and a paved access road (closed to cars) continues for over 2km (1¼ miles) to the summit. From the top you can scramble along the ridge to the east, known as Black Rock Mountain. To return, continue along the Scenic Drive, which ends a few miles outside the town of Bunclody.

Ballyhack Castle On a steep slope overlooking the Waterford estuary, about 32km (20 miles) west of Wexford, this large tower house was built around 1450 by the Knights Hospitallers of St. John, one of the two great military orders of the Crusades. The castle has been restored and turned into a heritage information center, with displays on the Crusader knights, medieval monks, and Norman nobles.

Off R733, Ballyhack, County Wexford. ✆ **051/389468.** www.heritageireland.ie. Free admission. June–Sept daily 10am–6pm.

Dunbrody Visitor Centre Housed in twin 18th-century grain mills, this intelligent, absorbing center tells the story of the Irish diaspora and the mass emigration that Ireland suffered over the course of centuries. It is an interesting

A TRIP THROUGH history: EXPLORING THE RING OF HOOK

The **Hook Peninsula** in southwest County Wexford is a picturesque place of rocky headlands and secluded beaches between Bannow Bay and Waterford Harbour. These were significant inlets in medieval times for travelers from Britain to Ireland, and the abundance of archaeological remains reflects that. The end of the peninsula, with its sturdy old lighthouse, is popular with birders as a site for watching the spring and fall passerine migration. The route described below will guide you through a driving or biking tour, and hikers can see most of the places listed from the Wexford Coastal Pathway.

Start your exploration of the peninsula at the town of **Wellington Bridge.** Just west of town on R733 is a roadside stop on the left by a cemetery; from here you can look across Bannow Bay to the ruins of **Clonmines**—a Norman village established in the 13th century. It's a fine example of a walled medieval settlement, with remains of two churches, three tower houses, and an Augustinian priory. You can drive to the ruins—just follow R733 another mile west to a left turn posted for the Wicklow Coastal Pathway, and continue straight on this road where the pathway turns right. The ruins are on private land, so you should ask permission at the farmhouse at the end of the road.

Continuing west on R733, turn left on R734 at the sign for the Ring of Hook, and turn right at the sign for **Tintern Abbey** (p. 253). The abbey was founded by the monks of Tintern in South Wales in the 13th century, but it has been much altered over the centuries. The grounds are beautiful and contain a restored stone bridge that spans a narrow sea inlet.

At **Baginbun Head,** a fine beach nestles against the cliffs, from which you can see the outline of the Norman earthwork fortifications on the head. Here the Norman presence in Ireland was first established with the victory of Norman forces over the Irish at the Battle of Baginbun.

The **tip of the peninsula,** with its line of low cliffs eroded in places for blowholes, has been famous for shipwrecks since Norman times. There has long been a **lighthouse** on this site; the present structure consists of a massive base, built in the early 13th century, and a narrower top dating from the 19th century.

The Ring of Hook road returns along the western side of the peninsula, passing the beaches at **Booley Bay** and **Dollar Bay.** On a promontory overlooking the town of Duncannon is a **fort** built in 1588 to protect Waterford Harbour from the Spanish Armada. Just north of Duncannon, along the coast at the village of **Ballyhack,** a ferry runs to County Waterford, and a Knights Hospitallers castle (see Ballyhack Castle, above) stands on a hill.

A visit to the Hook Peninsula wouldn't be complete without a stop at **Dunbrody Abbey,** in a field beside the road about 6.5km (4 miles) north of Duncannon. The abbey, founded in 1170, is a magnificent ruin and one of the largest Cistercian abbeys in Ireland. Despite its grand size, it bears remarkably little ornamentation. Tours are sometimes available; inquire at the visitor center across the road.

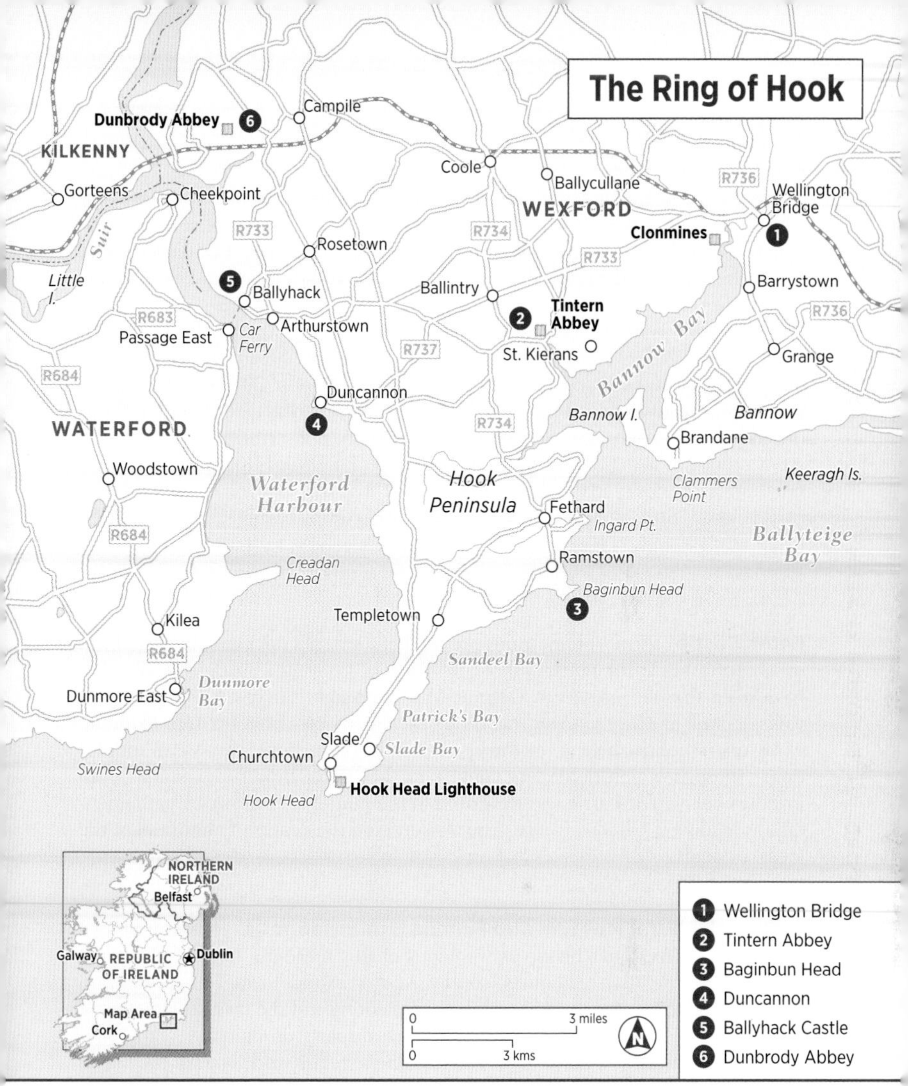

and sometimes heartbreaking tale that includes a turn-of-the-last-century New York street scene and an Irish-American hall of fame. The center is owned by the JFK Trust. As this book was being written, a €2.5-million renovation was underway to expand the center and turn it into a national center on emigration. Because of this, the prices and open hours listed below could change by the time of your visit. Call to check before heading out.

Moored in the quay adjacent to the building is the **SS *Dunbrody* Emigrant Ship** (p. 252), a beautifully constructed replica of a ship that was used to carry emigrants to America during the Great Famine.

The Quay, New Ross, County Wexford. ✆ **051/425239.** www.dunbrody.com. Admission €7.50 adults; €6 seniors; €4.50 students and children. Sept–June Mon–Fri 10am–5pm, Sat–Sun noon–5pm; July–Aug daily 9am–6pm.

Enniscorthy Castle Overlooking the River Slaney at Enniscorthy, 24km (15 miles) north of Wexford Town, this austere and solid-looking castle tower was built by the Prendergast family in the 13th century. It's said that the poet Edmund Spenser once owned it briefly. It's now owned and run by the local government, which has been renovating it at a tortuous pace over the course of several years. When finished, its displays will focus on the area's history and traditions, with rooms decorated as they would have been at various times in the castle's long history. However, as this book was being written, the museum was still closed for refurbishment as it has been for many years. According to the local council, it is due to reopen before summer 2012, but the opening has already been repeatedly delayed (it was initially scheduled to open in the summer of 2009), so we suggest you do not make a special trip without phoning first. Locals are skeptical about the likelihood of the castle opening anytime soon, and critical of the way the renovations are being conducted. We can get no final word from the council on new admission costs, so those listed below are those that were charged before the castle closed. Still, at least from the outside, it's a lovely castle.

Castle Hill, Enniscorthy, County Wexford. ✆ **054/35926.** Admission €4.50 adults; €3.50 seniors and students; €1 children; €11 families. June–Sept daily 10am–6pm; Oct–Nov and Feb–May daily 2–5:30pm; Dec–Jan Sun 2–5pm.

Ferns Castle Atmospheric ruins are all that's left of a once-grand castle built in 1221. Sitting at the north end of the village of Ferns, the castle is believed to have been the old fortress of Dermot MacMurrough. There's still a moat and walls, as well as a stone tower that offers excellent views from the top. If you do climb up, notice the hole at the top just to the left of the door. This was a "murder hole," through which defenders could pour hot oil or drop heavy stones onto invaders below. The castle was destroyed in the mid–17th century by parliamentarians led by Sir Charles Coote, who also ordered the deaths of almost all of the local residents.

Ferns, County Wexford. Free admission. Daily dawn–dusk.

Irish Agricultural Museum and Famine Exhibition ★ ☺ The importance of farming in Wexford's history is the focus of this museum, on the Johnstown Castle Demesne, 6km (3¾ miles) southwest of Wexford Town. In historic farm buildings, the museum contains exhibits on planting and the diverse activities of the farm household. There are also extensive displays on dairying, crafts, and Irish country furniture. Large-scale replicas illustrate the workshops of the blacksmith, cooper, wheelwright, harness maker, and basket maker. The section devoted to the famine is informative, eloquent, and as sobering as one might expect. Sadly, the 19th-century Gothic Revival castle on the grounds is not open to the public. Still, the grounds are perfect for picnics.

Johnstown Castle, Bridgetown Rd., off Wexford-Rosslare rd. (N25), Wexford, County Wexford. ✆ **053/917-1247.** www.irishagrimuseum.ie. Admission to museum €6 adults; €4 students and children; €20 families. Gardens €2 adults; €.50 children and students; or €6 by the car. Museum Apr–Nov Mon–Fri 9am–5pm, Sat–Sun 11am–4:30pm; Dec–Mar Mon–Fri 9am–1pm and 2–5pm. Gardens year-round daily 9am–5:30pm.

John F. Kennedy Arboretum Dedicated to the memory of the 35th U.S. president, this 240-hectare (593-acre) arboretum is about 32km (20 miles) west of Wexford and overlooks the simple thatched cottage where JFK's great-grandfather was born. The whole thing was initiated with financial help from a group of

THE RISING (& falling) OF VINEGAR HILL

Of the many rebel groups that took hold in the late 18th century, the Society of United Irishmen, founded in 1791, was most ahead of its time. Led by Wolfe Tone, it welcomed Catholics, Protestants, and dissenters alike in its effort to free Ireland from England's yoke. The British were deeply suspicious of the group's motives, not least because Tone was not shy about involving the French, England's enemy. In fact, in 1796, the French government sent 14,000 soldiers to join a United Irishmen uprising, but poor weather forced the boats back.

In 1798, the group tried again. Battles were fought in Kildare, Carlow, Wicklow, and Meath, and quickly won by English forces. In Wexford, though, feelings were very high, and the rebels were victorious. A detachment of 100 English-led soldiers was cut down at Oulart, and the city of Wexford burned. Wexford became the center of the battle in part because of the behavior of English-led forces. Throughout that spring there had been fury in Wexford because of torture of residents, and house burnings conducted by the loyalist North Cork Militia. Once the rebellion began, Wexford residents heard of summary executions of suspected United Irishmen in Wicklow and at the edge of Wexford. In the end, they knew they were fighting for their lives.

On May 29, led by Father John Murphy, a priest who reluctantly agreed to take over the leadership of the group, insurgents headed to Wexford Town. The group, armed with muskets and pikes, gathered size as it moved, and by the time it reached the town it had 15,000 fighters. The town fell quickly. Exhilarated, the group attempted to take the entire county, but its efforts to take other towns failed in places like Arklow and New Ross.

The English were shocked by the rebels' success at Wexford Town, but were soon emboldened by their subsequent failures, and they marched out to take them on. The troops arrived at the rebel encampment, on Vinegar Hill at the edge of Enniscorthy, on June 21. The rebels knew they were coming, and they prepared to take them on. Battle began at dawn, and lasted less than 2 hours. The rebels were mercilessly shelled, and their poor weapons were no match for the English artillery. More than 500 died in the battle, but that was nothing compared to what happened next.

Weeks of murder and atrocities followed, as loyalist troops raped and pillaged ruthlessly, killing an estimated 25,000 men, women, and children. Protestant leaders of the rebellion were beheaded, and their heads mounted on spikes outside the courthouse in Wexford Town. Father Murphy was stripped, flogged, hanged, and beheaded. His corpse was burned in a barrel. His head was spiked outside the local Catholic church, and Catholics in town were forced to open their windows so that they could smell his body burn.

The horrific massacre became a rallying cry for all subsequent Irish rebellions, and Wexford is forever associated with sacrifice and violence.

Vinegar Hill is at the east end of Enniscorthy, and although there's little there to memorialize the rebellion, it's a peaceful place with beautiful views. You reach it by crossing the bridge in town, and taking the first right after Treacy's Hotel, then following the signs. There's also an excellent hour-long walking tour that includes the 1798 history, with lots of fascinating details. Contact **Castle Hill Crafts** (✆ **054/36800**) for details.

The National 1798 Visitor Centre tells the story of Ireland's centuries-long struggle for independence from Great Britain.

Irish Americans, although the Irish government funds it now. Plants and trees from five continents grow here. There are play and picnic areas, and there's a small miniature railway as a sort of payback to the kids who must find it all a bit dull. A hilltop observation point (at 266m/872 ft.) presents a sweeping view of County Wexford and five neighboring counties, the Saltee Islands, the Comeragh Mountains, and parts of the rivers Suir, Nore, and Barrow.

Off Duncannon Rd. (R733), New Ross, County Wexford. ✆ **051/388171.** Admission €3 adults; €2.30 seniors; €1.50 students and children; €8 families. Apr and Sept daily 10am–6:30pm; May–Aug daily 10am–8pm; Oct–Mar daily 10am–5pm.

The SS *Dunbrody* Emigrant Ship is a replica of an 1845 vessel that ferried starving Irish peasants to the U.S. at the height of the Great Famine.

The National 1798 Visitor Centre ☺ Just south of Enniscorthy Castle, this visitor center, dedicated to the 1798 rebellion and its aftermath, uses interactive displays to give insight into the birth of modern democracy in Ireland. It's largely geared towards children, although it's not so childish that adults will be bored. Computers, a dramatic film about the uprising, and artifacts explain the events in an interesting way.

Millpark Rd., Enniscorthy, County Wexford. ✆ **054/923-7596.** www.1798centre.ie. Admission €6 adults; €3.50 seniors and students; €16 families. June–Aug Mon–Fri 9:30am–5pm; Sept–May Mon–Fri 9:30am–4pm.

SS *Dunbrody* Emigrant Ship ★ A magnificent, 458-ton, 52m (174-ft.) reconstruction of a tall ship built in 1845 and used to carry emigrants to the U.S. at the height of the Great Famine, this is an interesting way to step back into that turbulent history. Tours of the ship are fun and informative. At the start you're handed a replica of an 1849 ticket for a crossing to America (a nice touch) and then shown around the vessel by a series of actors in period costume, who tell you all about what life on board was like. Throw in a couple of authentic-seeming sounds and smells and the near-obligatory glossy video, and it all adds up to a satisfying, painlessly educational experience.

On the Quay, New Ross, County Wexford. www.dunbrody.com. ✆ **051/425239.** Admission €7.50 adults; €6 seniors; €4.50 students and children; €20 families. Tours Apr–Sept 10am–5pm; Oct–Mar 10am–4pm.

Tintern Abbey ★ In a lovely rural setting overlooking Bannow Bay, Tintern Abbey was founded in the 12th century by William Marshall, the Earl of Pembroke, as thanks to God after he nearly died at sea. The early monks were Cistercians from Tintern in South Wales (hence the name). The parts that remain—nave, chancel, tower, chapel, and cloister—date from the early 13th century, though they have been much altered since then. The grounds are extraordinarily beautiful and include a stone bridge spanning a narrow sea inlet. There's a small coffee shop on-site.

Saltmills, New Ross, County Wexford. ✆ **051/562650.** Admission €2.20 adults; €1.40 seniors; €1.20 students and children; €6 families. Mid-May to mid-Oct daily 10am–6pm. Signposted 19km (12 miles) south of New Ross off of R733.

Yola Farmstead A voluntary community project, this theme park depicts a Wexford farming community as it would have been 200 or more years ago. There are plenty of quaint thatched-roof buildings; bread and butter making are demonstrated; and craftspeople can be seen at work blowing and hand-cutting crystal at Wexford Heritage Crystal, a glass-production enterprise. It's quite touristy, but can be interesting. The **Genealogy Center** (✆ **053/31177**) is open daily 9am to 5pm. Consultation or one name search costs €25.

16km (10 miles) south of Wexford Town, 2.4km (1½ miles) from Rosslare Ferryport, Wexford-Rosslare rd. (N25), Tagoat, County Wexford. ✆ **053/913-2610.** Admission €6 adults; €4.50 children, seniors, and students; €15 families. May–Oct daily 10am–6pm; Mar–Apr and Nov Mon–Fri 10am–4:30pm.

Shopping

Shops in Wexford are open Monday to Thursday 9am to 5:30pm, and Friday and Saturday 9am to 6pm; some shops stay open until 8pm on Friday.

Barkers Established in 1848, this shop has an admirable selection of Waterford crystal, Belleek china, and Royal Irish Tara china, as well as Irish linens and international products such as Aynsley, Wedgwood, and Lladró. 36–40 S. Main St., Wexford, County Wexford. ✆ **053/912-3159.**

Byrne's Bookstore & World of Wonder This extensive and bustling emporium—spread out across three levels—offers much more than books, as the self-aggrandizing name implies. There's a long wall full of magazines and newspapers, a selection of stationery, and a slew of toys. 31 N. Main St., Wexford, County Wexford. ✆ **053/912-2223.**

Westgate Design Original Irish art, including paintings, drawings, and photographs, as well as a variety of locally made crafts fill this popular shop. 22 N. Main St., Wexford, County Wexford. ✆ **053/912-3787.**

Wexford Silver Pat Dolan and his sons create gold, silver, and bronze pieces by hand using traditional tools and techniques. They trace their silversmithing connections from 1647. A second workshop is in Kinsale (p. 309). 115 N. Main St., Wexford, County Wexford. ✆ **053/912-1933.**

Sports & Outdoor Pursuits

BEACHES County Wexford's beaches at **Courtown, Curracloe, Duncannon,** and **Rosslare** are ideal for walking, jogging, and swimming.

BICYCLING You can rent mountain bikes in Wexford Town at **Hayes Cycle Shop,** 108 S. Main St. (✆ **053/912-2462**). From Wexford, the road north up the coast through Curracloe to Blackwater is a scenic day trip. For complete 1- or 2-week cycling holidays in the Southeast, contact Bobbie Smith or Bill Passmore at **Celtic Cycling,** Lorum Old Rectory, Bagenalstown, County Carlow (✆ **059/977-5282;** www.celticcycling.com/lorum.html).

BIRD-WATCHING A good starting place for bird-watching in the region is the **Wexford Wildfowl Reserve** (p. 247); warden Chris Wilson can direct you to other places of interest.

The **Great Saltee Island** is excellent for watching seabirds, especially during May, June, and July, when it's mobbed with nesting parents and their young. Like something out of a Hitchcock feature, the cliffs on the island's southernmost point are packed to overflowing with raucous avian residents. You can get up close and personal with puffins, which nest in underground burrows, or graceful guillemots. Other species include cormorants, kittiwakes, gannets, and Manx shearwaters. The island is privately owned, but visitors are welcome on the condition that they do nothing to disturb the bird habitat and the island's natural beauty. From April to September, weather permitting, **Declan Bates** (✆ **053/29684**) provides boat rides to the island and back from the town of Kilmore Quay (about 16km/10 miles south of Wexford Town). He charges €100 minimum for the boat, or €20 per person for groups of at least five people.

Hook Head is a good spot for watching the spring and autumn passerine migration—the lack of sizable cliffs means that it isn't popular with summer nesting seabirds. In addition to swallows, swifts, and warblers, look out for the less common cuckoos, turtledoves, redstarts, and blackcaps.

While driving south from Gorey toward Ballycanew on R741, keep an eye out for a reddish **cliff** on the left, about 2km (1¼ miles) out of Gorey; this is a well-known peregrine aerie, with birds nesting until the early summer. The land is private, but you can watch the birds from the road.

Great Saltee Island, in County Wexford, is an excellent perch from which to watch nesting seabirds from May through July.

DIVING The Kilmore Quay area, south of Wexford Town, offers some of the most spectacular diving in Ireland, especially around the Saltee Islands and Conningbeg rocks. For all your diving needs, consult the **Pier House Diving Centre,** Kilmore Quay (✆ **053/29703;** scubabreaks@eircom.net).

GOLF In recent years, Wexford has blossomed as a golfing venue. One of the newest developments is an 18-hole championship seaside par-72 course at **St. Helens Bay Golf Club,** Kilrane (✆ **053/913-3234;** www.sthelensbay.com). Greens fees in high season are €45 on weekdays, €60 on weekends. Tennis courts and luxury cottages are available. The **Enniscorthy Golf Club,** Knockmarshall, Enniscorthy (✆ **054/923-3191;** www.enniscorthygc.ie), is an inland par-70 course with greens fees of €30 on weekdays, €40 on weekends.

HORSEBACK RIDING **Horetown House,** Foulksmills (✆ **051/565633**), offers riding lessons by the hour or in a variety of packages that include meals and lodging. Refurbished in 2007, this is one of the better residential equestrian centers in Ireland; it caters particularly to families and children. For more experienced riders, lessons in jumping and dressage are available. Training in hunting and admission to the hunt can also be arranged. Riding costs around €25 per hour; accommodations start at €100 for a double room, including an organic breakfast.

SAILING/FISHING The town of **Kilmore Quay,** south of Wexford Town on R739, is a center for sea angling in Wexford. The most popular rivers for fishing are the Barrow and the Slaney, where the sea trout travel upstream from mid-June to the end of August. **Blackwater Anglers** (✆ **053/912-7318**) offer fishing on a lake stocked with rainbow and brown trout from April to December. Dick Hayes runs **Harbour Thrills** (✆ **085/732-9787**), which runs boat trips, including journeys to and from Kilmore Quay.

WALKING Along the entire coastline, you'll see brown signs with a picture of a hiker on them. The signs mark the **Wexford Coastal Path,** which meanders along the coast via pristine beaches and country lanes. Unfortunately, the roads are often too busy for it to be a good idea to walk the whole route—especially on the bypass around Wexford Town. The markers are handy, however, for shorter walks between Wexford's beaches. In the northern part of the county, the section of beach from Clogga Head (County Wicklow) to Tara Hill is especially lovely, as is the walk to the top of Tara Hill, which offers views across sloping pastures to the sea. Farther south, the path veers off the roads and sticks to the beach from Cahore Point south to Raven Point and from Rosslare Harbour to Kilmore Quay.

There's a good coastal walk near the town of Wexford in the **Raven Nature Reserve,** an area of forested dunes and uncrowded beaches. To get there, take R741 north out of Wexford, turn right on R742 to Curracloe just out of town, and in the village of Curracloe, turn right and continue for just over a mile to the beach parking lot. The nature reserve is to your right. You can get there by car, driving a half-mile south, or walk the distance along the beach. The beach extends another 5km (3 miles) to Raven Point, where at low tide you can see the remains of a shipwreck, half-buried in the sand.

On the border between counties Wexford and Carlow, the long, rounded ridge of peaks are the **Blackstairs Mountains,** which allow for plenty of walks in an area unspoiled by tourism. Get a guidebook and maps from any sizable Wexford tourist office.

Where to Stay

VERY EXPENSIVE

Ferrycarrig Hotel This creamy white hotel takes full advantage of its enviable location at the very edge of the River Slaney. Most rooms have sweeping river views, and you can sip a cocktail on the deck watching the water traffic go by. Even the indoor pool has river views. Guest rooms are spacious and have a modern look, with crisp white comforters, and soft throws providing a burst of color. The restaurant and bar both serve good food, so you don't have to travel back to the town center for a meal if you'd rather not. The sauna, steam room, and spa treatments on offer should ease out any aches and pains.

Wexford Harbour Bridge, County Wexford. www.ferrycarrighotel.ie. ✆ **053/915-3652.** 102 units. €250 double. Rates include full breakfast. AE, MC, V. **Amenities:** Restaurant; bar; gym; indoor pool; steam room; beauty/spa treatments. *In room:* TV, hair dryer.

Marlfield House ★ Formerly the principal residence of the Earl of Courtown, this splendid Regency manor home, 65km (40 miles) north of Wexford Town, was built around 1850 as a grand country house, and is now a top-notch country hotel and restaurant. The large, traditionally decorated rooms have everything from CD players to four-poster beds. Most have hand-carved furniture draped in luxurious fabrics. Bathrooms tend to be quite spacious, and are stocked with thick towels, bathrobes, and Molton Brown toiletries. The public rooms and lounge are similarly grand, with crystal chandeliers and marble fireplaces. Marlfield is celebrated for its cuisine, which incorporates organically grown fruits and vegetables from the garden, and is served in the main dining area or in a fanciful sky-lit Victorian-style conservatory room.

Courtown Rd., Gorey, County Wexford. www.marlfieldhouse.com. ✆ **800/323-5463** in the U.S., or 055/942-1124. Fax 055/942-1572. 20 units. €230–€275 double; €455–€500 stateroom. Dinner from €55. Rates include full breakfast. AE, MC, V. Closed mid-Dec to Jan. **Amenities:** Restaurant; lounge; smoke-free rooms; tennis court; croquet lawn. *In room:* TV/DVD, CD player, hair dryer.

EXPENSIVE

Ballinkeele House ★ This grand 19th-century Irish manor B&B, built in 1840, is a wonderful place to appreciate Irish country-house living. As soon as you enter the majestic entrance hall with its Corinthian columns and fireplace, John and Margaret Maher see to it that you feel at home. Rooms are beautifully done in soft pastels, with heavy four-poster or half-tester beds and period touches everywhere. Dinner (book before noon) is served by candlelight in a chandeliered dining room, and it is excellent. Some 140 hectares (346 acres) of fields and woodlands surround the house, with gardens created around a pond, and strolling the grounds, you may encounter pheasants or foxes going about their business.

Signposted off the N11 north of Wexford at Oylgate, Ballymurn, Enniscorthy, County Wexford. www.ballinkeele.com. ✆ **053/913-8105.** Fax 053/913-8468. 5 units. €160–€180 double. Rates include full breakfast. Dinner €48. MC, V. Closed Dec–Jan. **Amenities:** Dining room; lounge. *In room:* TV, hair dryer, free Wi-Fi.

Kelly's Resort Hotel ★ ☺ Four generations of the Kelly family have turned this hotel into a popular family resort. It's been an honest-to-goodness pioneer in the country's hotel industry, being the first proper beachfront resort hotel; prices are all-inclusive for multiple-night stays, so you don't pay extra for meals or access to leisure facilities. It has plenty to keep you busy—an indoor swimming pool, spa, squash courts, and indoor tennis courts. In keeping with resort tradition, there's good dining at **La Marine** restaurant, and plenty of (sometimes cheesy) nighttime entertainment. Prices are a bit high, especially given that rooms are quite basic, if comfortable, but the all-inclusive factor is worth remembering. Prices drop considerably in spring and fall.

Wexford–Rosslare Harbour rd. (N25), about 16km (10 miles) south of Wexford Town, Rosslare, County Wexford. www.kellys.ie. ✆ **053/913-2114.** Fax 053/913-2222. 116 units. €835–€975 per person for 7 nights. Children's discounts available. AE, MC, V. **Amenities:** 2 restaurants; bar; miniature golf; gym; outdoor hot tub; 2 indoor pools; sauna; steam room; spa; beauty treatments; indoor tennis; squash. *In room:* TV, radio, hair dryer.

Riverside Park Hotel Set on the green banks of the River Suir in the bustling market town of Enniscorthy, this contemporary hotel has a warm facade, a bold stone tower centerpiece, and a circular atrium lobby. A flower-fringed terrace lures you to dine and relax by the river's edge. Guest rooms may be a bit colorful for some, with bold print fabrics, bright carpets, and vivid curtains. Rooms facing the river cost slightly more, but the view is beautiful. This place makes a great base from which to explore the Blackstairs Mountains and Wexford Town.

At the junction of N11 and N30 on the south edge of town, The Promenade, Enniscorthy, County Wexford. www.riversideparkhotel.com. ✆ **053/923-7800.** Fax 053/37900. 60 units. €125–€190 double. Rates include full Irish breakfast. AE, MC, V. **Amenities:** 2 restaurants; 2 bars; babysitting; discounts at nearby health club and golf course; Wi-Fi. *In room:* TV, hair dryer, free broadband Internet.

Talbot Hotel Wexford ★ ☺ Beautifully decorated with lots of warm red tones and highly polished wood, this is a good option in Wexford. The lobby and dining room are comfortable places to relax, with thickly cushioned chairs and plenty of sunlight. Bedrooms are midsize and contemporary, with all the modern conveniences. A nicely designed leisure center inside an adjacent 100-year-old grain mill features a pool, steam room, and sauna. Spa treatments are also available to work out the kinks, and the supervised children's play area means parents can relax while getting a massage. Advance online booking offers great deals.

On the Quay, Wexford Town, County Wexford. www.talbotwexford.ie. ✆ **053/912-2566.** Fax 053/912-3377. 132 units. €190–€230 double. Rates include full breakfast. AE, MC, V. **Amenities:** 2 restaurants; bar; children's playroom; gym; Jacuzzi; indoor pool; sauna; steam room; beauty/spa treatments. *In room:* TV, radio, hair dryer.

Woodbrook House ★ Hidden away at the end of a long drive through farmland and rolling hills a few miles outside the historic town of Enniscorthy, this 17th-century country house looks as if it stepped out of a Jane Austen book. In the vast central hall, a gorgeous, wrought-iron "flying staircase" curves upward with no support save for its clever engineering. Walls are done with elegant paint washes and *trompe l'oeil* to give the place an intelligent sense of history. Heavy wooden furniture has been well chosen to fit in with this look. Owners Giles and Alexandra FitzHerbert run the place with calm skill, while also raising their four children. They know a great deal about the area, and can help you plan your outings to get the most of them. Be sure to ask about special offers when you book, as discounts can be substantial.

Killanne, Enniscorthy, County Wexford. www.woodbrookhouse.ie. ✆ **054/925-5114.** 3 units. €150–€170 double. Rates include full breakfast. Dinner €40. MC, V. Closed Nov–Apr, but stays can be arranged during this time by contacting the management. **Amenities:** Lounge w/fireplace. *In room:* Radio, hair dryer.

MODERATE

Clonard House Set on a hillside overlooking Wexford Town, Clonard House is a Georgian country home (1792) with high ceilings and lots of architectural detail. It's attractively furnished with period antiques, and has a marvelous historical feel. At night you can unwind over an Irish coffee in the elegant drawing room before retiring to one of the nine bedrooms, most of which have four-poster beds with orthopedic mattresses. Breakfast is served in the charming dining room with period features.

Clonard Great, Wexford Town, County Wexford. ✆ **054/914-3141.** 9 units. €80–€100 double. Rates include full breakfast. MC, V. **Amenities:** Lounge. *In room:* TV, hair dryer.

Clone House This 250-year-old farmhouse is furnished with handsome antiques. A courtyard opens onto a garden in back, and you can walk through the fields to the bank of the River Bann. The owners pride themselves on their knowledge of the area (both the local region and Ireland as a whole), and they're very helpful when it comes to planning touring or outdoor activities. Ask about discounted rates if you plan to stay more than a couple of nights.

Ferns, Enniscorthy, County Wexford. www.clonehouse.ie. ✆ **053/936-6113.** 7 units, 5 with bathroom. €90 double. Rates include full breakfast. No credit cards. Closed Nov–Apr. **Amenities:** Smoke-free rooms. *In room:* TV (in some).

McMenamin's Townhouse At the western end of Wexford Town, opposite the railroad station, this Victorian-style town house offers warm hospitality at an affordable price. Guest rooms are a bit sparsely decorated, but still nicely furnished with Irish antiques and a mixture of wooden or brass beds. McMenamin's is run by Seamus and Kay McMenamin, who formerly ran a restaurant, and Kay puts her culinary skills to work by providing copious gourmet breakfasts complete with homemade breads and cereals.

3 Auburn Terrace, Redmond Rd., Wexford, County Wexford. www.wexford-bedandbreakfast.com. ✆ **053/914-6442.** Fax 053/46442. 6 units. €100 double. Children 11 and under half price. Rates include full breakfast. MC, V. **Amenities:** Babysitting; smoke-free rooms. *In room:* TV.

Where to Eat

MODERATE

Forde's Restaurant ★★ BISTRO This waterfront restaurant has become one of Wexford Town's most in-demand restaurants. In many ways, it's a classic bistro, both in looks and in terms of the menu. Starters include dishes such as homemade ravioli with brie and bacon, or Forde's prawn salad with tomato and chili sauce. Mains include saddle of spring lamb with rosemary and garlic stuffing or fresh guinea fowl roasted with a red wine demi glaze. The wine list is well chosen and (relatively) affordable, the crowd happy, the service professional.

The Crescent, Wexford, County Wexford. ✆ **053/912-3832.** www.fordesrestaurantwexford.com. Reservations recommended. Main courses €19–€29. AE, MC, V. Daily 6–10:30pm.

Mange2 FRENCH FUSION This attractive restaurant offers French cooking with a global twist. The mix won't be for everybody, but many will love the roast breast of pigeon, the warm smoked beef salad, or the pork loin marinated with tomato and maple. Veggie side dishes arrive crisp and steaming, wrapped in parchment packets. The wine list is modest and judicious. Fusion continues on the dessert menu, which might feature baked passion-fruit ricotta cake with orange ice cream.

100 S. Main St., County Wexford. ✆ **053/914-4033.** Reservations recommended. Dinner main courses €17–€25. MC, V. Tues–Sun 6pm–late.

Springsteen's Bar & Grill STEAKHOUSE This laid-back American-style steakhouse on Wexford's waterfront is a good choice if you're feeling a bit homesick during your travels. Its unfussy menu of grilled steaks, burgers, nachos, and chicken wings is served in a jovial atmosphere underneath the watchful eyes of black-and-white photos of America and Ireland. You might be surprised to discover that a frosty margarita and a burger can be just the thing on a rainy night in Ireland.

13–14 Commercial Quay, County Wexford. ✆ **053/912-4483.** www.springsteens.ie. Reservations recommended. Dinner main courses €17–€25. MC, V. Tues–Thurs 4–9:30pm; Fri–Sat 4–10pm; Sun 2–9pm.

INEXPENSIVE

Westgate Design DELI The restaurant inside this popular arts shop offers fresh-made sandwiches, wraps, hot platters, soups, and salads at thoroughly reasonable prices. The bread is made fresh, and you can eat your organic greens surrounded by original art. This is an excellent place to take a break in the afternoon for tea and cake.

22 N. Main St., Wexford, County Wexford. ✆ **053/912-3787.** www.westgatedesign.ie. All items €2.50–€10. MC, V. Daily 11am–5pm.

Wexford After Dark

THE PERFORMING ARTS

Opera fans troop to little Wexford each fall for the **Wexford Festival Opera** in October (see below), but you can catch interesting theatrical performances here year-round. Wexford is a town with a fine tradition of music and the arts.

The modern **Wexford Opera House** (✆ **053/912-2400;** www.wexford operahouse.ie), which opened in 2008, is an awkward addition to the Wexford skyline, with its large but rather garish copper-plated tower. Seen from the river, the tower stands in tragic juxtaposition to the gorgeous and iconic **Twin Churches** (p. 246). Controversially, the old Theatre Royal (dating from 1832) was demolished to make room for the new structure. Love or loathe what it's done to the town's skyline, it is impossible to deny that this state-of-the-art performance venue is, in terms of acoustics and sightlines, a great improvement on the cramped old theater it replaced. So it all comes down to your priorities in the end: sight or sound?

The biggest event in the calendar of the opera house is, unsurprisingly, the **Wexford Festival Opera.** Held over 2 weeks each October, this prestigious event attracts aficionados from all over Ireland and beyond. Opera lovers will be in heaven—but book early if there's something you want to see. Ticket sales are open from early June (although you can book a month early if you become a "friend" of the festival). Tickets start at around €10, rising to about €100 for the best seats. For more details call the Opera House box office at ✆ **053/912-2400** or visit **www.wexfordopera.com**.

There's always something interesting going on at the **Wexford Arts Centre,** Cornmarket, Wexford (✆ **053/912-3764;** www.wexfordartscentre.ie). Built as the market house in 1775, this building is a focal point for the arts in Wexford, and now houses three exhibition rooms and showcases a range of theatrical and artistic events. It's open year-round from 10am to 6pm daily.

To see professional Irish music and dancing, head 16km (10 miles) south of Wexford to the **Yola Farmstead** (p. 253), Wexford-Rosslare road (N25), Tagoat, County Wexford (✆ **053/913-2610**). For groups, by prior arrangement, the Farmstead stages traditional Irish banquets and *céilí* evenings of Irish music, song, and dance. If you're on your own, you still might be able to join in if a performance is planned. The average cost is around €32 per person.

PUBS

Antique Tavern It's worth a 24km (15-mile) trip from Wexford City to Enniscorthy to see this Tudor-style pub, off the main Dublin-Wexford road (N11). True to the name, the walls are lined with memorabilia from the Wexford area—old daggers, pikes, and lanterns—and the mood is friendly. 14 Slaney St., Enniscorthy, County Wexford. ✆ **054/923-3428.** www.theantiquetavern.com.

The Crown Bar Once a stagecoach inn, this tiny pub in the center of town has been in the Kelly family since 1841. Along with its historical overtones, it is known for its museum-like collection of antique weapons, including 18th-century dueling pistols and pikes from the 1798 rebellion. It's not always open during the day, so it's best to visit in the evening. Monck St., Wexford, County Wexford. ✆ **053/21133.**

Oak Tavern ★ More than 150 years old, this pub—originally a tollhouse—is 3km (2 miles) north of town, overlooking the River Slaney near the Ferrycarrig Bridge. There is a riverside patio for fine days, and traditional music sessions are held most evenings in the front bar. Wexford-Enniscorthy rd. (N11), Ferrycarrig, County Wexford. ✆ **053/912-0922.**

The Wren's Nest Near the John Barry Memorial on the harbor, 5 minutes from the bus and train station, this is a traditional pub, right down to its wooden floors and ceilings. The varied pub menu includes Wexford mussel platters, house pâtés, soups, salads, and vegetarian entrees. There is free traditional Irish music on Tuesday and Thursday nights. Custom House Quay, Wexford, County Wexford. ✆ **053/912-2359.**

COUNTY WATERFORD

Waterford City: 65km (40 miles) W of Wexford, 53km (33 miles) W of Rosslare Harbour, 158km (98 miles) SW of Dublin, 126km (78 miles) E of Cork, 153km (95 miles) SE of Shannon Airport

Waterford City (pop. 42,500) is the main seaport of southeast Ireland. Its unprotected proximity at the edge of the ferocious Atlantic Ocean makes it Ireland's Windy City, as the sea breeze always blows here. Its location has a lot to do with the fact that it is the oldest city in the country, founded by Viking invaders in the 9th century. In recent years, a major archaeological endeavor has excavated much of the ancient Viking city, and some of the more striking finds from these excavations can be seen in the **Waterford Treasures** exhibition at the Granary Museum.

Although the historic district around Reginald's Tower is intriguing, outside of that Waterford is largely a commercial center, dominated by its busy port. Because the rest of County Waterford is so beautiful, many travelers don't linger long in the capital city.

Coastal highlights south of Waterford include **Dunmore East,** a picturesque fishing village, and the charmingly old-fashioned **Portally Cove,** Ireland's only Amish-Mennonite community; **Dungarvan,** a major town with a fine harbor; **Ardmore,** an idyllic beach resort; and **Passage East,** a tiny seaport from which you can catch a ferry across the harbor and cut your driving time from

The seaport of Waterford, known as Ireland's windy city, is also the nation's oldest, founded by Vikings in the 9th century.

Waterford to Wexford in half. Of all the coastal towns in County Waterford, Ardmore most stands out. It has an ancient monastic site, a pristine Blue Flag beach, a stunning cliff walk, a fine craft shop, an excellent restaurant, and comfortable seaside accommodations.

In northwest County Waterford, the **Comeragh Mountains** provide many opportunities for beautiful walks, including the short trek to Mahon Falls. These mountains also have highly scenic roads for biking. Farther west, there's great fishing on the **Blackwater estuary.**

Waterford City Essentials

GETTING THERE Little **Waterford Airport,** off R675, Waterford (© **051/846600;** www.flywaterford.com), is served by **Aer Arran** (© **011/353-818-210-210** in the U.S., 818/210-210 in Ireland, or 0870/876-7676 in the U.K.; www.aerarann.com) from Manchester and Birmingham in northern England, and Luton in London.

Irish Rail offers daily service from Dublin and other points into Plunkett Station, at Ignatius Rice Bridge, Waterford (© **051/873401;** www.irishrail.ie).

Bus Éireann operates daily service into Plunkett Station Depot, Waterford (© **051/879000;** www.buseireann.ie), from Dublin, Limerick, and other major cities throughout Ireland.

Four major roads lead into Waterford: N25 from Cork and the south, N24 from the west, N19 from Kilkenny and points north, and N25 from Wexford.

The **Passage East Car Ferry Ltd.,** Barrack Street, Passage East, County Waterford (© **051/382480;** www.passageferry.ie), operates a car-ferry service across Waterford Harbour. It links Passage East, about 16km (10 miles) east of Waterford, with Ballyhack, about 32km (20 miles) southwest of Wexford. This shortcut saves about an hour's driving time between the cities. Crossing time averages 10 minutes. It offers continuous drive-on, drive-off service, with no reservations required. See "Wexford Town Essentials," earlier in this chapter, for fare and schedule information.

VISITOR INFORMATION The **Waterford Tourist Office** is at 41 The Quay, Waterford (✆ **051/875788;** www.waterfordtourism.com). It's open April to September Monday to Saturday 9am to 6pm, October Monday to Saturday 9am to 5pm, and November to March Monday to Friday 9am to 5pm. The year-round office in the courthouse, off the Square in Dungarvan (✆ **058/41741**), keeps comparable hours. The seasonal tourist office on the Square at Tramore (✆ **051/381572**) is open from mid-June to August Monday to Saturday 10am to 6pm.

CITY LAYOUT Waterford is a commercial city focused on its waterfront. The city center sits on the south bank of the Suir. Traffic from the north, west, and east enters from the north bank over the Ignatius Rice Bridge and onto a series of quays (Grattan, Merchants, Meagher, and Parade), although most addresses simply say "The Quay." Shops and attractions are concentrated near the quay area or on two thoroughfares that intersect it: The Mall and Barronstrand Street (changing their names to Broad, Michael, and John sts.). These streets were once rivers flowing into the Suir and, in fact, the original waterways continue to flow roughly 15m (49 ft.) beneath today's pavement.

GETTING AROUND Bus Éireann operates daily **bus service** within Waterford and its environs. The flat fare is €1.10. **Taxi** stands are outside Plunkett Rail Station and along the Quay opposite the Granville Hotel. If you need to call a taxi, try **Rapid Cabs** (✆ **051/858585**), **Metro Cabs** (✆ **051/857157**), or **Waterford Taxi Co-op** (✆ **051/877778**).

To see most of Waterford's sights it's best to walk. You can park along the quays, and pay at the nearest machine. However, you'll need a car to reach attractions outside of town.

To rent a car, contact **Budget Rent A Car,** Waterford Airport (✆ **051/873747**).

FAST FACTS If you need a drugstore, try **Gallagher's Pharmacy,** 29 Barronstrand St. (✆ **051/878103**), or **Mulligan's Chemists,** 40–41 Barronstrand St. (✆ **051/875211**).

In an **emergency,** dial ✆ **999. Garda Headquarters** (✆ **051/305300**) is the local police station. **Holy Ghost Hospital** is on Cork Road (✆ **051/374397**), and **Waterford Regional Hospital** is on Dunmore Road (✆ **051/848000**).

Among the resources for gay travelers is the **Gay and Lesbian Line Southeast** (✆ **051/879907**). The **Waterford Gay and Lesbian Resource Centre** is at the Youth Resources Centre, St. John's Park (✆ **087/638-7931**).

The **Voyager Internet Cafe,** 85 The Quay (✆ **051/843843**), isn't actually a cafe, but it does provide high-speed access with all the peripherals. It's open Monday to Saturday 10am to 9pm.

The **General Post Office** on Parade Quay (✆ **051/317312**) is open Monday to Friday 9am to 5:30pm, and Saturday 9am to 1pm.

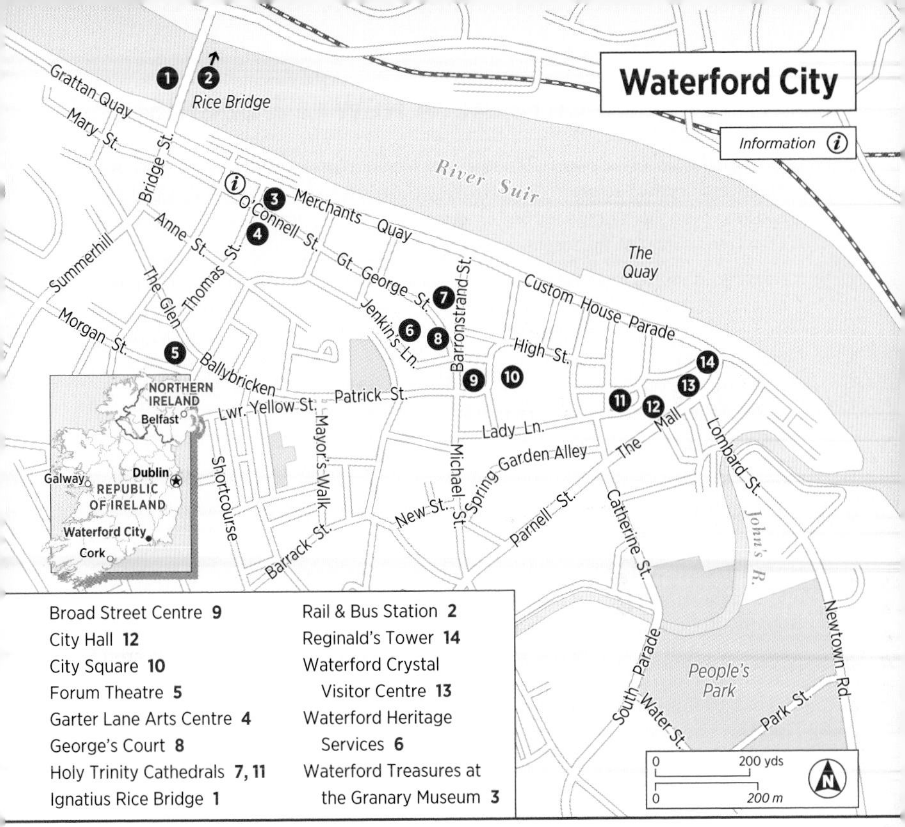

Exploring Waterford City

City Hall Headquarters of the local city government, this late-18th-century building houses local memorabilia, including the city's charter, granted in 1205. There's an absorbing display on the incredible life of Thomas Francis Meagher, a leader in an Irish insurrection in 1848; he was sentenced to death, but escaped to America. There he fought in the Civil War, earned the rank of brigadier general, and was eventually appointed governor of Montana. City Hall's other treasures include an 18th-century Waterford glass chandelier and priceless antique Waterford glasses.

The Mall, Waterford, County Waterford. ✆ **051/73501.** Free admission. Mon–Fri 9am–1pm and 2–5pm.

Garter Lane Arts Centre One of Ireland's largest arts centers, the Garter Lane occupies two buildings on O'Connell Street. Number 5, the site of the former Waterford Library, holds exhibition rooms and artists' studios, and no. 22a, the former Friends Meeting House, is home of the Garter Lane Theatre, with an art gallery and outdoor courtyard. The gallery showcases works by contemporary and local artists, plus a small but varied program of music, dance, and film screenings.

5 and 22a O'Connell St., Waterford, County Waterford. ✆ **051/855038.** www.garterlane.ie. Free admission to exhibitions. Concerts €10–€25; theater €12–€25; films €6–€9. Gallery Tues–Sat noon–6pm.

WATERFORD CRYSTAL: A NEW era BEGINS

In 2009, the global recession claimed its most famous Irish victim to date when the **Waterford Crystal Factory** in Waterford City closed after more than 2 centuries. It had long been the county's top visitor attraction, and the fourth-most-popular tourist site in the country, so its closure came as a huge blow.

However, as the old saying goes "from the ashes of disaster grow the roses of success," and in 2010 the crystal company found new owners, who promptly began work on a new visitor center.

When we called the closed factory in 2009, a sad-sounding man offered to make us a cup of tea and show us around himself if we cared to drop by. When we checked on them in 2011, the manufacturing facility was churning out 40,000 pieces of crystal a year, and the shiny new visitor center was about to open. The man who answered the phone sounded genuinely happy.

Just for that, we hope you'll stop by.

Holy Trinity Cathedrals Waterford has two impressive cathedrals, one Catholic and the other Protestant, both built by one equal-opportunity architect, John Roberts. Roberts lived 82 years (1714–96), fathered 22 children with his beloved wife, and built nearly every significant 18th-century building in and around Waterford. Holy Trinity on Barronstrand is the only baroque cathedral in Ireland and has 10 unique Waterford crystal chandeliers. It's open daily 7:30am to 7pm. The Anglican or Church of Ireland Holy Trinity Cathedral (conveniently nicknamed Christ Church) on Henrietta Street has a most peculiar spire and only clear glass, because its first bishop and rector disliked stained glass.

Barronstrand and Henrietta sts., Waterford, County Waterford.

Reginald's Tower Circular, topped with a conical roof, and with walls 3m (10 ft.) thick, this mighty tower stands at the eastern end of the Quay beside the river. It's said to have been built in 1003 by a Viking governor named Reginald and has never fallen into ruin, which makes it Ireland's oldest standing building in continuous use. Still dominating the Waterford skyline, it's particularly striking at night when fully floodlit. Over the centuries, it's been a fortress, a prison, a military depot, a mint, an air-raid shelter, and now a museum.

The Quay, Waterford, County Waterford. ✆ **051/304220.** Admission €3 adults; €2 seniors; €1 children. Combined ticket with Waterford Treasures (see below) available. June–Sept daily 10am–6pm; mid-Sept to May daily 10am–5pm.

Waterford Crystal Visitor Centre ★★ Since it was founded in 1783, Waterford has been a byword for the crystal of connoisseurs, and for good reason. The solid, faceted hand-carved crystal produced in Waterford is among the best in the world. For centuries Waterford's glittering product has been shipped around the world, to grace the drawing rooms and dining rooms of the wealthy and powerful. Only cataclysmic events have ever stopped that process: The devastating effects of the Irish famine forced the factory to close in 1851, but it was revived in 1947, then in 2009 the global recession forced the factory to close again, but it found new owners who opened a brand new center in 2010. As you might expect, the center, which is on the Mall in central Waterford, sparkles with a display of crystal carved into elaborate confections including glasses, globes, and chandeliers. In the shop, you can spend your way into the poorhouse in no time at all (don't look for any discounts at the factory—there are no seconds to be had—the advantage in shopping here is simply the wide selection). True fans will want to tour the factory to see the work firsthand.

The Mall, Waterford, County Waterford. ✆ **051/358398.** www.waterfordvisitorcentre.com. Free admission to gallery. Tours €12 adults; €8.50 seniors and students; free for children 11 and under; discounts available for groups. Tours Mar–Oct daily 8:30am–3:15pm; Nov–Feb Mon–Fri 9am–3:15pm. Reservations not required. Showrooms Mar–Oct daily 8:30am–6pm; Nov–Feb Mon–Fri 9am–5pm. Closed Mar 17.

Waterford Heritage Services Did your ancestors come from Waterford? If so, follow the small lane between George's and Patrick streets to this historic building adjoining St. Patrick's and get the trained staff to trace your local ancestry. Church registers dating from 1655, surveys, rolls, and census lists are used as resources.

St. Patrick's Church, Jenkins Lane, Waterford, County Waterford. ✆ **051/876123.** www.waterford-heritage.ie. Free admission; basic search fee €100 by appointment only. Mon–Thurs 9am–5pm; Fri 9am–2pm.

Waterford Treasures at the Granary Museum This impressive heritage center and museum, housed in a converted granary, unfolds Waterford's history from its earliest Viking origins. Along with an exceptional collection of Viking and medieval artifacts recovered in the region, there's also an ambitious state-of-the-art multimedia show including a three-dimensional film. There's so much to see and do that the exhibitions can seem like a circus with too many rings, more chaotic than enticing. If you move along at your own pace, however, you'll get the most out of it. You can always retreat to the gift shop and cafe for a breather.

Merchant's Quay, Waterford, County Waterford. ✆ **051/304500.** www.waterfordtreasures.com. Admission €7 adults; €5 seniors and students; €3 children; €10–€12 families. Combined ticket with Reginald's Tower (see above) available. June–Aug daily 9am–6pm; Sept–May Mon–Sat 10am–5pm, Sun 11am–5pm.

ATTRACTIONS FARTHER AFIELD IN COUNTY WATERFORD

Ardmore High Cross ★ Ardmore (Irish for "the great height") is a very ancient Christian site—St. Declan, its founder, is said to have been a bishop in Munster as early as the mid–4th century, well before St. Patrick came to Ireland. Tradition has it that the small stone oratory in a cemetery high above Ardmore marks his burial site. St. Declan's Oratory is one of several stone structures here

Walking Your Way Through Waterford

The best way to begin your exploration of Waterford is to take a Waterford City Walking Tour ★. Jack Burtchaell, well versed in the history, folklore, and witty anecdotes of the city, conducts an engaging hour-long tour of the old city, leaving daily from the reception area of the Granville Hotel on the Quay. Tours are offered daily at noon and 2pm from March through October and cost €6 for adults. For more information, call Waterford Tourist Services at ✆ 051/873711.

composing the ancient monastic settlement. The most striking is the perfectly intact 30m-high (98-ft.) round tower. There are also ruins of a medieval cathedral and, nearby, St. Declan's well and church. For a more in-depth exploration, pick up a copy of *The Pilgrim's Round of Ardmore, County Waterford,* at a local store for €3, or join the walking tour of ancient Ardmore, which leaves twice daily Monday to Saturday from the Tourist Information Office in the harbor. Contact the tourism office for times (see "Visitor Information," above).

Ardmore, County Waterford.

The Ardmore High Cross marks one of Ireland's oldest Christian sites, predating even the arrival of St. Patrick.

Lismore Castle ★ High above the River Blackwater, this turreted castle dates from 1185, when Prince John of England built a similar fortress on this site. Local lore says that Lismore Castle was once granted to Sir Walter Raleigh for £12 a year, although he never occupied it. One man who did live here was Richard Boyle, the first earl of Cork. He rebuilt the castle, including the thick defensive walls that still surround the garden, in 1626, but most of the present structure was rebuilt in the mid–19th century. You're free to wander the 3,200-hectare (7,904-acre) estate of gardens, forests, and farmland, but not the castle itself. It is the Irish seat of the Duke and Duchess of Devonshire, who won't let the general public in. But they're not above being entrepreneurs; in fact, if you've got the money, you can see it all, since the castle can be rented, complete with the duke's personal staff, to private groups for a minimum of €31,500 per week for up to 12 guests, during June through August. Included in the price are dinners, afternoon teas, and silver-service breakfasts. For booking information call ✆ **058/54424** in Ireland; if calling from another country, dial 011/353-5854-424. (Although, frankly, if you can afford that price, you've probably got a castle of your own.)

Lismore, County Waterford. ✆ **058/54424.** www.lismorecastle.com. Admission to gardens €8 adults; €4 children 15 and under. Mid-Mar to late Sept daily 11am–4:45pm. From Cappoquin, take N72 6.5km (4 miles) west.

Lismore Heritage Centre This interpretative center in the town's Old Courthouse tells the history of Lismore, a charming town founded by St. Carthage in the year 636. There's an interesting multimedia display on the town's unique treasures, including the Book of Lismore, which dates back 1,000 years, and the Lismore crosier (1116). Both were discovered hidden in the walls of Lismore Castle in 1814. The presentation also provides an excellent introduction to the surrounding area and its attractions. The center also offers several walking tours of Lismore town and cathedral, leaving daily at 11am and 3pm.

Lismore, County Waterford. ✆ **058/54975.** www.discoverlismore.com. Admission €5 adults; €4 seniors and students; €3.50 children; €15 families. May–Oct Mon–Fri 9:30am–5:30pm; Sat 10am–5:30pm; Sun noon–5:30pm.

A Walk to Mahon Falls

Mahon Falls is in the Comeragh Mountains, on R676 between Carrick-on-Suir and Dungarvan. At the tiny village of Mahon Bridge, 26km (16 miles) south of Carrick-on-Suir, turn west on the road marked for Mahon Falls, then follow signs for the falls and the COMERAGH DRIVE. In about 5km (3 miles), you reach a parking lot along the Mahon River (in fact, just a tiny stream). The trail, indicated by two boulders, begins across the road. Follow the stream along the floor of the valley to the base of the falls. From here you can see the fields of Waterford spread out below you, and the sea a glittering mirror beyond. Walking time is about 30 minutes round-trip.

Shopping

Waterford has a good selection of interesting little craft stores, plus three multilevel enclosed shopping centers: **George's Court,** off Barronstrand Street, **Broad Street Centre,** on Broad Street, and **City Square,** off Broad Street. Hours are usually Monday to Saturday from 9 or 9:30am to 6 or 6:30pm. Some shops are open until 9pm on Thursday and Friday.

The Book Centre This huge, four-level bookstore has all the books, newspapers, and magazines you need, as well as useful maps and CDs. You can also make a photocopy here or zap off a fax. 25 Barronstrand St., Waterford, County Waterford. © **051/873823.**

Kelly's Dating from 1847, this shop offers a wide selection of Aran knitwear, Belleek and Royal Tara china, Irish linens, and other souvenirs. 75-76 The Quay, Waterford, County Waterford. © **051/873557.**

Penrose Crystal Established in 1786 and revived in 1978, this has always been regarded as Waterford's *other* glass company, which turns out delicate handcut and engraved glassware carved with the stipple engraving process. A retail sales outlet is at Unit 8 of the City Square Shopping Centre. Both are open the usual hours, but the factory is also open Sunday 2 to 5:30pm from June to August. 32a John St., Waterford, County Waterford. © **051/876537.** www.penrosecrystal.com.

Sports & Outdoor Pursuits

BEACHES There are wide sandy beaches at Tramore, Ardmore, Clonea, or Dunmore East.

BICYCLING From Waterford City, you can ride 13km (8 miles) to Passage East and take the ferry (€3 with a bicycle) to Wexford and the beautiful Hook Peninsula. Or continue on from Passage East to Dunmore East, a picturesque seaside village with a small beach hemmed in by cliffs. The road from there to Tramore and Dungarvan is quite scenic. For a complete 1- or 2-week biking vacation in the Southeast, contact Don Smith at **Celtic Cycling,** Lorum Old Rectory, Bagenalstown, County Carlow (© **059/977-5282;** www.celticcycling.com/lorum.html). Prices start at around €700 per person.

FISHING The Colligan River is excellent for sea trout and salmon. For permit information, contact **Gone Fishing,** 42 Lower Main St., Dungarvan (© **058/43514**). The River Slaney, brimming with salmon and sea trout, can be fished from the old bridge in Enniscorthy.

GOLF County Waterford's golf venues include three 18-hole championship courses. **Waterford Castle Golf and Country Club,** The Island, Ballinakill, Waterford (✆ **051/871633;** www.waterfordcastle.com/golf), is a par-72 parkland course; greens fees are €50 to €55 on weekdays, €55 to €65 on weekends. **Faithlegg Golf Club,** Faithlegg House (✆ **051/380587;** www.faithlegg.com), a par-72 parkland course beside the River Suir, charges greens fees of €40 to €58 Monday to Thursday, €50 to €69 Friday to Sunday. **Dungarvan Golf Club,** Knocknagranagh, Dungarvan (✆ **058/41605;** www.dungarvangolfclub.com), a par-72 parkland course, has greens fees of €35 on weekdays, €45 on weekends. In addition, the 18-hole par-71 inland course at **Waterford Golf Club,** Newrath, Waterford (✆ **051/876748**), is 1.6km (1 mile) from the center of the city. Its greens fees are €40 on weekdays, €50 on weekends.

HORSEBACK RIDING Arrange to ride at **Killotteran Equitation Centre,** Killotteran, Waterford (✆ **051/384158**). Fees average around €25 per hour.

SAILING, WINDSURFING & SEA KAYAKING From May to September, the **Dunmore East Adventure Centre,** Dunmore East (✆ **051/383783;** www.dunmoreadventure.com), offers courses of 1 to 4 days that cost around €45 to €100 per day, including equipment rental. Summer programs for children are also available. This is a great spot for an introductory experience, but there isn't much wave action for thrill-seeking windsurfers.

Where to Stay

VERY EXPENSIVE

Waterford Castle ★★ There's something magical about taking a boat back home to your castle at the end of the night. Dating back 800 years, this is a deeply secluded castle on a private island in the River Suir, surrounded by woodland and an 18-hole championship golf course. It's 3km (2 miles) south of Waterford, accessible only by the castle's private car ferry. With an original Norman keep and two Elizabethan wings, it is the real thing, complete with leaded roof, mullioned windows, and fairy-tale turrets. Inside are oak-paneled walls, colorful tapestries, and huge stone fireplaces. The bedroom decor could use a freshening up given the price charged, but all rooms have firm mattresses and claw-foot bathtubs. The atmosphere is graciously informal; afternoon tea in the grand entrance hall is an event, as is dinner in the formal dining room (jackets requested for men).

The Island, Ballinakill, Waterford, County Waterford. www.waterfordcastle.com. ✆ **051/878203.** 19 units. €250–€450 double. Rates include full breakfast. AE, MC, V. **Amenities:** Restaurant; bar; concierge; 18-hole championship golf course; room service; tennis courts. *In room:* TV, CD player, radio, hair dryer.

EXPENSIVE

Treacy's Hotel Spa & Leisure Club ☺ With a great location on the waterfront at the foot of the Ignatius Rice Bridge, this is a family-friendly option right in the town center. Lounges and dining rooms are modern with creamy walls, and guest rooms are similarly contemporary and spacious. Family rooms have plenty of space for parents and two children; some even have bunk beds for the kids. Most rooms are surprisingly quiet, given the busy location and the child-friendly vibe. In the summer, there's a "kid's club" to keep the little ones busy while you head to the spa or museum. Prices are on the high side, unfortunately, but look out for online discounts that can make it more reasonable.

1 The Quay, Waterford, County Waterford. www.treacyshotelwaterford.com. ✆ **051/877222.** 130 units. €150–€180 double. Rates include service charge and full breakfast. MC, V. **Amenities:** 2 restaurants; 2 bars; babysitting; room service. *In room:* TV, hair dryer, Wi-Fi.

MODERATE

Foxmount Country House ★ ☺ This elegant, secluded, 17th-century country home is the perfect place to relax after a busy day of sightseeing. Rooms are attractively decorated, with soft colors and antique touches. Two adjacent guest rooms share a separate alcove—perfect for a family with kids. Four double rooms have private bathrooms. All have pastoral views. Margaret's breakfasts are bountiful affairs. The terrific Jack Meades pub (see below) is within walking distance.

Passage East Rd., Waterford, County Waterford. www.foxmountcountryhouse.com. ✆ **051/874308.** Fax 051/854906. 5 units. €130 double. Rates include full breakfast. No credit cards. Closed Nov–Feb. *In room:* TV, hair dryer.

Tannery Townhouse ★ Owned by the people behind the **Tannery** Restaurant (below), located just around the corner, the Tannery Townhouse comprises two stylish houses. Each has a classy, contemporary style, with big comfortable beds, louvered shutters, and neutral color schemes with splashes of vivid color often provided by crimson velvet bed throws. There's no big lobby and not a lot of services, but it has everything you need. Each morning fresh pastries are left outside your door, and you can brew your own fresh coffee or tea. The rooms are perfect for those who like a little privacy.

10 Quay St., Dungarvan, County Waterford (beside the library). www.tannery.ie. ✆ **058/45420.** 14 units. €110–€130 double. Rates include service charge and continental breakfast. AE, MC, V. *In room:* TV, hair dryer.

The Tower Hotel ☺ In a modern building on the Mall in central Waterford, this hotel balances a business-friendly attitude with a family-friendly approach. So the large, modern, well-designed rooms have work spaces and room for a child's cot (which the hotel will provide). There's a quiet, relaxing spa, and a children's play club. The in-house restaurant and bar are handy and nicely designed. It doesn't have a lot of personality, but it's a good, reliable option, with an indoor pool.

The Mall, Waterford, County Waterford. www.towerhotelwaterford.com. ✆ **051/862300.** Fax 051/870129. 135 units. €100–€180 double. Rates include service charge and full breakfast. MC, V. **Amenities:** 2 restaurants; bar; babysitting; room service. *In room:* TV, hair dryer.

INEXPENSIVE

Glencairn Inn ★★ 🎁 This intimate Victorian farmhouse B&B has a charming Gallic touch, provided by its friendly French owners. Rooms are tastefully decorated with buttermilk-colored walls and iron-and-brass beds, while the en suite bathrooms still have big, claw-foot bathtubs, perfect for soaking. The view outside is all rolling fields and pastures, and there's a sunny garden, where you can lounge with a book. Lovely though the guesthouse is, it's in the restaurant downstairs where the owners have really made their mark, in the excellent **Pastis Bistro** (see below). For guests, this means amazing breakfasts (omelets, freshly smoked salmon, homemade potato cakes . . .) and excellent dinners.

Glencairn, County Waterford (4.8km/3 miles from Lismore). www.glencairninn.com. ✆ **058/56232.** 4 units. €85 double. Rates include full Irish breakfast. 3-course fixed-price dinner €40. MC, V. Closed Christmas week. **Amenities:** Restaurant; bar; Wi-Fi. *In room:* TV.

Where to Eat

EXPENSIVE

La Boheme ★★ FRENCH This is a wonderful find, hidden away in an arched cellar underneath the headquarters of Waterford Chamber of Commerce. It exudes a kind of effortless class, without delivering too big a hit to the wallet, and it uses local ingredients to create classic French flavors. The menu changes constantly, but typical dishes include organic Clare Island roast wild pheasant with spinach stuffing, or chargrilled filet of Aged Irish Hereford beef with béarnaise sauce. Service is slick, professional, and attentive; but this is not the kind of top-tier restaurant where you have to sit up straight, or feel shy about asking for help with the rather dizzying wine list. A worthwhile splurge.

2 George's St., Waterford, County Waterford. ✆ **051/875645.** www.labohemerestaurant.ie. Reservations recommended. Main courses €28–€32. Fixed-price menus: 3 courses €35 (Tues–Fri and Sat until 7pm); 3-course early-bird €29 (Tues–Fri only); 5 courses €55; 7-course tasting menu €75. AE, MC, V. Tues–Sat 5:30–10pm; also Sun on Bank Holiday weekends.

Pastis Bistro ★★ FRENCH/MEDITERRANEAN The jewel in the crown of Stéphane and Fiona Tricot's Glencairn Inn (see above) is this exceptional little bistro, which has gathered quite a following among the diners of Waterford. Stéphane, who does most of the cooking, serves an inventive combination of Mediterranean fare with an Irish accent, using ingredients sourced locally where possible. Mains might include Cashel blue cheese ravioli, smoked wild Irish venison with local cauliflower in cream, or Irish quail and foie gras pie. The wine list is short, but every bit as well selected as one would expect from such knowledgeable hosts.

In the Glencairn Inn, Lismore, County Waterford. ✆ **058/56232.** www.glencairninn.com. Reservations recommended. Main courses €24–€29. MC, V. Thurs–Sat 7–9pm; Sun lunch 1–3pm.

The Tannery ★★ ECLECTIC EUROPEAN Until 1995 this impressive stone building on the quays was (as the name implies) a tannery; then it reappeared as a stylish contemporary restaurant and met instant success. The cuisine blends unlikely ingredients to create interesting, creative dishes that seem impossible on paper, but (at least for fusion fans) really work—quail and foie gras pie with raisins, seared scallops with parsnip and fennel dressing, or aged rib-eye with wild mushroom bread salad. It's not for all, but many love it.

Quay St., Dungarvan, County Waterford (beside the library). ✆ **058/45420.** www.tannery.ie. Reservations recommended. Main courses €22–€30. AE, MC, V. Tues–Fri and Sun 12:30–2:30pm; Tues–Sat 6:30–9:30pm; Sun 6:30–9pm (July–Aug only).

MODERATE

Bodega! CONTINENTAL If you're looking for the party place in Waterford, you've just found it. This place draws a young (20-something) crowd for the great food, lack of volume control, and convivial atmosphere. It's so popular you might need to book a couple of days in advance to be sure of a table. Choose from specials chalked onto the blackboard menu, which tends to be heavy on the seafood. Dishes are seasonal, but often include things local crabmeat and shrimp salad with baby spinach, homemade pâté with Guinness soda bread and cranberries, Waterford Angus steak frites, or the rack of Waterford lamb with herb crust. One note of caution—the restaurant is wheelchair accessible, but the toilets, unhelpfully, are not.

54 John St., Waterford, County Waterford. ✆ **051/844177.** www.bodegawaterford.com. Main courses lunch €5–€16, dinner €15–€27; 3 course fixed-price menu €30 (available per table only). Early-bird menus: 2 courses €21, 3 courses €26. MC, V. Mon–Fri noon–5pm; Mon–Wed 5:30–10pm; Thurs–Sat 5:30–10:30pm; late menu Fri–Sat 10:30pm–12:30am.

The Strand Seafood Restaurant SEAFOOD This intimate restaurant, attached to two pubs, has a well-deserved reputation for outstanding cuisine. If you can bring yourself to look up from your plate, the views of Hook Lighthouse and the Celtic Sea are stunning. Daily seafood specials augment the excellent regular menu. Grilled wild salmon with green-gooseberry sauce sounds risky but generously rewards all takers, and lemon sole stuffed with seafood mousse is gorgeous. Plates of crisp sautéed vegetables are liable to appear all by themselves. Alluring homemade desserts await the end of your meal.

In the Strand Inn, Dunmore East, County Waterford. ✆ **051/383174** or /383161. Reservations recommended. Main courses €22–€26. AE, MC, V. Daily 6:30–10pm.

Waterford After Dark

Waterford has two main entertainment centers. The 170-seat **Garter Lane Arts Centre Theatre,** 22a O'Connell St. (✆ **051/855038**), presents the work of local production companies such as the Red Kettle and Waterford Youth Drama. Visiting troupes from all over Ireland also perform contemporary and traditional works here. Performances are usually Tuesday to Saturday, and tickets average €12 to €25 for most events. Concerts—which tend toward the intimate, folky, and alternative—cost €10 to €25. There are also film screenings, which usually cost €9 for adults and €6 for children and seniors. The box office is open Tuesday to Saturday noon to 6pm, and accepts MasterCard and Visa.

When big-name Irish and international talents come to Waterford, they usually perform at the **Forum Theatre** at the Glen (✆ **051/871111;** www.forumwaterford.com), a 1,000-seat house off Bridge Street. Tickets average €10 to €25, depending on the event. The box office is open Monday to Friday 11am to 1pm and 2 to 4pm. In addition to concerts, stand-up comedy, and theatrical productions, there are special regular themed club nights, including "Traffik" (indie) every Saturday and "Bubble" (gay disco) on the first Friday of the month. The price for all club nights is €10.

Otherwise, Waterford's nightlife is centered in the hotel lounges and in the city's interesting assortment of pubs.

PUBS

Jack Meades ★ Waterford's most unusual pub is not in the city, but nestled beneath an old stone bridge in an area known as Halfway House, about 6km (3¾ miles) south. Dating from 1705, the pub is widely known by the locals as Meades Under the Bridge. As a public house with a forge, it was once a stopping-off point for coach travelers between Waterford and Passage East. The facade and interior—wooden beams and open fireplaces—haven't changed much over the years. There's a playground for kids, ducks to feed, and in July and August there's music with singalong sessions on Wednesday nights. All year, impromptu evening sessions can spring up at a moment's notice. From May to September, bar food is served daily. Cheekpoint Rd., Halfway House, County Waterford. ✆ **051/850950.** www.jackmeades.com.

The Munster ★ The flavor of old Waterford prevails in this 300-year-old building that is often referred to as Fitzgerald's (the name of the family that owns it). It is rich in etched mirrors, antique Waterford glass sconces, and dark-wood walls, some of which are fashioned out of timber from the old Waterford Toll Bridge. Among the many rooms are an original Men's Bar and a lively modern lounge that often features traditional Irish music on weekends. Bailey's New St., Waterford, County Waterford. ✆ **051/874656.**

T. & H. Doolan ★★ Once a stagecoach stop, this 170-year-old pub in the center of town is a favorite venue for evening sessions of ballad, folk, and traditional music. Lanterns light the whitewashed stone walls and a collection of old farm implements, crocks, mugs, and jugs. 32 George's St., Waterford, County Waterford. ✆ **051/841504.**

COUNTY KILKENNY

Kilkenny City: 48km (30 miles) N of Waterford, 81km (50 miles) NW of Wexford, 121km (75 miles) SW of Dublin, 137km (85 miles) SE of Shannon Airport, 148km (92 miles) NE of Cork, 61km (38 miles) NE of Cashel

With its remarkable collection of well-preserved castles, churches, monastic sites, and winding narrow lanes, lovely **Kilkenny City ★★** is a graceful medieval town. It's also a national hub for crafts and design, and its streets are dotted with shops selling pottery, woodwork, paintings, and jewelry. Its lively pub-and-entertainment circuit, including much-loved comedy festivals, makes this a top weekend getaway for the Irish. Its many charms make it popular with travelers, too, so it's not untouched by tourism, but it's not as overrun as Kerry, for example. In the off season, it reverts to its normal, sleepy self (with a pop. of just 11,000) and you can wander the streets in peace.

Like so many Irish towns, Kilkenny stands on the site of an old monastery from which it takes its name. A priory was founded here in the 6th century by St. Canice; in Gaelic, *Cill Choinnigh* means "Canice's Church." As the monastery grew, the town sprang up around it and prospered. It owes its appearance to its success in the Middle Ages. Then it was a prosperous walled city, and it served as an important governmental center during the 14th century. Much of its medieval architecture has been skillfully preserved, and the basic town plan has not changed much in the last 600 years.

The oldest house in town may well be **Kyteler's Inn** on St. Kieran Street. It was once the home of Dame Alice Kyteler, a wealthy woman accused of witchcraft in 1324. Facing execution, she escaped and disappeared into the countryside, never to be seen again, but her maid Petronilla was burned at the stake. Her home is now a pub and restaurant, decorated with effigies of witches.

Another building that stands out on the streetscape is the **Tholsel,** on High Street, with its curious clock tower and front arcade. It was originally (in 1761) a tollhouse or exchange. Later, it was a town meeting place where milk and sugar candy were sold, and dances, bazaars, and political meetings were held. Today, completely restored, it houses municipal archives.

The surrounding County Kilkenny countryside is dotted with rich river valleys, green pastures, hills, and picture-postcard villages. If you like monastic sites, take time to see the **Jerpoint Abbey,** on the River Nore just southwest of Thomaston on N9. It's an extraordinary Cistercian ruin that still has many elaborate medieval carvings on its walls; some even have traces of the original pigment.

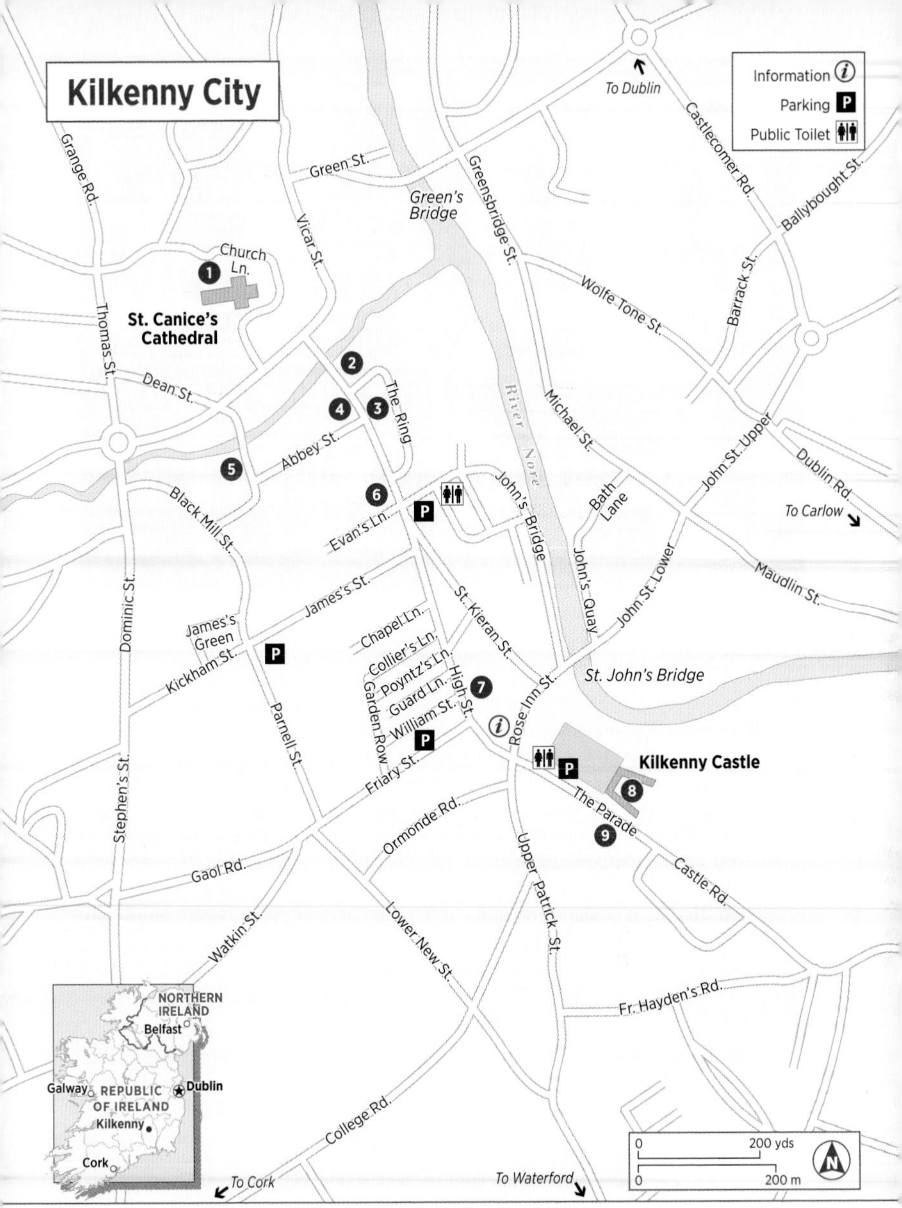

Black Abbey **5**
City Hall **7**
John Cleere's **4**
Kilkenny Castle **8**
Kilkenny Design Craft Centre **9**
Rothe House **6**
St. Canice's Cathedral **1**
St. Francis Abbey Brewery **3**
Watergate Theatre **2**

Colorful shop fronts in affluent Kilkenny City.

Also on the Nore is the picturesque village of **Inistioge ★**, about 24km (15 miles) southeast of Kilkenny City, with a tree-lined square and stone bridge with nine low arches spanning the river.

Abbey lovers will want to continue on to the tongue-twister town of Graiguenamanagh (its name means "village of the monks"), which holds the **Duiske Abbey.** Surrounded by peaceful views of Brandon Hill and the Blackstairs Mountains, Graiguenamanagh is at a bend of the River Barrow, about 32km (20 miles) southeast of Kilkenny City.

Kells, about 10km (6¼ miles) south of Kilkenny City (and not to be confused with the town of the same name in County Meath), is the only completely walled medieval town in Ireland. The thick city walls, seven towers, and some of the monastic buildings have all been well preserved.

Kilkenny City Essentials

GETTING THERE **Irish Rail** provides daily service from Dublin into the Irish Rail station on Carlow Road, Kilkenny (✆ **056/772-2024;** www.irishrail.ie).

Bus Éireann, McDonagh Station, Dublin Road, Kilkenny (✆ **056/776-4933;** www.buseireann.ie), operates daily service from Dublin and all parts of Ireland.

Many roads pass through Kilkenny, including the N9/N10 from Waterford and Wexford, the N8 and N76 from Cork and the southwest, the N7 and N77 from Limerick and the west, and the N9 and N78 from Dublin and points north and east.

VISITOR INFORMATION For information, maps, and brochures about Kilkenny and the area, contact the **Kilkenny Tourist Office,** Shee Alms House, Rose Inn Street, Kilkenny (✆ **056/775-1500**). It's open May to September Monday to Saturday 10am to 6pm; October to April, hours are Monday to Saturday 9:15am to 5pm.

CITY LAYOUT The main business district sits on the west bank of the River Nore. High Street runs the length of the city north to south, changing its name to Parliament Street at midpoint. It starts at the Parade, on the south end near Kilkenny Castle, and continues through the city to St. Canice's Cathedral at the northern end. Most of the city's attractions are along this route or on cross streets such as Patrick, Rose Inn, Kieran, and John. The tourist office can supply you with a good street map.

GETTING AROUND There is no bus service within Kilkenny. Local buses run to nearby towns on a limited basis, departing from the Parade. Check with **Bus Éireann** (✆ **056/776-4933;** www.buseireann.ie).

It's unlikely you will, but if you need a taxi, call **Nicky Power Taxi** (✆ 056/776-3000), **Billy Delaney Cabs** (✆ 056/772-2457), or **Kilkenny Taxi Service** (✆ 056/776-3017).

It's best not to drive once you're in town—Kilkenny's narrow medieval streets are only really navigable by locals, and you'll almost certainly get stuck. Park at one of the designated parking areas at the Parade, at the rail station, or at one of the shopping centers. Some parking is free, and other spaces have coin-operated machines, usually for €2 per hour. There's also a central multistory car park on Ormonde Street. If you need to rent a car to see the surrounding countryside, call **Barry Pender,** Dublin Road, Kilkenny (✆ **056/776-5777;** www.barrypender.ie).

The best way to see Kilkenny City is on foot. Plot your own route or join a guided walking tour (see below).

FAST FACTS If you need a drugstore, try **Boots the Chemist,** 36 High St. (✆ **056/777-1222**); **John O'Connell,** 4 Rose Inn St. (✆ **056/772-1033**); or **White's Chemist,** 5 High St. (✆ **056/772-1328**).

In an **emergency,** dial ✆ **999.** The local **Garda Station** is on Dominic Street (✆ **056/772-2222**).

If you need to access the Internet, try the **Kilkenny Library** at 6 John's Quay (✆ **056/779-4174;** kilkennylibrary.kilkenny.ie), open Tuesday and Wednesday 10:30am to 1pm, 2 to 5pm, and 7 to 9pm; Thursday and Friday 10:30am to 1pm and 2 to 5pm; and Saturday from 10:30am to 1pm. **Web-Talk,** 24 Rose Inn St. (✆ **056/775-0066**), is an Internet cafe with ISDN Internet access; it's open Monday to Saturday 10am to 10pm and Sunday 2 to 8pm, and charges €1.50 every 10 minutes and €6.50 an hour.

For information on upcoming events and festivals, visit **www.kilkenny.ie** or **www.kilkennycityonline.com**. When you're in town, check out the weekly *Kilkenny People* (**www.kilkennypeople.ie**), which also covers local happenings.

The **Kilkenny District Post Office,** 73 High St. (✆ **056/776-2327**), is open Monday to Friday 9am to 5:30pm (from 9:30am Tues), and Saturday 9:30am to 1pm.

Exploring Kilkenny City

Black Abbey ★ Nobody is sure why this Dominican church, founded in 1225, is named Black Abbey. It may be because the Dominicans wore black capes over their white habits, or perhaps because the Black Plague claimed the lives of eight priests in 1348. The Black Abbey's darkest days came in 1650, when Oliver Cromwell used it as a courthouse before destroying it; by the time he left, all that remained was the walls. The abbey was rebuilt, and opened in 1816 as a church, a new nave was completed in 1866, and the entire building was fully restored in 1979. Among the elements remaining from the original abbey are an alabaster sculpture of the Holy Trinity that dates from 1400, and a pre-Reformation statue of St. Dominic carved in Irish oak, which is believed to be the oldest such piece in the world. The huge Rosary Window, a stained-glass work of nearly 45 sq. m (484 sq. ft.) representing the 15 mysteries of the rosary, was created in 1892 by Mayers of Munich.

Abbey St. (off Parliament St.), Kilkenny, County Kilkenny. ✆ **056/772-1279.** Free admission; donations welcome. Apr–Sept Mon–Sat 7:30am–7pm, Sun 9am–7pm; Oct–Mar Mon–Sat 7:30am–5:30pm. No visits during worship.

The City of Marble

Kilkenny is sometimes known as the Marble City. That's because fine black marble was once quarried on the outskirts of town and, until 1929, some of the town's streets were paved in marble.

Kilkenny Castle ★★★ Standing majestically beside the River Nore on the south side of the city, this landmark medieval castle—built in the 12th century and remodeled in Victorian times—was the principal seat of the Butler family, whose members were the earls, marquesses, and dukes of Ormonde. In 1967, the castle was given to the Irish government to be restored to period splendor as an enduring national monument. From its sturdy corner towers to its battlements, Kilkenny Castle retains the imposing lines of an authentic fortress and sets the tone for the city. The exquisitely restored interior includes a library, drawing room, and bedrooms all decorated in 1830s style. The former servants quarters are now an art gallery with constantly changing exhibits. The old castle kitchen

Visitors are welcome to explore the interior and grounds of 12th-century Kilkenny Castle.

operates as a tearoom in the summer. The 20-hectare (49-acre) grounds include a riverside walk, extensive gardens, and a well-equipped children's playground. Access to the main body of the castle is by guided tour only, prefaced by an informative video on the rise, demise, and restoration of the structure. This is a very busy site, so arrive early (or quite late) to avoid waiting.

The Parade, Kilkenny, County Kilkenny. ✆ **056/770-4100.** www.kilkennycastle.ie. Admission €6 adults; €4 seniors; €2.50 children and students; €14 families. Mar daily 9:30am–5pm; Apr–May daily 9:30am–5:30pm; June–Aug daily 9am–5:30pm; Sept daily 9:30am–5:30pm; Oct–Feb daily 9:30am–4:30pm.

Rothe House This is a typical middle-class house from the Tudor period. Originally a merchant's home, built in 1594, it consists of three stone buildings divided by cobbled courtyards. It has an arcaded shop front and a remarkable timber ceiling. Purchased in 1961 by the Kilkenny Archeological Society, it was restored and opened to the public. Inside is a museum of sorts, filled with artifacts and period costumes. A family history research service for Kilkenny city and county has its offices here.

Parliament St., Kilkenny, County Kilkenny. ✆ **056/772-2893.** www.rothehouse.com. Admission €5 adults; €4 seniors and students; €3 children 15 and under. Combination tickets are available with St. Canice's Cathedral (not including cathedral round tower). Apr–Oct Mon–Sat 10:30am–5pm, Sun 3–5pm; Nov–Mar Mon–Sat 10:30am–4:30pm. Closed Dec 24–Jan 3.

St. Canice's Cathedral ★ At the northern end of the city, this is the church that gave Kilkenny its name, although the current structure is a relative newcomer—it was built in the 13th century on the site of a 6th-century church. The cathedral was built in early Gothic style, but has been much restored and altered over the years, not the least after Cromwell's gang defaced the building, using it as a stable for their horses. Restoration after that took more than a century to complete. It is noteworthy for its rich interior timber and stone carvings, its colorful glasswork, and the structure itself. Its roof dates from 1863, and its marble floor is composed of the four marbles of Ireland. On the grounds, amid the tombstones in the churchyard, is a massive round tower, 30m high (98 ft.) and 14m (46 ft.) in circumference; it is believed to be a relic of the ancient church (although its original conical top has been replaced by a slightly domed roof). If you want to climb to the tip of the tower, it will cost you a couple of euros and more calories than you can count (it's a steep and very narrow climb that is not for the faint of heart or the unfit). The steps that lead to the cathedral were constructed in 1614, and the carvings on the wall at the top of the stairs date from medieval times. Combination tickets providing admission to the cathedral and Rothe House are available, but be aware that these do not include access to the cathedral round tower.

Coach Rd., Irishtown, Kilkenny, County Kilkenny. ✆ **056/776-4971.** www.stcanicescathedral.com. Admission to cathedral only €4 adults; €3 seniors, children, and students. Admission to round tower €3 adults; €2.50 seniors, children, and students. Admission to cathedral and round tower €6 adults (no discounts). Combination tickets are available with Rothe House. Apr–May and Sept Mon–Sat 10am–1pm and 2–5pm, Sun 2–5pm; June–Aug Mon–Sat 9am–6pm, Sun 2–6pm; Oct–Mar Mon–Sat 10am–1pm and 2–4pm, Sun 2–4pm.

St. Francis Abbey Brewery Established in 1710 by John Smithwick, the brewery occupies a site that once belonged to the 12th-century Abbey of St. Francis. A popular local beer called Smithwick's is produced here, as are

Budweiser and Land Kilkenny Irish beer. A video presentation and free samples are offered in the summer.

Parliament St., Kilkenny, County Kilkenny. ✆ **056/772-1014.** Free admission. Presentation and tasting June–Aug Mon–Fri at 3pm.

ORGANIZED TOURS

Kilkenny City Sightseeing Tour This 13-stop double-decker tour bus runs seven times daily from Kilkenny Castle. Tickets are valid for 24 hours, so you can hop on and off at will.

Kilkenny Castle, The Parade, County Kilkenny. ✆ **01/458-0054.** www.city-sightseeing.com. Tickets €10 adults; €6 children; €8 seniors and students; €25 families. Daily June–Aug departs 10:30 and 11:30am, and 12:30, 2, 3, 4, and 5pm.

Tynan's Walking Tours Local historian Pat Tynan leads you through the streets and lanes of medieval Kilkenny, providing historical facts and anecdotes along the way. Tours depart daily from the tourist office, Rose Inn Street.

C/o Kilkenny Tourist Office, Rose Inn St., Kilkenny, County Kilkenny. ✆ **087/265-1745.** tynantours@eircom.net. Tickets €6 adults; €3 children; €5.50 seniors and students. Mar–Oct Mon–Sat 10:30am and 12:15, 1:30, 3, and 4:30pm; Sun 11:15am and 12:30pm; Nov–Mar group bookings only.

ATTRACTIONS FARTHER AFIELD IN COUNTY KILKENNY

Duiske Abbey ★ Duiske Abbey (1204) is a fine example of an early Cistercian abbey. It was suppressed in 1536, but its monks continued to occupy the site for many years. In 1774 the tower of the abbey church collapsed. In 1813 the roof was replaced and religious services returned to the church, but the abbey didn't approach its former glory until the 1970s, when a group of local people mounted a reconstruction effort. Now, with its fine lancet windows and a large effigy of a Norman knight, the abbey is the pride of Graiguenamanagh. The adjacent visitor center has an exhibit of Christian art and artifacts.

Graiguenamanagh, County Kilkenny. ✆ **059/972-4238.** Free admission; donations welcome. Daily 10am–5pm.

Dunmore Cave This gloomy series of chambers, formed over millions of years, contains some fine calcite formations. Known to humans for many centuries, the cave may have been the site of a Viking massacre in A.D. 928. Exhibits at the visitor center tell the story of the cave. It's about 11km (7 miles) from Kilkenny City.

Off Castlecomer Rd. (N78), Ballyfoyle, County Kilkenny. ✆ **056/776-7726.** Admission €3 adults; €2.30 seniors; €1.40 students and children. Mid-Mar to mid-June and mid-Sept to Oct daily 9:30am–5pm (last tour 4pm); mid-June to mid-Sept daily 9:30am–6:30pm (last tour 5pm); Nov to mid-Mar Wed–Sun and holidays 9:30am–5pm (last tour 3pm).

Jerpoint Abbey ★★ About 18km (11 miles) southeast of Kilkenny, this is an outstanding Cistercian monastery, founded in the latter half of the 12th century. Preserved in a peaceful country setting, one of the abbey's highlights is a sculptured cloister arcade. There is a splendid array of artifacts from medieval times, including unique stone carvings on ancient tombs and Romanesque architecture in the north nave. A tasteful interpretive center with an adjoining picnic garden makes this a perfect midday stop. Sheila Walsh, who often runs the front desk, is as friendly and knowledgeable as they come. She's also a font of information about the area. Ask her for details of where to find the mysterious ruins of the

Church of the Long Man, about 10 miles down the road. ***Tip:*** If you happen to be coming in spring or fall, plan your visit towards the end of the day. Wandering around these ancient places as the setting sun blushes the walls in peach and gold is an unforgettable experience.

On the N9, 2.4km (1½ miles) south of Thomastown, County Kilkenny. ✆ **056/772-4623.** Admission to Jerpoint Abbey €3 adults; €2.30 seniors; €1.50 children. Mar–May and mid-Sept to end of Oct daily 10am–5pm; June to mid-Sept daily 10am–6pm; Nov–Feb daily 10am–4pm.

The thick fortifications of Kells Priory have survived since the 13th century.

Kells Priory ★★ With its encompassing fortification walls and towers, as well as complex monastic ruins enfolded into the sloping south bank of the King's River, Kells is a glorious ruin. In 1193 Baron Geoffrey FitzRobert founded the priory and established a Norman-style town beside it. The current ruins date from the 13th to 15th centuries. The priory's wall has been carefully restored, and it connects seven towers, the remains of an abbey, and foundations of chapels and houses. You can tell by the thick walls that this monastery was well fortified, and those walls were built for a reason—it was frequently attacked. In the 13th century, it was the subject of two battles and burned to the ground. The priory is less than a half-mile from the village of Kells. If you have some time to spare, there's a footbridge behind it, which takes you on a beautiful walk across the river and intersects a riverside walk leading to a picturesque old mill.

Kells, County Kilkenny. Off N76 or N10. No phone. Free admission. From N76 south of Kilkenny, follow signs for R699/Callan and stay on R699 until you see signs for Kells.

Kilfane Glen and Waterfall The main place of interest in this small garden is the glen, created in true picturesque style, with an artificial waterfall and a rustic cottage. Views of the cottage and waterfall have been carefully composed, and the sound of water creates a counterpoint to the visual delights of the garden. An installation by the American artist James Turrell, *Air Mass,* is open to visitors, although the time of day it was intended to be seen—dusk—unfortunately doesn't correspond with the garden's hours in summer (the sun's still shining when they close at 6pm).

Thomastown, County Kilkenny. ✆ **056/772-4558.** www.kilfane.com. Admission €6 adults; €5.50 seniors; €5 students and children. July–Aug daily 11am–6pm. Other times by appointment.

Shopping

If you're an enthusiast of Irish crafts, Kilkenny City is well worth the trip. Its crafts scene is vibrant and lively, and it's difficult to leave empty-handed. The local tourist office provides a free **Craft Trail map** and lots of useful information on local artisans.

Kilkenny shopping hours are normally Monday to Saturday 9am to 6pm; many shops stay open until 9pm on Thursday and Friday.

Kilkenny is an excellent place in which to stock up on Irish crystal, woolens, and other handcrafted domestic goods.

The newest major addition to the shopping scene is **Market Cross,** a shopping center off High/Parliament Street (✆ **056/775-2666**), with its own multistory parking lot.

The Book Centre This shop offers a fine selection of books about Kilkenny and the area, as well as books of Irish interest. You can grab a quick daytime snack at the Pennefeather Cafe upstairs. 10 High St., Kilkenny, County Kilkenny. ✆ **056/776-2117.**

Kilkenny Crystal Established in 1969, this is the retail shop for Kilkenny's hand-cut crystal enterprise. The factory is on Callan Road (✆ **056/772-5132**), 16km (10 miles) outside of town, and it welcomes visitors. 19 Rose Inn St., Kilkenny, County Kilkenny. ✆ **056/772-1090.** www.kilkennycrystal.com.

Kilkenny Design Craft Centre The 18th-century coach house and stables of Kilkenny Castle have been wonderfully converted into shops and workshops for craftspeople. The center and the smaller shops collected nearby provide a showcase for handcrafted products—jewelry, glassware, pottery, clothing, linens, and furniture. There's also an excellent coffee shop and restaurant upstairs. Open Monday to Saturday from 10am to 7pm, and Sunday from 11am to 7pm (closed Sun Jan–Apr). Castle Yard, The Parade, Kilkenny, County Kilkenny. ✆ **056/772-2118.** www.kilkennydesign.com.

Liam Costigan This alumnus of the Kilkenny Design Centre produces fine handcrafted jewelry in gold and silver in this tiny studio. You can watch him work as you browse. Open Monday to Saturday 9am to 6pm. Colliers Lane, off High St., Kilkenny, County Kilkenny. ✆ **056/776-2408.**

P. T. Murphy This is Kilkenny's master jeweler. The shop is a very good source for Irish Claddagh and heraldic jewelry. 85 High St., Kilkenny, County Kilkenny. ✆ **056/772-1127.**

SHOPPING FARTHER AFIELD IN COUNTY KILKENNY

The Bridge Pottery Recently moved to a new studio in Burnchurch, this quirky enterprise is a dazzling kaleidoscope of Mediterranean colors and warm, earthen tones. Jugs, mugs, bowls, tiles, plates, even drawer handles—there's something here for every taste and budget, with prices ranging from just a few euros up to several hundred. Open Monday to Saturday from 10am to 5pm. Coals farm, Burnchurch, County Kilkenny. ✆ **056/772-9156.** www.bridgepottery.com.

Jerpoint Glass Studio At the last stop on the Craft Trail from Kilkenny to Stoneyford, you can witness the creation of Jerpoint glass, which you've probably been admiring in shops all across Ireland. The lines of the glasses, goblets, and pitchers are simple and fluid, highlighted with swirls of color. You can watch the glass being blown and then blow your budget next door at the shop, which includes an entire room of discounted seconds. The shop is open Monday to Saturday from 10am to 6pm and Sunday from noon to 5pm, while you can look in at the studio Monday to Thursday from 10am to 4:30pm, and Friday 10am to 2pm. Signposted from the N9 just south of Jerpoint Abbey, Stoneyford, County Kilkenny. ✆ **056/772-4350.** www.jerpointglass.com.

Nicholas Mosse Pottery In a former flour mill on the banks of the River Nore, this is the studio of Nicholas Mosse, a potter since age 7. Using hydropower from the river to fire the kilns, he produces colorful country-style earthenware from Irish clay, including jugs, mugs, bowls, vases, and plates. All are hand-slipped and hand-turned, then decorated by hand with cut sponges and brushes. An on-site museum displays antique Irish earthenware. There is also a cafe; it closes an hour before the shop. Open year-round Monday to Saturday from 10am to 6pm, and Sunday from 1:30 to 5pm. The Mill, Bennettsbridge, County Kilkenny. ✆ **056/772-7505.** www.nicholasmosse.com.

Stoneware Jackson Here's another fine pottery studio in Bennettsbridge, fast becoming a one-stop village for some of Ireland's most beautiful earthenware. The pieces are hand-thrown, featuring two-color glazing and Celtic motifs. Open Monday to Saturday from 10am to 6pm. Bennettsbridge, County Kilkenny. ✆ **056/27175.** www.stonewarejackson.com.

Sports & Outdoor Pursuits

BICYCLING For complete 1- or 2-week cycling holidays in the Southeast, contact Don Smith at **Celtic Cycling,** Lorum Old Rectory, Bagenalstown, County Carlow (✆ **059/977-5282;** www.celticcycling.com/lorum.html).

FISHING The **River Nore,** southeast of Kilkenny, is known for salmon and trout. For advice, permits, and supplies, visit the **Sports Shop,** 82 High St., Kilkenny (✆ **056/772-1517**).

Puffins, cormorants, and other seabirds jockey for space on the crowded beaches of Great Saltee Island during nesting season in late spring.

GOLF **Mount Juliet Golf and Country Club,** Thomastown, County Kilkenny (✆ **056/777-3000;** www.mountjuliet.ie), is an excellent course 16km (10 miles) south of Kilkenny City. The 18-hole, par-72 championship course, designed by Jack Nicklaus, charges greens fees of €80 to €100 on weekdays, and €100 to €120 on weekends. The price drops for Mount Juliet guests (see below), and reduced early and late rates are also available. Alternatively, try the 18-hole championship course at the **Kilkenny Golf Club,** Glendine, County Kilkenny (✆ **056/776-5400;** www.kilkennygolfclub.com), an inland par-71 layout, just 1.6km (1 mile) from the city. Greens fees are €35 Monday to Thursday, €40 Friday, and €45 weekends.

Where to Stay

VERY EXPENSIVE

Mount Juliet Estate ★★★ A private 3km (2-mile) lane wends its way beside the pastures of the Ballylinch Stud Farm to this exclusive hotel, an 18th-century manor house surrounded by 600 hectares (1,482 acres) of park. Mount Juliet is famous for its Jack Nicklaus–designed golf course, and is the home of Ireland's oldest cricket club. Guests can choose between the manor house, the Hunters Yard, and the Rose Garden lodges. Rooms are individually and sumptuously decorated with mahogany antiques and designer fabrics, and lounges are full of period pieces and original art.

The **Paddocks,** a cluster of 12 **self-catering luxury lodges,** are also available. Each has a fully equipped kitchen, and a lounge/dining room. Weekly rentals start at €2,400 for a two-bedroom lodge.

Thomastown, County Kilkenny. www.mountjuliet.ie. ✆ **056/777-3000.** Fax 056/777-3019. 32 units. €270–€350 double. AE, MC, V. **Amenities:** 3 restaurants; bar; concierge; 18-hole golf course; gym; Jacuzzi; indoor pool; room service; sauna; beauty/spa treatments; tennis courts; squash. *In room:* A/C, TV, hair dryer, minibar.

EXPENSIVE

Butler House ★ This elegant, historic building with a series of conical rooftops stands in 2 centuries—its front door faces busy Patrick Street, while its backyard overlooks secluded 18th-century gardens. Built in 1770 by the 16th Earl of Ormonde as part of Kilkenny Castle, it has a sweeping staircase, marble fireplaces, spacious modern guest rooms (some overlooking the castle), big bathrooms, and neutral color schemes with vivid splashes of bright color. Breakfast is served in the nearby Kilkenny Design Centre (p. 286), reached by walking across the guesthouse's gardens—lovely in summer, less so on a cold, rainy day.

16 Patrick St., Kilkenny, County Kilkenny. www.butler.ie. ✆ **056/776-0500.** Fax 056/776-5626. 13 units. €140–€180 double. Rates include full breakfast. AE, MC, V. **Amenities:** Restaurant; bar; babysitting. *In room:* TV, DVD, hair dryer, Wi-Fi (free).

Hotel Kilkenny ★★ ☺ Tucked away in a quiet residential neighborhood on the edge of town, this contemporary hotel is great for families. The whole place has been refurbished, and even the standard double rooms are big enough for a small family. Rooms are pleasantly furnished in a smart chocolate-and-cream palette, and there's good attention to detail (nice toiletries and bathrobes in the small bathrooms). There are lovely, well-tended gardens, and an excellent modern leisure center with an elaborate "kids' club," where you can drop the little ones off to play safely while you do a bit of shopping. But this kind of goodness doesn't come cheap.

College Rd., Kilkenny, County Kilkenny. www.hotelkilkenny.ie. ✆ **056/776-2000.** Fax 056/776-5984. 138 units. €220–€320 double. Rates include full breakfast. AE, MC, V. **Amenities:** Restaurant; bar; babysitting; children's playroom/activities; gym; Jacuzzi; indoor pool; sauna. *In room:* TV, hair dryer, free broadband Internet.

The Newpark Hotel ★ ☺ This hotel a mile north of the city center has a Victorian feel, but with elegant modern touches—rooms are done up in light wood with colorful Irish textiles, and the lounges have a stylish, contemporary look. The building is set amid 20 hectares (49 acres) of peaceful gardens and parkland. There's a good health club with an indoor pool, and a heated outdoor pool overlooking the gardens. If you need more help relaxing, stop by their Aveda spa for some pampering. In the summer, a kids club provides free daycare and babysitting. Check the website for good-value off-season specials.

Castlecomer Rd., Kilkenny, County Kilkenny. www.newparkhotel.com. ✆ **056/776-0500.** Fax 056/776-0555. 129 units. €100–€200 double. AE, MC, V. **Amenities:** Gym; Jacuzzi; indoor pool and children's pool; sauna/steam room; spa; beauty treatments. *In room:* TV, hair dryer, free high-speed Internet.

MODERATE

Abbey House This attractive Georgian (ca. 1750) building alongside the Little Argile River was once part of the Jerpoint Abbey's estate. The garden is a perfect spot to relax overlooking the Little Arrigle River, and the sitting room, complete with piano and stacks of books, suits both quiet reading and a round of songs. Owner Helen Blanchfield serves you tea and scones when you arrive, and then directs you to one of the comfortable rooms, all of which have firm, orthopedic beds and nice antique touches. Nearby, the village of Thomastown is a charming place to take a stroll.

Thomastown, County Kilkenny. On the N9, directly across from Jerpoint Abbey. www.abbeyhousejerpoint.com. ✆ **056/772-4166.** Fax 056/772-4192. 7 units. €80–€110 double. Rates include service charge and full Irish breakfast. AE, MC, V. Closed Dec 21–30. *In room:* TV.

Ballyduff House ★ ☺ This gorgeous Georgian manor house is tucked away in the countryside about 16km (10 miles) outside Kilkenny town. It's a rambling old structure, beautifully decorated with an eye for period style. The green lawns stretch out into acres of meadow reaching down to a peaceful river, where guests are welcome to fish and swim. You're welcome to explore the building, although the library is the best place of all, with shelves filled with enticing books, and lots of soft sofas to sink into. Beds are big and comfortable, and family rooms are especially spacious. The grounds have lots of space for children to ramble, and Brede will arrange pony rides for them if you ask in advance.

Thomastown, County Kilkenny. On R700, 5km (3 miles) from New Ross. www.ballyduffhouse.com. ✆ **056/775-8488.** 4 units. €100 double. Rates include full breakfast. No credit cards. **Amenities:** Lounge.

Kilkenny Ormonde Hotel ☺ This big hotel in the heart of Kilkenny town is a good option for families. Bedrooms are large and modern, decorated in soft, warm colors. Deluxe rooms come with both a queen-size bed and a single bed, while the family rooms (€150–€250) sleep four, with enough room for a cot or extra fold-down bed. There's also a large health club (complete with children's pool) connected to the hotel by an underground walkway. However, the hotel's central location means that it can be quite noisy, especially on weekends. If you're a light sleeper, ask for a quiet room when booking—on an upper floor if possible, and as far away from the nightclub as they can put you. The Ormonde also suffers from occasionally patchy service and underwhelming breakfasts.

Ormonde St., Kilkenny, County Kilkenny. www.kilkennyormonde.com. ✆ **056/772-3900.** Fax 056/772-3977. 118 units. €99–€129 double. Rates include full breakfast and VAT. AE, MC, V. **Amenities:** 3 restaurants; 2 bars; children's playroom; concierge; gym; Jacuzzi; indoor pool, children's pool, and volcano pool; room service; sauna/steam room; smoke-free rooms. *In room:* TV, hair dryer, minibar, free Wi-Fi.

Lawcus Farm Guesthouse ★★ This fabulously rustic, 200-year-old stone cottage at the edge of the King's River near the village of Kells cries out to be photographed. Owner Mark Fisher bought the place years ago to be near good fishing waters, and has gradually converted it by hand into a relaxing, modern country lodge, with walls warmly paneled in polished wood, brass bedsteads, and endless green views. He's added on a deck now, so that you can relax outside with a glass of wine and watch the sun set over the fields. Mark knows the best local places to hear traditional music, have a pint, catch some fish, or dine, and he's happy to share them. There are two family rooms now, with space for kids. There are no TVs or outside distractions. For those looking to get away from it all, this just might be the place.

Stonyford, County Kilkenny. Off the N10 on the Kells Rd. www.lawcusfarmguesthouse.com. ✆ **056/772-8949.** 5 units. €100 double; family rooms €150–€170. Rates include full breakfast. No credit cards. **Amenities:** Dining room; lounge. *In room:* Wi-Fi (free).

INEXPENSIVE

Aspect Hotel Kilkenny This modern hotel at the edge of Kilkenny town offers terrific value. Ultra-comfortable Hypnos beds, a pleasant, contemporary decor, a decent restaurant, and friendly staff at half the price you'd pay in the very center of town. The hotel is geared primarily toward business travelers, so has all the amenities you would expect including power showers, laptop safes, and free Wi-Fi. The only downside is that it's on a busy ring road, so there are no scenic views. But nobody's perfect.

Smithsland South, Springhill, Kilkenny, County Kilkenny. www.aspecthotelkilkenny.com. ✆ **056/778-3100.** Fax 056/778-3101. 80 units. €50–€80 double. Rates include service charge and full Irish breakfast. AE, MC, V. **Amenities:** Restaurant; bar. *In room:* TV, hair dryer, Wi-Fi (free).

SELF-CATERING

Clomantagh Castle ★★ Yet another one-of-a-kind rental property from the nonprofit Irish Landmark Trust, this huge, rambling establishment sleeps 10 and is ideal for a large family or group. Around it, a complex of buildings includes the ruins of a 12th-century church and an early-15th-century crenelated tower house attached to an 18th-century farmhouse. There are four large double bedrooms in the farmhouse, with a staircase leading to a fifth wonderfully medieval double bedroom in the tower. The decor throughout is pleasingly rustic, with fine period pieces and brass beds. There are several reception rooms and an enormous, well-equipped country kitchen with a flagstone floor, timbered ceiling, and Stanley range. Like all Irish Landmark Trust properties, Clomantagh Castle has no TV. Although the setting is rural, Kilkenny City is only about a 20-minute drive away.

Freshford, County Kilkenny. Contact the Irish Landmark Trust at www.irishlandmark.com. ✆ **01/670-4733.** Fax 01/670-4887. From €700 for 4 nights in low season, going up to €1,820 per week in high season. MC, V.

Where to Eat

In addition to the restaurants listed here, Kilkenny has a number of gorgeous old pubs, many of which serve reasonably priced food. See p. 287 for a few of our favorites.

EXPENSIVE

The Motte ★ MODERN CONTINENTAL This is a pretty place—the intimate dining room shimmers with gilt and candlelight, each table crowned by a bouquet of field flowers. The menu (based on locally produced meats and vegetables) changes constantly, but look out for fresh, home-baked breads, and main courses like sirloin in burgundy-butter sauce, or crispy stuffed duck. Sorbet precedes an excellent choice of diet-busting desserts, like velvety-rich chocolate cardamom truffle cake served with custard and a drizzle of raspberry sauce. Book a table well in advance and surrender your evening to conversation and good food.

Plas Newydd Lodge, Inistioge, County Kilkenny. ✆ **056/775-8655.** Reservations essential. 3-course fixed-price menu €40. MC, V. Wed–Sat 7–9:30pm.

Zuni ★ MODERN INTERNATIONAL Kilkenny Town is a favorite weekend getaway for Dubliners, and Zuni has hitched its wagon to that star. With its sleek design—leather banquettes, dark polished wood, creamy walls—it's one of the reigning local hot spots. The jet-setter menu features grilled steak, and dishes such as spiced duck breast with parsnip *dauphinoise,* or ahi tuna with bok choy, wasabi, and pickled ginger. Upstairs are 13 chic guest rooms available for €100 to €150 for a double. Ask about good-value specials combining 2 nights at a B&B with one dinner.

26 Patrick St., Kilkenny, County Kilkenny. ✆ **056/772-3999.** www.zuni.ie. Reservations required. Dinner main courses €18–€25. Early-bird menus (Sun–Fri): 2 courses €24, 3 courses €29. AE, MC, V. Tues–Sat 12:30–2:30pm; Mon–Sat 6:30–9:30pm; Sun 1–3pm and 6–9pm.

MODERATE

Café Sol ★★ SOUTHERN AMERICAN/MEDITERRANEAN This bright cafe with light streaming in through floor-to-ceiling windows is a cheerful place in both cuisine and appearance. It's open all day, starting with homemade scones and biscuits at breakfast time, moving on to a lunch menu stocked with comfort foods for busy Kilkenny shoppers and business folk—mainly homemade soups, salads, sandwiches, and hot plates. But the place really comes into its own at dinnertime, when the menu comes alive with zestier options, like Louisiana crab cakes with tomato salsa, chicken and mozzarella wrapped in phyllo, and steamed mussels with wine and garlic. ***Tip:*** This place has a laid-back definition for the term "early-bird": Its fixed-price menus are available until 9pm Sunday to Friday.

6 William St. (opposite the Town Hall), Kilkenny, County Kilkenny. ✆ **056/776-4987.** www.cafesolkilkenny.com. Reservations recommended for dinner. Main courses lunch €6–€12, dinner €17–€29. Early-bird menus (Sun–Fri until 9pm; Sat until 6:15pm): 2 courses €20, 3 courses €24. MC, V. Mon–Sat 11:30am–10pm; Sun noon–9pm.

Lautrecs MODERN INTERNATIONAL This atmospheric restaurant named after the artist Henri de Toulouse-Lautrec and decorated with prints of his work, is a romantic option with a happily varied menu. You could begin with an appetizer of goat cheese and red-onion confit baked in phyllo, and move on to one of their many pizzas, or try the marinated slow-roasted pork belly with duchess potato, roast rack of lamb with potato gratin, or pan-seared scallops with tiger prawns. The lunch menu is a low-fuss mix of pizzas, salads, and sandwiches.

9 Kieran St., Kilkenny, County Kilkenny. ✆ **056/776-2720.** www.lautrecs.com. Reservations recommended. Main courses lunch €5–€12, dinner €11–€23. MC, V. Mon–Fri 5–10pm; Sat–Sun 1–3pm and 5–10pm.

INEXPENSIVE

Kilkenny Design Centre Restaurant ★★ CAFETERIA Above the Kilkenny Design Centre gallery, this self-service restaurant is a classy place, with whitewashed walls, circular windows, beamed ceilings, and fresh, delicious food. The ever-changing menu is based on locally sourced ingredients, often featuring fresh local salmon, chicken and broccoli crumble made with Lavistown cheese, fresh green salads, and homemade soups. The fresh pastries and breads are tempting, as are the cheese scones.

Castle Yard, Kilkenny, County Kilkenny. ✆ **056/772-2118.** Main courses €13–€17. AE, MC, V. Year-round Mon–Sat 9am–5pm; May–Dec Sun 10am–5pm.

Marble City Bar and Tea Rooms TEAROOM A traditional tearoom tucked away in the basement of this picture-perfect old pub, discreetly hidden, like a little fortress of gentility. It's a thoroughly civilized affair, serving tea, cakes, sandwiches, and light meals all day while, upstairs, the pub serves heartier meals.

66 High St., Kilkenny, County Kilkenny. ✆ **056/776-1143.** Main courses €5–€10. AE, MC, V. Daily 9am–7pm.

The Water Garden TEAROOM Just outside Thomastown on the road to Kilkenny, this tearoom and small garden is operated by a local group that helps people with special needs or disabilities. The cafe serves lunch, tea, and baked goods; meals are prepared with organic vegetables and meats raised on the community farm. Lunches include sandwiches made with home-baked bread, soups, and a vegetable or meat pâté. Buy a ticket to the garden (admission €2.50) and you can take a stroll along a trickling stream; there's also a garden shop.

Ladywell, Thomastown, County Kilkenny. ✆ **056/772-4690.** Garden admission €2.50. Lunch €4–€8. No credit cards. Tues–Fri 10am–5pm; Sun 12:30–5pm. Closed Sun Christmas through Easter.

Kilkenny After Dark

To find out what's going on around town, pick up a copy of the local weekly paper *Kilkenny People.* Kilkenny is home to the small-but-mighty **Watergate Theatre,** Parliament Street (✆ **056/776-1674;** www.watergatetheatre.com), a 328-seat venue for local talent and visiting troupes in classic and contemporary plays, concerts, and ballets. Ticket prices average €10 to €20.

Across the street from the theater, **John Cleere's,** 28 Parliament St. (✆ **056/776-2573**), is a pub theater that's good for music and local productions.

For 2 weeks every August, the **Kilkenny Arts Festival** (✆ **056/775-2175;** www.kilkennyarts.ie) takes over the town. It is one of Ireland's largest and longest-running arts festivals, covering music, theater, dance, visual arts, literature, and film. There are also a variety of street theater performances on hand, so even if you don't plan to go to any of the scheduled events, you'll likely get caught up in the proceedings at some point. Check out the festival website for specific program details.

PUBS

Caislean Ui Cuain (The Castle Inn) ★★ A striking facade with a mural of old Kilkenny welcomes guests to this pub, founded in 1734 as a stagecoach inn. The interior is a pub lover's dream, with dark-wood furnishings and a paneled ceiling. Traditional music sessions—both scheduled and spontaneous—often start up, and many patrons and staff speak Irish. The Parade, Kilkenny, County Kilkenny. ✆ **056/776-5406.**

Eamon Langton's ★ No self-respecting Irishman—or anyone, for that matter—would pass through Kilkenny without stopping here for a pint. This is a classic traditional pub, with a lovely fireplace, etched mirrors, stained-glass windows, and burgundy-leather banquettes. On summer days, everyone heads to the back room—actually a lush, plant-filled conservatory with Gothic-style windows and a garden backed by the old city walls. Langton's has won plaudits for its pub grub, too, so bring your appetite. 69 John St., Kilkenny, County Kilkenny. ✆ **056/776-5133.**

Kyteler's Inn ★ This inn has served spirits for more than 650 years. The ground-floor restaurant (reasonably priced pub food served noon–3pm Mon–Sat) and bar are done in cozy, contemporary pine, so if you are in a medieval mood, head downstairs to the cellar, where a deep-set window overlooks Kieran's Well, which predates the inn itself, and where the original stone pillars still reach from floor to ceiling. This was once the home of Dame Alice Kyteler, a colorful character who made the tavern into a den of merrymaking. She also laid four husbands to rest in the Kilkenny graveyard. She was tried for being a witch and condemned to burn at the stake, but escaped and was never heard from again. Hungry for justice—or perhaps just because they'd already bought the kindling—the townsfolk burned her servant girl instead. The ghost of this unfortunate maid is said to haunt the place to this day, although, as the owners are quick to point out, you're more likely to see her after a few pints than when sober. Kieran's St., Kilkenny, County Kilkenny. ✆ **056/772-1064.** www.kytelersinn.com.

Marble City Bar and Tea Rooms ★ This central pub has a marvelous facade of carved wood, wrought iron, and polished brass, with flower boxes overhead—and the interior is equally inviting. Even if you don't stop for a drink here, you'll certainly want to take a picture. For a more genteel experience, try the new tearooms downstairs—they're open every day from 9am to 7pm. If you choose to have lunch here, a main course will set you back about €8. 66 High St., Kilkenny, County Kilkenny. ✆ **056/776-1143.**

Tynan's Bridge House 🎁 Before a man named Tynan turned it into a pub in 1919, this 225-year-old building was a pharmacy and grocery shop. Behind the horseshoe-shaped marble-top bar, side drawers marked CLOVES, ALMONDS, MACE, and CITRON are vestiges of those days, as is the 200-year-old scale with its little set of cup weights. It's all lit by nostalgic globe gas lamps, and adorned with brass fixtures and silver tankards. The crowd is a friendly but not intrusive mix of locals and visitors. An intricate old clock chimes the hour. 2 Horseleap Slip, St. John's Bridge, Kilkenny, County Kilkenny. ✆ **056/772-1291.**

8

COUNTY CORK

The largest of the 32 Irish counties, and one of the most diverse, Cork offers a brief course in all things Irish. It has lively small cities, quiet country villages, rocky hills, picturesque beaches, and long stretches of flat, green farmland. Here, modern tourism (this is where you find the Blarney Castle, after all) meets workaday Irish life, and somehow they manage to exist peacefully, side by side.

Cork has had a long and rebellious history, which has been for centuries tied intrinsically to Ireland's struggle for independence. It was founded by St. Finbarre in the 6th century, when he built a monastery on a swampy estuary of the River Lee. He gave the place the rather generic Gaelic name of *Corcaigh*—which, unromantically, means "marsh." Over the next 600 years, the little piece of swamp would ultimately become the crown in the Kingdom of South Munster, but by the end of the 12th century, the English had asserted their ownership of the region. Over the following centuries, Cork would change hands many times as the English and the Irish struggled for control. It resisted Cromwell's forces, only to lose to William of Orange.

Once firmly under English control, Cork thrived until the 18th century, when it was battered by the potato famine, which drained the region of its wealth and, ultimately, of its population.

British troops in Cork—nicknamed the "Black and Tans" for the color of their uniforms—were among the most repressive in Ireland. The county earned its nickname, "Rebel Cork," because it was a center of the 19th-century Fenian movement, and also played an active part in Ireland's 20th-century battle for independence. Most of Cork City, including the library, the City Hall, and most of the buildings on St. Patrick Street, were burned to the ground during the British occupation and the subsequent brutal civil war of the 1920s. The fighting here was long and ugly. Thomas MacCurtain, a mayor of Cork City, was killed by British forces in 1920. His successor, Terence MacSwiney, died in a London prison after a hunger strike lasting 75 days.

It would not be until the end of the 20th century that Cork would find its own true personality. It's now an affluent, foodie region of the country with a lovely stretch of coast and a laid-back personality. Its tough days seem long behind it.

The county's eponymous capital, Cork, is a university town, which keeps the population young and the arts scene ever evolving, and this also ensures that it has affordable restaurants and buzzing pubs and bars.

Colorful Kinsale, a pretty harbor town directly south of Cork City, has an outstanding gourmet restaurant scene and is well worth an overnight stay.

Slightly off the tourist trail, West Cork is the county's most remote and wild region, with strikingly rugged coastal landscapes where long sandy beaches stretch out beneath sheer cliffs.

PREVIOUS PAGE: **The formal herb gardens at Ballymaloe Cookery School, which helped to launch a culinary revolution in Ireland.**

The port of Cork City, a thriving town of 125,000 on the banks of the River Lee.

CORK CITY

Cork City (pop. 125,000) is developing a reputation as a kind of Dublin South. It's far smaller than the capital, but Cork is a busy, attractive, artsy place, and home to a major university that keeps the local population young. For travelers, it makes a great place to base yourself while your exploring the region, with its lively music scene and a burgeoning foodie culture that rivals Dublin's.

THINGS TO DO For visitors, Cork's offerings are wonderfully varied. You can fight the crowds at **Blarney Castle** to find out if kissing a rock can make you loquacious, explore an extraordinary collection of works by Irish artists at the **Crawford Art Gallery,** and climb to the top of the 300-year-old tower at **St. Anne's Church** to take in the sweeping views and ring the **Shandon Bells,** all before you begin a tour of the city's excellent restaurants.

SHOPPING Cork is an excellent place to find interesting Irish products to use while you're here, or take home with you. You can buy fresh local meat, breads, and produce at the **Old English Market,** or wrap yourself in locally made woolen blankets and sweaters at **Quills Woolen Market** (both are on St. Patrick St.). For local ceramics, pottery, and jewelry try the **Shandon Craft Centre,** which has free concerts in the summer (on John Redmond St.). And **Crafts of Ireland** on Winthrop Street is packed with works of local artisans.

RESTAURANTS & DINING In Cork, cuisine is at its best when it's fresh and local. Cork restaurants specialize in pairing meats from area farms and seafood straight from the docks, with innovative European and Asian cooking techniques. Try the local **lamb** in spring, tender **John Dory fish,** local **pork** (even the bacon is memorable), and organic, free-range **beef,** perfectly aged and grilled.

NIGHTLIFE & ENTERTAINMENT In late October, don't miss the Guinness Jazz Festival, one of Ireland's premier music festivals. The rest of the year you can catch traditional Irish music concerts at the **Triskel Arts Centre** on Main Street, and outstanding comedy at the **City Lights Comedy Club** on Coburg Street. Cork's pubs are known for their music scene—drop by **an Spailpin Fanac** on Main Street for live music. For a quiet drink, try the **Long Valley** on Winthrop Street.

County Cork
Ballymaloe Cookery School 15
Bantry House 5
Blarney Castle 11
Charles Fort 8
Cobh: The Queenstown Story 13
Derreen Gardens 3
Desmond Castle 10
Drombeg Stone Circle 6
Dursey Island 2
Fota Island Wildlife Park 12
Garinish Island (Ilnacullin) 4
Kinsale Museum 9
Michael Collins Memorial Centre 7
Mizen Head Signal Station 1
Old Midleton Distillery/ Jameson Heritage Centre 14
LIMERICK
TIPPERARY
WATERFORD
KERRY
CORK
Galty Mts.
Knockmealdown Mts.
Nagles Mts.
Boggeragh Mts.
Shehy Mts.
Caha Mts.
Macgillycuddy's Reeks
Mt. Eagle
The Paps
Knockboy
Killarney National Park
Tralee
Killarney
Bantry
Cork
Cobh
Blarney Castle
Cork Int'l
ATLANTIC OCEAN
CELTIC SEA
To Swansea
To Roscoff
NORTHERN IRELAND
REPUBLIC OF IRELAND
Belfast
Dublin
Galway
Map Area
0
10 miles
10 kms

Flying Within Ireland: Should You Bother?

In February 2011, tragedy befell Cork Airport when a Manx2 Airlines commuter plane crashed there in heavy fog, killing six. At this writing the investigation was still ongoing, but it did reinforce our general antipathy towards taking planes for short hops within Ireland. This isn't so much for safety reasons—the country has an excellent air safety record—but for the simple reason: Why would you bother? This is such a tiny country that taking internal flights just seems pointless to us. In almost all circumstances, you're better off driving, or going by train or coach.

Cork City Essentials

Cork is 258km (160 miles) SW of Dublin, 206km (128 miles) SE of Galway, 101km (63 miles) S of Limerick, 122km (76 miles) S of Shannon Airport, 126km (78 miles) W of Waterford, and 87km (54 miles) E of Killarney

GETTING THERE From Cork Airport, Kinsale Road (✆ **021/431-3131;** www.corkairport.com), 13km (8 miles) south of the city**, Aer Lingus** (✆ **0818/365-000** in Ireland, 516/622-4022 in the U.S., or 0871/718-5000 in the U.K.; www.aerlingus.com) operates flights to and from other European destinations, including London (Heathrow and Gatwick), Bristol, Glasgow, and Manchester in the U.K. **Ryanair** (✆ **0818/30-30-30** in Ireland, or 0871/246-0000 in Britain; www.ryanair.com) serves Cork from Dublin, plus London (Stansted and Gatwick) and Liverpool in the U.K.

There are **taxi** stands outside the arrivals hall of the airport. A journey to the city center should cost around €15.

Sky Link (✆ **021/432-1020;** www.skylinkcork.com), with its distinctive bright-yellow buses, provides a shuttle service direct from Cork airport to the city center. It takes 10 to 15 minutes and costs €5 one-way, €8 round-trip (€3.50/€6 students; €2.50/€5 kids aged 4–12; €12/€19 families). Departures are every 30 minutes from outside the arrivals hall. You can buy tickets from the driver or book online.

Bus Éireann (✆ **021/450-8188;** www.buseireann.ie) provides bus service from the airport to Parnell Place Bus Station in the city center; the fare is €4.10 one-way, €7 round-trip. The trip takes between 18 and 24 minutes, depending on time of day. Buses from all parts of Ireland arrive at **Bus Éireann's Passenger Depot,** Parnell Place, in the downtown area, 3 blocks from St. Patrick Street.

Iarnród Éireann (Irish Rail) (toll-free ✆ **1850/366222** or 01/836-6222; www.irishrail.ie) operates the train services in Ireland. Trains from Dublin, Limerick, and other parts of Ireland arrive at **Kent Station,** Lower Glanmire Road, Cork (✆ **021/455-7277**), on the city's eastern edge.

Fastnet Line (✆ **021/437-8892** in Ireland, or ✆ **0844/576-8831** from Britain) sails between Cork and Swansea in Wales four times weekly. The crossing takes about 14 hours; call or go online for detailed prices.

If you're approaching Cork from the east, take the Carrigaloe-Glenbrook ferry from Cobh across Cork Harbour. This ferry can save you an hour's driving time around the edge of Cork Harbour, and you'll bypass the generally heavy Cork City traffic. The ferry runs daily from 7am to 10pm.

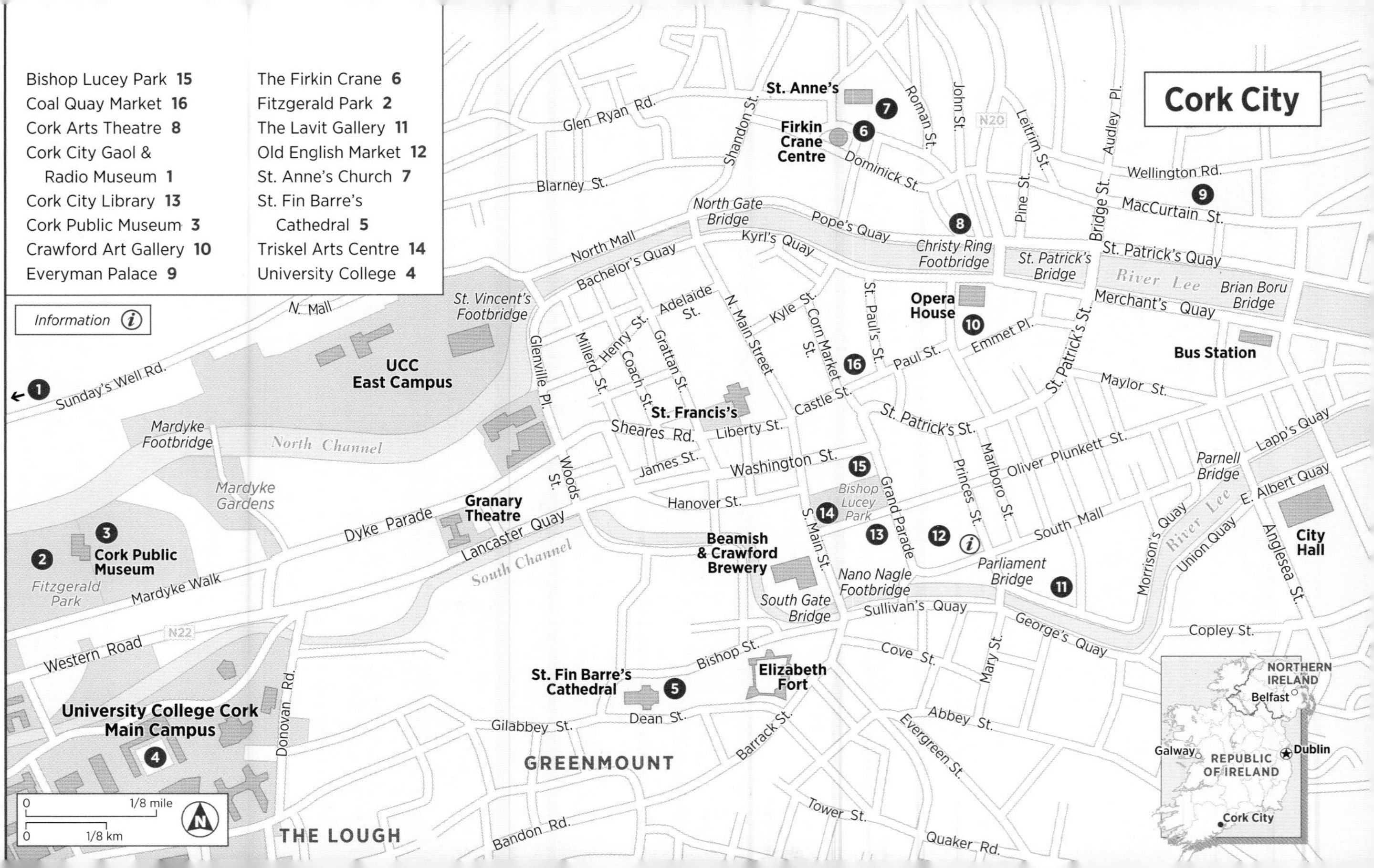
Cork City
Bishop Lucey Park 15
Coal Quay Market 16
Cork Arts Theatre 8
Cork City Gaol & Radio Museum 1
Cork City Library 13
Cork Public Museum 3
Crawford Art Gallery 10
Everyman Palace 9
The Firkin Crane 6
Fitzgerald Park 2
The Lavit Gallery 11
Old English Market 12
St. Anne's Church 7
St. Fin Barre's Cathedral 5
Triskel Arts Centre 14
University College 4
Information
St. Anne's
Firkin Crane Centre
Opera House
Bus Station
City Hall
St. Francis's
UCC East Campus
Granary Theatre
Beamish & Crawford Brewery
Elizabeth Fort
St. Fin Barre's Cathedral
Cork Public Museum
Fitzgerald Park
Mardyke Gardens
Mardyke Footbridge
University College Cork Main Campus
GREENMOUNT
THE LOUGH
River Lee
North Channel
South Channel
Bishop Lucey Park
Sunday's Well Rd.
N. Mall
North Mall
Bachelor's Quay
Glen Ryan Rd.
Blarney St.
Shandon St.
Roman St.
John St.
Leitrim St.
Pine St.
Audley Pl.
Bridge St.
Wellington Rd.
MacCurtain St.
Dominick St.
North Gate Bridge
Pope's Quay
Kyrl's Quay
Christy Ring Footbridge
St. Patrick's Bridge
St. Patrick's Quay
Brian Boru Bridge
Merchant's Quay
St. Vincent's Footbridge
Glenville Pl.
Millerd St.
Henry St.
Coach St.
Grattan St.
Adelaide St.
N. Main Street
Kyle St.
Corn Market St.
St. Paul's St.
Paul St.
Emmet Pl.
St. Patrick's St.
Maylor St.
Castle St.
Sheares Rd.
Liberty St.
James St.
Washington St.
Woods St.
Hanover St.
Grand Parade
Princes St.
Marlboro St.
Oliver Plunkett St.
South Mall
Parnell Bridge
Lapp's Quay
E. Albert Quay
Morrison's Quay
Union Quay
Anglesea St.
Dyke Parade
Lancaster Quay
Mardyke Walk
Western Road
N22
N20
S. Main St.
Nano Nagle Footbridge
Parliament Bridge
South Gate Bridge
Sullivan's Quay
George's Quay
Copley St.
Cove St.
Mary St.
Bishop St.
Dean St.
Gilabbey St.
Barrack St.
Abbey St.
Evergreen St.
Tower St.
Quaker Rd.
Bandon Rd.
Donovan Rd.
NORTHERN IRELAND
Belfast
Dublin
Galway
REPUBLIC OF IRELAND
Cork City
0 1/8 mile
0 1/8 km
N

Cars cost €5 one-way, €7 round-trip. For cyclists, the fare is €1 one-way, €1.50 round-trip. Discount tickets are available if you expect to make more than 10 trips. The journey lasts less than 5 minutes. For more information, contact **Cross River Ferries Ltd.,** Westland House, Rushbrooke, Cobh (✆ **021/420-2900;** www.scottcobh.ie).

Many main national roads lead into Cork, including N8 from Dublin, N25 from Waterford, N20 from Limerick, N22 from Killarney, and N71 from West Cork.

VISITOR INFORMATION For brochures, maps, and other information, visit the **Cork Tourist Office,** Tourist House, 42 Grand Parade, Cork (✆ **021/425-5100;** www.discoverireland.ie/southwest.aspx). Its hours are Monday to Saturday 9:15am to 5:30pm year-round. Online, consult the **Cork Guide** (www.cork-guide.ie).

CITY LAYOUT Cork's center is on an island, which lies between two branches of the River Lee. The city is divided into three sections:

FLAT OF THE CITY The city's downtown core is bounded by channels of the River Lee, and its main thoroughfare is **St. Patrick Street,** a graceful avenue lined with shops. A favorite meeting place here is by the statue of 19th-century priest Father Theobald Matthew, a crusader against drink who is fondly called the "Apostle of Temperance." The statue stands at the point where St. Patrick Street reaches St. Patrick's Bridge.

Nearby, the **South Mall** is a wide tree-lined street with attractive Georgian architecture and a row of banks, insurance companies, and legal offices, while the **Grand Parade** is a spacious thoroughfare that blends 18th-century bow-fronted houses with the remains of the old city walls. It has lots of offices and shops as well as the **Bishop Lucey Park.**

NORTH BANK St. Patrick's Bridge leads over the river to the north side of the city, a hilly, terraced area where St. Patrick Street becomes **St. Patrick's Hill.** And is it ever a hill, with an incline so steep that it's virtually San Franciscan. If you climb the stepped sidewalks of St. Patrick's Hill, you will be rewarded with a sweeping view of the Cork skyline.

East of St. Patrick's Hill, **MacCurtain Street** is a commercial thoroughfare that runs east, leading to Summerhill Road and up into the Cork hills to the residential districts of St. Luke's and Montenotte. West of St. Patrick's Hill is one of the city's oldest neighborhoods, **St. Ann's Shandon Church,** and the city's original Butter Market building.

SOUTH BANK South of the River Lee, South Bank encompasses the grounds of St. Finbarre's Cathedral, the site of St. Finbarre's 6th-century monastery, and also includes 17th-century city walls, the remains of Elizabeth Fort, and the City Hall (built in 1936).

GETTING AROUND **By Public Transportation** **Bus Éireann** operates bus service from Parnell Place Bus Station (✆ **021/450-8188;** www.buseireann.ie) to all parts of the city, its suburbs, and nearby towns. A local journey within Cork costs around €1.10; a return ticket to Blarney costs €5.60, and to Kinsale €11. City buses run frequently from 7am to 11pm Monday to Saturday, with slightly shorter hours on Sunday.

BY TAXI Taxis are readily available throughout Cork. The main taxi ranks are along St. Patrick Street, along the South Mall, and outside major hotels. To call for a taxi, try **ABC Taxis** (✆ **021/496-1961**), **Cork Taxi Co-Op** (✆ **021/427-2222**), or **Satellite Taxis** (✆ **1890/202020**).

BY CAR It's best to park and explore the city on foot or by public transport. Unless your hotel has a parking lot, it can be a hassle finding street parking. If you have to park in public areas, it costs around €2 per hour, whether you park in one of the city's two multistory parking lots, at Lavitt's Quay and Merchant's Quay, or on the street, where you still must pay to park. There are plenty of ground-level parking lots throughout the city.

Many international car-rental firms maintain rental desks at Cork Airport, including **Alamo** (✆ 021/2400-100), **Avis** (✆ 021/432-7460), **Budget** (✆ 021/431-4000), **Hertz** (✆ 021/496-5849), and **Murray's Europcar** (✆ 021/491-7300).

ON FOOT Because of the limited parking, the best way to see Cork is on foot, but don't try to do it all in a day. The South Bank and the central part, or flat, of the city can easily take a day to explore; save the Cork Hills and the North Bank for another day. You might want to follow the signposted Tourist Trail to guide you to the major sights.

[Fast FACTS] CORK CITY

For countrywide information, see chapter 15, "Planning your Trip to Ireland."

Drugstores Try **Murphy's Pharmacy,** 48 N. Main St. (✆ **021/427-4121**), or **Deasy's Pharmacy,** 99 Shandon St. (✆ **021/430-4535**).

Emergencies Dial ✆ **999.**

Gay & Lesbian Resources **Gay Cork** (**www.gaycork.com**) is a good central resource for the LGBT community in the city. It has a short but local listings section for local societies and support groups (everything from HIV/ AIDS advice to a gay hillwalkers' association). Also good are the **Southern Gay Men's Health Project,** 8 S. Main St. (✆ **021/427-8470** or -8471; www.gayhealthproject.com) and **Gay Cork**'s **Lesbian Line** (✆ **021/431-8318;** www.linc.ie), which is open Thursday 8 to 10pm.

Hospitals Try **Cork University Hospital,** Wilton Road (✆ **021/454-6400**), or Bon Secours Hospital, College Road (✆ **021/454-2807**).

Information See "Visitor Information," above.

Internet Access **Web Workhouse** (✆ **021/427-3090;** www.webworkhouse.com), 8 Winthrop St., offers Internet access 24 hours a day, 7 days a week. Charges range from €1.25 to €3 per hour, depending on the time of day. They also have an international call center, open daily from 10am to 10pm, and the facility to send and receive Western Union money transfers. On Saturday nights they run a gamer's night, allowing you to pay for up to 8 hours for €10. Alternatively, you could try **Wired to the World,** Thompson House, MacCurtain Street, and at 28 N. Main St. (✆ **021/453-0383;** www.wiredtotheworld.ie). The MacCurtain Street branch is open from 9am to 2am, 7 days a week; the North Main Street branch is open daily from 9am to midnight (opens 10am Sun). In addition to Internet access for €1 an hour, it also offers cheap international phone calls.

Library **Cork City Library** is at 57–61 Grand Parade (✆ **021/492-4900**).

Police The local **Garda Headquarters** is on Anglesea Street (✆ **021/452-2000**).

Post Office The **General Post Office,** on Oliver Plunkett Street (✆ **021/485-1042**), is open Monday to Saturday 9am to 5:30pm (opens 9:30am Tues).

Where to Stay

VERY EXPENSIVE

Hayfield Manor Hotel ★★★ ☺ This place is all about luxury, with elegant and spacious bedrooms that feel as if they've been dropped straight in from a private manor house. However, the period appearance is all smoke and mirrors—the building was built in 1996. The entire hotel is decorated with a warm palette of apricot and ocher, including the magnificent foyer with marble columns and a grand mahogany staircase. In the guest rooms, large windows and marble bathrooms set the tone, as well as big, orthopedic beds. Although less than a mile from the city center and near Cork's University College, Hayfield Manor is quite secluded. The fully equipped conservatory/health club is inviting, and, for such a posh hotel, it is surprisingly welcoming to pampered children. It offers everything from babysitting service to miniature bathrobes and cookies and milk at bedtime.

Perrott Ave., College Rd., Cork, County Cork. www.hayfieldmanor.ie. ✆ **021/484-5900,** or 800/525-4800 in the U.S. for reservations through Small Luxury Hotels of the World. 88 units. €160–€315 double; €590 suite. Rates include service charge and full Irish breakfast. AE, MC, V. Free parking. **Amenities:** 2 restaurants; bar; babysitting; concierge; Jacuzzi; indoor pool; room service; spa; steam room. *In room:* A/C, TV, CD player, hair dryer.

EXPENSIVE

The Gresham Metropole This elegant, historic hotel has been a local landmark for 100 years. It was renovated a few years ago, and now it has all you need—comfortable rooms neatly designed with neutral decor, firm beds, and luxurious fabrics; a good bar and restaurant; and a full recreation center with pool, sauna, and steam room. The lobby and bar are pleasant places to relax at the end of a long day, and the restaurant comes in handy (as does room service). It's often possible to get good discounts by booking online.

MacCurtain St., Tivoli, Cork, County Cork. www.gresham-hotels.com. ✆ **021/464-3700.** Fax 021/450-6450. 113 units. €100–€110 double; €180–€190 suite. Rates include breakfast. AE, DC, MC, V. **Amenities:** 2 restaurants; bar; gym; health club; hot tub; indoor pool; room service; sauna; steam room; free Wi-Fi. *In room:* TV, hair dryer.

The Imperial Hotel ★★ Since opening in 1845, the Imperial has played host to a number of distinguished guests, including Charles Dickens, Sir Walter Scott, and William Makepeace Thackeray. The Irish revolutionary leader, Michael Collins, stayed in room no. 115 the night before his assassination. With Waterford crystal chandeliers, marble floors, and brass fittings, the reception area and public rooms exude an aura of 19th-century grandeur. The guest rooms recently received an injection of much-needed attention, and are attractive enough with a warm, golden palette and dark-wood furniture. There are plenty of modern conveniences, and executive rooms have DVD players, dataports, minibars, and fax machines. The location couldn't be better either—right in the city center. ***Tip:*** This hotel tends to offer good deals on room-only rates; check the website.

South Mall, Cork, County Cork. www.flynnhotels.com/Imperial_Hotel. ✆ **800/44-UTELL** [448-8355] in the U.S., or 021/427-4040. Fax 021/427-5375. 88 units. €100–€160 double; €450 penthouse. Rates include full breakfast. AE, MC, V. Parking (designated spaces in Union Quay lot) €8 per day. **Amenities:** 2 restaurants; bar; cafe; concierge; room service. *In room:* TV, radio, high-speed Internet.

MODERATE

Hotel Isaacs This place offers a kind of stripped-down chic that makes the best of what it has and keeps prices reasonable. Exposed brick walls, huge picture windows, and excellent use of light all combine to make you forget the tired upholstery and weary carpet. Bedrooms are comfortable with pine furniture and individual color schemes. Superior rooms have air-conditioning and power outlets compatible with U.S. voltage. There's also the option of two- and three-bedroom self-catering apartments. The on-site restaurant, **Greenes,** serves good seafood. ***Tip:*** Heavily discounted rates are often available online.

48 MacCurtain St., Cork, County Cork. www.isaacs.ie. ✆ **021/450-0011.** 47 units, 11 self-catering suites. €70–€100 double; €85–€110 self-catering apartment. AE, MC, V. Free parking. **Amenities:** Restaurant; bar; room service; smoke-free rooms. *In room:* A/C (some rooms), TV, hair dryer, Wi-Fi.

The River Lee Hotel A much-needed renovation in 2010 has smoothed out a few tired edges at this hotel and generally given it a welcome upgrade. However, the place is still somewhat utilitarian. Most bedrooms have multiple beds—a double and a single, or two (or even three) singles. Huge, floor-to-ceiling windows give views of the leafy surroundings. The lobby is bright and modern, and there are nice touches, like the indoor swimming pool. However, the neighborhood is not Cork's finest, and the parking lot is a bit of a walk from the building. The best deals are to be had if you don't include breakfast here in your rate.

Western Rd., Cork, County Cork. www.doylecollection.com. ✆ **021/425-2700.** 182 units. €100–€150 per room. Breakfast €10. AE, DC, MC, V. Limited free parking. **Amenities:** Restaurant; bar; library; smoke-free rooms; spa; Wi-Fi (free). *In room:* TV, hair dryer.

INEXPENSIVE

Garnish House ★★ 🎁 This is the best B&B on the Western Road and, since B&Bs are wall-to-wall along the entire thoroughfare, that's saying something. Hansi Lucey is a wonderful innkeeper, the kind who makes a fuss about you as if you were a much-cherished friend. Fresh tea and scones await you upon arrival, and give an inkling of the excellent food you can expect at breakfast; in addition to the standard full Irish option you can choose from omelets, cinnamon toast, pancakes, or the house specialty—porridge with cream, honey, and either Irish whiskey or Baileys Irish Cream. Bedrooms are bright and spacious, and a few have whirlpool tubs. Family rooms sleep up to four. Self-catering options include a single-bed studio, a one-bedroom apartment, and a three-bed town house, all located across the street at comparable prices.

Western Rd., Cork, County Cork. www.garnish.ie. ✆ **021/427-5111.** Fax 021/427-3872. 14 units. €80–€110 double; €90–€120 self-catering apt. Rates include full breakfast. AE, DC, MC, V. Free parking. **Amenities:** Lounge; smoke-free rooms; free Wi-Fi. *In room:* TV, hair dryer.

Maranatha Country House ★★ 🎁 Tucked away in the forests outside Cork, this 19th-century manor house has beautiful, uniquely designed bedrooms. One room is fit for a princess, with a canopy of velvet and lavish florals; another evokes a cool forest; a third uses 365m (1,197 ft.) of fabric in its draperies alone. Traditional rules of decorating have been discarded in favor of whimsical effusiveness. The most luxurious quarters are in a huge ground-floor suite, which has a canopy bed and a large Jacuzzi. The breakfast conservatory houses an abundance of flowers, and the breakfast itself is plentiful and delicious.

Tower, Blarney, County Cork. www.maranathacountryhouse.com. ✆/fax **021/438-5102.** 6 units, all with private bathroom, 5 with shower only, 1 with Jacuzzi. €70–€80 double. 50% reduction for children 11 and under (sharing with parents). Rates include full breakfast. MC, V. Free parking. Closed mid-Dec to mid-Feb. **Amenities:** TV lounge; babysitting; smoke-free rooms. *In room:* Hair dryer.

Silver Springs Moran Hotel ★ On a hillside overlooking the River Lee 3km (2 miles) from the city center, this modern seven-story hotel is surrounded by 17 hectares (42 acres) of groomed gardens, and it has a great sense of style. The bedrooms, which have recently been refurbished, are outfitted with handcrafted Irish furniture and designer fabrics. Each has lovely views of either the river, city, or gardens. The exterior glass elevator offers lovely views of the countryside. There's plenty to do here with two good restaurants, a pool, a sauna, even tennis courts. One note of caution—this place is very popular with wedding receptions, so you may want to check whether all the guest facilities will be open to you if there's one during your stay.

Dublin Rd., Tivoli, Cork, County Cork. www.silverspringshotel.ie. ✆ **021/450-7533.** 109 units. €90–€110 double; €120–€180 suite. Rates include service charge and full breakfast. AE, DC, MC, V. Free parking. **Amenities:** 2 restaurants; bar; concierge; health club; Jacuzzi; indoor pool; room service; sauna; steam room; tennis courts; squash court. *In room:* TV, hair dryer.

Where to Eat

VERY EXPENSIVE

The Ivory Tower ★★ FUSION With its unattractive exterior, the Tower can be off-putting, but true foodies will persevere. This is all the brainchild of American-born Seamus O'Connell, a truly innovative chef who acquired a dedicated following here for his unusual and iconoclastic menus before decamping, most of the time, to a new venture in Dublin—although his ethos lives on. Ingredients are fresh and local, often sourced from local markets, and he builds on that foundation, adding extraordinary layers of flavor. The menu reads like a roster of unlikely combinations: swordfish with banana ketchup, hot smoked salmon with lemon geranium sauce, kumquats in Rioja wine. Not for the faint of heart, but it has many devoted fans.

The Exchange Bldgs., 35 Princes St. ✆ **021/427-4665.** Reservations required. Fixed 5-course dinner €60; surprise set menu €75; main courses €30–€40. AE, MC, V. Wed–Sat 6:30–11pm.

EXPENSIVE

Café Paradiso ★★ VEGETARIAN This outstanding vegetarian restaurant features organic local produce, complemented by Irish farmhouse cheeses. Lunches are light fare—understated but tasty sandwiches and fresh soups. For dinner, you might begin your meal with vegetable sushi with tempura, before moving on to sweet chili-glazed pan-fried tofu with Chinese greens in a coconut broth, or a braised turnip galette with portobello and pecan filling, red-wine sauce, and orange and caraway Brussels sprouts. For dessert, the praline-stuffed roasted pears with green apple sorbet and spiced caramel make an ideal finish. The well-selected wine list offers a number of choices by the glass or half-bottle.

16 Lancaster Quay, Western Rd. (across from Jurys hotel). ✆ **021/427-7939.** www.cafeparadiso.ie. Reservations recommended. Early-bird menus: 2 courses €24, 3 courses €30; fixed-price 3-course dinner €35; main courses €23–€25. AE, MC, V. Tues–Sat noon–3pm and 6:30–10:30pm. Closed Christmas week.

Jacques ★★ INTERNATIONAL Cork adores the effortlessly contemporary creations of sisters Eithne and Jacqueline Barry. Lately, the menu is highly influenced by Mediterranean and Asian ingredients, as seen in main dishes such as fresh monkfish with a leek risotto, preserved lemon, gremolata, and crispy pancetta. There are also classics such as sirloin steak and a modern spin on duck *à l'orange* served with chard and Gubbeen bacon. The small dining room, with its cheery lemon, tangerine, and green walls that are lined with modern artwork, is the perfect backdrop for the buzzy, fresh atmosphere.

9 Phoenix St. ✆ **021/427-7387.** www.jacquesrestaurant.ie. Reservations recommended. 3-course early-bird menu (5:30–7pm and after 9pm) €25; 2-course fixed-price dinner €24, 3 courses €30; dinner main courses €22–€27. AE, MC, V. Tues–Thurs 5:30–10:30pm; Fri–Sat noon–3pm and 5:30–10pm.

MODERATE

The Crawford Café ★★ COUNTRY HOUSE In a ground-floor room at the Crawford Art Gallery (p. 302), this popular bistro, decorated with oil paintings and statuary, is run by the Allen family of Ballymaloe House fame (p. 323). The dinner menu includes such traditional dishes as lamb braised with vegetables and rosemary, while the lunch menu features delightful salads, seafood, and an excellent spinach-and-mushroom crepe. All seafood is brought in fresh daily from Ballycotton Bay, and the fresh breads and baked goods are from Ballymaloe kitchens.

At the Crawford Art Gallery, Emmet Place. ✆ **021/427-4415.** www.crawfordartgallery.ie. Reservations recommended for parties of 6 or more. Fixed-price lunch €25; main courses €10–€15. MC, V. Mon–Fri 9:30am–4pm; Sat 9am–4pm. Lunch served noon–3pm.

Fenn's Quay Restaurant ★★ INTERNATIONAL This superbly restored 18th-century terrace house attracts a well-heeled clientele and is set to be a long-distance runner among Cork's many excellent restaurants. Bold, creative dishes furnish—but do not overwhelm—the menu, so that one may order chargrilled lamb chop with spiced couscous, *tzatziki*-and-mint pea purée, and cumin flatbread just as easily as a locally reared beef burger with spiced ketchup and rough-cut fries. The place gets jammed at lunchtime, when the prices offer good value, so be prepared to wait, or better yet, go for a leisurely dinner.

5 Sheares St. ✆ **021/427-9527.** Reservations recommended. Fixed-price menus €28–€42; dinner main courses €18–€28. MC, V. Mon–Sat 10am–10pm.

Greenes ★★ INTERNATIONAL Inside the Hotel Isaacs (p. 297) in central Cork, this is a beautiful and contemporary space, with soaring warehouse-style ceilings, exposed brick walls, and big windows overlooking a waterfall. The attraction here is the modern, understated cuisine, with perfectly grilled meats and fish. The early-bird menu is available all night on Mondays and Tuesdays, and there's also a full gluten-free menu. Call for details of their theater package, which includes a three-course meal and a ticket to a show at the Everyman (p. 309) for €45.

Hotel Isaacs, 48 MacCurtain St. ✆ **021/455-2279.** www.isaacs.ie. Reservations recommended. 3-course early-bird menu €27; dinner main courses €20–€29. AE, DC, MC, V. Mon–Thurs 6–10pm; Fri–Sat 6–10:30pm. Closed Sun. except for bank holiday weekends.

Jacob's on the Mall ★★ INTERNATIONAL Housed in what was once an old bathhouse, this stylish eatery is the talk of the town for its fresh ingredients and attention to detail. Spiced John Dory fish is served with basmati rice, wilted greens, and cucumber salsa; linguine comes with black olive tapenade and spinach, fennel, and anchovy crust; the breast of duck is served with roast butternut squash, buttered leeks, and ginger *jus*. The place is lovely, with tall windows flooding the dining room with light, and the service is reliably good.

30a South Mall. ✆ **021/425-1530.** Fax 021/425-1531. www.jacobsonthemall.com. Reservations recommended. Fixed-price 2-course menu €24–€28; main courses €18–€30. AE, MC, V. Mon–Sat 12:30–2:30pm and 6:30–10pm.

INEXPENSIVE

Idaho Cafe ★★ INTERNATIONAL This is a tiny place, with patrons squeezing in like sardines, and the attraction is the reliably good food. Lunchtime specials feature such items as Ummero bacon with minty new potatoes and cashews, or crabmeat and tuna quesadillas. Everything is made from fresh ingredients by people who understand that a bit of care in preparing even an inexpensive meal goes much appreciated. To find it, turn off St. Patrick Street, directly behind the Brown Thomas department store.

19 Caroline St. ✆ **021/427-6376.** Breakfast €2–€8; lunch main courses €9–€10. No credit cards. Mon–Sat 8:30am–5pm.

Quay Co-op ★★ VEGETARIAN/CAFETERIA The ground floor of this insider establishment is a whole-foods store that also sells fresh breads and cakes. The main attraction is on the second floor, reached by a narrow, steep staircase. Don't be put off by the inauspicious first impression—this self-service restaurant offers delicious hot and cold dishes, including soups, salads, pasta, pizza, chickpea burgers, and a variety of daily specials. There are also some vegan offerings on the menu. Everything is also available to go.

24 Sullivan's Quay. ✆ **021/431-7026.** www.quaycoop.com. Breakfast €3–€7.50; main courses €5–€11. MC, V. Mon–Fri 9am–9pm; Sat–Sun 9am–6pm.

Seeing the Sights

Blarney Castle and Stone ★★ While Blarney Castle is extremely touristy, it is still one of the most impressive castles in Ireland. It's about 8km (5 miles) from Cork City, and easily accessible from the city by bus. It was once huge, and the massive square tower that is all that remains of it has a parapet rising 25m (82 ft.). The origin of the famous Blarney Stone itself is unknown; theories (to be taken with a large pinch of salt) range from it having once been part of the Stone of Scone (held at Edinburgh Castle) presented to a local chieftain by Robert the Bruce; to being a fragment of the Wailing Wall in Jerusalem. It's wedged far enough underneath the battlements to make it uncomfortable to reach, but not far enough that countless tourists don't bend over backward, hang upside down in a parapet, and kiss it in hopes of increased loquaciousness. It's customary to tip the attendant who holds your legs (you might want to do it before he hangs you over the edge).

Blarney Castle, home of the infamous stone reputed to impart clever wit to anyone willing to hang upside down to kiss a rock.

After bypassing the stone, take a stroll through the gardens and a nearby dell beside Blarney Lake. The Badger Cave and adjacent dungeons penetrating the rock at the base of the castle can be explored by all but the claustrophobic with the aid of a flashlight.

R617, 8km (5 miles) northwest of Cork City, Blarney, County Cork. ✆ **021/438-5252.** www.blarneycastle.ie. Admission €10 adults; €8 seniors and students; €3.50 children 8–14; €24 families. May and Sept Mon–Sat 9am–6:30pm, Sun 9am–5:30pm; June–Aug Mon–Sat 9am–7pm, Sun 9am–5:30pm; Oct–Apr daily 9am–sundown. Last admission 30 min. before closing. Bus: Marked BLARNEY or TOWER from bus station on Parnell Place, Cork City.

Coal Quay Market This is Cork's open-air flea market, a trove of second-hand clothes, old china, used books, memorabilia, and—well, to be truthful—a lot of junk. It all happens on a street, now a little ragged, that was once Cork's original outdoor market.

Cornmarket St. Free admission. Mon–Sat 9am–5pm.

Cork Butter Museum ★ Started in 1770, Cork's butter exchange became the largest exporter of salted butter in the world, exporting around 500,000 casks of

THE GIFT OF gab (OR IS IT JUST BLARNEY?)

The much-beloved myth that being held upside down and backward from the top of a tall castle to kiss a rock brings you the ability to talk up a storm is actually quite new, although the Blarney association with the gift of gab goes back a long way. It is believed to have been Queen Elizabeth I who created it in the 16th century, in a fit of exasperation at the ability of then-Lord Blarney to prattle on at great length without actually ever agreeing to what she wanted. The custom of kissing the stone, though, is less than a century old. Nobody knows quite why it started, but around here they've got a thousand possible tales, some involving witches and others the crusaders, but don't believe them. It's all a bunch of . . .

the stuff each year by 1892. The exchange closed in 1924, and it now houses the Shandon Craft Centre and the Firkin Crane center (see below), a hot venue for contemporary dance performances. This museum is a quirky but rather charming celebration of butter and the role it has played in Irish life from medieval times to the present day. One for dairyphiles.

John Redmond St. ✆ **021/430-0600.** www.corkbutter.museum. Admission €4 adults; €3 seniors and college students; €1.50 children 12–17; free for children 11 and under. Mar–June and Sept–Oct daily 10am–5pm; July–Aug daily 10am–6pm; rest of year by appointment only.

Cork City Gaol and Radio Museum ★ Less than 2km (1¼ miles) west of the city center, this restored prison was infamous in the 19th and early 20th centuries, when it housed some of the greatest figures in the revolutionary movement. Today its exhibits celebrate the former prisoners, and colorfully explain the prison's history. Among those imprisoned here was Countess Constance Markiewicz (1868–1927), a Sinn Fein MP with an extremely colorful biography. She was the first woman elected to the British Parliament (although she refused to take her seat) and was sentenced to death for her part in the Easter Rising; when the sentence was commuted because of her gender, she told the court "I wish you had the decency to shoot me." She later became the first woman in Europe to hold a cabinet position. Included in the ticket price is entry to the **Radio Museum.** Based in the former prison governor's house, it incorporates the restored studio of Radio 6CX, which was on air between 1927 and 1930.

Depiction at the Cork City Gaol, where Irish revolutionaries served hard time in the 19th and 20th centuries.

Convent Ave., Sunday's Well. ✆ **021/430-5022.** www.corkcitygaol.com. Admission to Gaol or exhibition €8 adults; €7 seniors and students; €4.50 children; €24 families. Mar–Oct daily 9:30am–5pm; Nov–Feb daily 10am–4pm. Last admission 1 hr. before closing.

Cork Public Museum ★ This museum occupies a magnificent Georgian building in a park on the western edge of the city. Exhibits include models depicting early medieval times; artifacts recovered from excavations in the city, some dating 4,000 years; and a working model of an early flour mill with an unusual horizontal water wheel. There's an archive of photographs and documents relating to Cork-born Irish patriots Terence McSwiney, Thomas MacCurtain, and Michael Collins. Antique Cork silver, glass, and lace are on display.

Fitzgerald Park. ✆ **021/427-0679.** www.corkcity.ie. Free admission. Year-round Mon–Fri 11am–1pm and 2:15–5pm, Sat 11am–1pm and 2:15–4pm; also Apr–Sept Sun 3–5pm.

Crawford Art Gallery ★★★ The Crawford ranks among Ireland's best art galleries, with a strong collection led by works of Irish painters including Jack B. Yeats, Nathaniel Grogan, William Orpen, Sir John Lavery, James Barry, and Daniel Maclise. In the well-converted, 18th-century customhouse, the gallery also holds sculptures and handcrafted silver and glass pieces. A fine restaurant, the **Crawford Café** (p. 299), and bookstore are on the premises.

Emmet Place. ✆ **021/480-5042.** www.crawfordart gallery.ie. Free admission. Fri–Wed 10am–5pm; Thurs 10am–8pm. Last admission 15 min. before closing.

The Lavit Gallery Operated by the Cork Arts Society, this gallery, in an early-18th-century Georgian house overlooking the River Lee, promotes the area's contemporary arts scene in colorful, interesting fashion. The ground floor holds works by established artists, and the upper floor showcases up-and-coming talent.

5 Father Matthew St. ✆ **021/427-7749.** www.lavit gallery.com. Free admission. Tues–Fri 10:30am–6pm; Sat 10:30am–5pm.

The Crawford Art Gallery is devoted to paintings and sculptures by Irish artists.

Mutton Lane Mural ★ This giant mural along the walls of Mutton Lane depicts musicians performing the traditional Pana Shuffle, and is a vivid and colorful evocation of peace and community spirit. Painted by local artist Anthony Ruby in 2004, it incorporates a dedication that reads: "to everyone except George Bush."

Mutton Lane, off St. Patrick St.

Old English Market ★★ Ireland's best food market dates from a charter of King James I in 1610. The present building, finished in 1788, was damaged by fires in 1980 and 1986 and then brilliantly refurbished. Inside food stands brim with meats, fish, vegetables, and fruit, and you'll also find such traditional Cork

Founded by King James I in 1610, the Old English Market once forbade entry to the Irish.

delights as hot buttered eggs, tripe (animal stomach), *crubeens* (pigs' feet), and *drisheens* (local blood sausage). For the less adventurous, there are plenty of stands at which you can get coffee, fresh snacks, or lunch on the go; head to the **Joup** stand for hot soups made from local produce, or the prosaically named **Salad and Sandwich Bar** for good picnic supplies.

Grand Parade. Enter from St. Patrick St., Grand Parade, Oliver Plunkett St., or Princes St. www.corkenglishmarket.ie. Free admission. Mon–Sat 9am–6pm.

The red sandstone and limestone clock tower of St. Anne's distinguishes Cork's skyline.

St. Anne's Church ★★ Cork's prime landmark, also known as Shandon Church, is famous for its giant pepper-pot steeple and its eight melodious bells. No matter where you stand in the downtown area, you can see the stone tower, crowned with a gilt ball and a unique fish weather vane. Until recently, due to a quirk of clockworks, it was known as "the four-faced liar" because each of its four clock faces showed a different time, except on the hour, when they all managed to synchronize. Somewhat sadly, that charming quirk has been fixed. Built in 1722, the steeple has red sandstone (south) and limestone (west) walls, from which the colors of the Cork hurling and soccer teams are taken. A climb to the belfry rewards with the chance to play a tune on the famous Shandon Bells. Consequently, you might hear the bells of Shandon ringing at all times of the day. Continue on a sometimes-precarious climb up past the bells and you'll be further rewarded with spectacular views over the surrounding countryside.

Church St. ✆ **021/450-5906.** www.shandonbells.org. Admission €6 adults; €5 seniors and students. Mar–May and Oct Mon–Sat 10am–4pm, Sun 11:30am–3:30pm; June–Sept Mon–Sat 10am–5pm, Sun 11:30am–4:30pm; Nov–Feb Mon–Sat 11am–3pm. Last admission 30 min. before closing.

St. Fin Barre's Cathedral ★ This Church of Ireland cathedral sits on the spot St. Finbarre chose in A.D. 600 for his church and school. The current building dates from 1880 and is a fine example of early French Gothic style; its three giant spires dominate the skyline. The interior is highly ornamented with unique mosaic work. The bells were inherited from the 1735 church that previously stood on this site.

Bishop St. ✆ **021/496-3387.** www.cathedral.cork.anglican.org. Admission €4 adults; €2 seniors, students, and children. Apr–Sept Mon–Sat 9:30am–5:30pm, Sun 12:30–5pm; Oct–Mar Mon–Sat 9:30am–12:45pm and 2–5pm. Bank holiday opening varies.

University College, Cork (U.C.C.) A component of Ireland's National University, with about 7,000 students, this center of learning is housed in a pretty quadrangle of Gothic Revival–style buildings. Colorful gardens and wooded grounds grace the campus. Head to the visitor center to join a tour of the grounds, which takes in the Crawford Observatory, the Harry Clarke stained-glass windows in the Honan Chapel, and the Stone Corridor, a collection of stones inscribed with the ancient Irish Ogham style of writing.

Also at the university is the **Lewis Glucksman Gallery** (✆ **021/490-1844;** www.glucksman.org), a public art gallery and cultural institute that also comprises a shop and riverside restaurant. The building itself has earned or been on the short list for several architectural awards since its opening in 2004, and is as much of an attraction as the gallery's eclectic program of modern art, which changes roughly every quarter.

Western Rd. University: ✆ **021/490-1876.** http://visitorscentre.ucc.ie. University tours (by arrangement) €4; €15 families. Tours May–Oct Mon, Wed, Fri, and Sat 3pm. Glucksman Gallery: ✆ **021/490-1844.** www.glucksman.org. Free admission (suggested donation €5). Tues–Sat 10am–5pm; Sun 1–5pm.

BUS TOURS

In July and August, **Bus Éireann,** Parnell Place Bus Station (✆ **021/450-8188**), offers narrated half-day tours to Cork's major landmarks and buildings, including nearby Blarney. Fares start at around €10, and tours leave at 10:30am daily.

Cork City Tours These open-top buses let you hop on and hop off to explore the sights of Ireland's second city. They run all day in a loop from April through October (as frequently as every half-hour in July and Aug), so when you see something you want to explore, just get off and rejoin the tour later. Or you can stay on the bus and use the tour to get oriented. Tour highlights include the Cork City Gaol, St. Ann's Church, and U.C.C. (University College, Cork). You can buy your ticket on the bus if you get on at any of these stops, or buy a ticket and board the bus at the tourist office. The same company runs a **Cork "Outer Limits" tour,** which takes you into the suburbs, including **Blackrock,** a pretty enclave with a castle that has its own observatory. Combined tickets, which can be used on consecutive days, are available. Further details are available from the Cork Tourist Office.

✆ **021/430-9090.** www.corkcitytour.com. Either tour €14 adults; €12 seniors and students; €5 children 5–14; €34 families (up to 4 children). Combined ticket for both tours €20 adults; €18 seniors and students; €5 children 5–14; €40 families (up to 4 children). Mar–Oct daily, with hours and number of tours reflecting seasonal demand (usually 10am–4pm).

Sports & Outdoor Pursuits

SPECTATOR SPORTS

GAELIC GAMES Hurling and Gaelic football are both played on summer Sunday afternoons at Cork's **Pairc Ui Chaoimh Stadium,** Marina Walk (✆ **021/496-3311**). Check the local newspapers for details or log on to the Gaelic Athletics Association's site at www.gaa.ie.

GREYHOUND RACING Go to the dogs, as they say in Cork, only now in distinctly 21st-century style, at the **Cork Greyhound Stadium,** Curraheen Park, Cork (✆ **021/454-3095**), on Wednesday, Thursday, and Saturday at 8pm. Admission is around €10.

HORSE RACING The nearest racetrack is **Cork Racecourse,** Killarney Road, Mallow (✆ **022/50207;** www.corkracecourse.ie), approximately 32km (20 miles) north of Cork. Races are scheduled year-round, but particularly in mid-May, July, August, early October, and November. Admission is around €15 adults, €10 seniors and students, and free for children 13 and under (must be with an adult).

OUTDOOR PURSUITS

BICYCLING Although walking is probably the ideal way to get around Cork, you can rent a bike at **Cyclescene,** 396 Blarney St. (✆ **021/430-1183;** www.cyclescene.ie). It costs €15 to €20 per day or €80 per week, plus a refundable deposit of €100. Open Monday to Saturday 8:30am to 5:45pm.

FISHING The **River Lee,** which runs through Cork, the nearby **Blackwater River,** and the many area lakes present fine opportunities. Salmon licenses, lake fishing permits, tackle, and equipment can be obtained from **T. W. Murray,** 87 St. Patrick St. (✆ **021/427-1089**).

GOLF Local clubs that welcome visitors are the **Cork Golf Club,** Little Island (✆ **021/435-3451;** www.corkgolfclub.ie), 8km (5 miles) east of Cork, with greens fees of €85 weekdays, €95 weekends, and €50 early-bird; and **Douglas Golf Club,** Maryboro Hill, Douglas (✆ **021/489-5297;** www.douglasgolfclub.ie), 4.8km (3 miles) south of Cork, with greens fees of €50 weekdays, €55 weekends.

WALKING The **Old Railway Line** is a dismantled train route running from Cork to the old maritime town of Passage West. It is from here that Captain Roberts set out and crossed the Atlantic in the first passenger steamship, the *Sirius.* Following along the rails, a scenic walk affords the visitor excellent views of the inner harbor.

Shopping

St. Patrick Street is the main shopping thoroughfare, and many stores are scattered throughout the city on side streets and in lanes. In general, shops are open Monday to Saturday 9:30am to 6pm, unless indicated otherwise. In the summer many shops remain open until 9:30pm on Thursday and Friday, and some are open on Sunday.

Until recently, Cork had a lovely antiques quarter on Paul's Lane, but virtually all the shops that made the street unique have closed now, pushed out by higher rents and lack of local interest in anything old. It's all about the new now.

The main mall is **Merchant's Quay Shopping Centre,** Merchant's Quay and St. Patrick Street. This enclosed complex houses large department stores, such as **Marks and Spencer** (✆ **021/427-5555**), as well as small specialty shops, such as **Laura Ashley** (✆ **021/427-4070**).

Cork's best department store is **Brown Thomas,** 18 St. Patrick St. (✆ **021/480-5555**). It has three floors of the upscale items found in its sister shop in Dublin.

BOOKS

Mainly Murder Tucked between French Church and Academy streets, this tiny bookshop is a huge treasure-trove of whodunits for amateur sleuths. It stocks volumes on murder, mystery, and mayhem from Ireland, England, and many other English-speaking lands. 2A Paul St. ✆ **021/427-2413.**

Waterstone's With entrances on two streets, this large branch of the British-owned chain is always busy. It has a good selection of books about Cork and of Irish interest, as well as U.S. and other international titles. 69 St. Patrick St. ✆ **021/427-6522.**

CRAFTS

Crafts of Ireland Just a block off St. Patrick Street, this well-stocked shop presents an array of local crafts, including weavings, wrought iron, batik hangings, glass, graphics, pottery, toys, and Irish floral stationery. 11 Winthrop St. ✆ **021/427-5864.**

Meadows & Byrne This shop, with branches in many of Ireland's larger towns, offers attractive contemporary furniture, furnishings, and household items. It also has items of contemporary Irish design and crafts, including Jerpoint glass, Shanagarry and Jack O'Patsy pottery, and wrought-iron works by John Forkin. Academy St. ✆ **021/427-2324.** www.meadowsandbyrne.com.

Shandon Craft Centre Inside the Cork Butter Museum (p. 301), this is a general cooperative of local artisans. Sadly, their numbers have dwindled in recent years, but at the time of writing there were still a stained-glass worker, a jeweler, two ceramic workers, a glass cutter, and a stringed instrument maker in residence. More often than not you can watch the craftspeople at work while you browse their wares. In the summer, folk, traditional, jazz, and classical musicians offer **free concerts** from 1 to 2pm. Cork Butter Museum, John Redmond St. ✆ **021/450-3936.**

TWEEDS & WOOLENS

Blarney Woollen Mills About 10km (6¼ miles) northwest of Cork City, on the same grounds as the famous castle, this huge store (part of an Irish chain) in an 1824 mill is a one-stop source for Irish products: cashmere, crystal, wool—especially the distinctive Kelly green Blarney Castle–design wool sweaters, made on the premises. It's open until daily 6pm, year-round, often until 10pm in summer (although the 2012 hours hadn't been finalized at this writing). The mills are on the grounds of Blarney Castle, so if you're going on a tour from Cork, you're already there! Blarney, County Cork. ✆ **021/451-6111.** www.blarney.ie.

Quills Woolen Market For tweeds, woolens, and knits at the best prices, you might want to try this enterprise on Cork's busy main thoroughfare. It has branches in Killarney, Kenmare, and Sneem. 107 St. Patrick St. ✆ **021/427-1717.**

Cork After Dark

PUBS

An Bodhran There's Irish traditional music at this friendly pub every night starting at 9:30pm. The old-world decor includes stone walls, dark woods, and a huge stained-glass window. 42 Oliver Plunkett St. ✆ **021/427-4544.**

An Spailpin Fánac (The Migrant Worker) Opposite the Beamish Brewery, this is another of the city's choice spots for traditional Irish music Sunday to Thursday, starting at 9:30pm. It dates from 1779, and is a lovely, soothing place with low ceilings, exposed brick walls, flagstone floors, open fireplaces, a simple wooden bar, and woven rush seats. 28–29 S. Main St. ✆ **021/427-7949.**

The Hibernian This is a real insider's place, which everyone calls by its nickname, "the Hi-B." Located up a linoleum-covered flight of stairs (the entrance is beside the Minahan Chemist shop), it looks like a living room gone astray, with a mishmash of slightly threadbare upholstered armchairs and sofas strewn about at odd angles. The one-room bar is always crammed with a cross section of Cork—blue-collar types, students, artists, writers, eccentrics, and the beautiful, well-heeled set. 108 Oliver Plunkett St. (corner of Winthrop St.). ✆ **021/427-2758.**

BREWING UP loyalty

Ireland is known for its love of Guinness, but in Cork you're more likely to find locals drinking Murphy's or Beamish—the two locally brewed stouts. There is a definite sense of civic loyalty when it comes to drinking stout in this town. In fact, walk into any pub and order a "home and away" and you'll be presented with a pint of Murphy's and one of Guinness.

John Henchy & Sons It's worth a walk up steep Summerhill Road, a northeast continuation of busy MacCurtain Street, to reach this classic pub near the Arbutus Lodge hotel. Established by John Henchy in 1884, it looks much the same as it did then, with leaded-glass windows, thick red curtains, and a small snug (private room). The original Henchy family grocery store still operates adjacent to the pub. 40 St. Luke's. ✆ **021/450-7833.**

The Long Valley 🎁 This is one of those exceptional, family-run, old-fashioned bars that you fall in love with as soon as you enter—or even before. To the left of the entrance hallway is a snug with etched-glass doors and chased-silver doorknobs. Those doors came from the *Celtic,* a White Star ocean liner that ran aground in Cork Harbor. Inside the main bar is one long, low-slung room with a polished wooden bar running its full length. The barmen wear white butchers' coats, Victorian-style, and provide a constant supply of pints to the laid-back, predominantly 30-something crowd. 10 Winthrop St. ✆ **021/427-2144.**

CLUBS: COMEDY, DANCE & MUSIC

You're likely to have the last laugh every Friday and Saturday night from 9:30pm at **City Limits Comedy Club,** 2 Coburg St. (✆ **021/450-1206** for recorded information, or /450-7744 bar; www.thecomedyclub.ie). You can purchase tickets in advance at **www.tickets.ie**. Ticket prices vary depending on the act.

Club Classic You can expect an eclectic program from across the weekend at this ages 23-and-over venue. Classics and chart dominate on Fridays, with R&B, house, and special guest DJs on Saturdays. And if you're stuck for something to do on Sundays, entry is free and cocktails are cheap. The bar section is open from 4pm until 11:30pm, Monday to Wednesday; until 2am Saturday; and 1:30am Sunday. The full club is open Tuesday to Saturday, 11pm until 2am. 1 S. Main St. ✆ **021/490-5090.** www.clubclassic.ie. Cover €8–€10.

Havana Browns One of Cork's most popular nightclubs, attracting a young and trendy crowd. There are three bars, a dance floor, and DJs spinning a mixture of chart, R&B, and hip-hop, Open nightly from 11pm till 2am. Hanover St. ✆ **021/427-1969.** www.havana-browns.com. Cover €10 and up.

THE PERFORMING ARTS

Cork Opera House Just off Lavitt's Quay along the River Lee, this is southwest Ireland's major venue for opera, drama, musicals, dance, concerts, and stand-up comedy. Emmet Place. ✆ **021/427-0022.** www.corkoperahouse.ie. Tickets €17–€50; average €20–€36.

The Firkin Crane Dating from the 1840s, this unique rotunda was part of Cork's original Butter Exchange, and the building's name derives from Danish words pertaining to measures of butter. Although destroyed by fire in 1980, the

Coastal Kinsale is the cradle of Ireland's culinary renaissance.

site was rebuilt and opened as a cultural center in 1992. Today, it is dedicated to contemporary dance, and serves as a venue for new dance works and for touring national and international dance companies. Performances are occasional, with the best usually reserved for the Guinness Jazz Festival in October (see below). John Redmond St., Shandon. ✆ **021/450-7487.** www.firkincrane.ie. Tickets €10–€25.

Triskel Arts Centre Refurbished in 2011, this ever-growing arts center presents a variety of entertainment, from drama, poetry readings, and opera to traditional music concerts. There is also a full curriculum of daytime art workshops and gallery talks as well. The in-house restaurant is a stylish place to have a light meal or a cappuccino. Please note that, as part of the renovation, the telephone number below may have changed by the time you arrive; check online for listings and booking information. Tobin St., off S. Main St. ✆ **021/427-2022.** www.triskelart.com. Tickets €6–€20; most tickets around €15. Some performances are free.

THEATER

Cork Arts Theatre This not-for-profit theater in Carroll's Quay presents contemporary dramas and musicals in an intimate, 100-seat performance space. Most tickets cost around €10 to €15, and occasionally there are such egalitarian initiatives as "pay what you want" previews. The theater is fully accessible to those with limited mobility. Camden Court, Carroll's Quay. ✆ **021/450-5624.** www.corkartstheatre.com.

Everyman Palace This elegant, historic theater 2 minutes from the bus and train station is well known as a showcase for quality new plays, both Irish and international. The Irish National Ballet also performs here regularly. 17 MacCurtain St. ✆ **021/450-1673.** www.everymanpalace.com. Tickets €10–€40.

KINSALE & SOUTH CORK ★

Kinsale: 29km (18 miles) S of Cork, 87km (54 miles) SE of Killarney, 156km (97 miles) SE of Shannon Airport, 285km (177 miles) SW of Dublin, and 32km (20 miles) E of Clonakilty

Only 29km (18 miles) south of Cork City, **Kinsale** is a charming fishing village sitting on a picturesque harbor, surrounded by green hills. Considered the gateway to the western Cork seacoast, this artsy town of 3,000 residents supports

THE GUINNESS JAZZ festival

Held in Cork every year since 1978, this is Ireland's biggest and most prestigious jazz festival. Big names such as Ella Fitzgerald, Oscar Peterson, and Herbie Hancock have played here over the years, and thousands of musicians from all over the world take part annually. It's held at various venues around town in late October. Tickets can be purchased from the individual venues; check **www.guinnessjazzfestival.com** for full details. Tickets go on sale September 1; prices vary, some events are free.

dozens of little art galleries and craft shops filled with the work of regional artists. It also has made a name for itself as a foodie town, home to award-winning restaurants and pubs. Kinsale draws food lovers year-round, particularly in October during the 4-day **Gourmet Festival.**

With its narrow, winding streets, well-kept 18th-century houses, imaginatively painted shop fronts, window boxes overflowing with colorful flowers, and a harbor full of sailboats, Kinsale is enchanting. The downside of all this is that the secret is out: This is a tourist town, so add parking problems, crowds, and tour buses to the list of qualities making up the town's ambience.

In 1601, this was the scene of the Battle of Kinsale, a turning point in Irish history. In September of that year, a Spanish fleet anchored at Kinsale and came under attack by English forces. An Irish army marched across virtually the whole of Ireland to reach and help the Spanish troops, but they were routed in a battle on Christmas Eve. In response to their support of the Spanish, Catholics were banned by English administrators from the town of Kinsale—a banishment that lasted for a century.

Just off the coast of the Old Head of Kinsale—about 8km (5 miles) west of the town—a German submarine sank the *Lusitania,* which was on its way from New York to Liverpool, in 1915. The attack, which killed 1,200, ultimately brought America into World War I. Some of the victims are buried in a local cemetery.

Essentials

GETTING THERE **Bus Éireann** (✆ **021/450-8188;** www.buseireann.ie) operates regular daily service from Cork City to Kinsale. The arrival and departure point is the gas station on Pier Road, opposite the tourist office.

Kinsale is 29km (18 miles) south of Cork City on the Airport Road; if you're coming by car from the west, use the N71. From East Cork, Cross River Ferries Ltd. provides regular service across Cork Harbour (see "East Cork," later in this chapter).

VISITOR INFORMATION The **Kinsale Tourist Office,** Pier Road, Kinsale (✆ **021/477-2234;** www.kinsale.ie), is open year-round, generally during normal business hours.

GETTING AROUND Kinsale's streets are so narrow that walking is the best way to get around, and the town is so small that there is no local transport; if you need a taxi to outlying areas, call **Kinsale Cabs** (✆ **021/477-2642**) or **Cabs 3000** (✆ **021/477-3000**).

Seeing the Sights

Charles Fort ★ Southeast of the town itself, at the head of the harbor, this coastal landmark dates from the late 17th century. A classic star-shaped fort, it was constructed to prevent foreign naval forces from entering the harbor of Kinsale, then an important trading town. Additions and improvements were made throughout the 18th and 19th centuries, and the fort remained garrisoned until 1921. Across the river is James Fort (1602). The complex includes an exhibition center and cafe. ***Note:*** Charles Fort is sometimes closed in very bad weather, so call ahead if skies are stormy.

Off the Scilly rd., Summer Cove, County Cork. ✆ **021/477-2263.** www.heritageireland.ie. Admission €4 adults; €3 seniors; €2 students and children; €10 families. Tours available on request. Mid-Mar to Oct daily 10am–6pm; Nov to mid-Mar daily 10am–5pm. Last admission 1 hr. before closing.

Desmond Castle ★ Built around 1500 as a customhouse by the Earl of Desmond, this tower house has a dark history: Spanish troops occupied it during the battle of 1601, and the British later used it as a prison for captured American sailors during the War of Independence. Locally, it's known as "French Prison" because French prisoners were kept here during the mid–18th century. In a horrible accident, 54 French prisoners died here in a fire in 1747. During the Great Famine, the building was used as a workhouse for the starving populace. Now, in more peaceful times, the castle is a much more benign place. Today it is the home of the **International Museum of Wine,** celebrating the Irish emigrants who colonized the wine trade throughout the world after being forced to leave their own shores.

Cork St., Kinsale, County Cork. ✆ **021/477-4855.** Admission €3 adults; €2 seniors; €1 students and children; €8 families. Easter to late Sept daily 10am–6pm. Last admission 1 hr. before closing.

Kinsale Museum This small but enthusiastic museum in the historic Market House (1600) tells the town's story from its earliest days, with paintings, photos, and memorabilia highlighting such events as the Battle of Kinsale in 1601 and

The star-shaped fortress that guards the harbor of Kinsale dates to the late 1600s.

the sinking of the *Lusitania* in 1915. It's all you ever wanted to know about Kinsale, and so much more.

Market Sq., Kinsale, County Cork. ✆ **021/477-7930.** http://homepage.eircom.net/~kinsalemuseum. Admission €3.50 adults; €1.50 seniors and students; free for children. Apr–Sept daily 10am–6pm; Oct–Dec and Feb–Mar Mon–Fri 11am–1pm and 3–5pm.

WALKING TOUR: THE SCILLY WALK

1 Perryville House

The "official" start point for the Scilly Walk is the tourist office on Pier Road, but for us, this makes for a much more interesting and quirky place to begin. Perryville House sticks out like an architectural sore thumb on Long Quay, with its candy-pink frontage, Moorish iron verandas, and elaborate, French-style plasterwork above the front door. Now a hotel, this place owes its dainty mishmash of styles to a (somewhat enthusiastic) 19th-century renovation of a much older building. Pause, admire, and move on.

2 Spaniard Inn

Rounding a hairpin bend and entering Scilly, you'll pass the Spaniard Inn, one of the oldest pubs in the area. Built on the site of a ruined castle in 1650, it is named in honor of a local hero called Don Juan d'Aquila, the commander of a Spanish naval fleet who fought alongside the Irish at the Battle of Kinsale in 1601.

3 Scilly

Technically a separate village, Scilly is effectively a miniscule suburb of Kinsale, albeit one that retains a strong sense of its own identity. Pronounced "silly," its unusual name is thought to hark back to fishermen from the Scilly Isles (off the coast of Cornwall, England) who settled here during the 17th century.

4 James Fort

Take the right-hand road around the village, skirting along the coast, and join the marked pedestrian trail by the waterside. Along here there are lovely views across to Kinsale, and across the harbor you'll see the stout remains of James Fort. Named for King James I, it was built by the English shortly after the Battle of Kinsale, to guard the entrance to the port, and to ensure against further insurrection. It was captured by the forces of the (Protestant) King William I during his war with the deposed (Catholic) James II in 1690—part of the same conflict that is still commemorated today by the so-called "Orange marches" in Northern Ireland. Local lore has it that until the 19th century, access to this stretch of water was controlled by a chain, floating on timber kegs between the two shores, that could be drawn across the harbor at a moment's notice.

5 Summer Cove

Another tiny hamlet on the outskirts of Kinsale, Summer Cove is as sweet a place as its halcyon name suggests. Black and white toy town houses face the harbor, peppered with the occasional splash of green and red, as gulls circle overhead and the waves froth and bubble along the harbor walls.

There's not much to do here, but it would be a shame not to linger awhile on your way through to its most famous attraction.

6 Charles Fort

A short walk uphill from Summer Cove itself lies this impressive military structure. It was once the site of the medieval Ringcurran Castle, an important defensive position that was used by the Spanish during the Battle of Kinsale in 1601. After a lengthy battle, the allied Irish and Spanish troops were defeated by the English army, which reduced the castle to rubble. In 1678, a permanent fortress was built here, to reinforce the defenses of James Fort (see above). Named, like its counterpart, after the king of the day, Charles Fort remained in use as a barracks all the way up to the end of British rule in the early 20th century. It suffered extensive damage during the Civil War, and has only recently been restored to something like its former glory. The Scilly Walk ends here; if you continue to walk south along the sea, you'll find another path that follows the headland to the tip of Frower Point, which offers great views across the harbor to the Old Head of Kinsale.

An excellent place for a drink after the Scilly Walk, the Spaniard Inn draws sailors, musicians, and other jovial locals in droves.

Shopping

Boland's Kinsale Crafts This is a quality shop for made-in-Ireland goods, such as traditional Kinsale smocks, Aran sweaters, pottery, quilts, Irish leather belts, and jewelry. Pearse St., Kinsale, County Cork. ✆ **021/477-2161.**

Crackpots Pottery This shop holds a mix of functional and artistic pottery made by local artists. Some work is done on-site in the workshop; there's also a showroom and a good restaurant (p. 318). 3 Cork St., Kinsale, County Cork. ✆ **021/477-2847.**

Granny's Bottom Drawer Traditional Irish linens and lace are the ticket here. It's well stocked with tablecloths, pillowcases, Victorian table runners, and hand-crocheted place mats. 53 Main St., Kinsale, County Cork. ✆ **021/477-4839.**

Jagoes Mill Pottery Just over 3km (2 miles) from Kinsale, Irene Gahan Ryle runs a small pottery workshop in an 18th-century mill. Her work has a good balance of practicality and beauty, and it is only sold from the studio workshop and selected galleries. Jagoes Mill is open by appointment only, so call ahead if you'd like to visit. Jagoes Mill, Kinsale, County Cork. ✆ **021/477-2771.**

Kinsale Crystal Started in 1991 by a former Waterford Crystal master craftsman, this small workshop produces traditional full-lead, mouth-blown, and hand-cut crystal. Visitors are welcome to watch the process and purchase the sparkling results, which are sold nowhere else in Ireland. Market St., Kinsale, County Cork. ✆ **021/477-4493.** www.kinsalecrystal.ie.

Kinsale Silver Kinsale silver traces its origins back more than 300 years. The Dolan family runs this silversmith workshop, where you can watch as each piece is forged by hand, using traditional tools. Pearse St., Kinsale, County Cork. ✆ **021/477-4359.** www.kinsalesilver.com.

Sports & Outdoor Pursuits

BICYCLING Kinsale Harbour is perfectly designed for biking. To rent a bike, drop by the **Blue Haven,** Pearse Street (✆ **021/477-2209;** www.bluehaventransport.com). They have standard bikes for €10 per day, or electric cycles—with power-assisted gears that allegedly make light work of steep hills—for €25 per day. Safety gear is included with all rentals.

FISHING Kinsale is one of the southern Irish coast's sea-angling centers. There are numerous shipwrecks in the area for wreck fishing (not the least of them the *Lusitania,* near the Old Head of Kinsale). Try **Kinsale Angling** (the Ramparts, ✆ **021/477-4946;** www.kinsale-angling.com) for charter boats. They also run whale- and dolphin-watching trips. Prices vary wildly, so call or e-mail for details. Also the similarly named **Angling Kinsale,** Crohane (✆ **021/477-8054** or 086/103-6905), arranges sea fishing from Kinsale Harbor, as well as dolphin- and whale-watching expeditions. Prices vary widely, so call or e-mail for more information.

GOLF Embraced by the sea on three sides, the nothing-short-of-spectacular **Old Head Golf Links** (✆ **021/477-8444;** www.oldhead.com) is Tiger Woods's favorite Irish course. Named one of *Golf Magazine*'s "Top 100 Courses in the World," it is hauntingly beautiful, rain or shine. The course retains a resident environmentalist to ensure that crucial wildlife habitats are not disturbed. But golfing here costs big money: Greens fees are currently a whopping €200 for one 18-hole round, and €300 for 36 holes. If you really want to experience it but can't quite swing the price, come after 3pm, when rates go down to €115 for 18 holes (€95 in the off season). Caddy fees run €25 for a junior caddy or €40 for a senior caddy, and golf carts can be rented for €60.

If that's still too rich for your blood, there's a fine par-72 championship course at the **Fota Island Golf Club,** Carrigtwohill (✆ **021/488-3700;** www.fotaisland.ie), with greens fees of €65 to €85 in high season, and €50 to €80 in low season. Even less expensive is the **Kinsale Golf Club,** Kinsale (✆ **021/477-4722;** www.kinsalegolf.com), which has two courses, about 5km (3 miles) north of town. The 18-hole, par-71 Farrangalway course has greens fees of €35 Monday to Thursday, and €40 Friday to Sunday, while the smaller course at Ringenane charges €25 daily.

SAILING Yacht charters are available from **Kinsale Yacht Charters,** Castlepark Marina Centre, Kinsale, County Cork (✆ **087/271-0371;** www.kinsaleyachtcharter.com). From Kinsale it is possible to sail to Bantry Bay and back on a 1-week charter, or to the Dingle Peninsula on a 2-week charter. Prices run from about €1,885 to €3,540 per week, not including outboard or skipper, up to a heady €5,000 *per day,* for those to whom money is really no object.

Sovereign Sailing (✆ **021/477-4145;** www.sovereignsailing.com) offers a full range of yacht sailing options for all ages and levels of experience. Between March and November, full-day or half-day sails from Kinsale head out every day. Rates vary widely based on the kind of sailing you try. They also offer racing charter packages, but again, these don't come cheap.

Local sailors depart for the Mediterranean, Galway, and other open waters from the harbor in Kinsale, which began as a fishing village.

WALKING The **Scilly Walk** is a signposted pedestrian path along the sea that runs from Scilly, the community across the harbor from Kinsale, all the way to Charles Fort. (See p. 312 for a detailed description of the route.) If you continue to walk south along the sea from Charles Fort, you'll find another path that follows the headland to the tip of **Frower Point,** which offers great views across the harbor to the Old Head of Kinsale. The complete walk from Kinsale to Frower Point is 8km (5 miles) each way, and every part of it is quite rewarding. Drop in at the tourism office to pick up their leaflet about the walk, which includes a short but comprehensive guide and map.

One of the most pleasant ways to spend an hour in these parts is to take local resident Don Herily's excellent walking tour—or **Historic Stroll ★**, as he prefers to call it—of Kinsale town. Don and his fellow guide, Barry Moloney, have been leading visitors around the main sights since the mid-1990s, and their local knowledge is second to none. Highlights include the 12th-century St. Multose Church; a walk past Desmond Castle; and the harbor, where the 17th-century Battle of Kinsale is recounted with an enthusiasm only found in people who really love their subject. The tour starts outside the tourist office at 11:15am every day from April to October; on weekdays from May to September there's also an earlier tour at 9:15am. The cost is €6 adults, €1 children. You pay at the end or, in their words, "drop out for free if you're not delighted." (We doubt that happens very often.) For details, call ✆ **021/477-2873** or 087/250-0731, or check out www.historicstrollkinsale.com.

WATERSPORTS The **Oysterhaven Activity Centre** (✆ **021/477-0738;** www.oysterhaven.com), 8km (5 miles) from Kinsale, rents windsurfers, dinghies, and kayaks. The cost ranges from €20 to €40 for windsurfing kit, €12 to €20 for kayaks, and €30 to €45 for dinghys. They also run private windsurfing lessons for €80. They get pretty busy during summer, so call ahead to confirm opening times, and the hours during which equipment may be hired.

WHALE-WATCHING Whale-watching is a popular activity in summer, and one of the best companies to do it with is **Whale of a Time** (✆ **086/328-3250;** www.whaleofatime.ie), which uses rigid inflatable boats to cause less disruption to the creatures of the deep. Prices start from €35 to €70 per person. They also offer dolphin-watching trips in Cork Harbour for €35 per person. **Kinsale Angling** (see "Fishing," above) also offers dolphin-, whale-, and seal-watching trips, as does **Angling Kinsale** (✆ **021/477-8054;** www.anglingkinsale.com).

Where to Stay

MODERATE

Blindgate House ★ This small, contemporary hotel has a valuable combination of a central location and real sense of style. Its look is a good mix of contemporary dark-wood furnishings, natural fabrics in soothing neutral tones, polished wood floors, and serene lighting. Guest rooms are spacious and elegantly simple, while providing modern conveniences such as satellite TV and modem connections. All in all, you don't normally expect to find this level of designer savvy at this price level. It's a Zen haven amid the bustle of Kinsale town.

Blindgate, Kinsale, County Cork. www.blindgatehouse.com. ✆ **021/477-7858.** 11 units. €120 double. Rates include full breakfast. AE, MC, V. Free parking. Closed mid-Dec to mid-Mar. **Amenities:** Residents' lounge; babysitting; smoke-free rooms. *In room:* TV, radio, hair dryer.

The Blue Haven ★★ With a sophisticated design and a friendly attitude, this place is just about all a small inn should be. All the rooms are chic, with a creamy color scheme and a real sense of elegance. There's a highly rated—and very romantic—restaurant (see below) here, as well as a sophisticated, relaxing bar and a cafe that serves breakfast and light lunches, so you never have to leave the building if you don't want to. And if you must, the hotel can provide a Bentley to take you to and from the town center, the airport, or Cork City. Check the website for good 2-night deals, including dinner. ***Tip:*** If you want a canopy bed, request one of the rooms in the new wing, as these have more traditional decor.

3 Pearse St., Kinsale, County Cork. www.bluehavenkinsale.com. ✆ **021/477-2209.** 17 units. €110–€195 double. Rates include full breakfast. AE, MC, V. **Amenities:** Restaurant; cafe; bar. *In room:* TV.

Desmond House ★★ This beautiful Georgian town house in the center of Kinsale is a sophisticated, friendly place to stay. Bedrooms are decorated in soothing pastel tones of sky blue or powder-puff pink, with traditional antique furniture. They are also huge, by Irish standards—all have super-king-size beds (American king-size) and whirlpool baths. Three of the rooms have an additional single bed, making them a good size for families with small children. Breakfasts are excellent and the hosts are charming. Desmond House has unique booking arrangement, to protect you from the fluctuating international exchange rate: The amount you pay for your room is based on the exchange rate *at the time you booked*, but only if this works out cheaper. If it doesn't, you simply pay the current euro price.

42 Cork St., Kinsale, County Cork. www.desmondhousekinsale.com. ✆ **021/477-2209.** www.bluehavenkinsale.com. 4 units. €140 suite (2 people; extra guest €30). Discounts for 3 nights or more. Rates include full breakfast. MC, V. **Amenities:** *In room:* TV.

The Old Bank House ★★ This well-restored, waterside Georgian townhouse B&B, run by the same people behind the Blue Haven (see above), is a calming place with a kind of low-key luxury. Prices are a bit high for what you get, but the rooms and the views are lovely. Guest rooms aren't enormous, but they're not tiny either, and they're all tastefully decorated with heavy fabrics in tones of oatmeal or gray. Beds are large and comfortable, and much of the furniture is antique. Rooms at the front of the house overlook the sailboat-dotted harbor—views get significantly better the higher you go. ***Tip:*** Like its sister hotel, prices drop nearly by half in the autumn and winter, and you can find good offers on 2-night stays during the summer.

11 Pearse St. (next to post office), Kinsale, County Cork. www.oldbankhousekinsale.com. ✆ **021/477-4075.** 17 units. €110–€195 double. Rates include full breakfast. AE, MC, V. **Amenities:** Concierge. *In room:* TV.

The Old Presbytery ★ Noreen McEvoy runs this cozy B&B with an eye for detail and a real passion for hospitality. Set on a calm street, it is a labyrinth of half-staircases and landings, giving each room a private feel (though it can be tricky to find your way back if you leave for a while—we suggested they provide a free ball of twine for each guest, but failing that you'll just have to make do). Guest rooms are winningly decorated with brass and cast-iron beds, old armoires, and other antiques. Some have Jacuzzi tubs and one has its own sun room. Breakfasts here are fabulous. Two-bedroom self-catering suites, perfect for families or friends traveling together, are also available, although these carry a minimum 3-night stay in summer.

43 Cork St., Kinsale, County Cork. www.oldpres.com. ✆ **021/477-2027.** 10 units. €110–€170 double; €200 self-catering apt. per night. Rates include full Irish breakfast. MC, V. Free parking. *In room:* TV, hair dryer.

INEXPENSIVE

Walyunga This sweet, modern B&B with ocean views sits in the peaceful countryside 5 minutes' drive outside Kinsale. The noisiest things around here are the birds. Inside, all the guest rooms are nonsmoking, comfortable, and decorated with soft bedspreads and neutral tones. The spacious living room is a good place to meet other guests, and the breakfasts are great. Rooms have no TVs, but there's a shared set in the lounge. Make sure you ask for an en suite room if you'd rather not share a bathroom.

Sandycove, Kinsale, County Cork. www.walyunga.com. ✆ **021/477-4126.** 5 units. €60–€75 double. 25% discount for children 11 and under sharing room with parent. Rates include full Irish breakfast. MC, V. Closed Nov–Mar. **Amenities:** TV lounge.

Where to Eat

EXPENSIVE

The Blue Haven ★★ SEAFOOD Of all the restaurants in Kinsale, this hotel eatery has perhaps the biggest following, if only because there's something to suit most budgets and appetites. There are two places to eat: the atmospheric bar for first-rate bar food (seafood quiches, seafood pancakes, oak-smoked salmon) or the sky-lit restaurant for a full a la carte menu of fresh seafood, including Oysterhaven oysters, whole baked salmon on sweet potato mash, and filet of lemon sole with almond butter. Other specialties include Irish beef filet with horseradish *dauphinoise,* and local venison in season. The wines have Irish connections; they come from many of the French wineries that were started by Irish exiles.

3 Pearse St., Kinsale, County Cork. ✆ **021/477-2209.** www.bluehavenkinsale.com. Reservations recommended. Main courses at the bar €10–€26; fixed 3-course dinner €35; dinner main courses €20–€32. AE, MC, V. Restaurant daily 7–10pm. Bar daily 12:15–3pm and 6:30–10pm.

Jim Edwards ★ CONTINENTAL This classy, nautical "gastropub" is known as much for its refined menu as for its convivial atmosphere. Dishes are consistently elegant, and include things like roast duck with cassis and blackcurrant sauce, Kinsale oysters and lobster, medallions of monkfish with ginger and lime dressing, a variety of steaks, and a range of vegetarian dishes.

Market Quay, off Emmet Place, Kinsale, County Cork. ✆ **021/477-2541.** www.jimedwardskinsale.com. Reservations recommended for dinner. Dinner main courses €13–€33. AE, MC, V. Daily noon–11pm for bar food; lunch noon–2:30pm; dinner 5:30–10pm.

Jola's ★★ MODERN POLISH It's time to learn a new word: "Mo-Po" is short for Modern Polish, a sophisticated new breed of Eastern European–inspired cuisine that's become quite trendy in Europe over the last couple of years. The menu serves classic Irish dishes with a subtle Polish accent; dishes such as pierogi (a sort of Polish dumpling), and potato pancakes with pork goulash share the menu with more familiar local flavors, such as rack of lamb with basil and walnut pesto. There's also a decent wine list and a memorable selection of home-flavored vodkas. *Smacznego!* (That's Polish for *bon appétit.*)

18 Lower O'Connell St., Kinsale, County Cork. ✆ **021/477-3322.** www.jolasrestaurant.com. Dinner main courses €17–€26. MC, V. Daily 6–10pm.

Max's Wine Bar Restaurant ★ MODERN IRISH For more than 20 years, this old-world town house with outdoor dining space has been a local favorite. The fare ranges from light snacks to full meals—oysters and grilled mussels are a specialty. Other dishes include goat-cheese pastas, fresh soups, and roast lamb with lavender sauce.

Main St., Kinsale, County Cork. ✆ **021/477-2443.** Reservations recommended. Fixed-price early-bird 3-course dinner €24; dinner main courses €18–€30. MC, V. Mon and Wed–Sun 12:30–3pm (from 1pm Sun) and 6:30–10pm. No children after 8pm. Closed Nov–Feb.

MODERATE

Crackpots ★★ SEAFOOD We've been to countless restaurants where they'll gladly sell you souvenirs of your visit. Usually it's a T-shirt, or perhaps a jar of the house special sauce. But Crackpots is something we've never encountered before—an eccentric, yet winning combination of high-class restaurant and bijou pottery store (p. 313). Neither is done by half measures. It is consistently rated one of the best restaurants in Kinsale, and with good reason. Seafood forms the backbone of the menu; seared scallops are a specialty, served with saffron butter, wilted spinach, and Parma ham. Desserts have a retro quality; expect tiramisu, crème brûlée, and banoffee pie. It sounds like a bizarre combination, but somehow it all works.

3 Cork St., Kinsale, County Cork. ✆ **021/477-2847.** www.crackpots.ie. Reservations recommended. Fixed-price early-bird menu €22; main courses €14–€28. AE, MC, V. Mon–Sat 6–10pm; Sun noon–3pm.

Fishy Fishy Café ★★★ SEAFOOD There's nothing complicated about this marvelous place, which has long been one of our favorite restaurants in Kinsale: fresh seafood from local sources (they'll even tell you the names of who caught what if asked), fresh vegetables, farmhouse cheeses, imaginative salads, and homemade breads. The cold dishes are wonderful, but the chef's talents shine with the seafood chowder; warm salad of monkfish, salmon, and shellfish in sweet chili sauce; and the steamed local mussels with basil and lemon butter. Be forewarned that they don't accept bookings in the afternoon, so you can easily find yourself waiting 30 minutes at peak time. The owners also run a fish-and-chip shop and deli in town, with the cadenced name of **Fishy Fish Shop & Chippie,** near the St. Multose Church on Guardwell St. (Tues–Sat noon–4pm).

Crowley's Quay, Kinsale, County Cork. ✆ **021/470-0415.** www.fishyfishy.ie. Reservations not accepted for lunch. Main courses €16–€22. MC, V. Mar–Oct daily noon–9pm; Nov–Feb Sun–Wed noon–4pm, Thurs–Sat noon–9pm.

Pubs

The Bulman About 1.6km (1 mile) along the quay in the direction of Charles Fort, this pub draws a sweater-and-Wellington-boot contingent of fishermen and yachtsmen. There's also a smattering of artists, students, and expats, all of whom come for the pints and the lovely location. Twilight is great here—you can take your drink outside, listen to the waves lap against the wharf, and watch the gulls turn a shimmery orange as the sun sets. Summercove, Kinsale, County Cork. ✆ **021/477-2131.**

Daltons With its black frontage, bright red front door, and matching flower boxes, Daltons is hard to miss. That's just as well, because inside the atmosphere is so cheery and welcoming you'll be glad you came. There's a small selection of excellent pub food on offer, with seafood a particular specialty. 3 Market St., Kinsale, County Cork. ✆ **021/477-7957.**

The Greyhound Photographers are enchanted with the exterior of this pub, with its neat flower boxes, rows of stout barrels, and handmade signs. Inside it's cozy and known for hearty pub food—farmhouse soups, seafood pancakes, shepherd's pie, and Irish stew. Market Sq., Kinsale, County Cork. ✆ **021/477-2889.**

Lord Kinsale A touch of elegance prevails at this handsome pub, decorated with polished horse brass. It takes its name from the first Anglo-Norman baron who took charge of this Irish port in 1223. You'll often find evening singalongs here, and the soup-and-sandwich pub food is very good. There is

The view of Kinsale Harbour from the Spaniard Inn, named for Don Juan d'Aquila, who aided Irish revolutionaries in the early 1600s.

nightly live entertainment in the summer. Main St. and Market Quay, Kinsale, County Cork. ✆ **021/477-2371.**

The Spaniard Inn 🎁 High on Compass Hill overlooking the harbor, this atmospheric pub has picturesque whitewashed walls and a thatched roof, and if you have your pint outside while watching the sun set, somebody will probably take your picture. Inside, low ceilings create an intimate feel, and a fireplace warms the main room. Bar meals are available all day and the restaurant is open in the evening (we highly recommend the seafood chowder). Named for Don Juan d'Aquila, who rallied his fleet with the Irish in an unsuccessful attempt to defeat the English, the pub has live music on Monday, Wednesday, and Friday to Sunday nights in the summer, and Wednesday, Friday, and Saturday at other times of the year. Unsurprisingly, these nights tend to be the most crowded. Scilly, Kinsale, County Cork. ✆ **021/477-2436.** www.thespaniard.ie.

The White House With its Georgian facade, this is yet another pub that tempts many a visitor to take a photograph. Inside, along with the pub itself, there's a popular bistro, the **Restaurant d'Antibes,** with bright decor and a comfortable bar. They also have a few guest rooms (doubles €100–€180) for rent. End of Pearse St., Kinsale, County Cork. ✆ **021/477-2125.** www.whitehouse-kinsale.ie.

EAST CORK

Lying 24km (15 miles) east of Cork City, the harbor town of **Cobh** (pronounced *Cove,* meaning "haven" in Irish), was once Ireland's chief port of emigration, with three or four transatlantic liners calling each week. For thousands of Irish emigrants, particularly during the famine years and in the early part of the 20th century, Cobh was the last bit of Ireland they ever saw. It was also the last port of call for the Belfast-built RMS *Titanic* before it sank spectacularly in April 1912. Cobh is still a heavily industrialized port.

The county's major coastal town is **Youghal** (pronounced *Yawl*), near the Waterford border. A leading beach resort and fishing port, Youghal is loosely associated with Sir Walter Raleigh, who was once the mayor and is said to have planted Ireland's first potatoes here. From a tourist's-eye view, present-day Youghal is a moderately attractive, congested town with a grand stretch of beach just beyond the center.

Essentials

GETTING THERE If you're driving from Cork City, take the main Waterford road (N25) east. Exit at R624 for Fota and Cobh, or R632 for Shanagarry and Ballycotton. Midleton and Youghal have their own signposted exits. If you're coming from West Cork and want to bypass Cork City (a good idea during rush hour), take the car ferry operated by **Cross River Ferries Ltd.,** Atlantic Quay, Cobh (✆ **021/420-2900;** www.scottcobh.ie). It links Carrigaloe, near Cobh, with Glenbrook, south of Cork City. Ferries run daily from 7am to 10pm. Cars cost €5 one-way, €7 round-trip. For cyclists, the fare is €1 one-way, €1.50 round-trip. Discount tickets are available if you expect to make more than 10 trips. The journey lasts under 5 minutes.

Irish Rail (✆ **021/455-7277;** www.irishrail.ie) operates daily train service between Cork City and Cobh via Fota Island. **Bus Éireann** (✆ **021/450-8188;** www.buseireann.ie) also provides daily service from Cork City to Cobh and other points in East Cork.

Students cooking up a storm at Ballymaloe Cookery School, run by Ireland's most famous chef, Darina Allen.

VISITOR INFORMATION The **tourist office** (✆ **021/481-3301**) is open 9:30am to 5:30pm Monday through Friday, 1 to 5pm Saturday and Sunday, at the Old Yacht Club in the lower harbor at Cobh. **Seasonal tourist offices** operate at Distillery Road, Midleton (✆ **021/461-3702**), and Market Square, Youghal (✆ **024/20170**), from May or June through September. Hours are daily 9:30am to 5:30pm.

Seeing the Sights

Ballymaloe Cookery School ★ Professional and amateur cooks flock here from all over the world to sit near the whisk of Darina Allen. It all started with Darina's mother-in-law, Myrtle, whose evangelization of Ireland's bounty of fresh produce at Ballymaloe House restaurant (see below) elevated Irish "country house" cooking to gourmet status. The Allen family's success led to the founding of this cooking school, which offers dozens of courses ranging in length from a half-day to 12 weeks. Topics include cake making, tapas, sushi, vegetarian cuisine, family food, barbecue, and holiday cooking. Prices start at around €85 and rise to the stratosphere. The beautiful, extensive **gardens ★** on the grounds are open to visitors from May to September. Admission to the gardens is €6 adults; family discounts available. The **Cafe at the End of the Shop,** open 10am to 5pm every day, serves morning coffee, memorable light lunches, and afternoon tea.

Kinoith, Shanagarry, County Cork. ✆ **021/464-6785.** www.cookingisfun.ie. Half-day courses from €85–€110; 1- to 5-day courses €185–€895. Accommodations for students in self-catering cottages €30 sharing, €45 single per night (€105/€145 per week). Open year-round; schedule varies.

Cobh: The Queenstown Story ★★ Between the mid–19th and 20th centuries, more than 2.5 million people from across Ireland departed from Cobh (it was then known as Queenstown) for new lives in the United States, Canada, and Australia, so the city became synonymous with farewells. This intelligent heritage center commemorates Cobh's heartbreaking history as the last port of call for emigrants, many of them doomed to take convict ships to Australia, coffin ships to America, and transatlantic liners like the ill-fated *Titanic* and *Lusitania.* In a beautifully restored Victorian railway station, the center tells the story of the city, its harbor, and the Irish exodus in a series of displays, films, and exhibits. The center also has a restaurant, a shop, and a genealogical referral service.

Cobh Railway Station, Cobh, County Cork. ✆ **021/481-3591.** www.cobhheritage.com. Admission €7.50 adults; €6 seniors and students; €4 children 8–12; free for children 7 and under; €20 families. Daily Nov–Apr 9:30am–5pm, May–Oct 9:30am–6pm. Last admission 1 hr. before closing. Closed Christmas week.

Millions of starving peasants fled Ireland from Cobh when a potato blight devastated the island's main food source for several years straight.

Fota Island Wildlife Park & Arboretum Gardens ★★★ ☺ Wherever possible, the animals in this well-designed wildlife park a few miles outside Cork City roam free with no obvious barriers, mixing and mingling with other species and sometimes with human visitors. Only the cheetahs are behind conventional fencing. As with most zoos, it's got a share of rare and endangered zebras, ostriches, antelopes, and the like. Kangaroos, macaws, and lemurs roam over 16 hectares (40 acres) of grassland. Fota Island is also home to the Fota House and Arboretum Gardens—plantation-like estate, with a grand house built in 1820, and sprawling botanical gardens with exotic trees and plants. You can see part of the house for free, although tours of the rest are often laid on for just a few euros. A coffee shop, a small amusement park for young children, a tour train, picnic tables, and a gift shop are on the grounds.

Wildlife Park: Fota Island, Carrigtwohill, County Cork (16km/10 miles east of Cork on Cobh Rd.). ✆ **021/481-2678.** www.fotawildlife.ie. Tickets: Wildlife park €14 adults; €9 seniors, students, and children; €44–€56 families. House and Gardens: ✆ **021/481-5543.** www.fotahouse.com. €6 adults;

Take the *Titanic* Trail

Cobh (or Queenstown, as it was known back then) was the last port of call for the *Titanic,* and as such has sprung up a whole mini-industry for devotees of that ill-fated vessel. The popular *Titanic* Trail (✆ 021/481-5211; www.titanic-trail.com) is a walking tour of a variety of local sites most closely associated with the ship, and it uses them as a springboard for a broader overview of Cobh's maritime and emigrant history. In truth, some of the *Titanic* connections seem a little tenuous (see the actual building in which the White Star Line shipping company used to have an office—fancy that!), but fans will love it. If you're not one of them, console yourself with the thought of a complimentary Guinness at the end of the tour. The walk, which takes about an hour and 15 minutes, leaves from the Commodore Hotel, 4 Westbourne Place, every day from April to October at 11am. From June to August an extra tour leaves at 2pm. Tickets cost €9.50 adults, €4.75 kids 11 and under, and can be purchased on the day of the tour from the guide, or booked in advance on the number above. The same company also runs a Ghost Tour, which costs €15 per person; call or visit the website for details.

€4 seniors; €3 children; €15 families. Mon–Sat 10am–4:30pm; Sun 11am–4:30pm. Last admission 1 hr. before closing. Rail: Cork-Cobh line from Cork City to Fota station. Closed Dec 25–26.

The Old Midleton Distillery/Jameson Heritage Centre ★ This is sort of a Willy Wonka factory of booze. In a brightly colored building, with a huge copper vat out front, shining in the sun, this distillery and visitor center are all about smooth Irish whiskey. It's all done in a modern factory now, but the center of production for Jameson Whiskey still holds many of the original 1825 structures, all meticulously preserved. For the truly interested, there's a film to watch in the visitor center as well as a whiskey-making demonstration, followed by a tasting after the tour.

Distillery Rd., off Main St., Midleton, County Cork. ✆ **021/461-3594.** www.jamesonwhiskey.com. Admission €14 adults; €10 seniors; €11 students 18 and over; €8 children; €30 families. Daily 10am–6pm. Tours Apr–Oct 10am–4:30pm on request; Nov–Mar 11:30am, and 1:15, 2:30, and 4pm.

Shopping

Youghal Pottery This workshop offers a very good selection of pottery and ceramics in stoneware, earthenware, porcelain, and raku, all handmade on the premises. The shop also offers a selection of crafts, woolens, and textiles. There's also a handy tearoom, with views across the Blackwater River, and a heritage center. Foxhole, just off the N25 to Waterford, 1km (⅔ mile) north of Youghal. ✆ **024/91222.**

Where to Stay & Eat

EXPENSIVE

Ballymaloe House ★ Combining a Georgian farmhouse facade with the tower of a 14th-century castle, this ivy-covered enclave of hospitality run by the Allen family is on a working farm, complete with grazing sheep and cows. Ballymaloe is about 23km (14 miles) southeast of Cork City, less than 3km (2 miles) from Ballycotton Bay. Guest rooms are

The original distillery for Jameson Irish whiskey now runs tours and demonstrations, which end with a shot of the famous amber spirit.

The Friday buffet at Ballymaloe House, where Myrtle Allen inspired a culinary revolution based on traditional recipes and fresh local ingredients.

furnished in informal, comfortable, even rather rustic style. Make no mistake—the main attraction is the dining room, a pioneer of Ireland's "country house" culinary style. It is French-inspired and relies on local seafood and produce, accompanied by fresh vegetables from the garden. The kitchen's success has spawned an acclaimed **cooking school** (see above) and a shelf of Allen family cookbooks.

Shanagarry, Midleton, County Cork. www.ballymaloe.ie. ✆ **800/323-5463** in the U.S., or 021/465-2531. 33 units. €170–€250 double. Lunch averages €40; dinner averages €75. Rates include full breakfast. AE, DC, MC, V. **Amenities:** Restaurant; 9-hole golf course; outdoor pool; tennis courts. *In room:* Hair dryer.

MODERATE

Aherne's Townhouse and Restaurant ★★ In the heart of a busy seaside resort, this cozy restaurant with rooms has been penned into many travelers' journals because of its first-rate seafood. Comfortable and stylishly furnished, the guest rooms are all quite large by Irish standards. Most are more like hotel suites than rooms—each with king-size beds, antique desks, and designer fabrics. There are two bars and a relaxing sitting room, but the main reason to stay here is to be near the classic seafood restaurant. Its French-influenced cooking makes the most of the local catch—Blackwater salmon, giant prawn tails, rock oysters, and lobsters. Even the bar food is worth a detour—seafood pies, chowders, crab sandwiches, and crisp salads. Breakfasts here are a real indulgence, served in front of the fire.

163 N. Main St., Youghal, County Cork. www.ahernes.net. ✆ **024/92424.** Fax 024/93633. www.ahernes.net. 12 units. €150–€190 double; €172 studio. Bar lunch from €10; dinner main courses €28–€32. Rates include full breakfast. AE, DC, MC, V. **Amenities:** Restaurant; 2 bars; smoke-free rooms. *In room:* TV, hair dryer.

Bayview Hotel ★ It's hard to imagine a more romantic location for a seaside hotel, overlooking miles of spectacular coastline stretching out from Ballycotton Harbour. The capable owners John and Carnel O'Brien completely restored the place when they turned it into a hotel in the early 1990s. Rooms are bright and airy with modern furnishings and subtle, chocolate-and-cream tones. All have sea views. If you're in the mood to splurge, the hotel's restaurant is especially imaginative. Main dishes (which can be served in the garden if the weather's good) include filet of turbot with sautéed ceps and nut brown salsify in vanilla butter; ricotta and spinach ravioli in mushroom and tarragon sauce; or loin or pork with gingered carrots and scallion purée. Elaborate desserts include such concotions as iced Ovaltine and chocolate parfait with toffee popcorn, white chocolate sauce, and popcorn ice cream.

Ballycotton, County Cork. www.thebayviewhotel.com. ✆ **021/464-6746.** 35 units. €70–€175 double. Dinner main courses €28–€33. Rates include full breakfast. AE, MC, V. Closed Nov to early Apr. **Amenities:** Restaurant; bar; babysitting. *In room:* TV.

Harty's Restaurant ★ 🎁 CONTINENTAL In the little medieval village of Cloyne, this unfussy, whitewashed eatery is a great little restaurant. Owner/chef Eamon Harty's food is straightforward—chargrilled steaks; wild salmon with a cool cucumber sauce; and pan-fried fish cakes with lemon. As is true with all great chefs, Harty's success comes from choosing the freshest vegetables, ripest fruits, and highest-quality meats and fish, then knowing what to do with them. His homemade breads are heavenly, too.

Church St., Cloyne, near Midleton, County Cork. ✆ **021/465-2401.** www.hartysrestaurantcloyne.com. Dinner main courses €14–€33. MC, V. Daily 10:30am–9pm.

WEST CORK

For many, West Cork is Ireland's ultimate destination—not quite as crowded with tourists as Kerry, yet every bit as charming. It shares with Kerry a photo-friendly craggy topography and jagged coastline. It's impossible to make good time on the roads here, as they tend to be narrow and sinuous, twisting along rivers, through valleys, around mountains, and passing through lovely small towns. Those willing to slow down and go with the flow are amply rewarded. You'll probably come across at least one puzzling rural intersection that's completely unsignposted, and have to slow down for a herd of sheep slowly making its way down a country lane. In places, the public route that hugs the coast narrows to just one lane and delivers heart-stopping views. Over time, you may even come to think of the roads here as one of West Cork's great pleasures.

Some of the most beautiful coastal scenery (and severe weather) is on the islands. **Cape Clear ★**, home to a bird-watching observatory, is also a well-known Gaeltacht: Both schoolchildren and adults come here to work on their Gaelic skills each summer. **Dursey Island,** off the tip of the Beara Peninsula, is accessible by cable car. **Garinish Island** in Glengarriff is the site of Ilnacullin, an elaborate Italianate garden.West Cork is known for its enticing and colorful towns. A cluster of artists gives **Ballydehob** a creative flair. At the local butcher, colorful drawings of cattle, pigs, and chickens indicate what's available, and a mural on the outside wall of a pub depicts a *caleigh.* Other notable enclaves include the buzzy, seaside town of **Skibbereen** (meaning "Little Boat Harbor"), where impromptu traditional-music sessions are commonplace in its 22 pubs; the immaculate, flower-box-on-every-sill town of **Clonakilty;** the yachting town **Schull;** and **Barleycove,** a remote, wind-swept resort that's the last stop before Mizen Head and the sheer cliffs at the island's southernmost tip.

Essentials

GETTING THERE N71 is the main road into West Cork from north and south; from Cork and points east, N22 also leads to West Cork.

Bus Éireann (✆ **021/450-8188;** www.buseireann.ie) provides daily bus service to and from the principal towns in West Cork.

VISITOR INFORMATION Contact the **Skibbereen Tourist Office,** North Street, Skibbereen, County Cork (✆ **028/21766**). It is open year-round Monday to Friday 9:15am to 5:30pm, with weekend and extended hours May through September. There are **seasonal tourist offices** in the Square, Bantry (✆ **027/50229**), and Rossa Street, Clonakilty (✆ **023/883-3226**), operating from May or June through August or September. The **Beara Tourism & Development Association,** the Square, Castletownbere (✆ **027/70054;** www.bearatourism.com), is also open during the summer.

Exploring the Region

There is a magnificent **Sheep's Head Loop** drive that begins outside Bantry along the Goat's Path to Kilcrohane, then back through Ahakista, and on to Durrus. The north side is all sheer cliffs and stark beauty (the sunsets are incredible) while the more lush south-side road runs right alongside the wondrous Dunmanus Bay.

You may also want to explore **Dursey Island,** a barren promontory extending into the sea at the tip of the Beara Peninsula. It offers no amenities for tourists, but the adventurous will find beautiful seaside walks and a memorable passage from the mainland via cable car. To get there, take R571 past Cahermore to its terminus. As you sway wildly in the wooden cable car, reading the text of Psalm 91 (which has kindly been posted to comfort the nervous), you might wonder whether a ferry would have been a wiser option. It wouldn't. Apparently the channel between the island and mainland is often too treacherous to permit regular crossing by boat. There is no lodging on the island, so be sure you know when the last cable car departs for the mainland; for schedule information, call the Skibbereen Tourist Office at ✆ **028/21766.**

Unfortunately a number of formerly reliable historical tours of the area have recently gone out of business or put up their prices so much that we can no longer recommend them. However, **Dolores and Tim Crowley** (✆ **023/884-6107;** www.michaelcollinscentre.com) still run a wide variety of tours associated with Michael Collins and the civil war. Prices begin at around €6 per person.

Seeing the Sights

Bantry House ★★ On the edge of the town of Bantry, this Georgian house was built around 1750 for the earls of Bantry. It holds furniture and objets d'art from all over Europe, including Aubusson and Gobelin tapestries said to have been made for Marie Antoinette. The gardens, with original statuary, are beautifully kept—climb the steps behind the building for a panoramic view of the house, gardens, and Bantry Bay. The house also holds an informative exhibition on the ill-fated Spanish armada, which, led by the Irish rebel Wolfe Tone, attempted to invade the country near Bantry House in 1769. If you really love it, you can spend the night (€200–€300 double), or rent the self-catering gate lodge for €450 to €750 per week.

Bantry, County Cork. ✆ **027/50047.** www.bantryhouse.ie. Admission €10 adults; €8 seniors and students; €3 children 5–16; €24 families. Mid-Mar to Oct daily 10am–6pm.

Derreen Gardens ★ The benign climate of West Cork and Kerry has made this informal garden a site of great natural beauty on the breathtaking north coast of the Beara Peninsula. In the late 19th century, the garden was planted with American species of conifer, many of which have become venerable giants. One path follows the sweep of the shoreline through tunnels of rhododendron, while others wind through the dense foliage of the promontory, opening occasionally to a view of the mountains or an entrancing rocky glen. The garden is home to several rarities, most notably the New Zealand tree ferns that flourish in a small glade, among giant blue gum and bamboo.

Remembering Michael Collins

West Cork's most *and* least favorite son is the revolutionary Michael Collins (1890–1922), who was both born and assassinated in the county. Everyone here has an opinion about him. A hero to some, a traitor to others, Collins (who was immortalized in a movie starring Liam Neeson in 1996) was a larger-than-life, utterly charismatic man. The memory of Collins, sometimes referred to as "the Man Who Made Ireland," is preserved at the Michael Collins Memorial Centre and the ambush site near Macroom. For more on Collins, see "Who Was Michael Collins?" below.

The mysterious seaside Drombeg Stone Circle dates to 153 B.C.

Signposted 1.6km (1 mile) off R571 in Lauragh, County Kerry. ✆ **064/668-3103.** Admission €6 adults; €3 seniors, students, and children 15 and under; €18 families. Apr–July and Sept–Oct daily 10am–6pm; Aug Fri–Sun 10am–6pm (other times by appointment).

Drombeg Stone Circle ★★ This ring of 17 standing stones is the finest example of a megalithic stone circle in County Cork. Hills slope gently toward the sea nearby, and the builders could hardly have chosen a more picturesque spot. The circle dates from 153 B.C., and little is known about its ritual purpose. Just west of the circle are the remains of two huts and a cooking place; it is thought that heated stones were placed in a water trough (which can be seen adjacent to the huts), and the hot water was used for cooking. The cooking place dates from between A.D. 368 and 608.

Off R597 btw. Rosscarbery and Glandore, County Cork.

Ilnacullin (Garinish Island) ★★ Officially known as Ilnacullin, but usually referred to as Garinish, this little island is a beautiful and tranquil place. It used to be little more than a barren outcrop, whose only distinguishing feature was a Martello tower left over from the Napoleonic Wars. Then, in 1919, the English landscaper Harold Peto was commissioned to create an elaborately planned Italianate garden, with classical pavilions and myriad unusual plants and flowers. The island's unusually mild microclimate allows a number of subtropical plant species to thrive here; indeed, George Bernard Shaw is said to have written *St. Joan* under the shade of its palm trees. The island can be reached for a round-trip fee of €10 per person (€5 children) on a covered ferry operated by **Blue Pool Ferry,** the Blue Pool, Glengarriff (✆ **027/63333;** www.bluepoolferry.com), or **Harbour Queen Ferries,** the Harbour, Glengarriff (✆ **027/63116;** www.harbourqueenferry.com). Boats run back and forth about every 20 minutes. The island has a large restaurant and tearoom.

Glengarriff, County Cork. ✆ **027/63040.** www.heritageireland.ie. Admission (gardens) €4 adults; €3 seniors; €2 students and children; €10 families. Apr Mon–Sat 10am–6:30pm, Sun 1–6:30pm; May and Sept Mon–Sat 10am–6:30pm, Sun noon–6:30pm; June Mon–Sat 10am–6:30pm, Sun 11am–6:30pm; July–Aug Mon–Sat 9:30am–6:30pm, Sun 11am–6:30pm; Oct Mon–Sat 10am–4pm, Sun 1–5pm. Last landing 1 hr. before closing.

WHO WAS MICHAEL COLLINS?

Much of County Cork, and particularly the little town of Clonakilty, seems obsessed with Michael Collins, but when you learn a bit about him, you can understand why. Collins, also known as "the Big Fella," was one of the heroes of the Irish struggle for independence—the commander in chief of the army of the Irish Free State, which, under his command won the Republic's independence from Britain in 1921.

Collins was born in 1890 and, along with his seven brothers and sisters, was raised on a farm in Sam's Cross, just outside Clonakilty. He emigrated to England at 15 and, like many other young Irish men, found work in London. In his 20s, he joined the Irish revolutionary group, the Irish Republican Brotherhood (I.R.B.). He first came to fame in 1916, as one of the planners and leaders of the Easter Rising, fighting alongside Patrick Pearse at the General Post Office in Dublin. It may have roused passions among the population, but the Rising was a military disaster, and Collins—young but clever—railed against its amateurism. He was furious about the seizure of prominent buildings—such as the GPO—that were impossible to defend, impossible to escape from, and difficult to get supplies into.

After the battle, Collins was arrested and sent to an internment camp in Britain, along with hundreds of other rebels. There his stature within the I.R.B. grew, and by the time he was released, he had become one of the leaders of the Republican movement. In 1918, he was elected a member of the British Parliament, but like many other Irish members, refused to go to London, instead announcing that he would sit only in an Irish parliament in Dublin. Most of the rebel Irish MPs (including Eamon de Valera) were arrested by British troops for their actions, but Collins avoided arrest, and later helped de Valera escape from prison. Over the subsequent years, de Valera and Collins worked together to create an Irish state.

After lengthy negotiations and much bloodshed (Collins orchestrated an

Michael Collins Memorial Centre More a place of pilgrimage than a traditional attraction, the center is frequented by those who revere Collins rather than those who want to learn more about him. It's on the farm where he was born and raised—the old stone farmhouse in which Collins and his siblings were born still survives, although the larger farmhouse into which his family moved when Michael was 10 was burned to the ground in 1921 by the Black and Tans. The ambush site at Béal na mBláth, near Macroom, where he was assassinated, is kept as a shrine of sorts.

Signposted off N71, 5.6km (3½ miles) west of Clonakilty, Woodfield, County Cork. Free admission.

Mizen Head Signal Station ★★★ At Mizen Head, the southernmost point in Ireland, the land falls precipitously into the Atlantic breakers in a procession of spectacular 210m (700-ft.) sea cliffs. A suspension bridge permits access to the old signal station, now a visitor center, on a rock promontory, the southernmost point on the Irish mainland, with awe-inspiring views of the cliffs and the open sea. Whales, seals, dolphins, and seabirds contribute to the spectacle. No matter what the weather, it's worth a trip. On wild days, tremendous Atlantic waves assault the cliffs. On a clear day, seals bask on the rocks and gannets wheel over the sea and dive into the tranquil waters. The visitor center also has a assassination that essentially wiped out the British secret service in Ireland), Collins was sent by de Valera in 1921 to negotiate a treaty with the British government. In the meeting, British Prime Minister David Lloyd George agreed to allow Ireland to become a free republic, as long as that republic did not include the counties of Ulster (a move designed to appease the Unionists in Northern Ireland). Those largely Protestant counties would stay part of the United Kingdom. Knowing he could not get more at the time and hoping to renegotiate later, Collins reluctantly agreed to sign the treaty, deciding that it was time to stop the bloodshed. (Along with Lloyd George, Winston Churchill, then a government minister, also signed the treaty.) After signing the document Collins said, "I have just signed my death warrant."

As he'd expected, the plan tore the new Republic apart, dividing the group now known as the IRA into two factions—those who wanted to continue fighting for all of Ireland, and those who favored the treaty. Fighting soon broke out in Dublin, and the civil war was underway.

Collins had learned many lessons from the Easter debacle, and now his strategy was completely different. His soldiers operated as "flying columns," waging a guerrilla war against the enemy—suddenly attacking, and then just as suddenly withdrawing, thus minimizing their losses, and leaving the opposition never knowing what to expect next, but the battle stretched on for 10 months.

In August 1922, Collins was weary of the war, and was on a peace mission in his home county. After visiting various factions, and stopping at a pub near his mother's birthplace, he and his escort were on the road near Béal na mBláth when Collins was shot and killed. Precisely who killed him—whether it was his own men or the opposition—is not known. He had made, on his rapid rise to the top, too many enemies. He was 31 years old.

program of rather grown-up day courses throughout the year, in subjects such as bird-watching and local geology. They cost around €65 per person including lunch; check the website for details. As this book was being written, the Signal Station was just about to reopen after a major refurbishment program, which includes an improved visitor center, a lighthouse simulator, and new bridges and viewing platforms. It all sounds pretty spectacular.

On the way out to Mizen Head, you'll pass Barleycove Beach, one of the most beautiful beaches in southwest Ireland and a great place to explore.

Mizen Head, County Cork. ✆ **028/35115.** www.mizenhead.ie. Admission €6 adults; €3.50 children; free for children 4 and under; €18 families. Mid-Mar to May and Oct daily 10:30am–5pm; June–Sept daily 10am–6:30pm; Nov to mid-Mar Sat–Sun 11am–4pm. Take R591 to Goleen, and follow signs for Mizen Head.

Shopping

Bandon Pottery This attractive little shop, located behind artist Jane Forrester's home and studio, is full to bursting with colorful tableware, vases, bowls, and ornaments, all of which are handmade on-site. It's lovely stuff, and very unique, but because it's such a small operation the shop is only open when Jane

The Atlantic crashes off the 210m (700-ft.) sea cliffs at Mizen Head, the southernmost point in Ireland.

can be there, so make sure you call ahead to confirm opening hours before making a special trip (normally Mon–Sat from 11am–6pm). Ardkitt East, Enniskeane, County Cork. ✆ **023/884-7843** or 087/240-1738. www.bandonpottery.ie.

Courtmacsherry Ceramics Overlooking the sea, this studio and shop offers an array of porcelain animals and tableware, inspired by West Cork. Visitors are welcome to watch potter Peter Wolstenholme at work on new creations. Railway View, Courtmacsherry, County Cork. ✆ **023/884-6239.**

Quills Woollen Market This family-run enterprise in a small village deep in West Cork's Gaelic-speaking region has handmade sweaters and garments made from wool and goatskins. Main St., Macroom, County Cork. ✆ **026/43910.**

Rossmore Country Pottery This family-run studio produces a lovely range of practical domestic stoneware and a colorful collection of decorated earthenware flowerpots. Rossmore, County Cork (11km/6¾ miles from Clonakilty on Bandon-Bantry rd.). ✆ **023/883-8875.**

Sports & Outdoor Pursuits

BEACHES **Barleycove Beach** is a vast expanse of pristine sand with a fine view out toward the Mizen Head cliffs; despite the trailer park and holiday homes on the far side of the dunes, large parts of the beach never seem to get crowded. Take R591 to Goleen, and follow signs for Mizen Head. There is a public parking lot at the Barleycove Hotel.

Inchydoney Beach, on Clonakilty Bay, is famous for both its gorgeous beach and the salubrious **Inchydoney Lodge & Spa** (✆ **023/883-3143**) that specializes in thalasso (seawater) treatments. These hydrotherapy baths are meant to do pretty much everything from lowering your blood pressure, to relieving pain and breaking down cellulite. Treatments range from micro bubble jet color light therapy (rebalances the chakras, don't you know) to a green tea and fucus algae detox. Oh, and if you've ever wanted to bathe in chocolate cream, this is the place to do it. Most treatments cost €40 for 20 minutes. For more information, visit **www.inchydoneyisland.com**.

BICYCLING The **Mizen Head, Sheep's Head,** and **Beara peninsulas** offer fine roads for cycling, with great scenery and few cars. The Beara Peninsula is the most spectacular; the other two are less likely to be crowded with tourists during peak season. The loop around Mizen Head, starting in Skibbereen, is a good 2- to 3-day trip, and a loop around the Beara Peninsula from Bantry, Glengarriff, or Kenmare takes at least 3 days at a casual pace.

In Skibbereen, 18- and 21-speed bicycles can be rented from **Roycroft Cycles** (✆ **028/21235;** roycroftcycles@eircom.net); expect to pay around €70 per week, depending on the season. If you call ahead, you can reserve a lightweight mountain bike with toe clips at no extra cost.

BIRD-WATCHING **Cape Clear Island** is the prime birding spot in West Cork, and one of the best places in Europe to watch seabirds (see the box "Southern Exposure: An Excursion to Cape Clear Island," below). The best time for seabirds is July to September, and October is the busiest month for migratory passerines (and for bird-watchers, who flock to the island). There is a bird observatory at the **North Harbour,** with a warden in residence from March to November, and accommodations for bird-watchers; to arrange a stay, write to **Kieran Grace,** 84 Dorney Court, Shankill, County Dublin. **Ciarán and Mary O'Driscoll** (✆ **028/39153** or 087/268-0760; www.capeclearisland.eu), who operate a B&B on the island, also run boat trips for bird-watchers and have a keen eye for vagrants and rarities.

DIVING The **Baltimore Diving Centre,** Baltimore, County Cork (✆ **028/20300;** www.baltimorediving.com), provides equipment and boats to certified divers for exploring the many shipwrecks, reefs, and caves in this region. The cost starts at around €30 per dive if you bring your own gear, or €50 with hired equipment (plus €24 for a guide). Various 2-hour to 15-day certified PADI courses are available for all levels of experience.

FISHING The West Cork coast is known for its many shipwrecks, making this one of the best places in Ireland for wreck fishing. **Mark and Trish Gannon** of Courtmacsherry Sea Angling Centre, Woodpoint House, Courtmacsherry (✆ **023/46427;** www.courtmacsherryangling.ie), offer packages that include bed-and-breakfast in their idyllic stone farmhouse and a day's sea angling aboard one of their two Aquastar fishing boats. A day's fishing costs around €60 per person (€70 if you want to go out to a wreck). They also run dolphin- and whale-watching excursions for €35 per person, or €100 per hour for groups of up to 12.

Bird lovers from all over Europe patiently await a glimpse of the seabirds that flock to Cape Clear Island from July through September.

KAYAKING With hundreds of islands, numerous inviting inlets, and a plethora of sea caves, the coast of West Cork is a sea kayaker's paradise. **Lough Ine** offers warm, still waters for beginners, a tidal rapid for the intrepid, and access to a nearby headland riddled with caves that demand exploration. In Skibbereen, **Atlantic Sea Kayaking** (✆ **028/21058;** www.atlanticsea kayaking.com) specializes in guided trips around Galley Head in Clonakilty and Mizen Head. They also run family kayaking excursions, 2-day sea kayaking trips, and 1- to 5-day courses for those of varying levels of ability.

SAILING **Sail Cork** (East Hill, Cobh; ✆ **021/4811237;** www.sailcork.com) was founded in 1974 and runs courses on just about every aspect of sailing, yachting, and power boating, for all levels and ages. The variety is huge, but they include a half-day children's course on dinghy sailing (€25), a 1-day adult beginners course in power boating (€58), all the way up to weeklong trips for competent crew (mostly around €725). The course list on the website is exhaustive, so this should be your first port of call for details.

WALKING One of the most beautiful coastal walks in West Cork begins along the banks of **Lough Ine,** one of the largest saltwater lakes in Europe. Connected to the sea by a narrow isthmus, the lake is in a lush valley of exceptional beauty. To get there, follow signs for Lough Ine along R595 between Skibbereen and Baltimore; there is a parking lot at the northwest corner of the lake. The wide trail proceeds gradually upward from the parking lot through the woods on the west slope of the valley, with several viewpoints toward the lake and the sea beyond. Once you reach the hilltop, there is a sweeping view of the coast from Mizen Head to Galley Head. Walking time to the top and back is about 1½ hours.

Near Lauragh on the Beara Peninsula is the abandoned town of **Cummingeera,** at the base of a cliff in a wild, remote valley. The walk to the village gives you a taste for the rough beauty of the Caha Mountains, and a sense for the lengths to which people in pre-famine Ireland would go to find a patch of arable land. To get to the start of the walk, take the road posted for Glanmore Lake south from R571; the road is just over 1km (⅔ mile) west of the turnoff for Healy Pass. Follow the Glanmore Lake road 1km (⅔ mile), then turn right at the road posted for "stone circle"; continue 2km (1¼ miles) to the point where the road becomes dirt, and park on the roadside. From here, there is no trail—just walk up the valley to its terminus, about 2km (1¼ miles) away, where the ruins of a village hug the cliff's base. Where the valley is blocked by a headland, take the route around to the left, which is less steep. Return the way you came; the whole walk—4km (2½ miles)—is moderately difficult and takes 2 hours.

An easy seaside walk on the **Beara Peninsula** begins at Dunboy Castle, just over a mile west of Castletownbere on R572. This stretch of trail is part of the O'Sullivan Beara trail, which may eventually extend from Castletownbere to Leitrim. You can park your car along the road, by the castellated gatehouse, or drive up to the castle. The castle is a ruined 19th-century manor house overlooking the bay, with some graceful marble arches spanning the grand central hall. Just down the road are the sparse ruins of a medieval fortress. Beyond, the trail continues to the tip of Fair Head through rhododendrons, with fine views across to Bere Island. A walk from the gatehouse parking lot to the tip of Fair Head and back takes about 2 hours.

SOUTHERN EXPOSURE: AN excursion TO CAPE CLEAR ISLAND

Cape Clear Island, 13km (8 miles) off the mainland, is the southernmost inhabited point in Ireland. It can be bleak, with a craggy coastline and no trees to break the rush of sea wind, but that very barrenness appeals to many for its stark beauty, rough and irregular, but not without solace and grace. In early summer, wildflowers brighten the landscape, and in October, passerine migrants, some on their way from North America and Siberia, fill the air. Seabirds are present in abundance during the nesting season, especially from July to September. At any time, Cape Clear is unforgettable.

The first step (obviously) is getting there. In the high season (May–Sept), the *Cape Clear Xpress* is undoubtedly the quickest way to make the journey, with a crossing time of just 20 minutes (most ferries take more than double that). Sailings are frequent, but service is always subject to the seas and is more limited off season, so it's essential you call ahead first to confirm times for that day. The passage takes 20 minutes, and a round-trip ticket costs €15 for adults, €7 for children, and €40 for families. For inquiries, contact **Cape Clear Island Ferry Service** (✆ **028/39135** or 087/282-4008; www.capeclearferry.com). The ***Karycraft*** (✆ **028/28278** or 086/237-9032; www.capeclearferries.com) departs Schull daily in June, July, and August at 10:30am, and 2:30 and 4:30pm; and departs Cape Clear at 11:30am, and 3:30 and 5:30pm. In September, service is limited to one crossing daily, departing Schull at 2:30pm and Cape Clear at 5:30pm. The schedule for the rest of the year varies according demand and the weather, so call for details. Round-trip tickets cost €14 for adults, €5 for children, and €35 for families. Bikes are carried free.

Once you're on Cape Clear, there is much to see, including birds galore, seals, dolphins, the occasional whale, and ancient "marriage stones."

There's also a lot to do apart from hiking and sightseeing. **Cléire Lasmuigh,** Cape Clear Island Adventure Centre (✆ **028/39198;** info@lasmuigh.ie), offers outdoor programs, from snorkeling and sea kayaking to hillwalking and orienteering. Coastal cruises—for sea angling, scuba diving, or bird-watching—are the specialty of **Ciarán O'Driscoll** (✆ **028/39153**). There's no shopping mall, but local art, crafts, and books can be found in Harpercraft and the Back Room in Cotter's Yard, North Harbour. While you're at it, pick up a copy of Chuck Kruger's *Cape Clear Island Magic.* There's no better introduction to the wonder of this place.

Modest hostel, B&B, and self-catering accommodations are available by the day, week, or month. The island's **An Óige Youth Hostel** (✆ **028/41968;** www.anoige.ie/hostels/cape-clear) at the Old Coast Guard Station, South Harbour, is open year-round. Dorm accommodations cost from €17 per night adults, €15 children. They also have four- and six-bed private rooms from €80 and €116 per night. Most B&Bs are open year-round. They include **Ard na Gaoith** (contact Eileen Leonard, ✆ **028/39160;** ardnagaoithe@hotmail.com). For self-catering cottages by the day or week, contact **Ciarán O'Driscoll** (✆ **028/39153**). You can't miss the town's three pubs and two restaurants, which will keep you well fortified. (Also, the fruit scones baked at Cistin Chléire on North Harbour are fabulous.)

Cape Clear has a helpful website at **www.oilean-chleire.ie**, with further details on the history of the island, things to do, and accommodations.

The **Sheep's Head Way,** voted "Best Walk in Ireland" by *Country Walking* magazine, makes an 89km (55-mile) loop and incorporates numerous smaller day loops. The *Guide to the Sheep's Head Way,* available in most local stores and tourist offices, combines history, poetry, and topography in a fantastic introduction to the region. It is a rough place, and you won't find many tourists in its more remote reaches. There are treasures to be found, including several ancient ring forts and burial mounds, but you will have to work a little harder to locate them here than in regions long since "discovered."

One of Ireland's most beautiful spots, **Gougane Barra** (which means "St. Finbarre's Cleft") is a still, dark, romantic lake a little northeast of the Pass of Keimaneigh, 24km (15 miles) northeast of Bantry off R584 (also well signposted on the R584 Macroom-Glengarriff rd.). This is the source of the River Lee, where St. Finbarre founded a monastery in these deeply wooded mountains, supposedly on the small island connected by a causeway to the mainland. Though nothing remains of the saint's 6th-century community, the setting is idyllic, with rhododendrons spilling into the still waters where swans glide by. The island now holds an elfin chapel and eight small circular cells, dating from the early 1700s, as well as a modern chapel. Today Gougane Barra is a national forest park, and there are signposted walks and drives through the wooded hills. There's a small admission charge per car to enter the park.

WINDSURFING Weeklong courses and equipment rental are available at the **Oysterhaven Activity Centre** (p. 315) near Kinsale. There is a sheltered beach in Courtmacsherry where beginners can get started and another nearby beach that's good for wave jumping.

Where to Stay

MODERATE

Ballylickey Manor House ★★ With a stunning view of Bantry Bay, nestled amid sculpted lawns and gardens, and with a backdrop of mountains and moorlands, this 300-year-old manor house was built as a shooting lodge. It has five large suites and seven spacious, well-decorated cottages clustered around the swimming pool. The house has the feel of a country home, albeit a stylish one. It was regularly visited by the poet Robert Graves, who was the uncle of one of its current owners.

Bantry-Glengarriff rd. (N71), Ballylickey, County Cork. www.ballylickeymanorhouse.com. ✆ **027/50071.** Fax 027/50124. 14 units. €110–€130 double cottage; €130–€180 suites. Rates include full breakfast. AE, DC, MC, V. Closed Nov–Feb. **Amenities:** Restaurant; outdoor heated pool. *In room:* TV, hair dryer.

Longueville House Hotel ★★ ☺ Dating from 1720, this grand and beautiful country house is set amid acres of rolling farmland. It's saved from pomposity by the laid-back O'Callaghan family, who keep things down to earth. Guest rooms are furnished in old-world style with family heirlooms and period pieces. Most rooms have bucolic views of the surrounding farm, gardens, or the hotel's own vineyard. Reasonably priced family rooms are available, and there's a special children's menu at dinner. The **President's Restaurant** is one of the best in the area. Chef William O'Callaghan uses ingredients from the farm and transforms them into memorable dishes. A six-course tasting menu is available on

Wednesday to Friday nights (an even more elaborate eight-course meal is offered on Sat). In the summer, meals are also served in a sky-lit Victorian conservatory. Longueville House also hosts an occasional but appropriately rustic program of events, such as dawn chorus walks and mushroom hunts.

Killarney Rd. (N72), Mallow, County Cork. www.longuevillehouse.ie. ✆ **800/323-5463** in the U.S., or 022/47156. Fax 022/47459. 20 units. €160–€180 double; €200–€260 suite. Rates include full breakfast. 4-course fixed-price dinner €65; 8-course tasting menu €90; Sun lunch €40. Please inform of any food allergies when booking. AE, DC, MC, V. Closed mid-Feb to early Mar. **Amenities:** Restaurant; smoke-free rooms. *In room:* TV, hair dryer.

Rock Cottage ★ This B&B offers a wonderfully secluded, relaxing retreat in what was once Lord Bandon's hunting lodge. The spacious guest rooms in the tastefully restored Georgian building combine shades of elegance and comfort. Here's the best news: Your hostess, Barbara Klötzer, is a former head chef, and is now able to focus her culinary wizardry on a handful of lucky guests. Be aware, however, that this is very much a B&B, rather than an inn or hotel. The service can sometimes feel like a one-person show (you have to decide what you want for breakfast the night before, for example), although whether or not you think this is a bad thing really depends on the kind of experience you're looking for.

Barnatonicane (11km/6¾ miles from Durrus on R591), Schull, County Cork. www.rockcottage.ie. ✆ **028/35538.** 3 units. €140 double; self-catering cottage €860–€1,250 per week. Rates include full breakfast. 3-course dinner €45. MC, V. Free parking. *In room:* TV, hair dryer.

Sea View House ★★ This handsome seaside hotel is homey and full of interesting heirlooms, fine antiques, and an utter disregard for fads and trends. Instead, it sticks to old-fashioned principles of good service. The cheerily decorated rooms are individually furnished in a manner Grandma would like, with dark woods, busy fabrics, and mattresses firm enough to bounce a penny on. Request a room in the front of the house for peekaboo views of Bantry Bay through the leafy trees. The hotel is best known for its award-winning cuisine, the sort of hearty comfort food that's reassuringly still devoted to using marvelously fattening dollops of fresh cream, real butter, a slug of booze now and then, and salt. Half-board rates (which include dinner) work out marginally cheaper if you're planning to eat here.

Bantry-Glengarriff rd. (N71), Ballylickey, County Cork. www.seaviewhousehotel.com. ✆ **800/447-7462** in the U.S., or 027/50073. Fax 027/51555. 25 units. €150–€210 double. Dinner €45. Rates include full breakfast and service charge. Dinner €45. AE, MC, V. Closed mid-Nov to mid-Mar. **Amenities:** Restaurant; bar. *In room:* TV, hair dryer.

West Cork Hotel ★★ 🎁 This is the sort of comfy, old-style hotel that has a bit of style despite itself. Everything is designed to induce contentment and familiarity, and it's a testimony to its success that the public areas—particularly the buzzy pub—always draw a local crowd. Guest rooms are relaxing in the old-fashioned Irish way, with lots of traditional dark woods and mismatched patterns. The handsome yellow building at the Kennedy bridge is the first thing you see if you enter Skibbereen from the west on N71, or the last as you leave town if you're heading in the opposite direction. Family and room-only rates are good value, especially if you're planning a long stay.

Ilen St., Skibbereen, County Cork. www.westcorkhotel.com. ✆ **028/21277.** 30 units. €110–€120 double. Rates include full breakfast. AE, MC, V. Closed Dec 22–28. **Amenities:** Restaurant; bar. *In room:* TV.

INEXPENSIVE

Fortview House ★★ With pristine country-style rooms, antique pine furniture, wood floors, iron and brass beds, and crisp Irish linens, this place is a treasure. Beamed ceilings and a warm color palette add to the comfortable feeling, and the spacious, inviting sitting room completes the welcome. Violet Connell's breakfasts are legendary, with seven varieties of fresh-squeezed juices jostling for space on a menu that includes hot potato cakes, pancakes, kippers, and smoked salmon. If you prefer self-catering, there are two three-bedroom cottages (each sleeps six) on the Fortview grounds that rent for €350 per week in low season, rising to €750 per week in midsummer.

On R591 from Durrus toward Goleen, Gurtyowen, Toormore, Goleen, County Cork. www.fortviewhousegoleen.com. ✆ **028/35324.** 5 units. €100 double. Rates include full breakfast. No credit cards. Closed Nov–Feb. *In room:* TV.

Glebe Country House ★ Built in 1690 as a rectory, Glebe House is now a gracious guesthouse. The charming rooms, each comfortable and individually decorated, have views of the rose and herb gardens that wreath the house (though not all have private bathrooms). The spacious dining room provides a lovely setting for candlelit five-course dinners partly drawn from the house's garden. Dinners cost €35; book before noon and bring your own wine. The enticing breakfast menu includes waffles, scrambled eggs with rosemary shortbread, and "cheesy French toast" (a Glebe House specialty).

The Coach House apartments behind the main house offer comfortable self-catering accommodations. The ground floor, two-bedroom garden apartment sleeps five in two rooms. The ideal choice for families is the one-bedroom loft apartment that sleeps five, with a double and single bed in one room and a pullout sofa in the living room. Both apartments have linens, and each has a private patio-garden.

Balinadee (off Balinadee center), Bandon, County Cork. www.glebecountryhouse.ie. ✆ **021/477-8294.** Fax 021/477-8456. 4 units, 2 self-catering units. €90–€110 double. Rates include service charge and full Irish breakfast. €325–€570 per week self-catering apts. MC, V. **Amenities:** Dining room.

The Heron's Cove ★ Locals on the Mizen Head peninsula know the Heron's Cove as a terrific seafood restaurant (see below), but it's really what the Irish call a restaurant with rooms, and a very inviting place to stay at that. Its three sea-view rooms, with balconies overlooking a beautiful, sheltered cove, are tremendously appealing. The rooms are simple but comfortable; the family room sleeps four and costs only marginally more than a double. The atmosphere of the entire B&B is so friendly, it's almost familial. Enjoying a wonderful dinner with wine over sunset and then heading upstairs to your room for a moonlit view of the harbor is relaxing indeed.

Signposted in the center of Goleen, County Cork. www.heronscove.com. ✆ **028/35225.** Fax 028/35422. 5 units. €60–€90 double. Rates include full breakfast. AE, MC, V. **Amenities:** Restaurant. *In room:* TV, hair dryer.

Rolf's Country House A long-established family-run guesthouse overlooking the harbor and the Mizen peninsula, Rolf's is an appealing complex of cut-stone buildings. All guests have access to the open self-catering kitchen, although it is unlikely to compete with Rolf's Cafe Art and Restaurant. The art on the walls is part of a rotating exhibit of contemporary Irish painting and sculpture. There are also a number of private little bungalows available.

Green Acres: Farmstays in County Cork

With hundreds of acres of sheep pastures and farm land, Cork is a great place to stay on a working farm. The group Farmhouse Holidays lists hundreds of farm B&Bs around the country—dozens in County Cork alone—that offer inexpensive guest rooms, great breakfasts, fresh air, and the chance to glimpse real farm life.

Prices are often below €100 for a double room, and the eggs you eat for breakfast will probably have been collected that morning from the farm's hens.

Search by county on Farmhouse Holidays' website (www.irishfarmholidays.com) to see a list and photos of available options.

.5km (⅓ mile) off R595, signposted just outside Baltimore center, Baltimore, County Cork. ✆ **028/20289.** www.rolfscountryhouse.eu. €80–€100 double; bungalows €250–€300 2- or 3-night stays, rising to €500–€700 per week. AE, MC, V. **Amenities:** Restaurant. *In room:* Full kitchen.

SELF-CATERING

Ahakista ★ Simplicity, charm, and an alluring location on the Sheep's Head Peninsula (the least touristy of Cork's three peninsulas) make this recently restored stone cottage a magnificent getaway. It's a short walk to the two-pub farming and fishing village of Ahakista. The old-fashioned cottage has low-slung ceilings and a traditional, narrow staircase as well as fine views of Dunmanus Bay. It's perfect for walkers, as it's surrounded by 97km (60 miles) of marked walking paths along the wild coastline. The two-bedroom cottage has one double bed and one twin bed, plus a washing machine, a dryer, and a dishwasher.

Contact Elegant Ireland at www.elegant.ie. ✆ **01/475-1632.** Fax 01/475-1012. 1 cottage. €730–€1,265 per week in high season; €605–€1,045 in low season. MC, V. *In room:* TV, full kitchen.

Anne's Grove Gatelodge ★★ What could be more romantic than a tiny Gothic castle just big enough for two? This is an enchanting place with a living room warmed by a fireplace, a well-equipped kitchen, one double bedroom, and a bathroom. There are hardwood floors throughout the lodge, and the furnishings are rustic and inviting. It was built in 1853 by the distinguished architect Benjamin Woodward (who designed parts of both Trinity College and Oxford University), It was conceived as a medieval castle in miniature. The architectural lines of the rooms—leaded windows, doorways, and ceilings—all echo the classic Gothic arch. There is perhaps no dreamier base from which to explore northwest Cork, and the price is downright unbeatable. One word of caution, though: The bedroom is accessed via a spiral staircase and so is unsuitable for people with limited mobility.

Castleownroach, County Cork. Contact the Irish Landmark Trust at www.irishlandmark.com. ✆ **01/670-4733.** Fax 01/670-4887. 1 unit. €270–€474 per weekend in low season, rising to €595–€630 per week in high season. AE, MC, V at booking. *In room:* Kitchen.

Galley Head Lightkeeper's House ★★ This lighthouse keeper's house stands next to the lighthouse on the tip of breathtaking Galley Head, just south of Clonakilty. It's actually two connecting houses, which can be rented separately or together. The first has a fully equipped kitchen, sitting room, and lounge (or bedroom) with bathroom downstairs, and two bedrooms (one double, one twin) and a bathroom upstairs. The second has the same basic floor plan, minus the downstairs lounge and bathroom. Both houses have sturdy mahogany furnishings, oversize sofas and armchairs, a fireplace in *every* room, plus a dishwasher and washing machine. Its location feels remote, yet is still only a 20-minute drive from bustling Clonakilty. One of the lighthouse's best assets is its caretaker, Gerald Butler. He grew up in this house and is a marvelous storyteller and history buff and can give you a private tour of the lighthouse.

Galley Head, County Cork. Contact the Irish Landmark Trust at www.irishlandmark.com. ✆ **01/670-4733.** Fax 01/670-4887. 2 units. €472–€600 per weekend in low season, rising to €896–€924 per week high season. AE, MC, V at booking. *In room:* Kitchen, no TV.

Where to Eat

EXPENSIVE

Blairs Cove ★★ INTERNATIONAL This romantic restaurant has it all: a stone-walled, high-ceilinged dining room, open fireplaces, and windows overlooking majestic Dunmanus Bay. Owners Philip and Sabine de Mey have converted an old stone barn into one of the best dining experiences in southwest Ireland. Don't look for cutting-edge, break-the-mold fusion; this place is all about classic dishes done in a familiar way, only better than you've probably had them elsewhere. In 2009, **Options Bistro** was opened in an adjoining conservatory. The menu is a kind of seasonal, pared-down version of what you'd expect in the main restaurant. **Rooms** are available for nightly B&B, costing €90 to €130 for a double, depending on the time of year (weekends are top rate, year-round). Apartments and cottages are available for rent, starting at around €415 per week, rising to around €1,265 for the cottage in July and August.

Barley Cove Rd., Durrus, County Cork. ✆ **027/62913.** www.blairscove.ie. Reservations required. Early-bird menus €30–€40; dinner with starter buffet €58. MC, V. Tues–Sat 7:15–9:30pm. Closed Nov to mid-Mar.

Casino House ★★ INTERNATIONAL The views of Courtmacsherry Bay from this lovely restaurant are exquisite, and the interior is charming—Nantucket meets Provence. The food is similarly fine; the menu changes with the seasons, but starters might include goats cheese roulade with beet-root and orange salad; cream of carrot soup served with caramelized walnuts; or *piquillo* stuffed with crab, crème fraiche, and wild rocket. Main dishes might include leg sirloin steak with Burgundy sauce; salmon filet with sweet potato rosti, rhubarb and vanilla beurre blanc, or chef Michael Relja's melt-in-your-mouth sole with spring onions and wild rice. The international wine list includes many good-value options from Germany and Italy. Casino House also has a small self-catering cottage, starting at €85 per night.

16km (10 miles) from Kinsale on coast road (R600), Coulmain Bay, Kilbrittain, County Cork. ✆ **023/884-9944.** www.casinohouse.ie. Reservations recommended. Main courses €19–€28. MC, V. Tues–Sun 7–9pm; Sun 1–3pm. Closed Jan to mid-Mar.

Chez Youen ★★ SEAFOOD Overlooking the marina of this picturesque harbor town, the style of Frenchman Youen Jacob's restaurant (part of the Waterfront Hotel) evokes his native Brittany—with beamed ceilings, candlelight, and an open copper fireplace. Lobster is the specialty here, fresh from local waters, but the seafood platter, overflowing with fresh prawns, crab (three kinds!), oysters, lobster, and *moules marinieres* is amazing to behold. A smattering of classic meat dishes (steaks, and occasionally lamb and duck) round off the small but well-judged menu, and there's an excellent wine list.

The Pier, Baltimore, County Cork. ✆ **028/20600.** www.waterfronthotel.ie. Reservations required. Fixed-price 3-course dinner €50; dinner main courses €26–€55. Shellfish platter €55. AE, DC, MC, V. Mar–Oct Tues–Sat 6–10pm, Sun noon–4pm; Nov–Feb Fri–Sat 6–10pm.

The Heron's Cove ★ SEAFOOD This is a regular port of call for locals, who know they can count on it for excellent dining free of formality. The casual, modest dining room has a splendid view of a secluded cove, while the menu focuses on local seafood, with selections for vegetarians and carnivores alike. Typical dishes include pan-fried monkfish with walnut mayonnaise, or Danmanus Bay scallops with smoked bacon cream sauce. The menu usually includes lobster in the summer. For dessert, indulge in the Russian cheesecake, the house specialty. The cellar of 50 to 60 international wines is open for browsing; feel free to discuss the wines with other diners.

Signposted in the center of Goleen, County Cork. ✆ **028/35225.** www.heronscove.com. Reservations recommended. Main courses €20–€30. AE, DC, MC, V. May–Oct daily noon–10pm.

The Mews ★ MODERN IRISH This delightful restaurant combines artsy chic with exceptional local cuisine. The dining room uses original modern art as a backdrop for excellent seafood (fish cakes are particularly good, as is the prawn and chorizo linguine) and dishes such as the rack of lamb, chicken supreme stuffed with goats cheese, or steak with roast tomatoes and onion marmalade. Come at sunset for the best atmosphere, as golden light streams through the conservatory windows.

The Mews, Baltimore, County Cork. ✆ **028/20020.** Reservations recommended. Main courses €20–€29. No credit cards. Wed–Mon 7–10pm.

MODERATE

Good Things Café ★★ 🎁 CAFE One of our favorite restaurants in Cork, this tiny, unpretentious, bare-bones bistro was awarded a Michelin *Bib Gourmand* in 2010. The secret of their success is very simple: simple, delicious dishes, prepared with the freshest local produce. Even an omelet or salmon in pastry can be extraordinary here. They even truck in Murphy's Ice Cream from County Kerry. If you love the food, you could enroll in one of the courses offered at their **cooking school.** These include the €140 "Dozen Quickies in a Day," demonstration-based guide to preparing 12 easy gourmet meals; the "Of Course I Made It Myself" weekend master class costing €200; the rather self-explanatory 2-day "Happy Vegetarian" for €200; and the intensive, 5½-day "Kitchen Miracle Programme" for €975.

Ahakista Rd., Durrus, County Cork. ✆ **027/61426.** www.thegoodthingscafe.com. Main courses lunch €6–€20, dinner €21–€28; lobster €38. MC, V. Wed–Mon 10:30am–5pm and 6:30–8:30pm.

Mary Ann's ★★ PUB GRUB Dating from 1844, this rustic pub perched halfway up a hill is decorated with ships' wheels, lanterns, and bells—but you don't go to Mary Ann's for the cute decor. You go for the superlative pub menu of fresh seafood salads and West Cork cheese plates, as well as more ambitious dishes, such as scallops meunière or sirloin steak with garlic butter. On sunny days, sit outside in the attractive courtyard.

Castletownshend, Skibbereen, County Cork. ✆ **028/36146.** Reservations recommended for dinner. Main dishes €15–€23. AE, MC, V. Daily 12:30–2pm and 6–9pm. Closed holidays.

9

COUNTY KERRY

With its softly rolling green fields, long, sweeping seascapes, and vibrant little towns, it's easy to see why so many visitors make a beeline for County Kerry. Charming villages like colorful Kenmare and bustling historic towns like Killarney seem as familiar as the Irish folk songs written about them. Craggy mountain ranges punctuated by peaceful green valleys are just what you hope for when you come to Ireland.

Kerry's tremendous popularity has been great for local businesses, but during the summer it can mean that the spectacular rural scenery fairly bursts at the seams with millions of tourists. In July and August, tour buses struggle to share narrow mountain roads with local traffic, and at the best vantage points, the view is often blocked by two or three of the behemoths; it's easy to feel like the whole place is on the verge of being overrun. Luckily, it's still easy to escape the crowds. If you're driving along the congested Ring of Kerry and the crowds are getting to you, simply turn off onto a small country lane and chances are you'll find yourself alone and in the peaceful Irish wilderness within seconds. In the high season in Kerry, taking the road less traveled can be the best way to go.

Of course, not everybody minds the inevitable clutter and cacophony of the tourism industry. Those who enjoy the conviviality of the international crowds can stay on the main roads and soak up all the hubbub. Only you can decide which Ireland you want to experience.

THE IVERAGH PENINSULA

Millions of tourists who come to County Kerry each year are dependent upon the turn of a bus driver's wheel for their tour of the Iveragh Peninsula—which means they see nothing save for the famed two-lane road known as the Ring of Kerry. There's certainly plenty to see there, but it's worth mentioning that the 178km (110-mile) road traces only the edges. In total, the peninsula is nearly 1,813 sq. km (700 sq. miles) of wild splendor, which you'll only see if you're able to get off the tourist strip. Admittedly, almost everyone who gets this far feels compelled to "do" the Ring of Kerry, so once it's done, why not take an unplanned turn, get a little lost, and let serendipity lead you to the county's unspoiled heart?

Essentials

GETTING THERE **Bus Éireann** (✆ **064/663-0011;** www.buseireann.ie) provides limited daily service from Killarney to Cahersiveen, Waterville, Kenmare, and other towns on the Ring of Kerry. The best way to get to the Ring is by car, on N70 and N71. Several Killarney-based tour companies offer daily sightseeing tours of the Ring (see the section entitled "Killarney," later in this chapter).

PREVIOUS PAGE: **Sheep along the Healy Pass in County Kerry.**

VISITOR INFORMATION Stop in at the **Killarney Tourist Office,** Aras Fáilte, at the Town Centre Car Park, Beech Road, Killarney (✆ **064/663-1633;** www.killarney.ie), before you explore the area. It's open October to May Monday to Saturday 9:15am to 5:15pm, June and September daily 9am to 6pm, and July to August daily 9am to 8pm. During low season, the office occasionally closes for lunch from 1 to 2pm. The **Kenmare Tourist Office,** Market Square, Kenmare (✆ **064/664-1233**), is open daily June through September from 9:15am to 5:30pm, with extended hours in July and August. The rest of the year (Oct–Easter), it's open Monday to Saturday. More information is available online at www.kerrytourist.com.

> **Irish Only**
>
> **Parts of Kerry are in the Gaeltacht—or Irish-language section of the country. In some sections, town names are in Irish only, so we'll include the Irish names as well as the English names for the places likely to be affected.**

The Ring of Kerry ★★★

Undoubtedly Ireland's most popular scenic drive, the Ring of Kerry is the name for the small highway that skirts the edges of the Iveragh Peninsula, passing along the way a panorama of rugged coastline, tall mountains, and pristine lakes. What you won't find, at least in the summertime, is much in the way of peace. Bicyclists avoid the route because of the scores of tour buses thundering down it from early morning until late in the day. Most people traveling the route start and finish at its largest hub, Killarney, but the town of Kenmare makes for a more charming (and certainly more quiet) base.

The lovely town of Kenmare makes a good base if you're in the region to explore Killarney National Park.

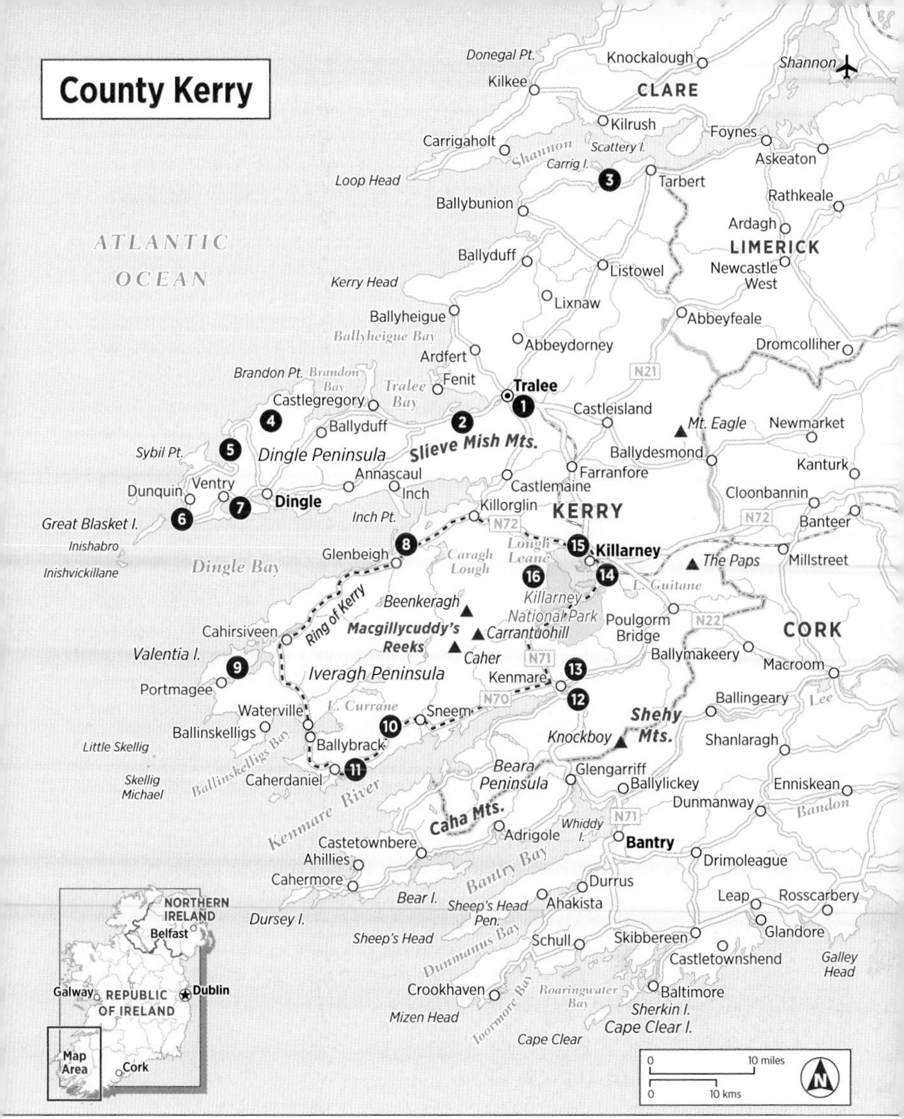

Blennerville Windmill **2**
Carrigafoyle Castle **3**
Derrynane House National Historical Park **11**
Eask Tower **7**
Gallarus Oratory **5**
Gap of Dunloe **16**
Ionad An Bhlascaoid Mhoir/ The Blasket Centre **6**
Kenmare Druid Circle **12**
Kerry Bog Village Museum **8**
Kerry County Museum **1**
Knockreer Estate **15**
Muckross House, Gardens, and Farms **14**
Seafari Eco-nature Cruises **13**
The Seanchaí: Kerry Literary & Cultural Centre **4**
The Skellig Experience **9**
Staigue Fort **10**

Beware of the GPS!

You can drive either way along the Ring of Kerry, but we recommend a **counter-clockwise** route for the most spectacular views. Drivers of very large vehicles also stick to this direction in order to avoid bottlenecks on the perilously narrow bends. This all worked fine for years—until modern technology intervened with the spread of GPS technology. Now some drivers unfamiliar with the route are being sent in a clockwise direction, thus causing all sorts of chaos, including some of the worst traffic jams ever seen on the Ring. These problems don't happen every day, but nonetheless, proceed with caution, and perhaps plan on taking a different route if you absolutely have to get somewhere on time.

Originally called Neidin (pronounced Nay-*deen,* meaning "little nest" in Irish), **Kenmare** is indeed a little nest of verdant foliage and colorful buildings nestled between the River Roughty and Kenmare Bay. It's an enchanting little place with flower boxes at every window, sparkling clean sidewalks, and lots of restaurants and plenty of places to stay.

From Kenmare to busy **Killarney,** the Ring road takes you through a scenic mountain stretch known as **Moll's Gap.** Killarney is best known for its glorious surroundings, in particular the spectacular landscapes of **Killarney National Park,** which includes the **Killarney Lakes** and the scenic **Gap of Dunloe.** The town itself, though, while colorful and bustling, is a victim of its own success. Tourism is more in-your-face here than perhaps anywhere else in Kerry, with generic leprechaun-laden souvenir shops and overpriced restaurants on every corner. So, to avoid becoming jaded, head out of town and get back on the road as quickly as possible. Along the way, you'll pass the lovely seaside town of **Portmagee,** which is connected by a bridge to leafy **Valentia Island.**

Departing Killarney, follow the signs for **Killorglin,** a smallish town that lights up in mid-August when it has a traditional horse, sheep, and cattle fair. It's officially called the **Puck Fair,** because local residents capture a wild goat (symbolizing the *puka* or *puki,* a mischievous sprite in Celtic legend) from the mountains and enthrone it in the center of town as a sign of unrestricted merrymaking. There's a whimsical statue of a goat by the river in honor of this town's love of the *puka.*

Continue on the N70, and glimpses of Dingle Bay will soon appear on your right. **Carrantuohill,** Ireland's tallest mountain at 1,041m (3,414 ft.), is to your left, and bleak views of open bog land constantly come into view.

The Ring winds around cliffs and the edges of mountains, with nothing but the sea below—another reason you will probably average only 50kmph (31 mph), at best. As you go along, you'll notice the remnants of many stone cottages dotting the fields along the way. Most date from the mid-19th-century Great Famine, when millions of people starved to death or were forced to emigrate. This area was hard hit, and the peninsula alone lost three-quarters of its population.

Glenbeigh is next on the Ring, and it's a sweet little seafront town with streets lined with palm trees and a sandy beach. It makes a good spot for a break, or you could continue along the sea's edge to **Cahersiveen,** where you can zip across to the little island of **Valentia.** In the 18th century, the Valentia harbor was notorious as a refuge for smugglers and privateers; it's said that John Paul

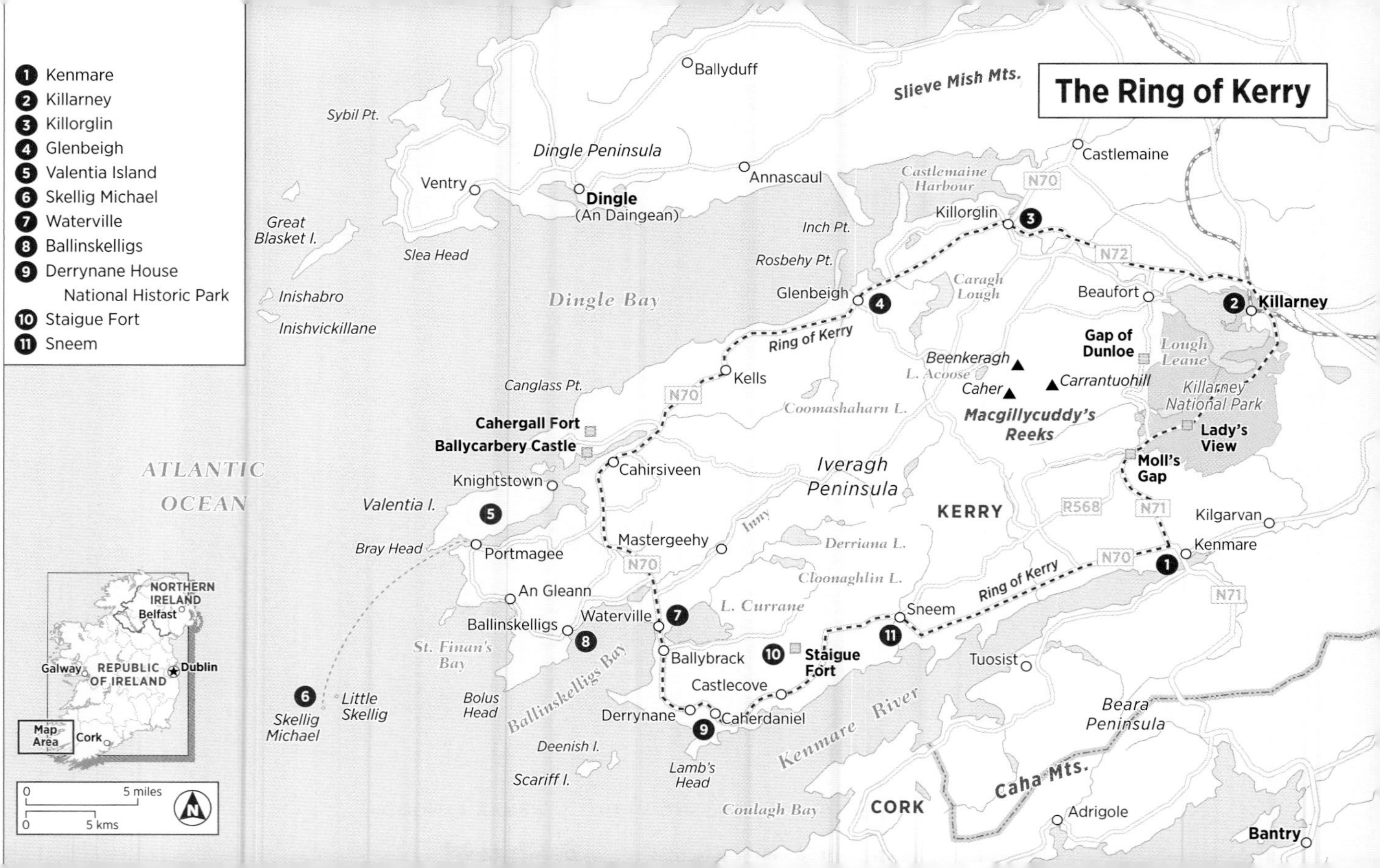
The Ring of Kerry
1 Kenmare
2 Killarney
3 Killorglin
4 Glenbeigh
5 Valentia Island
6 Skellig Michael
7 Waterville
8 Ballinskelligs
9 Derrynane House National Historic Park
10 Staigue Fort
11 Sneem
Ballyduff
Slieve Mish Mts.
Sybil Pt.
Dingle Peninsula
Castlemaine
Annascaul
Castlemaine Harbour
N70
Ventry
Dingle
(An Daingean)
Killorglin
Great Blasket I.
Inch Pt.
Slea Head
N72
Rosbehy Pt.
Caragh Lough
Beaufort
Glenbeigh
Inishabro
Dingle Bay
Killarney
Inishvickillane
Ring of Kerry
Gap of Dunloe
Lough Leane
Beenkeragh
L. Acoose
Kells
Carrantuohill
Canglass Pt.
Caher
Killarney National Park
Coomashaharn L.
Macgillycuddy's Reeks
Cahergall Fort
Lady's View
Ballycarbery Castle
Moll's Gap
ATLANTIC OCEAN
Cahirsiveen
Iveragh Peninsula
Knightstown
Valentia I.
KERRY
R568
N71
Kilgarvan
Inny
Bray Head
Mastergeehy
Derriana L.
Kenmare
Portmagee
Cloonaghlin L.
NORTHERN IRELAND
An Gleann
Belfast
L. Currane
Sneem
Waterville
Ballinskelligs
St. Finan's Bay
Ballybrack
Staigue Fort
Tuosist
Galway
REPUBLIC OF IRELAND
Dublin
Ballinskelligs Bay
Castlecove
Little Skellig
Bolus Head
Kenmare River
Beara Peninsula
Derrynane
Caherdaniel
Skellig Michael
Map Area
Cork
Deenish I.
Lamb's Head
Scariff I.
Caha Mts.
Coulagh Bay
CORK
Adrigole
0 5 miles
0 5 kms
N
Bantry

> **What's the Frequency, Kerry?**
>
> **In 1866, Valentia Island became the first place in Europe to have a permanent telegraph link with North America, via an undersea cable. A true feat of 19th-century engineering, the cable was used for precisely 100 years. You can still see the old receiving station (although it's just a shell) at the aptly named Telegraph Field, on the cliffs above Foilhomurrum Bay. A short distance away, a simple, black marble monument stands in muted commemoration of Ireland's role in bringing the world closer together.**

Jones, the Scottish-born American naval officer in the War of Independence, also anchored here quite often.

From Valentia you can hop a ferry to arguably the most magical site of the Ring of Kerry, an island just off its shore: **Skellig Michael,** a rocky pinnacle towering over the sea, where medieval monks built a monastery in exquisite isolation. Today, the ruins of their church, reached by way of rambling stone staircases up the sides of cliffs at the edge of the cobalt sea, still convey a sense of deep spirituality. Seabirds nest here in abundance, and more than 20,000 pairs of gannets inhabit neighboring **Little Skellig** during the summer nesting season. The crossing to the island can be rough, so you'll want to visit on as clear and calm a day as possible.

Head next for **Waterville,** an idyllic beach resort located between Lough Currane and Ballinskelligs Bay. For years it was a favorite retreat of Charlie Chaplin, and there's a statue of him near the beach.

If you follow the sea road north of town to the Irish-speaking village of **Ballinskelligs,** you'll see where the medieval monastery is slowly rotting away. There's a sandy Blue Flag beach just past the post office by Ballinskelligs Bay, and at the end of the beach are the remnants of a 16th-century castle.

Continuing on the N70, the next point of interest is **Derrynane,** at **Caherdaniel.** Derrynane is the former seat of the O'Connell clan and erstwhile home to Daniel O'Connell ("the Liberator" who freed Irish Catholics from the last of the English Penal Laws in the 19th century).

From there, watch for signs to **Staigue Fort,** about 3km (2 miles) off the main road. This well-preserved ancient stone fort is constructed of rough stones without mortar of any kind. The walls are 4m (13 ft.) thick at the base. Historians are not certain what purpose it served—it may have been a fortress, or just a kind of prehistoric community center—but experts think it probably dates from around 1000 B.C.

Sneem, the next village on the circuit, is a colorful little hamlet, where houses are painted in vibrant shades. The colors—blue, pink, yellow, and orange—burst out on a rainy day, like a little touch of the Mediterranean.

From here, you're no distance at all from your starting point, and you've made your way around the Ring.

SEEING THE SIGHTS

Derrynane House National Historic Park ★ On a comfortable estate along the Ring of Kerry coast between Waterville and Caherdaniel, this manor house was once the seat of the O'Connells and is where Ireland's Great Liberator, Daniel O'Connell, lived for most of his life. The Irish government maintains the house as a museum, filled with documents, illustrations, and memorabilia related to O'Connell's life. Some pieces are more interesting than others—take, for example, the chariot in which he traveled triumphantly through Dublin after his release from prison in 1844.

Caherdaniel, County Kerry. ✆ **066/947-5113.** Admission €3 adults; €2.10 seniors; €1 students and children; €8 families. Apr and Oct–Nov Wed–Sun and bank holidays 10:30am–5pm; May–Sept daily 10:30am–6pm. Last admission 45 min. before closing.

Kenmare Druid Circle ★ On a small hill near the central town market, this large Bronze Age druid stone circle is magnificently intact, with 15 standing stones arranged around a central boulder, which still bears signs (circular holes, a shallow dent at the center) of having been used in ceremonies. To find it, walk down to the market square and follow signs on the left side of the road. There's

EXPLORING THE mysterious SKELLIG ISLANDS

Craggy, inhospitable islands rising precipitously from the tumultuous sea, the **Skelligs ★★★** look extraordinary, holding onto the earth where gray skies meet stormy horizons about 14km (8⅔ miles) off the coast of the Iveragh Peninsula. Seen from the mainland, the islands appear impossibly steep and sharp angled. They must have seemed even more formidable in the 6th and 7th centuries, when simply getting to the islands would have been a dangerous prospect, and yet not only did a small community of devout monks build a community there, but they built it on the steepest, most wind-battered peaks of all. Over the course of many years, they carved 600 steps into the cliff face. Gradually they built monastic buildings amid the rocks hundreds of feet above the churning sea.

There is something tragic and beautiful about the remains of the ancient oratories and beehive cells, the largest of which is about 4×4m (13×13 ft.). Historians know very little about these monks and how they lived, although they were apparently influenced by the Coptic Church founded by St. Anthony in Egypt, and, like the saint, sought intense isolation. Records relating to the Skelligs indicate that, even here, all but completely hidden, the Vikings found the monastery, and punished it as they did all the Irish monastic settlements. Monks were kidnapped and killed in attacks in the 8th century, but the settlement always recovered. To this day, nobody knows why the monks finally abandoned the rock in the 12th century.

The passage to the islands by boat takes about 45 minutes, while the ascent up the steps is also time-consuming and only for the fit. The crossing cannot take place in bad weather, so you're strongly advised to call ahead if skies are gray.

Ferries from Valentia Island are run by **Des Lavelle** (✆ **087/237-1017** or 066/947-6124; http://indigo.ie/~lavelles), while those from Portmagee are run by **O'Keefe's** (✆ **066/947-7103**). The average cost is around €40 per person. There are also "unofficial" ways of reaching the islands (although they're very much at your own risk). For a negotiated fee, you can almost always find a fisherman who's willing to take you over, wait, and then bring you back. The crossing will be rougher, but certainly more adventurous.

no visitor center, and no admission fee; it's just sitting in a small paddock, passed by the sleepy traffic of everyday life.

Kenmare, County Kerry. Free admission (donation box).

Kerry Bog Village Museum This little cluster of thatched-roof cottages effectively demonstrates what life was like in Kerry in the early 1800s. The museum village has a blacksmith's forge and house, turf cutter's house, laborer's cottage, thatcher's dwelling, and tradesman's house. Stacks of cut turf are piled high by the road.

Ring of Kerry rd. (N71), Ballycleave, Glenbeigh, County Kerry. ✆ **066/976-9184.** www.kerrybogvillage.ie. Admission €6 adults; €5 seniors and students; €4 children. AE, DC, MC, V. Daily 8:30am–6pm.

Seafari Eco-nature Cruises and Seal-Watching Trips ☺ This is a good option for families who want to interest their kids in Kenmare Bay—aboard a 15m (49-ft.) covered boat. The 2-hour cruise covers 16km (10 miles) and is narrated by guides well versed in local history and wildlife, including dolphins, sea otters, and gray seals who frolic nearby. Boats depart from the pier next to the Kenmare suspension bridge. The family ticket includes coffee, tea, cookies, orange juice for the kids, and a drink of rum for the adults. From May to October, as many as four cruises may depart daily, depending on demand. Reservations are recommended.

Kenmare Pier, Kenmare, County Kerry. ✆ **064/664-2059.** www.seafariireland.com. Tickets €20 adults; €18 students; €15 children 12–18; €13 children 11 and under; €60 families with children 12 and under.

The Skellig Experience Just off the Ring of Kerry route (R765) on Valentia Island, this well-designed information center blends right into the terrain, its stark stone facade framed by grassy mounds based on the design of ancient archaeological sites. A series of displays tell the story of the lives of the monks

It's said that you haven't seen Ireland until you've stood amid the ruined monastic settlement atop Skellig Michael.

who once existed in near total isolation on Skellig Rocks, Skellig Michael, and Little Skellig. There's a section on the geology of the area and an informative bit on the seabirds that are now the islands' main inhabitants. Finally, you can take a (pricey) boat tour around the islands.

Skellig Heritage Centre, Valentia Island, County Kerry. ✆ **066/947-6306.** www.skellig experience.com. Exhibition and audiovisual €5 adults; €4 seniors and students; €3 children 11 and under; €14 families (2 adults, up to 2 children). Exhibition, audiovisual, and sea cruise €28 adults; €25 seniors and students; €15 children 11 and under; €8 additional child 13 and up; €72 families. Exhibition and minicruise of harbor (does not include Skellig Islands) €22 adults; €20 seniors and students; €11 children 11 and under; €7 child 12 and up; €60 families. May–June and Sept daily 10am–6pm; July–Aug daily 10am–7pm; Mar–Apr and Oct–Nov Mon–Fri 10am–5pm.

The beehive huts atop Skellig Michael, where 6th-century Christian monks lived, worked, and prayed in severe isolation from the mainland.

SHOPPING

Many good craft and souvenir shops lie along the Ring of Kerry, but those in **Kenmare** offer the most in terms of variety and quality. Kenmare shops are open year-round, usually Monday to Saturday 9am to 6pm. From May to September, many shops remain open until 9 or 10pm, and some open on Sunday from noon to 5 or 6pm.

Avoca Handweavers at Moll's Gap High on a mountain pass (288m/945 ft. above sea level) between Killarney and Kenmare, this isolated shop is an outpost of the famed County Wicklow weavers. As in all Avoca shops, the stock here features colorful, hand-woven blankets and throws, delicate knitted clothing, and pottery and jewelry in vivid colors. The excellent cafe makes a great place to stop for lunch or afternoon tea and cake. Closed from November to mid-March. Ring of Kerry rd. (N71), Moll's Gap, County Kerry. ✆ **064/663-4720.**

De Barra Jewellery Having taken over the family jewelry business a couple of years ago, talented young jeweler Shane de Barra has put his own stamp on things in this small, elegant shop on Kenmare's Main Street. His freshwater-pearl concoctions in silver or gold and his restrained beautiful touch on gold rings and bangles mark this place as special. Best of all, prices are reasonable. Main St., Kenmare, County Kerry. ✆ **064/664-1867.**

Kenmare Bookshop This shop specializes in books on Ireland—biographies and books by Irish writers, as well as maps and guides to the surrounding area. This is a good place for hikers to find survey maps and walking and specialist guides, and for sailors to track down marine charts. Shelbourne St., Kenmare, County Kerry. ✆ **064/664-1578.**

Quills Woolen Market This shop has two locations, both of which are good for chunky Aran hand knits, traditional Donegal tweed jackets, delicate Irish linen, Celtic jewelry, and hand-loomed knitwear. Market Sq. and Main St., Kenmare, County Kerry. ✆ **064/664-1078.** Also at South Sq., Sneem, County Kerry. ✆ **064/664-5277.**

With its brightly painted houses and shops, Sneem is worth a stop if you're exploring the Ring of Kerry.

SPORTS & OUTDOOR PURSUITS

GOLF **Waterville Golf Links,** Waterville (✆ **066/947-4102;** www.watervillegolflinks.ie), sits at the edge of the Atlantic. On huge sand dunes, bounded on three sides by the sea, this 18-hole championship course is one of the longest in Ireland (7,184 yards). Visitors are welcome. Greens fees start at €180 daily, cheaper for early birds.

Other challenging 18-hole courses on the Ring include **Dooks Golf Club,** Glenbeigh (✆ **066/976-8205;** www.dooks.com), a links par-70 course on the Ring of Kerry road, with greens fees of €85 (good discounts are available by booking online); and the expanded **Kenmare Golf Club,** Kenmare (✆ **064/664-1291;** www.kenmaregolfclub.com), a parkland par-71 course where greens fees run €40 weekdays, €45 weekends.

WALKING The low, long-distance path, the **Kerry Way,** traverses the extraordinary scenery of the Ring of Kerry. The first stage, from Killarney National Park to Glenbeigh, travels inland over rolling hills and past pastoral scenes. The second stage circles the Iveragh Peninsula via the towns of Cahersiveen, Waterville, Caherdaniel, Sneem, and Kenmare with a farther inland walk along the old Kenmare Road back to Killarney, for a total of 202km (125 miles). The route consists primarily of paths and "green roads" (old, unused roads built as make-work famine relief projects and now converted into walking paths). Maps outlining the route are available from the Killarney and Kenmare tourist offices (some are free, though the better ones cost a couple of euros), while good walking guides are available from bookstores in the area. For more information see **www.kerryway.net**.

WHERE TO STAY

Very Expensive

Park Hotel Kenmare ★★★ In a palm-filled garden beside Kenmare Bay, this imposing 19th-century building was originally built by the Great Southern Railway for first-class train travelers. Some things never change, and it's still a grand, luxury hotel for travelers. Fires crackle in the open fireplaces and original oil paintings decorate the walls. There's a set of armor at the top of the grand staircase surrounded by tapestries. Guest rooms have exquisite Georgian and Victorian furnishings, all beds have firm mattresses, rich fabrics, and peaceful waterfront or mountain views. The hotel restaurant has a romantic perspective, and is acclaimed for its modern Irish cuisine. The spa, **Sámas,** is famed for its creative use of the bucolic setting to induce relaxation. Activities run the gamut from lawn croquet to golf, tennis to salmon fishing. Obviously, none of this comes cheap, but then you expected that.

Kenmare, County Kerry. www.parkkenmare.com. ✆ **800/323-5463** in the U.S., or 064/664-1200. Fax 064/664-1402. 46 units. €350–€550 double; €846 suite. AE, DC, MC, V. Closed Nov 30–Dec 22 and Jan 4–Feb 12. **Amenities:** Restaurant; bar; babysitting; concierge; 18-hole golf course; room service; smoke-free rooms; tennis court. *In room:* TV, CD player, hair dryer, minibar.

Sheen Falls Lodge ★★★ Originally the 18th-century home of the Earl of Kerry, this salubrious resort sits beside a natural waterfall amid vast, sprawling grounds filled with smooth lawns and lush gardens. Guests enjoy horseback riding and private salmon fishing, among other activities. The lounges are decorated in lemony tones, with polished woodwork, open fireplaces, and original oil paintings. Staff members address guests by name, the bar feels like a drawing room, and the 1,000-volume library, with its green leather sofas and floor-to-ceiling bookshelves, is like an old-fashioned gentlemen's club. Guest rooms are spacious, decorated in rich, contemporary style; each overlooks the falls (stunning when floodlit at night) or the bay. There are also some self-catering cottages and villas available for those with deep pockets and a desire for privacy. It comes at a price, but this is the perfect Irish country-house atmosphere: elegant and yet relaxed.

Kenmare, County Kerry. www.sheenfallslodge.ie. ✆ **800/537-8483** in the U.S., or 064/664-1600. Fax 064/664-1386. 66 units. €420–€564 double; €636–€1,830 suite. Full breakfast €17–€24. AE, DC, MC, V. Closed Jan 2–Feb 1. **Amenities:** 2 restaurants; bar; concierge; gym; Jacuzzi; indoor pool; room service; spa; tennis. *In room:* A/C, TV/DVD, radio, hair dryer, minibar.

Moderate

Derrynane Hotel ★ Perched on a precipice between the mountainous coast and the open waters of the Atlantic, this contemporary hotel boasts one of the Ring's most dramatic and remote locations, next to the Derrynane National Park and midway between Waterville and Sneem. The guest rooms are basic (small, but well-organized, with the TV mounted on the wall), but you might forgive them for that once you take in the superb views. (Although, inevitably, rooms with sea views are more expensive.) There are a few amenities, including an outdoor swimming pool, should the weather be accommodating enough for a swim. You can book a local guide to take you on weekend walking trips. Well-equipped self-catering accommodations are also available year-round. Older travelers looking for an all-included deal may want to check out the Derrynane's Golden Breaks package, which is tailored for the over-55s with up to a week's full board at a discount.

Off Ring of Kerry rd. (N71), Caherdaniel, County Kerry. www.derrynane.com. ✆ **800/528-1234** or 066/947-5136. Fax 066/947-5160. 70 units. €70–€160 double. Rates include service charge and full Irish breakfast. 3-bedroom holiday cottages per 7 nights July–Sept €550–€1,600; Oct–Dec €450–€550; Christmas and New Year weeks €750. AE, DC, MC, V. Closed early Oct to Apr. **Amenities:** Restaurant; lounge. *In room:* TV.

Kenmare Bay Hotel & Resort ☺ This modern hotel on a hillside at the edge of Kenmare has sweeping views of the surrounding countryside. A major renovation and expansion a few years back spruced the place up considerably, and guest rooms are now sleek, with neutral paint and linens, and nicely modernized bathrooms. A cluster of self-catering cottages around the central building offers more options for travelers (check the website for bargains for these—recent offers have included a better-than-half-price deal). The hotel is exceptionally family friendly;

facilities for children range from a DVD corner in the restaurant, where kids can be deposited during dinner, to a full-fledged holiday camp program (check out the resort website for details). Those without children, however, may find it a bit too kid-centric. The Kenmare is also popular with tour groups, making it best suited to guests who value or need convenience more than peace and character. Sneem rd., Kenmare, County Kerry. www.kenmarebayhotel.com. ✆ **800/618-5343** in the U.S., or 064/667-9300. Fax 064/664-1541. 127 units. €130–€150 double. Rates include service charge and full breakfast. AE, DC, MC, V. Closed Nov–Mar. **Amenities:** Restaurant; bar; gym. *In room:* TV.

Sallyport House ★★ This country-house B&B has many things going for it—a great location, a 2-minute walk into Kenmare, and its extensive manicured grounds. It's a handsome manor with a sophisticated, luxurious feel. The spacious guest rooms are furnished with well-chosen antiques and have grand bathrooms. The rooms are made even more desirable by their gorgeous views of the surrounding countryside.

Glengarriff rd., Kenmare, County Kerry. www.sallyporthouse.com. ✆ **064/664-2066.** Fax 064/42067. 5 units. €100–€170 double. Rates include service charge and full breakfast. No credit cards. No children 11 and under. **Amenities:** Lounge. *In room:* TV, hair dryer.

Shelburne Lodge ★★ This Georgian farmhouse has been transformed into one of the most original, stylish, and comfortable B&Bs in Killowen. Every room has polished wood parquet floors, quality antique furnishings, contemporary art, and a luxurious but homey feel. The guest rooms are all large and gorgeously appointed, and breakfasts are virtually decadent.

Killowen, Cork Rd., Kenmare, County Kerry. www.shelburnelodge.com. ✆ **064/664-1013.** Fax 064/664-2067. 9 units. €100–€160 double. Rates include service charge and full breakfast. MC, V. Closed Dec–Feb. **Amenities:** Tennis court. *In room:* TV.

Tahilla Cove ★ This grand country house sprawls along the edge of the water in a secluded cove near Sneem. Owned by the same family for decades, this is a house of great character. The vast wooded acreage around the building gives it a feeling of seclusion, and the friendly Waterhouse family runs the place with unpretentious affability. The spacious bedrooms are comfortably and simply furnished and have private balconies, some with great views of Beara Peninsula (ask for a room with a sea view). You can borrow one of the boats and row out into the water, or go for a walk with the family's energetic spaniels—or bring your own dog! This is a dog-friendly hotel. **Dinners** here are like house parties, and are well worth staying for.

On the N70, follow signs, Sneem, County Kerry. www.tahillacove.com. ✆ **064/664-5204.** Fax 064/664-5104. 9 units. €80–€150 double. Discount for 5 nights. Rates include service charge and full breakfast. AE, MC, V. Closed Nov–Mar. **Amenities:** Wi-Fi. *In room:* TV, hair dryer, tea/coffeemaker.

SELF-CATERING

Iskeroon ★★ 🎁 In an arrestingly beautiful natural setting overlooking the sailboats of Derrynane Harbour and the Skelligs, this is a breathtaking place. Inside, the 1930s villa has been beautifully renovated, with flagstone floors and a deep blue palette, decorated with locally made furniture and tasteful art. There are plenty of extras, including in-room iPod docking stations and DVD players with a vast library of films. Until recently this was a full-fledged B&B; now the operation has been scaled back, although you're given a plentiful breakfast hamper on arrival. The self-catering apartments inside have their own kitchens, which may be a little on the small side, but have all you need. If you want even more independence, there two separate self-catering apartments in a converted coach house.

Bunavalla (near pier), Caherdaniel, County Kerry. www.iskeroon.com. ✆ **066/947-5119.** 2 units, both with private bathroom. €120 double (3-night minimum). Studio apts €480–€520 (1 week minimum). Rates include service charge and breakfast hamper (main house apts only). MC, V. Closed Nov–Feb. **Amenities:** Lounge, Wi-Fi (apts). *In room:* TV/DVD, iPod station.

WHERE TO EAT

Expensive

D'Arcy's Oyster Bar and Grill ★ CONTINENTAL In a two-story stone house at the top end of Kenmare, this restaurant has a homey atmosphere with a big open fireplace. The house specialty is Irish oysters, but there are plenty of other seafood options. The homemade breads and desserts are also excellent. Seven well-appointed guest rooms are upstairs, for those who fall in love with the place (€140 double).

Main St., Kenmare, County Kerry. ✆ **064/644-1589.** www.darcys.ie. Reservations recommended. Oysters €12 per half-dozen; main courses €18–€30. MC, V. Oyster bar daily noon–10pm. Grill daily 6–9:30pm. Closed Jan to mid-Mar.

Lime Tree ★★ MODERN IRISH Innovative cuisine is the focus at this Kenmare restaurant in an 1821 landmark renovated schoolhouse next to the Park Hotel. Paintings by local artists line the stone walls in the atmospheric dining room. The menu offers modern interpretations of classic Irish dishes and European cuisine; mains could include beef filet with colcannon and peppercorn *jus,* or roasted cod with couscous and sun-dried tomato dressing. Typical desserts include homemade praline ice cream and warm crepes with butterscotch sauce.

Shelbourne Rd., Kenmare, County Kerry. ✆ **064/664-1225.** www.limetreerestaurant.com. Reservations recommended. Main courses €19–€28. MC, V. Apr–Nov daily 6:30–10pm.

Mulcahy's MODERN/FUSION A good example of why Kenmare has become one of Ireland's foodie towns, Mulcahy's is dedicated to imaginative fusion cooking. Starters might include anything from pea soup to sushi, and Asian influences come to bear on Irish dishes like the Kerry lamb with pistachio crust. Everything is done imaginatively, with a bit of restraint.

16 Henry St., Kenmare, County Kerry. ✆ **064/664-2383.** Reservations recommended. Main courses €18–€30. MC, V. June–Sept daily 6–10pm, Sun noon–3pm; Oct–May Thurs–Mon 6:15–10pm. Closed 2 weeks in Nov.

Moderate

The Blue Bull TRADITIONAL IRISH Sneem is so small that if you blink, you miss it. Yet it has several good pubs, and this one serves excellent food. There are three small rooms, each with an open fireplace, plus a sky-lit conservatory in the back. Time-honored Irish fare, like smoked salmon and Irish stew, shares the menu with such dishes as salmon stuffed with spinach and Valencia scallops in brandy—all served to a backdrop of traditional Irish music on most nights. According to the pub's owners, the Blue Bull also holds the dubious honor of being Andrew Lloyd Webber's favorite place to eat in Ireland.

South Sq., Ring of Kerry rd. (N70), Sneem, County Kerry. ✆ **064/664-5382.** Reservations recommended. Main courses €10–€26. AE, MC, V. Bar food daily 11am–8pm. Restaurant Mar–Oct daily 6–10pm.

A quiet beach along the Ring of Kerry.

Packie's MODERN IRISH If you're looking for a stylish place to have a great meal that won't break the bank, this is it. There's always a buzz here, and the smart crowd fits in perfectly with the bistro look—colorful window boxes, slate floors, and stone walls filled with contemporary art. Everyone comes for the food: tried-and-true favorites such as Irish lamb stew, crisp potato pancakes, seafood sausages, and crab claws in garlic butter. Desserts are terrific, too.

Henry St., Kenmare, County Kerry. ✆ **064/664-1508.** Reservations recommended. Main courses €15–€30. MC, V. Mid-Mar to Dec Tues–Sat 6–10pm (also Mon 6–10pm in summer).

Inexpensive

Prego ★ ITALIAN When you're craving a break from all that heavy Irish food, head here for fresh, tasty Italian cuisine. The pasta is all homemade, and served with a light touch on the sauce. Salads are big and crisp, and the thin-crust pizzas are all made to order from scratch. All the classics are here and are well made.

18 Henry St., Kenmare, County Kerry. ✆ **064/664-2350.** All items €7–€16. MC, V. Daily 9am–10:30pm.

Purple Heather ★ IRISH This lovely little eatery is *the* place to lunch in Kenmare. The food consists of tearoom classics with a gourmet twist—wild smoked salmon or prawn salad, smoked trout pâté, vegetarian omelets, Irish cheese platters, and fresh homemade soups.

Henry St., Kenmare, County Kerry. ✆ **064/664-1016.** All items €6–€19. V. Mon–Sat 11am–5:30pm. Closed Sun, Christmas week, and bank holidays.

KILLARNEY

135km (84 miles) SW of Shannon, 309km (192 miles) SW of Dublin, 87km (54 miles) W of Cork, 111km (69 miles) SW of Limerick, 193km (120 miles) SW of Galway

Perhaps the busiest tourist hub in rural Ireland, Killarney's sidewalks are spacious enough in the winter, but in the summertime, they're absolutely packed, as the streets become one giant tour-bus traffic jam and horse-and-buggy drivers risk life and limb to push their way through. The locals are well practiced at

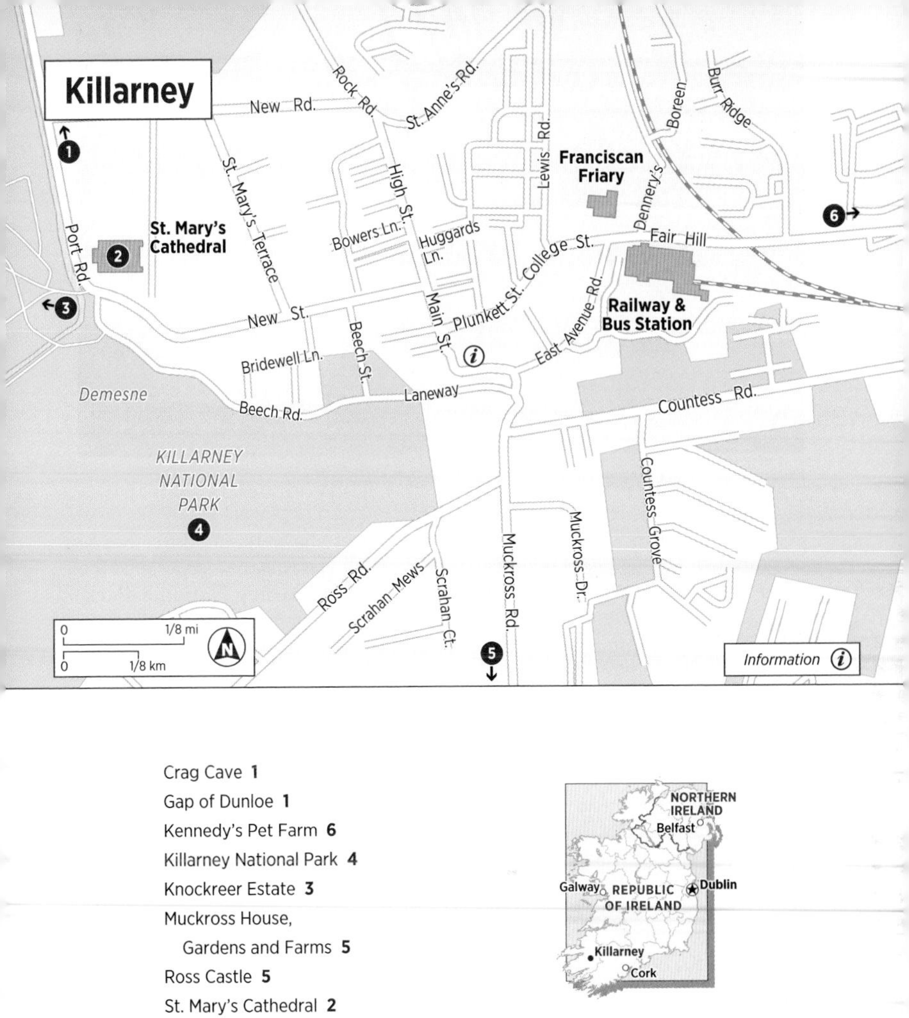

dispensing a professional brand of Irish charm, even as they hike up the hotel and restaurant prices to capitalize on the hordes descending from the buses. It all feels a bit cynical, with a few too many cheesy leprechaun-heavy gift shops for its own good. It's a bit much for some people, and hardly the bucolic, gentle Ireland that many are looking for. Luckily, it's easy enough to resist Killarney's gravitational pull and spend your time exploring the quieter countryside around it. You can always sneak into town from time to time for dinner or a night out in the pub with lots of people from your home nation.

Ironically, Killarney's popularity has little to do with the town itself; the attraction is the valley in which it nestles—a verdant landscape of lakes and mountains so spectacular that author and playwright Brendan Behan once said, "Even an ad man would be ashamed to eulogize it." Exploring its glories is

Killarney Lakes make for a placid and scenic boat ride in the national park.

certainly easy—just walk (or drive) from the town parking lot toward the cathedral and turn left. In a matter of minutes, you'll forget all that Killarney stress amid the quiet rural splendor of the 65-sq.-km (25-sq.-mile) **Killarney National Park.** Here the ground is a soft carpet of moss and the air is fragrant with wildflowers. Cars are banned from most of the ferny trails, so take a hike or hire a "jarvey," an old-fashioned horse-and-buggy available for hire at reasonable prices. Within the park's limits are two estates, **Muckross** and **Knockreer,** and the romantic remains of medieval abbeys and castles. At almost every turn, you'll see Killarney's own botanical wonder, the arbutus, or "strawberry tree," plus eucalyptus, redwoods, and native oak.

For many, the main attractions are the park's three lakes. The largest of these, the Lower Lake, is sometimes called Lough Leane or Lough Lein, which means "the lake of learning." It's more than 6km (3¾ miles) long and is dotted with 30 small islands. Nearby are the Middle Lake or Muckross Lake, and the smallest of the three, the Upper Lake. The most noteworthy of Killarney's islands, **Innisfallen,** seems to float peacefully in the Lower Lake. You can allegedly reach it by rowboat, available for rental at Ross Castle, but on our recent visits, the boathouse was unmanned all day, and trying to figure out just who was responsible for the boats proved impossible, so don't count on it. If you can get a boat and row yourself out, you'll find what's left of the monastery St. Fallen, which was founded in the 7th century and flourished for 1,000 years. It's said that Brian Boru, the great Irish chieftain, and St. Brendan the Navigator were educated here. From 950 to 1320, the *Annals of Innisfallen,* a chronicle of early Irish history, was written at the monastery; it's now in the Bodleian Library at Oxford University. Traces of an 11th-century church and a 12th-century priory can still be seen today.

Essentials

GETTING THERE **Aer Arann** (✆ **011/353-81821-0210** in the U.S., 818/210-210 in Ireland, or 0800/587-23-24 in the U.K.; www.aerarann.ie) offers regular flights from Dublin into Kerry County Airport, Farranfore, County Kerry (✆ **066/976-4644;** www.kerryairport.ie), about 16km (10 miles) north of Killarney. **Ryanair** (✆ **0818/303-030;** www.ryanair.com) flies direct from London (Luton or Stansted) to Kerry.

Irish Rail trains from Dublin, Limerick, Cork, and Galway arrive daily at the **Killarney Railway Station** (✆ **064/663-1067;** www.irishrail.ie), Railway Road, off East Avenue Road.

Bus Éireann operates regularly scheduled service into Killarney from all parts of Ireland. The bus depot (✆ **064/663-0011;** www.buseireann.ie) is adjacent to the train station at Railway Road, off East Avenue Road.

Kerry folk like to say that all roads lead to Killarney, and at least a half-dozen major national roads do. They include N21 and N23 from Limerick, N22 from Tralee, N22 from Cork, N72 from Mallow, and N70 from the Ring of Kerry and West Cork.

VISITOR INFORMATION The **Killarney Tourist Office,** Aras Fáilte, is at the town center on Beech Road (✆ **064/663-1633**). It's open October to May Monday to Saturday 9:15am to 5:15pm, June and September daily 9am to 6pm, and July to August daily 9am to 8pm. During low season, the office occasionally closes for lunch from 1 to 2pm. It offers many helpful booklets, including the *Tourist Trail* walking-tour guide and the *Killarney Area Guide,* with maps.

Useful local publications include ***Where: Killarney,*** a quarterly magazine distributed free at hotels and guesthouses. It is packed with current information on tours, activities, events, and entertainment.

TOWN LAYOUT Killarney is small, with a full-time population of about 7,000. The town is built around one central thoroughfare, Main Street, which, mercurially, changes its name to High Street at midpoint. The principal offshoots of Main Street are Plunkett Street, which becomes College Street, and New Street. The Deenagh River edges the western side of town and East Avenue Road edges the eastern side.

The busiest section of town is at the southern tip of Main Street, where it meets East Avenue Road. Here the road curves and heads southward out to the Muckross road and the entrance to Killarney National Park.

GETTING AROUND Killarney Town is so small and compact that there is no local bus service; the best way to get around is on foot. For a quick and easy tour, follow the signposted Tourist Trail for the highlights of the main streets. It takes less than 2 hours to complete. Pick up a booklet outlining the sights along the trail at the tourist office.

Taxi cabs line up at the rank on **College Square** (✆ **064/663-1331**). You can also phone for a taxi from **Killarney Cabs** (✆ **064/663-7444**), **Dave's Taxis** (✆ **087/679-8899**), or **Euro Taxis** (✆ **064/663-7676**).

There are a couple of large public parking lots near the town center, where parking costs upward of around €1.50 per hour. It's a good idea to leave your car in one of these unless you're heading out to Killarney National Park on the Muckross and Kenmare road (N71).

If you need to rent a car in Killarney, contact **Budget,** c/o International Hotel, Kenmare Place (✆ **064/663-4341;** www.budget.ie), and at Kerry Airport (✆ **066/976-3199;** www.budget.ie); or **Randles Bros.,** Muckross Road (✆ **064/663-1237**). **Avis** also has a branch at Kerry Airport (✆ **01/605-7500;** www.avis.ie), and at Shannon Airport (✆ **061/715-600;** www.avis.ie); and **Hertz** has branches at Cork Airport (✆ **021/496-5849;** www.hertz.ie) and Shannon Airport (✆ **061/471-369;** www.hertz.ie).

From Kenmare, the route through the Gap of Dunloe takes you past headspinning streams and ravines to the Upper Lake.

Horse-drawn **buggies,** called "jarveys," line up at Kenmare Place in Killarney Town. They offer rides to Killarney National Park sites and other scenic areas. Prices range from around €15 to upward of €50 per ride (up to four people), depending on the time and how far you go. For details, see "Organized Tours," below.

FAST FACTS If you need a drugstore, try **O'Sullivans Pharmacy,** 81 New St. (✆ **064/663-5886**), or **Donal Sheahan,** 34 Main St. (✆ **064/663-1113**).

In an emergency, dial ✆ **999.** The Killarney District Community Hospital is on St. Margaret's Road (✆ 064/663-1076). The Killarney Garda (Police) Station is on New Road (✆ 064/667-1160).

The **Killarney Public Library,** on Rock Road (✆ **064/663-2655**), provides Internet access from its bank of computers.

If you need to do your laundry, head for **Gleesons Launderette and Dry Cleaners,** Brewery Lane, off College Square (✆ **064/663-3877**).

The **Killarney Post Office,** New Street (✆ **064/663-1461**), is open Monday and Wednesday to Friday 9am to 5:30pm, Tuesday 9:30am to 5:30pm, and Saturday 9am to 1pm.

Seeing the Sights

THE TOP ATTRACTIONS

You can access **Killarney National Park ★★** (✆ **064/31947;** www.killarneynationalpark.ie) from several points along the Kenmare road (N71). The main entrance is at Muckross House, where the little visitor center is a good source for walking or driving maps and information on what to expect. There's also a pleasant cafe with indoor and outdoor seating if you need sustenance before setting out. Admission is free, and it's open all daylight hours year-round.

Just outside of town, the winding, rocky **Gap of Dunloe ★★** rises through mountains and wetlands about 10km (6¼ miles) west of Killarney. The route through the gap passes craggy hills, meandering streams, and deep gullies, and it ends in the park at Upper Lake. One of the best ways to explore the gap is by bicycle (see "Bicycling," under "Sports & Outdoor Pursuits," later in this chapter). Horse fanciers may want to take one of the excursions offered by **Corcoran's Tours,** 8 College St. (✆ **064/663-6666;** www.corcorantours.com), or

Dero's Tours, 22 Main St. (✆ **064/663-1251** or 663-1567; www.derostours.com). Combination horse/boat tours cost around €20 to €30 per person. If you'd rather have someone else handle the horse, you can take an 11km (6¾-mile) buggy tour. Excursions go from Kate Kearney's Cottage through the Gap of Dunloe to Lord Brandon's Cottage and back.

Knockreer Estate ★ The grand old house that once stood here burned down years ago, but the gardens are lovely, and 200-year-old trees mix with sweet wildflowers and azaleas for an attractive effect. There are beautiful views of the lake and the valley, and a pathway leads down to the River Deenagh. Main access to Knockreer is through Deenagh Lodge Gate, opposite the cathedral, in town.

Cathedral Place, off New St., Killarney, County Kerry. ✆ **064/663-1633.** Free admission to gardens. Daily dawn–dusk.

Muckross House and Gardens ★★ This rambling ivy-covered Victorian mansion was built for a wealthy landowner in 1843 and donated to the state in the 1930s. It is now a museum of sorts, of life in the county, showcasing locally made furniture, prints, art, and needlework, although it mixes them with non-Irish items like Oriental screens, Chippendale chairs, and Turkish carpets. But never mind, it's all an attractive international mixture and pleasant enough to explore. The gardens outside are lovely, and you can wander to the on-site restaurant and workshops, where local artisans demonstrate bookbinding, weaving, and pottery.

The ruin of the 15th-century **Muckross Abbey,** founded about 1448 and burned by Cromwell's troops in 1652, is also near the house. The abbey's central feature is a vaulted cloister around a courtyard that contains a huge yew tree, said to be as old as the abbey itself. W. M. Thackeray once called it "the prettiest little bijou of a ruined abbey ever seen."

Kenmare rd. (N71), Killarney, County Kerry. ✆ **064/667-0144.** www.muckross-house.ie. Admission house only €7 adults; €5.50 seniors; €3 students and children; €18 families. Combination ticket with Muckross Traditional Farms (below) €12 adults; €10 seniors; €6 students and children; €30 families. Daily July–Aug 9am–7pm, Sept–June 9am–5:30pm.

Muckross Traditional Farms ★★ ☺ Not far from the Muckross House estate, these farms are designed to demonstrate what traditional farm life was like in previous centuries in County Kerry. It's cleverly done—the farmhouses and barns are so authentically detailed that you feel as if you've dropped in on real farms. Work really does go on here, so farmhands work the fields, while the blacksmith, carpenter, and wheelwright ply their trades. Women draw water from the wells and cook meals in historically accurate kitchens. Children get a kick out of the animals, and it's interesting enough to keep adults from getting bored as well. ***Note:*** A combination ticket allows you to visit Muckross House for a small extra fee.

Kenmare rd. (N71), Killarney, County Kerry. ✆ **064/663-1440.** www.muckross-house.ie. Admission €7.50 adults; €6 seniors; €4 students and children; €20 families. Combination ticket with Muckross House and Gardens (above) €12 adults; €10 seniors; €6 students and children; €30 families. Apr and Sept–Oct Sat–Sun 1–6pm; May daily 1–6pm; June–Aug daily 10am–6pm; bank holidays 1–6pm.

Ross Castle ★ Just outside of Killarney Town, this 15th-century fortress still guards the edge of the Lower Lake. Built by the O'Donoghue chieftains, the castle was the last stronghold in Munster to surrender to Cromwell's forces in 1652. But it could not withstand time as well as the English army, and all that remains is a tower house, surrounded by a fortified *bawn* (walled garden) with

FOUR hikes IN KILLARNEY NATIONAL PARK

Within the park's 10,000-hectare (25,000-acre) limits are forest trails, bogs, moorland, landscaped gardens, four mountains, three major lakes, and two historic estates. It's also teeming with rare plants and wildlife. Venture into the woods and you'll be walking through the last natural habitat of the Irish red deer, and if you're very lucky, you might even see a white-tailed eagle, extinct in these parts for nearly 200 years until they were reintroduced in 2007. ***Note:*** Detailed maps for this and the other trails listed below are available at the visitor center at Muckross House. The following four trails are among our favorites:

- **Blue Pool Nature Trail.** This trail starts behind the Muckross Park Hotel and winds for an easy 2.4km (1.5 miles) along a path of coniferous woodland beside a small lake. The trail is named for the lake's unusually deep blue-green color, which is caused by copper deposits in the soil.
- **Cloghereen Nature Trail.** This is a wonderful idea. Incorporated into a small section of the Blue Pool trail (see above), this walk is fully accessible to blind visitors. A guide rope leads you along the route, which is lined by plants identified by scent and touch. An audio guide can be obtained from Muckross House for a small deposit.
- **Mossy Woods Nature Trail.** One of the park's gentler trails, this route starts from Muckross Lake and is just under 2km (1.3 miles) long. The moss-covered trees and rocks it passes are a major habitat for bird life. You'll also see several strawberry trees (arbutus) along the route, which is something of a botanical mystery. They're commonplace around these parts, but found almost nowhere else in Ireland, nor, indeed, the rest of Northern Europe. The route passes some incredible views of Torc Mountains and the memorably named MacGillycuddy's Reeks (p. 365).
- **Kerry Way.** Serious hikers might be interested in the Kerry Way, a long-distance trail that roughly follows the Ring of Kerry. The entire route is 202km (125 miles) long; detailed maps are available from the Killarney and Kenmare tourist offices. For more information on the route, see **www.kerryway.net**.

rounded turrets. The tower has been furnished in the style of the late 16th and early 17th centuries. While you can wander the grounds at will, you can only see inside the castle on a guided tour, and these tend to be a bit tedious, as the guides seem to scrounge around a bit for facts interesting enough to justify the ticket price. In good weather, the best way to reach it is via a lakeside walk (it's 3km/2 miles from Killarney to the castle). From the castle, you can take a boat tour of the lake, although these may irritate those allergic to touristy things.

Ross Rd., off Kenmare rd. (N71), Killarney, County Kerry. ✆ **064/663-5851.** Admission €6 adults; €4 seniors; €2 students and children; €14 family. Mid-Mar to late Oct daily 9:30am–5:45pm. Last admission 45 min. before closing. Closed late Oct to mid-Mar.

St. Mary's Cathedral Officially known as the Catholic Church of St. Mary of the Assumption, this limestone cathedral is designed in the Gothic Revival style, in the shape of a cross. Construction began in 1842, was interrupted by

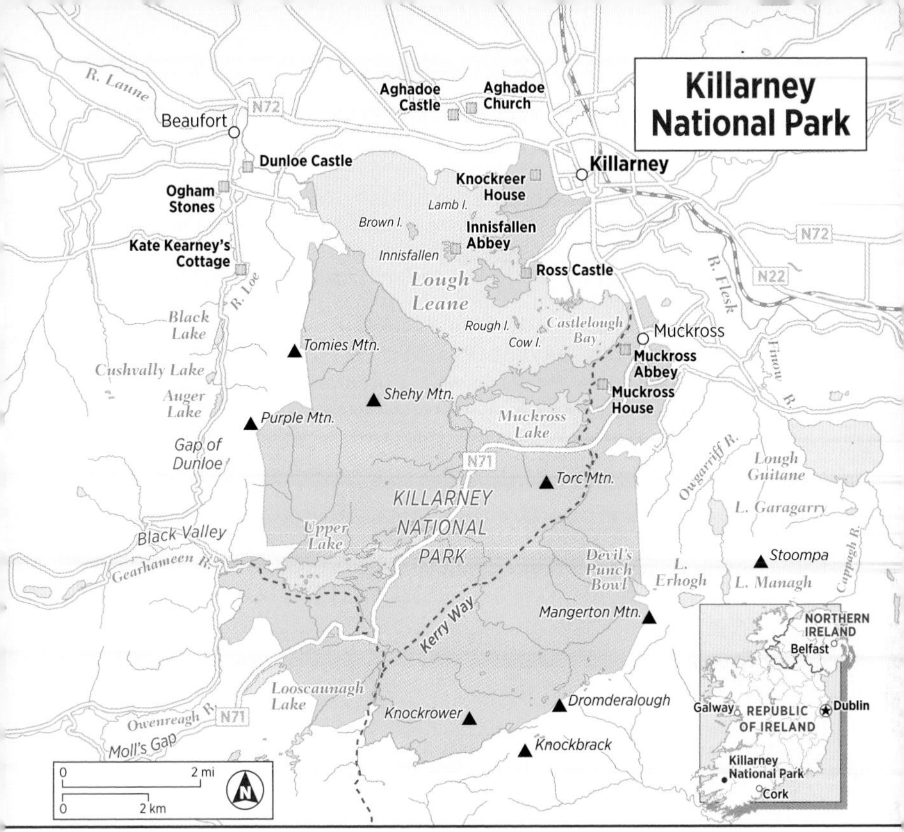

the famine, and concluded in 1855, although the towering spire wasn't added until 1912.

Cathedral Place, off Port Rd., Killarney, County Kerry. ✆ **064/663-1014.** Free admission; donations welcome. Daily 10:30am–6pm.

MORE ATTRACTIONS

Crag Cave ★ Although they are believed to be more than a million years old, these limestone caves were not discovered until 1983. Today, they're open for the wandering (via guided tour only, of course). The guides accompany you 3,753m (12,310 ft.) into the well-lit cave passage on a half-hour tour revealing massive stalactites and fascinating caverns. If you simply can't do without a souvenir fix, even here there's a crafts shop. There are also a children's play area (endearingly called **"Crazy Cave"**) and a cafe. It's very touristy, but interesting nonetheless.

Off Limerick rd. (N21), 24km (15 miles) from Killarney, Castleisland, County Kerry. ✆ **066/714-1244.** www.cragcave.com. Admission €12 adults; €9 seniors and students; €5 children; €30 families (2 adults, 2 children), €35 (2 adults, 4 children). "Crazy Cave" play area €8 for 2 hr. (children only). Mar–Dec daily 10am–6pm (until 6:30pm July–Aug); Jan–Feb Wed–Sun 10am–6pm.

Kennedy's Pet Farm ☺ At this 30-hectare (74-acre) dairy and sheep farm surrounded by mountain vistas, kids can watch cows being milked, piglets being fed, and peacocks strutting their stuff. Horse-drawn machinery is on display, and it's all good rural fun.

9.7km (6 miles) east of Killarney, off the main Cork rd. (N22), Glenflesk, Killarney, County Kerry. ✆ **064/775-4054.** www.killarneypetfarm.com. Admission €8. Price includes pony ride for children. Feb–Oct daily 10am–5pm.

ORGANIZED TOURS

In addition to Killarney's main sights, some bus tours also venture into the two prime scenic areas nearby: the Ring of Kerry and Dingle Peninsula. From May to September, tours are offered daily; prices range from around €20 to €30 per person. This list is far from exhaustive, but the following companies take tours outside Killarney: **Bus Éireann,** Bus Depot, Railway Road, off East Avenue Road (✆ **064/663-0011;** www.buseireann.ie); **Corcoran's Chauffeur Tours,** 8 College St. (✆ **064/663-6666;** www.corcorantours.com); and **Dero's Tours,** 22 Main St. (✆ **064/663-1251** or 663-1567; www.derostours.com). Both of the latter two also run 3-hour primer tours of Killarney and the area, including Muckross House, Ross Castle, the Killarney Lakes, the Gap of Dunloe and Torc Waterfall. It's not nearly enough time to see everything properly, but it's an easy option if all you want are the highlights. Both tours cost around €20, although when we last checked Dero's was slightly cheaper. Dero's also offer a daylong trip to the Gap of Dunloe, which can be upgraded to include a boat ride for €30, or a boat and jarvey ride for €50.

Bus Tours

In addition to the above, you might try this company for day trips to the Gap of Dunloe:

Gap of Dunloe Tours This tour takes you through the spectacularly scenic Gap of Dunloe. Starting with a bus trip from Killarney center, you can then choose either to walk the 11km (7 miles) from Kate Kearney's Cottage to Lord Brandon's Cottage (where you have lunch), or to travel by horse-drawn "jarvey." The day ends with a boat trip on the Killarney Lakes to Ross Castle. This is a good option for those who want a guided tour with a degree of freedom, but bear in mind that the price only covers the basic transport by bus and boat. You pay extra for a jaunting cart ride (€20 per person) and for lunch. In all, the tour lasts about 6 hours.

Tours depart from O'Connor's Pub, 7 High St., Killarney, County Kerry (or hotel pickup by arrangement). Tour can also be taken in reverse, starting at Ross Castle. ✆ **064/663-0200.** www.gapofdunloetours.com. Tour €30. Mar–Oct; call or reserve online.

Buggy Tours

The quaint horse-driven buggies known as "jaunting carts" or "jarveys" that constantly clip-clop down the lanes around the lakes are one of the most persistent and charming features of the Killarney landscape. If you decide to give them a try, note that jaunting-cart rates are set and monitored by the Killarney Urban District Council, so if you're quoted a price that seems outlandish, pass on by and try the next one. Current rates (per person, based on four people to a jaunting cart) run roughly from around €15 for a basic tour, or €20 for a tour including lake cruise, up to €80 for a 2-hour tour of the Muckross Estate, Lower Lake, and the Abbey. The buggies are arguably the best way to get around the national park, since cars are not allowed. The price depends on the destinations, which include Ross Castle, Muckross House and Gardens, Torc Waterfall, Muckross Abbey, Dinis Island, and Kate Kearney's Cottage, gateway to the Gap of Dunloe. You can hire a buggy at the park near Muckross House, or to arrange a tour in advance, contact **Killarney Jaunting Cars,** 10B Muckross Close, Killarney (✆ **064/663-3358;** www.killarneyjauntingcars.com).

Boat Tours

MV Lily of Killarney Tours Departing from the pier at Ross Castle, this enclosed water bus cruises the lakes for just over an hour. Make reservations. Old Weir Lodge, Muckross Rd., Killarney, County Kerry. ✆ **064/663-1068.** Tour €10 adults; €5 children 11 and under; €25 families. Apr–Oct daily 10:30am, noon, 1:45, 3:15, 4:30 and 5:45pm.

MV Pride of the Lakes Tours This enclosed boat offers daily sailings from the pier at Ross Castle. The trip lasts just over an hour, and reservations are suggested. Scotts Gardens, Killarney, County Kerry. ✆ **064/662-7737.** www.killarneylaketours.ie. Tour €10 adults; €5 children 11 and under; €25 families. Apr–Oct daily 11am, 12:30, 2:30, 4, and 5pm.

Shopping

Shopping hours are usually Monday to Saturday 9am to 6pm, but from May through September or October, most stores are open every day until 9 or 10pm. Although there are more souvenir and craft shops than you can shake a shillelagh at, here are a few of the best:

Christy's Irish Stores A branch of the highly successful County Cork–based enterprise, this large store on the corner of Plunkett Street in the center of town carries an array of wares ranging from cheesy leprechaun souvenirs to genuinely attractive hand-knit or hand-loomed sweaters, crystal, china, and pottery. Prices are reasonable. 10 Main St., Killarney, County Kerry. ✆ **064/663-3222.** www.christysirishstores.com.

Frank Lewis Gallery This gallery sells contemporary and traditional paintings, sculptures, and photographic work—much of it with a Kerry theme—by emerging artists. It's in a restored artisan's dwelling near the post office. 6 Bridewell Lane, Killarney, County Kerry. ✆ **064/663-1108.** www.franklewisgallery.com.

Killarney Art Gallery This shop-front gallery features original paintings by leading Irish artists from the Killarney area and elsewhere, as well as art supplies, Irish prints, and engravings. 4 Plunkett St., Killarney, County Kerry. ✆ **064/663-4628.** www.irishartcollector.com.

Killarney Bookshop Shop here for books on the history, legends, and lore of Killarney and Kerry. It also has a good stock of maps and other books of Irish and international interest. 32 Main St., Killarney, County Kerry. ✆ **064/663-4108.** www.killarneybookshop.ie.

Mucros Craft Centre On the grounds of Muckross House, this art studio and shop carries on local craft traditions in its weaver's workshop and pottery studio. There is also a wide selection of quality crafts from all over the country. Muckross House, Muckross Rd., Killarney, County Kerry. ✆ **064/663-1440.** www.muckross-house.ie.

Quill's Woollen Market This is one of the best spots in town for hand-knit sweaters of all colors and types, along with mohair and sheepskins. As well as this shop, there are branches in Sneem and Kenmare on the Ring of Kerry, in Cork City, and at Ballingeary, County Cork (the original shop). 1 High St., Killarney, County Kerry. ✆ **064/663-2277.**

Serendipity The shelves of this tidy shop feature a wide range of unusual crafts from local artisans, such as hand-thrown pottery from the likes of Nicholas

Mosse and Stephen Pearce, Jerpoint glass, and handcrafted jewelry. 15 College St., Killarney, County Kerry. ✆ **064/663-1056.**

Sports & Outdoor Pursuits

BICYCLING **Killarney National Park,** with its lakeside and forest pathways, trails, and roads, is a paradise for bikers. If you haven't brought your own wheels, you can rent whatever you need here, from 21-speed touring bikes to mountain bikes to tandems. Rental charges average around €15 per day, €80 per week. Bicycles can be rented from **David O'Sullivan's Cycles,** Lower New Street (✆ **064/663-1282;** www.killarneyrentabike.com). There are also smaller branches at the Outdoor Store, New Street and at the Beech Road Car Park; all can be reached on the same number. Most shops are open year-round daily from 9am to 6pm, until 8 or 9pm in the summer.

One great ride beginning in Killarney takes you through the Gap of Dunloe along a dirt forest road, where you'll see some of the best mountain scenery in the area. It can be made into a 56km (35-mile) loop if you return on N71. Ask at the bike rental store or the tourism office for more information.

FISHING Fishing for salmon and brown trout in Killarney's unpolluted lakes and rivers is a popular pastime around here. Brown-trout fishing is free on the lakes, but a permit is necessary for the rivers Flesk and Laune. A trout permit costs €8 to €15 per day.

Salmon fishing anywhere in Ireland requires a license; the cost is around €30 per day, €45 for 21 days. In addition, some rivers also require a salmon permit, which costs €10 to €15 per day.

Permits, tackle, bait, rod rental, and other fishing gear can be obtained from **O'Neill's,** 6 Plunkett St. (✆ **064/663-1970**). The shop also arranges the hire of boats and *ghillies* (fishing guides) for around €50 to €80 per day on the Killarney Lakes, leaving from Ross Castle.

GOLF Visitors are always welcome at the twin 18-hole championship courses of the **Killarney Golf & Fishing Club,** Killorglin Road, Fossa (✆ **064/663-1034;** www.killarney-golf.com), 5km (3 miles) west of the town center. Widely praised as one of the most scenic golf settings in the world, these courses, known as Killeen and Mahony's Point, have gorgeous lake and mountain settings. Greens fees are €70 to €130, depending on the course, and they don't increase on the weekend.

HORSEBACK RIDING Many trails in the Killarney area are suitable for horseback riding. Hiring a horse costs about €35 per hour at **Killarney Riding Stables,** N72, Ballydowney (✆ **064/663-1686;** www.killarney-trail-riding.com), and **Rocklands Stables,** Rockfield, Tralee Road (✆ **064/663-2592**). Lessons and weeklong trail rides can also be arranged.

WALKING There are four signposted nature trails in the **Killarney National Park.** The **Mossy Woods Nature Trail** starts near Muckross House, by Muckross Lake, and rambles 2.4km (1.5 miles) through yew woods along low cliffs. The **Old Boat House Nature Trail** begins at the 19th-century boathouse below Muckross Gardens and leads .8km (.5 mile) around a small peninsula by Muckross Lake. **Arthur Young's Walk** (4.8km/3 miles) starts on the road to Dinis, traverses natural yew woods, and then follows a 200-year-old road on the Muckross Peninsula. The **Blue Pool Nature**

MacGillycuddy's Reeks

This marvelously named range of mountains just west of Killarney is beautiful to look at—they were formed of red sandstone that was gradually shaved down by glaciers until they reached the gentle shape they hold today. The name, though, is a bit baffling. It turns out the mountains were named after an ancient clan that once predominated in this area—the Mac Gilla Machudas. The word "reek" is an old Irish term for a peaked hill. So these are the mountains of the Mac Gilla Machudas, just in case you were wondering.

Trail (2.4km/1.5 miles) travels from Muckross village through woodlands and past a small peaceful lake known as the Blue Pool. Maps of the four trails are available at the park's visitor center. In addition, the **Cloghereen Nature Trail** is a small section of the Blue Pool trail that's designed to be fully accessible to blind visitors. A guide rope leads you along the route, which is lined by plants identified by scent and touch. An audio guide can be obtained from Muckross House for a small deposit.

Rising steeply from the south shore of Muckross Lake, **Torc Mountain** provides spectacular views of the Killarney Lakes and nearby **MacGillycuddy's Reeks,** a moody mountain range. Start at the **Torc Waterfall** parking lot, about 6km (3¾ miles) south of Killarney, and follow the trail to the top of the falls. At a T-intersection, turn left toward the top parking lot, and almost immediately turn right on the Old Kenmare Road, which follows a small stream along the south slopes of Torc Mountain. After leaving the woods, you will see Torc Mountain on your right. Look for a crescent-shaped gouge in the side of the road, about 9m (30 ft.) across, with a small cairn at its far edge. This is the beginning of the path to the ridge top, marked somewhat erratically by cairns along the way. Return the way you came; the whole trip is just under 10km (6.2 miles), takes about 4 hours, and is moderately difficult.

If you prefer a little guidance, you could choose a guided walking tour of some length (from 1 day to a weekend to a full week). A number of walks and walking holidays of varying lengths are offered by **SouthWestWalks Ireland Ltd.,** 40 The Anchorage, Tralee, County Kerry (✆ **066/712-8733;** www.southwestwalksireland.com). Or you can arrange in advance to meet up with the **Wayfarers,** an international organization of passionate pedestrians, who schedule 5-week-long footloose circuits of the Ring of Kerry each spring, summer, and fall. To receive a schedule, contact the **Wayfarers,** 174 Bellevue Ave., Newport, RI 02840 (✆ **800/249-4620;** www.thewayfarers.com).

For long-distance walkers, the 202km (125-mile) **Kerry Way** is a signposted walking route that extends from Killarney around the Ring of Kerry (see "Four Hikes in Killarney National Park" and "Sports & Outdoor Pursuits," earlier in this chapter).

Spectator Sports

GAELIC GAMES The people of Killarney are passionately devoted to the national sports of hurling and Gaelic football, and games are played almost every Sunday afternoon during the summer at **Fitzgerald Stadium,** Lewis Road

(✆ **064/663-1700;** www.gaa.ie). For complete details, consult the local *Kerryman* newspaper or the Killarney Tourist Office.

HORSE RACING Killarney has two annual horse-racing meets, in early May and mid-July. Each event lasts for 3 or 4 days and draws large crowds. For more information, contact the **Killarney Racecourse,** Fossa (✆ **064/663-1125**), or the tourist office.

Where to Stay

EXPENSIVE

Aghadoe Heights Hotel & Spa ★★ A few miles outside of town, and with spectacular views of the Lower Lake, Aghadoe Heights is a jarringly modern structure sitting rudely by an ancient ruined church, but inside it's a five-star oasis of luxury. Rooms are spacious and calming in neutral tones, and they have big, orthopedic beds. Many rooms have breathtaking views of the lake and surrounding hills through floor-to-ceiling, wall-to-wall windows. The excellent **spa** is available at the push of a button. Guests can book a relaxing hour in the many steam rooms and saunas for €25. Breakfast is silver service, and the in-house **restaurant** specializes in modern Irish cuisine. You also can snack on a burger in the bar overlooking the lake. The hotel's Mercedes shuttle bus will take you into central Killarney for free.

Lakes of Killarney, Killarney, County Kerry. www.aghadoeheights.com. ✆ **064/663-1766.** Fax 064/663-1345. 74 units. €180–€220 double; €250–€560 suite. Rates include full breakfast. MC, V. Free parking. **Amenities:** Restaurant; bar; gym; Internet room; indoor pool; full-service spa. *In room:* TV/DVD, hair dryer, minibar.

Hotel Europe ★★ Part of the same group that operates the Dunloe Castle, this modern, five-story hotel has a picturesque setting right on the shores of the Lower Lake, adjacent to Killarney's two 18-hole championship golf courses and surrounded by mountain peaks. Tennis, boating, fishing, and horseback riding help round out the amenities. Views from lakeside rooms are spectacular, and most

Old-world gentility and a 21st-century spa afford the best of both worlds to guests at the Park Hotel Kenmare.

ENJOYING SPA life, IRISH STYLE

Times may be harder than they have been in recent years, economically speaking, but Ireland still has more than its share of top-rated spas. Nowhere is this truer than in County Kerry. In this region the best spas use exquisite natural settings to spectacular effect, and borrow their treatments from the Irish countryside. Everything from Irish spring water to Irish peat mud and Irish river stones can be used to coax forth beauty from tired, work-dulled skin and hair.

At the **Sámas spa** in the Park Hotel Kenmare (p. 350), which has won awards for its unique design, you can soak in the warm spa pool while gazing out over the mountains nearby. Spend an hour relaxing in the thermal suite (rock sauna, ice fountain, tropical mist shower), before moving on to your facial, wrap, or massage. The spa is for residents only, although they sometimes make exceptions when it's not too busy.

All guests at the **Aghadoe Heights Hotel & Spa** (above) outside Killarney are welcome to spend an hour in its exquisite thermal suite for a fairly small fee. With the wide array of steam rooms, saunas, tropical showers, cooling rooms, and hot tubs, it is a luxuriant 60 minutes. Once you're fully relaxed, you might sample one of the spa's numerous massages or facials, using Aveda products.

The spa at the **Sheen Falls Lodge** (p. 351) in Kenmare features a pool shaped like a flower—each petal forming a kind of private relaxation space. You can have a hot stone massage or facial and then float off in total relaxation.

The spa at the **Killarney Park Hotel** (below) is a modern, peaceful oasis, with a soothing pool and such exotic treatments as the 3-hour Absolute Spa Ritual for €270 in which you are rubbed with coconut before being wrapped in a milk-and-lavender essence and then massaged. It's purported to cure jet lag.

rooms have private balconies. A full-service spa, which opened in 2009, overlooks the sunken garden. Check the website for good package deals and special offers.

Off Killorglin rd., Fossa, Killarney, County Kerry. www.theeurope.com. ✆ **800/221-1074** in the U.S., or 064/667-1300. 206 units. €220–€290 double; €450 suite. Rates include full breakfast. V. Free parking. Closed Nov to mid-Mar. **Amenities:** 2 restaurants; bar; lounge; babysitting; gym; indoor pool; sauna; tennis. *In room:* TV, hair dryer.

Killarney Park Hotel ★★ With a handsome yellow neo-Georgian facade, this elegant four-story property is on the eastern edge of town near the tourist office. Public rooms are spacious and evoke a distinguished Victorian country house, with oil paintings, wainscot paneling, open fireplaces, and a sunlit conservatory-style lounge, as well as a high-end **spa.** The guest rooms have a traditional, conservative style, with quality provincial furnishings, designer fabrics, and marble-finished bathrooms. The restaurant is widely viewed as one of the best (and most expensive) in town. Breakfast is silver service, so come here for the true formal hotel experience.

Kenmare Place, Killarney, County Kerry. www.killarneyparkhotel.ie. ✆ **064/663-5555.** Fax 064/35266. 72 units. €220–€290 double. Rates include full breakfast. AE, DC, MC, V. **Amenities:** Restaurant; bar; babysitting; concierge; gym; Jacuzzi; indoor pool; room service; sauna/steam room; spa. *In room:* TV, hair dryer, minibar.

Muckross Park Hotel ★★ Deep in the Killarney National Park, this hotel cleverly mixes new and old architecture. In the process of incorporating a much older structure into the modern building, a lovely space is created. Its history does stretch back—Queen Victoria once lunched here, and George Bernard Shaw spent a summer here writing *Pygmalion*. Recently awarded five-star status, the hotel is furnished in country-house style, with wood-paneled walls, open fireplaces, and oil paintings in the public areas, and stone walls and low ceilings in the restaurant and bar. Rooms, which vary in size, are done in creamy colors with luxurious fabrics and some four-poster and half-tester beds. The latest addition is the extraordinary **Cloisters Spa,** beautifully designed with arched marble ceilings, a stunning pool, lots of space, and a peaceful ambience.

Muckross village, N71, Killarney, County Kerry. www.muckrosspark.com. ✆ **064/662-3400.** Fax 064/663-1965. 70 units. €200 double; €300 suites. Rates include full breakfast. AE, DC, MC, V. Free parking. Closed Nov–Feb. **Amenities:** Restaurant; bar; lounge; pool; full-service spa. *In room:* TV, hair dryer.

MODERATE

Earls Court House A 5-minute walk from the town center, Earls Court is the kind of genteel place where guests are greeted with tea and scones. The spacious guest rooms are tastefully furnished with Irish antiques, and have a distinct Victorian flair. Some have half-tester beds (with canopy covering just the head half of the bed), others king-size beds and sitting areas, and nearly all have private balconies—the second-floor rooms, in particular, have clear mountain views. Also available are reasonably priced suites (the four-poster suites have Jacuzzi baths) and wheelchair accessible rooms. The breakfast menu has a range of selections, from apple crepes to kippers and tomatoes.

Signposted off N71, Woodlawn Junction, Muckross Rd., Killarney, County Kerry. www.killarney-earlscourt.ie. ✆ **064/663-4009.** Fax 064/663-4366. 24 units. €100–€130 double; €130–€155 suite. Rates include service charge and full Irish breakfast. MC, V. Free parking. Closed Nov 6–Feb 5. **Amenities:** Room service. *In room:* TV, radio, hair dryer, broadband Internet, U.S. power sockets (some rooms).

Fairview House ★ Somewhere between boutique hotel and upmarket guesthouse, Fairview House is an airy, modern kind of place in the center of town. Rooms are spacious and comfortable, with polished wood floors, subtle cream and red colors, and enormous beds. Some rooms have Jacuzzi baths. There are also good-size family rooms as well as wheelchair-accessible rooms. The **restaurant** earns good reviews, as its head chef came from the late, lamented Cooperage, which was widely rated as one of the best restaurants in Killarney. ***Tip:*** Check the hotel's website for good deals, such as a one-third discount for online bookings.

College St., Killarney, County Kerry. www.fairviewkillarney.com. ✆ **064/663-4164.** 29 units. €90–€130 double. MC, V. **Amenities:** Restaurant; room service. *In room:* TV, hair dryer, free Wi-Fi.

Fuchsia House This modern house built in classic Victorian style is a darling guesthouse, beautifully run by Mary and Tommy Treacy. The owners are former teachers, and they've decorated the guest rooms in Provençal style, with wallpaper in delicate French designs, well-chosen fabrics in pastel colors, and classic prints on the walls. Families are welcome since all of the rooms have both a double and a single bed. Breakfast is served in a sunny conservatory, and the food is excellent.

Muckross Rd., Killarney, County Kerry. www.fuchsiahouse.com. ✆ **064/663-3743.** Fax 064/663-6588. 9 units. €80–€110 double. €5 per person reduction per night for 2 nights or more. Rates include full breakfast. MC, V. **Amenities:** Lounge; smoke-free rooms. *In room:* TV/DVD, hair dryer, free Wi-Fi.

Gleann Fia Country House Although it's only 1.6km (1 mile) from town, this modern, Victorian-style guesthouse feels pleasantly secluded, with thick forests surrounding it like a blanket. The house has an airy conservatory where you can relax over a cup of tea or, in the morning, choose from the extensive breakfast menu. The house has been thoughtfully and tastefully constructed to evoke old-world charm, rather than purposely built to be your average guesthouse. Rooms are spacious and have firm, comfortable beds, but the main attraction is the great outdoors. You can enjoy nature walks through the woods, along with peace and quiet to soothe your soul. Cheaper rates are available by booking in advance, or in the off season.

Deerpark, Killarney, County Kerry. www.gleannfia.com. ✆ **064/663-5035.** Fax 064/663-5000. 19 units. €80–€110 double. Rates include full breakfast. AE, MC, V. Free parking. **Amenities:** Lounge; smoke-free rooms. *In room:* TV.

Kathleen's Country House ★ About 1.6km (1 mile) north of town amid acres of sprawling gardens next to a dairy farm, this pleasant guesthouse is a two-story contemporary stone building with lots of big windows. Enthusiastic, efficient hostess Kathleen O'Regan-Sheppard has created attractive guest rooms with antique pine furniture and light floral fabrics, complemented by a collection of contemporary pastels and paintings. ***Note:*** The guesthouse is off a busy highway—ask for rooms at the back if you might be disturbed by road noise.

Madam's Height, Tralee rd. (N22), Killarney, County Kerry. www.kathleens.net. ✆ **064/663-2810.** Fax 064/663-2340. 17 units. €100–€111 double. Rates include full breakfast. AE, MC, V. Free parking. Closed Oct to late Apr. **Amenities:** Smoke-free rooms. *In room:* TV, hair dryer.

Killarney Royal ★ This small hotel neatly crosses the line between historic guesthouse and modern hotel, with beautiful attention to detail. Owner Margaret Scally grew up in the hotel business, and when she inherited the Royal, she renovated it in elegant style, with lots of cream and ivory tones and nice touches like delicate, carved-wood chairs and luxurious fabrics in the guest rooms. All the modern accouterments (phones, broadband, televisions) are also present.

College St., Killarney, County Kerry. www.killarneyroyal.ie. ✆ **064/663-1853.** Fax 064/663-4001. 29 units. €130–€200 double. Rates include full breakfast. AE, MC, V. Closed Nov–Feb. **Amenities:** Restaurant; lounge. *In room:* TV, hair dryer, high-speed Internet.

Randles Court ★ A former rectory dating from the early 20th century, this attractive yellow, gabled four-story house sits just outside Killarney Town on the road to Muckross House. With marble floors and chandeliers, and warmed by open fireplaces, the lounges and lobby are quite elegant. Rooms have traditional decor, including heavy armoires, antique desks, and vanities, and they're tastefully decorated in bright colors. ***Tip:*** Room-only rates can be quite a saving here.

Muckross Rd. (N71), Killarney, County Kerry. www.randleshotels.com. ✆ **800/4-CHOICE** (424-6423) in the U.S., or 064/663-5333. Fax 064/663-9301. 55 units. €130–€180 double. Rates include service charge and full breakfast. AE, DC, MC, V. Free parking. **Amenities:** Restaurant; bar; babysitting; fitness center; pool; room service; spa. *In room:* TV, hair dryer.

Where to Eat

VERY EXPENSIVE

Gaby's Seafood Restaurant ★★ SEAFOOD The walls at Gaby's are filled with commendations and awards, which could be a bit tacky if the food weren't so good. Gaby's is known for its succulent lobster, served grilled or in a house sauce of cream, cognac, and spices. Other choices include turbot with glazed pastry, black sole meunière, and a giant Kerry shellfish platter—a veritable feast of prawns, scallops, mussels, lobster, and oysters. Meat lovers may be offered a classic steak au poivre or rack of lamb with blue cheese and potato gateaux.

27 High St., Killarney, County Kerry. ✆ **064/663-2519.** www.gabysireland.com Reservations recommended. Main courses €25–€43. AE, DC, MC, V. Mon–Sat 6–10pm. Closed late Feb to mid-Mar and Christmas week.

MODERATE

Bricín ★ TRADITIONAL IRISH Seafood dishes and old-time Kerry *boxty* (a traditional dish of potato pancakes filled with chicken, seafood, curried lamb, or vegetables) are the trademarks of this relaxed restaurant above a craft-and-book shop. Don't be put off by the fact that you enter through the shop—the building dates from the 1830s, and the dining room has a pleasant rustic feel, with wood-paneled walls, turf fireplaces, and wood floors. The seafood is excellent and the service is charming.

26 High St., Killarney, County Kerry. ✆ **064/663-4902.** www.bricin.com. Reservations recommended for dinner. Fixed-price 2 course early-bird dinners €19–€29; fixed-price menus: 2 courses €26, 3 courses €35; dinner main courses €19–€26. AE, DC, MC, V. Mid-Mar to Easter Thurs–Sat 6–9:30pm; Easter–Oct Tues–Sat 6–9:30pm. Closed Nov to early Mar.

Treyvaud's ★ IRISH When this place opened a couple of years back, it immediately became one of the most popular lunch spots in town. Owned by two Irish brothers, it offers a clever mix of traditional Irish favorites for lunch (stews, steak pie, and sandwiches). For dinner, it raises the ante, focusing on fresh local ingredients (lamb, salmon, sea bass) creatively prepared. It all works and the crowds keep coming.

62 High St., Killarney, County Kerry. ✆ **064/663-3062.** www.treyvaudsrestaurant.com. Reservations recommended. Dinner main courses €16–€25. MC, V. Tues–Sat noon–10:30pm.

Pubs

Killarney Grand This large bar has a big following for its traditional music, played nightly from 9 to 11pm. After that, louder bands tend to play, and the crowd gets a little younger as the night goes on. Admission is free until 11pm, and rates vary after that. Main St., Killarney, County Kerry. ✆ **064/663-1159.** www.killarneygrand.com.

The Laurels One of the more popular "singsong" pubs in town, this place rings to the rafters with the lilt of Irish ditties. Ballad singers are booked nightly from April through October, starting at 9pm. Main St., Killarney, County Kerry. ✆ **064/663-1149.**

Molly Darcy's A delightful, quirky kind of place named after the owner's extraordinary-sounding grandmother (ask for the story), the emphasis here is on traditional pub food, freshly prepared. It's right on the edge of Killarney National Park. There's Irish dancing on Sunday evenings. Muckross Village, Muckross Rd., Killarney, County Kerry. ✆ **064/6634973.**

Traditional Irish music is a staple at O'Connor's pub in Killarney Town.

O'Connor's This is a terrific place to have a pint and catch a performance with an Irish theme. Depending on the night, you could hear traditional music, Irish stand-up comedy, literary readings, or a play. Performances start at 9:15pm. 7 High St., Killarney, County Kerry. ✆ **064/663-1115.**

Tatler Jack This traditional pub is a favorite gathering place for followers of Gaelic football and hurling. Traditional music or ballads are scheduled from June through September nightly from 9:30pm. Plunkett St., Killarney, County Kerry. ✆ **064/663-2361.** www.tatlerjack.com.

THE DINGLE PENINSULA

Dingle Town: 48km (30 miles) W of Tralee, 80km (50 miles) NW of Killarney

The quieter, smaller alternative to the Ring of Kerry, the Dingle Peninsula is a short drive away from Killarney. Locals say everything moves a little slower in Dingle, perhaps because everybody is taking in the extraordinary views. This is a unique place where all you can see for miles are undulating hills, craggy mountains, and a creamy shoreline curving at the edge of thick, fragrant woods. To call it "undiscovered" would be too generous—in the summer Dingle Town is packed with travelers—but it's not as ruthlessly jammed as the Ring of Kerry, and, from time to time, even in the high season, you can find yourself blissfully alone amid its natural beauty.

Essentials

GETTING THERE Regular bus service runs between Dingle and Tralee on **Bus Éireann** (✆ **066/712-3566** for the nearest travel center in Tralee; www.buseireann.ie), where you can connect with daily coach services to and from all parts of Ireland. The boarding and drop-off point is on Upper Main Street.

If you're driving from Tralee to Dingle, follow R559, or take R561 from Castlemaine.

VISITOR INFORMATION The **Dingle Tourist Office** is on Main Street, Dingle (✆ **066/915-1188**). It is open seasonally, usually mid-April through October. Regular hours are Monday to Saturday 9am to 5pm (extended and Sun hours in peak summer season).

For extensive, detailed tourist information on the Dingle Peninsula, see www.ringofkerrytourism.com or **www.dingle-peninsula.ie**.

GETTING AROUND Dingle Town has a population of only 1,200 and thus is too small for a local bus service. **Bus Éireann** (✆ **066/712-3566** for the nearest travel center in Tralee) provides service from Dingle to other towns on the peninsula. For local taxi or minibus service, contact **Dial a Dingle Cab** (✆ **087/222-2248**). The best way to get around little Dingle Town, with its narrow, winding, hilly streets, is to walk. The street along the waterfront is Strand Street, and aside from that, it has three other main streets—Green Street, John Street, and Main Street. Once you've figured those out, the rest will follow easily.

To see the sights beyond the town, drive west along R559 or take one of the sightseeing tours suggested below.

Impressions

I walked up this morning along the slope from the east to the top of Sybil Head, where one comes out suddenly on the brow of a cliff with a straight fall of many hundreds of feet into the sea. It is a place of indescribable grandeur, where one can see Carrantuohill and the Skelligs and Loop Head and the full sweep of the Atlantic, and over all, the wonderfully tender and searching light that is seen only in Kerry. One wonders in these places why there is anyone left in Dublin, or London, or Paris, when it would be better, one would think, to live in a tent or hut with this magnificent sea and sky, and to breathe this wonderful air, which is like wine in one's teeth.

—John Millington Synge (1871–1909), Irish playwright

The coastal town of Dingle is also known by its Irish name, An Daingean.

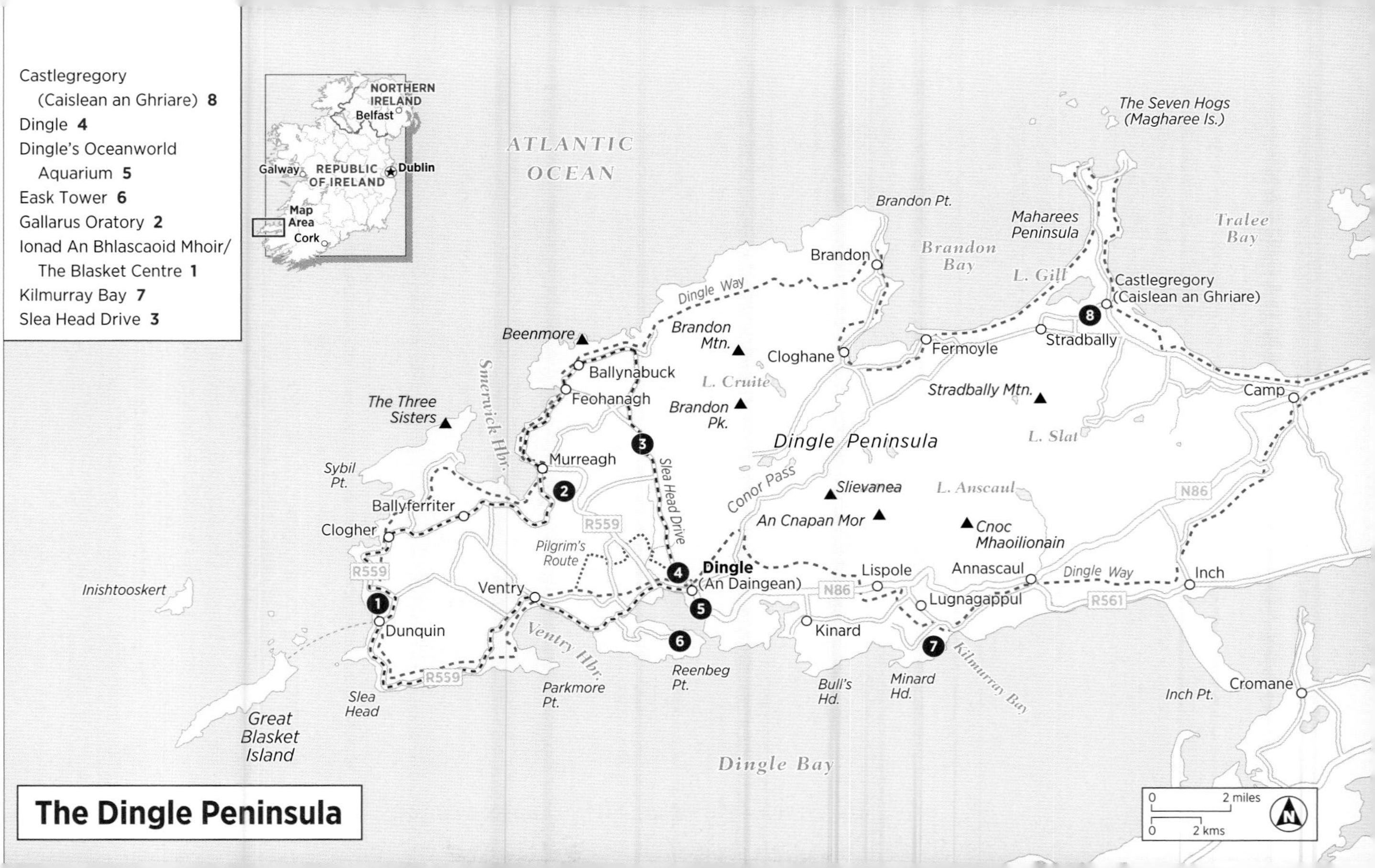
The Dingle Peninsula
Castlegregory (Caislean an Ghriare) 8
Dingle 4
Dingle's Oceanworld Aquarium 5
Eask Tower 6
Gallarus Oratory 2
Ionad An Bhlascaoid Mhoir/ The Blasket Centre 1
Kilmurray Bay 7
Slea Head Drive 3
NORTHERN IRELAND
Belfast
REPUBLIC OF IRELAND
Dublin
Galway
Map Area
Cork
ATLANTIC OCEAN
The Seven Hogs (Magharee Is.)
Tralee Bay
Brandon Pt.
Maharees Peninsula
Brandon Bay
L. Gill
Castlegregory (Caislean an Ghriare)
Brandon
Dingle Way
Beenmore
Brandon Mtn.
Cloghane
Fermoyle
Stradbally
Camp
Ballynabuck
L. Cruite
Stradbally Mtn.
Feohanagh
Brandon Pk.
The Three Sisters
Smerwick Hbr.
L. Slat
Dingle Peninsula
Murreagh
Slea Head Drive
Conor Pass
Sybil Pt.
Slievanea
L. Anscaul
N86
Ballyferriter
An Cnapan Mor
Cnoc Mhaoilionain
Clogher
R559
Pilgrim's Route
Dingle (An Daingean)
Lispole
Annascaul
Dingle Way
Inch
R559
Ventry
N86
Lugnagappul
R561
Inishtooskert
Dunquin
Kinard
Ventry Hbr.
Kilmurray Bay
R559
Reenbeg Pt.
Parkmore Pt.
Bull's Hd.
Minard Hd.
Cromane
Slea Head
Inch Pt.
Great Blasket Island
Dingle Bay
0 2 miles
0 2 kms
N

YOU SAY "DINGLE," I say "AN DAINGEAN"

If you're planning on visiting the Dingle Peninsula in County Kerry, things might get a little confusing, given that, technically speaking, it no longer exists. The whole region has been embroiled in heated controversy after the Irish government ruled in 2005 that as it was in an Irish-language area, Dingle must have a Gaelic name. Since nobody could remember what Dingle's Irish name originally was, the government helpfully invented one for it. Cute little Dingle, it decreed, would now be called "An Daingean," which translates as "the Fortress."

Aside from being less than catchy, the new name caused an explosion of outrage among Dingle residents and business owners who had grown up in Dingle, lived in Dingle all their lives, and didn't want to live in An Daingean now.

Surveys found that more than 90% of An Daingean residents wanted to be Dingle residents. Meetings were held. Voices were raised. In a move clearly not decided to calm tempers, the government minister responsible for the name change threatened to kick Dingle out of the Gaeltacht (the government-supported Irish-language region) if it refused to change all road signs from "Dingle" to "An Daingean." It even forbade it to keep the word "Dingle" on any signs, no matter how tiny the print size. Being dropped from the Gaeltacht would cost Dingle millions in government support.

Given that the minister involved is Eamon O Cuiv, the grandson of Irish rebel and founding prime minister Eamon de Valera (also a vociferous supporter of the Irish language), it's possible that this all should have come as no surprise. But residents were still furious.

In 2006, road signs were changed, and "Dingle" disappeared from government maps, but nearly all private businesses kept the Dingle in their names. A local artist built a huge, wooden Hollywood-style sign on a hill above the town reading DINGLE. It was short-lived, but the battle was far from over. Locals called for a referendum, and it seemed that every window in Dingle Town had a sticker calling for both names to be represented on road signs and maps. In October 2006, a vote was held over whether to change the name back; the motion carried, with a grand total of just 81 votes against. But because it had no legal basis under Irish law, the government still refused to agree. Recently, locals have begun spray painting "Dingle" onto signs that only used the Irish name, only for it to be washed off—and then sprayed right on again.

So it seems that, at least for now, your kids will likely be visiting Fungie the An Daingean Dolphin during your visit.

FAST FACTS In an **emergency,** dial ✆ **999.** The **Dingle Hospital** is on Upper Main Street (✆ **066/915-1455**). The local **Garda Station** is at Holy Ground, Dingle (✆ **066/915-1522**).

The **Dingle Dry Cleaners** is on Mail Road (✆ **066/915-0680**).

Internet access is available from the **Old Forge Internet Cafe,** Holy Ground (✆ **066/915-0523**).

In & About Dingle Peninsula is a newspaper-style publication distributed free at hotels, restaurants, shops, and the tourist office. It lists events, attractions, activities, and more.

Exploring the Town

Dingle ***(An Daingean)*** is a charming, brightly colored little town at the foot of steep hills and on the edge of a gorgeous stretch of coast. There's not much to do here, but it has plenty of hotels and restaurants and makes a good base for exploring the region. The town's most famous resident is a dolphin that adopted the place years ago and has been bringing in dolphin-loving tourists ever since. Its busiest time is in August, when the Dingle Races bring in crowds from throughout the area to watch the horses run every other weekend. (The racetrack is just outside of town on the N86.) In the last week of August, the Dingle Regatta fills the harbor with traditional Irish currach boats in a vivid display of color and history.

When leaving Dingle, heading west takes you on the **Slea Head Drive,** a gorgeous stretch of road known for its collection of ancient sites. At any tourist information center, you can get a guide to the various ruined abbeys and old forts along the way. (***Note:*** This is serious Gaeltacht territory, so under new Irish rules, all signs—even road hazard signs—are in Gaelic only.)

Not far from Dingle, **Gallarus Oratory** is a beautifully preserved, early Christian church building. With a shape much like an overturned boat, it's made of stone with no mortar and was so well constructed that it's completely watertight after more than 1,000 years. The oratory is signposted on the R559 near Ballyferriter. There's a visitor center that charges a few euros for parking and has little to offer besides a short film, so if that doesn't interest you, skip the center, park elsewhere, and walk up to the oratory—access is free.

A few miles away, the village of **Ballyferriter** ***(Baile an Fheirtearaigh)*** is named after a local rebel named Piaras Ferriter. He was a poet and soldier who fought in the 1641 rebellion and ultimately became the last area commander to surrender to Oliver Cromwell's English troops. Just north of the village, you can follow signs to the moody ruins of the Dún an Oir Fort, a defensive citadel dating from the Iron Age. There's also a small memorial to 600 Spanish and Irish troops who were massacred here by the English in 1580. Most were beheaded; the nearby site where their remains were buried is still known locally as "the Field of the Heads."

The village of **Dunquin** ***(Dún Chaion),*** stunningly situated between Slea Head and Clogher Head, is where you catch ferries (**© 066/335-3805;** www.blasketislands.ie) to the **Blasket Islands** ***(Na Blascaodaí).*** Until they were evacuated in 1953, the islands were famous for having an entirely Gaelic-speaking population. These days it's inhabited only by seals and seabirds. If you're up to it, there's a 13km (8-mile) walk to the west end of Great Blasket and back, and it passes sea cliffs and beaches of ivory sand; you can stop along the way at the only cafe on the island. Ferries depart Dunquin every hour from 10am (check return times on the day). The round-trip costs €25.

Slea Head, at the southwestern edge of the peninsula, has pristine beaches, great walks, and extensive archaeological remains. **Dunbeg Fort** (**© 066/915-9755;** www.dunbegfort.com) sits on a rocky promontory just south of Slea Head, its walls rising from the cliff edge. Although much of the fort has fallen into the sea, the place is well worth a visit at the bargain-basement rate of €3 per person.

Back on the mainland and on the north side of the peninsula, **Castlegregory** ***(Caislean an Ghriare)*** is a seaside village with two wide, sandy beaches. It's known for its good diving waters, and scuba divers and watersports fans flock to the place in summer. It's a bit bustling for isolationists, who are better off heading to tiny **Cloghane (*An Clochán*)** on the southern edge of Brandon Bay. With a population of 270 and a lovely beach, it's got much to offer. It also is a good place for climbers interested in tackling nearby **Mount Brandon (*Cnoc Bhréannain*),** which is Ireland's second-highest mountain (951m/3,120 ft.). The mountain is a good all-day climb and has gorgeous views, but don't try it without a map and compass and some experience scaling considerable heights.

Dingle's Oceanworld Aquarium ☺ This is a nicely designed aquarium, although it's quite small, given the ticket price. As is the norm at such places, there are lots of sea critters in creatively designed tanks. There's an aquarium tunnel you can walk through with the fish swimming above and around you, and members of the young staff carry around live lobsters, crabs, starfish, and other "inner space" creatures and introduce them up close to kids. This is a compact, hands-on, interactive place that is a good way of rewarding your kids for being so patient while you took pictures of a pile of rocks back up the road.

Dingle Harbour, Dingle, County Kerry. ✆ **066/915-2111.** www.dingle-oceanworld.ie. Admission €12 adults; €9 seniors; €7 children; €35 families. MC, V. Daily 10am–5pm.

Kids can shake hands with lobsters, crabs, and other sea creatures at Dingle's Oceanworld Aquarium.

Eask Tower Built in 1847 as a famine-relief project, this is a remarkable edifice, a 12m (39-ft.) tower built of solid stone nearly 5m (16 ft.) thick, with a wooden arrow pointing to the mouth of the harbor. It is certainly interesting to look at, but the main

The Atlantic batters the cliffs that hem in the Dingle Peninsula along the Slea Head Drive.

reason for making the 1.6km (1-mile) climb to the summit of Carhoo Hill is not to see the tower, but the incredible views of Dingle Harbour, Connor Pass, and, on the far side of the bay, the peaks of the Iveragh Peninsula. This is a great place to get your bearings, but save a trip here for a clear day.

Carhoo Hill, Dingle, County Kerry. Free admission. From Dingle, follow Slea Head Rd. 3.2km (2 miles), turn left at road signposted for Colâiste Ide, and continue another 3.2km (2 miles).

Ionad An Bhlascaoid Mhoir/The Blasket Centre ★ On the westerly tip of the Dingle Peninsula, this visitor center is dedicated to the remote Blasket Islands. The largest of the islands, Great Blasket, was once an outpost of Irish civilization and a nurturing ground for Irish-language writers, but its inhabitants abandoned the island in 1953. The center explains in interesting style the cultural and literary traditions of the Blaskets and the history of Corca Dhuibhne, the Gaeltacht area. There's a bookshop specializing in local literature, and a handy cafe with views of the Blaskets. The **Blasket Island Ferry** (✆ **086/335-3805**) charges €20 to €35 round-trip to the islands (depending on when you go), or €40 including an "eco-marine adventure tour," on which you could spot anything from puffins and terns to dolphins and even, or so we're told, whales. You can catch the ferry at the harbor in Dunquin; sailings are hourly from 10am to 5pm.

Dunquin, County Kerry. ✆ **066/915-6444.** www.heritageireland.ie. Admission €4 adults; €3 seniors; €2 children and students; €10 families. Apr to late Oct daily 10am–6pm. Last admission 45 min. before closing.

Sightseeing Tours

Fungie the Dolphin Tours ★ ☺ The story of Fungie is both strange and heartwarming. The bottlenose dolphin was first spotted by Dingle's lighthouse keeper in 1984, as it escorted fishing boats out to sea and then back again at the end of their voyages, day after day. The sailors named him and he became a harbor fixture. Fishermen took their children out to swim with him, and he seemed to love human contact. It is a rare case of a wild dolphin essentially domesticating itself. Now people come from miles around to have a few minutes' time with Fungie and the fishermen ferry them out to meet him. Trips last about 1 hour and depart regularly, roughly every 2 hours in the low season and as frequently as every half-hour in high season. Fungie swims right up to the boats, which stay out long enough for you to take in views of the picturesque bay. Wonderful though this tour can be, however, one does have to wonder how much longer Fungie will be drawing in the crowds, given that he's been at it for 25 years—and nobody quite knows how old he is (best estimates put him well into his thirties). Fungie is such a hit with kids that we'll keep listing the tour until the old fellow stops showing up. We understand he's as hale and hardy as ever, but it would be wise to call ahead first before making a special journey. If you want to get closer and more personal with Fungie, you can also arrange an early morning dolphin swim (see "Up Close with Fungie," later in this chapter).

The Pier, Dingle, County Kerry. ✆ **066/915-2626** or 915-1967. www.dingledolphin.com. Tour starting at €16 adults; €8 children 11 and under. No charge if dolphin not seen. Daily 10am–6pm, weather permitting.

Sciuird Archaeological Adventures For serious history buffs, these are a great opportunity to get deeper insight into ancient local history. Led by a local historian, the tours last about a half-day and involve a short bus journey and some easy walking. Four or five monuments, from the Stone Age to medieval times, are

A landmark in Dingle, An Droichead Beag is a hotbed for live traditional Irish music.

on the route. All tours, limited to 8 to 10 people, start from the top of the pier. Reservations are required, at least a day or so in advance if possible. Holy Ground, Dingle, County Kerry. ✆ **066/915-1606.** archeo@eircom.net. Tour €20 per person. Apr–Sept daily 10:30am and 2pm; the rest of the year by appointment.

Shopping

Brandon Gallery This gallery displays and sells the work of local artist Michael Flaherty. His oil paintings, in a bold impasto style, are influenced by the local landscape and much in demand. Open daily from 10am to 6pm. Clappagh Cross, Brandon, County Kerry. ✆ **066/713-8233.** www.michaelflaherty.net.

Brian de Staic Brian de Staic specializes in Celtic jewelry, handcrafted and engraved with ancient Celtic symbols or the letters of the Ogham alphabet, an ancient Irish form of writing. Hours are Monday to Saturday from 9am to 6pm. Green St., Dingle, County Kerry. ✆ **066/915-1298.** www.briandestaic.com.

Greenlane Gallery This art gallery holds a good selection of quality contemporary Irish paintings on its whitewashed walls—watercolors, sculpture, and ceramics. Hours are Wednesday to Friday from 11am to 4pm (5pm Sat). Green St., Dingle, County Kerry. ✆ **066/915-2018.** www.greenlanegallery.com.

Holden Leathergoods Talented leather craftsman Conor Holden creates exquisite handcrafted, silk-lined leather handbags, baggage, briefcases, and belts. Open Monday to Saturday from 8:30am to 6:30pm and Sunday 10:30am to 5pm (in low season, open Mon–Fri 9am–5pm). The Old School House, signposted 4.8km (3 miles) west of town on the Ventry rd. (R559), off the Slea Head Dr., Burnham, Dingle, County Kerry. ✆ **066/915-1796.** www.holdenleathergoods.com.

Louis Mulcahy Pottery North of Dunquin, this is the studio where Louis Mulcahy produces a sophisticated range of pottery from local clay. The finished products include everything from unique tableware to teapots, platters, and lamps. Furniture and handmade silk lampshades are also available, as is a selection of Lisbeth Mulcahy's tapestries and weavings. The Mulcahys also have a shop and cafe in Ballyferriter Village, just down the road, with more distinctive painted housewares. Summer opening hours are 9am to 7pm weekdays, 10am to 7pm weekends (cafe daily 10am–5pm); winter hours are 9am to 5:30pm weekdays (cafe open 9am–6pm), 10am to 5:30pm weekends (cafe open 10am–6pm). Clogher, Ballyferriter, County Kerry. ✆ **066/915-6229.** www.louismulcahy.com.

The Weavers' Shop Weaver Lisbeth Mulcahy creates fabrics and tapestries inspired by the local landscape. She uses wool, Irish linen, cotton, and alpaca in her scarves, throws, tapestries, and napkins. Everything is gorgeous and pricey. Open October to May Monday to Saturday from 9am to 6pm; June to September Monday to Saturday from 9am to 9pm, Sunday from 10am to 6pm. Green St., Dingle, County Kerry. ✆ **066/915-1688.** www.lisbethmulcahy.com.

Sports & Outdoor Pursuits

BEACHES The Dingle Peninsula has some of the most dramatic beaches in Ireland. The most famous is **Inch Strand**—a 5km-long (3-mile) creamy stretch of sand dunes in the town of Inch *(Inse)*—but one of the most striking is **Kilmurray Bay at Minard ★★** where, in the shadow of Minard Castle, giant sandstone boulders form a beach unlike anything you've ever seen. It's definitely not safe for swimming, but ideal for a picnic.

Like Minard, **Trabeg Beach** confronts the southwest storms of the Atlantic head on. Here, during ebb tide, you will find exquisite wave-sculptured, maroon sandstone shapes below sheer rock cliffs, and small sea caves lined with veins of crystalline quartz. The beauty of the rock sculptures combined with the roar of the surf is magical.

Some of the calmest beaches in this area for swimming are east of Castlegregory, on the more protected west side of Tralee Bay. The beach at **Maherabeg** has a coveted European Blue Flag (meaning it is exceptionally unpolluted and environmentally safe), and the beaches of **Brandon Bay** are particularly scenic—great for walking and swimming.

BICYCLING Mountain bikes can be rented at **Foxy John Moriarty,** Main Street, Dingle (✆ **066/915-1316**). Alternatively, the staff at the **Mountain Man Outdoor Shop,** Strand Street, Dingle (✆ **066/915-2400;** www.themountainmanshop.com), can handle the arrangements for you. The cost is normally around €15 per day, or €55 per week. Employees at

The ruins of Minard Castle on Kilmurray Bay on the Dingle Peninsula.

Turquoise waters lap this beach on the Dingle Peninsula.

both shops know the area well, and can suggest a number of day trips or overnight touring options. Foxy John's has the added advantage of also being a pub, although you might want to save your pints until after your bike ride. One possible day trip is to take the road out to the tip of the peninsula past Slea Head and Clogher Head. The scenery is outrageously beautiful and the journey is hilly, but not ridiculously so.

BIRD-WATCHING In summer, the small, uninhabited islands surrounding Great Blasket attract flocks of nesting seabirds, including vast numbers of storm petrels. From Clogher Head north of Dunquin at the western extremity of the Dingle Peninsula, rare autumn migrants can sometimes be seen. Inch Peninsula, extending into Castlemaine Harbour south of Inch town, is a wintering ground for brent geese, which arrive in late August and move on in April; there is also a large wigeon population in the fall.

DIVING On the North Dingle Peninsula, **Waterworld,** Harbour House, Scraggane Pier, Castlegregory, County Kerry (✆ **066/713-9292;** www.waterworld.ie), is a diving center that offers packages including diving, room, and board at good rates. Classes for beginners are available. The house is a short boat ride from most of the diving sites.

GOLF Sixteen kilometers (10 miles) west of Dingle Town, on the western edge of the Dingle Peninsula, overlooking the Atlantic, the **Dingle Golf Club (Ceann Sibéal),** Ballyferriter (✆ **066/915-6255;** www.dinglelinks.com), welcomes visitors to play its 18-hole, par-72 course. Greens fees for 18 holes are €30 to €65 daily, depending on the season.

HORSEBACK RIDING At **Dingle Horse Riding,** Ballinaboula House, Dingle (✆ **066/915-2199;** www.dinglehorseriding.com), rides are available along nearby beaches or through the mountains. A 1-hour mountain ride starts at €30. Half-day, full-day, and 3- to 5-day packages, including accommodations, meals, and riding, can be arranged.

SAILING The **Dingle Sailing Centre,** The Marina, Dingle (✆ **066/915-2603;** www.saildingle.com), offers an array of courses taught by experienced, certified instructors. Summer courses cost from about €130 to €200.

SEA ANGLING For packages and day trips, contact Nick or Maureen O'Connor at **Angler's Rest,** Ventry (✆ **066/915-9947;** www.iol.ie/~avalon), or Seán O'Conchúir (✆ **066/915-5429**), representing the **Kerry Angling Association.**

Spectacular views await hikers along the Dingle Way.

WALKING The **Dingle Way** begins in Tralee and circles the peninsula, covering 153km (95 miles) of gorgeous mountain and coastal landscape. The most rugged section is along Brandon Head, where the trail passes between Mount Brandon and the ocean. The views are tremendous, but the walk is long (about 24km/15 miles, averaging 9 hr.) and strenuous, and should be attempted only by experienced walkers and in good weather. The section between Dunquin and Ballyferriter (also 24km/15 miles) follows an especially lovely stretch of coast. For more information, see *The Dingle Way Map Guide,* available in local tourist offices and shops.

Another good walk is the ascent up **Mount Brandon.** The approach from the west is a more gradual climb, but the walk from the eastern, Cloghane side is far more interesting and passes the pastoral beauty of the Paternoster Lakes. The road to the trail head is signposted just past Cloghane on the road to Brandon town; drive about 5km (3 miles) on this road to a small parking lot and the Lopsided Tea House. Be sure to bring plenty of water and food, gear for wind and rain, and a good map. The trail climbs through fields, past an elaborate grotto, and along the slope of an open hillside where red-and-white poles clearly mark the way. As you round the corner of the high open hillside, the Paternoster Lakes and Brandon come into view. The walk through this glacial valley toward the base of the mountain is the most beautiful part—if the weather's bad, you won't have wasted your time if you turn around before reaching the summit.

The only seriously strenuous leg is the climb out of this valley to the ridge, a short but intense scramble over boulders and around ledges. Once you reach the ridge top, turn left and follow the trail another .4km (.25 mile) or so to the summit. You can return the way you came or continue south along the ridge, returning to Cloghane on the Pilgrim's Route, an old track that circumnavigates the Dingle Peninsula. Although this is a day hike (about 4 hr. to the summit and back), and very well marked, it shouldn't be taken lightly and certainly isn't for amateurs—bring all necessary supplies and let someone know when you expect to return. Information on routes and weather conditions is available at the Cloghane visitor center.

UP close WITH FUNGIE

It is extremely rare for a wild dolphin to choose voluntarily to live among people rather than with his own kind, but for some 25 years, a dolphin named Fungie has chosen to live with Dingle's human population. In fact, he likes people so much that diving into the water to swim with him has become a popular local pastime, and one that he seems to enjoy as much as the human visitors. He can swim about 40kmph (25 mph), but he slows down to the pace of an Australian crawl when you're out there, and amuses himself by leaping over the human swimmers' heads. If you want to swim with Fungie, contact **John Brosnan** (✆ **066/915-1967**) to book a time. He'll rent you the necessary gear for the cold Irish waters (semi-dry suit, mask, snorkel, boots, and fins, all in one duffel—€25 per person), and then ferry you out by boat. The 2-hour escorted swim also costs €25. For obvious reasons (it's out in the sea), only adults can swim with Fungie, although children will certainly enjoy watching.

Hidden Ireland Tours, Dingle (✆ **251/478-7519** in the U.S., or 087/258-1966; www.hiddenirelandtours.com), offers a week of easy to moderate guided hiking through some of Ireland's most beautiful scenery. It takes in parts of the Kerry Way, Killarney National Park, the Beara Peninsula in County Cork, Skellig Michael, and the Dingle Peninsula. The cost, including luggage transfers and accommodations, runs around €2,300 per person. Hikes are available April to September.

A twisty, misty, one-lane mountain road, the Conor Pass is one of Ireland's most beautiful drives.

WINDSURFING The beaches around Castlegregory offer a variety of conditions for windsurfing. Those on the eastern side of the peninsula are generally calmer than those to the west. Equipment can be hired from **Jamie Knox Watersports,** Brandon Bay, Castlegregory, County Kerry (✆ **066/713-9411;** www.jamieknox.com), on the road between Castlegregory and Fahamore. The cost runs from €15 for 1 hour to €70 for the whole day. They also offer lessons for surfers of all skill levels; a 2-hour beginner's taster costs €40 adults, €30 kids 15 and under.

Where to Stay

EXPENSIVE

Dingle Skellig Hotel ☺ This three-story hotel has an idyllic location next to Dingle Bay on the eastern edge of town. The look of the place is all polished pine and tasteful contemporary touches. Most guest rooms are done in neutral colors with floral touches, although some have slightly lurid color combinations. Many have gorgeous views. This is a family hotel in the classic sense, complete with children's playroom—in the summer, there are evening cabaret performances and children's entertainment. Rooms for visitors with disabilities are available at a reduced rate.

Annascaul Rd., Dingle, County Kerry. www.dingleskellig.com. ✆ **066/915-0200.** Fax 066/915-1501. 111 units. €130–€240 double; €180–€500 suites. Rates include full breakfast. AE, MC, V. Free parking. Open year-round; Jan–Feb Fri–Sun only. **Amenities:** Restaurant; bar; lounge; gym; Jacuzzi; indoor pool; room service; spa; steam room. *In room:* TV, radio, hair dryer.

MODERATE

Benners Hotel One of the few hotels out here open year-round, Benners is right in the heart of town. The lovely Georgian doorway with a fanlight at the front entrance sets the tone for this old-world hostelry. The 250-year-old hotel blends traditional Irish charm with modern comforts. Its style is a bit old-fashioned, but rooms are comfortable and furnished with antiques, including some four-poster beds.

Main St., Dingle, County Kerry. www.dinglebenners.com. ✆ **066/915-1638.** Fax 066/915-1412. 52 units. €120–€230 double. Rates include service charge and full Irish breakfast. AE, DC, MC, V. **Amenities:** Restaurant; 2 bars. *In room:* TV, hair dryer.

Greenmount House ★★ This modern bungalow on a hill above Dingle isn't much to look at from the outside, but don't be fooled. Inside it's a stylish place, with lush colors and clever design. Each of the spacious guest rooms has its own sitting area and large bathroom—some are split-level, a few have balconies, and some have sea views. Breakfasts, ranging from smoked salmon omelets to ham-and-pineapple toasted sandwiches, have won awards for owners Mary and John Curran.

John St., Dingle, County Kerry. www.greenmount-house.com. ✆ **066/915-1414.** 12 units. €100–€160 double. Rates include full breakfast. MC, V. Closed Dec 20–26. **Amenities:** Smoke-free rooms. *In room:* TV.

Milltown House Tucked away near a tidal inlet just outside of Dingle, Milltown House is a simple, white-and-black 19th-century house, but it's a good guesthouse to know about. The spacious guest rooms have sitting areas and orthopedic beds. Some have sea views and the others overlook the garden. Two rooms are wheelchair accessible. The nonsmoking sitting room—with easy chairs and an open fire—is comfortable, while the conservatory breakfast room (with a lavish breakfast menu) looks out on Dingle Bay. Film buffs might want to request room no. 2—it's where Robert Mitchum stayed while filming *Ryan's Daughter.*

Milltown (off Ventry rd.), Dingle, County Kerry. www.milltownhousedingle.com. ✆ **066/915-1372.** Fax 066/915-1095. 10 units. €130–€170 double. Rates include full breakfast. MC, V. Closed mid-Nov to late Apr. *In room:* TV, hair dryer.

Pax Guest House ★ This former retirement home has been transformed into a comfortable B&B with homey touches. On a green hill overlooking Dingle Bay, Pax House's sunny balcony takes in sweeping views as far as Slea Head. The furniture is heavy pine (some four-poster beds), and the decor is bright and cheerful. This peaceful place is a real getaway.

Pax House is signposted on the N86, Dingle, County Kerry. www.pax-house.com. ✆ **066/915-1518.** Fax 066/915-2461. 12 units. €120–€180 double. Rates include full breakfast. MC, V. Free parking. *In room:* TV, radio, hair dryer.

SELF-CATERING

The Captain's House ★ Jim and Mary Milhench own and run this dapper little B&B in the middle of Dingle. The name is inspired less by the location (the house is landlocked, except for a river running through the manicured yard) than by Jim's former career as a sea captain. It's a place we've long recommended, but recently we were sad to hear that the B&B side of things has had to be scaled back due to Jim's health. Accommodations now come mainly in the form of two well-equipped holiday apartments (mostly self-catering, although a continental breakfast is provided). The apartments have private patios with views of the town and mountains, and a grill that guests are free to use. The Captain's House remains a friendly place to stay, filled with character, and we hope Jim is better soon.

The Mall, Dingle, County Kerry. ✆ **066/915-1531.** Fax 066/915-1079. 2 units. €100–€110 suite. Rates include continental breakfast. AE, MC, V. Closed Dec–Jan. *In room:* TV.

Where to Eat

MODERATE

The Chart House ★★ MODERN COUNTRY This popular restaurant (be sure to book ahead) has an inviting bistro atmosphere with lots of polished pine and warm, rose-colored walls. The cooking here is an ambitious blend of Irish dishes and outside influences. Main courses might include steak filet with black pudding mash, or pork with brandied apples. With unusual food and excellent service, it has carved out quite a reputation.

The Mall, Dingle, County Kerry. ✆ **066/915-2255.** Reservations required. Fixed-price 3-course dinner €35; main courses €15–€28. MC, V. Wed–Mon 6:30–10pm. Closed Jan 8–Feb 12.

Doyle's Seafood Bar ★★ SEAFOOD This popular seafood restaurant is a great, laid-back place to try fresh local fish. Start with a plate of Kerry oysters, or perhaps a grilled prawn salad; then move on to a perfectly prepared seafood linguine, or perhaps a spicy fish stew, made with spinach, white wine, and saffron. The early-bird menu (served until 7:30pm) is excellent value, and more than just the limited selection one usually finds with such deals.

5 John St., Dingle, County Kerry. ✆ **066/915-2674.** www.doylesofdingle.ie. Reservations required. Early-bird menus: 2 courses €22, 3 courses €27; dinner main courses €25–€30. MC, V. Mon–Sat 5–9:30pm.

Lord Bakers SEAFOOD/PUB GRUB The ages-old decor in this pub restaurant combines a stone fireplace and cozy alcoves with a more modern, sunlit conservatory and a few Art Deco touches. The menu offers standard bar food, but juices it up with things like crab claws in garlic butter, Kerry oysters, seafood Mornay, and steaks. Dinner specialties are more elegant, including sole stuffed with smoked salmon and spinach in cheese sauce, lobster, and rack of lamb.

Main St., Dingle, County Kerry. ✆ **066/915-1277.** www.lordbakers.ie. Reservations recommended for dinner. Bar food €10–€16; 3 course early-bird menu €26; dinner main courses €16–€30. AE, MC, V. Fri–Wed 12:30–2pm and 6–9:30pm.

INEXPENSIVE

An Cafe Liteartha CAFE/TEAROOM "The Literary Cafe" is a self-service cafe in an excellent bookstore. This is heaven for those interested in Irish history, literature, maps, and . . . scones. The cafe sells fresh soups, sandwiches, salads, and seafood, and scones and cakes that melt in your mouth. It's an ideal spot for a quiet lunch or snack in the middle of town.

Dykegate St., Dingle, County Kerry. ✆ **066/915-2204.** All items €3–€6. No credit cards. Mon–Sat 9am–6pm (later in summer).

Pubs

An Droichead Beag/The Small Bridge Sitting directly on a bridge, with a cool stone floor and a friendly rustic atmosphere, this pub draws crowds year-round for sessions of traditional Irish music, usually starting at 9:30pm. It's not very big, so arrive early if you want even standing room! Lower Main St., Dingle, County Kerry. ✆ **066/915-1723.**

Dick Mack's The titular Dick Mack (a much-loved Dingle character) died some years ago, but his family carries on his name. Dick ran the place as a pub and shoeshine shop, and his small leather shop is still in its regular place. This is a favorite among locals, as its quirky nature has attracted celebrities such as Robert Mitchum, Timothy Dalton, and Paul Simon, whose names are commemorated with stars on the sidewalk just outside. Green St., Dingle, County Kerry. ✆ **066/915-1960.** dickmacks.homestead.com.

O'Flaherty's This big barn of a pub is true Dingle. Old posters and news clippings line the walls, alongside poems by local authors and favorite Gaelic phrases. In the evenings, excellent traditional-music sessions fill the place from wall to wall. Bridge St., Dingle, County Kerry. ✆ **066/915-1983.**

TRALEE

32km (20 miles) NW of Killarney

Forget the visions of bucolic splendor conjured up by its singsong name; with a population of 22,000, Tralee is three times the size of Killarney, and it feels like it. This is more a workaday town than a tourist center, and there's not much here for visitors to do. In fact, it can feel a bit rough at times—especially on weekend nights, when the town's many bars are packed, and walking the streets can feel a bit of a health hazard. However, it has quite a few good hotels, and it makes a handy base for exploring Kerry. Locals tend to outnumber visitors here most of the year, except during the **Rose of Tralee festival** in August. The town is the permanent home of the National Folk Theatre of Ireland, **Siamsa Tire,** which operates year-round, but is most active during July and August.

Essentials

GETTING THERE **Aer Arann** (✆ **011/353-81821-0210** in the U.S., 818/210-210 in Ireland, or 0870/876-76-76 in the U.K.; www.aerarann.ie) offers regular flights from Dublin into **Kerry County Airport,** Farranfore, County Kerry (✆ **066/976-4644;** www.kerryairport.ie), about 24km (15 miles) south of Tralee. **Ryanair** (www.ryanair.com) flies direct from Dublin and London (Luton or Stansted) to Kerry.

Buses from all parts of Ireland arrive daily at the **Bus Éireann Depot,** John Joe Sheehy Road (✆ **066/716-4700;** www.buseireann.ie).

Trains from major cities arrive at the **Irish Rail Station,** John Joe Sheehy Road (✆ **066/712-3522;** www.irishrail.ie).

COULD YOU BE THE rose OF TRALEE?

A 19th-century song about a pretty local girl named Mary O'Connor is at the root of this now-famous beauty contest. William Mulchinock's tear-jerker of a song about the girl he was stopped by fate from marrying so caught the public's imagination that more than 100 years later, it is still performed in Irish pubs worldwide. Thus, in 1959 was the idea born for a contest to find the prettiest girl in Tralee and crown her.

Every August, the town fills with pretty girls, those who make them beautiful, and those who want to look at them. The contest rules are fairly generous in terms of just who is Irish, not to mention Traleean—the rules require contestants to be of Irish birth *or ancestry,* so past winners have been from places as far flung as the U.S. and Australia. The festival lasts 5 days, during which time the entire town becomes somewhat obsessed with it—restaurants, pubs, and theaters all get involved in hosting events related to the Rose of Tralee. In recent years they've also added a men's section, the "Escort of the Year."

If you want to join in the fun, or if you know a pretty girl with an Irish last name, contact the **Rose of Tralee Festival Office** (✆ **066/712-1322;** www.roseoftralee.ie).

Four major national roads converge on Tralee: N69 and N21 from Limerick and the north, N70 from the Ring of Kerry and points south, and N22 from Killarney, Cork, and the east.

VISITOR INFORMATION The **Tralee Tourist Office,** Ashe Memorial Hall, Denny Street (✆ **066/712-1288**), offers information on Tralee and the Dingle Peninsula. It is open year-round Monday through Friday 9am to 1pm and 2 to 5pm, with weekend and extended hours in the spring and summer. There is also a good cafe on the premises. For Tralee tourist information online, explore **www.tralee.ie** and **www.tralee-insight.com**.

GETTING AROUND The best way to get around Tralee's downtown area is to walk. If you prefer to take a taxi, call **Tralee Radio Taxis,** Monavelley (✆ **066/712-5451;** www.traleeradiotaxis.com), or **Dimo Cabs,** 47 Ashe St. (✆ **066/712-5555**).

FAST FACTS If you need a drugstore, try **O'Carroll's Pharmacy,** 106 Rock St. (✆ **066/712-1181**), or **Boots,** 5 Central Plaza (✆ **066/719-0540**) or 5 Abbey Court (✆ **066/719-0540**).

In an **emergency,** dial ✆ **999. Bon Secours Hospital** is on Strand Street (✆ **066/714-9800**). **Tralee General Hospital** is on Killarney Road (N22; ✆ **066/718-4000**). The local **Garda Station** is off High Street (✆ **066/710-2300**).

Seeing the Sights

Tralee is not really a pretty town, but it has some attractive Georgian architecture and a few sights worth seeing. Mostly, though, it's a good place to load up on supplies and gas up the car before heading into the countryside. A fairly short drive away, the town of **Listowel** is a neatly laid out Georgian town on the River Feale. It's also home to the **Kerry Literary and Cultural Centre,** which has a small but interesting exhibit on local writers. Nearby, **Carrigafoyle Castle** stands its ground as it has for 500 years.

Blennerville Windmill ★ Just 5km (3 miles) west of Tralee and reaching 20m (66 ft.) into the sky, this must surely be the most photographed object in Tralee. This picturesque windmill at the edge of a river still works, and that makes it quite rare in this part of the world. Built in 1800, it flourished until 1850, when it was largely abandoned. After decades of neglect, it was restored, and is now fully operational, producing 5 tons of ground whole-meal flour per week. The visitor complex has an emigration exhibition center, an audiovisual theater, craft workshops, and a cafe.

This active windmill near Tralee still grinds 5 tons of whole-meal flour each week.

R559, Blennerville, County Kerry. ✆ **066/712-1064.** Admission €5 adults; €4 seniors and students; €3 children 6 and over; free for children 5 and under; €15 families. Apr–May and Sept–Oct daily 9:30am–5:30pm; June–Aug 9am–6pm.

Carrigafoyle Castle ★ This rugged medieval castle entirely surrounded by water outside of Listowel dates from the 15th century. Its name comes from the Gaelic *Carragain Phoill* (or "Rock of the Hole"), and probably describes its location in the channel between the land and Carrig Island. It was once the seat of the O'Connor clan, who ruled most of the Kerry clan for a century or so—it was besieged by English forces in the late 16th century and taken again by Cromwell less than a century later. Today you can climb the stone staircase to the top of the tower for magnificent views.

2km (1¼ miles) west of Ballylongford, County Kerry. No phone. Free admission.

Kerry County Museum ★ ☺ This huge facility is designed to give an in-depth look at 7,000 years of life in County Kerry. There are supersize versions of all the usual visitor center offerings: historic displays, photos, a film, mannequins in period garb—all the bases are covered. They really go to town with the sections covering the Middle Ages, which include a reconstruction of medieval town streets, complete with sounds, smells, and other special effects. There's also a whole section devoted to the Fitzgerald family, powerful Anglo-Normans who founded the town in the 13th century. The rest of the museum chronologically examines Kerry music, history, legends, archaeology, and, um, soccer, through interactive and hands-on exhibits.

Ashe Memorial Hall, Denny St., Tralee, County Kerry. ✆ **066/712-7777.** www.kerrymuseum.ie. Admission €8 adults; €6.50 seniors and students; €5 children; €22 families. May–Aug daily 9:30am–5:30pm; Sept–Apr Tues–Sat 9:30am–5pm. Bank Holiday weekends Sun–Mon 10am–5pm (other days stay the same). Last admission 1 hr. before closing.

The Seanchaí: Kerry Literary and Cultural Centre ★ This small museum is cleverly designed to draw attention to Kerry's rich literary history by introducing you to its impressive slate of writers, living and dead. There are all kinds of interactive displays, films to watch, and explanations of the works of writers such as the poet Brendan Kennelly and the novelist Maurice Walsh, who wrote *The Quiet Man*. There are regular literary readings held here (call ahead or check the website for listings) and lots of events in the summer. The museum hosts the prestigious Writers' Week literary festival each June, which attracts top writers from Europe and the Americas.

24 The Square, Listowel, County Kerry. ✆ **068/22212.** www.kerrywritersmuseum.com. Free admission. Guided tours €4 adults; €3 seniors, students, and children. June–Sept daily 9:30am–5:30pm; Oct–May Mon–Fri 10am–4pm. Last tour 1 hr. before closing.

Sports & Outdoor Pursuits

GOLF The **Tralee Golf Club,** Fenit/Churchill Road, West Barrow, Ardfert (✆ **066/713-6379;** www.traleegolfclub.com), overlooking the Atlantic 13km (8 miles) northwest of town, is an Arnold Palmer–designed course. One of Ireland's newer, and most spectacularly situated courses. Greens fees are a pricey €180, although this also allows you to play a second round within a week of the first.

About 40km (25 miles) north of Tralee in the northwest corner of County Kerry is Bill Clinton's favorite Irish course, the **Ballybunion Golf Club ★**, Ballybunion, County Kerry (✆ **068/27146;** www.ballybuniongolfclub.ie). This facility offers the chance to play on two challenging 18-hole seaside links, both on cliffs overlooking the Shannon River estuary and the Atlantic. Tom Watson has rated the Old Course one of the finest in the world, while the Cashen Course was designed by Robert Trent Jones, Sr. Greens fees are €50 to €180 or €180 for golf on both courses within 1 week.

HORSEBACK RIDING If you'd like to see the Tralee sights from horseback, you can't do better than to hire a horse from **Eagle Lodge Equestrian Centre,** Gortatlea (✆ **066/713-7266**). Prices start at around €25 per hour for 1- or 2-hour rides on the Slieve Mish Mountains and Queen Scotia's Glen.

Spectator Sports

DOG RACING Greyhounds race year-round on Tuesday and Friday starting at 8pm at the **Kingdom Greyhound Racing Track,** Oakview, Brewery Road (✆ **066/712-4033**). Admission is around €10 per person; the fee includes a program.

HORSE RACING Horse racing takes place twice a year (in early June and late Aug) at **Tralee Racecourse,** Ballybeggan Park (✆ **066/712-6490,** or 712-6188). Post time is usually 2:30pm. Tickets to races start at around €12 for adults, €6 for seniors and students, and are free for children 13 and under.

Where to Stay

MODERATE

Abbey Gate Hotel ★ This modern three-story hotel is ideally located within walking distance of Tralee's prime attractions, shops, and pubs. Its lobby and public rooms are sleek and contemporary, while guest rooms—though quite small—are tastefully decorated with comfortable beds and bright colors. The **bar,** with its polished paneling and open fireplace, is perhaps the best room in the place.

Maine St., Tralee, County Kerry. www.abbeygate-hotel.com. ✆ **066/712-9888.** Fax 066/712-9821. 100 units. €110–€200 double. AE, DC, MC, V. Limited parking. **Amenities:** 2 restaurants; bar; room service. *In room:* TV, hair dryer.

Ballygarry House Hotel ★★ Just south of town, this country inn is surrounded by well-tended gardens and shaded by sheltering trees, making it feel like a real hideaway. The guest rooms vary in size; each is classically decorated with dark-wood reproductions and luxurious fabrics in neutral tones. The lobby and lounges are steeped in elegant comfort, with lots of big sofas and club chairs to sink down into. **Brooks** restaurant is a classy option for relaxing at the end of the day, and the excellent spa, **Nádúr,** is a soothing, modern oasis. Guests have the run of the thermal suite (a series of rooms/treatments ranging from steam to sauna to hot tub), which soothes away the cares of your traveling day.

Tralee-Killarney rd., Leebrook, Tralee, County Kerry. www.ballygarryhouse.com. ✆ **066/712-3322.** Fax 066/712-7630. 46 units. €130–€190 double. Rates include service charge and full Irish breakfast. AE, MC, V. Closed Dec 20–28. **Amenities:** Restaurant; bar; full-service spa. *In room:* TV.

Ballyseede Castle Hotel ★ This 15th-century castle 3km (2 miles) east of Tralee comes complete with a live-in ghost and was once the chief garrison of the Fitzgeralds, the earls of Desmond. A hotel for 20 years, it has a marvelously regal look. The lobby has Doric columns and a hand-carved oak staircase, while drawing rooms have ornate plasterwork and marble fireplaces. Guest rooms are a mixed bag—some are elegantly appointed, others are a bit old-fashioned and faded. With wood paneling and a towering alcohol cabinet, the **Library Bar** is impressive. The **restaurant** is highly rated and known for its extensive wine cellar.

Tralee-Killarney rd., Tralee, County Kerry. www.ballyseedecastle.com. ✆ **877/905-6789** in the U.S., or 066/712-5799. Fax 066/712-5287. 12 units. €110–€200 double. MC, V. **Amenities:** Restaurant; bar. *In room:* TV, hair dryer.

Grand Hotel Allegedly built on the site of a great medieval castle (of which no trace remains), the Grand is a cheerful, friendly place in the middle of Tralee town. The decor is traditional without being stuffy—the building has been restored sympathetically to its original Victorian design, typified by rooms such as the **Pikeman Bar,** with its wide, hammered-glass front and acres of polished walnut. The bedrooms are bright and modern, and the autumnal color schemes nicely reflect the heritage theme. Good last-minute deals and package offers are often available online, so check the website before booking.

Denny St., Tralee, County Kerry. www.grandhoteltralee.com. ✆ **066/712-1499.** 43 units. €100–€130 double. AE, MC, V. **Amenities:** Restaurant; bar; babysitting. *In room:* TV, hair dryer, Wi-Fi.

Manor West Hotel ★★ Your first sight of Manor West isn't very promising—it sits at the edge of Tralee in a shopping center on a busy highway surrounded by parking lots—but, inside, this modern, attractive hotel has plenty to offer. Rooms are contemporary, quiet, and comfortable with plenty of elegant touches. The **Harmony** spa offers marvelous Elemis treatments, while the gym and pool give you a place to work off the rich dinners from the **Walnut Room** restaurant. However, this isn't the best place to stay if you don't have a car, as it's a long walk or cab ride into town. ***Note:*** Although you're not exactly drowning in breakfast offerings around here, the room-only rate can be a vastly cheaper option. Check online before you book.

Killarney Rd., Tralee, County Kerry. www.manorwesthotel.ie. ✆ **800/618-5343** in the U.S., or 066/719-4500. Fax 066/719-4545. 77 units. €110–€130 double; €130–€170 suites. Rates include full breakfast. AE, DC, MC, V. **Amenities:** Restaurant; bar; gym; indoor pool; sauna/steam room; spa. *In room:* TV, hair dryer, free high-speed Internet, minibar.

Meadowlands Hotel ★ Another find in the Tralee burbs—so probably best suited to those with their own cars—the Meadowlands is a cozy, welcoming sort of hotel. Although the building looks quite modern from the outside, the interior is tastefully furnished in country-house style. The spacious bedrooms are decorated in warm tones of cream, peach, and summery yellow; beds are firm and comfortable. All bedrooms have (adjustable) air conditioning—quite unusual in these parts. The restaurant specializes in fresh fish, as well it should since it's supplied from the owner's own fishing fleet.

Oakpark, Tralee, County Kerry. www.meadowlandshotel.com. ✆ **066/718-0444.** 58 units. Fax 066/718-0964. €100–€150 double; €200 suite. Rates include full breakfast. AE, MC, V. **Amenities:** Restaurant (seafood); bar; guest lounge. *In room:* A/C, TV, hair dryer, broadband Internet (some rooms).

INEXPENSIVE

The Shores ★★ This modern house offers sweeping views of Tralee Bay from virtually every window. Inside, furnishings are eminently tasteful, with a creamy, light color scheme, and well-chosen antiques adding touches of simple beauty. One downstairs room has a private entrance and a fireplace. All rooms have firm orthopedic mattresses, with crisp white cotton and cream lace linen. There's a sun deck and a private beach for when the sun shines, and a guest library and video rentals for when it does not. Breakfast options are extensive, with smoked salmon and waffles as alternatives to the standard fried eggs and bacon. For those in search of additional privacy, a self-catering cottage is available for weekly rental.

.8km (½ mile) west of Stradbally on the Conor Pass rd., Cappatigue, Castlegregory, County Kerry. www.theshorescountryhouse.com. ✆ **066/713-9196.** 6 units. €70–€90 double. Rates include full breakfast. Fixed-price dinner €35. MC, V. Closed Dec–Jan. **Amenities:** Smoke-free rooms. *In room:* TV.

SELF-CATERING

Illauntannig Island Cottage For those who really want to get away from it all, this cottage is perfectly located. Illauntannig is one of the seven Maharees Islands, about 1.6km (1 mile) offshore from Scraggane Bay, on the north shore of the Dingle Peninsula. This is the only cottage on the island, and with its four bedrooms, one bathroom, a sitting room with fireplace, and a sunny kitchen, it feels like a snug, safe place. Make no mistake—you'll be roughing it, with oil lamps substituting for electric lighting and drinking water imported from the mainland. The basic necessities are provided, with gas-powered refrigeration and hot water, but your only companions will be seabirds and cows—the island's only year-round residents. Bob Goodwin, a venerable seaman with a wealth of knowledge on local birds and history, will check in on you every day by two-way radio, and can take you to the mainland as often as necessary for supplies. He can also arrange fishing trips. You can spend your days exploring the small island, which holds the evocative remains of a 6th-century monastery, but little else except exquisite wind-swept views of the deep blue sea.

Contact Bob Goodwin, Maharees, Castlegregory, County Kerry. jfcourtney@eircom.net. ✆/fax **066/713-9443.** 1 cottage. €600–€700 per week. Rates include transport to and from the island, bedding, and all utilities. No credit cards. Closed Nov–Mar.

Kerry Cottages ★★ ☺ Deep in the heart of Kerry, these 10 cottages are off a back road, a few minutes on foot to the beach and another 20 minutes or so to little Castlegregory village. All the cottages have polished pine furnishings, terra-cotta floors (carpeting upstairs), and whitewashed walls. The smallest is a cozy two-bedroom retreat with a small private garden; six cottages have three bedrooms and little backyards. The Sands is the largest house, with five bedrooms, each with a private bathroom. Second-story bedrooms in the larger cottages have great sea views. Each place is equipped with a washer-dryer and dishwasher, and the kitchens have all you need to prepare most meals. There's a small playground area for kids, with a swing set and slide. Rates vary seasonally; the cottages are an especially good value outside the summer season.

Castlegregory, Dingle Peninsula, County Kerry (1.6km/1 mile from Castlegregory). www.kerrycottages.com. ✆ **01/284-4000.** Fax 01/284-4333. Book through Kerry Cottages, 3 Royal Terrace W., Dún Laoghaire, County Dublin. 10 cottages. €395–€895 per week for a 3-bedroom cottage; €550–€1,350 for a 5-bedroom cottage. MC, V. *In room:* TV, kitchen, no phone.

Where to Eat

The Tankard SEAFOOD Right on the water's edge, the restaurant's wide picture windows provide gorgeous views of the seafront amid a chic, contemporary decor. The menu focuses on local seafood—lobster, scallops, prawns, and black sole are all house specialties. It also features local meat, including rack of lamb, duck, quail, and steak. Bar food is available all day, but this restaurant is at its best in the early evening, especially at sunset.

10km (6¼ miles) northwest of Tralee, Kilfenora, Fenit, County Kerry. ✆ **066/713-6349.** Reservations recommended. Main courses €16–€33; fixed-price Sun lunch €22. AE, DC, MC, V. Bar food daily 2–10pm. Restaurant daily noon–4pm and 6–10pm.

Tralee After Dark

Siamsa Tire ★, the National Folk Theatre of Ireland, is at Town Park (✆ **066/712-3055;** www.siamsatire.com). Founded in 1974, Siamsa (pronounced *Sheem*-sha) offers a mixture of Irish music, dance, and mime. Its folk programs depict old folk tales and utilize farmyard activities, such as thatching a cottage roof, flailing sheaves of corn, and twisting a *sugan* rope. It also offers dramatic performances and musical concerts (traditional and classical) by amateur and professional companies. They also host touring shows of a more popular kind and film screenings. Admission to the main shows costs from around €16 to €30 for adults, €14 to €23 for seniors, students, and children. Call ahead for reservations.

PUBS

Harty's Lounge Bar This pub—celebrated as the meetinghouse where the Rose of Tralee festival was born—is known for its good traditional pub food, such as steak-and-Guinness pie, shepherd's pie, and Irish stew. 30 Lower Castle St., Tralee, County Kerry. ✆ **066/712-5385.**

Kirby's Olde Brogue Inn This big barn of a pub is properly rustic, with decor heavy on farming implements. There's an excellent menu here, and traditional music and folk ballads when the right people show up. Rock St., Tralee, County Kerry. ✆ **066/712-3221.** www.kirbysbrogue.com.

Oyster Tavern This tavern has probably the nicest location of any pub in the Tralee area, just 5km (3 miles) west of downtown, overlooking Tralee Bay. The pub grub includes seafood soups and platters. Fenit Rd., The Spa, Tralee, County Kerry. ✆ **066/713-6102.**

10

TIPPERARY, LIMERICK & CLARE

With miles of emerald green farmland and the stunning drama provided by the Rock of Cashel, Tipperary is a peaceful place, while Limerick swirls and eddies through the flatland of the Shannon River valley, and Clare simply explodes with variety, from the lunar landscape of the Burren to a dramatic coastline.

In fact, Limerick, despite its marvelous name and the 50,000 bad jokes and dirty songs for which it can arguably be blamed, is a rather quiet, bucolic county. Tipperary has very little to dazzle you aside from the **Rock of Cashel,** which is simply spectacular and worth a trip across the country all on its own. Clare, on the other hand, with its desolate, rocky Burren and majestic Cliffs of Moher, is just showing off.

So what we're saying, we suppose, is stop in at Limerick for a photo or two, head to the Rock, and then hurry on to Clare for the real razzle-dazzle.

COUNTY TIPPERARY

Clonmel: 174km (108 miles) SW of Dublin, 182km (113 miles) SE of Galway, 79km (49 miles) SE of Limerick, 103km (64 miles) SE of Shannon Airport, 48km (30 miles) NW of Waterford, 145km (90 miles) E of Killarney

In many ways County Tipperary is a bit mysterious. Everybody's heard of it, but few have actually been. It's a bit out of the way—too far from most major tourist hot spots for an easy day trip—and its tourist attractions are few. This works to its advantage, though, since far from the tour buses and the clicking of camera shutters, you may just find the Ireland everyone is looking for: welcoming, unspoiled, green, and peaceful.

GETTING THERE **Irish Rail** runs several trains a day into Clonmel from Limerick and Waterford. It serves Clonmel Station, Thomas Street, Clonmel, Tipperary (✆ **052/612-1982;** www.irishrail.ie). The station is a 10-minute walk from the town center.

There are more **buses** than trains to Clonmel, and **Bus Éireann** operates daily bus service to Limerick, Wexford, and Rosslare, into Clonmel Train Station, Thomas Street, Clonmel (✆ **052/612-1982;** www.buseireann.ie).

If you're **driving** from Dublin and points north, take the N7 or N76; if you're coming from the west, take the N24.

VISITOR INFORMATION The **Clonmel Tourist Office** is at 6 Sarsfield St., Clonmel (✆ **052/612-2960**). It's open year-round Monday to Saturday 9:30am to 5:30pm. The **Cashel Tourist Office** is at the Heritage Centre, Main Street, Cashel (✆ **062/62511**), open daily 9:30am to 5:30pm from March to October and 9:30am to 5:30pm Monday to Friday

PREVIOUS PAGE: **Poulnabrone, an ancient dolmen in the limestone karst landscape of the Burren, County Clare.**

from November to February. A **seasonal office** is at Castle Street, Cahir (✆ **052/714-1453**), open June to August Monday to Saturday 9:30am to 6pm.

Exploring the Area

Clonmel, the capital of Tipperary, is the unassuming gateway to the region. A working town, largely unspoiled by tourism, Clonmel (whose name in Gaelic, *Cluaín Meala,* means "Meadows of Honey") makes a strategic, pleasant base in the Southeast. Looking at the pretty rural town, poised on the banks of the Suir, it's hard to believe that it once withstood a Cromwellian siege for 3 brutal months.

Whether you're staying in Clonmel or just passing through, several scenic drives converge here: the **Comeragh or Nire Valley Drive** deep into the Comeragh Mountains, which rise from the south banks of the Suir; the **Knockmealdown Drive,** through the historic village of Ardfinnan and the Vee Gap (see below); and the **Suir Scenic Drive.** All are signposted from Clonmel.

North of Clonmel and deep in the Tipperary countryside, **Cashel,** with its monastic buildings and dramatic setting, is not to be missed. Because it's on the main N8 road, most people pass through en route from Dublin to Cork. If your travels don't take you to Cashel, a side trip from Waterford is worth the drive. In particular, the following two scenic routes are well worth a detour.

At Cahir, head north through the scenic **Galtee Mountains ★** to the Glen of Aherlow. The pristine 11km (7-mile) Glen of Aherlow is a secluded and scenic pass between the plains of counties Tipperary and Limerick.

If you're driving south into Waterford, you might want to travel via the **Vee Gap.** This 18km-long (11-mile) road winds through the Knockmealdown Mountains from Clogheen to Lismore and Cappoquin in County Waterford. It's a dramatic drive, which peaks at the Tipperary-Waterford border, where the two slopes of the pass converge to frame the patchwork fields of the Galtee Valley far below. At this point, numerous walking trails lead to the nearby peaks and down to the mountain lake of **Petticoat Loose**—named after a, shall we say, lady of flexible morals. A more edifying local character was Samuel Grubb, of Castle Grace, who so loved these slopes that he left instructions to be buried upright overlooking them. And so he was. The rounded stone cairn you might notice off the road between Clogheen and the Vee Gap is where he stands in place, entombed, facing the Golden Vale of Tipperary.

Ahenny High Crosses You're likely to have this little-known and rarely visited site to yourself, except for the cows whose pasture you will cross to reach it. The setting is idyllic and gorgeous on a bright day. The well-preserved Ahenny high crosses date from the 8th or 9th century. Tradition associates them with seven saintly bishops, all brothers who were said to have been waylaid and murdered. Their unusual stone "caps," thought by some to be bishops' miters, more likely suggest the transition from wood crosses, which would have had small roofs to shelter them from the rain. Also note their intricate spiral and cable ornamentation in remarkably high relief, which may have been inspired by earlier Celtic metalwork.
Kil Crispeen Churchyard, Ahenny, County Tipperary. 8km (5 miles) north of Carrick-on-Suir, signposted off R697. Box for donations.

Athassel Priory Although it is in ruins, many delightful details from the original medieval priory that once stood here still remain. This was an Augustinian priory, founded in the late 12th century, and it was once elaborately decorated.

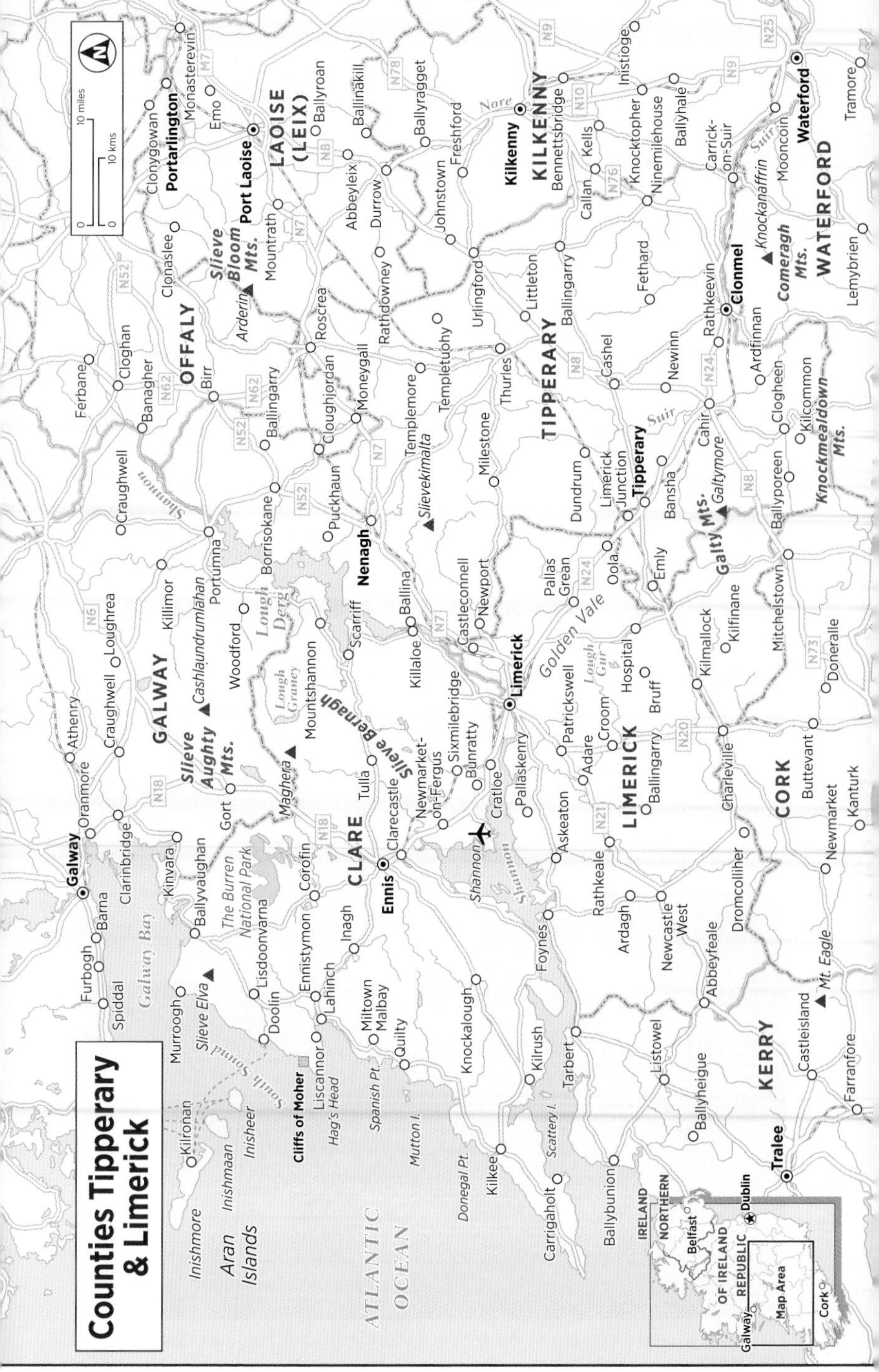

Counties Tipperary & Limerick
10 kms
10 miles
OFFALY
LAOISE (LEIX)
KILKENNY
GALWAY
CLARE
LIMERICK
TIPPERARY
WATERFORD
CORK
KERRY
ATLANTIC OCEAN
Galway
Oranmore
Athenry
Craughwell
Loughrea
Clarinbridge
Kinvara
Gort
Ballyvaughan
Galway Bay
Barna
Furbogh
Spiddal
Murroogh
Slieve Elva
Doolin
Lisdoonvarna
The Burren National Park
Corofin
Ennistymon
Lahinch
Liscannor
Cliffs of Moher
Hag's Head
Miltown Malbay
Quilty
Spanish Pt.
Mutton I.
Inagh
Ennis
Clarecastle
Tulla
Newmarket-on-Fergus
Sixmilebridge
Bunratty
Cratloe
Shannon
Knockalough
Kilrush
Kilkee
Donegal Pt.
Scattery I.
Carrigaholt
Tarbert
Foynes
Askeaton
Pallaskenry
Rathkeale
Ardagh
Newcastle West
Abbeyfeale
Dromcolliher
Listowel
Ballybunion
Ballyheigue
Tralee
Castleisland
Farranfore
Mt. Eagle
Newmarket
Kanturk
Buttevant
Charleville
Doneralle
Mitchelstown
Kilmallock
Kilfinane
Bruff
Hospital
Lough Gur
Croom
Adare
Patrickswell
Ballingarry
Limerick
Golden Vale
Pallas Grean
Oola
Emly
Galty Mts.
Galtymore
Bansha
Tipperary
Limerick Junction
Dundrum
Cahir
Ballyporeen
Clogheen
Kilcommon
Knockmealdown Mts.
Ardfinnan
Clonmel
Rathkeevin
Comeragh Mts.
Knockanaffrin
Lemybrien
Newinn
Cashel
Fethard
Ballingarry
Littleton
Thurles
Templetuohy
Milestone
Urlingford
Johnstown
Freshford
Templemore
Slievekimalta
Castleconnell
Newport
Ballina
Killaloe
Nenagh
Puckhaun
Moneygall
Cloughjordan
Roscrea
Rathdowney
Borrisokane
Scarriff
Mountshannon
Lough Derg
Lough Graney
Slieve Bernagh
Maghera
Woodford
Portumna
Cashlaundrumlahan
Killimor
Slieve Aughty Mts.
Shannon
Banagher
Birr
Ferbane
Cloghan
Clonaslee
Slieve Bloom Mts.
Arderin
Mountrath
Abbeyleix
Durrow
Ballinakill
Ballyroan
Ballyragget
Port Laoise
Emo
Portarlington
Clonygowan
Monasterevin
Kilkenny
Nore
Bennettsbridge
Kells
Callan
Knocktopher
Ninemilehouse
Inistioge
Ballyhale
Carrick-on-Suir
Suir
Mooncoin
Waterford
Tramore
Inishmore
Inishmaan
Inisheer
Aran Islands
Kilronan
South Sound
NORTHERN IRELAND
REPUBLIC OF IRELAND
Belfast
Dublin
Galway
Cork
Map Area
N6
N7
N8
N9
N10
N18
N20
N21
N24
N25
N52
N62
N73
N76
N78

The main approach is over a low stone bridge and through a gatehouse. The church entrance is a beautifully carved doorway at its west end, while to the south of the church is the cloister, its graceful arches eroded by time. Look for a carved face protruding from the southwest corner of the chapel tower, about 9m (30 ft.) above ground level.

3km (2 miles) south of Golden, County Tipperary. Take signposted road from Golden, on the N74; the priory is in a field just east of the road.

The Bolton Library In this library, you'll see what is supposedly the smallest book in the world, as well as other rare, antiquarian, and unusual books dating as far back as the 12th century. The works by Dante, Swift, Calvin, Newton, Erasmus, and Machiavelli are displayed alongside silver altarpieces from the cathedral on the Rock of Cashel.

On the grounds of St. John the Baptist Church, John St., Cashel, County Tipperary. ✆ **062/61944.** Admission €2; free for young children. Mon–Fri 10am–4:30pm.

Brú Ború Heritage Centre ★ At the foot of the Rock of Cashel, this modern complex adds a musical element to the historic Cashel area. Operated by Comhaltas Ceoltoiri Éireann, Ireland's foremost traditional-music organization, Brú Ború presents daily performances of authentic Irish traditional music at an indoor theater. Many summer evenings feature concerts in the open-air amphitheater. A subterranean "Sounds of History" exhibition gives an audio tour of Ireland through the ages. A gift shop, restaurant, and self-service snack bar are also on hand.

Rock Lane, Cashel, County Tipperary. ✆ **062/61122.** www.comhaltas.ie. Free admission to center. Show €20 adults; €10 children. Combined dinner and show tickets €50 adults; €25 children. "Sounds of History" exhibition €5 adults; €3 children. Daily 9am–5pm (later on show nights). Shows mid-June to mid-Sept Tues–Sat 9pm.

Cahir Castle ★★ On a rock in the middle of the River Suir, this remarkably complete medieval fortress can trace its history from the 3rd century, when a fort

Cahir Castle occupies the site of a 3rd-century fortress, but Normans built the current structure in the 14th century.

St. Patrick reputedly baptized King Aengus in the 5th century here at the Rock of Cashel.

was first built on the rock—hence the town's Gaelic name, "City of the Fishing Fort." The present structure, which belonged to the Butler family for 600 years, 1375 to 1961, is Norman. It has a massive keep, high walls, spacious courtyards, original gateways with portcullis still intact, and a fully restored great hall. The interpretive center has an engaging 20-minute video introduction to the region's major historic sites, and you can take a guided tour of the castle grounds. But do take the time to walk through the castle buildings, which are not included in the tour.

Cahir, County Tipperary. ✆ **052/744-1011.** Admission €3 adults; €2.40 seniors; €1.50 students and children; €8 families. Mid-Mar to mid-June daily 9:30am–5:30pm; mid-June to Aug daily 9am–6:30pm; Sept to mid-Oct daily 9:30am–5:30pm; mid-Oct to mid-Mar daily 9:30am–4:30pm. Closed Dec 24–30.

Ormond Castle This mid-15th-century castle built by Sir Edward MacRichard Butler on a strategic bend of the River Suir has lain in ruins for centuries. What still stands, attached to the ancient battlements, is the last surviving Tudor manor house in Ireland. Trusting that "if he built it, she would come," Thomas Butler constructed an extensive manor in honor of his most successful relation, Queen Elizabeth I. He was to be disappointed. Elizabeth never dropped by, but many others have, especially since the Heritage Service partially restored this impressive piece of Irish history. The manor's plasterwork, carvings, period furniture, and collection of original 17th- and 18th-century royal charters will make you glad you bothered to visit and wonder why Good Queen Bess never did.

Signposted from the center of Carrick-on-Suir, Carrick-on-Suir, County Tipperary. ✆ **051/640787.** Free admission. End of Apr to Sept daily 10am–6pm. Closed Oct–Apr. Last admission 45 min. before closing.

The Rock of Cashel ★★★ When you're near the town of Cashel, the first thing you'll see is the extraordinary, dramatic outline of this craggy abbey at the top of the hill at the town center. It dominates views for miles around. An outcrop of limestone reaching 60m (197 ft.) into the sky, "the Rock" tells the tales of 16 centuries. It was the castled seat of the kings of Munster at least as far back as A.D. 360, and it remained a royal fortress until 1101, when King Murtagh O'Brien granted it to the church. Among Cashel's many great moments was the legendary baptism of King Aengus by St. Patrick in 448. Remaining on the rock are the ruins of a two-towered chapel, a cruciform cathedral, a 28m (92-ft.) round tower, and a cluster of other medieval monuments. Inside the cathedral, extraordinary and detailed ancient carvings survive in excellent condition. The views of and from the Rock are spectacular. Forty-five-minute guided tours are available on request.

Cashel, County Tipperary. ✆ **062/61437.** www.cashel.ie/attractions/rock.htm. Admission €6 adults; €4 seniors; €2 students and children; €14 families. Daily Mid-Mar to early June and mid-Sept to mid-Oct 9:30am–5.30pm; early June to mid-Sept 9am–7pm; mid-Oct to mid-Mar 9am–4.30pm. Last admission 45 min. before closing.

Swiss Cottage The earls of Glengall used the Swiss Cottage as a hunting and fishing lodge as far back as 1812. It's a superb example of *cottage orné:* a rustic house embodying the ideal of simplicity that so appealed to the Romantics of the early 19th century. The thatched-roof cottage has extensive timberwork, usually not seen in Ireland, and is believed to have been designed by John Nash, a royal architect. The interior has some of the first wallpaper commercially produced in Paris. A guided tour (the only way to see the building) lasts approximately 40 minutes.

Off Dublin-Cork rd. (N8), Cahir, County Tipperary. ✆ **052/41144.** Guided tour €3 adults; €2.10 seniors; €1.30 students and children; €8 families. Mid-Apr to end of Oct daily 10am–6pm. Reduced opening in late Oct; call to confirm. Last admission 45 min. before closing.

Sports & Outdoor Pursuits

BICYCLING For complete 1- or 2-week cycling holidays in the Southeast, contact Don Smith at **Celtic Cycling,** Lorum Old Rectory, Bagenalstown, County Carlow (✆ **059/977-5282;** www.celticcycling.com/lorum.html).

BIRD-WATCHING As many as 15 species of Irish water birds—including mute swans, coots, gadwalls, and gray herons—can be seen at the **Marlfield Lake Wildfowl Refuge,** several miles west of Clonmel in Marlfield. On your way, you will pass signposts for **St. Patrick's Well,** less than 1.6km (1 mile) away, a tranquil spot with an effervescent pool of reputedly healing crystalline water. In the middle of the pool rises an ancient Celtic cross. The legend that Patrick visited here seems more solidly rooted than most such claims.

FISHING The **River Suir,** from Carrick-on-Suir to Thurles, was once one of the finest salmon rivers in Europe, but recent excessive trawling at its mouth has threatened its stock. It's still a decent salmon river, especially in the February run and from June to September. Trout (brown and rainbow) are in abundance here in the summer. Here you'll find some of the least expensive game fishing in Ireland; single weekday permits cost around €40. Trout permits are issued by local fishing clubs, and prices vary. The fishing season lasts from St. Patrick's Day to the end of September. Get in touch with the local tourist offices for more details. To orient yourself and to consider your options, pick up a copy of *Angling on the Suir,* a helpful pamphlet put out by the Tourist Office. The **River Nore** and the nearby **River Barrow** are also known for good salmon and trout fishing.

HORSEBACK RIDING Once the most popular riding center for miles around, Melodys Nire Valley Equestrian Centre closed its doors after 30 years. At the moment there are no stables that we know of offering trekking and trail riding in the Nire Valley—really the best riding territory in this part of Ireland—but a little farther afield you could try the **Clonmel Equestrian Centre,** Mongarrif, Clonmel, County Tipperary (✆ **087/244-6302**).

SWIMMING If you're staying in the area, you're welcome to swim at the **Clonmel Civic Swimming Pool** (✆ **052/21972**), near the Market Place, which also has a handy gym and sauna. It's open Monday to Friday 9am to 9:45pm, Saturday and Sunday 10am to 7:45pm. Call for specific public swimming hours, as it might not be open for general access at all times of day.

TENNIS The courts of the **Hillview Sports Club,** Mountain Road, Clonmel (✆ **052/21805;** www.hillviewsportsclub.com), may be used by visitors.

WALKING **R668** between Clogheen and Lismore is a scenic stretch of road, and some great walks begin at the **Vee Gap,** a dramatic notch in the Knockmealdown Mountains. About 2km (1¼ miles) north of R669 and R668, you reach the highest point in the gap; there is a parking lot, as well as a dirt road continuing down to a lake nestled into the slope below. This is Bay Lough, and the dirt road used to be the main thoroughfare over the gap; it now offers a fine walk to the shores of the lake, with outstanding views of the valley to the north. For a panoramic perspective of the region, start walking due east from the gap parking lot to the summit of Sugarloaf Hill; the hike is extremely steep, but well worth the effort—the views from the ridge are superb.

In the Clonmel area, there are excellent river and hill walks, some more challenging than others. The most spectacular is the ascent of famed **Slievenamon,** a mountain rich in myth. Inexpensive, detailed trail maps for at least a half-dozen walks are available at the Clonmel Tourist Office on Sarsfield Street, Clonmel. Also available is a free leaflet guide to the birds, butterflies, and flora of nearby **Wilderness Gorge.**

The **Galtee Mountains,** northwest of the Knockmealdowns, offer some great long and short walks. One beautiful route on a well-defined trail is the circuit of **Lake Muskry,** on the north side of the range. To get there, take R663 west out of Bansha, and follow signs for the town of Rossadrehid. To get to the trail, ask for directions in Rossadrehid; there are several turns, and the landmarks change frequently because of logging. The trail leads you up a glaciated valley to the base of a ring of cliffs where the crystalline waters of Lake Muskry lie; from here you can walk around the lake, take in the tremendous views of the valley, and return the way you came. Walking time to the lake and back is 3 hours.

Another option on this walk is to continue up past the lake to the top of the ridge, and from there along the ridge top to Galtymore, a prominent dome-shaped peak about 5km (3 miles) west of Lake Muskry. It is a beautiful but extremely demanding walk, about 6 hours to Galtymore and back. This is only one of many extraordinary walks in the Glen of Aherlow. Trail maps and all the information and assistance you need are available at the **Glen of Aherlow Fáilte Society,** just behind the Coach Road pub, Coach Road, Newtown (✆ **062/56331;** www.aherlow.com). It's open daily June to October from 9am to 6pm, with variable hours at other times of year.

Where to Stay

EXPENSIVE

Cashel Palace Hotel ★ Originally built in 1730 as a residence for Church of Ireland archbishops, this mammoth redbrick Palladian mansion has been a hotel for over 30 years. It has an ideal location right in the middle of Cashel town, yet within its own walled grounds, and recent owners have updated the property and filled it with antiques and designer fabrics. The house is a proud display of lofty, corniced ceilings, Corinthian pillars, mantelpieces of Kilkenny marble, and a paneled early Georgian staircase of red pine. Guest rooms have a warm, traditional look and vast bathrooms, while the 10 rooms in the Mews House are smaller and more modern. The **Bishop's Buttery** restaurant has splendid views of the floodlit Rock, while well-tended gardens hold mulberry bushes that were planted in 1702 to commemorate the coronation of Queen Anne. Be sure to ask if you want a room with a view of the Rock of Cashel, but be aware that these are more expensive.

Main St., Cashel, County Tipperary. www.cashel-palace.ie. ✆ **062/62707.** Fax 062/61521. 23 units. €140–€176 double; €220 suite. Rates include service charge and full Irish breakfast. AE, MC, V. **Amenities:** Restaurant; bar; babysitting. *In room:* TV, hair dryer.

Hotel Minella ★ The attractive centerpiece of this sprawling hotel complex along the River Suir was built in 1863, but there have been many additions since then. Its riverbank location and attractive landscaping provide an appeal beyond the somewhat incongruous mix of architectural styles. Once you're inside, its warm, welcoming atmosphere takes over. The standard guest rooms are furnished traditionally in dark wood and prints. Bedrooms are dressed in rich colors, with big comfortable beds; and some have their own Jacuzzis or steam rooms in the bathrooms (the latter are especially spacious and luxurious). Perhaps the chief appeal of this hotel is its state-of-the-art **health and fitness club,** where you can also get a massage—you could easily spend several days using the facilities.

1.6km (1 mile) east of Clonmel center on the south bank of the River Suir, Coleville Rd., Clonmel, County Tipperary. www.hotelminella.ie. ✆ **052/612-2388.** 90 units. €130–€180 double; €200–€350 suite. Rates include service charge and full breakfast. AE, MC, V. **Amenities:** Restaurant; bar; 2 lounges; babysitting; outdoor hot tub; indoor Jacuzzi; indoor pool; room service; sauna; smoke-free rooms; aromatherapy steam room; all-season tennis court. *In room:* TV, free high-speed Internet.

Mobarnane House This elegant, splendidly restored 18th-century farmhouse was opened in 2000 as a B&B and immediately became popular with discerning travelers in search of a period setting, tranquil surroundings, and warm hospitality. Richard Craik-White is a terrific chef, and his wife, Sandra, is a warm hostess. Dinner is a convivial affair, served at a communal table. Guest rooms are prettily decked out in cream or blue, furnished with mahogany pieces and antiques. The best two rooms have mountain views and their own sitting rooms; the other two face the lake and are equally pretty but not as large. Unfortunately, prices are rather high for what's on offer. Still, if money is no object and peace is your desire, this could be the place.

Fethard, County Tipperary. www.mobarnanehouse.com. ✆ **052/31962.** 4 units. €150–€190 double. 4-course dinner €45 (Mon–Sat, book 24 hr. in advance). 20% reduction for 3 or more nights. Rates include service charge and full breakfast. MC, V. Closed Nov–Feb. Not suitable for those with limited mobility. No young children. *In room:* TV.

MODERATE

Dundrum House Hotel Located 10km (6¼ miles) northwest of Cashel, this Georgian country manor is nestled in the fertile Tipperary countryside, surrounded by sprawling grounds and gardens. Originally built as a residence in 1730 by the Earl of Montalt, it was later used as a convent school, and then transformed into a hotel in 1978. It is furnished with heirlooms, vintage curios, Victorian pieces, and reproductions. Each room is individually decorated with a traditional and slightly dated feel, some with four-poster beds, armoires, and other traditional furnishings. Enormous family rooms make this place good for those travelling with kids. Look for exceptional weekend specials on offer all year. The hotel's bar is especially appealing, in a former chapel with stained-glass windows.

Dundrum, County Tipperary. www.dundrumhousehotel.com. ✆ **062/71116.** Fax 062/71366. 86 units. €100–€150 double. Self-catering apts. and vacation homes also available. AE, MC, V. **Amenities:** Restaurant; bar; 18-hole championship golf course; gym; indoor pool; sauna. *In room:* TV, radio, hair dryer.

Kilcoran Lodge Hotel A former hunting lodge nestled amid wooded grounds, this old Victorian treasure is on a hillside set back from the main road a few miles west of Cahir. The public areas retain their old-world charm, with open fireplaces, grandfather clocks, antique tables and chairs, brass fixtures, and tall windows framing expansive views of the Suir Valley and Knockmealdown Mountains. Guest rooms are basically but comfortably appointed and have modern bathrooms. The bar is noted for its excellent daytime menu, which includes Irish stew, traditional boiled bacon and cabbage, homemade soups, and hot scones. ***Tip:*** You can normally find significantly reduced room-only rates and good special offers on the hotel's website.

Dublin-Cork rd. (N8), Cahir, County Tipperary. www.kilcoranlodgehotel.com. ✆ **800/447-7462** in the U.S., or 052/41288. Fax 052/41994. 22 units. €60–€130 double. Rates include service charge and full breakfast. AE, MC, V. **Amenities:** Restaurant; bar; lounge; gym; Jacuzzi; indoor pool; sauna. *In room:* TV, radio, hair dryer.

Roundwood House ☺ Just outside County Tipperary in County Laois, Roundwood House has an insouciant, put-up-your-feet casual elegance. Good taste pervades the splendid 18th-century Palladian country villa, set amid secluded woods, pasture, and gardens. The six guest rooms in the main house are spacious and decorated with an eye for charm and simplicity. The two on the second floor share a large central play area ideal for families with children. The Yellow House, across the herb garden and courtyard from the main building, has been tastefully restored to offer four double rooms. If you're looking for privacy, there are three self-catering cottages available, including the original gatehouse. ***Note:*** The nearest TV is a long walk away.

4.8km (3 miles) northwest of Mountrath, on R440 toward the Slieve Bloom Mountains, Mountrath, County Laois. www.roundwoodhouse.com. ✆ **057/873-2120.** Fax 057/873-2711. 10 units. Main house €130 double; Yellow House €120 double. Rates include full Irish breakfast. Self-catering cottages €180–€380 3 nights up to €280–€500 per week. 5-course dinner Tues–Sat (book by 2pm) €50; 3-course supper Sun–Mon €35; 6pm children's dinner €10. AE, DC, MC, V.

INEXPENSIVE

Bansha House The guest rooms in this small Georgian manor house are pleasant, with sturdy country furniture and, perhaps, a bit too much pink in the color scheme. However, through a cruel twist of fate, the largest rooms lack private bathrooms. The self-catering Primrose Cottage, which sleeps five, is perfect for families and folks who want to do their own cooking. The town of Bansha sits at the base of the magnificent Galtee Mountains, which dominate the skyline on a clear day and make this an ideal base for walking, cycling, or just taking in the scenery. The adjacent Bansha House Stables are professional horse breeders.

Bansha, County Tipperary. www.tipp.ie/banshahs.htm or banshahouse@eircom.net. ✆ **062/54194.** Fax 062/54215. 8 units, 5 with private bathroom. €90 double; cottage €500–€600 per week. Rates include full breakfast. Dinner €27. MC, V. Closed Dec 20–28.

Kilmaneen Farmhouse This sweetly decorated, relaxing farmhouse B&B is a real find. Set amid a beautiful mountainous terrain, it's run with aplomb by Kevin and Ber O'Donnell. Those who love fishing love Kilmaneen, as you can cast for trout here, into either the Suir or the Tar, without any permit required. You will be provided with a fisherman's hut for tying flies, storing equipment, and waders. Kevin is trained in mountaineering and leads trekking and walking tours into the nearby Knockmealdowns, Comeraghs, or Galtee mountains. If you decide you want to stay a week, there's a fully equipped guest cottage, cozy enough for two and spacious enough for five. It rents for anywhere from €250 to €500 per week, depending on the season and number of occupants. The main farmhouse can also be hired on a self-catering basis for €400 to €600 per week. Finding your way here can be tricky, so call ahead and ask for detailed directions.

Newcastle, County Tipperary. www.kilmaneen.com. ✆ **052/613-6231.** 3 units, 2 with shower only. €80 double. Rates include full breakfast. Evening buffet €25 Mon–Sat (book 24 hr. in advance). MC, V. *In room:* TV (some).

Mr. Bumbles Above Declan Gavigan's Mr. Bumbles restaurant (see below), with their own exterior staircase, these four rooms are basic but bright. They are meticulously clean and have firm beds. The family room sleeps three. If you crave a night off from the social rituals of the standard B&B and want an excellent breakfast, this is the place. Better yet, it's possible to negotiate a B&B-and-dinner combination, which all but guarantees sweet dreams.

Richmond House, Kickham St., Clonmel, County Tipperary (top of Clonmel Market Place). www.mrbumbles.ie. ✆ **052/612-9188.** 4 units, all with shower only. €60 double. Rates include full breakfast. MC, V. **Amenities:** Restaurant. *In room:* TV.

SELF-CATERING

Coopers Cottage ★ This adorable Victorian cottage is perfect for a family wanting to explore the southeastern counties of Tipperary, Waterford, and Kilkenny. Stella and Eamonn Long have lovingly restored and renovated this vine-covered 19th-century cooper's cottage, once Eamonn's family home, into a comfortable, tasteful hideaway. With exposed beams, polished wood floors, and a wood-burning stove, the Longs have created a house full of light, with spectacular views of the Galtee Mountains. The house, which has three bedrooms and sleeps six, comes with absolutely everything, and there's even a barbecue and a modest fenced-in garden, with a patio for sunny days.

1.6km (1 mile) off N24 at Bansha, Raheen, Bansha, County Tipperary. www.dirl.com/tipperary/bansha/coopers.htm. ✆ **062/54376.** 1 cottage. €400–€550 per week. No credit cards. *In room:* TV, kitchen.

Where to Eat

VERY EXPENSIVE

Chez Hans ★★ CONTINENTAL/SEAFOOD In a former Gothic chapel in the shadow of the mighty Rock of Cashel, this restaurant's cathedral-style ceiling, stone walls, and candlelight create a perfect setting for a memorable meal. The menu draws from local produce and seafood for dishes such as Kilmore Quay scallops with couscous salad and salsa verde, cassoulet of seafood, Dunmore East lobster, rack of Tipperary lamb, and roast duck with orange sauce, colcannon, and pesto. The flavors are luxurious, the portions generous, the crowd appreciative.

Rockside, Cashel, County Tipperary. ✆ **062/61177.** www.chezhans.net. Reservations required. Main courses €29–€45. MC, V. Tues–Sat 6:30–10pm. Closed last 2 weeks in Jan and last 2 weeks in Sept.

MODERATE

Befani's ★★ MEDITERRANEAN/TAPAS This laid-back, elegant restaurant has become quite a local favorite since it opened a few years ago. Befani describes itself as "a taste of the Mediterranean in Clonmel," and it certainly takes its message to heart. Local produce complements traditional Mediterranean flavors, so you could just as easily find a Cashel blue cheese risotto on the menu as, say, an olive oil and garlic roasted chicken, chargrilled vegetable pizza, or Moroccan-style lamb shank. There's also a tapas menu that balances local cuisine with hints of the global village: a simple bruschetta, fried calamari, or Thai king prawns in a lemon grass and chili tempura. The restaurant also runs an attractive guesthouse, with double rooms for a fully reasonable €70 per night.

6 Sarsfield St., Clonmel, County Tipperary. ✆ **052/617-7893.** www.befani.com. Reservations recommended. Main courses €17–€23. AE, MC, V. Mon–Sat 9–11am and 12:30–10pm (tapas 12:30–10pm); Sun 12:30–9:30pm.

Mr. Bumbles ★★ INTERNATIONAL With its natural woods, bright colors, and bistro feel, this split-level restaurant is inviting and the food first-rate. Many dishes are grilled or pan-seared local seafood and beef. Wild sea trout, Tipperary sirloin, or filet are often on the menu. The presentation is nicely done, and portions are generous. The French house wines are fairly reasonable at roughly €14 per bottle, and the international wine list is also strong. Recently, Mr. Bumbles has been running an extremely popular two-course lunch deal for €10—wryly dubbed "the Credit Crunch Lunch." The way the economy's heading at the moment, we wouldn't be at all surprised if the deal's still on when you get there.

Richmond House, Kickham St., Clonmel, County Tipperary. ✆ **052/612-9188.** www.mrbumbles.ie. Reservations recommended. Fixed-price early-bird menus: 2 courses €20, 3 courses €24; main courses €19–€27. MC, V. Mon–Sat noon–2:30pm and 6–10pm; Sun noon–3pm and 6–9:30pm.

Pubs

Gerry Chawkes Chawkes is a Clonmel landmark, a shrine not so much to stout as to sport. A fanatic of hurling and racing (dogs and horses), Gerry Chawke has made his pub a cult place, lined with fascinating sports memorabilia. Athletic clubs from throughout Ireland make a point of stopping here, as do local politicians in recovery from council meetings. 3 Gladstone St. Upper, Clonmel, County Tipperary. ✆ **052/612-1149.**

Railway Bar ★ 🎁 You'll need on-the-ground directions to find Kitty's, which is what locals call this pub in a cul-de-sac behind the train station. Your efforts will be worthwhile, especially on weekends, when a traditional-music session is likely to break out. No one is paid or even invited to play here; they just show up. Often, there are so many musicians and so many wanting to hear them that the music spills outside, down the lane. No frills here—just the best Irish music around, and a pub out of the who-knows-when past. Clonmel, County Tipperary. No phone.

Tierney's ★★ This place has been the Tipperary pub of the year so many times that we've lost count. It's a remarkably classy pub, with dark carved wood, shiny brass railings, and stained glass. It goes on and on from one level to another, with small lounges, big dining rooms, and little nooks. Upstairs, a full-service restaurant has several dining rooms, each with its own character, and outside there's a walled beer garden for times when the weather is kind. 13 O'Connell St., Clonmel, County Tipperary. ✆ **052/612-4467.**

COUNTY LIMERICK

24km (15 miles) E of Shannon Airport, 198km (123 miles) SW of Dublin, 105km (65 miles) N of Cork, 111km (69 miles) NE of Killarney, 105km (65 miles) S of Galway

In such a tiny country, a population approaching 90,000 is enough to make gritty Limerick City the third-largest city in the Republic. Strategically located on the banks of the River Shannon, the town was founded as a Viking settlement in the 10th century and grew in importance over the centuries. For many years, it struggled with endemic poverty, but today it is a busy place with a serious focus on business, and its shiny new office buildings stand as evidence—although this city's new economy has been hit quite brutally by the recession.

Adare is one of Ireland's prettiest towns, though its predominant house style is English.

Limerick is working hard to throw off the grim legacy bestowed by Frank McCourt's best-selling book *Angela's Ashes,* which described in excruciating detail a childhood spent there in poverty and unimaginable horribleness. Still, despite the effort to scrub itself up, the city suffers from a crime problem so serious that the Irish who once wryly dubbed this place "Stab City" have started calling it "Slab City." In 2008 it was the murder capital of Europe while Ireland was named the safest country in the same report.

The tourist board tries to put a positive spin on things, and we recognize that they are making efforts to clean the place up. But this still feels like a rough old town, and the area where its most impressive sights are located—the riverside Medieval Heritage Precinct dominated by the 13th-century **King John's Castle**—is no exception, so use extra caution when carrying handbags or pricey cameras, and pay to park in a parking lot rather than on the street.

Happily, the countryside around Limerick City is much less scary—most of it is green, bucolic river basin and pleasant farmland. The picture-postcard village of Adare is definitely worth a visit (although you'll see everything from the end of a row of tour buses), as are Lough Gur, gorgeous Glin Castle, and Rathkeale.

Essentials

GETTING THERE From the United States, Aer Lingus, British Airways, and Continental operate regularly scheduled flights into **Shannon Airport,** off the Limerick-Ennis road (N18), County Clare (✆ **061/712000;** www.shannonairport.com), 24km (15 miles) west of Limerick. Aer Lingus and Ryanair operates flights to London, Birmingham, and Bristol in England. A taxi from the airport to the city center costs about €35; you can catch one at the airport or prebook with **Shannon Airport Cabs** (✆ **061/333-366;** www.shannonairportcabs.com).

Bus Éireann (✆ **061/313333;** www.buseireann.ie) provides the Shannonlink bus service from Shannon Airport to **Colbert Station,** Limerick's railway station, on Parnell Street. The fare is approximately €7 one-way. Bus services from all parts of Ireland come to this station.

Irish Rail operates direct trains from Dublin, Cork, and Killarney, with connections from other parts of Ireland. They arrive at Limerick's **Colbert Station,** Parnell Street (✆ **061/315555;** www.irishrail.ie).

Limerick City can be reached on N7 from the east and north; N20, N21, N24, and N69 from the south; and N18 from the west and north.

VISITOR INFORMATION The **Limerick Tourist Information Centre** is on Arthur's Quay, Limerick (✆ **061/317522**). It is open Monday to Friday 9:30am to 5:30pm, Saturday 9:30am to 1pm, with expanded and weekend hours in summer. Ask for a free copy of the *Shannon Region Visitors Guide,* which is packed with helpful information about activities and events.

Another office is located in the **Adare Heritage Centre,** Main Street, Adare (✆ **061/396225;** www.adareheritagecentre.ie). It is open Monday to Saturday year-round (except Christmas, St. Stephen's Day [Dec 26], and New Year's Day) 9am to 1pm and 2 to 5pm (until 6pm and on Sun during the summer).

For good all-around visitor information on the Web, see **www.limerick.com** or **www.limerick.ie**.

GETTING AROUND **Bus Éireann** (✆ **061/313333**) operates local bus service around Limerick and its environs; fares start at around €1.50. Buses depart from Colbert Station, Parnell Street.

Taxis line up outside Colbert Station, at hotels, and along Thomas and Cecil streets, off O'Connell Street. To reserve a taxi, call **Economy Cabs** (✆ **061/411422**), **Fixed Price Taxis** (✆ **061/313131**), or **Top Cabs** (✆ **061/417417**).

Driving around Limerick can be a little confusing because of the profusion of one-way streets—it's best to park your car and walk to see the sights. However, you might want to drive to King's Island for King John's Castle (there's a free parking lot opposite the castle). If you need to park downtown, head for the lot at **Arthur's Quay,** which is convenient for sightseeing and shopping, and well signposted. Parking in the city costs around €1.50 per hour.

If you need to rent a car in Limerick city, contact **Irish Car Rental** (Ennis Rd., Limerick; ✆ **1850/206088** or 061/206025; www.irishcarrentals.com). Most major international car-rental firms maintain desks at Shannon Airport (see the "County Clare" section, later in this chapter).

THERE ONCE WAS A poet FROM LIMERICK . . .

To find out how a genre of bawdy pub poetry came to be associated with this unassuming Irish town requires looking back nearly 300 years. Nobody really knows who wrote the first sharply worded, five-line poem, but the style gained popularity in the 18th century and is credited to a group of poets who lived in the town of Croom in County Limerick. Known as the *Fili na Maighe,* or the "Gaelic poets of the Maigue," the poets wrote sardonic, quick-witted poems in Irish that soon became all the rage. Their style was adopted across the region, and within a century, everybody was doing it. Most anthologies on the subject list 42 poets and Irish scholars in the county in the 19th century, who were known for composing limericks, most with themes of romance, drinking, personal squabbles, and politics.

But it's possible that the true rise of the limerick came as a result of an 18th-century battle of wills between a poet and pub owner, Sean O'Tuama, and his friend Andrias MacCraith. Boyhood friends O'Tuama and MacCraith grew up in County Limerick and were well educated. The two fell out quite spectacularly (nobody remembers over what) and then wrote a series of castigating verses about each other. These became enormously popular, and the modern limerick was born. In retrospect, they're kind of cute, although the meter was sometimes a little stretched. As MacCraith once wrote:

O'Tuama! You boast yourself handy,
At selling good ale and bright brandy
But the fact is your liquor
Makes everyone sicker,
I tell you this, I, your good friend, Andy.

On foot, the city's streets are fairly easy to figure out, and the main central street has a changing name—it's Rutland Street in the north and O'Connell Street and Quinlan Street in the south. Most tourist sights are in the north on King's Island, which is the oldest part of the city, although some are to the south around Pery Square (where the architecture is grand Georgian buildings) and on the river's edge. A good way to hit the high points is to pick up a booklet outlining the Tourist Trail at the tourist office and in bookshops.

FAST FACTS If you need a drugstore, try **Hogan's Pharmacy,** 45 Upper William St. (✆ **061/415195**). After-hours service is available by calling ✆ **088/526800.** You could also try **Boots the Chemist** at 4–5 William St. (✆ **061/416-598**).

In an **emergency,** dial ✆ **999. St. John's Hospital** is on St. John's Square (✆ **061/415822**). The local **Garda Headquarters** is on Henry Street (✆ **061/212400**).

The main **Post Office** is on Cecil Street (✆ **061/212055**) and there's another at 39 Upper William St. (✆ **061/409805**).

Seeing the Sights

Hunt Museum ★ Part of the reason to come to this museum is just to see the building—the grand, 18th-century Old Custom House, where the elegant Palladian facade is a copy of the Petit Trianon at Versailles. The museum's 2,000-work collection of ancient, medieval, and modern treasures—the finest outside of

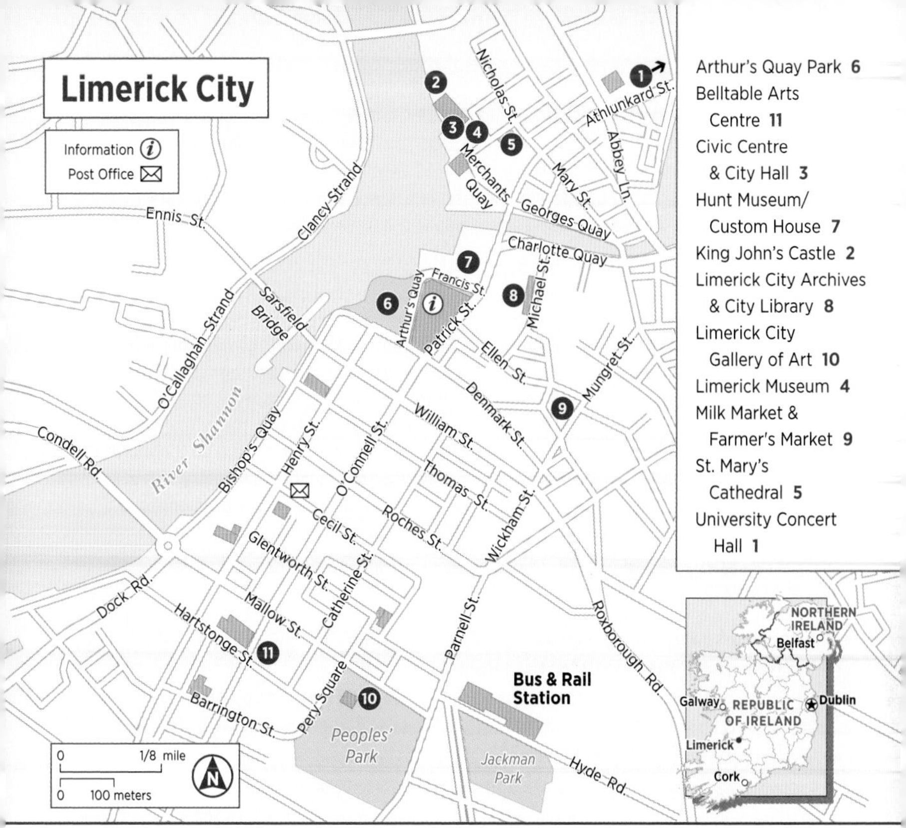

Dublin's National Museum—includes ancient Irish metalwork and medieval bronzes, ivories, and enamels. There are also paintings by Renoir, Picasso, and Jack Yeats. The collection was once privately owned by the late John and Gertrude Hunt, antiques dealers and consultants who willed their collection to Ireland in the 1970s. Free guided tours are available (check at the front desk), and there are tours for kids as well. The in-house restaurant serves snacks and full meals.

The Custom House, Rutland St., Limerick. ✆ **061/312833.** www.huntmuseum.com. Admission €8 adults; €6.25 seniors and students; €4.25 children; €18 families. Mon–Sat 10am–5pm; Sun 2–5pm.

King John's Castle ✋ This stern riverside fortress is the centerpiece of Limerick's historic area. It dates from 1210, and may have been ordered built by King John of England. The low-slung gray-stone structure is a good example of medieval architecture, with distinctive rounded gate towers and thick curtain walls. Over the years, the castle has not always fared well, though. In an astonishing piece of historical vandalism, its ancient courtyard was filled up with cheap, modern houses during the mid–20th century. Happily they're gone now, and a recent €7-million restoration has put the castle back into better condition—but unfortunately, there's just not much to see here. Aside from a poorly explained archaeological excavation in the courtyard, the rest of the structure has little to offer. Access to the actual castle structure is limited, and what you can see is not well used. Worse, the big, modern visitor center serves mainly to ruin views of the castle, and it justifies the high admission price with a sprawling display of mannequins in period costumes and one of the most overwrought and historically simplified visitor center films you'll see on your Irish trip. The simple fact is, King John's Castle costs more than it's worth.

Nicholas St., Limerick. ✆ **061/411201.** Admission €9 adults; €7 seniors and students; €5.50 children; €21 families. Daily 10am–5pm. Last admission 1 hr. before closing.

Limerick City Gallery of Art This gallery houses a permanent collection, including fine paintings by Jack B. Yeats, brother of the poet W. B. Yeats. It regularly hosts traveling exhibitions, including some from the Irish Museum of Modern Art. The gallery building is the lovely neo-Romanesque Carnegie Building, dating from 1903. On some evenings, it hosts literary readings or classical music concerts, so check local listings to see if one is scheduled during your stay. As this book was being written, the gallery was undergoing renovation, which, while not changing the exhibits inside, should make it even shinier than ever.

Leprechauns

The word "leprechaun" comes from the Irish *leath bhrógan,* meaning "shoemaker." In folklore, leprechauns were often depicted as shoemakers by trade. Today the word is sometimes employed to sum up the more crass side of the tourism industry. It is also used by some Northern Irish Unionists as a pejorative term for Gaelic.

Pery Sq., on the corner of Mallow St. in the People's Park, Limerick. ✆ **061/310633.** www.gallery.limerick.ie. Free admission. Mon–Wed and Fri 10am–6pm; Thurs 10am–7pm; Sat 10am–5pm; Sun 2–5pm. Closed Dec 24–30 and Jan 1.

Limerick Museum This small museum is overshadowed by the Hunt Museum, but for history buffs it's worth a stop for its insight into the town's background, with displays on Limerick's archaeology, natural history, civic treasures, and traditional crafts of lace, silver, furniture, and printing. Also on view are historical paintings, maps, prints, and photographs, as well as the city's original charter, signed by Oliver Cromwell (and, later, King Charles II), and a sword presented by Queen Elizabeth I.

Castle Lane, at Nicholas St., Limerick. ✆ **061/417826.** www.limerickcorp.ie/citymuseum. Free admission. Tues–Sat 10am–1pm and 2:15–5pm. Closed Sat on bank holiday weekends.

St. Mary's Cathedral This cathedral sits on a site that was originally a palace belonging to one of the kings of Munster, Donal Mor O'Brien, who donated the land to the church in 1172. The current building is much newer than that, but still contains a 12th-century Romanesque doorway, a pre-Reformation stone altar, and a huge stone slab said to be the coffin lid of Donal Mor O'Brien's grave. It also has original 15th-century **misericords** (supports for standing worshippers).

Bridge St., Limerick. ✆ **061/310293.** www.cathedral.limerick.anglican.org. Donation €2. June–Sept Mon–Sat 9am–5pm; Oct–May Mon–Sat 9am–4:30pm.

Shopping

Shopping hours in Limerick are Monday to Saturday 9:30am to 5:30pm. Many stores also stay open until 9pm on Thursday and Friday.

At the corner of Ellen and Wickham streets, in the heart of Limerick's old Irishtown, the old **Milk Market** is an informal bazaar selling everything from pottery to french fries. It holds two weekly markets worth knowing about: a **Farmer's Market** Saturdays from 7am to 2pm, and an **Arts and Crafts Market** Fridays from 11am to 4pm.

Arthur's Quay Centre This four-story shopping center overlooking Arthur's Quay Park houses dozens of shops, including both workaday chains and small boutiques selling handicrafts. Open Monday to Wednesday 9am to 7pm, Thursday and Friday 9am to 9pm, Saturday 9am to 6pm. Arthur's Quay, Limerick. ✆ **061/419888.** www.arthursquay-shopping.com.

Brown Thomas This is the Limerick branch of Ireland's native upscale department store. Its prices aren't the lowest, but it sells Aran knitwear, Donegal tweeds, and designer clothing. O'Connell St., Limerick. ✆ **061/417222.** www.brownthomas.com.

Cruises Street Shopping Centre The centerpiece of Limerick's downtown shopping district, this is a cleverly designed village-style mall on a pedestrianized street. There are plenty of stores for everyone here. Cruises St. (off Patrick St.), Limerick. No phone.

O'Mahoney's This quaint old bookshop has stood here for more than a century, and, along with all the latest hardbacks and paperbacks, it's also a good place to get information about Limerick and its surrounding countryside. 120 O'Connell St., Limerick. ✆ **1890/686868** or 061/418155. www.omahonys.ie.

Sports & Outdoor Pursuits

FISHING If you're looking for endless fish tales, an excellent guide, the best local tackle, and pure, all-around entertainment, it's hard to beat Paddy Guerin at the **Kingfisher Angling Centre** in nearby Castleconnell (15-min. drive from Limerick; ✆ **061/377407;** www.ireland360.com/kingfisher). He's even got a pub where you can tell your own tales at the end of the fishing day. In Limerick itself, get information, licenses, permits, and equipment at the **Fishing, Shooting and Archery Store,** The Milk Market, Carr Street (✆ **061/413484**). **Celtic Angling,** in nearby Ballingarry, Adare (✆ **069/68202;** www.celticangling.com), sells all the supplies you need. They also offer daylong salmon-fishing excursions on the Shannon, including pickup from Limerick City, equipment, and licenses. A day's fishing will cost on average €190 to €375 for one person, plus €60 to €145 for each additional person in a group; equipment rental is included in the price. (Owner Paddy Dunworth also offers guided sightseeing trips and hillwalking excursions; check the website for details.)

GOLF The par-70 inland course at the **Limerick Golf Club,** Ballyclough (✆ **061/415146;** www.limerickgolfclub.ie), 4.8km (3 miles) south of Limerick, has greens fees of €50 weekdays, €70 weekends. The par-71 inland course at **Castletroy Golf Club,** Castletroy, County Limerick (✆ **061/335753;** www.castletroygolfclub.ie), 4.8km (3 miles) east of Limerick, charges greens fees of €30 Monday to Thursday, €40 Friday to Sunday.

HORSEBACK RIDING The county's fields provide good turf for horseback riding. Rates run about €25 to €30 per hour. The **Clonshire Equestrian Centre,** Adare, County Limerick (✆ **061/396770;** www.clonshire.com), offers riding for all levels, horsemanship classes, and instruction for cross-country riding, dressage, and jumping. Clonshire is also home to the Limerick

Foxhounds; in the winter, it's a center for hunting in the area. Per-hour rates average upwards of €40 for adults, €30 for students and children 17 and under. Riding and board packages are available.

Where to Stay

EXPENSIVE

Absolute Hotel & Spa Owned by the same company behind the wonderful **Aghadoe Heights** in Killarney (p. 366), the Absolute is a stylish place to stay with a real modern elegance. Although the building itself is modern, the interior decor plays on a kind of 19th-century chic, with exposed brick walls and huge black-and-white photos of Limerick 100 years ago. The comfortable bedrooms are decorated in soothing tones of oatmeal and mahogany, with flatscreen TVs with built-in Internet access. Bathrooms look great, but have only showers (no tubs), and can be a bit form-over-function—the doors are opaque frosted glass, and offer somewhat limited privacy. The lounges and Riverbank restaurant have large windows with fine views of the River Shannon. (***Note:*** we have heard one or two complaints about noise from the bar, especially on weekends, so light sleepers should ask for rooms well away from it.)

Sir Harry's Mall, Limerick, County Limerick. www.absolutehotel.com. ✆ **061/463-600.** Fax 061/463-601. 99 units. €100–€190 double; €170–€210 suite. Rates include full breakfast. MC, V. **Amenities:** Restaurant; bar; full-service spa. *In room:* A/C, TV, hair dryer, high-speed Internet access.

Clarion Hotel Limerick Built in 2002, this is Limerick's sleekest modern hotel. Its white tower stands out amid the low-slung buildings—you won't have trouble finding it. Along with the Absolute (above), it provides a badly needed dose of modernity compared to the city's other, largely old-fashioned, hotels. Rooms are big and decorated in shades of coffee and cream, and those high up among its 17 floors have excellent views. It has all the latest accouterments, and does it all with great style. The restaurant has floor-to-ceiling windows overlooking the river, and the bar has a trendy vibe.

Steamboat Quay, Limerick, County Limerick. www.clarionhotellimerick.com. ✆ **061/444100.** Fax 061/444101. 158 units. €95–€150 double. AE, DC, MC, V. **Amenities:** Restaurant; bar; gym; pool; sauna. *In room:* TV, hair dryer, minibar, high-speed Internet access.

MODERATE

Castle Oaks House ★★ This gracious, two-story Georgian manor house at the edge of the River Shannon was once a convent. It still retains a few original touches, including stained-glass windows, and the banquet hall is in the old chapel. The comfortable guest rooms are quite feminine, furnished with soft pastel fabrics, and well-chosen antiques. There's also a complex of self-catering vacation homes on the grounds. Each has three bedrooms, sleeping up to five, and are available for about €400 to €600 per week, depending on the season. The hotel will help you arrange activities, including fishing or horseback riding.

9.7km (6 miles) east of Limerick City, off Dublin rd. (N7), Castleconnell, County Limerick. www.castleoaks.ie. ✆ **800/223-6510** in the U.S., or 061/377666. 20 units. €90–€120 double; €120–€220 suite. Rates include full breakfast. AE, DC, MC, V. **Amenities:** Restaurant; bar; gym; Jacuzzi; indoor pool; spa treatments; steam room; tennis court. *In room:* TV.

Where to Eat

EXPENSIVE

Freddy's Bistro ★ MODERN IRISH The old coach house that holds this pleasant, upscale restaurant conveys a great sense of history, while the restaurant itself is reliably relaxed and friendly. The menu changes regularly here, but always combines local produce and meats in traditional dishes such as fresh local mussels in chardonnay and dill, duck pâté with Cumberland sauce, grilled filet steak, or braised lamb shank with roasted root vegetables and honey *jus*. The steaks are particularly good, perfectly cooked, and served with inventive sauces.

Theatre Lane, Limerick. ✆ **061/418749.** www.freddysbistro.com. Reservations recommended. Main courses €16–€29; early evening fixed-price menu €28, available 5:30–7pm (use term "early evening" when making reservation). AE, MC, V. Tues–Sat 5:30pm–closing.

MODERATE

Copper and Spice ★ INDIAN/THAI This good Indian restaurant is a refreshing change from all that Irish cuisine. The modern dining room sets a brilliant backdrop for Seema Conroy's superb cooking: terrific breads, tantalizing curries, wonderful veggie pakoras. All the usual favorites are on offer in pleasant, modern surroundings.

2 Cornmarket Row, Limerick. ✆ **061/313620.** www.copperandspice.com. Reservations recommended. Main courses €11–€24; early-bird 3-course dinners €18–€25, available 5–7pm (last orders 7:15pm, table must be vacated by 8pm). AE, MC, V. Daily 5–10:30pm.

Curragower Seafood Bar ★ 🎁 SEAFOOD This place is stripped down to the bare bones, and its entire focus is on seafood. There are hearty seafood chowders in the winter, and crab claws on ice in the summer. Savor huge Irish oysters in season, and prawns and Atlantic salmon all the time. The restaurant's terrace has good views of King John's Castle. There's live traditional music here on Wednesday nights from 9pm.

Clancy's Strand, Limerick. ✆ **061/321788.** www.curragower.com. Main courses €11–€24. MC, V. Daily noon–11pm.

Limerick City After Dark

PUBS

The Locke Established in 1724 near the river, this is one of Limerick's oldest and most popular pubs. It's a lovely, rambling place, with open fires roaring, and nooks and crannies for quiet conversations over a pint. It's known for its traditional Irish music—played on Sunday and Tuesday year-round. It's a good place to come on a summer's evening, when there is outdoor seating and Japanese lanterns strung along a cobbled walkway lend a romantic, festive air. The pub also has a comfortable restaurant that serves Irish and Mediterranean cuisine. 2A-3 Georges Quay, Limerick. ✆ **061/413733.** www.lockebar.com.

Vintage Club In one of Limerick's older sections near the quays, this pub used to be a wine cellar, and the decor reflects it: barrel seats and tables, oak casks, dark-paneled walls, and a beer garden. It's not fancy, but it's good old-fashioned Limerick. 9 Ellen St., Limerick. ✆ **061/410694.**

W.J. South's This timeless old pub has a black-and-white-checkerboard floor; a high, white marble bar; and a succession of Victorian mahogany arches behind the bar, which frame bottles, mirrors, and curios. The pub's crowd is a mixture of locals and tourists, and they keep things buzzing here year-round. The Crescent, Limerick. ✆ **061/318850.**

THE PERFORMING ARTS

Belltable Arts Centre By day, this building is open for gallery exhibits of modern Irish artists, while at night, there's a mixture of local professional theatrical productions and art-house film screenings. There's also a popular bar and a good coffee shop. Most shows run Monday to Saturday at 8pm, but call ahead to confirm showtimes. 69 O'Connell St., Limerick. ✆ **061/319866.** www.belltable.ie. Tickets €6 cinema, €8–€25 theater and dance, €12–€20 live music. Discounts are available if you book at least 2 weeks in advance.

Dolan's Warehouse This is a popular venue for touring international rock bands, and a good place to see Irish bands as well. Everybody from Evan Dando to Kasabian has played here, and the eclectic lineup is well worth checking out. There are actually three venues here—**Dolan's Pub and Restaurant,** which has traditional Irish music by local or visiting bands every night; the Warehouse itself, where the big acts play; and a more intimate bar and performance space upstairs, imaginatively called **Upstairs.** 3 Dock Rd., Limerick. ✆ **061/314483.** www.dolanspub.com. Tickets €6–€26.

University Concert Hall On the grounds of the University of Limerick, this 1,000-seat hall offers a broad program of national and international solo stars, variety shows, and ballet. It also books the Irish Chamber Orchestra, RTE Concert Orchestra, University of Limerick Chamber Orchestra, Limerick Singers, and European Community Orchestra. A list of events is available from the tourist office. Most performances start at 8pm, but call ahead for details. You can also buy tickets to the **University of Limerick Arena** through the same website; this is the university's sports complex, which occasionally hosts matches and other special events worth looking out for (for example, the Harlem Globetrotters were about to arrive on our last visit). University of Limerick, Plassey, County Limerick. ✆ **061/331549.** www.uch.ie. Tickets €15–€40.

Elsewhere in County Limerick

If you're seduced by charming Irish villages, you'll want to head to the lovely village of **Adare ★★**, which is full of picturesque thatched-roof cottages, beautiful gardens, ivy-covered medieval churches, and lots and lots of tour buses. Yes, this place has been seriously discovered by the tour-bus crowds (even by May, which is still officially off season, the roads can get clogged at times), but it's still worth a stop.

Adare Heritage Centre If you make it to Adare, drop by this small but friendly heritage center artfully tucked away in a stone building. It has a walk-through display on Adare's colorful history, as well as a small cafe and several crafts shops, with a fairly good selection of pottery and linen. Main St., Adare, County Limerick. ✆ **061/396666.** www.adareheritagecentre.ie. Daily 9am–6pm (closed at lunchtime).

Foynes Flying Boat Museum ★★ This one isn't just for aviation buffs—history fans will fall for it, too. This was the first Shannon Airport—predecessor to the modern runways of Shannon Airport in County Clare—restored as an absorbing museum. It commemorates an era begun on July 9, 1939, when Pan Am's luxury flying boat *Yankee Clipper* landed at Foynes, marking the first commercial

If the Story Fitz . . .

Between Adare and Limerick, the small town of Patrickswell is home to the bijou Honey Fitz Theatre (✆ 061/385386; www.loughgur.com), the main venue for the Lough Gur Storytelling Festival, a weekend-long event in late October that celebrates the art of the good yarn, through a program of music, drama, and poetry (events are also held at the Lough Gill Interpretive Centre). Honey Fitz was the nickname of John Fitzgerald (1863–1950), grandfather to President John F. Kennedy. According to the biographer Robert Dallek, Fitz had a reputation for being "the only politician who could sing *Sweet Adeline* sober and get away with it." The theater was opened in 1994 by Fitzgerald's granddaughter, Jean Kennedy Smith (who was then U.S. ambassador). *Sweet Adeline* was sung during the ceremony.

passenger flight on the direct route between the United States and Europe. On June 22, 1942, Foynes was the departure point for the first nonstop commercial flight from Europe to New York. This is also where bartender Joe Sheridan invented Irish coffee in 1942. (At a festival each Aug., there's a contest to select the world Irish-coffee-making champion.) The complex includes a 1940s-style cinema and cafe, the original terminal building, and the radio and weather rooms with original transmitters, receivers, and Morse code equipment.

Foynes, County Limerick. ✆ **069/65416.** www.flyingboatmuseum.com. Admission €9 adults; €7 seniors and students; €5 children 5–13; €25 families; free for children 4 and under. MC, V. Mar–Oct daily 10am–5pm. Last admission 1 hr. before closing. 37km (23 miles) east of Limerick on N69.

Glin Castle ★ Lilies of the valley and ivy-covered ash, oak, and beech trees line the driveway leading from the village of Glin to this gleaming-white castle, home to the knights of Glin for the past 700 years. The vast estate sprawls over 160 hectares (395 acres) of sloping lawns, gardens, farmlands, and forests. The centerpiece of it all is, naturally, the castle—which is really a Georgian house with Gothic details. The castle operated as a hotel until 2009, when, to our great dismay, it closed as a result of the recession (although you can still book overnight stays as a group of at least six). The building itself is not normally open to the public, but visits can be arranged; call ahead for details.

Limerick-Tarbert rd. (N69), Glin, County Limerick. ✆ **068/34173.** Free admission to gardens. Approx. 40km (25 miles) east of Limerick City on N69.

Lough Gur ★ The lovely lake known as Lough Gur is surrounded by an unusual preponderance of ancient sites, most of which are well signposted on the R512, the drive that skirts around the lake's edge. There's much to see here, and it might be best to stop at the visitor center first for information and a map to the sites, although it's a little expensive for what it offers, so you may prefer to explore on your own. Lough Gur was occupied continuously from the Neolithic period to late medieval times. Archaeologists have uncovered foundations of a small farmstead built around the year 900, a lake island dwelling built between 500 and 1000, a wedge-shaped tomb that was a communal grave around 2,500 B.C., and the extraordinary Grange Stone Circle, which is a 4,000-year-old site with 113 upright stones forming the largest prehistoric stone circle in Ireland. The lake itself is a great place to explore and have a picnic.

11km (6¾ miles) SE of Limerick City on R512, Lough Gur, County Limerick. ✆ **061/385186.** www.loughgur.com. Museum and audiovisual presentation €5 adults; €3 seniors, students, and children; €13 families. Visitor center mid-May to Aug daily 10am–5pm (last admission 4:30pm); site open year-round.

WHERE TO STAY

Very Expensive

Adare Manor ★ This 19th-century Tudor Gothic mansion, nestled on the banks of the River Maigue, has been masterfully restored and refurbished as a deluxe resort, with 15th-century carved doors; Waterford crystal chandeliers; ornate fireplaces; and spacious, antiques-filled guest rooms. The hotel's fine restaurant is known for its stellar cuisine and service. Virtually every known countryside activity, from horseback riding to salmon fishing to fox hunting, can be arranged. And the 18-hole championship golf course designed by Robert Trent Jones, Sr., has legions of fans. The hotel also offers some rather ordinary looking, three-bedroom suburban-style homes it calls "villas" for families or groups.

> Impressions
>
> ***In Ireland, the inevitable never happens and the unexpected constantly occurs.***
>
> **—Sir John Pentland Mahaffy**

Adare, County Limerick. www.adaremanor.com. ✆ **800/462-3273** in the U.S., or 061/605200. Fax 061/396124. 63 units. €280–€505 double; €350–€600 villas. AE, DC, MC, V. **Amenities:** 2 restaurants; bar; babysitting; concierge; 18-hole golf course; gym; indoor pool; room service; sauna; spa treatments. *In room:* TV, hair dryer, minibar.

Expensive

Dunraven Arms ★★ On the banks of the River Maigue, this 18th-century inn is a charming country retreat 16km (10 miles) south of Limerick City with an old-world ambience. Lounges and dining rooms have open fireplaces and antiques, while guest rooms are lavishly decorated in golden tones with comfortable beds and luxurious fabrics. Half are in the original house, half in a new wing, but all are furnished in traditional style, with Victorian accents and period pieces. It's not all old-fashioned style, as there's a thoroughly modern recreation center with a huge pool as well. Book in advance online as Internet specials often drop the nightly rate on a double to under €100.

Main St. (N21), Adare, County Limerick. www.dunravenhotel.com. ✆ **800/447-7462** in the U.S., or 061/605900. Fax 061/396541. 86 units. €155 double; €260–€395 suite. Rates include full breakfast. AE, MC, V. **Amenities:** Restaurant; bar; gym; indoor pool; room service; steam room. *In room:* TV, radio, hair dryer, Wi-Fi.

Echo Lodge ★ Built in 1884 as a parochial house, then converted for use as a convent before being turned into a hotel, this is a lovely place to stay and eat. Owner Daniel Mullane's world travels are evident in the furnishings, colors, and fabrics, all of which come together in harmony. Beds are comfortable, and guest rooms are designed with subtle flair. The **Mustard Seed** restaurant (see below) is a destination in itself, with a menu that presents a creative mix of organic local produce, brilliantly prepared.

13km (8 miles) from Adare, off the Newcastle West rd. from the center of Ballingarry, County Limerick. www.mustardseed.ie. ✆ **069/68508.** 18 units. €130–€330 double. Rates include full breakfast. AE, MC, V. Closed Feb 1–15. **Amenities:** Restaurant. *In room:* TV, hair dryer, Wi-Fi.

Inexpensive

Adare Country House ★ This sweet little B&B, a stone's throw from the center of Adare, is run with charm by hosts Denis and Eileen Moroney. The modern, comfortable bedrooms are tastefully decorated in classically influenced color schemes of pale blue and yellow, with polished wood floors and paintings by Eileen herself. Breakfasts are excellent.

Adare, County Limerick. www.adarecountryhouse.com. ✆ **061/395986.** 10 units. €70 double. Rates include full breakfast. AE, MC, V. **Amenities:** Guest lounge. *In room:* TV, Wi-Fi.

Fitzgerald's Woodlands House Hotel This family-run hotel has been around for over 25 years and has its charms, not least of which are the spacious rooms and the huge leisure center. Bedrooms are pleasantly decorated in white with red accents, but a little basic, and the decor could use updating in places. Still, beds are comfortable and covered in fluffy duvets. The staff is friendly and helpful, and there's a good in-house restaurant and friendly pub. The big swimming pool tends to get crowded, but we cannot fault the in-house spa treatments such as a Fijian Bobo massage, scalp and shoulder hot-oil ritual, and coconut cream body glow.

Adare, County Limerick. www.woodlands-hotel.ie. ✆ **061/605100.** 94 units. €70–€150 double. Rates include full breakfast. AE, MC, V. **Amenities:** 2 restaurants; bar; Jacuzzi; pools; sauna; full-service spa; steam room. *In room:* TV, hair dryer, Wi-Fi.

WHERE TO EAT

Expensive

The Mustard Seed at Echo Lodge ★★★ MODERN INTERNATIONAL Most food critics place this elegant rural spot among the top restaurants in the country. The chef uses fresh, organic herbs and vegetables from the restaurant's own gardens, and all meats are sourced from local organic producers, so the food is as fresh as it can be. The cooking style is an intelligent mixture of European styles with an Irish touch, evidenced in such dishes as pan-seared Irish beef on wild mushroom polenta with Parmesan crackling, or breast of Barbary duck on buttered greens with lime-and-vanilla mash and chocolate oil. Dinner here is a memorable event.

At the Echo Lodge hotel, 13km (8 miles) from Adare, off the Newcastle West rd. from the center of Ballingarry, County Limerick. ✆ **069/68508.** www.mustardseed.ie. Fixed-price 4-course dinner €64 (daily 7–9:30pm); 3-course early-bird menu €38 (summer only, Sun–Thurs 4:45–5:45pm). AE, MC, V. Closed Feb 1–15.

The Wild Geese ★★★ MODERN INTERNATIONAL The emphasis here is simple, but perfect: Start with superb local ingredients and build on that. This is clear in dishes such as the steamed Kenmare mussels served in a white-wine sauce, the Clare crabmeat soufflé, or grilled Irish salmon with baby corn salad. In season, you will find unforgettable dishes such as rack of Adare lamb with rosemary-and-thyme potato gratin, or wild pheasant stuffed with currants. Service is impeccable, and because of that, the atmosphere is relaxed and filled with a sense of anticipation.

Rose Cottage, Adare, County Limerick. ✆ **061/396451.** www.thewild-geese.com. Reservations required. Early-bird menus (Tues–Fri 6:30–7:30pm, Sat 6:30–7pm) €29–€35; main courses €25–€30; fixed-price Sun lunch menus €20–€25. AE, MC, V. Tues–Sat 6:30pm–closing; also May–Sept Sun 5:30pm–closing. Closed Dec 24–Jan 2.

PUBS

Finnegan's First opened in 1776, this historic alehouse is as old as the U.S. The name is borrowed from *Finnegan's Wake,* which is why the decor has a Joycean theme. There are plenty of picnic tables in the rose garden for summer days, Irish music on most weekends, and good cheap food served year-round. Dublin rd. (N7), about 8km (5 miles) east of Limerick City, Annacotty, County Limerick. ✆ **061/337338.** finnegansbar@eircom.net.

O'Shaughnessy's This is a lovely, cozy place, just outside the gates to Glin Castle (above). Although it doesn't look that remarkable from the outside, a rustic, cottagelike atmosphere prevails within. The pub has been in the same family for generations; catch the landlord in a chatty mood and he'll tell you all manner of funny tales (so far as we know, all good ones) about their illustrious neighbors. By the entrance to the Glin Castle Estate, Limerick-Tarbert rd. (N69), Glin, County Limerick. ✆ **068/34115.**

COUNTY CLARE

Ennis: 67km (42 miles) S of Galway, 27km (17 miles) NW of Shannon Airport, 37km (23 miles) NW of Limerick, 235km (146 miles) SW of Dublin, 133km (83 miles) NW of Cork

With its miles of pasture and green, softly rolling fields, Clare seems, at first, a pleasantly pastoral place. But head to the coast and a dramatic landscape awaits you, with plunging cliffs and crashing waves. Or turn north, and you'll find the vast stony wilderness of the **Burren.**

Like its neighbors Kerry and Galway, Clare has a remarkable coastline, including the spectacular **Cliffs of Moher** and quaint seaside towns such as **Lahinch** and **Kilkee.** At its southern tip the boating paradise of Lough Derg brings in water cruisers and sailboats. At the edges of the lake **Killaloe** is a darling village at the foot of the Slieve Bernagh Hills, and home to a picturesque marina. Killaloe Cathedral dates from the 13th century, and has extensive carving on its doorway. The stone cross near the door dates to early Christian times and is carved with Irish Ogham scripts and Scandinavian runes. The grounds also hold a 12th-century oratory.

> **Hey, Girl!**
>
> **In countries with large populations of Irish decent, it's popular for people to name their daughters Colleen. However, it's rare to meet a girl in Ireland named Colleen, as this Gaelic word means simply, "girl."**

Traditional Irish music is always on heavy rotation in Clare, which is well known for a vibrant music scene, especially in the charming villages of **Doolin, Miltown Malby, Fanore,** and **Ennistymon.** This is also an excellent place for those fascinated by the country's ancient history, as it's littered with historic and prehistoric sites, from the **Poulnabrone Dolmen** to **Bunratty Castle,** with its better-than-you-probably-expected folk park.

County Clare Essentials

GETTING THERE From the United States, Delta Airlines, Aer Lingus, and Continental operate regularly scheduled flights into **Shannon Airport,** off the Limerick-Ennis road (N18), County Clare (✆ **061/712000;** www.shannon airport.com), 24km (15 miles) west of Limerick. Aer Lingus operates domestic flights from Dublin.

County Clare

Aillwee Cave 1
Bunratty Castle & Folk Park 18
Bunratty Winery 19
Burren Centre 7
Burren Smokehouse 3
Clare Heritage and Genealogical Centre 10
Clare Museum 13
Cliffs of Moher 5
Corcomroe Abbey 2
Craggaunowen—The Living Past Experience 15
Doolin Ferry Co. 4
Dromoland Castle 14
Dysert O'Dea Castle and Clare Archaeology Centre 11
East Clare Heritage Centre 16
Ennis Friary 12
Gleninsheen Wedge Tomb 8
Knappogue Castle 17
Lahinch Seaworld & Leisure Centre 6
Poulnabrone Dolmen 9

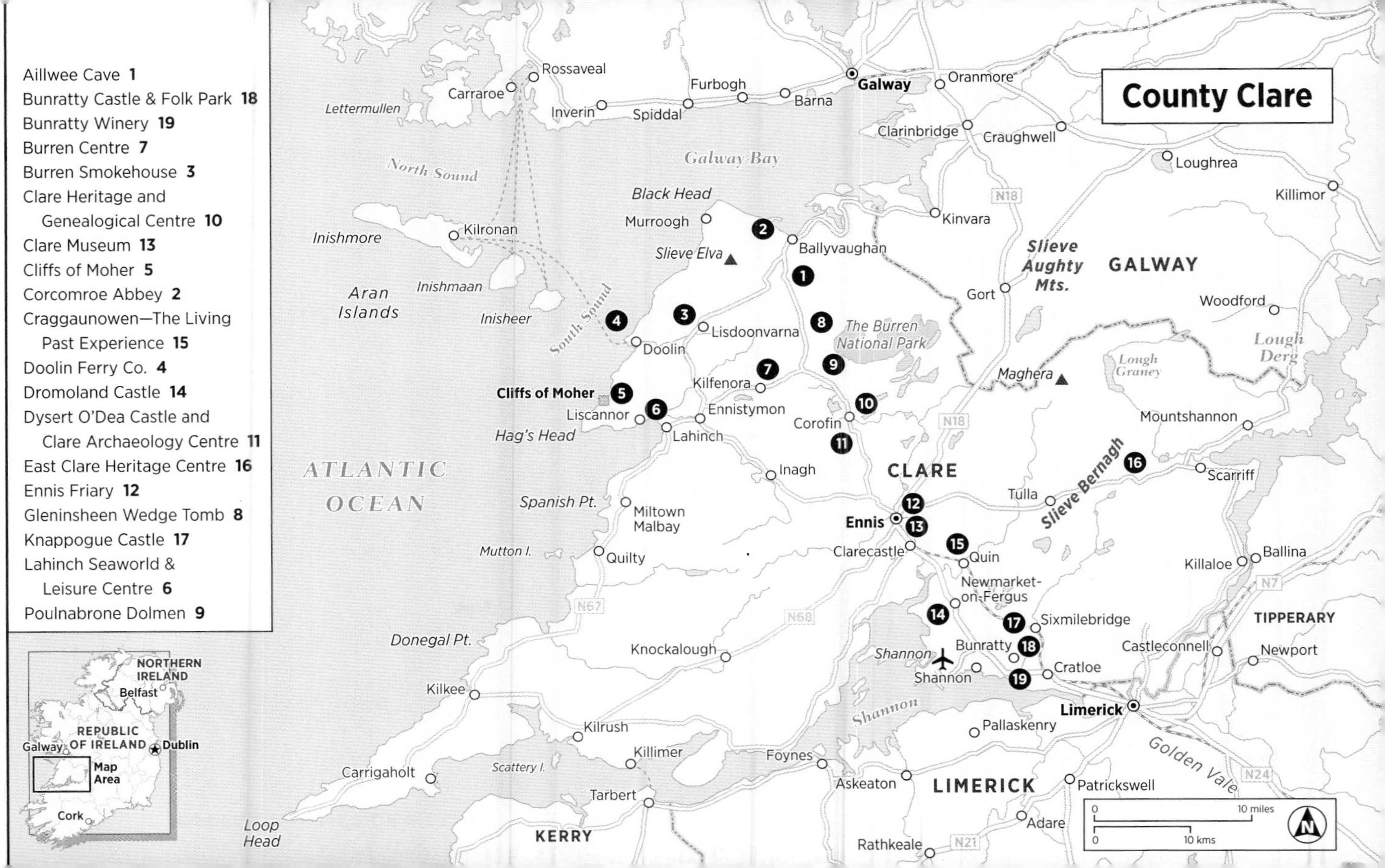

The harbor of Killaloe, on the banks of Lough Derg.

Irish Rail provides service to **Ennis Rail Station,** Station Road (✆ **065/684-0444;** www.irishrail.ie), and Limerick's **Colbert Station,** Parnell Street (✆ **061/315555**), 24km (15 miles) from Shannon.

Bus Éireann provides bus services from all parts of Ireland into **Ennis Bus Station,** Station Road (✆ **065/682-4177;** www.buseireann.ie), and other towns in County Clare.

By car, County Clare can be reached on N18. Shannon Airport has offices of the following international rental firms: **Car Hire** (✆ **061/206025;** www.carhire.ie), **Avis** (✆ **061/715600;** www.avis.ie), **Budget** (✆ **061/471361;** www.budget.ie), and **Hertz** (✆ **061/471369;** www.hertz.ie). Several local firms also maintain desks at the airport; among the most reliable is **Dan Dooley Rent-A-Car** (✆ **061/471098;** www.dandooley.ie).

From points south, County Clare can be reached directly, bypassing Limerick, on the **Tarbert-Killimer Car Ferry.** It crosses the Shannon River from Tarbert, County Kerry, to Killimer, County Clare. Trip time for the drive-on/drive-off service is 20 minutes; no reservations are needed. Crossings from Tarbert are on the half-hour; from Killimer, on the hour. Ferries operate year-round except Christmas Day. From Killimer departures are April to September Monday to Saturday 7am to 9pm and Sunday 9am to 9pm (with additional sailings May–Sept at half past the hour from 10:30am–5:30pm daily), and October to March Monday to Saturday 7am to 7pm and Sunday 9am to 7pm. From Tarbert departures are April to September Monday to Saturday 7:30am to 9:30pm and Sunday 9:30am to 9:30pm (with additional sailings May–Sept on the hour from 11am–6pm daily), and October to March Monday to Saturday 7:30am to 7:30pm and Sunday 9:30am to 7:30pm. Summer fares for cars with passengers are €18 one-way and €28 round-trip; for foot passengers and cyclists, fares are €5 one-way and €7 round-trip. For more information, contact **Shannon Ferry Ltd.,** Killimer/Kilrush, County Clare (✆ **065/905-3124;** www.shannonferries.com). The Killimer Ferry terminal has a gift shop and restaurant, and daily hours are 9am to 9pm.

VISITOR INFORMATION There's a **tourist office** in the arrivals hall of Shannon Airport (✆ **061/471644**). Hours coincide with flight arrivals and departures.

The **Ennis Tourist Office,** Authors Row, Ennis, County Clare (✆ **065/682-8366**), is about 1.6km (1 mile) south of town on the main N18 road. It's open year-round Monday to Saturday 9:30am to 1pm and 2 to 5pm, with weekend and extended hours April to October.

Seasonal tourist offices in County Clare are at the Cliffs of Moher (✆ **065/708-1171**); O'Connell Street, Kilkee (✆ **065/905-6112**); and Town Hall, Kilrush (✆ **065/905-1577**). These offices are usually open from May or June until early September.

Because Lough Derg unites three counties (Clare, Galway, and Tipperary), there are several sources of information about that area. They include **Shannon Development Tourism,** Shannon, County Clare (✆ **061/361555;** www.discoverireland.ie/shannon); **Failte Ireland West,** Forster Street, Galway (✆ **091/537700;** www.discoverireland.ie/west); and **Tipperary Lake Side,** The Old Church, Mill Street, Borrisokane, County Tipperary (✆ **067/27155;** www.tipperarylakeside.com). Seasonal information offices include the **Nenagh Tourist Office,** Connolly Street, Nenagh, County Tipperary (✆ **067/31610**), open early May to early September; and the **Killaloe Tourist Office,** The Lough House, Killaloe, County Clare (✆ **061/376866**), open May to September. You can also find visitor information at any Limerick tourist office, or online at **www.countyclare.com**.

From Shannon Airport to Ennis

The 24km (15-mile) road from Shannon Airport to Ennis, a well-signposted section of the main Limerick-Galway road (N18), is a much-traveled route with the feel of a proper highway—something that you didn't encounter previously much in these shores, but which is becoming more and more ubiquitous. On the whole, though, the Irish countryside is still a land of *boreens* (country single-lane roads), so don't get too comfortable.

To reach the village of **Bunratty,** with its 15th-century medieval castle (which is inevitably besieged by tour groups in the summer), turn right on the N18 and proceed for 8km (5 miles). Or you could turn left, heading toward Ennis, and pass through the charming river town of **Newmarket-on-Fergus,** with its grand **Dromoland Castle.**

The county town of Clare, **Ennis** (pop. 19,000) is a busy market town, and one of the largest towns in this part of the country. Unfortunately, it not only sits on the banks of a river—the River Fergus—but on the busy N18, meaning that the traffic congestion is appalling and the exhaust fumes a perpetual menace. Ennis is a sprawling place, with lots of unspectacular suburbs, but its center is easily explored on foot, especially if you stop by the tourist office and pick up a walking tour and map before you set out. You can still see the town's medieval layout—its winding narrow lanes date back centuries, as does its 13th-century friary. The statue in the town center is of Daniel O'Connell, a beloved Irish politician whose overwhelming election to the British Parliament in 1828 forced Britain to end its ban of Catholic parliamentarians. The statue near the courthouse is of Eamon de Valera, who represented Clare in the Irish Parliament and later became president of Ireland.

Seeing the Sights

Bunratty Castle and Folk Park ★ ☺

Though it was built in 1425, Bunratty Castle is remarkably intact, furnished with medieval antiques, and open to visitors.

Long before you reach Bunratty, the gray stone walls of this rugged, 15th-century fortress dominate the views from the main road. Standing fiercely beside the O'Garney River, Bunratty Castle (1425) is an exceptionally complete medieval castle and thus offers a rare perspective on living in a castle in those troubled times. The ancient stronghold has been restored with period-appropriate furniture, stained glass, luxurious tapestries, and other art. The castle you see today was the fourth castle built on this spot, and it was largely built by the MacNamara family in 1425, but in an earlier incarnation it was a home of the English royal family, until it was destroyed by the Irish chieftains of Thomond in 1332. After the current structure was completed, it was ultimately taken over by the powerful O'Brien family clan, the largest in North Munster. They ruled from here and lived a life of luxury. In their time, the castle was surrounded by lush gardens in which thrived thousands of deer. After Ireland fell to Cromwell, the castle was taken over by a variety of English families, until the last abandoned it in 1804 and moved into Bunratty House, which is also available for tours.

Today the castle is a kind of historical theme park, crawling with tourists in the high season. By day, the building's inner chambers and grounds are open for tours; at night, the Great Hall serves as a candlelit setting for medieval banquets and entertainment (p. 431).

Around the castle is the 8-hectare (20-acre) theme park, Bunratty Folk Park. While it is, as you might expect, extremely touristy, it's also done well. The re-creation of 19th-century Irish villages includes thatched cottages, farmhouses, kitchen gardens, and an entire village street, with a school, post office, pub, grocery store, print shop, and hotel—all open for browsing and shopping. Fresh scones are baked in the cottages, and craftspeople ply such trades as knitting, weaving, candle making, pottery, and photography. It's all a bit cute, and yet it's quite fun, too. In the summer there's a *Céilidh* (traditional Irish party) in the folk park nightly. The evening starts with a three-course meal, followed by a 40-minute show featuring storytelling, folk music, and dancing (7pm nightly; €50 adults, €25–€38 children 6–12, children 5 and under free; call ahead to book). You can while away a very enjoyable afternoon exploring the castle, great house, and folk park, and kids will find its living history fascinating.

Limerick-Ennis rd. (N18), Bunratty, County Clare. ✆ **061/361511.** www.shannonheritage.com. Admission €16 adults (€12 Nov–Feb); €10 students; €9 children; €34 families. June–Aug Mon–Fri 9am–5:30pm, Sat 9am–6pm (last admission to Folk Park 5:15pm); Sept–May daily 9am–5:30pm (last admission to Folk Park 4:15pm). Last admission to castle 4pm year-round.

Bunratty Winery In a coach house dating from 1816, this winery produces traditional medieval wines including mead—a drink made from honey, fermented grape juice, water, matured spirits, and herbs, a historical favorite of the upper classes. The winery is also one of only two distilleries officially licensed to brew Irish potcheen, a heady potato moonshine that was so popular and pernicious, it was banned in 1661—and was only made legal again in 1997. Most of the products are made for Bunratty Castle's medieval-style banquets (p.431), but visitors are welcome at the working winery to watch the production in progress and taste the brew.

Bunratty, County Clare. ✆ **061/362222.** homepage.eircom.net/~bunrattywinery. Free admission. Mon–Fri 9:30am–5:30pm.

Clare Museum In the same building as the Ennis tourist office, this interesting little museum does a good job of explaining and illustrating the colorful history of the county. Through a combination of films, drawings, and artifacts, the exhibition stretches back 6,000 years and can make a good early stop to a first-time tour of the county. The museum has recently abolished admission charges—an increasingly rare gesture, and a welcome one.

Arthur's Row, Ennis, County Clare. ✆ **065/682-3382.** www.clarelibrary.ie/eolas/claremuseum. Free admission. Tues–Sat 9:30am–1pm and 2–5:30pm. Last admission 12:30 and 4:30pm.

TAKING A (MOON) shine TO POTCHEEN

"Keep your eyes well peeled today, the excise men are on their way, searching for the mountain tay, in the hills of Connemara . . ."

Potcheen, also known as Irish moonshine whiskey, is a potent drink traditionally brewed from grain or potatoes. It was banned by the English crown in 1661, an act that effectively criminalized thousands of distillers overnight. Unsurprisingly, that didn't stop people from making the stuff, and after 336 years on the wrong side of the law, potcheen was finally made legal again in 1997.

One 17th-century writer said of potcheen that "it enlighteneth ye heart, casts off melancholy, keeps back old age and breaketh ye wind." Its usefulness didn't stop there, evidently, as history records the drink being used as everything from a bath tonic to a substitute for dynamite.

Potcheen has long been used in fiction as a symbol of Irish nationalism, its contraband status rich with rebellious overtones. The traditional folk song "The Hills of Connemara" describes potcheen being secretly distributed under the noses of excise men, and it was a popular subject for Irish poets in the 19th century. Indeed, the first film to be made entirely in the Irish language—*Poitin* (1977)—was a violent tale about a potcheen moonshiner harassed by local ne'er-do-wells.

There are currently just two licensed potcheen distilleries in the world: Bunratty Winery (see above) and Knockeen Hills in Waterford. In 2008, the European Union awarded the drink "Geographical Indicative" protection, which means that only the genuine Irish product is allowed to carry the name (the same status enjoyed by champagne and Parma ham). Like most liquors it can be drunk straight, on the rocks, or with a mixer, but at anything from 80 to a massive 180 proof, newly legal potcheen packs a mean punch, so enjoy . . . cautiously.

Craggaunowen—The Living Past Experience Through an old fortified castle and re-creations of ancient sites such as a *crannog* (a fortified island) and a ring fort, the Craggaunowen Project offers a timeline of Ireland's past from the Neolithic period to the Middle Ages. There are reconstructed Bronze Age dwellings (often inhabited by craftspeople demonstrating ancient weaving techniques and the like); working demonstrations of cooking and farming methods; pottery making; and even a herd of rare sheep of a breed native to Ireland since prehistoric times. It's interesting to explore, and certainly makes up in charm for what it lacks in razzmatazz, although it's not as effective as it might be at conveying any real sense of living history. Still, it's worth a visit, especially for history buffs and those curious about what such sites looked like.

About 16km (10 miles) from Ennis, signposted off R469, Quin, County Clare. ✆ **061/360788.** www.shannonheritage.com. Admission €9 adults; €7 seniors and students; €5.50 children; €22 families. May–Sept daily 10am–5pm. Last admission 1 hr. before closing.

Dysert O'Dea Castle and Clare Archaeology Centre ★★ In an area rich in archaeological sites, this center cleverly links them all together. The center is in a castle that was built in 1480 by Diarmaid O'Dea on a rocky outcrop of land. Like many others, it was badly damaged by Cromwell's gang, and hundreds of years would pass before it would be restored and opened to the public in 1986. Today it holds good exhibitions on the history of the area, and acts as a starting point for a trail that wanders through the 25 historical and archaeological sites nearby, including a church founded by St. Tola in the 8th century, with a unique doorway with a border of 12 heads carved in stone. The O'Deas, the former chieftains of the area, are buried underneath it. There's also a round tower from the 10th or 12th century, a 12th-century high cross, a holy well, a 14th-century battlefield, and a stone fort believed to date from the Iron Age.

R476 to Corofin, County Clare. ✆ **065/683-7401.** www.dysertcastle.com. Admission €4 adults; €3.50 seniors and students; €2.50 children; €10 families. May–Sept daily 10am–6pm.

East Clare Heritage Centre/Holy Island Tours In the 10th-century church of St. Cronan, this center provides genealogical research and explains the heritage and history of the East Clare area through a series of exhibits and an audiovisual presentation. A pier across the road is the starting point for a 15-minute excursion in an eight-seat boat on Lough Derg to nearby Inishcealtra (Holy Island), a 7th-century monastic settlement. The remains include a tall round tower that has long since lost its pointed roof, as well as four chapels, hermit cells, and graves that date from the settlement's earliest days.

Off the Portumna-Ennis rd. (R352), Tuamgraney, County Clare. Center ✆ **061/921351.** Island tours ✆ **086/874-9710.** www.eastclareheritage.com. Admission to the center €3 adults; €2 children. Holy Island Tours €10 adults; €5 seniors and children. Center daily Mon–Fri 10am–5pm; Holy Island Tours Apr–Sept daily 10am–5pm, weather permitting (at other times according to demand).

Ennis Friary ★ When you walk around Ennis Friary, it can be hard to get a sense of scale, but if it helps you to understand it, consider that records show that in 1375 it was the home and workplace for 350 friars and 600 students. Founded in 1241, this Franciscan abbey, a famous seat of learning in medieval times, made Ennis a focal point of western Europe for many years. It was finally forced to close in 1692, and thereafter fell into ruin, but it's been partly restored, and contains many beautifully sculpted medieval tombs, decorative fragments, and carvings, including the famous McMahon tomb, with its striking representations of

THE LOUGH DERG drive

In the southern section of the county where Clare, Limerick, and Tipperary meet, Lough Derg creates a stunning waterscape. Often called an inland sea, Lough Derg is the Shannon River's largest lake and widest point: 40km (25 miles) long and almost 16km (10 miles) wide. It is a popular place for the Irish to spend summer weekends.

The road that circles the lake for 153km (95 miles), the **Lough Derg Drive,** is one continuous photo opportunity, where panoramas of hilly farmlands, gentle mountains, and glistening waters are unspoiled by commercialization. The drive is a collage of colorful shoreline towns, starting with **Killaloe ★**, County Clare, and **Ballina,** County Tipperary. They're so close that they are essentially one community—only a splendid 13-arch bridge over the Shannon separates them. In the summer, its pubs and bars are filled with weekend sailors.

Kincora, on the highest ground at Killaloe, was the royal settlement of Brian Boru and the other O'Brien kings, although no trace of any of their buildings survive. Killaloe is a picturesque town with lakeside views at almost every turn and restaurants and pubs perched on the shore, but don't overlook Ballina's legendary nightlife.

Eight kilometers (5 miles) inland from Lough Derg's lower southeast shores is **Nenagh,** the chief town of north Tipperary. It lies in a fertile valley between the Silvermine and Arra mountains.

On the north shore of the lake in County Galway, **Portumna** is worth a visit for its lovely forest park and castle.

Memorable little towns and harborside villages like **Mountshannon** and **Dromineer** dot the rest of the Lough Derg Drive. Some towns, like **Terryglass** and **Woodford,** are known for atmospheric old pubs where spontaneous sessions of traditional Irish music are likely to break out. Others, like **Puckane** and **Ballinderry,** offer unique crafts.

The best way to get to Lough Derg is by car or boat. Although there is limited public transportation in the area, you will need a car to get around the lake. Major roads that lead to Lough Derg are the main Limerick-Dublin road (N7) from points east and south, N6 and N65 from Galway and the west, and N52 from the north. The Lough Derg Drive, which is well signposted, is a combination of R352 on the west bank of the lake and R493, R494, and R495 on the east bank. Find out about boating and swimming on the lake in "Sports & Outdoor Pursuits" (below).

the Passion. The nave and chancel are the oldest parts of the friary, but other structures, such as the 15th-century tower, transept, and sacristy, are also rich in architectural detail. It's run by the Irish historical preservation group, Dúchas, which offers entertaining and informative tours in the summer. ***Note:*** Recently the friary's opening hours have been variable—call before making a special trip. Abbey St., Ennis, County Clare. ✆ **065/682-9100.** Admission €3 adults; €2 seniors; €1 children and students; €8 families. Easter to mid-Oct daily 10am–5pm. Last admission 45 min. before closing.

Knappogue Castle & Walled Gardens ★★ Midway between Bunratty and Ennis, this regal castle was built in 1467 as the home of the MacNamara clan, who, along with the O'Briens, dominated the area for more than 1,000 years. Oliver Cromwell used the castle as a base in the mid–17th century while pillaging the countryside and thus, unlike many castles, it was largely left intact. The original Norman structure includes elaborate late-Georgian and Regency wings added in the mid–19th century. Early in the 20th century, it fell into disrepair, but was rescued by Texan Mark Edwin Andrews, a former U.S. assistant secretary of the navy. He and his wife, Lavone, an architect, worked closely with area historical societies and returned the castle to its former glory, even furnishing it with 15th-century furniture. The Andrewses were the last private owners of the house, as they turned it over to the Shannon Development group in 1996. The restored Victorian walled gardens were opened to the public shortly afterward, and today they supply the castle with fresh herbs for the medieval banquets held nightly during the summer months (p. 431).

Quin, County Clare. ✆ **061/368103.** Admission €6 adults; €3.50 seniors and students; €3.40 children. Early May to Aug daily 10am–4:30pm. Last admission 4pm.

Shopping

Bunratty Village Mills On the grounds of the Bunratty Castle Hotel, dozens of fine shops are laid out like a 19th-century village. These include stores offering crafts and housewares, clothing, music, and books—a good place to shop for quality souvenirs, from named and independent brands. Main St., Bunratty, County Clare. ✆ **061/364321.**

Custy's Traditional Music Shop Bring the melodious sounds of County Clare home with you. The selection here includes a full range of traditional-music tapes and CDs, instruments, books, and photos. Cooks Lane, O'Connell St., Ennis, County Clare. ✆ **065/682-1727.** www.custysmusic.com.

The Ennis Bookshop This well-stocked bookstore has one of those gorgeous old shop fronts that make it hard to resist popping in for a browse. The local history section is one of the best in the region. 13 Abbey St., Ennis, County Clare. ✆ **065/682-9000.** www.ennisbookshop.ie.

Gift Venue This spacious china store, formerly known as the Belleek Shop, also sells top branded Irish crystal, and stylish designer tableware from Louise Kennedy. 36 Abbey St., Ennis, County Clare. ✆ **065/686-7891.** www.giftvenue.com.

McKernan Scarves A husband-and-wife team, Eugene and Anke McKernan weave and sell a colorful array of distinctive wool scarves, jackets, vests, and blankets, all by hands. They work on the premises, and you can pop into the workshop and watch the weaving happen. Open daily 10am to 6pm. Handweavers, Main St., Tuamgraney, County Clare. ✆ **061/921527.** www.mckernanscarves.com.

Puckane Crafts A rustic, thatched-roof cottage serves as the shop of Adele Starr's artisan wares. There are Celtic and rural scenes and pieces with heraldic and religious themes. She stocks Jerpoint glass, as well as works by potter Nicholas Mosse and designs by Louise Kennedy. These all make great souvenirs. Open Monday to Saturday from 10am to 6pm, Sunday 2 to 6pm. R493, Puckane, Nenagh, County Tipperary. ✆ **067/24229.**

Sports & Outdoor Pursuits

BOATING & OTHER WATERSPORTS If you enjoy boating, tubing, water-skiing, windsurfing, canoeing, or other water activities, this is the place for you.

River cruising is big business in this part of the country, and there are plenty of ways to do it—if you're an experienced cruiser you can rent a barge or cruiser and make your own way, or you can rent a cruiser or barge complete with crew, or take a cabin on a shared cruiser. It all depends on your

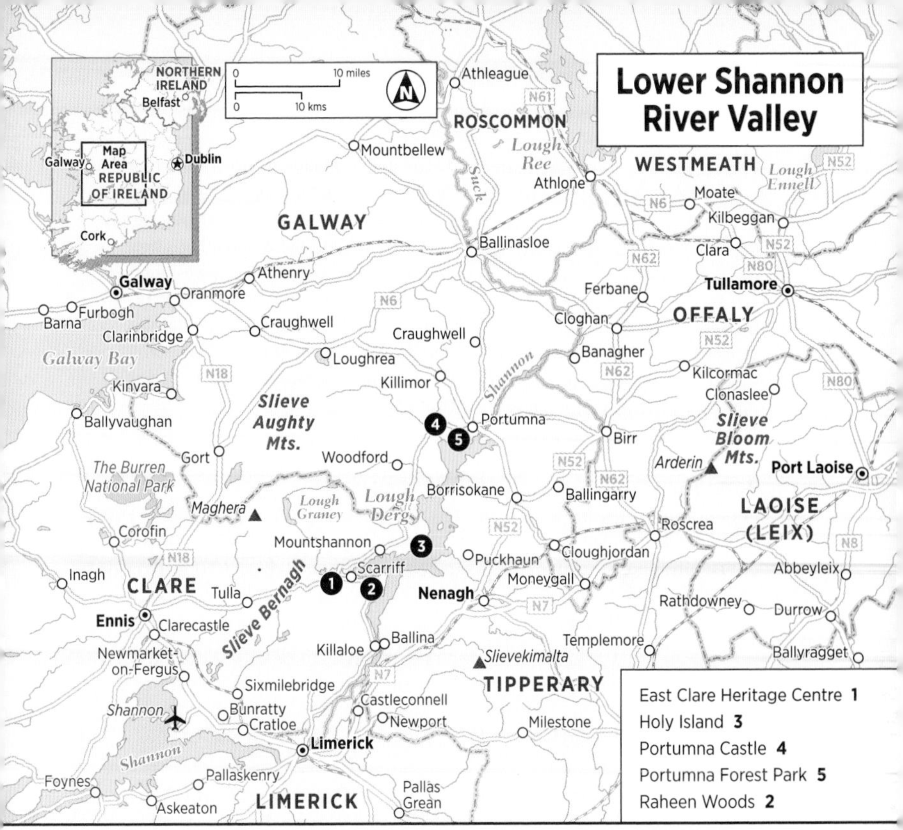

level of expertise, and the depth of your pockets. Numerous companies rent cabin cruisers along this stretch of the river including **Emerald Star Line,** The Marina, Carrick-on-Shannon, County Leitrim (✆ **071/962-7633;** www.emeraldstar.ie); and **Shannon Castle Line,** The Marina, Williamstown Harbour, Whitegate, County Clare (✆ **061/927042;** www.shannon cruisers.com).

Whelan's Boat Hire, 25 Abbey St., Killaloe, County Clare (✆ **061/376159;** whelans@killaloe.ie), rents 6m (20-ft.) lake boats with outboard engines for sightseeing or fishing in the waters of Lough Derg. Prices include fuel, fishing gear, life jackets, and rainwear. In the summer, Whelan's offers river tours that provide plenty of local history and lore.

GOLF Shannon may be the only airport in the world with its own championship golf course. The 18-hole, par-72 championship course at the **Shannon Golf Club,** Shannon Airport (✆ **061/471849;** www.shannongolf.com), may not be the quietest course in Ireland, but

Irish Troopers

During the years of America's western expansion, about one-third of the U.S. Cavalry was comprised of soldiers born in Ireland. On June 25, 1876, almost 130 Irishmen rode with Custer's 7th Cavalry into a Sioux camp along the Little Big Horn River.

it's the handiest. Greens fees are €55 weekdays, €65 weekends and bank holidays, with early and late tee times from €25. Within 1km (⅔ mile) of the terminal, it is bounded on one side by the Shannon River, and on the other by busy runways.

More peaceful choices in the area include the par-71 **Dromoland Golf Club,** Newmarket-on-Fergus, County Clare (✆ **061/368444;** www.dromolandgolf.com), with greens fees of €45 to €70, depending on the time of year. The par-71 parkland course at the **Ennis Golf Club,** Drumbiggle, Ennis, County Clare (✆ **065/682-4074;** www.ennisgolfclub.com), charges greens fees of €35 weekdays, €40 weekends.

The Mass Hole

To say golf is a religious experience in Ireland is not blasphemous. Actually, it's quite appropriate. Only in Ireland can you experience the unique hazard of the Mass hole. When the celebration of Mass was outlawed during penal times, secret Masses were often held in hidden dales, culverts, and gorges, out of sight of the British. Some golf links incorporate such places into their courses.

The **East Clare Golf Club,** Scariff/Killaloe Road, Bodyke, County Clare (✆ **061/921322;** www.eastclare.com), is an 18-hole championship course. Greens fees are €30 weekdays, €35 weekends.

SWIMMING Lough Derg in the southern part of the county is known for clear, unpolluted water that's ideal for swimming, particularly at **Castle Lough, Dromineer,** and **Portumna Bay.** Portumna Bay has changing rooms and showers.

WALKING There are some excellent walks in **Portumna Forest Park,** in **Raheen Woods,** and along the shoreline of **Lough Derg.** For a touch of scenic wilderness, walk a portion of the **Slieve Bloom Way,** a circular 34km (21-mile) signposted trail that begins and ends in Glenbarrow, County Laois.

Where to Stay

VERY EXPENSIVE

Dromoland Castle ★ This vision of turrets and towers makes for a fairy-tale night, albeit at prices fit for a king (or at least an ex-president). About 15 minutes' drive from Shannon Airport, the castle dates from 1686, and stands amid extensive parklands and gardens where deer roam freely. The drawing rooms and stately halls have all the wood and stone carvings, medieval suits of armor, rich oak paneling, and oil paintings your heart could desire. The guest rooms are lavishly decorated with designer fabrics and reproduction furniture. Service is excellent, if rather stiff and self-conscious, although that's not a surprise given the kind of guests they get here. In 2004, George W. Bush stayed here while attending the E.U.-U.S. Summit.

Limerick-Ennis rd. (N18), Newmarket-on-Fergus, County Clare. www.dromoland.ie. ✆ **800/346-7007** in the U.S., or 061/368144. Fax 061/363355. 100 units. €450–€540 double; €725–€880 suite. Full Irish breakfast €29. AE, DC, MC, V. **Amenities:** 2 restaurants; bar; babysitting; concierge; 18-hole golf course; room service; tennis courts; fishing and boating equipment; walking/jogging trails. *In room:* TV, hair dryer.

EXPENSIVE

Bunratty Castle Hotel ★ This manor house adjoining Bunratty Castle isn't a castle at all—instead it's a gracious country-house hotel with a sunny yellow facade, offering comfort and convenience with a touch of elegance. Recently renovated, it's got a fresh new feel. The public rooms are nicely done, with an antique marble altar as a reception desk. The spacious guest rooms have orthopedic king-size beds draped in neutral fabrics with occasional bright touches. There's also a spa, where you can soak away the cares of world travel.

Bunratty, County Clare. www.bunrattycastlehotel.com. ✆ **061/478-700.** Fax 061/364-891. 80 units. €100–€175 double. Rates include full breakfast. AE, MC, V. **Amenities:** Restaurant; bar; babysitting; spa. *In room:* A/C, TV, hair dryer.

Old Ground Hotel Long a focal point in the busy market town of Ennis, this ivy-covered hotel dates from 1749, and was once both the town hall and the jail. It's simply but elegantly decorated, with creamy yellows in the lobby, and neutral tones in the guest rooms, livened by soft, russet bed covers. There are lots of memorable touches—look out for a fireplace dating to 1553; it once warmed Lemaneagh Castle. On summer evenings, cabaret-style entertainment is offered in the pub.

O'Connell St., Ennis, County Clare. www.flynnhotels.com. ✆ **065/682-8127.** Fax 065/682-8112. 114 units. €140–€170 double; €200–€275 suite. Rates include full breakfast. AE, MC, V. **Amenities:** 2 restaurants; bar; lounge. *In room:* TV, hair dryer.

MODERATE

Lakeside Hotel ☺ On the southern banks of Lough Derg, shaded by ancient trees, this two-story country house–style hotel has a lovely setting. In fact, this is by a long way its greatest selling point, as guest rooms could do with a face-lift, and breakfast is underwhelming; but the views of the lake and gardens are stunning. Make sure you stipulate a lake view, although these cost extra (they also tend to be a little quieter). The excellent on-site leisure center is a big attraction for families; among its facilities are two kids' pools, a waterslide, and child care (weekdays).

Killaloe, County Clare. www.lakeside-killaloe.com. ✆ **800/447-7462** in the U.S., or 061/376122. Fax 061/376431. 46 units. €100–€130 double; €20 supplement for lake views. Rates include full breakfast. AE, MC, V. **Amenities:** Restaurant; bar; babysitting; gym; Jacuzzi; indoor pool; smoke-free rooms; steam room; tennis court. *In room:* TV.

INEXPENSIVE

Avarest Bunratty ★ If you're looking for a cozy retreat within a very short drive of the airport, you can hardly do better than this cheery B&B. Bedrooms are clean, comfortable, and modern, with semi-orthopedic beds and power showers in the bathrooms. Breakfasts are delicious and, blessedly, offer more than just the fried-egg-and-bacon option one is often limited to at B&Bs in this price range. The owners successfully cultivate the kind of friendly, welcoming atmosphere that leaves you wanting for nothing. ***Note:*** The Avarest has no restaurant, but the owners can recommend places nearby.

Hurlers Cross, Bunratty, County Clare. www.avarest.ie. ✆ **061/360278.** 5 units. €70–€80 double. 25% reduction for kids 2–12 when sharing with parent. Rates include service charge and full breakfast. MC, V. **Amenities:** Internet access. *In room:* TV, Wi-Fi (free).

RENTING A cottage IN THE IRISH COUNTRYSIDE

For an area of such popularity, much of County Clare has surprisingly few hotels. In many ways, that's part of its allure—its lakes and forests are unspoiled by condos, motels, and fast-food joints—but it still has left travelers in the lurch over the years.

When the "Rent an Irish Cottage" program was pioneered here almost 30 years ago, the idea was simple: Build small rental cottages designed in traditional style, with exteriors of white stucco, thatched roofs, and half doors.

Aside from the turf fireplaces, all of the interior furnishings, plumbing, heating, and kitchen appliances are modern.

Built in groups of 8 to 12, the cottages are on picturesque sites in remote villages such as Puckane, Terryglass, and Whitegate, overlooking or close to Lough Derg's shores. As there are no restaurants or bars on-site, you shop in local grocery stores, cook your own meals, and mix with locals in pubs at night. In other words, it's a chance to become part of the community.

Rates range from around €350 to €1,500 per cottage per week, depending on the size (one to six bedrooms) and time of year. Rental rates include bed linens and color TV; towels and metered electricity are extra.

One of the loveliest cottage settings belongs to **Mountshannon,** County Clare, a cluster of 12 pastel-toned, one- and two-story cottages on the shores of Lough Derg at Mountshannon Harbour. Grouped like a private village around a garden courtyard, the three-bedroom cottages cost €310 to €690 per week, depending on the time of year. Also on the shores of Lough Derg are 12 cottages in a country village setting in **Terryglass,** County Tipperary. Rates for three-bedroom cottages are the same as above.

For more information, contact **Rent an Irish Cottage,** 51 O'Connell St., Limerick, County Limerick (✆ **061/411109;** www.rentacottage.ie).

Bayly Farm 🎁 In a wisteria-covered Georgian farmhouse just a couple of miles from Lough Derg, owners Desmond and Jacqueline Bayly have created a relaxed atmosphere on the grounds of a working farm. The house is surrounded by miles of pasture, and guests are welcome to explore the grounds and the nearby river (Desmond can even give you a map to all the farm's beauty spots). On cold days you can relax in the drawing room by the fire. Guest rooms are spacious and beautifully decorated with quality antiques. All have lovely, bucolic views. Bathrooms are a mix of wonderful antiques and modern fittings (including underfloor heating)—and most rooms are en suite. Breakfast is hearty, as you'd expect on a farm, and the price is right.

Ballinaclough, Nenagh, County Tipperary. www.balyfarm.ie. ✆ **067/31499.** 3 units. €70–€80 double. Rates include full breakfast. No credit cards. Dinner €35, book in advance. *In room:* Hair dryer.

Glocca Morra This friendly B&B a few miles outside Killaloe offers comfortable rooms and spectacular views of the lake and surrounding countryside. The owner is happy to share information about the area, and will lure you to have hearty breakfasts, including delicious scrambled eggs and smoked salmon and fresh-baked muffins. Rooms are simply and pleasantly decorated, and many have polished wood floors. The area is quiet, but light sleepers may be disturbed by noise from other rooms, as rooms are not soundproof. ***Note***: There are no TVs in rooms, although there is a TV and DVD player in the lounge.

9km (6 miles) north of Killaloe on the main road, Ogonnelloe, County Clare. www.gloccamorra.com. ✆ **061/923172.** 4 units. €70 double. Rates include full breakfast. AE, DC, MC, V. Closed Nov–Feb. **Amenities:** Lounge; smoke-free rooms. *In room:* TV.

Where to Eat

MODERATE

Brogan's PUB FOOD This place is big but friendly, with plenty of tables, even when it's busy at lunchtime. The food is classic Irish, with lots of stews, meat pies, and fish and chips. It's marginally better for lunch than dinner, as it feels more like a restaurant than a pub.

24 O'Connell St., Ennis, County Clare. ✆ **065/682-9480.** Main courses €8–€22. No credit cards. Daily 10am–10pm.

The Cherry Tree Restaurant ★★★ 🎁 MODERN CONTINENTAL This lovely waterside restaurant in enchanting Killaloe is the destination restaurant of the midlands, and it has scooped a number of prestigious European awards in the past few years. The dining room is colorful and inviting, and the cooking is sophisticated. Seafood is a strong suit, but everything on the menu begins with fine local ingredients: Barbarie duck with orange relish, organic salmon with sautéed prawns, and roast wild venison with apples are the kind of dishes you're likely to find on the constantly changing menu. The atmosphere is elegant but relaxed, and the service is attentive but not overpowering. Book well in advance.

Lakeside, Ballina, Killaloe, County Clare. ✆ **061/375688.** www.cherrytreerestaurant.ie. Reservations recommended. Main courses €18–€28; early-bird menus: 2 courses €21, 3 courses €26; 3-course fixed-price dinner €39. AE, MC, V. Tues–Sat 6–10pm; Sun 12:30–3pm. Closed Sun–Wed in winter season.

Cruise's Pub and Restaurant GRILL Another marvelously historic restaurant (dating from 1658), this one has low beamed ceilings, crackling fires in open hearths, lantern lighting, and a rough flagstone floor strewn with sawdust. It's a casual place with a traditional pub menu, including dishes like Irish stew, steaks, and seafood. On warm days, you can sit outside in the courtyard overlooking the friary.

Abbey St., Ennis, County Clare. ✆ **065/684-1800.** Reservations recommended. Main courses €10–€26. MC, V. Daily 12:30–10pm.

Goosers ★ SEAFOOD With a thatched roof and mustard-colored exterior, this popular (read: often jampacked) pub and restaurant sits on the Ballina side of the Shannon, looking out at the river. Its two informal rooms have open fireplaces, stone floors, and beamed ceilings, and you sit on *sugan* chairs (traditional wood chairs with twisted straw rope seats). There's picnic-table seating outside in good weather. The bar-food menu includes traditional dishes such as bacon and cabbage, and Irish stew, while the restaurant focuses on local seafood—lobster, oysters, sole, and monkfish—simply prepared.

Ballina, County Clare. ✆ **061/376791.** Reservations recommended for dinner. Bar food €6–€23; dinner main courses €22–€34. AE, MC, V. Restaurant Mon–Sat 6:30–10pm; Sun 12:30–2:30pm and 6:30–10pm; bar food daily 12:30–10pm. No children after 8pm.

Lantern House CONTINENTAL High on a hillside just north of Killaloe, the biggest draw of this country-house restaurant is its panoramic views of Lough Derg. The owners here extend a warm welcome, and the candlelit dining room exudes old-world charm, with a beamed ceiling, wall lanterns, and lace tablecloths. The menu changes frequently, but good options usually include poached local salmon, pan-fried sole, or grilled sirloin steak. There are also rooms to rent here, although they're slightly overpriced at €90 (double).

Ogonnelloe, County Clare. ✆ **061/923034.** Reservations recommended. Main courses €10–€25. MC, V. Daily 6–9pm. Closed Mon Nov to mid-Feb.

Tulsi ★ INDIAN The latest in a small chain of Indian restaurants that includes popular branches in Dublin and Galway, Tulsi is a good place to stop for authentic Indian food. All the favorites are here; if you like your food spicy, opt for a chicken chili masala or *jalfrezi;* for something less likely to leave you gasping for air, the *badami korma* (chicken or lamb in an aromatic yogurt and nut sauce) or *tandoori tikka masala* (chargrilled chicken or lamb in a creamy tomato sauce) are delicious.

Carmody St., Ennis, County Clare. ✆ **065/684-8060.** Main courses €9–€16. MC, V. Mon–Sat 5–11pm; Sun 1–10pm.

INEXPENSIVE

Country Choice ★ CAFE If you're looking for picnic provisions or food for the road, this is the place to find it. You can fill your basket with sweet local marmalade, rich farmhouse cheeses, and freshly baked loaves of bread. Out back, you can linger over a cup of coffee at the cafe and listen in on all the local gossip. There's an inexpensive lunch menu, and fresh baked goods are served in the morning. The wine selection is, well, more of a display than a list; you simply pick out any of the bottles that are for sale in the shop and they serve it to you (plus €5 corkage).

25 Kenyon St., Nenagh, County Tipperary. ✆ **067/32596.** www.countrychoice.ie. Lunch main courses €5–€12. No credit cards. Mon–Sat 9am–5:30pm (lunch served 12:30–3:30pm).

Molly's Bar and Restaurant CONTINENTAL Next to the Killaloe bridge, this brightly colored pub and restaurant offers expansive views of Killaloe Harbour. Inside is a cheerful clutter with shelves lined with old plates, vintage clocks, and pine and mahogany furnishings. The food is a similarly casual mix of light fare and heavier dinner selections, and good options on our visit included the fresh local salmon and huge chargrilled steaks. Outdoor seating is available on picnic-style tables. There's live music, traditional and modern, Thursday to Sunday evenings, as well as a disco and sports bar in the basement.

Ballina, Killaloe, County Clare. ✆ **061/376632.** Reservations recommended for dinner. All items €7–€22. AE, MC, V. Daily 12:30–11:30pm.

MEDIEVAL BANQUETS

The medieval banquets at Bunratty and Knappogue castles can be booked in the United States through a travel agent or by calling ✆ **800/CIE-TOUR** (243-8687). Or, book online at **www.shannonheritage.com** and receive a discount for either one. The banquets are undeniably touristy but fun nevertheless, and even the locals have been known to attend once in a while. ***Note***: Book early; these banquets sell out months in advance.

Bunratty Castle ★★ IRISH Every evening a full medieval banquet is re-created in this sturdy castle, complete with music, song, and merriment. Seated at long tables in the magnificent baronial hall, guests sample chicken with apple and mead sauce, or spare ribs with honey and whiskey (nobody minds if you eat with your fingers). Drinks include mulled wine, claret, and flagons of ale and mead. To add to the fun, at each banquet, a "lord and lady" are chosen from the participants to reign over the 3-hour proceedings, and someone else is thrown into the dungeon.

Castle Limerick–Ennis rd. (N18), Bunratty, County Clare. ✆ **061/360788.** www.shannonheritage.com. Reservations required. Dinner and entertainment €60 adults; €45 children 10–12; €30 children 6–9; free for children 5 and under. MC, V. Daily 5:30 and 8:45pm.

Knappogue Castle ★ IRISH Once the stronghold of the MacNamara clan, this 15th-century castle is smaller and has a more intimate feel than Bunratty (and, unlike most banquet venues, is wheelchair accessible). However, their assertion that the menu consists of real dishes "as served during the period" is dubious, given that it includes such famous "medieval fare" as chicken supreme and lemon cheesecake. And there's a vegetarian option, for those medieval vegetarians. Still, it might not be authentic, but it can be really fun. Post-dinner entertainment consists of a colorful 35-minute show telling the history of Ireland through music and dance. ***Tip:*** As with the Bunratty Castle banquet, above, there is a discount for booking online.

Quin, County Clare. ✆ **061/360788.** www.shannonheritage.com. Reservations required. Dinner and entertainment €57 adults; €43 children 10–12; €29 children 6–9; free for children 5 and under. MC, V. May–Oct daily 6:30pm.

Clare After Dark

Brandon's Bar Irish music aficionados will probably already have heard of this place, as it's one of the best places to see live music in the region. Its music program is seriously eclectic; on one night you could hear traditional folk here, and the next heavy metal, indie, electro-clash, or new wave. 70 O'Connell St., Ennis, County Clare. ✆ **065/682-8133.**

Cois na hAbhna This traditional arts center (the name is pronounced *Cush*-na *How*-na) stages lively sessions of music, song, and dance, followed by Irish dancing with audience participation. Snacks are traditional as well—the likes of tea and brown bread. Traditional dance sessions are run seasonally on Wednesdays from 9pm to midnight. Call for the most current schedule of *Céilís* and other events. Galway Rd., Ennis, County Clare. ✆ **065/682-4276.** www.coisnahabhna.ie. Admission around €8, depending on the event.

The Derg Inn On the south bank of Lough Derg at the edge of Tipperary, this is one of the lake's better watering holes. The decor is . . . well, everything. There are horse pictures, china plates, books, beer posters, vintage bottles, lanterns, you name it. Find your way through the eclectic mix and you can have a well-poured pint, accompanied by traditional music on Wednesday and Sunday evenings. The menu here is also excellent and not unsophisticated—the pâté with homemade mango chutney and garlic bread is divine. Terryglass, County Tipperary. ✆ **067/22037.** www.derginn.ie.

Durty Nelly's Established in 1620 next door to Bunratty Castle, this ramshackle, thatched-roof cottage was originally a watering hole for the castle guards. Now it's a favorite haunt of locals and tourists looking for a pint after the medieval banquets at the castle. It's likely the decor—old lanterns, sawdust on the floors, and open turf fireplaces—hasn't changed much in centuries. This is a good spot for a substantial pub lunch or a full dinner in one of the two restaurants. Spontaneous Irish music sessions break out here on most evenings. Limerick-Ennis rd. (N18), Bunratty, County Clare. ✆ **061/364861.** www.durtynellys.ie.

Paddy's Pub From the harbor on south Lough Derg, it's a short walk up a winding lane to this small, dark pub. A fine display of antiques and nightly traditional music in summer make it a jewel among Lake Derg's pubs. Casual pub food (burgers and sandwiches) makes it a good option. Poker fans may want to come down on Friday, when an intense game of Texas hold 'em is open to anyone with €10. Terryglass, County Tipperary. ✆ **067/22147.** www.paddysbar.ie.

Durty Nelly's pub in Bunratty, County Clare, lies right in the shadow of Bunratty Castle.

The Burren ★★★

The extraordinary otherworldly landscape of the region known simply as the Burren is difficult to describe. Carved by nature from bare carboniferous limestone, the view manages to be both desolate and beautiful. Sheets of rock jut and undulate in a kind of moonscape as far as you can see. Amid the rocks, delicate wildflowers somehow find enough dirt to thrive, and ferns curl gently around boulders, moss softens hard edges, orchids flower exotically, and violets brighten the landscape. With the flowers come butterflies that thrive on the rare flora. Even Burren animals are unusual: The pine marten (small weasels), stoat (ermine), and badger, all rare in the rest of Ireland, are common here.

The Burren began to get its strange and unforgettable appearance 300 million years ago when layers of shells and sediment were deposited under a tropical sea. Many millions of years later, those layers were exposed by erosion and poor prehistoric farming methods, and since then, it's all been battered by the Irish rain and winds, producing all that you see today. About 7,000 years ago, when this landscape was already very old indeed, humans first began to leave their mark here, in the form of Stone Age burial monuments, such as the famed **Poulnabrone Dolmen** and **Gleninsheen wedge tomb.**

Lisdoonvarna, on the western edge, is a charmingly old-fashioned spa town that has long been known for its natural mineral springs. Each summer, it draws thousands of people to bathe in its sulfuric streams, iron creeks, and iodine lakes.

One of the best ways to explore the Burren is to take the R480. Through a series of corkscrew turns, the road curves from **Corofin** through gorgeous scenery to **Ballyvaughan,** a delightful little village overlooking the blue waters of Galway Bay.

EXPLORING THE REGION

Burren National Park ★★★ spreads across 1,653 hectares (4,083 acres) and continually acquires more land as it becomes available. The remarkable rocky land is dotted with picturesque ruined castles, tumbling cliffs, rushing rivers, lakes, barren rock mountains, and plant life that defies all of nature's conventional rules. The park is particularly rich in archaeological remains from the Neolithic through the medieval periods—dolmens and wedge tombs (approx. 120 of them), ring forts (500 of those), round towers, ancient churches, high crosses, monasteries, and holy wells. The park is centered at Mullaghmore Mountain, but there is, as of yet, no official entrance point and no admission charges or restrictions to access.

With its unique terrain and meandering walking paths, the Burren lends itself to **walking.** One of the best ways to amble through the limestone pavements and terraces, shale uplands, and lakes is to follow the **Burren Way.** The 42km (26-mile) signposted route stretches from Ballyvaughan to Liscannor, and you can pick it up in the park, walk a stretch of it, and then head back to your car, if you wish. An information sheet outlining the route is available from any tourist office. **Burren Guided Walks and Hikes** offers a wide selection of guided walks, hikes, and rambles. For more information contact Mary Howard at ✆ **065/707-6100,** or visit www.burrenguidedwalks.com.

Aillwee Cave ★ This deep cave was undiscovered for thousands of years until a local farmer followed a dog into it 50 years ago. Inside he found a huge cavern with 1,000m (3,280 ft.) of passages running straight into the heart of a mountain. He kept it to himself for decades before eventually spreading the word. Professional cave explorers later uncovered its magnificent bridged chasms, deep caverns, a frozen waterfall, and hollows created by hibernating brown bears. Brown

"Green roads," built by starving farmers during the Great Famine, now make excellent walking trails through the Burren.

bears have been extinct in Ireland for 10,000 years. Guided tours are excellent here—generally led by geology students from area universities. There's a scary moment when they turn out the lights for a minute so you can experience the depth of the darkness inside. Tours last approximately 30 minutes, and are conducted continuously. On-site, there's also a craft shop, a farm shop, a cheese-making enterprise called Burren Gold Cheese, and the new **Burren Bird of Prey Centre** (✆ **065/707-7036;** www.birdofpreycentre.com), a working aviary designed to mimic the natural habitat of the buzzards, falcons, eagles, and owls that live there. Visitors can observe the birds, learn about the center's breeding program, and watch flying demonstrations in an open-air arena at noon and 3pm daily (also at other times in summer).

In early spring, wildflowers poke up from between the limestone slabs of the Burren.

Ballyvaughan, County Clare. ✆ **065/707-7036.** www.aillweecave.ie. Admission (joint ticket with Burren Bird of Prey Centre) €17 adults; €15 seniors and students; €10 children; €39 families. Sept–June daily 10am–5:30pm; July–Aug daily 10am–6:30pm.

The Burren Centre This is a fine place to acquaint yourself with all facets of the area. Using films, landscape models, and interpretive displays, it highlights the local geology, flora, and fauna. There's a tearoom and a shop stocked with locally made crafts and products.

R476 to Kilfenora, County Clare. ✆ **065/708-8030.** www.theburrencentre.ie. Admission to exhibition €6 adults; €5 seniors and students; €4 children; €20 families. Mid-Mar to May and Sept–Oct daily 10am–5pm; June–Aug daily 9:30am–6pm. Last admission 30 min. before closing.

Wildflower spotting in the Burren.

Clare Heritage and Genealogical Centre Housed in a former Church of Ireland edifice built in 1718, this small but engaging heritage center has exhibits on Clare farming, industry, commerce, language, and music, as well as a handy tearoom and gift shop. If you're named Kelly, Murphy, or Walsh (among others) and researching your family roots, you might also want to stop by its well-equipped genealogical research center. You can make use of the records they hold here, but if you're *really* interested in building your family tree, the staff will undertake a full-fledged family history report for between €195 and €425 or more, depending on how much work is required.

Aillwee Cave was unknown in modern times until a farmer stumbled into it in the mid–20th century.

Church St., Corofin, County Clare. ✆ **065/683-7955.** www.clareroots.com. Museum admission €4 adults; €3.50 seniors, students, and children. Genealogical Centre year-round Mon–Fri 9am–5:30pm. Museum Apr–Oct daily 9:30am–5:30pm.

Corcomroe Abbey Set jewel-like in a languid, green valley bounded by rolling hills, the jagged ruins of this Cistercian abbey are breathtaking. The abbey was founded in 1194 by Donal Mór O'Brien, and his grandson, a former king of Thomond, is entombed in the abbey's northern wall. There are some interesting medieval and Romanesque carvings in the stone, including one of a bishop with a crosier. Corcomroe is a lonely spot, except for on Easter morning, when people come from miles around to celebrate Mass. It's quite a sight if you happen to be around.

Just off the main Galway-Ballyvaughan rd. (N67) near Oughtmama, County Clare. Free admission.

Poulnabrone Dolmen ★ This portal tomb is an exquisitely preserved prehistoric site. Its dolmen (or stone table) is huge, and surrounded by a natural pavement of stones. The tomb has been dated back 5,000 years. When it was excavated in the 1980s, the remains of 16 people were found, including a newborn baby. The greatest mystery remains how the gigantic stones were moved and

Take Green Roads Through the Burren

"Green roads" are former highways that crisscross the Burren landscape in inaccessible areas. Most of these unpaved roads were created during the Great Famine as make-work projects for starving locals, although some are ancient roads of indeterminate origin. These old, unused roads are now popular with hikers, and some are signposted. They're also famous for harboring rare and beautiful wildflowers, such as orchids and deep blue gentians.

FALLING IN love WITH LOVE IN LISDOONVARNA

If you've been looking for love in all the wrong places, clearly you've never been to Lisdoonvarna. This adorable little County Clare town lives for love. There's a Matchmaker Pub on the main street. The are three people in town who still officially call themselves matchmakers—Willie Daly, a horse whisperer, and his daughters, Claire and Marie, who are the fourth generation of the Daly family to carry on the tradition.

Every autumn, the entire town gets involved in the matchmaking business, when it throws the month-long **Lisdoonvarna Matchmaking Festival.** Thousands of lovelorn singletons descend upon the town looking for "the One," and all of Lisdoonvarna cheers them on.

Throughout the town, up and down each street, and in every atmospheric corner, every available space is used for mixers, minglers, and . . . well, more mixers. The locals stir the pot as much as possible, holding romantic breakfasts, romantic dinners, romantic games, romantic dances, romantic horse races (?)—well, it *is* Ireland, after all.

To find out more about Lisdoonvarna, visit its marvelously kitsch website, **www.matchmakerireland.com**, or Willie's own website, **www.williedaly.net**.

lifted—the capstone alone weighs 5 tons. You'll have no trouble finding this sight—just look for all the tour buses. At times they literally block the road. What must the locals think?

R480, 8km (5 miles) south of the Aillwee Caves, County Clare. Free admission.

WHERE TO STAY

Expensive

Gregans Castle Hotel ★★ Not a castle at all, but an ivy-covered, stone manor house, this hotel is filled with light and offers lovely views of the Burren and Galway Bay. Owned and managed by the Hayden family, Gregans demonstrates decades of attention to detail. The drawing room and expansive hallways are filled with heirlooms, and the walls are decorated with Raymond Piper's mural paintings of the Burren. Guest rooms are spacious and elegantly decorated in muted colors with comfortable orthopedic beds. On a sunny day, you can play croquet on the lawn or feed the hotel's donkeys and ponies. The kitchen is led by a talented chef who turns fresh local produce into extraordinary meals—it's well worth the cost for dinner here. Afterward, you can linger over drinks around the fire in the lounge. Unfortunately, prices are a bit high for what's on offer here.

Ballyvaughan-Lisdoonvarna rd. (N67), Ballyvaughan, County Clare. www.gregans.ie. ✆ **800/323-5463** in the U.S., or 065/707-7005. Fax 065/707-7111. 22 units. €245–€320 double; €365–€450 suite. Children 13–17 sharing with parent €50; 6–12 €30; 5 and under €20. Rates include full breakfast. AE, MC, V. Closed Nov–Mar. **Amenities:** Restaurant; bar. *In room:* TV, hair dryer, Wi-Fi (in premier suites only).

Inexpensive

Fergus View ★ The views from this lovely, rambling house are extraordinary—rolling hills, undulating green fields, colorful gardens. Inside there's a fire crackling at the hearth, and a warming cup of tea after your long drive. The guest rooms are sweet and not particularly frilly, although they are a bit small. Owner Mary Kelleher goes out of her way to make guests feel at home, and has compiled one of the best local guides to the region that we've seen. She's also converted a small stone lodge nearby into attractive self-catering accommodations for up to five people.

Kilnaboy, Corofin, County Clare. www.fergusview.com. ✆ **065/683-7606.** Fax 065/683-7192. 6 units. €72 double. Rates include full breakfast. No credit cards. Closed end of Oct to Easter. 3.2km (2 miles) north of Corofin on road to Kilfenora. **Amenities:** Smoke-free rooms.

Rusheen Lodge ★ On the main road just south of Ballyvaughan village, this award-winning bungalow-style guesthouse is completely surrounded by flowering gardens. The innkeeper is Karen McGann, whose grandfather, Jacko McGann, discovered the nearby Aillwee Caves. Rooms are decorated with a traditional touch, and have firm beds covered in floral fabric. Breakfast, served in a bright, pastel-toned dining room, can include fresh-caught local fish.

Knocknagrough, Ballyvaughan, County Clare. www.rusheenlodge.com. ✆ **065/707-7092.** Fax 065/707-7152. 9 units. €90–€100 double; €120–€190 suite. Rates include full breakfast. AE, MC, V. Closed Dec–Feb. **Amenities:** Wi-Fi. *In room:* TV, hair dryer.

WHERE TO EAT

An Fulacht Fia ★ MODERN IRISH This gorgeous little restaurant overlooking Galway Bay has a reputation that extends much further than the fringes of Ballyvaughn village. But the food served here is local—almost everything's sourced from within the Burren itself—and the end result is a creative and finely judged menu. Typical dishes may include pistachio-crusted Burren rack of lamb served with juniper berries and thyme *jus,* or hazelnut-coated salmon filet with creamed leeks and citrus butter. The wine list is excellent, though it will hurt your wallet a bit.

Coast Rd., Ballyvaughan, County Clare. ✆ **065/707-7300.** www.anfulachtfia.ie. Reservations recommended. Early-bird dinners: 2 courses €21, 3 courses €26; main courses €18–€25. MC, V. Mon–Sat 5:30–9pm; Sun 7:30–9pm. Early-bird dinner daily 5–6:30pm. Reduced hours in winter; call ahead.

AFTER DARK

Vaughn's This is a music pub with a countrywide reputation for attracting excellent traditional bands and stellar Irish dancing. Summers are the busiest times (things quiet down quite a bit in the off season). The barn next door is used for dancing on Thursday at 10pm and Sunday at 9pm. The traditional Irish food served here is good and affordable. Main St., Kilfenora, County Clare. ✆ **065/708-8004.** www.vaughanspub.ie.

The Clare Coast

One of Ireland's most photographed places, the **Cliffs of Moher ★** draw thousands of visitors to Clare's remote reaches every day of the year—rain or shine. Rising to vertiginous heights 210m (689 ft.) above the Atlantic and stretching along about 8km (5 miles) of coastline, the cliffs are undeniably impressive. In bad weather, access to the cliffs is (understandably) limited, as the wind can blow very hard here and it's a long way down. When the weather is fine, there's a guardrail to offer you a small sense of security as you peek over the edge, though some foolhardy visitors treat it with startling disdain, climbing over it for a better view of the sheer drop (although a fierce new anti-climb policy is intended to put a stop to that). It's all well worth a visit, but be aware that in the high season, the crowds can rather spoil the effect.

Farther along the Clare Coast, **Lahinch** is an old-fashioned Victorian seaside resort, with a wide beach and long promenade curving along the horseshoe bay. Golfers will already know all they need to know about this town, as it's renowned for its golf course. Dubbed by fans the "St. Andrews of Ireland," it is the paradigm of Irish links golf and is ranked among the 50 best courses in the world by *Golf* magazine.

Nearby, the secluded fishing village of **Doolin** is the unofficial capital of Irish traditional music. Its quaint old pubs and restaurants ring with the sound of fiddle and accordion all year long. Doolin is also a departure point for the short boat trip to the beautiful and isolated **Aran Islands** (p. 471).

The Clare Coast is dotted with **seaside resorts** with varying degrees of crowds and beauty, and the best include places such as **Kilrush, Kilkee, Miltown Malbay,** and **Ennistymon.** This part of the county is a marvelous place to take amusing pictures of signs denoting the presence of tiny villages and beauty spots with quirky names like Puffing Hole, Intrinsic Bay, Chimney Hill, Elephant's Teeth, Mutton Island, and Lover's Leap.

SEEING THE SIGHTS

Cliffs of Moher ★ These high cliffs plunging down to the Atlantic offer unforgettable views. This is a dramatic place, where the soundtrack is provided by the roar of waves crashing against the cliff walls far below and the faint cries of nesting seabirds. On a clear day, you can see the Aran Islands in Galway Bay as misty shapes off in the distance. Understandably, this is also dead center on the tourist track, with a constant throng of tour buses and cars clogging the parking lot

The crashing waves of the Atlantic drown out the sound of the tour buses at the spectacular Cliffs of Moher.

The Cliffs of More . . . Money

After the construction of a glossy €30-million visitor center a few years ago, prices at the Cliffs of Moher were bound to increase. And so they have. First it was parking charges, which increased over the course of a few years from €2.50 to €4.50, then to €6, and finally €8. In 2011, the cliffs introduced a new "family-friendly" per-person charge of €6 to replace the parking charges. The new charge includes parking and admission to the controversial visitor center and cliff "Experience." Children under 16 years old get in for free. So now, a couple—who just want to park and see the cliffs—rather than paying €8 for the privilege, will pay a "family-friendly" €12 instead.

As this book is being written you could still opt to pay €8 to park your car (which suddenly, given the new charges, seems almost cheap) and not go to the visitor center at all, but you have to ask for that option, and it is not advertised on-site. The group who run the cliff says it intends to eliminate the option in the near future, and move over fully to the per-person charge.

It's all become a little absurd, frankly. We are talking about a natural wonder here, created by winds and waves, and this seems dangerously close to naked profiteering. For what it's worth, access to the cliffs is actually free. Under Irish law, you cannot be charged for visiting the cliffs on foot. Because of this, some visitors have begun rejecting the parking charge and finding places to park nearby, then hiking up to the cliffs for a quick peek before racing back to their cars. But before you try this, bear in mind that the local government has banned all parking on the side of the road near the cliffs, and this law is zealously enforced. We've heard of several visitors coming back to their cars to find €50 parking tickets.

below. In recent years, a large modern visitor center has opened, changing the landscape and adding little to the wonders wrought by nature. Now there are more souvenir shops and a "Cliffs of Moher Experience" including a film—why this is necessary when the real thing is right outside, we simply do not know. Now a per-person price is being introduced for parking and access to the visitor center, and the fees situation has become a bit outrageous. (See "The Cliffs of More. . . Money" box above.) ***Tip:*** If you visit the cliffs after the visitor center closes, it's much more peaceful. And free.

R478, 11km (6¾ miles) north of Lahinch, County Clare. ✆ **065/708-6146.** www.cliffsofmoher.ie. Admission and parking €6 adults; children 15 and under free. Visitor center Mar 9am–6pm; Apr and Oct 9am–6:30pm; May and Sept 9am–7pm; June 9am–7:30pm; July–Aug 9am–8:30pm; Nov–Feb 9am–5pm. Cliffs open at all times.

Lahinch Seaworld and Leisure Centre ☺ This small but well-designed aquarium has all the usual kid pleasers, including slithery conger eels, ferocious sharks, and rubbery rays. There's a touch pool where they can get up close and personal. If you are then inspired to take to the water yourself, the leisure center next door charges very reasonable rates. They also have a sauna, steam room, Jacuzzi, and—smart move, this—a fully supervised child care and play zone.

The Promenade, Lahinch, County Clare. ✆ **065/708-1900.** www.lahinchseaworld.com. Admission to aquarium or pools (same rates, but ticket doesn't cover both) €9 adults; €8 seniors and students; €7 children 5–15; €5 children 2–4; €30 families. Aquarium daily 10am–6pm (last entry 5:30pm).

SPELUNKING IN THE caves AROUND DOOLIN

The area around Doolin is well known among cavers for its many intriguing potholes and caves. The area is riddled with them—the ground underneath your feet may look solid, but it's really like Swiss cheese. If you're interested in joining the spelunkers, you can stop by the tourist office and pick up brochures from local caving guides, as well as maps.

The most extraordinary single cave is **Poll na gColm,** just northeast of Lisdoonvarna. This is one of Ireland's longest caves, and its caverns wander for miles through underground passageways, vaults, and natural wonders.

For divers, there's a cluster of underwater caves just north of Doolin's harbor called the **Green Holes of Doolin** that are said to be simply extraordinary. You can get a peek at what divers will see at an area known as "Hell," where the roof of a cave has worn away, and the water rushes through an open cavern into a series of undersea pathways.

Novices should definitely not go caving on their own without training or guides. To get one or both of those, check out **www.caving.ie**.

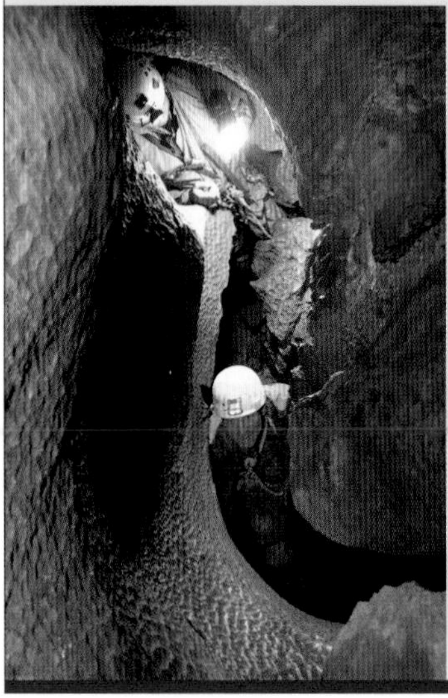

Scattery Island ★ This unspoiled island with a fantastic name is located in the Shannon Estuary near Kilrush, and holds atmospheric monastic ruins dating from the 6th century. A high, round tower and several churches are all that is left of an extensive settlement that was founded by St. Senan. To visit the island, contact one of the boat operators who arrange the 20-minute ferry rides—frequency depends on demand, and even in summer there may be only one trip per day. Or ask at the Information Centre (in Kilrush, just past the pier) when the next ferry departs. Here's an interesting little scrap of trivia associated with Scattery Island: Although it's a ruin, St. Senan's is what's known as a titular diocese—meaning that the pope still appoints it a bishop, although they don't actually do anything. The current incumbent is also the bishop of Brooklyn. Merchants Quay, Kilrush, County Clare. ✆ **065/905-1577** (Kilrush Tourism Office), or ✆ **065/682-9100** (Ennis Friary). Free admission. Ferry prices vary; usually around €15 round-trip.

GETTING TO THE ARAN ISLANDS

Doolin Ferry Co. Although the three fabled islands—Inishmore, Inishmaan, and Inisheer—are usually associated with Galway, the isles are actually closer to Doolin (roughly 8km/5 miles, or 30 min. in a boat). Ferries run back and forth to the islands daily during the high season. (For more information about the Aran Islands, see "The Aran Islands" in chapter 11.)

The Pier, Doolin, County Clare. ✆ **065/707-4455.** www.doolinferries.com. Inishmore, Inishmaan, or Inisheer round-trip €40 adults; €20 children. Interisland ferry round-trip €20 adults, €10 children; one-way €10 adults, €5 children. Student and family discounts available. Operates Mar–Oct; call for current schedule.

SHOPPING

Burren Smokehouse Get all of the smoked salmon you've ever dreamed of at this excellent smokehouse, where the freshest fish is prepared in traditional ways. You can watch the fish being prepared, and then buy some to take home. Doolin Rd., Lisdoonvarna, County Clare. ✆ **065/707-4432.** www.burrensmokehouse.ie.

Doolin Crafts Gallery This shop is the brainchild of two artisans: Matthew O'Connell, who creates batik work with Celtic designs on wall hangings, cushion covers, and scarves; and Mary Gray, who hand fashions gold and silver jewelry inspired by the Burren. There is a good coffee shop on the premises. Ballyvoe, Doolin, County Clare. ✆ **065/707-4309.** www.doolincrafts.com.

Traditional Music Shop In this town known for its traditional music, this shop is a center of attention. It's got Irish traditional music on CDs, plus books and instruments. Ballyreen, Doolin, County Clare. ✆ **065/707-4407.** www.irishmusicdoolin.com.

SPORTS & OUTDOOR PURSUITS

BIRD-WATCHING The **Bridges of Ross,** on the north side of **Loop Head,** is one of the prime autumn bird-watching sites in Ireland, especially during northwest gales, when several rare species have been seen with some consistency. The **lighthouse** at the tip of the head is also a popular spot for watching seabirds.

DOLPHIN-WATCHING The Shannon Estuary is home to about 70 bottlenose dolphins, one of four such resident groups of dolphins in Europe. Two-hour cruises run by **Dolphinwatch** leave daily May to September from Carrigaholt. Advance booking is essential (✆ **065/905-8156;** www.dolphinwatch.ie). Fees start at €24 for adults, €12 for children ages 4 to 15, and €6 for children 3 and under. They also run 4-hour sunset cruises (€40 per person), although these are usually adults-only events.

GOLF **Doonbeg Golf Club,** Doonbeg (✆ **065/905-5600;** www.doonbeggolfclub.com), has links designed by golf pro Greg Norman in a breathtaking setting. The magnificent 15th hole ends in a funnel-shaped green surrounded by sky-high dunes. With a helipad and a complex that includes a country club, hotel, and cottages, Doonbeg has quickly become a haunt for

Atlantic winds and stunning views are a constant distraction at the seaside Lahinch Golf Course.

the moneyed set, so it should come as no surprise that greens fees are a hefty €160 to €190 per person.

Also famous, and just as pricey, is **Lahinch Golf Club,** Lahinch (✆ **065/708-1003;** www.lahinchgolf.com). It has two attractive 18-hole links courses, and the "Old Course"—the longer championship links course—is the one that has given Lahinch its far-reaching reputation. This course's elevations, especially at the 9th and 13th holes, make for great views, but it also makes wind an integral part of play. Watch the goats, Lahinch's legendary weather forecasters; if they huddle by the clubhouse, it means a storm is approaching. Visitors are welcome to play, especially on weekdays; greens fees are €165 for the Old Course, €83 for a 9-hole game. On the newer Castle Course, however, the rate is a much more affordable €55.

SURFING If you've always wanted to try it, here's your chance: **Lahinch Surf School** (✆ **065/708-2061** or 087/960-9667; www.lahinchsurfschool.com) is set up in a hut on Lahinch promenade, and they specialize in getting people suited up and out on the waves—whether you surf every weekend or have never hit a board in your life. They're friendly and know their stuff; besides, surfing is good for you, apparently. Wet suits, surfboards, and lessons included. Private lessons cost around €100 to €140, depending on the time of year; group lessons cost around €40.

Students look forward to their next break at the Lahinch Surf School.

WHERE TO STAY

Very Expensive

Moy House ★ This unusual 19th-century tower house overlooking the bay about 1.6km (1 mile) outside the little town of Lahinch is beautiful inside and out. Rooms have comfortable modern beds covered in crisp Irish linens and are decorated with original paintings and period antiques. Some have wooden floors, and some bathrooms are beautifully designed (a glass panel in one lets you look down into an old well), and stocked with covetable bath products. Fresh, local produce is used in the kitchen, and dining in is worthwhile, although it's a bit of a splurge. Unfortunately, prices have got a bit high here in recent years given what's on offer.

Miltown Malbay Rd., Lahinch, County Clare. www.moyhouse.com. ✆ **065/708-2800.** Fax 065/708-2500. 9 units. €225–€280 double; €270–€360 suite. Children sharing with 2 adults €70 each. 4-course dinner €55. Rates include service charge and full breakfast. AE, MC, V. *In room:* TV, hair dryer.

Moderate

Aran View House Dating from 1736, this rambling three-story Georgian house stands on a hill surrounded by farmland just north of Doolin. Its prime location affords panoramic views of the gorgeous Clare coastline. Inside the decor is a bit old-fashioned, with colorful carpets and mahogany furnishings. Some bedrooms could use a face-lift, although they're big and generally comfortable, and some have four-poster beds. A handful of self-catering cottages offer a bit more space or privacy.

Doolin, County Clare. www.aranview.com. ✆ **065/707-4420** or 707-4061. Fax 065/707-4540. 19 units. €110 double. Children sharing with 2 adults €20. Rates include full breakfast. AE, MC, V. Closed Nov–Mar. **Amenities:** Restaurant; bar. *In room:* TV, hair dryer.

Ballinalacken Castle Country House ★ This is a beautifully located hotel, just below the crest of a hill, overlooking the misty Aran Islands. The hotel itself is not a castle, but it sits next to the atmospheric ruins of Ballinalacken Castle. The main hotel building was built in the 1840s, but most of the guest rooms are in a modern wing. If you love architectural detail, ask for a room in the old house, which has high ceilings, marble fireplaces, and, in room no. 16, sweeping views of hills and sea. All rooms are traditionally furnished and quite spacious.

Doolin, County Clare. www.ballinalackencastle.com. ✆ **065/707-4025.** 12 units. €130–€160 double; €130–€170 double with four-poster beds; €180–€200 suite. Rates include full breakfast. AE, DC, MC, V. Closed Nov–Apr 15. **Amenities:** Restaurant. *In room:* TV, hair dryer.

Inexpensive

Doonmacfelim Guest House On Doolin's main street a few hundred feet from Gus O'Connor's Pub (see below), this modern two-story guesthouse is a great value. It's close to the center of everything, but the house is surrounded by a farm, and thus quite peaceful. Guest rooms are spacious and simply furnished, with nice country views.

Doolin, County Clare. www.doonmacfelim.com. ✆ **087/125-0303.** 8 units. €70–€80 double. Rates include full breakfast. MC, V. **Amenities:** Tennis court. *In room:* Hair dryer.

Self-Catering

Loop Head Lightkeeper's House ★★ Here is yet another of the many splendid properties run by the Irish Landmark Trust (ILT). This is a comfortingly solid old house next to a lighthouse at the very tip of remote Loop Head, just

Rollicking Irish music jams at Gus O'Connor's Pub pack in crowds from all around Ireland.

southwest of Kilkee. Once home to the keeper of the lighthouse, it offers astonishing views and a real historical feel. Downstairs are a kitchen, sitting room, two bathrooms, and a double bedroom. Upstairs are two more bedrooms (one double, one twin) and a small sitting room. Nice touches are everywhere: sturdy mahogany furnishings, brass beds, oversize armchairs, fireplaces, and deep windowsills. Unsurprisingly the views are stunning; on a clear day you can see as far of the Cliffs of Moher and Dingle Bay. It's a 20-minute drive from bustling Kilkee, a little seaside resort with old-fashioned appeal. As with all ILT properties, there is no TV, but there is a radio. Bring bottled water for drinking.

Loop Head, about 4.8km (3 miles) from Kibaha, County Clare. Contact the Irish Landmark Trust www.irishlandmark.com. ✆ **01/670-4733.** Fax 01/670-4887. €330 for 2 nights in low season, going up to €1,000 per week in high season. AE, MC, V at booking.

WHERE TO EAT

Barrtrá Seafood Restaurant ★★ SEAFOOD With windows overlooking Liscannor Bay, this is a good place to bite into fresh seafood and take in gorgeous views. The food is simple but well prepared. Starters include avocado and crab salad and duck leg confit with orange and black currant sauce, while main dishes include monkfish and scallop brochette, or a "seafood symphony" of cod, prawns, monkfish, mussels, and crab in white-wine sauce. It's not fancy, but it's friendly and the food is reliably tasty. Sunset here is a wonder.

Barrtrá, Lahinch, County Clare. ✆ **065/708-1280.** www.barrtra.com. Reservations recommended. Fixed-price dinner €42; main courses €18–€26. AE, MC, V. Daily 1–2pm and 6–10pm. Closed Jan–Feb; always call ahead during off season.

Stonecutters Kitchen ☺ BISTRO This chirpy restaurant in Doolin is pitched at families. The crowd-pleasing menu reads a little like pub grub without the pub—good, hearty stuff such as fish pies, tasty stews, and burgers. Kids can either order from a special menu or have half-size adult portions, and there's a play area where they can run amok. We're not quite talking Chuck E. Cheese's here, but it's fair to say you might not like this place if your kid-tolerance isn't high.

Doolin, County Clare. ✆ **065/707-5962.** www.stonecutterskitchen.com. Main courses €10–€15; kids menu main courses €6–€10. MC, V. Daily 12:30–9:30pm. Always call ahead during off season.

DOOLIN'S TRADITIONAL MUSIC PUBS

Gus O'Connor's Pub ★★ Amid a row of thatched fishermen's cottages and a 10-minute walk from the seafront, this country pub brings people in from miles around. While this keeps the evening buzzing, it also means that it can get very crowded, especially on weekend nights. Along with its historical charm (it dates from 1832), Gus O'Connor's has a deserved international reputation for its lively Irish traditional-music sessions. If you're hungry, it serves good meals, too. Fisher St., Doolin, County Clare. ✆ **065/707-4168.** www.gusoconnorsdoolin.com.

McGann's 🎁 Sure, Gus O'Connor's is more famous than this place, but McGann's is also jammed with tourists. On many nights, there are no locals in Gus's at all—they're just up the road, downing pints of Guinness and listening to just-as-wonderful traditional music at this friendly pub. Feel free to join them. Roadford, Doolin, County Clare. ✆ **065/707-4133.** www.mcgannspubdoolin.com.

11

GALWAY, WESTMEATH & OFFALY

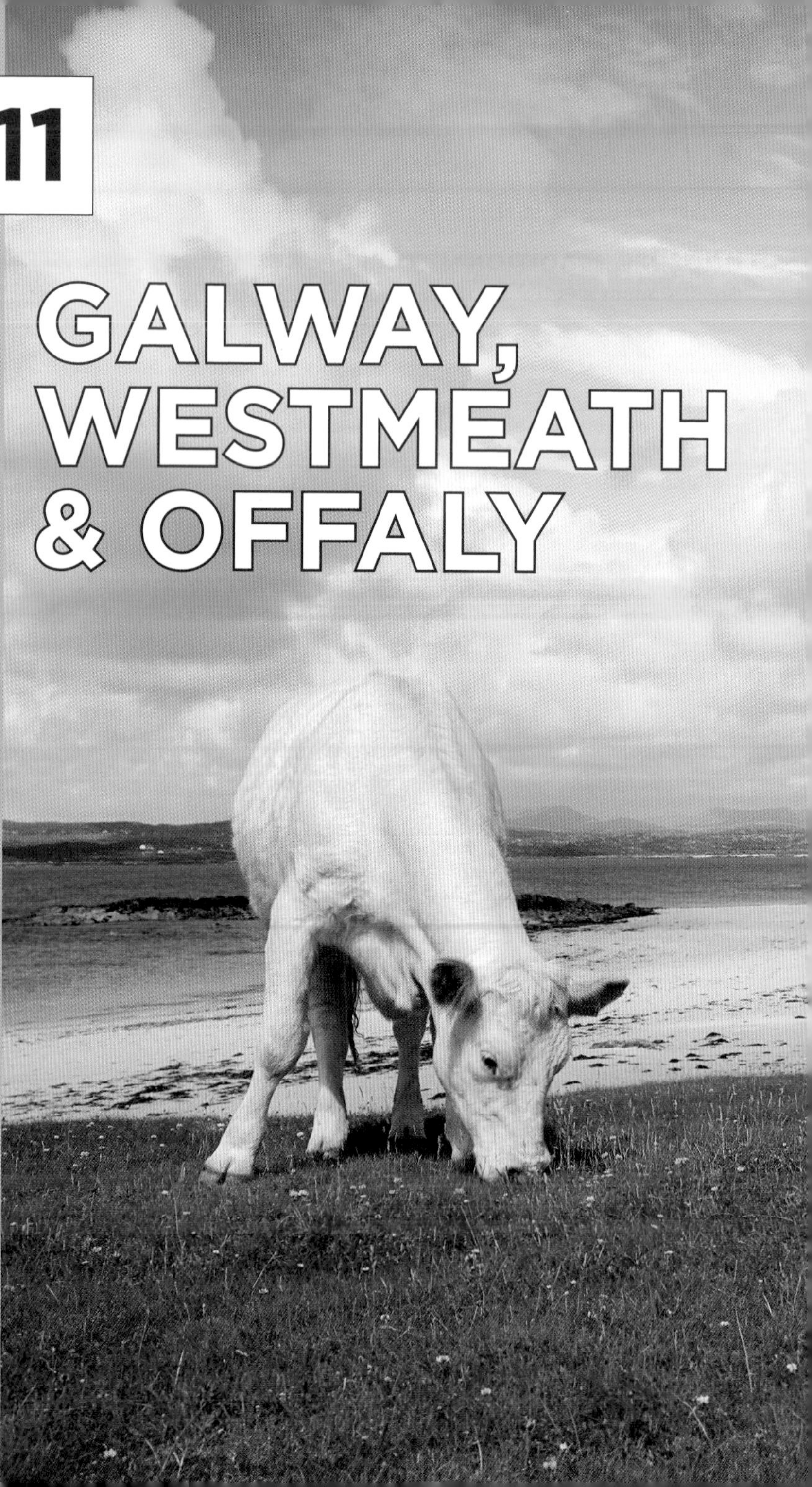

For many travelers to Ireland, Galway is the farthest edge of their journey. Part of the reason they draw the line here is because the county looks so otherworldly—with its bleak bogs; wind-swept, heather-clad moors; and extraordinary light—they think that it must be the end of all that's worth seeing in Ireland (if not the end of the world). It isn't, of course, as County Mayo has picturesque rocky coasts and Donegal a kind of exquisite isolation, but Galway is just far enough from the touristy bustle to feel far away.

The history of this area—the southernmost portion of the region known as Connaught—is as hard as the rocky soil. In the 17th century, after Oliver Cromwell and his armies mercilessly ravaged the rest of the country, he famously said the Irish could go "to hell or Connaught," and ordered Irish landowners to give up their property and live west of the Shannon River. In so doing, he condemned them to a life of destitution. While English landlords divvied up Ireland's most fertile lands, Connaught was so rocky and barren it held no interest for them. Many years later, it was here that the Great Famine of 1845 to 1849 took its largest toll. Entire towns in Connemara became ghost towns as tens of thousands of people either starved or emigrated.

These days, there's virtually nothing left here to remind you of Connaught's gloomy history. This region is bustling and affluent, its villages brightly painted. The land Cromwell thought contemptible is green and haunting, and much loved by hunters and anglers. Its natural beauty and wild soul make this an unforgettable place to visit.

THE GALWAY BAY COAST

Even for those who have seen it many times, driving up the spectacular Galway Bay coast is breathtaking, with the Aran Islands in soft focus and the heather-covered foothills of Connemara beside you. Departing Galway City, and certainly once you pass Spiddal, you have the sense of passing through a gateway into Ireland's wild west, a land strikingly remote, melancholy, and moody. Count on it taking about 40 minutes from Galway to Rossaveal, and another 40 minutes to Carna, at the northernmost tip of the bay, and be prepared for every traffic sign to be in Gaelic.

Galway Bay Coast Essentials

GETTING THERE & AROUND The best way to see the sights along the Galway Bay coast is to drive. From Galway City, follow the coast road (R336). From Galway City to Inverin, it's about 32km (20 miles).

PREVIOUS PAGE: **Livestock is not an uncommon sight on the beaches of County Galway.**

VISITOR INFORMATION Contact or visit **Ireland West Tourism,** Aras Fáilte, Foster Street, Galway, County Galway (✆ **091/537700;** www.discoverireland.ie/west). Hours are May, June, and September daily 9am to 5:45pm; July and August daily 9am to 7:45pm; October to April Monday to Friday 9am to 5:45pm, and Saturday 9am to 12:45pm. Seasonal offices, open from late April through September, are at Clifden (✆ **095/21163**) and Salthill (✆ **091/520500**).

Exploring the Coast

Head west into Connemara, following signs for the coast road (R336). The road winds its way along the edge of the headland to the busy, unromantic modern beach resort, **Salthill *(Bóthar na Trá),*** a summer favorite of Irish families, which is somewhat reminiscent of the New Jersey shore in the U.S., or Blackpool in England. It has a boardwalk and a fine beach, plus lots of bars, fast food, amusement rides, and game arcades, which can be good if you've got children looking for an alternative to historic sights (so long as you don't mind the crowds). Farther along the scenic road are charming little historic towns including Gaelic-speaking **Spiddal *(An Spidéal),*** which is also an ideal spot to shop for locally made Aran knit sweaters and other handicrafts.

The road continues as far as **Inverin *(Indreabhán),*** then turns northward, with signposts for **Rossaveal *(Ros an Mhíl).*** From Rossaveal, you can make the shortest sea crossing from the Galway mainland to the Aran Islands (see "The Aran Islands" section, p. 471), and on a sunny day, you might want to combine this coastal drive with a trip to the islands.

If you continue on R336, you'll leave the Galway Bay coast and travel past the rocky and remote scenery approaching the center of Connemara. Along the way you'll pass **Ros Muc,** site of the **Padraig Pearse Cottage.** This simple, rather bleak thatched-roof structure served as a retreat for Dublin-based Pearse

Salthill is a popular beach town for Irish families.

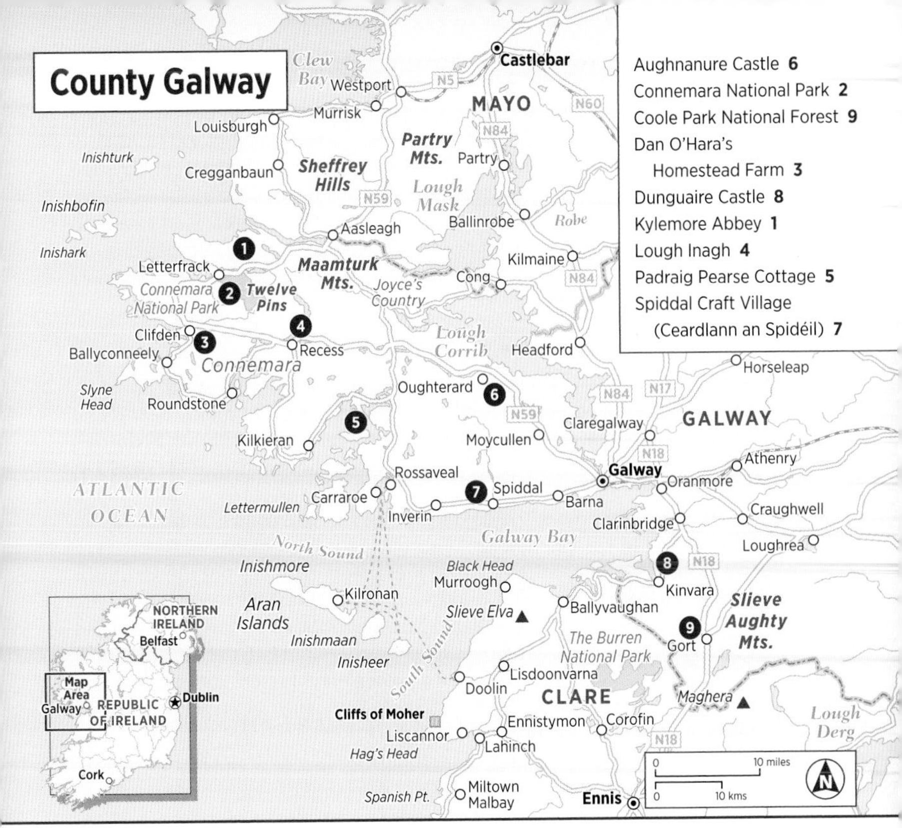

(1879–1916), who was one of the leaders of Ireland's 1916 Easter Rising. He used his time here to improve his knowledge of the Irish language. Now a national monument, the cottage contains documents, photographs, and other memorabilia. Admission is €2 for adults. It's open from mid-June to mid-September daily 9:30am to 5:30pm.

At this point, you can continue north into the heartland of Connemara or retrace your route to Galway.

Shopping

Ceardlann an Spidéil/Spiddal Craft Village Rather than one shop, this is actually a cluster of cottage shops for local craftspeople, and a good place to find unique pottery, woven wool, and jewelry. The art galleries feature hand-carved stone crafts, sculpture, paintings, and posters, and there's a good coffee shop on the premises. For a snack, lunch or light meal, the **Builín Blasta Café** (**© 091/558-559**), is a good option. They also sell fresh bakery goods to take away. The shops are open Monday to Saturday from 9:30am to 6:30pm and Sunday from 2 to 5:30pm in July and August, and Monday to Saturday from 9:30am to 5:30pm September through June. Phone numbers for the individual artists are listed on the website. Coast Rd., Spiddal, County Galway. www.ceardlann.com.

Standún A fixture on the Connemara coast since 1946, this shop has long been known as a good source for authentic *bainin* sweaters, handcrafted by local women from the Aran Islands and the surrounding Connemara countryside. Along with these chunky white knits, it also offers tweeds, sheepskins, linens, glassware, china, pottery, jewelry, books, and maps. It also has a good cafe with panoramic views of Galway Bay and the Aran Islands. Open from March to December Monday to Saturday from 9:30am to 6:30pm. Coast Rd., Spiddal, County Galway. ✆ **091/553108.** www.standun.com.

Sports & Outdoor Pursuits

FISHING As you might surmise, this area is prime territory for sea fishing, especially for mackerel, pollock, cod, turbot, and shark. To find a boat-rental service in the area where you plan to stay, contact the **Inland Fisheries Ireland,** Teach Breac, Earl's Island, County Galway (✆ **091/563118;** www.wrfb.ie), for recommendations. A fishing license costs around €36 per day or €50 for 3 weeks. Rental of rods and reels plus bait is likely to run another €35 to €50 per day.

Those who prefer trout fishing might want to check out the **Crumlin Lodge Fisheries,** Inverin, County Galway (✆ **091/593105**). This fishery has a lake stocked with sea-reared rainbow trout and allows two fish per person to be taken per day. Prices range from around €16 to €50, depending on whether you fish from a bank or a boat; *ghillies* (guides) are available for approximately €40 extra. Fishing starts at 9am daily; reservations must be made at least a day in advance.

SWIMMING The Silver Strand at Barna and the beach at Spiddal are clean, sandy, and ideal for swimming.

Where to Stay

Cloch na Scíth/Kellough Thatched Cottage The trio of guest rooms in Nancy Hopkins Naughton's centuries-old thatched farmhouse are warm and welcoming, with antique pine furniture, polished wood floors, and patterned quilts. The whole house is open to guests and is full of antiques and keepsakes. Tomas Naughton, Nancy's husband, is both a talented painter and an all-Ireland *sean-nos* (traditional a cappella Gaelic) singer. Nancy bakes a fresh corn cake in the open hearth each day and leaves it out for her guests to have with tea. A small sandy beach is minutes away by foot. In addition, there is an inviting **self-catering thatched stone cottage,** built by Tomas's great-grandfather. It rents for €295 to €560 per week, depending on the season. It has two bedrooms, a kitchen-dining-living room with a woodstove, a spacious sunroom, and one-and-a-half bathrooms.

15km (9⅓ miles) from Galway center, just east of Spiddal, Coast Rd., Kellough, Spiddal, County Galway. www.thatchcottage.com. ✆ **091/553364.** 3 units. €72–€76 double. Rates include full breakfast. No credit cards. **Amenities:** Smoke-free rooms. *In room:* No phone.

Connemara Coast Hotel ★ Only 10km (6¼ miles) west of Galway City and with Galway Bay at its back door, this friendly, midsize hotel has a lot going for it. The guest rooms are nicely decorated in neutral colors, but that's not what will lure you here—the big draw is that each room has a picture-window view of the Aran Islands or Clare hills. Some have turf-burning fireplaces and some have private verandas. It's an attractive, laid-back seafront hotel that makes a good hub for your journey. There are two restaurants, and the hotel pub, **Sin Sceal Eile (That's Another Story),** offers traditional entertainment most nights.

Coast Rd., Furbo, County Galway. www.connemaracoast.ie. ✆ **091/592108.** Fax 091/592065. 112 units. €180–€300 double. Rates include full breakfast. AE, DC, MC, V. **Amenities:** Restaurant; bar; gym; Jacuzzi; indoor pool; smoke-free rooms; steam bath; 2 tennis courts. *In room:* TV.

The Twelve Named for the famous Twelve Pins mountain range of Connemara, this old-world roadside inn has revamped itself in recent years into a luxurious, modern, four-star boutique guesthouse. Most guest rooms have comfortable king-size or twin beds, and some have fold-out sofa beds for families traveling with children. Beds are covered in fluffy comforters and soft bedspreads; windows have peaceful views. The **West Restaurant** downstairs is one of the best in the area. Its menu features fresh local seafood and produce; try the marinated salmon carpaccio, or the lobster, crab, and prawn terrine. This is a pet-friendly hotel; just call ahead if you want to bring your dog. Check the website for good special offers and inclusive deals.

> Impressions
>
> ***I have a total irreverence for anything connected with society except that which makes the roads safer, the beer stronger, the food cheaper, the old men and old women warmer in the winter and happier in the summer.***
>
> **—Brendan Behan (1923–64)**

Coast Rd., Bearna Village, Barna, County Galway. www.thetwelvehotel.ie. ✆ **091/597000.** Fax 091/597003. 48 units. €150–€300 double; €175–€550 suites. Rates include full breakfast. AE, MC, V. **Amenities:** Restaurant; bar; room service; smoke-free rooms. *In room:* TV/DVD player, minibar, MP3 docking station.

Where to Eat

Boluisce SEAFOOD This is one of the few restaurants in little Spiddal. In a friendly, homey dining room, locals and visitors fill its seats each night to feast on the freshest possible seafood. Dishes include fresh Galway Bay lobster Thermidor, grilled organic salmon with scallion mashed potatoes, and a seafood platter of fresh crab, Atlantic prawns, smoked salmon, and an oyster. They also serve steaks and stir-fries to those not in the mood for fish.

Coast Rd., Spiddal, County Galway. ✆ **091/553286.** www.boluisce.com. Reservations recommended. Dinner main courses €11–€24. AE, MC, V. Mar 17–Sept daily 12:30–9pm; Oct–Mar 16 Thurs–Sun 12:30–3pm and 6–9pm.

GALWAY CITY ★

92km (57 miles) N of Shannon Airport, 219km (136 miles) W of Dublin, 105km (65 miles) NW of Limerick, 209km (130 miles) NW of Cork, 193km (120 miles) N of Killarney

A thriving, artsy city on Ireland's rugged western coast, Galway still has its winding medieval lanes, but it also has a cosmopolitan core. Stone-clad cafes and pastel-colored boutiques draw tourists to the cobbles of Quay Street, while crowds pack in everywhere for the Galway Races and the Galway Arts Festival. Traditional Ireland lingers here—you can sip a creamy Guinness at a pub and watch fiddlers and singers hold court by turf fires. Then amble to the sea and stroll the seaweed-dappled shore of Galway Bay.

Artsy shops and pubs line the cobblestone streets of thriving, prosperous Galway.

Things to Do Central Galway is condensed and very walkable. The city's hub is busy Eyre Square (pronounced Air Square), which is a few minutes' walk from everywhere. Arty types should strike out immediately for the city's charming medieval quarter, with its tiny art galleries and coffee shops. History buffs will want to stop by St. Nicholas' Church, where it's said Columbus prayed before one of his journeys in search of the New World.

Shopping Galway is known for its good shopping, but the way the stores are scattered around town can make it hard to find what you want. If you're looking for locally made Claddagh rings and Aran sweaters, try the tiny malls of small shops clustered in historic buildings, such as the **Cornstore** on Middle Street, the **Grainstore** on Lower Abbeygate Street, and the **Bridge Mills,** a 430-year-old mill building beside the River Corrib.

Restaurants & Dining In Galway seafood is the main attraction—during the boom times, the best restaurants all had helipads, for the millionaires from Dublin who flew to Galway by helicopter for business lunches featuring fresh local **oysters**, still salty from the sea. While you're in town, look out for sweet Irish **prawns**, or tender pan-fried local **trout**. Try the ivory tinged smoked **haddock** and tangy Galway **mackerel**.

Nightlife & Entertainment You cannot swing a cat (please don't try this) in Galway without hitting a charming, traditional Irish pub, particularly around Eyre Square. Head to the Medieval Quarter or down near the quays for the oldest, less touristy pubs. Most nightclubs in the city are virtually empty until the pubs close at 11pm, and the best are in the suburb of Salthill.

Essentials

GETTING THERE **Aer Arann** (✆ **011/353-81821-0210** in the U.S., 818/210-210 in Ireland, or 0870/876-7676 in the U.K.; www.aerarann.ie) flies from Dublin into Galway Airport (Carnmore, about 16km/10 miles east of the city; ✆ **091/755569;** www.galwayairport.com) four times daily. They also

Bridge Mills **10**
Corrib Princess **1**
Druid Theatre **11**
Eyre Square
Shopping Centre **8**
Ferry to Aran Islands **15**
Galway Arts Centre **9**
Galway Cathedral **2**
Galway City Museum **13**
Galway Irish Crystal
Heritage Centre **4**
Lynch's Castle **7**
Lynch Memorial Window **6**
Nora Barnacle House **3**
St. Nicholas'
Collegiate Church **5**
Spanish Arch **14**
Taibhdhearc Theatre **12**

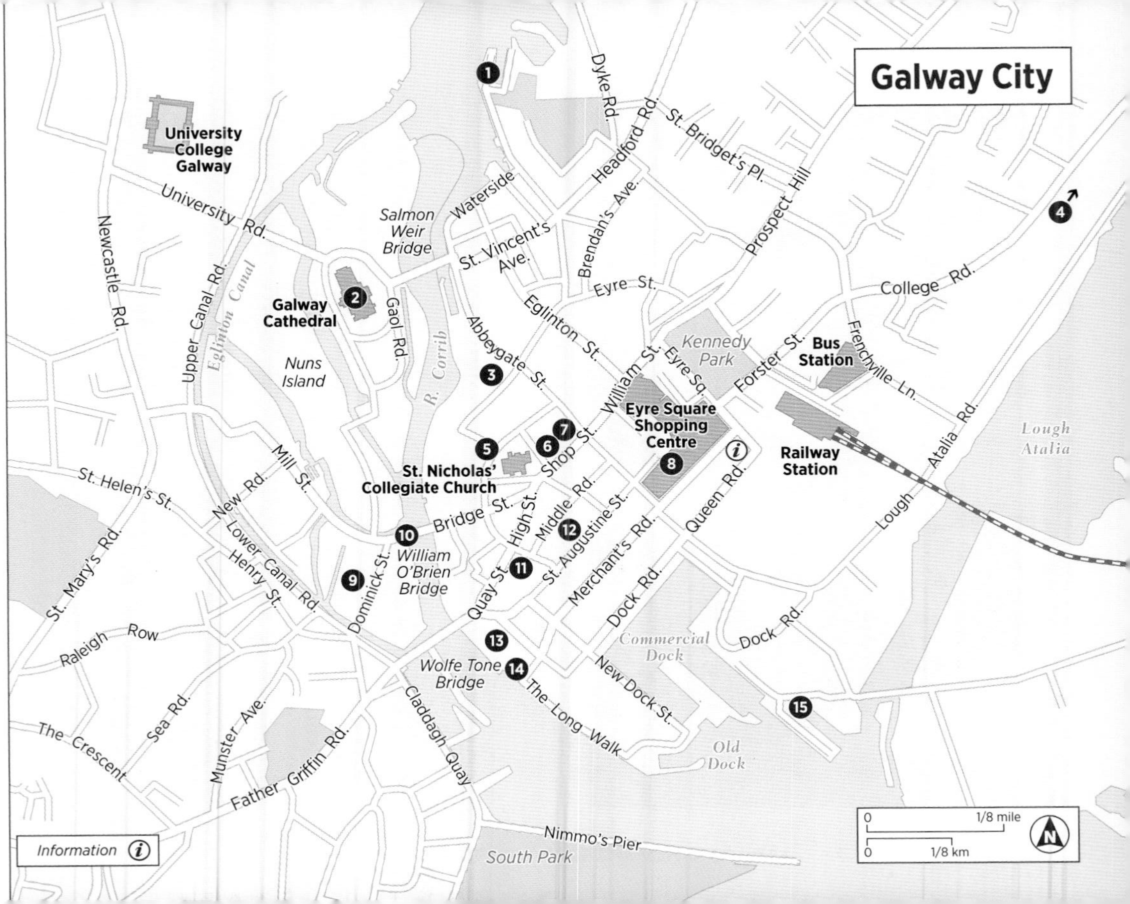

The bustling streets in Galway, known since the 15th century as the City of Tribes.

fly direct to Galway from London, Manchester, and Edinburgh in the U.K. A taxi to the city center costs about €20; the occasional bus, if it coincides with your arrival, can be a handy alternative. It costs upwards of €5 and drops you off at Galway Rail Station.

Irish Rail trains from Dublin and other points arrive daily at **Ceannt Station** (✆ **091/561444;** www.irishrail.ie), off Eyre Square, Galway.

Buses from all parts of Ireland arrive daily at **Bus Éireann Travel Centre,** Ceannt Station, Galway (✆ **091/562000;** www.buseireann.ie).

As the gateway to west Ireland, Galway is the terminus for many national roads. They lead in from all parts of Ireland, including N84 and N17 from the north points, N63 and N6 from the east, and N67 and N18 from the south.

VISITOR INFORMATION For information about Galway and the surrounding areas, contact or visit **Ireland West Tourism (Aras Fáilte),** Foster Street (✆ **091/537700;** www.discoverireland.ie/west). Hours are May, June, and September daily 9am to 5:45pm; July and August daily 9am to 7:45pm; and October to April Monday to Friday 9am to 5:45pm, Saturday 9am to 12:45pm. For further detailed information on events and news in Galway, consult **www.galway.net**.

CITY LAYOUT The core of downtown Galway lies between Eyre Square on the east and the River Corrib on the west. The main thoroughfare begins west of Eyre Square. Its name changes—from William to Shop, Main Guard, and Bridge—before it crosses the River Corrib and changes again. If that sounds confusing, well, it is a bit. But the streets are all short and well marked, and it's fairly simple to find your way around the city center.

GETTING AROUND Galway has excellent local bus service. Buses run from the **Bus Éireann Travel Centre** (✆ **091/562000**) or Eyre Square to various suburbs, including Salthill and the Galway Bay coastline. Fares start at around €1.50.

There are taxi ranks at Eyre Square and all the major hotels in the city. If you need to call a cab, try **Galway Taxis** (✆ **091/561111**), **Big-O Taxis** (✆ **091/585858**), or **City Taxis** (✆ **091/525252**).

A town of medieval arches, alleyways, and cobblestone lanes, all surrounded by more modern suburbs, central Galway is best explored on foot (wear comfortable shoes). Once you check in at your hotel or guesthouse, park your car and tour by walking. (To see the highlights, follow the signposts on the Tourist Trail of Old Galway. A handy booklet, available at the tourist office and at most bookshops, provides historical and architectural details.) If you must bring your car into the center of town, park it and then walk. There is free parking in front of Galway Cathedral, but most street parking uses a pay-to-park system. It costs around €1 per hour. Multistory parking garages average €1.80 per hour or €15 per day.

Galway Airport has two main car-rental firms, **Avis** (✆ **091/786440;** www.avis.ie) and **Budget** (✆ **091/564570;** www.budget.ie).

FAST FACTS If you need a drugstore, try **Boots the Chemist,** 35 Shop St. (✆ **091/561022**); **Whelan's Chemist,** Williamsgate Street (✆ **091/562291**); or **Newcastle Pharmacy,** 41 Newcastle Rd. (✆ **091/524934**).

In an **emergency,** dial ✆ **999. University College Hospital** is on Newcastle Road (✆ **091/544544**). There's also **Merlin Park Regional Hospital** (✆ **091/757631**). The local **Garda Station** is on Mill Street (✆ **091/538000**).

For information, gay and lesbian travelers might contact the **Galway Lesbian Help Line** (✆ **091/564611**) or the **Gay Help Line** (✆ **091/566134**).

For Internet access in Galway, try **Net Access,** in the heart of the city in the Olde Malte Arcade, High Street (✆ **091/395725;** www.netaccess.ie). The **Galway Library/An Leabhar,** in the Hynes Building,

THE CLADDAGH ring

The delicate **Claddagh** (pronounced *Clod*-uh) ring has become synonymous with Ireland and its diaspora. It originated here, or more precisely, just over the Father Griffin Bridge, on the west bank of the River Corrib, in the town of Claddagh. It's now a residential satellite to Galway, but in ancient times it was a kingdom with its own laws, fleet, and customs. The earliest known Claddagh ring was made in the 17th century for a wedding.

The ring features two hands holding a heart topped by a crown. The hands are said to represent friendship, the crown loyalty, and the heart love—the three ingredients of a perfect marriage. Originally, the ring was a wedding band worn facing out for engagement and facing in for marriage. Though no longer widely worn as a symbol of marriage, it is still frequently worn as a friendship ring and makes a lovely memento.

Thomas Dillon's jewelry store on Quay Street claims to be the original creator of the Claddagh ring—it's been selling them since 1750.

Augustine Street (✆ **091/561666**), is open Monday 2 to 5pm, Tuesday to Thursday 11am to 8pm, Friday 11am to 5pm, and Saturday 11am to 1pm and 2 to 5pm.

The **Post Office,** 3 Eglinton St. (✆ **091/534727**), is open Monday to Saturday 9am to 5:30pm (from 9:30am Tues).

Galway Tribes

By the 15th century, 14 wealthy merchant families ruled the Galway Town, giving it the nickname it still bears today—"City of Tribes." These families, mostly of Welsh and Norman origin, ruled as an oligarchy, and you still see storefronts and businesses bearing these names today: Athy, Blake, Bodkin, Browne, Darcy, Deane, Font, Ffrench, Joyce, Kirwan, Lynch, Martin, Morris, and Skerret.

Where to Stay

VERY EXPENSIVE

The G ★ Designed by the hat designer Philip Treacy, this over-the-top hotel looks like a cross between *Barbarella* and *My Fair Lady.* There are psychedelic touches (the Pink Salon is the color of Pepto-Bismol with a white-and-black spiral carpet and purple sofas) and a bit of disco chic (the otherwise subtle taupe-and-white grand salon has huge glass baubles hanging overhead). The restaurant, Matz, offers modern Irish cuisine in a Technicolor dining room. Bedrooms are calmer, in soothing white with touches of coffee and cream; beds are luxuriant with soft pillows and lush linens. Bathrooms are sensational, many have showers built for two, and all have excellent bath products. The service is outstanding—a team of butlers attend to your every whim, and the room service menu is long and varied, featuring dishes from the Italian-Irish in-house restaurant. The **ESPA spa** is oh-so-sophisticated, and it's all very Manhattan. It's about a 15-minute walk from central Galway. It was included in Condé Nast's Gold List for 2009, and there is no place trendier on Ireland's west coast.

Wellpark, Galway, County Galway. www.theghotel.ie. ✆ **091/865200.** Fax 091/865203. 101 units. €120–€300 double; €320–€590 suites. Rates include full breakfast. AE, MC, V. **Amenities:** Restaurant; bar; smoke-free rooms; spa. *In room:* Satellite TV, DVD/CD player, hair dryer, Wi-Fi.

The Volvo Ocean Cup floods the streets of Galway with sailors and spectators.

Glenlo Abbey Hotel ★★ About 3km (2 miles) outside of Galway on the main Clifden road, this secluded, sprawling stone hotel overlooks Lough Corrib in a sylvan setting, surrounded by a 9-hole golf course. Dating from 1740, this was originally the ancestral home of the Ffrench and Blake families, 2 of the 14 families who ruled the city for centuries. The building has retained its grandeur in the public areas, with hand-carved wood furnishings, hand-loomed carpets, ornate plasterwork, and an extensive collection of Irish art and antiques. The guest rooms, which have lovely views of Lough Corrib and the countryside, are luxuriously decorated with traditional furnishings, as well as marbled bathrooms.

Bushy Park, Galway, County Galway. www.glenlo.com. ✆ **091/526666.** Fax 091/527800. 46 units. €200–€290 double; €620 suite. Rates include breakfast. Dinner from around €50 per person. AE, DC, MC, V. Free parking. **Amenities:** 2 restaurants; 2 bars; concierge; 9-hole golf course; room service. *In room:* TV, hair dryer, free Wi-Fi.

EXPENSIVE

Galway Harbour Hotel This modern hotel has borrowed a lot from boutique hotels, and its design has clean lines, along with lots of blond wood and neutral colors. Rooms are large and quiet, and there are family rooms with plenty of space for kids. It's well located within walking distance of Eyre Square, so it's not at all bad for the price, but there are flaws. Some beds are a bit uncomfortable, and the bathrooms are quite plain and have painfully bright lighting. The recently renovated restaurant and bar are both pleasant places to hang out. ***Note:*** Keep an eye on the hotel's website—very good deals can be found online.

New Dock Rd., Galway, County Galway. www.harbour.ie. ✆ **091/569466.** Fax 091/569455. 96 units. €90–€180 double. No service charge. Rates include full breakfast. AE, MC, V. Free parking at nearby lot. **Amenities:** Restaurant; bar; Internet room; smoke-free rooms. *In room:* TV, CD player, hair dryer, free Wi-Fi.

Hotel Meyrick Locations don't get much more central than this: Perched on the edge of Eyre Square, the Hotel Meyrick is right in the center of the action in Galway. Combining splendid Victorian architecture with spacious modern design, this is a well-priced option, with frequent online bargains. Most rooms are spacious and designed in neutral shades of cream with comfortable king-size beds. However, they could do with a makeover, and we've heard some reports of patchy service. The in-house **Oyster Grill Restaurant** specializes in modern Irish cuisine. The **Square Spa** on the upper floors of the hotel allows you to overlook the city while you relax or exercise.

Eyre Sq., Galway, County Galway. www.hotelmeyrick.ie. ✆ **091/564041.** 97 units. €135–€214 double; €210–€300 suites. Rates include full breakfast. AE, MC, V. Free parking at nearby lot. **Amenities:** Restaurant; bar; smoke-free rooms. *In room:* TV, hair dryer, broadband Internet.

The House Hotel ★★ This four-story stone building in Galway's historic area, next to the Spanish Arch, was formerly a warehouse, and is now a boutique loft hotel. From its low-key lobby with polished oak floors, columns, and big windows, to its subtle, contemporary rooms, it's a comfortable, modern alternative. Rooms are divided into categories like "comfy," "classy," and "swanky," and they pretty much do what it says on the label. The swanky rooms are definitely, well, the swankiest. The comfy rooms (and bathrooms) can be very small. All have good beds, soft linens, lots of sunlight, high ceilings, and a refreshing urban feel. The design has won accolades, and it prides itself on service.

Spanish Parade, Galway, County Galway. www.thehousehotel.ie. ✆ **091/538900.** Fax 091/568262. 45 units. €150–€220 double. AE, DC, MC, V. **Amenities:** Restaurant; bar. *In room:* TV, hair dryer, minibar, broadband Internet.

Park House Hotel ★ With a steady, old-fashioned approach to luxury, the Park House is a reliable option in central Galway. For 30 years, its warmly lit frontage has been welcoming travelers into the tastefully decorated lobby. Rooms are spacious and classically decorated with plaid bedspreads and colorful throw pillows. Privacy is one of the things this hotel does especially well—no two rooms directly face each other, ensuring peace and quiet for all guests. Superior rooms are arranged around a roof garden, which adds a nice touch. All rooms have free broadband—a relative rarity in Ireland. The **Park Room Restaurant** is an award-winning, luxurious operation (see below), and its traditional style fits perfectly with this rock-steady hotel's ethos.

Foster St., Eyre Sq., Galway, County Galway. www.parkhousehotel.ie. ✆ **091/564924.** Fax 091/569219. 84 units. €120–€220 double; €200–€260 suite. Rates include full breakfast. AE, MC, V. **Amenities:** Restaurant; bar; smoke-free rooms. *In room:* TV, DVD/CD player, hair dryer, broadband Internet.

The Radisson Blu Hotel & Spa ☺ A recent renovation has transformed this once-bland hotel into a more modern, interesting place to stay with a great location near Eyre Square. All rooms are fairly spacious and well equipped with comfortable king-size beds, desks, modern bathrooms, and plenty of electronic gadgets for business travelers. Neutral colors dominate, creating a soothing palette with cream walls, white comforters, and softly hued bedspreads. The sun pours into the in-house bar through huge windows, and the hotel restaurant is justifiably popular with locals. You can chill out in the Spirit One spa, or work out in the well-equipped fitness club, and swim in the elegant pool. This is a child-friendly hotel, with family rooms (bigger than normal rooms, with extra beds), kid-size hot-water bottles to warm their toes, and a "toy library" where they can check out toys during their stay.

Lough Atalia Rd., Galway, County Galway. www.radissonhotelgalway.com. ✆ **091/538300.** Fax 091/538380. 282 units. €160–€300 double; €200–€700 suites. AE, DC, MC, V. **Amenities:** Restaurant; bar; gym; pool; spa. *In room:* TV, hair dryer, minibar, Wi-Fi.

MODERATE

Menlo Park This reasonably priced modern hotel just outside the city center is a good alternative with comfortable, good-size rooms and a quiet location. Its setting of lush lawns and gardens makes it popular for weddings, although the hotel building is rather nondescript. Guest rooms are not big, but they're not cramped either, with large beds (most have doubles, but some have kings). Each has a bold color design with deep blue or maroon "statement" walls, and matching accent throws and cushions. The good, if not fancy, in-house restaurant and bar mean you don't have to head back into the town center at night if you don't want to, which is just as well because it's a little more than a mile away.

Headford Rd., Galway, County Galway. www.menloparkhotel.com. ✆ **01850/381127.** 70 units. €90–€150 double. Rates include breakfast. MC, V. **Amenities:** Restaurant; bar, room service; parking (free). *In room:* TV, hair dryer, Wi-Fi (free).

INEXPENSIVE

Barnacle's Quay Street House This cheap and cheerful guesthouse and hostel is bright, attractive, and friendly—what more do you need? The interior of this 16th-century house has been completely modernized, but it still has marvelous fireplaces and lots of character. Bedrooms are done in sunny yellows, and there's a communal kitchen if you are weary of restaurants. The clientele tends to be young, mostly college students filling the shared dorm rooms, but the four-bed rooms are also good for families traveling on a budget. All are welcome, and the location is central. Book early in the high season, as the place tends to fill up quickly.

10 Quay St., Galway, County Galway. www.barnacles.ie. ✆ **091/568644.** 10 units. €38–€52 dorm beds; €35–€82 double. Rates include continental breakfast. MC, V. **Amenities:** Lounge; Wi-Fi (free).

Devondell ★ You'd be hard-pressed to find a better B&B in Galway than Berna Kelly's much-lauded house in the Lower Salthill residential area, about 2km (1¼ miles) from Galway's city center. It's a modern house, and guest rooms are spacious and done up with period furnishings and crisp Irish linens. Breakfasts are exceptional, with cereal, fresh fruit, yogurt, cheese, hash browns, kippers, eggs, and French toast. Devondell is walking distance from the seafront.

47 Devon Park, Lower Salthill, County Galway. www.devondell.com. ✆ **091/528306.** 4 units. €80–€90 double. Rates include full breakfast. MC, V. Free parking. Closed Dec–Feb. *In room:* TV.

Sleepzone Around the corner from the train station, this is the flagship branch of the popular Sleepzone chain, which has been earning praise from the budget travel industry for several years now. Options here range from dorms that sleep up to 10, to private double en suite rooms. Rooms are clean and modern, and the hostel has better facilities than most of Galway's budget hotels—including free Wi-Fi. Those who can't quite face staying in a hostel might consider renting one of the two **Sleepzone Townhouses.** Each contains three bedrooms, a kitchen, and a lounge. You can book the rooms individually, but they're designed for families or groups of friends to take the whole house. Town houses costs €150 to €225 per night Sunday to Thursday, and €225 to €275 per night on Friday and Saturday.

Bothar na mBan (btw. Prospect Hill and St. Vincent's Ave.), Galway, County Galway. www.sleepzone.ie. ✆ **091/566-999.** €20–€32 dorms; €60–€78 double. MC, V. **Amenities:** Wi-Fi and computer room.

Where to Eat

EXPENSIVE

Kirwan's Lane ★★ CONTINENTAL This stylish, inviting restaurant is widely acclaimed, and for good reason. The dining room is rustic chic, with pine furnishings and walls painted warm ocher and vivid red. It's a particularly good value at lunchtime, when the constantly changing menu might include a starter of smoked haddock and clam chowder, or ox tongue pancetta with truffle smoked potatoes. The dinner menu features dishes with fresh local produce, game, and seafood, including crab, guinea fowl, and woodcock, all beautifully presented.

Kirwan's Lane. ✆ **091/568266.** Reservations recommended. Main courses €18–€30. AE, MC, V. Daily 12:30–2:30pm and 6–10pm. Closed Sun Sept–June.

The Malt House ★★ MODERN IRISH This long-established place on High Street has developed something of a new lease of life since new owners came in a few years ago. Once rather starched and formal, it's now relaxed and cool. The dining room is bright and spacious, with chic contemporary art. The food is upmarket Irish bistro dishes with an international twist, and an emphasis on locally sourced ingredients–chicken breast with pearl barley and corn risotto, scallops with suckling pig and potato cake or steak and chips with caramelized onions and pepper sauce. Lunch strikes a more traditional note (fish and chips, beef and mushroom pie, BLT salad), and it's decidedly cheaper too.

High St. ✆ **091/567866.** www.themalthouse.ie. Reservations recommended. Dinner main courses €19–€28. AE, MC, V. Mon–Sat 12:30–3pm and 6:30–10:30pm.

Park Room Restaurant ★ CONTINENTAL Half a block east of Eyre Square, at the back of the Park House Hotel, this fine restaurant has an old-world decor of stained glass, dark woods, and oil paintings, and a sophisticated cooking approach. Entrees include grilled prime sirloin steak au poivre, and pan-fried trout with shrimp and dill butter. The seafood is exceptional; the ambience is pleasantly upscale.

Forster St., Eyre Sq. ✆ **091/564924.** Reservations recommended. Main courses €20–€33. AE, MC, V. Daily 12:30–3pm and 6–10pm.

Vina Mara CONTINENTAL Tucked into Galway's medieval quarter, this charming little eatery is extremely popular with local diners. While it emphasizes European cooking techniques, it uses regionally-sourced ingredients (meat, seafood, and produce). The result is fresh and modern. The menu changes frequently, but starters might include organic smoked haddock and leek tortellini, or Irish prawn tempura. Mains could include roast cod with green pea risotto, or grilled Irish trout with chorizo. Desserts are irresistible, and there are many good wines by the glass.

19 Middle St. ✆ **091/561610.** www.vinamara.com Reservations recommended. Main courses €15–€25. AE, MC, V. Daily 12:30–3pm and 6–10:30pm.

MODERATE

Ard Bia at Nimmo's ★★ WINE BAR/SEAFOOD This is one of Galway's trendy tables—a place to see and be seen that manages to serve fantastic food while constantly admiring itself. It's ideal for a festive, buzzy meal out. Pass the stone facade, climb a winding stairway, and you'll find yourself in a wonderfully romantic dining room, particularly on a starry night when you can see the moon through the skylights. The menu changes according to season and tends to feature seafood in the summer and game during the winter. It usually includes items such as grilled Galway mackerel with mussels and squid, roast breast of free-range duck with almond couscous, or Burren smoked trout pâté. Dessert could be burned honey and blood orange *panna cotta,* or chocolate mousse. The wines are terrific, too. Be sure to reserve your table in advance.

Long Walk, Spanish Arch. ✆ **091/561114.** www.ardbia.com. Reservations recommended. Main courses €16–€22. MC, V. Wed–Sat 6–10:30pm.

Brannagans IRISH This jolly, affordable restaurant is where Galway goes when it wants to relax with some fries and a beer. Upstairs from the Townhouse Bar, the mood here is lively and friendly. The menu is not adventurous, but the food is well cooked, and the service is sharp. The food crosses the Atlantic and comes back again—you can have "voodoo wings" as a starter, and then move on to the roasted Irish salmon with colcannon, the creamy fish pie, or the sausages ("bangers") and mashed potatoes. Nothing is fussy here. It's tasty and filling and the beer is nicely chilled.

Quay St., above the Townhouse Bar. ✆ **091/534496.** www.brannagans.ie. Main courses €12–€20. AE, MC, V. Tues–Sat 6–11pm.

G.B.C. (Galway Bakery Company) ★ BISTRO With a distinctive Old Galway shop-front facade, this building is two eateries in one: a ground-level self-service coffee shop and a full-service bistro upstairs. The restaurant menu lists a straightforward and unfussy selection of dishes, from steaks, seafood, and burgers to pasta and chicken fajitas. Baked goods, particularly the homemade brown bread, are an added attraction. Prices are reasonable and the service is good. The coffee shop serves memorably good breakfasts and light lunches that won't break the bank.

7 Williamsgate St. ✆ **091/563087.** www.gbcgalway.com. Coffee-shop items under €8; 3 course fixed-price dinner (from 4pm) €20; dinner main courses €13–€17. AE, DC, MC, V. Coffee shop daily 8am–9pm. Restaurant Sun–Thurs noon–8pm; Fri–Sat noon–9pm.

McDonagh's FISH AND CHIPS/SEAFOOD For superfresh seafood, served in an authentic maritime atmosphere, this is Galway's best choice. The place is divided into three parts: a traditional "chipper" for fish and chips, a smart restaurant in the back, and a fish market where you can buy raw seafood. The McDonaghs, fishmongers for more than four generations, buy direct from local fishermen every day, and it shows; crowds line up every night to get in. The menu includes salmon, trout, lemon or black sole (or both), turbot, and silver hake, all cooked to order. In the back restaurant, you can crack your own prawns' tails and crab claws in the shell, or tackle a whole lobster.

22 Quay St. ✆ **091/565001.** www.mcdonaghs.net. Reservations not accepted June–Aug. Main courses €8–€20 (seafood platter €35); fish and chips about €9. AE, MC, V. Restaurant Mon–Sat 5–10pm. Fish and chip takeout Mon–Sat noon–11pm; Sun 4–10pm.

INEXPENSIVE

Busker Brownes ★ CAFE/BAR A modern cafe in a medieval building, Busker Brownes is a favorite of locals and travelers for its funky decor that mixes ancient stonework with modern tables and art, as well as for its big breakfasts and homemade, inexpensive lunches and dinners. It offers everything from steaks and hamburgers to Irish stew. It also stays open late—one of a few Galway eateries to do so.

Upper Cross St. ✆ **091/563377.** www.buskerbrownes.com. Main courses €10–€19. MC, V. Mon–Sat 10:30am–11:30pm; Sun 12:30–11:30pm.

Seeing the Sights

Many of Galway's top attractions are outdoors and free of charge. In the center of town, for example, on Shop Street, is **Lynch's Castle,** dating from 1490 and renovated in the 19th century. It's now a branch of the Allied Irish Bank, and you can walk in and look around. The stern exterior is watched over by a handful of amusing gargoyles.

Close to the city docks, you can still see the area where Spanish merchants unloaded cargo from their galleons. The **Spanish Arch** was one of four arches built in 1594, and the **Spanish Parade** is a small open square, which, like Eyre Square, is great for people-watching.

Galway Arts Centre ★★ Once the home of W. B. Yeats's patron, Lady Gregory, this attractive town house for many years housed local governmental offices. Today it offers an excellent program of concerts, readings, and exhibitions by Irish and international artists, returning, in a way, to a form Lady Gregory would have appreciated. A second building, used primarily for performances and workshops, is located at 23 Nuns Island (same phone).

47 Dominick St. ✆ **091/565886.** www.galwayartscentre.ie. Free admission to exhibits. Mon–Sat 10am–6pm.

Galway Cathedral ★ It's easy to understand why this church's nickname is so short and simple, given that its official name is "Cathedral of Our Lady Assumed into Heaven and St. Nicholas." Its walls are fine-cut limestone from local quarries and its floors are Connemara marble. It's not particularly old, as it was built in the 1960s. Contemporary Irish artisans designed the statues, stained-glass windows, and mosaics.

University and Gaol rds., beside the Salmon Weir Bridge on the river's west bank. ✆ **091/563577.** www.galwaycathedral.org. Free admission; donations welcome. Daily 8:30am–6pm.

Galway City Museum ★ This little museum offers a fine collection of local documents, photographs, city memorabilia, examples of medieval stonework, and revolving exhibits.

Off Spanish Arch. ✆ **091/532460.** www.galwaycitymuseum.ie. Free admission. June–Sept daily 10am–5pm; Oct–May Tues–Sat 10am–5pm.

Galway Irish Crystal Heritage Centre ★★ Visitors to this distinctive crystal manufacturer can watch the craftsmen at work—blowing, shaping, and hand-cutting the glassware—and then go shop for the perfect pieces to take back home. Glassmaking demonstrations are continuous on weekdays. The shop and restaurant are open daily.

East of the city on the main Dublin rd. (N6), Merlin Park, Galway, County Galway. ✆ **091/757311.** www.galwaycrystal.ie. Free admission. Mon–Fri 9am–5:30pm; Sat 10am–5:30pm; Sun 11am–5pm.

Nora Barnacle House ★ Just across from the St. Nicholas church clock tower, this restored 19th-century terrace house was once the home of Nora Barnacle, who later would become the wife of James Joyce. It contains letters, photographs, and other exhibits on the lives of the Joyces and their connections with Galway.

Bowling Green. ✆ **091/564743.** Admission €2.50 adults; €2 seniors, students, and children 6–12; children 5 and under free. Daily 10am–1pm and 2–5pm.

Tragic Tale of Lynch's Window

One block away from Eyre Square on Market Street, the Lynch Memorial Window sits in a wall above a built-up Gothic doorway. It commemorates the tragic story of the 16th-century Galway mayor James Lynch FitzStephen, who condemned his own son to death for the murder of a Spanish merchant. After finding no one to carry out the deed, he executed the boy himself. The act destroyed him and he retreated into a life of seclusion.

In July, September, and October, the Galway Races draw spectators from all across Europe.

St. Nicholas' Collegiate Church ★★ This is Galway's oldest church—it's said that Christopher Columbus prayed here in 1477 before sailing away on one of his attempts to reach the New World. Established about 1320, it has changed from Roman Catholic to Church of Ireland and back again at least four times and is currently under the aegis of the latter denomination. Inside are a 12th-century crusader's tomb with a Norman inscription, a carved font from the 16th or 17th century, and a stone lectern with barley-sugar twist columns from the 15th century. Guided tours, conducted by Declan O Mordha, a knowledgeable and enthusiastic church representative, depart from the south porch according to demand, except on Sunday morning.

Lombard St. ✆ **091/564648.** www.stnicholas.ie. Free admission to church; donations of €2 adults, €1.30 seniors and students requested. Tours €3; reservations required. Daily Mar–Dec 9am–7pm; daily Jan–Feb 9am–5pm.

Cruises & Tours

Corrib Princess This 157-passenger, two-deck boat cruises along the River Corrib, with commentary on points of interest. The trip lasts 90 minutes, passing castles, historical sites, and assorted wildlife. There is a full bar and snack service. You can buy tickets at the dock or at the *Corrib Princess* desk in the tourist office.

Woodquay. ✆ **091/592447.** www.corribprincess.ie. Cruise €15 adults; €13 seniors and students; €8 children; €35 families. May–Sept daily 2:30 and 4:30pm; also 12:30pm July–Aug.

Sports & Outdoor Pursuits

SPECTATOR SPORTS

GREYHOUND RACING The hounds race year-round every Thursday, Friday, and Saturday at the newly redeveloped **Galway Greyhound Track,** College Road, off Eyre Square (✆ **091/562273**). Doors open 7pm and admission is €10 adults, €5 seniors and students, and €.50 children.

HORSE RACING This is one of the most famous racetracks in Europe—the subject of fable and song—and when (in July, Sept, and Oct) horses pound the track at the **Galway Racecourse,** Ballybrit (✆ **091/753870;** www.galwayraces.com), less than 3km (2 miles) east of town, it's an event known simply as the **Galway Races.** It brings in horse lovers and high rollers from around the country, and is well worth catching. Admission is around €20 to €40 (€2 kids 13 and under), depending on the event and day of the week.

Going to the Galway Races

Galway horses are famous for their speed, small size, and beauty, so it's no surprise that the races here are the best in Ireland and among the best in Europe. There are records of organized horse racing in Galway as far back as the 13th century, and in 1764 there was a well-known 5-day race at Knockbarron near Loughrea. Almost a century later, the Galway Racecourse opened officially. To this day, races in Galway are extremely popular, and people come from around the country to experience the frivolity (music is usually performed around the racecourse), the pomp (women are known to get dressed to the nines), and the exhilaration of the race itself. Tickets aren't expensive and it's a truly Irish event well worth catching if you happen to be in town when the races are on. See www.galwayraces.com for more details.

OUTDOOR PURSUITS

BICYCLING To rent a bike, contact **Richard Walsh Cycles,** Headford Road, Woodquay (✆ **091/565710**).

FISHING Set beside the River Corrib, Galway City and nearby Connemara are popular fishing centers for salmon and sea trout. For the latest information on requirements for licenses and local permits, check with the **Inland Fisheries Ireland,** Teach Breac, Earl's Island, Galway (✆ **091/563118;** www.wrfb.ie). The extraordinarily accessible organization also provides free consultation for overseas anglers on where to go at different times of the season for salmon or trout, where to find the best *ghillies* (guides), and which flies and gear to use. Maps and brochures are available on request. For gear and equipment, try **Duffy's Fishing,** 5 Main Guard St. (✆ **091/562367**), **Freeney Sport Shop,** 19 High St. (✆ **091/568794**), or **Great Outdoors Sports Centre,** Eglinton Street (✆ **091/562869**).

GOLF Less than 3km (2 miles) west of the city is the 18-hole, par-69 seaside course at **Galway Golf Club,** Blackrock, Galway (✆ **091/522033;** www.galwaygolf.com). Greens fees are €30 (closed to nonmembers Sun).

HORSEBACK RIDING Riding enthusiasts head to **Aille Cross Equestrian Centre,** Aille Cross, Loughrea, County Galway (✆ **091/841216;** www.aille-cross.com), about 32km (20 miles) east of Galway. Run by personable Willy Leahy (who has appeared often on American television), this facility is one of the largest in Ireland, with 50 horses and 20 Connemara ponies. For about €25 to €40 an hour, you can ride through nearby farmlands, woodlands, forest trails, and along beaches.

Shopping

Given its status as both a tourist hub and a vibrant arts community, it's unsurprising that Galway has fairly good shopping. Some of the best is in tiny malls of small shops clustered in historic buildings, such as the **Cornstore** on Middle Street, the **Grainstore** on Lower Abbeygate Street, and the **Bridge Mills,** a 430-year-old mill building beside the River Corrib. **Eyre Square Centre,** the downtown area's largest shopping mall, with around 50 shops, incorporates a section of Galway's medieval town wall into its complex.

Most shops are open Monday to Saturday 9 or 10am to 5:30 or 6pm. In July and August, many shops stay open late, usually until 9pm on weekdays, and some also open on Sunday from noon to 5pm.

Here's a sampling of some of Galway's best shops:

ANTIQUES & CURIOS

Cobwebs This sweet little shop across from the Spanish Arch offers jewelry, antique toys, curios, and rarities from Ireland and beyond. 7 Quay Lane. ✆ **091/564388.** www.cobwebs.ie.

The Winding Stair Three floors crammed with antiques—just the place to pick up an Art Nouveau lamp, painted wooden chest, or church pew. 4 Mainguard St. ✆ **091/561682.**

BOOKS

Charlie Byrne's Bookshop This is an atmospheric bookshop, with a marvelously haphazard, collegiate feel. Most of the books are secondhand, with a good selection of paperbacks, should you need to stock up, and plenty of Irish-interest titles. There are also some surprising finds, with a fair selection of titles in archaeology, art history, the cinema, and music. Cornstore Mall, Middle St. ✆ **091/561766.** www.charliebyrne.com.

Kenny's Book Shop and Galleries Ltd. A Galway fixture for more than 50 years, this shop is an attraction unto itself. It's a friendly, busy shop with plenty of old maps, prints, engravings, and books on all topics—many on local history, as well as whole sections on Yeats and Joyce—wedged in every available crevice. Kenny's is famous for its antiquarian department, its bookbinding workshop, and an ever-changing gallery of local artworks. Lisobun Retail Park, Tuam Rd. ✆ **091/709350.** www.bookshop.kennys.ie.

CRYSTAL, CHINA & SOUVENIRS

Galway Irish Crystal This factory outlet on the loop (or "ring road") around Galway Town has lots of hand-cut crystal, and a center that explains where it all comes from and how it's made. Dublin Rd., Merlin Park. ✆ **091/757311.** www.galwaycrystal.ie.

Treasure Chest With an artful exterior that seems to have stepped straight out of Wedgwood, this is a pleasant one-stop shop for Royal Tara and Royal Doulton china, Irish Dresden and Lladró figures, and Belleek china. It also carries Irish designer clothing, Aran knitwear, lingerie, and swimwear, not to mention touristy souvenirs. 31–33 William St. and Castle St. ✆ **091/563862.** www.treasurechest.ie.

HANDICRAFTS

Design Concourse If you're looking for local handicrafts, this is a good choice, as it's filled with the work of dozens of talented Irish craftspeople. Its offerings include woodwork, jewelry, furniture, and glass. Kirwan's Lane. ✆ **091/566927.**

Twice as Nice A sweet, old-fashioned shop, this little gem is filled with fine white linens and cottons for the bedroom and dining room, as well as antique linens and sumptuous christening gowns. 5 Quay St. ✆ **091/566332.**

JEWELRY

Fallers of Galway Dating from 1879, Fallers has long been a prime source of Claddagh rings, many of which are made on the premises. It also sells Celtic crosses, some inlaid with Connemara marble, as well as gold and silver jewelry and crystal. Williamsgate St. ✆ **800/229-3892** in the U.S. (for catalogs), or 091/561226. www.fallers.com.

Hartmann & Son Ltd. The Hartmann family, which started in the jewelry business in the late 1800s in Germany, brought their skills and wares to Ireland in 1895, and opened this shop just off Eyre Square in 1942. They enjoy a far-reaching reputation as watchmakers, goldsmiths, and makers of Claddagh rings. 29 William St. ✆ **091/562063.** www.hartmanns.ie.

Thomas Dillon's Claddagh Gold This colorful little shop claims to be the original creator of the Claddagh ring, and it could be right—it's been selling them since 1750. The tiny boutique on Quay Street is an excellent place to get your Claddagh, or other gold and silver jewelry. Quay St. ✆ **800/229-3892** in the U.S. (for catalogs), or 091/566365. www.claddaghring.ie.

MUSIC & MUSICAL INSTRUMENTS

P. Powell and Sons This family-run shop sells traditional Irish music, instruments, and recordings. The Four Corners, Williams St. ✆ **091/562295.**

TWEEDS, WOOLENS & CLOTHING

Brown Thomas The local branch of one of Ireland's oldest and most upscale department stores, owned by the same people as London's Selfridges. Galway's best-dressed fashionistas have this place on speed dial. 18–21 Eglinton Bldgs. ✆ **091/565254.** www.brownthomas.com.

Faller's Sweater Shop This shop has a huge supply of knitwear made by Irish artisans from the wool of Irish sheep. Prices are quite good. 25 High St. ✆ **091/564833.**

Mac Eocagain/Galway Woollen Market This is an excellent resource if you're shopping for traditional Aran hand-knits and colorful hand-loomed sweaters and capes, as well as linens, lace, and sheepskins. Each item has two prices, one including value-added tax (VAT) and one tax-free for non–European Union (E.U.) residents. 21 High St. ✆ **091/562491.**

O'Máille (O'Malley) Established in 1938, this shop became famous in the 1950s for outfitting the entire cast of *The Quiet Man* and has done a fabulous business ever since in quality Irish tweeds, knitwear, and traditional Aran knits. 16 High St. ✆ **091/562696.** www.omaille.com.

Galway City After Dark

PUBS

An Pucan A block east of Eyre Square, this old-fashioned nautical-theme pub hosts good Irish traditional music (daily from 9pm). It's an Irish-language pub, though, so the eavesdropping is terrible if you're not bilingual. 11 Forster St. ✆ **091/561528.** www.anpucan.ie.

Crane Bar In the southwestern part of Galway, at the corner of an open market area called "the Small Crane," this rustic pub is known for its nightly musical entertainment. From 9pm every night, there's blues, country-and-western, or traditional Irish music, and even occasional poetry slams. Downstairs the music is free; upstairs it will cost you from nothing (most nights) to about €20, depending on who's playing. 2 Sea Rd. ✆ **091/587419.** www.thecranebar.com.

The Quays pub features an eclectic range of music.

Front Door This sunny, laid-back pub is a good place to linger over a pint and the newspaper. Its many windows let the sun pour in, and the staff couldn't care less how long you stay. It's a lovely, relaxed place. High St. © **091/563757.** www.frontdoorpub.com.

Murty Rabbitt's This place dates from 1872 and hardly appears to have changed since then, with lanterns hanging in the corners and pictures of old Galway on the walls. Run by the fourth generation of the Rabbitt family (whose great-grandpa started it with money he'd made in the California gold rush), it's a block east of Eyre Square. 23-25 Forster St. © **091/566490.**

The Quays If this unusual pub looks a bit theological, that's because its entire interior was imported from a French medieval church—stained glass, carved wood, Gothic arches, pews, and all. Evening music ranges from traditional Irish to '70s retro to Dixieland, and usually starts at 9pm. Quay St. and Chapel Lane. © **091/568347.**

CLUBS

Nightclubs in Galway tend to be wastelands until 11pm, and then packed up until 2am when most close. Expect to pay cover charges in a range of about €5 to €20, which doesn't include drinks. There are plenty of options if you've got dancing on your mind, including **Halo,** 36 Abbeygate St. Upper (© **091/565976;** www.halonightclub.com) and **Karma**, Eyre Square (© **091/500330;** www.karma.ie), both of which are popular with a young, twenty-something crowd. In nearby Salthill, new dance clubs with hot guest DJs are popping up all the time. One reliably good option is **Liquid** (© **091/527155**).

Fridays and Saturdays are gay nights at the **Attic @ Liquid,** Liquid, Salthill (© **091/527155**).

MEDIEVAL BANQUET

A half-hour drive from Galway, **Dunguaire** is a splendid 16th-century castle where, in the summer, you can attend a medieval banquet with a show featuring works by Irish writers like Synge, Yeats, and Gogarty. Banquets cost €56 adults,

Book well in advance for tickets to the renowned vanguard Druid Theatre.

€42 children 9 to 12 years old, €28 children 6 to 8 years old. Call ✆ **061/360788** or visit www.shannonheritage.com for reservations. Dunguaire is in south County Galway on the Ballyvaughan road (N67), near Kinvara, approximately 26km (16 miles) from Galway. The castle is open to visitors daily from 10am to 5pm, after which there are two banquet seatings—one at 5:30pm and one at 8:45pm. Banquets are held every night from May to September; many nights book up months in advance.

THEATER

The creative theater group, **Druid Theatre,** performs in two venues in Galway—in a recently refurbished, former grain warehouse at Chapel Lane (✆ **091/568660;** www.druidtheatre.com), and at the Town Hall Theatre (✆ **091/569777;** www.tht.ie). Performances are unique and original, focusing on Irish folk dramas and Anglo-Irish classics. This is widely viewed as one of Ireland's best theaters, and so its shows are frequently either sold out or on tour; book well in advance. Tickets run €15 to about €40. The Town Hall Theatre also hosts an eclectic program of concerts and film screenings.

Taibhdhearc Theatre Pronounced *Thive*-yark, this is a 108-seat, year-round venue for Irish-language plays. In summer, it presents a program of traditional music, song, dance, and folk drama. The box office is open Monday to Saturday from 1 to 6pm (until 8pm on show nights); most shows start at 8pm. Middle St. ✆ **091/563600.** www.antaibhdhearc.com (website in Gaelic). Tickets €10–€17.

Galway Suburbs

On the main road south (N18) of Galway are two small fishing villages, **Clarenbridge** and **Kilcolgan.** Each year at the end of September, the villages host the annual **Galway Oyster Festival ★**. Launched in 1954, the 5-day festival is packed with traditional music, song, dancing, sports, art exhibits, and, above all, oyster-tasting events and oyster-opening competitions.

If you continue south on N18 for another 16km (10 miles), you'll see signs to the quietly beautiful **Coole Park National Forest** (✆ **091/631804;** www.coolepark.ie). This was once a country home of the dramatist and arts patron Lady Gregory, who, along with W. B. Yeats and Edward Martyn, founded the Abbey Theatre. Sadly, her house no longer stands, but her influence is memorialized in a tree on the grounds on which the following people carved their initials while visiting with her: George Bernard Shaw, Sean O'Casey, John Masefield, Oliver St. John Gogarty, W. B. Yeats, and Douglas Hyde, the first president of Ireland. Clearly, this is an exceptional place. There's a visitor center, as well as a tearoom, picnic tables, and plenty of nature trails to wander. The visitor center is open daily 10am to 5pm late March to May and September, with extended hours from 10am to 6pm June to August. The last admission is 15 minutes before closing (1 hr. for the audiovisual presentations). Admission is free.

Not too far away from the home of his friend, W. B. Yeats had his own summer home in Gort at **Thoor Ballylee** (✆ **091/631436**). The restored 16th-century Norman tower house served as the inspiration for his poems "The Winding Stair" and "The Tower." In the interpretive center, an audiovisual presentation examines the poet's life. Also on the grounds are the original Ballylee Mill, partially restored, and a bookshop specializing in Anglo-Irish literature. The site is on the N18 at Gort. Admission is €6 for adults, €5.50 for seniors and students, €2.50 for children 12 and over, €1.50 for children 11 and under, and €12 for families. It's open from May to September daily 10am to 6pm. It's also home to the **Tourist Information Office** (✆ **091/631436**), open May to September daily 9:30am to 5pm. Please note that at this writing Thoor Ballylee was closed for refurbishment after suffering flood damage. It's expected to be fully up and running long before you read this, but all the same it may be wise to call before setting out if you're traveling a long way.

Not too far away from Yeats's and Lady Gregory's summer homes, west off the main road, between Gort and Kilcolgan, **Dunguaire Castle,** Kinvara (✆ **061/360788;** www.shannonheritage.com), sits on the south shore of Galway

Oliver St. John Gogarty made his home in Dunguaire Castle, where Yeats and Lady Gregory were frequent guests.

A horse and buggy trundles past the ruins of Dún Aengus on Inishmore, Aran Islands.

Bay. Once the royal seat of the 7th-century King Guaire of Connaught, the castle was taken over later by the legendary Oliver St. John Gogarty, Irish surgeon, author, poet, and wit. Together the three must have had a kind of Bloomsbury society west in the summertime, when all of Dublin's greatest literary minds decamped to their manor homes. Today Dunguaire's greatest appeal is the exquisite view from its battlements of the nearby Burren and Galway Bay. Admission is €6 for adults, €3.50 for seniors and students, €3.40 for children, and €15 for families. It's open daily from May through September 10am to 5pm (last admission 4pm). There are **medieval banquets** here on summer evenings (above). Dunguaire is on the N67 just east of Kinvara.

WHERE TO EAT

Moran's Oyster Cottage ★★ SEAFOOD Presidents, prime ministers, movie stars, and locals all find their way here, because the food is legendary. For six generations, the Morans have been catching salmon and shucking oysters and preparing them to perfection. The wild smoked salmon is exquisite—sheer velvet. Willie Moran believes in a small menu, fresh and wild and with nothing in the way. Ambience? It's a thatched cottage with 36 swans and a blue heron outside the front door.

The Weir, Kilcolgan, County Galway. ✆ **091/796113.** www.moransoystercottage.com. Main courses €11–€24; lobster €39. AE, MC, V. Mon–Sat 10:30am–11:30pm; Sun noon–11:30pm.

Paddy Burke's ★ SEAFOOD Platters of local oysters and mussels are served throughout the day at this homey tavern, with its lemon color and thatched roof. You can pick your favorite spot to relax in the half-dozen rooms and alcoves with stone walls, open fireplaces, potbellied stoves, and traditional *sugan* chairs (wood chairs with twisted rope seats). In good weather, there is seating in a back garden. Lunch and snack items range from seafood soups and chowders to sandwiches, salads, and omelets. In the evening, you can also order full meals, with choices such as Atlantic plaice and crab with prawn sauce, and honey roast duck with mead sauce. The tavern is on the main road, 16km (10 miles) south of Galway City.

Ennis-Galway rd. (N18), Clarenbridge, County Galway. ✆ **091/796226.** www.paddyburkesgalway.com. Reservations recommended for dinner. Main courses €17–€25; bar menu around €3 per item. AE, DC, MC, V. Mon–Sat 10:30am–10:30pm; Sun noon–9:30pm.

THE ARAN ISLANDS

When you see the ghostly shapes of these islands floating 48km (30 miles) out at sea like misty Brigadoon, you instantly understand why the **Aran Islands** have been the subject of fable and song for thousands of years.

The islands—***Inis Mór* (Inishmore),** ***Inis Meain* (Inishmaan),** and ***Inis Oirr* (Inisheer)**—are outposts of Gaelic culture and language. Life on the islands is deeply isolated—to this day, many of the 1,500 inhabitants maintain a somewhat traditional life, fishing from currachs (small crafts made of tarred canvas stretched over timber frames), living in stone cottages, relying on pony-drawn wagons to get around, and speaking Gaelic.

They still wear the classic, creamy, hand-made *bainin* sweaters that originated here, as there's nothing better for keeping out the chill.

> **Impressions**
>
> ***I have heard that, at that time, the ruling proprietor and magistrate of the north island used to give any man who had done wrong a letter to a jailer in Galway, and send him off by himself to serve a term of imprisonment.***
>
> **—J. M. Synge (1871–1909), *The Aran Islands***

Sadly, though, the constant flow of tourists has had an impact on island life, and many islanders now spend their time running tourist-related businesses. In fact, visiting in the high season—particularly in July and August—can be a disappointment, since the small, rocky islands are not suited to being overrun by crowds, and at that time of year, visitors arrive by the boatload.

Most visitors debark from the ferries at Kilronan, Inishmore's main town and a very easy place in which to arrange or rent transportation. The mode is up to you: Horse-drawn buggies can be hailed like taxis as you step off the boat, minivans stand at the ready, and bicycle-rental shops are within sight.

Of the islands, Inishmore is the largest and easiest to reach from Galway, and the one that best handles the large groups of tourists. Its easy transport means you can escape the crowds if you wish, or, if you play well with others, there are plenty of pubs and restaurants. If that all seems far too noisy, you might prefer Inishmaan or Inisheer, both of which are smaller and quieter, and arguably more beautiful than Inishmore.

A resident of Inishmore repairs his thatched roof.

All the islands are rather strange looking, with a ring of rocks around their outer edges and, inside, small farms surrounded by soft green grass and wildflowers. The most dramatic landscape is to be found on the western sides where huge cliffs plummet dizzily into the frothing sea below.

There are some excellent geological sights out here, including the magnificent **Dún Aengus ★★**, a vast, 2,000-year-old stone fortress on Inishmore, on the edge of a cliff that drops 90m (295 ft.) to the sea. Its original purpose is unknown—some think it was a military structure, others say it was a vast ceremonial theater. From the top, there are spectacular views of Galway Bay, the Burren, and Connemara.

Also on Inishmore, a heritage center, **Ionad Arann,** Kilronan (✆ **099/61355;** www.visitaranislands.com), explores the history and culture of the islands. Exhibits examine the harsh landscape, Iron Age forts, and early churches. In addition, the 1932 film *Man of Aran,* directed by Robert Flaherty, is shown six times daily. The center is open April to May and September to October daily 11am to 5pm, and from June to August daily 10am to 7pm. Admission to the center is €4.50 for adults, €3 for students, €2.50 for seniors and children, and €9.25 for families. Discounted combination tickets to the center and film are available. The cafe serves soups, sandwiches, and pastries throughout the day.

Getting There

Here are the best ways to arrange an excursion to the Aran Islands from Galway City (for more information about the Aran Islands, including getting there from Doolin in County Clare, see "The Clare Coast" in chapter 10):

Aer Arann Islands The fastest way to get from the mainland to the Aran Islands is on this local airline, which has small planes departing from Connemara Airport, approximately 29km (18 miles) west of Galway City to the islands every day in the high season. Flight time is 10 minutes. Alternatively, you could try one of the new scenic routes, a 30-minute trip that takes in the islands together with the **Cliffs of Moher** (p. 438). It costs €385 for an eight-seater aircraft; no individual fares are available. You can book your flight at the Galway Tourist Office or at Aer Arann Reservations. A range of specials are usually offered, combining flights with bus/accommodations, and so forth.

Connemara Airport, Inverin, County Galway. ✆ **091/593034.** Fax 091/593238. www.aerarannislands.ie. Round-trip fare €45 adults; €37 students; €25 children 11 and under. MC, V. Apr–Sept daily 8:30am, 10am, 11:30am, 4pm, and 5:30pm; Oct–Mar daily 9am, 11:30am, and 4:30pm.

Aran Island Ferries This company, with a number of offices in Galway center, offers extensive, year-round daily service to all three Aran Islands. Most boats leave from Rossaveal in Connemara, 37km (23 miles) west of the city, for the 40-minute trip. Island Ferries provides bus connection service from its Victoria Place office 90 minutes before sailing time. During peak summer season, there are daily excursions from Galway Dock, which cost up to about €7 more than tickets from Rossaveal.

37–39 Foster St., Galway, County Galway. ✆ **091/568903.** Fax 091/568538. www.aranislandferries.com. Round-trip fare starts at €25 adults; €20 seniors and students; €13 children 5–12; 10% discount for online booking. Round-trip bus fare €7 adults; €6 seniors and students; €4 children. From Rossaveal Apr–Oct 10:30am, 1pm (until early Oct), and 6:30pm. From Inishmor Apr–Oct daily 8:15am, noon and 5pm; also 5pm in June, 5pm and 6:30pm July–Aug; Nov–Mar daily 8:15am and 5pm.

Where to Stay & Eat

The **Inishmore tourist office** (✆ **099/61263**), on the waterfront near the ferry pier in Kilronan, can help you book a room if you haven't reserved in advance.

Kilmurvey House ★ This has been *the* place to stay on Inishmore since Dún Aengus fell into ruin. The 18th-century stone family home of the "Ferocious" O'Flahertys forms the core of this most hospitable and pleasant guesthouse, with 12 diverse rooms, all comfortable and impeccably clean. It's a friendly place, where an array of delights awaits you at breakfast. An optional four-course dinner is served with advance reservations. Kilmurvey House lies just below Dún Aengus, Inishmore's prime attraction. A handful of shops, cafes, and restaurants, as well as a Blue Flag (safe to swim) white-sand beach, are within a short stroll.

8km (5 miles) from the ferry on the coast rd., Kilmurvey, Kilronan, Inis Mór, Aran Islands, County Galway. www.kilmurveyhouse.com. ✆ **099/61218.** 12 units. €110 double. Rates include full breakfast. MC, V. Closed Nov to Easter.

Man of Aran Cottage In the traditional thatched seaside cottage constructed in 1934 for the filming of *Man of Aran,* Joe and Maura Wolfe's cozy B&B overlooking Kilmurvey Bay is friendly and unpretentious, with comfortable rooms—decorated with simple pine furniture and whitewashed walls—and tranquil views. The biggest draw may well be its first-class **restaurant,** open Monday to Saturday 12:30 to 3pm and 7:30 to 10pm. The menu draws upon the organic vegetables and herbs grown in the cottage garden, and fresh seafood.

Kilmurvey, Kilronan, Aran Islands, County Galway. www.manofarancottage.com. ✆ **099/61301.** 5 units. €80 double with shared bathroom; €90 double with private bathroom. Rates include full breakfast. Reservations required for dinner. Fixed-price dinner €35. No credit cards. **Amenities:** Restaurant.

Radharc An Chlair ★ Leaving the ferry and walking onto tiny Inisheer, you're met by Peadar Poil and given a lift up to the house—wait for it—on his tractor. Peadar's wife, Brigid, runs a spit-and-polish B&B operation and the guest rooms are all comfortable and cozy. She is a superb cook and a terrific baker, so even a scone and a cup of tea here are a pleasure.

Inis Oirr, Aran Islands, County Galway. ✆ **099/75019.** 6 units. €70 double. Rate includes full breakfast. MC, V. Closed Christmas.

CONNEMARA

If you look for Connemara on road signs, you may be looking forever, because it's not a city or county, but rather an area or region. Like the Burren in County Clare, the boundaries are a bit hazy, but most agree that Connemara is west of Galway City, starting at Oughterard and continuing toward the Atlantic. You know it when you see it, as it is an area of heartbreaking barrenness and unique beauty, with dark bogs and tall jagged mountains punctuated by curving glassy lakes dotted with green islands.

The desolate landscape is caused, in part, by an absence of trees that were felled and dragged off long ago for building ships, houses, and furniture. Connemara is part of the **Gaeltacht,** or Irish-speaking area, so many signs are in Gaelic only. Traditional music thrives here, as do handicrafts and cottage industries.

It's a varied place—in fact, you could say that there are two Connemaras. South of the Galway-Clifden road is a vast bog-mantled moorland dotted with lakes, and with a low, indented, rocky coastline. North of the Galway-Clifden road, tall quartzite domes and cones form the Maumturks and the Twelve Bens (also called the Twelve Pins), rising toward the breathtaking Killary fiord—the

The Spooky Shortcut

If you're planning a drive across the Connemara National Park to Clifden, you may want to make a shortcut across the rough but beautiful "bog road" more prosaically known as the R341. Unless you're travelling at night, that is. A hotel manager in these parts once told us that many locals consider the road to be haunted, and won't take it after dark. It's certainly dark and scary, and we wouldn't take it in bad weather.

only fiord in the 6,000 or so islands that make up the British Isles—near where Mayo takes over from Galway. Oscar Wilde wrote, "Connemara is a savage beauty." Now you can see that for yourself.

Connemara Area Essentials

GETTING THERE & GETTING AROUND From Galway City, **Bus Éireann** (✆ **091/562000;** www.buseireann.ie) provides daily service to Clifden and other small towns en route. The best way to get around Connemara is to drive, following N59 from Moycullen and Oughterard. Or you can take a guided tour (see "Sightseeing Tours," below). Clifden is 65km (40 miles) west of Galway City.

VISITOR INFORMATION Contact or visit **Ireland West Tourism,** Aras Fáilte, Foster Street, Galway, County Galway (✆ **091/537700;** www.discover ireland.ie/west). See "Visitor Information" in the beginning of this chapter for hours. The **Oughterard Tourist Office,** Main Street, Oughterard (✆ **091/552808;** www.connemarabegins.com), is open year-round Monday to Friday from 9am to 5pm, with extended hours in the summer season. In addition, a **seasonal office,** open Monday to Saturday 9am to 5pm between March and October, is maintained at Clifden (✆ **095/21163**).

A white-sand beach with turquoise water at Roundstone in Connemara.

Clifden's lively harbor, on Clifden Bay.

Exploring the Area

The seaside town of **Clifden** ***(An Clochán)*** has an enviable location at the edge of the blue waters of Clifden Bay, where miles of curving, sandy beaches skirt the rugged coastline. It's a small, attractive Victorian town with colorful shop fronts and church steeples thrusting skyward through a veil of trees. With its plentiful restaurants, shops, hotels, and pubs, it makes a handy base for exploring the area, so it's quite touristy. If you prefer a quieter location, you might want to look at one of the many smaller towns and villages in the area, such as the small fishing port of **Roundstone** ***(Cloch na Rón)*** ★ about 24km (15 miles) away, which, while still relatively peaceful, is also equipped with all of the essentials: pristine beaches, comfortable guesthouses, good restaurants, shops to explore, and more than its share of natural charm.

From Roundstone, you can head on to the little community of **Letterfrack** ***(Leitir Fraic)*** at the edge of Connemara National Park, close to the extraordinary Gothic Kylemore Abbey. The tiny village, founded by Quakers, has a

Going to the Bogs

Connemara's **bog lands** began forming 2,500 years ago. During the Iron Age, the Celts preserved butter in the bog. Today, with one-third of Connemara classified as bog, the turf (or peat) that's cut from the bog remains an important source of fuel. Cutting and drying turf is an integral part of the rhythm of the seasons in Connemara. Cutting requires a special tool, a spade called a *slane,* which slices the turf into bricks about 46 centimeters (18 in.) long. The bricks are first spread out flat to dry, and then stacked in pyramids for further drying. If you spend enough time in Ireland, you'll get used to the strong, smoky smell of burning turf. You can always tell when turf is burning in a home's fireplace—the smoke coming out of the chimney is blue and sweet scented.

handful of pubs and B&Bs in a glorious natural setting. It's near the bright white sands of **Glassillaun Beach** and **Lettergesh,** where horses raced across the sand in the film *The Quiet Man.*

THE TOP ATTRACTIONS

Aughnanure Castle ★ Standing on an outcrop of rock surrounded by forest and pasture, this sturdy fortress is a well-preserved Irish tower castle, with an unusual double bawn (a fortified enclosure) and a still-complete watchtower that you can climb. It was built around A.D. 1500 as a stronghold of the "Ferocious" O'Flaherty clan, who dominated the region and terrified their neighbors in their day. The castle's fireplaces are so big that you could fit a double bed in them.

32km (20 miles) west of Galway City, signposted off N59, Clifden rd., Oughterard, County Galway. ✆ **091/552214.** Admission €3 adults; €2 seniors; €1 students and children. Late Apr to Oct daily 9:30am–6pm.

Connemara National Park ★★★ ☺ This lovely national park spreads over 2,000 hectares (4,940 acres) of mountains, bogs, and grasslands. There's an excellent visitor center just south of the crossroads in Letterfrack, which can give you tips and general information on the park's landscape, population of wild things, and scenic walking trails. It's worth taking one of these up some of the Twelve Bens, or through the peaceful *Gleann Mór* (Big Glen), with its River Polladirk. The center also offers sustenance in the form of tea, sandwiches, and freshly baked goods. During July and August, Tuesday and Thursday are "nature days" for children; on Monday, Wednesday, and Friday, there are guided walks for the whole family. Call the center for information on these and other special programs.

Clifden-Westport rd. (N59), Letterfrack, County Galway. ✆ **095/41054.** www.connemaranationalpark.ie. Free admission. Park open year-round. Visitor center Mar–Oct 9am–5:30pm.

Dan O'Hara's Homestead Farm If you're intrigued by the unique Connemara landscape and want more insight into how Connemara farmers find soil to till on this rocky land, you may want to head to this small farm. It is set up under

Stocky Connemara ponies are ideally suited to the rugged landscape along the coast of County Galway.

AN excursion TO INISHBOFIN

The island of **Inishbofin** is a small emerald-green gem that lies 11km (6¾ miles) off the northwest coast of Connemara and offers seclusion and spectacular beauty, provided the skies are clear enough to deliver the unforgettable views of and from its shores. Once the domain of monks, then the lair of pirate queen Grace O'Malley, later Cromwell's infamous priest prison, and currently home to 180 year-round residents, Inishbofin is well worth a day's expedition or even a 2-day stay for those looking for peace and quiet.

Numerous ferries to the island operate from the port of Cleggan (13km/8 miles northwest of Clifden off N59) daily April through October. **Inishbofin Island Discovery,** Cloonamore, Inishbofin Island, County Galway (✆ **095/45819** or 44878; www.inishbofinislanddiscovery.com), sails between the island and Cleggan on the mainland, several times a day. Tickets cost €20, €15 students 12 and older, €10 children age 6 to 12, and €5 children age 3 to 5. ***Note:*** Reservations are *essential.*

pre-famine conditions and reflects daily life in the 1840s, with local people using traditional tilling and farming methods. There are also some cleverly designed reconstructions of ancient dwellings and fortifications that give real insight into how things looked then. And, as ever in Ireland, hidden away on the land is an authentic megalithic tomb and a dolmen. For those who like the peace and quiet here too much to tear themselves away, there are a farmhouse B&B and some self-catering cottages.

About 6.5km (4 miles) east of Clifden off N59, Lettershea, Clifden, County Galway. ✆ **095/21246.** www.connemaraheritage.com Admission €8 adults; €7 seniors and students; €4 children; €20 families. Apr–Oct daily 10am–6pm. Last admission 1 hr before closing.

Kylemore Abbey ★★ This extraordinary Gothic abbey sits at the base of a heavily wooded hill overlooking the mirrorlike waters of Kylemore Lake. The exterior of the main building—a vast, crenelated 19th-century house—is a splendid example of neo-Gothic architecture. The inside is not so impressive—in 1920, its owners donated it to the Benedictine nuns, and the sisters have run a convent boarding school here ever since, using the building as a utilitarian structure. Only the grounds and a tiny section of the house are open to the public, but the grounds are attraction enough. The highlight is the recently restored Gothic chapel, an exquisite cathedral in miniature with a plain, somber cemetery to one side; a lavish Victorian walled garden; and the breathtaking views of it all from across the lake. The complex includes a decent **restaurant** that serves produce grown on the nuns' farm, as well as tea and good scones, a shop with a working pottery studio, and a visitor center. The abbey is most atmospheric when the bells are rung for midday office or for vespers at 6pm. ***Note:*** Ticket prices are often discounted here in the winter.

Kylemore, County Galway. ✆ **095/52000.** www.kylemoreabbey.com. Admission €12 adults; €9 seniors; €8.50 students; free for children 9 and under; €24–€33 families. Abbey and grounds daily Jan 11am–4pm, Feb 11am–5pm (late Feb from 10:30am), Mar–Apr and Nov 10am–5pm, May–Jun 9am–6pm, Jul–Aug 9am–7pm, Sept–Oct 9:30am–5:30pm, Dec 10am–4:30pm. Times may vary with weather and light. Last admission 30 min. before closing.

SIGHTSEEING TOURS

Several companies offer sightseeing tours of Connemara from Galway or Clifden.

Bus Éireann Departing from the bus station in Galway, this 8-hour tour of Connemara takes in Maam Cross, Recess, Roundstone, and Clifden, as well as Kylemore Abbey, Leenane, and Oughterard. It's available in the summertime only.

Ceannt Station, Galway, County Galway. ✆ **091/562000.** www.buseireann.ie. €23 adults; €16 seniors and students; €12 children. June–Aug Mon–Fri 8:30 and 11:15am, 1pm, 5:30pm, and 6:15pm; Sat 10am; Sun 10:15am, 12:50 and 6:15pm.

Connemara Walking Centre This company's expert local guides lead walking tours of Connemara, with an emphasis on history and archaeology, as well as scenery. The walks cover different sections—from the Renvyle Peninsula and Roundstone Bog to the Kylemore Valley, the Maumturk Mountains, and Sky Road. Weeklong walking trips are based at Dun Gibbons, a center dedicated to exploring Connemara's countryside. All walks assemble at Island House in Clifden and include bus transportation to the walking site. Tours run from March to October and cost from €20. Advance reservations are required.

The Island House, Market St., Clifden, County Galway. ✆ **095/21379.** Tours from €20. Tours offered Mar–Oct; call for times and a detailed price list.

Corrib Cruises Departing from the pier at Oughterard, this company's sightseeing boat cruises across Lough Corrib, Ireland's largest lake, stopping at some of its 365 islands. One visits **Inchagoill Island,** with its 12th-century monastery that was inhabited until the 1940s. Another trip goes to the island and to Cong in County Mayo, site of **Ashford Castle** (p. 506). The Cong-Oughterard round-trip cruise can start at either place. In fact, there are currently four different day cruises on offer, as well as an evening "Irish Hour" (happy hour) cruise.

Oughterard, County Galway. ✆ **091/557798.** www.corribcruises.com. 2-hr. round-trip cruises to island start at €20 adults; €15 seniors; €10 children age 12–16; €5 children age 5–11; and free for children 4 and under. Cruises run May–Sept daily 11am and 2:45pm. Be sure to book ahead and to confirm times.

Shopping

Avoca Handweavers The Connemara branch of the famous Wicklow weavers is in a lovely, isolated location 10km (6¼ miles) north of Clifden on an inlet of the bay, surrounded by colorful flower gardens. Inside are the Irish chain's trademark colorful woven clothes and blankets, as well as locally made marble

Connemara Pony

The **donkey** is a trademark of this region, and the long-eared creatures still work on many farms. But more famous is the sturdy little horse known as the **Connemara pony,** the only horse breed native to Ireland (although it's had an infusion of Spanish blood over the centuries). Often raised in tiny fields with limestone pastures, these animals have great stamina and are invaluable for farming and pulling equipment. The Connemara pony is also noted for its gentle temperament, which makes it ideal for children's riding.

souvenirs, pottery, jewelry, and music. There's an excellent cafe as well, which makes a good place for lunch. Open April through October daily from 9:30am until at least 6pm. Clifden-Leenane rd. (N59), Dooneen Haven, Letterfrack, County Galway. ✆ **095/41058.** www.avoca.ie.

Connemara Marble Visitor Centre Connemara's unique green marble is quarried, cut, shaped, and polished here. Estimated by geologists to be about 500 million years old, the marble ranges from lime green to dark emerald. On weekdays you'll see craftspeople at work hand-fashioning jewelry, paperweights, ashtrays, Celtic crosses, and other giftware. Open daily from 9am to 5:30pm. 13km (8 miles) west of Galway City on Galway-Clifden rd. (N59), Moycullen, County Galway. ✆ **091/555102.**

Fuchsia Crafts Wedged in the center of Oughterard's main thoroughfare, this small pink shop sells crafts produced throughout Ireland, including products made from pressed Irish peat, bronze sculptures, and recycled art cards of Connemara scenes, as well as pottery, crystal, jewelry, knitwear, and much more. Open daily 9am to 10pm from June through September; daily 9am to 7pm in April, May, and October; and Monday to Saturday 9am to 6pm from November through March. The Square, Oughterard, County Galway. ✆ **091/552644.**

Millars Connemara Tweed Ltd. This is the home of the colorful Connemara tweeds. Although most people just buy skeins of wool or hand-woven materials—plus ready-made ties, hats, caps, scarves, blankets, and bedspreads—there are also rush baskets, Aran *crios* belts, plus an art gallery of regional paintings. Open Monday to Saturday from 9am to 6pm, with extended summer hours. Main St., Clifden, County Galway. ✆ **095/21038.**

O'Dalaigh Jeweller This family-run jewelry shop has handmade, one-of-a-kind pieces with a sophisticated Celtic theme. Along with affordable silver pieces, there is some gorgeous gold jewelry, some based on designs found carved on stones at Newgrange, and some truly unique engagement and wedding rings. Main St., Clifden, County Galway. ✆ **095/22119.** www.celticimpressions.com.

Síla Mag Aoide Designs (Sheila Magee) Although inspired by ancient Celtic images and designs, Sheila Magee's work is original and contemporary. In addition to a wide selection of her handmade silver jewelry, her shop offers a range of works, including watercolor prints and art cards of Connemara scenes, baskets, and handmade frames. Open daily from 9am to 9pm May to September, with shorter off-season hours. The Monastery, Michael Killeen Park, Roundstone, County Galway. ✆ **095/35912.** www.thehouseofmagaoide.com.

Sports & Outdoor Pursuits

BICYCLING Bicycles can be rented year-round from **Mannion Cycles,** Bridge Street, Clifden, County Galway (✆ **095/21160**). The rate for a regular touring bike in high season starts at around €10 per day. Touring bikes can also be hired from May through October at the **Little Killary Adventure Company,** Leenane, County Galway (✆ **095/43411;** www.killary.com). They go for €18 per day.

DIVING You can rent equipment and receive instruction at **Scubadive West,** Renvyle, County Galway (✆ **095/43922;** www.scubadivewest.com).

Fishing is superb on the grounds of Ballynahinch Castle, where the day often ends with a fish-weighing ceremony in the inn's pub.

FISHING Lough Corrib is renowned for brown-trout and salmon fishing. Brown-trout fishing is usually good from the middle of February, and salmon is best from the end of May. The mayfly fishing begins around the middle of May and continues for up to 3 weeks.

Angling on Lough Corrib is free, but a state license is required for salmon. For advice on where to obtain one, contact the **Inland Fisheries Ireland,** Teach Breac, Earl's Island, County Galway (© **091/563118;** www.wrfb.ie).

For salmon and sea trout, the **Ballynahinch Castle Hotel** at Ballynahinch, Recess, County Galway (© **095/31006;** www.ballynahinch-castle.com), is an angler's paradise. State fishing licenses, tackle hire and sales, maps, and advice are available at the hotel.

At **Portarra Lodge,** Tullykyne, Moycullen, County Galway (© **091/555-051;** www.portarralodge.com), packages are available, including B&B accommodations in a modern guesthouse on the shores of Lough Corrib, dinners, and boats and tackle. Michael Canney is an avid angler and a great guide to this part of Galway. A double room with full breakfast costs €70 per night. Weekly packages that include half-board, boat, and *ghillie* are also available.

GOLF Visitors are welcome at the 18-hole, par-72 championship seaside course of the **Connemara Golf Club,** Ballyconneely, Clifden, County Galway (© **095/23502;** www.connemaragolflinks.com), nestled in the heart of Connemara and overlooking the Atlantic. Greens fees from May to September are €65 weekdays, €75 weekends; from October to April, they're €50 weekdays, €60 weekends.

The **Oughterard Golf Club,** Oughterard, County Galway (© **091/552131;** www.oughterardgolfclub.com), is an 18-hole, par-70 inland course. Greens fees are €25 weekdays, €35 weekends.

HORSEBACK RIDING See the beaches of Connemara from horseback on a trek with the **Cleggan Riding Centre,** Clegan, County Galway (© **095/44746;** www.clegganridingcentre.com). The center offers beach and mountain treks, and the most popular is a 3-hour ride to Omey Island at low tide. Prices start at around €50. Or explore with **Connemara and Coast Trails,** Loughrea, County Galway (© **091/841216;** www.connemara-trails.com). Rides are for experienced and beginning riders alike. Riding starts at around €20 per person per hour.

WALKING If you feel like stretching your legs, head to the town of **Leenane,** which is the start of any number of exhilarating walks. One of the best takes you to the picturesque Aasleagh Waterfall (*Eas Liath*) east of the Killary Harbor. Another walk around that harbor, Ireland's only fiord, follows the Green Road. It was once the primary route from the Rinvyle Peninsula to

LOUGH INAGH & THE walk TO MAUM EAN ORATORY

Lough Inagh, nestled between the Maumturk and the Twelve Bens mountains in the heart of Connemara, is in a spectacularly beautiful valley, where mountain slopes rise precipitously from the valley floor and small streams cascade into the lake in a series of sparkling waterfalls. The R344 cuts through the valley, linking Recess to the south and Kylemore Lake to the north.

The **Western Way,** a walking route that traverses the high country of Galway and Mayo, follows a quiet country road above the R344 through the Lough Inagh Valley. To reach the beginning of the walk, drive north on the R344, turning right on a side road—the sign for Maum Ean—about 200m (656 ft.) before the Lough Inagh Lodge Hotel. Continue on this side road for about 6km (3¾ miles) to a large gravel parking lot on the left. Park here, and follow the well-worn trail 2km (1.25 miles) to the top of the pass, through glorious mountain scenery.

This short (4km/2.5-mile) walk follows the Western Way to the top of a mountain pass that has long been associated with St. Patrick and is now the site of a small oratory, a hollow in the rock known as **Patrick's Bed,** a life-size statue of the saint, and a series of cairns marking the Stations of the Cross. Together, these monuments make a striking ensemble, strangely eerie when the mists descend and conceal the far slopes in their shifting haze. On a clear day, there are great views, with the Atlantic Ocean and Bertraghboy Bay to the southwest and another range of mountains to the northeast. The round-trip walking time is about 1 hour.

Leenane, and is now largely a sheep track. The path passes a ghost town (an abandoned pre-famine village) on the far side of the harbor, where the fields rise at a devilishly steep slope from the ruined cottages clustered at the water's edge. There are excellent walking trails in the **Connemara National Park,** some of which lead up the sides of the Twelve Bens. You can get maps at the park's visitor center.

WATERSPORTS Hobie Cat sailing and sailboarding can be arranged at the **Little Killary Adventure Company,** Leenane, County Galway (✆ **095/43411;** www.killary.com). Rates start at around €60 per day (two sessions), which entitles you to use the watersports equipment and participate in all the center's supervised sporting activities, including kayaking, water-skiing, hill and coastal walking, rock climbing, archery, and more.

Where to Stay

EXPENSIVE

Ballynahinch Castle ★★ Set on an enchanting 140-hectare (346-acre) estate at the base of Ben Lettery, one of the Twelve Bens mountains, this turreted, gabled manor house overlooks the Owenmore River. Dating from the 16th century, it once served as a base for the "Ferocious" O'Flaherty chieftains. It was also said to be home to the sea pirate Grace O'Malley. The ambience can be best described as country-house casual; the place feels luxurious, yet there's little stuffiness. The guest rooms are tastefully decorated in cream and ocher with a traditional look. Many have fireplaces and four-poster beds (all with orthopedic mattresses). This is a sportsman's lodge, renowned for top-notch trout and salmon fishing. Each evening, the day's catch is weighed in and recorded at the Fishermen's Bar, usually creating a cause for celebration.

Recess, County Galway. www.ballynahinch-castle.com. ✆ **095/31006.** Fax 095/31085. 40 units. €190–€330 double; €260–€315 suite. Rates include full breakfast. AE, DC, MC, V. Closed Feb. **Amenities:** Restaurant; bar; babysitting; limited room service; tennis courts. *In room:* TV, hair dryer.

Cashel House Hotel ★ About 20 minutes outside Clifden in the tiny seaside town of Cashel, this lovely, old-fashioned hotel is a virtual haven of peace. The same family has owned and run the place for years—the older staff will happily recount their memories of when General Charles de Gaulle came to stay in the 1960s. The owner is personally responsible for the magical gardens that surround the low, wide-windowed building. Bedrooms are large, with separate seating areas and picture windows. The king-size beds are firm and the bathrooms modern. The floral motif is carried from the gardens through to the wallpaper, curtains, and bedding, but it's all tastefully done. Dinner in the big dining room is excellent Continental cuisine, but you will pay (€60 per person) for the privilege of trying it (beware if staff members offer you anything—tea, for example—as nothing comes free and it will all appear on your bill in the end). There's plenty to keep you busy here—a private beach, tennis courts, fishing areas, stables with riding lessons and trekking, and signposted walking paths, but it's still a quiet, mature place for quiet, mature people.

Cashel Bay, Cashel, County Galway. www.cashel-house-hotel.com. ✆ **800/323-5463** or 800/735-2478 in the U.S., or 095/31001. Fax 095/31077. 32 units. €170–€315 double; €285–€355 master suite. Rates include full breakfast. AE, MC, V. Closed Jan. **Amenities:** Restaurant; bar; smoke-free rooms; tennis court. *In room:* TV, hair dryer.

EXPENSIVE

Abbeyglen Castle ★★ On a hilltop overlooking Clifden and the bay, this is a splendidly informal Irish castle hotel—it's the kind of place where a parrot in reception confuses staff by making the sound of the telephone ringing, and the piano bar brings guests together in a house-party atmosphere. The grand public areas have candelabra chandeliers, arched windows, and vintage settees. Guest rooms are large and comfortable, with beautiful fabrics. The personable staff can arrange fishing trips, packed lunches, and local activities. Dinner is part of the fun here and the food is excellent, with virtually all produce sourced locally. On Tuesdays, the restaurant serves a traditional Irish menu, and there's live traditional music.

Sky Rd., Clifden, County Galway. www.abbeyglen.ie. ✆ **095/21201.** Fax 095/21797. 45 units. €160–€195 double. Rates include full breakfast. AE, MC, V. Closed early Jan to Feb. **Amenities:** Restaurant; bar; miniature golf; Jacuzzi; outdoor pool; sauna; spa; tennis court. *In room:* TV.

Currarevagh House ★ A tranquil country house on the shores of Lough Corrib just outside the tiny town of Oughterard, Currarevagh (pronounced Curra-reeva) offers quiet, unpretentious elegance. Its three guest lounges have turf fires burning on cool days, with soft sofas into which you can sink while reading a book from the house's extensive library. Rooms are designed in traditional style with country chic touches—big windows are enveloped in floral fabrics, comfortable beds stacked with thick blankets, and antique dressers provide a homey touch. Each morning, a lavish breakfast is set in the dining room, with fresh eggs and bacon from local farms, and in the evening a five-course meal features seafood caught that day. Afternoon tea in the drawing room, with tender scones and tiny cakes, is an event.

Lower Sky Rd., Clifden, County Galway. www.currarevagh.com. ✆ **091/552312.** 12 units. €160 double. Rates include full breakfast. MC, V. **Amenities:** Restaurant, bar. *In room:* TV, hair dryer.

Delphi Lodge ★★ Part of an exquisite landscape of crystal lakes and trickling rivers, hardwood forests, and mountain slopes, the Delphi has always been an anglers' hideaway. The rooms are spacious and masculine, furnished with an informally elegant touch, all with peaceful lake and mountain views. Guests are either here for fishing or relaxation. Dinners (€50 per person for four courses) are excellent, with an emphasis on the catch of the day, and eaten at elegant, long dining table. The library and lounge are warmed by wood-burning fireplaces; there's an honor bar where you make your own cocktails in the evening. Owner Peter Mantle can supply you with everything you need to fish—permits, licenses, and equipment rental. ***Note:*** Rooms do not have locks, but the staff keeps a close eye on who comes in and out of the building. All cancellations incur a €30 penalty fee.

The Delphi Estate and Fishery, Leenane, County Galway. www.delphilodge.ie. ✆ **095/42222.** Fax 095/42296. 12 units, 5 cottages. €200 double. Rates include full Irish breakfast. 2- and 3-bedroom self-catering cottages €450–€650 per 3 nights or €800–€1,250 per week, plus metered utility bills. AE, MC, V. Closed Christmas and New Year's holidays. **Amenities:** Restaurant (guests only); honor bar. *In room:* TV.

Dolphin Beach House ★★ This is a stylish, restful place to base yourself about 19km (12 miles) from Clifden. The 19th-century house has been beautifully restored, and the spacious bedrooms have soaring ceilings, heated floors, antique furnishings, pristine bed linens, and spellbinding views. It all combines for a feeling of homespun luxury, with the beach just a stone's throw away. Meals are fashioned mainly from ingredients produced on the estate; you can even collect your own eggs for breakfast on a walk down to the beach. Dinner is available for €40 (though it must be booked in advance).

Lower Sky Rd., Clifden, County Galway. www.dolphinbeachhouse.com. ✆ **095/21204.** Fax 095/22935. 8 units. €130–€180 double. Rates include full breakfast. MC, V. Closed Nov–Feb. **Amenities:** Restaurant. *In room:* TV.

Lough Inagh Lodge ★ Standing alone on the shore of the tranquil Lough Inagh, this handsome fishing-and-sporting lodge has an enviable location. Without another building in sight, you can soak up the tranquillity, with only the splashing of fish in the lake to break the silence. Inside, the public rooms strike a note of warm hospitality, with open log fires in the library and oak-paneled bar. Spacious guest rooms have a similarly traditional look, with period furnishings; most have separate dressing rooms. Request a room in the front of the house for views of the lake and the Twelve Bens.

Recess, County Galway. www.loughinaghlodgehotel.ie. ✆ **800/323-5463** or 800/735-2478 in the U.S., or 095/34706. Fax 095/34708. 12 units. €150–€240 double. Dinner €46. Rates include full breakfast. AE, MC, V. Closed Jan–Feb. **Amenities:** Restaurant; bar. *In room:* TV, hair dryer.

Renvyle House ★★ This grand old house sits on the wild Atlantic shoreline. It was purchased in 1917 by Oliver St. John Gogarty, the famed Irish poet, wit, surgeon, and politician, who fondly called this secluded seascape and mountain setting "the world's end." That's putting it mildly: It really is off the beaten track,

Aran Sweaters

The distinctive chunky, creamy Irish "fisherman's sweaters" known as Aran knit sweaters originated in this region. Using the oat-colored wool from the native sheep, the semi-waterproof sweaters were first knitted by the women of the nearby Aran Islands for their husbands and sons to wear while out at sea. Each family had a different stitch or pattern. Years ago, the patterns were not only a matter of aesthetics; they served as the chief way to identify men who had drowned in the treacherous waters off the coast. Today these sweaters are hand-knitted in the homes of Connemara and the nearby Aran Islands, then sold in the many craft shops throughout the region.

about 10 minutes' drive from the Connemara National Park—not ideal for a quick overnight, but perfect for a stay of a few days or longer. Many have found it worth the trek. W. B. Yeats honeymooned here, and Churchill was a frequent guest. Today it retains a turn-of-the-20th-century ambience, particularly in its public areas. Guest rooms vary in size and decor, from grand rooms with balconies to cozy attic rooms. Most have a masculine decor with red or gold plaid and hunter green carpeting. Along with sporting amenities, it hosts event weekends, including murder-mystery weekends, fly-fishing clinics, and painting weekends.

Renvyle, County Galway. www.renvyle.com. ✆ **095/43511.** 65 units. €115–€350 double. Rates include full Irish breakfast. AE, DC, MC, V. Closed Jan–Feb 15. **Amenities:** Restaurant; bar; 9-hole golf course; outdoor pool; 2 tennis courts. *In room:* TV.

Zetland Country House Hotel ★ This fine fishing lodge in Cashel, about 20 minutes' drive from Clifden, is another good option for anglers. The unusual building was constructed in 1856 as a sporting lodge for a wealthy family. The guest rooms, many of which look out onto the bay, are decorated with antique and reproduction furniture and neutral fabrics. However, the place could do with a face-lift, and some may find the whole effect more stuffy and old-fashioned than charmingly retro. Seafood and game are specialties of the **restaurant,** and vegetables and fruit come from the inn's own gardens. The view from the dining room is spectacular. The Zetland owns the Gowla Fishery, a private sea-trout fishery with 14 lakes and 6.5km (4 miles) of river, so if you don't catch anything here, you'll have some explaining to do. ***Note:*** The hotel has recently changed hands; although we've not yet been for a re-visit, word so far is positive—as is the fact that they've lowered some prices (though not, sadly, for the high season).

Cashel Bay, Cashel, County Galway. www.zetland.com. ✆ **800/448-8355** in the U.S., or 095/31111. Fax 095/31117. 19 units. €120–€200 double. Dinner main courses €29; 4-course fixed-priced menu €49. Rates include full breakfast. AE, MC, V. Closed Nov–Mar. **Amenities:** Restaurant; tennis court. *In room:* TV, hair dryer.

INEXPENSIVE

Connemara Gateway Just outside the village of Oughterard, this contemporary two-story inn sits near the upper shores of Lough Corrib and across the road from an 18-hole golf course. Behind the rambling modern exterior, a cheery down-to-earth lobby features lots of plants and homey bric-a-brac. Guest rooms have a smart, if slightly clinical look, with local tweed fabrics and plaids, plain oak dressers and headboards, and scenes of Connemara on the walls. This place is all about what you can do outside, and there are endless activities at the touch of a button—from organized tours to pony treks to fishing trips.

Galway-Clifden rd. (N59), Oughterard, County Galway. www.connemaragateway.com. ✆ **091/552328.** Fax 091/552332. 62 units. €90 double. Rates include full breakfast. AE, DC, MC, V. **Amenities:** Restaurant; bar; indoor pool; sauna; smoke-free rooms; tennis court. *In room:* TV.

Doonmore Hotel ☺ This seasoned waterfront hotel in a prime location on Inishbofin has stunning views of the sea and of nearby Inishshark and High Island. Small boats dot the bay, and there is a seal colony just beyond the hotel's front doors. The rooms are basic, but the wide range of options is handy for families, as there are plenty of spacious family units with children's bunk beds. The unpretentious rooms in the modern wing are clean, full of light, and furnished with simple pine furniture. The older rooms in the original hotel building are worn but comfortable. The hotel is a short walk from the ferry, and the owners can arrange all you need for sea angling and scuba diving.

Inishbofin Island, County Galway. www.doonmorehotel.com. ✆ **095/45804.** 25 units. €80–€100 double. Rates include full breakfast. AE, MC, V. Closed Nov–Mar. **Amenities:** Restaurant; bar. *In room:* TV.

Errisbeg Lodge Conveniently near to Roundstone, yet blessedly isolated between mountainside and sea, Errisbeg Lodge has a truly spectacular setting. Jackie and Shirley King's family land starts high on Errisbeg Mountain and slopes down to the sea, forming a haven for rare species of wildflowers and birds, and the dark blue Atlantic uncoils from glorious sandy beaches. Guest rooms are rustic and spare, with stucco walls, inexpensive pine furniture, and beds topped with farmhouse floral comforters. All rooms have either mountain or ocean views. There are two deserted beaches within walking distance, and miles of hills to roam. This is not a fancy place, but the hosts are welcoming and the scenery is a draw in itself.

Just over 1.6km (1 mile) outside of Roundstone on Clifden rd., Roundstone, County Galway. www.errisbeglodge.com. ✆ **095/35807.** 5 units. €90–€100 double. Rates include full breakfast. No credit cards. Closed Dec–Jan. **Amenities:** Smoke-free rooms.

Glen Valley Farm At the base of a remote glaciated valley, this award-winning B&B redefines "secluded." The entrance drive follows the base of the valley for over 1.6km (1 mile) before you arrive at the house, which has sweeping views across to the far line of hills. Rooms are simple and the decor old-fashioned, but the house is in a serene, restful setting. The spectacular Western Way walking trail passes near the house and follows the hills along Killary Harbour, with unforgettable views—there's no better place to watch the sun set.

Signposted 5.6km (3½ miles) west of Leenane on the Clifden rd., Glencroff, Leenane, County Galway. www.glenvalleyhouse.com. ✆ **095/42269.** Fax 095/42365. 4 units, 2 with private bathroom. €70 double with private bathroom; €66 double with shared bathroom. MC, V. Closed Nov–Feb. **Amenities:** TV (in guest lounge).

Where to Eat

MODERATE

High Moors ★ 🎁 MODERN CONTINENTAL Just outside of Clifden, a narrow country road leads to this modern bungalow-style restaurant, high on a hill with panoramic views of the Atlantic and the wild countryside. A homey ambience prevails, and the food and menu are simple, based on whatever is fresh at the markets.

The dishes include such classics as breast of chicken with basil and tomato, filet of pork with three spices, and roast leg of Connemara lamb with red currant and rosemary. Try to book a table for sunset—the views are incredible. The attached **Steam Coffee House** (✆ **095/30600**) is a great place for a coffee break.

Off the Ballyconneely rd., Dooneen, Clifden, County Galway. ✆ **095/21342.** Reservations recommended. Main courses €14–€20. AE, MC, V. Wed–Sun 6:30–10pm. Closed Nov–Easter.

O'Dowd's Seafood Restaurant SEAFOOD This homey, traditional restaurant overlooking the harbor has been serving up steaming plates of seafood since 1840. The decor is rustic but nobody minds, as everyone is here for the food: seafood chowder, crab claws in garlic butter, fresh oysters, steamed mussels, fish curry, and grilled Connemara smoked salmon in cheese sauce with tagliatelle. There are also a couple of meat options such as lamb stew and chargrilled steak.

Roundstone Harbour, Connemara, County Galway. ✆ **095/35809.** www.odowdsrestaurant.com. Reservations recommended. 2-course fixed-price dinner €20; main courses €13–€22. AE, DC, MC, V. Apr–Sept daily noon–10pm; Oct–Mar daily noon–3pm and 6–9pm.

Station House Restaurant ★ MODERN CONTINENTAL Locals flock to this restaurant, hidden away in the courtyard at the rear of the Clifden Station House Hotel. The draw is the imaginative cooking that manages to infuse even the simplest dish with zest and originality. The chef loves to chargrill and smoke, which heightens the taste of the rich flavors he prefers in dishes like the blackened turbot, served with smoked oysters and grilled mushrooms. Desserts are delectable, too.

At the rear of the Station House Hotel, on the N59, Clifden, Connemara, County Galway. ✆ **095/21699.** www.clifdenstationhouse.com/restaurant-dining-galway. Reservations recommended. Main courses €16–€24. AE, MC, V. Wed–Sun 6:30–9:30pm. Closed Oct–Apr.

EASTERN GALWAY, WESTMEATH & OFFALY

Birr: 24km (15 miles) E of Portumna. Athlone: 97km (60 miles) E of Galway

Eastern Galway segues smoothly into Offaly and Westmeath, and the rugged countryside becomes a bit softer and greener as you head inland. This is farming country, and pastures stretch as far as the eye can see, punctuated by historic sites and small farming communities. The early Christian settlement of **Clonmacnoise** ***(Cluain Mhic Nóis)*** occupies a beautiful stretch of land by the river, with its stone chapels and mysterious round towers. Farther along, you might want to stop by the town of **Birr** ***(Biorra),*** known for its magnificent and historic gardens, and **Banagher** ***(Beannchar na Sionna),*** a sleepy, working town with a picturesque harbor—although in recent years, sadly, it's got a little rougher and more run-down than it used to be. Later, the river winds and curls its way to **Athlone** ***(Baile Átha Luain),*** a vibrant, colorful university town where the buildings are all brightly painted, and there's plenty to do and see. It also has excellent restaurants, coffee shops, historic pubs, and a popular marina for mooring and hiring boats.

Essentials

GETTING THERE & GETTING AROUND The best way to get here is by car. Although there's some public transportation, you're still best off with a car in order to see the smaller towns and remote sites. Major roads that lead to this

Clonmacnoise, an early Christian settlement north of Shannonbridge in County Offaly.

area are the main Galway-Dublin road (N6) from points east and west, N62 from the south, and N55 and N61 from the north. You can also boat through the region along the Shannon River, which cuts a swath through the region.

VISITOR INFORMATION Information on this area can be obtained from the **Ireland West Tourism Office,** Foster Street, Galway (✆ **091/537700;** www.discoverireland.ie/west). Hours are May, June, and September daily 9am to 5:45pm; July and August daily 9am to 7:45pm; and October to April Monday to Friday 9am to 5:45pm, Saturday 9am to 12:45pm. The **East Coast & Midlands Tourism Office,** Clonard House, Dublin Road, Mullingar, County Westmeath (✆ **044/934-8650**), is open Monday to Friday 9am to 5:45pm, plus Saturday during peak season.

Seasonal tourist information points are generally open from May or June to September at signposted sites in **Athlone,** at the Athlone Castle (✆ **090/649-4630;** www.athlone.ie), **Ballinasloe** (✆ **090/964-2604**), **Birr** (✆ **057/912-0110**), and **Clonmacnoise** (✆ **090/967-4134**).

Seeing the Sights

Athlone Castle ★ Built in 1210 for King John of England, this mighty stone fortress sits on the edge of the Shannon atop the ruins of an earlier fort built in 1129 as the seat of the chiefs of Connaught. Athlone Castle protected the town for centuries. It was besieged for almost 6 months in 1641, and again in 1690, but it fell in 1691 after an intense bombardment by forces sent by William of Orange. The Dutch military commander who took the town, Godard van Glinkel, was rewarded for his efforts with the earldom of Athlone. Today the castle is a national monument, adapted as a visitor center and museum. There are displays on the history of the area, and on the great Irish tenor (and local boy) John McCormack. The castle's original medieval walls have been preserved, as have two large cannons dating from the reign of George II and a pair of 25cm (10-in.) mortars cast in 1856.

Athlone, County Westmeath. ✆ **090/649-2912.** Admission €6 adults; €3.60 seniors and students; €1.90 children; €17 families. May to mid-Oct daily 10am–5pm. On the riverbank, signposted from all directions.

Battle of Aughrim Interpretative Centre Via a high-tech, three-dimensional audiovisual presentation, this center re-creates the Battle of Aughrim, which took place on July 12, 1691. On that day, the army of James II of England confronted the forces of his son-in-law, William of Orange, in a bloody battle. The confrontation involved 45,000 soldiers from eight countries and cost 9,000 lives, changing the course of Irish and European history. (For more about the conflict between William and James, see "The Making of Ireland," in chapter 2.) The center, which holds a bookshop, craft shop, and cafe, is in Aughrim village, adjacent to the battlefield, which is signposted. Aughrim is on the main Dublin-Galway road, about 19km (12 miles) west of the Shannonbridge/Clonmacnoise area.

Galway-Dublin rd. (N6), Aughrim, near Ballinasloe, County Galway. ✆ **090/967-3939.** Admission €5 adults; €4 seniors and students; €3 children 11 and under; €12 families. June to late Aug Tues–Sat 10am–1pm and 2–6pm; Sun 2–6pm.

Birr Castle Demesne ★★ The 17th-century castle is not open to the public, but people come here anyway, just to see the extraordinary gardens. The demesne (or estate) of the Parsons family, now the earls of Rosse, wraps around a peaceful lake and along the banks of the two rivers. The box hedges have been featured in the *Guinness Book of Records* as the tallest in the world, and the hornbeam cloisters are lovely. The grounds contain an astronomical exhibit, with a 19th-century reflecting telescope that was once the largest in the world. Recently restored by the Historic Science Centre, the telescope is used twice daily, at noon and 3pm. During the summer, there are often exhibits on the history of Birr Castle and its residents.

Birr, County Offaly. ✆ **057/912-0336.** www.birrcastle.com. Admission €9 adults; €7.50 students and seniors; €5 children 5–12; free for children 4 and under; €25 families. Mid-Mar to Oct daily 9am–6pm; Nov–Feb daily noon–4pm. Courtyard Café mid-Mar to Oct daily 10am–2:30pm. Take N52 37km (23 miles) southwest of Tullamore.

Charleville Castle ★ Now, *this* is a castle. Designed in 1798 by Francis Johnston, this spooky, Gothic, crenelated masterpiece took 12 years to build. Today it's considered one of the best of Ireland's early-19th-century castles, and those who believe in such things say it is haunted. (It appeared on the TV show *Ghost Hunters* in 2008). It has fine limestone walls and plenty of towers, turrets, and battlements. Inside there's spectacular plasterwork and hand-carved stairways, as well as secret passageways and dungeons. Charleville is run by volunteers, so opening times can be a little unpredictable. Tours run every day in the summer, and there are occasional night tours—but call ahead, particularly if you're planning to visit in the off season. Prices are a little on the high side, but the money is very obviously needed for restoration work. The fact that the staff, so dedicated and enthusiastic, are all unpaid, makes paying that little bit extra a lot easier to justify.

Off Birr Rd. (N52), Tullamore, County Offaly. ✆ **057/932-3040** (recorded information) or 087/766-4110 (volunteer duty officer). info@charlevillecastle.com. Guided tour €16 adults; €8 students age 17–18; €4 children 6–16; free for children 5 and under. Evening tours (prebooking only) €16 adults. Apr to end Aug 1–6pm. Other times vary.

Clonmacnoise ★★★ Resting somberly on the east bank of the Shannon, this is one of Ireland's most profound ancient sites. St. Ciaran founded the monastic community of Clonmacnoise in A.D. 548 at the crucial intersection of the Shannon and the Dublin-Galway land route, and it soon became one of Europe's great centers of learning and culture. For nearly 1,000 years, Clonmacnoise flourished under the patronage of Irish chiefs. The last high king, Rory O'Conor, was buried here in 1198. Clonmacnoise was raided repeatedly by native chiefs, Danes, and Anglo-Normans, until it was finally destroyed by English troops in 1552. Previously the monks always had something to rebuild, but this time the English carried away everything—the roofs from the buildings, the doors, even the panes from the windows. By the time they'd finished, according to a report written by a monk from that time, "There was not left a bell, small or large, an image or an altar, or a book, or a gem, or even glass in a window, from the wall of the church out, which was not carried off." Today you can see what was left of the cathedral, a castle, eight churches, two round towers, three sculpted high crosses, and more than 200 monumental slabs, including some stones on which the old carvings can still be seen with thoughtful messages in ancient Celtic writing saying things like, "A prayer for Daniel." The visitor center has a well-designed exhibition, a slightly childish film, and pleasant tearooms.

On R357, 6.5km (4 miles) north of Shannonbridge, County Offaly. ✆ **090/967-4195.** Admission €6 adults; €4 seniors; €2 students and children 8 and over; free for children 7 and under; €14 families. Nov to mid-Mar daily 10am–5:30pm; mid-Mar to mid-May and mid-Sept to Oct daily 10am–6pm; mid-May to mid-Sept daily 9am–7pm. Last admission 45 min. before closing.

Locke's Distillery Museum Established in 1757, this 18th- and 19th-century enterprise was one of the oldest licensed pot-still whiskey distilleries in the world. After producing whiskey for almost 200 years, it closed in 1953; over the past 15 years, a local group has restored it as a museum. In 1998, a major exhibition space opened in the restored front grain loft to display a host of distilling artifacts. A 35-minute tour will not only tell you how whiskey was distilled using old techniques and machinery, but also inform you about the area's social history. The tour ends with a sample of Kilbeggan Irish Whiskey. It's midway between Dublin and Galway, making it a good stop-off point while you're on a cross-country journey or touring in the area. There's an on-site restaurant and craft shop.

On N6, east of Athlone, Kilbeggan, County Westmeath. ✆ **057/933-2134.** www.lockesdistillerymuseum.ie. Admission €7 adults; €5.75 seniors and students; €16 families. Apr–Oct daily 9am–6pm; Nov–Mar daily 10am–4pm.

Portumna Castle ★ Built in 1609 by Earl Richard Burke, this massive, noble structure on the northern shores of Lough Derg is a particularly fine manor house. Had it not been gutted by fire in 1826, who knows what billionaire might own it now? The fire spared much of the impressive exterior, including its Dutch-style decorative gables and rows of stone mullioned windows. The ground floor is open to the public, as are the recently restored walled kitchen and gardens.

Off N65, Portumna, County Galway. ✆ **090/974-1658.** Admission to castle €3 adults; €2 seniors; €1 children and students; €8 families. Free admission to gardens. Late Apr to late Sept daily 9:30am–6pm; Oct Sat–Sun 9:30am–6pm. Closed last week in Oct. Last admission 45 min. before closing.

Portumna Forest Park ★★ On the shores of Lough Derg, this 560-hectare (1,383-acre) park is east of the town, off the main road. It offers trails and signposted walks, plus viewing points and picnic areas.

Off N65, Portumna, County Galway. Free admission. Daily dawn–9pm.

Tullynally Castle and Gardens A turreted and towered Gothic Revival manor, this creamy white castle home is dazzling. It has been the home of the Pakenham family, the earls of Longford, since 1655. The highlights include a great hall that rises two stories, with a ceiling of plaster Gothic vaulting, filled with family portraits, china, and antique furniture. There's a strangely fascinating collection of workaday 19th-century gadgets. Frustratingly, the building itself is only open to prebooked groups (and with a minimum charge of €250 it's unrealistic but all for the largest ones). However, the 12-hectare (30-acre) grounds are an attraction in themselves, with woodland walks, a linear water garden, a Victorian grotto, and an avenue of 200-year-old Irish yew trees. Tullynally is near Lough Derravaragh, an idyllic spot featured in the legendary Irish tale *The Children of Lir.* There are also a cafe and a plant shop on the grounds.

About 32km (20 miles) east of Longford and 21km (13 miles) north of Mullingar, off the main Dublin-Sligo rd. (N4), Castlepollard, County Westmeath. ✆ **044/966-1159.** www.tullynallycastle.com. Admission to gardens €6 adults; €3 children; €16 families. Castle building is only open for prebooked group tours—call in advance for information. Garden May–Aug Thurs–Sun and holidays 1–6pm.

SIGHTSEEING CRUISES

Viking Tours Head to Clonmacnoise on this company's 71-passenger Viking replica ship. The 4½-hour trip includes a 1-hour stopover at the monastic site. For no particular reason, the crew dress themselves in Viking attire for the journey, and passengers are encouraged to dress up as well—Viking clothing is provided should you be so inclined. Advance booking required.

7 St. Mary's Place, Athlone, County Westmeath (office address). ✆ **090/647-3383.** www.vikingtoursireland.ie. €10 adults; €5 children; €30 families. July–Sept daily at 9am.

Sports & Outdoor Pursuits

BICYCLING Bikes can be rented from **D.B. Cycles & Babyland,** Unit 3, Magazine Road, Athlone, County Westmeath (✆ **090/649-2280**), for around €12 per day or €70 per week.

BOATING The following companies rent cabin cruisers, usually for a minimum of 1 week, along this section of the Shannon: **Athlone Cruisers,** Jolly Mariner Marina, Athlone, County Westmeath (✆ **090/647-2892;** acl@wmeathtc.iol.ie); and **Silverline Cruisers,** The Marina, Banagher, County Offaly (✆ **057/915-1112;** www.silverlinecruisers.com). Crafts range from four to six berths; rates average €1,000 to €2,000 per week in high season.

GOLF **Birr Golf Club,** The Glens, Birr, County Offaly (✆ **057/912-0082;** www.birrgolfclub.com), is an 18-hole course on 45 hectares (111 acres) of parkland countryside; the greens fees are €25 weekdays, €35 weekends.

In the Athlone area is the 18-hole **Athlone Golf Club,** Hodson Bay, Athlone, County Westmeath (✆ **090/649-2073;** www.athlonegolfclub.ie), with greens fees of €30 weekdays, €35 weekends; and the 18-hole championship **Mount Temple Golf Club,** Moate, County Westmeath (✆ **090/648-1841;** www.mounttemplegolfclub.com), 8km (5 miles) east of Athlone, with greens fees of €20 weekdays, €25 weekends. The **Glasson Golf Hotel & Country Club,** Glasson, County Westmeath (✆ **090/648-5120;** www.glassongolfhotel.ie), is on the shores of Lough Ree, 10km (6¼ miles) north of Athlone. Greens fees are €65 Monday to Thursday, €70 Friday and Sunday, and €75 Saturday.

Lovely parkland and woodland golfing in the Lough Derg area is offered at 18-hole clubs such as **Portumna Golf Club,** Ennis Road, Portumna, County Galway (✆ **090/974-1059;** www.portumnagolfclub.ie), with greens fees of €30 weekdays, €35 weekends.

HORSE RACING The horse racing runs from July to September at the **Kilbeggan Racecourse,** Loughnagore, Kilbeggan, County Westmeath (✆ **057/933-2176;** www.kilbegganraces.com), off the main Mullingar road (N52), 1.6km (1 mile) from town. Tickets cost €15, €25 families (two adults with children aged 15 or under).

Where to Stay

VERY EXPENSIVE

Temple Country House & Spa ★★ This 250-year-old manor has recently undergone a wide-ranging renovation, more than doubling the number of rooms, and expanding and improving its famed spa. The result is a clever mix of modern and historic architecture, and even more devotion to peace and relaxation. Days are spent wandering the countryside and indulging in spa treatments (the house has its own line of skin-care products), and taking yoga or chi kung classes. At mealtimes Temple's acclaimed low-fat gourmet cooking—nothing chaste and deprived here, just well-prepared, tasty food without the fat—allows indulgence without guilt. The spacious rooms are comfortably and attractively appointed, if not overtly luxurious. Weekends at Temple Country House tend to be booked solid 2 months in advance; plan to book at least 3 weeks ahead for a midweek stay. Temple is an adults-only hotel.

Horseleap, Moate, County Westmeath. www.templespa.ie. ✆ **057/933-5118.** Fax 0506/35008. 25 units. €130–€190 double; €200–€290 suite. AE, MC, V. Free parking. **Amenities:** Restaurant; bike rental; sauna/steam room; spa. *In room:* TV.

Wineport Lodge ★★★ On weekends, this contemporary cedar lodge on Lough Ree is a haven for stressed-out Dubliners, who travel an hour to get here, and are rewarded with peace and quiet. Every room is named for a wine or wine region (Bollinger, Loire Valley, Tuscany), and all have panoramic views of the lake. The modern decor (sleek walnut furnishings, cream linens) and spacious bathrooms (with heated floors) ensure that you feel cosseted and cared for. To feel even more so, you can indulge in an array of beauty and massage treatments. Dining here is also an event and, as you might imagine, the wine list is excellent.

Glasson, Athlone, County Westmeath. www.wineport.ie. ✆ **090/643-9010.** 10 units. €180–€220 double. €200–€240 suite. AE, MC, V. Free parking. **Amenities:** Restaurant. *In room:* TV, hair dryer.

MODERATE

Brosna Lodge Hotel Although it sits on the main thoroughfare in Banagher, a busy river town near Clonmacnoise, this simple, two-story hotel has a warm country atmosphere, thanks to a beautiful, flower-filled front garden and enthusiastic innkeeper-owners Pat and Della Horan. The public areas are furnished with traditional period pieces and antiques, and there's a busy pub and restaurant. Guest rooms are bright and airy with simple decor, and most overlook the gardens or the town.

Main St., Banagher, County Offaly. www.brosnalodge.com. ✆ **057/915-1350.** 14 units. €100 double. Rates include full breakfast. MC, V. Free parking. **Amenities:** Restaurant; bar; lounge. *In room:* TV.

INEXPENSIVE

The Bastion ★★ In the heart of Athlone's Left Bank district, surrounded by good restaurants and just up the street from Athlone Castle, the Bastion is a marvelously contradictory place—the outside of the building is brightly painted in red and blue, but inside, it's all sophisticated pale hues, dark-wood floors, minimal furniture, and peace and quiet. Brothers Vinny and Anthony McCay have converted an old draper's shop into a lovely, relaxing place, with crisp white linens, comfortable beds, and modern art. Bathrooms are a bit of a squeeze, but they're perfectly adequate. In the morning, a big buffet breakfast of cereal, fresh bread, Irish cheeses, and fruit is served in the comfortable dining room—a healthy break from the usual B&B eggs and bacon. There are no TVs or telephones in rooms—you're here to relax. ***Note:*** There are lots of steep staircases here, so it's not for those with limited mobility.

2 Bastion St., Athlone, County Westmeath. www.thebastion.net. ✆ **090/649-4954.** Fax 090/649-3648. 6 units. €65–€80 double. Rates include continental breakfast. MC, V. *In room:* No phone.

Where to Eat

Most small towns in this area have little in the way of restaurant life. In some villages, the only place in town making food at all is the pub. But **Athlone** has a vibrant restaurant scene, with increasingly sophisticated restaurants and lots of coffee shops on its Left Bank, while **Shannonbridge** is improving as well. Along with the choices below, see the hotels listed above, as most have excellent restaurants.

EXPENSIVE

Crookedwood House ★★ MODERN IRISH An attractive country house with a fine restaurant and rooms to rent, Crookedwood is a good place to know about. Noel Kenny is a talented chef who delights in giving earthy flavors a kick. Dishes usually include things like grilled rack of lamb with an herb crust, or seafood in chardonnay. Guest rooms are spacious and nicely furnished, and best of all, they allow you to just fall into bed after one of those fabulous meals. Eight overnight accommodations are also available for €140 double (including full breakfast).

Crookedwood, Mullingar, County Westmeath. ✆ **044/72165.** Fax 044/72166. www.crookedwoodhouse.com. Early dinner Tues–Sat 6:30–7:30pm €26; main courses €22–€29. MC, V. Mon–Sat 6:30–10pm; Sun noon–2pm.

Left Bank Bistro ★ FUSION This smart little bistro is as sassy and bright as they come. The menu circles the earth, starting with Irish filet of beef with horseradish butter and moving on to Asia for prawns in wonton wraps and Italy for grilled chicken with Parmesan polenta. The food is good, the service cheerful and professional, the crowd happy and buzzing. ***Tip:*** The early-bird menu is actually available all night (except Sat, when it stops at 7:30pm).

Fry Place, Athlone, County Westmeath. ✆ **090/649-4446.** www.leftbankbistro.com. Reservations required. Main courses €18–€28; 3-course early-bird menu €28. AE, MC, V. Tues–Sat 10am–9:30pm.

MODERATE

Hatter's Lane ★ ☺ CONTINENTAL This warm and friendly restaurant right next to the excellent Gertie Browns pub has just the right casual but attractive Irish country feel. The food is a little of everything, from baked cod and grilled halibut to Malaysian chicken and grilled lamb kabobs, all served in large enough portions to please the heartiest appetite.

Strand St., Athlone, County Westmeath. ✆ **090/647-3077.** Main courses €9–€19. MC, V. Tues–Sat noon–5pm and 6–10pm.

INEXPENSIVE

A Slice of Life ★ CAFE This sunny, welcoming coffee shop just across from the Bastion guesthouse (above) serves breakfast rolls and croissants, sandwiches made to order, lots of vegetarian options, and soups made fresh each day. It's a great place for lunch, or for a cup of tea and a slice of cake. The staff members are so friendly, you'll want to take them home.

Bastion St., Athlone, County Westmeath. ✆ **090/649-3970.** www.asliceoflife.ie. Main courses €3–€6. No credit cards. Mon–Sat 8:30am–6pm.

Pubs

Gertie Browns This big, rambling pub on Athlone's Right Bank, just off the river, is a friendly place where everybody seems to know everybody else. A fire blazes at the hearth, a band sometimes strikes up an impromptu performance by the door, the Guinness is cold, and the atmosphere is warm. 9 Costume Place, Athlone, County Westmeath. ✆ **090/647-4848.**

Killeen's A few miles from Clonmacnoise, tucked into the little village of Shannonbridge, this is another good Irish boozer that has outgrown its pub-and-grocery-store origins. Along with a relaxed mood and friendly regulars come turf fires, excellent pints of Guinness, and faultless Irish coffees. Shannonbridge, County Offaly. ✆ **090/967-4112.**

Moran's Overlooking the Woodford River, this place (correct pronunciation is *Mor*-ins) is a traditional, old-style Irish pub, peddling groceries and pints with equal friendliness. It has plenty of shaded, outdoor seating with lovely views of the water. Woodford, County Galway. ✆ **090/974-9063.**

Sean's Bar 🎁 A fine place to shoot the breeze with the locals, or just to enjoy the live music (usually traditional) that's played nightly, Sean's Bar has low ceilings, good beer on tap, and friendly regulars. There's been a competition underway for years between this humble old pub and the Brazen Head in Dublin over which is the oldest pub in Ireland. The *Guinness Book of World Records* weighed in on Sean's side in 2004, and not long afterward, on an Irish radio program, the owner of the Brazen Head conceded that given its ancient walls and written evidence that it has been a pub through centuries, Sean's won—but only just. So there you have it. This ancient building—long and narrow with low ceilings and a fireplace at one end—has been a public house for more than 1,000 years. It doesn't look anything like that old from the outside, as the building has been much added to over the centuries, but fragments of the original walls were discovered during renovation work, and there are records of every owner to the year 900. That's a little something to think about as you're sipping your pint. 13 Main St., Athlone, County Westmeath. ✆ **090/649-2358.** www.seansbar.lightholderproductions.com.

12

MAYO, SLIGO & THE NORTH SHANNON VALLEY

The strikingly beautiful landscape of Galway continues to the strikingly beautiful landscape of southern Mayo without fanfare. Like Galway, Mayo is marked by dramatic scenery, which terminates in rocky cliffs plunging down into the opaque blue waters of the icy sea.

If you head farther north, you'll reach the smooth pastures of County Sligo. The main appeal here is not its towns, which tend to be functional farm communities, but the countryside. This is the landscape that soothed W. B. Yeats's soul and inspired his poetry. Sligo's unspoiled marvels are still a healing tonic. The county is filled with fairy-tale castles and mysterious prehistoric sites, but its biggest gift to you is peace.

Heading inland from Sligo, you'll reach the upper Shannon River valley, with its sprawling lakes, promising fresh trout and salmon, and nearly limitless watersports in the summer.

COUNTY MAYO

Ballina: 101km (63 miles) N of Galway, 193km (120 miles) N of Shannon Airport, 246km (153 miles) NW of Dublin, 311km (193 miles) NW of Cork

Serenely beautiful, County Mayo sits in the shadow of its more famous neighbor, Galway, and doesn't seem to mind. For experienced Ireland travelers, Mayo is a kind of Galway Lite—its rugged coastal scenery is similar to that of Galway, but it has less of the traffic or tourist overload from which Galway suffers in the summer. This is peaceful, pleasant Ireland, with striking seascapes and inland scenery that ranges from lush and green to stark, desertlike, and mountainous. It's an unpredictable place, where the terrain changes at the turn of a steering wheel. This region was hit so hard by the potato famine that, in some ways, it's only now recovering. Starvation and emigration emptied it then, and that emptiness is still noticeable. It feels, as you leave Galway, as if it all goes quiet.

For some, the county's most familiar history is cinematic; Mayo was the setting for the 1951 John Ford film *The Quiet Man,* starring John Wayne and Maureen O'Hara. The setting for the film was the town of **Cong.** There's little to see there except for the scant remains of the stone cottage used in the film, which has been gradually torn apart over the years by people who want to bring home one of its stones. (We strongly request that you do not take anything except photographs—as do the locals.) Guided tours of the locations used in the

Irish Only: Brush Up Your Gaeltacht

Parts of Mayo are in the Gaeltacht, or Irish-language section of the country. In some sections, this means town names are in Irish only, so we'll include the Irish names as well as the English names for the places likely to be affected. Confusingly, most maps are still in English only.

PREVIOUS PAGE: **A cottage in County Sligo at the base of Ben Bulben.**

film are available from the **Quiet Man Movie Club.** They have to be booked by a group of four; the all-in cost is €200 for a half-day or €300 for a full-day tour, and cover up to 193km (120 miles) round-trip. Contact Paddy Rock (✆ **087/243-9760;** paddy@quietmanmovieclub.com or info@culchiefestival.com) for more information. Among Mayo's other attractions are the mysterious 5,000-year-old settlement at **Céide Fields,** the religious shrine at **Knock,** and some of Europe's best fishing waters at **Lough Conn, Lough Mask,** and the **River Moy. Ballina *(Béal an Átha),*** Mayo's largest town, calls itself the home of the Irish salmon. And **Westport** is a little resort town guaranteed to steal your heart.

County Mayo Essentials

GETTING THERE Several airlines serve **Ireland West Airport Knock,** Charlestown, County Mayo (✆ **094/936-8100;** www.irelandwestairport.com). From Dublin you can fly **Aer Arann** (✆ **011/353-81821-0210** in the U.S., 0818/210-210 in Ireland, or 0870/876-7676 in the U.K.; www.aerarann.ie); from the U.K., **Aer Lingus** flies from London Gatwick (✆ **0818/365-000** in Ireland; www.aerlingus.com); **Ryanair** (**0818/303-030** in Ireland; www.ryanair.com) flies from London Luton and Stanstead; and **bmibaby** (✆ **1890/340-122** in Ireland; www.bmibaby.com) serves Knock from Manchester and Birmingham. The U.K. airline **Flybe** (✆ **01392/268-529** in the U.K.; www.flybe.com) also flies from Edinburgh.

Irish Rail (✆ **096/20229;** www.irishrail.ie) and **Bus Éireann** (✆ **096/71800;** www.buseireann.ie) provide daily service from Dublin and other cities into Ballina, Westport, and Castlebar, with bus connections into smaller towns. There is also express service from Galway into most Mayo towns.

From Dublin and points east, the main N5 road leads to many points in County Mayo; from Galway, take N84 or N17. From Sligo and points north, take N17 or N59. To get around County Mayo, it's best to rent a car. Firms with outlets at Ireland West Airport include **Avis** (✆ **094/936-7707;** www.avis.ie), **Budget** (✆ **090/662-4668;** www.budget.ie), **Hertz**

Westport is a handsome, vibrant town on Clew Bay in County Mayo.

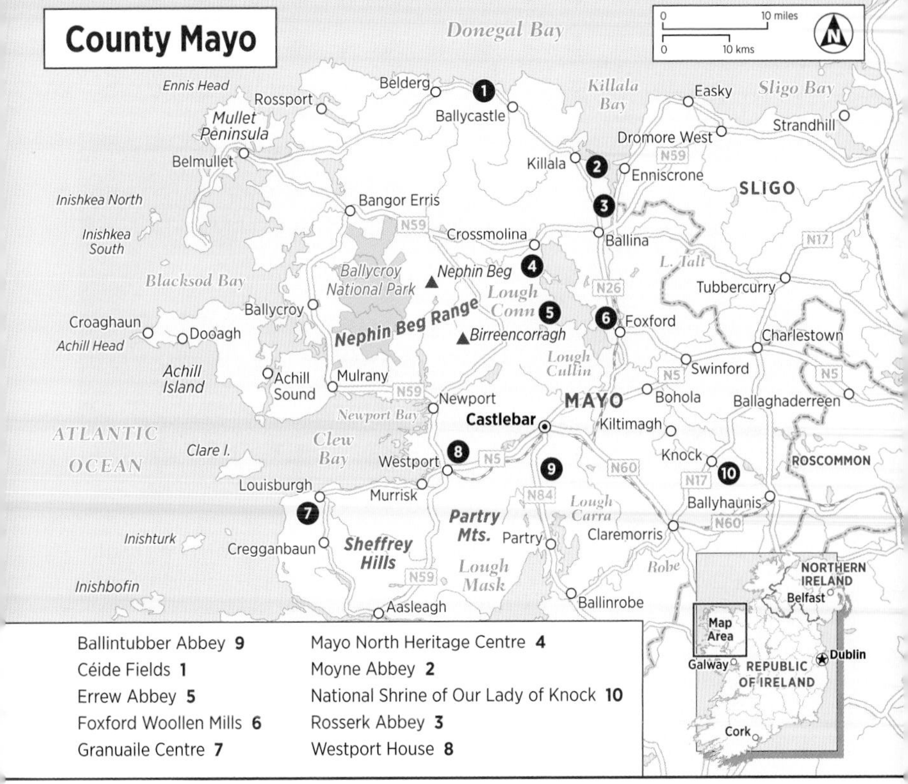

(✆ **094/936-7333;** www.hertz.ie), and **Irish Car Rentals** (✆ **061/206-094;** www.irishcarrentals.com.ie).

VISITOR INFORMATION For year-round information, visit or contact the **Westport Tourist Office,** The Mall, Westport (✆ **098/25711;** www.westporttourism.com). It's open Monday to Saturday from 9am to 6pm (1pm on Sat Nov–Apr). There is no longer a tourism office at Ireland West Airport.

Seasonal tourist offices, open from May or June to September or October, are the **Ballina Tourist Office,** Cathedral Road, Ballina, County Mayo (✆ 096/70848); **Castlebar Tourist Office,** Linenhall Street, Castlebar, County Mayo (✆ 094/902-1207); **Knock Village Tourist Office,** Knock (✆ 094/938-8193); **Cong Village Tourist Office** (✆ 094/954-6542); and **Achill Tourist Office,** Achill Sound (✆ 098/45384).

Exploring the County

Because it's a rural county with no major cities or many large towns, County Mayo feels a bit like a place without a center. Towns like Castlebar, Claremorris, Westport, and Ballinrobe in the southern part of the county, and Ballina in the northern reaches, make good places to stop, refill the tank, and have lunch, but they offer little to make you linger. The county's attractions lie in the countryside, and in smaller communities like Foxford, Ballycastle, Louisburgh, and Newport.

With its sandy beaches and heathery bogs, Achill Island is a beautiful refuge from civilization.

County Mayo's loveliest town, **Westport (*Cathair na Mairt*) ★**, nestles on the shores of Clew Bay. Once a major port, it was designed by Richard Castle with a tree-lined mall, rows of Georgian buildings, and an octagonal central mall where a vibrant market adds zest to the town on Thursdays.

Southeast of Westport, **Croagh Patrick,** a 750m (2,460-ft.) mountain, dominates the views of western Mayo for miles. St. Patrick is said to have spent the 40 days of Lent praying here in the year 441. To commemorate that, on the last Sunday of July, thousands of Irish people make a pilgrimage to the site, which has become known as St. Patrick's Holy Mountain.

Heading west, the rugged, bog-filled, sparsely populated coast makes for scenic drives to secluded outposts. Leading the list is **Achill Island (*An Caol*) ★**, a heather-filled bog land with sandy beaches and spectacular views of waves crashing against rocky cliffs. The drive from the mainland and then across the island to the little town of Keel requires patience and skill, but rewards you with a camera filled with photos. **Clare Island,** once the home of Mayo's legendary "Pirate Queen," Grace O'Malley, is another scenic isle, south of Achill in Clew Bay.

Like the drive to Achill Island, the road from Ballina along the edge of the northern coast to Downpatrick Head is breathtaking. It passes through **Killala** (***Cill Alaidh*** or ***Cill Ála***), a small, secluded harbor village that came close to changing the course of Ireland's history. In 1798, the French General Amable Humbert landed here with 1,100 troops in an attempt to help the Irish defeat the British forces. After several surprisingly successful fights with troops under British command, particularly a thorough routing at Castlebar, Humbert had attracted thousands of Irish volunteers who fought by his side. At that point, the British sent General Cornwallis (the same general who surrendered to Washington at Yorktown in 1781) to take him on in Longford, with thousands of well-armed troops. The battle lasted only half an hour before Humbert surrendered. The French soldiers were treated honorably, but the Irish volunteers who had fought with Humbert, and anybody suspected of sympathizing with him, were slaughtered.

Outside Killala on the road R314 to **Ballina (*Béal an Átha*)** are several ruined friaries worth a stop for those who love the blurred beauty of ancient abbeys. **Moyne Abbey** was established in the mid-1400s and destroyed by

A lone columnar outpost in the open sea, Downpatrick Head stands strong against the Atlantic's toughest blows.

Richard Bingham, the English governor of Connaught, in the 16th century. It's a peaceful place, and you can see why the monks chose it. The same is true, even more so, of **Rosserk Abbey** about 3km (2 miles) away. Sitting at the edge of the River Rosserk, the abbey is in much better shape than the Moyne: Its chapel windows are well preserved. You can climb a winding stone stair to look out across the bay. The piscina of the church (once used for washing altar vessels) is still here, carved with angels, and on its lower-left-hand column is a delightful detail: a tiny, elegant carving of a round tower that recalls its 23m-tall (75-ft.) counterpart in nearby Killala. The Rosserk Abbey was built at the same time as the Moyne and also destroyed by Bingham's troops.

Riverside Rosserk Abbey is beautifully preserved, with views across the bay.

Ballintubber Abbey ★ This abbey is a survivor—one of few Irish churches in continuous use for almost 800 years. Founded in 1216 by Cathal O'Connor, king of Connaught, it has endured fires, numerous attacks, illnesses, and anti-Catholic pogroms. Although Oliver Cromwell's forces so thoroughly dismantled the abbey that they even carried off its roof in 1653 in an effort to finally suppress it, clerics continued discreetly conducting religious rites. Today it's an impressive church, with 13th-century windows on the right side of the nave and a doorway dating to the 15th century. It was completely restored in 1966. A helpful visitor center illuminates its troubled and fascinating history. Guided tours are available weekdays from 10am to 5pm; there's no charge but donations of €4 per person are requested.

Off the main Galway-Castlebar rd. (N84), about 32km (20 miles) west of Knock, Ballintubber, County Mayo. ✆ **094/903-0934.** www.ballintubberabbey.ie. Free admission; donations welcome. Daily 9am–midnight.

Céide Fields ★★ In a breathtaking setting, above huge chalk cliffs that plunge hundreds of feet into a deep blue sea, ancient people once lived, worked, and buried their dead—a fact that nobody knew until the 1930s, when a local farmer named Patrick Caulfield noticed stones piled in strange patterns in his fields. More than 40 years later, his son Seamus, by then an archaeologist, explored his father's discovery (he became a scientist in part because he wanted to understand the stones he'd played among as a child). Under the turf, he found Stone Age fields, megalithic tombs, and the foundations of a village. Standing amid it now, you can see a pattern of farm fields as they were laid out 5,000 years ago (predating the construction of the Egyptian pyramids). Preserved for millennia beneath the bog, the site is both fascinating and inscrutable; to a casual observer, it's all little more than piles of stones, but the visitor center makes it meaningful in a series of displays, films, and tours. The pyramid-shaped center itself is designed to fit in with the dramatic surroundings—you can see the building for miles. It also contains a **cafeteria,** which comes as a relief since this site is 20 hilly, rocky kilometers (12 miles) of winding roads from anywhere.

On R314, the coastal road north of Ballina, btw. Ballycastle and Belderrig, Ballycastle, County Mayo. ✆ **096/43325.** www.museumsofmayo.com/ceide.htm. Admission €4 adults; €3 seniors; €2 students and children; €10 families. Easter to May and Oct daily 10am–5pm; June–Sept daily 10am–6pm.

At Céide Fields, a seaside bog preserved the remains of a Stone Age farm settlement for more than 5,000 years.

A TRIP TO CLARE island

Lying just about 5km (3 miles) off the Mayo coast, just beyond Clew Bay, **Clare Island** is a place of unspoiled splendor. Inhabited for 5,000 years and once quite populous—1,700 people lived there in the early 19th century—Clare is now home to 150 year-round islanders, plus perhaps as many sheep. But the island is best known as the haunt of Grace O'Malley, the "Pirate Queen" who controlled the coastal waters 400 years ago (for more on O'Malley, see the box below).

O'Malley's modest castle and the partially restored Cistercian Abbey where she is buried are among the island's few attractions. The rest of the draw is its remote natural beauty. Two ferry services operate out of Roonagh Harbour, 29km (18 miles) south of Westport; fares run about €15 round-trip for the 15-minute journey: **O'Malley's Ferry Service,** aboard the *Island Princess* (✆ **098/25045;** www.omalleyferries.com), and **Clare Island Ferries,** aboard the *Pirate Queen* (✆ **098/23737;** www.clareislandferry.com).

If you want a proper tour of the island, look for Ludwig Timmerman's 1974 Land Rover. Ludwig is notoriously uncontactable, but if you should see him around, he offers cordial, informative tours from June to August. Otherwise, your transport options are rented mountain bikes or your own feet.

Errew Abbey This atmospheric, ruined 13th-century Augustinian church sits on a tiny peninsula in Lough Conn. The cloister is well preserved, as is the chancel with altar and piscina. There's also an oratory with massive stone walls in fields adjacent to the abbey—on the site of a church founded in the 6th century, and known locally by the marvelous, tongue-twistery name *Templenagalliaghdoo,* which means "Church of the Black Nun."

Signposted about 3.2km (2 miles) south of Crossmolina on the Castlebar rd., then 5km (3 miles) down a side road, County Mayo. No phone. Free admission.

Foxford Woollen Mills Visitor Centre Founded in 1892 by a local nun to provide work for a community ravaged by the effects of the Irish famine, Foxford Woollen Mills brought prosperity to the area through the worldwide sales of beautiful tweeds, rugs, and blankets. Using a multimedia presentation, the center tells the story of this local industry, then offers an on-site tour of the working mills. Tours run every 20 minutes and last approximately 45 minutes. A restaurant, shop, exhibition center, art gallery, heritage room, and other craft units (including a doll-making workshop) are also part of the visit.

Off the Foxford-Ballina rd. (N57), 16km (10 miles) south of Ballina, St. Joseph's Place, Foxford, County Mayo. ✆ **094/925-6104.** www.museumsofmayo.com/foxford.htm. Admission €4 adults; €3 seniors, students, and children; €9 families. May–Oct Mon–Sat 10am–6pm, Sun noon–6pm; Nov–Apr Mon–Sat 10am–6pm, Sun 2–6pm. Last tour 30 min. before closing.

Granuaile Centre ★ This interesting center (pronounced *Graw-nya-wayl*) in an old, converted church, is dedicated to the life and story of one of Ireland's great female heroes, Grace O'Malley (1530–1600). Known by the ferocious sobriquet "the Pirate Queen," she led battles against the English and ruled the seas in these parts. (See "Local Hero: Pirate Grace O'Malley," below.) Parts of the center also address the Great Famine that killed an estimated 100,000 people in County Mayo.

Louisburgh, County Mayo. ✆ **098/66341.** Admission €4 adults; €2 seniors and students; students and children free if accompanied by parents. June to mid-Sept Mon–Sat 10am–6pm.

Mayo North Heritage Centre If you're tracing your Mayo family tree, you'll want to stop in here. The data bank includes indexes to church registers of all denominations, plus school records, leases, and wills. There's a somewhat incongruous adjacent museum, with displays of rural household items, farm machinery, and farm implements. The lovely **Enniscoe Gardens** adjoin the center; combined tickets to the center and gardens are a good deal. There is a handy tearoom on the premises should you need a break.

On Lough Conn, about 3.2km (2 miles) south of Crossmolina, off R315, Enniscoe, Castlehill, Ballina, County Mayo. ✆ **096/31809.** www.mayo.irish-roots.net. Museum admission €5 adults; €3 children; €8 families. Combined ticket with gardens €6 adults; €4 children; €15 families. Oct–May Mon–Fri 9am–4pm; June–Sept Mon–Fri 9am–6pm, Sat–Sun 2–6pm.

National Shrine of Our Lady of Knock/Church of the Apparition ★ This is Ireland's version of Lourdes, and Catholic pilgrims (mostly Irish Catholic) come here in droves. It all dates from a day in August 1879 when two young local girls said they saw Joseph, Mary, and St. John standing in bright light in front of the southern tower of the parish church. Soon, 13 other witnesses claimed to have seen the same thing, and the Church declared it a miracle. Before long, miracles were occurring fast and furious, as sick and lame visitors claimed to be healed after visits to the church. Knock came to the world's attention in 1979, when Pope John Paul II visited the shrine. There's not much to the town of Knock on the whole—it sits unspectacularly at the intersection of the N17 and R323 (it's not even on some maps of Ireland, it's so small)—but it's filled with increasingly large, modern religious structures, including a huge circular basilica that seats 7,000 and contains artifacts or furnishings from every county in Ireland.

RoolaBoola Childrens Arts Festival

Now in its 13th year, RoolaBoola is a festival of children's theater, film, and arts workshops at the Linenhall Arts Centre in Castlebar. The festival has been growing in prominence over the last few years and now attracts professional theater companies from all over the world. What particularly appeals about this festival is that, although the plays are aimed very firmly at children, they are intelligent, well-produced pieces of theater that don't talk down to their audience. Recent productions have included a children's opera about the Pied Piper's boyhood and a funny and sensitive play about the Kindertransport. There are also film screenings and workshops, some of which don't need to be prebooked. Expect to pay about €6 to €10 per ticket. Family tickets cost €25 and admit four to any show; a few activities are free. For more information and details on how to book, call the box office at ✆ 094/902-3733 or 902-8886, or visit the festival website, www.thelinenhall.com/roola-boola. The festival program runs for a week in late October, and the program is usually announced in early September.

Lord Altamont, a wealthy descendant of Pirate Queen Grace OMalley, resided at lovely Westport House, now open to the public.

The grounds also hold a folk museum (displays include original letters pertaining to the apparition) and a religious bookshop.

On the N17 Galway rd., Knock, County Mayo. ✆ **094/938-8100.** www.knock-shrine.ie. Free admission to shrine. Museum €4 adults; €3 seniors and children age 5 and over; €3.50 students; free for children 4 and under. Shrine and grounds year-round daily 8am–6pm or later. Museum May–Oct daily 10am–6pm; Nov–Apr. Daily noon–4pm.

Westport House ☺ At the edge of the town of Westport, this late-18th-century residence is the home of Lord Altamont, the marquis of Sligo, and a descendant, it is said, of Pirate Queen Grace O'Malley—thus, the bronze statue of her on the grounds. The work of Richard Cassels and James Wyatt, the house has a graceful staircase of ornate white Sicilian marble, unusual Art Nouveau glass and carvings, family heirlooms, and silver. The grandeur of the residence is undeniable, but purists might be put off by the fact that the sprawling gardens are quite a commercial enterprise these days, with a **Pirate Adventure Park,** swan-shaped pedal boats on the lake, a kid-size train tooting its way through the gardens, a children's zoo, an aviary, and more. And if you don't mind paying up to €40 extra per person, you can also take part in various 2-hour activity sessions, including laser clay pigeon shooting and archery, although some of these require a group of at least five.

Westport, County Mayo. ✆ **098/25430** or 27766. www.westporthouse.ie. Admission to house and gardens €12 adults; €8.50 seniors and students; €6.50 children. House, gardens, and adventure park €24 adults; €18 seniors and students; €17 children; €75 families. House and gardens: Mar and Oct Sat–Sun only 10am–4pm; mid-Apr through June and Sept daily 10am–6pm; July–Aug daily 10am–7pm. Open for special events only Nov–Feb (call or see website for listings). Adventure Park: May–June daily noon–6pm; July–Aug daily noon–7pm. Mar to mid-Apr, Sept, and Oct by pre-booking only; closed Nov to Feb, except school holidays.

Sports & Outdoor Pursuits

FISHING The waters of the River Moy and loughs Carrowmore and Conn are known for good fishing, particularly for salmon and trout. For general information about fishing in County Mayo, contact the **Inland Fisheries Ireland,** Abbey Street, Ballina (✆ **096/22788;** www.fishinginireland.info). To arrange a day's fishing, contact **Cloonamoyne Fishery ★**, Castlehill, near Crossmolina, Ballina (✆ **096/51156** or 087/314-8449; www.cloonamoynefishery.com). Managed by an Irish-born former New Yorker, Barry Segrave, this professional angling service will advise and equip you to fish the local waters—for brown trout on loughs Conn and Cullin; for salmon on loughs Beltra, Furnace, and Feeagh; and for salmon and sea trout on the rivers Moy and Deel. The fishery rents fully equipped boats and tackle, teaches fly-casting, and provides transport to and from all fishing. Daily rates are €40 for a rowboat, €60 for a boat with engine, and €120 for a boat with engine and *ghillie* (guide).

County Mayo is also home to the **Pontoon Bridge Hotel Fly Fishing School,** Pontoon, County Mayo (✆ **094/925-6120;** www.pontoonbridge.com), where you don't need to be a hotel guest to enjoy the fishing or the courses. Daily rates for fishing on loughs Conn and Cullin are €40 for a rowboat, €60 for a boat with engine, and €120 for a boat with engine and *ghillie.* For fishing on the River Moy the fee is €30 to €40 per rod, per day, or €130 to €250 for fishing on private water. You will also need to buy a permit, which can be arranged by the hotel. The Fly Fishing School offers a 1-day course in the art of fly-casting, as well as fly-tying, tackle design, beginners courses, and other information necessary for successful game fishing. Fees are around €120 per person. Courses run daily year-round if there is demand. The recently expanded Pontoon Bridge Hotel also runs painting and cooking classes.

Permits and state fishing licenses can be obtained at the **Mayo Angling Advice Centre,** at the Tiernan Bros. fishing tackle shop, Upper Main Street, Foxford, County Mayo (✆ **094/945-6731;** www.tiernanbrothers.8k.com). It also offers a range of services, including boat hire and *ghillies.*

For fishing tackle, try, **Kingfisher Bates,** Pier Road, Enniscrone, County Mayo (✆ **096/36733**), or **Ridge Pool Tackle Shop,** Cathedral Road, Ballina, County Mayo (✆ **096/72656**). On Achill Island, get sea-angling gear at **O'Malley's Island Sports** on the main road (next to the post office) in Keel (✆ **098/43125**). O'Malley's can also arrange boat hire and bike hire.

GOLF County Mayo's 18-hole golf courses include a par-71 inland course at **Castlebar Golf Club,** Rocklands, Castlebar, County Mayo (✆ **094/902-1649;** www.castlebargolfclub.ie), has greens fees of €25 weekdays and €35 weekends (couples get a €20 discount). They sometimes run special deals that include a meal at the clubhouse for very little extra, especially out of season. The par-73 championship course at **Westport Golf Club,** County Mayo (✆ **098/28262;** www.golfwestport.com), charges varied greens fees of €30 weekdays (except on Wednesdays, when the fee is €25), €50 weekends. On the shores of Clew Bay, the challenging and scenic course winds around the slopes of Croagh Patrick Mountain.

LOCAL hero: PIRATE GRACE O'MALLEY

Grace O'Malley, the "Pirate Queen," was born in 1530 on Clare Island. She was, by all accounts, ahead of her time. A heroine, adventurer, pirate, gambler, mercenary, traitor, chieftain, and noblewoman, she is remembered now with affection, although at the time she was feared and despised. Even as a child, she was fiercely independent. When her mother refused to let her sail with her father, she cut off her hair and dressed in boys' clothing. Her father called her *"Grainne Mhaol,"* or "Bald Grace," later shortened to Granuaile (pronounced *Graw-nya-wayl*), a nickname she'd carry all her life.

At 16, Grace married Donal O'Flaherty, second in line to the O'Flaherty clan chieftain, who ruled all of Connacht. A few years later, her career as a pirate began when the city of Galway, one of the largest trade centers in the British Isles, refused to trade with the O'Flahertys. Grace used her fleet of fast galleys to waylay slower vessels on their way into Galway Harbour. She then offered safe passage for a fee in lieu of pillaging the ships.

She is most fondly remembered for refusing to trade her lands in return for an English title, a common practice of the day.

When the English captured her sons in 1593, she went to London to try and secure their release. In an extraordinary turn of events, she actually secured a meeting with Queen Elizabeth. History records that, just as remarkably, the two women got on quite well (although legend has it that Grace initially tried to smuggle a knife in with her, in case things went differently). A deal was struck; Elizabeth agreed to release her sons, and to return some captured lands, if Grace would agree to renounce piracy. This she did, and returned to Ireland, triumphant.

The truce did not last, however. She got her sons back, but not her property. She took up piracy again and continued it until her death from natural causes in 1600.

To this day, the Irish think of Granuaile as a national hero, and a defender of the Gaelic way of life.

KAYAKING Courses for adults and children are at the **Atlantic Adventure Centre,** in Lecanvey, just outside of Westport, County Mayo (✆ **098/64806;** www.atlanticadventurecentre.com). Most of the kayaking is done at the Blue Flag beaches at Old Head, Bertra, and Carramore. Very reasonable accommodations rates are available for campers. The adventure center has all you need for a wide range of activities, from canoeing to rock climbing. Call for details.

The windy beaches of Achill Island are a magnet for surfers and windsurfers.

WALKING The region to the east of the Mullet peninsula has a spectacular array of sheer sea cliffs and craggy islands. The small, secluded beach at **Portacloy,** 14km (8⅔ miles) north of Glenamoy on the R314, is a good starting point for a dramatic walk. On a sunny day, its aquamarine waters and fine-grained white sand recall the Mediterranean more than the North Atlantic. At its western edge, there is a concrete quay. From here, head north up the steep green slopes of the nearest hill. Don't be too distracted by the fantastic view or adorable little sheep: The boggy slopes on which you are walking end precipitously at an unmarked cliff edge—the walk is not recommended for children. Exercise caution and resist the urge to try to get a better view of the mysterious sea caves or to reach the outermost extent of the coast's promontories. Instead, use a farmer's fence as a guide and head west toward the striking profile of **Benwee Head,** about 2.4km (1½ miles) away. Return the same way to have a swim in the chilly, tranquil waters of Portacloy.

WINDSURFING & OTHER WATERSPORTS The constant wind off the Atlantic Ocean means that Achill Island is ideal for windsurfing, hang gliding, or any activities that involve a breeze. If you want to try it out, talk with Richie O'Hara at **McDowell's Hotel & Activity Centre** (Slievemore Road, near Dugort; ✆ **098/43148**). He also gives surfing instructions and advice on rock climbing, and rents out canoes and surfboards. For other options, contact the useful Atlantic Adventure Centre (see above).

Where to Stay

VERY EXPENSIVE

Ashford Castle ★★★ Turrets, towers, drawbridge, and battlements: Ashford has them all. The structure dates from the 13th century, when it was built for the De Burgo (Burke) family. Later it became a country residence of the Guinness clan. A hotel since 1939, it has been enlarged and updated over the years. It drew worldwide media attention in 1984 when President Ronald Reagan stayed here during his visit to Ireland; in 2001, the Irish actor Pierce Brosnan held his wedding here. Reflected in the glassy waters of Lough Corrib, the castle sits regally amid vast forested, flowering grounds. The fairy tale continues inside with antiques, medieval armor, carved oak paneling, and museum-quality paintings. Bedrooms convey an air of privilege with heavy fabrics, soft carpets, and big, comfortable beds. The restaurant serves respectable European cuisine with a stiffly formal attitude—jacket and tie are required for men after 7pm. There are two bars—the jovial **Dungeon** and the **Prince of Wales Cocktail Bar,** which has the air of a men's club. Check online before booking, as specials are often offered outside of the high season.

Cong, County Mayo. www.ashford.ie. ✆ **800/346-7007** in the U.S., or 092/954-6003. Fax 092/954-6260. www.ashford.ie. 83 units. €376–€476 double; €650–€950 staterooms and suites. Rates include service charge. AE, DC, MC, V. **Amenities:** Restaurant; 2 bars; babysitting; concierge; 9-hole golf course; gym; Jacuzzi; room service; sauna; spa; tennis court. *In room:* TV, hair dryer, minibar.

EXPENSIVE

Enniscoe House ★★ This is a terrific place for unwinding and escaping the real world. Overlooking Lough Conn and surrounded by an extensive wooded estate, complete with nature walks, this two-story Georgian country inn is owned and run by Susan Kellett, a descendant of a family who settled on the lands in the 1660s. Inside Enniscoe is truly magnificent, with delicate plasterwork, lovely fireplaces, and a grand staircase. Guest rooms are individually furnished; those at the front of the house are particularly impressive, with hand-carved armoires and canopied beds. All rooms have views of parkland or the lake. Meals feature locally caught fish and vegetables and herbs from the adjacent garden. Enniscoe also has its own fishery (see Cloonamoyne Fishery under "Fishing" in "Sports & Outdoor Pursuits," above). Self-catering apartments are available.

3.2km (2 miles) south of Crossmolina, off R315, next to the North Mayo Heritage Centre, Castlehill, near Crossmolina, Ballina, County Mayo. www.enniscoe.com. ✆ **800/223-6510** in the U.S., or 096/31112. Fax 096/31773. 6 units. €220–€260 double. Self-catering cottages €480–€800 per week. Dinner €50. Rates include full breakfast. AE, MC, V. Closed Nov–Mar. **Amenities:** Smoke-free rooms. *In room:* TV.

Mount Falcon Castle ★★ This sternly beautiful gray-stone manor house has a striking setting just south of Ballina amid lush forests and lakes. It was built in 1876 by the same man responsible for the exterior of Ashford Castle, and was renovated in 2006 in luxurious style. The expansion tripled the number of guest rooms and also changed the property from one of near total isolation to a somewhat busier place, by adding three private home developments to the estate. A spa with a heated pool has been added for hotel guests, and the house's kitchen has been turned into a 72-seat **restaurant** with an attractive bar. Forty-five modern, chalet-style self-catering suites are also available. They are located in three separate parts of the estate, in groups of 12 to 17 units, with views overlooking the lake, forest, or a private courtyard.

Foxford rd. (N57), Ballina, County Mayo. www.mountfalcon.com. ✆ **800/223-6510** in the U.S., or 096/74472. Fax 096/74473. 32 units. €180–€240 double; €480 suite. Rates include full breakfast. Self-catering lodges €420–€720 per night. AE, DC, MC, V. Closed Feb–Mar and Christmas week. **Amenities:** Restaurant; bar; pool; spa; tennis court. *In room:* TV, hair dryer.

Newport House Hotel ★★ Close to the Clew Bay coast, this ivy-covered Georgian mansion house is a lovely place to stay. Its architectural detail is excellent and includes fine, ornate plasterwork on the soaring ceilings and a sky-lit dome above the cascading central staircase. It all feels a bit like a lavish period film—with heavy antique furnishings and big oil paintings. The guest rooms are divided between the main house and two smaller courtyard buildings, one of which used to belong to Sean Lemass, who was taoiseach (prime minister) during John F. Kennedy's visit in 1963. The rooms are spacious and elegant, with sash windows, high ceilings, and original paintings and prints. The **restaurant** is a destination in itself and a place of pilgrimage for food lovers (half-board rates are available). As the hotel sits at the edge of Newport Town along the Newport River, it's an excellent base for salmon anglers, and packages that include a day's fishing are sometimes posted on the hotel's website. All that said, though, prices are still a bit high for what's on offer here.

Newport, County Mayo. www.newporthouse.ie. ✆ **800/223-6510** in the U.S., or 098/41222. Fax 098/41613. 18 units. €228–€496 double. Rates include full breakfast. AE, DC, MC, V. Closed Oct–Feb. **Amenities:** Restaurant; bar. *In room:* TV, hair dryer.

MODERATE

The Bervie ★★★ Standing strong at the edge of the sea, the Bervie seems to cradle you protectively within its sturdy walls. Once a coast guard station, the whitewashed building has been a hotel for two generations. Owner Elizabeth Barrett was born and raised here, where her mother ran a guesthouse for decades. A few years back, Elizabeth and her husband, John, took over and upgraded the building and made it into what it is today—a snug, relaxing, attractive place to stay. Many rooms have views of the sea (it's just a few feet away), and all are decorated in soothing tones with distinctive, locally made furniture and art. The large, relaxing lounge is filled with tastefully appointed chairs and sofas and is heated by an open fireplace. The sunny breakfast room has dramatic views of the sea and the cliffs across the bay. Breakfasts are out of this world, including homemade cereals, Elizabeth's delectable jams, and a variety of egg options, including light and fluffy scrambled eggs with smoked salmon. Excellent dinners are also available if you book in advance.

From Westport, take the N59 to Achill Island, then the R319 across the island to the village of Keel, where the Bervie is signposted, County Mayo. www.bervie-guesthouse-achill.com. ✆ **098/43114.** Fax 098/43407. 14 units. €100–€130 double. Dinner from €45. Rates include full breakfast. MC, V. Closed Nov–Mar. **Amenities:** Smoke-free rooms. *In room:* TV.

INEXPENSIVE

Drom Caoin ★ ☺ From Mairin Maguire-Murphy's comfortable home, a short walk from the center of Belmullet, there are panoramic views of Blacksod Bay and Achill Island. Two of the guest rooms have recently been renovated into self-catering apartments that can be rented by the night or week, with or without breakfast. It's a great concept—you can cook your own meals and enjoy the extra space of a suite. The other two bedrooms are small, with compact bathrooms. Breakfast is something to look forward to here—omelets, fresh fish, and toasted cheese are offered periodically, and the fresh scones are delicious.

Belmullet, County Mayo. www.belmullet-accommodation.com. ✆/fax **097/81195.** 4 units, 2 with shower only. From €74–€80 double; €70–€80 apartment. B&B; €450–€550 apt. by the week (without breakfast). 33% reduction for children. MC, V. **Amenities:** Wi-Fi (free). *In room:* TV.

Where to Eat

MODERATE

Achill Cliff House SEAFOOD With sweeping views of the bay and the Minaun Cliffs beyond, the restaurant in the Achill Cliff House hotel in Keel is one of a few good options on Achill Island. As it's just a few yards from the sea, the menu leans toward seafood, with fresh mussels and seafood chowder both good options as starters. For main courses, there are grilled plaice, Clew Bay oysters, and fresh Atlantic lobster. All entrees come with generous portions of fresh vegetables, as well as the decadent house garlic-cheese potatoes. Service is relaxed and friendly, and the mood is one of infectious holiday pleasure. If you decide to spend the night, bedrooms here are basic but comfortable, with modern en suite bathrooms; prices range from €70 to €100 for a double, depending on the time of year.

Main St., Keel, Achill Island, County Mayo. ✆ **098/43400.** www.achillcliff.com. Fixed-price 3-course dinner €27; main courses €21–€26. MC, V. Daily 6:30–10pm.

An Port Mor ★ SEAFOOD/MODERN IRISH This gorgeous, friendly little place has won a string of awards, and one bite will tell you why. Locally sourced seafood is a specialty, all fresh and expertly prepared. You may start with Inishturk crab and gruyere cheese tart, before going on to filet of Achill Island sea trout in a white-wine cream and chive sauce, or Clew Bay scallops cooked with lemon, saffron, and fennel. The atmosphere is laid-back, and the slightly over-the-top, faux-Mediterranean decor adds to the jovial feel (it's left over, apparently, from the restaurant's previous incarnation as an Italian trattoria).

Bridge St., Westport, County Mayo. ✆ **098/26730.** www.anportmor.com. Main courses €15–€28. MC, V. Daily 6–10pm.

The Helm MODERN IRISH This dependable local eatery occupies a handsome position overlooking the harbor in Westport. The food is tasty and unpretentious—typical mains include pork chops in cream sauce, filet steak or a classic roast rack of lamb—though fresh seafood is the real specialty, which, given that they have their own fishing boat, makes sense. The catch of the day might include monkfish medallions or black sole with lemon and herb butter. It can get pretty busy here on weekends, so do book ahead.

The Harbour, Westport, County Mayo. ✆ **098/26398.** www.thehelm.ie. Main courses €15–€20. MC, V. Daily 6–10pm.

INEXPENSIVE

La Bella Vita ★ ITALIAN Its name means "the Beautiful Life," and this relaxed feel-good Italian wine bar-cum-restaurant delivers with good pasta, risotto, veal, poultry, and game in a romantic atmosphere, complete with open fires and candlelight. Start with the antipasti or bruschetta, and leave room for one of the homemade desserts. The food is complemented by a great wine list.

High St., Westport, County Mayo. ✆ **098/29771.** Reservations not accepted. Main courses €8–€17. MC, V. Tues–Sun 6–10pm.

SLIGO & YEATS COUNTRY

Sligo Town: 219km (136 miles) NE of Shannon Airport, 217km (135 miles) NW of Dublin, 76km (47 miles) NE of Knock, 60km (37 miles) NE of Ballina, 140km (87 miles) NE of Galway, 118km (73 miles) N of Athlone, 337km (209 miles) N of Cork

Sligo Town (pop. 18,000) is a thriving farm town on the south side of the River Garavogue, surrounded on three sides by mountains, the most famous of which are Ben Bulben to the north and Knocknarea to the south. A gray and somber town, with a mix of historic and less interesting modern architecture, Sligo is undergoing something of a renaissance—albeit one that has, like the rest of the country, hit difficult times due to the economic crisis. Roughly half of the town center has been refurbished in the past decade. From a visitor's perspective, the focus of this has been Sligo's new "Left Bank," where cafes and restaurants spill onto the waterfront promenade whenever weather permits. If you do find your way blocked by construction in this town (and we frequently have) it will also affect you in terms of driving, as closed streets require confusing roadway diversions, but it's a small enough place that it's really impossible to be lost for long.

Sligo Town isn't busy, historic, or pretty enough to require much of your time, but it is a handy place to base yourself if you want to explore the bucolic farmland that has become, thanks to the impressive energy of the County Sligo tourism offices, "Yeats Country." Although he was born in Dublin, the poet W. B. Yeats spent so much time in County Sligo that it became a part of him, and he a part of it—literally, as he is buried here. As you'll quickly discover, every hill, cottage, vale, and lake seems to bear a plaque indicating its relation to the poet or his works.

When you plan your itinerary, allow plenty of time to explore the countryside that so inspired him.

Sligo Town Essentials

GETTING THERE **Aer Arann** (✆ **011/353-81821-0210** in the U.S., 0818/210-210 in Ireland, or 0870/876-76-76 in the U.K.; www.aerarann.ie) operates two daily flights from Dublin into little **Sligo Airport,** Strandhill, County Sligo (✆ **071/916-8280;** www.sligoairport.com), 8km (5 miles) southwest of Sligo Town. The flight takes about 40 minutes. The bus to Sligo Town from the airport will cost you around €4, while you can expect a taxi to cost around €15 to €20.

Irish Rail, with its station on Lord Edward Street (✆ **071/916-9888;** www.irishrail.ie), operates daily service into Sligo from Dublin.

Bus Éireann, also pulling into Lord Edward Street (✆ **071/916-0066;** www.buseireann.ie), operates daily bus service to Sligo from Dublin, Galway, and other points, including Derry in Northern Ireland. A one-way adult ticket from Dublin to Sligo costs around €20.

Four major roads lead to Sligo: N4 from Dublin and the east, N17 from Galway and the south, N15 from Donegal to the north, and N16 from County Fermanagh in Northern Ireland.

VISITOR INFORMATION For information about Sligo and the surrounding area, contact the **Failte Ireland North West,** Aras Reddan, Temple Street, Sligo (✆ **071/916-0336;** www.discoverireland.ie/northwest). It's open year-round Monday to Friday 9am to 5pm, with weekend and extended hours April to August. The most comprehensive local Internet source for Sligo can be found at **www.sligotourism.ie**.

TOWN LAYOUT Edged by Sligo Bay to the west, Sligo Town is bisected by the Garavogue River, with most of its commercial district on the river's south bank. **O'Connell Street** is the main north-south artery, and the main east-west thoroughfare is **Stephen Street,** which becomes Wine Street and then Lord Edward Street. The **Tourist Office** is in the southwest corner of the town on Temple Street, 2 blocks south of O'Connell Street. Three bridges span the river; the **Douglas Hyde Bridge,** named for Ireland's first president, is the main link between the two sides.

County Sligo
Carrowkeel Passage Tomb Cemetery 7
Carrowmore Megalithic Cemetery 6
Drumcliff & Yeats's Grave 2
Glencar Lake & Waterfall 1
Knocknarea 4
Lough Gill Drive 5
Parke's Castle 3
NORTHERN IRELAND
Map Area
Belfast
Galway
REPUBLIC OF IRELAND
Dublin
Cork
Donegal Bay
Inver Bay
Killybegs
DONEGAL
Ballintra
Ballyshannon
Tullaghan
Bundoran
Lower Lough Erne
Inishmurray
Cliffoney
Lough Melvin
Dartry Mts.
Benbulben
Glencar L.
Enniskillen
L. Macnean
Drumcliff
Rosses Point
Sligo Bay
Manorhamilton
Belcoo
Easky
Ballycastle
Strandhill
Sligo
Killala Bay
Dromore West
Lough Gill
Dromahair
Upper Lough Erne
Killala
Enniscrone
Knockalongy
Ballysadare
Collooney
Glengavlen
Slieve Gamph (Ox Mts.)
Drumkeeran
Riverstown
SLIGO
LEITRIM
CAVAN
Crossmolina
Ballina
L. Talt
Ballymote
Lough Arrow
Lough Allen
Iron Mts.
Ballyconnell
MAYO
Castlebaldwin
Ballyfarnon
Tubbercurry
Drumshanbo
Ballinamore
Lough Conn
Lough Key
Lough Oughter
Ballinafad
Curlew Mts.
Foxford
Birreencorragh
Charlestown
Lough Gara
Boyle
Carrick-on-Shannon
Lough Cullin
Swinford
Drumsna
Mohill
Arva
Brosna
0
10 miles
10 kms
Bohola
Ballaghaderreen
ROSCOMMON
Lough Boderg
LONGFORD
N15
N16
N4
N59
N17
N26
N5
N61
A47
A46
A4
A32
A509
N87

GETTING AROUND There is no public transport in the town of Sligo. During July and August, **Bus Éireann** (✆ **071/916-0066**) runs from Sligo Town to Strandhill and Rosses Point.

Taxis line up at the taxi stand on Quay Street. If you prefer to call for a taxi, try **A&C Taxis** (✆ 071/913-8333), **A-Taxis Cabs** (✆ 086/064-4277), or **Zero Cabs** (✆ 071/915-4555).

You'll need a car to see the sights outside Sligo Town. If you need to hire one, contact **Avis,** Sligo Airport (✆ **01/605-7500**), or **Hertz,** Sligo Airport (✆ **071/914-4068**).

The best way to see the town is on foot. Follow the signposted route of the Tourist Trail. The walk takes approximately 90 minutes. From mid-June to September, the **Tourist Office,** Temple Street, Sligo (✆ **071/916-1201**), offers guided tours; contact the office for details and reservations.

FAST FACTS In an **emergency,** dial ✆ **999. St. John's Hospital** is at Ballytivan, Sligo (✆ **071/914-2606**), or you can try **Sligo County Hospital,** The Mall (✆ **071/914-2620**). The **Garda Station** is on Pearse Road (✆ **071/915-7000**).

Need to check your e-mail? There are Internet-accessible PCs at the **County Sligo Library,** on Stephen Street (✆ **071/914-2212**), which is open Tuesday to Friday 10am to 5pm, and Saturday 10am to 1pm and 2 to 5pm.

The **Sligo General Post Office,** Wine Street (✆ **071/915-9273**), is open Monday to Friday 9am to 5:30pm and Saturday 9am to 1pm.

Seeing the Sights in Sligo Town

The Model The Model is one of the region's leading creative hubs, although in our opinion, its major expansion in 2010 severely marred the aesthetic appeal of this arts center (oh, the irony) by grafting a stark modernist facade onto the former 19th-century schoolhouse. Still, its impressively diverse program features something for everyone of an artistic bent, including exhibitions by local and international artists, concerts, film screenings, poetry readings, and lectures. However, the best part of it all is the permanent gallery, which houses the Niland Collection. Among the Niland gems are works by Jack Yeats (1871–1957), brother of William and dedicatee of an entire room at the National Gallery of Ireland in Dublin (p. 149); Paul Henry (1877–1958), a noted Northern Irish landscape painter; and Estella Solomons (1882–1968), who in addition to being one of the foremost portrait painters of her generation, also played a significant role in the War of Independence.

The Mall, Sligo, County Sligo. ✆ **071/914-1405.** www.themodel.ie. Free admission to permanent collection; tickets to other events free to €25. Tues–Sat 11am–5:30pm (Thurs until 8pm); Sun noon–5pm.

Sligo Abbey Founded as a Dominican house in 1252 by Maurice Fitzgerald, Earl of Kildare, Sligo Abbey was the center of early Sligo Town. It thrived for centuries, and flourished in medieval times when it was the burial place of the chiefs and earls of Sligo. But, as with other affluent religious settlements, the abbey was under constant attack, and it was finally destroyed in 1641. Much restoration work has been done in recent years, and the cloisters contain outstanding examples of stone carving; the 15th-century altar is one of few intact medieval altars in Ireland.

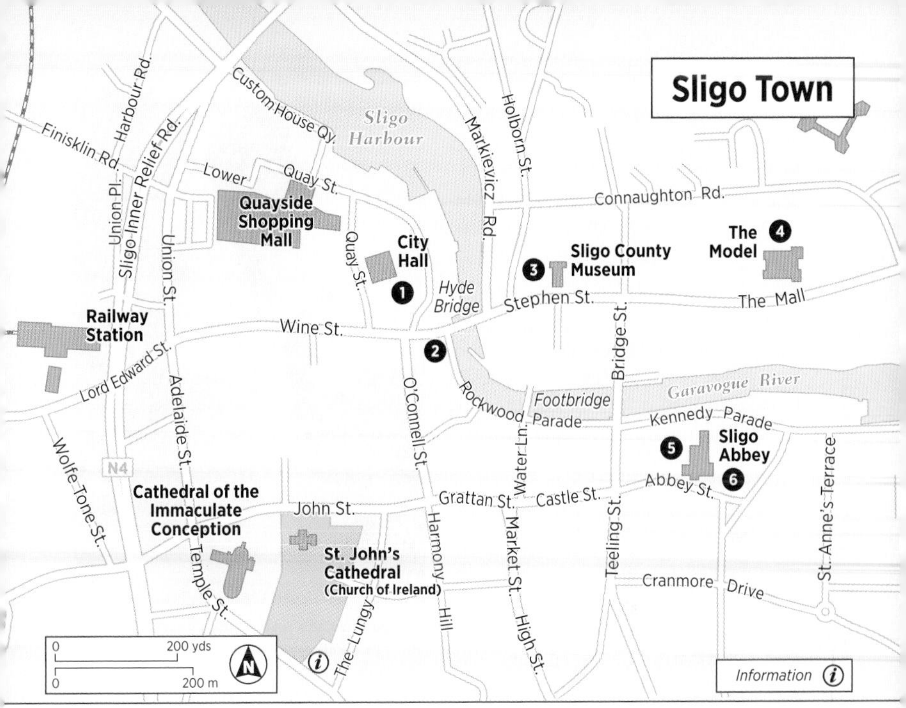

City Hall **1**
Hawk's Well Theatre **6**
The Model **4**
Sligo Abbey **5**
Sligo County Museum **3**
Yeats Memorial Building **2**

Abbey St., Sligo, County Sligo. ✆ **071/914-6406.** Admission €3 adults; €2 seniors; €1 students and children; €8 families. Mid-Apr to mid-Oct daily 10am–6pm; mid-Oct to early Nov Fri–Sun 9:30am–4:30pm. Last admission 45 min. before closing.

Sligo County Museum ★ In a 19th-century church mansion, this museum has quite a good exhibit related to Sligo's Stone Age history and archaeological finds in the area. Leaping forward millennia, another section is devoted to the Yeats family, with a display of William Butler Yeats's complete works in first editions, poems on broadsheets, letters, and his Nobel Prize in Literature (1923). There's also a collection of oils, watercolors, and drawings by Jack B. Yeats (W. B. Yeats's brother) and John B. Yeats (William and Jack's father).

There is a permanent collection of 20th-century Irish art, including works by Paul Henry and Evie Hone.

Stephen St., Sligo, County Sligo. ✆ **071/914-7190.** Free admission. Tues–Sat 10am–noon and 2–4:50pm. Closed Oct–May.

Yeats Memorial Building In a 19th-century redbrick Victorian building, this memorial contains an extensive library with items of special interest to Yeats scholars. The building is also headquarters of the Yeats International Summer School and the Sligo Art Gallery, which exhibits works by local, national, and international artists. The latest addition is a handy cafe. Douglas Hyde Bridge, Sligo, County Sligo. ✆ **071/914-2693.** www.yeats-sligo.com. Free admission. Mon–Fri 10am–5pm.

In Sligo Town, the Yeats Memorial Building houses a library devoted to William Butler's life and work.

SIGHTSEEING TOURS & CRUISES

Lough Gill Cruises On this tour, you cruise on Lough Gill and the Garavogue River aboard the 72-passenger *Wild Rose* water bus while listening to the poetry of Yeats. Trips to the Lake Isle of Innisfree are also scheduled. An onboard bar serves refreshments.

Blue Lagoon, Riverside, Sligo, County Sligo. ✆ **071/916-4266.** www.roseofinnisfree.com. Lough Gill cruise from €15 adults; €7.50 children 11 and over. Innisfree cruise €17 adults; €8.50 children 11 and over. June–Sept Lough Gill cruise daily 2:30 and 4:30pm, Innisfree tour daily 11am, 12:30, 1:30, 3:30, and 4:30pm. Apr–May and Oct (Sun only) cruise and tour schedule subject to demand; call ahead.

Shopping in Sligo Town

Most Sligo shops are open Monday to Saturday 9am to 6pm, and some may have extended hours during July and August.

The Cat & the Moon This shop offers uniquely designed crafts from throughout Ireland, ranging from beeswax candles and baskets to modern art, metal and ceramic work, wood turning, hand weaving, Celtic jewelry, and furniture. An expanded gallery displays a large variety of paintings, limited-edition prints, and occasionally sculpture. 4 Castle St., Sligo, County Sligo. ✆ **071/914-3686.** www.thecatandthemoon.com.

Kate's Kitchen Kate's has an outstanding delicatessen section, with gourmet meats, cheeses, salads, pâtés, and breads baked on the premises, all ideal makings for a picnic. Don't miss the handmade Irish chocolates and preserves. Hopper & Pettit stocks potpourri, soaps, and natural oils, as well as Crabtree & Evelyn products. 3 Castle St., Sligo, County Sligo. ✆ **071/914-3022.** www.kateskitchen.ie.

Michael Kennedy Ceramics This shop features the work of one of Ireland's foremost ceramic artists, Michael Kennedy, who produces pottery and porcelain with layers of textured markings and drawings that form a maze of intricate patterns. He then applies glazes that reflect the strong tones and shades of the Irish countryside in vases, jars, and dishes. Market Cross, Sligo, County Sligo. ✆ **071/914-8844.** www.michaelkennedyceramics.com.

M. Quirke Michael Quirke started out as a butcher, but a few years ago he traded his cleaver for woodcarving tools and transformed his butcher shop into a craft studio. Step inside and watch as he transforms chunks of native timbers into Ireland's heroes of mythology, from Sligo's Queen Maeve to Cúchulainn, Oisin, and other folklore characters. He also carves chess sets and other Irish-themed wood items. The price of an individual carving averages €90. Wine St., Sligo, County Sligo. ✆ **071/914-2624.**

Wehrly Bros. Ltd Established in 1875, this is one of Sligo's oldest shops, noted for a fine selection of jewelry and watches, as well as cold-cast bronze sculptures of Irish figures, silverware, Claddagh rings, Waterford crystal, Belleek china, and Galway crystal. 3 O'Connell St., Sligo, County Sligo. ✆ **071/914-2252.**

Exploring the Surrounding Countryside

The area around Sligo Town is known for its ancient burial grounds and pagan sites, some dating from the Stone Age. As you drive down country lanes, you'll often spy a **dolmen** (ancient stone table) in pastures with sheep or ponies grazing casually around it. The presence of so many burial sites and of the stacked stones of mysterious ancient religions makes this a particularly fascinating section of the country. Some are open to the public, but most are not, and the Irish are passionate about property rights, so don't go clambering over a fence for a better photo without getting permission first.

To plunge in at the deep end of ancient sites, stop by the vast and strangely beautiful **Carrowmore** (see listing below). It's a huge Neolithic cemetery that once contained as many as 200 passage tombs, some predating Newgrange by

The rocky, remote climb to Carrowkeel is rewarded by the experience of standing alone in a Stone Age burial ground.

This Megalithic burial ground at Carrowmore encompasses the oldest known piece of free-standing stone architecture.

500 years. From Carrowmore, you can see the hilltop cairn grave of **Knocknarea** as a lump atop the large hill in the distance. Local legend has it that this is the grave of the "fairy queen" Queen Maeve (Queen Mab in Shakespeare plays). If you have the energy to make the relatively gentle 30-minute climb to the top, the views are extraordinary. (Knocknarea is on the same road as Carrowmore—follow signs for MESCAN MEADHBHA CHAMBERED CAIRN.) From Carrowmore and Knocknarea, it's about an hour's drive to the Neolithic mountaintop cemetery of **Carrowkeel,** which offers an unforgettable experience. After a breathtaking ascent on foot, you'll find yourself alone with the past. The tombs face Carrowmore below and are aligned with the summer solstice.

At the foot of Knocknarea is **Strandhill,** 8km (5 miles) from Sligo Town. This delightful resort area stretches into Sligo Bay, with a sand-duned beach and a patch of land nearby called Coney Island, which is usually credited with lending its name to the New York beach amusement area. Across the bay is another resort, Rosses Point.

Northwest of Sligo Bay, 6km (3¾ miles) offshore, lies the uninhabited island of **Inishmurray ★**, which contains the haunting ruins of a very early monastic settlement. Founded in the 6th century and destroyed by the Vikings in 807, the monastery of St. Molaise contains in its circular walls the remains of several churches, beehive cells, altars, and an assemblage of "cursing stones" once used to bring ruin on those who presumably deserved it. For transportation to the island, ask at the tourism office, or call **Keith Clarke** (✆ **087/254-0190**) or **Joe McGowan** (✆ **087/667-4522;** joemcgowan@sligoheritage.com). Aside from this ancient history and waterfront beauty, most of the rest of Sligo's attractions are associated in some way with the poet William Butler Yeats, as you'll note below.

Carrowkeel Passage Tomb Cemetery ★★ Atop a hill overlooking Lough Arrow, this ancient cemetery is gorgeous, isolated, and frequently empty. Its 14 cairns, dolmens, and stone circles date from the Stone Age (3,000 B.C.), and it's easy to feel that history, standing among the cold, ageless rocks. The walk up from the parking lot takes about 20 minutes, so be ready to get a little exercise. But it's worth the effort. This is a simple site—no visitor center, no tea shop, no admission fee—nothing but ancient mystery.

West off the N4 (signposted on N4), btw. Sligo Town and Boyle, County Sligo. Free admission.

Carrowmore Megalithic Cemetery ★★★ Here, at the dead center of the Coolera Peninsula, sits a massive passage grave that once had a Stonehenge-like stone circle of its own. Encircling that were as many as 200 additional stone circles and passage graves arranged in an intricate and mysterious design. Over the years, some of the stones have been moved, but more than 60 circles and passage graves still exist, although the site spreads out so far that many of them are in adjacent farms. Look out for your first dolmen in a paddock next to the road about a mile before you reach the site. The dolmens were the actual graves, once covered in stones and earth. Some of these are open to visitors—you can get a map to them from the visitor center. On the main site, Tomb 52A (which was only excavated in 1998) is estimated to be 7,400 years old, making it the earliest known piece of free-standing stone architecture in the world. This is one of the great sacred landscapes of the ancient world. It's all well presented, and the excellent visitor center has good exhibits and guided tours.

Carrowmore Visitors Centre (signposted on N4 and N15), County Sligo. ✆ **071/916-1534.** Admission €3 adults; €2 seniors; €1 students and children; €8 families. Daily 10am–6pm. Last admission 1 hr. before closing. Both visitor center and site closed mid-Oct to Apr.

Drumcliff & Yeats's Grave ★ Eight kilometers (5 miles) north of Sligo Town, Drumcliff is a small, stone church that somehow manages to dominate the valley in which it sits—drawing your eye with its tall steeple and its ancient Celtic crosses. When Yeats died in 1939 in France, he asked that, "If I die here, bury me up there on the mountain, and then after a year or so, dig me up and bring me privately to Sligo." True to his wishes, in 1948 his body was moved here, to the church where his great-grandfather had been a rector. As you walk into the graveyard, Yeats's grave is marked with a dark, modest stone just to the left of the church. He's buried alongside his young wife, Georgie Hyde-Lee (when they married in 1917 he was 52 and she was 23). The moving epitaph ("Cast a cold eye on life, on death . . .") comes from his poem "Under Ben Bulben." The church sits atop the 6th-century foundations of the monastery St. Columba, and the round tower on the main road dates from that earlier building. The high cross in the churchyard is from the 11th century, and its faded eastern side shows Christ, Daniel in the lions' den, Adam and Eve, and Cain murdering Abel. On the simpler west side, there's

"Cast a cold eye on life, on death/Horseman, pass by!" reads the stone on Yeats's grave.

a scene of the crucifixion. The little visitor center has a few gifts and doodads, and an excellent tea shop with marvelous cakes, good hearty sandwiches, and fresh hot soup.

Drumcliff Churchyard, Drumcliff (off N15), County Sligo.

The Lough Gill Drive ★★ This 42km (26-mile) drive-yourself tour around Lough Gill is well signposted. Head 1.6km (1 mile) south of town and follow the signs for **Lough Gill,** the beautiful lake that figured so prominently in Yeats's writings. Within 3.2km (2 miles) you'll be on the lower edge of the shoreline. Among the sites are **Dooney Rock,** with its own nature trail and lakeside walk (inspiration for the poem "Fiddler of Dooney"); the **Lake Isle of Innisfree,** made famous in Yeats's poetry and in song; and the **Hazelwood Sculpture Trail,** a unique forest walk along the shores of Lough Gill, with 13 wood sculptures.

The storied Innisfree is one of 22 islands in Lough Gill. You can drive the lakeside circuit in less than an hour, or you can stop at the east end and visit **Dromahair ★**, a delightful village on the River Bonet, in County Leitrim. The road along Lough Gill's upper shore brings you back to the northern end of Sligo Town. Continue north on the main road (N15), and you'll see the graceful profile of **Ben Bulben** (519m/1,702 ft.), one of the Dartry Mountains, rising off to your right.

County Sligo and County Leitrim.

Parke's Castle ★ On the north side of the Lough Gill Drive, on the County Leitrim side of the border, Parke's Castle stands out as a lone outpost amid the natural tableau of lake view and woodland scenery. Named after an English family that gained possession of it during the 1620 plantation of Leitrim (when land was confiscated from the Irish and given to favored English families), this castle was originally the stronghold of the O'Rourke clan, rulers of the Kingdom of Breffni. Beautifully restored using Irish oak and traditional craftsmanship, it exemplifies the 17th-century fortified manor house. In the visitor center, informative

Yeats memorialized the serene shoreline of Lough Gill.

Yeats's grave lies near a church parking lot, but some consider Ben Bulben his rightful headstone.

exhibits and a splendid audiovisual show illustrate the history of the castle and introduce visitors to the rich, diverse sites of interest in the surrounding area. The tearoom offers enticing pastries.

Lough Gill Dr., County Leitrim. ✆ **071/916-4149.** Admission €3 adults; €2 seniors; €1 students and children; €8 families. Late Apr to Sept daily 10am–6pm. Last admission 45 min. before closing.

Sports & Outdoor Pursuits

BEACHES For walking, jogging, or swimming, there are safe sandy beaches with promenades at **Strandhill, Rosses Point,** and **Enniscrone** on the Sligo Bay coast.

BICYCLING With its lakes and woodlands, Yeats Country is particularly good biking territory. To rent a bike, contact **Flanagans Cycles,** Market Square, Sligo (✆ **071/914-4477**).

FISHING For fishing gear and tackle, see **Barton Smith,** Hyde Bridge, Sligo (✆ **071/914-6111**). For boat rental, see **Kingfisher Bates,** Pier Road, Enniscrone (✆ **096/36733**).

GOLF With its seascapes, mountain valleys, and lakesides, County Sligo is known for challenging golf courses. Leading the list is **County Sligo Golf Club ★**, Rosses Point Road, Rosses Point (✆ **071/917-7134;** www.countysligogolfclub.ie), overlooking Sligo Bay under the shadow of Ben Bulben mountain. It's an 18-hole, par-71 championship seaside links famed for its wild, natural terrain and constant winds. Greens fees range from around €40 to €125 weekdays and €50 to €150 weekends, depending on the time of year.

Eight kilometers (5 miles) west of Sligo Town is **Strandhill Golf Club,** Strandhill (✆ **071/916-8188;** www.strandhillgc.com), a seaside par-69 course with greens fees of €40 weekdays, €50 weekends. On Mondays from April to October (except bank holidays), you can get 18 holes plus coffee and a hearty "Golfer's Grill" meal for €30.

In the southwestern corner of the county, about 40km (25 miles) from Sligo Town and overlooking Sligo Bay, the **Enniscrone Golf Club,** Enniscrone (✆ **096/36297;** www.enniscronegolf.com), is a seaside par-72 course. Greens fees are €60 weekdays, €75 weekends.

HORSEBACK RIDING An hour's or a day's riding on the beach, in the countryside, or over mountain trails can be arranged at **Sligo Riding Centre,** Carrowmore (✆ **087/230-4828;** www.sligoridingcentre.com), or at **Woodlands Equestrian Centre,** Loughill, Lavagh, Tubbercurry, County Sligo (✆ **071/918-4207**). Rates average €20 to €40 per hour.

Where to Stay

EXPENSIVE

Clonalis House ★ This sweetly decorated manor house is a lovely, elegant place to stay. Bedrooms are charming—decorated with antique furniture, marble fireplaces, and oil paintings with frilly gold frames hanging atop floral wallpaper. Beds are four poster or half-tester (of course) and there are sweeping views out over the grounds. Hostess Marguerite O'Conor Nash creates delicious home-cooked breakfasts, served at a communal oak table. She's an accomplished chef—so it's worth booking a place for dinner (book a day in advance). There are four self-catering cottages on the grounds if you prefer a little more independence.

> Impressions
>
> ***Being Irish, I have an abiding sense of tragedy which sustains me through temporary periods of joy.***
>
> **—W. B. Yeats**

On the N60 west of Castlerea, County Roscommon. www.clonalis.com. ✆ **094/962-0014.** €170–€200 double. 10% discount for 2 nights or more. Self-catering cottages €340–€400 per week. Rates include full breakfast. Dinner. €48 (Tues–Sat 8pm, 24 hr. notice.) MC, V. Closed Oct–Mar. **Amenities:** Games room; tennis court. *In room:* No TV, no phone.

Cromleach Lodge ★★ Thirty-two kilometers (20 miles) south of Sligo Town, this lovely, modern sprawling hotel, nestled in the quiet hills above Lough Arrow, is run by Moira and Christy Tighe. Though not a period house, it's decorated to feel like one. Views from the restaurant, lounges, and most guest rooms deliver a stunning panorama of lakeland and mountain scenery. Guest rooms are large by Irish standards and feature sitting areas, oversize orthopedic beds, designer fabrics, and original oil paintings. Deluxe rooms have underfloor heating and balconies. There's also an award-winning **restaurant** (see below). The hotel was renovated and extended in 2008, with the addition of 60 new rooms and a spa. ***Tip:*** Cromleach Lodge can be a good option for families with young children; kids under 3 can stay in their parent's room at no extra charge, fold-out child beds are available to hire for €10 per night, and with a small amount of notice they can arrange babysitting too.

Ballindoon, Castlebaldwin, County Sligo. www.cromleach.com. ✆ **071/916-5155.** 130 units. €90–€284 double. Rates include full breakfast. AE, DC, MC, V. Closed Nov–Jan. **Amenities:** 2 restaurants; bar; 2 lounges; sauna; smoke-free rooms; spa; Wi-Fi. *In room:* TV, minibar.

MODERATE

Sligo Park Hotel With a glass-fronted facade and sky-lit atrium lobby, this is Sligo's most contemporary hotel, set back from the road amid sprawling parkland, and surrounded by lovely gardens, with distant views of Ben Bulben to the north. The decor in the lobby is modern and creative, with a good use of color, and sleek contemporary furniture. The guest rooms are more generic but inoffensive, with pastel-toned floral fabrics, quilted headboards, and orthopedic beds. The leisure center is a big draw, with a gorgeous indoor pool and plenty to keep you busy.

Pearse Rd. (just over 1.6km/1 mile south of Sligo on the Dublin rd./N4), Sligo, County Sligo. www.leehotels.ie. ✆ **071/919-0400.** Fax 071/916-9556. or www.sligoparkhotel.com. 136 units. €100–€115 double. Rates include service charge and full breakfast. DC, MC, V. **Amenities:** 2 restaurants; bar; gym; Jacuzzi; indoor pool; sauna/steam room; smoke-free rooms; tennis court. *In room:* TV, DVD player (some rooms), radio, hair dryer, Wi-Fi.

Temple House ★★★ A grand manor house tucked away amid pastures, forest, and terraced gardens, Temple House is where you can live out your country-house dream. Overlooking a lake and the ruins of a Knights Templar castle, the house impresses with its sheer size and historic authenticity. The Perceval family has lived here since 1665, and recently a new generation, the wonderful Roderick and Helena, has taken over. They artfully juggle raising their two young children with caring for their guests and running their working farm. Guest rooms are enormous—one is so big that it's called "the Half Acre Room"—and filled with heirlooms. Beds are firm and comfortable, and all the bathrooms are modern. The walled garden a short walk from the house supplies the vegetables served with the evening meals and the fruit offered at breakfast. Book a place for dinner, where the atmosphere is intentionally like a relaxed manor-house party—guests meet for drinks around the fire in the drawing room and dine together at the vast table. Breakfast includes homemade cereals, fresh fruit compote, and yogurt. There are also two charming self-catering guesthouses for those who want a bit more privacy.

Ballymote, County Sligo. www.templehouse.ie. ✆ **071/918-3329.** Fax 071/918-3808. 6 units. €140–€190 double. Self-catering cottage from €280 for 2 nights, rising to €800 for 5 nights (5-night minimum rental Jul–Aug). Rates include full breakfast. 4-course dinner €45 (not available Sun). AE, MC, V. Free parking. Closed Dec–Easter. **Amenities:** Smoke-free rooms; Wi-Fi.

Where to Eat

VERY EXPENSIVE

Knockmuldowney INTERNATIONAL Four stories high, with a forbidding entrance, a monumental stone staircase, and thrusting turrets, Markree Castle is formidable. Inside, there's an equally extraordinary looking restaurant—a regal 60-seat room under lavish 19th-century Louis Philippe–style plasterwork, inside a grand, stone castle. You dine like a king here, but unfortunately the food doesn't always reach royal status. The menu can dazzle with its use of local produce and game in dishes such as thyme-marinated Irish lamb in Madeira *jus,* or fresh scallops and crabmeat lasagna, but it can also disappoint with a provincial cooking style and unprofessional staff. This place has its fans and its enemies. Some love its unpredictability and localism, and love the food; others say they received dreadful service and hated the place. But even many of the latter say it might be worth it just to dine in that gorgeous room. If you want to see more of the place, a double room costs €130 to €260 per night.

Collooney, County Sligo. ✆ **071/916-7800.** www.markreecastle.ie/knockmuldowney.php. Reservations required. Main courses €24–€36; fixed-price dinner €35. AE, DC, MC, V. Daily 7–9pm; Sun 1–3pm. Closed several days at Christmas.

Moira's at Cromleach Lodge ★★★ MODERN CONTINENTAL It's worth the 32km (20-mile) drive south of Sligo Town to dine at this lovely country house overlooking Lough Arrow. The panoramic views are secondary, however, to Chef Moira Tighe's food, which has won a fistful of prestigious awards. The menu changes nightly, depending on what is freshest and best from the sea and garden. It may include such dishes as pan-fried fish of the day with lobster tartare and champagne sauce, or grilled filet of beef with shallot-and-pancetta ragout and garlic confit mash. Desserts are characterized by an imaginative and expertly judged combination of flavors, such as Armagnac parfait with poached baby pear, mixed-nut biscotti and red-wine syrup, or a Florentine cone of mango mousse with marinated fruit and Greek yogurt ice cream. The dining room is wisely arranged so that every table can share in the magnificent view of the grounds. If you love it so much, you may want to spend the night (see above).

Ballindoon, Castlebaldwin, County Sligo. ✆ **071/916-5155.** www.cromleach.com. Reservations required. Main courses €27–€35; fixed-price Sun lunch €35. AE, MC, V. Daily 6:30–9pm. Closed Nov–Jan.

INEXPENSIVE

Montmartre ★ FRENCH This compact little restaurant is renowned in these parts for its authenticity. It serves up classic, beautifully presented French cuisine, often using seasonal, local ingredients. The seafood is particularly good here, including fresh lobster (if you can bear to see your main course plucked from the tank). The wine list is excellent; predominantly French (no surprises there), but with a few well-chosen New World options. Service, however, is patchy; the impeccably turned-out French staff are either charming or aloof, and the service can be glacially slow, so it's best not to eat here if you're in a hurry. Still, this place does have a lot of fans.

1 Market Yard, Sligo, County Sligo. ✆ **071/916-9901.** Reservations recommended. Main courses €12–€25. MC, V. Tues–Sat 5–11pm.

Tobergal Lane CAFE/TAPAS/BISTRO A popular lunch spot in Sligo, this is a rather cool, modern place. Breakfasts (languidly served until late afternoon) include pancakes and a variety of rather health-conscious nut-berry-and-yogurt combinations, or you could opt for a croissant from the in-house bakery. The lunch menu is filled out by a variety of reasonably priced sandwiches, panini, salads, and soups. In the evening there's a modest selection of tapas, or classic dishes including steaks and burgers. At weekends there's live music—usually jazz. ***Tip:*** Come before 7pm for the early-bird dinner menu; at three courses for €15, it's an exceptionally good value.

Tobergal Lane, off O'Connell St., Sligo, County Sligo. ✆ **071/914-6599.** Reservations recommended. Bakery items €3–€4; breakfast €4–€7.50; lunch main courses €5–€14; fixed-price 3-course early-bird dinner €15; tapas €5–€10; fixed-price 4-course dinner €50 for 2 people; dinner main courses €12–€18. MC, V. Daily 10am–10pm. Closed Mon in winter and certain bank holidays; call to confirm.

Sligo After Dark

PUBS

The Crossbar In the heart of County Sligo's rich traditional music scene, this bright yellow pub stands at the center of the little village of Gurteen. There's always a lively buzz from the local crowd, drawn by the congeniality of owners

Adrian Tansey and Pauline Walsh and the warmth of the open fireplace. (They also serve food, although we've never eaten here.) This is the preferred hangout of the Sligo Gaelic football team, with the requisite big-screen television to air major sporting events. Gurteen, County Sligo. ✆ **071/918-2203.**

Stanford's Village Inn Five generations of the McGowan family have run this old tavern, and not much has changed over the years. There are several comfortable bars with open fires, and there's a delightful blend of old stone walls, vintage pictures, and oil lamps. If you're driving around Lough Gill from Sligo, this 160-year-old pub is a great midway stop for a drink or a snack. Main St., Dromahair, County Leitrim. ✆ **071/916-4140.** www.stanfordsinn.com.

The Thatch Established in 1638 as a coaching inn, this is the kind of pub that makes you feel as if you've stepped right into a picture postcard. Its thatched roof and whitewashed exterior have withstood modernization without losing charm. Irish traditional music usually starts at 9pm on Thursday and Sunday year-round and Tuesday through Sunday in August. Dublin-Sligo rd. (N4), about 8km (5 miles) south of Sligo, Ballisodare, County Sligo. ✆ **071/916-7288.**

THE PERFORMING ARTS

Blue Raincoat Theatre This is Sligo's award-winning theater company. It is one of only three professional Irish acting companies that own their own theaters (the Abbey in Dublin and the Druid in Galway are the others). During July and August, the Blue Raincoat often presents lunchtime performances of Yeats's plays, as well as other Sligo-related productions. Evening shows usually start at 8pm. Lower Quay St., Sligo, County Sligo. ✆ **071/917-0431.** www.blueraincoat.com. Tickets average €10–€15.

Hawk's Well Theatre The premier stage of Ireland's northwest region, this modern 350-seat theater presents a varied program of drama, comedy, ballet, opera, and concerts of modern and traditional music. It derives its name from *At the Hawk's Well,* a one-act play by Yeats. The theater occasionally produces shows, but mostly books visiting professional and local companies. The box office is open Monday to Saturday 10am to 6pm; most shows start at 8pm. Johnston Court, Sligo, County Sligo. ✆ **071/916-1518.** www.hawkswell.com. Tickets average €10–€25.

THE MIDLANDS: ROSCOMMON, LEITRIM & CAVAN

Roscommon: 82km (51 miles) NE of Galway, 147km (91 miles) NW of Dublin; Longford: 129km (80 miles) NW of Dublin, 44km (27 miles) NE of Athlone; Carrick-on-Shannon: 56km (35 miles) SE of Sligo; Cavan: 105km (65 miles) NW of Dublin

The northern region of the Republic sprawls across three counties, with vast green parks and luxurious manor houses dolloped generously across it like clotted cream on a scone.

In **County Roscommon** you can spend days wandering through places like the grand Strokestown Park House, which, with its sobering Irish Famine Museum, tells of both the haves and the have-nots of Ireland's recent past. Head to the town of **Boyle** to wonder at the ancient carvings on the worn walls of Boyle Abbey and explore the green and pleasant baths within the wilds of Lough Key Forest Park before heading off to discover the lost worlds of Roscommon Castle.

In **County Leitrim** the town of **Carrick-on-Shannon** sits beautifully at one of the great ancient crossing places of the Shannon River. **County Cavan** is a lovely place to drive through, with thick forests, miles of farmland, and a distinctive form of local crystal that makes a memorable souvenir.

Essentials

GETTING THERE & GETTING AROUND The best way to get to and around the Upper Shannon area is by car. Although there is public transportation to major towns, you will need a car to get to most of the attractions. Among the main roads that lead to this area are the main Dublin-Sligo road (N4), the main Dublin-Cavan road (N3), N5 and N63 from Castlebar and the west, and N61 and N55 from the south.

VISITOR INFORMATION Information on **County Roscommon** is available from the **Ireland West Tourism Office,** Foster Street, Galway (✆ **091/537700;** www.discoverireland.ie/west). Hours are May, June, and September daily 9am to 5:45pm; July and August daily 9am to 7:45pm; and October to April Monday to Friday 9am to 5:45pm and Saturday 9am to 12:45pm. Information on **County Cavan** is available from the **Cavan Tourist Office,** Farnham Street, Cavan, County Cavan (✆ **049/433-1942;** www.cavantourism.com), open May through September Monday to Friday 9am to 6pm, Saturday 10am to 2pm; on **County Leitrim** from the **North-West Tourism Office,** Aras Reddan, Temple Street, Sligo (✆ **071/916-1201**), open Easter through September Monday to Friday 9am to 6pm, Saturday 9am to 5pm, and Sunday 9am to 3pm, with extended hours in July and August; and also from the tourist office on the Quay at **Carrick-on-Shannon** (✆ **071/962-0170**), open May through September Monday to Saturday 9:15am to 5:30pm and Sunday 10am to 2pm.

Seasonal information points, operating from June to August, are signposted in Boyle (✆ **071/966-2145**), Longford (✆ **043/46566**), and Roscommon (✆ **090/662-6342**).

Exploring the Area

Boyle Abbey ★ Sitting forlornly in a corner of bustling central Boyle, rugged old Boyle Abbey looks sad and forgotten. Time has truly passed it by. Founded in 1161 by Cistercian monks from Mellifont, and once a large and architecturally beautiful place, the abbey was a haven of otherworldliness for 500 years until it was savagely destroyed in the mid-1600s by English soldiers suppressing Irish Catholicism. As part of their efforts, they murdered the resident monks and converted the structure into a military garrison. After they left it, it was abandoned to decay. Today the ruins form a complex fossil clearly imprinted with both the serene and violent aspects of the abbey's history. The 13th-century nave in the northern section of the structure still has distinctive capitals on its columns, some carved with faces, others with fanciful creatures and dragons. There's a *sheela-na-gig* (an erotic pagan symbol) tucked in one corner of the nave, according to the abbey's own information, but despite enthusiastic searching, we were unable to find the sexy little wench. The interpretive center, housed in the restored gatehouse, is informative and thoughtfully designed. At this writing, conservation work was underway at the abbey, but it remains open to visitors.

N4, Boyle, County Roscommon. ✆ **071/966-2604.** Admission €3 adults; €2 seniors; €1 students and children; €8 families. Free if conservation work underway. Easter to late Sept daily 10am–6pm (last admission 45 min. before closing).

Cavan Crystal Craft & Design Centre ★ One of the country's top crystal companies, this establishment is known for its delicate glassware, mouth-blown and hand-cut by skilled craftspeople. Visitors are invited to watch as the master blowers fashion the molten crystal into intricate shapes and designs, which are then finished by master cutters. Handily enough, the completed products are sold in the center's shop. Bring your credit card, and don't make any sudden moves in this fragile place.

Dublin rd. (N3), Cavan, County Cavan. ✆ **049/433-1800.** www.cavancrystaldesign.com. Free admission. Mon–Fri 9:30am–6pm; Sat 10am–5pm; Sun noon–6pm.

Clonalis House ★ This great house stands on land that has belonged to the O'Conor clan for more than 1,500 years. The O'Conors were the kings of Connaught, and this is the current home of the O'Conor Don, a direct descendant of the last high king of Ireland. The house, built in 1880, is a combination of Victorian, Italianate, and Queen Anne architecture, with mostly Louis XV–style furnishings, plus antique lace, horse-drawn farm machinery, and other memorabilia. Its primary attraction, though, is the O'Conor clan collection of portraits, documents, and genealogical tracts 2,000 years old. Displays include an ancient harp said to have belonged to Turlough O'Carolan (1670–1738), a blind Irish bard who composed tunes still played today. The grounds, with terraced and woodland gardens, hold the O'Conor inauguration stone, similar to the Scottish Stone of Scone, held at Edinburgh Castle. You have to see the house by guided tour, but if you really want to see the place to the fullest effect, you can stay the night (p. 520).

On the N60 west of Castlerea, County Roscommon. ✆ **094/962-0014.** www.clonalis.com. Admission €7 adults; €6 students and seniors; €5 children 7–12. June–Aug Mon–Sat 11am–5pm. Last tour 1 hr. before closing.

Lough Key Forest Park ★ ☺ Stretching for miles along the shores of Lough Key, encompassing lush woodlands, a glassy lake, and a dozen islands, this park holds nature walks, ancient monuments, ring forts, a central viewing tower, picnic grounds, a cafe, and a shop. All of it was privately owned until 1957, when it was sold to the Irish Land Commission. Sadly, Rockingham House, the mansion designed by John Nash, burned down in the 1950s, but even without it, there's plenty to see and do. In addition to cypress groves and wildflower meadows, there are bog gardens filled with unusual peat-loving plants and shrubs. Wildlife, including deer, otters, and shy hedgehogs, has the run of the place. The ruins of a 12th-century abbey can be seen on Trinity Island, while on Castle Island, a 19th-century castle stands there, as if taunting you for not living someplace this beautiful. Powerboats and rowboats are available to rent if you want a closer look. Pony and cart rides are a good way to explore the park without breaking a sweat, and the **Lough Key Experience** takes you through a 9m-high (30-ft.) tree canopy walk and a section of Victorian tunnel. There's plenty for kids here, too, with the **Adventure Kingdom,** a vaguely castle-themed playground, and **Boda Borg,** a rather peculiar indoor problem-solving game. If you're planning to do more than just the basics here, the day passes can be a significant saving, covering admission to everything at a cost of €18 adults, €17 seniors and students, €21 children, and €60 for families.

Enter from the main Dublin-Sligo rd. (N4), 3km (2 miles) east of Boyle, County Roscommon. ✆ **071/967-3122.** www.loughkey.ie. Admission to park €5 per car charged Apr–Sept only. Lough Key Experience €7.50 adults; €6 seniors; €5 children 5–17; €20 families. Boda Borg €13 2-hr. pass, €17 day pass (min 3 people, discount for groups of 5). Adventure Play Kingdom €5 children.

Strokestown: A Kind of Atonement

The somber and informative Famine Museum at Strokestown could be seen as a kind of atonement for the behavior of Major Denis Mahon, the landlord at Strokestown in the 1840s. When a blight killed the country's potato crop, setting off widespread famine, Mahon and his land agents could have done many things to help the hundreds of starving peasants who lived and worked on the property, but instead they evicted them as soon as it became clear they would not be able to pay their rent. He even went so far as to charter ships to send them away from Ireland. In 1847 Major Mahon was shot to death near Strokestown, and two men were hastily (and dubiously) convicted of the crime. But it seems clear that many hungry people had motives.

Apr–June daily 10am–6pm; July–Aug Mon–Fri 10am–6pm, Sat–Sun 10am–8pm; Mar and Sept–Oct Thurs–Sun 10am–6pm; Nov–Feb Fri–Sun 10am–5pm. Extended opening late Dec to early Jan. Boda Borg last admission 2 hr. before closing; Experience and Play Kingdom 1 hr. before closing. Park year-round daily dawn–dusk.

Strokestown Park House, Gardens, and Famine Museum ★★★ Strokestown Park House was the seat of the Pakenham-Mahon family from 1600 to 1979, and the vast estate, which stretches for miles in every direction, was granted to Nicholas Mahon by King Charles II after the Restoration in appreciation of his support of the House of Stewart during the bloody English Civil War. It was quite a reward. The original house, completed in 1697, was considered to be too small and unimposing by Nicholas's grandson, Thomas. So he hired Richard Cassels (also known as Richard Castle) to build him something bigger and more impressive. The result is this 45-room Palladian house. The north wing houses Ireland's last existing galleried kitchen (where the lady of the house could observe the culinary activity without being part of it). The south wing is an elaborate vaulted stable so magnificent that it has been described as an "equine cathedral."

To see the other end of the economic scale, head out into the old stable yards to the excellent **Irish Famine Museum ★★**. Anyone who wants to understand the effects and causes of the deadly potato blight of the 1840s will want to visit this exhibition. It chronicles the twists of fate, catastrophic mistakes, and callous disregard that caused widespread starvation and mass deaths. The cruel irresponsibility of the landowners and the British government of Ireland in ignoring the spreading death and disease is exposed in jaw-dropping detail. This has been called one of the most important museums in Ireland, and that is not overstating it.

The Irish Famine Museum explores the effects of the potato blight that ravaged this region in the mid-19th century.

On the main Dublin-Castlebar rd. (N5), Strokestown Park, Strokestown, County Roscommon. ✆ **071/963-3013.** www.strokestownpark.ie. Admission to house, garden, and museum €12 adults; €11 seniors, students, and children; €25 families. Separate admission to each sight €8 adults; €4 seniors, students, and children; €16 families. Mar 17–Oct daily 11am–6pm; Nov–Mar 16 daily 11am–5pm.

Sports & Outdoor Pursuits

BOATING Dozens of companies rent out cabin cruisers on the Shannon. **Carrick Craft,** The Marina, Carrick-on-Shannon, County Leitrim (booking line ✆ **028/3834-49993** from the U.S., or 01/278-1666; www.carrickcraft.com), and **Emerald Star Line,** The Marina, Carrick-on-Shannon,

County Leitrim (✆ **071/962-7633;** www.emeraldstar.ie), are two that get particularly good word of mouth.

FISHING Head to Roscommon Town and stop by the Tourist Office (Library Building, Abbey St.; ✆ **090/662-6342;** www.discoverireland.ie/west) and ask for a map of the (unfortunately named) **Suck Valley Way.** The walk along the river passes some of the best fishing in Ireland, according to local fishermen. With the right equipment, you could catch rudd, tench, pike, and perch.

GOLF The **Slieve Russell Hotel Golf Club,** Cranaghan, Ballyconnell, County Cavan (✆ **049/952-6444;** www.slieverussell.ie), charges greens fees of €39 (€49 Sat) for nonguests of the hotel. Guests of the hotel (see below) pay €30 (€40 Sat).

Two other 18-hole courses in the area are **County Cavan Golf Club,** Arnmore House, Drumellis, County Cavan (✆ **049/433-1541;** www.cavangolf.ie), with greens fees of €25, or €20 before midday every day; and **County Longford Golf Club,** Dublin Road, Longford (✆ **043/334-6310;** www.countylongfordgolfclub.com), with greens fees of €20 weekdays, €25 weekends.

HORSEBACK RIDING **Moorlands Equestrian & Leisure Centre,** Drumshanbo, County Leitrim (✆ **071/964-1500;** www.moorlands.ie), offers lessons (indoors or outdoors), as well as trail rides along Lough Allen and the nearby hills. Children are welcome. During the off season, courses in equestrian science are offered. Book lessons or trail rides at least a day in advance. Mountain walking, watersports, and accommodations are also offered.

Where to Stay & Eat

EXPENSIVE

Lough Rynn Castle Seat of the Clements, the earls of Leitrim, this new hotel is in a grand 19th-century stone castle, surrounded by a vast, sprawling estate of woodland, ornamental gardens, open pastures, and lakes. It will entrance history buffs and garden lovers. Its perfectly restored terraced walled garden dates from 1859, and is designed in the manner of a Victorian pleasure garden. Inside it's all a certain kind of luxury: silk wallpaper, Chippendale chairs, polished antiques, and floral carpets—you get the picture. Beds are big and piled high with cushions and linens; some are four-poster, many are antiques. Views are pastoral, and the mood throughout is formal. There are many handsome guest lounges where you can have tea and relax, and the hotel restaurant is in a simply gorgeous historic room.

South of Carrick-on-Shannon, on the outskirts of Mohill, 5.2km (3¼ miles) from the main Dublin-Sligo rd. (N4), County Leitrim. www.manorhousehotels.com. ✆ **01/295-8900.** 42 units. €125–€300 double. Rates include full breakfast. AE, DC, MC, V. **Amenities:** Restaurant; bar; 18-hole golf course. *In room:* TV, fridge, hair dryer.

Slieve Russell Hotel ★ ☺ Set amid vast parklands, lakeland, and gardens, this impressive resort hotel is a popular destination among the Irish. (The easy, 2-hr. drive from the capital means it's big with Dubliners.) It's a well-designed modern building with the feel of a historic hotel—the public areas have huge open fireplaces, marble staircases, and wrought-iron trim. Guest rooms vary—some are traditional in style, less attractive, and small, others are modern and bigger. It seems to be random selection of which kind you get, so hope for the best. They'll accommodate you if they can, but if they're booked up, that's what you get. ***Tip:*** Check the website for good half-board offers; sometimes it's barely more than a standard double room.

Ballyconnell, County Cavan. www.slieverussell.ie. ✆ **049/952-6444.** 222 units. €130–€270 double. Rates include full breakfast. DC, MC, V. Free parking. **Amenities:** 3 restaurants; 2 bars; babysitting; concierge; 18-hole championship golf course; exercise room; Jacuzzi; indoor pool; room service; sauna/steam room; spa; 4 tennis courts; 2 squash courts. *In room:* TV, hair dryer, minibar.

MODERATE

Farnham Estate Hotel ★★ Once the seat of the earls of Farnham, Cavan aristocracy since the 16th century, this grand country pile has been gradually transformed into a peaceful, luxurious retreat. The renovations have not always been sympathetic to the old building—most bedrooms are in a new, uncompromisingly contemporary 21st-century wing, with sleek lines, subtle spotlighting, and a modern, glass reception area. Bedrooms are spacious and elegant, with large, beds and flatscreen TVs. There's a state-of-the-art **spa** and a golf course. It's all surrounded by rolling parkland, forest, and more than 4 miles of nature trails.

Farnham Estate, Cavan, County Cavan. www.farnhamestate.com or www.radissonblu.ie/farnham-estate-hotel. ✆ **049/437-7700.** Fax 049/437-7701. 158 units. €130–€160 double; €180–€260 suites. Rates include full breakfast. AE, MC, V. **Amenities:** Restaurant; 2 bars; golf course; swimming pool; sauna; spa. *In room:* Flatscreen TV, Wi-Fi.

Ross Castle and House ★★ Ross Castle is a 16th-century fortified tower said to be haunted by a lovesick bride-to-be named Sabrina, whose lover, Orwin, drowned in Lough Sheelin en route to their wedding. Along with a ghost, this comfortable castle contains four guest rooms, including one family room. Rooms are spacious and pleasantly decorated in country-house style. Nearby, Ross House is a sprawling manor house with seven elegant guest rooms. The oldest sections of the building date from the mid–17th century. The farm is noted for its brown trout and is stocked with pike and perch. Look out for discounts and specials online.

Mount Nugent, County Cavan. www.ross-castle.com. ✆ **043/81286.** 16 units. €120–€150 double. Dinner €22. MC, V. **Amenities:** Babysitting; Jacuzzi; sauna; tennis court. *In room:* TV (house only).

A Pub

There are many good pubs in this area, but don't miss the sweet, ivy-covered **Derragarra Inn,** Butlersbridge, County Cavan (✆ **049/433-1003**), for a drink or a meal. Relax by the turf fireplace or in the garden, overlooking the River Annaly. It's 6km (3¾ miles) north of Cavan Town.

13

COUNTY DONEGAL

Beyond Sligo, the topography changes and the roads twist and turn through tortuous corkscrews. When the signs change into Gaelic, and the landscape opens up into great sweeping views of rocky hills and barren shores, and a freezing mist blows in off the sea, you've reached Donegal. The austere beauty of this county can be almost too bleak, but it is also unforgettable. On a sunny day, you can stand at the edge of the sea at Malin Head and, despite the sun, the wind and the sea spray will blow a chill right through you—it feels as if you're standing at the edge of the world. Its natural wonders include the magnificent Slieve League cliffs and the remote beaches tucked into the bays and inlets of its sharply indented coast.

The towns of Donegal are perhaps the least developed for tourism in Ireland. Few tourists make it this far. Buildings are made of cold stone, and villages perch on the slopes of precipitous hillsides. When you stop to take a wander, you can't help but worry whether the car's brakes will hold. But take the chance. The people in Donegal are as nice as can be, and meeting them is worth the trip in itself. Of course, fewer tourists mean fewer amenities. It's harder to find good restaurants and modern guesthouses. In addition, you'll have to contend with road signs that vary from cryptic to nonexistent. You will spend half your time lost. But Ireland is a small place; wherever you're headed, you'll get there eventually. And you're bound to have plenty of adventures along the way.

DONEGAL TOWN

222km (138 miles) NW of Dublin, 283km (176 miles) NE of Shannon Airport, 66km (41 miles) NE of Sligo, 69km (43 miles) SW of Derry, 180km (112 miles) W of Belfast, 205km (127 miles) NE of Galway, 403km (250 miles) N of Cork, 407km (253 miles) NE of Killarney

Overseen by a low, gloomy castle at the edge of the picturesque estuary of the River Eske on Donegal Bay, Donegal Town (pop. 3,200) is a small country burg. As recently as the 1940s, the town's central mall (called "the Diamond") was used as a market for trading livestock and goods. Today the marketing is done in the form of tweeds and tourist goods, as the Diamond is surrounded by little crafts shops and somewhat dingy small hotels. Although Donegal Town makes for a pleasant enough stop after miles of empty countryside, it's not the best place to spend the night as most of its hotels are old-fashioned and there are more interesting hostelries in the surrounding countryside. If you're here at the end of June, though, stop by the lively Donegal Arts Festival, which fills the town with traditional Irish singing, dancing, and storytelling.

PREVIOUS PAGE: **A farmstead along the coast at Malin Head.**

Essentials

Donegal Town.

GETTING THERE **Aer Arann** (✆ **011/353-81821-0210** in the U.S., 818/210-210 in Ireland, or 0870/876-76-76 in the U.K.; www.aerarann.ie) flies once daily from Dublin and twice a week from Glasgow to tiny **Donegal Airport,** Carrickfinn, Kincasslagh, County Donegal (✆ **074/954-8284;** www.donegalairport.ie), near Letterkenny, and about 65km (40 miles) northwest of Donegal Town on the Atlantic coast.

Bus Éireann (✆ **074/912-1309;** www.buseireann.ie) operates daily bus service to Donegal Town from Dublin, Derry, Sligo, Galway, and other points. The pickup and boarding point is in front of the Abbey Hotel on the Diamond.

If you're driving from the south, Donegal is reached on N15 from Sligo or A46 or A47 from Northern Ireland; from the east and north, it's N15 and N56; from the west, N56 leads to Donegal Town.

VISITOR INFORMATION The **Donegal Tourist Office,** Quay Street (✆ **074/972-1148**), is open Easter through September Monday to Friday 9am to 5pm, Saturday 10am to 6pm, and Sunday noon to 4pm, with extended hours in July and August. For online tourist information, go to **www.donegaltown.ie**.

TOWN LAYOUT The town is laid out around the triangular central mall called the Diamond, where the roads from Killybegs, Ballyshannon, and Ballybofey converge. **Main Street** and **Upper Main Street,** which form the prime commercial strip, extend northeast from the Diamond.

GETTING AROUND Easily walked, Donegal has no local bus service within the town. Taxis park in the Diamond, or call **Jim Johnston** (✆ **074/972-1349**) or **Brendan McBrearty** (✆ **074/972-3420**).

There is a pay parking lot along the quay beside the tourist office and off Main Street.

A booklet outlining the signposted walking tour of Donegal Town is available at the tourist office and most bookshops.

FAST FACTS In an **emergency,** dial ✆ **999.** Donegal **District Hospital** is on Upper Main Street (✆ **074/972-1019**). The local **Garda Station** is on Quay Street (✆ **074/972-1021**).

Donegal County Library, Mountcharles Road (✆ **074/972-5329**), is open Monday, Wednesday, and Friday 3 to 6pm, and Saturday 11am to 1pm and 2 to 6pm. Internet access is free (for the time being), but there is a limit of 1 hour per session. Book ahead.

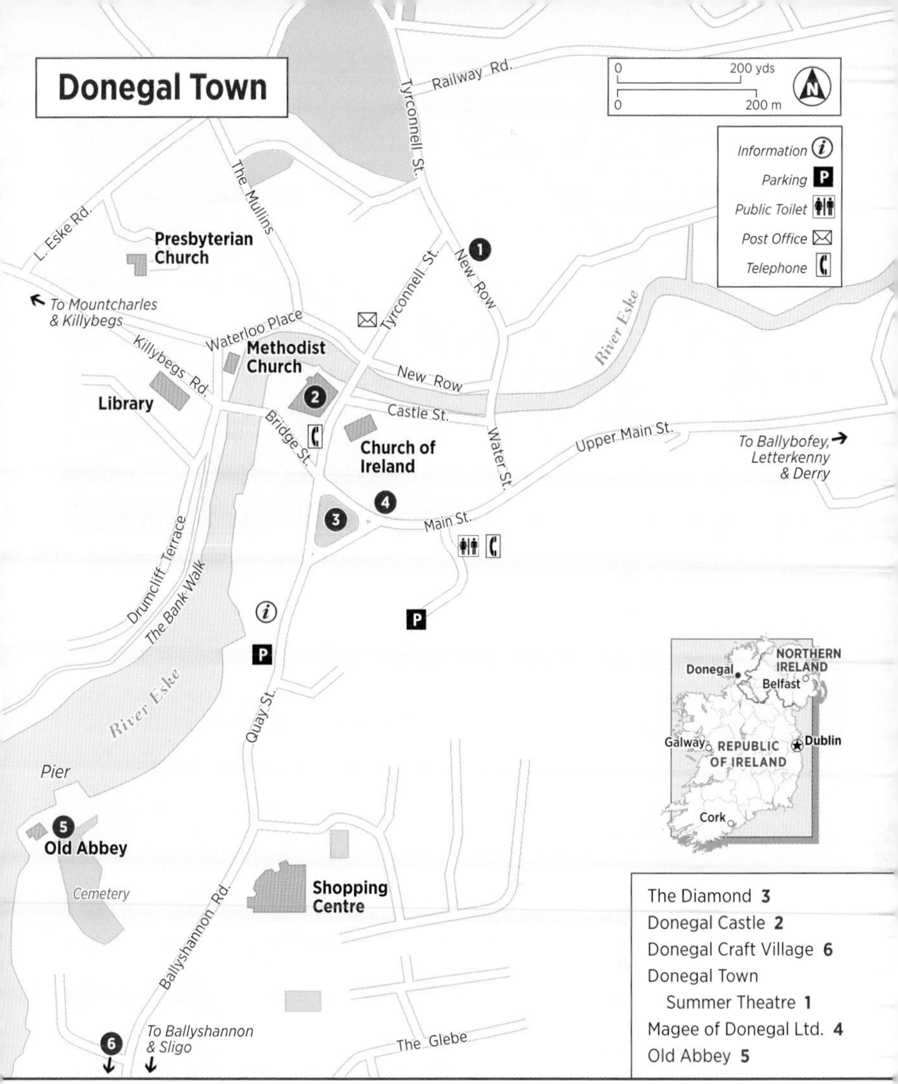

The **Donegal Post Office** on Tirconnail Street (✆ **074/972-1024**) is open Monday to Friday 9am to 5:30pm, Saturday 9am to 1pm.

Exploring Donegal Town

The center of town—physically and metaphorically—the **Diamond** is a market square dominated by an obelisk erected in memory of four early-7th-century Irish clerics from the local abbey who wrote the first recorded history of Gaelic Ireland, *The Annals of Ireland.*

Lough Derg and its many islands lie about 16km (10 miles) east of Donegal. Legend has it that St. Patrick spent 40 days and 40 nights fasting in a cavern at this secluded spot, and since then it has been revered as a place of penance

Four generations of the Barnes family have run Biddy O'Barne's, which promises a roaring fire, live music, and perfect pours.

and pilgrimage. From June 1 to August 15, thousands of Irish people take turns coming to Lough Derg to do penance for 3 days at a time, remaining awake and eating nothing but tea and toast. It's considered one of the most rigorous pilgrimages in all of Christendom. To reach the lake, take R232 to Pettigo, then R233 for 8km (5 miles).

Donegal Castle Built in the 15th century on the banks of the River Eske, this solid, grey-stone castle was once the chief stronghold for the O'Donnells, a powerful Donegal clan. In the 17th century, during the Plantation period, it was taken over by Sir Basil Brook, who added an extension with 10 gables, a large bay window, and smaller mullioned windows in Jacobean style. Much of the building has survived the centuries, and both the interior and exterior of the castle were beautifully restored in the 1990s. In the summer, free guided tours are often available.

Castle St., Donegal. ✆ **074/972-2405.** Admission €4 adults; €3 seniors; €2 students and children; €10 families. Easter to mid-Sept daily 10am–6pm; mid-Sept to early Apr Thurs–Mon 9:30am–4:30pm. Last admission 45 min. before closing.

Old Abbey Sitting in a peaceful spot where the River Eske meets Donegal Bay, this ruined Franciscan monastery was founded in 1474 by the first Red Hugh O'Donnell and his wife, Nuala O'Brien of Munster. It was generously endowed by the O'Donnell family and became an important center of religion and learning. Great gatherings of clergy and lay leaders assembled here in 1539. It was from this friary that some of the scholars undertook to salvage old Gaelic manuscripts and compile *The Annals of the Four Masters* (1632–36). Enough remains of its glory—ruins of a church and a cloister—to give you an idea of what once was.

The Quay, Donegal. Free admission.

SIGHTSEEING CRUISES

Donegal Bay Waterbus New and improved, this 160-seat boat has replaced the older, smaller version. The modern two-deck boat makes daily tours of Donegal Bay. The guided tour lasts 90 minutes and passes the Old Abbey and Seal

Island, home to a colony of about 200 noisy seals. (***Warning:*** The guide never seems to take a break, and the detailed commentary is nonstop.) The views are wonderful. Sailing times are usually morning and afternoon or evening, but are dependent upon weather and the tides. Tickets can be obtained from the ticket office on the pier.

The Pier, Donegal Town. ✆ **074/972-3666.** www.donegalbaywaterbus.com. €15 adults; €10 seniors; €9 children 4–17; free for children 3 and under. Closed Oct–Mar 17.

Shopping

Most Donegal shops are open Monday to Saturday from 9am to 6pm, with extended hours in summer and slightly shorter hours in winter.

Donegal Craft Village This cluster of artisans' shops in a rural setting about 1.6km (1 mile) south of town provides a creative environment for an ever-changing group of craftspeople and a range of ancient and modern trades: porcelain, ceramics, weaving, wood sculpture, jewelry, and metalwork. You can browse from shop to shop and see the artists at work. The coffee shop serves baked goods, snacks, and lunch in the summer. The studios are open year-round Monday to Saturday 10am to 6pm and Sunday noon to 6pm. Ballyshannon Rd., Donegal. ✆ **074/972-2225.** www.donegalcraftvillage.com.

Forget-Me-Not/The Craft Shop This shop features a wide selection of gifts both usual and unusual. Items include handmade jewelry, Celtic art cards, Donegal county banners and hangings, Irish traditional music figures, tweed paintings, bog oak sculptures, and beaten-copper art. The Diamond, Donegal. ✆ **074/972-1168.** www.forgetmenot.ie.

Magee of Donegal Ltd. Established in 1866, this shop is *the* name for fine Donegal hand-woven tweeds, including beautiful suits, jackets, overcoats, hats, ties, and even material on the bolt. The Diamond, Donegal. ✆ **074/972-2660.** www.mageedonegal.com.

Melody Maker Music Shop If you're enchanted by the traditional and folk music of Donegal, stop in here for tapes, recordings, and posters. This is also the main ticket agency for the southwestern section of County Donegal, handling tickets for most concerts and sports nationwide. Castle St., Donegal. ✆ **074/972-2326.** www.donegalmusicshop.com.

William Britton & Sons Established in 1874, this shop stocks antique jewelry, silver, crystal, clocks, sports-related sculptures, pens, and watches. W. J. Britton is a registered appraiser and a fellow of the National Association of Goldsmiths of Great Britain and Ireland. Main St., Donegal. ✆ **074/972-1131.**

DONEGAL TOWN summer FESTIVAL

If you're heading this way in early July, you may want to check out **www.donegaltown.ie** for details of the town's annual Summer Festival. The program is an enthusiastic mixture of free concerts (from local bands that, in all probability, you've never heard of) and family-friendly fun and games. The festival lasts 4 days, with the biggest events scheduled over a weekend.

Sports & Outdoor Pursuits

BICYCLING The north side of Donegal Bay offers great cycling roads—scenic but very hilly. For long-distance bikers, one good but arduous route from Donegal Town follows the coast roads west to Glencolumbkille (day 1), continues north to Ardara and Dawros Head (day 2), and then returns to Donegal (day 3). It takes in lots of spectacular coastal scenery along the way. Rental bikes are available from the **Bike Shop,** Waterloo Place (✆ **074/972-2515**). The cost varies based on the kind of bike, but starts at around €10 a day, €60 a week.

FISHING For advice and equipment for fishing in Lough Eske and other local waters, contact **Doherty's Fishing Tackle,** Main Street (✆ **074/972-1119**). The shop stocks a wide selection of flies, reels, bait, and fishing poles. It's open Monday to Saturday 9am to 6pm.

WALKING Crossing Boyce's Bridge on the Killybegs road will bring you to the beginning of the **Bank Walk** to your left. This 2.5km (1.5-mile) walk is delightful, following the west bank of the River Eske as it empties into Donegal Bay. It offers great views of the Old Abbey, Green Island, and Donegal Bay.

Where to Stay

VERY EXPENSIVE

Harvey's Point Country Hotel ★ About 6km (3¾ miles) northwest of town, this elegant, rambling, Swiss-style lodge sits in splendid isolation on the shores of Lough Eske at the foot of the Blue Stack Mountains. The enormous guest rooms (each room's size is listed on the hotel website), which have sweeping views of either the lake or the mountains, are elegantly decorated with mahogany furniture, creamy wallpaper, and plush linens. Bathrooms are spacious and modern. The excellent **restaurant** was recently expanded down to the edge of the lough, so ask for a table by the window and enjoy sunset on the water.

Tullan Strand-Bundoran, a moody beach on Ireland's wildest coast.

Hikers along the Slieve League, the country's most dramatic coastal walk.

Lough Eske, Donegal, County Donegal. www.harveyspoint.com. ✆ **074/972-2208.** 20 units. €180–€390 double; €580–€700 suite. Rates include service charge, tax, and full breakfast. AE, DC, MC, V. Closed Mon–Fri Nov–Mar. **Amenities:** Restaurant; bar; lounge; bike rental; boat rental. *In room:* TV, hair dryer, minibar, broadband Internet.

Solis Lough Eske Castle ★★ About 5km (3 miles) northeast of town, this meticulously restored 19th-century castle is a regal option. Outside it's an impressive, stone-turreted building; inside it's an elegant country house with fires burning in the many fireplaces, a library where you can retire with a whiskey, and a gallery bar where you can mingle with other guests. Rooms have been done in classic style, with ivory wall coverings, masculine coffee-and-cream fabric color schemes, big, comfortable beds, and views of either the lake or the mountains (although the less expensive rooms have views of the castle courtyard). Bathrooms are spacious and marble, each one individually designed, some with claw-foot tubs. The restaurant has cream-colored, button-back sofa banquettes and picture windows overlooking the countryside. There's a small spa, a sauna, and a sunlit indoor pool as well.

Lough Eske, Donegal, County Donegal. www.solisloughheskecastle.ie. ✆ **074/972-5100.** 99 units. €220–€300 double. Rates include service charge, full breakfast, and tax. AE, DC, MC, V. **Amenities:** Restaurant; bar; pool; sauna; spa. *In room:* TV, hair dryer, Wi-Fi.

MODERATE

Mill Park Hotel ★ A few minutes' walk from Donegal Town center, this modern hotel and wellness center is a great option in its price range. The large guest rooms are neatly, if a bit colorfully, decorated with modern furnishings and fabrics in yellow and russet hues. The lobby and lounge are lovely, with polished wood floors and nicely chosen rustic decor. The restaurants (including an upscale traditional Irish restaurant and a modern cafe-bar with lighter Mediterranean-style cuisine) are good options, and the health center is a real bonus, with a beautifully designed pool and gym. There are great deals to be had by booking online in advance.

Killybegs Rd., Donegal, County Donegal. www.millparkhotel.com. ✆ **074/972-2880.** Fax 074/972-2640. 115 units. €110–€200 double. Rates include full breakfast. AE, DC, MC, V. **Amenities:** 2 restaurants; bar; gym; Jacuzzi; indoor pool; spa; steam room. *In room:* TV, hair dryer.

INEXPENSIVE

Sheep cling to the hillsides of the Atlantic-battered Slieve League.

Ard na Breatha ★ Just a mile or so outside of Donegal Town, at the top of a hill and surrounded by peaceful green countryside, this friendly guesthouse has comfortable rooms and huge and hearty breakfasts. Built on a working farm, it's a welcoming place with a fire crackling in the hearth in the lounge, and gorgeous views of the Blue Stack Mountains. The split-level dining room overlooks Donegal Town in the near distance. Bedrooms are decorated in casual, country-house style, with wood or iron beds, fluffy wool rugs, and antique pine dressers. The excellent in-house **restaurant** offers local and organic modern-Irish cuisine, and a wide array of breakfast options—the food here is outstanding.

Drumrooske Middle, Donegal Town, County Donegal. www.ardnabreatha.com. ✆ **074/972-2288.** 10 units. €80 double. Rates include service charge and full breakfast. MC, V. **Amenities:** Restaurant; bar; lounge. *In room:* TV, hair dryer.

Rhu-Gorse ★ Finding your way to this little guesthouse just outside of Donegal Town isn't easy, but your efforts will be well rewarded. A modern home of stature and character, beautifully set at the foot of the Blue Stack Mountains, Rhu-Gorse has a North Woods feel, with a big stone fireplace, open beams, thick duvets on soft beds, and country chic pine furniture. But the main attraction is the extraordinary view from each window—sweeping scenes of Lough Eske and the encircling mountains.

Lough Eske Dr. (8km/5 miles outside of Donegal), Lough Eske, Donegal, County Donegal. www.lougheske.com. ✆/fax **074/972-1685.** 3 units. €85 double. Rates include full breakfast. MC, V. Free parking. Closed Nov–Apr. *In room:* TV.

Where to Eat

As in many towns in northwest Ireland, the best restaurants here are in hotel dining rooms. However, the following are also good choices.

The Harbour SEAFOOD This family-friendly restaurant on Quay Street emphasizes freshness (the seafood comes from Killybegs each day, and the sources of all the meats and eggs are listed on the menu). The lengthy and varied menu includes everything from fish to pizza. Options include roast salmon in a champagne butter sauce, monkfish with buttered mash, and Irish sirloin steak with creamy chasseur sauce.

Quay St., Donegal. ✆ **074/972-1702.** Main courses €11–€25. MC, V. Daily 4–10pm.

The Weaver's Loft CAFE Upstairs from Magee's tweed shop, this 60-seat self-service restaurant with its huge mural of Donegal conveys the feel of times past. The menu changes daily, but usually includes prawn, cheese, and fruit salads, as well as tasty sandwiches, soups, cakes, and tarts.

Magee Shop, The Diamond, Donegal. ✆ **074/972-2660.** Main courses €5–€10. AE, MC, V. Mon–Sat 9:45am–5pm.

Donegal After Dark

Nightlife in Donegal Town is very low-key, but if you're in town during July and August, try to take in a performance of the Donegal Drama Circle at the **Donegal Town Summer Theatre,** O'Cleary Hall, Tirconaill Street (no phone). Performances are held on Tuesday, Wednesday, and Thursday at 9pm and feature works by Donegal-based playwrights. No reservations are necessary; admission prices start at around €5 for adults, €3 for students.

PUBS

Biddy O'Barnes You have to detour into the Blue Stack Mountains and the scenic Barnesmore Gap, 11km (6¾ miles) northeast of Donegal Town, to visit this pub, which has been in the same family for four generations. Passing through the front door—with its etched-glass window and iron latch—is like entering a country cottage, with blazing turf fires, stone floors, wooden stools, and benches. On most evenings, there's a spontaneous music session. Donegal-Ballybofey rd. (N15), Barnesmore, County Donegal. ✆ **074/972-1402.** www.biddysobarnes.com.

The Olde Castle Bar There is an old-Donegal aura at this little pub, which has a welcoming open fireplace, etched glass, and whitewashed walls. The bartenders are friendly and there's a good menu of pub food. Castle St., Donegal. ✆ **074/972-1262.** www.oldecastlebar.com.

The Schooner Inn Given the name, it's somewhat unsurprising that this pub is decorated with model ships and seafaring memorabilia. There is music on most summer evenings, with traditional Irish music on Monday and Saturday, folk music on Wednesday, and singing acts on Thursday, Friday, and Sunday. Upper Main St., Donegal. ✆ **074/972-1671.**

THE DONEGAL BAY COAST

The Donegal Bay coast extends for 80km (50 miles) from Bundoran (32km/20 miles S of Donegal Town) to Glencolumbkille (48km/30 miles W of Donegal Town)

The rugged coastline around Donegal Bay is wild and beautiful. The rocky land careens toward the dark blue Atlantic, where the roads end just short of the icy water. Roads corkscrew so tightly that it will almost make you dizzy, and the main speed limit is the one you impose on yourself, as speeds much above 55kmph (35 mph) are dangerous. That's just as well, since the spectacular views will cause you to stop again and again to take in the rolling hills, jagged mountains, bright green fields, and crashing seas. There's plenty to see and do here, as there are excellent beaches and watersports, as well as seaport towns, folk museums, and craft centers.

The towns along the way are varied: To the south of Donegal Town, **Bundoran *(Bun Dobhráin)*** is a tacky seaside town with little to offer to anyone except the surfers who make the most of its famously rough surf, while **Ballyshannon *(Béal Átha Seanaidh)*** is a busy, pretty hill town that many use as a base for exploring the surrounding countryside. In the summer, **Rossnowlagh *(Ross Neamblach)*** is nicer and also has a fine beach. To the north of Donegal Town, the coastal scenery is breathtaking, especially once you pass the little town of **Killybegs *(Ceala Beaga).*** The mountains reach right to the sea, creating the breathtakingly rugged coastline for which Donegal is famed. Killybegs itself is a fishing town known for its handmade carpets, while nearby, near the foot of the striking Slieve League cliffs, **Kilcar *(Cill Chártha)*** is a manufacturing center for warm Donegal tweed.

> **Irish Only**
>
> **Along with counties Mayo and Kerry, Donegal is in the Gaeltacht, or Irish-language, section of the country. Increasingly, road signs in these regions are being changed into Irish only. We're including the Irish names as well as the English names for the places where you're likely to encounter this.**

Area Essentials

GETTING THERE & AROUND **Aer Arann** (✆ **818/210-210** in Ireland, or 0870/876-76-76 in the U.K.; www.aerarann.com) operates daily flights from Dublin and twice-weekly flights from Glasgow (Scotland) to Donegal Airport, Carrickfinn, Kincasslagh, County Donegal (✆ **074/954-8284**), about 65km (40 miles) north of Killybegs.

Bus Éireann (✆ **074/912-1309;** www.buseireann.ie) runs daily bus service to Killybegs and Glencolumbkille, on the northern half of the bay, and to Ballyshannon and Bundoran, on the southern half of the bay.

The best way to get to and around Donegal Bay is by car. Follow the N15 route on the southern half of the bay, the N56 route on the northern half of the bay.

VISITOR INFORMATION The official Donegal tourism website, **www.donegaldirect.ie**, is a good all-round resource. It has a hotel-booking tool, which includes a list of up-to-date special offers, comprehensive entertainment listings, and a useful section of suggested driving routes with maps. Otherwise, you could contact the **North West Tourism Office,** Aras Reddan, Temple Street, Sligo (✆ **071/916-1201;** www.discoverireland.ie/northwest); the **Letterkenny Tourist Office,** Derry Road, Letterkenny (✆ **074/912-1160**); or (the diminutive) **Bundoran Tourist Office,** The Bridge, Bundoran, County Donegal (✆ **071/984-2539**). The first two are open daily year-round; the third is open daily from June through August and Thursday to Sunday in September.

Southern Donegal Bay

To reach the southern section of Donegal Bay from Sligo, take the N15 road up the Atlantic coast, and at about 32km (20 miles) north, you'll come to **Bundoran,** the southern tip of County Donegal and a major beach resort. A victim of its own success, Bundoran is littered with tacky amusement arcades, fast-food restaurants, and cheap souvenir stands, and offers little to warm your heart, unless you're toting a surfboard—its waves draw surfers from throughout Europe. In recent years, Bundoran has tried to rebrand itself as kind of the Las Vegas of northwest Ireland, complete with an annual Elvis festival in November. Whether you find this to be a good or bad thing depends entirely on your tolerance for kitsch.

Continuing up the coast, you'll pass **Ballyshannon.** Dating from the 15th century, it has a charming town center with a distinctive clock tower where its two main streets meet; it's another favorite with beachgoers, and is known for its lively pubs and traditional music. In late July or early August, the **Ballyshannon Folk Festival** brings music to the streets day and night.

County Donegal

Abbey Mills **10**
Ardara Heritage Centre **12**
Catsby Cave **9**
Doe Castle **2**
Donegal Historical Society Museum **11**
Fort Dunree Military Museum **5**
Glebe House & Gallery **4**
Glencolumbkille Folk Park **13**
Glenveagh National Park **3**
Greencastle Maritime Museum **7**
Grianan of Aileach **6**
Lough Derg **8**
The Workhouse **1**

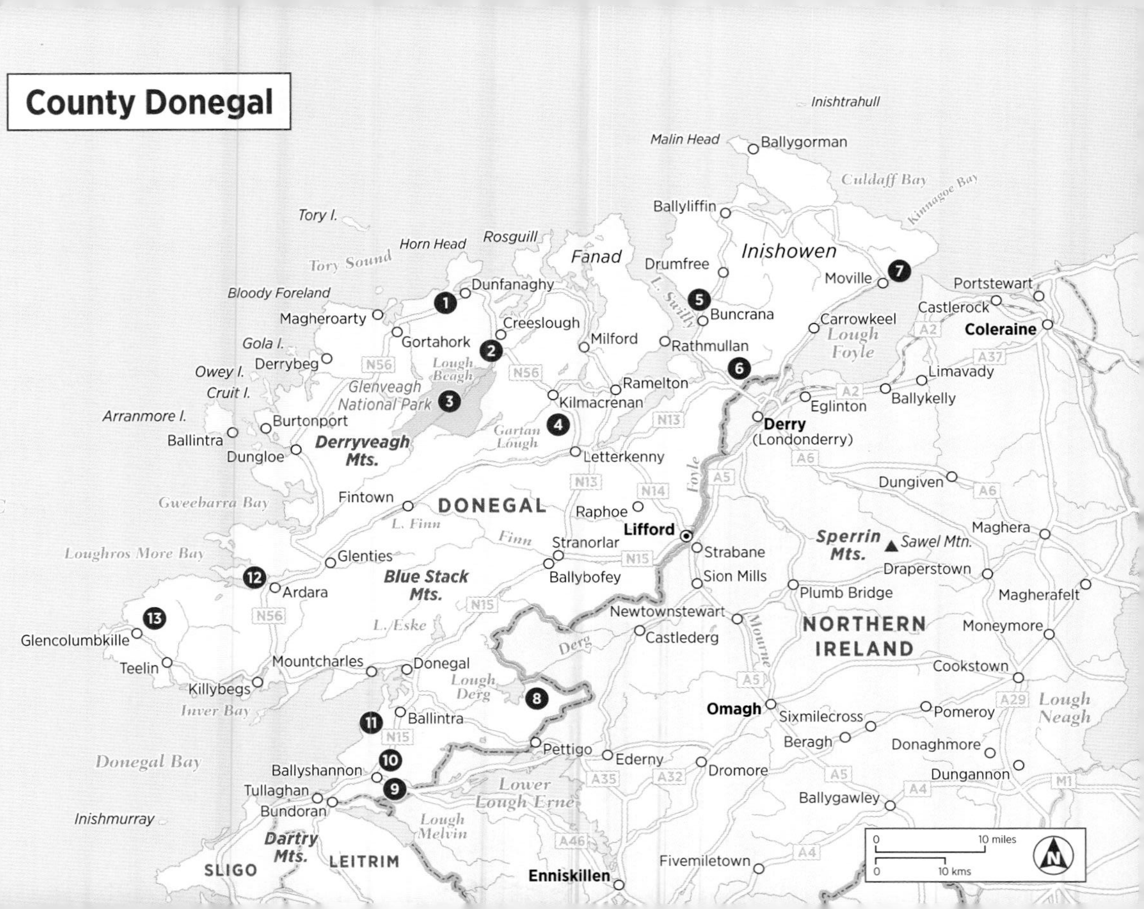

Two kilometers (1¼ miles) northwest of Ballyshannon, **Abbey Mills** is a heritage center inside a restored portion of the grand Cistercian Assaroe Abbey, which was founded in 1184 and mostly lies in ruins. However, the great mill wheel has been rebuilt and is driven by water from the Abbey River just as in ancient days. Some 50m (164 ft.) away, at the edge of the Abbey River, **Catsby Cave** is a grotto where a rough-hewn altar still stands. Here, Mass was celebrated in secrecy during the so-called "penal years" (17th–19th c.), when Catholic rituals were illegal.

If it's a sunny day, you may want to leave the main road and head for the coastal resort of **Rossnowlagh,** with its gorgeous Blue Flag beach. At over 3km (2 miles) long and as wide as the tides allow, it's a flat sandy stretch shielded by flower-filled hills and ideal for walking. You'll see horses racing on it occasionally, and this spot is a splendid vantage point for watching sunsets over the sea.

Overlooking the beach from a hilltop is the **Donegal Historical Society Museum,** Rossnowlagh (✆ **071/985-1342;** www.donegalhistory.com), inside a somber Franciscan friary. Its small exhibit on local history is limited in scope, but the place itself—vast gardens overlooking the sea and peaceful woodlands—is extraordinary. There's a tearoom with outdoor seating and a shop with religious objects. It's open daily from 10am to 5pm. There's no admission charge, but donations are welcome.

From Rossnowlagh, return to the main road via the **Donegal Golf Club** (see "Sports & Outdoor Pursuits," below) at Murvagh, a spectacular setting nestled on a rugged sandy peninsula of primeval dune land, surrounded by a wall of dense woodlands. From here, the road curves inland to Donegal Town.

SHOPPING

Britton and Daughters In a cottage across from the Sandhouse Hotel, this workshop is a source of unusual crafts, including glass hand-etched with local scenes and Celtic, nautical, and wildlife designs; carved rocks (heads, Celtic designs, dolphins, and so on); and posters. Off the Ballyshannon-Donegal rd., Rossnowlagh, County Donegal. ✆ **071/985-2220.**

SPORTS & OUTDOOR PURSUITS

BEACHES Donegal Bay's beaches are wide, sandy, clean, and flat—ideal for walking. The best are **Rossnowlagh** and **Bundoran.**

GOLF The Donegal Bay coast is home to two outstanding 18-hole championship seaside golf courses. **Donegal Golf Club,** Murvagh, Ballintra, County Donegal (✆ **074/973-4054;** www.donegalgolfclub.ie), is 5km (3 miles) north of Rossnowlagh and 11km (6¾ miles) south of Donegal Town. It's a par-73 course with greens fees of €50 weekdays, €65 weekends.

The **Bundoran Golf Club,** off the Sligo-Ballyshannon road (N15), Bundoran, County Donegal (✆ **071/984-1302;** www.bundorangolfclub.com), is a par-69 course designed by Harry Vardon. The greens fees are €45 weekdays, €55 weekends.

SURFING Bundoran is popular with surfers for its steady waves, and has hosted the European Surfing Championships. Rossnowlagh also has excellent surf, and attracts lots of surfers. When the surf is up, you can rent boards and wet suits locally from around €5 per hour per item.

WHERE TO STAY

Expensive

Sandhouse Hotel Perched at the edge of the Blue Flag beach at Rossnowlagh, this is a friendly, homey hotel with exceptional sea views. Warmed by open fireplaces, the public rooms are decorated with antiques and local art, while a sunlit, plant-filled conservatory offers sweeping views of the sea. Guest rooms are a bit old-fashioned in style, and vary in size; all are decorated with a slightly haphazard mixture of antiques and replicas. Beds are comfortable, but have cheap-looking nylon bedspreads, but views from the sea-facing rooms are outstanding. The restaurant is excellent, and specializes in fresh Donegal Bay seafood. You can relax in the small spa or just walk along the 3.2km (2 miles) of soft sand right outside the door.

Off the Ballyshannon-Donegal rd. (N15), Rossnowlagh, County Donegal. www.sandhouse-hotel.ie. ✆ **800/44-UTELL** (448-8355) in the U.S., or 071/985-1777. Fax 071/985-2100. 64 units. €130–€190 double. Rates include full Irish breakfast. AE, MC, V. Closed late Dec to Jan. **Amenities:** Restaurant; bar; lounge; Jacuzzi; marine spa; steam room; tennis court. *In room:* TV, hair dryer, broadband Internet.

Moderate

Fitzgerald's Hotel This small, family-run hotel overlooking Donegal Bay is popular for its reasonable prices and no-nonsense approach. The owners actually promote the hotel's nonacceptance of both tour groups and private functions (a rare boast indeed), but that all adds to the hotel's personable atmosphere. Bedrooms are spacious, with slightly out-dated contemporary decor that does look tired in places, but the **restaurant** is one of the best places to eat in the otherwise unlovely town of Bundoran.

Bundoran, County Donegal. www.fitzgeraldshotel.com. ✆ **071/984-1336.** Fax 071/984-2121. 16 units. €80–€150 double. Rates include full Irish breakfast. MC, V. Closed late Nov to early Feb and Sun–Tues in Oct and Nov. **Amenities:** Restaurant; Wi-Fi. *In room:* TV, hair dryer.

Inexpensive

Ard-na-Mara ★★ A beautiful country home nestled between the Blue Stack Mountains and Rossnowlagh's Blue Flag beach, Ard-na-Mara is a relaxing getaway with panoramic views of the sea. The hotel is a 3-minute walk from the beach, so it's perfect in the summertime. Rooms are simply but pleasantly decorated, so this place is a good low-cost alternative to the more expensive hotels in the area.

Rossnowlagh Rd., Rossnowlagh, County Donegal. www.ardnamara-rossnowlagh.com. ✆ **071/985-1141.** 7 units. €90 double; €25 children 12 and under. Rates include full Irish breakfast. MC, V. Closed late Dec to Jan. *In room:* TV, hair dryer.

WHERE TO EAT

Heron's Cove MODERN IRISH One of an expanding breed of so-called "restaurants with rooms," Heron's Cove is technically a B&B, although the restaurant is really the business end of things here. Chef Dierdre Clinton (awarded the title "Irish Chef of the Year" in 2008) specializes in unpretentious modern cookery. Steaks and seafood lead the way in the glossy dining room, with polished wood floors and padded chairs draped in white linen, and the wine list is above average. The menu changes with the seafood seasons, but opt for the summer

In the 6th century, St. Columba established a monastery here at Glencolumbkille.

pudding if it's being offered for dessert (it's not pudding as most of us know it, but a light cake crust stuffed with seasonal fruit; it's alarmingly purple, but quite delicious). Attractively decorated guest rooms cost around €90 per night for a double.

On the main Ballyshannon-Rossnowlagh rd., Creevy, County Donegal. ✆ **071/982-2070.** www.heronscove.ie. Reservations recommended. Dinner main courses €18–€26. MC, V. Mon–Tues 6–9:30pm; Wed–Sat 6–10pm; Sun 2 lunch sittings, 12:30pm and 3pm, then 6–9:30pm.

SOUTHERN DONEGAL BAY AFTER DARK

In summer **Rossnowlagh** is a hub of social activity. People flock to the **Sandhouse Hotel** (see above) on the beach for the nautical atmosphere of the Surfers Bar.

Farther south, the **Thatch Bar** at Dorrian's Imperial Hotel, Main Street, Ballyshannon, County Donegal (✆ **071/985-1147;** www.dorriansimperialhotel.com), holds nightly sessions of Irish traditional music in summer. It also has one of those straight-from-a-postcard Irish exteriors that are impossible to pass without stopping to take a photo. Inside, you can stay in one of the chintz-draped bedrooms for around €85 a night for a double.

Northern Donegal Bay

From Donegal Town, follow the main road (N56) for a slow, spectacularly scenic drive along the northern coast of Donegal Bay, where the road winds along past sheer cliffs, craggy rocks, bog land, panoramic mountain and sea views, and green pastures. You'll often see the distinctive thatched-roof cottages typical of this area—with rounded roofs held down by ropes (called *sugans*) fastened beneath the eaves to help the thatch resist the strong sea winds. It's only 48km (30 miles) from Donegal Town to gorgeous Glencolumbkille, the traditional end of the west coast drive, but these are some of the most winding roads you'll ever drive, so it can take an hour or more.

Your first stop could be at **Killybegs *(Ceala Beaga)***—where, if you arrive around sundown, you can watch the fishing boats unloading the day's catch—or at Studio Donegal in **Kilcar *(Cill Chártha)*** if you're interested in picking up Donegal tweed at a bargain (see "Shopping," below).

Spectacular photo ops await at **Slieve League *(Sliabh Liag)* ★★**, with its perilously high sea cliffs crashing down into the waters below. (Take the turnoff for the Bunglass viewing point at Carrick.) Once at the cliffs, you must decide whether you want to merely gaze at their 300m (984-ft.) splendor or to brave a wind-buffeted walk along the treacherous ridge. (This walk should only be for the fearless and fit. Including the climb up and then back down, the hike is about 10km/6.25 miles and takes 4 or 5 hr.)

Just before you come to Killybegs, the N56 road swings inland and northward, and the landscape becomes desolate and wild. Continue on the coastal road west to discover the extraordinary beauty of **Glencolumbkille *(Gleann Cholm Cille)* ★★**, a 5,000-year-old Atlantic outpost. Here the dark bogs disappear, replaced by a lush green valley. It is said that St. Columba established a monastery here in the 6th century and gave his name to the glen (its Gaelic name—*Gleann Cholm Cille*—means "Glen of Columba's Church"). Those interested in the history of the place will want to stop by the **Glencolumbkille Folk Park ★** (✆ **074/973-0017;** www.gleanncholmcille.ie). Built by the people of Glencolumbkille in the form of a tiny village, or *clachan,* this modest theme park of thatched cottages reflects life in this remote corner over centuries. There are miniature playhouses to entertain the children, while a tearoom serves traditional Irish stews and *brútin* (a stew of hot milk and potatoes). Hearty Guinness cake is a house specialty. In the *sheebeen,* a shop of traditional products, check out the local wines made from fuchsia, heather, seaweed, and tea. Admission and tour are €4 for adults, €2.50 for seniors and children, and €11 for families. It's open Monday through Saturday from 10am to 6pm and Sunday noon to 6pm, Easter through September.

To continue touring from Glencolumbkille, follow the signs directing you to the charming, hilly town of **Ardara *(Árd an Rátha),*** reached over a mountainous terrain. The road follows another breathtaking drive, through **Glengesh Pass,** a narrow, sinuous, scenic roadway that rises to a height of 270m (886 ft.) before plunging, in a tortuously zigzag pattern of hairpin curves, into the valley below. The road leads eventually to tiny Ardara, a stone village known for its tweed and woolen craft shops (see "The Atlantic Highlands," below).

SHOPPING

Folk Village Shop Part of Glencolumbkille's folk park mentioned above, this is well worth a visit in its own right for smart shopping. The well-stocked shelves of this whitewashed cottage feature the arts and crafts of members of the local community—hand-knit sweaters and other woolen items, turf-craft art, books, jewelry, and assorted cottage industry souvenirs. Since the Folk Village operates as a charitable trust, purchases are not subject to VAT (sales tax), so you save some money and help a good cause by shopping here. Glencolumbkille, County Donegal. ✆ **074/973-0017.**

Lace House A combination crafts shop and information bureau, this is where you go for almost everything in Glencolumbkille, including advice and good conversation. It also sells lovely local crafts, including woolen knitted items and the titular lace. Glencolumbkille, County Donegal. ✆ **074/973-0116.**

Studio Donegal Started in 1979, this hand-weaving enterprise is distinguished by its knobby tweed, subtly colored in tones of beige, oat, and ash. You can walk around the craft shop and the mill and see the caps, jackets, and cloaks in the making. Kilcar is on the R263 between Killybegs and Glencolumbkille, about 32km (20 miles) west of Donegal Town. Glebe Mill, Kilcar. ✆ **074/973-8194.** www.studiodonegal.ie.

Taipeis Gael The name means "Gaelic Tapestry," and it refers to a group of artists who create unique Irish tapestries using natural dyeing, carding, spinning, and weaving skills handed down from generation to generation. The completed tapestries are influenced by Gaelic culture, music, and folklore. There are week-long tapestry-making courses during the summer months, should you want to try it yourself. Malin Beg, Glencolumbkille, County Donegal. ✆ **074/973-0325.** taipeisgael@eircom.net.

SPORTS & OUTDOOR PURSUITS

BEACHES Glencolumbkille has two fine beaches: One is the flat, broad, sandy beach at the end of Glencolumbkille village, where the R263 swings left; the lesser known gem is a tiny beach surrounded by a horseshoe of cliffs, accessible from the small road signposted to Malin More (off the R263) about 1.6km (1 mile) southwest of town.

BICYCLING If you're very fit, the north side of Donegal Bay has great cycling roads—tremendously scenic if very hilly. One good but arduous route from Donegal Town follows the coast roads west to Glencolumbkille (day 1), continues north to Ardara and Dawros Head via Glengesh Pass (day 2), and then returns to Donegal (day 3). It takes in some of the most spectacular coastal scenery in Ireland along the way, but takes place on small winding roads that must be shared with cars. Rental bikes are available in Donegal from the **Bike Shop** (✆ **074/972-2515**), Waterloo Place, Donegal, for roughly €10 per day.

FISHING Surrounded by waters that hold shark, skate, pollock, conger, cod, and mackerel, **Killybegs** is one of the most active centers on the northwest coast for commercial and sport sea fishing. **Brian McGilloway** (✆ **087/220-0982;** www.killybegsangling.com) operates full-day fishing expeditions on the 12m (39-ft.) MV *Meridian,* from Blackrock Pier. Prices average €55 per person per day, plus €15 for rods and tackle, or around €450 to €700, depending on what you want to catch, for a party of 8 to 10 (8 is preferable for comfort). The daily schedule and departure times vary according to demand; reservations are required.

WALKING The peninsula to the west of Killybegs boasts some of the most spectacular coastal scenery in Ireland, and much of it is accessible only from the sea or on foot. The grandeur of the **Slieve League ★★** cliffs makes the hills popular with hikers, but only attempt them with a good map, hiking boots, and basic provisions. The best way to visit this natural monument is to hike from the Bunglass lookout point to Trabane Strand in Malin Beg, a few miles southwest of Glencolumbkille. This walk crosses the notorious "One Man's Pass," a vertigo-inducing narrow ridge with steep drops on both sides. The distance from Bunglass to Trabane Strand is 15km (9⅓ miles), and you will have to arrange a pickup at the end. The summits of the Slieve League, rising almost 600m (1,968 ft.) above the sea, are often capped in clouds, and you should think twice about undertaking the walk if there is danger of losing visibility along the way.

Another lesser known walk that is just as spectacular is the coastal walk between Glencolumbkille and the town of **Maghera** (not so much a town as a small cluster of houses). Glen Head, topped by a Martello tower, overlooks Glencolumbkille to the north. This walk begins with a climb to the tower and continues along the cliff face for 24km (15 miles), passing only one remote outpost of human habitation along the way, the tiny town of **Port.** For isolated sea splendor, this is one of the finest walks in Ireland, but only experienced walkers with adequate provisions should undertake the walk, and only in fine weather.

WHERE TO STAY & EAT

The Blue Haven ★ CONTINENTAL On a broad, open sweep of Donegal Bay between Killybegs and Kilcar, this modern sky-lit restaurant offers 180-degree views of the bay from a bank of windows. It's an ideal place to stop for a meal while touring. The bar-food menu, available throughout the day, offers soups, sandwiches, and omelets. The dinner menu includes grilled fresh salmon, T-bone and sirloin steaks, and vegetarian tortillas. You can stay the night in one of 15 bright and sunny rooms, with views of Donegal Bay for €100 (double).

Largymore, Kilcar, County Donegal. www.bluehaven.ie. ✆ **074/973-8090.** Dinner reservations required. Dinner main courses €11–€26. MC, V. Daily 6–9:30pm; Sun 12:30–4pm.

Bruckless House ★ Clive and Joan Evans have restored their mid-18th-century farmhouse with such care and taste that every room is a delight. Furniture and art they brought back from their years in Hong Kong add a special elegance. All the guest rooms are spacious and bright. The gardens here sprawl for more than 15 acres, and have taken first prize in County Donegal's country garden competition at least twice in recent years. They are dazzling in the spring and summer. Inside and out, Bruckless House is a gem. Be sure to ask Clive to introduce you to his fine Connemara ponies that he raises and treasures. The **Gate House Lodge** can be rented as a self-catering cottage. It sleeps up to four people, and has its own private garden. The price ranges from €200 per week in the low season to €450 per week in July and August.

Signposted on N56, 19km (12 miles) west of Donegal, Bruckless, County Donegal. www.bruckless.com. ✆ **074/973-7071.** 4 units, 1 with private bathroom. €120 double with bathroom; €100 double with shared bathroom. Rates include full Irish breakfast. AE, MC, V. Closed Oct–Apr. **Amenities:** Smoke-free rooms. *In room:* No phone.

Dún Ulún House ★ This is a friendly and diverse hostelry with a B&B and two cottages, each with its own personality. The main building is unremarkable, but the extraordinary beauty of the seaside it overlooks makes it memorable. The rooms (with orthopedic beds) are cozy and comfortable, decorated with quilts and throw rugs. Then there's the cottage with an open fire in the kitchen and basic, functional furnishings in the bedrooms (rates are €25 per person per night). There's also a separate self-catering cottage across the street, which rents by the week for €250 to €400 plus electricity. If you like Irish music, this could be your place: The owners have a band made up of five family members who play traditional music.

R263 (1.6km/1 mile west of Kilcar), Kilcar, County Donegal. dunulunhouse@eircom.net. ✆ **074/973-8137.** 10 units, 9 with private bathroom. €75 double. Rates include full breakfast. MC, V. Free parking. *In room:* TV.

Kilclooney dolmen, in County Donegal's Atlantic Highlands, Ireland's wildest and most desolate region.

Kitty Kelly's ★ SEAFOOD/CONTINENTAL You can't miss this 200-year-old farmhouse restaurant on the coastal road out of Killybegs—just look for a bright pink building with a green door next to Fentra Beach. Inside the place is packed with old-world charm, and the fresh seafood is exceptional, arriving each day, fresh off the boat. Look out for the daily specials, which are often the best thing on the menu.

Largy, Killybegs, County Donegal (5km/3 miles west of Killybegs on coast road). www.kittykellys.com. ✆ **074/973-1925.** Fixed-price 3-course menu €40; dinner main courses €25 (includes coffee). AE, MC, V. Daily 7–9:30pm.

PUBS

Harbour Bar This popular meeting place in Killybegs holds an Irish-music night on Tuesdays during July and August. Main St., Killybegs, County Donegal. ✆ **074/973-1049.**

THE ATLANTIC HIGHLANDS

The Atlantic Highlands start at Ardara, 40km (25 miles) NW of Donegal Town, 16km (10 miles) N of Killybegs

This is the most isolated part of Donegal, which is the most isolated county in Ireland, so it doesn't get much more rugged, exhilarating, and, well, *isolated* than this. There is a point when you're driving through the highlands, where the signs drop all pretense at bilingualism and switch to Gaelic. This is disconcerting, because most maps are in English, and the Gaelic names and the English names of places frequently are not even distant relatives. It's disorienting—one minute you know exactly where you are and the next you haven't a clue. It's as if somebody has stolen your compass. At that moment, which often occurs on a mountainside by a rushing stream amid rocky terrain where there's no space to pull the car over and stare more closely at the useless map, you're in the true Donegal. With its breathtaking coastal scenery, mountain ranges, and the lunar landscape of its rocky beaches, you could fill your camera's memory card here.

The best place to start a tour of Donegal's Atlantic Highlands is at **Ardara *(Árd an Rátha)*** ★, an adorable village about 40km (25 miles) northwest of Donegal Town. From there, weave your way up the coast, turning inland when a place lures you to do so. This drive can take 4 hours or 4 days, depending on your schedule and interests. ***Our advice:*** Take your time. You may never come this way again, and you will want to remember every moment.

Atlantic Highlands Essentials

GETTING THERE & AROUND **Aer Arann** (✆ **011/353-81821-0210** in the U.S., 818/210-210 in Ireland, or 0870/876-76-76 in the U.K.; www.aerarann.ie) operates regularly scheduled flights from Dublin to **Donegal Airport,** Carrickfinn, Kincasslagh, County Donegal (✆ **074/954-8284**), in the heart of the Atlantic coast.

Bus Éireann (✆ **074/912-1309;** www.buseireann.ie) operates daily bus service to Ardara and Glenties from Donegal Town.

The best way to get to and around Donegal's Atlantic Highlands is by **car,** starting on the main N56 route, but don't expect a freeway—at times the N56 is so narrow, it's difficult for two cars to pass. Signs are infrequent and occasionally in Gaelic, so pay close attention when you pass them. It's easy to miss a turn if you're lulled into complacency.

VISITOR INFORMATION Contact the **North West Tourism Office,** Aras Reddan, Temple Street, Sligo (✆ **071/916-1201;** www.discoverireland.ie/northwest); the **Letterkenny Tourist Office,** Derry Road, Letterkenny (✆ **074/912-1160**); or the **Donegal Tourist Office,** Quay Street, Donegal (✆ **074/972-1148;** www.donegaltown.ie). The first two are open year-round; the third is open from Easter through September.

Exploring the Region

Looking as if it were carved from stone, charming little **Ardara** is known for its exceptional tweed and wool creations. Astride a narrow river in a steep gulch, it is a pleasant place to stop, chat with the locals, and do a bit of shopping or maybe have a cup of tea in its small but useful heritage center. If you happen to arrive in June, you may be lucky enough to catch the **Ardara Weavers Fair,** which has been going on since the 18th century, and features spectacular works in wool.

Heading north from Ardara, the landscape rolls across green hills and splashes into clear lakes. There are two little resort towns here—**Naran *(An Fhearthainn)*** and **Portnoo**—which are favorites with Irish families in the summer. They have lovely beaches, particularly Naran which has an excellent Blue Flag beach. A little farther along is the neat-as-a-pin little town of **Glenties *(Na Gleanta),*** which unsurprisingly has been the winner several times of the Irish Tidy Towns competition. It's excellent for fishing and for walks. The playwright Brian Friel set his play *Dancing at Lughnasa* here.

From here, the road curves inland to towns like **Gweedore *(Gaoth Dobhair),*** where Gaelic is the primary language and the countryside is increasingly desolate, but you're just a few miles from the gorgeous **Glenveagh National Park** and **Mount Errigal,** Donegal's highest mountain. The park is strewn with lakes and thick forest, and is home to rare golden eagles. At the edge of the park, Glenveagh Castle is a good place to meet other travelers, a bit of a relief after a long time driving empty roads.

Out along the coast, the road passes through Dungloe to an area known as the **Rosses,** extending from Gweebarra Bridge as far north as Crolly. It's a hard and rock-strewn land, but strangely beautiful, punctuated by mountains, rivers, and glassy lakes. Along the way, you'll pass **Burtonport** ***(Ailt an Chorrain),*** and it's said that more salmon and lobster are landed here than at any other port in the country.

The coastal area north of the Rosses, between Derrybeg and Gortahork, is known as the **Bloody Foreland,** from the fact that its rocks take on a ruddy color when lit by the setting sun. If you can arrange to be driving through such far-flung terrain at sunset on a clear day, you are in for a treat.

Next you'll approach the top rim of Donegal, dominated by a series of small peninsulas like fingers of land jabbing out into the sea. **Horn Head** ***(Corrán Binne)*** is the most extraordinary of these, with breathtaking cliffs towering 180m (590 ft.) above the sea. But roads on this headland are a bit perilous in places, and definitely not for those uncomfortable with heights. At the base of the peninsula, **Dunfanaghy** ***(Dún Fionnachaidh)*** is one of the prettiest little towns you'll pass, with a great beach, much favored by Irish families. After Horn Head, the next peninsula to the east is **Rosguill** ***(Ros Goill).*** The 16km (10-mile) route around this peninsula is much less traumatic than the one around Horn Head, and is called the Atlantic Drive. This leads you to yet another peninsula, the **Fanad,** with a 73km (45-mile) circuit between Mulroy Bay and the glassy waters of Lough Swilly. The village of **Rathmelton** ***(Ráth Mealtain)*** is another one of those distinctive Irish villages that seems to have been hewn from the rocky hillside. It is tiny and eminently photographic, with its gray Georgian warehouses reflected in the mirrorlike water of the lake. It was once a bustling place, apparently, but then the rail line was rerouted to Letterkenny, and it all went quiet here. A few miles away, along a winding waterfront road, the village of **Rathmullan** ***(Ráth Maoláin)*** is an excellent stopping point, with a couple of good hotels, an evocative ruined abbey, and a beautiful stretch of flat, sandy beach on which to stroll or ride horses.

Ardara Heritage Centre Ardara has long been a center for weaving, and this center's varied displays represent the history of tweed production in the region. A video provides an outline of nearby places of interest. The staff is eager to help, and the cafe serves inexpensive teas, soups, and simple meals.

On N56 in the center of Ardara, County Donegal. ✆ **074/954-1704.** Admission €3 adults; €1.70 seniors and students; €1.20 children 13 and under. Easter–Sept Mon–Sat 10am–6pm; Sun 2–6pm.

Doe Castle This little tower house is so complete, it looks as if you could move in today and set up well-fortified housekeeping. A battlement wall with round towers at the corners encloses the central tower; the view from the battlements across the bay is superb. Built in the early 16th century, the castle was extensively restored in the 18th century and inhabited until 1843. It's a lovely little place, surrounded on three sides by the waters of Sheep Haven Bay, and on the fourth by a moat carved into the bedrock that forms its foundation. If the entrance is locked, you can get the key from the caretaker in the house nearest the castle.

5.6km (3½ miles) off N56; turnoff signposted just south of Creeslough, County Donegal. Free admission.

Glebe House and Gallery ★ Sitting in woodland gardens on the shores of Lough Gartan, about 6.5km (4 miles) southwest of Glenveagh, this Regency-style house was built as a rectory in the 1820s. It was owned until recently by English artist Derek Hill. Hill donated the house and his art collection to the

Irish government. The house is decorated with Donegal folk art, Japanese and Islamic art, Victoriana, and William Morris papers and textiles. The stables were converted into an art gallery housing the 300-item Hill Collection of works by Picasso, Bonnard, Yeats, Annigoni, and Pasmore.

18km (11 miles) northwest of Letterkenny on the Churchill rd. (R251), Church Hill, County Donegal. ✆ **074/913-7071.** Admission €3 adults; €2.20 seniors; €1.30 students and children; €8 families. Easter week only 10am–6pm, then late May and June Sat–Thurs 11am–6:30pm; July–Aug daily 11am–6:30pm. Last tour 1 hr. before closing. Closed Sept–Easter.

Glenveagh National Park and Castle ★★★ This thickly wooded valley is a lush forest paradise, with the lavish Glenveagh Estate at its core. It is beautiful and pleasant now, but its history is dark. This was originally the home of the infamously cruel landlord John George Adair, who evicted scores of struggling tenant farmers in the freezing winter of 1861, ostensibly because their presence on his estate was ruining his view. If the tale is true, it's a form of divine justice that his estate now belongs to all of the people of Ireland. In keeping with his reputation, Adair didn't donate the property to anybody. He sold it to the distinguished Philadelphia art historian Henry McIlhenny, and then McIlhenny donated the land and house to the Irish nation. Today the fairy-tale setting includes woodlands, herds of red deer, alpine gardens, a sylvan lake, and the highest mountain in Donegal, Mount Errigal. There's a visitor center with a little shop, and a charming tearoom in the castle. ***Tip:*** You can take a shuttle bus from the visitor center to the castle for a round-trip fare of €3.

Main entrance on R251, Church Hill, Letterkenny, County Donegal. ✆ **074/913-7090.** www.glenveaghnationalpark.ie or www.heritageireland.ie. Free admission to park. Castle €5 adults; €3 seniors; €2 students and children; €10 families. Mar–Oct daily 10am–6:30pm (last admission 5pm); Nov–Feb daily 9am–5pm (last admission 4pm).

Once the home of a brutal English landlord, Glenveagh Castle and its lush gardens now belong to the Irish people.

The Workhouse ★ This simple stone structure was one of 100,000 workhouses in Ireland during the Great Famine, which killed around a million people across the country. This one was constructed in 1844, just before the height of the famine, and it provided meals and a roof for more than 300 people. Exhibits here portray the life of workhouse inmates, local famine history, and the history of Dunfanaghy. There's also a craft center and cafe.

Just west of Dunfanaghy on N56, County Donegal. ✆ **074/913-6540.** www.dunfanaghyworkhouse.ie. Admission €4.50 adults; €3 seniors and students; €2.50 children; €10 families. Mon–Sat 10am–1pm.

Shopping

Ardara is a hub of tweed and woolen production. Most shops are open Monday to Saturday 9am to 5:30pm, with extended hours in summer. Unless otherwise noted, shops are on the main street of the town (N56).

C. Bonner & Son With 500 hand-knitters throughout County Donegal and 50 weavers in its factory, C. Bonner & Son produces a wide selection of hand-knit and hand-loomed knitwear, including linen-cotton and colorful sheep-patterned lamb's-wool sweaters, all for sale here in its factory outlet. Also for sale is a broad selection of crafts and gifts, including sheepskins, pottery, wool hangings, linens, crystal, and china. Closed January and February. Glenties Rd., Ardara, County Donegal. ✆ **074/954-1196.** Also at Front St., Ardara, County Donegal. ✆ **074/954-1303.**

C. Kennedy & Sons Ltd. Established in 1904, this family-owned knitwear company employs about 500 home workers who hand-knit or hand-loom *bainin* sweaters, hats, scarves, and jackets in native Donegal patterns and colors. The shop also sells turf crafts, pottery, and dolls. Ardara, County Donegal. ✆ **074/954-1106.**

Eddie Doherty A hand-weaver with over 40 years experience, Eddie weaves throws, scarves, caps, and shawls in a variety of colors and designs, some of which reflect the colors of the Donegal landscape. The loom is on display and the weaving is demonstrated to visitors. Ardara, County Donegal. ✆ **074/954-1304.** www.handwoventweed.com.

John Molloy In the heart of wool and weaving country, this factory shop is well stocked with hand-knits, homespun fashions, sports jackets, tweed scarves and rugs, and all types of caps, from kingfisher to *ghillie* styles. There's even a bargain bin. Factory tours are available as are weaving demonstrations. Ardara, County Donegal. ✆ **074/954-1133.** Also at Glencolumbkille ✆ **074/973-0282.** www.johnmolloy.com.

Sports & Outdoor Pursuits

BEACHES The western coast of Donegal has lots of pristine and secluded beaches. If you like populated beaches, several of them spread around Dawros Head, including **Traighmore Strand** in Rossbeg, and the Blue Flag beaches in Portnoo and Navan. **Magheroarty,** near Falcarragh on the northern coast, has a breathtaking beach, unspoiled by crowds or development. The same goes for **Tramore** beach on the western side of Horn Head near Dunfanaghy; you have to hike a short distance, but the rewards are seclusion and miles of creamy sand. Other peaceful sandy beaches ideal for walking and jogging include **Carrigart, Downings, Marble Hill,** and **Port na Blagh.**

BIRD-WATCHING **Horn Head,** a nesting site for many species of seabirds, has a huge nesting population of razorbills. **Malin Head,** at the end of the Inishowen Peninsula, is a good site for watching migrating species in late autumn.

FISHING The rivers and lakes in this area produce salmon, sea trout, and brown trout, and the coastal waters yield flounder, pollock, and cod. Fishing expeditions are offered by charter boats, fishing boats, and trawlers. For details, contact the **North Western Regional Fisheries Board,** Abbey Street, Ballina, County Mayo (✆ **096/22788;** www.northwestfisheries.ie or www.cfb.ie).

GOLF One of Ireland's most challenging golf courses is the **Rosapenna Golf Club,** Atlantic Drive, Downings, County Donegal (✆ **074/915-5000;** www.rosapenna.ie), an 18-hole championship seaside par-70 links course that was laid out in 1983 by Tom Morris of St. Andrews. It also has the newer Sandy Hills links, which was named the top course in Britain and Ireland by *Golf World* magazine in 2008. Greens fees are €60 at the Tom Morris course and €85 at Sandy Hills. There's a €10 discount if you book your tee time online.

Other 18-hole courses in this part of Donegal are **Dunfanaghy Golf Club,** Dunfanaghy, County Donegal (✆ **074/913-6335;** www.dunfanaghygolfclub.com), a seaside par-68 course with greens fees of €30 weekdays, €40 weekends; **Narin & Portnoo Golf Club,** Narin-Portnoo, County Donegal (✆ **074/954-5107;** www.narinportnoogolfclub.ie), a par-69 seaside course with greens fees of €45 weekdays, €60 weekends; and **Portsalon Golf Club,** Portsalon, County Donegal (✆ **074/915-9459;** www.portsalongolfclub.com), a seaside par-69 course with greens fees of €40 weekdays, €50 weekends.

HORSEBACK RIDING **Dunfanaghy Stables,** Arnold's Hotel, Dunfanaghy, County Donegal (✆ **074/913-6208;** www.dunfanaghystables.com), specializes in trail riding on the surrounding beaches, dunes, and mountain trails. An hour's ride averages €30 adults, €25 children. Between May and September they also offer guided trail riding holidays, which include all meals and 7 nights stay at **Arnold's Hotel** (see below), for between €1,140 and €1,240 per person.

WALKING A section of the **Ulster Way** passes through Donegal between the towns of Falcarragh to the north and Pettigo to the south, on the border with Fermanagh. This trail traverses some remote and wild terrain, passing Mount Errigal and Glenveagh Park before heading south into the Blue Stack Mountains, so should not be undertaken without a good map, proper attire, and supplies.

There are some incredible walks on **Hook Head,** signposted off N56 just west of Dunfanaghy. Follow Hook Head Drive to the concrete lookout point. From here you can walk out to a ruined castle on the headland and continue south along a line of impressive quartzite sea cliffs that glitter in the sun as though covered with glass. This is a moderately difficult walk.

The **Ards Forest Park** is on a peninsula jutting out into Sheep Haven Bay, about 5.6km (3½ miles) south of Dunfanaghy on N56. The park is mostly forested and includes an area of dunes along the water. There are signposted nature trails, and you can buy a guidebook as you enter the park.

Where to Stay

EXPENSIVE

Castle Grove ★ This beautiful white manor house sits like a jewel in a crown of sweeping green grounds originally designed by the famed Lancelot "Capability" Brown in the 18th century. Its lounges are done in a traditional style, with big fireplaces in the lounges. Guest rooms are large and decorated with antiques; all have peaceful, bucolic views. Breakfasts are grand here, and usually include fresh fish options, as well as homemade breads and cereals. There are boats you can borrow for fishing or rowing on the lake, there are stables with horses for trekking, and the house has an arrangement for guests to use three nearby golf courses.

Ballymaleel, off Ramelton Rd., Letterkenny, County Donegal. www.castlegrove.com. ✆ **074/915-1118.** Fax 074/915-1384. 14 units. €160–€190 double. Rates include full breakfast. MC, V. **Amenities:** Restaurant; bar; lounge; access to nearby golf courses; tennis courts; rowing. *In room:* TV.

Rathmullan House ★★★ On the western shores of Lough Swilly, Donegal's great sea lake, just outside of the sweet little village of Rathmullan, this secluded, sprawling country mansion is surrounded by extensive gardens and mature trees. The mostly Georgian (ca. 1760) mansion has beautifully appointed lounges where you can relax by a crackling fire. Rooms in the well-designed new wing are even more desirable than those in the original section, with polished wood floors, modern decor, gas fireplaces, and big claw-foot tubs in the spacious bathrooms. Small cottages are also available for those seeking more privacy. All rooms have orthopedic beds, and two are wheelchair accessible. The award-winning breakfast buffet is copious and imaginative, and dinner in the **restaurant** is a memorable event, especially if you like fresh local seafood or tender steak. ***Tip:*** The family rooms, which are interconnecting suites that sleep five, only cost about €50 to €80 more than a double.

Lough Swilly, Rathmullan, County Donegal. www.rathmullanhouse.com. ✆ **800/223-6510** in the U.S., or 074/915-8188. Fax 074/915-8200. 34 units. €190–€270 double. Rates include full Irish breakfast. Dinner €45–€55. MC, V. **Amenities:** Restaurant; bar; indoor pool; steam room; 2 tennis courts. *In room:* TV, hair dryer.

MODERATE

Fort Royal Hotel ★ Built in 1819, this rambling, three-story country house sits amid lush gardens and woodlands, with a small sandy beach on the western shore of Lough Swilly, just north of the Rathmullan village. Both the public areas and the guest rooms are decorated in a country-house style, with a mix of antiques and new pieces, and oil paintings of Donegal. Beds are covered in plaid or print bedspreads in blue or russet hues. Most have huge windows to take in the views of the lake or the colorful gardens. The restaurant specializes in seafood brought in that day by local fishing boats. It doesn't get fresher than that.

Rathmullan, County Donegal. www.fortroyalhotel.com. ✆ **800/447-7462** in the U.S., or 074/915-8100. Fax 074/915-8103. 11 units. €130–€180 double. Rates include full breakfast. AE, V. Closed Nov–Easter. **Amenities:** Restaurant; bar; lounge; golf course; tennis court; Wi-Fi. *In room:* TV.

Rosapenna Golf Hotel At the very edge of Sheephaven Bay, this contemporary two-story hotel is a favorite with golfers, who flock here for the 18-hole links course. (Greens fees are €30 to guests.) Nongolfers come for the scenery, the seclusion, and the hotel's location on a peaceful beach at the edge of the bay. The deluxe guest rooms, dining rooms, and lounges all have panoramic views of land and sea. Bedrooms are decorated in country casual style, with pillows, bedspreads, and curtains in floral patterns.

Atlantic Dr., Downings, County Donegal. www.rosapenna.ie. ✆ **074/915-5301.** Fax 074/915-5128. 53 units. €150–€175 double; €190–€220 suite. Rates include full breakfast. AE, MC, V. Closed late Oct to mid-Mar. **Amenities:** Restaurant; bar; 18-hole golf course; indoor pool; 2 tennis courts. *In room:* TV.

Shandon Hotel ☺ This family-owned hotel lures both couples looking for a spa getaway and families with children, with its pool, playground, spa, and excellent restaurant. At the foot of green rolling hills and overlooking Sheephaven Bay, the views here are extraordinary. All guest rooms have sea views and are spacious, with white walls, printed bedspreads and curtains. The restaurant specializes in fresh local seafood, and the bar is a great place for a post-dinner drink. But the main attraction is the setting—even the spa whirlpool tub is arranged to make the most of the view.

Marble Hill Strand, Sheephaven Bay, Dunfanaghy, County Donegal. www.shandonhotel.com. ✆ **074/913-6137.** 70 units. €130–€160 double. Rates include full Irish breakfast. MC, V. **Amenities:** Restaurant; gym; indoor pool; spa; steam room. *In room:* TV, hair dryer.

INEXPENSIVE

Ardeen House ★ This pretty white country house sits on peaceful grounds at the edge of the town of Ramelton overlooking Lough Swilly. Let the friendly owners know when you're arriving, and they'll have tea and fresh scones waiting when you get there. There's a snug lounge with a fireplace, while guest rooms are spacious and pleasantly decorated in neutral colors, with creamy white quilts, and a mix of antiques. Breakfast is served around the long dining table, and includes fresh fruits, homemade brown bread, and scones, as well as the usual eggs and bacon. There's also a lovely self-catering cottage with exposed stone walls and an open fireplace that rents for €350 to €500 per week.

Ramelton, County Donegal. www.ardeenhouse.com. ✆ **074/915-1243.** 5 units. €80–€90 double. Rates include full breakfast and taxes. MC, V. Closed Oct–Apr. **Amenities:** Smoke-free rooms. *In room:* No phone.

Arnold's Hotel Right across the road from Sheephaven Bay, this family-run place offers warm hospitality, sweeping views of the Atlantic, and endless outdoor activity. Brothers Derek and William Arnold run the place, acting as desk clerks, porters, waiters, horse wranglers, and whatever else is needed. Rooms are comfortable and attractive, if slightly bland, although those above the restaurant can smell of food. Arnold's is an ideal base for touring northwest Donegal and for exploring Glenveagh National Park. Golf, fishing, and pony trekking can all be arranged at the front desk. ***Tip:*** Check the website for good room-only and package deals.

Dunfanaghy, County Donegal. www.arnoldshotel.com. ✆ **800/44-UTELL** (448-8355) in the U.S., or 074/913-6208. 30 units. €80–€120 double. Rates include full breakfast. AE, MC, V. Closed Nov–Mar 15. **Amenities:** Restaurant. *In room:* TV.

SELF-CATERING

Donegal Thatched Cottages ★★ This cluster of cottages is spectacularly located on Cruit Island, an enchanting landscape of rock and sand just off the Donegal coast near Dungloe. Accessible by a small bridge, Cruit is a narrow finger of land pointing out into the Atlantic, dwarfed by its neighbors Aranmore and Owey islands. The cottages are on the Atlantic side, which alternates rocky headlands with unspoiled beaches; on the lee side, a quiet beach extends for miles. There's a great seaside walk along the western side of the island, which takes in a series of half-moon beaches. Each cottage has three bedrooms and is built according to a traditional plan, resembling many rural homes here, with wooden and tiled floors, high ceilings, and a great loft bedroom on the second floor. Although the location is remote, there are pubs and restaurants within a short driving distance.

Cruit Island, c/o Conor and Mary Ward, Rosses Point, County Sligo. Signposted opposite Viking House Hotel on Kincasslagh Rd., 9.5km (6 miles) north of Dungloe, Cruit Island. www.donegalthatchcottages.com. ✆ **071/917-7197.** 10 cottages. €340–€855 per cottage per week, plus €20 per person cover charge. Towels €20 per week. Turf for fire €20 per week. Weekend discounts available. MC, V. *In room:* TV, kitchen, no phone.

Termon House ★★★ 🎁 The setting of this remote seaside cottage is spectacular, directly on a wind-swept beach that calls out to be explored. Within walking distance of the wee village of Maghery, the house sleeps six people upstairs in three handsome bedrooms; downstairs there's a sitting room, a parlor, and a country-style kitchen with a Stanley range and a big farmhouse table. The house is full of treasures—sturdy mahogany furnishings, oversize sofas and armchairs, stone fireplaces, and deep windowsills with cushioned seats, perfect for relaxing with a book. As with all Irish Landmark Trust properties, there's no TV.

Termon House, Maghery (near Dungloe), County Donegal. Contact the Irish Landmark Trust at www.irishlandmark.com. ✆ **01/670-4733.** Fax 01/670-4887. €460 for 4 nights in low season, going up to €1,295 per week in high season. MC, V. *In room:* Kitchen.

Where to Eat

Dining in hotel restaurants is often a good idea. **Rathmullan House** (see above) has an excellent restaurant if you're in the mood to splurge.

The Mill Restaurant ★★ INTERNATIONAL This is deservedly one of the hottest dining destinations in this part of Donegal. The draw is the cooking, which is all about pairing ingredients to achieve disarming results. All the seafood dishes are exceptional, especially the Doe Castle mussels. Desserts are simple and elegant, and the wine list is well chosen. You can also spend the night in one of the Mill's immaculate guest rooms (€100 double).

Figart (.8km/½ mile past village of Dunfanaghy, beside lake), County Donegal. ✆ **074/913-6985.** www.themillrestaurant.com. Reservations recommended for dinner. Fixed-price dinner €44; dinner main courses €18–€27. MC, V. Tues–Sat 7–9pm; Sun 12:30–2pm and 7–9pm. Closed mid-Dec to Mar.

Water's Edge MODERN IRISH As its name implies, this restaurant is at the edge of picturesque Lough Swilly, and the dining room is designed to make the most of that setting with walls that consist almost entirely of windows. The modern exterior belies the traditional dining room, with beamed ceilings, an open fireplace, and watercolors of Donegal landscapes. The menu focuses on fresh Irish seafood and meats, including wild salmon and perfectly grilled steaks. More basic bar food is also served all day. If you like the place you can spend the night in one of the adorable, creamy white guest rooms (€120 double).

The Ballyboe, Rathmullan, County Donegal. ✆ **074/915-8182.** www.thewatersedge.ie. Reservations recommended for dinner. Dinner main courses €11–€27. MC, V. Easter–Sept daily noon–10pm.

Pubs

Most of the pubs in this Irish-speaking area are prone to sudden outbreaks of traditional Irish music in summer, which can be a good or bad thing, depending upon your perspective. Two places especially renowned for music are the **Lakeside Centre,** in the village of Dunlewey (in Gaelic: *Dún Lúiche*; ✆ **074/953-1699;** www.dunleweycentre.com), which also has a historic homestead garden, and **Leo's Tavern ★**, Meenaleck, Crolly (✆ **074/954-8143;** www.leostavern.com), which also has an excellent restaurant. The highly successful Irish group Clannad and the vocalist Enya (all part of the talented Brennan family) got their starts at Leo's.

The don't-miss pub in Ardara is **Nancy's ★** (✆ **074/954-1187**) on Front Street, which has to be one of the smallest pubs in Ireland. It's an old Victorian house with the pub in the sitting room. As the crowd pours in, other rooms open up in hospitality.

THE INISHOWEN PENINSULA

Buncrana: 113km (70 miles) NE of Donegal Airport, 84km (52 miles) NE of Donegal Town, 19km (12 miles) NW of Derry, 145km (90 miles) NE of Sligo, 359km (223 miles) NE of Shannon, 259km (161 miles) NW of Dublin

To drive around the Inishowen is to traverse desolate seascapes, intimidating mountains, restful valleys, and impenetrable woodlands. This is a world apart, where residents treasure the legends of Ireland and still observe its ancient traditions. If you've made it this far, well done! You join the hardy, lucky few who have discovered the rugged, peaceful beauty of Inishowen.

Inishowen Peninsula Essentials

GETTING THERE & AROUND Operated by local company Foyle Coaches, **North West Busways** (✆ **074/938-2116;** www.foylecoaches.com) offers service between Letterkenny and Moville, via Cardonagh and Buncrana, and there's daily Dublin-Inishowen service (via Derry) on offer by **John McGinley Luxury Coach Travel** (✆ **074/913-5201;** www.johnmcginley.com).

The best way to get to and around the Inishowen Peninsula is by car, following the signposted 161km (100-mile) Inishowen route.

VISITOR INFORMATION Contact the **North West Tourism Office,** Aras Reddan, Temple Street, Sligo (✆ **071/916-1201;** www.discoverireland.ie/northwest); the **Letterkenny Tourist Office,** Derry Road, Letterkenny (✆ **074/912-1160**); or the **Inishowen Tourism Society,** The Diamond, Cardonagh, County Donegal (✆ **074/937-4933;** www.visitinishowen.com). The latter's website has excellent hotel and guesthouse listings if you want more options. All the tourist offices are open year-round Monday to Friday 9:30am to 5:30pm, with extended summer hours.

Seeing the Sights

To an extent, driving around the northernmost point of Ireland is worth doing just so you can say you did. You stood on Malin Head and felt the icy mist come in on a wind that hit you like a fist, and you balanced yourself on the rocky edge of the country and looked out at the true north. You have felt the satisfaction that comes from knowing there is no farther to go.

Luckily, though, there's more to Inishowen than that. The **Inishowen (*Inis Eoghain*)** Peninsula reaches out from Lough Foyle to the east and Lough Swilly to the west toward Malin Head, its farthest point. Around the edges are ancient sites, beautiful beaches, and charming villages. At its center are gorgeous views, mountains, and quiet, vivid green pastures. If you are looking to get lost, this is a great place to do it.

But it won't be easy. Inexplicably, despite its clear need to be off the beaten path, and even with a decided dearth of traffic, the Inishowen Peninsula circuit is very well signposted, with all directions clearly printed in English and Irish, miles and kilometers.

To make a loop around the peninsula, start in the bustling little town of **Moville (*Bun an Phobail*),** which is a good place to stock up on gas and picnic provisions, and after a few miles of coastal road, you'll soon find yourself driving through **Greencastle (*An Cáisleá Nua*),** which holds the quirky Maritime Museum and Planetarium. From there, it's a short drive to the picturesque Inishowen Head. Follow signs off the main road onto a small side road, which you can take to the end, and then you walk the rest of the way to the headland. It's a bit eerily isolated, but the views are stupendous—on clear days, you can see all the way to the Antrim Coast. Back along the main road, look for a turnoff for **Culdaff (*Cúil Dabhcha*),** a sleepy waterfront village with a pretty beach. On its main street, the Clonca Church is a solid 17th-century structure with a high cross carved on one side with the biblical tale of loaves and fishes, and on the other with Celtic designs.

From Culdaff, it's about a 20-minute drive north to the pretty town of **Malin (*Málainn*),** with its stone bridge and village green. From Malin, it's another 20-minute drive to **Malin Head (*Cionn Mhélanna*),** a satisfyingly remote place at the end of the road where, even on a sunny day, the wind often howls and the temperature can be 10° colder than it is just 20 miles south. The farther north you go, the tinier the road becomes, the hillier and wilder the terrain, and the fewer the signs; a few corkscrew turns later and you'll be wondering where you are, but persevere. There are not really many places to go here, so follow your instincts and the few signs, and meander past the small cluster of houses until you

A rugged beach on Culdaff Bay.

reach rocky **Banba's Crown *(Fíor-cheann Éireann),*** the farthest point of the headland. Here, winds permitting, you can wander down to the rocky edge of the land and catch a glimpse of some old concrete huts built in World War II as lookout points. To the west of them is **Hell's Hole,** a natural land formation where waves crash deafeningly against the craggy shore. To the east, a path leads to a hermit's cave known as the **Wee House of Malin.**

The Culdaff Bay lighthouse.

Finding your way back to the main road without any signs is half the battle, and once you've done it, you're soon around the top of the peninsula and headed down the other side, through the **Gap of Mamore,** a mountain pass that rises 240m (787 ft.), then slowly descends on a corkscrew path to sea level, past a series of small, scenic villages to busy **Buncrana,** an excellent place to rest and have a meal. From the northern end of the seafront, you can find the old stone Castle Bridge that leads to **O'Doherty's Keep,** a simple, ruined tower house that served as the headquarters of the O'Doherty clan from the 15th century until it was destroyed 300 years later. The ruins next to it are all that's left of the castle that the English built to replace it. Appropriately, they are privately owned and inaccessible to the public; the O'Doherty grounds, on the other hand, can be explored for free.

About 16km (10 miles) south of Buncrana, the hilltop fort known as ***Grianan of Aileach*** is an beautifully preserved ring fort. It was built as a temple of the sun around 1700 B.C., and from the mid–5th century A.D. to the early 12th century A.D., it was the royal residence of the O'Neills, the chiefs of this area.

After you've toured the Inishowen, head south through **Letterkenny** (***Leitir Ceanainn;*** pop. 5,000). The largest town in the county, it's on a hillside overlooking the River Swilly. There you can pick up the N56, the main road, and drive to the twin towns of **Ballybofey** and **Stranorlar.** Change here to N15, which takes you to yet another scenic Donegal drive, the **Barnesmore Gap,** a vast open stretch through the Blue Stack Mountains, which leads you into Donegal Town and points south.

Fort Dunree Military Museum Perched on a cliff overlooking Lough Swilly, Fort Dunree is a military and naval museum that incorporates a Napoleonic Martello tower into more recent World War I defenses. It features a wide range of exhibitions, an audiovisual center, and a cafeteria housed in a restored forge. There are also displays on the wildlife of the area and the history of the fort itself. Even if you have no interest in military history, it's worth a trip for the extraordinary views.

Signposted on the coast road north of Buncrana, County Donegal. ✆ **074/936-1817.** www.dunree.pro.ie. Admission €6 adults; €4 seniors and children. Daily 10:30am–6pm.

Greencastle Maritime Museum and Planetarium This compact maritime museum, in the harbor home of a busy fishing fleet, is housed in the old 1857 coast guard station. Outside are grand views of Lough Foyle above a monument to those lost while working at sea. The museum's modest rambling exhibits focus on the everyday struggles, as well as the historical events, from armada wrecks and famine-era emigration to the heroism of the Irish lifeboat-rescue teams. There's even an incongruous Mesolithic exhibit. A small coffee, craft, and souvenir shop is at hand. Proving there's a little bit of everything here, a planetarium has three shows daily; call ahead to confirm times.

Harbour, Greencastle, County Donegal. ✆ **074/938-1363.** www.inishowenmaritime.com. Admission to museum €5 adults; €3 seniors, children, and students. Admission to museum and planetarium €10 adults; €6 seniors, children, and students. Easter–Oct Mon–Sat 9:30am–5:30pm, Sat–Sun noon–5:30pm; Nov–Easter Mon–Fri 9:30am–5pm.

Sports & Outdoor Pursuits

BEACHES **Ballyliffin, Buncrana, Greencastle,** and **Moville** have safe, sandy beaches ideal for swimming or strolling.

GOLF The Inishowen is a major center for golf in Ireland, and it has four 18-hole golf courses. Two are at the **Ballyliffin Golf Club,** Ballyliffin, County Donegal (✆ **074/937-6119;** www.ballyliffingolfclub.com). The "Old Links" is a par-71 course with greens fees of €60; the "Glashedy Links" course costs €70. The **North West Golf Club,** Fahan, Buncrana, County Donegal (✆ **074/936-1027;** www.northwestgolfclub.com), founded in 1890, is a par-69 seaside course with greens fees of €30 weekdays, €35 weekends. **Greencastle Golf Course,** Greencastle, County Donegal (✆ **074/938-1013**), is a par-69 parkland course with greens fees of €25 weekdays, €35 weekends.

WATERSPORTS The Inishowen's long coastline, sandy beaches, and combination of open ocean and sheltered coves provide great opportunities for watersports. The northwest coast presents some of the most challenging surfing conditions in Europe. For advice and specific information, contact the **Irish Surfing Association,** Easkey Surf and Information Centre, Easkey, County Sligo (✆ **096/49428;** www.isasurf.ie).

Where to Stay & Eat

Ballyliffin Lodge ★ ☺ This boutique hotel in Ballyliffin village has sweeping views of Malin Head and the famous Inishowen coastline, and is popular with golfers for its two links courses, including one designed by Nick Faldo. Others are lured by its relaxing atmosphere, including its spa and leisure facilities. This is the kind of hotel where you can spend whole days without walking off the grounds. Guest rooms are fairly spacious, with a tasteful coffee-and-caramel color scheme and big windows. More expensive rooms have small balconies, just big enough for a table and chairs. The **Rock Crystal Spa** draws regulars all the way from Dublin for its relaxing treatments. Ballyliffin is a child-friendly hotel, with plenty of activities to keep the little ones busy.

Ballyliffin, County Donegal. www.ballyliffinlodge.com. ✆ **074/937-8200.** 40 units. €120–€160 double; €160–€260 suite. Rates include full breakfast. AE, MC, V. **Amenities:** Restaurants; bar; 2 links golf courses; gym; pool; sauna/steam room; spa. *In room:* TV, hair dryer, high-speed Internet.

Carlton Redcastle Hotel & Spa ★ On the shores of Lough Foyle, this elegant spa hotel offers a mix of old-world charm and modern luxury that hits just the right notes. Guest rooms are decorated in soothing contemporary style, in muted shades of taupe and charcoal. Many have views of the water, while others offer green countryside or golf course views. The comfortable orthopedic beds are wrapped in designer fabrics, and all bathrooms are marble. The **spa** will help you relax away all your cares, and you can work off some steam in the well-equipped gym. The indoor pool is beautifully designed with huge windows overlooking the water. ***Note:*** Rooms near the bar are noisy, so ask for a room far away from it if you're a light sleeper.

Redcastle, Moville, County Donegal. www.carltonredcastle.ie. ✆ **074/938-5555.** 71 units. €120–€170 double; €160–€260 suite. Rates include full breakfast. AE, MC, V. **Amenities:** 2 restaurants; bar; 9-hole golf course; gym; Jacuzzi; sauna/steam room; spa; tennis court. *In room:* TV, hair dryer, high-speed Internet.

Cosy Cottage CAFE This friendly, inexpensive eatery in Moville is often packed, largely because it's one of very few restaurants the little town has to offer. The menu is straightforward pub-style food: sausages and mash, steak and fries, chicken *goujons* (nuggets), deep-friend scampi. It's nothing fancy, but it's a pleasant place to grab a quick meal without spending a bundle. The owners also have cheap and cheerful self-catering flats you can rent in town for €150 to €250 a week

Bath Terrace Lane, Moville, County Donegal. www.thecosycottage.com. ✆ **074/938-5740.** Main courses €6–€12. MC, V. Mon–Sat noon–2pm and 6–8pm.

Kealy's Seafood Bar ★ SEAFOOD Right across the road from the pier in Greencastle, Tricia Kealy's friendly, always-buzzing little fish house is worth a special journey for the fresh local seafood. The chef knows what to pair with just-off-the-boat fish—poached hake in saffron sauce, plaice in anchovy butter, cod with Stilton—which makes dining here a surprisingly refined experience, given that the look of the place is not at all fancy. If you prefer, sidle up to the bar for an afternoon treat of fish chowder or smoked salmon on brown bread.

Greencastle, County Donegal. ✆ **074/938-1010.** Reservations recommended for dinner. Fixed-price dinner €40; dinner main courses €23–€50. AE, MC, V. Wed and Thurs 7–9pm; Fri–Sun 12:30–2:45pm and 7–9pm. Bar food daily 12:30–3pm. No children after 9pm. Closed Mon–Tues and 2 weeks in Nov.

The Red Door ★ MODERN EUROPEAN On vast grounds overlooking Lough Swilly, this lovely old Georgian house (built in 1785) has an elegant but cozy atmosphere throughout its two dining rooms. The food is unpretentious and crowd-pleasing, and led by what's in season: starters could be fresh crab and apple salad, or seared scallops with spicy chorizo sausages. Mains might be steak with colcannon (potatoes mashed with cabbage), or roast spring lamb with asparagus. Portions are generous and the atmosphere congenial. The wine list is a little pricey, but there are some good options for under €30 per bottle.

Fahan, County Donegal. ✆ **074/936-0289.** Reservations required. Main courses €14–€24. MC, V. Thurs–Sat 6–10pm; Sun 1–4:30pm and 5:30–10pm.

The Strand On a hillside overlooking Pollen Strand, with views of nearby Malin Head, this modern, family-run hotel is surrounded by tree-lined gardens. The decor throughout the hotel is contemporary, with wide windows and traditional touches. Guest rooms are neatly, though not imaginatively, appointed with beech wood furniture, plaid fabrics, and neutral carpets. Bathrooms are modern but smallish. The restaurant is popular with locals—it often hosts Irish music and is a good place to have a pint after dinner.

Ballyliffin, Clonmany, County Donegal. www.ballyliffin.com. ✆ **074/937-6107.** Fax 074/937-6486. 21 units. €90–€100 double. Rates include full breakfast. MC, V. **Amenities:** Restaurant; bar. *In room:* TV, hair dryer.

NORTHERN IRELAND

14

The terms Ulster, Northern Ireland, "the six counties," and "the North" are used interchangeably in Ireland for this small, ruggedly beautiful, and historically troubled land. The fact that nobody knows quite what to call it is somehow appropriate given the seemingly endless struggle that has gone on for the soul of this place.

For many years, visitors to Ireland avoided the North, for obvious reasons. In fact, the vast majority of people in the Republic of Ireland have never crossed the border into Ulster, and that's a pity. This is a colorful, exciting region, with vibrant towns and a countryside of breathtaking beauty. The way the locals treat you may come as a surprise—in fact, we'll go out on a limb and say that rural Northern Ireland is, in many ways, friendlier to visitors than the Republic. In part because of its relatively low tourism numbers, you'll find you are very welcome here, whereas, in the southern counties, the overwhelming flow of visitors has taken a toll on that famous Irish *faílte* (welcome).

Belfast and **Derry,** the North's only cities of any size, are both quite manageable, with winding streets and grand historical monuments. But the main draw here is the magnificent countryside: the cool greens of the **Glens of Antrim,** the rugged **Mourne Mountains,** and the famously craggy coastline culminating in the extraordinary lunar **Giant's Causeway.**

Still, the Troubles are obviously the elephant in the Northern Irish living room. It would be a unique visit that ignored politics entirely, whether it's the unforgiving murals in west Belfast or the strident graffiti that startles you in even the most bucolic village. Everybody picks a side in the Sisyphean effort to claim this rocky soil for God and country. But whose God and which country? Herewith, a quick rundown of the history of it all.

The strife in Northern Ireland can be traced back 800 years. In fact, there's an apocryphal story about a phone call between two friends—an Irish politician and an English parliamentarian—at the start of the Irish civil war in the 1920s. According to lore, the Englishman asked his Irish friend, "Is it true that there's an uprising in Ireland?" and the Irishman replied, "Aye, 'tis true." "When did it start?" the Englishman asked. "When Strongbow invaded Ireland," the Irishman said. "When will it end?" asked the Englishman. "When Cromwell gets out of hell." The story alludes to the fact that when the English first invaded Ireland in the 12th century, they were led by the Earl of Pembroke, nicknamed "Strongbow." They never really left, and some Irish have never quit trying to get rid of them.

Over the centuries, the British waged a largely futile effort to make Ireland, and the Irish, British. Their tactics included outlawing the Irish language, banning Catholicism, and barring Catholics from landownership; finally, in the mid-1600s, Oliver Cromwell's New Model Army went for the more basic approach of killing them in droves. British families were brought over to take their land—essentially, physically replacing Irish Catholics with British Protestants—in a

PREVIOUS PAGE: **Giant's Causeway, Northern Ireland's UNESCO World Heritage Site in County Antrim.**

An Creagán Visitors' Centre **12**
Andrew Jackson Cottage **26**
Ards Peninsula **35**
Armagh Astronomy Centre **51**
Armagh County Museum **30**
Beaghmore Stone Circles **11**
Belleek Visitors Centre **7**
Benburb Valley Park **53**
Carrick-A-Rede Rope Bridge **19**
Carrickfergus Castle **25**
Castle Coole **6**
Castle Espie **33**
Castle Ward **38**
Castlewellan Forest Park **49**
Crom Estate **8**
Devenish Island **5**
Down Cathedral **40**
Drum Manor Forest Park **10**
Drumena Cashel **48**
Dundrum Castle **41**
Dunluce Castle **23**
Dunluce Centre **22**
Enniskellen Castle **4**
Explore Erne **1**
Exploris **36**
Florence Court **2**
Giant's Causeway & Visitor Centre **20**
Giant's Ring **29**
The Glens of Antrim **24**
Gortin Glen Forest Park **13**
Grant Ancestral Home **9**
Gray's Printers' Museum **16**
Greencastle Fort **45**
Grey Abbey **34**
Irish Linen Centre **31**
Legananny Dolmen **44**
Lough Neagh Discovery Centre **30**
Marble Arch Caves **3**
Mount Stewart House **28**
The Mountains of Mourne **47**
Murlough Nature Reserve **42**
Navan Fort **52**
Nendrum Monastic Site **32**
Old Bushmills Distillery **21**
Peatlands Park **54**
Portaferry Castle **37**
Silent Valley Mountain Park **46**
Sperrin Heritage Centre **18**
St. Patrick Heritage Centre/
Down County Museum **39**
Tollymore Forest Park **43**
Rathlin Island Bird Sanctuary **18**
Ulster Folk & Transport Museum **27**
Ulster American Folk Park **14**
Wilson Ancestral Home **15**

Northern Ireland counties shown are the historic counties. UK counties were reorganized after 1973.

Northern Ireland
SCOTLAND
Culdaff Bay
Kinnagoe Bay
Rathlin I.
Mull of Kintyre
Giant's Causeway
Ballintoy
Fair Head
Torr Head
Portrush
Bushmills
Ballycastle
Moville
Portstewart
Castlerock
Coleraine
Armoy
Cushendun
North Channel
To Troon
Lough Foyle
Ballymoney
Cushendall
Red Bay
Limavady
Trostan
Ballykelly
Antrim Mts.
To Cairnryan
Carnlough Bay
Carnlough
Glenarm
To Stranraer
DERRY (LONDONDERRY)
Garvagh
Kilrea
Bann
ANTRIM
Dungiven
Broughshane
Sperrin Mts.
Sawel Mtn.
Maghera
Ballymena
Larne
Island Magee
Draperstown
Magherafelt
Ballyclare
Whitehead
Randalstown
Carrickfergus
Moneymore
Antrim
Greenisland
Belfast Lough
Newtownabbey
Belfast Int'l
Glengormley
Bangor
Donaghadee
To Douglas, Heysham, Liverpool
Cookstown
TYRONE
Lough Neagh
Crumlin
BELFAST
Newtownards
Pomeroy
Sixmilecross
Comber
Ards Peninsula
Coal Island
Lagan
Strangford Lough
Dungannon
Lisburn
Killinchy
Portavogie
Saintfield
Ballygawley
Craigavon
Lurgan
Augher
Portadown
Dromore
Ballynahinch
Killyleagh
Aughnacloy
Portaferry
Strangford
Tandragee
DOWN
Armagh
Banbridge
Downpatrick
Scarva
ARMAGH
Middletown
Markethill
Castlewellan
Dundrum
Ardglass
Monaghan
Keady
Rathfriland
Newcastle
Dundrum Bay
Newry
Mourne Mts.
MONAGHAN
IRISH SEA
Ballybay
Slieve Gullion
Warrenpoint
Castleblayney
Forkhill
Annalong
Omeath
Cootehill
Carlingford
Kilkeel
Carlingford Lough
Inniskeen
Greenore
Shercock
Dundalk
Fane
Carrickmacross
Louth
Bailieborough
Dundalk Bay
Dromiskin
Castlebellingham
Kingscourt
LOUTH
Dunany Point
Virginia
Ardee
Dunleer
L. Ramor
Nobber
Mullagh
Clogherhead
Oldcastle
MEATH
Collon
Tullyallen
Kells (Ceanannus Mór)
Knowth
Drogheda
Slane
Newgrange
IRELAND
NORTHERN
Map Area
Belfast
OF IRELAND
REPUBLIC
Galway
Dublin
Cork
A2
A44
A26
A37
A54
A6
A29
A42
A36
A8
A505
A5
A4
M1
A3
A1
A49
A7
A21
A50
A28
A25
A2
N54
N2
N1
N52
18
20
19
22
21
23
24
17
11
10
12
25
26
27
28
29
30
34
33
32
35
9
54
31
53
36
37
44
52
51
50
38
39
40
49
41
48
42
43
47
46
45

process the Irish called "planting." The descendants of those British settlers, generally speaking, form the Protestant population of Northern Ireland today.

After centuries of struggle, Ireland finally won independence of a sort from Britain in 1921, in the aftermath of the 1916 Rebellion. After much arguing, it was decided that the island would be divided. Twenty-six Irish counties would form an independent, free state (now the Republic of Ireland), while six counties in the Ulster province with predominantly Protestant populations would become Northern Ireland and remain a part of the United Kingdom.

When the six counties were detached from the rest of the island, two conflicting ideological bodies emerged: Unionists, associated with the Protestant majority, who want to remain a part of the United Kingdom, and nationalists, associated with the Catholic minority, who want the whole of Ireland united as one independent nation. Of course, being a Unionist or a nationalist doesn't imply approval of the violence. In fact, the overwhelming majority of Northern Irish people, regardless of whether they want British rule or Irish rule, oppose the use of violence.

After the division, the British police and government in Ulster were quite brutal toward the Catholic minority. Things came to a head in the late 1960s when the minority Catholic population began an intense civil rights campaign. Their marches and demonstrations were crushed by the authorities, sometimes with disproportionate levels of violence, thus setting the stage for the reemergence of the Irish Republican Army, a violent paramilitary nationalist group that first appeared early in the 20th century. This modern battle between the British authorities and the Irish resistance that became known as the Troubles began in 1969 and would not end for nearly 30 years.

Throughout the 1970s, violence was a fact of everyday life in Northern Ireland. By the 1980s, the violence was sporadic, if still shocking, and in the 1990s, the Northern Irish people—stunned by the sheer horror of an IRA bombing in the town of Omagh that killed 29 civilians on a busy shopping street—had had enough.

With the personal involvement of U.S. President Bill Clinton urging them to find a peaceful solution to their disagreements, on May 22, 1998, Northerners and their fellow islanders in the Republic voted to accept the Belfast Agreement,

The North: To Go or Not to Go?

The North is not for everyone. It's not a peaceful place, but it is a beautiful and fascinating one. This is not a war zone—even with the changing political landscape and the sporadic outbreaks of violence Ulster is generally safe for travelers.

Because of that, our advice is: Go. But go cautiously. And follow these basic rules:

- **Don't discuss the political situation or religion with anyone you don't know well.**
- **Don't get involved in political arguments. Ever.**
- **Don't travel deep into West Belfast.**
- **Consider touring the Shankill and Falls roads with an organized tour, rather than on your own.**
- **If you think a neighborhood looks unsafe, turn around and walk away.**
- **Most of Northern Ireland is perfectly safe for visitors, and you're very unlikely to see any violence at all. But remain alert and aware just the same.**

universally known as the "Good Friday Agreement." It dismantled the claims of both Ireland and Britain to the North and acknowledged the sovereign right of the people of Northern Ireland to take charge of their political destiny, effectively separating their government from London.

For nearly a decade after that peace agreement was signed, there was virtually none of the terrorism that once shattered the peace, but the issues that divide the people remained unresolved.

In 2009, violence flared again in this region, in a series of brutal murders and attacks on British soldiers, on people involved on one side or the other of the political landscape, and even on some who seemed to have no involvement in the struggle at all.

By 2011, the situation seemed calmer, but it was clear that nothing had really been settled. A spate of low-level violence continued, and a spinoff faction of the IRA, which calls itself the "Real IRA," took responsibility for most of the attacks. Tensions remained high

Still, from a visitor's perspective, the violence has always been remarkably contained. Like diplomats, foreigners have always had a kind of immunity. Derry and Belfast at their worst have always been safer for visitors than almost any comparable American city, and the Ulster countryside was then, and is now, as idyllic and serene as Vermont. When we've marveled at this, more than one Northern Irish person has told us, "It isn't your fight."

Keeping Your Irish Up

If you want to brush up on your knowledge of Northern Ireland, Newshound (www.nuzhound.com) is an indispensable resource. Run by American expat John Fay, this is an extremely well-organized catalog of news articles culled from Irish newspapers, covering everything from the Troubles to dining and shopping in Belfast. A vast array of articles about the Republic (click "NewsoftheIrish") includes culture, travel, and even dining reviews from Dublin to Donegal. The site is intelligent, user-friendly, and searchable.

NORTHERN IRELAND ESSENTIALS

Visitor Information

The **Belfast Visitor Welcome Center** is at 47 Donegall Place, Belfast (✆ **028/9024-6609;** www.discovernorthernireland.com or www.gotobelfast.com). In addition, there are more than 30 tourist information centers (TICs) scattered around the province, most of which are open year-round. The obliging personnel will make sure you see the highlights. Local accommodations may be booked in any TIC, and most are hooked up to online reservations systems that can secure reservations throughout all of Ireland and the United Kingdom. To make your own reservations anywhere in Ireland using a credit card, you can call the toll-free number (✆ **0800/6686-6866**).

Getting to the North

BY AIR Belfast has two airports—**Belfast International Airport** (✆ **028/9448-4848;** www.belfastairport.com) and **Belfast City Airport** (✆ **028/9093-9093;** www.belfastcityairport.com). **Continental** (✆ **800/231-0856;**

VISITING NORTHERN IRELAND: a checklist

- There is no marked land border. You don't need a separate visa or your passport when visiting from the Republic.
- Road signs are in **miles,** not kilometers. Signs around the border usually show both, but the switchover can be confusing.
- The currency is the **British pound,** although the euro is accepted unofficially in some border areas. The easiest and cheapest way to get the local currency is to stop at an ATM.
- Your cellphone company will treat Northern Ireland as the U.K., so if possible let them know in advance that you'll be going. They can help you save money on international roaming charges.
- Don't forget to check that your travel insurance and any car-rental agreements are equally valid in Northern Ireland.
- Not every difference is an inconvenience; unlike in the Republic (where there are no postal codes), Northern Irish hotels, restaurants, and attractions almost always list postal codes on their websites, which are extremely useful if your rental car has a GPS navigation system. You might want to make note of a few before you go.

www.continental.com) offers scheduled flights from New York to Belfast International.

A range of carriers provide service into both airports, including **easyJet** (✆ **0871/244-2366** in Britain; www.easyjet.com) from Liverpool, London, and many cities in continental Europe.

Service to **City of Derry Airport** (✆ **028/7181-0784;** www.cityofderryairport.com) is provided by **Ryanair** (✆ **0871/246-0000;** www.ryanair.com) from London Stansted, Birmingham, Liverpool, and Glasgow.

BY FERRY Ferry services into Belfast include **Norfolk Line Irish Ferries** (✆ **0844/499-0007** in Britain, or 01/819-2999 in Ireland; www.norfolkline.com), which takes 8 hours from Liverpool, and the **Isle of Man Steam Packet Co.** (✆ **08722/992-992;** www.steam-packet.com), which takes 2 hours and 45 minutes from Douglas, on the Isle of Man (summer service only). In addition, **Stena Sealink** (✆ **08705/707070;** www.stenaline.com) operates fast craft (105 min.) and ferry service (3 hr., 15 min.) from Stranraer, Scotland, to Belfast, and from Larne to the port of Fleetwood in the north of England; **P&O European Ferries** (✆ **08716/645-645;** www.poferries.com) from Fleetwood, Troon, and the Scottish port of Cairnryan to Larne.

BY CRUISE SHIP Cruise ships call at the deepwater facilities at Lisahally or at Queen's Quay in the city center. For the latest information on cruises to Derry Port, contact the tourist office.

BY TRAIN Trains on the **Irish Rail** (✆ **1850/366222;** www.irishrail.ie) and **Northern Ireland Railways** (✆ **028/9066-6630;** www.translink.co.uk) systems travel into Northern Ireland from Dublin's Connolly Station daily. They arrive at Belfast's **Central Station,** East Bridge Street (✆ **028/9089-9411**). Monday to Saturday, eight trains a day connect Dublin and Belfast;

on Sunday, it's five. The trip takes about 2 hours. Trains for Derry, Larne, Bangor, and Portadown depart from **Great Victoria Street Station** (Glengall St.; ✆ **028/9043-4424**). You can also use the U.K.-based **National Rail Enquiries** information line (✆ **08457/48-49-50;** www.nationalrail.co.uk). It's a useful one-stop resource for train times, although it can only help with journeys that start or end within Northern Ireland.

BY BUS **Ulsterbus** (✆ **028/9066-6630;** www.translink.co.uk) runs buses from the Republic to Belfast and towns across Northern Ireland. Belfast has two bus stations: The main **Europa Bus Centre** is behind the Europa Hotel and near the Great Victoria Street Station, while the **Laganside Bus Centre,** mainly used for buses into the surrounding counties, is on Oxford Street. The express bus from Dublin to Belfast takes under 3 hours and runs hourly Monday to Saturday, less frequently Sunday.

BY CAR You can easily reach Northern Ireland from the Republic of Ireland. Odds are you'll find it hard to identify the border at all since the big border crossings are long gone. Main roads to Northern Ireland from the Republic include N1 from Dublin (which is regularly under extensive construction), N2 from Monaghan, N3 from Cavan, N14 and N15 from Donegal, and N16 from Sligo. ***Important note:*** If you are renting a car and taking it across the border, make certain that all your insurance coverage is equally valid in the North and in the Republic. Don't forget to check any coverage provided by your credit card as well.

Getting Around in the North

BY TRAIN Belfast is the hub for **Northern Ireland Railways** (also known as Translink; ✆ **028/9066-6630**), with two principal rail stations: **Great Victoria Street Station,** on Great Victoria Street, and **Belfast Central Station,** on East Bridge Street. Most trains depart from Belfast Central. The three main routes in the North's rail system are north and west from Belfast to Derry via Ballymena; east to Bangor, tracing the shores of Belfast Lough; and south to Dublin via Newry.

BY BUS **Ulsterbus** (✆ **028/9033-3000;** www.translink.co.uk) runs daily scheduled service from Belfast to major cities and towns throughout Northern Ireland. From the **Laganside Bus Centre,** Donegall Quay, Belfast (✆ **028/9032-0011**), buses leave for destinations in the North, including Belfast International Airport and the Larne ferries, as well as the Republic. Bus service in the North is thorough and will get you to most towns of any size, although small villages are less well-served.

BY SIGHTSEEING TOUR From June to August, **Ulsterbus** operates full- and half-day coach tours from the Europa Bus Centre, Glengall Street, Belfast. The tours run to places such as the Glens of Antrim, Causeway Coast, Fermanagh Lakelands, Sperrin Mountains, the Mountains of Mourne, and Armagh. There are also tours to specific attractions, such as the Giant's Causeway, Old Bushmills Distillery, Navan Centre in Armagh, and the

Watch Where You Light Up

As in the Republic of Ireland, smoking has been banned in public places, including restaurants and bars, in Northern Ireland.

Ulster-American Folk Park in Omagh. For more information, visit or phone the Ulsterbus/Translink tourism office at the Europa Bus Centre, Glengall Street (✆ **028/9033-7004;** www.ulsterbustours.com).

BY CAR The best way to travel around the Northern Ireland countryside is by car. The roads are not always in great condition (although this is largely the result of ongoing construction programs that will ultimately improve them), but they are well signposted. Your biggest problem will be other drivers—Northern Ireland has an appalling record of road accidents, and many people drive far too fast here—but the same attention to safety that you exhibit when driving at home will bear similar rewards here. Generally speaking, distances between towns and villages here are quite small. If you want to rent a car, **Avis** (✆ **028/9024-0404**), **Budget** (✆ **028/9023-0700**), **Europcar** (✆ **028/9031-3500**), and **Hertz** (✆ **028/9073-2451**) have offices in Belfast, and most have branches at the airports. If you rent a car in the Republic, you can drive it in the North as long as you make sure the rental company's insurance will cover you.

[Fast FACTS] NORTHERN IRELAND

Area Code The area code for all of Northern Ireland is **028.** Drop the "0" when dialing from outside of Northern Ireland.

Business Hours Banks are generally open Monday to Friday 10am to 12:30pm and 1:30 to 3 or 4pm; they're closed on holidays. In Belfast and Derry City, banks tend not to close for lunch. Most shops are open Monday to Saturday 9 or 9:30am to 5 or 5:30pm, with one early-closing day a week, usually Wednesday or Thursday. Shops in tourist areas are likely to be open Sunday and to have extended hours, especially in the summer months.

Currency Since Northern Ireland is a part of the United Kingdom, it uses the **pound sterling (£),** not the euro.

Electricity The Northern Irish system operates on 240 volts. To use standard American 110-volt appliances, you'll need both a transformer and a plug adapter. Note that they are not the two-pin round plugs standard throughout Europe.

Embassies & Consulates The **U.S. Consulate General** is at Danesfort House, 223 Stranmillis Rd., Belfast BT9 5GR (✆ **028/9038-6100;** www.usembassy.org.uk/nireland).

Emergencies Dial ✆ **999** for fire, police, and ambulance.

Gas (Petrol) Filling up the tank is far cheaper in the Republic, so do it before you cross the border. In the North, the approximate price of 1 liter of unleaded gas is £1.30. There are approximately 4 liters to the U.S. gallon, which makes the price of a gallon of unleaded gas positively astronomical by comparison.

Mail United Kingdom postal rates apply, and mailboxes are painted red. Most post offices are open weekdays 9am to 5pm, and Saturday 9am to 1pm. From Northern Ireland to the United States or Canada, airmail letters not exceeding 20 grams cost 97p and postcards 50p and take about 5 to 7 days.

Newspapers & Magazines For listings of upcoming cultural events throughout Northern Ireland, check the free bimonthly *Arts Link* brochure, published by the Arts Council of Northern Ireland and available at any Northern Ireland Tourist Board office.

Parking Because of long-standing security concerns, parking regulations are more restrictive and more relentlessly enforced in the North than in the Republic. Look out for signs warning you where to park and not park. Never park on double red or double yellow lines.

Police To reach the **Police Service of Northern Ireland (PSNI),** as the Northern Irish police force is known, dial ✆ **999** or 112 anywhere in the North.

Safety Contrary to the media image, the North has one of the lowest levels of crime in western Europe. Historically, serious crimes such as homicide and robbery have been associated with terrorism and the Troubles, but those are usually targeted to specific people or areas. Nonetheless, there are some crime problems in cities, so use care to avoid pickpockets in shopping areas of Belfast, and always lock your car whenever you leave it, whether you're in a city or the countryside.

Taxes **VAT (value-added tax)** of 20% is included in the price of almost everything, except B&B accommodations. The percentages vary with the category of the services and purchases. It is usually already included in the prices you're quoted by hotels and the prices you see marked on merchandise tags. VAT is included in the hotel prices we've quoted in this guide. Many shops offer tax-free shopping options, such as "Cashback," and are pleased to explain the details. Vouchers from the North can be presented at the Dublin or Shannon airports before departure from Ireland. For further information, contact **HM Revenue and Customs,** Belfast International Airport (✆ **028/9441-3439** or 9442-3439; www.hmrc.gov.uk).

Telephone To reach Northern Ireland from anywhere but the Republic of Ireland or Great Britain, dial the U.K. country code (44) and then 28 (the area code minus the initial 0), and finally the local eight-digit number. From the Republic of Ireland, omit the country code; dial 048 and then the local eight-digit number. From Great Britain, dial 028 and the eight-digit number. For local calls within Northern Ireland, simply dial the eight-digit local number.

BELFAST

166km (103 miles) N of Dublin, 340km (211 miles) NE of Shannon, 201km (125 miles) E of Sligo, 422km (262 miles) NE of Cork

For those who remember a Belfast plagued by violence in the 1970s and 1980s, thinking of the city in terms of tourism rather than terrorism can be difficult, but things *have* changed here. Nearly half a million people—a third of Northern Ireland's population—live in Belfast, and while most of them live in neighborhoods segregated by religion, you rarely see signs of tension in the city center. Central Belfast has been repaired and polished, and it is a pleasure to wander its narrow lanes, to linger in its historic pubs, and to dine in the Michelin-starred restaurants it couldn't have dreamed of 25 years ago.

Things to Do The elaborate Victorian **City Hall** is a great place to start exploring the city. Don't miss the leafy and historic **University Quarter.** And no trip to Belfast is complete without a tour of the **Peace Wall** and the murals on

Belfast's City Hall on Donegall Square.

the **Falls and Shankill roads**—it's important to see both sides of modern life in Belfast.

Shopping In central Belfast, the streets and Victorian arcades around Donegall Place are filled with gift boutiques and jewelry shops. Look out for good buys on Belleek china, linen, and crystal. For chain stores try the Westfield Castlecourt Shopping Centre on Royal Avenue or the grand, glass-domed Victoria Square shopping center.

Restaurants & Dining Belfast's varied restaurant scene has been making waves in the last few years. Its two star chefs (Michael Deane and Paul Rankin) are famed for their use of fresh Irish produce and innovative cooking techniques to create one-of-a-kind dishes. Happily, there's plenty of affordable, traditional Irish cuisine in Belfast's pubs as well.

Nightlife & Entertainment Most visitors to Belfast are drawn to the historic pubs hidden down pedestrianized lanes around **Donegall Place.** These are great places to have a pint and chat with the locals. There's also a fast-growing new generation of hip modern bars mostly clustered in the **University Quarter,** where the music is cutting edge.

Note: The sectarian areas, with the famous political murals, are just to the west of the city center. The best known are on the Shankill and Falls roads. It's generally safe to drive the roads and photograph the murals, but it's a bit safer to take one of the Black Cab tours (p. 577).

Essentials

GETTING THERE For details, see "Getting to the North," in the section earlier. Belfast has two airports—Belfast International and Belfast City—and gets considerable sea traffic at Belfast Harbour and at Larne (30 min. from Belfast by train, bus, or car).

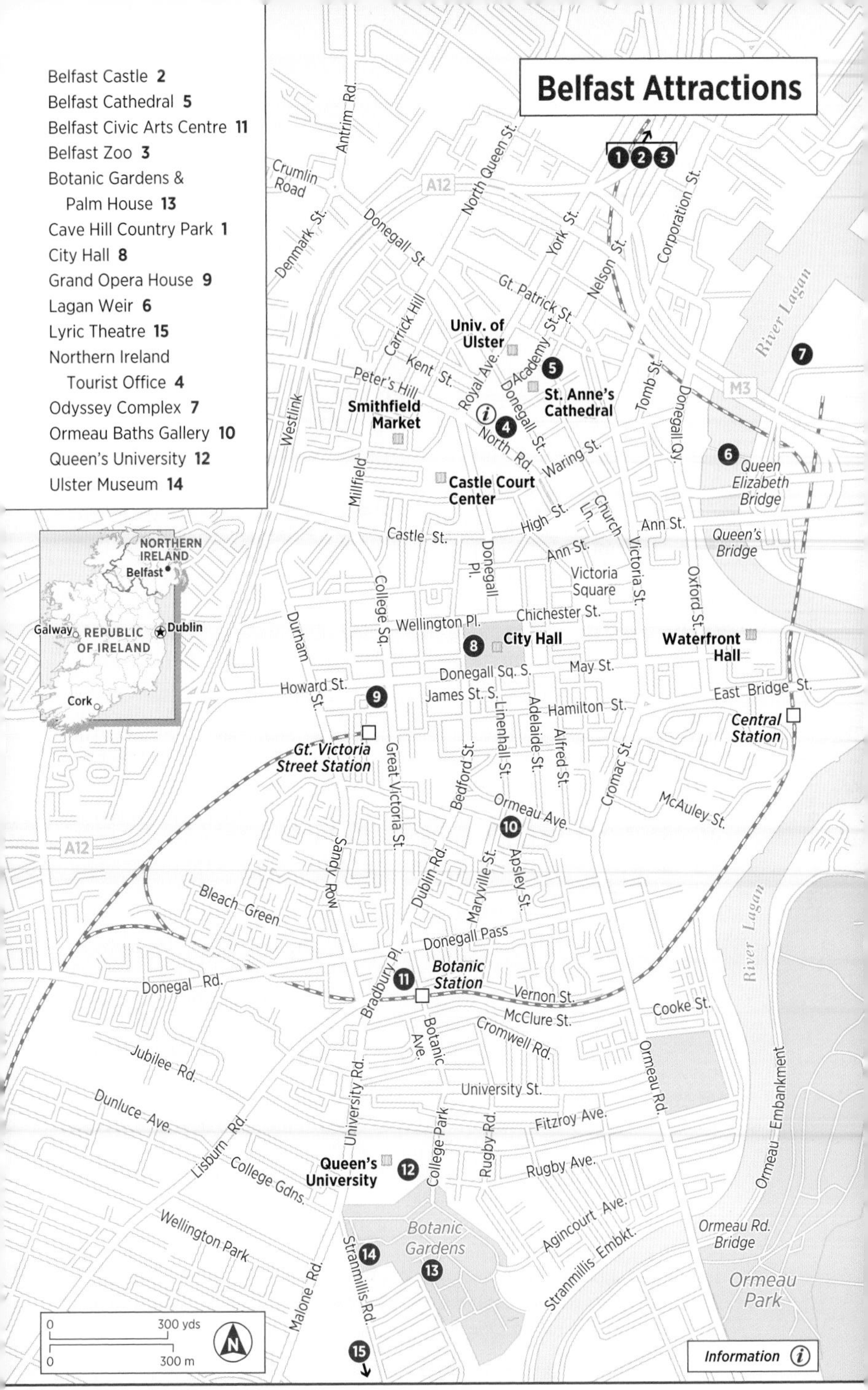

Belfast Attractions
Belfast Castle 2
Belfast Cathedral 5
Belfast Civic Arts Centre 11
Belfast Zoo 3
Botanic Gardens & Palm House 13
Cave Hill Country Park 1
City Hall 8
Grand Opera House 9
Lagan Weir 6
Lyric Theatre 15
Northern Ireland Tourist Office 4
Odyssey Complex 7
Ormeau Baths Gallery 10
Queen's University 12
Ulster Museum 14
NORTHERN IRELAND
Belfast
Galway
REPUBLIC OF IRELAND
Dublin
Cork
Antrim Rd.
Crumlin Road
A12
North Queen St.
Denmark St.
Donegall St.
York St.
Corporation St.
Nelson St.
Gt. Patrick St.
River Lagan
Carrick Hill
Univ. of Ulster
Academy St.
Kent St.
Royal Ave.
St. Anne's Cathedral
Peter's Hill
Smithfield Market
Donegall St.
Tomb St.
M3
Donegall Qy.
North Rd.
Waring St.
Westlink
Queen Elizabeth Bridge
Millfield
Castle Court Center
Church Ln.
High St.
Ann St.
Castle St.
Queen's Bridge
Donegall Pl.
Ann St.
Victoria Square
College Sq.
Victoria St.
Oxford St.
Durham St.
Wellington Pl.
Chichester St.
City Hall
Waterfront Hall
Donegall Sq. S.
May St.
Howard St.
James St. S.
East Bridge St.
Linenhall St.
Adelaide St.
Hamilton St.
Central Station
Gt. Victoria Street Station
Great Victoria St.
Alfred St.
Bedford St.
Cromac St.
McAuley St.
Ormeau Ave.
A12
Sandy Row
Dublin Rd.
Maryville St.
Apsley St.
Bleach Green
Donegall Pass
Bradbury Pl.
Botanic Station
Donegal Rd.
Vernon St.
Cooke St.
McClure St.
Botanic Ave.
Cromwell Rd.
Jubilee Rd.
University Rd.
University St.
Ormeau Rd.
Ormeau Embankment
Dunluce Ave.
Fitzroy Ave.
Rugby Rd.
College Park
Lisburn Rd.
Queen's University
Rugby Ave.
College Gdns.
Agincourt Ave.
Wellington Park
Botanic Gardens
Ormeau Rd. Bridge
Stranmillis Rd.
Stranmillis Embkt.
Malone Rd.
Ormeau Park
0
300 yds
0
300 m
N
Information

From Belfast International Airport, nearly 31km (19 miles) north of the city, your best option is the **Translink Airbus** to the Europa bus center downtown. It leaves every half-hour (every 15 min. in peak time), and costs around £7 per person for a one-way ticket, £10 round-trip. A taxi will run closer to £25 to £30.

Belfast City Airport is 6km (3¾ miles) from the city center, and is affordably reached by taxi, which should cost roughly £8 to get into the city. You can also take Citybus no. 21 from the airport terminal or the local train from the Sydenham Halt train station directly across from the airport, both for £2.

Queen's University, south of the city center.

VISITOR INFORMATION Brochures, maps, and other data on Belfast and the North are available from the **Belfast Welcome Centre,** at 47 Donegall Place (✆ **028/9024-6609;** www.gotobelfast.com). It's open June through September Monday to Saturday 9am to 7pm and Sunday noon to 5pm; October through May, hours are Monday to Saturday 9am to 5:30pm. The tourist information desk at **Belfast City Airport** (✆ **028/9045-7745**) is open year-round Monday to Friday 5:30am to 10pm, Saturday 5:30am to 9pm, and Sunday 5:30am to 10pm. The desk at **Belfast International Airport** (✆ **028/9442-2888**) is open March to September daily whenever the airport is open, October to February daily 6:30am to 11pm. Also check **www.belfast.net**, a comprehensive guide to the city, featuring tourism, news, accommodations, events, and nightlife listings.

GETTING AROUND **Metro,** Donegall Square West, Belfast (✆ **028/9066-6630;** www.translink.co.uk), is the renamed local bus service provider in Belfast. Buses depart from Donegall Square East, West, and North, plus Upper Queen Street, Wellington Place, Chichester Street, and Castle Street, and from bus stops throughout the city. An information kiosk is located on Donegall Square West, and you can download timetables from the website. Fares are determined by the number of zones traversed. The maximum fare for city-center travel is £1.30. Multiple-trip tickets, day tickets, and 7-day passes offer significant savings.

If you've brought a **car** into Belfast, it's best to leave it parked and take public transportation or walk around the city. If you must drive and want to park your car downtown, look for a blue P sign that shows a parking lot or a parking area. Belfast has a number of "control zones," indicated by a pink-and-yellow sign, where no parking is permitted. In general, on-street parking is limited to an area behind City Hall (south side), St. Anne's Cathedral (north side), and around Queen's University and Ulster Museum.

Taxis are available at all main rail stations, ports, and airports, and in front of City Hall. Most metered taxis are London-type black cabs with a yellow disc on the window. Other taxis may not have meters, so you should ask about the fare to your destination in advance. Except for inexpensive service down the Shankill Road and the Falls Road (still driven by local residents, as normal Belfast taxis have for years refused to drive down these roads), Belfast taxi fares are on the high side, with a £3 minimum and an additional £1.10 per mile.

Small and easily traversed, central Belfast is best explored **walking.** The city is divided into small quarters: The **city center** spreads out from around the impressive, domed City Hall building and bustling Donegall Square. This is the best place for shopping, particularly along Donegall Place, which extends north from the square, onto Royal Avenue. Bedford Street, which travels south from the Donegall Square, becomes Dublin Road, which, in turn, leads south to the **University Quarter,** the leafy area around Queen's University. This is where you'll find the Botanic Gardens, art galleries, and museums, as well as a buzzing nightlife scene. Heading north from Donegall Place, it's a short distance to the **Cathedral Quarter,** which surrounds Donegall Street, and holds, as the name implies, the city's most important cathedrals, as well as many vast Victorian warehouses. Finally there's the **Golden Mile**—the area around Great Victoria Street beyond Bradbury Place. It's considered the city's best address for restaurants and pubs, although it's a bit hyperbolically named. As one local said to us, "It's not a mile and it's not golden. But it's nice enough."

FAST FACTS The **U.S. consulate general** is at Danesfort House, 223 Stranmillis Rd., Belfast BT9 5GR (✆ **028/9038-6100;** www.usembassy.org.uk/nireland).

In an **emergency,** dial ✆ **999** for fire, police, and ambulance. Central hospitals include Belfast City Hospital (✆ **028/9032-9241**) on Lisburn Road, and Mater Hospital (✆ **028/9074-1211**) on Crumlin Road near Antrim Road.

For Internet access, head to the **Belfast Welcome Centre,** 47 Donegall Place (✆ **028/9024-6609;** www.gotobelfast.com), which has an Internet cafe; connections cost around £2 per hour. Or try the **Revelations Internet Cafe** (✆ **028/9032-0337;** www.revelations.co.uk) at 27 Shaftesbury Sq., where Internet connection is £1.10 for 15 minutes, and you can have a nice cup of joe while you're at it.

The main post office, the **Belfast GPO (General Post Office),** is at Castle Place, at the intersection of Royal Avenue and Donegall Place. It's open Monday to Friday 9am to 5:30pm, and Saturday 9am to 7pm.

Seeing the Sights

To discover the most historic parts of Belfast, you might try **Old Town: 1660–1685** (✆ **028/9024-6609**), a walking tour that traces the old city walls and explores the oldest part of the city at 2pm Saturdays (£5). From May to September, the **Historical Pub Tours of Belfast** (✆ **028/9268-3665**) departs twice a week from the Crown Liquor Saloon on Great Victoria Street and then travels on to six of the city's pubs. Tours are Thursday at 7pm and Saturday at 4pm, take 2 hours, and cost £6, not including drinks.

Black Cab Tours transport visitors safely through formerly troubled neighborhoods to see the Belfast Murals.

Belfast Castle Northwest of downtown and 120m (394 ft.) above sea level stands Belfast Castle, whose 80-hectare (198-acre) estate spreads down the slopes of Cave Hill. Dating from 1870, this was the family residence of the third marquis of Donegall, and it was built in the style of Britain's Balmoral castle. After a relatively brief life in private ownership, in 1934 it was given to the city, which used it largely for private functions for more than 50 years before opening it to the public in 1988. It's a lovely place to visit, with sweeping views of Belfast and the lough. Its cellars contain a nifty Victorian arcade, with a bar, a bistro, and a shop selling antiques and crafts. According to legend, a white cat was meant to bring the castle residents luck, so look around for carvings featuring the creature.

Signposted off Antrim Rd., 4km (2½ miles) north of the city center, County Antrim. ✆ **028/9077-6925.** www.belfastcastle.co.uk. Free admission and parking. Castle Mon–Sat 9am–10pm; Sun 9am–6pm.

Belfast Cathedral The foundation stone on this monumental cathedral was laid in 1899, but it would be more than a century later before it was finally completed, and even now it awaits a steeple. Crisscrossing architectural genres from Romanesque to Victorian to modern, the huge structure is more attractive inside than out. Carvings representing life in Belfast top the 10 pillars in the nave. Its most impressive features, though, are the delicate mosaic ceilings of the tympanum and the baptistery, both designed by sisters Gertrude and Mary Martin over the course of 7 years, and made of thousands of pieces of glass.

Donegall St., Belfast. ✆ **028/9033-2328.** Free admission; donations accepted. Mon–Fri 10am–4pm.

Belfast Zoo ☺ In a picturesque mountain park on the slopes of Cave Hill just outside of town and overlooking the city, this zoo was founded in 1920 as Bellevue Gardens and has been modernized completely in recent years. It emphasizes conservation and education, and focuses on breeding rare species, including

Cave Hill Country Park encompasses ancient burial markers, five caves, and many sites from which to take in panoramic views.

Hawaiian geese, Indian lions, red lechwe (a kind of antelope), and golden lion tamarins.

8km (5 miles) north of the city on A6, Antrim Rd., County Antrim. ✆ **028/9077-6277.** www.belfastzoo.co.uk. 2 price tiers; lower prices apply Oct–Mar. Admission £6.90–£8.50 adults; £3.50–£4.30 children 4–18; free for seniors and children 3 and under. Apr–Sept daily 10am–7pm; Oct–Mar daily 10am–4pm. Bus: 1A, 1B, 1C, 1D, 1E, 1F, 1G, or 2A.

Cave Hill Country Park ☺ This park atop a 360m (1,181-ft.) basalt cliff offers panoramic views, walking trails, and archaeological and historical sights. The park gets its name from five small caves thought to have been Neolithic iron mines; several other ancient sites are scattered about the place, often unmarked. These include stone cairns, dolmens, and McArt's Fort—the remains of an ancient defensive hill fort in which Wolfe Tone and his fellow United Irishmen planned the 1798 rebellion. It's mostly gone now, but you can explore the ruins, which sit atop the park's most famous viewpoint. The **Cave Hill Visitor Centre,** on the second floor of Belfast Castle (see above), contains a diverting exhibition on the history of the park, and the castle itself. At the moment, the park is under construction to improve the walking paths, but the work should be done by the time you visit.

Off Antrim Rd., 6.5km (4 miles) north of city center, County Antrim. www.belfastcity.gov.uk/parksandopenspaces. Parking at Belfast Castle or Belfast Zoo (above). Bus 1A, 1B, 1C, 1D, 1E, 1F, or 1G.

Touring the Troubles

For many years, Belfast was best known for its most conflicted neighborhoods, where in the 1970s protests occurred daily, and in the 1980s violence was the norm. Now that peace has grudgingly descended upon the Catholic Falls Road and its nearby parallel, the Protestant Shankill Road, there's a growing industry around exploring the city's most infamous sectarian neighborhoods. The best tours are given by the various "Black Cabs," which take groups of one to five people in London-style cabs through the neighborhoods, past the barbed wire, towering fences, and partisan murals, as guides explain their significance. There are a number of these tour groups, and quality varies considerably, but the 2-hour **Black Taxi Tour** (✆ **0800/052-3914;** www.belfasttours.com) is highly recommended. Its drivers are relaxed, patient, and amazingly unbiased (our driver let us guess at the end of the tour whether he was Catholic or Protestant . . . we guessed wrong). The fare is £25 for the first two passengers, or £10 per person for three or more passengers.

CHOOSING sides: UNDERSTANDING NORTHERN IRELAND'S DIVISIONS

To understand Northern Ireland, you first must understand who is involved in the sectarian game, because the battle between **Republicans** (those who believe the North should become part of the Republic of Ireland; also called nationalists or "the Catholics," depending on who's talking), and the **Loyalists** (those who are loyal to the British crown and think the North should stay, as it is now, part of the United Kingdom; also called Unionists or "the Protestants") defines this region to this day. The problem is that both sides have splintered over the last decade, and so it's hard to keep up with who's who.

The Republicans are now divided among devotees of the IRA (the Irish Republican Army), the "Real" IRA (a splinter faction that branched off from the IRA), and Sinn Fein (also splintered from the IRA, and now its political face). Supporters for this side often have the green, white, and orange Irish flag hanging from their homes and businesses.

The Loyalists are divided among a variety of paramilitary groups, including the UDA (Ulster Defence Association), the UDF (Ulster Defence Force), and the UVF (Ulster Volunteer Force). Much of the violence in the last decade has been the result of turf wars between those Protestant groups. Supporters of that side often have the British Union Jack flag flying from their homes and businesses.

These days, many, though not all, of these groups are more involved in organized crime than political struggle, and all of them have been lumped together by pundits under the new term "Irish mafia." Massive bank robberies (all of Northern Ireland's currency was withdrawn and reissued within 1 week in 2005 after a gang suspected to be connected with the IRA stole £22 million in a bank heist), importation and sales of illegal weaponry, and drugs are all blamed on the same factions that once battled for political power here. Most Irish people will tell you that they're sick of the lot of them—however, don't ask unless you know the person you're talking to. It's an extremely sensitive subject that should not be brought up casually. If you're really curious, take one of the Black Cab tours (see "Touring the Troubles," above) and you can ask your driver questions to your heart's content.

City Hall ★ Standing as a symbol to Belfast's Industrial Revolution preeminence, this is a glorious explosion of granite, marble, and stained glass, and looking even better after a recent renovation. It was built in classical Renaissance style in 1906. Its creamy white walls are Portland stone and its soft green dome is copper. Several statues dot the grounds—a grim-faced statue of Queen Victoria stands in front of it, looking as if she wishes she were anyplace else. Bronze figures around her represent the textile and ship-building industries that powered Belfast's success. There's also a memorial to the victims of the *Titanic* disaster. Inside the building is even better, with an elaborate entry hall heavy with marble, but lightened by stained glass, and a rotunda with a soaring painted ceiling—and it all somehow manages not to be too tacky. There are often exhibitions upstairs as well as a handy coffee shop. To learn all the building's details, take a free guided tour—ask in the lobby.

Donegall Sq., Belfast. ✆ **028/9027-0456.** Free admission. Guided tours June–Sept Mon–Fri 11am, and 2 and 3pm, Sat 2:30pm; Oct–May Mon–Sat 11am and 2:30pm. Otherwise by arrangement.

Cultúrlann McAdam Ó Flaich ★ This warm and welcoming place on the Falls Road is the center for Irish language and culture. Inside a redbrick former church, it holds a tourist information desk, but the biggest attraction is the shop, which sells a good selection of books about Ireland, as well as Irish crafts and CDs of Irish music. Its pleasant cafe is a good place to stop for a cup of coffee. It holds regular "Gaeltacht experience" evenings, with traditional Irish food and music.

216 Falls Rd., Belfast. ✆ **028/9096-4180.** www.culturlann.ie. Free admission. Mon–Fri 9:30am–5:30pm; Sat 10am–5:30pm.

Falls Road ★★ Scarred by decades of conflict, the Catholic Falls Road is a compelling place, as are all political hotbeds. It is quite safe—the residents are used to sightseers wandering through to photograph the political murals, and most people are welcoming. It's an ordinary enough *looking* neighborhood—houses have flowers in the windows and kids play in the streets. The big skyscraper you can see down the road is the Divis Tower—it's all residential save for the top two floors, which were taken over by the British military in the 1970s, and used as a watchtower. Just past the tower begins the long, tall, imposing wall of wood, concrete, and metal that has become known as the "Peace Line." It has divided the Catholics of Falls Road from the Protestants of Shankill Road for 30 years. Its huge metal gates are open during the day, but some are still closed at night. In some sections, the fence is more than 6m (20 ft.) tall. It has become a sort of Berlin Wall of Ireland, and locals and visitors draw pictures and write

A mural honoring hunger striker Bobby Sands in the Catholic Falls Road neighborhood.

The Odyssey Complex houses a science center, ice hockey arena, IMAX theater, and other amusements.

messages of peace on it. On the corner of Falls and Sevastopol Street is the surprisingly small Sinn Fein headquarters—at one end of the building is a mural of the late hunger striker Bobby Sands, arguably the most famous political mural in Belfast. The theme of the murals on the Falls Road can be quite wide-ranging these days; there are some protesting against causes such as the Iraq war and the Israeli/Palestinian conflict, in addition to matters closer to home.

From Donegall Sq., travel north along Donegall Place and turn left on Castle St., then head straight ahead on Divis St. across the busy Westlink to the Falls Rd.

Odyssey Complex ☺ This enormous entertainment, education, and sports center on the east bank of the river is bursting with activities and has been popular since it opened in 2001. For kids, its hands-on science center—**W5**—is a hypermodern, interactive learning environment where children can compose their own music on an air harp, create tornadoes, learn how robots are built, and try to make one of their own. Also in the complex are an arena where the Belfast Giants ice hockey team plays, an IMAX cinema, video-game arcades, and lots of bars, restaurants, and cafes. On a rainy day, there's probably no better place to go to keep everyone amused and dry.

> Impressions
>
> ***We make out of the quarrel with others, rhetoric, but of the quarrel with ourselves, poetry.***
>
> **—W. B. Yeats**

5-min. walk across the weir from the Lagan Lookout, Belfast. ✆ **028/9046-7700.** www.theodysseyarena.com. Admission to W5 £8 adults; £6 children 4–18; £23 families. Mon–Sat 10am–6pm; Sun noon–6pm.

Palm House & Belfast Botanical Gardens Dating from 1828, these gardens were established by the Belfast Botanic and Horticultural Society. Ten years later, they gained a glass house, or conservatory, designed by noted Belfast architect Charles Lanyon. Now known as the Palm House, this unique structure contains a good variety of tropical plants, including sugar cane, coffee, cinnamon, banana, aloe, ivory nut, rubber, bamboo, guava, and spindly birds of paradise. If the weather's fine, stroll in the outdoor rose gardens, first established in 1927.

Signposted from M1/M2 (Balmoral exit), Stranmillis Rd., County Antrim. ✆ **028/9032-4902.** Free admission. Palm House and Tropical Ravine Apr–Sept Mon–Fri 10am–noon, daily 1–5pm; Oct–Mar Mon–Fri 10am–noon, daily 1–4pm. Gardens daily 8am–sunset. Bus: 61, 71, 84, or 85.

Ormeau Baths Gallery ★ Occupying the site of, and partly incorporating, the old Victorian swimming baths designed by Robert Watt, Ormeau Baths Gallery opened in 1995 as the city's principal exhibition space for contemporary visual art. This striking and versatile facility can program multiple simultaneous exhibitions in a variety of mediums, and has become the premier showcase for the best of Northern Irish contemporary art.

18A Ormeau Ave., Belfast. ✆ **028/9032-1402.** www.ormeaubaths.co.uk. Free admission. Tues–Sat 10am–5:30pm. Last admission 5pm.

Queen's University This is Northern Ireland's most prestigious university, founded by Queen Victoria in 1845 to provide nondenominational higher education. The main, 19th-century Tudor Revival building may remind you of England's Oxford, as its design was based on that of the Founder's Tower at Magdalen College. But that's hardly all there is to this university, which sprawls through 250 buildings, where 17,500 students are studying at any given time. Most of the buildings are of interest only for those rushing to chemistry class, but the whole neighborhood around the university is a quiet, attractive place to wander, and University Square on the north side of campus is simply beautiful. At one end of the square is the Union Theological College, which dates from 1853 and housed the Northern Ireland Parliament after the partition of Ireland.

Visitor Centre, University Rd., Belfast. ✆ **028/9033-5252.** www.qub.ac.uk/vcentre. Free admission. May–Sept Mon–Sat 10am–4pm; Oct–Apr Mon–Fri 10am–4pm. Bus: 8A, 8B, or 8C.

A mural pays tribute to Queen Elizabeth II in the Protestant Shankill Road neighborhood.

Red Hand of Ulster

Around Belfast, and all of Northern Ireland, you'll frequently come across representations of a red hand. It's carved in door frames, painted on walls and ceilings, and even planted in red flowers in gardens. Known as the Red Hand of Ulster, it is one of the symbols of the region. According to one version of the old tale, the hand can trace its history from a battle between two men competing to be king of Ulster. They held a race (some say by boat, others say it took place on horseback) and agreed that the first man to touch Ulster soil would win. As one man fell behind, he pulled his sword and cut off his right hand, then with his left, flung the bloody hand ahead of his competitor, winning the right to rule.

Shankill Road ★★ Almost as soon as you turn onto Protestant Shankill Road, you pass a building that has been entirely painted with the Union Jack flag. A few blocks down the road, and off to the right, you'll see a cluster of enormous murals, including one celebrating Oliver Cromwell, who massacred Irish Catholics in an effort to conquer the island. Shankill is indefinably grimmer than the Falls Road—it's more down at heel and you'll see more boarded-up shops, but the people are generally friendly. Shankill murals seem to be darker than those on the Falls, where many murals are about solidarity with the downtrodden; here, they're all about the corruption of Catholics, with a display of painted weaponry, although some of the more aggressive murals were removed in 2010.

The Shankill Rd. runs parallel to the Falls Rd. To reach it from Donegall Sq., head north along Donegall Place and Royal Ave., then turn left on Peter's Hill and cross the Westlink rd.

Ulster Museum ★★ Built in the grand classical Renaissance style, with an Italian marble interior, this excellent museum crams in 9,000 years of Irish history with exhibits on art, furniture, ceramics, costume, industrial heritage, and a permanent display of products "Made in Belfast." A recent renovation has improved its displays considerably, making it a brighter more spacious and interesting place. One of the best-known exhibits is the collection of gold and silver jewelry recovered by divers in 1968 off the Antrim coast from the 1588 wreckage of the Armada treasure ship *Girona*. Check out the "Early Ireland" gallery, which has an extensive, cleverly displayed collection of prehistoric artifacts of stone and bronze from Northern Ireland's many ancient archaeological sites. There's also an exceptional collection

The Ulster Museum explores 9,000 years of Irish history.

of historic fine arts, including Belleek pottery, a vast assemblage of Irish silver, and formal costume.

Signposted from M1/M2 (Balmoral exit); next to the Botanic Gardens, Stranmillis Rd., Belfast. ✆ **028/9044-0000.** http://www.nmni.com/um. Free admission, except to major special exhibitions. Tues–Sun 10am–5pm. Bus: 8. Rail: Botanic station.

Shopping

Belfast is a surprisingly good place to shop. Start at Donegall Place, where the streets are lined with shops, and the Victorian arcades are filled with gift shops and jewelry stores. Good buys are to be had on Belleek china, linen, and crystal from County Tyrone. Continue your spree at **Craftworks Gallery,** Bedford House, Bedford Street (✆ **028/9024-4465**), a one-stop shop for crafts from throughout the region. The gallery can supply a free copy of the brochure *Crafts in Northern Ireland,* detailing local crafts and where to find them. It is just behind Belfast City Hall. Or you could head to the excellent **Wicker Man,** 44–46 High St. (✆ **028/9024-3550,** www.thewickerman.co.uk), which has a good stock of crafts. You'll find both Irish crafts and traditional Irish music at **Cultúrlann McAdam Ó Fiaich** (216 Falls Rd.; ✆ **028/9023-9303**).

The main shopping street is **Royal Avenue,** home of several well-known chain stores, while the **Westfield Castlecourt Shopping Centre** on Royal Avenue and the glass-domed **Victoria Square** shopping center are Belfast's main downtown multistory shopping malls.

Belfast's leading department stores are **Anderson & McAuley** and **Marks & Spencer,** both on Donegall Place, and **Debenham's** in the Castlecourt Shopping Centre on Royal Avenue. Other shops to look for include the following:

Archive's Antiques Centre This labyrinth of collectibles sprawls across three floors filled with military memorabilia, books, Irish silver, and china. Open Monday to Friday 10:30am to 5:30pm, Saturday 10am to 6pm. 88 Donegall Pass, Belfast. ✆ **028/9023-2383.**

The Bureau Belfast's premier boutique for men's fashions, carrying such trendy labels as Paul Smith, Stone Island, and Etro. A nice little tidbit about this place is that on the day they opened, in the height of the Troubles, their neighbors were a derelict burger joint and a newly bombed-out cafe. How times have changed. 44 and 46–50 Howard St., Belfast. ✆ **028/9032-6100.** www.thebureaubelfast.com.

Good Vibrations Something of a legend in the Belfast music scene, this much-loved record store is finally open again after nearly 20 years out of business. It's owned by local boy and former punk music mogul, Terri Hooley, who ran Good Vibrations as a combined shop and independent music label from the '70s until the early '90s; Bill Clinton was among those who sent letters of good luck when it was announced the shop would reopen in 2008. Expect to find a strong range of collectibles, rock, jazz—and punk, of course. Winetavern St. No phone. www.goodvibesbelfast.com.

Kozo Paper This wonderful little shop specializes in paper and stationery crafts from Asia and the Far East. Their range of handmade paper—from Japan, India, China, and Nepal, among other places—is exquisite. They also do a great line in photo albums and journal books, which are bound on-site by the Cathedral Bindery. Open Tuesday to Friday 12:30 to 5:30pm and Saturday 10am to 5pm. 18 North St., Belfast. ✆ **028/9033-2321.**

No Alibis Crime fiction is the mainstay of this quirky, absorbing little independent bookstore. Oddly, it's also a major source of books devoted to American politics. There's a snug little reading area at the back, where you can browse your purchases over a cup of coffee. 83 Botanic Ave., Belfast. ✆ **028/9031-9607.** www.noalibis.com.

Oakland Antiques On Belfast's antiques row, Donegall Pass, this is the biggest shop of them all, with an impressive array of Edwardian, Georgian, and Victorian silver, porcelain, and more. Open Monday to Saturday 10am to 5:30pm. 135 Donegall Pass, Belfast. ✆ **028/9023-0176.** www.oaklandantiques.co.uk.

Rojo A must for dedicated followers of footwear, this small fashion boutique has an incredible range of designer shoes. Big names such as Gucci, Prada, and Kenzo share the shelves with a small but perfectly formed range of original designs. 613 Lisburn Rd., Belfast. ✆ **028/9066-6998.** www.rojoshoes.co.uk.

Rusty Zip A retro store with a decidedly groovy interior, this place sells all manner of vintage gear, from jeans and flares, to big collar shirts and miniskirts. Think Austin Powers with a Belfast twang. 28 Botanic Ave., Belfast. ✆ **028/9032-6100.**

St. George's Market This is Belfast's original "variety market," dating from the 19th century and now standing across from the new Waterfront Hall. The market was completely restored in 1999 and is a colorful outlet for fresh fruit, flowers, fish, vegetables, clothing, crafts, and lots more. Open Tuesday and Friday starting at 8am. May St. at Oxford St., Belfast. ✆ **028/9043-5704.**

Smyth's Irish Linens If you want to stock up on fine Irish linen damask tablecloths, napkins, and handkerchiefs, head for this shop in the heart of the city's prime shopping thoroughfare. It also stocks other traditional gift items and offers VAT-free export. 65 Royal Ave., Belfast. ✆ **028/9024-2232.**

The Steensons This is the main showroom of Bill and Christina Steenson, both celebrated Irish goldsmiths. On display and for sale is the widest collection anywhere of their unique gold and silver jewelry, as well as work by a select number of top designers from elsewhere in the country. Bedford St. (behind Belfast City Hall), Belfast. ✆ **028/9024-8269.** www.thesteensons.com.

Tom Caldwell Gallery Come here for a selection of paintings, sculptures, and ceramics by Irish artists, as well as handcrafted furnishings, rugs, and cast-iron candelabras. Open Monday to Friday from 9:30am to 5pm, Saturday from 10am to 1pm. 40 Bradbury Place, Belfast. ✆ **028/9032-3226.** www.tomcaldwellgallery.com.

Utopia This is one of those gift shops that tries hard to be all things to all people. Consequently the stock is a little eclectic (if you were hoping to find Belleek china and a Robin Hood–themed chess set on the same shopping trip, this is the store for you). However, it manages not to resort too much to the leprechaun-and-Guinness fridge magnet school of souvenirs. Open Monday to Friday from 10am to 5pm, Saturday from 10am to 1pm. Fountain Centre, College St., Belfast. ✆ **028/9024-1342.** www.utopiaonline.co.uk.

The Wicker Man This is head and shoulders above the average emporium for Celtic-themed knickknacks. The rather utilitarian exterior conceals an excellent range of affordable art and Irish-made souvenirs. There's also an exhibition space, showcasing the work of a different local artist every month—usually worth a look in itself. The name, in case you didn't know, refers to an ancient Celtic rite in which people were (supposedly) burned alive inside a giant wicker effigy. Open

Monday to Saturday from 9am to 5:30pm (Thurs until 9pm) and 1 to 5:30pm on Sunday. 44–46 High St., Belfast. ✆ **028/9024-3550.** www.thewickerman.co.uk.

Workshops Collective A clearinghouse of sorts for local artists, this shop in the University Quarter allows you to purchase paintings, sculpture, crafts, and furniture directly from the artists who made them. The works are ever changing and range from the interesting to the I-wouldn't-have-that-in-my-house. 1a Lawrence St., Belfast. ✆ **028/9020-0707.**

Sports & Outdoor Pursuits

FISHING The 9km (5½-mile) stretch of the Lagan River from the Stranmillis weir to Shaw's Bridge offers decent coarse fishing, especially on summer evenings. From May to July, Lough Neagh has good shore and boat fishing. For fishing equipment and contacts try **Get Hooked,** 49 Suffolk Rd., Belfast (✆ **028/9062-3431**). For info, tackle, and bait, try the **Village Tackle Shop,** 55a Newtownbreda Rd., Belfast (✆ **028/9049-1916**).

GOLF The Belfast area offers four 18-hole courses within 6km (3¾ miles) of the city center. Some 5km (3 miles) southwest of the city, there's the **Balmoral Golf Club,** 518 Lisburn Rd., Belfast (✆ **028/9038-1514;** www.balmoralgolf.com), with greens fees of £27 weekdays (except Wed), £40 weekends and Wednesdays. About 6km (3¾ miles) southwest of the city center the **Dunmurry Golf Club,** 91 Dunmurry Lane, Dunmurry, Belfast (✆ **028/9061-0834;** www.dunmurrygolfclub.co.uk), costs £27 weekdays, £30 weekends. About 4.8km (3 miles) south of the city center is the **Belvoir Park Golf Club,** 73 Church Rd., Newtownbreda, Belfast (✆ **028/9064-6714;** www.belvoirparkgolfclub.com), £65 weekdays, £75 weekends; and 4.8km (3 miles) north, the **Fortwilliam Golf Club,** Downview Avenue, Belfast (✆ **028/9037-0770;** www.fortwilliam.co.uk), £22 weekdays, £29 weekends (quaintly, we think, women are charged a few pounds less). Weekdays are usually better for visitors, and each club has preferred weekdays. Phone ahead. Club pros offer lessons, usually for about £25 per hour; book at least 2 days ahead.

HORSEBACK RIDING Saddle up at the **Drumgooland House Equestrian Centre,** 29 Dunnanew Rd., Seaforde, Downpatrick, County Down (✆ **028/4481-1956** or 07718/658-666). It offers half- and full-day forest treks and beach rides starting at around £35. Full equestrian holidays are available.

Where to Stay

EXPENSIVE

Culloden Estate and Spa ★ Not in the city itself, but 8km (5 miles) east on the shore of Belfast Lough, in County Down, this elegant hotel sprawls across acres of secluded gardens and woodlands. The grey stone manor house was originally built as a palace for the bishops of Down, and it has grand style, with fine antiques, plasterwork and paintings, Louis XV chandeliers, an unexpectedly modern spa, and exceptional service. Guest rooms are spacious with large, comfortable beds, and are done up in neutral colors that vary from room to room. The Mitre Restaurant is somewhat formal without being stuffy, and specializes in French-influenced Irish cuisine.

142 Bangor Rd., Holywood, County Down. www.hastingshotels.com. ✆ **028/9042-1066.** Fax 028/9042-6777. 79 units. £160–£230 double. Full breakfast £20. AE, DC, MC, V. Free valet parking. **Amenities:** Restaurant; bar; babysitting; bicycle rental; concierge; gym; Jacuzzi; indoor pool; room service; spa; beauty treatments; steam room; tennis court. *In room:* TV, hair dryer.

Merchant Hotel ★★ This luxurious, elegant hotel has guest rooms draped in rich fabrics and equipped with the latest business technology. In a former bank building that was converted into a hotel with exquisite attention to detail, the hotel gets just about everything right. The Great Room restaurant is a beautiful space—its soaring ceilings, gilded plasterwork frieze, Corinthian columns, and marble floors make a breakfast of eggs and bacon seem entirely wrong, and champagne and caviar seem so right. Guest rooms will horrify minimalists, with silk wallpaper, designer carpets in vivid colors, and king-size beds. This place is all about service and luxury, so for a mere £80 you can be taken to or picked up at the airport in the hotel's chauffeur-driven Bentley. Good discounts are available online, in advance.

35–39 Waring St., Belfast, County Antrim. www.themerchanthotel.com. ✆ **028/9023-4888.** Fax 028/9024-7775. 26 units. £220 deluxe double. Rates include breakfast. AE, DC, MC, V. Free valet parking. **Amenities:** 2 restaurants; bar; concierge; room service. *In room:* TV, hair dryer, Wi-Fi.

MODERATE

Europa Hotel ★ This elegantly efficient hotel is a favorite of business travelers. Former U.S. President Bill Clinton has stayed here (one suite is named after him), and for good reason—the lobby is warm and welcoming, with Irish art on the walls and a fire crackling in the hearth. Hotel workers are as friendly as Belfastians get. The guest rooms are spacious and contemporary, filled with mahogany furnishings, rich fabrics, and marble bathrooms. The downsides are the restaurants and bar, which lack the style displayed effortlessly in the rest of the hotel, and can feel chain-hotelish. But the food is acceptable if not stellar, and the price is right. Book in advance and doubles are under £100.

Great Victoria St., Belfast, County Antrim. www.hastingshotels.com. ✆ **028/9027-1066.** Fax 028/9032-7800. 272 units. £90–£180 double. Luxury suites available. Continental breakfast £15; full breakfast £18. AE, DC, MC, V. Valet parking £16. **Amenities:** 2 restaurants; bar; babysitting; concierge; access to nearby health club; room service. *In room:* TV, hair dryer, Wi-Fi.

Malmaison Belfast ★★ This hotel—part of the sophisticated British Malmaison chain—is so trendy and decked out in eggplant-and-black hues that one British newspaper described it as looking like "Dracula's living room." Created from two classically ornate 19th-century warehouses, it manages to offer a kind of cozy sophistication. Rooms are not huge, but will be home sweet home to those who think modern is the way to go. The color scheme includes neutral walls with black touches and blood-red crushed-velvet covers on the firm orthopedic beds. All the latest gadgetry awaits your moments of idleness, including plasma TVs, DVDs, and free Internet service. The bar and brasserie are (surprise, surprise) sleek and modern in design, with an emphasis on black (it makes everybody look thinner, you know).

34–38 Victoria St., Belfast, County Antrim. www.malmaison.com. ✆ **800/525-4800** in the U.S., or 028/9022-0200. Fax 028/9022-0220. 59 units. £100–£160 double. AE, DC, MC, V. **Amenities:** Brasserie; bar; health club; 24-hr. room service; smoke-free rooms. *In room:* TV/DVD, CD player, hair dryer, minibar, Wi-Fi.

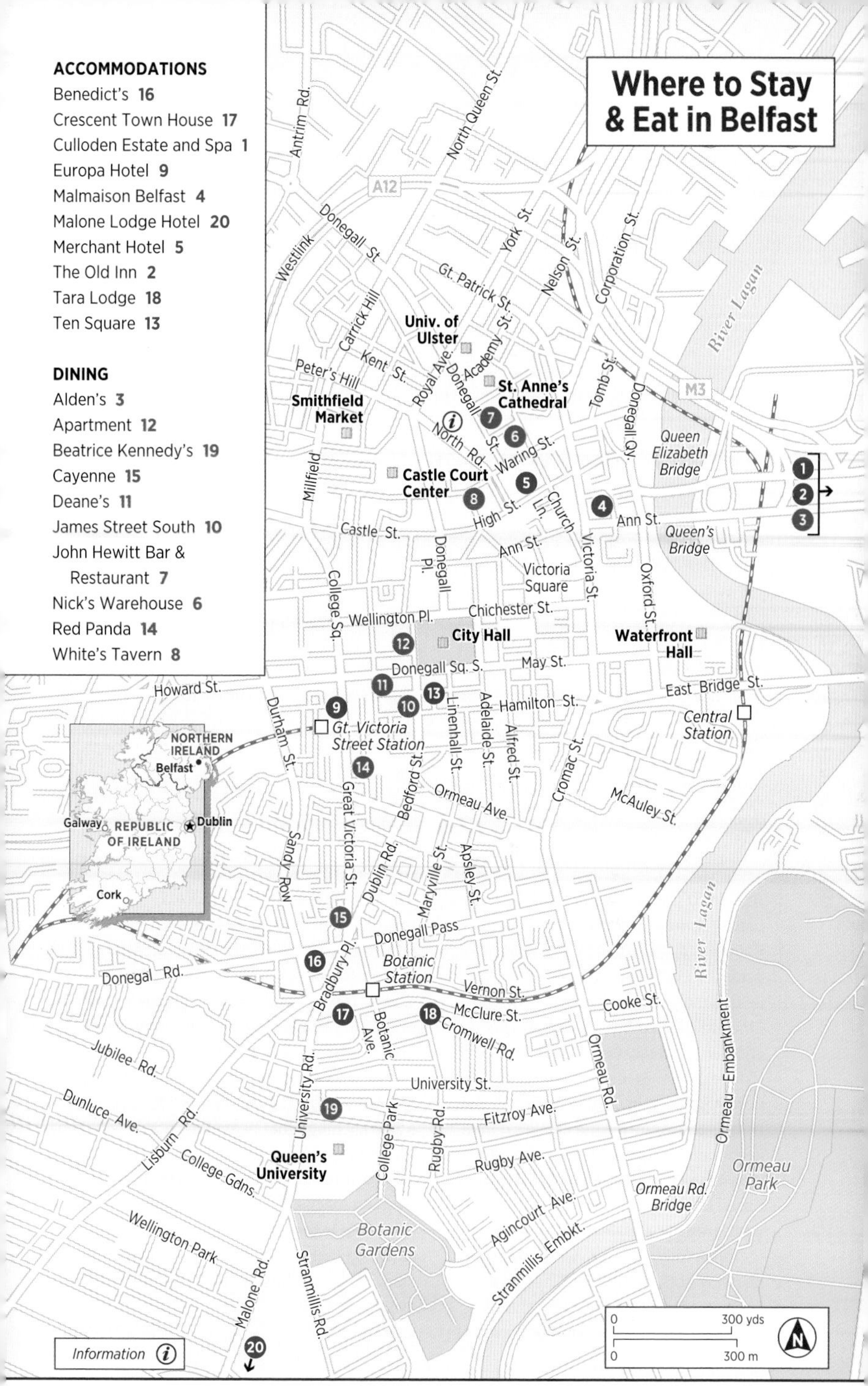

Where to Stay & Eat in Belfast
ACCOMMODATIONS
Benedict's 16
Crescent Town House 17
Culloden Estate and Spa 1
Europa Hotel 9
Malmaison Belfast 4
Malone Lodge Hotel 20
Merchant Hotel 5
The Old Inn 2
Tara Lodge 18
Ten Square 13
DINING
Alden's 3
Apartment 12
Beatrice Kennedy's 19
Cayenne 15
Deane's 11
James Street South 10
John Hewitt Bar & Restaurant 7
Nick's Warehouse 6
Red Panda 14
White's Tavern 8
Antrim Rd.
North Queen St.
A12
Donegall St.
Westlink
York St.
Gt. Patrick St.
Nelson St.
Corporation St.
River Lagan
Carrick Hill
Univ. of Ulster
Academy St.
Kent St.
Royal Ave.
Peter's Hill
St. Anne's Cathedral
Smithfield Market
Tomb St.
M3
Donegall Qy.
Queen Elizabeth Bridge
North Rd.
Waring St.
Millfield
Castle Court Center
Church Ln.
High St.
Ann St.
Queen's Bridge
Castle St.
Donegall Pl.
Victoria Square
Victoria St.
Oxford St.
College Sq.
Wellington Pl.
Chichester St.
City Hall
Waterfront Hall
May St.
Donegall Sq. S.
East Bridge St.
Howard St.
Durham St.
Linenhall St.
Adelaide St.
Hamilton St.
Alfred St.
Central Station
Gt. Victoria Street Station
Cromac St.
Bedford St.
Ormeau Ave.
McAuley St.
NORTHERN IRELAND
Belfast
Galway
REPUBLIC OF IRELAND
Dublin
Cork
Sandy Row
Great Victoria St.
Dublin Rd.
Maryville St.
Apsley St.
Donegall Pass
Botanic Station
Bradbury Pl.
Donegal Rd.
Vernon St.
Cooke St.
McClure St.
Cromwell Rd.
Botanic Ave.
Jubilee Rd.
University Rd.
University St.
Ormeau Rd.
Ormeau Embankment
Dunluce Ave.
Fitzroy Ave.
College Park
Rugby Rd.
Lisburn Rd.
Queen's University
Rugby Ave.
College Gdns.
Ormeau Park
Ormeau Rd. Bridge
Agincourt Ave.
Wellington Park
Botanic Gardens
Stranmillis Embkt.
Malone Rd.
Stranmillis Rd.
Information
0 300 yds
0 300 m
N

The Old Inn ★★ When the author C. S. Lewis wrote about this historic coaching inn of North County Down, about 10 minutes' drive from central Belfast, it was already very old. Records date it from 1614, and those hoping for a historic place to stay should look no further. Its **Parlour Bar and Lounge** are still topped by thatched roofs, and its crackling fire has warmed the toes of former president George H. W. Bush. You can stay in one of the large, beautifully decorated rooms, many with polished wood floors and some with excellent antiques, or isolate yourself in the private cottage, which comes with its own fireplace. The food in its main restaurant has won plaudits, but there's cheaper fare in the relaxing bistro and Parlour Bar.

Main St., Crawfordsburn, County Down. www.theoldinn.com. ✆ **028/9185-3255.** Fax 028/9185-2775. 32 units. £100–£125 double; £225 cottage. Rates include full Irish breakfast. AE, MC, V. **Amenities:** 2 restaurants; bar. *In room:* TV, hair dryer.

Ten Square ★ This funky boutique hotel aims to emulate the exotic luxury of Shanghai's Pudong district with small bedrooms and low-slung beds with pure white linens, mahogany furniture, and coir carpet. Armoires, shutters, and double doors are all inlaid with white opal glass. The overall feel is one of elegant minimalism. The hotel's **Grill Room & Bar** serves modern Irish cuisine in a lavishly designed contemporary setting with an exotic feel with dark, polished wood floors, dim lighting, and arched doorways. The emphasis there is on Irish meats, especially steak. Service here is efficient, and there are discounts available online in advance.

10 Donegall Sq., Belfast, County Antrim. www.tensquare.co.uk. ✆ **028/9024-1001.** Fax 028/9024-3210 23 units. £140–£180 double. Rates include breakfast. AE, MC, V. Street parking only. **Amenities:** 2 restaurants; 2 bars; concierge. *In room:* TV, hair dryer, minibar, high-speed Internet.

Your Own Private Hideaway

Hoping to stay somewhere off the beaten path? The **Irish Landmark Trust** (in the Republic ✆ **01/670-4733;** www.irishlandmark.com), our favorite source of unique rental accommodations on the Emerald Isle, has just the ticket. The charming **Ballealy Cottage** sits just 8km (5 miles) from Belfast International Airport in Ballealy, in County Antrim. It was built as the lodge for the castle's gamekeeper and is tucked deep in the Randalstown Forest on the magnificent Shanes Castle Estate. The house has an endearingly irregular architectural style in high Victorian folly tradition, with octagonal chimney pots, hipped rooflines, mullioned transom windows, and countless gables. Inside, there is a hodgepodge of half-landings, shuttered windows, mahogany antiques, and enough books and interesting objets d'art to keep even the most curious guest engaged for weeks. The house sleeps five to seven people in three bedrooms with lovely old brass beds. It is surrounded by the forest and its wildlife (deer regularly visit the cottage yards). The dining room features a Stanley range that heats the entire house (there's also a modern electric oven range in the kitchen, along with a washing machine). But the best room in the house is the enormous bathroom where a giant claw-foot tub takes center stage. Rates change month to month, but average around £650 per week in high season.

INEXPENSIVE

Benedict's ★ This is one of a new generation of ultrahip small hotels that are springing up in central Belfast. The rooms are clean and modern, with huge beds and Jacuzzi baths, and the staff is pleasant and helpful. The downside is the noise—the bar and restaurant are both very popular nightspots (the bar has a DJ or live music every night). However, rooms are located on the third floor, above the quieter guests-only bar, so it's not as bad as it could be. This place is more likely to suit someone looking for a party atmosphere, rather than those looking for peace and quiet. The **restaurant** runs a "beat the clock" deal every night between 5:30 and 7pm, where the time you order dictates the price you're charged.

7–21 Bradbury Place, Shaftesbury Sq., Belfast, County Antrim. www.benedictshotel.co.uk. ✆ **028/9059-1999.** 17 units. £80–£90 double. AE, MC, V. **Amenities:** Restaurant; bar; free Wi-Fi. *In room:* TV, hair dryer.

Crescent Town House As the name implies, this stylish hotel fills a huge converted Victorian town house just south of the city center. Using deep purple as an accent color, the rooms have a modern decor, with chrome and leather touches alongside blonde wood and neutral fabrics. Basic doubles are more simply equipped, but deluxe doubles have plasma-screen TVs, datapoints, and other extras. The brasserie serves modern Irish cuisine, while **Bar Twelve** has a laid-back, publike atmosphere, and attracts locals as well as guests. ***Note:*** The first floor can be noisy because of the bar; light sleepers should get rooms on higher floors.

13 Lower Crescent, Belfast, County Antrim. www.crescenttownhouse.com. ✆ **028/9032-3349.** 17 units. £85–£110 double. Rates include full breakfast. AE, MC, V. **Amenities:** Restaurant; bar. *In room:* TV, hair dryer.

Malone Lodge Hotel Tucked away in the leafy university neighborhood south of the city center, the Malone has plenty of fans drawn by its unfussy but efficient style. Rooms are large and elegant with a soothing cream and taupe color scheme. They are divided into rooms, suites, and apartments—the latter have tiny kitchens and comfortable living rooms, and are great for families traveling with children. All are well equipped with televisions, power showers, Wi-Fi—and there's an award-winning restaurant and bar as well. The staff is reliably friendly and helpful.

60 Eglantine Ave., Belfast, County Antrim. www.malonelodgehotel.com. ✆ **028/9038-8000.** Fax 028/9038-8088. 50 units. £80–£95 double. Rates include breakfast. AE, MC, V. Free parking. **Amenities:** Restaurant; bar. *In room:* Satellite TV, hair dryer, Wi-Fi.

Tara Lodge ★★ 🎁 This small hotel in the Queen's Quarter, just outside the city center, offers stylish, comfortable, and (relatively) inexpensive, boutique-style accommodations. Rooms are on the small side, but the space is intelligently used, with firm, comfortable beds and subtle lighting. All rooms have modern touches, including flatscreen TVs and Wi-Fi. The breakfasts are excellent, especially (when you're sick of eggs and bacon) the homemade porridge. There's no in-house restaurant, but there are good restaurants and pubs in easy walking distance, and staff are happy to recommend their favorites. Book in advance for £10 off the normal price.

36 Cromwell Rd., Botanic Ave., Belfast, County Antrim. www.taralodge.com. ✆ **028/9059-0900.** 28 units. £85 double. Rates include breakfast. AE, MC, V. Free parking. **Amenities:** Free Wi-Fi. *In room:* TV/DVD, hair dryer, Wi-Fi.

Where to Eat

Over the last decade or so, the restaurant scene in Belfast has changed considerably—expanding from a longtime reliance on traditional meat-and-potatoes meals to a more international approach. There's no particular restaurant quarter, although there are plenty of eateries on the Golden Mile, and the **Odyssey Complex** (p. 580) holds a dozen or so eating places, many of which are geared to families with kids.

EXPENSIVE

Alden's ★★ MODERN IRISH This modern eatery is a favorite with Belfast foodies, drawn by its elegant but unfussy look and feel, and cooking that merges fresh Irish produce with French cooking style. Start with something suitably complex to put you in the right frame of mind—perhaps the seared Irish scallops with Parma ham and *puy* lentils, then move on to a main such as whole plaice with prawns and capers, or rib-eye steak with bacon and scallion mash. Desserts are wonderful, the wine list intelligent, the staff eager to please.

229 Upper Newtownards Rd., Belfast. ✆ **028/9065-0079.** www.aldensrestaurant.com. Reservations recommended. Main courses £12–£22. AE, DC, MC, V. Mon–Fri noon–2:30pm; Mon–Thurs 6–10pm; Fri–Sat 6–11pm.

Beatrice Kennedy ★★ TRADITIONAL IRISH This is a sweet place in the University Quarter, with bare wood floors, neatly folded white linens, and a friendly staff and a laid-back atmosphere. After a fire damaged the restaurant in 2011, it was renovated in stellar style. The menu is rich with traditional dishes that have been given a modern twist. You could start with salt and chili prawns with *napa* slaw and chili jam, or seared scallops with beet-root crisps. For a main course you could try chargrilled, dry-aged Irish rib-eye with cracked pepper cream. Or local hake with crushed potatoes and prawn butter.

44 University Rd., Belfast. ✆ **028/9020-2290.** www.beatricekennedy.co.uk. Main courses £18–£20. MC, V. Tues–Sat 5–10:30pm; Sun 12:30–2:30pm and 5–8:30pm.

Cayenne ★★ MODERN IRISH Owned by the Northern Ireland celebrity chef Paul Rankin, Cayenne is known for pairing the best local produce with exotic ingredients in a lively environment. The wide-ranging menu changes constantly, but offers seasonal dishes such as starters like the salt and chili squid or the crispy duck salad. Mains can include dishes such as braised neck of lamb with Spanish sausage and fondant potatoes, or roast venison with hot-and-sour cabbage and sherry vinegar cream. The wine list was recently recession-proofed, so now includes more affordable bottles that Rankin promises are still high quality. The service is absolutely excellent. Save room for the dessert.

7 Lesley House, Shaftesbury Sq., Belfast. ✆ **028/9033-1532.** www.cayenne-restaurant.co.uk. Reservations required. Main courses £14–£25. AE, DC, MC, V. Mon–Fri noon–2:15pm; Mon–Thurs 6–10pm; Fri–Sat 6–11pm; Sun 5–8:45pm.

Deane's ★★★ FUSION The titular Michelin star–winning chef Michael Deane presides over the stove at this sleek modern restaurant for dinner from Wednesday to Sunday, while the once very formal dining space has been taken down a notch so that it focuses on food rather than the knot in your (no-longer-required) tie. Deane's cooking is modern and sublime, a hip melding of Asian style, with Irish and U.K. ingredients and classic French touches. For a starter, try the foie gras parfait with Armagh apple chutney. Mains change all the time but can include aged sirloin with triple-cooked chunky fries, or braised shoulder of English lamb. The six-course tasting menu (£65) is exceptional if money is no object. There are four other (cheaper) Deane's restaurants in and around Belfast, including a seafood bar next door and a deli-bistro (44 Bedford St.). All are well worth your time.

38–40 Howard St., Belfast. ✆ **028/9033-1134.** Reservations required. www.michaeldeane.co.uk. Main courses £17–£20. AE, DC, MC, V. Mon–Sat noon–3pm and 5:30–11pm.

James Street South ★★★ MODERN IRISH With its chic, minimalist interior, decorated with modern artwork and narrow mirrors on cream walls and brightened by the floor-to-ceiling arched windows overlooking James Street South, this is one of the city's hot restaurants. The terrific cooking delivers modern classics with an Irish twist. The menu changes constantly but can include dishes such as roast turbot with razor clams and lobster bouillabaisse, or loin of Antrim lamb with white asparagus and saffron *jus*. Don't pass on a side order of champ—mashed potatoes with spring onions and lots of butter. Portions are generous; the wine list excellent.

21 James St. S., Belfast. ✆ **028/9043-4310.** www.jamesstreetsouth.co.uk. Reservations required. Main courses £12–£20. AE, MC, V. Mon–Fri noon–2:45pm; Mon–Sat 5:45–10:45pm.

MODERATE

Apartment ★ INTERNATIONAL This is one for the trendy crowd. Calling itself "Belfast's only style bar," this hot spot is filled with all the brushed chrome and brown leather your stylish heart desires. It's more bar than restaurant by night, but by day it's the reverse. The food is an affordable mix of modern bistro classics with a heavily Asian influence, so chargrilled steaks, pizza, and salads share the menu with dishes such as pork chops with sour apple salsa, or wok-fried chicken tempura with lemon. The food is good, but wear your Manolos.

2 Donegall Sq. W., Belfast. ✆ **028/9050-9777.** www.apartmentbelfast.com. Main courses £8–£15. MC, V. Mon–Sat noon–9pm; Sun noon–6pm.

Nick's Warehouse ★★ MODERN IRISH In an old warehouse between St. Anne's Cathedral and the tourist office, this extremely popular place offers a world-spanning menu of rib-sticking, soulful, hearty food. The titular owner Nick Price gets his influences from everywhere—you might see Scandinavian dishes on the menu alongside Mediterranean ones—but he is clearheaded enough to be true to each individual dish. There's a relaxed wine bar downstairs and a classy dining room upstairs, with brick walls and an open kitchen. Appetizers include smoked salmon with potatoes and creamed horseradish. Main courses include sirloin steaks, lamb chops with honey-and-ginger sauce, and whole baked sea bass.

35 Hill St., Belfast. ✆ **028/9043-9690.** www.nickswarehouse.co.uk. Reservations recommended. Main courses £7–£19. AE, DC, MC, V. Mon–Fri noon–2:30pm; Mon–Sat 6–9:30pm (drinks until midnight).

INEXPENSIVE

John Hewitt Bar & Restaurant ★ MODERN IRISH This centrally located bar is always buzzing; its well-dressed, young crowd seems to find time to hang out, day and night. It's a good place for lunch, as the menu leans toward upscale Irish traditional pub food with dishes like grilled pork and black-pepper sausages and mashed potatoes, or grilled salmon, and steak and ale pie with baby potatoes. It also has some of the best Guinness in town. Happily, as it aims to be true to the socialist principles of its namesake Irish politico, prices are extremely reasonable. 51 Donegall St., Belfast. ✆ **028/9023-3768.** www.thejohnhewitt.com. Main courses £5–£8. MC, V. Mon–Sat noon–3pm; Fri noon–6pm (drinks until midnight).

Red Panda CHINESE This small chain of upscale Chinese restaurants is relentlessly popular, and this location, on the Golden Mile, may be the busiest of all. The attraction is the authentic food in bright, pleasant surroundings. The menu has all the usual favorites, and it's a great break from the hearty Irish fare you'll find elsewhere.

60 Great Victoria St., Belfast. ✆ **028/9080-8700.** Main courses £6–£8. MC, V. Mon–Sat noon–3pm and 6–10pm.

White's Tavern ★ TRADITIONAL IRISH This may well be Belfast's favorite place to have lunch. One of the city's many historic pubs, White's is tucked away on a lane between Rosemary and High streets. It's hard to find, but worth ferreting out as it's got all the low beams and wood floors you might hope for. The food is warming, traditional dishes like Irish stew, sausage and mashed potatoes, and fish and chips.

2–12 Wine Cellar Entry, Belfast. ✆ **028/9024-3080.** www.whitestavern.co.uk. Main courses £5–£8. No credit cards. Mon–Sat noon–6pm (drinks until midnight).

Belfast After Dark

PUBS & CLUBS

Belfast has a plethora of historic pubs where the crowds tend to be local and friendly, but the big news here in recent years has been its fast-growing new generation of hip modern bars geared toward the young and trendy. The late-night places are mostly clustered in the University Quarter, while the pubs are spread around town. If you're drawn to traditional pubs, several of the best are hidden away in the pedestrian lanes off Donegall Place.

The licensing laws in Northern Ireland aren't as strict as they used to be. Pub hours are generally Monday to Saturday from 11:30am to 11pm and Sunday from 12:30 to 2:30pm and from 7 to 10pm, although some open until 1am, especially on Friday and Saturday; bars stay open later. Nightclubs tend not to get busy until after the pubs close; admission ranges from £3 to £15.

Apartment If you feel like a good cocktail in sophisticated surrounds with a 20- to 30-something crowd of Belfast's beautiful people, then this is the place. It has dubbed itself Belfast's "only style bar," and its smooth, sophisticated style clearly appeals to Belfast's best DJs, as they are regularly at the turntables. Upscale, city-center style is the name of the game here. 2 Donegall Sq., Belfast. ✆ **028/9050-9777.** www.apartmentbelfast.com.

Bar Bacca/La Lea Essentially two bars in one, this has been Belfast's most stylish nightclub for several years now. It's a sensory experience, with classic architecture, soaring ceilings, and an Eastern bent—a huge Buddha head hangs above the dance floor, incense burns, and bodies dance the night away. The private bar evokes a decadent Bedouin tent. There's a strict door policy—you'll have a better chance of getting in if you're dressed to kill. 43 Franklin St., Belfast. ✆ **028/9023-0200.**

The ornately detailed Victorian interior of the Crown Liquor Saloon, a National Trust property.

Crown Liquor Saloon Dating from 1826, this is the jewel in Northern Ireland's crown of pubs. Opposite the Europa Hotel and the Grand Opera House, this gas-lit old alehouse has what many architecture buffs believe to be the finest example of Victorian Gothic decor in the country. Owned by the National Trust and run by Bass Ireland, it has it all: stained-glass windows, pounded tin ceiling, elaborate tile floor, etched and smoked glass dividing the wooden cubicle seating, a beveled mirror with floral and wildlife decorations, scalloped lamps, and a long bar with inlaid colored glass and marble trim. Don't even get us started on the gorgeous mosaic exterior. The 10 dark-wood private rooms are guarded by mythological beasts with shields. There are gunmetal plates for striking matches, little windows to peep discreetly through, and an antique system of bells that once summoned service. Great Victoria St., Belfast. ✆ **028/9027-9901.** www.crownbar.com.

Empire Music Hall This is a grand place—a converted Victorian church that has become legendary on the Irish music and bar scenes. It has three floors of bars and music, with different styles represented on different nights—jazz on Tuesday, Irish traditional on Wednesday, blues Thursday, and rock Friday and Saturday nights. There's also a semiregular comedy club on Tuesdays; call ahead or check the website for details. 42 Botanic Ave., Belfast. ✆ **028/9024-9276.** www.thebelfastempire.com.

Irene & Nan's The young and trendy crowd into this elaborately decorated bar every night. Its name is an homage to two glamorous retirees who hung out in a nearby pub for many years. Taking their style to heart, this place drowns in designer chic with a slight 1950s retro theme. The mezzanine floor is the most sumptuous, but the music is excellent on all levels. If you're hungry, the in-house bistro is not bad at all. 12 Brunswick St., Belfast. ✆ **028/9023-9123.** www.ireneandnansbelfast.co.uk.

John Hewitt Bar & Restaurant This centrally located joint—named after a local socialist hero—is an exquisitely rare thing: a modern bar with no televisions and no gaming machines. During the day and early in the evening, the low rumble of conversation is the loudest thing you'll hear here. In the evening, there's often live music, including folk several nights a week and jazz on Fridays. The food is good here, too. This one is for the grown-ups. 51 Donegall St., Belfast. ✆ **028/9023-3768.** www.thejohnhewitt.com.

Limelight & Katy Daly's This is where pub and club morph into one venue. Rock bands regularly perform in its music club space, while the stripped-down pub is one of the best places in Belfast to hang out, take in the music, and down a few pints. The crowd is youngish, and the mood is usually friendly and untrendy. 17–19 Ormeau Ave., Belfast. ✆ **028/9032-5942.** www.cdcleisure.net.

Milk Bar Club In the city's Cathedral Quarter, this is one of Belfast's hottest clubs, with music 7 nights a week and a devoted 20-something clientele. Inside, you'll find a riot of color, energy, and noise—everything from house and disco to R&B. On weekends it has a fierce doorman policy—you'll need to look fancy. 10–14 Tomb St., Belfast. ✆ **028/9027-8876.**

Morning Star This beautifully restored old pub tucked away in Pottinger's Entry arcade is a nice, traditional pub. It dates from 1810, and may be even older. It was once the final stop of the Dublin-to-Belfast stagecoach; its horseshoe-shaped bar may be a result of that history. It still has its original facade and the wooden snugs in which weary stagecoach travelers once rested. Along with evening drinking, it's a good place for lunch as well. 17–19 Pottinger's Entry, Belfast. ✆ **028/9023-5986.** www.themorningstarbar.com.

Pat's Bar For a taste of Belfast's harbor atmosphere, join the sailors, dockers, and businesspeople at this pub at the gates of Prince's Dock. Cross its red-tile floor to the antique hand-carved beech bar, and then relax in its pinewood surroundings. There's an interesting collection of memorabilia—much of it given to the bar's owner by sailors—clogs, swords, a telescope, and a bayonet. There's traditional Irish music on Friday and Saturday night at 9pm. 19 Prince's Dock St., Belfast. ✆ **028/9074-4524.**

Robinson's Bar This trendy, modern bar next door to the Crown Liquor Saloon attracts Belfast's young and beautiful. The top floor (the Loft) has a modern vibe, with a big dance floor and top local and national DJs spinning tunes late into the night. Downstairs is a hip bistro, and below that a more traditional saloon pub, where you can have a quiet(er) drink. 38–42 Great Victoria St., Belfast. ✆ **028/9024-7447.** www.robinsonsbar.co.uk.

Rotterdam This small, traditional place in the Cathedral Quarter eschews modern annoyances—you'll find no TVs above the bar here. Instead, there are roaring fires and good pub food, as well as excellent pints of Guinness. This is one of the better music pubs in town, so expect jazz on Tuesdays, blues on Wednesdays, acoustic on Thursdays, and a mix of good sounds on the weekend. This bar has been battling demolition for several years; developers planned to knock it down and build a luxury housing development, but as this book went to press it was open and thriving. 54 Pilot St., Belfast. ✆ **028/9074-6021.**

White's Tavern Tucked into a historic cobblestone trading lane in the city center, this old tavern was established in 1630 as a wine shop. It's full of old

Belfast's oldest tavern, White's dates to 1630.

barrels and hoists, ornate snugs, brick arches, large copper measures, framed newspaper clippings of 200-year-old vintage, quill pens, and other memorabilia. It's a good pub for conversation and browsing, and it features traditional music as well as quiz nights, darts, and theme nights. 2-4 Winecellar Entry (btw. High and Rosemary sts.), Belfast. ✆ **028/9033-0988.**

THE PERFORMING ARTS

Several sources provide up-to-date listings of shows and concerts. *That's Entertainment* is free and widely available at tourist offices and pubs, as are the *Big List* and *Artslink*. There's always the *Belfast Daily Telegraph* and the *Irish News*. You could also try **www.gotobelfast.com** and **www.belfast.net**.

With its distinctive bronze dome, the **Waterfront Hall** dominates the Lagan skyline (Oxford St., Laganside; ✆ **028/9033-4455** for credit card reservations, or 9033-4400 for program information; www.waterfront.co.uk). The state-of-the-art conference center and concert venue attracts international performers. On the Golden Mile near the Europa Hotel, the **Grand Opera House** (Great Victoria St.; ✆ **028/9024-1919;** www.goh.co.uk) first opened its doors in 1895. A central part of Belfast's cultural scene, it offers the finest opera, drama, and musicals in town. The **Ulster Hall** (Bedford St.; ✆ **028/9032-3900** or 9033-4455; www.ulsterhall.co.uk) hosts touring music groups, comedy, and drama, and is home to the Ulster Orchestra. The basement of the **Empire Music Hall,** 42 Botanic Ave. (✆ **028/9032-8110;** www.thebelfastempire.com), is home to a varied music program, with regular jazz, blues, salsa, and acoustic sessions nightly. Ticket prices range from nothing to hardly anything (£3). The **Odyssey** (2 Queen's Quay; ✆ **028/9073-9074;** www.odysseyarena.com) on the waterfront has a 10,000-seat arena where touring rock groups from Oasis to Destiny's Child have performed. The complex also holds dozens of restaurants and bars, so there's plenty to keep you busy before the show.

Theaters include the **Lyric Theatre** (Ridgeway St.; ✆ **028/9038-5673;** www.lyrictheatre.co.uk) for new plays by Irish and international playwrights.

Tickets, which cost from around £8 to £30 for most events, can be purchased in advance from **www.ticketmaster.ie**. (You can always arrange to have tickets purchased online delivered to your hotel.)

THE GAY & LESBIAN SCENE

The gay and lesbian scene in Belfast is very low-key and always has been. The handful of gay pubs and bars are generally friendly places, though; once you've been around a bit and people recognize you, you'll find a warm welcome. The scene is getting more cosmopolitan all the time.

Widely viewed as the heart of the scene is **Kremlin** (96 Donegall St.; ✆ **028/9031-6060;** www.kremlin-belfast.com), a clever, Soviet-themed bar open 7 nights a week but best known for its Saturday-night party, "Revolution." It's split into three areas: a cocktail bar, a disco bar, and a club section, where resident DJs and visiting acts play live. Theme nights encompass everything from the Wizard of Oz to the Kremlin State Fair, complete with games, circus acts, and cotton candy. We're not sure what Lenin would have thought, but it's all in the spirit of open-minded fun.

The castle at Carrickfergus is considered to be Ireland's oldest, from 1180.

The gay scene goes public each year in late July or early August for Belfast's small but enthusiastic Pride celebration (**www.belfastpride.com**). For general information about GLBT life in Belfast check out the **Gay Belfast** website (**www.gaybelfast.net**), or search for Northern Ireland on the **Gay Ireland** website (**www.gay-ireland.com**).

SIDE TRIPS FROM BELFAST

Carrickfergus

19km (12 miles) NE of Belfast

Just outside Belfast off the M3 motorway, the castle town of Carrickfergus offers a nice break from the hustle and bustle of the city, and some fresh sea air. Locals like to say that Carrickfergus was thriving when Belfast was a sandbank, and looking around its winding medieval streets at the edge of the sea, it's easy to believe. In 1180 John de Courcy, a Norman, built a massive keep at Carrickfergus, the first real Irish castle, to guard the approach to the strategically critical Belfast Lough. Even today, although the town spreads for several miles in each direction along the shore, the huge, forbidding castle is still its center. The narrow streets across from the castle follow the historic winding pattern of medieval roads, and you can still find some of the old city walls.

Stop into the **Carrickfergus Tourist Information Office,** Heritage Plaza, Antrim Street, Carrickfergus, County Antrim (✆ **028/9336-6455**); it's open all year Monday to Friday 9am to 5pm.

Andrew Jackson Cottage This one-story cottage with earthen floor and open fireplace was the ancestral home of Andrew Jackson, seventh president of the United States. His parents emigrated to the United States in 1765. The house now contains a display on Jackson's life and career and Ulster's connections with America.

Boneybefore, Carrickfergus, County Antrim. ✆ **028/9335-8049.** Free admission. June–Sept Mon–Fri 10am–1pm, daily 2–6pm; by appointment only the rest of the year.

Carrickfergus Castle ★ ☺ This impressive Norman castle looms darkly over the entrance to Belfast Lough, where William of Orange landed on June 14, 1690, en route to the Battle of the Boyne. The central keep inside dates to the 12th century, the thick outer walls were completed 100 years later, and the gun ports are a relatively new addition, only 400 years old. The castle has withstood sieges by Edward the Bruce in 1315 and King John in 1210, though it was temporarily captured by the French in 1760. The outside is more impressive than the inside, which has been largely dedicated to inspiring the imagination of children. The use of waxwork figures inside (riding horses, threatening to shoot people over the walls) is a bit over-the-top, and it's a shame that, in the interest of safety, the keep's upper windows are glassed in, making it impossible to photograph the lovely view (or even to see it properly). Much of the remains of the castle walls were closed to the public on our visit, so we couldn't take in the view from there. Still, kids will love it, although those without little ones may want to take a photo and drive on. In the summer, medieval banquets, a medieval fair, and a crafts market are held, adding a touch of play and pageantry.

Marine Hwy., Antrim St., Carrickfergus, County Antrim. ✆ **028/9335-1273.** Admission £3 adults; £1.50 seniors and children; £8 families. Apr–Sept Mon–Sat 10am–6pm, Sun noon–6pm; Oct–Mar Mon–Sat 10am–4pm, Sun 2–4pm.

Cultra

11km (6¾ miles) E of Belfast

Ulster Folk & Transport Museum ★ ☺ This 70-hectare (173-acre) site brings together many parts of Ulster's past in a sprawling outdoor folk museum. The museum includes a collection of 19th-century buildings saved from the bulldozer's path and moved here intact from their original sites. You walk among

Joining the National Trust

Several of Ulster's best sites are managed by the National Trust, a not-for-profit organization that preserves historic buildings and areas of natural beauty across the U.K. (including Northern Ireland) and keeps them accessible to the public. Although admission to National Trust sites is usually just a few pounds, taking out a yearly membership gives you unlimited free admission to all of them, which can represent a saving if you plan to visit more than just one or two. If you also happen to be visiting Britain on your trip—or within the same year—it could be a wise investment. The current membership costs are £48 for individuals, £80 for couples, and £82 for families. You can sign up for membership at any National Trust property, or join in advance online at www.nationaltrust.org.uk. Alternatively, American visitors can join the U.S. wing of the National Trust, the Royal Oak Foundation. Call ✆ 212/480-2889 or visit www.royal-oak.org for more information.

farmhouses, mills, and churches; and explore rural schools, a forge, a bank, a print shop, and more. Actors in period dress reenact tasks of daily life—cooking over an open hearth, plowing the fields with horses, thatching roofs, and practicing traditional Ulster crafts such as textile making, spinning, quilting, lace making, printing, spade making, and shoemaking. The transport museum's collection ranges from donkey carts to DeLoreans, and there is a permanent exhibition on the *Titanic*.

153 Bangor Rd. (11km/6¾ miles northeast of Belfast on the A2), Cultra, Holywood, County Down. ✆ **028/9042-8428.** www.uftm.org.uk. Day ticket to both museums £8 adults; £4.50 seniors, students, and children; £21 families. Mar–Sept Tues–Sun 10am–5pm; Oct–Feb Tues–Fri 10am–4pm, Sat–Sun 11am–4pm.

The Ards Peninsula

The Ards Peninsula, beginning about 16km (10 miles) east of Belfast, curls around the western shore of **Strangford Lough ★**. This is a place of great natural beauty, as well as a bird sanctuary and wildlife reserve. Two roads traverse the peninsula: A20 (the Lough road) and A2 (the coast road). The Lough road is the more scenic.

At the southern tip of the Lough, car ferry service connects Portaferry with the Strangford Ferry Terminal (✆ **028/4488-1637**), in Strangford, on the mainland side. It runs every half-hour, weekdays 7:30am to 10:30pm, Saturday 8am to 11pm, Sunday 9:30am to 10:30pm. No reservations are needed. A one-way trip takes 5 minutes and costs £5.80 for a car and driver, £1 for each additional passenger.

The **Portaferry Tourist Information Office,** The Stables, Castle Street (✆ **028/4272-9882**), is open Monday to Saturday 10am to 5:30pm, Sunday 1 to 6pm. There are two National Trust properties in this area, one on the Ards Peninsula and the other just across the lough at Portaferry.

An ancient dolmen in a field on the Ards Peninsula.

Castle Espie ★ ☺ This marvelous wildlife center, owned and managed by the Wildlife and Wetlands Trust, is home to a virtual UN of rare migratory geese, ducks, and swans. Some are so accustomed to visitors that they will eat grain from their hands, so children can have the disarming experience of meeting Hooper swans eye to eye. Guided trails are designed for children and families, and the center sponsors activities and events year-round. A favorite of birdwatchers in search of waterfowl, the center has thousands of pale-bellied brents in early winter. The book and gift shop is enticing, there's an excellent play area for kids, and the restaurant serves good lunches and home-baked cakes.

78 Ballydrain Rd., Comber, County Down. ✆ **028/9187-4146.** Admission £5.60 adults; £4.50 seniors and students; £3 children. Daily 10:30am–4:30pm; slightly later in summer. 21km (13 miles) southeast of Belfast, signposted from the A22 Comber-Killyleagh-Downpatrick rd.

Castle Ward ☺ About 2km (1¼ miles) west of Strangford village is this grand manor house dating from 1760. A hybrid of architectural styles melding Gothic with classical, it sits on a 280-hectare (692-acre) country estate of formal gardens, woodlands, lakelands, and seashore. Inside, kids can dress up in period clothes and play with period toys, or they can ride a tractor-trailer out to see the farm animals. There's a theater in the stable yard that hosts operatic performances in summer. ***Note:*** If you don't mind skipping the inside of the house, you can visit the grounds for about half the house ticket price.

Strangford, County Down. ✆ **028/4488-1204.** www.nationaltrust.org.uk. Admission to house, gardens, and grounds £10 adults; £5 children. Grounds Apr–Sept daily 10am–8pm; Oct–Mar daily 10am–4pm. House Mar–Oct daily 11am–5pm.

Exploris ☺ This cheery, kid-focused aquarium concentrates on sea life native to Strangford Lough and the Irish Sea. Inside, the mixture of displays ranges from the educational-but-arguably-dull (models of the Strangford Lough ecosystem) to the more lively (giant aquariums filled with local and regional sea life) to the downright fun (the seal sanctuary). Along with its splashy occupants, the aquarium complex contains a cafe where you can rest and a gift shop where you can buy fish-related key rings, as well as a park, picnic area, and children's playground.

Castle St., Portaferry, County Down. ✆ **028/4272-8062.** www.exploris.org.uk. Admission £7 adults; £4.50 children. Apr–Aug Mon–Fri 10am–6pm, Sat 11am–6pm, Sun noon–6pm; Sept–Mar Mon–Fri 10am–5pm, Sat 11am–5pm, Sun 1–5pm.

Giant's Ring 🎁 This massive, mysterious, prehistoric earthwork, 180m (590 ft.) in diameter, has at its center a megalithic chamber with a single capstone. Ancient burial rings like this one were long thought to be protected by fairies, and thus were left untouched, but this one was quite an exception—in the 19th century, it was used as a racetrack, with the high embankment around it serving as grandstands. Today, its dignity has been restored and it is a place of wonder for the few who visit; sadly, it is largely neglected by tourists.

Ballynahatty, County Down. 6km (3¾ miles) southwest of Belfast center, west off A24; or 1.6km (1 mile) south of Shaw's Bridge, off B23. Free admission.

Grey Abbey The impressive ruins of Grey Abbey sit amid a beautifully landscaped setting, perfect for a picnic. Founded in 1193 by the Cistercians, it contained one of the earliest Gothic churches in Ireland. This is a particularly plain Cistercian ruin (some of their abbeys were quite elaborate). Amid the ruined choirs, there is a fragmented stone effigy of a knight in armor, possibly a likeness of John de Courcy, husband of the abbey's founder, Affrica of Cumbria. There's also a small visitor center.

Greyabbey, County Down. No phone; for information contact the NI Environment Agency at ✆ **028/9181-1491.** Free admission. Easter–Sept daily 10am–6pm; Oct–Easter Sun only noon–4pm.

Legananny Dolmen This renowned, impressive granite dolmen (Neolithic tomb) on the southern slope of Slieve Croob looks, in the words of archaeologist Peter Harbison, like "a coffin on stilts." This must be one of the most photographed dolmens in Ireland, and you must see it up close to fully appreciate its size. The massive capstone seems weightlessly poised on its supporting uprights.

Slieve Croob, County Down. Take A24 from Belfast to Ballynahinch, B7 to Dromara, and then ask for directions.

Mount Stewart House Once the home of Lord Castlereagh, this 18th-century house sits on the eastern shore of Strangford Lough. Its lush gardens hold an impressive array of rare and unusual plants. Inside, the art collection is excellent, including the *Hambletonian* by George Stubbs and family portraits by Batoni, Mengs, and Lazlo. The Temple of the Winds, a rare 18th-century banqueting house, is also on the estate, but is only open on public holidays.

On the east shore of Strangford Lough, southeast of Newtownards, 24km (15 miles) southeast of Belfast, on A20, Newtownards, County Down. ✆ **028/4278-8387.** www.nationaltrust.org.uk. House and garden admission £7.10 adults; £4 children. House Mar–Oct (except Easter week) daily noon–6pm. Lakeside gardens daily all year 10am–6pm.

Nendrum Monastic Site Hidden away on an isolated island, this site dates from the 5th century, when it was founded by St. Mochaoi (St. Mahee). This site is much older than Grey Abbey across the water, and the remains of the ancient community are fascinating. Foundations show the outline of ancient churches, a round tower, and beehive cells. There are concentric stone ramparts and a sundial, reconstructed from long-broken pieces. Its visitor center shows informative videos and has informative exhibits. The road to Mahee Island crosses a causeway to Reagh Island and a bridge still protected by the 15th-century Mahee Castle.

Signposted from Lisbane, on the A20 south of Comber, County Down. ✆ **028/9754-2547.** Free admission. Site 24 hr. Visitor center Apr–Sept Tues–Sat 10am–7pm, Sun 2–7pm; Oct–Mar Sat 10am–4pm, Sun 2–4pm.

Portaferry Castle This is little more than a small, 16th-century tower house, but together with another tower house in Strangford it once controlled all the ship traffic through the Narrows. It's a piece of history right beside the visitor center, so it's worth popping your head in for a peek.

Castle St., Portaferry, County Down. Free admission. Easter–Sept Mon–Sat 10am–5pm; Sun 2–6pm.

SPORTS & OUTDOOR PURSUITS

BICYCLING If you want to explore the area on two wheels, you can rent bicycles for roughly £10 to £15 a day. Cycle rental by the day or week, and delivery in the North Down/Ards area, are available from **Mike the Bike,** 53 Frances St., Newtownards (✆ **028/9181-1311**). He also rents kayaks, if you feel like a splash. If you want some guidance and companionship, contact Tony Boyd at **Iron Donkey,** 15 Ballyknocken Rd., Saintfield (✆ **028/9081-3200;** www.emeraldtrail.com).

DIVING The nearby loughs and offshore waters are a diver's dream—remarkably clear and littered with wrecks. To charter a diving expedition in Strangford Lough, contact **Des Rogers** (✆ **028/4272-8297**). One of Europe's finest training centers, **DV Diving,** 138 Mount Stewart Rd., Newtownards, County Down (✆ **028/9186-1686** or 9146-4671; www.dvdiving.co.uk), offers diving courses.

FISHING For info, tackle, and bait, try the **Village Tackle Shop,** 55a Newtownbreda Rd., Belfast (✆ **028/9049-1916**), or **H. W. Kelly,** 54 Market St., Downpatrick, County Down (✆ **028/4461-2193**). Sea-fishing trips from Portaferry into the waters of Strangford Lough and along the County Down coast are organized by Peter and Iris Wright at **Norsemaid Sea Enterprises,** 152 Portaferry Rd., Newtownards, County Down (✆ **028/9181-2081**). Reservations are required. To outfit yourself and fish for rainbow trout year-round, visit **Ballygrangee Trout Fishery,** Mountstewart Road, Carrowdore, County Down (✆ **028/4278-8883** or 07714/956-775).

GOLF Several well-established courses are just a short drive from Belfast in north County Down. They include the **Bangor Golf Club,** Broadway, Bangor (✆ **028/9127-0922;** www.bangorgolfclubni.co.uk), with greens fees of £26 weekdays, £34 weekends; **Downpatrick Golf Club,** 43 Saul Rd., Downpatrick (✆ **028/4461-5947;** www.downpatrickgolfclub.org.uk), with greens fees of £23 weekdays, £28 weekends; and the 71-par **Scrabo Golf Club,** 233 Scrabo Rd., Newtownards (✆ **028/9181-2355;** www.scrabo-golf-club.org), with greens fees of £19 weekdays, £24 weekends.

WHERE TO STAY

Moderate

Portaferry Hotel ★ Set in a designated conservation area and incorporating a terrace dating from the mid–18th century, the Portaferry Hotel retains the charm of a seasoned waterside inn while providing the amenities of a modern hotel. A recent renovation brought in more sleek, neutral color schemes, along with (unfortunately) higher prices that, nice though it is, are somewhat hard to justify. Many rooms have excellent views of the lough, though, and if you can get a deal by booking online in advance, it's a pleasant enough place to stay. The hotel restaurant is handy, if a little pricey.

The Strand, Portaferry (47km/29 miles from Belfast), County Down. www.portaferryhotel.com. ✆ **028/4272-8231.** 14 units. £70–£110 double. Rates include full breakfast. AE, DC, MC, V. **Amenities:** Restaurant; bar; Internet access. *In room:* TV, radio, hair dryer.

Inexpensive

Ballycastle House Mrs. Margaret Deering's home is a charming 300-year-old farmhouse that has been sweetly (if a bit fussily) refurbished. The guest rooms are quite girly, with floral bedspreads and curtains, startlingly pink walls and lots of draped fabric. All offer restful rural views. Margaret makes a warm and welcoming host, and breakfasts are fresh and delicious, although choice is rather limited. A two-bedroom self-catering cottage is also available starting at £375 per week.

20 Mountstewart Rd. (8km/5 miles southeast of town on A20), Newtownards, County Down. www.ballycastlehouse.com. ✆/fax **028/4278-8357.** 3 units. £60–£75 double. Children's and senior discounts available. Rates include full breakfast. No credit cards. **Amenities:** Smoke-free rooms. *In room:* Hair dryer.

Edenvale House ★ Just down the road from Mount Stewart House, with views of Strangford Lough and the Mourne Mountains, this elegant and welcoming Georgian country house is a beautiful option. Request one of the two front guest rooms, since they are the most spacious—with either a four-poster or king-size bed, good-size bathrooms, large dressing rooms, and far-reaching views across the lough. The other guest room is smaller but extremely attractive, with garden views and a small shower-only bathroom. Breakfasts—served at a communal dining room table—are exceptional, with fresh eggs from the owners' chickens, local bacon, and homemade bread. The entire house is smoke-free. ***Note:*** Edenvale House accepts payment in euros as well as sterling.

130 Portaferry Rd., Newtownards, County Down (3.2km/2 miles from Newtownards on A20). www.edenvalehouse.com. ✆ **028/9181-4881.** 3 units, 1 with shower only. £90 double. Rates include full breakfast. MC, V. Closed Christmas. *In room:* TV, hair dryer, Wi-Fi (free).

Killyleagh Castle Towers ★★ This is for those people who always wanted to spend more time in a castle. These three gatehouse towers in the small, picturesque town of Killyleagh rent by the week. Built in the 1620s, the fanciful stone towers have spiral staircases and roof terraces. The two smaller towers sleep four; the larger tower sleeps five. Rooms range from small and snug to barely more spacious.

High St., Killyleagh, County Down. ✆ **028/4482-8261.** 3 units. £300–£450 per week. MC, V.

Old School House Inn This handy guesthouse just south of Castle Espie near Nendrum is a personable place with comfortable, homey rooms, a friendly staff, and a good restaurant. Relax in your well-appointed room before heading downstairs to sample fresh oysters from the inn's oyster farm. Each bedroom is named after an American president of Ulster descent. Who knew there were 12 of them?

Ballydrain Rd., Comber (on the road to Nendrum), County Down. www.theoldschoolhouseinn.com. ✆ **028/9754-1182.** 12 units. £80 double. Rates include full breakfast. MC, V. **Amenities:** Restaurant. *In room:* TV, hair dryer.

WHERE TO EAT

Primrose Bar and Restaurant BISTRO The Primrose—an erstwhile blacksmith shop—is divided into a casual bistro and a more upscale restaurant. The bistro is popular for its steaks, burgers, open-faced prawn sandwiches, and fresh-baked bread. The restaurant offers finer fare, including grilled salmon with sesame crust and soy stir-fry vegetables, or pork medallions with apple and cinnamon. There's a nice fire blazing on chilly days, and, as the locals say, the *craic* is good (there's a good time to be had).

30 Main St., Ballynahinch, County Down. ✆ **028/9756-3177.** www.primrosebar.co.uk. Dinner main courses £7–£14. AE, MC, V. Bar daily noon–11pm. Restaurant Fri–Sun noon–2:30pm and 5–9pm.

Downpatrick

37km (23 miles) SE of Belfast

The charming town of Downpatrick is closely identified with St. Patrick. Legend has it that when Patrick came to Ireland in A.D. 432 to begin his missionary work, strong winds blew his boat here. He'd meant to sail up the coast to County Antrim, where as a young slave he had tended flocks on Slemish Mountain. Instead, he settled here and converted the local chieftain Dichu and his followers to Christianity. Over the next 30 years, Patrick roamed through Ireland carrying out his work, but this is where he died, and some believe he is buried in the graveyard of Downpatrick Cathedral, although there's no proof. Because of all of this, the town tends to be crowded, largely with Catholic pilgrims, around St. Patrick's Day, but the constant activities and religious fervor are worth witnessing.

For information in the Down District, stop into the **St. Patrick Visitor Centre,** 53A Market St., Downpatrick, County Down (✆ **028/4461-2233;** www.saintpatrickcentre.com). It's open October to March Monday to Saturday 10am to 5pm; April to September Monday to Saturday 9:30am to 5:30pm, and Sunday 1 to 5:30pm. A "St. Patrick's Country" bus tour is offered according to demand and can be booked through this office.

Down Cathedral Excavations show that Downpatrick was a *dún* (or fort), perhaps as early as the Bronze Age, and its earliest structures were built on the site where this church now sits. Ancient fortifications ultimately gave way to a series of churches, each built atop the ruins of the previous incarnation, over 1,800 years. The current cathedral is an 18th- and 19th-century reconstruction of its 13th- and 16th-century predecessors. Just south of the cathedral stands a relatively recent monolith inscribed with the name "Patric." By some accounts, it roughly marks the grave of the saint, who is said to have died at Saul, 3km (2 miles) northeast. The tradition identifying this site as Patrick's grave seems to go back no further than the 12th century, though, when John de Courcy reputedly transferred the bones of saints Brigit and Columba here to lie beside those of St. Patrick.

The Mall, Downpatrick, County Down. ✆ **028/4461-4922.** Free admission. Mon–Sat 9:30am–4:30pm; Sun 2–5pm.

St. Patrick Heritage Centre/Down County Museum ☺ Next to the cathedral and sharing an extensive 18th-century jail complex, the St. Patrick Centre and the County Museum provide some intriguing glimpses into the rich history of this area. The surprisingly high-tech exhibits put everything into context. There's a 180-degree film (which, according to the center, can give some people motion sickness). You'll also be introduced to some of the county's more notable figures, from St. Patrick to a handful of prisoners sent off to Australia in the 19th century.

The Mall, Downpatrick, County Down. ✆ **028/4461-5218.** www.saintpatrickcentre.com. Free admission, except for some special events. June–Aug Mon–Sat 9:30am–6pm, Sun 10am–6pm; Oct–Mar Mon–Sat 10am–5pm (usually closed Sun); St. Patrick's Day (Mar 17) 9:30am–7pm; Apr–May and Sept Mon–Sat 9:30am–5:30pm, Sun 1–5:30pm.

Lisburn

16km (10 miles) SE of Belfast

There's a nice museum in this small town a short distance from Belfast.

Irish Linen Centre and Lisburn Museum Using multimedia presentations to re-create historical factory scenes, this museum traces the history of Irish linen. Given the rather stodgy subject matter, it's surprisingly interesting. You can see linen in all stages of production, and watch skilled weavers at work on restored 19th-century looms in the workshop. If you're a big fan of linen and want to give over a whole day to it, you can book a place on an **Irish Linen Tour** (£10 per person) by calling the Banbridge Gateway Tourist Information Centre (✆ **028/4062-3322**).

Market Sq., Lisburn, County Antrim. ✆ **028/9266-3377.** Free admission. Mon–Sat 9:30am–5pm.

Lough Neagh

16km (10 miles) W of Belfast

Lough Neagh, at 396 sq. km (153 sq. miles), is the largest lake in the 6,000 or so islands in the British Isles. Ancient Irish lore maintains the lake was created by the mighty giant Fionn MacCumhail (Finn McCool) when he flung a chunk of earth into the sea to create the Isle of Man. But before you think about taking a dip, consider this: The lake's claim to fame is its eels. Yep, the waters are positively infested with the slimy creatures. Hundreds of tons of eels are taken from Lough Neagh and exported each year, mainly to Germany and Holland. The ages-old eel-extraction method involves "long lines," baited with up to 100 hooks. As many as 200 boats trailing these lines are on the lake each night (the best time to go fishing for eels). So, maybe take a rain check on that swim.

If you're not entirely creeped out by that, however, you can take a **boat trip** on the lovely lake. Boats depart regularly from the nearby **Kinnego Marina** (✆ **028/3832-7573**), signposted from the main road. They last about 45 minutes and cost about £10 for adults, £7 for children.

Lough Neagh Discovery Centre ★ Midway between Belfast and Armagh city, this center on the southern shore of the lake at Oxford Island is a sprawling nature reserve with lush reed beds, verdant woodlands, and gorgeous wildflower meadows. The center has historical and geographic exhibits, walking trails, bird-watching observation points, and bucolic picnic areas. For a closer look at everything in sight, the center has binoculars for hire.

Oxford Island, Craigavon, County Armagh. ✆ **028/3832-2205.** Free admission. Apr–Sept daily 10am–6pm; Oct–Mar Wed–Sun 10am–5pm.

County Armagh

65km (40 miles) SW of Belfast

County Armagh is a green rolling stretch of gentle hills and small villages. It is also one of Northern Ireland's most rebellious Republican regions—there are police watchtowers atop some hills, occasional barracks (mostly empty these days), and until a couple of years ago, you could expect to hear the rhythmic thumping of military helicopters flying over.

Armagh is also the county where, in March 2009, the peace in Northern Ireland was sorely tested when a Catholic policeman was murdered by members of an IRA splinter group. Shortly afterwards, two British soldiers were shot outside their barracks while paying for a pizza delivery. Thankfully, this didn't lead to the sort of tit-for-tat retaliation seen in the past—and condemnation was loud from all sides—but it does point to the fact that very real tensions still exist under the surface here. Peace or no peace, you'll certainly notice that sectarian graffiti is omnipresent. That said, however, remember that none of this is directed at visitors. There's no reason to avoid this scenic, forested county.

Small and manageable **Armagh City** is a handsome cathedral city. Its name, from the Irish *ard Macha* (Macha's height) refers to the pagan queen Macha who is said to have built a fortress here. It's no coincidence that St. Patrick chose to base himself here when he was spreading Christianity—it was a bold challenge to the native paganism. The simple stone church that he built in the 5th century is now the giant Church of Ireland cathedral—clearly, his plan worked, at least to some extent. There are actually two St. Patrick cathedrals in Armagh City—one Catholic and one Protestant—and each is the seat of its primate.

The town has the kind of dignity you might expect in a seat of religion, with grand public buildings, huge churches, and big Georgian town houses along the Mall. Buildings, doorsteps, and sidewalks are made of delightful pink, yellow, and red local limestone that make the city glow even on a dull day.

Stop into the **Armagh Tourist Information Centre,** the Old Bank Building, 40 Upper English St., Armagh (✆ **028/3752-1800**); it's open all year, Monday to Saturday 9am to 5pm and Sunday 2 to 5pm.

A short distance outside the city, the small town of Bessbrook has historic cottages, the forests of Slieve Gullion, and ancient Navan Fort, the most important archaeological site in Ulster.

Armagh Astronomy Centre and Planetarium ☺ On your way up College Hill from the Mall, you'll pass the 200-year-old Armagh Observatory, still in service but closed to the public. Farther up the hill stands the Astronomy Centre and Planetarium complex, whose Astropark (a scale model of the universe kids can walk through) and Digital Theatre offer an array of exhibits and shows, with hands-on learning opportunities for children. Planetarium shows must be prebooked and, for some reason, you have to pick up your ticket at least half an hour before it starts. ***Note:*** Call ahead to check winter opening hours, as they tend to vary.

College Hill, Armagh, County Armagh. ✆ **028/3752-3689.** www.armaghplanet.com. Admission to show and exhibition area £6 adults; £5 seniors and children; £20 families. July–Aug daily 11:30am–5pm; Sept–June Mon–Sat 11:30am–5pm. Showtimes vary; typically 1 show daily on weekdays and 5 on Sat. Some shows unsuitable for children under 8.

Armagh County Museum The Armagh museum is in a building that looks like a diminutive Greek temple. Its collection documents local life across the millennia, and ranges from prehistoric axe heads to wedding dresses to a grim cast-iron skull that once rested atop the Armagh gallows. In addition to natural history specimens and folklore items, the museum also has an art collection, with works by George Russell and John Luke, as well as maps, photographs, and a research library.

The Mall East, Armagh. ✆ **028/3752-3070.** www.armaghcountymuseum.org.uk. Free admission. Mon–Fri 10am–5pm; Sat 10am–1pm and 2–5pm.

Armagh Public Library Founded in 1771 by Archbishop Richard Robinson, the library has an inscription in Greek above its door that translates as "the Medicine Shop for the Soul." As small-town libraries go, this one is exceptional, as it contains Robinson's collection of 17th- and 18th-century books, engravings, and maps, as well as a 1726 first edition of *Gulliver's Travels* annotated by Swift himself. It was stolen in a robbery in 1999, but recovered 2 years later and returned to its rightful home.

43 Abbey St., Armagh. ✆ **028/3752-3142.** www.armaghrobinsonlibrary.org. Free admission. Mon–Fri 10am–1pm and 2–4pm.

Benburb Valley Park, Castle, and Heritage Centre ★ The sweet village of Benburb sits on the dramatic banks of the River Blackwater, a favorite for canoeists and anglers. The park at the edge of town follows the river to a tree-lined gorge where a partially restored 17th-century castle high on a cliff keeps an eye on the scene. From there, a half-mile walk brings you to the Benburb Valley Heritage Centre, a restored linen mill, and the Benburb Castle, all within the grounds of a Servite monastery. It's a historical smorgasbord.

89 Milltown Rd., Benburb, County Armagh. ✆ **028/3754-8170.** Park free admission. Castle and Heritage Centre admission £2.70. Park daily until dusk. Castle and Heritage Centre Apr–Sept Mon–Sat 10am–5pm. 11km (6¾ miles) northwest of Armagh; take B128 off A29.

The Mall Just to the east of the town center, this park has an interesting history. It was used for such low activities as horse racing and cock fighting until the 18th century, when an archbishop converted it into a lush park surrounded by Georgian buildings. The courthouse at its northern end was destroyed by an IRA bomb in 1993, but then rebuilt. It dates from 1809, and was designed by a local architect, Francis Johnston, who went on to create much of Dublin's famous Georgian architecture. Opposite the courthouse, the gloomy Armagh Gaol (jail), was built in 1780 and remained in use until 1988.

The Mall, east of the town center, Armagh.

Navan Fort ★ ☺ Believed to have been the royal and religious capital of Ulster from 1150 B.C. until the spread of Christianity, the Navan Fort is a mysterious place. Its central circular earthwork enclosure holds a smaller circular structure, and it all encloses an Iron Age burial mound. Even today, scientists do not really know what it was used for, although they know that it was all set on fire around 95 B.C., possibly as part of a ritual. Unfortunately, the extremely useful interpretive center at the site is sometimes closed due to lack of funding. However, if you happen to catch it open, it's an excellent resource with exhibits and multimedia presentations to explain the history and prehistory of the site. A book, gift shop, and cafe are also on hand.

The Navan Centre, 81 Killylea Rd., Armagh. ✆ **028/3752-9644.** Admission £6 adults; £4 children. April–Sept daily 10am–5:30pm; Oct–Mar daily 10am–3pm. 3.2km (2 miles) from Armagh on A28, signposted from Armagh center.

Peatlands Park As the name implies, Peatlands Park is a park filled with peat. It's a big park—more than 240 hectares (593 acres)—and the peat bogs and small lakes are quite lovely. The whole thing is a nature reserve, so you wander through it on a well-designed system of walking paths, or, slightly more fun on rainy days, you ride through it on a narrow-gauge railway. Nature walks and events are offered through the year.

33 Derryhubbert Rd. (11km/6¾ miles southeast of Dungannon, at exit 13 off M1), The Birches, County Armagh. ✆ **028/3885-1102.** Free admission to park. Rail ride £1. Vehicle access to park daily 9am–dusk. Railway Easter–Aug daily 1–6pm.

St. Patrick's Church of Ireland Cathedral ★ Built on the site of St. Patrick's 5th-century church, the Anglican cathedral dates from the 13th century, although much of the structure was built in the 1830s. Inside the church are the remains of an 11th-century Celtic cross, and a strange granite carved figure known as the Tandragee Idol, which dates from the Iron Age. A stone slab on the exterior wall of the north transept marks the spot where Brian Boru, the high king of Ireland who died in the last great battle with the Vikings in 1014, is buried.

Cathedral Close, Armagh. ✆ **028/3752-3142.** Free admission; donations accepted. Apr–Oct daily 10am–5pm; Nov–Mar daily 10am–4pm. Guided tours June–Aug Mon–Sat 11:30am and 2:30pm.

St. Patrick's Roman Catholic Cathedral ★ Built at the same time as the current structure of the Anglican church—in the mid-1800s—the cathedral is a grand Gothic Revival building dominating its portion of the town. It stands on a hill and is reached via stone stairs. Outside it's gray and hulking, but inside is another story, as vividly painted mosaics bathe it in color. Unfortunately, a renovation in the 1980s added some modern touches that stand out starkly against its otherwise perfect 19th-century authenticity.

Cathedral Rd., Armagh. ✆ **028/3752-2802.** Free admission; donations accepted. Daily 8am–dusk.

St. Patrick's Trian Visitor Complex ☺ In the old Second Presbyterian Church in the heart of Armagh, this modern visitor complex provides an informative and engaging introduction to Armagh, the "motherhouse" of Irish Christianity. Its dramatic presentations, including the *Armagh Story* and *The Land of Lilliput* (complete with a giant Gulliver beset by Lilliputians), are entertaining for the whole family. This is a good first stop to get your bearings in local history and culture. There is a craft courtyard and a cafe, as well as a visitor genealogical service, if you have local roots.

40 English St. (off Friary Rd., a 10-min. walk from town), Armagh. ✆ **028/3752-1801.** www.saintpatrickstrian.com. Admission £4.50 adults; £2.50 children. Sept–June Mon–Sat 10am–5pm, Sun 2–5pm; July–Aug 10am–5:30pm, Sun 2–6pm. Closed Jan 1 and Dec 25–26.

THE CAUSEWAY COAST & THE GLENS OF ANTRIM

106km (66 miles) from Larne to Portstewart on the coastal A2; Larne: 40km (25 miles) from Belfast

The most extraordinary stretch of countryside in Northern Ireland, the evocatively named Glens of Antrim are really nine green valleys stretching north and west from Belfast, and curving around toward Donegal. The names of the glens are all based on local legends, and although the meanings are largely lost to the ages, the popular translations are Glenarm (glen of the army), Glencloy (glen of the hedges), Glenariff (ploughman's glen), Glenballyeamon (Edwardstown glen), Glenaan (glen of the rush lights), Glencorp (glen of the slaughter), Glendun (brown glen), Glenshesk (sedgy glen), and Glentaisie (Taisie's glen).

Many modern residents of this region are descendants of the ancient Irish and the Hebridean Scots, so this is one of the strongholds in Northern Ireland of the Gaelic tongue. To this day, the glen people are known to be great storytellers.

The quiet seaside town of Cushenden in County Antrim.

The area's attractions are formidable, and include the awe-inspiring **Giant's Causeway,** the picturesque **Carrick-A-Rede Rope Bridge,** and **Old Bushmills Distillery.** For bird-watchers, the coastal moors and cliffs and the offshore nature reserve on **Rathlin Island** are prime destinations. Each August, the seaside town of **Ballycastle** plays host to one of Ireland's oldest traditional gatherings, the Oul' Lammas Fair.

VISITOR INFORMATION The principal **tourist information centers** in North Antrim are at Narrow Gauge Road, **Larne** (✆ **028/2826-0088**); Sheskburn House, 7 Mary St., **Ballycastle** (✆ **028/2076-2024**); **Giant's Causeway Information Centre,** 44 Causeway Rd. (✆ **028/2073-1855**); and Dunluce Centre, Sandhill Drive, **Portrush** (✆ **028/7082-3333**). All but the Dunluce Centre are open year-round; hours vary seasonally. Summer hours, at minimum, are Monday to Friday 9:30am to 5pm, Saturday 10am to 4pm, and Sunday 2 to 6pm.

Exploring the Coast

The **Antrim Coast** is 97km (60 miles) long, stretching north of **Larne** and west past Bushmills and the Giant's Causeway to **Portrush.** If you start in gorgeous **Glenarm,** with its castle walls and barbican gate, and head north along the coast from there, the route takes in sweeping views of midnight-blue sea against gray unforgiving cliffs and deep green hillsides. As you arc around the northern headlands, the road passes through the National Trust village of **Cushendun ★**, with its tea shops and perfect Cornish-style cottages, and a string of bustling beach towns at the foot of rocky cliffs **(Portstewart, Portballintrae, Portrush, Ballycastle).** Along the way the coastal drive meanders under bridges and stone arches, passing crescent bays, sandy beaches, harbors, and huge rock formations. The ocean gleams beside you as you curve along its craggy shoreline, and the light creates intense colors. In the spring and autumn, you can often have the road all to yourself. In **Carnlough,** a quiet village with a glassy harbor, you can climb the white stone bridge and walk along a path for about a mile to the Cranny Falls waterfall. Later, for spectacular views, turn off the main coastal road at Cushendun onto the **Torr Head Scenic Road** (it's signposted), although note that this narrow, rugged, cliff-side road is not for those with fears of heights. It climbs in seemingly perilous fashion to the tops of hills that are bigger than you might think, and on a clear day, you can see all the way to the Mull of Kintyre in Scotland. Arguably the best views are to be had at **Murlough Bay** (follow the signs off the scenic road). In the late spring and summer, you can take a ferry from **Ballycastle** to **Rathlin Island,** where seals and nesting birds make their homes at the **Kebble National Reserve.** Near Ballycastle, the town of **Ballintoy** is a picture postcard waiting to happen, stretched out at the edge of **White Park Bay,** with its wide, sandy beach at the foot of rocky hills. Finally, you can take in the eerily lunar **Giant's Causeway**—a true natural wonder.

It's best not to look down as you cross the ocean on the Carrick-a-Rede rope bridge.

Seeing the Sights

Carrick-A-Rede Rope Bridge ★★★

Eight kilometers (5 miles) west of Ballycastle off the A2 road, this open rope bridge spans a chasm 18m (59 ft.) wide and 24m (79 ft.) above the sea between the mainland and a small island. Local fishermen put up the bridge each spring to allow access to the island's salmon fishery, but visitors

Views along the Torr Head Scenic Drive.

can use it for a thrilling walk and the chance to call out to each other, "Don't look down!" (By the way, that is excellent advice.) If you are acrophobic, stay clear; if you don't know whether you are, this is not the place to find out. ***Note:*** The 19km (12-mile) coastal cliff path from the Giant's Causeway to the rope bridge is always open and is worth the exhaustion.

Larrybane, County Antrim. ✆ **028/2076-9839.** www.nationatrust.org.uk. Admission £5 adult; £2.80 children. Mar–May and Sept–Oct daily 10am–6pm; June–Aug daily 10am–7pm; Nov–Dec daily 10:30am–3:30pm. Last admission 45 min. before closing.

Dunluce Castle ★ Between the Giant's Causeway and the bustling seaside town of Portrush, the coastline is dominated by the hulking skeletal outline of what must have been a glorious castle. This site was the main fort of the Irish MacDonnells, chiefs of Antrim. From the 14th to the 17th century, it was the largest and most sophisticated castle in the North, with a series of fortifications built on rocky outcrops extending into the sea. This was the power base of the north coast for 400 years. In 1639, part of the castle fell into the sea, taking some of the servants with it; soon after, it was allowed to fall into ruin. The site incorporates two of the original Norman towers dating from 1305. The visitor center shows an audiovisual presentation with background on the site.

87 Dunluce Rd. (5.6km/3½ miles east of Portrush off A2), Bushmills, County Antrim. ✆ **028/2073-1938.** www.northantrim.com/dunlucecastle.htm. Admission £2. Apr–Sept daily 10am–6pm; Oct–Mar daily 10am–5pm. Last admission 30 min. before closing.

Dunluce Centre ★ ☺ Rainy days do happen, and when they do in County Antrim, this is where you take the kids. This family-oriented entertainment complex will keep them busy all day with the Darklight Laser Show, a 4-D cinema, and a "fun house" with games and clowns. There are also a viewing tower with panoramic views of the coast, a Victorian-style arcade of shops, and a restaurant with a children's play area. Some attractions incur additional costs.

Dunluce Rd., Bushmills, County Antrim. ✆ **028/7082-3333.** www.dunlucecentre.co.uk. Admission £5. Apr 2–11 and July–Aug daily 11am–6pm; rest of Apr, May–June, and Sept–Oct Sat–Sun noon–5pm.

Giant's Causeway ★★★ A World Heritage Site, this natural rock formation is extraordinary. Sitting at the foot of steep cliffs, and stretching out into the sea, it is a natural formation of thousands of tightly packed basalt columns. The tops of the columns form flat steppingstones all of which are perfectly hexagonal. They are all about 30 centimeters (12 inches) in diameter; some are very short, others are as tall as 12m (39 ft.). Scientists believe they

One of the thousands of mysterious hexagonal stone columns that create the surface of the Giant's Causeway.

The Old Bushmills Distillery reputedly has been making spirits as far back as 1276.

were formed 60 or 70 million years ago by volcanic eruptions and cooling lava. The ancients, on the other hand, believed the rock formation to be the work of giants. To reach the causeway, you walk from the parking area down a steep path for nearly 1.6km (1 mile), past amphitheaters of stone columns and formations with fanciful names like Honeycomb, Wishing Well, Giant's Granny, King and his Nobles, and Lover's Leap. If you wish, you can then climb up a wooden staircase to Benbane Head to take in the views, and then walk back along the cliff top. There is a regular shuttle service (£2) down from the visitor center for those who can't face the hike. ***Note:*** The causeway itself is never closed—even after the visitor center shuts down, you can still walk down the path on your own. Also, the local council makes a lot of money charging for parking in the official parking lot, but you can park for free on some nearby streets. A controversial new £6-million visitor center was under construction at the causeway in 2011 and due to open in summer 2012. New visitor centers usually mean increased parking prices, so prices here could well go up by the time you visit. Also the construction has eliminated much of the handy, free street parking, so use common sense when parking, and ensure that wherever you park, you park legally.

Causeway Rd., Bushmills, County Antrim. ✆ **028/2073-1582.** Free admission (parking £6). Visitor center daily 10am–5pm (sometimes open later in summer).

Old Bushmills Distillery ★★ Licensed to distill spirits in 1608, but with historical references dating from as far back as 1276, this ancient distillery is endlessly popular. Visitors can tour the working sections and watch the whiskey-making process, starting with fresh water from the adjacent River Bush and continuing through distilling, fermenting, and bottling. At the end of the tour, you can sample the wares in the Potstill Bar, where you can learn more about the history of the distillery. Tours last about 25 minutes. The Bushmills coffee shop serves tea, coffee, homemade snacks, and lunch.

Main St., Bushmills, County Antrim. ✆ **028/2073-3218.** www.bushmills.com. Admission £6.50 adults; £5.50 seniors and students; £3.50 children 8–17; £20 families; children 7 and under not allowed on tours. Apr–Oct tours offered frequently throughout the day Mon–Sat 9:30am–5:30pm, Sun noon–5:30pm (last tour leaves 4pm); Nov–Mar tours offered Mon–Sat at 10:30am, 11:30am, and 1:30, 2:30, and 3:30pm, Sun at 1:30, 2:30, and 3:30pm. Closed Good Friday, July 12, Dec 25, and Jan 1.

GOING TO THE birds: A TRIP TO RATHLIN ISLAND

Want to get close to nature? Plan a trip to **Rathlin Island ★**, 9.7km (6 miles) off the coast north of Ballycastle. The tiny island is 6km (3¾ miles) long, and less than 1.5km (1 mile) wide and almost completely treeless, with a rugged coast of 60m-high (197-ft.) cliffs, a small beach, and crowds of seals and seabirds in spring and summer. Once you get there you'll realize that it's not quite as isolated as it seems—it has a resident population of 100, plus a pub, a restaurant, and several guesthouses, should you miss the last boat to shore. This is a favorite bird-watching spot, especially in spring and early to midsummer when the birds are nesting. Given that there's little else to do here except to take in the scenery, it's no surprise that the island's biggest draw is bird-watching at the **Kebble National Nature Reserve** on the western side of the island, and the **RSPB West Lighthouse Viewpoint** (✆ **028/2076-3948;** free admission, by appointment only, Apr–Aug), where you can spot guillemots, kittiwakes, razorbills, and colorful puffins.

Boat trips operate daily from Ballycastle pier; crossing time is 50 minutes. The round-trip fare is £11 for adults, £5.50 for children, free for kids 4 and under. The number and schedule of crossings vary from season to season and from year to year, and are always subject to weather conditions, but there are usually several crossings a day. It's best to book well in advance online or by phoning the ticket office (✆ **028/2076-9299;** www.rathlinballycastleferry.com).

On the island, a minibus (summer only) will take you from Church Bay to the West Light Platform and the Kebble Nature Reserve for roughly £3.50 adults, £3 children, round-trip. Bicycles can be rented from **Soerneog View Hostel** (✆ **028/2076-3954**) for £10 per day.

For more information, call ✆ **028/2076-3948.**

A Shopping Stop

The Steensons This is the workshop-showroom of Bill and Christina Steenson, two of the most celebrated goldsmiths in Ireland. On display and for sale is a small, impressive selection of their pieces, as well as a sampling of the work of other distinguished contemporary Irish goldsmiths and silversmiths. Open Monday to Saturday 9:30am to 5:15pm. Toberwine St., Glenarm, County Antrim. ✆ **028/2884-1445.** www.thesteensons.com.

Sports & Outdoor Pursuits

ADVENTURE SPORTS The **Ardclinis Activity Centre,** High Street, Cushendall, County Antrim (✆ **028/2177-1340;** www.ardclinis.com), offers a range of year-round outdoor programs and courses. They include everything from rock climbing and mountain biking to windsurfing and rafting. Half-day, full-day, and weeklong activities for ages 8 and older are provided, as well as 5- and 6-night scenic walking and cycling tours. It's best to book at least several weeks ahead. The center will arrange local B&B or hostel accommodations.

FISHING The best time to fish in the North Antrim Glens is July to October, both for salmon and for sea trout. The rivers of choice are the Margy, Glenshesk, Carey, and Dun. For locally arranged game fishing, contact **Gillaroo Angles,** 7 Cooleen Park, Jordanstown, Newtownabbey, County Antrim (✆ **028/9086-2419**). For info, tackle, and bait, try **Red Bay Boats,** Coast Road, Cushendall (✆ **028/2177-1331**).

GOLF North Antrim boasts several notable courses, including champion pro golfer Darren Clarke's home course, the **Royal Portrush Golf Club,** Dunluce Road, Portrush (✆ **028/7082-2311;** www.royalportrushgolfclub.com). Royal Portrush has two links courses, including the celebrated Dunluce Course, ranked number three in the United Kingdom. Greens fees here are £125 weekdays, £140 weekends, and £35 weekdays, £40 weekends on the smaller Valley Links course. However, they will only let you play if you're already a member of a recognized golf club and have a playing handicap. Also in play is a very strict dress code, so, you know, be on your best behavior. Just over the border in County Londonderry is the **Portstewart Golf Club,** 117 Strand Rd., Portstewart (✆ **028/7083-2015;** www.portstewartgc.co.uk). Of its three links courses, the par-72 Strand Course is the celebrated one here. Some days and times are more accessible than others for visitors, so call ahead for times and fees, which range from £10 to £95 for 18 holes, depending on the course you choose and the day of the week.

PONY TREKKING **Watertop Farm Family Activity Centre,** 188 Cushendall Rd., Ballycastle (✆ **028/2076-2576;** www.watertopfarm.co.uk), offers pony trekking and other outdoor activities, daily in July and August and weekends in late June and early September. In the Portrush area, contact **Maddybenny Riding Centre,** Loguestown Road, Portrush (✆ **028/7082-3394;** www.maddybenny.com); Maddybenny also has a B&B, which has appeared in several best-of lists for farmhouse B&Bs in Ireland over the last decade. Rooms run around £70 for a double. Also, in Castlerock, there's **Hill Farm Riding and Trekking Centre** (✆ **028/7084-8629**). Fees are typically around £15 per hour-long trek.

WALKING The **Ulster Way,** 904km (560 miles) of marked trail, follows the North Antrim Coast from Glenarm to Portstewart. The **Moyle Way** offers a spectacular detour from Ballycastle south to Glenariff. Maps and accommodations listings for both ways are in the free NITB booklet *The Ulster Way: Accommodation for Walkers.* Or pick up a copy of *Walking the Ulster Way,* by Alan Warner (Appletree Press, 1989). The NITB also offers *An Information Guide to Walking,* full of useful information for avid pedestrians.

Last but far from least is the **Causeway Coast Path.** It stretches from Bushfoot Strand, near Bushmills, in the west to Ballintoy Harbour in the east. Short of sprouting wings, this is the best way to take in the full splendor of the North Antrim Coast.

Where to Stay

EXPENSIVE

Bushmills Inn ★★ In the center of the famous whiskey-making village of the same name, this elegant and historic inn dates from the 17th century. Some of the guest rooms are in the original coaching inn and the others are in the newer mill house; the coaching inn has old-world charm, with open turf fireplaces, gas lamps, and antique furnishings. Guest rooms here are comfortable, with country-pine furniture, floral wallpaper, and vintage prints. The newer mill house rooms have less character, but they are considerably more spacious and modern. In converted stables, the hotel restaurant offers an excellent take on Irish cuisine in a relaxed environment.

9 Dunluce Rd., Bushmills, County Antrim. www.bushmills-inn.com. ✆ **028/2073-3000.** 32 units. £160–£230 double. Family rooms available. Rates include full breakfast. MC, V. **Amenities:** Restaurant; bar; babysitting; smoke-free rooms. *In room:* TV, hair dryer.

MODERATE

Londonderry Arms Hotel At the foot of Glencloy, this ivy-covered former coaching inn dates from 1848 and sits in the heart of a delightful coastal town with views of the harbor. The inn recently expanded and a surprising degree of continuity was achieved between the original Georgian structure and the newer wing. Each room has its own character, but all are done in traditional style in shades of cream and white, with colorful bed covers and curtains, and dull, utilitarian carpet. Bathrooms are not fancy but have all you need. The restaurant downstairs is respected for its traditional Irish cuisine. ***Historical note:*** At one point Sir Winston Churchill owned this building through a family inheritance. (He slept in room no. 114.)

20 Harbour Rd., Carnlough, County Antrim. www.glensofantrim.com. ✆ **800/44-PRIMA** (447-7462) in the U.S., or 028/2888-5255. Fax 028/2888-5263. 35 units. £60–£105 double. Rates include full breakfast. High tea £14; dinner £22. AE, DC, MC, V. **Amenities:** Restaurant; bar. *In room:* TV, radio.

Magherabuoy House Hotel Nestled amid gardens at the edge of Portrush, this attractive country-manor-style hotel now owned by the Best Western group offers panoramic views of the seacoast, while staying well away from the town's hubbub. The traditional decor of the public rooms—dark woods, gilded mirrors, and open fireplaces—is toned down a notch in the guest rooms, which are comfortable and homey, with fluffy comforters in neutral colors, modern pine headboards, and watercolors of seascapes on the walls. ***Note***: Significant discounts are available online if you book ahead.

41 Magheraboy Rd., Portrush, County Antrim. www.magherabuoy.co.uk. ✆ **028/7082-3507.** Fax 028/7082-4687. 40 units. £70–£120 double. Rates include full breakfast. AE, DC, MC, V. **Amenities:** 2 restaurants; bar/nightclub; gym; Jacuzzi. *In room:* TV.

Whitepark House ★★ Sitting above gorgeous Whitepark Bay, this is a unique, warm, and welcoming place to stay. Owners Bob and Siobhán Isles have filled their 18th-century home with art and pictures from their travels around the world, but their hearts are clearly right here. The bedrooms are luxuriously decorated with rich fabrics and good, firm mattresses. Rooms are spacious and have sweeping views of the sea. All rooms have new bathrooms. Guests can chat in the pleasant living room by the warming fireplace, in the light-filled conservatory, or at the breakfast table over one of Bob's excellent Irish breakfasts. No wonder the inn has received a number of prestigious awards.

A2 coast rd. to Whitepark Bay, Ballintoy, County Antrim. www.whiteparkhouse.com. ✆ **028/2073-1482.** 3 units. £100 double. Rates include full Irish breakfast. MC, V. **Amenities:** Lounge w/ fireplace; smoke-free rooms.

INEXPENSIVE

The Meadows This family-run guesthouse, a 10-minute walk from Cushendall, provides spacious, well-designed, affordable guest rooms in a lovely coastal setting. The views of the sea (even of Scotland off in the distance on clear days) are splendid. Rooms are simply decorated, but pleasant, and beds are comfortable. Breakfasts are excellent. There's a family room, and one unit is fully adapted for travelers with disabilities. The owner, Anne Carey, is knowledgeable about the area and happy to help.

81 Coast Rd., Cushendall, County Antrim. www.themeadowscushendall.com. ✆ **028/2177-2020.** 6 units, all with shower only. £50 double. Family rates negotiable. Rates include service charge and full Irish breakfast. V. **Amenities:** Smoke-free rooms. *In room:* TV.

Sanda Perched high at the mouth of Glenariff, the "Queen of the Glens," Sanda affords spectacular views. The two guest rooms are modest and immaculate. The beds are very firm, and a pleasant lounge, complete with TV and a stack of books about the area, is available to guests. Hosts Donnell and Elizabeth O'Loan are knowledgeable and articulate about the region's ancient sites, as well as its current attractions.

29 Kilmore Rd., Glenariff, County Antrim. www.sandabnb.com. ✆ **028/2177-1785.** 2 units, both with shower only. £50 double. Family rates negotiable. Rates include service charge and full Irish breakfast. No credit cards. Closed Dec–Feb. **Amenities:** TV lounge; smoke-free rooms.

SELF-CATERING

Bellair Cottage ★ This century-old whitewashed farmhouse and attached barn have been converted into an inviting traditional home away from home. The three-bedroom house (sleeping up to six) occupies a secluded setting high on Glenarm Glen, with a stone-walled garden. The kitchen has its original open fireplace, and the master bedroom is lovely. For an extended working holiday or summer break, Bellair is a good size for two people, giving each a private workplace. The nearby North Antrim Coast is all the inspiration any writer, painter, photographer, or gazer could ask for. You can book activities through **Rural Cottage Holidays (RCH)**—horseback riding, day boats, trekking, rock climbing, or bicycling. This cottage is very popular, so check the Cottages in Ireland website for other options—many of them more affordable and just as beautiful—in the area.

Glenarm, County Antrim. www.cottagesinireland.com. Contact RCH at ✆ **028/9024-1100.** Fax 028/9024-1198. 1 cottage. £300–£420 per week. Also available for 2- or 3-day stays. MC, V. *In room:* TV, fridge, full kitchen, no phone.

Tully Cottage ★ This old farm cottage has been lovingly restored and tastefully appointed. Although it has two bedrooms and is just large enough to accommodate four people quite comfortably, it is the perfect love nest or honeymoon nook. Elevated and secluded, it affords spectacular views of Glenarm Glen and the North Channel down to the Mull of Galloway. The beds are firm, the tub is spacious, the fireplace works, and the kitchen is well equipped. Glenarm makes a good base for exploring the North Antrim Coast. Horse riding, day boats, trekking, and rock climbing can be arranged in advance; bicycles can be waiting for you at the cottage, all through RCH.

Glenarm, County Antrim. www.cottagesinireland.com. Contact RCH at ✆ **028/9024-1100.** Fax 028/9024-1198. 1 cottage. £250–£380 per week. Also available for 2- to 3-day stays. MC, V. *In room:* TV/DVD, radio, fridge, kitchen.

Where to Eat

Coast ITALIAN This big, boisterous Italian joint offers all the usual Italian fare, big plates of bland-but-fine pasta, and crisp, stone-baked pizzas. It also has a selection of steak and seafood dishes if you just aren't in the mood for Italian and everybody else is. Prices are very reasonable.

6 Harbour Rd., Portrush, County Antrim. ✆ **028/7082-3311.** Main courses £6–£10. AE, MC, V. Mon–Fri 5–9:30pm; Sat 4–10:30pm; Sun 3–9:30pm. Closed Mon–Tues during low season.

The Harbour Bistro BISTRO The menu at this vast and cacophonous restaurant and bar has a good selection of imaginatively prepared seafood (try the glazed monkfish and scampi with piped mash and white-wine cream), but also offers steaks and other meat dishes. It's almost always crowded, sometimes overwhelmingly so. Still, the food is good, and the atmosphere is buzzy.

6 Harbour Rd., Portrush, County Antrim. ✆ **028/7082-2430.** Main courses £10–£15. AE, MC, V. Mon–Fri 5–10pm; Sat 5–10:30pm; Sun 4–9pm.

Londonderry Arms Hotel IRISH This rambling old hotel in Carnlough sits right on the waterfront and is beloved for its home-style Irish food. Stews, roasts, baked chicken, and soups are all freshly made, and sold at thoroughly reasonable prices (£4–£9). That's why this rustic, amiable place in the middle of nowhere gets so crowded at lunchtime.

20 Harbour Rd., Carnlough, County Antrim. ✆ **028/2888-5255.** Main courses £7–£14. MC, V. Daily 7:30–8:30am, 11:30am–3pm, and 5–9pm.

The Ramore Oriental Restaurant ASIAN This big, modern restaurant is the main eatery in the same big complex that includes Coast and the Harbour Bistro (see above). The menu is a real hodgepodge of influences, including Chinese, Japanese, and Thai. Dishes can include Thai surf and turf (steak with lobster, coconut sauce, and prawn rolls), an Asian spin on lamb hot pot, and wok-fried sea bass with sweet-and-sour sauce.

6 Harbour Rd., Portrush, County Antrim. ✆ **028/7082-6969.** www.ramorerestaurant.com. Main courses £10–£15. AE, MC, V. Wed–Thurs 6–9:30pm; Fri–Sat 6–10pm; Sun 5:30–9:30pm.

Smuggler's Inn Country House ★ IRISH Surrounded by lovely gardens and across from the entrance to the Giant's Causeway, this casual family restaurant has wide-windowed views of the coast, which are particularly beautiful at sunset. The menu emphasizes local ingredients and creative sauces: baked salmon with mashed potatoes, grilled Irish venison, or roast North Antrim duck with peach brandy. Comfortable, un-fussy guest rooms are is also available (£50–£90 double).

306 Whitepark Rd., Giant's Causeway, County Antrim. ✆ **028/2073-1577.** Reservations required. Main courses £8–£15. MC, V. Daily noon–2:30pm and 4–9pm.

Sweeney's Public House Wine Bar ★ PUB GRUB This is a good, all-round option for when you're sick of fussy dinners. Laid-back and often packed with locals, Sweeney's serves tasty, traditional pub food—burgers, fried fish, and pies—at reasonable prices. Service can get overwhelmed on busy weekend nights, though.

6b Seaport Ave., Portballintrae, County Antrim. ✆ **028/2073-2405.** Reservations recommended for dinner. Main courses £6–£14. No credit cards. Mon–Sat 12:30–8pm; Sun 12:30–2:30pm and 5–8pm.

Pubs

J. McCollam Known to locals as John Joe's or McCollam's Bar, this has been the hottest scene in Cushendall for traditional music and Antrim atmosphere for nearly a century. You have to be willing to wedge yourself in, but you're not likely to have any regrets. There's a trad session every Friday night year-round. Mill St., Cushendall, County Antrim. ✆ **028/2177-1992.** www.mccollamsbar.com.

M. McBride's Opened in 1840, Mary McBride's was the smallest pub or bar in Europe until it expanded to include a bistro and restaurant. The old record-holding pub is still intact, so squeeze in and partake of the legend. Traditional music tends to break out in the pub's conservatory, while the Riverside Bistro serves light lunches and dinners (noon–9pm). The Waterside Restaurant, specializing in seafood, has a dinner menu (6–9pm) that features Torr Head lobster and Cushendun salmon; main courses run £6 to £17. 2 Main St., Cushendun Village, County Antrim. ✆ **028/2176-1511.**

O'Malley's 🎁 This is a favored fisherman's haunt and a great place to have a drink and kick back without being up to your elbows in tourists. The bar is off the wood-paneled lobby of the Edgewater Hotel, facing the magnificent beach at Portstewart. The Edgewater Hotel, 88 Strand Rd., Portstewart, County Derry. ✆ **028/7083-3314.**

THE MOURNE MOUNTAINS

48km (30 miles) SW of Belfast

South and west from Downpatrick, the rolling foothills of the Mournes make a promise that the mountains beyond fulfill. These are the highest mountains in Northern Ireland and the rocky landscape here is breathtaking—all gray granite, yellow gorse, purple heather, and white stone cottages. Remote and traversed by few roads, the mountains—complete with barren, wind-swept moors—are left to hikers and walkers. The ancestral home of the Brontës is here, in ruins. But it's not desolate. There are forest parks, sandy beaches, lush gardens, and, of course, pubs.

The region is dominated by the massive cold, barren peak of **Slieve Donard** (839m/2,752 ft.). From the top, the view takes in the full length of Strangford Lough, Lough Neagh, the Isle of Man, and, on a crystalline day, the west coasts of Wales and Scotland. (The recommended ascent of Slieve Donard is from Donard Park on the south side of Newcastle.) If that's too high for you, head to the heart of the Mournes, to the exquisite **Silent Valley Reservoir** (Silent Valley; ✆ **028/9074-6581;** car £4.50, or £1.60 adults, 60p children; Mar–Sept daily 10am–6:30pm, Oct–Apr daily 10am–4pm), where there are easy, well-marked paths around the lake and a coffee shop with an information center to keep it all from feeling too far from civilization.

Besides walking and climbing and sighing at the splendor of it all, there's **Newcastle,** a lively, traditional seaside resort with a golden sand beach and one of the finest golf courses in Ireland. It makes a good base for exploring the area, but if it's too urban for you (pop. 7,200), there are small coastal towns strung along the A2—**Kilkeel, Rostrevor,** and **Warrenpoint**—that have more bucolic charms. If you make it to the town of **Dundrum,** you could find the streets filled with musicians, fire-eaters, and jugglers, all drawn by the annual **All Ireland Busking Competition.** The month (and, indeed, location) tends to hop around, however, so it's kind of pot luck as to when you might stumble across them.

The landscape around the Mourne Mountains, Ireland's highest peaks.

Wherever you stay, the mountains are the main attraction, and in Ireland you can't have cliffs and sea without soaring birds, fairy-tale castles, and mysterious dolmens. Finally, if your idea of nightlife has more to do with stars than bars, the Mourne Mountains provide a luminous getaway.

Essentials

GETTING THERE If you're driving up from Dublin, turn east off the Dublin-Belfast road at Newry and take A2, following the north shore of Carlingford Lough, between the mountains and the sea. It's a drive you won't soon forget.

VISITOR INFORMATION For information in the Down District, stop into the **St. Patrick Visitor Centre,** 53A Market St., Downpatrick, County Down (**✆ 028/4461-9000**), open October to March, Monday to Saturday 10am to 5pm; April to September, Monday to Saturday 9:30am to 6pm and Sunday 1 to 6pm.

There's also the **Newcastle Tourist Information Centre,** 10–14 Central Promenade, Newcastle, County Down (**✆ 028/4372-2222;** www.downdc.gov.uk). It's open Monday to Saturday 10am to 5pm and Sunday 2 to 6pm, with extended summer hours (daily 9:30am–7pm). A coach tour of the Mournes, offered according to demand, can be booked here. Or get information and maps at the **Mourne Heritage Trust Centre,** 10–14 Central Promenade, Newcastle, County Down (**✆ 028/4372-4059;** www.mournelive.com), open all year Monday to Friday 9am to 5pm. It offers guided mountain walks Mondays and Saturdays when the weather cooperates.

Seeing the Sights

Castlewellan Forest Park ★ Surrounding a fine trout lake and watched over by a magnificent private castle, this forest park just begs for picnics and outdoor activities. Woodland walks, a lakeside sculpture trail, formal walled gardens, and excellent trout fishing (brown and rainbow) await. The real draw is the National Arboretum, begun in 1740 and now grown to 10 times its original size. The largest of its three greenhouses features aquatic plants and a collection of free-flying tropical birds. The town of Castlewellan, elegantly laid out around two squares, is a short distance away.

6.5km (4 miles) northwest of Newcastle on A50, The Grange, Castlewellan Forest Park, Castlewellan, County Down. ✆ **028/4377-8664.** Free admission. Parking £4.50. Daily 10am–dusk. Coffeehouse summer 10am–5pm.

Drumena Cashel (Stone Fort) The walls of this irregularly shaped ancient stone-ring fort—a farmstead dating from the early Christian period—were partially rebuilt in the mid-1920s and measure 2.7m (9 ft.) to 3.6m (12 ft.) thick. The *souterrain* (underground stone tunnel) is T-shaped and was likely used in ancient times for cold storage. In the extreme, it likely provided some protection from Viking raiders. There were once thousands of such fortifications in Ireland and this is one of the better-preserved examples in this region.

3km (2 miles) southwest of Castlewellan, off A25, County Down.

Dundrum Castle ★ The site of an early Irish fortification (of which nothing is visible now), the oldest visible portions of this castle's striking and extensive ruins date from the 12th century. The enormous keep was built in the 13th century, as was the gatehouse. It was the home of the Maginnis family until the 17th century, when it was captured by Oliver Cromwell's army, which destroyed it in 1652. The hilltop setting is lovely, and the views from the keep's parapet are panoramic. This was once one of the mightiest of the Norman castles in Northern Ireland (second only to Carrickfergus), and it still commands the imagination, if nothing else.

6.5km (4 miles) east of Newcastle, off A2, Dundrum, County Down. ✆ **028/9181-1491.** No phone. Free admission. Mid-Apr to May and Sept Tues–Sun 10am–5pm; Jun–Aug daily 10am–5pm.

Greencastle Fort The first castle on this site, built in 1261, faced its companion, Carlingford Castle, across the lough. It was a two-story rectangular tower surrounded by a curtain wall with corner towers. Very little survives. Most of what you see is from the 14th century. It served as a royal garrison until it was destroyed by Cromwell's forces in 1652.

6.5km (4 miles) southwest of Kilkeel, Greencastle, Cranfield Point, Mouth of Carlingford Lough, County Down. No phone. Admission £1.40. Apr–Sept Tues–Sat 10am–1pm and 1:30–7pm, Sun 2–7pm; Oct–Mar Tues–Sat 10am–1pm and 1:30–4pm, Sun 2–4pm.

Murlough Nature Reserve Sand dunes, heath land, and forest, surrounded by estuary and sea, make for a lovely outing on a clear, bright day, but you'll want to bring a windbreaker and some binoculars; this is a prime habitat for a host of waders and seabirds. Take a picnic, and you may find your dessert on the dunes, which are strewn with wild strawberries in the summertime.

On the main Dundrum-Newcastle rd. (A2), southeast of Dundrum, County Down. ✆ **028/4375-1467.** Free admission. Parking £3 car, £1 motorcycle. Daily dawn–dusk. Facilities available mid-Mar to mid-Apr, mid-May to mid-June, and late Sept to early Oct Sat–Sun 10am–6pm; late Apr to early May and mid-June to mid-Sept daily 10am–6pm.

Silent Valley Mountain Park ☺ More than 90 years ago, the 36km (22-mile) dry-stone Mourne Wall was built to enclose Silent Valley, which was dammed to create the Silent Valley Reservoir, to this day the major source of water for County Down. The 36km (22-mile) **Mourne Wall trek ★★** follows the Mourne Wall, a 2.4m (8-ft.) granite fence built over 18 years between 1904 and 1922, which threads together 15 of the range's main peaks. The steep path is more than most hikers want to take on, and certainly shouldn't be attempted in a single day, but it is a fine, long walk for experienced ramblers, and offers wonderful views. A good alternative is the more modest walk from the fishing port of Kilkeel to the Silent Valley and Lough Shannagh. An even less strenuous alternative is to drive to the Silent Valley Information Centre and take the shuttle bus to the top of nearby Ben Crom. The bus runs daily in July and August, weekends only in May, June, and September, and costs £2.50 round-trip, £1 for children. The park also offers a restaurant, gift shop, children's playground, and picnic area.

6km (3¾ miles) north of Kilkeel on Head Rd., Silent Valley, County Down. ✆ **028/9074-6581.** Admission £4.50 per car (£6 for a minivan). Information Centre Apr–Sept daily 10am–6:30pm; Oct–Mar daily 10am–4pm.

Tollymore Forest Park All that's left of the once-glorious Tollymore House is a delightful 480-hectare (1,186-acre) wildlife and forest park. The park offers a number of walks along the Shimna River, noted for its salmon, or up into the north slopes of the Mournes. The forest is a nature preserve inhabited by a host of local wildlife, including badgers, foxes, otters, and pine martens. Don't miss the trees for the forest—there are some exotic species here, including magnificent Himalayan cedars and a 30m-tall (98-ft.) sequoia in the arboretum.

Off B180, 3.2km (2 miles) northwest of Newcastle, Tullybrannigan Rd., Newcastle, County Down. ✆ **028/4372-2428.** Free admission. Parking £4. Daily 10am–dusk.

Sports & Outdoor Pursuits

BICYCLING The Mourne roads are narrow and often bordered by 1.7m-high (5½-ft.) dry-stone walls. The foothills of the Mournes around Castlewellan are ideal for cycling, with panoramic vistas and very little traffic. In these parts, the perfect year-round outfitter is **Ross Cycles,** 44 Clarkhill Rd. (✆ **028/4377-8029**), signposted from the Clough-Castlewellan road, .8km (½ mile) out of Castlewellan; the shop carries light-frame, highly geared mountain bikes for the whole family, with helmets and children's seats. All cycles are fully insured, as are their riders. You can park and ride, or request local delivery. Daily rates are around £7 to £10, and family and weekly rates are available.

FISHING The best time to fish for trout and salmon is August to October. Some sizable sea trout can be seen on the Whitewater River in the Mournes, and not all of them get away. The **Burrendale Hotel** in Newcastle (✆ **028/4372-2599**) and the **Kilmorey Arms Hotel** in Kilkeel (✆ **028/4176-2220**) offer special holiday breaks for game anglers. For further information, as well as tackle, bait, and outfitting needs, try **Four Seasons,** 47 Main St., Newcastle (✆ **028/4372-5078**).

GOLF **Royal County Down ★**, Newcastle, County Down (✆ **028/4372-3314;** www.royalcountydown.org), is nestled in huge sand dunes with the Mountains of Mourne in the background. This 18-hole, par-71 championship course was created in 1889 and is considered one of the best in the British Isles; the Annesley links are worth a try, too. Greens fees are £150 to £165 Monday to Saturday, €180 Sunday (In winter prices drop to £50–£100). Not too far away, the **Kilkeel Golf Club,** Mourne Park, Ballyardle, Kilkeel (✆ **028/4176-5095;** www.kilkeelgolfclub.org), is a beautiful parkland course on the historic Kilmorey Estate. The best days for visitors are weekdays except Tuesday, and greens fees are £25 weekdays, £30 weekends.

HORSEBACK RIDING The **Mount Pleasant Trekking and Horse Riding Centre** (✆ **028/4377-8651;** www.mountpleasantcentre.com) offers group trekking tours into Castlewellan Forest Park for around £12 an hour. For riding in the Tollymore Forest Park or on local trails, contact the **Mourne Trail Riding Centre,** 96 Castlewellan Rd., Newcastle (✆ **028/4372-4351;** www.mournetrailridingcentre.co.uk). It has quality horses and offers beach rides for skilled riders. Prices start at £18 an hour.

WATERSPORTS For canoeing, rock climbing, and a variety of other intrepid activities, contact **One Great Adventure,** The Grange Yard, Castlewellan Forest Park, Castlewellan, County Down (✆ **0844/770-5477; 028/4372-2882;** www.onegreatadventure.com).

Where to Stay

EXPENSIVE

The Slieve Donard Spa and Resort ★★ From this turreted, redbrick Victorian hotel on the seafront, you look across Dundrum Bay to where the Mountains of Mourne sweep down to the sea. Outside, you can walk along the 6.5km (4-mile) sandy strand to the foot of them. When the hotel was built in 1897, there were coal fires in every bathroom. These days, the renovated public areas and well-appointed guest rooms incorporate every modern convenience. Front rooms overlooking the sea are especially appealing, and a new spa offers relaxing treatments with spectacular views. The pool is gorgeous.

Downs Rd., Newcastle, County Down. www.hastingshotels.com. ✆ **028/4372-1066.** Fax 028/4372-4830. 178 units. £185–£260 double. Children's discount available. Rates include full breakfast. AE, DC, MC, V. **Amenities:** Restaurant; bar; gym; Jacuzzi; indoor pool; spa; steam room. *In room:* TV, hair dryer, minibar.

MODERATE

Burrendale Hotel and Country Club ☺ This meticulously maintained, modern hotel enjoys a fine location between the Mournes and the shore, and is a 15-minute walk from Newcastle Centre and the Royal County Down Golf Course. The spacious contemporary rooms are neat as pins. In addition, so much attention has been paid to the needs of guests with limited mobility that the Burrendale is a past recipient of the British Airways award for disabled access and amenities, both in the hotel and in the country club. If you're traveling with kids, the family rooms have the space you need. Good online deals are available if you book in advance.

51 Castlewellan Rd., Newcastle, County Down. www.burrendale.com. ✆ **028/4372-2599.** Fax 028/4372-2328. 69 units. £140–£160 double; £170 suite. Rates include full buffet breakfast. AE, DC, MC, V. **Amenities:** Restaurant; bar; babysitting; gym; indoor pool; room service; beauty treatments; smoke-free rooms. *In room:* TV, radio, hair dryer.

Glassdrumman Lodge Country House and Restaurant ★★ "Simple elegance" is the mark Graeme and Joan Hall set in establishing this extraordinary place, and they have achieved just that. Poised between sea and mountains, with splendid views of each, Glassdrumman Lodge is encrusted with awards for fine dining and elegant accommodations. Here is a place that knows what good service is all about: Shoes are shined and cars cleaned overnight. Some of the light-filled rooms have working fireplaces, and room no. 4 has a grand view of the sea. Fabrics are floral, and the attitude is old-fashioned formality. The lodge is only 3km (2 miles) from the Silent Valley. The **restaurant** specializes in organic produce and ingredients, and is an attraction in itself.

85 Mill Rd., Annalong, County Down. www.glassdrummanlodge.com. ✆ **028/4376-8451.** Fax 028/4376-7041. 10 units. £145–£170 double. Rates include full breakfast. MC, V. **Amenities:** Restaurant; bar; room service; smoke-free rooms. *In room:* TV, hair dryer, Wi-Fi.

INEXPENSIVE

Beach House This simple, friendly B&B is literally a stone's throw from the beach, overlooking the deep blue waters of Dundrum Bay. Guest rooms are basic, but pleasant enough, with bright bedspreads. Rooms are reliably clean and comfortable. Bathrooms are tiny, but have everything you need. The lounge and dining room make good use of the building's Victorian origins, with polished wood floors and whitewashed columns, and big windows thrown open in the summer. Owners John and Myrtle are helpfulness itself.

11 Downs Rd., Newcastle, County Down. beachhouse22@tiscali.co.uk. ✆ **028/4372-2345.** 3 units. £80–£90 double. Rates include full breakfast. MC, V. Free parking. **Amenities:** Smoke-free rooms. *In room:* TV, Wi-Fi.

Briers Country House ★ Mary Bowater has lovingly converted her 200-year-old house into an award-winning B&B, keeping its old-world charm. The house is surrounded by acres of gardens, where the Bowaters grow most of their own fruit and vegetables. They also make the breads and preserves served in their full-service **restaurant,** where breakfasts are excellent. The home-style guest rooms are relaxing and have good views. The house is in the foothills of the Mourne Mountains, beside the Tollymore Forest Park.

39 Middle Tollymore Rd. (2.5km/1½ miles from the beach at Newcastle, off B180), Newcastle, County Down. www.thebriers.co.uk. ✆ **028/4372-4347.** 8 units. £60–£65 double. Rates include full breakfast. 3-day and weekly rates available. MC, V. **Amenities:** Restaurant; smoke-free rooms. *In room:* TV, hair dryer.

Dufferin Coaching Inn ★★ The brightly painted exterior of this former bank building is a good indication of the cheery personalities of the owners, Morris and Kitty Crawford, who run this place with infectious enthusiasm. The bedrooms have four-poster beds and other furniture handmade by Kitty of wood, metal, and marble. Walls are bedecked with William Morris prints, and beds have matching covers. Bathrooms are spacious and carefully decorated. If you feel like a pint, the Dufferin Arms next door is lively.

31 High St., Killyleagh, County Down. www.dufferincoachinginn.com. ✆ **028/4482-1134.** 7 units. £65–£90 double. Rates include full breakfast. MC, V. **Amenities:** *In-room:* TV.

Kilmorey Arms Hotel ★ In this pleasant seaside resort, the Kilmorey Arms was a delightful 200-year-old inn, but after a recent renovation it's now a delightful *modern* hotel, with a colorful, contemporary look. Rooms are spacious, simply decorated, and well equipped. The hotel bar is a popular local hangout, so it's a good place to mix and mingle with nontourists. However, it can be a bit loud at night, so if noise bothers you, ask for a room away from the bar. In their favor, after a wide-ranging renovation, prices were not raised unreasonably, and it offers real value for money.

41 Greencastle St., Kilkeel, County Down. www.kilmoreyarmshotel.co.uk. ✆ **028/4176-2220.** Fax 028/4176-5399. 26 units. £100 double. Children's and senior discounts available. Rates include full breakfast. MC, V. **Amenities:** Restaurant; bar; nightclub; smoke-free rooms. *In room:* TV.

SELF-CATERING

Hanna's Close ★★ ☺ Hanna's Close is a meticulously restored *clachan*, or medieval-style extended-family settlement, founded in 1640 and restored in 1997. On a low bluff over a lovely shallow stream, facing the spectacular Mountains of Mourne, this born-again *clachan* is so quiet that there's little to wake you other than singing birds. The cottages, which sleep from two to seven, have everything you'll need, including central heating, open fireplaces, and a wood-burning stove. They are ideal for families with kids 4 years and over, though the steep steps and rustic character of the cottages won't suit everyone.

Aughnahoory Rd., Kilkeel, County Down. www.cottagesinireland.com. Contact Cottages in Ireland at ✆ **028/9036-0500.** 7 cottages. £140–£260 per 2 nights, rising to €445 per week, per cottage. Booking fee £19. Additional charge for heat and electricity. V. *In room:* Fridge, kitchen.

Where to Eat

Most of the dining in the Mournes, with or without frills, gourmet or generic, happens in hotels, guesthouses, and pubs. When your stomach growls, in addition to the suggestions here, you may also consider the accommodations listed above and the pubs listed below.

The Duke Restaurant ★ MODERN This humble but quality restaurant above the Duke Bar in Warrenpoint has fans around the country. The chef specializes in using local seafood and produce in innovative ways. Dishes are often influenced by Asian cuisine and could include seared chili beef with crunchy vegetables, or turbot with butternut squash risotto. Seafood is a particular strong point, as the restaurant makes good use of its proximity to Kilkeel's fishing port. The steaks are reliably good, too. The wine list offers house white and red for around £12 a bottle, along with pricier options.

Above the Duke Bar, 7 Duke St., Warrenpoint (9.7km/6 miles on A2 from Newry), County Down. Reservations recommended. ✆ **028/4175-2084.** Dinner main courses £12–£15. MC, V. Tues–Sat 6–10pm; Sun 5:30–9pm.

Sea Salt BISTRO/ECLECTIC This bright and cheerful Newcastle bistro is a good place to go for a light bite or an imaginatively prepared main meal. By day it's a delicatessen, serving fresh sandwiches, panini, soups, and nibbles. By night it's a popular bistro, especially on Friday and Saturday nights when a tapas menu is served. The tasty seafood chowder is famous among locals.

51 Central Promenade, Newcastle, County Down. ✆ **028/4372-5027.** Reservations recommended weekends. Main courses £5–£7. MC, V. Mon–Thurs 10am–5pm; Fri 10am–9pm; Sat–Sun 9am–9pm.

Pubs

Harbour Inn You won't find a quainter "wee" harbor on the Down Coast than Annalong, and the Harbour Inn, as its name suggests, is right on the dock. The black guillemots tend to outnumber the people here, and on a warm day, picnic tables sit out front for the dockside happy hour. There's an inviting lounge and full restaurant serving lunch, tea, dinner, and snacks. A local band plays every Saturday night. 6 Harbour Dr., Annalong Harbour, Annalong, County Down. ✆ **028/4376-8678.**

Jacob Halls If there's a chill in the air, you'll leave it behind in Jacob Halls, with its three massive fires blazing at the first suggestion of frost. This well-worn pub is a hub of hospitality. There's live music Thursday to Sunday, and pub grub from lunch on. Greencastle St., Kilkeel, County Down. ✆ **028/4176-4751.**

The Percy French The Percy French has stood watch over the gates of the Slieve Donard Hotel for a century. It's named after the famed Irish composer who died in 1920, leaving behind these words as an epitaph:

Remember me is all I ask—and yet

If remembrance proves a task—forget.

Forgetting is not a real option, however, as long as this fine old faux-Tudor pub pours a good pint and serves hearty fare. The same beamed roof encloses both the lounge and a full-service restaurant with a traditional Irish menu. There's a band playing oldies (1960s–1980s) music on Saturday, and a disco every Friday. Downs Rd., Newcastle, County Down. ✆ **028/4372-3175.**

DERRY CITY

118km (73 miles) NW of Belfast, 63km (39 miles) SW of Portrush, 113km (70 miles) NW of Armagh, 98km (61 miles) NE of Enniskillen, 232km (144 miles) NW of Dublin, 354km (220 miles) NE of Shannon

Standing on a hill on the banks of the Foyle estuary, strategically close to the open sea, Derry was long a favorite Irish target for invaders: In 1566, Queen Elizabeth I sent English troops to take the town, and Derry was nearly destroyed in 1608 by Sir Cahir O'Doherty. Always, the city resisted ferociously. In 1609, King James I decided to settle the problem once and for all by giving much of Derry to Protestant English and Scottish families, casting out the native Catholics. At the same time, London workers' guilds sent over hundreds of builders to reconstruct the ruined medieval town (and, not coincidentally, add even more Protestant residents, thus changing the religious mix once and for all). Subsequently the town changed its name from "Derry" to "Londonderry"—a move that has kept the city's true identity a source of controversy ever since. Londonderry remains the official name of the city in Ulster, but it's called Derry a few miles away in the Republic of Ireland and by most residents. Over the years, those not wanting to step on toes have come to write the town's name as "Derry/Londonderry," and to say it as "Derry-stroke-Londonderry." That led a local radio DJ to coin the nickname "Stroke City," a bit of a double-entendre (get it wrong and someone will have a stroke).

The city's greatest beauty—aside from its setting amid rolling green hills—is its noble 17th-century **walls,** about 1.6km (1 mile) in circumference and more than 5m (16 ft.) thick. You can climb the steps to the top of the walls and walk

Bloody Sunday Monument **2**
Cathedral of St. Columb (C.O.I.) **10**
Central Library **7**
Derry Craft Village **5**
The Fifth Province **11**
Genealogy Centre **12**
Guild Hall **3**
Millennium Forum **6**
Playhouse **9**
St. Eugene's Cathedral (R.C.) **1**
Tower Museum **4**
Workhouse Museum and Library **8**

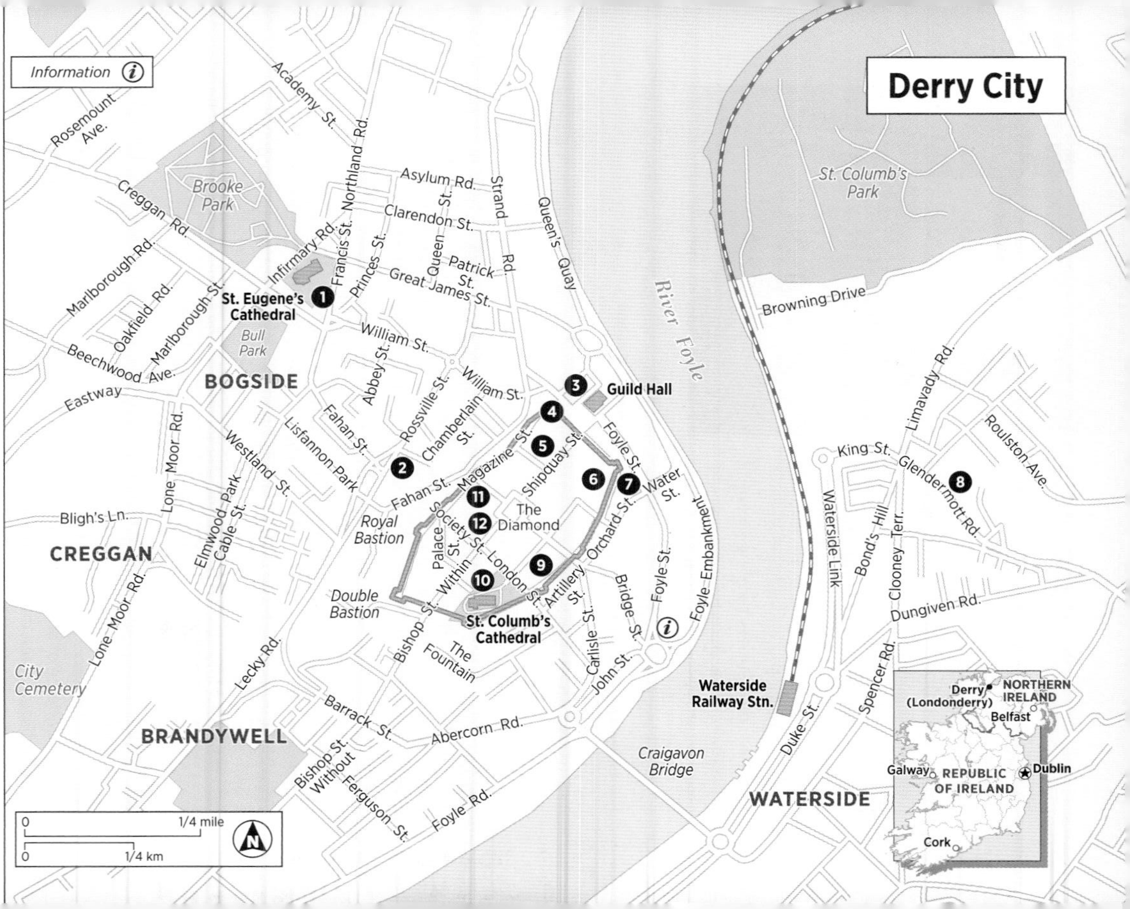

all the way around the town center. Although they were the focus of attacks and repeated sieges, the walls remain solid and unbroken to this day. Derry is a pretty, vibrant hill town—a pleasure to walk and easy to traverse. Historians believe the town's design was modeled on the French Renaissance community Vitry-Le-Francois, which is similarly designed like a Roman military camp—with two main streets forming a central cross and ending in four city gates. The architecture within the walls is largely medieval, while the rest of the city's architecture is Georgian, with big, brick-fronted town houses and imposing public buildings.

Derry's *Hands Across the Divide* sculpture, celebrating peace between Catholics and Protestants in Northern Ireland.

Within Ireland, though, Derry is not known for its architecture, but for the fact that, in the 1960s and 1970s, the North's civil rights movement was born here, and baptized in blood on the streets. The "Bloody Sunday" massacre in 1972, in which British troops opened fire on a peaceful civil rights march, killing 14, shocked the world and led to years of violent unrest. In the **Bogside,** as the neighborhood at the bottom of the hill west of the walled section is known, the famed mural reading "You Are Now Entering Free Derry" remains as a symbol of those times.

Happily, much of that sectarian strife seems to be behind Derry now, and it is emerging as a promising center of culture and commerce. Symbolic of the changes in Derry is the ***Hands Across the Divide*** sculpture that you pass as you cross the Craigavon Bridge into town. Erected 20 years after Bloody Sunday, it is a bronze sculpture of two men reaching out toward one another.

For travelers, Derry is strategically located at the edge of the picturesque Inishowen Peninsula, while the Giant's Causeway and the North Antrim Coast,

New World, Old Argument . . .

To see evidence of how far back this titular dispute goes, one has to look no further than a United States road atlas. Near Manchester, New Hampshire, is a small old town called Derry. In the early 19th century there was a dispute over its name, so a group of residents set up a new town just to the south called—you guessed it—Londonderry. Whether anybody thought of Stroke City back then is unclear. The fact that even its name is controversial is excellent symbolism of the city's tenuous position, all but straddling the border between Ulster and the Republic of Ireland. Drive into the suburbs and suddenly the currency changes to the euro—but that's the only way you can tell that you are in a different country.

the Northwest Passage and the Sperrins, and Glenveagh National Park in Donegal are all within an hour's drive. This makes the town an ideal base of operations from which to explore one of Ireland's most unspoiled regions.

> **Coin of the Realm**
>
> **When we're in the Derry area (on the border between Ulster and the Republic of Ireland), we carry two change purses—one for euros and one for pence—because we never know which we'll need.**

Essentials

GETTING THERE **By Plane** Service to **City of Derry Airport** (✆ **028/7181-0784;** www.cityofderryairport.com) is provided by **Ryanair** (✆ **0818/303030** in Ireland, 0871/246-0000 in the U.K.; www.ryanair.com) from London's Stansted Airport and other destinations in Europe. **Aer Arann** (✆ **818/210-210** in Ireland, or 0870/876-76-76 in the U.K. [including Northern Ireland]; www.aerarann.com) operates flights between Derry and Dublin. The no. 43 Limavady **bus** stops at the airport. A **taxi** for the 13km (8-mile) journey to the city center costs about £10 and should take roughly half an hour. If you're landing in either of the Belfast airports, without a connection to Derry, the **Airporter** coach can take you straight to Derry (£18 one-way). Call ✆ **028/7126-9996** or visit www.airporter.co.uk for information.

BY CRUISE SHIP Derry City is a port of call for an increasing number of cruise ships, including six-star luxury liners, which call at the deepwater facilities at Lisahally or at the city center's Queen's Quay. For the latest information on cruises to Derry Port, contact the visitor information center in Derry (✆ **028/7126-7284**).

BY TRAIN **Northern Ireland Railways** (✆ **028/9066-6630;** www.translink.co.uk) operates frequent trains from Belfast and Portrush, which arrive at the **Northern Ireland Railways** Londonderry/Derry Station—referred to everyone, somewhat more simply, as **Waterside Railway Station** (✆ **028/7134-2228**), on Duke Street, on the east side of the Foyle River. A free Linkline bus brings passengers from the train station to the city center.

It's possible to travel by train from Dublin, but you'd have to take the train to Belfast and transfer. The whole journey costs about £40 one-way, and takes about 4 hours, depending on the transfers. For more information, contact **Irish Rail/Iarnród Éireann** (✆ **1850-366-222;** www.irishrail.ie).

A cannon on the medieval ramparts of Derry.

BY BUS The fastest bus between Belfast and Derry, the no. 212 Maiden City Flyer, operated by **Ulsterbus** (✆ **028/9066-6630;** www.translink.co.uk), takes a little over 90 minutes. Ulsterbus also has service from Portrush and Portstewart. From the Republic, **Bus Éireann** (✆ **091/562000;** www.buseireann.ie) offers

THE APPRENTICE BOYS & THE siege OF DERRY

Changing Derry's name and planting it with Protestants didn't immediately end the city's troubles. In December 1688, after backing the English Parliament during the civil war, Derry was attacked by Catholic forces led by the Earl of Antrim. At one point in the battle, messengers from the earl were sent into the city, ostensibly for talks, but it was a trick to distract the city leaders as the earl's troops prepared to attack. At the last minute, some of the town's apprentice boys saw the ruse for what it was, and locked the city gates—thus saving the town, but setting off the Great Siege of Derry. For months, the town's population endured attacks, disease, and starvation as the earl's troops waited them out. By the time they were rescued, nearly a quarter of the city's residents had died.

The apprentice boys were seen as Protestant heroes, and have been celebrated by the town ever since in marches and parades held every summer, although these have been widely associated with conflict between Protestants and Catholics.

three buses a day from Galway's **Bus Éireann Travel Centre,** Ceannt Station, Galway, via Sligo and Donegal; three buses daily to and from Cork; and eleven from Dublin. **Lough Swilly Bus Service** (✆ **028/7126-0731**) serves Derry from a number of towns in County Donegal, including Dunfanaghy and Letterkenny.

VISITOR INFORMATION The **Derry Visitor and Convention Bureau and Tourist Information Centre** is at 44 Foyle St., Derry (✆ **028/7126-7284;** www.derryvisitor.com). It's open year-round, Monday to Friday 9am to 5pm and Saturday 10am to 5pm; also Sunday 10am to 4pm from March to October.

GETTING AROUND **Ulsterbus,** Foyle Street Depot, Derry (✆ **028/7126-2261**), operates local bus service to the suburbs. There is no bus service within the walls of the small, easily walkable city. The black London-style **taxis** you'll see are known in Derry and Belfast as "people's taxis," and they pick up multiple passengers going in the same direction for very cheap fares (they first appeared during the Troubles when buses would not serve the violence-prone areas and are now local institutions). However, they primarily serve nationalist areas outside the walls and will not go to most areas of interest to tourists. Use any of the other taxis available throughout the city, which are plentiful and reasonably priced.

There are taxi stands at the **Ulsterbus Depot,** Foyle Street (✆ **028/7126-2262**), and at the **Northern Ireland (Waterside) Railway Station,** Duke Street, Waterside (✆ **028/7134-2228**). To call a cab, contact **Sackville Taxis** (✆ **028/7137-1666**), **Derry Taxis** (✆ **028/7126-0247**), or **Foyle Taxis** (✆ **028/7126-3905**).

Local car-rental offices include **Europcar** (✆ **028/7181-2773**) and **Hertz** (✆ **028/7181-1994**) at the City of Derry Airport.

The focal point of Derry is the **Diamond,** a large square holding a war memorial in the center of the city. Four streets radiate out from the Diamond: Bishop, Ferryquay, Shipquay, and Butcher. Each extends for several blocks and ends at a gateway (Bishop's Gate, Ferryquay Gate, Shipquay Gate, and Butcher's Gate) cut into the thick city walls.

Two bridges connect the east and west banks of the River Foyle. The Craigavon Bridge, built in 1933, is one of the few examples of a double-decker bridge in the British Isles. The Foyle Bridge, Ireland's longest bridge, opened in 1984 and provides a dual-lane highway about 3.2km (2 miles) north of the Craigavon Bridge. West of the river are two major areas: the walled inner city and, beyond that, the area known as the Bogside. The streets near the waterfront are known as Waterside, and it's where most of the better hotels and many restaurants are located. Also in Waterside is a small grassy viewing point called the **"Top of the Hill,"** where you can enjoy spectacular eagle's-eye views of the city and its splendid environs. You'll never find your own way there, so take a taxi and bring your map. Short of a helicopter tour, this is the best way to get your initial bearings.

FAST FACTS In an emergency, dial ✆ **999** for fire, police, and ambulance. **Altnagevin Hospital** is on Glenshane Road (✆ **028/7134-5171**). The main **police station** is on Strand Road (✆ **028/7136-7337**).

In the city center, the **Bank of Ireland** (✆ **028/7126-4992**) is on Shipquay Street, and the **Ulster Bank** (✆ **028/7126-1882**) is at Waterloo Place. Both are open Monday to Friday 9:30am (10am on Wed) to 4:30pm. The **Northern Bank** (✆ **028/7126-5333**) at Shipquay Place is open Saturday 9:30am to 12:30pm, in addition to the typical weekday hours.

You can access the Internet from computer terminals at the **Central Library,** 35 Foyle St. in the city center (✆ **028/7127-2300**), for £3 per hour.

The main **post office,** 3 Custom House St. (✆ **028/7136-2563**), is open Monday 8:30am to 5:30pm, Tuesday to Friday 9am to 5:30pm, and Saturday 9am to 12:30pm.

Seeing the Sights

The Derry Visitor and Convention Bureau sponsors **Inner City Walking Tours,** June to September Monday to Friday. Tours depart the Tourist Information Centre (44 Foyle St.) at 10:30am and 2:30pm; tickets are £4 adults, £3 seniors and children. Alternatively, Martin McCrossan's colorful **City Tours** (✆ **028/7127-1996;** www.derrycitytours.com) group offers informative walking tours year-round. Tours set out from 11 Carlisle Rd. daily at 10am, noon, and 2pm, but call ahead to book a place. The cost is £4 adults.

Finally, if you're tired of walking, Martin McGowan will take you by horse-drawn carriage through the old city and unravel its history as you go. Excursions cost around £35 for 90 minutes. Call **Charabanc Tours** (✆ **028/7127-1886**) for details and reservations from May to October.

The Bogside ★★ Just outside the walled city center, the Bogside was developed in the 19th and early 20th centuries as a home to Catholic workers. By the 1960s, it was overcrowded and rife with poverty and unemployment, making it ripe for revolution. In the late 1960s and 1970s, protests were regular events here as Derry became the center of the Catholic civil rights movement. In 1969, protests morphed into riots, and the "Battle of the Bogside" unfolded over the course of 3 days, while fires burned and rocks were hurled at local police officers. At the end of it, the British government decided to base armed soldiers in Derry to keep

Derry's Bogside neighborhood, site of the Bloody Sunday massacre.

the peace. By then, relations between Catholics and the Protestant local government had broken down entirely. The 30,000 residents of the neighborhood declared their area as "Free Derry," independent of British and local government. They painted murals arguing their cause on the walls of their houses and barricaded the soldiers and police out of the area. The Bogside was so dangerous for outsiders that even the military wouldn't go there without armored vehicles. Thus, on a Sunday in January 1972, the civil rights march that attracted 20,000 marchers shouldn't have attracted particular attention, until British troops suddenly opened fire on the marchers, killing 14, in one of the worst atrocities of the Troubles. The soldiers later said they'd been fired upon first, but subsequent investigations found little or no evidence of that. (In 2010, after a 12-year inquiry, the British government finally accepted this to be the case and apologized.) Relations between soldiers and residents remained very poor for some time. The day of the incident was known as "Bloody Sunday," and it galvanized the IRA into further acts of violence throughout the region. Tensions remained through the 1970s and 1980s, but calmed in the 1990s.

Most of the Bogside has been redeveloped, with modern buildings replacing the old Victorian structures, and most who lived there in the 1960s have moved elsewhere. But the Free Derry corner remains near the house painted with the mural reading "You Are Now Entering Free Derry." Nearby is a memorial to the IRA members who died in hunger strikes in the 1970s. On Rossville Street, where the Bloody Sunday shootings happened, a memorial has been erected commemorating those killed.

The Bogside, Derry.

Cathedral of St. Columb ★ Within the city walls, near the Bishop's Gate, this cathedral, built as a Church of Ireland edifice between 1628 and 1633, is a prime example of the so-called "Planters Gothic" style of architecture. It was the first cathedral built in Europe after the Reformation, although several sections were added afterward, including the impressive spire and stained-glass windows depicting scenes from the siege of 1688 and 1689. The chapter house contains a display of city relics, including the four massive original padlocks for the city gates, and an audiovisual presentation that provides background on the history of the building and the city. On the porch, a small stone inscribed *"In Templo Verus Deus Est Vereo Colendus"* (The true God is in His temple and is to be truly worshipped) is part of the original church built on this site in 1164. There's an old mortar shell on the porch as well—it was fired into the churchyard during the great siege; in its hollow core it held proposed terms of surrender. The flags around the chancel window were captured during the siege.

London St., Derry. ✆ **028/7126-2746.** £1 donation requested. Mar-Oct Mon-Sat 9am-5pm; Nov-Feb Mon-Sat 9am-1pm and 2-4pm.

Derry Genealogy Centre This heritage library and Genealogy Centre, in the heart of the old walled city, can help you research your Derry roots. Derry was one of the main ports for the exodus of thousands of emigrants for the New World in the 18th and 19th centuries; records show that Ulster men and women became the second-most-numerous group in the Colonial population and played

CLIMBING THE walls THAT CIRCLE DERRY

One of the best ways to explore Derry is via its old stone walls. Climb the stairs to the top and you can circle the entire walled city in about 30 minutes. Steps off of the parapets are frequent, so you'll never get stuck up there. If you start at the **Diamond,** as the square in the center of the walled section is called, and walk down Butcher Street, you can climb the steps at **Butcher's Gate,** which, during the Troubles, was a security checkpoint between the Bogside and the city. Walk to the right across **Castle Gate,** which was built in 1865, and on to **Magazine Gate,** which was once near a powder magazine. Shortly afterward you'll pass **O'Doherty's Tower,** which houses the worthwhile Tower Museum. From there you can see the brick walls of the Guildhall. Farther along, you'll pass **Shipquay Gate,** which once was very near the port, back when the waters passed closer to the town center. The walls turn uphill from there, past the Millennium Forum concert hall, and up to **Ferryquay Gate,** where in 1688, local apprentice boys, anticipating an attack, barred the gate against attacking forces, thus saving the town. Next you'll pass **Bishop's Gate,** and notice a tall brick tower just outside the gate—it's all that remains of the **Old Gaol** (jail), where the rebel Wolfe Tone was imprisoned after the unsuccessful uprising in 1798. Farther along, the **Double Bastion** holds a military tower with elaborate equipment used to keep an eye on the Bogside—it's usually splashed by paint hurled at it by Republicans. From there you can easily access the serene churchyard of **St. Columb's Cathedral.** From the next stretch of wall, you have a good view over the political murals of the Bogside down the hill. A bit farther along the wall, an empty plinth stands where once there was a statue of Rev. George Walker, a governor of the city during the siege of 1699. It was blown up by the IRA in 1973. The small chapel nearby is the **Chapel of St. Augustine** (1872), and the building across the street from it with metal grates over the windows is the **Apprentice Boys' Memorial Hall.** Walk but a short way farther, and you're back to Butcher's Gate.

an important role in the settlement of the West. ***Note:*** The center has few staff, so call ahead. Or, if you can't make it, check out their website—it's one of the most useful Irish genealogy websites we've seen.

Harbour Museum, Harbour Sq., Derry. ✆ **028/7126-9792.** www.rootsireland.ie. Mon–Fri 9am–5pm.

Guild Hall ★ Just outside the city walls, between Shipquay Gate and the River Foyle, this Tudor Gothic–style building looks much like its counterpart in London. The site's original structure was built in 1890, but it was rebuilt after a fire in 1908 and again after a series of sectarian bombings in 1972. The hall is distinguished by its huge, four-faced clock and its stained-glass windows, made by Ulster craftsmen, that illustrate almost every episode of note in the city's history. The hall is used as a civic center for concerts, plays, and exhibitions.

Shipquay Place, Derry. ✆ **028/7137-7335.** Free admission. Mon–Fri 9am–5pm; Sat–Sun by appointment. Free guided tours July–Aug.

St. Eugene's Cathedral ★★ Designed in the Gothic Revival style, this is Derry's Catholic cathedral, in the heart of the Bogside district just beyond the city walls. The foundation was laid in 1851, but work continued until 1873. The spire was added in 1902. It's built of local sandstone and is known for stained-glass windows by the famed makers of stained glass, Meyer and Co. of Munich, depicting the Crucifixion.

Francis St., Derry. ✆ **028/7126-2894.** www.steugenescathedral.com. Free admission. Mon–Sat 7am–9pm; Sun 7am–6:30pm.

Tower Museum ★★ In O'Doherty Tower, a medieval-style fort, this award-winning museum presents the history of the city, from its geological formation to the present day. Visitors are invited to walk through time, and a series of exhibits and audiovisual presentations provoke their imaginations along the way. The tower's collection of historical artifacts includes items salvaged from the Spanish Armada, ravaged by storms off the Irish coast in 1588. The Tower Museum, a must for all visitors who want to understand Derry, is just inside the city walls next to Shipquay Gate and includes a new Spanish Armada museum.

Union Hall Place, Derry. ✆ **028/7137-2411.** Admission £4.50 adults; £2.65 seniors, students, and children; £9.50 families. July–Aug Mon–Sat 10am–5pm, Sun 2–5pm; Sept–June Tues–Sat 10am–5pm.

The Workhouse Museum and Library ★ This compact museum on the Waterside, only minutes from central Derry, sits inside a building that was one of the much-feared 19th-century workhouses. In their day, they were notorious for disease, misery, and death. Built to keep the poor from starving to death, workhouses were actually little more than concentration camps. The story told here is

Oh, Danny Boy . . .

About 19km (12 miles) east of Derry is another Georgian enclave, the town of Limavady in the Roe Valley. It was here that Jane Ross wrote down the tune of a lovely song she heard played by a fiddler passing through town. It became the famous "Londonderry Air," otherwise known as "Danny Boy."

both grim and moving. There's also an exhibit on the role played by the city of Derry during World War II.

23 Glendermott Rd., Waterside, Derry. ✆ **028/7131-8328.** Free admission. Mon–Thurs and Sat 10am–5pm.

Shopping

The city center offers the best shopping options, including two modern multistory malls: the **Richmond Centre,** facing the Diamond at the corner of Shipquay and Ferryquay streets; and the newer **Foyleside Shopping Centre,** just outside the walls. **London Street,** beside St. Columb's Cathedral, is Derry's antiques row, where most of the city's antiques and curio shops cluster.

In general, shops are open Monday to Saturday 9am to 5:30pm. Shops in the two large shopping centers are open Monday to Wednesday and Saturday 9am to 5:30pm, Thursday and Friday 9am to 9pm. In the summer, some shops are open on Sunday.

Austins This is the city's landmark three-story, Victorian-style department store, specializing in fashions, perfumes, china, crystal, and linens. It's the island of Ireland's oldest department store, established in 1839. The coffee shop on the third floor looks out on a panorama of the city. The Diamond, Derry. ✆ **028/7126-1817.** www.austinsstore.com.

Derry Craft Village In the heart of the inner city near the Tower, this shopping complex reflects Old Derry, with architecture of the 16th to 19th centuries. It houses crafts shops, artists' workshops, and a tearoom. Shipquay St. (enter on Shipquay or Magazine St.), Derry. ✆ **028/7126-0329.**

The Donegal Shop For those not traveling on to Donegal, which is known for its wool and knitted textiles, this is a good place to stock up on colorful sweaters, blankets, hats, and other fine wool products. 8 Shipquay St., Derry. ✆ **028/7126-6928.**

Sports & Outdoor Pursuits

BICYCLING Whether you want to rent a bike and do your own exploring or sign up for a cycling tour of County Derry and County Donegal, **An Mointean Rent-a-Bike and Cycle Tours,** 245 Lone Moor Rd., Derry (✆ **028/7128-7128**), offers excellent service. Rental of mountain or touring bikes costs from about £15 a day, £50 a week. Package tours with bed-and-breakfast included are also available.

FISHING The Foyle System of rivers makes this a promising area for snagging brown and sea trout (Apr to early July and Sept) and a variety of salmon (Mar–Sept). In addition, there is a stocked lake at Glenowen. Call **Glenowen Fisheries Co-operative** (✆ **028/7137-1544**) for bookings. You can outfit yourself and get useful information at **Rod and Line,** 1 Clarendon St., Derry (✆ **028/7126-2877**). If you're looking for an experienced local *ghillie* (guide) or boatman, contact **Glenowen Fisheries Co-operative** (✆ **028/7137-1544**), or the **Faughan Angler's Association,** 26a Carlisle Rd., Derry (✆ **028/7126-7781**). For a game-fishing rod license (currently £15 per season), contact the **Loughs Agency,** 22 Victoria Rd., Derry (✆ **028/7134-2100;** www.loughs-agency.org).

GOLF Derry has two 18-hole parkland courses: the **City of Derry Golf Club,** 49 Victoria Rd. (✆ **028/7134-6369;** www.cityofderrygolfclub.com), with greens fees of £30 weekdays, £40 weekends; and the very inexpensive **Foyle International Golf Centre,** 12 Alder Rd., Derry (✆ **028/7135-2222;** www.foylegolfcentre.co.uk), which charges greens fees of £17 weekdays, £20 weekends. It is always best to phone ahead.

HORSEBACK RIDING **Ardmore Stables,** 8 Rushall Rd., Ardmore (✆ **028/7134-5187** or 0778/482-4080; www.ardmorestables.com), offers lessons, trail rides, and pony trekking. Across the border, only 6.5km (4 miles) from Derry in County Donegal, **Lenamore Stables,** Muff, Inishowen (✆ **4077/938-4022;** www.lenamorestables.net), also offers lessons and trekking, and has guest accommodations.

WALKING Just outside the city, off the main Derry-Belfast road, the **Ness Woods** have scenic walks, nature trails, and the North's highest waterfall.

Where to Stay

EXPENSIVE

Everglades Hotel ★★ On a hill overlooking the east bank of Lough Foyle in the prosperous Waterside district, this three-story contemporary hotel takes its name from Florida's Everglades, with the tenuous connection that, like much of Florida, the hotel is built on reclaimed waterfront land. Guest rooms are luxuriously decorated in quality contemporary furnishings and smart designer fabrics. The hotel restaurant is popular with Belfast families celebrating special occasions. Afternoon tea (£7) is served daily from 2 to 5pm, and the scones are fresh and tender. The laid-back **Library Bar** features live jazz on weekends.

Prehen Rd., Derry, County Derry. www.hastingshotels.com/everglades-hotel. ✆ **028/7132-1066.** 64 units. £100–£170 double. Rates include full breakfast. AE, DC, V. Free parking. **Amenities:** Restaurant; bar; room service; smoke-free rooms. *In room:* TV, hair dryer.

MODERATE

Beech Hill Country House Hotel ★ This country-house hotel in a residential neighborhood outside the city center dates from 1729, and it has an elegant antiquarian air. Antiques and marble fireplaces decorate the public areas, and some of the pleasant guest rooms have four-poster beds with frilly floral covers. The hotel restaurant is the elegant **Ardmore** (see below). The hotel's wooded grounds are great to wander. Check online for really good Web-only deals, which can be as cheap as £85 per night.

32 Ardmore Rd., Derry, County Derry. www.beech-hill.com. ✆ **800/44-PRIMA** (447-7462) in the U.S., or 028/7134-9279. Fax 028/7134-5366. 27 units. £85–£140 double; £170–£235 suites. Rates include full breakfast. AE, MC, V. Free parking. **Amenities:** Restaurant; bar; lounge; minigym. *In room:* A/C (in some), TV, hair dryer.

City Hotel ★ This modern hotel in the town center has an excellent location, overlooking the waters of the River Foyle. Guest rooms are contemporary in style with neutral modern decor, comfortable beds, and plenty of space. It's targeted primarily at business travelers, so it offers all the conveniences you might hope for, including a handy (if not spectacular) restaurant, a bar, and a swimming pool. But its main attraction is that great spot, right in the middle of the action.

Queens Quay, Derry, County Derry. www.cityhotelderry.com. ✆ **028/7136-5800.** 145 units. £85–£154 double. Rates include full breakfast. MC, V. Free parking. **Amenities:** Restaurant; bar; indoor pool. *In room:* TV.

Clarence House ★ This well-kept brick Victorian guesthouse is great for families, as it has rooms of all sizes—from twins to doubles to family rooms. Guest rooms are comfortable, and the owner is friendly enough that he has a loyal group of regular visitors—it's a favorite of British and Irish television crews.

15 Northland Rd., Derry, County Derry. ✆ **028/7126-5342.** 11 units, 7 with private bathroom. £65 double with bathroom; £60 double with shared bathroom. Children's discount available. Rates include full breakfast. MC, V. Limited free parking. **Amenities:** Babysitting. *In room:* TV, hair dryer.

A Note on Prices

Derry prices for both accommodations and dining are exceptionally reasonable. The fact that Derry has hardly any expensive hotels or restaurants does not mean that it lacks quality lodging or dining. The city simply offers more for less and is, for the foreseeable future at least, a real bargain.

Da Vinci's Hotel This new modern hotel about a mile outside the town center is part of the Ramada chain, but it doesn't look like it. In a spacious loft-style riverfront building, it combines exposed brick walls, big windows, and wood floors to give it a great Manhattan-in-Eire look. Guest rooms are spacious and decorated in neutral tones with bright splashes of color; most have big arched windows. With a good restaurant (the **Grill Room**, listed below) and a lively bar, you get a lot for your money here. ***Tip:*** Book online in advance for discounts as deep as 50%.

15 Culmore Rd., Derry, County Derry. www.davincishotel.com. ✆ **028/7127-9111.** 70 units. £80–£100 double. Rates include full breakfast. MC, V. Free parking. **Amenities:** Restaurant; bar; Wi-Fi. *In room:* TV, hair dryer, broadband Internet.

Tower Hotel It doesn't get much more central than this—this modern hostelry is the only hotel inside the old city walls. Its rooms are a sleek turn on the usual modern chain hotel, with well-chosen furnishings, comfortable beds, neutral linens, and quite a few bells and whistles. There's a handy Mediterranean-style bistro, as well as a cafe and bar and a workout facility.

The Diamond, Butcher St., Derry, County Derry. www.towerhotelderry.com. ✆ **028/7137-1000.** Fax 028/7137-1234. 93 units. £70–£110 double. Rates include full breakfast. MC, V. Free parking. **Amenities:** Restaurant; cafe/bar; free Wi-Fi. *In room:* TV.

INEXPENSIVE

The Saddlers House and the Merchant's House ★★ Peter and Joan Pyne have beautifully restored two architectural gems into award-winning B&Bs. The Saddlers House is a rambling Victorian mansion with spacious rooms, simply but tastefully decorated. The elegant Merchant's House is a grand late-Georgian structure revived with such care that it's won conservation awards. The pair also own a couple of self-catering cottages (starting at £90 per night). Joan and Peter are cheerful hosts—their door is (sometimes literally) always open. A full Irish breakfast is served in both Saddlers House and the Merchant's House, as well as a more healthy cereal, yogurt, and homemade fruit compote. Both houses are just a few minutes' walk from the walled city center. Visit the Saddlers House website for info on all the properties.

Saddlers House, 36 Great James St., Derry, County Derry. www.thesaddlershouse.com. ✆ **028/7126-9691.** Fax 028/7126-6913. 7 units, 3 with private bathroom. £55 double with bathroom; £50 double with shared bathroom. Merchant's House, 16 Queen St., Derry. ✆ **028/7126-9691.** Fax 028/7126-6913. 5 units, 1 with private bathroom. £55 double with bathroom; £50 double with shared bathroom. Children's and senior discounts available. Rates include full breakfast. MC, V. *In room:* TV.

Travelodge This chain hotel may lack character, but it's a reliable affordable option. The spacious rooms are simply decorated in warm tones with basic modern furniture. Its family rooms—which easily hold two adults and two children—are a blessing for those traveling with little ones. There's nothing special or memorable about this place, but it's handy and cheap. A 2-night minimum stay applies on weekends during the summer.

22–24 Strand Rd., Derry, County Derry. www.travelodgederry.co.uk. ✆ **0870/191-1733** or 0871/984-6234. Fax 028/7127-1277. 40 units. £45–£85 double. Continental breakfast £8. AE, MC, V. Free parking. **Amenities:** 2 restaurants; bar; complimentary access to nearby fitness center. *In room:* TV, hair dryer.

White Horse Hotel This hotel, once an old inn and now part of the Best Western chain, is a favorite of tour operators. Its countryside setting 6km (3¾ miles) northeast of the city on the Limavady road is peaceful, and there's frequent bus service into Derry. Rooms are spacious and well appointed in a homey style, although there are neither bells nor whistles here. If you're an AARP member, ask about their seniors discount.

68 Clooney Rd., Campsie, County Derry. www.whitehorsehotel.biz. ✆ **028/7186-0606.** Fax 028/7186-0371. 56 units. £45–£120 double. Rates include full breakfast. Weekly and weekend discounts available. AE, DC, MC, V. Free parking. **Amenities:** Restaurant; bar. *In room:* TV.

Where to Eat

EXPENSIVE

Ardmore Room Restaurant ★ CONTINENTAL Lunch in this pretty dining room at the Beech Hill Hotel draws many business types, who relax in what was once a billiard room overlooking gardens, while enjoying a superb meal. In the evening, there's a soft, romantic ambience. The food is a Continental take on Irish cuisine, so expect dishes such as Irish venison Wellington with spinach and mushroom mousse, grilled Irish rib-eye steak with red-wine sauce, pan-fried Atlantic salmon with tomato fondue and shaved fennel. There's an extensive international wine list, as well as a selection of excellent home-baked specialty breads.

Beech Hill Country House Hotel, 32 Ardmore Rd. ✆ **028/7134-9279.** www.beech-hill.com. Reservations recommended. Main courses £17–£24. MC, V. Daily noon–2:30pm and 6–9:30pm.

La Sosta ITALIAN This family-run Italian restaurant is an excellent choice when you have spaghetti on your mind. The menu carries all the usual pasta suspects, plus fresh salads and good meat dishes. The well-made sauces betray the chef's Italian roots. Service is friendly and the atmosphere family friendly and relaxed.

45a Carlisle Rd., Derry. ✆ **028/7137-4817.** www.lasostarestaurant.co.uk. Main courses £12–£20. AE, MC, V. Mon–Sat 5:30–9:30pm; Sun noon–2:30pm and 5:30–9pm.

Satchmo's Restaurant ★ INTERNATIONAL In the elegant Everglades Hotel, Satchmo's combines fresh local produce with classical cooking styles to produce memorable meals. Dishes are mostly modern takes on classics such as medallions of pork with champ and black pudding, venison with sweet potato fondants and wild mushrooms, or the filet of sea bass with roast tomato and tapenade. After dinner you can relax with a brandy in the library bar. The ambience here is formal, and the dress code seems to be mostly suit and tie for men. It's a good way to treat yourself after a hard day's sightseeing.

Everglades Hotel, Prehen Rd., Derry. ✆ **028/7132-1066.** Reservations recommended. Main courses £11–£22. AE, DC, MC, V. Daily 6:30–9:30pm; Sun 12:30–2:30pm.

MODERATE

Brown's Bar and Brasserie ★ MODERN IRISH Behind the unassuming exterior of this Waterside area row house, you will find some of the finest food in Derry. The decor is warm, streamlined, and minimalist—conducive to quiet conversation. The innovative menu changes constantly but usually blends the best of modern Irish with strong French influences, and an emphasis on fresh and, when possible, organic ingredients. Dishes can include roast hake with creamed leeks and Donegal crab, 24-hour braised Loch Erne lamb shoulder with smoked bacon and cabbage, or sirloin steak with celeriac and parsnip gratin.

1 Bond's Hill, Waterside, Derry. ✆ **028/7134-5180.** www.brownsrestaurant.com. Reservations recommended. Main courses £14–£21. MC, V. Tues–Fri noon–2:30pm; Tues–Thurs 5:30–10pm; Fri–Sat 5:30–10:30pm; Sun noon–2pm.

Da Vinci's Grill Room INTERNATIONAL The glow of candlelight and rich Renaissance reds and blues romantically warm the rough stone walls and arched doorways at this restaurant in Da Vinci's Hotel, but it's the food that will coax you a short distance (5-min. drive) from Derry center. Choose from delights such as grilled sea bass with jalapeno mash and mango salsa, or dry-aged Irish sirloin with peppercorn sauce. Sunday lunch (£14 for three courses) is extremely good value. Stop in to see the magnificent mahogany central bar and its towering three-faced clock. Da Vinci's also has good, affordable rooms (see above).

15 Culmore Rd., Derry, County Derry. ✆ **028/7127-9111.** Reservations recommended. Main courses £11–£16. AE, MC, V. Mon–Sat 5:30–9:30pm; Sun 12:30–2:30pm and 5–8:30pm.

Gaslight Grill ★ INTERNATIONAL The good, honest food at this popular restaurant draws enthusiastic crowds of local diners. Although generally modern European in tone, the menu has a particularly North American accent, especially when it comes to the satisfying, meatier entrees. Burgers may come with smoked applewood cheese and onion marmalade made with Guinness, and the sirloin steak may be served with a Jack Daniel's and blue cheese sauce. There's also a good selection of seafood and pasta dishes. Service is just attentive enough, and the atmosphere is lively.

31–33 Foyle St., Derry. ✆ **028/7126-0708.** www.thegaslightgrill.com. Reservations recommended. Main courses £10–£20. MC, V. Mon–Sat 5–10pm; Sun 1–3pm and 4–9pm.

Mange 2 ★ FUSION A family-owned restaurant that colors outside all the lines most restaurants stay in between, Mange 2 is both romantic and relaxed, bright by day and candlelit at night, friendly but not intrusive. Its mixed-bag menu of Continental/Asian fusion changes regularly, but is reliably good and made with fresh local produce. Think Jamaican-style pork filet with lyonnaise potatoes, or filet of sea bream with spinach and mushroom cream. This is one of the best restaurants in Derry.

110–115 Strand Rd., Derry. ✆ **028/7136-1222.** www.mange2derry.com. Main courses £11–£17. AE, MC, V. Mon–Fri 11:30am–3pm and 5:30–10pm; Sat–Sun 10:30am–3pm and 5:30–10pm.

O'Brien's American Steakhouse & Grill ★ NORTH AMERICAN This is a loud, bright, extroverted piece of Americana in the middle of central Derry. Big TVs blast music videos or sports, staff are young and cheerful, clientele are known to drink a bit, and the food is cheap and very good. Considering what you get—huge steaks served on sizzling platters with large salads and gigantic mounds of potatoes—prices are beyond reasonable. This place is a steal.

59 Strand Rd., Derry. ✆ **028/7136-1527.** Reservations not accepted. Main courses £8–£17. AE, MC, V. Mon–Fri noon–10pm; Sat 4–11pm; Sun 2–10pm.

Quaywest Wine Bar & Restaurant INTERNATIONAL This is one of the trendier options in Derry—you might want to wear your high heels to this one. The mix of bar and restaurant leans more heavily toward bar as the night goes on, but the food is always excellent, and the international menu travels from Morocco to Mexico and back again.

28 Boating Club Lane, Derry. ✆ **028/7137-0977.** www.quaywestrestaurant.com. Reservations recommended. Main courses £12–£15. MC, V. Mon–Sat 5–11pm; Sun noon–10:30pm.

INEXPENSIVE

Badger's PUB GRUB This comfortable corner pub and restaurant is just the place to enjoy a simple, satisfying dinner before the theater, or to settle into after your day's adventures for a drink and a chat. With stained glass and wood paneling, the two levels have a Victorian feel, but were designed with a modern appreciation of light and openness. It's a popular meeting spot for locals who come for the friendly service, the steak-and-Guinness pie, and the hot sandwiches known as "damper melts."

16–18 Orchard St., Derry. ✆ **028/7136-0763.** Reservations not accepted. Dinner main courses £5–£10. MC, V. Mon–Thurs noon–7pm; Fri–Sat noon–9:30pm; Sun noon–4pm.

Fitzroy's BRASSERIE This laid-back, brightly colored bistro is open all day and is a great option for a quick, easy meal at reasonable prices. It tends to have a buzzing crowd of regulars, and it's easy to see why. Food is a casual mix of cultures, from chicken and bacon *ciabatta* sandwiches to Cajun chicken to pasta, along with plenty of vegetarian options.

2–4 Bridge St., Derry. ✆ **028/7126-6211.** www.fitzroysrestaurant.com. Reservations recommended. Main courses £5–£7 lunch, £7–£10 dinner. MC, V. Mon–Tues 10am–8pm; Wed 10am–10pm; Thurs–Sat 9:30am–10pm; Sun noon–8pm.

Derry After Dark

One thing to keep in mind as you're sketching out your after-dark plans is that Derry is a youthful city—roughly 40% of its population is under 30. This fact, coupled with a legal drinking age of 18, means that the night scene is driven by the young. On weekends, after 1 or 2am when the clubs empty, the city center can seem a rather loud and volatile place.

THE PERFORMING ARTS

Derry has long been associated with the arts, especially theater, poetry, and music. While its financial resources have been modest, its commitment remains inventive and tenacious. The **Millennium Forum,** Newmarket Street (✆ **028/7126-4455** box office; www.millenniumforum.co.uk), inside the city walls, has added a cultural meeting place and superb theater space to the local mix.

Other principal venues for concerts, plays, and poetry readings are the **Guild Hall,** Shipquay Place (✆ **028/7137-7335**), and the **Playhouse,** 5–7 Artillery St. (✆ **028/7126-8027;** www.derryplayhouse.co.uk), as well as the **Nerve Centre,** 7–8 Magazine St. (✆ **028/7126-0562;** www.nerve-centre.org.uk), which has a cinema and two concert and theater amphitheaters. The **Verbal Arts Centre,** Stable Lane and Mall Wall, Bishop Street Within (✆ **028/7126-6946;** www.verbalartscentre.co.uk), is devoted to promoting literature through readings and spoken-word events. Ticket prices range from free to about £15.

PUBS

Derry pubs are an important part of the local fabric, and hanging out in one is a good way to meet locals. Boozers are tied into the local music scene, so you'll frequently find bands playing. There are even pub debating contests, in the midst of which you'll hear Irish eloquence at its well-lubricated best. Here's a small sampling of Derry's more-than-ample pub options.

Along **Waterloo Street,** just outside the city walls, is a handful of Derry's most traditional and popular pubs, known for their live music and simply as the place to be. The **Dungloe,** the **Gweedore,** and **Peador O'Donnells** are three well-established hot spots. Walk from one end of Waterloo to the other—an act that will take you all of 2 minutes—and you'll likely find the bar for you.

The Clarendon This inviting bar offers more quiet and calm than most of Derry's bars. It's a congenial pub for those who are past 30 and are somewhere beyond the sonic boom. You can have a conversation here, as well as a drink. 48 Strand Rd., Derry. ✆ **028/7126-3705.**

River Inn Two adjoining bars combine to form the oldest pub in Derry. The downstairs River Inn inhabits cellars opened to the thirsty public in 1684. Thursday is cocktail night. 37 Shipquay St., Derry. ✆ **028/7137-1965.**

Sandino's Cafe Bar This tiny place is quite trendy, and is where many of the city's more literary folk settle in for the evening. Its "South of the Border" theme refers to the United States' Mexican border, not to the North's border on the Republic. Bands play most nights. Water St., Derry. ✆ **028/7130-9297.** www.sandinos.com.

THE CLUB SCENE

Provided you're under 25, there are several places where you'll want to be seen if not heard. Two multi-entertainment complexes stand out; the first is **Strand,** 31–35 Strand Rd. (✆ **028/7126-0494**), with a classy bar serving mostly pub grub and an open venue for bands. On weekend nights, the tables in the bar are moved aside and the Strand morphs into a nightclub for the 20-plus crowd. Then there's **Earth,** 1 College Terrace (✆ **028/7136-0556**), which has long been the city's main nightclub. It's near the university, so expect a young crowd.

THE SPERRIN MOUNTAINS

65km (40 miles) E to W along the Derry-Tyrone border

Southeast of Derry, the Sperrin Mountains rise up out of County Tyrone, reaching their highest point at Sawel, from which you can see as far as the Foyle Estuary and across the Northern Ireland countryside to Lough Neagh and the Mournes. This is splendid, wide-open, walking country, home to golden plover, red grouse, and thousands upon thousands of fluffy white sheep.

In the Sperrins, you won't be likely to find the tallest, oldest, or most famous anything. Even the highest peak in the range—Sawel, at 661m (2,168 ft.)—is an easy climb. This is Ireland in a minor key. It is a corner of Ireland largely unsung, but also unspoiled. You'll see mostly wildflowers here, rather than formal gardens, and cottages rather than castles. All the same, gold has been found in these mountains. Poetry, too. The Nobel-winning poet Seamus Heaney grew up on the edge of the Sperrins and found words to suit their subtle splendor.

Unless you come to farm, chances are you'll spend your time exploring the dark-russet blanket bogs and purple heathland, the gorse-covered hillsides, and the forest parks, whether on foot, cycle, or horseback. There are salmon and trout to be fished from Foyle. There are also a few historical museums. As for minor destinations for a morning walk or an afternoon drive, there's no shortage of standing stones (about 1,000 have been counted), high crosses, dolmens, and hill forts—more reminders that every last bit of bog on this island has its own slew of stories, if only we could hear them told.

VISITOR INFORMATION There are four nationally networked tourist information centers in County Tyrone. The **Cookstown Centre,** Burn Road, Cookstown (✆ **028/8676-9949**), is open weekdays 9am to 5:30pm, with weekend and extended hours Easter to September. The **Killymaddy Centre,** Ballygawley Road (off A4), Dungannon (✆ **028/8776-7259**), is open Monday to Friday 9am to 5pm, Saturday 10am to 4pm. The **Omagh Centre,** 1 Market St., Omagh (✆ **028/8224-7831**), is open weekdays 9am to 5pm, weekends 10am to 4pm (an hour later in July and Aug). The **Strabane Centre,** Abercorn Square, Strabane (✆ **028/7188-3735**), is open Monday to Saturday 9am to 5pm (half an hour later in July and Aug).

Seeing the Sights

An Creagán Visitors' Centre Beautifully designed to fit in with the craggy countryside around, this visitor center is an excellent place to get your bearings when you first arrive in the Sperrins. Besides viewing interpretive exhibitions on the region, you can find cycling and trekking routes, rent bicycles, and have a meal in the restaurant. The center owns self-catering cottages nearby, which could make a great base. Call for more information.

A505 (20km/13 miles east of Omagh), Creggan, County Tyrone. ✆ **028/8076-1112.** www.an-creagan.com. Admission £1.50 adults; £1 children. Apr–Sept daily 11am–6:30pm; Oct–Mar Mon–Fri 11am–4:30pm.

Beaghmore Stone Circles In 1945, six stone circles and a complex assembly of cairns and alignments were uncovered here, in remote moorland north of Evishbrack Mountain and near Davagh Forest Park on the southern edge of the Sperrins. The precise function of this intriguing concentration of Bronze Age

The green and woody precincts of Gortin Glen Forest Park.

stonework is unknown, but it may have involved astronomical observation and calculation.

17km (11 miles) northwest of Cookstown, signposted from A505 to Omagh, County Tyrone.

Drum Manor Forest Park Once a private estate, this extensive park and woodland has numerous trails and three old walled gardens, one of which has been designed as a butterfly garden. Also on the grounds are a pond that attracts a variety of wildfowl, a heronry, and a visitor center with exhibits on local wildlife.

4km (2½ miles) west of Cookstown on A505, County Tyrone. ✆ **028/8676-2774.** Admission £3.40 per car; pedestrians £1 adults, 50p children. Daily 10am–dusk.

Gortin Glen Forest Park ★★ Nearly 400 hectares (988 acres) of conifers make up this nature park. The woodlands are a habitat to a variety of wildlife, including a herd of Japanese silka deer. A forest drive offers splendid views of the Sperrins. Here are also a nature center, wildlife enclosures, trails, and a cafe. For those planning to arrive on foot, the Ulster Way (p. 613) passes through the park.

B48 (11km/6¾ miles north of Omagh), Cullion, County Tyrone. ✆ **028/8164-8217.** Parking £3; pedestrians £1 adults, 50p children. Daily 9am to 1 hr. before sunset.

Grant Ancestral Home This farm cottage was the home of the ancestors of Ulysses S. Grant, 18th president of the United States. Grant's maternal great-grandfather, John Simpson, was born here and emigrated to Pennsylvania in 1738 at the age of 22. The cottage has two rooms with mud floors and has been restored and furnished with period pieces. The site includes a visitor center with an audiovisual presentation, a tearoom, and various exhibits, including a collection of typical 18th-century agricultural implements.

32km (20 miles) southeast of Omagh off A4, Dergina, Ballygawley, County Tyrone. ✆ **028/8555-7133.** Admission £1 adults; 50p seniors and children. Apr–Sept Mon–Sat noon–5pm; Sun 2–6pm.

Gray's Printers' Museum Although a museum and print shop are housed together here, the two are unrelated. The shop, maintained by the National

Trust, dates from 1760 and holds an exhibit of 19th-century hand-operated printing presses. John Dunlop, founder of the first daily newspaper in the U.S. and printer of the American Declaration of Independence, learned his trade here. An audiovisual show provides insight into how the presses operated and the part Dunlop played in America's early days. The museum, operated by the local district council, is a venue for changing exhibits germane to the history and culture of the region. Access to the printing press is through the museum. ***Note:*** Opening times are a little fluid, so call ahead to check.

49 Main St., Strabane, County Tyrone. ✆ **028/7188-0055.** Tours £3.20 adults; £1.90 children; £8.30 families. Museum Tues–Fri 11am–5pm; Sat 11:30am–5pm. Guided tours of printing press Apr–Sept Tues–Sat 2–5pm. Last admission 45 min. before closing.

Sperrin Heritage Centre ★ ☺ A range of computerized presentations and other exhibits introduce the history, culture, geology, and wildlife of the region. This is a gold-mining area, and for a small additional fee (around 80p) you'll get a chance to try your hand at panning for gold. A cafeteria, craft shop, and nature trail share the grounds.

274 Glenelly Rd. (east of Plumbridge off B47), Cranagh, County Tyrone. ✆ **028/8164-8142.** Admission £3 adults; £2 children. Apr–Sept Mon–Fri 11:30am–5:30pm; Sat 11:30am–6pm; Sun 2–6pm.

Ulster American Folk Park ★★ ☺ This outdoor museum presents the story of emigration from this part of rural Ireland to America in the 18th and 19th centuries. There are reconstructions of the thatched cottages that emigrants left behind and replicas of the log cabins that became their homes on the American frontier. The park developed around the homestead where Thomas Mellon was born in 1813. He emigrated to Pittsburgh and prospered to the point where his son Andrew became one of the world's richest men. The Mellon family donated part of the funding to build this excellent park. Walk-through exhibits include a forge, weaver's cottage, schoolhouse, famine cabin, and full-scale replica of an emigrant ship with original buildings from the ports of Derry, Belfast, and Newry. A self-guided tour of all the exhibits, which are staffed by interpreters in period costume, takes about 2 hours. Musical events tie in with the Ulster-American theme, such as a bluegrass music festival in September.

2 Mellon Rd. (4.8km/3 miles north of Omagh on A5), Castletown, Camphill, Omagh, County Tyrone. ✆ **028/8224-3292.** www.nmni.com/uafp. Admission £6.50 adults; £4 seniors and children 5–16. Mar–Sept Tues–Sun 10am–5pm; Oct–Feb Tues–Fri 10am–4pm, Sat–Sun 11am–4pm. Last admission 1½ hr. before closing.

Wilson Ancestral Home This small thatched, whitewashed cottage on the slopes of the Sperrin Mountains was the home of Judge James Wilson, grandfather of Woodrow Wilson, 28th president of the United States. James Wilson left the house in 1807 at the age of 20. It contains some of the family's original furniture, including a tiny out-shot bed (sleeping nook) in the kitchen close to the fire, larger curtained beds, and a portrait of the president's grandfather over the fireplace. Wilsons still occupy the farmhouse next door. ***Note:*** Opening hours are subject to change; phone in advance.

28 Spout Rd., off Plumbridge Rd., Dergalt, Strabane, County Tyrone. ✆ **028/8224-3292.** Free admission. July–Aug Tues–Sun 2–5pm.

Sports & Outdoor Pursuits

BICYCLING The Sperrin countryside is ideal for cycling. Bicycles can be rented by the day or week from the **An Creagán Visitors' Centre** (see above). Bike rentals run roughly £10 a day, £35 a week.

BIRD-WATCHING The Sperrins are home to golden plovers, peregrines, ravens, grouse, and hen harriers. **Sawel Mountain,** the highest of the Sperrins, is a great place to take out your binoculars and field guide.

FISHING The **Foyle System** of rivers, from Derry to Omagh and Limavady to Dungiven, makes this a promising area for brown and sea trout (Apr to early July and Sept) and a variety of salmon (Mar–Sept). There's also some good coarse fishing available north and west of Omagh, on the Baronscourt Lakes and on the Strule and Fairy Water rivers. The necessary permits, equipment, and good advice are available from **C. A. Anderson & Co.,** 64A Market St., Omagh (✆ **028/423118226-8053**); **Mourne Valley Tackle,** 50 Main St., Newtownstewart (✆ **028/8166-1543**); and **North West Country Sports,** 19 Butcher St., Strabane (✆ **028/2206007188-3981**).

GOLF Several 18-hole courses are located in County Tyrone, all within a modest drive from the heart of the Sperrins: **Strabane Golf Club,** 33 Ballycolman Rd., Strabane (✆ **028/7138-2007;** www.strabanegolfclub.co.uk), with greens fees of £16 weekdays, £20 on weekends; **Newtownstewart Golf Club,** 38 Golf Course Rd., Newtownstewart (✆ **028/8166-1466;** www.newtownstewartgolfclub.com), with greens fees of £18 weekdays, £25 weekends; **Omagh Golf Club,** 83a Dublin Rd., Omagh (✆ **028/8224-3160;** www.omaghgolf.co.uk), with greens fees of £20 weekdays, £25 weekends; and **Killymoon Golf Club,** 200 Killymoon Rd., Cookstown (✆ **028/8676-3762;** www.killymoongolfclub.com), with greens fees of £15 Monday, £21 Tuesday through Friday, and £26 weekends.

HORSEBACK RIDING For private lessons or country trail rides, contact the magnificently named **Tullywhisker Riding School,** 51 Brocklis Rd., Strabane (✆ **028/8165-8015**).

WALKING Whether you're on foot, wheels, or horseback, be sure to traverse the **Glenshane Pass** between Mullaghmore (545m/1,788 ft.) and Carntogher (455m/1,492 ft.), and the **Sawel Mountain Drive** along the east face of the mountain. The vistas along these routes through the Sperrins will remind you of why you've gone out of your way to spend time in Tyrone.

Where to Stay

MODERATE

Grange Lodge ★ Norah and Ralph Brown are the gracious hosts of this handsome Georgian guesthouse, which began life as a 17th-century settler's hall. Set high on a hill atop an 8-hectare (20-acre) estate, it's a classy, tranquil retreat and a good base for day trips throughout County Tyrone. Guest rooms are attractive and comfortable, but everyone stays here for the food. Norah has won all sorts of culinary awards, and her lovingly prepared, home-style meals have achieved near-cult status in this otherwise gastronomically challenged part of the North. At breakfast, don't miss the house specialty: porridge infused with Bushmills Whiskey and cream. And book a place for **dinner,** too (£35). Or, if you're really inspired, join one of her 4-hour cookery courses (£75).

7 Grange Rd. (signposted 1.6km/1 mile south of M1, Junction 15), Moy, Dungannon, County Tyrone. www.grangelodgecountryhouse.com. ✆ **028/8778-4212.** Fax 028/8778-4313. 5 units. £85 double. Rates include full breakfast. MC, V. Closed Dec 20–Feb 1. **Amenities:** Smoke-free rooms. *In room:* TV.

INEXPENSIVE

Greenmount Lodge ☺ This large, first-rate guesthouse is set on a 60-hectare (148-acre) farm. All the rooms are nicely appointed, and you'll find pretty quilts on the beds and armchairs in the rooms; three are family units, and one ground-floor room is fully accessible for those with limited mobility. Mrs. Frances Reid, the friendly hostess, is a superb cook; both breakfasts and evening meals are a home-style delight.

58 Greenmount Rd. (13km/8 miles southeast of Omagh on A5), Gortaclare, Omagh, County Tyrone. www.greenmountlodge.com. ✆ **028/8284-1325.** Fax 028/8284-0019. 9 units. £60 double. Children's discount available. Rates include full breakfast. Dinner £16. MC, V. **Amenities:** Babysitting. *In room:* TV, Wi-Fi.

SELF-CATERING

Sperrin Clachan ★ This restored *clachan,* or family cottage compound, sits beside the Sperrin Heritage Centre in the beautiful Glenelly Valley. It makes an ideal base for exploring the natural riches and cultural legacy of the Sperrin region, as well as the city of Derry, only 40km (25 miles) to the north. Each cottage has everything you'll need to set up house, including central heating and an open fireplace. There are four cottages in all; each sleeps two to five people. In addition to these, Rural Cottage Holidays offers a wide array of other traditional cottages in the region, including the award-winning, four-star Glenelly Cottages.

Glenelly Valley, Cranagh, County Tyrone. www.cottagesinireland.com. Contact RCH at ✆ **028/9036-0500.** 4 cottages. From £160–£220 for 2 nights, rising to £470–£520 per week in high season. MC, V. Free parking. *In room:* TV, fridge, kitchen.

Where to Eat

Mellon Country Hotel ★ INTERNATIONAL Just over 1km (⅔ mile) north of the Ulster-American Folk Park, this old-world country inn has had a modern makeover, and now has a sleek new interior. Its handy restaurant offers simple, hearty fare—burgers, soup, salads, and ploughman's platters—as well as seafood dishes. The house specialty is Tyrone black steak, a locally bred hormone-free beef. Food is available all day on a hot and cold buffet, and you can also order a late breakfast or afternoon tea. There are a few nicely decorated rooms, should you choose to stay the night, starting at £80 for a double.

134 Beltany Rd., Omagh, County Tyrone. ✆ **028/8166-1224.** www.melloncountryhotel.com. Dinner main courses £8–£20. AE, MC, V. Mon–Sat noon–3pm and 5–10pm; Sun noon–3pm and 4:30–9pm.

THE FERMANAGH LAKELANDS

Enniskillen: 134km (83 miles) SW of Belfast, 98km (61 miles) SW of Derry, 84km (52 miles) W of Armagh, 44km (27 miles) SW of Omagh, 174km (108 miles) NW of Dublin, 271km (168 miles) NE of Shannon

In the extreme southwest corner of Northern Ireland, County Fermanagh is a resort area dominated by **Lough Erne,** a long, narrow lake with 154 islands and countless coves and inlets.

The **Shannon-Erne Waterway,** linking the lough to the Shannon system, enhances the lure of Lough Erne as a boating destination. Were you to cruise the whole length of the waterway between the village of Leitrim and Lough Erne, you'd travel 65km (40 miles), past 16 lochs, three lakes, and the Woodford River, all of which are ripe for aquatic exploration.

The hub of this lakeland paradise, wedged between the upper and lower branches of Lough Erne, is **Enniskillen,** a delightful resort town that was the medieval seat of the Maguire clan and a major crossroads between Ulster and Connaught. Both Oscar Wilde and Samuel Beckett were once students here at the royal school.

At the northern tip of the lake is **Belleek,** sitting right across the border in the Republic of Ireland, and known the world over for its trademark delicate bone chinaware. At the southern end of the lake is County Cavan and another slice of border with the Irish Republic. The surrounding countryside holds diverse attractions, from stately homes at Florence Court and Castle Coole to the Marble Arch Caves.

In medieval times, a chain of island monasteries stretched across the waters of Lough Erne, establishing it as a haven for contemplatives. Even allowing for less lofty minds, the Fermanagh Lakelands are still a peaceful place to get away from it all and to gaze, in a phrase from Hopkins, at the "pied beauty" of it all.

VISITOR INFORMATION The **Fermanagh Tourist Information Centre,** Wellington Road, Enniskillen, County Fermanagh (✆ **028/6632-3110**), is open weekdays year-round from 9am to 5:30pm (until 7pm July–Aug). From Easter to September, it's also open Saturday 10am to 6pm and Sunday 11am to 5pm. For an introduction to the Fermanagh Lakelands on the Web, take a look at **www.fermanaghlakelands.com**.

Exploring the Lakelands

TOURING THE LAKES & ISLANDS

Erne Tours Ltd., Enniskillen (✆ **028/6632-2882;** www.ernetoursltd.com), operates cruises on Lower Lough Erne. The MV *Kestrel,* a 56-seat cruiser, departs from the Round "O" Jetty, Brook Park, Enniskillen. Trips, including a stop at Devenish Island, last just under 2 hours. Call for reservations and to confirm times. The fare starts at £10 for adults, £9 for seniors, £6 for children 13 and under, or £28 for a family of four.

The **Share Holiday Village,** Smith's Strand, Lisnaskea (✆ **028/6772-2122;** www.sharevillage.org), operates cruises on Upper Lough Erne. The 1½-hour trips are conducted onboard the *Inishcruiser,* a 57-passenger ship. The fares are about the same as those for Erne Tours, and the boat is fully wheelchair accessible. Call for times and precise prices. Share Holiday Village also offers other watersports activities and self-catering, family-friendly cottages (called "chalets").

Numerous charter boat companies in the area will allow you to travel privately for a day or a week on narrow boats, barges, or yachts. Prices vary from a few hundred pounds to much more, for the more elegant options. For a good list of options, go to **www.fermanaghlakelands.com** and click on "Find Something to Do," or call the tourist office to request a brochure.

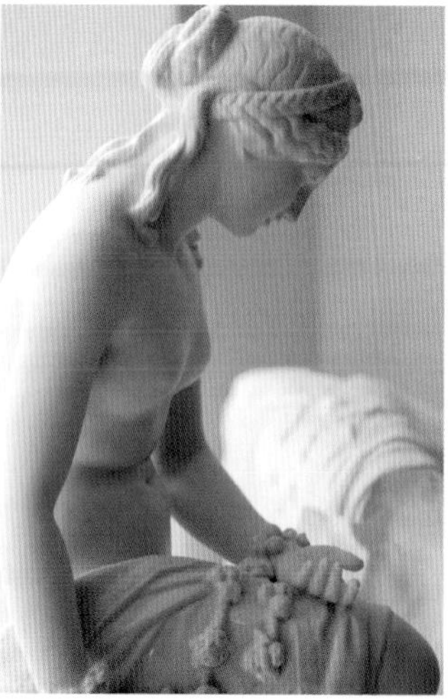

Porcelain from Belleek Pottery in the Fermanagh Lakelands.

Independent boatmen offer ferry crossings to some of the many islands in Lough Erne. White Island, Devenish Island, and Boa Island are all rich in archaeological and early Christian remains. Devenish Island has Lough Erne's most important island monastery, founded in the 6th century by St. Molaise. The extensive remains include a 12th-century round tower, which you can climb to take in the view and get a feel for the tiny space inside. From April to September, a ferry runs to Devenish Island from Trory Point, 6km (3¾ miles) from Enniskillen on A32; journey time is about 12 minutes.

On White Island, seven stone figures remain from a vanished 10th-century monastery inside a ruined 12th-century church. From April through August, a ferry runs to White Island, departing from Castle Archdale Marina (for times, call Mr. Bradshaw at ✆ **028/6862-1892,** or 0836/787123 mobile), 16km (10 miles) from Enniskillen on the Kesh road; journey time is about 18 minutes. Departures April through June are on weekends only, every hour on the hour from 11am to 6pm with the exception of 1pm. In July and August, the ferry runs daily, with the same sailing times. The round-trip fare is no more than a few euros. In the cemetery at the west end of Boa Island, there are two ancient Janus (looking both ways) idols, which are thought to date from the 1st century. Boa Island is connected to the shore by bridges.

Though it's possible to visit all three islands in a single day, it's a bit ambitious. Begin with Devenish, then visit White, and, if time permits, finish up with Boa.

SEEING THE SIGHTS

Belleek Visitors Centre ★★ The fine Parian china produced in the tiny village of Belleek is recognized worldwide for its quality. While you'll find pieces in shops all over the north of Ireland, this is the flagship store. In the visitor center, in a Victorian-era china-making factory, you can browse to your heart's content in the spacious shop, or head to the free museum and learn the history of this china-making town and see its best works. Depending on the exchange rate, prices tend to be considerably less than you'll find elsewhere, and shipping by UPS is available. If you want to learn even more about Belleek, take one of the informative 30-minute tours of the china factory. If you prefer to relax and ponder the china in peace, you might spend that same time lingering over a cup of tea and a slice of cake in the cheery tearoom. ***Note:*** Belleek is just inside the Ulster border, so prices will be in British pounds.

Follow signs in Belleek, County Fermanagh. ✆ **028/6865-9300.** www.belleek.ie. Free admission. Tours £4 adults; £2 seniors; £3 children. Jan–Feb Mon–Fri 9am–5:30pm; Mar–June Mon–Fri 9am–5:30pm, Sat 10am–5:30pm, Sun 2–5:30pm; July–Sept Mon–Fri 9am–6pm, Sat 10am–6pm, Sun noon–5:30pm; Oct Mon–Fri 9am–5:30pm, Sat 10am–5:30pm, Sun noon–5:30pm; Nov–Dec Mon–Fri 9am–5:30pm, Sat 10am–5:30pm. Tours every 30 min. Fri last tour 3pm.

Castle Coole ★ On the east bank of Lower Lough Erne, this quintessential neoclassical mansion was designed by James Wyatt for the Earl of Belmore and completed in 1796. Its rooms include a lavish state bedroom hung with crimson silk, said to have been prepared for George IV (1762–1830). Other features include a Chinese-style sitting room, magnificent woodwork, fireplaces, and furniture dating from the 1830s. A nearly 600-hectare (1,482-acre) woodland estate surrounds the house. A classical music series runs from May to October.

2.4km (1½ miles) southeast of Enniskillen on the main Belfast-Enniskillen rd. (A4), County Fermanagh. ✆ **028/6632-2690.** www.nationaltrust.org.uk. House admission £4.60 adults; £1.80 children; £12 families. Grounds £2.50 adults; £1.25 children; £6.25 families. House Mid-Mar to May and Sept Sat–Sun 11am–5pm (and all week during Easter week only); June Fri–Wed 11am–5pm; July–Aug daily 11am–5pm. Last admission 30 min. before closing. Grounds Mar–Sept 10am–7pm; Oct–Feb 10am–4pm.

Crom Estate ★★ This nearly 800-hectare (1,976-acre) nature reserve is a splendid National Trust property, with forest, parks, wetlands, fen meadows, and an award-winning lakeshore visitor center. There are numerous trails, with concealed places for observing birds and wildlife. You can rent a rowboat and row your way out to the islands. There's also a 19th-century castle on the estate,

BUYING belleek

If you're not a china expert, but you still want to bring back some Belleek pieces from your trip, here are a few tips to ensure that your purchases become heirlooms.

- The Belleek Heirloom Centre has the best selection of patterns from which to choose, giving you lots of options and a wide price range.
- At the center, all the china is displayed around the room. You walk around looking at all the pieces, then note the item numbers of those pieces you like. You take the numbers to the central counter, and they bring boxed china pieces to you.
- Make sure they pull the pieces out of the boxes so you can be sure they are what you expected.
- Take the pieces from the sales assistant and look at them closely. This is delicate china, and it can have tiny imperfections that you can only see by getting up close and personal.
- Be particularly conscious of the bottom of the piece—look for tiny hairline cracks. We bought a lovely Belleek vase once that looked perfect, but leaked through a nearly invisible crack.
- If it looks good to you and you love it—buy it!

though sadly it's not open to visitors. The estate is also a great place to fish for bream and roach. Permits and day tickets are available at the gate lodge. During the summer, there are frequently special programs and guided nature walks on weekends. The estate has several cottages available for rent by the week (£250–£800). Call or check the National Trust website for more information.

Newtownbutler, County Fermanagh. ✆ **028/6773-8118.** www.nationaltrust.org.uk. Admission £3 adults; £1 children; £8 families. Mid-Mar to May and Sept–Oct daily 10am–6pm; June–Aug daily 10am–7pm. Visitor center Mid-Mar to Sept daily 11am–5pm; Oct Sat–Sun 11am–5pm. Last admission 1 hr. before closing. Closed Nov to mid-Mar. 34km (21 miles) south of Enniskillen. Take A4 and A34 from Enniskillen to Newtownbutler, then take the signposted right turn onto a minor road.

Devenish Island ★★ This is the most extensive of the ancient Christian sites in Lough Erne. In the 6th century, St. Molaise founded a monastic community here, to which the Augustinian Abbey of St. Mary was added in the 12th century. In other words, this is hallowed ground, hallowed all the more by the legend that the prophet Jeremiah is buried somewhere nearby—if you can figure that one out. The jewel of Devenish is the perfectly intact, 12th-century round tower, which was erected with Vikings in mind. The island is a marvelous mélange of remnants and ruins, providing a glimpse into the lake's mystical past. While you're in the spirit, be sure to explore Boa and White islands, with their extraordinary carved stone figures, and bring your camera (see the introduction to this section for details on island hopping).

2.4km (1½ miles) downstream from Enniskillen. ✆ **028/6862-1588.** Admission to round tower £2.25; seniors and children £1.20. Ferry from Trory Point (6.5km/4 miles from Enniskillen on A32) Easter to mid-Sept at 10am and 1, 3, and 5pm; other sailing times based on demand. Round-trip fare £3 adults; £2 children. Closed mid-Sept to Easter.

Enniskillen Castle ★★ Dating from the 15th century, this magnificent stone fortress sits overlooking Lough Erne on the western edge of Enniskillen. It incorporates three museums: the medieval castle, with its unique twin-turreted Watergate tower, once the seat of the Maguires, chieftains of Fermanagh; the county museum, with exhibits on the area's history, wildlife, and landscape; and the museum of the famous Royal Inniskilling Fusiliers, with a collection of uniforms, weapons, and medals dating from the 17th century. Other exhibits include life-size figurines and 3-D models of old-time castle life.

Castle Barracks, Enniskillen, County Fermanagh. ✆ **028/6632-5000.** www.enniskillencastle.co.uk. Admission £3.50 adults; £2.50 seniors, students, and children, £9.50 families. Mar–June and Sept–Oct Tues–Fri 10am–5pm, Mon and Sat 2–5pm; July–Aug Tues–Fri 10am–5pm, Sat–Mon 2–5pm; Nov–Mar Mon 2–5pm, Tues–Fri 10am–5pm. Also bank holidays observed in both Northern Ireland and the Republic, 10am–5pm.

Explore Erne ☺ Just outside Belleek village, this exhibition offers an engaging multimedia introduction to Lough Erne. It covers its geologic formation and the lives, ancient and modern, lived along its reedy banks. Science, myth, and history blend to tell the story of this legendary, alluring lake.

Erne Gateway Centre, off main Enniskillen-Belleek rd., Corry, Belleek, County Fermanagh. ✆ **028/6865-8866.** Admission £1 adults; 50p seniors and children; £2.50 families. July–Sept daily 11am–5pm.

Florence Court ★★ This 18th-century Palladian mansion is set among dramatic hills, 13km (8 miles) southwest of Upper Lough Erne and Enniskillen.

Florence Court, in the Fermanagh Lakelands.

Originally the seat of the earls of Enniskillen, its interior is rich in rococo plasterwork and antique Irish furniture, while outside there's a fine walled garden, an icehouse, and a waterwheel-driven sawmill. The forest park offers a number of trails, one leading to the top of Mount Cuilcagh (nearly 660m/2,165 ft.). There's also a tearoom, where you can recover from the climb.

Florence Court, off A32, County Fermanagh. ✆ **028/6634-8249.** www.nationaltrust.org.uk. Admission to house £4.60 adults; £2 children; £11 families. Grounds only £3.25 adults; £1.75 children; £7.75 families. House mid-Apr to Sept daily 11am–5pm (closed Tues May–June and Fri Sept). Mid-Mar to mid-Apr and Oct Sat–Sun 11am–5pm. Gardens and park Jan–Feb and Nov–Dec daily 1am–4pm; Mar–Oct daily 11am–7pm. Also open all public holidays. Last admission 1 hr. before closing.

Marble Arch Caves ★★★ ☺ West of Upper Lough Erne and 19km (12 miles) from Enniskillen near the Florence Court estate, these UNESCO-listed caves are among the finest in Europe for exploring underground rivers, winding passages, and hidden chambers. Electrically powered boat tours take visitors underground, and knowledgeable guides explain the origins of the amazing stalactites and stalagmites. Tours last 75 minutes and leave at 15-minute intervals. The caves are occasionally closed after heavy rains, so phone ahead before making the trip.

Marlbank, Florence Court, off A32, County Fermanagh. ✆ **028/6634-8855.** www.marblearchcaves.net. Admission £8.50 adults; £5.75 seniors and students; £5.50 children 17 and under; £18 families. Reservations recommended. Mid-Mar to June and Sept daily 10am–4:30pm (last tour at 4:30pm); July–Aug daily 10am–5pm (last tour at 5pm).

Shopping

Enniskillen has fine shops along its main street, which changes its name five times (East Bridge, Townhall, High, Church, Darling, Ann) as it runs the length of the town. Most shops are open Monday to Saturday 9:30am to 5:30pm.

The largest shopping complex in Enniskillen is the **Erneside Shopping Centre** (✆ **028/6632-5705;** www.ernesideshopping.com), a modern bi-level mall on Shore Road, just off Wellington Road. It stays open until 9pm on Thursday and Friday. The other principal towns for shopping in the area are **Irvinestown** and **Lisnaskea.**

The town's former butter market offers a nifty shopping experience. Dating from 1835, it has been restored and transformed into the **Buttermarket, Enniskillen Craft and Design Centre,** Down Street. There are various craft stores and workshops here, with occasional traditional music, craft fairs, and street theater to enliven the atmosphere.

Sports & Outdoor Pursuits

BICYCLING Several of the watersports and activity centers in the area, such as **Lakeland Canoe Centre** (see "Watersports," below), also rent bicycles. Bicycles are also available from **Corralea Activity Centre,** Belcoo

(✆ **028/6638-6123**), and **Belleek Bicycle Hire,** Belleek Cottages, Fermanagh (✆ **028/6865-81**). Daily bike rental runs around £7 to £10. For cycle tours with **Kingfisher Cycle Trail,** contact Pat Collum at the Tourist Information Centre, Wellington Road, Enniskillen (✆ **028/6632-3110;** www.cycletoursirelandkingfishercycletrail.com).

BIRD-WATCHING These lakelands are prime bird-watching territory. To mention a few, you'll find whooper swans, great-crested grebes, golden plovers, curlews, corncrakes, kingfishers, herons, merlins, peregrines, kestrels, and sparrow hawks. On Upper Lough Erne, the primary habitats are the reed swamps, flooded drumlins, and fen; on the lower lake, the habitats of choice are the less visited islands and the hay meadows. Two important preserves are at the Crom Estate (see "Seeing the Sights," above) and the Castlecaldwell Forest and Islands.

BOATING Lough Erne is an explorer's dream, and you can take that dream all the way to the Atlantic if you want. The price range for fully equipped, four- to eight-berth cruisers is around £700 to £1,135 per week, including VAT, depending on the season and the size of the boat. The many local cruiser-hire companies include **Erne Marine,** Bellanaleck (✆ **028/6634-8267** or 077/0812-7700), and **Carrickcraft,** Lurgan (✆ **028/3834-4993;** www.cruise-ireland.com).

On Lower Lough Erne, north of town, you can hire motorboats from **Manor House Marine,** Killadeas (✆ **028/6862-8100;** www.manormarine.com). Charges average £60 to £85 for a half-day, and £85 to £125 for a full day, depending on the size of the boat (maximum eight people). You'll have to pay a refundable deposit before heading out.

FISHING The **Fermanagh Lakes** are an angler's heaven. If you can't catch a fish here, you will really have to question your technique. The best time for salmon is February to mid-June; for trout, mid-March to June or mid-August until late September. As for coarse fishing, about a dozen species await your line in the area's lakes and rivers. If you've left time for advance planning and consultation, contact the **Fisheries Conservancy Board,** 1 Mahon Rd., Portadown (✆ **028/3833-4666**). For on-the-spot info, tackle, and bait, try **Trevor Kingston,** 18 Church St., Enniskillen (✆ **028/6632-2114**). For locally arranged game fishing, call or drop in on **Melvin Tackle,** Main Street, Garrison, County Fermanagh (✆ **028/6865-8194**). All necessary permits and licenses are available at the **Fermanagh Tourist Information Centre** (see "Visitor Information," p. 645).

GOLF There are two 18-hole courses in the Lakelands, both in Enniskillen. The **Enniskillen Golf Club,** in the Castle Coole estate (✆ **028/6632-5250;** www.enniskillengolfclub.com), charges greens fees of £20 weekdays, £25 weekends. The **Castle Hume Golf Club,** Castle Hume (✆ **028/6632-7077;** www.castlehumegolf.com), is 5km (3 miles) north of Enniskillen, with greens fees of £25 to £35 weekdays, £35 to £45 weekends, depending on the number of holes played.

HORSEBACK RIDING Pony trekking and riding lessons are available from **Drumhoney Stables,** Lisnarick (✆ **028/6862-1892**). There is also a large equestrian center at **Castle Leslie** (see "Where to Stay," below), where you can combine riding on the 400-hectare (1,000-acre) private estate with a stay at the castle or at its renovated Hunting Lodge.

WALKING The southwestern branch of the **Ulster Way** follows the western shores of Lough Erne, between the lake and the border. The area is full of great walks. One excellent 11km (6.75-mile; 3–7 hr.) hike is from a starting point near Florence Court and the Marble Arch Caves (see "Seeing the Sights," above) to the summit of **Mount Cuilcagh** (656m/2,152 ft.). A trail map is included in the Northern Ireland Tourist Board's *Information Guide to Walking.*

WATERSPORTS The **Lakeland Canoe Centre,** Castle Island, Enniskillen (✆ **028/43770714;** www.onegreatadventure.com), is a watersports center based on an island west of downtown. For a full day of canoeing and other sports, including archery, cycling, dinghy sailing, and windsurfing, prices start roughly at £15 per day. Camping and simple accommodations are also available at a modest cost. (***Note:*** at this writing the Centre was closed due to severe weather damage, though it's expected to be fully back up and running by 2012.) The **Share Holiday Village,** Smith's Strand, Lisnaskea (✆ **028/6772-2122;** www.sharevillage.org), offers sailing, canoeing, windsurfing, and banana skiing. Costs start at around £10 per person. Other watersports centers include the **Boa Island Activity Centre,** Tudor Farm, Kesh (✆ **028/6863-1943;** www.tudorfarm.com).

Where to Stay

EXPENSIVE

Castle Leslie ★★ 🎁 A stay here is one of Ireland's true luxuries, if you can afford it. The sprawling estate stretches over hundreds of acres, and curls around three lakes and through ancient hardwood forests. The manor house is as comfortable and elegant as a vintage Chanel slipper. Each guest room has unique features—a claw-foot tub in an alcove near the bed, a spectacular view in a bay window, or a four-poster bed—and all are named after former residents of the mansion. While there are a few luxurious guest rooms in the castle itself (at a premium, inevitably), most rooms are in the recently renovated **Hunting Lodge.** Rooms in this more modern building are stylish and comfortable, with lovely views of the grounds. If you prefer more privacy, you can rent a cottage on the estate (€320–€380 per night). If the excellent cuisine inspires you, there's a **cooking school** on-site.

Castle Leslie: A Piece of Irish History

Castle Leslie might just look like another posh castle hotel, but it's a little piece of Irish history, politics, and current events. This majestic place has welcomed a dazzling list of luminaries over the years, from historical figures (W. B. Yeats was a houseguest, and Winston Churchill was a cousin of the Leslie family); to celebrities (Paul McCartney and Heather Mills were married here in 2002). Because the owners were great collectors, it's a place of hidden treasures. Strolling around you'll wander past Wordsworth's harp, the Bechstein grand piano on which Wagner composed *Tristan and Isolde,* and Winston Churchill's baby clothes, among many other things.

Glaslough, County Monaghan. www.castleleslie.com. ✆ **047/88109.** Fax 047/88256. 30 units. €3,320–€5,120 double. Rates include all meals and most activities. MC, V. **Amenities:** 2 restaurants; bar; spa; tennis courts. *In room:* TV, hair dryer, Wi-Fi.

Manor House Country Hotel ☺ Dating from 1860, this three-story Victorian mansion has a varied history that includes a stint as a base for American forces during World War II. The public areas are decorated with antiques and ornate plasterwork, and from the windows you have lovely views of Lough Erne. Rooms are a bit dull but nice enough, furnished in traditional style, with darkwood furniture and big beds; a few have four-posters or half-canopy beds. This is a good option for families with children, as it has kid-friendly facilities including family rooms, a swimming pool, minigolf, and a supervised playroom.

Killadeas, Irvinestown, Enniskillen, County Fermanagh. www.manor-house-hotel.com. ✆ **028/6862-2200.** 81 units. £140–£150 double; £195–£325 suite. Rates include full breakfast. AE, MC, V. **Amenities:** Restaurant; 2 bars; supervised children's playroom; miniature golf; gym; indoor pool; sauna/steam room; beauty treatments; tennis court. *In room:* TV.

INEXPENSIVE

Belmore Court Motel If you're just looking for a bed on which to crash, this three-story motel has a variety of options at rock-bottom prices. It's the same motel principle as in the United States: bland decor, no amenities, but rates that you really can't beat. Most rooms have kitchenettes, and about a third of the units have two bedrooms or a suite setup of bedroom and sitting room. Some have kitchens. Guest rooms are nondescript but inoffensive, done in pastel colors, with standard furnishings in light wood, and writing desks. The motel is on the eastern edge of town, within walking distance of all the major sights and shops. There's also a 30-room budget **hotel** in the same complex.

Temp Rd., Enniskillen, County Fermanagh. www.motel.co.uk. ✆ **028/6632-6633.** Fax 028/6632-6362. 31 units. £65–£75 double; £95–£140 family room (up to 2 children, discounts for multiple-night stays.). Full breakfast £5; continental breakfast £3. AE, MC, V. *In room:* TV, kitchenette.

Where to Eat

Franco's ★ INTERNATIONAL Next to the Buttermarket in three converted and restored buildings once part of Enniskillen's working waterfront, this casual restaurant blends old-world ambience and the legacy of the sea with contemporary recipes and fresh local ingredients. The Italian-American menu includes plenty of pasta and pizza options, as well as alternatives including barbecue dishes and shish kabob.

Queen Elizabeth Rd., Enniskillen, County Fermanagh. ✆ **028/6632-4424.** www.francosrestaurant.co.uk. Reservations not accepted. Dinner main courses £9.50–£15. AE, MC, V. Mon–Sat noon–11pm; Sun noon–10:30pm. (Sept–Oct opens 5pm Mon–Tues.)

Snaffles Brasserie ★ BISTRO This surprisingly affordable restaurant at Castle Leslie's Hunting Lodge is a relaxed and elegant complement to this grand old estate. The contemporary, oak-beamed dining room looks out through huge windows over the estate. The cuisine is classic brasserie food with a hint of internationalism; the menu changes constantly but includes dishes such as filet of beef with mushroom and duck liver duxelles, puff pastry and Madeira *jus,* or pan-fried cod with cockles and mussels in garlic butter sauce. The children's menu (€12 for two courses) is simple and unpretentious.

Glaslough, County Monaghan. Drive through the center of Glaslough to castle gates. ✆ **047/88100.** www.castleleslie.com. Reservations required. Main courses €23–€35. AE, MC, V. Daily 5:30–9pm.

Enniskillen After Dark

Many or even most of the pubs and hotels in the area offer live entertainment, especially in the summer and on weekends.

If you're looking for Victorian style, try **Blakes of the Hollow ★**, 6 Church St., Enniskillen (✆ **028/6632-2143**). The pub opened in 1887 and has been in the Blake family ever since, retaining its original Victorian decor and ambience, with a long marble-topped mahogany bar and pinewood alcoves.

Check out what's on at the **Ardhowen Theatre,** Dublin Road, Enniskillen (✆ **028/6632-5440;** www.ardhowentheatre.com). Also known as the Theatre by the Lakes because of its enviable position overlooking Upper Lough Erne, this 300-seat theater presents a varied program of concerts, drama, cabaret, jazz, gospel, blues, and other modern music. Tickets run from around £10 to £20 for most performances; curtain time is usually 8pm.

PLANNING YOUR TRIP TO IRELAND

15

GETTING THERE

By Plane

About half of all visitors from North America arrive in Ireland on direct transatlantic flights to **Dublin Airport** (**DUB; ✆ 01/814-1111;** www.dublinairport.com), **Shannon Airport** (**SNN; ✆ 061/471369;** www.shannonairport.com), or **Belfast International Airport** (**BFS; ✆ 028/9448-4848;** www.belfastairport.com). The other half fly first into Britain or Europe, then backtrack into Ireland by air or sea.

In the Republic, there are seven smaller regional airports, all of which offer service to Dublin and several of which receive some (very limited) European traffic. They are Cork, Donegal, Galway, Kerry, Knock, Sligo, and Waterford. In Northern Ireland, the secondary airports are Belfast City Airport and Derry City Airport. Airline service to these smaller airports changes frequently, so be sure to consult your preferred airline or travel agent as soon as you begin to sketch your itinerary.

By Ferry

If you're traveling to Ireland from Britain or the Continent, traveling by ferry is a good alternative to flying. Several car and passenger ferries offer reasonably comfortable furnishings, cabin berths (for longer crossings), restaurants, duty-free shopping, and lounges.

Prices fluctuate seasonally and depend on your route, your time of travel, and whether you are on foot or in a car. It's best to check with your travel agent for up-to-date details, but just to give you an idea, the lowest one-way adult fare in high season on the cruise ferry from Holyhead to Dublin starts at around €30. A car usually costs €75 to €150.

Irish Ferries (www.irishferries.ie) operates from Holyhead, Wales, to Dublin, and from Pembroke, Wales, to Rosslare, County Wexford. For reservations, call **Scots-American Travel** (**✆ 800/247-7268** in the U.S.; www.scotsamerican.com) or **Irish Ferries** (**✆ 0870/517-1717** in the U.K., or 0818/300-400 in the Republic of Ireland; 353/818-300-400 in Northern Ireland; www.irishferries.com). **Stena Line** (**✆ 01/204-7777;** www.stenaline.com) sails from Holyhead to Dun Laoghaire, 13km (8 miles) south of Dublin; from Fishguard, Wales, to Rosslare; and from Stranraer, Scotland, to Belfast, Northern Ireland. **P&O Irish Sea Ferries** (**✆ 352/3420-808-294** in the U.S., 0871/664-2121 in Britain, or 01/407-3434 in Ireland; www.poferries.com) operates from Liverpool to Dublin and from Cairnryan, Scotland, to Larne, County Antrim, Northern Ireland.

GETTING AROUND

By Car

Although Ireland has a reasonably extensive network of public transportation, there are many advantages to having your own car there. Trains tend not to go to charming small towns and villages, and great houses and castles tend to be miles from any major town. Buses are slow and service to places off the beaten track can be infrequent.

PREVIOUS PAGE: **A hiker looks over the Atlantic from a green road in the Burren, County Clare.**

In the summer, weekly rental rates on a manual-transmission compact vehicle begin at around €160 and ascend steeply. Rates are much cheaper out of season.

Unless your stay in Ireland extends beyond 6 months, your own valid driver's license (provided you've had it for at least 6 months) is all you need to drive in Ireland. Rules and restrictions for car rental vary slightly and correspond roughly to those in other European nations and the U.S., with two important distinctions. Most rental-car agencies in the Republic won't rent to you (1) if you're 24 and under or 75 and over (there's no upper age limit in the North) or (2) if your license has been valid for less than a year.

DRIVING LAWS, TIPS & WARNINGS Highway safety has become a critical issue in Ireland during the past several years. The number of highway fatalities is high for such a small nation—Ireland is ranked as the second-most dangerous country in Europe in which to drive (second only to Greece). In an effort to rein in the Irish drivers, the Republic now uses a penalty "points" system similar to that in the U.K. and the U.S. While visitors won't have points added to their licenses, they may still be penalized with fines if they speed or commit driving infractions.

All distances and speed limits on road signs in the Republic of Ireland are in **kilometers,** while in Northern Ireland they are in **miles.** Take care if you're driving around the borderlands—the border is unmarked, so you can cross over from one side to the other without knowing it. It's easy to get confused and speed accidentally.

If you're not used to driving in rural areas on the left-hand side of the road, take precautions. Try to avoid driving after dark; stay off the road when driving conditions are compromised by rain, fog, or heavy traffic. Getting used to left-side driving, left-handed stick shift, narrow roads, and a new landscape are enough for the driver to manage, so it's helpful if you can have somebody along to navigate, or rent a GPS navigation device with your car—most major rental firms offer them.

Roundabouts (what Americans call traffic circles or rotaries) are found on most major roads and take a little getting used to. Remember always to yield to traffic coming from the right as you approach a roundabout and follow the traffic to the left, signaling before you exit the circle.

One signal that could be misleading to U.S. drivers is a flashing amber light at a pedestrian traffic light. This almost always follows a red light and it means yield to pedestrians, but proceed when the crossing is clear.

There are relatively few types of roads in the Republic. **National (N)** roads link major cities on the island. Though these are the equivalent of U.S. highways, they are rarely more than two lanes in each direction, and are sometimes as small as one U.S.-size lane. Most pass directly through towns, making cross-country trips longer than you'd expect. **Regional (R)** roads have one lane of traffic traveling in each direction, and generally link smaller cities and towns. Last are the rural or unclassified roads, often the most scenic back roads. These can be poorly signposted, very narrow, and a bit rough, but travel through beautiful countryside.

In the North, there are two **Major Motorways (M),** equivalent to interstates, as well as a network of lesser A- and B-level roads. Speed limits are posted.

ROAD RULES IN A nutshell

1. Drive on the left side of the road.
2. Road signs are in kilometers, except in Northern Ireland, where they are in miles.
3. On motorways, the left lane is the traveling lane. The right lane is for passing.
4. Everyone must wear a seat belt by law. Children must be in age-appropriate child seats.
5. Children 11 and under are not allowed to sit in the front seat.
6. When entering a roundabout (traffic circle), give way to traffic coming from the right.
7. The speed limits are 50kmph (31 mph) in urban areas; 80kmph (50 mph) on regional and local roads, sometimes referred to as non-national roads; 100kmph (62 mph) on national roads, including divided highways (called dual carriageways); and 120kmph (75 mph) on freeways (called motorways).

Both the North and the Republic have severe laws against drunk driving, and the legal blood alcohol limit is very low. Even one pint of beer can put you over the limit. The general rule is: Do not drink and drive.

RENTALS Try to make car-rental arrangements well in advance of your departure. Ireland is a small country, and in high season it can completely run out of rental cars—but before it does, it runs out of affordable rental cars. Discounts are common in the off season, of course, but it's also possible to negotiate a decent deal for July and August if you reserve in advance.

Major international car-rental firms are represented at airports and cities throughout Ireland and Northern Ireland. They include **Alamo-Treaty** (✆ 871/384-1086; www.goalamo.com), **Auto-Europe** (✆ 800/358-1229; www.autoeurope.com), **Avis** (✆ 21/428-1111 in Ireland; 800/230-4898 in the U.S.; www.avis.ie), **Budget** (✆ 90/662-7711; 800/527-0700 in the U.S.; www.budget.ie), **Hertz** (✆ 01/870-5777; 800/654-3001 in the U.S.; www.hertz.ie), **Murrays Europcar** (✆ 61/206086; 800/800-6000 in the U.S.; www.europcar.ie), **National** (✆ 800/227-7368 in the U.S.; www.nationalcar.com), **Payless** (✆ 800/729-5377 in the U.S.; www.paylesscar.com), and **Dan Dooley/Kenning Rent-a-Car** (✆ 62/53103; 800/331-9301 in the U.S.; www.dan-dooley.ie).

When comparing prices, always ask if the quoted rate includes the 13.5% government tax (VAT), the €15 airport pickup fee (assuming you pick up your car right upon arrival), CDW (collision damage waiver), and theft insurance. If you have your own auto insurance, you may be covered; check your existing policy before you pay for additional coverage you may not need. If you rent a car in the Republic, it is best to return it to the Republic, and if you rent it in the North, return it in the North. (Most firms charge extra for cross-border drop-offs.)

If you rent with a credit card that claims to provide free protection, be sure to call your card's customer service line to make certain there are no restrictions on that coverage in Ireland. Visa *does not* offer insurance protection for car rentals in Ireland. And MasterCard and American Express—even gold cards—have limited their protection on Irish rentals. Be certain that your information is current. Always confirm the details of your coverage when you charge your car rental to your credit card. If you are renting a car in the Republic and taking it into the North (or vice versa), be sure to ask the car-rental firm if the CDW and theft insurance covers cross-border transport. If not, you may be required to buy extra insurance.

PARKING You're better off without a car in Dublin. Traffic, a shortage of parking places, and one-way streets conspire to make you regret having wheels. In Dublin, virtually all streets are pay to park. Look for signs directing you to ticket machines; there should be one each block or so. Some larger towns also have multistory car parks; in central Dublin they average about €2 per hour and €23 for 24 hours.

By contrast, parking in most villages and small towns is easy and usually free. Look out for public parking lots—they're often free and are clearly marked at the edge of town centers.

In Belfast and other large cities in the North, some special security measures are always in place. Control zone signs indicate that no unattended vehicle can be left there at any time. That means if you are a single traveler, you cannot leave your car; if you are a twosome, one person must remain in the car while it's parked. Also, unlocked cars anywhere in the North are subject to a fine, for security reasons.

By Train

Iarnród Éireann (**Irish Rail;** ✆ **1850/366222** or 01/836-6222; www.irishrail.ie) operates the train services in Ireland. Train travel is generally the fastest way to get around the country. Most lines radiate from Dublin to other principal cities and towns. From Dublin, the journey time to Cork is 3 hours; to Belfast, 2 hours; to Galway, 3 hours; to Limerick, 2¼ hours; to Killarney, 4 hours; to Sligo, 3¼ hours; and to Waterford, 2¾ hours.

> **Ticket Talk**
>
> **When buying travel tickets—air, ferry, or train—ask for either a "single" (one-way) or a "return" (round-trip).**

Iarnród Éireann also offers an enticing array of weekend-to-weeklong holiday packages or **RailBreaks** to practically every corner of Ireland, north as well as south.

In addition to the Irish Rail service between Dublin and Belfast, **Translink** (✆ **028/9066-6630;** www.nirailways.co.uk) operates routes from Belfast that include Coleraine and Derry, in addition to virtually all 21 localities in Northern Ireland. The same organization runs the Belfast city service, called **Citybus.**

By Bus

Bus Éireann (✆ **01/836-6111;** www.buseireann.ie) operates an extensive system of express bus service, as well as local service, to nearly every town in Ireland. Express routes include Dublin to Donegal (4¼ hr.), Killarney to Limerick (2½ hr.), Limerick to Galway (2 hr.), and Limerick to Cork (2 hr.). The Bus Éireann website provides timetables and fares for bus service throughout Ireland.

Irish Rail Routes

MONEY-SAVING RAIL & BUS passes

For extensive travel by public transport, you can save money by purchasing a rail/bus pass or a rail-only pass. The options include the following:

- **Eurailpass:** Of the dozens of different Eurailpasses available, some are valid for unlimited rail travel in 17 European countries—but none include Britain or Northern Ireland. Other passes let you save money by selecting fewer countries. In the Irish Republic, the Eurailpass is good for travel on trains, Expressway coaches, and the Irish Continental Lines ferries between France and Ireland. Passes that let you travel throughout continental Europe and the Republic of Ireland, start at around €400 ($570) for 2 weeks of travel. The pass must be purchased 21 days before departure for Europe by a non–European Union resident. For further details or for purchase, call **Rail Pass Express** (✆ **800/722-7151;** www.eurail.com). It's also available from **STA Travel** (✆ **800/781-4040;** www.sta.com) and other travel agents.
- **BritRail Pass + Ireland:** Includes all rail travel throughout the United Kingdom and Ireland, including a round-trip ferry crossing on Stena Line. A pass is good for any 5 days of unlimited travel within a 30-day period. But they don't come cheap. Passes start at $450 and go up from there. They must be purchased before departure for Ireland or the United Kingdom from **BritRail** (✆ **866/BRITRAIL** [274-8724]; www.britrail.com).

Similarly, **Translink** provides detailed information on services within Northern Ireland (✆ **028/9066-6630;** www.nirailways.co.uk/atulsterbus.asp). Bus travel in both countries is affordable, reliable, and comfortable, but slow.

By Plane

Because Ireland is such a small country, it's unlikely you'll be flying from place to place within it. If you do need to get somewhere very quickly, the main domestic carrier is **Aer Arann** (✆ **818/210-210** in Ireland, 011/353-81821-0210 in the U.S., or 0800/587-23-24 in the U.K.; www.aerarann.com). It operates flights to airports in Dublin, Belfast, Cork, Derry, Donegal, Galway, Kerry, and Knock. **Aer Lingus** (✆ **818/365-000** in Ireland, 800/474-7424 in the U.S., or 0871/1718-5000 in the U.K.; www.aerlingus.com) also operates some domestic flights.

TIPS ON ACCOMMODATIONS

In this guide, we use our own system of zero to three stars for rating places to stay, based on quality of amenities, atmosphere, and the most subjective, overall value for money. Cost is only a factor inasmuch as it affects value. For example, an expensive hotel may rate only one star, while a moderately priced guesthouse rates two stars if it delivers an exceptional experience for the money. See the "Where to Stay" sections throughout this book for recommendations.

For even more information about staying in Ireland, *Be Our Guest* is a comprehensive guide to the hotels, country houses, castles, and inns of Ireland, published by the Irish Hotel Federation. It is available from the Irish Tourist Board.

Major Irish Bus Routes

It's also online at **www.irelandhotels.com**, which is a handy, searchable site, with options to sort hotels by feature (TV in all rooms, elevators, babysitting, and so on).

Those looking for something exclusive should try **Ireland's Blue Book** (www.irelands-blue-book.ie), which lists a collection of upscale manor house hotels and castles.

Bed & Breakfasts

You receive a personal touch when you stay in someone's home, and more often than not, this is a real bonus. For anyone on a budget who is touring the country and spending only a night or two in each location, B&Bs are often hard to beat.

While most B&Bs are regulated and inspected by Ireland's Tourism Quality Services (look for the shamrock seal of approval), many operate outside the regulation system. Those without governmental supervision or approval are not necessarily worse than those stamped with the green shamrock. Approval involves an annual fee and some restrictions that some B&B owners choose not to accept.

In the high season it's a good idea to make your reservation weeks in advance. However, you can often find a room at a B&B when you arrive out of season. In a moderately priced B&B, the average cost for a room with private bathroom is roughly €45 per person per night. Obviously, some B&Bs charge less than this, and some charge more. While each year more and more B&Bs accept credit cards, but many still do not—ask in advance.

In the North, the Northern Ireland Tourist Board inspects each of its recommended B&Bs annually. Its *Information Guide to Bed & Breakfast* is available free from the NITB. The NITB also sells a useful comprehensive annual listing titled *Where to Stay in Northern Ireland.*

Hidden Ireland

Hidden Ireland is essentially a collection of particularly elegant and unique B&Bs. These private houses offer you the opportunity to experience life in a castle or in a historic manor house, including some of Ireland's oldest and grandest buildings. Expect to pay anywhere from €150 to €345 a night for a double room in one of these places. To explore this option, contact the Hidden Ireland, PO Box 31, Westport, County Mayo (✆ **01/662-7166,** or 800/688-0299 in the U.S.; www.hidden-ireland.com).

Farmhouse B&Bs

Many of Ireland's small, family-run farms offer an inexpensive alternative to hotels and guesthouses, especially for families with small children. The **Irish Farm Holidays Association** (✆ **071/982-2222;** www.irishfarmholidays.com) produces an annual guide to farmhouse accommodations, and we've included a number in this guide.

Self-Catering

If you want to stay awhile and establish a base, you might consider renting an apartment, town house, or cottage. Self-catering is a huge business in Ireland, and the range on offer is impressive. The minimum rental period is usually 1 week, although shorter periods are negotiable in the off season. Families and small groups often find self-catering works out to be significantly less expensive than staying in hotels. However, in the high season, in both the Republic and the North, a cottage sleeping seven could cost anywhere from around €350 to more than €1,000 per week. Both Tourism Ireland and the Northern Ireland Tourist Board prepare helpful annual guides to self-catering cottages.

Among the self-catering companies worth checking out is **Trident Holiday Homes,** 15 Irishtown Rd., Irishtown, Dublin 4 (✆ **01/201-8440;** www.tridentholidayhomes.ie). For alluring seaside properties in west County Cork, try **Cashelfean Holiday Houses,** Durrus, County Cork (✆ **027/62000;** www.cashelfean.com). In the west of Ireland a selection of traditional Irish cottages, fully equipped to meet modern expectations, is offered by **Rent an Irish Cottage PLC,** 85 O'Connell St., Limerick, County Limerick (✆ **061/411109;** www.rentacottage.ie). Finally, for self-catering in the stunning countryside of Northern Ireland and Donegal, try **Cottages in Ireland** (✆ **028/9036-0500;** www.cottagesinireland.com).

Youth Hostels

Some Irish hostels are broadening their scope and redesigning to attract travelers of all ages, as well as families. Many have private rooms and, although they cost a fraction of even a modest bed-and-breakfast, quite a few are attractive and in extraordinarily beautiful locations. We've included the best of these in this guide.

AnÓige, the Irish Youth Hostel Association, 61 Mountjoy St., Dublin 7 (✆ **01/830-4555;** www.anoige.ie), runs dozens of exquisitely located hostels in Ireland, many of them in buildings of real character.

In the North, **YHANI** (Youth Hostels Association of Northern Ireland), 22–32 Donegall Rd., Belfast BT12 5JN (✆ **028/9032-4733;** www.hini.org.uk), runs similar hostels in often extraordinary locations.

The Bottom Line on Beds

RATES In recent years, as the Irish economy has crumbled, hotel prices have become more unstable. Generally there's been a downward trend in prices across the Republic and Northern Ireland. However, in the summer, prices can spike up and fall within the course of a week. We recommend booking well ahead to get the best prices. And please note that, especially in cities, if you book a month or two in advance, you can often get a better rate at a four-star hotel than at a two-star guesthouse. The most expensive hotels have been offering in-advance discounts of up to 70%. So before you book that cheap hotel with no services, just have a peek at your dream hotel's prices and see if it's not as cheap if not cheaper for at least some of your time in the country.

The price categories used throughout this guide indicate the cost of a double room for two per night, including tax but not service charges:

Very Expensive	€251 and up
Expensive	€176 to €250
Moderate	€100 to €175
Inexpensive	Under €100

Note: Many hotels span more than one of these categories, and in those cases, we've done our best to put them into the price category you're most likely to encounter on your visit.

Keys to the Castle

Dream of spending your vacation like a king or queen? Two companies specialize in self-catering accommodations in Ireland's historic and architecturally significant properties—including elegant Georgian manor houses, stately country mansions, lighthouses, and castles. The Irish Landmark Trust, 25 Eustace St., Dublin 2 (✆ 01/670-4733; www.irishlandmark.com), rescues historic but neglected properties all over the island and restores them into fabulous hideaways, complete with period furnishings. It's a not-for-profit institution, so prices are hard to beat. Elegant Ireland, 15 Harcourt St., Dublin 2 (✆ 01/473-2505; www.elegant.ie), can put you up in anything from an upscale seaside bungalow to a medieval castle that sleeps 20. As most properties are privately owned, they are priced according to what the market will bear. Bargains are harder to come by, and deals are more likely in the off season.

Some hotels and B&Bs list their prices per person, but we find that confusing so in this guide we've used the price a double room would cost for two people spending 1 night. If you're traveling on your own, expect to play slightly more than half the price of a double.

Children staying in their parent's room are usually charged at 20% to 50% of the adult rate.

TERMINOLOGY The Irish use the phrase "en suite" to indicate a room with private bathroom. A "double" has a double bed, and a "twin" has two single beds. An "orthopedic" bed has an extra-firm mattress. Queen- and king-size beds are not common except in large, deluxe hotels.

RESERVATIONS Foreign visitors to Ireland should always have at least their first night's room booked, as they will be required to give an address at Immigration when they arrive at the airport.

If you arrive in Ireland without a room reservation for some nights of your stay, and you're not sure where to look, try the local tourist office, which can help with its computerized reservation service known as **Gulliver.** In Ireland or Northern Ireland, you can also call the Gulliver line directly (✆ **00800/668-668-66**). This is a nationwide and cross-border "free-phone" facility for credit card bookings, operated 8am to 11pm from Monday to Friday, and 8am to 10pm weekends. Gulliver is also accessible from the United States (✆ **011-800/668-668-66**) and on the Web at **www.gulliver.ie**.

QUALITY & VALUE Despite the various systems of approval, regulation, and ratings, accommodations in Ireland are quite uneven in quality and cost. Often these variations are due to location; a wonderful, budget B&B in an isolated area of countryside can be dirt-cheap, while a mediocre guesthouse in Dublin or Cork can cost much more.

In any given lodging, the size and quality of the rooms can vary considerably, often without any corresponding variation in cost. This is particularly true of single rooms, which can approach Victorian boardinghouse standards in some guesthouses. Don't be discouraged by this, but know what you're getting into so you're not disappointed. If you have complaints, state them at once and unambiguously—doing so may bring an immediate resolution (ask for a lower rate or a better room).

Note: Many lodgings close for a few days or more on and around Christmas, even when they announce that they are open year-round. If you plan to visit Ireland during the Christmas holidays, double-check that the hotels, restaurants, and attractions you're counting on will be open.

[FastFACTS] IRELAND

Area Codes Area codes in Ireland range from one digit (the Dublin area code is "1") to three. Area codes are included in all listings in this guide. Within Ireland, you dial 0 before the area code. Outside of Ireland, however, you do not dial 0 before the area code.

Business Hours **Banks** are open 10am to 4pm Monday to Wednesday and Friday, and 10am to 5pm Thursday. **Post offices** (also known as **An Post**) in larger city centers are open from 9am to 5:30pm Monday to Friday and 9am to 1:30pm Saturday. The GPO on O'Connell Street in Dublin is open 8:30am to 6pm Monday to Saturday. Post offices in small towns often close for lunch from 1 to 2:30pm. **Museums and sights** are generally open 10am to 5pm Tuesday to Saturday and 2 to 5pm Sunday. **Shops** generally open 9am to 6pm Monday to Friday, with late opening on Thursday until 7 or 8pm, and Saturday from 10am to 5pm. In Dublin's city center, most department stores and many shops are open noon to 6pm Sunday.

In **Northern Ireland,** bank hours are Monday to Friday 9:30am to 4:30pm. Post offices are open 9:30am to 5:30pm Monday to Friday and Saturday 9am to 1pm. Some in smaller towns close for an hour at lunchtime. Shopping hours are much the same as in the Republic, with some smaller shops closing for an hour at lunchtime.

Car Rental See "By Car" under "Getting Around," earlier in this chapter.

Cellphones See "Mobile Phones," below.

Crime See "Safety," later in this section.

Disabled Travelers For travelers with disabilities, Ireland is a mixed bag. Its modern buildings and cities are generally accessible, but many of its buildings are historic, and those often lack wheelchair access. Trains can be accessed by wheelchairs but only with assistance. If you plan to travel by train in Ireland, be sure to check out Iarnród Éireann's website (www.irishrail.ie), which includes services for travelers with disabilities. A mobility-impaired liaison officer (✆ **01/703-3299**) can arrange assistance for travelers with disabilities if given 24-hour notice prior to the departure time.

If you're conducting research prior to your trip, one of the best Irish-based online resources is **www.disability.ie**.

For advice on travel to Northern Ireland, contact **Disability Action,** Portside Business Park, 189 Airport Rd. W., Belfast BT3 9ED (✆ **028/9029-7880;** www.disabilityaction.org). The Northern Ireland Tourist Board also publishes a helpful annual *Information Guide to Accessible Accommodation,* available from any of its offices worldwide.

Finding accessible lodging can be tricky in Ireland. Many of the buildings here are hundreds of years old, and older hotels, small guesthouses, and landmark buildings still have steps outside and in. The **National Rehabilitation Board of Ireland,** 24–25 Clyde Rd., Ballsbridge, Dublin 4 (✆ **01/608-0400**), publishes several guides to accessible guesthouses, the best of which is *Guide to Accessible Accommodation in Ireland*).

Many travel agencies offer customized tours and itineraries for travelers with disabilities. Among them are **Flying Wheels Travel** (✆ **507/451-5005;** www.flyingwheels travel.com), **Access-Able Travel Source** (✆ **303/232-2979;** www.access-able.com), and **Accessible Journeys** (✆ **800/846-4537** or 610/521-0339; www.disabilitytravel.com).

Doctors Healthcare in Ireland is comparable to that in other European nations. In the Irish system, private doctors and hospitals provide care and patients purchase healthcare insurance. Contact the **International Association for Medical Assistance to Travelers (IAMAT;** ✆ **716/754-4883,** or 416/652-0137 in Canada; www.iamat.org) for tips on health in Ireland, and for lists of doctors.

Drinking Laws You must be age 18 or over to be served alcoholic beverages in Ireland. Restaurants with liquor licenses are permitted to serve alcohol during the hours when meals are served. Hotels and guesthouses with licenses can serve during normal hours to the public; overnight guests, referred to as "residents," can be served after closing hours. Children are allowed in pubs that serve food during daylight hours. Alcoholic beverages by the bottle can be purchased at stores displaying OFF-LICENSE signs and at most supermarkets, but only during legal drinking hours. Ireland has very severe laws and penalties regarding driving while intoxicated, and the legal blood-alcohol limit is low—even one pint can put some people over the limit.

Driving Rules See "Getting Around," earlier in this chapter.

Electricity The Irish electric system operates on 220 volts with a plug bearing three rectangular prongs. The Northern Irish system operates on 240 volts. To use standard American 110-volt appliances, you'll need both a transformer and a plug adapter. Most new laptops have built-in transformers, but some do not, so beware. Attempting to use only a plug adapter is a sure way to fry your appliance or, worse, cause a fire.

Embassies & Consulates The **American Embassy** is at 42 Elgin Rd., Ballsbridge, Dublin 4 (✆ **01/668-8777**); the **Canadian Embassy** is at 7–8 Wilton Terrace, Third Floor, Dublin 2 (✆ **01/417-4100**); the **British Embassy** is at 29 Merrion Rd., Dublin 2 (✆ **01/205-3700**); and the **Australian Embassy** is at Fitzwilton House, Seventh Floor, Wilton Terrace, Dublin 2 (✆ **01/664-5300**). In addition, there is an **American Consulate** at Danesfort House, 223 Stranmillis Rd., Belfast BT9 5GR (✆ **028/9038-6100**).

Emergencies For the **Garda (police),** fire, ambulance, or other emergencies, dial ✆ **999.**

Family Travel To locate accommodations, restaurants, and attractions that are particularly kid-friendly, look for the "Kids" icon ☺ throughout this guide.

Gasoline In Ireland, gas is called petrol and it is sold by the liter. At press time, the cost of a liter of petrol was about €1.40, which means a gallon of gas was around €5.60.

Insurance For information on traveler's insurance, trip cancellation insurance, and medical insurance while traveling, please visit www.frommers.com/planning.

Internet & Wi-Fi Wi-Fi is widespread in Irish cities, but rural areas are still not well served. The best B&Bs do provide it, but in some far-flung areas (Donegal, the North, and parts of Galway) it's still quite rare in rural B&Bs, and even some four-star hotels. Internet cafes are less common than they used to be, although you'll still find PCs you can use in hotels, hostels, libraries, and tourist information offices, especially in larger towns and more tourist-centered areas.

Language Ireland has two official languages: English and Gaelic (which is also known as Irish). All native Irish can speak English. Gaelic is growing in popularity, and there is a strong national movement to preserve and expand use of the language. Areas of the country where Gaelic is protected and promoted are known as the **Gaeltacht** and include Donegal, Galway, and parts of Kerry. In these regions, signs are in Gaelic only (no English translation is provided). As Gaelic is a complex and ancient language that you will not be able to figure out on your own, don't hesitate to ask for help (in English) if you get lost—despite the government's best efforts, everybody in Gaeltacht regions speaks English.

LGBT Travelers Ireland has come a long way since homosexuality was legalized in 1993 (1982 in the North), but gay and lesbian visitors should be aware that this is still a deeply conservative country. With rare exceptions, gay communities are low-key, and even in such ostensibly liberal places as Dublin and Galway, gay bashing is not unheard of. Things have improved a great deal, but proceed with caution.

There's a burgeoning gay community in Dublin. The *Gay Community News (GCN),* a monthly free newspaper of comprehensive Irish gay-related information, is available in gay venues and bookshops. *In Dublin,* the city's leading event listings guide, dedicates several pages to gay events, club info, and a helpful directory. Two small magazines have recently emerged—*Free!* and *Scene City*—and both contain city maps with gay venues highlighted.

Among the best resources on the Web are **Gay Ireland Online** (www.gay-ireland.com) and **Outhouse** (www.outhouse.ie). These include events listings, advice sections, useful contacts, and discussion forums.

Mail In Ireland, mailboxes are painted green with the word POST on top. In Northern Ireland, they usually look the same but are painted red, with a royal coat of arms symbol. From the Republic, an airmail letter or postcard to the United States or Canada, not exceeding 25 grams, costs €.85 and takes 5 to 7 days to arrive. From Northern Ireland to the United States or Canada, airmail letters not exceeding 20 grams cost 97p and postcards 50p and also take about 5 to 7 days.

Mobile Phones The three letters that define much of the world's wireless capabilities are GSM (Global System for Mobiles), a big, seamless network that makes for easy cross-border cellphone use throughout Europe and dozens of other countries worldwide. In the U.S., T-Mobile and AT&T Wireless use this quasi-universal system; in Canada, Microcell and some Rogers customers are GSM, and all Europeans and most Australians use GSM.

If your cellphone is on a GSM system, and you have a world-capable multiband phone, you can make and receive calls while you're in Ireland. Just call your wireless operator and ask for "international roaming" to be activated on your account. Unfortunately, per-minute charges can be very high. Other options include **renting** a phone in Ireland. You can either rent a phone from any number of overseas sites, including kiosks at airports and at car-rental agencies, or rent one before you leave home.

As another option, you can purchase a "pay as you go" SIM card from an Irish phone company and use that in your own phone, topping it up whenever you need to. There's a Vodafone shop in Dublin airport where you can purchase an Irish SIM card. This allows you to pay in-country rather than international rates for calls you receive while you're there.

Disposable phones are less common in Ireland and the U.K. than in some other countries, although some supermarkets do sell them.

If you buy a disposable phone or an Irish SIM card, local calls may be as low as 10¢ per minute, and in Ireland incoming calls are free.

Money & Costs The Republic of Ireland uses the single European currency known as the **euro** (€). Euro notes come in denominations of €5, €10, €20, €50, €100, €200, and €500. The euro is divided into 100 cents; coins come in denominations of €2, €1, 50¢, 20¢, 10¢, 5¢, 2¢, and 1¢.

As part of the United Kingdom, Northern Ireland uses the British **pound sterling** (£). The British pound is not accepted in the Republic, and the euro is not accepted in the North—if you're traveling in both parts of Ireland, you'll need some of both currencies, although shops right on the border tend to accept both. For those traveling between Great Britain and Northern Ireland, although the pounds issued in Northern Ireland are legal tender in Great Britain and vice versa, the paper money actually *looks* different, and you may find that cabdrivers and small business owners in the North won't accept bills issued in Great Britain and vice versa. In that case, you can change the money into locally issued versions at any large central bank, free of charge.

The British currency used in Northern Ireland has notes in denominations of £5, £10, £20, £50, and £100. Coins are issued in £2, £1, 50p, 20p, 10p, 5p, 2p, and 1p denominations.

Note for all international travelers: The values of most currencies have been fluctuating a great deal lately, so it is best to begin checking exchange rates well in advance of your visit to get a feel for where they will stand for your trip.

The easiest and best way to get cash away from home is from an ATM (automated teller machine), sometimes referred to as a "cash machine" or a "cashpoint." The **Cirrus** and **PLUS** ATM networks span the globe; look at the back of your bank card to see which network you're on. Be sure you know your personal identification number (PIN) and daily withdrawal limit before you depart. ***Note:*** Remember that many banks impose a fee every time you use a card at another bank's ATM, and that fee can be higher for international transactions (up to $5 or more). In addition, the bank from which you withdraw cash may charge its own fee. For international withdrawal fees, ask your bank.

Large towns usually have an ATM, but in rural counties—especially Galway, Clare, and Limerick—ATMs can be few and far between. We once drove 50 miles looking for an ATM in Clare before finally finding one, so stock up on cash if you're headed out to the countryside. If you're having difficulty locating an ATM, some convenience stores have their own (usually indicated by a sign outside), although these usually incur an extra charge of a couple of euros.

Most Republic and Northern Ireland ATMs accept PINs of four to six digits, but they often do not have alphanumeric keypads. If your PIN features letters (for example: STAN37), use a telephone dial to figure out the numeric equivalents (or better yet, memorize it before you leave home).

THE VALUE OF THE EURO VS. OTHER POPULAR CURRENCIES

Euro €	US$	C$	UK£	A$	NZ$
1.00	1.40	1.35	.85	1.35	1.90

Frommer's lists exact prices in the local currency. The currency conversions quoted above were correct at press time. However, rates fluctuate, so before departing consult a currency exchange website such as **www.oanda.com/currency/converter** to check up-to-the-minute rates.

WHAT THINGS COST IN IRELAND	EURO €
Taxi from the airport to Dublin	20–30.00
Double room, moderate	100–200.00
Double room, inexpensive	50–100.00
Cup of coffee	2.25
Pint of beer	3.50
Movie ticket	8.50
Bus fare	1.20
Moderate three-course meal for one	30.00
Gallon of gas	5.60

Credit cards are another safe way to carry money. They also provide a convenient record of all your expenses, and they generally offer relatively good exchange rates. You can withdraw cash advances from your credit cards at banks or ATMs, provided you know your PIN. Keep in mind that you'll pay interest from the moment of your withdrawal, even if you pay your monthly bills on time. Also, note that many banks now assess a 1% to 3% "transaction fee" on **all** charges you incur abroad (whether you're using the local currency or your native currency). Visa and MasterCard are the most widely accepted credit cards in Ireland. American Express and Diners Club are accepted by most major hotels, but are less commonly accepted elsewhere. Cards are widely accepted at shops and restaurants, although small rural businesses and some B&Bs do not accept them.

Traveler's checks are not widely accepted in Ireland. You'll probably have to change the checks at a bank and pay a fee for the privilege. That said, the most popular traveler's checks are offered by **American Express** (✆ **800/807-6233** or 800/221-7282 for cardholders—this number accepts collect calls, offers service in several languages, and exempts Amex gold and platinum cardholders from the 1% fee), **Visa** (✆ **1800-411-055** toll-free in Ireland), and **MasterCard** (✆ **800/622-7747**).

For help with currency conversions, tip calculations, and more, download Frommer's convenient Travel Tools app for your mobile device. Go to www.frommers.com/go/mobile and click on the "Travel Tools" icon.

Newspapers & Magazines The *Irish Independent* is the country's bestselling newspaper, and it's published daily (**www.independent.ie**). Other major daily newspapers include the *Irish Examiner* and the *Irish Times.* The *Dubliner Magazine* is a slick, monthly news and entertainment magazine with listings, arts and culture information, and a useful website (**www.thedubliner.ie**). In *Dublin Magazine* (**www.indublin.ie**) is a popular arts-and-entertainment listings magazine.

Passports See **www.frommers.com/planning** for current discussions and news about passports. See "Embassies & Consulates," above, for whom to contact if you lose yours while traveling in Ireland. For additional, country-specific information, please contact the following agencies:

For Residents of Australia Contact the **Australian Passport Information Service** at ✆ **131-232,** or visit the government website at www.passports.gov.au.

For Residents of Canada Contact the central **Passport Office,** Department of Foreign Affairs and International Trade, Ottawa, ON K1A 0G3 (✆ **800/567-6868;** www.ppt.gc.ca).

For Residents of New Zealand Contact the **Passports Office** at ✆ **0800/225-050** in New Zealand or 04/474-8100, or log on to www.passports.govt.nz.

For Residents of the United Kingdom Visit your nearest passport office, major post office, or travel agency or contact the **United Kingdom Passport Service** at ✆ **0870/521-0410** or search its website at www.ukpa.gov.uk.

For Residents of the United States To find your regional passport office, either check the U.S. State Department website (**www.state.gov**) or call the **National Passport Information Center** toll-free number (✆ **877/487-2778**) for automated information.

Petrol Please see "Gasoline," p. 666.

Police In the Republic of Ireland, a law enforcement officer is called a **Garda,** a member of the *Garda Síochána* ("Guardian of the Peace"); in the plural, it's **Gardaí** (pronounced *Gar*-dee) or simply "the Guards." Dial ✆ **999** to reach the Gardaí in an emergency. Except for special detachments, Irish police are unarmed and wear dark blue uniforms. In Northern Ireland you can also reach the police by dialing ✆ **999.**

Safety By U.S. standards, Ireland is very safe, but, particularly in the cities, it's not safe enough to warrant carelessness. Travelers should take normal precautions to protect their belongings from theft and themselves from harm. In the countryside, you're unlikely to encounter any problems with crime, but keep valuables in the trunk of your car all the same. In Dublin and Belfast, you'll need to be wary of the usual tourists' plague: pickpockets, purse snatchers, and car thieves. Also, in recent years, some of Dublin's busiest thoroughfares have been the scenes of brutal attacks at night. To alert visitors to potential dangers, the Dublin Police (called the **Garda**) publish a small leaflet, *A Short Guide to Tourist Security,* which is available at tourist offices and other public places. The booklet advises you not to carry large amounts of money or important documents like your passport or airline tickets when strolling around.

Most advice is standard for travel anywhere: Do not leave cars unlocked or cameras, binoculars, or other expensive equipment unattended. Take special care if you'll be out in Dublin late at night when the pubs and nightclubs close. Ask at your hotel which areas are safe and which are not. Take a taxi back to your hotel if you're out after about 11pm.

In Northern Ireland, safety has to be a somewhat greater concern because of the political unrest that has prevailed there for the past 30 years, but violence has diminished. Occasionally flare-ups do happen, and there were a number of incidents in 2011. Outbreaks of violence often occur during the Orange marching season in the late summer. Still, visitors rarely, if ever, have problems with sectarian strife, since they are simply not the target of it.

Senior Travel Mention the fact that you're a senior when you first make your travel reservations—although most of the major U.S. airlines have canceled their senior discount and coupon book programs, many hotels still offer discounts for seniors. In most cities, people over the age of 60 qualify for reduced admission to theaters, museums, and other attractions.

Seniors, known throughout Ireland as **OAPs** (old-age pensioners), enjoy a variety of discounts and privileges. Native OAPs ride the public transport system free of charge, but the privilege does not extend to tourists. Visiting seniors can avail themselves of other discounts, though, particularly on admission to attractions and theaters. Always ask about an OAP discount if special rates are not posted.

Tourism Ireland is helpful, and can offer advice on how to find the best accommodations, travel, and so forth. It publishes lists of reduced-rate hotel packages for seniors; contact it for details.

Members of **AARP** (formerly known as the American Association of Retired Persons), 601 E St. NW, Washington, DC 20049 (✆ **888/687-2277;** www.aarp.org), get discounts on hotels, airfares, and car rentals. AARP offers members a wide range of benefits, including *AARP The Magazine* and a monthly newsletter. Anyone 50 and over can join. Similarly, **SAGA Tours** (✆ **800/343-0273** or 617/262-2262) operates tours to Ireland specifically geared to seniors or anyone 50 and over.

Smoking Ireland and Northern Ireland both have broad antismoking laws that ban smoking in all public places, including bars, restaurants, and hotel lobbies. However, most restaurants and pubs have covered outdoor smoking areas.

Student Travel If you're interested in studying here, contact your university to find out if it has a partnership program in Ireland. To get basic info on whether or not you need a student visa and how to get one, get in touch with the Irish Department of Foreign Affairs Visa Section, Hainault House, 69–71 St. Stephen's Green, Dublin (✆ **01/478-0822**). U.S. firms offering educational travel programs to Ireland include Academic Travel Abroad (✆ **800/523-4293;** www.academictravel.com) and North American Institute for Study Abroad (✆ **570/275-5099**).

If you do spend a semester or two in Ireland, contact the Union of Students in Ireland Travel (✆ **01/602-1906;** www.usit.ie). It's great for arranging travel from and around Ireland at the cheapest rates. Its notice boards are filled with flat shares, language classes, jobs, and cheap flights.

If you're looking for less structured knowledge, try spending a week in Glencolmcille, County Donegal, studying the Irish (Gaelic) language, dancing, archaeology, Celtic pottery, or tapestry weaving at Oideas Gael (✆ **074/973-0248;** www.oideas-gael.com).

If you're traveling internationally, you'd be wise to arm yourself with an **International Student Identity Card (ISIC),** which offers substantial savings on rail passes, plane tickets, and entrance fees. It also provides you with basic health and life insurance and a 24-hour helpline. The card is available from **STA Travel** (✆ **800/781-4040** in North America; www.sta.com or www.statravel.com, or www.statravel.co.uk in the U.K.), the biggest student travel agency in the world. If you're no longer a student but are still age 25 or under, you can get an **International Youth Travel Card (IYTC)** from the same people, which entitles you to some discounts (but not on museum admissions). **Travel CUTS** (✆ **800/592-2887** in the U.S. or 1866/246-9762 in Canada; www.travelcuts.com) offers similar services for both Canadians and U.S. residents. Irish students may prefer to turn to **USIT** (✆ **01/602-1906;** www.usit.ie), an Ireland-based specialist in student, youth, and independent travel.

Taxes As in many European countries, sales tax is called VAT (value-added tax) and is often already included in the price quoted to you or shown on price tags. In the Republic, VAT rates vary—for hotels, restaurants, and car rentals, it is 13.5%; for souvenirs and gifts, it is 21%. In Northern Ireland, the VAT is 20% across the board. VAT charged on services such as hotel stays, meals, car rentals, and entertainment cannot be refunded to visitors, but the VAT on products such as souvenirs is refundable.

Telephones In the Republic, the telephone system is known as Eircom; in Northern Ireland, it's British Telecom. Every effort has been made to ensure that the numbers and information in this guide are accurate at the time of writing. **Overseas calls** from Ireland can be quite costly, whether you use a local phone card or your own calling card.

To call Ireland from home: Dial the international access code (011 from the U.S., 00 from the U.K., 0011 from Australia, or 0170 from New Zealand). Then dial the country code (353 for the Republic, 44 for the North). Next, dial the local number, remembering to omit the initial 0, which is for use only within Ireland (for example, to call the County Kerry number 066/12345 from the United States, you'd dial 011-353-66/12345).

To make local calls: To dial a local number within an area code, drop the initial 0. To dial a number within Ireland, but in a different area code, use the initial 0. Local calls from a phone booth require a Callcard (in the Republic) or Phonecard (in the North). Both are prepaid computerized cards that you insert into the phone instead of coins. They can be purchased in a range of denominations at phone company offices, post offices, and many retail outlets (such as newsstands). There's a local and international phone center at the General Post Office on O'Connell Street in Dublin.

To make **international calls** from within Ireland, first dial 00 and then the country code (U.S. and Canada 1, U.K. 44, Australia 61, New Zealand 64). Next you dial the area code and local number. For example, to call the U.S. number 212/000-0000 from Ireland, you'd dial ✆ 00-1-212/000-0000. The toll-free international access code for **AT&T** is ✆ 1-800-550-000, for **Sprint** it's ✆ 1-800-552-001, and for **MCI** it's ✆ 1-800-55-1001. ***Note:*** To dial direct to Northern Ireland from the Republic, simply replace the 028 prefix with 048.

For **directory assistance,** dial the toll-free number ✆ **11811** if you're looking for a number inside Ireland. In Northern Ireland, try ✆ **118888.** From the United States, the (toll) number to call is ✆ **00353-91-770220.**

Time Ireland follows Greenwich Mean Time (1 hr. earlier than Central European Time) from November to March, and British Summer Time (the same as Central European Time) from April to October. Ireland is 5 hours ahead of the eastern United States. Ireland's latitude makes for longer days and shorter nights in the summer, and the reverse in the winter. In June, the sun doesn't fully set until around 11pm, but in December, it is dark by 4pm.

Tipping For porters or bellhops, tip €1 per piece of luggage. For taxi drivers, hairdressers, and other providers of service, tip as you would at home, an average of 10% to 15%.

For restaurants, the policy is usually printed on the menu—either a gratuity of 10% to 12% is automatically added to your bill or it's left up to you. Always ask if you are in doubt. As a rule, bartenders do not expect a tip, except when table service is provided.

Toilets Public restrooms are usually simply called "toilets" or are marked with international symbols. In the Republic of Ireland, some of the older ones still carry the Gaelic words FIR (MEN) and MNA (WOMEN). Among the newest and best-kept restrooms are those found at shopping malls and department stores. Free restrooms are available to customers of sightseeing attractions, museums, hotels, restaurants, pubs, shops, and theaters. Most of the newer gas stations (called "petrol stations" in Ireland) have public toilets, and a few have baby-changing facilities.

VAT See "Taxes," on p. 671.

Visas Citizens of the United States, Canada, Australia, and New Zealand entering the Republic of Ireland or Northern Ireland for a stay of up to 3 months do not need a visa, but a valid **passport** is required.

For citizens of the United Kingdom, when traveling on flights originating in Britain, the same rules apply as they would for travel to any other member state of the European Union (E.U.).

For information about Irish Visas go to **http://travel.state.gov** and click on "Visas." If you have any doubts about your eligibility, contact the Irish Embassy in your home country. A full list of countries who qualify for the Irish Visa waiver program can be found by going to **www.citizensinformation.ie** and clicking on "Travel and Recreation," "Travel to Ireland," then "Visas for Tourists Visiting Ireland."

Water Tap water throughout the island of Ireland is generally safe. However, some areas in the west of Ireland have been battling with out-of-date water-purification systems. This is rare, but keep an eye out for signs warning you that water is not drinkable, and always carry a large bottle of water with you.

Wi-Fi See "Internet & Wi-Fi," earlier in this section.

Women Travelers Women should expect few if any problems traveling in Ireland. Women are accepted traveling alone or in groups in virtually every environment, and gone are the days when women were expected to order half-pints of beer in pubs, while men were allowed to order the bigger, more cost-effective pints of ale. In fact, the only time you're likely to attract any attention at all is if you eat alone in a restaurant at night—a sight that is still relatively uncommon in Ireland outside of the major cities. Even then, you'll not be hassled.

If you drink in a pub on your own, though, expect all kinds of attention, as a woman drinking alone is still considered to be on the market—even if she's reading a book, talking on her cellphone to her fiancé, or doing a crossword puzzle. So be prepared to fend them off. Irish men almost always respond well to polite rejection, though.

In cities, as ever, take a cab home at night, and follow all the usual advice of caution you get when you travel anywhere. Essentially, don't do anything in Ireland that you wouldn't do at home.

Index

C

D

H

I

J

N

O

P

T

U

Y

Accommodations

Restaurants

Pubs

Photo Credits

p. i: © Wojtek Buss / AGE Fotostock; p. iii, iv, v, vi: © Anthony Woods; p. 1: © nagelestock.com / Alamy; p. 2: © Photolibrary; p. 3: © Dennis Flaherty / Alamy; p. 6: © Michael McLaughlin; p. 7, top: © Grianne Flynn; p. 7, bottom: © Arco Images GmbH / Alamy; p. 8: © The Irish Image Collection / AGE Fotostock; p. 9: © Declan Masterson; p. 11, left: © Anthony Woods; p. 11, right: © Adafir / Alamy; p. 12: © Anthony Woods; p. 13: © Grianne Flynn; p. 14: © Michael McLaughlin; p. 15: © Mira / Alamy; p. 16: © The Irish Image Collection / AGE Fotostock; p. 17, top: © Courtesy Park Hotel Kenmare; p. 17, bottom: © Courtesy Gregans Castle; p. 19: © Courtesy Temple House; p. 20: © Anthony Woods; p. 21, left: © Courtesy Ballymaloe House, Photo by Keewi Photography; p. 21, right: © Stefano Lunardi / Marka / AGE Fotostock; p. 22: © Anthony Woods; p. 23, left: © Michael McLaughlin; p. 23, right: © Michael McLaughlin; p. 23, bottom: © Stephen Rafferty / Eye Ubiquitous / Alamy; p. 25: © Stephen Emerson / Alamy; p. 26: © Courtesy the Merchant Hotel; p. 29: © Michael McLaughlin; p. 30: © Michael McLaughlin; p. 31: © Ancient Art & Architecture Collection Ltd / Alamy; p. 35: © Victor Ginesi; p. 39: © 19th era / Alamy; p. 42: © An Post/Maxwell Photography; p. 44, left: © Carl Mydans//Time Life Pictures/Getty Images; p. 44, right: © Barry Batchelor / AFP / Newscom; p. 47: © Vivi Film/Cartoon Saloon / The Kobal Collection; p. 48: © James Horan; p. 49: © Stefano Lunardi / Marka / AGE Fotostock; p. 50: © Stephen Rafferty / Eye Ubiquitous / Alamy; p. 58: © The Irish Image Collection / AGE Fotostock; p. 62: © James Horan; p. 64: © Anthony Woods; p. 65: © Anthony Woods; p. 67: © Michael McLaughlin; p. 68: © Michael McLaughlin; p. 72: © Victor Ginesi; p. 73: © Michael McLaughlin; p. 76, left: © James Horan; p. 76, right: © Anthony Woods; p. 78: © James Horan; p. 80: © Richard Cummins / The Irish Image Collection / AGE Fotostock; p. 81: © Anthony Woods; p. 82: © Peter McCabe / The Irish Image Collection / AGE Fotostock; p. 84: © Anthony Woods; p. 86: © Gareth McCormack / Lonely Planet Images; p. 87: © Hon F. Lau / Alamy; p. 89, top: © Michael McLaughlin; p. 89, bottom: © Grianne Flynn; p. 92: © Michael McLaughlin; p. 93: © Michael McLaughlin; p. 98: © Michael McLaughlin; p. 99: © Anthony Woods; p. 105: © James Horan; p. 106, top: © James Horan; p. 106, bottom: © James Horan; p. 107: © James Horan; p. 141: © The Print Collector / Alamy; p. 145: © James Horan; p. 146: © James Horan; p. 147, left: © James Horan; p. 147, right: © James Horan; p. 148, left: © Anthony Woods; p. 148, right: © Jim Cole / Alamy; p. 151, top: © James Horan; p. 151, bottom: © Anthony Woods; p. 153: © James Horan; p. 154, left: © James Horan; p. 154, right: © Howard Davies / Alamy; p. 157: © James Horan; p. 159: © An Post/Maxwell Photography; p. 160: © James Horan; p. 162: © Anthony Woods; p. 166: © James Horan; p. 169: © Anthony Woods; p. 171: © Anthony Woods; p. 172: © James Horan; p. 176: © James Horan; p. 177: © James Horan; p. 178: © James Horan; p. 180: © Anthony Woods; p. 183: © Anthony Woods; p. 184: © Anthony Woods; p. 185: © Courtesy of The Clarence Hotel; p. 188: © Courtesy Abbey Theatre, Photo by Ros Kavanagh; p. 192: © Anthony Woods; p. 195: © Anthony Woods; p. 196: © Anthony Woods; p. 197, top: © Anthony Woods; p. 197, bottom: © Anthony Woods; p. 200: © Anthony Woods; p. 202: © Anthony Woods; p. 204: © Anthony Woods; p. 207: © Anthony Woods; p. 209: © Anthony Woods; p. 210: © Anthony Woods; p. 211: © Anthony Woods; p. 213, top: © Anthony Woods; p. 213, bottom: © Anthony Woods; p. 223: © Anthony Woods; p. 231: © Jim Cole / Alamy; p. 232: © Declan Masterson; p. 237: © Anthony Woods; p. 240: © Anthony Woods; p. 244: © Anthony Woods; p. 246: © Anthony Woods; p. 252, top: © Anthony Woods; p. 252, bottom: © Anthony Woods; p. 254: © Anthony Woods; p. 261: © David Lyons / Alamy; p. 266: © Richard Cummins / SuperStock; p. 274: © K. Loos / Arco Images GmbH / Alamy; p. 276: © Anthony Woods; p. 279: © isifa Image Service s.r.o. / Alamy; p. 280: © J. De Meester / Arco Images GmbH / Alamy; p. 281: © Kevin Schafer / Alamy; p. 288: © Christopher Gallagher / The Garden Picture Library / Alamy; p. 290: © Adina Tovy / Robert Harding Picture Library Ltd / Alamy; p. 301: © Anthony Woods; p. 302: © Anthony Woods; p. 303, top: © Rick Senley / Loop Images / Photolibrary; p. 303, bottom: © Anthony Woods; p. 304: © Richard Cummins / The Irish Image Collection / AGE Fotostock; p. 309: © Christian Handl / Imagebroker / AGE Fotostock; p. 311: © Anthony Woods; p. 313: © Liam White / Alamy; p. 315: © Anthony Woods; p. 319: © Michael Leonhard / Alamy; p. 321: © Courtesy Ballymaloe Cookery School; p. 322: © Anthony Woods; p. 323, left: © Enzo Cositore / Alamy; p. 323, right: © Courtesy Ballymaloe House, Photo by Keewi Photography; p. 327: © Anthony Woods; p. 330: © Anthony Woods; p. 331: © The Irish Image Collection / SuperStock ; p. 340: © H. & D. Zielske / Look / Alamy; p. 342: © Anthony Woods; p. 348: © David Lyons / Alamy; p. 349: © David Lyons / Alamy; p. 350: © Anthony Woods; p. 354: © Anthony Woods; p. 356: © Anthony Woods; p. 358:

© Andrew McConnell / Alamy; p. 366: © Courtesy Park Hotel Kenmare; p. 371: © Anthony Woods; p. 372: © Anthony Woods; p. 376, top: © Courtesy Dingle Oceanworld Aquarium; p. 376, bottom: © Anthony Woods; p. 378: © Anthony Woods; p. 379: © Anthony Woods; p. 380: © Gareth McCormack / Alamy; p. 381: © Lilian Henglein / Cultura RM / Alamy; p. 382: © Frank van der Zwan / Alamy; p. 387: © Anthony Woods; p. 392: © Ingolf Pompe / Look / AGE Fotostock; p. 396: © Avico Ltd / Alamy; p. 397: © Anthony Woods; p. 404: © Anthony Woods; p. 418: © nagelestock.com / Alamy; p. 420: © Michael McLaughlin; p. 432: © Robert Knight/ Eye Ubiquitous / Alamy Images; p. 433: © Michael McLaughlin; p. 434, top: © Michael McLaughlin; p. 434, bottom: © Michael McLaughlin; p. 435: © Courtesy Aillwee Caves; p. 438: © Michael McLaughlin; p. 440, left: © Michael McLaughlin; p. 440, right: © Michael McLaughlin; p. 442, top: © Michael McLaughlin; p. 442, bottom: © Courtesy Lahinch Surf School; p. 444: © Blaine Harrington III / Alamy; p. 446: © The Irish Image Collection / AGE Fotostock; p. 448: © Michael McLaughlin; p. 452: © Michael McLaughlin; p. 454: © Michael McLaughlin; p. 456: © Courtesy Volvo Ocean Race, Photo by Rick Tomlinson; p. 463: © The Irish Image Collection/Design Pics/ Newscom; p. 467: © Steppenwolf / Alamy Images; p. 468: © Courtesy Druid Theatre, Photo by Robert Day; p. 469: © Michael McLaughlin; p. 470: © Michael McLaughlin; p. 471: © Michael McLaughlin; p. 474: © Michael McLaughlin; p. 475: © Michael McLaughlin; p. 476: © Michael McLaughlin; p. 480: © Alberto Paredes / Alamy; p. 487: © Grianne Flynn; p. 494: © The Irish Image Collection / AGE Fotostock; p. 496: © David Lyons / Alamy; p. 498: © Michael McLaughlin; p. 499, top: © Michael McLaughlin; p. 499, bottom: © Michael McLaughlin; p. 500: © Michael McLaughlin; p. 503: © The Irish Image Collection / AGE Fotostock; p. 505: © Michael McLaughlin; p. 506: © Gareth McCormack / Alamy; p. 514: © Michael McLaughlin; p. 515: © Michael McLaughlin; p. 516: © Michael McLaughlin; p. 517: © Michael McLaughlin; p. 518: © Michael McLaughlin; p. 519: © Michael McLaughlin; p. 527: © Courtesy Stroketown Park; p. 530: © David Lyons / Alamy; p. 532: © Grianne Flynn; p. 534: © Grianne Flynn; p. 536: © Grianne Flynn; p. 537: © Grianne Flynn; p. 538: © Grianne Flynn; p. 544: © Michael McLaughlin; p. 548: © Grianne Flynn; p. 551: © Grianne Flynn; p. 558: © Tony Lilley / Alamy; p. 559: © Michael Foyle / Alamy; p. 562: © Britain on View / Photolibrary; p. 572: © Victor Ginesi; p. 574: © Victor Ginesi; p. 576: © Victor Ginesi; p. 577: © Victor Ginesi; p. 579: © Victor Ginesi; p. 580: © Steffan Hill / Alamy; p. 581: © Peter Evans / Alamy; p. 582: © Courtesy National Museums Northern Ireland; p. 593: © H & D Zielske / Look-foto / Photolibrary; p. 595: © Victor Ginesi; p. 596: © Victor Ginesi; p. 598: © Victor Ginesi; p. 608: © J Orr / Alamy; p. 609, top: © JoeFox / Alamy; p. 609, bottom: © Victor Ginesi; p. 610: © Ken Gibson / Photolibrary; p. 611: © Victor Ginesi; p. 618: © The Irish Image Collection / SuperStock ; p. 626: © JoeFox CountyDerry / Alamy; p. 627: © Victor Ginesi; p. 630: © Victor Ginesi; p. 641: © Rob Whitworth / Alamy; p. 646: © Grianne Flynn; p. 649: © Grianne Flynn; p. 654: © Eoin Clarke / Lonely Planet Images.

NOTES